THE
Culinary Arts
COOK

Institute®
BOOK

Culinary Arts Institute®

Fourth Printing July 1986

Copyright © 1985 by
Advance Publishers
3706 Silver Star Road
Orlando, Florida 32808

All rights reserved under the International and Pan-American Copyright Conventions. Manufactured in the United States of America and published simultaneously in Canada.

ISBN: 0-8326-0580-8

CONTENTS

Note: Certain recipes in this book call for specialized equipment. These recipes are clearly indicated by the following symbols:

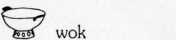 wok   crock

 chafing dish   food processor

 fondue pot   grill

 crêpe pan

APPETIZERS

Fried Cheese

Kefalotyri or kasseri cheese, sliced lengthwise in ¼-inch-thick wedges (about 1 pound for 4 people)
2 egg yolks minced with 2
tablespoons water
Flour
Olive oil
2 lemons, cut in quarters

1. Dip cheese slices into egg-yolk mixture, then into flour, coating each side evenly. Shake off excess flour.
2. In a 10-inch skillet, heat a ¼-inch layer of olive oil. When the oil begins to smoke, add the cheese. Fry first on one side, then on the other.
3. Remove from skillet and squeeze some lemon juice on each slice. Serve immediately. Allow 2 slices for each person.

Olive Canapés

1 pound Greek olives, pitted
2 tablespoons olive oil
4 hard-cooked eggs, mashed
Pinch dry mustard
1 clove garlic, crushed in a garlic press
Pepper to taste
Egg yolks, hard-cooked and chopped for garnish
Scallions (green part), minced for garnish

1. Put olives and olive oil into a blender; purée. Blend in remaining ingredients except yolks and scallions.
2. Serve on **crackers,** or mound in a dish and serve crackers separately. Garnish with egg yolks and scallions.
1 CUP

Onion-Chive Butter

1 tablespoon sliced green onion
1 tablespoon snipped chives
½ cup butter (at room temperature)

1. Blend onion, chives, and butter.
2. Form into a roll about 1 inch in diameter. Chill.
3. Cut into small disks.
ABOUT ⅔ CUP

Individual Chicken Terrines

½ cup thinly sliced small carrots
¼ cup brandy
2 pounds boned chicken, coarsely chopped
1 small onion
1 small carrot
1 teaspoon salt
¼ teaspoon nutmeg
1 egg, lightly beaten
2 teaspoons vegetable oil
2 tablespoons ice water
1½ tablespoons matzo meal or white cornmeal
Vegetable oil
Watercress
Cucumber Sauce, if desired (page 54)

1. Simmer carrot slices in brandy in a covered saucepan just until tender (about 3 minutes). Remove carrots with a slotted spoon; reserve. Mix a quarter of the chicken with brandy; remove from heat and let stand 45 minutes. Drain.
2. Mince remaining chicken, the onion, and carrot in a food processor or blender; remove to a mixing bowl. Stir in marinated chicken, salt, nutmeg, egg, oil, and ice water; mix well. Sprinkle matzo meal over mixture; mix well.
3. Layer the carrot slices in bottom of 8 lightly oiled 6-ounce custard cups. Spoon chicken mixture over carrots, smoothing top of mixture. Cover cups tightly with aluminum foil; place in a baking pan. Pour boiling water into baking pan, halfway up sides of custard cups.
4. Bake at 325°F 40 to 45 minutes, or until mixture is set. Remove cups from water. Remove foil. Let stand 5 minutes.
5. Terrines can be served hot, or refrigerated until chilled and served cold. To unmold, run knife around edge of cups and invert on individual plates. Garnish with watercress. Serve with Cucumber Sauce, if desired.
8 SERVINGS

Note: For a luncheon entrée, follow directions above, using six 10-ounce glass dishes. Bake until mixture is set.

Individual Chicken Terrines

Shrimp Paste à la Creole

Peppery Peanut Butter and Coconut Sandwiches

Peppery Peanut Butter and Coconut Sandwiches

8 slices white bread
6 tablespoons peanut butter
2 tablespoons butter, softened

1 teaspoon Tabasco
½ cup fresh grated or chopped flaked coconut

1. Remove crusts from bread. Flatten each slice with a rolling pin and cut into 3 strips.
2. Combine peanut butter, butter, and Tabasco.
3. Spread peanut butter mixture on bread; dip in coconut. Roll each bread strip to form a pinwheel.
4. Chill thoroughly before serving.

2 DOZEN APPETIZERS

Chicken Liver Spread

½ pound chicken livers
1 cup milk
¼ cup rendered chicken fat or margarine
1 medium onion, cut in quarters
3 hard-cooked eggs, peeled

and cut in half
½ pound cooked ham or cooked fresh pork, cut up
¼ teaspoon salt
¼ teaspoon pepper
⅛ teaspoon garlic powder (optional)

1. Soak livers in milk 2 hours. Drain livers and discard milk.
2. Melt fat in skillet. Add livers and onion and cook over medium heat until tender.
3. Combine livers, pan drippings, and all remaining ingredients. Grind or mince.
4. Add extra melted chicken fat or margarine, if desired, to make spread of desired spreading consistency.

ABOUT 4 CUPS

Shrimp Paste à la Creole

Fresh shrimp
Court Bouillon for Fish and Shellfish (see page 43)
¼ cup butter, melted
1 garlic clove, crushed in a

garlic press
⅛ teaspoon ground mace
⅛ teaspoon pepper
Tabasco to taste

1. Cook enough shrimp in bouillion to make 4 cups shelled shrimp.
2. Put shrimp, hot melted garlic, mace, pepper, and Tabasco into container of an electric blender; process 10 seconds.
3. Serve on **toasted cassava** or **Melba toast.**

Eggplant Appetizer

1 large eggplant
1 medium onion, minced
1 garlic clove, crushed in a garlic press
1 teaspoon chopped parsley
½ teaspoon freshly dried

mint
½ cup olive oil
1 tablespoon wine vinegar (or more to taste)
Juice of 1 large lemon
Salt and pepper to taste

1. To prepare eggplant, place in a baking pan and prick top in four or five places with a fork.
2. Bake at 350°F about 45 minutes, or until skin is wrinkled and the surface is soft.
3. Cool eggplant slightly and cut in half. Scoop out the flesh and place in a blender. Add onion, garlic, parsley, and mint. Blend until well mixed.
4. Combine olive oil, vinegar, and lemon juice. Add to the eggplant mixture and blend well. Season with salt and pepper.
5. Chill. Serve with **toasted French** or **pita bread.** May also be used as a dip for fresh vegetables, or served separately as a first course.

ABOUT 4 CUPS

Crisp Cheese Crackers

¼ cup sesame seed
2 cups all-purpose flour
Salt (optional)
½ teaspoon ground red pepper
1½ cups grated kefalotyri

cheese
¾ cup butter, softened
¼ cup olive oil
2 egg yolks, beaten, for brushing
Sesame seed

1. Combine ¼ cup sesame seed, flour, salt, red pepper, and cheese. Work in butter and oil, using hands. Mix until dough holds together.
2. Roll dough out on lightly floured board. Cut into small diamond shapes. Transfer to cookie sheets. Brush with egg.
3. Bake at 350°F about 12 minutes, or until golden.
ABOUT 3 DOZEN

Sesame Seed Dip

½ cup tahini (sesame seed paste)
2 tablespoons olive oil (or more to taste)
¾ cup water
Juice of 1 lemon

2 garlic cloves, crushed in a garlic press
½ cup walnuts
Salt and pepper to taste
¼ cup sesame seed, toasted

1. In a blender, combine all the ingredients except sesame seed until smooth and milky white in color. Refrigerate.
2. Garnish with sesame seed. Serve with **crackers** or as a vegetable dip.
ABOUT 1¾ CUPS

Anchovy Fillets

½ pound anchovy fillets preserved in salt
Wine vinegar (2 or more

cups)
2 tablespoons olive oil

1. Separate fillets. Scrape scales and as much of the salt as possible from each fillet.
2. Soak in wine vinegar 5 to 10 minutes, changing as often as necessary until the vinegar remains clear.
3. Drain fillets on paper towels.
4. Arrange fillets on a serving platter. Drizzle with 1 tablespoon fresh vinegar and the olive oil.
5. Serve as an hors d'oeuvre or in anchovy salad.

Marrow Canapés

8 large marrow bones, cut in 2-inch pieces
Salted water
½ cup butter

1 loaf cocktail-size black bread, cut in thick slices
¼ cup minced parsley
Ground red pepper

1. Using a thin sharp knife, loosen marrow from bones and remove. Soak marrow in salted water for 24 hours. Drain.
2. Cut marrow into ½-inch-thick rounds and poach in simmering water until tender (2 to 3 minutes). Remove with a slotted spoon. Drain on paper towels.
3. Melt butter in a skillet. Fry slices of bread on both sides.
4. Spread slices with marrow. Sprinkle with parsley and red pepper.
5. Place under broiler for a moment. Serve hot.
12 TO 15 PIECES

Fried Calf, Lamb, or Chicken Livers

1 pound livers, cut in small pieces (do not cut chicken livers)
1½ cups flour, seasoned with

pepper for dredging
Olive oil for frying
2 lemons, quartered
Salt to taste

1. Rinse livers in cool water. Drain on absorbent paper.
2. Dip livers in flour. Shake off excess.
3. In a deep skillet, heat olive oil to smoking. Brown livers on both sides over medium heat.
4. Squeeze lemon juice on each piece. Season with salt. Serve at once.
4 SERVINGS

Barbecued Lamb Innards

1 large intestine
Innards (heart, liver, kidneys, lungs, and sweetbreads) from a milk-fed calf
Salt to taste
1 tablespoon vinegar
¾ cup olive oil
Juice of 2 to 3 lemons

2 garlic cloves, crushed in a garlic press
2 teaspoons pepper
2 teaspoons oregano
1 teaspoon thyme
2 lamb casings, washed and drained
Pepper to taste

1. Rinse intestine in lukewarm water. Using a long spit, turn inside out. Rub salt over surface. Wash thoroughly in lots of lukewarm water.
2. Put innards in a large bowl. Cover with lukewarm water. Add salt and vinegar. Let stand ½ hour. Drain. Discard membranes and connective tissues. Cut into pieces.
3. Combine olive oil, lemon juice, garlic, 2 teaspoons pepper, oregano, and thyme. Add innards. Marinate in refrigerator 4 to 6 hours, turning occasionally.
4. Drain innards, reserving marinade. Knot one end of casing, then stuff with innards and knot other end.
5. Put a skewer beside the filled casing. Tie to the skewer with the empty casing by turning the casing around the length of the skewer.
6. Charcoal-broil over embers heated until they are white, turning about every 10 minutes and brushing frequently with the marinade. Cook until tender (about 2½ hours). Remove from spit. Cut into 2-inch pieces. Sprinkle with pepper. Serve hot.
10 TO 20 PIECES

Purée of Anchovies

1 can (2 ounces) flat anchovy fillets, drained
3 slices stale white bread
Water

½ cup sour cream or mayonnaise
1½ teaspoons vinegar

1. Mince or pound anchovy fillets.
2. Moisten bread with enough water to cover; then squeeze dry. Break into bits or mince with a fork. Blend in sour cream and vinegar to make a smooth purée. Serve as a spread with **dark bread rounds.**
ABOUT 1 CUP

Chilled Artichoke Plate

4 medium artichokes
Chicken Stock (see page 48)
¼ cup lemon juice
1 teaspoon salt
½ pint cherry tomatoes

¾ cup Mock Béarnaise
Sauce (page 49)
1 pound fresh asparagus, cut
in 2-inch pieces

1. Snip tips from artichoke leaves with scissors. Simmer artichokes in 1 inch of the stock with lemon juice and salt in a large covered saucepan until tender (about 45 minutes). Lift from pan with tongs; let cool. Refrigerate until chilled.
2. Carefully scoop seeds from tomatoes, using small end of a melon-ball cutter. Fill tomatoes with ¼ cup of the sauce; refrigerate.
3. Scrape choke from artichoke bottoms. Place artichokes in center of individual plates and dollop each with 2 tablespoons sauce. Arrange raw asparagus pieces and tomatoes attractively on plates. Serve immediately.
4 SERVINGS

Tangerine Yakatori

½ cup tangerine or orange
juice
¼ cup dry white wine
3 tablespoons light soy sauce
½ bunch green onions, cut
in 1-inch pieces

2 large tangerines or oranges,
peeled, sectioned, and
seeded
2 large whole chicken
breasts, skinned, boned,
and cut in 1 x ¼-inch strips

1. Combine all ingredients in a mixing bowl. Refrigerate covered 2 hours, stirring occasionally. Drain; reserve marinade.
2. Thread ingredients alternately on wooden skewers. Broil 4 inches from heat until chicken is done (about 3 minutes on each side).
3. Heat marinade until bubbly. Serve in individual cups as a dipping sauce.
4 SERVINGS

Spring Cottage Cheese Spread

1 carton (12 to 14 ounces)
cottage cheese
½ cup sour cream
8 radishes, shredded
3 tablespoons sliced green

onion
½ teaspoon salt
Lettuce leaves
Radish roses
Rye or French bread

1. Mix cottage cheese with sour cream. Add radishes, onion, and salt; toss to mix well.
2. Mound on lettuce leaves. Garnish with radish roses. Surround with bread.
ABOUT 2⅓ CUPS

Seviche

1¼ pounds whitefish fillets,
skinned and cut in 2 x
¼-inch strips
1 cup fresh lemon juice
2 green chiles, seeded and
minced
1 teaspoon snipped fresh or
½ teaspoon dried oregano
leaves
1 tablespoon snipped fresh
or 1½ teaspoons dried coriander leaves
1 tablespoon olive oil

1 teaspoon salt
¼ teaspoon freshly ground
pepper
2 large tomatoes, peeled,
seeded, and chopped
1 medium green pepper,
finely chopped
1 small yellow onion, finely
chopped
¼ cup fresh lime juice
Radish slices
Ripe olives

1. Place fish in a shallow glass bowl; pour lemon juice over it. Refrigerate covered 6 hours, stirring occasionally. Drain; discard lemon juice.
2. Mix remaining ingredients except radish slices and olives with fish in a medium bowl. Refrigerate 30 minutes.
3. Serve on chilled plates; garnish with radish slices and olives. Or spoon into **fluted lemon shells.**
8 SERVINGS (½ CUP EACH)

Crab Meat and Bean Sprouts with Omelet Strips

2 eggs
3 tablespoons water
1 tablespoon dry sherry
1 tablespoon light soy sauce
1 tablespoon light soy sauce
1 tablespoon walnut or
vegetable oil
4 green onions, chopped
¾ cup chopped green
pepper

1 cup sliced fresh
mushrooms
2 cups drained fresh or
canned bean sprouts
1 tablespoon light soy sauce
8 ounces fresh or 1 can (7 ¾
ounces) crab meat, drained
and flaked
1 teaspoon toasted sesame
seed

1. Beat eggs with water, sherry, and 1 tablespoon soy sauce. Heat half the walnut oil in a small skillet. Cook egg mixture in skillet until set but still moist on top; remove to plate and cut egg into strips.
2. Heat remaining walnut oil in a wok or medium skillet. Cook and stir vegetables and 1 tablespoon soy sauce until vegetables are just tender (about 3 minutes). Add crab meat and omelet strips; cook and stir until thoroughly heated (about 1 minute). Sprinkle with toasted sesame seed. Serve immediately.
4 SERVINGS

Mushroom Cheese Mold

2 packages (8 ounces each) cream cheese, softened
½ pound Cheddar cheese, shredded (about 2 cups)
1 clove garlic, crushed
1½ teaspoons brown mustard
¼ teaspoon salt
1 can (3 to 4 ounces) mushroom stems and pieces, drained and chopped
¼ cup finely chopped onion
2 tablespoons finely diced pimento
2 tablespoons finely chopped parsley
Sliced mushrooms (optional)
Parsley (optional)

1. Combine cheeses, garlic, mustard, and salt in a bowl. Add chopped mushrooms, onion, pimento, and parsley; mix well.
2. Turn mixture into a lightly buttered 3-cup mold. Refrigerate until firm.
3. Unmold onto serving platter. Garnish with sliced mushrooms and parsley, if desired. Serve with crackers.
3½ CUPS SPREAD

Avocado Cocktail Dip

1 large ripe avocado
2 teaspoons lemon juice
1 small slice onion
¼ cup mayonnaise
6 drops of Tabasco
Salt to taste
Potato chips

1. Halve and peel avocado, reserving 1 shell. Cube avocado and put into container of an electric blender. Add lemon juice, onion, mayonnaise, Tabasco, and salt. Process until puréed.
2. To serve, pile avocado mixture into reserved shell; place on a serving dish and surround with potato chips for dipping.
ABOUT 1 CUP

Corn Fritters

1 cup fresh corn kernels
½ cup butter
1 cup all-purpose flour
4 eggs
Corn oil for frying, heated to 365°F

1. Cook corn until soft in boiling salted water in a saucepan; drain thoroughly, reserving 1 cup liquid. Melt butter with corn liquid in saucepan, add flour, and cook, stirring rapidly, until mixture is smooth and rolls away from the sides of pan.
2. Remove from heat and add the eggs, one at a time, beating well after each addition. Stir in cooked corn.
3. Drop batter by spoonfuls into heated oil and fry until golden and well puffed. Drain on absorbent paper. Serve hot.
ABOUT 30 FRITTERS

Mushroom Cheese Mold

Fresh
Sweet
Cherry
Appetizer
Tray

Fresh Sweet Cherry Appetizer Tray

Fresh sweet cherries
Assorted cheeses (Cheddar,
  Swiss, Gouda, Kuminost)
Sweet gherkins, thickly sliced

Salami, thinly sliced
Cream cheese
Horseradish
Parsley

1. Wash cherries just before serving and put into a serving bowl.
2. Cut some of the Cheddar and Swiss cheeses into ½-inch cubes and put, along with sliced gherkins, onto party picks. Slice remaining cheeses.
3. Soften cream cheese at room temperature and season with a small amount of horseradish. Spread on salami slices and shape into cornucopias, fastening with wooden picks. Garnish with parsley.
4. Arrange all appetizers on a large tray with the cherries.

Vegetable Mélange with Mustard Sauce

1 large yellow squash or
  zucchini, pared and minced
3 medium carrots, minced
¼ cup minced onion
¼ cup minced dill pickle
4 ounces Swiss cheese,
  minced

⅓ cup prepared mustard
⅓ cup dill pickle juice
1 teaspoon sugar
½ teaspoon curry powder
1 garlic clove, minced
Lettuce cups

Combine squash, carrot, onion, pickle, and cheese in a medium bowl. Mix remaining ingredients, except lettuce cups; pour over vegetables and stir to coat well. Refrigerate until well chilled. Serve in lettuce cups.

6 SERVINGS

Tomato Toast

¼ cup finely chopped onion
2 tablespoons butter or margarine
Italian-style tomatoes (canned), drained
1 teaspoon sugar
⅛ teaspoon salt
1 egg yolk, fork beaten
¼ to ½ teaspoon Worcester-shire sauce
¼ cup shredded Parmesan cheese
4 slices white bread, toasted, crusts removed, and toast cut in quarters
Snipped fresh parsley or crushed dried basil or oregano

1. Add onion to heated butter in a heavy saucepan and cook until tender, stirring occasionally.
2. Force enough of the drained tomatoes through a sieve to yield 1½ cups. Add to onion with sugar and salt; cook, stirring occasionally, until liquid evaporates and mixture is thick (about 25 minutes).
3. Stir a small amount of tomato mixture into egg yolk; blend thoroughly and return to saucepan. Cook and stir 5 minutes.
4. Mix in Worcestershire sauce and half of cheese; spread generously on toast quarters. Sprinkle half of appetizers with the remaining cheese and half with the parsley.
5. Broil appetizers 3 to 4 inches from heat until bubbly. Serve hot.
16 APPETIZERS

Haitian Rarebit

8 kaiser rolls
16 slices American or Cheddar cheese
½ cup sweet pickle relish
1 cup chopped cooked ham, chicken, beef, or tongue
8 tablespoons butter or margarine, melted

1. Split rolls. On bottom half of each roll, place in the following order: 1 slice cheese, 1 tablespoon sweet pickle relish, 2 tablespoons chopped meat, and another slice cheese. Replace top of roll.
2. Generously brush top and bottom of sandwiches with melted butter.
3. Place rolls in a large skillet over medium heat. Cover with a lid slightly smaller than the skillet and weight it down over the rolls. Brown both sides until cheese melts. Serve immediately.
8 SERVINGS

Shrimp Dunk

1 can or bottle (12 ounces) beer plus ½ cup water
1 small onion, sliced
Top and leaves of 1 stalk celery
1 tablespoon salt
3 or 4 peppercorns
1 bay leaf
1 garlic clove
1 pound very large shelled shrimp, uncooked

1. Combine ingredients except shrimp in a large saucepan. Cover; heat to boiling. Boil 10 minutes.
2. Add shrimp. Cover and boil 5 minutes, or just until shrimp turn pink. Remove from heat; chill in cooking liquid.
3. Serve cold with dunking bowls of cold beer. Serve as hors d'oeuvres or as a summertime main entrée.
25 TO 30 SHRIMP

Acra

5 dried Italian pepper pods or 1 small piece hot pepper
1 tablespoon coarse salt
6 peppercorns
½ medium onion, chopped
2 garlic cloves
1 egg
1 cup finely grated malanga root*
Peanut oil for frying, heated to 365°F

1. In a mortar, pound together to a paste the pepper pods, salt, peppercorns, onion, and garlic.
2. Add seasoning paste and egg to grated malanga root; beat until light.
3. Drop mixture by spoonfuls into heated oil and fry until golden. Drain on absorbent paper.
20 FRITTERS

*Malanga root can be found in Puerto Rican markets.

Eggplant Fritters

3 long thin eggplants
1 tablespoon lime juice
Salt, pepper, and cayenne or red pepper to taste
1½ cups all-purpose flour
(about)
¾ cup beer (about)
Oil for deep frying heated to 365°F
Salt

1. Slice eggplants into eighteen ½-inch rounds. Season with lime juice, salt, and ground peppers. Marinate 15 minutes.
2. Make a batter the consistency of whipping cream by mixing flour with beer.
3. Dip and coat eggplant slices in batter. Fry in heated oil until golden brown. Drain on absorbent paper. Sprinkle lightly with salt. Serve hot.
18 FRITTERS

Artichoke Fritters: Follow recipe for Eggplant Fritters. Substitute **artichoke hearts** or **bottoms** for eggplant rounds.

Marinated Mushrooms

1 pound small fresh mushrooms
⅔ cup vegetable oil
½ cup beer
¼ cup minced green onion with tops
2 tablespoons lemon juice
1 tablespoon chopped parsley
1 large garlic clove, minced
½ teaspoon salt
Dash pepper

1. Wash mushrooms, remove stems, and pat dry. Reserve stems for later use.
2. Combine remaining ingredients in a shallow glass or ceramic dish. Add mushrooms. Cover and let stand at room temperature about 3 hours, stirring occasionally.
3. Place mushrooms, cup side up, on a broiler pan. Spoon some marinade over each. Broil 3 inches from heat about 2 minutes, or until lightly browned. Serve warm with picks.
40 TO 50 MUSHROOMS

Note: Marinated Mushrooms may also be served cold. Marinate in refrigerator. Do not broil. Turn into a serving bowl with marinade; serve with picks. Canned button mushrooms may also be used when serving this dish cold.

Clam and Walnut Stuffed Mushrooms

20 large mushrooms
½ cup butter or margarine
1 clove garlic, minced
1 can (10 ounces) minced or
whole baby clams, drained
1 cup soft bread crumbs
½ cup chopped walnuts
¼ cup chopped parsley
¼ teaspoon salt
¼ teaspoon black pepper
Walnut halves (optional)
Parsley sprigs (optional)

1. Rinse mushrooms and pat dry. Remove stems and chop (about 1 cup); set aside.
2. Melt butter in a large skillet. Use about 3 tablespoons of melted butter to brush on mushroom caps. Place caps in a shallow pan.
3. To butter remaining in skillet, add garlic and reserved chopped mushroom stems; sauté 2 minutes. Add clams, bread crumbs, nuts, parsley, salt, and pepper; mix well.
4. Spoon stuffing into mushroom caps, piling high.
5. Bake at 350°F about 12 minutes, or until hot.
6. If desired, garnish with walnut halves and parsley sprigs.
20 STUFFED MUSHROOMS

Beet Relish

1 can (16 ounces) whole
beets, drained
¼ cup prepared horseradish
¼ cup sugar
¼ cup vinegar
¼ cup water
1 tablespoon grated onion
1 teaspoon salt
⅛ teaspoon pepper

1. Grate or mince beets.
2. In casserole or other container with a cover, mix beets with remaining ingredients. Cover.
3. Store in refrigerator for at least 1 day before serving.
ABOUT 2 CUPS

Broiled Fish Quenelles

2 pounds skinned fish fillets
(all trout or a combination
of trout, whitefish, or pike)
½ cup chopped onion
⅓ cup chopped carrot
1 egg, beaten
2 teaspoons vegetable oil
1½ teaspoons salt
1½ teaspoons matzo meal or
white cornmeal
3 tablespoons ice water
Watercress

1. Place all ingredients except 1 tablespoon of the ice water and watercress in a blender or food processor; purée until the consistency of a paste. Add remaining ice water if necessary (mixture should hold together and be easy to handle).
2. Form fish mixture into oval patties, using ½ cup for each. Place on a lightly oiled cookie sheet.
3. Broil 4 inches from heat until patties are well browned and slightly puffed (8 to 10 minutes on each side). Serve immediately. Garnish with watercress.
8 SERVINGS

Crab Meat Quiche

1 unbaked 9-inch pie shell
2 eggs
1 cup half-and-half
½ teaspoon salt
Dash ground red pepper
¾ cup (3 ounces) shredded
Gruyère cheese
1 tablespoon flour
1 can (7½ ounces) Alaska
King crab, drained and
flaked

1. Prick bottom and sides of pie shell. Bake at 450°F 10 minutes, or until delicately browned.
2. Beat together eggs, half-and-half, salt, and red pepper.
3. Combine cheeses, flour, and crab; sprinkle evenly in pie shell. Pour in egg mixture.
4. Bake, uncovered, at 325°F 45 minutes, or until tip of knife inserted 1 inch from center comes out clean. Let stand a few minutes. Cut into wedges to serve.
16 APPETIZERS

German Beer Cheese

½ pound Cheddar cheese
½ pound Swiss cheese
2 teaspoons Worcestershire
sauce
1 teaspoon dry mustard
1 small garlic clove, mashed
½ cup beer (about)

1. Shred cheeses finely. Or put through a meat grinder, using finest blade.
2. Add Worcestershire sauce, dry mustard, garlic, and enough beer to make a mixture of spreading consistency.
3. Turn into a 3-cup rounded bowl or mold; pack firmly. Chill. Unmold and serve at room temperature with **small rye rounds** or **crackers.**
3 CUPS

Wine-Cheese Canapés

½ cup whipped unsalted butter
cream cheese
4 teaspoons Roquefort cheese
2 tablespoons sauterne
Parsley, minced
4 toasted bread rounds
Pimento-stuffed olive slices
2 packages (3 ounces each)
Paprika
Clear Glaze (see recipe)

1. Whip together butter and Roquefort cheese. Spread onto toasted bread rounds.
2. Whip cream cheese with sauterne.
3. Pipe a swirl of the mixture onto each canapé. Roll edges in minced parsley. Top with pimento-stuffed olive slice; sprinkle.
4. Glaze and chill.

Clear Glaze: Soften **1 envelope unflavored gelatin** in **⅔ cup cold water** in a bowl. Pour **1 cup boiling water** over softened gelatin and stir until gelatin is dissolved. Chill until slightly thickened. To glaze canapés: Place canapés on wire racks over a large shallow pan. Working quickly, spoon about 2 teaspoons of slightly thickened gelatin over each canapé. (Have ready a bowl of ice and water and a bowl of hot water. The gelatin may have to be set over one or the other during glazing to maintain the proper consistency.) The gelatin should cling slightly to canapés when spooned over them. Any drips may be scooped up and reused.
ABOUT 24 CANAPÉS

Mushrooms à la Grecque

1 pound fresh mushrooms or 2 cans (6 to 8 ounces each) whole mushrooms
⅓ cup olive oil
⅓ cup dry white wine or apple juice
¼ cup water
1 tablespoon lemon juice
¾ cup chopped onion
1 large clove garlic, minced
1½ teaspoons salt
1 teaspoon sugar
½ teaspoon coriander seed (optional)
¼ teaspoon black pepper
2 cups carrot chunks
½ cup pimento-stuffed olives

1. Rinse, pat dry, and halve fresh mushrooms or drain canned mushrooms; set aside.
2. In a large saucepan combine oil, wine, water, lemon juice, onion, garlic, salt, sugar, coriander, and black pepper. Bring to boiling; add carrots.
3. Cover and simmer for 15 minutes. Add mushrooms and olives. Return to boiling; reduce heat. Cover and simmer for 5 minutes.
4. Chill thoroughly, at least overnight.
5. To serve, thread mushrooms, carrot chunks, and olives on skewers or spoon into a bowl. Serve as hors d'oeuvres.
8 TO 10 HORS D'OEUVRE PORTIONS

Liver Pâté

1½ cups chopped onion
4 drops Tabasco
1 cup chopped celery
1¼ teaspoons salt
1½ cups chicken stock
1½ pounds chicken livers, membranes removed
1 cup dry white wine
1 teaspoon paprika
2 envelopes unflavored gelatin
⅛ teaspoon ground allspice or cloves
½ cup cold water
¼ teaspoon garlic powder
Assorted vegetable relishes

1. Simmer onion and celery in stock and wine in an uncovered saucepan until liquid is reduced to 2 cups (about 15 minutes). Stir in paprika, allspice, garlic powder, Tabasco, and salt; simmer 2 minutes. Stir in livers; simmer covered until livers are tender (about 15 minutes). Drain; discard liquid.
2. Sprinkle gelatin over cold water; let stand 3 minutes. Set over low heat, stirring occasionally, until gelatin is dissolved (about 5 minutes).
3. Purée half the livers and vegetables along with half the gelatin mixture in a food processor or blender. Repeat with remaining ingredients, combine the two mixtures.
4. Pour mixture into a lightly oiled 1½-quart mold or bowl or ten 6-ounce custard cups. Chill until set (about 4 hours).
5. Serve from mold, or unmold onto platter and accompany with assorted vegetables.
10 TO 12 SERVINGS

Puff Shrimp with Orange Ginger Sauce

Orange Ginger Sauce (see recipe)
Fat for deep frying heated to 375°F
2 pounds medium raw shrimp (20 to 25 per pound)
3 egg yolks
½ cup white wine
¾ cup all-purpose flour

1 teaspoon salt
¼ teaspoon pepper
3 egg whites

Orange Ginger Sauce:
1 cup orange marmalade
2 tablespoons soy sauce
¼ cup sherry
1 piece whole ginger root
1 clove garlic, minced

1. Prepare and cool Orange Ginger Sauce.
2. Fill a deep saucepan or automatic deep fryer one-half to two-thirds full with fat for deep frying; heat slowly to 375°F.
3. Shell and devein raw shrimp and set aside.
4. Beat together in a bowl egg yolks, wine, flour, salt, and pepper until smooth.
5. Beat egg white until stiff, not dry, peaks are formed. Fold egg whites into egg yolk mixture.
6. Dry shrimp thoroughly and dip into batter, coating well.
7. Deep-fry one layer deep in heated fat 2 to 3 minutes on each side, or until golden brown. Remove from fat with a slotted spoon. Drain on absorbent paper. Be sure temperature of fat is 375°F before frying each layer. Serve shrimp hot accompanied with the Orange Ginger Sauce for dipping.
8. For Orange Ginger Sauce, combine in a saucepan marmalade, soy sauce, sherry, ginger root, and minced garlic. Stir over low heat until mixture bubbles. Remove from heat. Cool. Remove ginger before serving.
40 TO 50 APPETIZERS

Savory Cheese Custards

1 large yellow onion
¼ teaspoon salt
1½ teaspoons poppy seed
1 cup instant nonfat dry-milk solids
2 cups water
2 teaspoons Worcestershire

sauce
2 teaspoons Dijon mustard
¼ teaspoon salt
2 eggs
2 ounces Jarlsberg or Parmesan cheese, finely shredded

1. Bake onion at 400°F until tender when pierced with a fork (about 1½ hours). Let cool. Peel onion and chop finely (about 1½ cups). Mix onion with ¼ teaspoon salt and the poppy seed; spoon mixture into the bottom of 4 ramekins or custard cups.
2. Process dry-milk solids, water, Worcestershire sauce, mustard, ¼ teaspoon salt, and eggs in a food processor or blender until very smooth.
3. Pour mixture into ramekins; sprinkle cheese over mixture. Place ramekins in a shallow baking pan; pour 1 inch boiling water into pan.
4. Bake at 325°F 30 to 40 minutes, or until custard is set and a knife inserted between center and edge comes out clean. Serve warm, or refrigerate and serve cold.
4 SERVINGS

Pickled Shrimp

1 can or bottle (12 ounces) beer
¼ cup oil
1 tablespoon lemon juice
1 teaspoon sugar
1 teaspoon salt
½ teaspoon each dill seed, dry mustard, and celery salt

¼ teaspoon tarragon
⅛ teaspoon ground red pepper
2 bay leaves, halved
2 medium onion, chopped
1 package (10 ounces) small to medium frozen cooked shrimp, thawed

1. Place all ingredients except shrimp in a saucepan. Simmer 10 to 15 minutes, or until onions are just tender.
2. Add shrimp; remove from heat. Turn into a small casserole. Cover and refrigerate at least 1 day.
3. Remove bay leaves; drain off marinade. Let guests spoon shrimp and onions onto **cocktail rye rounds.**
ABOUT 25 APPETIZERS

Note: With larger shrimp to be served on fancy picks, use only one onion and slice it. Remove onion before serving. Recipe may also be made with uncooked shrimp. Add them 4 to 5 minutes before end of cooking time; cover and simmer until shrimp turn pink. Continue as in above recipe.

Chili Nuts

1 package (12 ounces) shelled raw peanuts
2 tablespoons peanut or

vegetable oil
2 teaspoons chili powder
1 teaspoon salt

1. Combine ingredients in a large baking pan; spread thinly.
2. Bake at 325°F minutes. Cool on waxed paper.
2 CUPS

Shrimp Spread

½ cup butter or margarine, softened
2 green onions with some tops
2 parsley sprigs
¼ teaspoon salt
⅛ teaspoon garlic powder
Dash pepper

1 package (12 ounces) frozen cooked shrimp, thawed
½ cup beer
1 tablespoon capers (optional)
Fancy crackers or tiny cream puffs

1. Using a food processor or blender, process butter, onions, parsley, and seasonings until vegetables are minced and mixture is smooth. (With blender, prepare in 2 or 3 batches.)
2. Add shrimp, beer, and capers. Process to a smooth paste.
3. Serve at room temperature on crackers or in tiny cream puffs. Use a rounded teaspoon for each. One half recipe of Shrimp Spread fills one recipe Appetizer Puffs (see page 21).
⅔ CUPS SPREAD FOR ABOUT 7 DOZEN CRACKERS OR TINY CREAM PUFFS

Egg Rolls

Skins:
1½ cups flour
½ teaspoon salt
2 eggs, fork beaten
1½ cups water

Filling:
¼ pound cooked roast pork, cut in 1 inch cubes
6 medium shrimp, shelled and cooked
3 green onions, trimmed and cut in 1-inch pieces

½ cup water chestnuts, drained
3 stalks celery, cut in 3-inch pieces
4 to 6 leaves Chinese cabbage
½ cup bean sprouts, drained
2 tablespoons peanut oil
1 tablespoon soy sauce
1 tablespoon sherry
½ teaspoon salt
½ teaspoon sugar

1. For skins, with **steel blade** of food processor in bowl, add flour and salt.
2. Combine lightly beaten eggs and water. With machine on, add liquid ingredients through the feed tube and process a few seconds until batter is smooth.
3. Lightly grease a 7- or 8-inch skillet with peanut oil and heat over medium heat until it smokes. Quickly pour exactly 2 tablespoons batter into the center of the pan and rotate to evenly spread the batter into a 5-inch circle. Cook about 2 minutes, until the edges of the pancake begin to curl. Remove to a plate and cover with a damp cloth. Repeat procedure until all batter is used, stacking skins on plate. If not using a well-seasoned pan, it will be necessary to lightly grease the skillet before making each skin.
4. Let skins cool completely before filling and rolling.
5. For filling, using **steel blade,** separately process pork and shrimp, using quick on/off motions, until coarsely chopped. Set aside.

6. Still using **steel blade,** process green onions until finely chopped. Set aside.
7. Using **shredding disc,** separately shred water chestnuts and celery, removing each from bowl; pack celery vertically in the feed tube, filling it as full as possible.
8. To slice Chinese cabbage, lightly roll together 2 to 3 leaves of cabbage and place vertically in feed tube. Slice with **slicing disc,** using light pressure.
9. Combine shredded celery, sliced Chinese cabbage, and bean sprouts in a bowl. These ingredients must be blanched before proceeding. To do so, cover with boiling water, stir a few times only, and remove to a colander. Immediately rinse with cold water and drain thoroughly. Roll ingredients in a towel to remove any excess moisture. Set aside.
10. Heat peanut oil in a wok. Add chopped pork and shrimp and stir-fry to heat through. Add remaining ingredients and stir-fry very briefly to heat through. Remove to a colander and let cool completely.
11. For rolls, skins and fillings must be completely cooled for successful egg rolls.
12. Place 2 to 3 tablespoons of filling slightly below the center of the skin. Fold the bottom side up to cover filling. Fold in sides and roll the skin. Brush the top edge with unbeaten egg white and seal like an envelope.
13. To cook, heat ¼-inch peanut oil in a large skillet and fry on both sides until lighly browned. Drain on paper towels.
ABOUT 15 EGG ROLLS

Note: Egg rolls can be made in advance. To reheat, place in 325°F oven for 10 to 15 minutes.

Appetizer Puffs

1 cup beer
½ cup butter or margarine
½ teaspoon salt
1 cup all-purpose flour
4 eggs

1. Heat beer, butter, and salt to boiling in a saucepan.
2. Add flour at once. Beat vigorously with a wooden spoon until mixture leaves sides of pan and forms a smooth ball.
3. Add eggs, one at a time, beating until smooth.
4. Drop mixture by rounded teaspoonfuls onto a greased cookie sheet, 1 inch apart.
5. Bake at 450°F 10 minutes. Turn oven control to 350°F and bake 5 to 10 minutes more, or until lightly browned and puffed.
6. Cool. Split and fill with desired filling.
ABOUT 40 PUFFS

Pickled Mushrooms

4 pounds small mushrooms
4 cups boiling water
1½ tablespoons salt

Marinade:
1¾ cups water
15 peppercorns
2 bay leaves
2½ tablespoons salt
¾ cup sugar
¾ cup vinegar

1. Cut the mushroom stems off even with the caps.
2. Cook over medium heat in boiling water with salt until they sink to the bottom, about 10 to 15 minutes.
3. Remove mushroom caps; place in small sterilized jars.
4. Make marinade. Boil water with peppercorns and bay leaves for 30 minutes. Add salt and sugar. Stir until dissolved. Add the vinegar, bring to boiling.
5. Pour hot marinade over mushroom caps. Close the jars. Keep refrigerated 2 or 3 days before serving.
4 PINTS

Herbed Stuffed Mushrooms

¾ pound mushrooms, chopped
¼ teaspoon salt
⅛ teaspoon freshly ground pepper
1½ teaspoons snipped fresh or ½ teaspoon dried basil leaves
1 tablespoon snipped parsley
½ cup chopped onion
8 large mushrooms, stems removed and sliced into rounds; reserve caps
2 tablespoons brandy
1 tablespoon clarified butter
Parsley for garnish (optional)

1. Process ¾ pound mushrooms, the salt, pepper, basil, parsley, and onions in a food processor or blender until thick and smooth. Layer ½ cup of the mushroom mixture in bottom of a baking dish.
2. Mix sliced mushroom stems, brandy, and butter. Fill reserved mushroom caps with mixture; place filled caps in baking dish. Spoon remaining mushroom mixture around mushrooms.
3. Bake at 400°F 20 minutes. Garnish with parsley.
4 SERVINGS

Oysters Rockefeller

2 tablespoons butter or margarine
2 tablespoons flour
½ teaspoon salt
⅛ teaspoon pepper
1 cup milk (use light cream for richer sauce)
1 egg, well beaten
2 dozen oysters in shells
2 tablespoons sherry
2 tablespoons butter or margarine
1 tablespoon finely chopped
onion
1 pound fresh spinach, cooked, drained, and finely chopped
1 tablespoon minced parsley
½ teaspoon Worcestershire sauce
6 drops Tabasco
¼ teaspoon salt
Few grains ground nutmeg
¼ cup shredded Parmesan cheese

1. For sauce, heat 2 tablespoons butter in a saucepan. Blend in flour, salt, and pepper; heat and stir until bubbly.
2. Gradually add the milk, stirring until smooth. Bring to boiling; cook and stir 1 to 2 minutes longer.
3. Stir the egg into white sauce; set aside.
4. Pour **coarse salt** into a 15 x 10 x 1-inch jelly roll pan to a ¼-inch depth. Open oysters and arrange the oysters, in the shells, on the salt; sprinkle ¼ teaspoon sherry over each.
5. Heat 2 tablespoons butter in a heavy skillet. Add the onion and cook until partially tender. Add the chopped spinach, 2 tablespoons of the white sauce, parsley, Worcestershire sauce, and Tabasco to the skillet along with salt and nutmeg; mix thoroughly. Heat 2 to 3 minutes.
6. Spoon spinach mixture over all of the oysters; spoon remaining white sauce over spinach. Sprinkle each oyster with cheese.
7. Bake at 375°F 15 to 20 minutes, or until tops are lightly browned.
4 TO 6 SERVINGS

Herbed Stuffed Mushrooms

Chili con Queso Dip

1 cup chopped onion
2 cans (4 ounces each) green chilies, chopped and drained
2 large cloves garlic, mashed
2 tablespoons cooking oil
1 pound process sharp Cheddar cheese, cut into chunks
1 teaspoon Worcestershire sauce
¼ teaspoon paprika
¼ teaspoon salt
½ cup tomato juice

1. Sauté onion, green chilies, and garlic in oil in cooking pan of chafing dish over medium heat until onion is tender.
2. Reduce heat to low, and add remaining ingredients, except tomato juice. Cook, stirring constantly, until cheese is melted.
3. Add tomato juice gradually until dip is the desired consistency. Place over hot water to keep warm.
4. Serve with **corn chips.**
3¼ CUPS DIP

Feet in Aspic

1½ pounds pigs' feet or calves' feet
½ pound lean pork or veal shanks
3 carrots, pared
1 onion, cut in quarters
2 stalks celery or 1 small celery root
2 bay leaves
5 peppercorns
3 whole allspice
2 cloves garlic, crushed (optional)
Water
1 tablespoon salt
½ cup chopped fresh parsley
⅓ cup vinegar
Lemon wedges
Parsley sprigs

1. Have the butcher skin and split pigs' feet.
2. Cook pigs feet, pork, vegetables, bay leaves, peppercorns, allspice, garlic, and water to cover in a covered saucepot 2 hours on low heat. Skim off foam and add salt, parsley, and vinegar; cook 2 hours.
3. Strain off the stock; set aside. Take out pigs' feet and carrots. Discard onion and spices. Dice meat and slice carrots.
4. Arrange sliced carrots on bottom of an oiled 2-quart mold. Put meat on top of carrots in mold. Add parsley. Pour stock into mold.
5. Chill until set, at least 4 hours. Skim off fat.
6. Unmold onto platter. Garnish with lemon wedges and parsley sprigs.
8 SERVINGS

Fresh Mushrooms in Sour Cream

1 pound fresh mushrooms, sliced
⅔ cup sliced green onions with tops
2 tablespoons butter or margarine
1 tablespoon fresh lemon juice
1 tablespoon flour
1 cup sour cream
2 tablespoons chopped fresh dill or 1 tablespoon dill weed
¼ teaspoon salt
⅛ teaspoon pepper
Small rounds of rye or Melba toast

1. Sauté mushrooms and onions in butter and lemon juice for 4 minutes. Stir in flour. Cook slowly, stirring 1 minute. Add sour cream, dill, salt, and pepper. Cook and stir 1 minute.
2. Serve warm on toast.
ABOUT 2 CUPS

Flybanes

8 hard-cooked eggs
4 small tomatoes
Salt and pepper
Mayonnaise
Lettuce

1. Peel the eggs. Cut off both ends so eggs will stand evenly. Stand the eggs on a small tray; they will serve for mushroom stems.
2. Cut the tomatoes in halves lengthwise. Remove cores. Sprinkle with salt and pepper. Put each tomato half over an egg as a mushroom cap. Dot the caps with mayonnaise. Garnish the tray with lettuce.
8 FLYBANES

Pickled Watermelon Rind

3 pounds watermelon rind
Salted water (use 3 tablespoons salt for each quart of water)
2 pounds sugar
3 cups distilled white vinegar
6 pieces stick cinnamon (3 inches each)
2 tablespoons whole allspice
2 tablespoons whole cloves
2 tablespoons whole mustard seed

1. Cut rind into 1-inch cubes; trim off outer green skin and bright pink flesh.
2. Soak overnight in enough salted water to cover. Drain.
3. Heat sugar and vinegar to boiling.
4. Tie spices in cheesecloth bag.
5. Add spice bag and melon rind to vinegar mixture. Cook, uncovered, until melon is transparent, about 45 minutes.
6. Discard spice bag.
7. If desired, add a few drops red or green food coloring to the rind.
8. Pack watermelon rind tightly into hot, sterilized jars. Pour boiling syrup over watermelon to within ⅛ inch from top, making sure vinegar solution covers rind. Seal each jar at once.
3 PINTS

Dill Pickles

3 pounds 4-inch cucumbers
2 cloves garlic, crushed
1 cup distilled white vinegar
5 cups water
½ cup salt
3 tablespoons dried dill weed

1. Scrub cucumbers.
2. Place a layer of dill on bottom of a large ceramic bowl or crock. Cover with half the cucumbers. Add another layer of dill, then the remaining cucumbers. Add garlic. Top with a final layer of dill.
3. Mix vinegar, water, and salt. Pour over dill and cucumbers. Add more water, if needed, to cover completely.
4. Cover bowl with a china plate to hold pickles under the brine. Let stand in a cool place 4 days.
5. Seal in sterilized jars.
4 PINTS PICKLES

Crab Meat Newburg Appetizer

2 tablespoons butter or margarine
2 tablespoons flour
½ teaspoon salt
2 cups milk
2 cups (8 ounces) shredded Cheddar cheese
2 cans (7½ ounces each) Alaska King crab, drained and flaked
3 hard-cooked eggs, grated
½ cup finely chopped onion
Dash ground red pepper
1 tablespoon snipped parsley

1. Melt butter in a saucepan. Add flour and salt. Gradually add milk, stirring until thickened and smooth.
2. Add cheese, stirring until blended. Blend in remaining ingredients, except parsley. Put into a 1½-quart casserole.
3. Bake, covered, at 325°F 15 minutes, or until heated through. Sprinkle with parsley. Serve with **Melba toast** or **toast-points.**
25 SERVINGS

Swedish Meat Balls I

1 cup (3 slices) fine, dry
  bread crumbs
1 lb. ground round steak
½ lb. ground pork
½ cup mashed potatoes
1 egg, beaten
1 teaspoon salt

½ teaspoon brown sugar
¼ teaspoon pepper
¼ teaspoon allspice
¼ teaspoon nutmeg
⅛ teaspoon cloves
⅛ teaspoon ginger
3 tablespoons butter

1. Set out a large, heavy skillet having a tight-fitting cover.
2. Set out bread crumbs.
3. Lightly mix together in a large bowl ½ cup of the bread crumbs and steak, pork, potatoes, egg and a mixture of salt, brown sugar, pepper, allspice, nutmeg, cloves, and ginger.
4. Shape mixture into balls about 1 in. in diameter. Roll balls lightly in remaining crumbs.
5. Heat the butter in the skillet over low heat.
6. Add the meat balls and brown on all sides. Shake pan frequently to brown evenly and to keep balls round. Cover and cook about 15 minutes, or until meat balls are thoroughly cooked.
ABOUT 3 DOZEN MEAT BALLS

Eggs with Anchovies

4 hard-cooked eggs
Lettuce leaves
16 anchovy fillets

2 tablespoons mayonnaise
1 dill pickle, sliced
1 tomato, sliced

1. Peel the eggs; cut in halves.
2. Arrange eggs, yolks up, on a dish covered with lettuce leaves.
3. Place 2 anchovy fillets over each egg to form an "X."
4. Garnish with mayonnaise, pickle, and tomato slices.
8 EGG HALVES

Mustard Butter

½ cup butter (at room
  temperature)

½ cup prepared mustard

1. Beat the butter with the mustard until creamy.
2. Spread on toast rounds to serve with **sardines or herring.**
1 CUP

Lombardy Green Tart

1 package (10 ounces) frozen chopped spinach, thawed
2 cups low-fat cottage cheese
1 medium zucchini, minced
2 stalks celery, minced
1 bunch green onions, green part only, minced
2 tablespoons snipped parsley
2 teaspoons snipped fresh or
1 teaspoon dried marjoram leaves
2 teaspoons snipped fresh or 1 teaspoon dried thyme leaves
4 eggs, lightly beaten
½ teaspoon salt
⅛ teaspoon freshly ground pepper
Lettuce leaves

1. Press all liquid from spinach.
2. Combine all ingredients, except lettuce leaves, in a bowl. Mix thoroughly. Spoon mixture into a lightly oiled 9-inch pie plate.
3. Bake at 375°F 45 minutes. Cut into wedges to serve. Serve hot, or refrigerate until chilled and serve on lettuce.
6 SERVINGS

Lombardy Green Salad: Follow recipe for Lombardy Green Tart. Omit eggs, baking, and lettuce. Serve chilled on a bed of **fresh spinach leaves.**

Pork Pâté

1½ pounds ground fresh pork
½ pound salt pork, diced
5 medium onions, quartered
2 pounds sliced pork liver
3 eggs, beaten
1½ teaspoons salt
½ teaspoon black pepper
1 teaspoon marjoram
½ teaspoon allspice
1 tablespoon beef flavor base
½ pound sliced bacon

1. Combine fresh pork and salt pork in a roasting pan. Roast at 325°F 1 hour, stirring occasionally.
2. Remove pork from pan and set aside. Put onions and liver into the pan. Roast 20 minutes, or until liver is tender. Discard liquid in pan or use for soup.
3. Combine pork, liver, and onion. Grind twice.
4. Add eggs, dry seasonings, and beef flavor base to ground mixture; mix well.
5. Line a 9x5x3-inch loaf pan (crosswise) with bacon slices. Pack ground mixture into pan. Place remaining bacon (lengthwise) over top of ground mixture.
6. Bake at 325°F 1 hour. Cool in pan.
7. Remove pâté from pan. Chill.
8. To serve, slice pâté and serve cold with **dill pickles** and **horseradish**.
ABOUT 4 POUNDS

Chicken Fritters Guadeloupe

2 cups minced cooked chicken
3 tablespoons finely chopped parsley
2 tablespoons finely chopped chives
3 tablespoons fresh bread crumbs
1 tablespoon grated onion
1 tablespoon curry powder
Salt to taste
¼ teaspoon cayenne or red pepper
¼ cup Dijon mustard
½ cup dry bread crumbs
1 egg, beaten with 1 teaspoon peanut oil
Oil for frying, heated to 365°F

1. Mix chicken with parsley, chives, fresh bread crumbs, onion, and seasonings. Shape mixture into walnut-size balls, roll in dry bread crumbs, then in beaten egg, and again in bread crumbs. Chill in refrigerator.
2. Just before serving, fry in hot oil until golden brown. Drain on absorbent paper and serve hot.
ABOUT 20 FRITTERS

Cocktail Meatballs

1 large onion, minced
2 tablespoons olive oil
1½ pounds freshly ground round steak (half each of lamb and veal)
3 tablespoons cracker meal
2 cups firm-type bread, crust removed
2 eggs
6 tablespoons chopped
parsley
2 teaspoons oregano, crushed
1½ teaspoons mint
2 tablespoons vinegar
Salt and pepper to taste
Flour
Olive or corn oil for deep frying heated to 365°F

1. Brown half of onion in 2 tablespoons oil in a small frying pan. Mix with the uncooked onion and add to meat in a large bowl. Add the remaining ingredients except flour and oil. Toss lightly with two forks to mix thoroughly.
2. Dust hands with flour. Roll a small amount of meat at a time between palms, shaping into a ball.
3. To heated fat in deep fryer, add the meatballs a layer at a time. Fry until browned on all sides (about 12 minutes). Serve hot.
30 to 40 MEATBALLS

Cocktail Meatballs

Fish Fondue

12 frozen fish sticks
1 pound mussels (shelled and cooked)
½ pound shrimp (cleaned and cooked)
½ pound lobster meat (cleaned and cooked)
1 quart vegetable (or peanut) oil

Dill mustard sauce
¼ cup beef broth
3 tablespoons dry mustard
2 tablespoons mayonnaise
1 teaspoon dill

Tartar Sauce
¼ cup mayonnaise
½ teaspoon dry mustard
2 tablespoons pickle relish

Chili Sauce
¼ cup ketchup
2 tablespoons chili sauce

Batter
1 cup all-purpose flour
¼ teaspoon salt

Dip
6 eggs, beaten
½ cup milk

1. Heat oil in fondue pot to 375°F.
2. Spear bite-sized fish and dip fish first into egg-milk mixture, then roll in flour batter.
3. Dip fish carefully into hot oil and cook until golden brown, about 30 seconds to 1 minute.
4. Remove from fondue fork, dip in sauce and enjoy.
6 SERVINGS

Ham and Egg Rolls

6 hard-cooked eggs
12 thin slices cooked ham
Lettuce leaves
Mayonnaise
Pickles

1. Peel the eggs; cut in halves.
2. Roll each half of egg in a slice of ham. Secure with wooden pick.
3. Arrange lettuce leaves around ham and egg rolls on serving plate. Decorate with mayonnaise and garnish with pickles.
12 ROLLS

Feta Cheese Triangles

1 pound feta cheese, crumbled
2 egg yolks
1 whole egg
3 tablespoons chopped
parsley
Dash finely ground pepper
¾ pound butter, melted and kept warm
1 pound filo

1. Mash feta cheese with a fork. Add egg yolks, egg, parsley, and pepper.
2. Melt butter in a saucepan. Keep warm, but do not allow to brown.
3. Lay a sheet of filo on a large cutting board. Brush with melted butter. Cut into strips about 1½ to 2 inches wide. Place ½ teaspoon of the cheese mixture on each strip about 1 inch from base. Fold to form a triangle. Continue until all cheese mixture and filo have been used.
4. Place triangles, side by side, in a shallow roasting pan or baking sheet.*
5. Bake at 350°F about 20 minutes, or until golden brown. Serve at once.
ABOUT 100 PIECES

Note: Feta Cheese Triangles freeze well. Before serving, remove from freezer and let stand 15 to 20 minutes. Bake at 325°F until golden brown.

*Pan must have four joined sides; otherwise butter will fall to bottom of the oven and burn.

Feta Cheese Triangles

Fish Fondue

1   **Gourmet Gouda Spread**
2   **Peekaboo Appetizers**
3   **Cheddar-Sausage Rolls**
4   **Avocado Rye Rounds**
5   **Sailor's Borsch**
6   **Rémoulade with Scallops**

Gourmet Gouda Spread

1 round baby Gouda cheese
(8 to 10 ounces) at room
temperature
3 tablespoons blue cheese
2 tablespoons dry white

wine
2 tablespoons butter
1 teaspoon prepared mustard
¼ teaspoon Worcestershire
sauce

1. Cut top off Gouda cheese through red wax. Scoop out cheese, leaving a ¼-inch shell. Refrigerate shell.
2. Combine Gouda and blue cheese in a small bowl; mix in wine, butter, mustard, and Worcestershire sauce. Fill shell with cheese mixture. Chill several hours or overnight.
3. Before serving, bring to room temperature. Accompany with crackers or party rye bread slices.
ABOUT 1 CUP CHEESE SPREAD

Peekaboo Appetizers

1 can (7¾ ounces) salmon,
drained and flaked
⅓ cup sour cream
⅓ cup finely chopped green
pepper
2 tablespoons finely chopped

onion
¼ teaspoon dill weed
¼ teaspoon salt
3 sticks pie crust mix
½ cup sour cream
Toasted sesame seed

1. Combine salmon, ⅓ cup sour cream, green pepper, onion, dill weed, and salt in a bowl.
2. Meanwhile, prepare pastry according to package directions. Form into 3 balls; roll each into a 12x6-inch rectangle and cut into 18 squares. Place about 1 teaspoon filling in center of each square; bring corners together over filling and press pastry edges together. Place on a buttered baking sheet.
3. Bake at 450°F 12 minutes, or until lightly browned.
4. To serve, spoon about ½ teaspoon sour cream on each appetizer and top with sesame seed. Serve hot or cold.
54 APPETIZERS

Cheddar-Sausage Rolls

1 cup (4 ounces) shredded
Cheddar cheese, at room
temperature
3 tablespoons sour cream

6 slices summer sausage,
about 4½ inches in
diameter

1. Combine cheese and sour cream in a small bowl.
2. Remove casings from sausage. Spread a scant 2 tablespoons cheese mixture on each slice of sausage. Place one slice of sausage on top of another, overlapping one half of the way. Roll sausage firmly and wrap. Repeat twice to form 3 rolls. Chill.
3. To serve, cut into ½-inch slices.
ABOUT 1½ DOZEN APPETIZERS

Avocado Rye Rounds

½ cup cottage cheese
½ avocado, peeled and cut
in pieces
1 tablespoon grated fresh
onion
2 teaspoons fresh lemon
juice
½ teaspoon Worcestershire

sauce
3 drops Tabasco
¾ cup chopped cooked
chicken
¼ cup chopped celery
Party rye bread slices,
toasted and buttered
Pimento

1. Put cottage cheese and avocado into an electric blender or a bowl and blend or beat until fairly smooth. Blend in onion, lemon juice, Worcestershire sauce, and Tabasco. Stir in chicken and celery. Cover; chill several hours or overnight.
2. To serve, spread about 1 tablespoon avocado mixture on each rye toast slice. Garnish with pimento.
ABOUT 2 DOZEN APPETIZERS

Sailor's Borsch

1 can (46 ounces) tomato
juice
1 tablespoon beef stock base
1 teaspoon salt
1 can or jar (16 ounces)
sliced beets

⅓ cup coarsely chopped
parsley
2 tablespoons red wine
vinegar
1 carton (8 ounces) plain
yogurt

1. Heat 1 cup tomato juice, beef stock base, and salt in a saucepan. Stir until beef stock base and salt are dissolved.
2. Combine 1 cup tomato juice with beets and liquid, parsley, and vinegar in an electric blender or bowl; blend or beat until beets are finely chopped. Combine both mixtures with remaining tomato juice. Chill.
3. Top each serving with a dollop of yogurt.
ABOUT 2 QUARTS SOUP

Note: Borsch may be served hot. Yogurt may be stirred in just before serving, if desired.

Rémoulade with Scallops

1 cup sour cream
1½ teaspoons prepared
mustard
1½ teaspoons chopped
capers
1½ teaspoons parsley flakes
1 teaspoon snipped chives

1 small clove garlic, crushed
in a garlic press
Butter
1 package (12 ounces) frozen
scallops, thawed and
drained

1. Turn sour cream into a bowl. Gently blend in mustard, capers, parsley flakes, chives, and garlic. Cover and chill several hours or overnight.
2. Heat desired amount of butter in a skillet, add scallops, and sauté about 5 minutes, or until lightly browned. Serve on wooden picks with the sauce.
ABOUT 1 CUP SAUCE

Daisy Canapés

8 rounds bread
⅓ cup softened butter
1½ ounces anchovy paste
4 hard-cooked eggs

1. Spread untoasted rounds of bread with butter and then with anchovy paste.
2. Cut narrow strips out of hard-cooked egg whites.
3. Arrange in petal fashion on paste and place sieved hard-cooked egg yolk in center.
MAKES 8 CANAPÉS

Half-and-Half Canapés

½ cup flaked cooked salmon
2 tablespoons mayonnaise
1½ tablespoons lemon juice
¼ teaspoon salt
Dash pepper
8 toast rounds
3 tablespoons softened butter
½ cup mashed avocado
8 strips pimiento

1. Mix salmon, mayonnaise, ½ tablespoon lemon juice, salt and pepper.
2. Spread toast rounds with softened butter.
3. Spread half of each round with salmon mixture, the other half with avocado mixed with remaining lemon juice.
4. Mark the division with a pimiento strip.
MAKES 8 CANAPÉS

Olive Pinwheels

6 tablespoons ground boiled ham
2 tablespoons mayonnaise
1 teaspoon horseradish
1 loaf sandwich bread
4 tablespoons butter
6 stuffed olives

1. Combine ham, mayonnaise and horseradish.
2. Remove all crusts from bread.
3. Cut a ¼-inch lengthwise slice from bread.
4. Spread with softened butter and with ham mixture.
5. Place olives in a line crosswise at one end of the bread; roll bread starting at the end of slice.
6. Wrap in plastic wrap or waxed paper; chill for several hours.
7. When ready to serve, cut crosswise into slices any thickness desired.
MAKES 6 TO 8 PINWHEELS

Curried Cheese Canapés

½ lb. sharp Cheddar cheese
2 tablespoons butter
½ teaspoon curry powder
1 teaspoon grated onion
Madeira wine
Crisp crackers

1. Grind or grate the cheese and blend with softened butter, curry powder, onion and enough wine to make of spreading consistency.
2. Spread on crackers or Melba toast rounds and top each with a cocktail onion.
MAKES 30 CANAPÉS

Shrimp Canapés

8 cooked jumbo shrimp split from head to tail
½ cup French dressing
16 toast rounds
4 tablespoons lemon mayonnaise
1½ ounces caviar
Parsley

1. Marinate shrimp in French dressing for 1 hour.
2. Spread toast rounds with lemon mayonnaise.
3. Place shrimp, flat side down, on toast.
4. Fill curve formed by shrimp with caviar.
5. Garnish with tiny sprig of parsley at the head of shrimp.
SERVES 8

Tomato-and-Egg Canapés

8 rounds bread
2 tablespoons mayonnaise
Sliced tomatoes
Hard-cooked eggs, sliced
Salt
4 stuffed green olives, sliced

1. Toast rounds of bread on one side and spread the untoasted side with mayonnaise.
2. Add thin slices of tomato, then slices of hard-cooked egg.
3. Sprinkle very lightly with salt and garnish with a slice or two of stuffed olives.
MAKES 8 CANAPÉS

Sardine Canapés

1 can (3¾ oz.) sardines
2 tablespoons mayonnaise
1 teaspoon catchup
1 teaspoon prepared horseradish
¼ teaspoon salt
¼ teaspoon paprika
Dash Worcestershire sauce
Crackers, Melba toast or toast rounds

1. Drain and mash sardines.
2. Combine with other ingredients except crackers and mix to a spreading consistency.
3. Spoon 1 teaspoon of mixture onto each cracker.
MAKES ABOUT 36

Party Spread

1 pkg. (8 oz.) cream cheese
¼ cup butter, softened
1 teaspoon paprika
¼ teaspoon dry mustard
½ teaspoon onion salt
1½ teaspoons caraway seeds
2 teaspoons capers, drained
1 teaspoon prepared mustard
2 teaspoons minced onion

1. Blend cream cheese and butter together.
2. Blend in remaining ingredients and chill several hours to blend flavors.
3. Spread on thinly sliced pumpernickel or rye bread or crackers.
MAKES ABOUT 1⅓ CUPS

Hot Crab Spread

1 package (8 ounces) cream cheese, softened
1 tablespoon milk
2 teaspoons Worcestershire sauce
1 can (7½ ounces) Alaska King crab, drained and flaked, or 1 package (6 ounces) frozen crab meat, thawed, drained, and flaked
2 tablespoons chopped green onion
2 tablespoons toasted slivered almonds

1. Combine cream cheese, milk, Worcestershire sauce, crab, and green onion. Place in small individual casseroles. Sprinkle with almonds.
2. Bake, uncovered, at 350°F 15 minutes. Serve with **assorted crackers.**
2 CUPS

Tangy Cheese Dip

4 ounces Muenster cheese or other semisoft cheese, finely shredded (1 cup)
3 ounces blue cheese, crumbled

1 package (3 ounces) cream cheese, softened
⅛ teaspoon garlic powder
¾ cup beer (about)

1. After shredding, let Muenster cheese stand at room temperature at least 1 hour.
2. Using an electric blender or food processor, blend cheeses and garlic. Gradually add enough beer to make a mixture of dipping consistency.
3. Serve at room temperature with crackers for dipping.
ABOUT 2 CUPS

Fabulous Cheese Mousse

¼ cup cold water
1 tablespoon unflavored gelatin
3 pkgs. (1¼ oz. each) Roquefort cheese
2 pkgs. (1⅓ oz. each) Camembert cheese

1 egg yolk, slightly beaten
1 tablespoon sherry
1 teaspoon Worcestershire sauce
1 egg white
½ cup heavy cream, whipped

1. Soften gelatin in the cold water; dissolve completely over low heat.
2. Force the cheeses through a fine sieve, then blend in the egg yolk, sherry and Worcestershire sauce.
3. Beat until smooth.
4. Add dissolved gelatin to cheese mixture and beat until smooth. (Cheeses and other ingredients may be mixed in electric blender if desired.)
5. Beat egg white until rounded peaks are formed; fold into cheese mixture along with the whipped cream.
6. Turn into a 1-pint fancy mold which has been rinsed with cold water.
7. Chill until firm and unmold on chilled serving plate.
8. Serve with crackers.
MAKES 1-PINT MOLD

Mosaic Sandwiches

16 slices white bread
16 slices brown bread

Any desired canape spread or canape butter

1. Slice bread ¼ inch thick.
2. Cut into fancy shapes: hearts, diamonds, spades or clubs, and spread half of them with desired filling.
3. With a smaller cutter cut out the center of remaining pieces in the same shape as the original. For example, if the original shape was a heart, cut a heart shape out of center.
4. Insert white heart into brown bread and brown heart into white bread.
5. Place each on corresponding shape spread with filling.
MAKES 16 SANDWICHES

Stuffed Grape Leaves

1 jar (32 ounces) grapevine leaves
1 quart water
½ cup olive oil
3 medium onions, finely chopped
1½ cups long-grain rice
Juice of 2 lemons
2 tablespoons pine nuts

1 tablespoon dried black currants
2 teaspoons dill
2 teaspoons mint
¼ cup minced parsley
Salt and pepper to taste
Water (about 1 cup)
Olive oil (about 1 cup)

1. To prepare grapevine leaves, rinse leaves thoroughly in cold running water to remove brine.
2. Bring 1 quart water to a boil. Add leaves and parboil 3 minutes. Drain.
3. Select 4 or 5 heavy leaves and line bottom of a medium-size Dutch oven. Set aside.
4. To prepare filling, heat ½ cup olive oil in a medium skillet. Add onion and cook until translucent. Remove with a slotted spoon.
5. In a saucepan, parboil rice in 1 cup water until liquid is absorbed.
6. Combine rice, onion, lemon juice, pine nuts, currants, dill, mint, and parsley. Season with salt and pepper. Cool.
7. To fill grapevine leaves, place a leaf on a working surface, rough side up with stem pointing toward you. Place about a teaspoon of the rice mixture at the base of the leaf. Lift the bottom sides of the leaf up onto the filling. Fold both the right and left sides of the leaf over the filling. Roll up, tucking the edges in.
8. Place the stuffed grape leaves side by side in the Dutch oven to cover the bottom. Put a second layer on top of the first one. Continue to do this until all the stuffed leaves have been put in.
9. Add water and olive oil to cover. Place an inverted plate on the grape leaves. Bring to boiling. Cover Dutch oven, lower heat, and simmer 1 hour. Taste a stuffed grape leaf to see if rice is tender. If necessary, continue cooking.
10. Cool in liquid. Remove carefully with a spoon. Chill in refrigerator 24 hours before serving. Serve cold.
ABOUT 50 STUFFED GRAPE LEAVES

Note: Stuffed Grape Leaves will keep 10 days in the refrigerator.

Crusty Roll Tempters

6 crusty rolls
1 cup chopped cooked ham
1 cup finely shredded
  cabbage
2 hard-cooked eggs, chopped
¼ cup chopped green
  pepper
¼ cup pimiento strips
½ cup chopped salted
  peanuts
2 tablespoons chopped
  pickled onion
¼ cup mayonnaise
¾ teaspoon salt
¼ teaspoon pepper

1. Cut rolls lengthwise through center; scoop out centers to within ¼ inch of crust.
2. Butter inside if desired.
3. Mix remaining ingredients together.
4. Fill the lower halves of rolls generously with ham mixture.
5. Place scooped-out upper section of rolls over filling; cut into halves.
SERVES 6

Cream Cheese Cone Sandwiches

9 slices bread
3 tablespoons butter,
  softened
1 pkg. (8 oz.) cream cheese
2 teaspoons cherry jelly
Red food coloring
2 teaspoons orange
  marmalade
Yellow food coloring
1 teaspoon water
Green food coloring

1. Spread bread slices with butter; trim off crusts.
2. Roll to form cones and fasten with wooden picks.
3. Place on baking sheet and toast in 400°F. oven about 10 minutes.
4. Remove wooden picks.
5. Divide cream cheese into 3 parts.
6. To one part, add cherry jelly and red coloring to give a light pink shade.
7. To second part, add marmalade and enough yellow coloring to give an orange-yellow shade.
8. To third part, add water and green coloring.
9. Using a pastry tube, swirl each color into 3 of the cones.
SERVES 9

Chicken-Mushroom Sandwiches

1 cup minced cooked
  chicken
½ cup (4-oz. can)
  mushrooms, chopped
¼ cup salted almonds,
  chopped
3 tablespoons salad dressing
2 tablespoons chopped green
  olives
¼ teaspoon salt
⅛ teaspoon paprika
6 frankfurter buns, cut in
  halves

1. Combine the filling ingredients and blend well.
2. Spread between halves of buns.
SERVES 6

Crab Meat in Rolls

8 finger rolls
1½ cups flaked crab meat
1½ cups diced celery
2 hard-cooked eggs, chopped
½ teaspoon salt
¼ teaspoon pepper
Dash Tabasco sauce
3 tablespoons lemon juice
½ cup salad dressing

1. Make a lengthwise cut in center of top of each roll, spread apart and remove soft part.
2. Mix crabmeat, celery, eggs, salt, pepper, Tabasco sauce, lemon juice and salad dressing together and fill center of rolls.
3. Place rolls on crisp lettuce to serve.
SERVES 8

Creamy Shrimp Dip

1 package (8 ounces) cream
  cheese, softened
1 can (10¾ ounces) con-
  densed cream of shrimp
  soup
2 tablespoons chopped green
onion
1 teaspoon lemon juice
¼ teaspoon curry powder
Dash garlic powder
4 drops Tabasco
Raw vegetables

1. Combine cream cheese, soup, green onion, lemon juice, curry powder, garlic powder, and Tabasco with a beater just until blended; do not overbeat. Chill.
2. Serve as a dip with raw vegetable pieces.
ABOUT 2½ CUPS DIP

Creamy
Shrimp
Dip

Avocado Sandwiches on Sour Dough

2 avocados, thinly sliced and salted
¼ cup butter (½ stick), softened
½ teaspoon oregano leaves
¼ teaspoon each chervil,

parsley flakes, and grated lemon peel
Dash onion powder
8 slices sour dough or Italian bread, diagonally cut

1. Prepare avocado slices.
2. Cream butter with seasonings. Spread thinly over bread.
3. Top with avocado slices. Serve with white wine.

8 SERVINGS

Canapé Suggestions

Place sliced smoked salmon or turkey on toast rounds, garnish with white grapes and mayonnaise.

Spread toast rounds with Egg Butter. Cover with sliced smoked ham. Garnish with sliced stuffed olives.

Place thinly sliced tongue on toast rounds. Spread with tomato purée and garnish with olive slice.

Place rings of hard-cooked egg whites on toast rounds. Fill centers of rings with caviar, anchovy rolls, or sliced stuffed olives. Garnish with sieved hard-cooked egg yolks.

Mix 3 ounces caviar with 4 teaspoons minced onion. Spread on toast rounds and garnish with cream cheese or strips of pimiento.

Cook 8 cleaned cooked shrimp in 2 tablespoons butter. Add ¼ teaspoon curry powder, ⅛ teaspoon dry mustard, 1 teaspoon sherry wine. Serve hot on small bread croustades or packaged appetizer shells.

Spread toast fingers with prepared mustard and top with whole sardines marinated in lemon juice.

Spread toast with butter, then with cream cheese. Garnish with strips of pimiento or sprinkle with sieved pimiento.

Spread crackers with mayonnaise, cover with thin slices of cucumber and garnish with rosettes of snappy cheese spread and sprigs of parsley.

Spread bread fingers with cream cheese or with equal parts of Roquefort and cream cheese. Top with walnut meats.

Spread toast triangles with Egg Butter, then with pickled beets pressed through ricer. Sprinkle with a few drops of French dressing and garnish with sieved egg yolks.

Spread rounds of whole-wheat bread with Mustard Butter. Top with slice of tomato and sprinkle with salt. Or spread with Chive Butter and top tomato with slice of cucumber and a dash of paprika.

Make tomato aspic, adding minced cucumber and minced celery. Chill in ½-inch layer and cut into rounds. Serve on crackers.

Spread toast generously with thick mayonnaise. Dip into minced watercress and sprinkle with salt. Garnish with minced hard-cooked egg white.

Spread toast squares with mixture of ¼ cup each of peanut butter and raspberry jam and 2 tablespoons butter.

Spread toast with mixture of strawberry jam and nut meats.

☞ Chili Pinwheels

1 can (about 15½ ounces) kidney beans
½ teaspoon chili powder
½ pound ground beef
⅓ cup chopped onion
¼ cup chopped green
pepper
2 tablespoons ketchup
2 dashes Tabasco
Salt and pepper
8 dinner crepes (see below)

1. Drain and mash beans. Blend in chili powder. Set aside.
2. Sauté beef with onion and green pepper. When onion and green pepper are tender, remove from heat and drain off any liquid. Stir ketchup, Tabasco, and bean mixture into drained meat. Season with salt and pepper to taste.
3. For bite-size snacks or hors d'oeuvres, assemble by jelly-roll method (below).
4. Bake at 375°F 15 minutes. Cool 5 minutes and slice.
8 ROLLS

Chili Turnovers: Follow recipe for Chili Pinwheels for filling. Assemble by turnover method (below). Bake at 375°F 15 minutes; serve hot. These can be picked up and eaten like a sandwich.

Jelly-Roll Method: Spread crêpe with filling according to recipe. Lift edge and fold under. Roll up firmly.

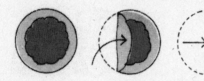

Turnover Method: Using a slotted spoon, place filling on one half of the crêpe leaving a ¼- to ½-inch border. Moisten the back of a spoon with sauce from the filling. Run moistened spoon along rim of crêpe. Fold crêpe in half and press along rim to seal.

☞ Dinner Crêpes

1 cup all-purpose flour
⅛ teaspoon salt
3 eggs
1½ cups milk
2 tablespoons melted butter or oil

1. Sift flour and salt. Add eggs, one at a time, beating thoroughly. Gradually add milk, mixing until blended. Add melted butter or oil and beat until smooth. (Or mix in an electric blender until smooth.)
2. Let batter stand for 1 hour before cooking crêpes.
ABOUT 18 CRÊPES

☞ Fried Cheese Roll

6 (1-ounce) wedges Gruyère cheese
6 dinner crêpes (see below)
2 eggs, beaten
⅓ cup fine dry bread crumbs, seasoned or plain
Oil for frying heated to 375°F

1. Coarsely shred 1 wedge of cheese over 1 crêpe to within 1 inch of crêpe edges. Fold two opposite sides of crêpe over 1 inch. Continue folding as directed in egg-roll method (below). Dip rolls into eggs. Coat thoroughly with bread crumbs.
2. Fry in 375°F oil until golden brown (about 5 minutes). Cool slightly. Cut into 1-inch pieces and serve.
6 CHEESE ROLLS

Egg-Roll Method: Place filling in a line down the center of the crêpe, leaving enough space at either end of the filling to fold crêpe up and over the filling. Lift edge and tuck around and under filling. Roll up firmly.

☞ Chili-Nut Log

8 ounces process sharp Cheddar cheese spread (at room temperature)
2 tablespoons butter or margarine (at room temperature)
½ teaspoon minced onion
¼ teaspoon minced garlic
1 tablespoon chili powder
Dash cayenne pepper
2 tablespoons lemon juice
⅓ cup finely chopped walnuts or pecans
3 dinner crêpes (opposite)
Melted butter or margarine
2 tablespoons chopped parsley

1. Combine cheese, 2 tablespoons butter, onion, garlic, chili powder, cayenne, lemon juice, and nuts. Mix until well blended. Shape into 3 or 4 logs. (If mixture is too soft to work with, refrigerate for 10 to 15 minutes.)
2. Place log at one end of crêpe and roll up. Brush outside of crêpe with melted butter and roll in parsley. Refrigerate 10 minutes, slice, and serve with picks.
3. Store in refrigerator up to 1 week, or store in freezer.
3 LOGS

Cocktail Frank Wrap-Ups

2 dinner crêpes (see page 36) 1 package (5½ ounces)
1 teaspoon prepared mustard   cocktail frankfurters

1. Spread each crêpe on one side with ½ teaspoon mustard. Cut each crêpe in 8 wedges. Starting from wide edge, roll up a frankfurter in each wedge. Place seam side down in a shallow baking pan.
2. Bake at 375°F 10 minutes. Spear with wooden picks and serve with **bottled cocktail sauce.**
16 APPETIZERS

1 Chili Pinwheels
2 Chili Turnovers
3 Fried Cheese Roll
4 Chili-Nut Log
5 Cocktail Frank Wrap-Ups

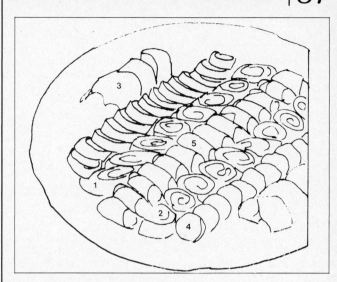

Crêpe Appetizer Platter

Sardine Spread

½ cup butter or margarine, softened
1 can (3½ oz.) sardines

1 tablespoon lemon juice
⅛ teaspoon paprika

1. Cream the softened butter.
2. Remove skins from sardines and mash sardines with lemon juice and paprika.
3. Beat into the butter.
MAKES 1 CUP

Nippy Beef Spread

1 package (3 ounces) vacuum-packed wafer-sliced beef, finely chopped
1 package (8 ounces) cream cheese (at room

temperature)
2 tablespoons prepared horseradish
1 teaspoon Worcestershire sauce

Combine ingredients for spread. Serve with wafer crêpes.
1½ CUPS SPREAD

Note: Spread can be stored in a covered container in the refrigerator for 1 week, or it can be frozen.

Wafer Crêpes

2½ cups dinner crêpe batter (page 36)
Cooking oil

1. Heat a skillet or griddle over medium heat, and brush with oil.
2. Pour ½ tablespoon batter in skillet, but do not swirl the pan. Pour 3 or 4 more crêpes, turn when brown, and brown on other side. Place crêpes on ungreased baking sheet.
3. Bake at 350°F about 15 minutes, turning over halfway through baking. Remove from baking sheet and serve with dips, spreads, or cheese.
ABOUT 8 DOZEN WAFERS

Yule Sandwich Log

Prepare sandwich fillings: – Deviled ham – peanut butter; egg-bacon; avocado-pineapple; and cheese-shrimp. Prepare cranberry-cheese frosting. Remove crusts from unsliced sandwich loaf and cut lengthwise into 5 slices. Butter 4 slices of bread and spread each with one of the 4 fillings, reserving the cranberry-cheese mixture for top and sides of loaf. Stack the 4 slices and top with the remaining slice of bread. Press loaf firmly together and wrap in plastic wrap. Chill in refrigerator 1 hour. Frost loaf with cranberry-cheese mixture, making lengthwise ridges with a spatula. Garnish platter with cinnamon pear halves placed on lettuce leaves, using maraschino cherries for "bell clappers."

Deviled Ham – Peanut Butter Filling: Combine **⅓ cup peanut butter** with **1 can (3 oz.) deviled ham**, **¼ cup salad dressing** and 3 tablespoons chopped dill pickle.
MAKES ¾ CUP

Egg-Bacon Filling: Combine **2 hard-cooked eggs,** chopped, **⅓ cup crumbled cooked bacon** and **3 tablespoons salad dressing.**
MAKES ¾ CUP

Avocado-Pineapple Filling: Combine **⅓ cup mashed avocado, 2 tablespoons drained, crushed pineapple, 1 teaspoon lemon juice, 1 tablespoon salad dressing** and **dash salt.**
MAKES ½ CUP

Cheese-Shrimp Filling: Combine **½ cup pimiento cream cheese, ½ teaspoon chili sauce, ⅓ cup finely chopped shrimp** and **½ teaspoon lemon juice.**
MAKES ⅔ CUP

Cranberry-Cheese Frosting: Combine **3 packages (3 oz. each) cream cheese** and **⅓ cup strained cranberry sauce.** Beat with electric beater until smooth and fluffy.
MAKES 1¾ CUP

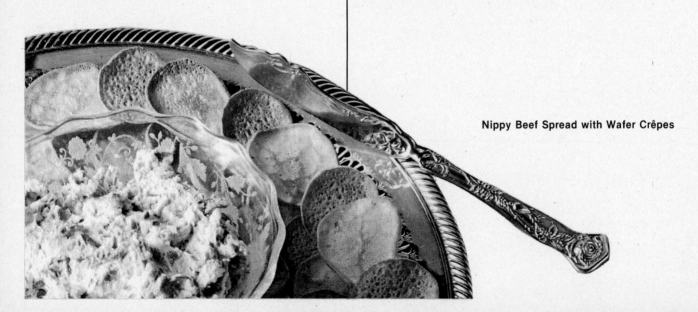

Nippy Beef Spread with Wafer Crêpes

Canapé Butters

All these butters are prepared as follows: Cream butter thoroughly. Grind fish, meat, or vegetables to a paste and combine with the seasoning and butter. If mixture is not entirely smooth, rub through a sieve. Spread on toast rounds and garnish appropriately or use as a base for sandwich fillings.

Shrimp Butter

1 cup butter
1 cup minced cooked shrimp
¼ teaspoon salt
Dash paprika
1 tablespoon lemon juice

Chive Butter

½ cup butter
¼ cup chives
4 drops Worcestershire sauce

Anchovy Butter

1 cup butter
½ cup minced anchovies or
  4 tablespoons anchovy
  paste
2 teaspoons lemon juice
4 drops onion juice
Variations:
Substitute herring, bloaters, crawfish, lobster, smoked salmon, whitefish or sardines for the anchovies.

Horseradish Butter

½ cup butter
¼ cup grated horseradish

Mustard Butter

½ cup butter
¼ cup prepared mustard

Ham Butter

½ cup butter
¼ pound cooked ham
2 hard-cooked eggs, chopped
Dash pepper

Egg Butter

½ cup butter
4 hard-cooked egg yolks
Few grains cayenne
6 drops Worcestershire sauce

Cheese Butter

½ cup butter
¼ cup grated Parmesan
  cheese or 1½ ounces
Roquefort or ½ cup snappy
  cheese spread

Pimiento Butter

½ cup butter
¼ cup mashed pimiento
2 teaspoons India relish,
  drained

Dried Beef Butter

½ cup butter
3-4 ounces dried beef
Few drops Tabasco sauce

Olive Butter

¼ cup butter
2 tablespoons chopped
olives
¼ teaspoon lemon juice

Chili Butter

¼ cup butter
2 tablespoons chili sauce,
drained

Guacamole

1 small clove garlic
2 large ripe avocados, peeled
2 tablespoons lemon juice
1 teaspoon chili powder
  (optional)
Salt to taste

1. Using **steel blade,** mince garlic. Add avocado and remaining ingredients and process to desired consistency. (Remember to use quick on/off motions if a coarse, chunky consistency is desired.)
2. Serve as a dip with tortilla chips, on lettuce as a salad, or as a filling for tacos.
ABOUT 2 CUPS DIP

Note: If not served immediately, refrigerate in a covered bowl with avocado pits immersed in guacamole. This will help prevent the avocado from darkening on standing.

Hawaiian Sandwiches

1 cup minced, cooked
  chicken
½ cup moist, shredded
  coconut
¼ cup salad dressing
2 tablespoons finely chopped
celery
½ teaspoon lemon juice
½ teaspoon salt
6 frankfurter buns, cut in
  halves

1. Combine the filling ingredients and blend well.
2. Spread between halves of buns.
SERVES 6

Liver-Bologna Spread

¼ pound liverwurst sausage,
  mashed
¼ pound bologna, chopped
  fine
1 hard-cooked egg, chopped
fine
1 sweet pickle, chopped fine
¼ teaspoon dry mustard
1 tablespoon lemon juice
Mayonnaise to moisten

Combine all ingredients in a bowl with enough mayonnaise to moisten to spreading consistency.
MAKES 1½ CUPS

Blue Cheese in a Melon

½ pound blue cheese   ¼ cup heavy cream
1 pkg. (8 oz.) cream cheese   1 ripe cantaloupe

1. Thoroughly blend the blue and cream cheese together; beat in the cream until fluffy.
2. Using a melon-ball cutter, scoop melon balls from ripe cantaloupe.
3. Spoon cheese dip into cantaloupe shell.
4. Serve with assorted crackers and melon balls on cocktail picks.

Tuna in a Cucumber

1 can (7 oz.) tuna   ½ teaspoon salt
1 pkg. (3 oz.) cream cheese   ¼ teaspoon pepper
1 tablespoon mayonnaise   1 tablespoon pickle relish
1 tablespoon lemon juice   3 small cucumbers

1. Thoroughly blend first 7 ingredients together. Chill.
2. Core the cucumbers to remove centers.
3. Stuff tuna mixture into cavities and chill.
4. Slice and serve on assorted crackers.

Jellied Mélange

2 tablespoons unflavored   chicken
   gelatin   ½ cup chopped cooked ham
½ cup cold water   ½ cup chopped celery
3¾ cups hot chicken broth   1 pimiento, minced
2 tablespoons onion juice   Mayonnaise
1 cup chopped cooked   Parsley

1. Soften gelatin in cold water for 5 minutes and dissolve in hot broth.
2. Add onion juice.
3. Cool; when mixture begins to thicken, stir in chicken, ham, celery and pimiento and pour into small molds. Chill.
4. Serve on lettuce garnished with mayonnaise and parsley.
SERVES 8

Shrimp Melange: Omit ham, use tomato juice instead of chicken broth and chopped, cleaned cooked shrimp instead of chicken.

Stuffed Celery Rings

1 medium bunch celery   French dressing
Tangy cheese spread

1. Cut the top from bunch celery.
2. Wash and dry each stalk.
3. Fill smallest stalks with cheese spread, then fill next smallest stalks and press firmly against first stalks.
4. Continue filling and pressing stalks together until all the celery is formed into a bunch. Tie firmly with string; chill.
5. Slice crosswise into thin slices and serve on lettuce or watercress. Sprinkle with French dressing.
SERVES 8

Note: If desired, use Roquefort spread instead of tangy cheese spread.

Tomato Sandwich Hors d'Oeuvres

8 tablespoons deviled ham   4 large tomatoes
3 tablespoons mayonnaise   Parsley
½ teaspoon minced onion

1. Combine the ham, mayonnaise and onion.
2. Rinse, dry and cut each tomato into four ¼-inch crosswise slices.
3. Spread deviled ham mixture on half the tomato slices and top each with a second tomato slice to make sandwiches.
4. Garnish with mayonnaise and a sprig of parsley and serve as a first course.
SERVES 8

Banana Hors d'Oeuvres

2 large, firm, ripe bananas   1 pkg. (3 oz.) cream cheese
½ cup lemon juice   ⅓ cup finely chopped nuts

1. Peel bananas; cut crosswise into 1-inch pieces.
2. Marinate in lemon juice 1 hour, turning pieces occasionally.
3. Drain; spread pieces with cream cheese and roll in nuts.
MAKES 8 HORS D'OEUVRES

SAUCES, STOCKS &
DRESSINGS

Four Thieves Sauce

2 tablespoons butter
2 tablespoons flour
1½ cups chicken broth
Salt and freshly ground pepper to taste
1 egg yolk
3 tablespoons Four Thieves Vinegar (below)
1 egg white, beaten stiff but not dry

1. Melt butter in a saucepan over medium heat. Add flour and, stirring constantly with a whisk, make a lightly browned roux. Continue to stir rapidly with a whisk while gradually adding broth. When all the broth is added, boil 4 minutes to reduce the liquid. Season with salt and pepper.
2. Remove from heat and beat a small amount of hot sauce into egg yolk; return mixture to saucepan. Cool thoroughly.
3. Blend sauce into vinegar. Just before serving, fold in beaten egg white.
4. Serve sauce with cold fish or poultry.

Four Thieves Vinegar

Several sprigs each of narrow-leaved basil, rosemary, sage, and marjoram
10 cloves
1 cinnamon stick
10 peppercorns, cracked
2 garlic cloves
1 bay leaf
Thyme sprig
2 tablespoons salt
8 dried Italian pepper pods
3½ cups wine vinegar
2 garlic cloves

1. Stem the basil, rosemary, sage, and marjoram and put into a 1-quart jar along with the spices, 2 garlic cloves, bay leaf, thyme, salt, and pepper pods. Pour vinegar into jar; cover. Allow to stand 1 month in a sunny window, then strain through wet cheesecloth.
2. Put a garlic clove into each of 2 decorative 1-pint bottles; cover tightly.

Court Bouillon for Fish and Shellfish

1 onion
1 leek
1 carrot
3 celery stalks
5 parsley sprigs
1 basil sprig
2 tablespoons olive oil
2 quarts boiling water
Bouquet garni
6 peppercorns, cracked
2 whole cloves
6 dried Italian pepper pods or 1 whole pink hot pepper
½ cup amber rum

1. Finely chop fresh vegetables and herbs together.
2. Heat oil in a large saucepan, add chopped mixture, and cook until lightly browned. Add boiling water, bouquet garni, peppercorns, cloves, pepper pods, and rum. Cover; boil 30 minutes. Boil uncovered to reduce volume by half.
3. Strain and cool before using.
ABOUT 1 QUART

Green Goddess Salad Dressing

1 cup mayonnaise
½ cup thick sour cream
3 tablespoons tarragon vinegar
1 tablespoon lemon juice
⅓ cup finely chopped parsley
3 tablespoons finely chopped onion
3 tablespoons mashed anchovy fillets
1 tablespoon chopped chives
2 teaspoons chopped capers
1 clove garlic, crushed in a garlic press or minced
⅛ teaspoon salt
⅛ teaspoon pepper

1. Blend all ingredients thoroughly.
2. Cover bowl tightly and chill in refrigerator 3 to 4 hours.
3. Serve on Green Goddess Salad.
ABOUT 2½ CUPS DRESSING

Mayonnaise

2 egg yolks
½ teaspoon salt
¼ teaspoon white pepper
½ teaspoon dry mustard
Wine or tarragon vinegar (about 3 tablespoons)
1½ cups olive oil

1. Beat egg yolks until thick and lemon colored. Beat in salt, pepper, dry mustard, and half of the vinegar.
2. Beating constantly, trickle in ⅓ cup olive oil, add ½ teaspoon vinegar, and trickle in remaining olive oil. Check for consistency.
3. If the Mayonnaise is too thick, add vinegar drop by drop and mix by hand until the appropriate consistency is achieved. Adjust seasoning.
ABOUT 1½ CUPS

Note: If Mayonnaise curdles, wash beater. Beat an egg yolk until thick in a small bowl. Slowly add curdled mixture, beating constantly to form a new emulsion. Another egg yolk may be necessary. If so, beat again until thick, add mixture slowly.

Cucumber Sauce

1 medium cucumber, pared, seeded, and finely chopped
Chicken Stock (page 48)
1½ cups Low-Fat Yogurt (page 47)
1 tablespoon snipped fresh

or 1½ teaspoons dried dill weed
¼ teaspoon salt
Dash freshly ground white pepper

1. Simmer cucumber in 1 inch of stock in a covered saucepan until tender (about 5 minutes); drain off and discard stock.
2. Mix cucumbers with remaining ingredients. Serve cold, or heat and serve warm.
ABOUT 2 CUPS

Note: Snipped coriander or mint can be used in place of dill in this recipe.

Mustard Sauce

¾ cup sour cream
⅓ cup mayonnaise
2 tablespoons prepared

mustard
¼ teaspoon salt
¼ teaspoon sugar

1. Mix all ingredients well.
2. Serve with cold pork, ham, or hard-cooked eggs.
ABOUT 1¼ CUPS

Sour Cream Sauce

2 hard-cooked eggs
1 cup sour cream
1 teaspoon prepared mustard or dill

¼ teaspoon sugar
¼ teaspoon salt
⅛ teaspoon pepper

1. Press eggs through a sieve. Add sour cream and beat with a mixer at medium speed 3 minutes. Add mustard, sugar, salt, and pepper. Beat 1 minute at high speed.
2. Serve with ham or veal.
1½ CUPS

Mushroom Sauce

1 pound mushrooms, sliced
1 large onion, chopped
1 cup chicken or meat broth or bouillon
3 tablespoons flour

2 tablespoons melted butter
½ cup sour cream
1 teaspoon lemon juice
Salt and pepper

1. Simmer mushrooms with onion in bouillon 15 minutes.
2. Blend flour into batter. Stir into mushrooms. Bring to boiling, stirring.
3. Remove from heat. Stir in sour cream, lemon juice, and salt and pepper to taste.
3 CUPS

Tartar Sauce

2 hard-cooked eggs
2 tablespoons finely chopped mushrooms
2 tablespoons salad oil
2 teaspoons prepared mustard
2 teaspoons pickle liquid

¼ teaspoon salt
¼ teaspoon sugar
½ cup mayonnaise
½ cup sour cream
¼ cup finely chopped dill pickles

1. Mash cooked egg yolks. Chop whites separately.
2. Sauté mushrooms in oil. Blend in mashed egg yolks, mustard, pickle liquid, salt, and sugar.
3. Blend mayonnaise into sour cream. Add chopped egg whites, egg yolk mixture, and pickles; mix well.
ABOUT 2 CUPS

French Dressing Antillaise for Salads

½ cup olive oil
1 teaspoon salt
½ teaspoon freshly ground pepper
2 garlic cloves
Tarragon, dill, or oregano to

taste
5 parsley sprigs
2 scallions or green onions, finely chopped
1 tablespoon wine vinegar

1. Pour oil into a salad bowl; add remaining ingredients. With a pestle or wooden spoon, rub herbs against the side of the bowl and mix with oil.
2. For salad, marinate your choice of **celery pieces, chickpeas, onion slices, cherry tomatoes, sliced mushrooms, sliced cooked beets,** or **beans** (never more than two) in dressing for at least 1 hour before serving.
3. To serve, toss chilled **salad greens** with marinated vegetables.

Salad with French Dressing Antillaise

Green Onion Sauce

1 cup sour cream
3 tablespoons sliced green
  onion
1 egg yolk, beaten
2 tablespoons prepared

mustard
1 teaspoon lemon juice
½ teaspoon sugar
¼ teaspoon salt

1. Combine sour cream, green onion, egg yolk, prepared mustard, lemon juice, sugar, and salt.
2. Serve hot or cold.
ABOUT 1½ CUPS

Cold Horseradish Sauce

6 ounces prepared cream-
  style horseradish
1 large apple, pared and
  shredded

1½ cups sour cream
½ teaspoon sugar
¼ teaspoon salt

1. Mix horseradish with apple. Add sour cream; stir in sugar and salt.
2. Serve with cold meat, hard-cooked eggs, and fish.
ABOUT 2½ CUPS

Mock Crème Fraîche

1½ cups Neufchatel cheese   6 tablespoons Low-Fat Yogurt

1. Mix cheese and yogurt in a blender or food processor until smooth and fluffy. Place in small jars; cover tightly.
2. Set jars in a warm place (100°F) for 2 hours; see Note. Cool and refrigerate. Stir before using.
ABOUT 2 CUPS

Note: Use an oven thermometer in making Mock Crème Fraîche, as temperature is very important. A gas oven with a pilot light will be about 125°F. Turn electric oven to as warm a setting as necessary to maintain temperature. Mock Crème Fraîche can be refrigerated up to 3 weeks.

Green Peppercorn Sauce

1 cup Chicken Stock (page
  48)
2 tablespoons brandy
1 tablespoon arrowroot
Cold water
¼ pound fresh mushrooms,
  chopped

¼ cup Mock Crème Fraîche
  (above)
½ teaspoon salt
¼ teaspoon freshly ground
  pepper
2 tablespoons drained green
  peppercorns

1. Heat stock and brandy.
2. Mix arrowroot with a little cold water; stir into stock. Simmer, stirring constantly, until stock has thickened (about 4 minutes). Stir in remaining ingredients. Heat thoroughly. Serve immediately.
ABOUT 2½ CUPS

Vinegar and Oil Dressing with Tomato

1 tablespoon imported
  mustard (Dijon, preferably)
2 tablespoons red wine
  vinegar, or more to taste
½ cup olive oil
1 large tomato, peeled and
  diced
2 whole scallions, minced
2 tablespoons minced parsley
1 tablespoon chopped capers
1 teaspoon dill

Put mustard and vinegar into a small bowl. Add olive oil while stirring with a whisk. Add remaining ingredients; mix well. Refrigerate several hours before serving.
1¾ CUPS

Madeira Sauce

¼ cup chopped celery
¼ cup chopped carrot
2 tablespoons chopped green
  onion
1 tablespoon cooking oil
1 quart water
2 beef bouillon cubes
1 chicken bouillon cube

½ bay leaf
Pinch ground thyme
Few grains freshly ground
  black pepper
1 tablespoon tomato sauce
¼ cup water
2 tablespoons flour
⅓ cup Madeira

1. Cook celery, carrot, and onion in hot oil in a large saucepot until dark brown, but not burned.
2. Stir in 1 quart water, bouillon cubes, bay leaf, thyme, and pepper. Bring to boiling, and simmer until liquid is reduced by half.
3. Strain the liquid. Stir in tomato sauce and bring to boiling.
4. Vigorously shake ¼ cup water and flour in a screw-top jar. While stirring the boiling mixture, slowly add the flour mixture. Cook 1 to 2 minutes, then simmer about 30 minutes, stirring occasionally.
5. Just before serving, stir Madeira into sauce and bring sauce to boiling.
ABOUT 1½ CUPS SAUCE

Vinaigrette Dressing

1 tablespoon fresh lemon
  juice
1 tablespoon olive or
  vegetable oil
¼ cup Chicken Stock (page
  48)
2 teaspoons snipped parsley
1 teaspoon snipped fresh or

½ teaspoon dried basil
  leaves
2 teaspoons distilled white
  vinegar
1 teaspoon Dijon mustard
1 small garlic clove, minced
⅛ teaspoon salt
Freshly ground white pepper

Measure all ingredients into a jar with a tight cover; shake vigorously. Refrigerate dressing until chilled. Shake before serving.
ABOUT ½ CUP

Madeira Sauce

1 cup Chicken Stock (page 48)
Juice of 1 lemon
1 teaspoon Worcestershire sauce
¼ teaspoon salt
⅓ cup Madeira wine
1 tablespoon arrowroot
Cold water
1 tablespoon snipped parsley

1. Heat stock, lemon juice, Worcestershire sauce, salt, and Madeira in a small saucepan.
2. Mix arrowroot with a little cold water; stir into stock mixture. Simmer, stirring constantly, until thickened (about 3 minutes). Stir in parsley. Serve immediately.
ABOUT 1½ CUPS SAUCE

Cumberland Sauce

½ cup fresh cranberries
2 teaspoons grated orange peel
1 large navel orange, peeled and finely chopped
2 tablespoons brandy
½ cup port wine
¼ cup orange juice
¼ cup Beef Stock
1 teaspoon prepared mustard

1. Process cranberries, orange peel and chopped orange, and brandy in a food processor or blender until finely ground.
2. Transfer mixture to a saucepan; stir in remaining ingredients. Simmer uncovered until sauce is of medium thick consistency (about 15 minutes). Serve hot, or refrigerate and serve cold.
3. Serve over duck, pork, ham, or over cottage cheese or fruit salads.
ABOUT 1½ CUPS

Cauliflower Sauce

¾ pound cauliflower
Chicken Stock (page 48)
½ teaspoon salt
¼ teaspoon freshly ground white pepper
2 tablespoons dry white wine
1 teaspoon snipped fresh or ½ teaspoon dried thyme leaves
2 ounces Swiss cheese, shredded
Snipped parsley (optional)

1. Remove leaves and tough stalks from cauliflower; separate into flowerets. Simmer cauliflower, covered, in 1 inch of stock until tender (about 8 minutes); drain.
2. Purée cauliflower with remaining ingredients, except cheese and parsley, in a food processor or blender. Heat thoroughly over low heat. Stir in cheese; heat, stirring constantly, until cheese is melted (about 2 minutes).
3. Stir parsley into sauce, if desired, and serve immediately as a sauce or soup.
ABOUT 1⅓ CUPS

Low-Fat Yogurt

1 quart 2% milk
¼ cup instant nonfat dry-milk
2 tablespoons low-fat natural yogurt

1. Mix milk and dry-milk solids in a medium saucepan. Heat to scalding (150°F); cool to 110°F. Stir in yogurt.
2. Transfer mixture to a glass or crockery bowl. Cover with plastic wrap; wrap bowl securely in a heavy bath towel. Set in warm place (100° to 125°F)* for 4 to 6 hours, until yogurt has formed.
3. Place several layers of paper toweling directly on yogurt; refrigerate covered until cold.
ABOUT 1 QUART

*A gas oven with a pilot light will be about 125°F; however, use an oven thermometer, as temperature is very important. Turn an electric oven to as warm a setting as necessary to maintain temperature.
   Excess liquid and a coarse texture will result if temperature is too high. Liquid can be drained with a nylon baster. Blend yogurt in a food processor or blender to restore texture.

Note: This recipe can be made using skim or reconstituted dry milk, although the product will not be as rich.
   Purchased low-fat natural yogurt can be substituted in any recipe.

Yogurt

2 to 3 tablespoons prepared yogurt
1 quart skimmed or whole milk
½ cup instant nonfat dry milk

1. Allow yogurt to reach room temperature.
2. Bring milk to scalding, then cool to 110° to 115°F. Add dry milk and mix.
3. Dilute yogurt with ½ cup of the milk; mix with the milk. Pour into a bowl.
4. Cover. Wrap with large towel. Set in a warm place 6 to 8 hours (an oven with a pilot light is a good place). When semisolid, store in refrigerator.
ABOUT 1 QUART

Beef Stock

1 pound lean beef stew cubes
1 pound lean veal stew cubes
½ pound beef soup bones
3 carrots, cut in 2-inch pieces
1 tomato, quartered and seeded
2 medium yellow onions, quartered
1 stalk celery, cut in 2-inch pieces
1 garlic clove, minced
1 teaspoon salt
Bouquet garni:
  1 teaspoon dried thyme leaves
  1 bay leaf
  2 sprigs parsley
Water

1. Place meats, vegetables, garlic, salt, and bouquet garni in an 8-quart Dutch oven. Pour in water to cover (about 3 quarts). Simmer covered 2 to 2½ hours. Cool slightly.
2. Strain stock through a double thickness of cheesecloth into a storage container. Taste for seasoning. If a more concentrated flavor is desired, return stock to saucepan and simmer 20 to 30 minutes, or dissolve **1 to 2 teaspoons instant beef bouillon** in the stock.
3. Store covered in refrigerator or freezer. Remove solidified fat from top of stock before using.
2 TO 2½ QUARTS

Note: Refrigerated stock is perishable. If not used within several days, heat to boiling, cool, and refrigerate or freeze to prevent spoilage. Stock can be kept frozen up to 4 months.

Chicken Stock

5 pounds chicken backs and wings, or stewing chicken, cut up
3 carrots, cut in 2-inch pieces
2 medium yellow onions, quartered
1 stalk celery, cut in 2-inch pieces
2 teaspoons salt
Bouquet garni:
  ¾ teaspoon dried thyme leaves
  ¾ teaspoon dried rosemary leaves
  1 bay leaf
  4 sprigs parsley
  2 whole cloves
Water

1. Place chicken, vegetables, salt, and bouquet garni in an 8-quart Dutch oven. Pour in water to cover (about 4 quarts). Simmer covered 2 to 2½ hours.
2. Strain stock through a double thickness of cheesecloth into a storage container. Taste for seasoning. If more concentrated flavor is desired, return stock to saucepan and simmer 20 to 30 minutes, or dissolve 1 to 2 teaspoons instant chicken bouillon in the stock.
3. Store covered in refrigerator or freezer. Remove solidified fat from top of stock before using.
3 TO 3½ QUARTS

Note: Refrigerated stock is perishable. If not used within several days, heat to boiling, cool, and refrigerate or freeze to prevent spoilage. Stock can be kept frozen up to 4 months.

Fish Stock

2 pounds fresh lean fish with heads and bones, cut up
1 medium yellow onion, quartered
½ teaspoon salt
1 cup dry white wine
Water
Bouquet garni:
4 sprigs parsley
1 bay leaf
½ teaspoon dried thyme leaves
1 sprig celery leaves
2 peppercorns

1. Rinse fish under cold water. Place fish, onion, salt, wine, and bouquet garni in a 3-quart saucepan. Pour in water to cover (about 1½ quarts). Simmer covered 2 hours. Cool slightly.
2. Strain stock through a double thickness of cheesecloth into a storage container. Taste for seasoning. Add a small amount of salt and lemon juice, if desired. If a more concentrated flavor is desired, return stock to saucepan and simmer 30 to 45 minutes.
3. Store covered in refrigerator or freezer.
ABOUT 1 QUART

Note: Use white firm-fleshed fish such as halibut, cod, flounder, or lemon sole. Frozen fish can be used if necessary.
  Refrigerated stock is highly perishable. If not used within 2 days, heat to boiling, cool, and refrigerate or freeze to prevent spoilage. Stock can be kept frozen up to 2 months.

Butter

1 cup whipping cream (preferably at least several days old)
Salt (optional)
Herbs (optional)

1. Place the blade and bowl of food processor in freezer to chill.
2. Pour whipping cream into chilled bowl and process two to three minutes, or until butter is formed.
3. Turn mixture into a sieve to remove buttermilk; reserve the buttermilk for cooking or drinking.
4. If desired, add salt or herbs to butter and blend.
5. Remove butter from bowl and pack into desired container. Cover and chill thoroughly to harden.
MAKES ¼ POUND

Candied Cranberries

2 cups fresh cranberries
1 cup sugar

1. Wash cranberries and spread over bottom of a shallow baking dish. Sprinkle with sugar and cover tightly.
2. Bake at 350°F 1 hour, stirring occasionally.
3. Chill before serving.

Mock Hollandaise Sauce

½ cup Neufchatel cheese   Dash salt
3 tablespoons Low-Fat Yogurt   Juice of ½ lemon
 (page 47)

1. Mix all ingredients in a blender or food processor until smooth and fluffy.
2. Cook over simmering water until hot and thickened. Serve immediately or refrigerate and serve cold. Stir before using.
¾ CUP

Mock Béarnaise Sauce: Stir **1½ teaspoons snipped fresh** or **½ teaspoon dried tarragon leaves** and **½ teaspoon minced shallots** into sauce before heating.

Mock Mayonnaise: Stir **1½ teaspoons Dijon mustard** and **½ teaspoon sugar** into sauce before heating. Refrigerate until cold.

Note: The above sauces can be refrigerated up to 3 weeks.

Medium White Sauce

2 tablespoons butter   ⅛ teaspoon pepper
2 tablespoons flour   1 cup milk (use light cream
½ teaspoon salt   for a richer sauce)

1. Heat butter in a saucepan. Blend in flour, salt, and pepper; heat and stir until bubbly.
2. Gradually add the milk, stirring until smooth. Bring to boiling; cook and stir 1 to 2 minutes longer.
ABOUT 1 CUP

Thick White Sauce: Follow recipe for Medium White Sauce. Use 3 to 4 tablespoons flour and 3 to 4 tablespoons butter.

Thin White Sauce: Follow recipe for Medium White Sauce. Use 1 tablespoon flour and 1 tablespoon butter.

Béchamel Sauce: Follow recipe for Medium White Sauce. Substitute **½ cup chicken broth** for ½ cup milk; use ½ cup cream for remaining liquid needed. Stir in **1 tablespoon minced onion.**

Italian Dressing

6 tablespoons olive oil
3 tablespoons wine vinegar
1 clove garlic, crushed in a
garlic press
¼ teaspoon salt
⅛ teaspoon pepper

1. Place all ingredients in a screw-top jar, shake well, and chill.
2. Just before serving, beat or shake thoroughly.
ABOUT 1½ CUP DRESSING

Anchovy Dressing: Follow recipe for Italian Dressing. Add **1 teaspoon prepared mustard** and **2 finely chopped anchovy fillets** to jar before shaking.

Tomato Sauce Creole

⅓ cup peanut oil
2 medium onions, thinly sliced
6 Italian plum tomatoes, peeled, seeded, and finely chopped
½ cup beef stock
Salt and freshly ground pepper to taste
3 drops Tabasco
1 garlic clove, crushed in a garlic press

1. Heat oil in a saucepan, add onion, and cook over low heat until translucent but not browned. Add tomato, stock, and seasonings; stir with a wooden spoon until tomato pulp is cooked to a fine purée.
2. Serve with rice or grilled meats.

Spicy Cranberry Sauce

2 cups (about ½ pound) cranberries
1 cup sugar
1 cup water
1 piece (3 inches) stick cinnamon
⅛ teaspoon salt

1. Sort and wash cranberries.
2. Combine sugar, water, cinnamon stick, and salt in a 1-quart saucepan and stir over low heat until sugar is dissolved.
3. Bring to boiling; boil uncovered for 5 minutes. Add the cranberries. Continue to boil uncovered without stirring, about 5 minutes, or until skins pop. Cool and remove cinnamon stick.
4. Serve with meat or poultry.
ABOUT 2 CUPS SAUCE

Spicy Cranberry Sauce

Blue Cheese Sour Cream Dressing

1 package blue cheese salad dressing mix
1 package (3 ounces) cream
cheese, softened
1 cup sour cream

1. Prepare salad dressing following package directions.
2. Blend dressing with cream cheese in a bowl. Stir in sour cream until dressing is of desired consistency.
3. Serve dressing with **fruit and vegetable salad.**
ABOUT 1½ CUPS DRESSING

Tomato Meat Sauce

¼ cup olive oil
½ cup chopped onion
½ pound beef chuck
½ pound pork shoulder
7 cups canned tomatoes with
liquid, sieved
1 tablespoon salt
1 bay leaf
1 can (6 ounces) tomato paste

1. Heat olive oil in a large saucepot. Add onion and cook until lightly browned. Add the meat and brown on all sides. Stir in tomatoes and salt. Add bay leaf. Cover and simmer about 2½ hours.
2. Stir tomato paste into sauce. Simmer, uncovered, stirring occasionally, about 2 hours, or until thickened. If sauce becomes too thick, add ½ **cup water.**
3. Remove meat and bay leaf from sauce (use meat as desired). Serve sauce over **cooked spaghetti.**
ABOUT 4 CUPS SAUCE

Tomato Sauce with Ground Meat: Follow recipe for Tomato Meat Sauce. Brown ½ **pound ground beef** in **3 tablespoons olive oil,** breaking beef into small pieces. After removing meat from sauce, add ground beef and simmer 10 minutes longer.

Tomato Sauce with Mushrooms: Follow recipe for Tomato Meat Sauce. Clean and slice ½ **pound mushrooms.** Cook slowly in 3 tablespoons melted butter until lightly browned. After removing meat from sauce, add mushrooms and simmer 10 minutes longer.

Tomato Sauce with Chicken Livers: Follow recipe for Tomato Meat Sauce. Rinse and pat dry ½ **pound chicken livers.** Slice livers and brown in **3 tablespoons olive oil.** After removing meat from sauce, add livers and simmer 10 minutes longer.

Tomato Sauce with Sausage: Follow recipe for Tomato Meat Sauce. Brown about ½ **pound Italian sausage,** cut in 2-inch pieces, in **1 tablespoon olive oil.** After removing meat from sauce, add sausage and simmer 10 minutes longer.

Blue Cheese Sour Cream Dressing

English Mustard Sauce

1 tablespoon flour	1 tablespoon cider vinegar
1 teaspoon dry mustard	1 tablespoon butter
⅛ teaspoon salt	1 tablespoon prepared
⅛ teaspoon pepper	mustard
½ cup water	

1. Combine the flour, dry mustard, salt, and pepper in a heavy saucepan. Gradually add the water and vinegar; cook, stirring, until boiling; cook 1 to 2 minutes longer.
2. Remove from heat; stir in butter and mustard. Serve hot.
ABOUT ½ CUP

Béchamel Sauce

2 tablespoons butter	broth, or chicken broth
3 tablespoons flour	Salt and pepper to taste
1½ cups hot milk, beef	½ cup whipping cream

Melt butter over medium heat; stir in flour. Using a whisk, stir rapidly until smooth. Gradually add milk or other liquid, stirring constantly. Bring sauce to a rapid boil and boil 4 minutes, or until sauce is thick and reduced to half its original volume. Season with salt and pepper. Reduce heat and stir in cream. Heat thoroughly, but do not boil.
ABOUT 1⅔ CUPS

Creole Barbecue Sauce

1 can (28 ounces) Italian plum tomatoes, drained	¼ cup lime juice
1 medium onion, finely chopped	1 teaspoon salt
⅔ cup olive oil	⅛ teaspoon dried basil
2 garlic cloves, crushed in a garlic press	Dash pepper
	Bouquet garni
	5 drops Tabasco

1. Chop tomatoes; put tomato and onion into a saucepan and cook uncovered over medium heat for 15 minutes.
2. Force tomato mixture through a fine sieve into another saucepan. Discard remaining solids.
3. Add remaining ingredients to saucepan. Stir until blended. Simmer uncovered about 1 hour, stirring occasionally.
4. Brush sauce over meat for barbecuing.
ABOUT 3½ CUPS

Bolognese Meat Sauce

2 tablespoons butter	¼ pound ground lean pork
1 medium onion, finely chopped	¼ cup tomato sauce or tomato paste
1 small carrot, finely chopped	½ cup white wine
1 small stalk celery, finely chopped	1 cup beef broth or stock
¾ pound ground beef	½ teaspoon salt
	¼ teaspoon pepper

1. Melt butter in a skillet. Stir in onion, carrot, and celery. Cook until tender. Add meat and cook over low heat 10 to 15 minutes.
2. Add tomato sauce, wine, ¼ cup broth, salt, and pepper; mix well. Simmer about 1¼ hours. Stir in remaining broth, a small amount at a time, while the sauce is simmering. Sauce should be thick.
ABOUT 2½ CUPS SAUCE

French Dressing

¾ cup salad oil or olive oil	¾ teaspoon salt
¼ cup lemon juice or cider vinegar	¼ teaspoon paprika
1 tablespoon sugar	¼ teaspoon dry mustard
	¼ teaspoon pepper

1. Combine in a screw-top jar salad or olive oil, lemon juice or cider vinegar, sugar, salt, paprika, dry mustard and pepper.
2. Cover jar tightly and shake vigorously to blend well. Store in covered container in refrigerator.
3. Shake well before using.
ABOUT 1 CUP DRESSING

Anchovy French Dressing: Follow recipe for French Dressing. Use lemon juice. Omit salt and add 4 minced **anchovy fillets.** Shake well.

Lorenzo French Dressing: Follow recipe for French Dressing. Add ¼ cup finely chopped **watercress** and 2 tablespoons **chili sauce.** Shake well.

Olive French Dressing: Follow recipe for French Dressing. Add ½ cup chopped **stuffed olives** and shake well.

Tangy French Dressing: Follow recipe for French Dressing. Add 3 to 4 tablespoons **prepared horseradish** and shake well.

Curried French Dressing: Follow recipe for French Dressing. Add ¼ teaspoon **curry powder** and shake well.

Fruit Juice French Dressing: Follow recipe for French Dressing. Substitute **orange** or **pineapple juice** for the lemon juice or vinegar, or use 2 tablespoons of each fruit juice.

Creamy French Dressing: Follow recipe for French Dressing. Add ¼ cup **thick sour cream** and blend well.

Garlic French Dressing: Cut into halves 1 clove **garlic**; add to completed dressing. Chill dressing about 12 hours before using to allow flavors to blend. Remove garlic before serving or when flavor of dressing is sufficiently strong.

Roquefort French Dressing: Follow recipe for French Dressing. Blend together until smooth 3 ounces (about ¾ cup) crumbled **Roquefort cheese** and 2 teaspoons **water**. Add dressing slowly to cheese, blending after each addition.

Honey-Lime French Dressing: Follow recipe for French Dressing. Substitute **lime juice** for the lemon juice or vinegar. Blend in ½ cup **honey** and ¼ teaspoon grated **lime peel**.

Vinaigrette French Dressing: Follow recipe for French Dressing. Add 2 tablespoons finely chopped **dill pickle**, 1 tablespoon chopped **chives**, and **1 hard-cooked egg** chopped. Shake well.

Italian Dressing: Follow recipe for French Dressing. Use olive oil. Omit lemon juice or vinegar and add 6 tablespoons **wine vinegar**. Reduce salt to ½ teaspoon. Omit sugar, paprika and dry mustard. Shake well.

Tomato Soup French Dressing: Follow recipe for French Dressing. Add ⅔ cup (about one-half 10½-to 11 ounce can) **condensed tomato soup**, 1 tablespoon chopped **onion** and ½ teaspoon **marjoram**. Shake well.

Honey French Dressing: Follow recipe for French Dressing. Use lemon juice. Blend in ½ cup **honey** and ¼ teaspoon grated **lemon peel**. For added flavor, add ½ teaspoon **celery seed** and shake well.

Chiffonade French Dressing: Follow recipe for French Dressing. Add 1 **hard-cooked egg**, chopped, 2 tablespoons finely chopped **ripe olives**, and 4 teaspoons finely chopped **parsley**. Shake well.

Tarragon French Dressing: Follow recipe for French Dressing. Use olive oil. Substitute **tarragon vinegar** for lemon juice or cider vinegar. Decrease sugar to 1 teaspoon. Add 1 clove **garlic**, cut into halves, ¼ teaspoon **Worcestershire sauce** and ⅛ teaspoon **thyme**. Shake well.

Cream Sauce

2 tablespoons butter
2 tablespoons flour
1 cup milk
1 cup half-and-half
½ teaspoon salt
Dash nutmeg

1. Melt butter in a saucepan and blend with flour.
2. Gradually stir in milk and half-and-half.
3. Season with salt and nutmeg.
4. Cook, stirring constantly, until sauce boils and thickens.
5. Cover with a sheet of waxed paper on surface and keep warm until ready to use.
2 CUPS SAUCE

Cheese Sauce for Broccoli

2 tablespoons butter or margarine
2 tablespoons flour
½ teaspoon salt
1 cup milk
¼ cup dry white wine, such as sauterne
½ cup grated pasteurized process Swiss cheese
Dash each white pepper and nutmeg
1 tablespoon chopped pimento (optional)

1. Melt butter and blend in flour and salt.
2. Add milk, stirring until smooth; cook and stir until sauce boils and is thickened.
3. Add wine, cheese, pepper, nutmeg, and pimento, if desired. Stir over low heat until cheese is melted.
4. Spoon hot sauce over **cooked broccoli spears**.
ABOUT 1½ CUPS SAUCE

Creamy Fruit Mayonnaise

⅓ cup mayonnaise
⅓ cup sour cream
1 tablespoon honey
1 tablespoon lemon juice
1 tablespoon orange juice
¼ teaspoon salt

Combine mayonnaise, sour cream, honey, juices, and salt, blending well.
ABOUT ¾ CUP FRUIT MAYONNAISE

Garlic Mayonnaise

4 garlic cloves, crushed in a garlic press
¼ teaspoon salt
2 egg yolks
Olive oil (about 1 cup)
Juice of ½ lemon, or more to taste
Salt and white pepper

1. Combine garlic, salt, and egg yolks.
2. Slowly add oil, a drop at a time, beating vigorously until 2 to 3 tablespoons have been added. Add remaining oil in a steady stream, beating constantly.
3. Add lemon juice, beating well. Season with salt and pepper.
ABOUT 1½ CUPS

Tomato Sauce

3 tablespoons butter
1 large onion, chopped
2 pounds fresh ripe
tomatoes, peeled and
chopped
2 teaspoons sugar

2 whole cloves
1 bay leaf
1 garlic clove, crushed in a
garlic press
1 teaspoon vinegar
Salt and pepper to taste

1. Melt butter in a saucepan; add onion and cook until translucent.
2. Add tomatoes and remaining ingredients.
3. Simmer uncovered 20 minutes.
3 CUPS

Note: A variation served during Lent is Anchovy Tomato Sauce. To prepare, use **olive oil** instead of butter, decrease sugar to 1 teaspoon, increase vinegar to 2 teaspoons; and add **½ tube anchovy paste** or **1 can (2 ounces) anchovies**, drained and cut into small pieces.

Avocado Cocktail Sauce

1 cup sliced avocado
1 tablespoon lemon juice
⅓ cup mayonnaise
Few grains salt

¼ cup chili sauce or tomato
catchup
½ teaspoon Worcestershire
sauce

Combine ingredients and mix well.
MAKES 1⅔ CUPS

Cocktail Sauce for Avocados

½ cup heavy cream
½ cup chili sauce
½ cup mayonnaise

1 tablespoon Worcestershire
sauce
3 tablespoons lemon juice

Whip cream and fold in remaining ingredients. Serve with avocados.
MAKES 2 CUPS

Savory Onion Topper

3 cups chopped sweet
Spanish onion
3 tablespoons butter

1¼ cups chili sauce
¼ cup bottled meat sauce

1. Sauté onion in butter in a skillet until tender. Mix in chili sauce and meat sauce; heat thoroughly.
2. Serve over grilled or broiled hamburgers.
ABOUT 2½ CUPS SAUCE

Sauce for Grapefruit Cup

½ cup heavy cream,
whipped

1 cup Tomato Sauce
1 tablespoon lemon juice

1. Fold whipped cream into tomato sauce, add lemon juice and beat well.
2. Serve on grapefruit sections.
MAKES 1½ CUPS

Cucumber Sauce

1 cucumber, grated
½ cup chili sauce
1 teaspoon onion juice

2 tablespoons lemon juice
Few grains pepper
2 drops Tabasco sauce

Combine ingredients and serve on seafood.
MAKES 1½ CUPS

Fruit Sauce

1 cup Currant Jelly
½ cup boiling water

1 tablespoon chopped
orange peel

Combine ingredients and beat. Serve hot.
MAKES 1¼ CUPS

Grapefruit Mint Cocktail

1 cup Mint Jelly
1½ cups water

1¼ cups sugar

1. Melt mint jelly in double boiler and beat with egg beater.
2. Boil water and sugar together 10 minutes and add to mint jelly.
3. Chill and pour over grapefruit sections.
MAKES 2½ CUPS

Burger with Savory Onion Topper

Onion Confetti Relish

2 cups chopped sweet
  Spanish onion (1 large)
½ green pepper, diced
3 tablespoons diced pimento
½ cup vinegar
¼ cup water
¼ cup sugar
2 teaspoons caraway seed
½ teaspoon salt

1. Combine onion with green pepper and pimento.
2. Combine vinegar, water, sugar, caraway seed, and salt. Bring to boiling and simmer 5 minutes. Pour over onion mixture. Refrigerate several hours.
3. Serve with grilled or broiled hamburgers.
2½ CUPS RELISH

Honey Sauce

¼ cup pineapple syrup
¼ cup lemon juice
¼ cup honey

Combine ingredients, chill and pour over fruit.
MAKES ¾ CUP

Honeydew Melon Cocktail Sauce

1 cup sugar
¾ cup boiling water
⅓ cup orange juice
⅓ cup lime juice
2 tablespoons lemon juice

1. Boil sugar and water together 5 minutes, cool and add fruit juices.
2. Pour over honeydew melon balls.
MAKES 1¾ CUPS

Mayonnaise Sauce

½ cup chili sauce
½ cup mayonnaise
2 drops Tabasco sauce
½ teaspoon A-1 Sauce
¼ teaspoon salt
1 teaspoon lemon juice

Mix ingredients and chill thoroughly. Serve on fish cocktails.
MAKES 1 CUP

Pineapple Grapefruit Juice

⅔ cup canned pineapple
  syrup
⅓ cup grenadine syrup
⅓ cup grapefruit juice

Combine syrups with fruit juice, chill and pour over fruit cocktail.
MAKES 1⅓ CUPS

Baltimore Sauce

1 tablespoon prepared
  horseradish
½ cup tomato catchup or
  chili sauce
3 tablespoons lemon juice
1 teaspoon Worcestershire
  sauce
½ teaspoon celery salt

1. Combine ingredients and mix thoroughly.
2. Chill and serve over seafood.
MAKES ¾ CUP

Use **½ cup minced celery** instead of celery salt if desired.

Chili Cocktail Sauce

⅓ cup chili sauce
⅔ cup mayonnaise
2 tablespoons pineapple
syrup
2 tablespoons lemon juice

Combine ingredients, chill and serve.
MAKES 1¼ CUPS

Cocktail Sauce

¼ cup mayonnaise
2 tablespoons French
  dressing
2 tablespoons chili sauce
1 tablespoon chopped
  pimento
2 teaspoons chopped olives
Salt and pepper

Combine ingredients, chill and serve with avocado cocktail.
MAKES ½ CUP

Horseradish Cocktail Sauce

1 cup tomato catchup
¼ cup chili sauce
1 tablespoon lemon juice
Few drops Tabasco sauce
1 tablespoon prepared
  horseradish
¼ teaspoon salt
Dash pepper

Combine ingredients and mix well.
MAKES 1⅓ CUPS

Manhattan Sauce

2 teaspoons prepared
  horseradish
3 tablespoons tomato
  catchup
2 tablespoons vinegar
¼ cup lemon juice
¼ teaspoon Tabasco sauce
1 teaspoon salt

Combine horseradish, catchup, vinegar, lemon juice, Tabasco sauce and salt.
MAKES ⅔ CUP

Basic Molasses Barbecue Sauce

Mobile Sauce

¼ cup mayonnaise
¼ cup tomato catchup
2 tablespoons fresh tomato

2 tablespoons minced green pepper
2 tablespoons chili sauce

Combine ingredients, chill and serve.
MAKES ¾ CUP

Basic Molasses Barbecue Sauce

¼ cup cornstarch
4 cups lemon juice (about 2 dozen lemons)
2 cups cooking oil
1 jar (12 ounces) light or dark molasses

¼ cup salt
1 tablespoon black pepper
6 bay leaves, broken in pieces
3 cloves garlic, minced

1. Combine cornstarch and lemon juice in a saucepan. Cook and stir over low heat until mixture bubbles and thickens. Cool.
2. Using rotary or electric beater, beat in remaining ingredients until thoroughly blended and thickened.
3. Store in refrigerator until needed.
ABOUT 2 QUARTS SAUCE

Sea Food Sauce

1 cup mayonnaise
2 tablespoons anchovy paste
2 tablespoons chili sauce
2 tablespoons tarragon

vinegar
¼ cup tomato catchup
Lemon juice and pepper, if needed

Combine ingredients, chill and serve.
MAKES 1⅔ CUPS

SALADS

Fruited Carrot Salad

4 carrots
1 cup unsweetened pineap-
    ple juice
2½ cups orange juice
Lettuce cups
Snipped mint

1. Pare carrots into strips with a vegetable peeler. Place in a shallow glass dish; pour fruit juices over. Refrigerate covered 6 hours or overnight, stirring occasionally.
2. Drain carrots, spoon into lettuce cups, and garnish with mint.
4 SERVINGS

Beet Salad

1 16 ounce can sliced beets
    (about 2 cups, drained)
½ cup vinegar
¼ cup reserved beet liquid
2 tablespoons sugar
1½ teaspoons salt
1 teaspoon caraway seeds
⅛ teaspoon freshly ground
    pepper

1. Drain contents of can sliced beets, reserving liquid.
2. Place the beets into a 1-quart bowl and add a mixture of vinegar, beet liquid, sugar, salt, caraway seeds, and pepper.
3. Toss beets lightly in this salad marinade. Cover bowl and place into refrigerator to marinate 1 or 2 days; carefully turn beets occasionally.
4. Serve beets with some of the marinade.
4 OR 5 SERVINGS

Beet Salad with Horseradish: Follow recipe for Beet Salad. Add 1 or 2 tablespoons **freshly grated horseradish** or ¼ cup **prepared horseradish** to beets with the seasonings.

Tomato Aspic

4 cups tomato juice
⅓ cup chopped celery leaves
⅓ cup chopped onion
2½ tablespoons sugar
1¼ teaspoons salt
1 bay leaf
½ cup cold water
2 envelopes unflavored
    gelatin
2½ tablespoons cider vinegar

1. Set out a 1-quart mold.
2. Pour tomato juice into a saucepan.
3. Add celery leaves, onion, sugar, salt and bay leaf to tomato juice.
4. Simmer, uncovered 10 minutes, stirring occasionally.
5. Meanwhile, pour water into a small bowl.
6. Sprinkle gelatin evenly over water.
7. Let stand until softened.
8. Lightly oil the mold with salad or cooking oil (not olive oil); set aside to drain.
9. Remove tomato juice mixture from heat and strain into a large bowl. Immediately add the softened gelatin to hot tomato juice mixture and stir until gelatin is completely dissolved.
10. Add cider vinegar and stir well.
11. Pour tomato-juice mixture into the prepared mold. Cool; chill in refrigerator until firm.
12. Unmold onto chilled serving plate.
6 TO 8 SERVINGS

Pimento Cheese-Avocado Salad

Salad:
4 ripe avocados
Lemon juice
1 jar (7 ounces) whole
    pimentos, drained
⅓ cup fresh parsley, cleaned
    and trimmed (3 tablespoons
    chopped)
1 package (8 ounces) cream
    cheese, cut in quarters
1 tablespoon capers
Pinch cayenne pepper
½ teaspoon salt
⅛ teaspoon pepper
Salad greens

Dressing:
1 whole pimento, drained
½ cup mayonnaise
½ cup sour cream
¼ teaspoon salt
⅛ teaspoon pepper
2 tablespoons lemon juice

1. For salad, cut avocados into halves, peel, and remove pits. Enlarge the pit cavities with a spoon, reserving scooped-out avocado. Score the surfaces of cavities with a fork. Brush surface (except cavities) with lemon juice.
2. Pat pimentos dry with a paper towel. Keep pimentos in one piece. Line the avocado cavities with the pimentos and trim evenly around the edges. Set leftover pimento aside.
3. Using **steel blade** of food processor, process parsley until chopped. Set aside.
4. Using **plastic blade** of food processor, process cream cheese until smooth. Add 2 tablespoons chopped parsley, scooped-out avocado, leftover pimento, capers, cayenne pepper, salt, and pepper. Process until thoroughly blended.
5. Fill the lined avocado with the cheese mixture, spreading it smoothly on the top. Cover and chill thoroughly.
6. For dressing, using **plastic blade,** add all ingredients to the bowl and process until thoroughly blended. Chill thoroughly.
7. When ready to serve, halve each filled avocado shell lengthwise and arrange quarters on crisp salad greens. Serve with dressing on the side.
8 SERVINGS

Tomato Aspic

Salade Niçoise

Salad Dressing, below
3 medium-sized cooked
  potatoes, sliced
1 package (9 ounce) frozen
  green beans, cooked
1 clove garlic, cut in half
1 small head Boston lettuce
2 cans (6½ or 7 ounces
  each) tuna, drained
1 mild onion, quartered and
thinly sliced
2 ripe tomatoes, cut in
  wedges
2 hard-cooked eggs,
  quartered
1 can (2 ounces) rolled anchovy fillets, drained
¾ cup pitted ripe olives
1 tablespoon capers

1. Pour enough salad dressing over warm potato slices and cooked beans (in separate bowls) to coat vegetables.
2. Before serving, rub the inside of a large shallow salad bowl with the cut surface of the garlic. Line the bowl or a large serving platter with the lettuce.
3. Unmold the tuna in center of bowl and separate into chunks.
4. Arrange separate mounds of the potatoes, green beans, onion, tomatoes, and hard-cooked eggs in colorful grouping around the tuna. Garnish with anchovies, olives, and capers.
5. Pour dressing over all before serving.
6 TO 8 SERVINGS

Salad Dressing: Combine in a jar or bottle ½ cup olive oil or salad oil, 2 tablespoons red wine vinegar, a mixture of 1 teaspoon salt, ½ teaspoon pepper, and 1 teaspoon dry mustard, 1 tablespoon finely chopped chives, and 1 tablespoon finely chopped parsley. Shake vigorously to blend well before pouring over salad.
ABOUT ⅔ CUP

Oriental Cucumber Salad

10 baby cucumbers (about 3
  inches long), sliced in very
  thin rounds
1 bunch green onions, tops
  only, finely chopped
2 teaspoons honey or sugar
2 teaspoons toasted sesame
  seed
½ cup distilled white vinegar
½ teaspoon sesame oil
5 tablespoons light soy sauce
Salad greens

1. Arrange cucumber and onion in a shallow glass dish. Shake remaining ingredients except salad greens in a covered jar; pour over the vegetables. Refrigerate for 2 hours, stirring occasionally.
2. Drain cucumber and onion; marinade can be strained and refrigerated for use again. Serve salad on lettuce or other salad greens.
4 SERVINGS

Garden Vegetables in Sweet Seasoned Vinegar

1½ cups very thinly sliced
  baby cucumbers
2 cups very thinly sliced
  broccoli stalks
½ cup cider vinegar
½ teaspoon salt
¼ teaspoon freshly ground
  pepper
1½ teaspoons sugar
Salad greens

1. Arrange vegetable slices in a shallow glass dish. Shake remaining ingredients except salad greens in a covered jar;

pour over vegetables. Refrigerate covered 30 minutes; stir occasionally. Drain; marinade can be strained and refrigerated for use again.
2. Serve vegetables on salad greens.
4 SERVINGS

Cucumber Salad

2 medium-size (about 1¼
  pounds) cucumbers, washed
  and pared
2 teaspoons salt
3 tablespoons vinegar
3 tablespoons water
½ teaspoon sugar
¼ teaspoon paprika
¼ teaspoon pepper
½ clove garlic, minced
¼ teaspoon paprika

1. Slice cucumbers thinly into a bowl.
2. Sprinkle salt over the cucumber slices.
3. Mix lightly and set cucumbers aside for 1 hour.
4. Meanwhile, mix vinegar, water, sugar, ¼ teaspoon paprika, pepper and garlic together and set aside.
5. Squeeze cucumber slices, a few at a time (discarding liquid), and put into a bowl. Pour the vinegar mixture over the cucumbers and toss lightly. Sprinkle ¼ teaspoon paprika onto cucumbers.
6. Chill the salad in refrigerator for 1 to 2 hours.
6 TO 8 SERVINGS

Cucumber Salad with Sour Cream: Follow recipe for Cucumber Salad. Blend in 1 cup **thick sour cream** after the vinegar mixture.

Cucumber Salad with Onions: Follow recipe for Cucumber Salad or variation. Omit garlic. Cut off root ends from 3 or 4 fresh **green onions or scallions.** Trim green tops down to 2- or 3-inches, removing any wilted or bruised parts; peel and rinse. Slice onions by holding on hard surface and cutting across all with sharp knife. Add sliced onions to cucumber slices before adding the vinegar mixture.

Shrimp Salad

1½ cups cooked shrimp,
  sliced in half lengthwise
½ cup diced cooked
  potatoes
2 hard-cooked eggs, sliced
½ cup chopped celery
¼ cup chopped green onions
½ cup mayonnaise or salad
  dressing
½ cup sour cream
½ teaspoon chili powder
Salt to taste
Lettuce leaves
Lemon wedges

1. Combine all ingredients, except lettuce and lemon wedges, and stir gently until evenly mixed and coated with dressing.
2. Refrigerate at least 1 hour before serving.
3. When ready to serve, place on lettuce leaves. Serve with lemon wedges.
6 SERVINGS

Note: Shrimp salad also makes a delicious avocado filling.

Orange-Pea Salad

2 packages (10 ounces each) frozen green peas
1⅓ cups chopped celery
½ teaspoon dried leaf tarragon
¼ cup sour cream
2 teaspoons grated orange peel
2 tablespoons thawed frozen orange juice concentrate
1 teaspoon salt
½ teaspoon sugar
Salad greens
Orange sections

1. Cook peas according to package directions. Drain and cool. Mix with celery, tarragon, sour cream, orange peel, orange concentrate, salt, and sugar. Chill.
2. Line a serving bowl with salad greens, spoon in pea salad, and garnish with orange sections.
6 SERVINGS

Italian Potato Salad I

1 package (2 pounds) frozen southern-style hash brown potatoes
1 package (9 ounces) frozen Italian green beans
1 teaspoon seasoned salt
¼ teaspoon pepper
⅔ cup bottled creamy Italian dressing
½ cup chopped celery
½ cup pitted ripe olives, cut
in half crosswise
2 hard-cooked eggs, diced
2 tablespoons chopped green onion
½ teaspoon salt
1 cup cherry tomatoes, cut in half
1 cup shredded Provolone cheese (about 4 ounces)
Romaine leaves

1. Thaw hash brown potatoes.
2. Cook Italian green beans, following package directions, until just tender; drain.
3. Combine potatoes and beans in a bowl. Sprinkle with seasoned salt and pepper. Chill.
4. Combine dressing, celery, olives, eggs, onion, and salt in a large bowl. Add chilled vegetables and toss to coat with dressing. Lightly mix in tomatoes and cheese. Chill thoroughly to blend flavors, at least several hours.
5. To serve, spoon salad into a bowl lined with romaine.
ABOUT 10 SERVINGS

Luscious Rock Lobster Salad

3 6- to 8-ounce frozen rock lobster tails (or use 3 6-ounce cans rock lobster meat)
1½ quarts water
1½ teaspoons salt
1 cup diced celery
½ cup slivered unblanched almonds
1 tablespoon minced
scallions or onion
¾ cup mayonnaise
2 tablespoons cream
2 tablespoons lemon juice
¼ teaspoon sugar
¼ teaspoon salt
¼ teaspoon crushed dried tarragon leaves
⅛ teaspoon white pepper

1. If using canned rock lobster, chill in the can in refrigerator. Drain and cut into chunks when ready to prepare salad.
2. To Cook Frozen Rock Lobster Tails – Bring water and salt to boiling in a heavy sauce pot or kettle.
3. Add frozen or thawed rock lobster tails to kettle. Cover; bring water again to boiling, reduce heat and simmer for

7 to 12 minutes.
4. Drain tails, cover with cold water and drain again. Using scissors or a sharp knife, cut through thin shell or underside of each tail. Insert fingers under meat and carefully pull it out. Cool meat; chill in refrigerator. Cut into chunks when ready to prepare salad.
5. To Complete Salad – Prepare celery, almonds and minced scallions or onion.
6. Put into a large bowl, reserving about 2 tablespoons of the almonds for garnish. Add the rock lobster meat.
7. Blend together mayonnaise, cream, lemon juice, sugar, ¼ teaspoon salt, tarragon leaves and white pepper.
8. Add to the ingredients in the bowl, toss lightly to mix thoroughly. Chill.
9. Serve in a chilled salad bowl; garnish with reserved almonds and **ripe olives**.
6 SERVINGS

Garbanzo Salad

1 can (15 ounces) garbanzos, drained
¼ cup chopped parsley
1 can or jar (4 ounces) pimentos, drained and chopped
3 green onions, chopped
¼ cup wine vinegar
2 tablespoons olive or salad oil
1 teaspoon salt
½ teaspoon sugar
¼ teaspoon pepper

Combine all ingredients in a bowl; cover and refrigerate until chilled.
ABOUT 6 SERVINGS

Cucumber Mousse

1 package (3 ounces) lime-flavored gelatin
¾ cup boiling water
1 cup cottage cheese
1 cup mayonnaise or salad
dressing
2 tablespoons grated onion
¾ cup grated cucumber
1 cup slivered almonds

1. Dissolve gelatin in boiling water. Stir in cottage cheese, mayonnaise, and onion until well blended. Fold in cucumber and almonds.
2. Pour mixture into a 1-quart mold. Refrigerate until set.
4 TO 6 SERVINGS

Beer-Curried Fruit

½ cup packed brown sugar
1 tablespoon cornstarch
2 to 3 teaspoons curry powder
¾ cup beer
¼ cup butter or margarine
1 tablespoon grated orange peel
1 can (30 ounces) cling peach slices, drained
1 can (29 ounces) cling pear halves or slices, drained
2 cans (11 ounces each) mandarin oranges, drained
2 bananas, thinly sliced

1. In a large saucepan, combine sugar, cornstarch, and curry powder. Stir in beer. Cook, stirring constantly, until thickened and clear.
2. Add butter and orange peel; stir until melted.
3. Add peaches, pears, and mandarin oranges. (If using pear halves, cut into slices.) Cover and simmer about 10

minutes. Stir in bananas.

4. Turn into a serving dish, chafing dish, or warming dish. Sprinkle with **flaked coconut.**

7 CUPS

Tangy Cabbage Mold

1 envelope unflavored gelatin
¼ cup cold water
¼ cup sugar
2 tablespoons lemon juice
½ teaspoon salt

1 can or bottle (12 ounces) beer
1½ cups shredded cabbage (about ¼ of a 2-pound head)
½ green pepper, shredded

1. Soften gelatin in cold water in a saucepan. Stir over low heat until dissolved.
2. Add sugar, lemon juice, and salt; stir until dissolved. Add beer. Chill until partially thickened.
3. Stir in cabbage and green pepper.
4. Turn into a 3½-cup mold, a shallow 1½-quart oblong casserole (8x6 inches), or 6 individual molds.

6 SERVINGS

Beermato Aspic

1 can (18 ounces) tomato juice (2¼ cups)
1 can or bottle (12 ounces) beer
⅓ cup chopped onion
⅓ cup chopped celery leaves (optional)

2½ tablespoons sugar
1 tablespoon lemon juice
½ teaspoon salt
1 bay leaf
2 envelopes unflavored gelatin
¼ cup cold water

1. Combine tomato juice (reserve ¼ cup), beer, onion, celery leaves, sugar, lemon juice, salt, and bay leaf in a saucepan. Simmer, uncovered, 10 minutes.
2. Meanwhile, sprinkle gelatin over cold water and reserved tomato juice in a large bowl; let stand to soften.
3. Strain hot tomato juice mixture into bowl; stir until gelatin is completely dissolved.
4. Pour into a lightly oiled 1-quart mold. Chill until firm. Unmold onto crisp **salad greens.**

8 SERVINGS

Note: For individual aspics, turn mixture into 8 oiled ½-cup molds. Chill until firm.

Beermato Aspic

Avocado Crab Salad, Paella Style

2 cans (5 ounces each) lobster (or use fresh lobster)
2 dozen small clams*
1 clove garlic, crushed
1 tablespoon butter or margarine
2 tablespoons dry sherry
¼ teaspoon saffron, crushed
Dash pepper
1¼ cups uncooked rice
¾ cup small pimento-stuffed olives
2 ripe avocados

1. Drain and remove bones from lobster (see note below).
2. Cook clams gently in boiling salted water to cover until the shells open.
3. Remove clams and cook shrimp in the same liquid, 3 to 5 minutes, covered.
4. Chill the shellfish, strain and measure 2½ cups of the fish broth into a medium sauce pan. Add garlic, butter or margarine, dry sherry, saffron, and pepper.
5. Bring to boiling and add uncooked rice.
6. Cover and cook over low heat about 15 minutes, or until rice kernels are soft and broth is absorbed.
7. Shell the chilled shrimp. (If using freshly cooked lobster, shell and cut meat into pieces; reserve 2 claws for garnish.)
8. Combine rice, clams, shrimp and lobster in a large mixing bowl. Add pimento-stuffed olives.
9. Mix lightly with a fork and chill thoroughly.
10. When ready to serve avocados, peel, halve, remove seeds and brush lightly with lemon juice.
11. Turn salad mixture into serving bowl and arrange avocado, cut in wedges, over top. (Garnish with lobster claws, if available.)
12. Serve the salad with **olive oil, herbed mayonnaise, salad dressing** or **tartar sauce,** as desired.
6 TO 8 SERVINGS

Note: If using fresh lobster meat, cook lobsters (about 1¼ pounds each) in 3 quarts boiling water and 3 tablespoons salt. Cover pot and cook lobsters over low heat about 20 minutes. Remove lobsters and use the same liquid to cook the clams and shrimp (one shellfish at a time). Reserve the cooking liquid.

*If desired, 1 dozen mussels may be substituted for 1 dozen small clams.

Chicken Mousse Amandine

½ cup dry white wine, such as sauterne
2 envelopes unflavored gelatin
3 egg yolks
1 cup milk
1 cup chicken broth
½ cup (about 3 ounces) almonds, finely chopped
3 cups ground cooked chicken
¼ cup mayonnaise
2 tablespoons minced parsley
2 tablespoons chopped green olives
1 teaspoon lemon juice
1 teaspoon onion juice
½ teaspoon salt
½ teaspoon celery salt
Few grains paprika
Few grains cayenne pepper
½ cup chilled heavy cream
Sprigs of parsley

1. Place a small bowl and a rotary beater in refrigerator to chill.
2. Pour wine into a small cup and sprinkle gelatin evenly over wine; set aside.
3. Beat egg yolks slightly in top of a double boiler; add milk gradually, stirring constantly.
4. Stir in the chicken broth gradually. Cook over simmering water, stirring constantly and rapidly until mixture coats a metal spoon.
5. Remove from heat. Stir softened gelatin and immediately stir it into the hot mixture until gelatin is completely dissolved. Cool; chill in refrigerator or over ice and water until gelatin mixture begins to gel (becomes slightly thicker). If mixture is placed over ice and water, stir frequently; if placed in refrigerator, stir occasionally.
6. Blend almonds and chicken into chilled custard mixture along with mayonnaise, parsley, olives, lemon juice, onion juice, and a mixture of salt, celery salt, paprika, and cayenne pepper.
7. Using the chilled bowl and beater, beat cream until of medium consistency (piles softly).
8. Fold whipped cream into chicken mixture. Turn into a 1½-quart fancy mold. Chill in refrigerator until firm.
9. Unmold onto chilled serving plate and, if desired, garnish with sprigs of parsley.
8 SERVINGS

Dubonnet Chicken Salad Mold

2 envelopes unflavored gelatin
1 cup cranberry juice cocktail
1 cup red Dubonnet
1 cup red currant syrup
1 envelope unflavored gelatin
¾ cup cold water
1 tablespoon soy sauce
1 cup mayonnaise
1½ cups finely diced cooked chicken
½ cup finely chopped celery
¼ cup toasted blanched almonds, finely chopped
½ cup whipping cream, whipped
Leaf lettuce
Cucumber slices, scored
Pitted ripe olives

1. Soften 2 envelopes gelatin in cranberry juice in a saucepan; set over low heat and stir until gelatin is dissolved. Remove from heat and stir in Dubonnet and currant syrup.
2. Pour into a 2-quart fancy tube mold. Chill until set but not firm.
3. Meanwhile, soften 1 envelope gelatin in cold water in a saucepan. Set over low heat and stir until gelatin is dissolved.
4. Remove from heat and stir in soy sauce and mayonnaise until thoroughly blended. Chill until mixture becomes slightly thicker. Mix in chicken, celery, and almonds. Fold in whipped cream until blended.
5. Spoon mixture into mold over first layer. Chill 8 hours or overnight.
6. Unmold onto a chilled serving plate. Garnish with lettuce, cucumber, and olives.
ABOUT 10 SERVINGS

Avocado Crab Salad, Paella Style

Christmas Eve Salad

1 cup diced cooked beets
1 cup diced tart apple, not peeled
1 cup orange sections
1 cup sliced bananas
1 cup diced pineapple (fresh or canned)
Juice of 1 lime
Oil and Vinegar Dressing
Shredded lettuce
½ cup chopped peanuts
Seeds from 1 pomegranate

1. Drain beets well. Combine beets, apple, oranges, bananas, and pineapple. Refrigerate until ready to serve.
2. Add lime juice to beet-fruit mixture. Add desired amount of dressing and toss until evenly mixed and coated with dressing.
3. To serve, make a bed of shredded lettuce in salad bowl. Mound salad on top. Sprinkle with peanuts and pomegranate seeds.
8 TO 10 SERVINGS

Hot Potato Salad

6 medium boiling potatoes (2 pounds)
10 slices bacon (½ pound)
½ cup chopped onion
½ cup beer
1 to 1½ tablespoons sugar
1 to 1½ teaspoons salt
1 teaspoon celery seed

1. Place unpeeled potatoes in a large saucepan; add water to cover. Heat to boiling. Boil, uncovered, for 20 minutes, or until tender. Peel and cube; turn into a serving dish.
2. Meanwhile, cook bacon until crisp; leave drippings in skillet. Crumble bacon over potatoes.
3. Add onion to skillet. Sauté until tender. Add beer, sugar, salt, and celery seed. Heat to boiling, stirring occasionally. Pour over potatoes; toss lightly.
6 SERVINGS

Asparagus Vinaigrette

1 envelope herb-flavored oil-and-vinegar salad dressing mix
Tarragon-flavored white wine vinegar
Water
Salad oil
2 tablespoons chopped
parsley
1 tablespoon finely chopped chives
2 teaspoons capers
1 hard-cooked egg, finely chopped
Cooked asparagus spears, chilled

1. Prepare salad dressing mix as directed on package, using vinegar, water, and salad oil.
2. Using 1 cup of the dressing, mix well with parsley, chives, capers and egg. Chill thoroughly.
3. To serve, arrange chilled asparagus in six bundles on a chilled serving plate lined with **Boston lettuce.** Garnish each bundle with a **pimento strip.** Complete platter with **cucumber slices** and **radish roses.** Mix dressing well before spooning over asparagus.
6 SERVINGS

Guacamole I

2 very ripe avocados
1 medium fresh tomato
1 small onion, chopped (about ⅓ cup)
2 tablespoons lemon juice
1 teaspoon salt
1 to 2 teaspoons chili powder

1. Peel avocados and mash pulp, leaving a few small lumps throughout.
2. Peel and chop tomato and add to mashed avocado. Add onion, lemon juice, salt, and chili powder to taste. If not serving immediately, refrigerate in covered bowl, with avocado pits immersed in guacamole; this is said to help keep avocado from darkening on standing.
3. Serve on lettuce as a salad, as a "dip" with tostada chips, or as a condiment to top taco fillings.
ABOUT 2 CUPS GUACAMOLE

Note: If you prefer a smoother guacamole, ingredients may be blended to desired consistency.

Guacamole II

2 large ripe avocados
3 tablespoons lemon juice
1 medium tomato
1 slice onion
1 small green chili
1 small clove garlic, minced
⅛ teaspoon coriander
Salt

1. Halve avocados, peel, remove pits, and cut avocado into pieces. Put into an electric blender with lemon juice.
2. Peel, halve, and seed tomato. Add to blender along with onion, chili, garlic, coriander, and salt to taste. Blend.
3. Serve as a dip with **corn chips, cauliflowerets,** and **carrot** and **celery sticks.**
ABOUT 3 CUPS DIP

Broccoli Salad

1 pound broccoli
3 tablespoons olive oil
3 tablespoons lemon juice
1 medium clove garlic
¼ teaspoon salt
⅛ teaspoon pepper

1. Trim off leaves and bottoms of broccoli stalks, and split thick stems lengthwise. Cook, covered, in a small amount of salted water until just tender. Drain and chill.
2. Combine olive oil, lemon juice, garlic, salt, and pepper. Drizzle over thoroughly chilled broccoli and serve.
ABOUT 3 SERVINGS

Cauliflower Salad: Follow recipe for Broccoli Salad. Substitute **1 medium head cauliflower** for broccoli. Peel and dice **1 boiled potato;** combine with cauliflower and chill. Substitute **wine vinegar** for the lemon juice and add ¼ teaspoon oregano.

Green Bean Salad: Follow recipe for Broccoli Salad. Clean and cook **½ pound green beans** and substitute for broccoli. Use wine vinegar instead of lemon juice.

Asparagus Salad: Follow recipe for Broccoli Salad. Clean and cook **1 pound asparagus** and substitute for the broccoli.

Peach Wine Mold

Cauliflower Acapulco

1 large head cauliflower

Marinade (see below)
1 can (15 ounces) garbanzos, drained
1 cup pimento-stuffed olives
Pimentos, drained and cut lengthwise in strips
Lettuce
1 jar (16 ounces) sliced pickled beets, drained and chilled
1 large cucumber, thinly sliced and chilled
Parsley sprigs
Radish roses
Guacamole I (see page 66)

1. Bring 1 inch of salted water to boiling in a large saucepan. Add cauliflower, cover, and cook about 20 minutes, or until just tender; drain.
2. Place cauliflower, head down, in a deep bowl and pour marinade over it. Chill several hours or overnight; occasionally spoon marinade over all.
3. Shortly before serving, thread garbanzos, olives, and pimento strips onto wooden picks for decorative kabobs. Set aside while arranging salad.
4. Drain cauliflower. Line a chilled serving plate with lettuce and place cauliflower, head up, in the center. Arrange pickled beet and cucumber slices around the base, tucking in parsley sprigs and radish roses.
5. Spoon and spread guacamole over cauliflower. Decorate with kabobs. Serve cold.
6 TO 8 SERVINGS

Marinade: Combine **1½ cups vegetable oil, ½ cup lemon juice, 1½ teaspoons salt,** and **1 teaspoon chili powder.** Shake marinade well before using.

Peach Wine Mold

1 can (29 ounces) sliced peaches
1 package (6 ounces) lemon-flavored gelatin
1½ cups boiling water
1 cup white wine
⅓ cup sliced celery
⅓ cup slivered blanched almonds
Curly endive

1. Drain peaches thoroughly, reserving 1¼ cups syrup. Reserve and refrigerate about 8 peach slices for garnish. Cut remaining peaches into pieces; set aside.
2. Pour gelatin into a bowl, add boiling water, and stir until gelatin is dissolved. Stir in reserved syrup and wine. Chill until partially set.
3. Mix peaches, celery, and almonds into gelatin. Turn into a 1½-quart fancy mold. Chill until firm.
4. Unmold salad onto a serving plate. Garnish with curly endive and reserved peach slices.
ABOUT 8 SERVINGS

Rooster's Bill

1 medium jícama*
1 large orange
¼ cup chopped onion
Juice of 1 lemon
1 teaspoon salt
1 teaspoon chili powder
½ teaspoon oregano, crumbled

1. Wash, pare, and chop jícama into ½-inch chunks.
2. Pare and section orange, reserving juice, and add to jícama; pour orange juice over fruit chunks. Add onion, lemon juice, and salt and stir until evenly mixed. Let stand at least 1 hour in refrigerator before serving.
3. When ready to serve, sprinkle with chili powder and oregano.
4 TO 6 SERVINGS

*3 large tart crisp apples may be substituted for jícama.

Sweet-Sour Beans in Tomato Shells

⅓ cup cider vinegar
2½ tablespoons dark brown sugar
½ teaspoon salt
1 can (16 ounces) diagonally
sliced green beans, drained
1 tablespoon finely chopped onion
6 tomato shells, chilled
1 tablespoon basil, crushed

1. Pour a mixture of the vinegar, brown sugar, and salt over the beans and onion in a bowl; toss lightly. Set in refrigerator to marinate 1 hour, tossing occasionally.
2. Sprinkle the inside of each tomato shell with crushed basil and **salt.** Spoon beans equally into tomato shells. Garnish with crisp **bacon curls.**
6 SERVINGS

Vegetable Platter Vinaigrette

1 pound fresh green beans halved
1 small head cauliflower Salt
Chicken Stock (see page 48) Freshly ground pepper
1 cup Vinaigrette Dressing 1 medium red onion, thinly
(see page 46) sliced
1 pint cherry tomatoes,

1. Steam green beans and whole cauliflower in separate covered saucepans in 1 inch of stock until tender (about 15 minutes). Drain. Mix beans with ½ cup dressing; refrigerate covered 3 hours, stirring occasionally.
2. Drain beans and tomatoes; reserve dressing. Place cauliflower in center of a platter; arrange beans and tomatoes around cauliflower. Sprinkle vegetables lightly with salt and pepper. Arrange onion slices over beans and tomatoes. Cut cauliflower into wedges to serve. Pass reserved dressing.
8 TO 10 SERVINGS

California Fruit Plate

2 cups low-fat cottage cheese 2 tablespoons honey
8 fresh figs, cut in quarters 4 lemon wedges
2 cups fresh raspberries

1. Place ½ cup cottage cheese on each of 4 salad plates.
2. Surround cottage cheese with 8 quarters of fig; sprinkle raspberries over figs.
3. Drizzle honey over fruit and cottage cheese. Squeeze lemon over all.
4 SERVINGS

Macaroni Picnic Salad

1 package (16 ounce) elbow 1 cup mayonnaise
macaroni (4 cups) ⅓ cup sweet pickle liquid
1 cup each sliced radishes, ¼ cup spicy brown mustard
sliced celery and sliced 1 teaspoon prepared
sweet gherkins horseradish
2 tablespoons chopped 1 teaspoon salt
onion ⅛ teaspoon white pepper

1. Cook macaroni in boiling salted water following directions on package.
2. Drain in colander.
3. Combine the macaroni in a large bowl with radishes, celery, sweet gherkins and chopped onion.
4. Mix mayonnaise, sweet pickle liquid, brown mustard, horseradish, salt, and white pepper thoroughly in a small bowl.
5. Toss dressing with macaroni mixture. Chill.
6. When ready to serve salad, garnish with **salad greens, radish roses** and **gherkin fans.**
ABOUT 8 SERVINGS

Macaroni Picnic Salad

Pineapple-Mint Salad

1 can (20 ounces)
  unsweetened pineapple
  chunks, drained
2 cups low-fat cottage cheese
½ bunch mint, snipped

Bibb lettuce
1 cup sliced celery
Mint sprigs
8 orange slices

1. Dice 1 cup of the pineapple; mix with cottage cheese and snipped mint.
2. Arrange lettuce leaves on a platter or individual plates; mound pineapple mixture on lettuce. Arrange remaining pineapple and the celery around mounds of pineapple mixture. Garnish with mint sprigs and orange slices.
4 TO 6 SERVINGS

Cucumber Salad

2 cups plain yogurt
1 scallion, chopped
1 teaspoon mint
½ teaspoon salt
Freshly ground pepper

Pinch dill
1 garlic clove, crushed in a
  garlic press
4 cucumbers, pared and thinly sliced

Mix yogurt with scallion, salt, pepper, dill, and garlic. Add cucumber and toss to coat with dressing. Refrigerate 1 hour.
6 SERVINGS

Potato Salad

½ cup olive oil
3 tablespoons wine vinegar
1 teaspoon oregano, crushed
2 tablespoons chopped
  parsley

1 medium onion, finely
  sliced
5 large red potatoes
Salt and pepper to taste

1. Combine olive oil, vinegar, oregano, parsley, and onion. Mix well. Set aside to marinate.
2. Scrub potatoes. Boil them in salted water in their jackets. When just tender (about 40 minutes), remove and plunge into cold water so they can be handled at once. Peel while hot and cut into even slices.
3. Pour the dressing over the potatoes; toss lightly. Add salt and pepper.
6 SERVINGS

Fruit Salad with Ice Cream Topping

4 pears, cored
1 large melon wedge
1 can Mandarin orange
  wedges
½ can pineapple

Green grapes (optional)
2 pints vanilla ice cream
1 cup fresh orange juice
Orange rind

1. Cut the pears and melon wedge in pieces and mix with the canned fruits.
2. Pour in a little of the syrup from the cans. Cover and let salad stand in refrigerator until chilled.
3. Divide the ice cream into 8 dishes.
4. Distribute fruit on top of ice cream.
5. Just before serving, pour on the fresh orange juice. Sprinkle with finely slivered orange rind or coconut.
SERVES 8

Anchovy Potato Salad

Dressing
1 cup olive oil
½ cup wine vinegar
¼ teaspoon sugar
1 teaspoon dill
1 teaspoon marjoram
Pepper to taste

Salad
8 Anchovy Fillets or 1 can (2
  ounces) anchovies preserved
  in olive oil, drained

1 bunch escarole, torn in
  bite-size pieces
2 potatoes, boiled and diced
1 small jar pickled beets,
  drained and diced
2 green peppers, cleaned
  and thinly sliced
4 scallions, minced
3 hard-cooked eggs, sliced,
  for garnish
1 teaspoon capers for garnish
Salt and pepper to taste

1. For dressing, combine all ingredients in a jar. Shake well. Refrigerate 1 or 2 hours before serving.
2. For salad, combine anchovies with remaining ingredients, except eggs, capers, salt, and pepper. Add the salad dressing and toss to coat. Garnish with eggs and capers. Season with salt and pepper.
4 TO 6 SERVINGS

Cucumber and Tomato Salad

3 firm-ripe homegrown
  tomatoes, cut in wedges
3 pickle cucumbers (as
  straight as possible), pared
  and sliced ¼ inch thick
4 scallions, finely chopped
¼ pound feta cheese,
  crumbled

Kalamata olives (about 8)
Oregano and freshly dried
  dill, a generous pinch of
  each
Salt and pepper to taste
3 tablespoons wine vinegar
⅓ cup olive oil

1. In a salad bowl, combine tomatoes, cucumbers, scallions, cheese, and olives. Season with oregano, dill, salt, and pepper.
2. Combine vinegar and olive oil in a small jar; shake well. Add to salad and toss.
6 TO 8 SERVINGS

Lobster Salad

6 cups diced fresh lobster
  meat, chilled
3 hard-cooked eggs, mashed
  through a sieve
1 large scallion, minced
1 small leek, finely chopped
2 teaspoons tarragon
½ teaspoon thyme

2 garlic cloves, crushed in a
  garlic press
2 cups mayonnaise
1 tablespoon capers
Juice of 1 lemon
Cucumber, sliced paper thin
Tomato wedges for garnish

1. Combine all ingredients except cucumber and tomato. Adjust seasoning.
2. Spoon into heated **pastry shells,** a **lobster** cavity, or on a bed of **lettuce.** Garnish with cucumber slices and tomato wedges.
ABOUT 12 SERVINGS

Fruit Salad with Ice Cream Topping

Piquant Perfection Salad

1½ cups boiling water
1 package (6 ounces) lemon-flavored gelatin
1 can (8 ounces) crushed pineapple in juice
Water
1 can or bottle (12 ounces) beer
3 medium carrots, shredded (about 1½ cups)
½ small head cabbage, finely shredded (about 3 cups)

1. Pour boiling water over gelatin; stir until dissolved.
2. Drain pineapple, thoroughly pressing out and reserving juice. Add enough water to juice to measure ¾ cup.
3. Add juice and beer to gelatin. Chill until partially thickened.
4. Stir in carrots, cabbage, and pineapple. Turn into a shallow pan or oiled 6½-cup ring mold or any 1½-quart mold. Chill until set.
5. Dip mold briefly in hot water; invert on a serving platter.
6. Serve with a dressing of **1 cup mayonnaise** blended with **2 tablespoons beer.**
12 HALF-CUP SERVINGS

Piquant Perfection Salad

Russian Salad

⅓ cup olive oil
3 tablespoons vinegar
1 cup diced cooked carrots
1 cup diced cooked beets
2 potatoes, cooked and diced
1 cup french-cut green
beans, cooked and diced
1 cup cooked peas
¼ cup minced parsley
Mayonnaise
Salt and pepper to taste
2 teaspoons capers

1. Mix olive oil and vinegar and pour over vegetables; allow to marinate 1 to 2 hours. Drain. Discard dressing.
2. Mix vegetables and parsley with enough mayonnaise to bind together (about 1 cup). Season with salt and pepper. Garnish with capers to serve.
6 SERVINGS

Warsaw Salad

1 cup mayonnaise
⅓ cup sour cream
1 tablespoon prepared mustard
2 cups julienne beets, cooked or canned
1½ cups kidney beans, cooked or canned
1½ cups cooked or canned
peas
1 cup diced dill pickles
6 ounces (about 1¼ cups) cooked crab meat
3 scallions, chopped
1 hard-cooked egg, sliced
Carrot curls and radish roses to garnish

1. Combine mayonnaise, sour cream, and mustard in a large bowl.
2. Add remaining ingredients, except egg, carrots, and radishes; toss gently to mix.
3. Garnish with egg slices, carrot curls, and radish roses.
8 TO 12 SERVINGS

Raw Broccoli Salad

3 cups raw bite-size pieces broccoli spears
½ cup Low-Fat Yogurt (see page 47)
½ teaspoon freshly ground
pepper
2 ounces Cheddar cheese, shredded
1 large carrot, cut in thin slices

Mix broccoli with yogurt, salt, and pepper. Spoon mixture on 4 salad plates. Sprinkle tops of salads with cheese; arrange carrot slices around salads.
4 SERVINGS

Sauerkraut Salad with Carrots and Apples

¼ cup salad or olive oil
1½ teaspoons sugar
1 teaspoon caraway seed
½ teaspoon salt
1 teaspoon vinegar
1 pound sauerkraut, drained
2 medium tart apples, peeled, cored, and diced
¾ cup grated carrot

1. Combine oil, sugar, caraway seed, salt, and vinegar.
2. Rinse and drain sauerkraut well; chop. Stir into oil mixture.
3. Add apples and carrot; toss to mix.
ABOUT 6 SERVINGS

Rose Salad

10 small potatoes (about 2½ pounds), cooked
¼ cup olive oil
3 tablespoons lemon juice or vinegar
1 tablespoon water
1 tablespoon sugar
1 teaspoon salt
¼ teaspoon pepper
2 cups shell beans, cooked
or canned
¼ pound sauerkraut, drained
4 stalks celery, sliced lengthwise
6 cups shredded red cabbage
Boiling water
3 tablespoons tarragon vinegar
4 cooked or canned beets, sliced

1. Slice potatoes. Mix olive oil, lemon juice, 1 tablespoon water, sugar, salt, and pepper. Pour over potatoes. Add beans, sauerkraut, and celery.
2. Add red cabbage to boiling water. Let stand 2 minutes. Drain well. Stir in tarragon vinegar; mix until cabbage is pink.
3. Mound red cabbage in center of a large platter. Arrange beet slices in cabbage to form a rose.
4. Place potatoes and other vegetables around edges. Use **celery** for rose stem. Garnish with **lettuce leaves.**
8 TO 12 SERVINGS

Potato Salad with Wine

2 pounds potatoes
2 teaspoons salt
Boiling water
1 cup white wine
1 stalk celery
⅓ cup olive oil

¼ cup chopped fresh dill
¼ cup chopped parsley
3 tablespoons lemon juice
2 tablespoons chopped
  chives
¼ teaspoon pepper

1. Cook potatoes with salt in enough boiling water to cover until tender, about 30 minutes. Peel and slice; put into a bowl.
2. Pour wine over potatoes; let stand 30 minutes.
3. Cook celery in a small amount of boiling water until soft. Press celery through a sieve. Combine 2 tablespoons cooking liquid and puréed celery, oil, dill, parsley, lemon juice, chives, and pepper.
4. Add celery mixture to potatoes; mix.
6 SERVINGS

Red Cabbage-Apple Salad

3 cups shredded red cabbage
1 red apple, cut in 1½ x
  ¼-inch strips
1 sweet red pepper, cut in
  1½ x ¼-inch strips
2 tablespoons cider vinegar

¼ cup apple juice
¼ teaspoon caraway seed
⅛ teaspoon salt
⅛ teaspoon freshly ground
  pepper
Salad greens

Mix all ingredients except salad greens in a medium bowl. Refrigerate covered 2 hours. Serve on salad greens or individual plates.
4 SERVINGS

Northwest Fruit Slaw

Beet Mousse

8 medium beets
1 tablespoon vinegar
1½ teaspoons unflavored
  gelatin
¼ cup orange juice
½ cup instant nonfat dry-

milk solids
2 to 3 ice cubes
1½ teaspoons prepared
  horseradish
Salad greens

1. Cut greens from beets; discard. Simmer beets in 2 inches water and vinegar until tender (about 30 minutes). Slip off skins. Cut thin slice from bottoms of beets; hollow out centers with melon-baller, leaving ½-inch shells; reserve centers. Refrigerate beets until chilled.
2. Sprinkle gelatin over orange juice in a small saucepan; let stand 5 minutes. Set over low heat, stirring occasionally, until gelatin is dissolved (about 3 minutes). Pour gelatin mixture into a food processor or blender; add beet centers and dry-milk solids. Process, adding ice cubes one at a time, until mixture is the consistency of thick whipped cream. Stir in horseradish. Fill beets with mixture; refrigerate until serving time. Serve on salad greens.
4 SERVINGS

Green Bean and Onion Salad

1 pound small boiling onions
1½ pounds fresh green
  beans
Chicken Stock (see page 48)
½ cup Mock Crème Fraîche
  (see page 46)
¼ cup low-fat cottage cheese
2 tablespoons snipped fresh
  chives

1 teaspoon snipped fresh or
  ½ teaspoon dried thyme
  leaves
1 teaspoon snipped fresh or
  ½ teaspoon dried marjoram
  leaves
Salt
Freshly ground pepper
Juice of ½ lemon

1. Simmer onions and beans in 1 inch of stock in a covered saucepan until tender (15 to 18 minutes). Drain; refrigerate covered until chilled (about 2 hours).
2. Mix remaining ingredients except salt, pepper, and lemon juice; refrigerate covered until chilled.
3. Arrange vegetables on a platter; sprinkle lightly with salt and pepper. Squeeze lemon juice over. Spoon sauce over or pass sauce separately.
6 SERVINGS

Northwest Fruit Slaw

1 can (16 ounces) light sweet
  cherries
1 can (16 ounces) dark sweet
  cherries
3 fresh Anjou, Bosc, or Com-
  ice pears

2 cups finely shredded
  cabbage
Creamy Fruit Mayonnaise
  (page 53)
Lettuce

1. Drain cherries and remove pits. Reserve a few cherries for garnish. Core and dice 1 pear. Core and slice remaining pears into wedges for garnish.
2. Combine cabbage, cherries, and diced pear. Add Creamy Fruit Mayonnaise and toss lightly to coat fruit and cabbage.
3. Line a serving bowl with lettuce and spoon in salad. Garnish with pear wedges and reserved cherries.
ABOUT 8 SERVINGS

Haitian Rock Lobster Salad

8 rock lobster tails
Court Bouillon for Fish and
  Shellfish (page 43)
4 cups rice
16 cherry tomatoes, washed
  and stemmed
1 cup cubed pared cucumber
3 celery stalks, diced
1 cup cubed fresh pineapple

1 cup small Greek black
  olives
¼ cup capers
1 cup French Dressing An-
  tillaise for Salads (page 44)
4 hard-cooked eggs, peeled
  and quartered
¾ cup amber rum

1. Simmer lobster tails in court bouillon 20 minutes. Belly
side down on a board, split the tail lengthwise with a sharp
knife and keep warm in the bouillon until serving time (see
Note).
2. Toss rice with vegetables, pineapple, olives, and capers.
Add dressing and toss again.
3. Mound the rice mixture on a large silver platter, garnish
with hard-cooked egg quarters, and edge platter with drained
cooked lobster tails.
4. At the table, warm rum, ignite it, and pour it flaming
over the lobster.
8 SERVINGS

Note: If you have room in the freezer, save the court bouillon
to use as a base for Béchamel Sauce for fish or for a
chowder.

Greek Salad in Peppers

1 large tomato, chopped
1 green onion, sliced
⅛ teaspoon salt
1 teaspoon snipped fresh or
  ½ teaspoon dried basil
  leaves
1 tablespoon fresh lemon

juice
4 small green peppers, cored
½ cup crumbled feta cheese
8 anchovies, drained and
  rinsed
8 lemon wedges

1. Mix tomato, onion, salt, basil, and lemon juice;
refrigerate covered 1 hour.
2. Spoon half the tomato mixture into green peppers; layer
cheese over tomatoes. Spoon remaining tomato mixture
over cheese. Arrange 2 anchovies over top of each pepper. Serve with lemon wedges.
4 SERVINGS

Turnip-Carrot-Cabbage Slaw

1 cup shredded white turnip
1 cup shredded carrot
2 cups finely shredded
  cabbage
¼ cup finely chopped onion

¼ cup chopped parsley
¼ teaspoon salt
⅛ teaspoon pepper
3 tablespoons mayonnaise

1. Toss vegetables together gently with a mixture of salt,
pepper, and mayonnaise until vegetables are evenly coated.
2. Chill, covered, in refrigerator until ready to serve.
ABOUT 6 SERVINGS

Sardine-Egg Salad-Stuffed Tomatoes

6 tomatoes
2 cans (3¾ ounces each)
  Norwegian sardines
6 hard-cooked eggs, diced
2 tablespoons capers

¼ cup sour cream
2 tablespoons mayonnaise
1 tablespoon caper liquid
½ teaspoon dry mustard
¼ teaspoon salt

1. Rinse tomatoes (peel if desired) and chill thoroughly in
refrigerator.
2. Drain 1 can of sardines, remove tails, and cut the sardines into pieces; reserve the other can of sardines for completing the salad. Lightly toss the sardines for completing
the salad. Lightly toss the sardines with the eggs and capers.
3. Combine the sour cream, mayonnaise, caper liquid, dry
mustard, and salt. Add to egg-sardine mixture and toss lightly to mix well. Chill thoroughly.
4. When both the mixture and tomatoes are thoroughly
chilled, cut a slice from the top of each tomato. Using a
spoon, remove seeds. Invert shells to drain. Sprinkle insides
with **seasoned salt** before stuffing. Fill center of tomatoes
with the egg-sardine mixture.
5. Choose greenest **lettuce leaves** and use to line salad
plates. Set tomatoes on lettuce. Place one sardine across
each stuffed tomato and garnish with sprigs of **watercress.**
6 SERVINGS

Pickled Pepper Salad

2 cups sliced pickled red
  peppers
¾ cup chopped celery
½ cup sliced ripe olives
8 anchovy fillets, chopped

2 tablespoons olive oil
2 tablespoons wine vinegar
¼ teaspoon oregano
⅛ teaspoon salt
¼ teaspoon pepper

1. Gently combine the red peppers, celery, olives, and anchovy fillets. Mix oil, vinegar, oregano, salt, and pepper;
pour over the red pepper mixture. Toss gently.
2. Serve very cold.
6 TO 8 SERVINGS

Red Kidney Bean Salad

1 can (16 ounces) kidney
  beans
¼ cup wine vinegar
3 tablespoons olive oil
¼ teaspoon oregano
¼ teaspoon salt

⅛ teaspoon pepper
¼ cup sliced celery
2 tablespoons chopped
  onion
Lettuce cups

1. Thoroughly rinse and drain kidney beans.
2. Combine vinegar, oil, oregano, salt, and pepper; mix
with beans. Blend in celery and onion; chill.
3. Serve in crisp lettuce cups.
ABOUT 4 SERVINGS

Stuffed Eggplant Salad

2 large eggplants
4 medium tomatoes, peeled and diced
⅓ cup thinly sliced green onion
⅓ cup olive or salad oil
½ cup fresh lemon juice
¼ cup chopped parsley
1 tablespoon sugar
2½ teaspoons salt
2 teaspoons oregano
¼ teaspoon ground black pepper

1. Wash and dry eggplants; place on a cookie sheet. Bake in a 375°F oven 35 to 45 minutes, or until tender when pierced with a fork. Cool.
2. Cut a thin lengthwise slice from the side of each eggplant; carefully spoon out pulp. Chill shells.
3. Dice pulp and put into a bowl. Add tomatoes, green onion, oil, lemon juice, parsley, sugar, salt, oregano, and pepper; toss to mix. Chill.
4. Before serving, drain off excess liquid from salad mixture. Spoon salad into shells.
6 SERVINGS

Green Salad

1 large head lettuce, or an equal amount of another salad green (curly endive, romaine, escarole, chicory,
or dandelion greens)
1 clove garlic
Italian Dressing (see page 50)

1. Wash lettuce in cold water, removing core, separating leaves, and removing any bruised leaves. Drain; dry thoroughly and carefully. Tear lettuce into bite-size pieces, put into a plastic bag, and chill 1 hour.
2. Just before serving, cut garlic in half and rub a wooden bowl. Put greens in bowl and pour on desired amount of dressing. Turn and toss the greens until well coated with dressing and no dressing remains in the bottom of the bowl.
ABOUT 6 SERVINGS

Green Salad with Anchovy Dressing: Follow recipe for Green Salad. Add **2 tomatoes,** cut in wedges, **¼ cup diced celery,** and **½ cup chopped ripe olives** to lettuce in bowl. Toss with **Anchovy Dressing.**

Mixed Salad: Follow recipe for Green Salad. Add **¼ cup chopped cucumber, ¼ cup chopped celery, ¼ cup sliced radishes,** and **¼ cup chopped ripe olives** to lettuce before tossing with dressing.

Italian Potato Salad II

2 medium potatoes, boiled, peeled, and diced
⅓ cup chopped celery
½ cup diced pared cucumber
½ cup chopped ripe olives
2 tablespoons minced onion
¾ cup Italian Dressing (page 50)
¼ teaspoon oregano

1. Lightly toss together the potatoes, celery, cucumber, olives, and onion. With a fork, thoroughly but carefully blend in the dressing mixed with oregano.
2. Cover the salad. Chill about 1 hour before serving.
ABOUT 4 SERVINGS

Fresh Bean Sprout Salad

1 pound fresh bean sprouts, rinsed (see Note)
2 medium carrots, shredded
1 tablespoon toasted sesame
seed
2 teaspoons vegetable oil
⅓ cup distilled white vinegar
2 teaspoons sugar

1. Mix bean sprouts and carrots in a shallow glass dish.
2. Shake remaining ingredients in a covered jar; pour over vegetables.
3. Refrigerate covered 1½ hours; stir occasionally. Serve in shallow bowls.
4 TO 6 SERVINGS

Note: If fresh bean sprouts are not available, you can substitute **1 large pared, seeded, shredded cucumber.**

Greek Salad

Salad Dressing:
⅓ cup olive oil
¼ cup wine vinegar
½ teaspoon salt
1 teaspoon oregano

Salad:
1 large head romaine,
  trimmed and torn in pieces
1 cucumber, pared and cut
  in 3½-inch pieces
1 small bunch radishes,
  cleaned and trimmed
2 small green peppers,
  trimmed and cored
1 can (8 ounces) whole
  beets, drained
4 tomatoes
⅓ pound feta cheese
Greek olives
Anchovy fillets (optional)

Greek Salad

1. For salad dressing, mix all ingredients and refrigerate.
2. For salad, put romaine pieces in a large salad bowl.
3. Using **slicing disc** of food processor, slice cucumber, radishes, green pepper, and beets.
4. Cut tomatoes into quarters.
5. Using **plastic blade** of food processor, process feta cheese, using quick on/off motions, until crumbled.
6. Combine prepared salad ingredients with romaine in a bowl, sprinkle with crumbled feta cheese, and top with olives and, if desired, anchovy fillets. Pour salad dressing over salad and serve.
8 SERVINGS

Stuffed Eggplant Salad

2 large eggplants
4 medium tomatoes, peeled
  and diced
⅓ cup thinly sliced green
  onion
⅓ cup olive or salad oil
½ cup fresh lemon juice
¼ cup chopped parsley
1 tablespoon sugar
2½ teaspoons salt
2 teaspoons oregano
¼ teaspoon ground black
  pepper

1. Wash and dry eggplants; place on a cookie sheet. Bake in a 375°F oven 35 to 45 minutes, or until tender when pierced with a fork. Cool.
2. Cut a thin lengthwise slice from the side of each eggplant; carefully spoon out pulp. Chill shells.
3. Dice pulp and put into a bowl. Add tomatoes, green onion, oil, lemon juice, parsley, sugar, salt, oregano, and pepper; toss to mix. Chill.
4. Before serving, drain off excess liquid from salad mixture. Spoon salad into shells.
6 SERVINGS

Stuffed Eggplant Salad

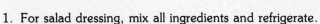

Bacon-Bean Salad

⅔ cup cider vinegar
¾ cup sugar
1 teaspoon salt
1 can (16 ounces) cut green
  beans
1 can (16 ounces) cut wax
  beans
1 can (16 ounces) kidney
  beans, thoroughly rinsed
  and drained
1 medium onion, quartered
  and finely sliced
1 medium green pepper,
  chopped
½ teaspoon freshly ground
  black pepper
⅓ cup salad oil
1 pound bacon, cut in 1-inch
  squares
Lettuce (optional)

1. Blend vinegar, sugar, and salt in a small saucepan. Heat until the sugar is dissolved and set aside.
2. Drain all beans and toss with onion, green pepper, vinegar mixture, and ground pepper. Pour oil over all and toss to coat evenly. Store in a covered container in refrigerator.
3. When ready to serve, fry bacon until crisp; drain on absorbent paper. Toss the bacon with bean mixture. If desired, serve the salad on crisp lettuce.
ABOUT 12 SERVINGS

Note: If desired, omit bacon.

Shrimp and Avocado Salad

1 cup wine vinegar
⅓ cup water
½ cup lemon juice
1 cup salad oil
¼ cup chopped parsley
2 cloves garlic, minced
1 tablespoon salt
¼ teaspoon freshly ground
  black pepper
1 tablespoon sugar
1 teaspoon dry mustard

1 teaspoon thyme, crushed
1 teaspoon oregano, crushed
2 pounds large cooked
  shrimp, peeled and
  deveined
3 small onions, sliced
⅓ cup chopped green
  pepper
2 ripe avocados, peeled and
  sliced

1. For marinade, combine vinegar, water, lemon juice, oil, parsley, and garlic in a bowl or a screwtop jar. Add a mixture of salt, pepper, sugar, dry mustard, thyme, and oregano; blend thoroughly.
2. Put shrimp, onions, and green pepper into a large shallow dish. Pour marinade over all, cover and refrigerate 8 hours or overnight.
3. About 1 hour before serving, put avocado slices into bowl. Pour enough marinade from shrimp over the avocado to cover completely.
4. To serve, remove avocado slices and shrimp from marinade and arrange on crisp **lettuce** in a large serving bowl.
ABOUT 8 SERVINGS

Greek-Style Lamb-and-Olive Salad

Greek-Style Salad Dressing:
½ cup olive or salad oil
1 cup red wine vinegar
3 to 4 tablespoons honey
1½ teaspoons salt
⅛ teaspoon dry mustard
2 teaspoons crushed dried
  mint leaves
¼ teaspoon crushed oregano
¼ teaspoon crushed thyme
¼ teaspoon anise seed

Salad:
1½ pounds roast lamb,
  trimmed of fat and cut in
  strips
Curly endive
1 large cucumber, pared and
  sliced
4 medium tomatoes, sliced
  and quartered
1 cup pitted ripe olives

1. For dressing, mix oil, vinegar, honey, salt, dry mustard, mint, oregano, thyme, and anise.
2. Pour the dressing over cooked lamb in a bowl, cover, and marinate in refrigerator at least 1 hour, or until thoroughly chilled.
3. To serve, arrange curly endive in a large salad bowl. Toss cucumber, tomatoes, and olives with some of the dressing and turn into salad bowl. Spoon meat over vegetables and pour more dressing over all.
6 SERVINGS

Sauerkraut Slaw

2 cups (16-ounce can)
  sauerkraut, drained and
  snipped with scissors
1 onion, chopped (about ½
  cup)
1 green pepper, sliced (about
  ¾ cup)

1 unpared red apple, diced
  (about 1 cup)
⅓ to ½ cup sugar
1 can (16 ounces) sliced
  tomatoes or tomato
  wedges, drained
Seasoned pepper

1. Combine sauerkraut, onion, green pepper, apple, and sugar in a serving bowl; toss until well mixed. Cover and refrigerate.
2. Before serving, overlap tomato slices around edge of bowl. Sprinkle slices with seasoned pepper.
8 TO 12 SERVINGS

Mixed Vegetable Salad

1 cup diced cooked potatoes
1½ cups cooked sliced
  carrots
1½ cups cooked whole or
  cut green beans (fresh,
  frozen, or canned)
1½ cups cooked green peas
  (fresh, frozen, or canned)
1 cup sliced or diced cooked
  beets
Bottled Italian-style salad

dressing
Lettuce
1 cup sliced celery
1 small onion, chopped
2 hard-cooked eggs, chopped
¾ cup small pimento-stuffed
  olives
¾ cup mayonnaise
¼ cup chili sauce
1 teaspoon lemon juice

1. Put potatoes, carrots, beans, peas, and beets into separate bowls. Pour salad dressing over each vegetable; chill thoroughly.
2. To serve, drain vegetables and arrange in a lettuce-lined salad bowl along with celery, onion, eggs, and olives.
3. Blend mayonnaise, chili sauce, and lemon juice. Pass with the salad.
ABOUT 8 SERVINGS

Beef Salad Acapulco

3 cups cooked beef strips
¾ cup salad oil
½ cup red wine vinegar
1½ teaspoons salt
¼ teaspoon ground pepper
⅛ teaspoon cayenne pepper
1 tablespoon chili powder

Salad greens
Avocado slices, brushed with
  marinade
Onion and green pepper
  rings
Tomato wedges
Ripe olives

1. Put beef strips into a shallow dish. Combine oil, vinegar, salt, pepper, cayenne pepper, and chili powder in a bottle; cover and shake vigorously. Pour over beef strips. Cover; marinate several hours or overnight.
2. Remove beef from marinade and arrange on crisp greens on chilled salad plates. Garnish with avocado slices, onion rings, green pepper rings, tomato wedges, and ripe olives. Serve the marinade as the dressing.
4 TO 6 SERVINGS

Shrimp and Avocado Salad

Molded Spinach Cottage Cheese on Platter

1 package (10 ounces) frozen chopped spinach
2 envelopes unflavored gelatin
¾ cup water
2 chicken bouillon cubes
2 tablespoons lemon juice
1½ cups creamed cottage cheese
½ cup sour cream
½ cup sliced celery
⅓ cup chopped green pepper
2 tablespoons minced green onion

1. Cook and drain spinach, reserving liquid. Add enough water to liquid to make ½ cup. Set spinach and liquid aside.
2. Soften gelatin in ¾ cup water in a saucepan; add bouillon cubes. Set over low heat; stirring occasionally, until gelatin and bouillon cubes are dissolved. Remove from heat; stir in spinach liquid and lemon juice. Set aside.
3. Beat cottage cheese until fairly smooth with mixer or in electric blender. Blend with sour cream and then gelatin mixture. Stir in spinach, celery, green pepper, and onion. Turn into a 5-cup mold. Chill until firm.
4. Unmold onto a chilled large platter. If desired, arrange slices of summer sausage around the mold.

6 TO 8 SERVINGS

Cinnamon Waldorf Molds

⅓ cup red cinnamon candies
3 cups water
2 packages (3 ounces each) cherry-flavored gelatin
1 tablespoon lemon juice
2 cups chopped celery
2 cups chopped unpared red apples
1 cup miniature marshmallows
½ cup chopped walnuts
Lettuce

1. Heat cinnamon candies and water to boiling in a saucepan. Remove from heat and add gelatin and lemon juice; stir until gelatin and candies are dissolved.
2. Chill until slightly thickened.
3. Mix in celery, apples, marshmallows, and walnuts. Spoon into 6 to 8 individual fancy molds or turn into a 1½-quart mold. Chill until firm.
4. Unmold onto lettuce.

6 TO 8 SERVINGS

Vegetable Salad with Yogurt Dressing

¾ cup Low-Fat Yogurt (page 47)
2 tablespoons snipped parsley
½ cup finely chopped dill pickle
½ cup chopped tomato
1 teaspoon salt
1 cup sliced radishes
1 medium zucchini, shredded
2 medium carrots, shredded
1 large beet, shredded

1. Mix yogurt, parsley, pickle, chopped tomato, and salt; refrigerate covered 1 hour.
2. Arrange radish slices around edge of a serving plate. Arrange zucchini, carrots, and beet decoratively in center of plate. Serve yogurt mixture with salad.

4 SERVINGS

Tossed Supper Salad

Dressing:
1 cup salad oil
½ cup cider vinegar
1 teaspoon salt
1 teaspoon sugar
½ teaspoon onion salt
¼ teaspoon crushed tarragon
¼ teaspoon paprika
¼ teaspoon dry mustard
¼ teaspoon celery salt
⅛ teaspoon garlic salt
⅛ teaspoon ground black pepper

Salad:
2 cans (6½ or 7 ounces each) tuna
½ head lettuce
1 cup spinach leaves, washed
1 cup diced celery
¾ cup chopped green pepper
½ cup cooked green peas
4 sweet pickles, chopped
4 radishes, thinly sliced
2 hard-cooked eggs, sliced
2 tablespoons chopped pimento
2 tomatoes, rinsed and cut in eighths
1 teaspoon salt
Tomato wedges
Ripe olives

1. For dressing, put oil and vinegar into a jar; mix salt, sugar, and seasonings; add to jar, cover, and shake well. Refrigerate until needed. Shake before using.
2. For salad, drain tuna well and separate into small chunks; put into a bowl. Toss tuna with ½ cup prepared dressing; cover and refrigerate 1 to 2 hours.
3. Tear lettuce and spinach into pieces and put into a large bowl. Add celery, green pepper, peas, pickles, radishes, eggs, and pimento; add the tuna with its dressing and tomatoes. Sprinkle with salt. Toss lightly until ingredients are mixed and lightly coated with dressing; add more dressing, if desired.
4. Garnish with tomato wedges and ripe olives.

8 TO 10 SERVINGS

Shrimp Salad with Coral Dressing

2 cups cooked, peeled, and
  deveined shrimp
1½ cups cooked rice
½ cup sliced celery
½ cup chopped unpeeled
  cucumbers
¼ cup chopped chives
⅓ cup mayonnaise
¼ cup sour cream

1 tablespoon chili sauce
¼ teaspoon onion salt
⅛ teaspoon pepper
1½ teaspoons tarragon
  vinegar
Salad greens
Horseradish (optional)
Lemon wedges

1. Toss shrimp, rice, celery, cucumbers, and chives together.
2. Blend ingredients for dressing. Pour over shrimp mixture and toss thoroughly. Chill.
3. Serve on salad greens. Top with a little horseradish, if desired, and garnish with lemon wedges.
4. Accompany with champagne.
6 SERVINGS

Ham Mousse

1 pound chopped ham
2 small chopped cucumbers
1 bunch chopped dill
1 cup heavy cream
2½ teaspoons prepared mustard
2 teaspoons unflavored gelatin
6 tablespoons cold water
2 tomatoes

1 frozen turkey roll (1 pound)
1 can white asparagus with tips (1 pound)
1 package frozen peas (cooked according to directions)
1 can creamed mushrooms (8 ounces)

1. Mix the chopped ham, cucumber and dill.
2. Beat the cream to a light foam and season with the mustard.
3. Melt the gelatin in ¼ cup cold water in a double boiler.
4. Stir the melted gelatin and the chopped ham into the cream. Pour into a water-rinsed ring mold, and place the mousse in the refrigerator to set.
5. Dip the tomatoes in hot water, remove the skin and cut them in halves.
6. Carve the turkey roll in even slices. Place the ham mousse in the middle of a large round dish. If the ring mold is dipped in hot water for a moment it will slide out easily. Put the asparagus in the middle of the mousse and arrange turkey slices in groups around the mousse. Surround with tomatoes and peas. Distribute the creamed mushrooms on the turkey slices.
SERVES 8 TO 10

Chef's Fruit Salad

Cinnamon-Buttered Raisins:
1 tablespoon butter or margarine, melted
½ cup dark raisins
½ cup golden raisins
½ teaspoon ground cinnamon

Salad:
Salad greens

1 quart shredded salad greens
6 cups mixed fruit
Creamy Lemon Celery-Seed Dressing or Celery-Seed Salad Dressing
1½ cups Swiss cheese strips
1½ cups cooked ham or turkey strips

1. For Cinnamon-Buttered Raisins, melt butter in a skillet. Mix in raisins and cinnamon. Set over low heat 5 minutes, stirring frequently. Cool.
2. Line a salad bowl with salad greens. Add shredded greens.
3. Arrange fruit in bowl. Spoon some of the desired dressing over all. Top with cheese and ham strips alternated with Cinnamon-Buttered Raisins. Serve with remaining dressing.
ABOUT 6 SERVINGS

Creamy Lemon Celery-Seed Dressing; Blend thoroughly **1½ cups mayonnaise, ¼ cup unsweetened pineapple juice, 1 teaspoon grated lemon peel, 1 tablespoon lemon juice, ½ teaspoon celery seed,** and **few drops Tabasco.** Cover and refrigerate at least 1 hour to blend flavors.
ABOUT 1½ CUPS DRESSING

Celery-Seed Salad Dressing: Combine in a small bowl **¼ cup sugar, ⅓ cup light corn syrup, ¼ cup cider vinegar, 1½ to 2 teaspoons celery seed, 1 teaspoon dry mustard, 1 teaspoon salt, few grains white pepper,** and **1 teaspoon grated onion.** Beat with a rotary beater until mixture is thoroughly blended. Add **1 cup salad oil** very gradually, beating constantly. Continue beating until mixture thickens. Cover and chill thoroughly. Shake before serving.
2 CUPS DRESSING

Garden-Green Salad Mold

1 package (3 ounces) lime-flavored gelatin
¼ teaspoon salt
1 cup boiling water
1 cup cold water
1 ripe medium avocado
1 tablespoon lemon juice

2 cups finely shredded cabbage
½ cup thinly sliced radishes
½ cup thinly sliced green onions with tops
Crisp greens

1. Put gelatin and salt into a bowl; add boiling water and stir until completely dissolved. Blend in cold water. Chill until slightly thickened.
2. Mash avocado and stir in lemon juice; blend thoroughly with gelatin. Mix in cabbage, radishes, and green onions.
3. Turn into a 1-quart mold or individual molds and chill until firm. Unmold onto chilled serving plate and garnish with salad greens.
ABOUT 8 SERVINGS

Stewed Tomato Aspic

1 envelope unflavored gelatin
½ cup cold water
1 can (16 ounces) stewed tomatoes
1 tablespoon sugar
¼ teaspoon salt
1 tablespoon cider vinegar

1½ teaspoons prepared horseradish
1½ teaspoons grated onion
¼ teaspoon Worcestershire sauce
2 hard-cooked eggs, cut in quarters
Salad greens

1. Sprinkle gelatin over water to soften.
2. Turn tomatoes into a saucepan and break up any large pieces with a spoon. Stir in sugar, salt, vinegar, horseradish, onion, and Worcestershire sauce and heat to boiling. Add softened gelatin and stir until dissolved.
3. Chill gelatin until slightly thickened.
4. Arrange egg quarters around bottom of a 3- or 4-cup mold. Spoon slightly thickened gelatin mixture into mold. Chill until firm.
5. Unmold and garnish with crisp greens.
4 TO 6 SERVINGS

Smogasbord Pear Salads

Smorgasbord Pear Salads

6 fresh Bartlett pears   Celery-Olive Filling
Shrimp Filling   Salad Greens
Zippy Cheese Filling

1. Halve and core pears. Fill 4 halves with Shrimp Filling, 4 with Zippy Cheese Filling, and 4 with Celery-Olive Filling.
2. Arrange filled pear halves on salad greens in a large shallow bowl or on a serving platter.
12 SALADS

Shrimp Filling: Chop **1 cup cooked deveined shrimp** and combine with **¼ cup chopped celery, 2 tablespoons chopped parsley, 2 teaspoons instant minced onion, ½ teaspoon salt,** and **⅓ cup mayonnaise.**

Zippy Cheese Filling: Combine **1 cup cottage cheese, 1 tablespoon drained capers,** and **1 tablespoon chopped pimento-stuffed olives.**

Celery-Olive Filling: Combine in a small bowl **1 cup cooked sliced celery, ¼ cup ripe olives,** cut in wedges, and **1 tablespoon diced pimento.** Put into a jar with a lid **⅓ cup salad oil, 2 tablespoons vinegar, ½ teaspoon salt,** and **1½ teaspoons sugar;** cover and shake to blend. Pour over celery mixture. Let marinate 2 hours, stirring occasionally.

Hearty Bean Salad

1 can (15 ounces) kidney   relish
   beans, drained   ½ cup shredded sharp Ched-
2 hard-cooked eggs, diced   dar cheese
¼ cup chopped onion   ½ cup sour cream
½ cup diced celery   Lettuce
⅓ cup drained sweet pickle

1. Mix kidney beans, eggs, onion, celery, relish, and cheese in a large bowl. Add sour cream and toss together lightly; chill.
2. Serve the salad on lettuce.
4 TO 6 SERVINGS

Rice Salad with Assorted Sausages

⅓ cup white wine vinegar   3 cups finely shredded red
1 teaspoon lemon juice   cabbage
¼ teaspoon French mustard   ½ cup raisins
1 teaspoon salt   ½ cup walnut pieces
¼ teaspoon ground black   Greens
   pepper   Link sausage (such as brat-
⅓ cup salad oil   wurst, smoky links, and
3 cups cooked enriched   frankfurters), cooked
   white rice, cooled

1. Put vinegar into a bottle. Add lemon juice, mustard, salt, and pepper. Cover and shake. Add oil and shake well.
2. Combine rice, cabbage, raisins, and walnuts in a bowl; chill.
3. When ready to serve, shake dressing well and pour over salad; toss until well mixed.
4. Arrange greens on luncheon plates, spoon salad on greens, and accompany with assorted sausages.
6 TO 8 SERVINGS

Green Goddess Salad

Green Goddess Salad Dressing (page 43)

Salad greens (such as lettuce, curly endive or escarole)

1. Prepare and chill green goddess salad dressing.
2. Rinse salad greens, discard bruised leaves, drain and dry.
3. Using as much of each green as desired, tear into pieces enough greens to yield about 2 quarts. Put into a large plastic bag or vegetable freshener. Chill in refrigerator.
4. When ready to serve, turn salad greens into a chilled bowl. Add the dressing and gently turn and toss until greens are evenly coated.
5. Serve immediately.
6 TO 8 SERVINGS

Green Goddess Salad with Crab Meat: Follow recipe for Green Goddess Salad. Drain, remove and discard bony tissue, and separate contents of 2 6½-ounce cans **crab meat** (about 2⅔ cups, drained). Lightly toss crab meat with salad greens.

Tomato-Cream Slaw

1 cup sour cream
¼ cup mayonnaise
½ cup tomato sauce
2 tablespoons cider vinegar

2 tablespoons sugar
1 teaspoon celery seed
1 small head cabbage, coarsely shredded

1. Combine in a bowl, the sour cream, mayonnaise, tomato sauce, vinegar, sugar, and celery seed. Refrigerate at least 1 hour for flavors to blend and dressing to chill.
2. Put shredded cabbage into a bowl and chill.
3. Just before serving, pour the dressing over the cabbage and toss lightly to mix.
ABOUT 6 SERVINGS

Salade à la Crème

1 quart mixed greens (such as iceberg, Boston, or Bibb lettuce, romaine, escarole, or chicory)
½ cup sour cream
2 tablespoons chopped

parsley
2 tablespoons dry white wine (such as chenin blanc)
½ teaspoon salt
⅛ teaspoon freshly ground pepper

1. Using only perfect leaves, wash, dry, tear into pieces, and chill greens before combining with dressing. Cold, dry leaves ensure a crisp salad.
2. Combine sour cream, parsley, wine, salt, and pepper.
3. At serving time, transfer greens to a large bowl, add dressing, and toss well.
ABOUT 6 SERVINGS

Red Vegetable Salad

1 pint cherry tomatoes, stems removed, cut in half
20 radishes, sliced
1 small red onion, sliced
3 tablespoons wine vinegar
2 teaspoons salad oil

1 teaspoon salt
2 teaspoons snipped fresh mint
⅛ teaspoon freshly ground white pepper
Lettuce leaves

1. Combine all ingredients except lettuce leaves in a medium bowl; refrigerate covered 2 hours, stirring occasionally.
2. Serve vegetables on lettuce.
4 TO 6 SERVINGS

Red Vegetable Salad

Garbanzo Bean Salad

2 cans (15 ounces each) garbanzos, drained (about 4 cups)
1 cup cut celery
2 green peppers, diced or slivered
2 or 3 tomatoes, peeled and cut in small pieces
½ cup finely chopped sweet onion
1 cup radish slices
¼ cup snipped parsley
1 cup quartered pitted ripe olives
1 envelope Italian salad dressing mix
2 teaspoons Worcestershire sauce
1 teaspoon ground coriander
¾ teaspoon lemon pepper marinade

1. Combine the vegetables and olives in a bowl; toss lightly and refrigerate to chill.
2. Meanwhile, prepare salad dressing following package directions, using wine vinegar and adding Worcestershire sauce and remaining ingredients with the mix. Shake thoroughly before using.
3. About 1 hour before serving, toss salad ingredients lightly with dressing until well mixed, then chill.
10 TO 12 SERVINGS

Piquant Cucumber Slices

2 tablespoons sugar
1 teaspoon salt
⅛ teaspoon white pepper
1 teaspoon celery seed
¼ cup cider vinegar
1 tablespoon lemon juice
1 cucumber, rinsed (do not pare)
¼ cup coarsely chopped onion
2 tablespoons chopped parsley

1. Combine the sugar, salt, white pepper, celery seed, vinegar, and lemon juice in a bowl; blend thoroughly.
2. Score cucumber by drawing tines of a fork lengthwise over entire surface. Cut into ⅛-inch slices.
3. Add cucumber to vinegar mixture with onion and parsley; toss to coat evenly.
4. Chill thoroughly, turning several times.
ABOUT 4 SERVINGS

Wilted Lettuce

1 large head lettuce
6 slices bacon, diced
½ cup water
¼ cup cider vinegar
2 tablespoons heavy cream
1 tablespoon sugar
¼ teaspoon salt

1. Tear lettuce into pieces into a bowl; set aside.
2. Fry bacon until crisp in a skillet; reserve ¼ cup drippings. Drain bacon on absorbent paper; set aside.
3. Stir the remaining ingredients into drippings in skillet. Heat mixture just to boiling, stirring constantly.
4. Immediately pour vinegar mixture over the lettuce and toss lightly to coat thoroughly. Top with the bacon.
ABOUT 8 SERVINGS

Marinated Fruit Salad

2 apples
3 pears
3 peaches
1 pineapple
Confectioners sugar
¼ cup rum or Cointreau

1. Pare, core and slice apples and pears. Halve, pit, peel and slice peaches. Cut pineapple into chunks.
2. Place fruit in a bowl and sprinkle with confectioners sugar to taste. Sprinkle with rum or Cointreau.
3. Cover the bowl tightly and chill for at least 6 hours so the sugar draws out fruit juices.
SERVES 8

Bacon-Bean Salad

⅔ cup cider vinegar
¾ cup sugar
1 teaspoon salt
1 can (16 ounces) cut green beans
1 can (16 ounces) cut wax beans
1 can (16 ounces) kidney beans, thoroughly rinsed and drained
1 can (16 ounces) lima beans
1 medium-sized onion, quartered and finely sliced
1 medium-sized green pepper, chopped
½ teaspoon freshly ground black pepper
⅓ cup salad oil
1 pound bacon, cut in 1-inch squares (optional)

1. Blend vinegar, sugar, and salt in a small saucepan. Heat until the sugar is dissolved. Remove from heat and set aside.
2. Drain all beans and toss with onion, green pepper, vinegar mixture, and the pepper. Pour oil over all and toss to coat evenly. Store in a large covered container in refrigerator.
3. When ready to serve, fry bacon until crisp; drain on absorbent paper. Toss the bacon with bean mixture.
ABOUT 12 SERVINGS

Roquefort-Vegetable Salad

Crisp salad greens
1 small onion, sliced
1 cup sliced raw cauliflower
1 can (16 ounces) cut green beans, chilled and drained
1 can (13 to 15 ounces) green asparagus spears, chilled and drained
Roquefort-Mayonnaise Dressing, below

1. Half-fill six individual salad bowls with the greens. Arrange vegetables on greens.
2. Accompany with a bowl of the dressing garnished with snipped **parsley.**
6 SERVINGS

Roquefort-Mayonnaise Dressing: Blend **3 ounces cream cheese,** softened, in a bowl with **3 ounces Roquefort cheese,** crumbled. Stir in ½ **cup light cream,** ½ **cup mayonnaise,** ½ **teaspoon Worcestershire sauce,** ¼ **teaspoon garlic powder,** and ¼ **teaspoon dry mustard.** Beat until fluffy and chill.
ABOUT 1½ CUPS DRESSING

Avocados Stuffed with Cauliflower Salad

2 cups very small, crisp raw
  cauliflowerets
1 cup cooked green beans
½ cup sliced ripe olives
¼ cup chopped pimento
¼ cup chopped onion

Oil and Vinegar Dressing
Salt to taste
6 small lettuce leaves
3 large ripe avocados
Lemon wedges

1. Combine all ingredients, except lettuce, avocados, and lemon wedges; stir gently until evenly mixed and coated with dressing.
2. Refrigerate at least 1 hour before serving.
3. When ready to serve, peel, halve, and remove pits from avocados. Place a lettuce leaf on each serving plate; top with avocado half filled with a mound of cauliflower salad. Serve with lemon wedges.
6 SERVINGS

Piquant Pepper-Cabbage Slaw

¼ to ⅓ cup sugar
2 tablespoons flour
1 teaspoon salt
2 teaspoons dry mustard
2 eggs, fork beaten
1 cup milk, scalded
¾ cup cider vinegar

2 tablespoons butter or
  margarine
1 teaspoon celery seed
1 head chilled cabbage,
  finely shredded
1 green pepper, chopped
1 red pepper, chopped

1. Mix sugar, flour, salt, and dry mustard together in top of a double boiler. Blend in the eggs and milk. Cook over boiling water about 5 minutes, stirring frequently.
2. Stir in the vinegar, a small amount at a time. Cook and stir until mixture begins to thicken, then mix in butter and celery seed. Remove from heat; cool and chill thoroughly.
3. To serve, toss the cabbage and peppers with enough dressing to coat evenly (store remaining dressing); mound onto fresh **spinach leaves.**
ABOUT 8 SERVINGS

German Potato Salad

12 slices bacon, diced and
  fried until crisp (reserve 6
  tablespoons drippings)
3 medium-sized onions,
  chopped (2 cups)
1 cup less 2 tablespoons
  cider vinegar

1½ tablespoons sugar
1½ teaspoons salt
¼ teaspoon pepper
2 to 3 lbs. potatoes, cooked,
  peeled, and cut in ¼-inch
  slices

1. Heat bacon drippings in a skillet. Add onion and cook until tender, stirring occasionally. Stir in vinegar, sugar, salt, and pepper; heat to boiling. Mix in bacon.
2. Pour over potato slices in a serving dish and toss lightly to coat evenly. Garnish with snipped **parsley** and **paprika.** Serve hot.
ABOUT 6 SERVINGS

Avocados Stuffed With Cauliflower Salad

Crunchy Peanut Cole Slaw

3 cups finely chopped green
  cabbage
1 cup finely chopped red
  cabbage
1 cup finely chopped celery
1 cup coarsely chopped
  cauliflower
1 cup sour cream
1 cup mayonnaise
1 tablespoon sugar
1 teaspoon salt
1 tablespoon tarragon
  vinegar

½ cup finely chopped
  cucumber
¼ cup finely chopped green
  onion
¼ cup finely chopped green
  pepper
1 tablespoon butter or
  margarine
½ cup coarsely chopped
  salted peanuts
2 tablespoons shredded
  Parmesan cheese

1. Toss the green and red cabbage, celery, and cauliflower together and chill.
2. Combine the sour cream, mayonnaise, sugar, salt, vinegar, cucumber, green onion, and green pepper for the salad dressing and chill thoroughly.
3. Melt butter in a small skillet; add peanuts and heat several minutes until lightly browned. Remove from heat and immediately stir in the Parmesan cheese. Set aside.
4. Just before serving, toss chilled vegetables with the dressing and top with the peanut mixture.
8 SERVINGS

German Potato Salad

Shades o' Green Salad

French Dressing (page 52)
3 ounces (about 3 cups) spinach
4 stalks Pascal celery
½ green pepper
1 cucumber, rinsed

½ head lettuce
2 tablespoons chopped chives
6 green olives
1 small avocado

1. Chill 6 individual salad bowls in refrigerator.
2. Prepare and chill French dressing.
3. Remove and discard tough stems, roots and bruised leaves from spinach.
4. Wash, drain and pat dry. Use part of the spinach to line the salad bowls. Set remainder aside.
5. Cut celery, pepper and cucumber into pieces or slices.
6. Rinse lettuce, drain and pat dry.
7. Tear lettuce and reserved spinach into pieces. Toss vegetables with lettuce, spinach and chives.
8. Add about ⅓ cup of the French dressing; toss lightly to coat greens evenly. (Store remaining dressing in a covered container in refrigerator.)
9. Arrange individual portions of salad in bowls.
10. Pit and slice olives.
11. Rinse, peel, cut into halves lengthwise, remove pit and slice avocado.
12. Garnish salads with avocado and olive slices.
6 SERVINGS

SOUPS

Creamy Cheddar Cheese Soup

2 tablespoons butter
2 tablespoons chopped
  onion
⅓ cup all-purpose flour
1¼ teaspoons dry mustard
¼ teaspoon garlic powder
¼ teaspoon paprika
2 teaspoons Worcestershire

sauce
1½ quarts milk
3 tablespoons chicken
  seasoned stock base
1½ cups sliced celery
2½ cups (10 ounces) shredded Cheddar cheese

1. Melt butter in a 3-quart saucepan. Add onion and sauté until tender. Stir in flour, mustard, garlic powder, paprika, and Worcestershire sauce.
2. Remove from heat; gradually add milk, stirring constantly. Add chicken stock base and celery; mix well. Cook over low heat, stirring occasionally, until thickened. Add cheese and stir until cheese is melted and soup is desired serving temperature; do not boil.
3. Serve topped with **chopped green pepper, pimento strips, toasted slivered almonds,** or **cooked crumbled bacon.**
ABOUT 2 QUARTS

Mulligatawny Soup

1 broiler-fryer chicken (2½ to
  3 pounds), cut in pieces
1 package soup greens (or
  see Note)
1 onion, peeled and
  quartered
1 teaspoon salt
1 bay leaf
1 cup water

5 thick slices lean bacon,
  diced
4 tomatoes, peeled and
  chopped
⅓ cup flour
2 teaspoons curry powder
Cayenne pepper
½ cup half-and-half

1. Put chicken, soup greens, onion, salt, bay leaf, and water into an electric cooker.
2. Cover and cook on Low 4 hours.
3. Remove chicken from cooker and set aside. Strain broth and reserve 1 cup. Pour remaining broth into cooker.
4. Fry bacon in a skillet until lightly browned. Add chopped tomato and cook 2 minutes. Stir in flour and curry powder. Add reserved chicken broth gradually, stirring constantly until mixture comes to boiling. Add to broth in cooker.
5. Remove chicken meat from skin and bones and cut in strips. Add to cooker; stir.
6. Cover and cook on High 2 hours.
7. Add cayenne and half-and-half to cooker; mix well.
8. Serve soup with **toasted bread cubes.**
ABOUT 8 SERVINGS

Note: For soup greens, use all or a choice of the following vegetables: carrot, celery, leek, onion, parsnip, turnip; and herbs: parsley, tarragon, thyme.

Mulligatawny Soup

Corn Soup I

½ cup finely chopped onion
2 tablespoons butter
1 quart beef stock or canned
  beef broth
2½ cups cooked whole
  kernel golden corn

3 tomatoes, peeled, halved,
  and seeded
Salt and pepper
1 cup whipping cream
Sour cream

1. Melt butter in a large saucepan. Add onion and cook until soft. Add corn, tomato sauce, and stock. Bring to boiling, reduce heat, and simmer about 10 minutes to blend flavors, stirring frequently.
2. Remove from heat and stir in cream. Season to taste with salt and pepper. Serve hot.
6 TO 8 SERVINGS

Brussels Sprout Soup

4 packages (10 ounces each)
frozen Brussels sprouts
7 bouillon cubes
5 cups boiling water
8 slices bacon, diced
2 cloves garlic, minced
6 cups milk
¾ cup uncooked rice
1 teaspoon oregano leaves,
crushed

2 teaspoons salt
½ teaspoon pepper
1 package (10 ounces) frozen
peas and carrots
1 teaspoon salt
2 cups water
¾ cup shredded Parmesan
cheese
Assorted crackers

1. Set out a large saucepot or Dutch oven and a saucepan.
2. Partially thaw frozen Brussels sprouts.
3. Make chicken broth by dissolving bouillon cubes in boiling water. Set aside.
4. Fry in saucepot or Dutch oven the bacon and garlic.
5. Add 3 cups of the broth to saucepot with milk, uncooked rice, and a mixture of oregano leaves, salt and pepper.
6. Bring to boiling, reduce heat and simmer covered 15 minutes.
7. Add to saucepot the frozen peas and carrots. Bring to boiling, reduce heat and simmer about 10 minutes, or until vegetables are tender.
8. Meanwhile, coarsely chop the partially thawed Brussels sprouts. Combine in saucepan the remaining 2 cups of broth, salt and 2 cups water.
9. Bring to boiling and add the chopped Brussels sprouts. Return to boiling and simmer uncovered 10 minutes, or until tender.
10. Add Brussels sprouts with their cooking liquid to rice mixture. Stir in shredded Parmesan cheese. Accompany with assorted crackers.
ABOUT 20 SERVINGS

Split Pea-Vegetable Soup

1¼ cups dried green split
peas, rinsed
1 quart water
2 leeks, washed thoroughly
and cut in large pieces
1 large onion, peeled and
cut in large pieces
4 green onions, diced
2 carrots, pared and diced
2 tablespoons butter

¼ pound fresh mushrooms,
cleaned and diced
1 cup defrosted frozen cut
okra
1 cup defrosted frozen whole
kernel corn
1 teaspoon salt
Few grains pepper
1 can (about 13 ounces)
chicken broth

1. Put split peas into an electric cooker. Add water, cover, and let stand overnight.
2. The next day, add leek, onion, and carrot to cooker; mix.
3. Cover and cook on High 5 hours.
4. Heat butter in a skillet. Add mushrooms and cook until lightly browned.
5. Add browned mushrooms, okra, corn, salt, pepper, and broth to vegetable mixture; stir.
6. Cover and cook on High 1 hour.
7. Serve garnished with **sour cream** and **snipped parsley.**
ABOUT 2½ QUARTS SOUP

Norwegian Fruit Soup

1 quart water
2 tablespoons rice
½ cup finely chopped apple
1 cup pitted dark sweet cherries and juice
½ cup red raspberry fruit

syrup
¼ cup lemon juice
2-inch piece stick cinnamon
1 tablespoon cold water
1 teaspoon cornstarch

1. Bring 1 quart water to boiling in a deep saucepan.
2. Add 2 tablespoons rice to water so boiling will not stop. Boil rapidly, uncovered, 15 to 20 minutes, or until a kernel is entirely soft when pressed between fingers. Drain rice, reserving liquid.
3. Rinse and finely chop enough apple to yield ½ cup.
4. Put cherries into a bowl.
5. Add fruit syrup and lemon juice.
6. Return the rice water to the saucepan. Add the apple and cinnamon stick.
7. Cook over medium heat 4 to 5 minutes, or until apple is tender. Add the drained rice and the cherry mixture. Remove the cinnamon. Simmer 5 minutes.
8. Blend together cold water and cornstarch to form a smooth paste.
9. Blend cornstarch mixture into soup. Bring to boiling. Continue to cook 3 to 5 minutes. Cool soup slightly.
10. Serve soup warm or cold. If serving soup cold, garnish with **whipped cream.**
ABOUT 3½ CUPS SOUP

Raisin Fruit Soup: Follow recipe for Norwegian Fruit Soup. Omit cherries. Increase red raspberry syrup to 1 cup. Add to the syrup mixture 1 cup (about 5 ounces) dark seedless **raisins.**

Blender Pea Soup

1 can (17 ounces) green peas
(undrained)
1½ cups milk
2 tablespoons butter or
margarine
2 teaspoons flour

½ teaspoon salt
½ teaspoon nutmeg
¼ teaspoon sugar
1 small onion, peeled and
quartered

1. Put peas with liquid into an electric blender container. Add 1 cup milk, butter, flour, salt, nutmeg, and sugar. Cover and blend thoroughly. Remove cover and add onion, a quarter at a time, continuing to blend.
2. Pour mixture into an electric cooker.
3. Use the remaining ½ cup milk to rinse out blender (cover blender and turn on, then off). Pour into cooker.
4. Cover and cook on Low 1 hour.
ABOUT 1 QUART SOUP

Easy Beer-Cheese Soup

2 cans (10½ ounces each) condensed cream soup, such as celery, mushroom, or chicken
1 teaspoon Worcestershire sauce
¼ teaspoon seasoned salt
¼ teaspoon paprika
2 cans or bottles (12 ounces each) beer
2 cups shredded Cheddar cheese (8 ounces)
Garnish (optional)

1. In a saucepan, mix soup and seasonings. Add beer gradually while stirring. Heat to simmering.
2. Add cheese. Heat slowly, stirring constantly, until cheese is melted.
3. Pour into soup bowls or cups. Garnish as desired with **croutons, bacon bits, minced parsley,** or **chives.**
7 CUPS; ABOUT 8 SERVINGS

Picnic Green Pea Soup

2 tablespoons chopped onion
¼ cup sliced celery
1 tablespoon butter or margarine
1 can (11¼ ounces) con-
densed green pea soup
1 soup-can water
1 can (8 ounces) tomatoes, drained and chopped
Thyme croutons

1. Cook onion and celery in butter until tender. Blend in soup; gradually add water, stirring constantly. Add tomatoes and heat, stirring occasionally.
2. Garnish with croutons.
ABOUT 3 SERVINGS

Thyme Croutons: Cut **1 slice white bread** into cubes. Heat 2 tablespoons **butter or margarine** in a skillet; add bread cubes and brown them, stirring constantly. Add a dash of **ground thyme.**

Picnic Green Pea Soup

Pacific Seafood Chowder

1½ pounds North Pacific halibut, fresh or frozen
1 can (7½ ounces) Alaska King crab or 1 package (6 ounces) frozen Alaska King crab
3 medium potatoes
1 large sweet Spanish onion
¾ cup chopped celery
¼ cup chopped green pepper
2 cloves garlic, minced
¼ cup butter or margarine
2 cans (16 ounces each) tomatoes
2 cups clam-tomato juice
1½ teaspoons salt
¼ teaspoon pepper
¼ teaspoon thyme
¼ teaspoon marjoram
1 dozen small hard-shell clams
Snipped parsley

1. Defrost halibut, if frozen. Cut into 1-inch chunks. Drain canned crab and slice. Or defrost, drain, and slice frozen crab. Pare potatoes and cut into ½-inch pieces. Peel and thinly slice onion.
2. Sauté onion, celery, green pepper, and garlic in butter in a saucepot. Add tomatoes with liquid, clam-tomato juice, and seasonings. Cover and simmer 30 minutes. Add halibut, potatoes, and clams. Cover and simmer about 10 minutes, or until halibut and potatoes are done and clam shells open. Add crab and heat through.
3. Sprinkle with parsley. Serve with buttered crusty bread.
ABOUT 8 SERVINGS

Sweet-Sour Trahana

2 eggs, slightly beaten
½ cup plain yogurt
½ cup milk
1 teaspoon salt
1½ cups all-purpose flour
Semolina (about 1½ cups)

1. Blend eggs, yogurt, milk, and salt. Add flour and semolina, a little at a time, to form a stiff dough.
2. Knead for about 5 minutes (dough will be very sticky). Divide into small portions. Roll with hands into balls. Place on a clean cloth.
3. Flatten each piece as thin as possible. Let dry undisturbed on trivets at least 12 hours.
4. Cut into small pieces. Turn pieces over and continue drying for another 12 hours or more.
5. When completely dry, mash into crumbs with rolling pin. Spread on a baking sheet.
6. Bake at 200°F for 2 hours.

Note: The weather affects the drying of the trahana. When it is humid, allow more time for drying. Homemade trahana is far superior to the commercially made product. Store in an airtight jar indefinitely.

Sweet Trahana: Follow recipe for Sweet-Sour Trahana; omit yogurt and increase milk to 1 cup.

Sour Trahana: Follow recipe for Sweet-Sour Trahana; omit milk and increase yogurt to 1 cup.

Pacific
Seafood
Chowder

Chinese Chicken-Mushroom Soup

1 pound chicken breasts	4 cups hot water
½ teaspoon salt	1 tablespoon cornstarch
1 tablespoon cooking oil	3 tablespoons cold water
10 medium-size mushrooms, sliced	1 tablespoon soy sauce
4 chicken bouillon cubes	2 tablespoons lemon juice

1. Bone chicken breasts, remove skin, and cut into ¼-inch-wide strips, 1½ to 2 inches long. Sprinkle with salt and let stand 30 minutes.
2. Heat oil in a wok and sauté mushrooms a few minutes until golden. Remove from wok. Dissolve bouillon cubes in hot water and set aside.
3. Mix cornstarch with cold water. Stir in soy sauce. Combine with chicken bouillon in the wok. Bring to boiling, add chicken pieces, and simmer, covered, 5 minutes.
4. Add mushrooms and lemon juice to soup, adding more salt, if necessary. Heat gently without boiling.
5. Serve with a thin **lemon slice** in each bowl.
5 SERVINGS

Beef Sub Gum Soup

½ pound beef round, cut into small cubes	bouillon
1 tablespoon cooking oil	2 cups water
1 can (20 ounces) Chinese vegetables, drained	¼ cup uncooked rice
	2 tablespoons soy sauce
2 cans (10½ ounces each) condensed beef broth or	⅛ teaspoon pepper
	1 egg, beaten

1. In a large wok, brown beef in hot oil. Chop vegetables and add to the browned meat with remaining ingredients, except egg.
2. Bring soup to boiling, stirring to blend. Cover and simmer 40 minutes.
3. Remove soup from heat and slowly stir in the egg. Let stand until egg is set.
ABOUT 6 SERVINGS

Quick Canned Soup with a Zest

1 can (10½ ounces) condensed meat and vegetable soup, any flavor	⅔ cup beer
	⅔ cup water

Combine ingredients in a saucepan; heat to simmering. Simmer 2 to 3 minutes.
2 SERVINGS

Split Pea Soup

1 pound dried split peas, rinsed	½ cup sliced celery
	2 teaspoons salt
1½ pounds smoked ham hocks	6 whole peppercorns
	1 bay leaf
1 cup chopped onion	1½ quarts water

1. Put all ingredients into an electric cooker.
2. Cover and cook on Low 8 to 10 hours.
3. Remove ham hocks and dice meat; reserve ham. Discard bay leaf and peppercorns.
4. Pour soup, about one quarter at a time, into an electric blender and blend until smooth. Return soup to cooker, mix in ham, and keep hot until serving time.
6 TO 8 SERVINGS

Seashore Beer Soup

1 can (10¾ ounces) condensed tomato soup	beer
	¼ teaspoon garlic salt
1 can (11 ounces) condensed green pea soup	1 can (4½ ounces) tiny shrimp
1 can or bottle (12 ounces)	1 cup half-and-half or cream

1. Place condensed soups in saucepan; stir in beer. Add garlic salt.
2. Heat to simmering, stirring until smooth. Simmer 3 to 4 minutes.
3. Just before serving, add undrained shrimp and half-and-half. Heat to serving temperature; do not boil.
6 SERVINGS

Yellow Pea Soup with Pork

¾ pound (about 1⅔ cups) yellow peas	¾ cup coarsely chopped onion
2½ quarts cold water	1 teaspoon salt
1 1-pound piece smoked shoulder roll	1 teaspoon whole thyme
	¼ teaspoon sugar
3 quarts water	

1. Rinse, sort (discarding imperfect peas) and put peas into a large saucepan.
2. Pour 2½ quarts cold water over the peas.
3. Cover and set peas aside to soak overnight.
4. The next day, set out shoulder roll.
5. Put the shoulder roll, water and onion into a large sauce pot.
6. Simmer 1½ to 2 hours, or until meat is tender.
7. Remove meat and set aside. Skim off fat from liquid, leaving about 2 tablespoons. Drain the peas and add to the broth with salt, whole thyme, and sugar.
8. Simmer 1½ to 2 hours, or until peas are tender. If necessary, skim off shells of peas as they come to the surface.
9. Serve soup with thin slices of the meat.
ABOUT 2½ QUARTS SOUP

Ham-Bean Soup

2 quarts water
1 pound (about 2 cups) dried Great Northern or pea beans
3 tablespoons butter
2 cups finely chopped onion
½ cup finely chopped celery
2 teaspoons finely chopped garlic
3 cans (about 10 ounces each) condensed chicken broth
Water
1 ham shank (about 4

pounds) or 2 ham hocks (about 1½ pounds)
1 can (about 16 ounces) tomatoes or 4 to 6 medium-sized firm ripe tomatoes, peeled and chopped
2 whole cloves
1 bay leaf
¼ teaspoon freshly ground black pepper
2 cups shredded Cheddar cheese (about 8 ounces)

1. Bring water to boiling in a 6-quart saucepot. Add beans gradually to water so that boiling continues. Boil 2 minutes. Remove from heat and set aside 1 hour.
2. Drain beans, reserving liquid. Return beans to saucepot along with 4 cups of cooking liquid.
3. Melt butter in a large skillet. Add onion, celery, and garlic; cook 5 minutes, stirring occasionally. Turn contents of skillet into saucepot.
4. Combine chicken broth with enough water to make 6 cups. Pour into saucepot.
5. Peel skin from ham shank and cut off excess fat. Add shank and skin to saucepot along with tomatoes, cloves, bay leaf, and pepper. Bring to boiling, reduce heat, and simmer 2 to 2½ hours, or until ham is tender.
6. Remove ham shank and skin; cool. Transfer soup to a large bowl; remove bay leaf and cloves. Cut meat into pieces and return to soup. Refrigerate, then skim off fat.
7. Transfer soup to saucepot and bring to simmer. Add cheese and stir until melted.
ABOUT 4 QUARTS SOUP

Note: Soup may be stored in the refrigerator and reheated, or cooled and poured into freezer containers and frozen. Thaw and reheat over low heat.

Egg and Lemon Soup with Sour-Dough Noodles

1½ quarts chicken broth
1 cup trahana (see Note)
Salt and pepper to taste

2 eggs, separated
Juice of 2 lemons

1. Bring broth to boiling; boil 6 minutes. Add trahana, salt, and pepper. Simmer covered 10 minutes.
2. In a small bowl, using a wire whisk, beat egg whites until frothy. In another bowl, beat egg yolks. Combine. Slowly beat in lemon juice, then 1 cup hot broth. Add to soup. Serve immediately.
ABOUT 2½ CUPS

Note: There are three varieties of trahana dough – sour, sweet, sweet-sour. It may be made at home (see recipe for Sweet-Sour Trahana and variations) or purchased at a Greek grocery store.

Bean Soup

1 cup large dried white beans
2 quarts water
1 cup sliced celery (½-inch pieces)
2 cups chopped onion
4 medium carrots, cut in

½-inch slices
½ cup chopped parsley
1 tablespoon tomato paste
1 cup olive oil
1 tablespoon oregano, crushed
3 tablespoons wine vinegar

1. Bring beans to a boil in the water. Reduce heat and simmer 1 hour.
2. Add remaining ingredients. Simmer 2 hours more.
3. Add **salt** and **pepper** to taste. Serve with **toasted bread.**
6 TO 8 SERVINGS

Lentil Soup

1 package (16 ounces) dried lentils
2 quarts water
½ cup olive oil
1 cup chopped celery
½ cup grated carrot

1 onion, quartered
1 tablespoon tomato paste
3 garlic cloves, peeled
2 bay leaves
Salt and pepper to taste
Vinegar

1. Rinse lentils several times. Drain.
2. In a kettle put lentils, water, olive oil, celery, carrot, onion, tomato paste, garlic, bay leaves, salt, and pepper. Bring to a boil. Reduce heat and simmer covered 2 hours. Adjust salt and pepper.
3. Serve with a cruet of vinegar.
6 TO 8 SERVINGS

Fresh Cabbage Soup

5 slices bacon, diced
1 pound cabbage, chopped
2 carrots, sliced
2 potatoes, sliced
1 stalk celery, sliced
1½ quarts water

2 tablespoons flour
2 tablespoons butter or margarine (at room temperature)
Salt and pepper

1. Fry bacon until golden but not crisp in a 3-quart saucepan.
2. Add vegetables and water. Simmer 30 minutes, or until vegetables are tender.
3. Blend flour into butter; stir into soup. Bring soup to boiling, stirring. Season to taste with salt and pepper. If desired, serve with dumplings or pierogi.
6 TO 8 SERVINGS

Caraway-Cabbage Soup

Caraway-Cabbage Soup

3 tablespoons butter or margarine
1 head (2 pounds) cabbage, coarsely chopped
5 cups chicken stock
1 teaspoon caraway seed
¼ teaspoon pepper
1 can or bottle (12 ounces) beer
⅓ cup flour
1 cup cream, half-and-half, or milk
Salt

1. Melt butter; add cabbage. Cook slowly, stirring often, until limp.
2. Add stock, caraway seed, and pepper. Cover and simmer about 1 hour, adding beer during last 10 minutes.
3. Mix flour and a little cream to a smooth paste; add remaining cream. Stir into soup. Cook, stirring constantly, until bubbly and slightly thickened. Season to taste with salt.
12 CUPS; 8 TO 12 SERVINGS

Meat Broth

2 pounds beef shank or short ribs, or pork neckbones
1 pound marrow bones
3 quarts water
1 large onion, quartered
2 leaves cabbage
2 sprigs fresh parsley or 1
tablespoon dried parsley flakes
1 carrot, cut up
1 parsnip, cut up
1 stalk celery, cut up
5 peppercorns
1 tablespoon salt

1. Combine beef, bones, and water in a 6-quart kettle. Bring to boiling. Boil 15 minutes, skimming frequently.
2. Add remaining ingredients. Simmer rapidly about 1½ hours, or until meat is tender.
3. Strain off broth. Chill quickly. Skim off fat.
4. Remove meat from bones. Set meat aside for use in other dishes. Discard bones, vegetables, and peppercorns.
5. Return skimmed broth to kettle. Boil rapidly about 15 minutes, or until reduced to about 6 cups. Store in refrigerator until needed.
ABOUT 1½ QUARTS

Meat Stock: Prepare Meat Broth as directed. Chill. Lift off fat. Boil until reduced to 3 cups, about 45 minutes.

Cold Cucumber-Beet Soup

1 small bunch beets with beet greens (about 1 pound)
1½ quarts water or chicken broth
1 teaspoon salt
2 medium cucumbers, pared and diced
6 radishes, sliced
6 green onions with tops, sliced
2 tablespoons fresh lemon juice
2 cups sour cream or
buttermilk
1 dill pickle, minced (optional)
3 tablespoons chopped fresh dill or 4 teaspoons dill weed
Salt and pepper
1 lemon, sliced
2 hard-cooked eggs, chopped or sliced
12 large shrimp, cooked, peeled, and deveined (optional)

1. Scrub beets and carefully wash greens. Leave beets whole; do not peel. Put beets and greens into a kettle with water and salt. Bring to boiling. Cover. Reduce heat, and cook slowly until tender, about 30 minutes, depending on size of beets. Drain, reserving liquid in a large bowl.
2. Peel and chop beets, mince the greens.
3. Add beets and greens to reserved liquid along with cucumber, radish, green onion, lemon juice, sour cream, pickle (if desired), and dill. Season with salt and pepper to taste; mix. Chill.
4. Serve garnished with lemon slices and hard-cooked egg and, if desired, whole shrimp.
ABOUT 2 QUARTS SOUP

Avocado Yogurt Soup

1 cup avocado pulp (2 to 3 avocados, depending on size)
⅔ cup unsweetened yogurt
⅔ cup beef stock, or bouillon made with ⅔ cup water and 1 bouillon cube,
then chilled
1 tablespoon lemon juice
1 teaspoon onion juice or grated onion
½ teaspoon salt
Dash Tabasco

1. Put avocado pulp and yogurt into an electric blender and blend until evenly mixed. Adding gradually, blend in beef stock, lemon juice, onion juice, salt, and Tabasco. Chill well.
2. Serve soup in chilled bowls.
4 TO 6 SERVINGS

Farm-Style Leek Soup

2 large leeks (1 pound) with part of green tops, sliced
2 medium onions, sliced
1 large garlic clove, minced
¼ cup butter or margarine
4 cups chicken stock or bouillon
2 cups uncooked narrow or medium noodles (3 ounces)
1 can or bottle (12 ounces) beer
1½ cups shredded semisoft cheese (Muenster, brick, process, etc.)
Salt and pepper

1. Cook leek, onion, and garlic in butter for 15 minutes, using low heat and stirring often.
2. Add stock. Cover and simmer 30 minutes.
3. Add noodles. Cover and simmer 15 minutes, or until noodles are tender.
4. Add beer; heat to simmering. Gradually add cheese, cooking slowly and stirring until melted. Season to taste with salt and pepper.

6 SERVINGS, ABOUT 1½ CUPS EACH

Minestrone

6 cups water
1¼ cups (about ½ pound) dried navy beans, rinsed
¼ pound salt pork
3 tablespoons olive oil
1 small onion, chopped
1 clove garlic, chopped
¼ head cabbage
2 stalks celery, cut in ½-inch slices
2 small carrots, pared and cut in ½-inch slices
1 medium potato, pared and diced
1 tablespoon chopped parsley
½ teaspoon salt
¼ teaspoon pepper
1 quart hot water
¼ cup packaged precooked rice
½ cup frozen green peas
¼ cup tomato paste
Grated Parmesan cheese

1. Bring the 6 cups water to boiling in a large saucepot. Gradually add the beans to the boiling water so the boiling does not stop. Simmer the beans 2 minutes, and remove from heat. Set aside to soak 1 hour.
2. Add salt pork to beans and return to heat. Bring to boiling, reduce heat, and simmer 1 hour, stirring once or twice.
3. While beans are simmering with salt pork, heat the olive oil in a skillet, and brown the onion and garlic lightly. Set aside.
4. Wash the cabbage, discarding coarse outer leaves, and shred finely.
5. After the beans have simmered an hour, add the onion, garlic, celery, carrots, potato, cabbage, parsley, salt, and pepper. Slowly pour in 1 quart hot water and simmer about 1 hour, or until the beans are tender.
6. Meanwhile, cook the rice according to package directions. About 10 minutes before the beans should be done, stir in the rice and peas. When the peas are tender, stir in the tomato paste. Simmer about 5 minutes. Serve sprinkled with cheese.
ABOUT 6 SERVINGS

Roman Egg Soup with Noodles

4 cups chicken broth
1½ tablespoons semolina or flour
1½ tablespoons grated Parmesan cheese
⅛ teaspoon salt
⅛ teaspoon pepper
4 eggs, well beaten
1 cup cooked noodles
Snipped parsley

1. Bring chicken broth to boiling.
2. Meanwhile, mix semolina, cheese, salt, and pepper together. Add to beaten eggs and beat until combined.
3. Add noodles to boiling broth, then gradually add egg mixture, stirring constantly. Continue stirring and simmer 5 minutes.
4. Serve topped with parsley.
4 SERVINGS

Roman Egg Soup with Spinach: Follow recipe for Roman Egg Soup with Noodles; omit noodles. Add **½ pound chopped cooked fresh spinach** to broth before adding egg mixture.

Zuppa di Pesce: Royal Danieli

3 pounds skinned and boned fish (haddock, trout, cod, salmon, and red snapper)
1 lobster (about 1 pound)
1 pound shrimp with shells
1 quart water
½ cup coarsely cut onion
1 stalk celery with leaves, coarsely cut
2 tablespoons cider vinegar
2 teaspoons salt
¼ cup olive oil
2 cloves garlic, minced
1 bay leaf, crumbled
1 teaspoon basil
½ teaspoon thyme
2 tablespoons minced parsley
½ to 1 cup dry white wine
½ cup chopped peeled tomatoes
8 shreds saffron
1 teaspoon salt
½ teaspoon freshly ground black pepper
6 slices French bread
¼ cup olive oil

1. Reserve heads and tails of fish. Cut fish into bite-size pieces.
2. In a saucepot or kettle, boil lobster and shrimp 5 minutes in water with onion, celery, vinegar, and 2 teaspoons salt.
3. Remove and shell lobster and shrimp; devein shrimp. Cut lobster into bite-size pieces. Set lobster and shrimp aside.
4. Return shells to the broth and add heads and tails of fish. Simmer 20 minutes.
5. Strain broth, pour into saucepot, and set aside.
6. Sauté all of the fish in ¼ cup oil with garlic, bay leaf, basil, thyme, and parsley 5 minutes, stirring constantly.
7. Add to reserved broth along with wine, tomatoes, saffron, 1 teaspoon salt, and the pepper. Bring to boiling; cover and simmer 10 minutes, stirring occasionally.
8. Serve with slices of bread sautéed in the remaining ¼ cup olive oil.
ABOUT 2½ QUARTS SOUP

"Little Hats" in Broth

½ cup (4 ounces) ricotta or cottage cheese
2 tablespoons grated Parmesan cheese
½ cup finely chopped cooked chicken
1 egg, slightly beaten
⅛ teaspoon salt
Few grains nutmeg
Few grains pepper
2 cups sifted all-purpose flour
¼ teaspoon salt
2 eggs
3 tablespoons cold water
2 quarts chicken broth or bouillon

1. Combine cheeses, chicken, 1 egg, ⅛ teaspoon salt, nutmeg, and pepper; set aside.
2. Combine flour and ¼ teaspoon salt in a large bowl. Make a well in the center of the flour. Place 2 eggs, one at a time, in the well, mixing slightly after each one is added. Gradually add the water; mix well to make a stiff dough. Turn dough onto a lightly floured surface and knead until smooth and elastic (5 to 8 minutes).
3. Roll dough out to about 1/16 inch thick. Cut into 2½-inch circles. Place ½ teaspoon of the chicken-cheese mixture in the center of each round. Dampen the edges with water, fold in half, and press together to seal. Bring the two ends together, dampen, and pinch together.
4. Bring the chicken broth to boiling. Add pasta and cook 20 to 25 minutes, or until pasta is tender. Pour broth and pasta into soup bowls, and serve immediately.
8 SERVINGS

Lettuce Soup

2 tablespoons butter or margarine
2 tablespoons flour
1 can (about 10 ounces) condensed chicken broth
1 soup can water

½ small head lettuce, cored and coarsely chopped
¼ cup thinly sliced celery
1 tablespoon chopped watercress
Salt and pepper

1. Melt butter in a saucepot; stir in flour and cook until bubbly.
2. Gradually stir in chicken broth and water; bring to boiling, stirring constantly. Cook 1 minute.
3. Stir in lettuce, celery, and watercress. Season with salt and pepper to taste. Cook until vegetables are crisp-tender, about 5 minutes.
ABOUT 3 SERVINGS

Black Bean Soup

1 pound dried black beans, washed
2 quarts boiling water
2 tablespoons salt
5 cloves garlic
1½ teaspoons cumin (comino)

1½ teaspoons oregano
2 tablespoons white vinegar
10 tablespoons olive oil
½ pound onions, peeled and chopped
½ pound green peppers, trimmed and chopped

1. Put beans into a large, heavy saucepot or Dutch oven and add boiling water; boil rapidly 2 minutes. Cover tightly, remove from heat, and set aside 1 hour. Add salt to beans and liquid; bring to boiling and simmer, covered, until beans are soft, about 2 hours.
2. Put the garlic, cumin, oregano, and vinegar into a mortar and crush to a paste.
3. Heat olive oil in a large skillet. Mix in onion and green pepper and fry until onion is browned, stirring occasionally. Thoroughly blend in the paste, then stir in the skillet mixture into the beans. Cook over low heat until ready to serve.
4. Meanwhile, mix a small portion of **cooked rice, minced onion, olive oil,** and **vinegar** in a bowl; set aside to marinate. Add a soup spoon of rice mixture to each serving of soup.
ABOUT 2 QUARTS SOUP

Gazpacho

1 clove garlic
2 cups chopped peeled fresh tomatoes
1 large cucumber, pared and chopped
½ cup diced green pepper
½ cup chopped onion

1 cup tomato juice
3 tablespoons olive oil
2 tablespoons vinegar
Salt and pepper
Dash Tabasco
½ cup crisp croutons

1. Cut garlic in half and rub onto bottom and sides of a large bowl. Add tomatoes, cucumber, green pepper, onion, tomato juice, olive oil, and vinegar to bowl and stir until evenly mixed. Season to taste with salt, pepper, and Tabasco.
2. Chill in refrigerator at least 1 hour before serving.
3. Serve soup in chilled bowls. Top each serving with a few croutons.
8 TO 10 SERVINGS

Brown Vegetable Stock

2 pounds mixed vegetables (carrots, leeks, onions, celery, turnips, etc.)
¼ cup butter or margarine
2½ quarts water

½ teaspoon salt
½ teaspoon thyme
3 sprigs parsley
½ bay leaf
Dash of pepper

1. Chop vegetables. Brown in butter.
2. Add water and seasonings. cover.
3. Simmer 1½ hours or until vegetables are tender.
4. Strain and chill.
ABOUT 2 QUARTS STOCK

White Vegetable Stock: If a lighter, clearer stock i desired, omit butter and do not brown vegetables.

Red and White Bean Soup

2 cups dried navy beans, soaked overnight
2 cups chopped onion
1 tablespoon salt
10 whole peppercorns
1 stalk celery with leaves, sliced
¼ cup minced parsley or 2 tablespoons dried parsley

½ teaspoon crushed thyme or basil
2 cups chopped potato
¼ cup flour
1 can (15 ounces) tomato sauce
1 can (14 ounces) brown beans in molasses sauce

1. Drain soaked beans, reserving liquid. Add enough water to bean liquid to measure 6 cups. Combine in a large saucepan soaked beans, bean liquid, onion, salt, peppercorns, celery, parsley, and thyme. Heat to boiling; simmer 45 minutes.
2. Stir in potato. Simmer 20 minutes or until tender.
3. In a separate saucepan, stir flour into melted butter; cook until bubbly. Gradually add tomato sauce; mix well.
4. Stir tomato mixture and brown beans into soup. Simmer 5 minutes.
8 SERVINGS

Chili Soup

½ pound ground beef
1 cup chopped onion
5 cups water
1 can (28 ounces) tomatoes
1 can (15 ounces) tomato sauce
1 clove garlic, crushed

1 tablespoon chili powder
1 teaspoon salt
1 teaspoon cumin
½ teaspoon oregano
1 cup uncooked macaroni
1 can (about 15 ounces) kidney or chili beans

1. Brown meat in a large saucepan; drain off fat. Stir in onion; cook 1 minute.
2. Add water, tomatoes, tomato sauce, garlic, chili powder, salt, cumin, and oregano. Simmer 30 minutes.
3. Add remaining ingredients; cook until macaroni is done (about 10 to 15 minutes).
8 TO 10 SERVINGS

Rock Lobster Bouillabaisse

¼ cup olive oil
1 cup chopped celery
1 onion, chopped
1 clove garlic, chopped
½ teaspoon thyme
1 bay leaf
1 can (28 ounces) tomatoes (undrained)
1 bottle (8 ounces) clam juice
1 cup dry white wine
¼ cup chopped parsley
1½ pounds fish fillets (turbot, flounder, cod, or halibut), cut in 2-inch pieces
1 pound frozen South African rock lobster tails
Salt and pepper

1. Heat olive oil in a saucepot and sauté celery, onion, and garlic until tender but not brown. Add thyme, bay leaf, tomatoes, clam juice, wine, and parsley. Cover and simmer 15 minutes.
2. Add fish to saucepot. Cut each frozen rock lobster tail into 3 pieces, crosswise through hard shell, and add to stew. Simmer 10 minutes.
3. Season to taste with salt and pepper. Remove bay leaf.
4. Ladle into large bowls and serve with slices of **French bread.**
6 SERVINGS

Sherried Chicken Chowder

10 cups water
1 broiler-fryer chicken (about 2½ pounds)
1 carrot, coarsely chopped
1 stalk celery, coarsely chopped
1 onion, halved
4 whole cloves
2 teaspoons salt
1 teaspoon crushed tarragon
1 bay leaf
½ cup uncooked barley or rice
½ teaspoon curry powder
¼ cup dry sherry
1 cup half-and-half

1. Place water, chicken, carrot, celery, onion halves studded with cloves, salt, and tarragon in Dutch oven or saucepot. Bring to boiling; simmer 1 hour, or until chicken is tender.
2. Remove chicken; cool. Discard skin; remove meat from bones; chop.
3. Strain stock. Discard cloves and bay leaf. Reserve stock and vegetables. Skim fat from stock.
4. Purée vegetables and 1 cup stock in an electric blender.
5. Return stock to Dutch oven; bring to boiling. Stir in barley and puréed vegetables. Simmer 1 hour, or until barley is tender. Stir in chicken, curry, sherry, and half-and-half.
8 SERVINGS

Mixed Vegetables Soup

3 cups beef broth or 3 beef bouillon cubes dissolved in 3 cups boiling water
1 small potato, diced
2 carrots, diced
1 tomato, chopped
1 green onion, sliced
½ cup shredded cabbage or ½ cup sliced zucchini
½ teaspoon Beau Monde seasoning or seasoned salt
1 tablespoon minced parsley

1. Combine broth, potato, and carrot in a saucepan; bring to boiling. Simmer 30 minutes.
2. Add remaining ingredients; cook 5 minutes, or until cabbage is crisp-tender.
4 SERVINGS

Meatball Soup

1 pound ground beef
1 onion, chopped
1½ quarts water
1 can (16 ounces) tomatoes
3 potatoes, cubed
2 carrots, sliced
2 stalks celery, sliced
3 sprigs fresh parsley, minced, or 2 tablespoons dried
½ cup uncooked barley
2 teaspoons salt
½ teaspoon crushed thyme or basil
¼ teaspoon garlic powder
¼ teaspoon pepper
1 bay leaf
1 teaspoon Worcestershire sauce
1 beef bouillon cube

1. Shape beef into tiny meatballs. Brown meatballs and onion in a large saucepan, or place in a shallow pan and brown in a 400°F oven. Drain off excess fat.
2. Add remaining ingredients. Bring to boiling, simmer 1½ hours, or until vegetables are tender.
8 SERVINGS

Gazpacho Garden Soup

3 large tomatoes, chopped
1 clove garlic, crushed
1 small cucumber, chopped
1 green pepper, chopped
½ cup sliced green onions
¼ cup chopped onion
¼ cup minced parsley
1 teaspoon crushed rosemary
¼ teaspoon crushed basil
½ teaspoon salt
¼ cup olive oil
¼ cup salad oil
2 tablespoons lemon juice
2 cups chicken broth or 3 chicken bouillon cubes dissolved in 2 cups boiling water, then cooled

1. Combine all ingredients except chicken broth in a large bowl. Toss gently.
2. Stir in chicken broth; chill.
3. Serve in chilled bowls with garnishes suggested in Gazpacho.
6 SERVINGS

Vegetarian Chowder

4 cups sliced zucchini
½ cup chopped onion
⅓ cup butter or margarine
⅓ cup flour
2 tablespoons minced parsley
1 teaspoon crushed basil
1 teaspoon salt
⅛ teaspoon pepper
3 cups water
1 chicken bouillon cube
1 package (10 ounces) evaporated milk
1 can (16 ounces) tomatoes, broken up, or 3 tomatoes, skinned and chopped
1 cup shredded Monterey Jack cheese (optional)

1. Sauté zucchini and onion in butter in a large saucepan. Stir in flour, parsley, basil, salt, and pepper.
2. Gradually add water, stirring constantly. Add remaining ingredients. Bring to boiling; simmer 10 to 15 minutes.
3. If desired, stir in Monterey Jack cheese.
6 TO 8 SERVINGS

Egg and Lemon Soup

1½ quarts chicken stock (homemade or canned)
1½ cups uncooked parboiled rice
1 whole egg
3 egg yolks
Juice of 2 lemons
Salt and pepper to taste

1. Heat stock in a saucepan. Add rice and simmer, covered, until tender (about 20 minutes).
2. Beat egg and yolks until light. Beating constantly, slowly add lemon juice.
3. Measure 2 cups hot chicken stock and add, tablespoon by tablespoon, to egg mixture, beating constantly to prevent curdling. Add this mixture to the remaining hot chicken stock with rice. Season with salt and pepper.
4. Serve at once.
6 SERVINGS

Egg and Lemon Soup

Pioneer Potato Soup

1 quart chicken stock
4 potatoes, chopped (about 4 cups)
2 cups sliced carrots
½ cup sliced celery
¼ cup chopped onion
1 teaspoon salt
½ teaspoon marjoram, dill weed, or cumin
⅛ teaspoon white pepper
1 cup milk or half-and-half
2 tablespoons flour
Garnishes: paprika, sliced green onions, crisply cooked crumbled bacon, chopped pimento, snipped chives or parsley, or grated Parmesan cheese

1. Combine all ingredients except milk, flour, and garnishes in a large saucepan. Bring to boiling; simmer 30 minutes.
2. Gradually add milk to flour, stirring until smooth. Stir into soup.
3. Bring soup to boiling; boil 1 minute, stirring constantly.
4. Garnish as desired.
4 TO 6 SERVINGS

Potato Soup with Sour Cream: Follow recipe for Pioneer Potato Soup. Before serving, stir in **½ cup sour cream.** Heat; do not boil.

Puréed Potato Soup: Follow recipe for either Pioneer Potato or Potato Soup with Sour Cream, omitting the flour. Purée in an electric blender before serving. Reheat, if necessary.

French Cauliflower Soup

1 head cauliflower, cut in flowerets
5 cups chicken stock or 5 chicken bouillon cubes in 5 cups water
½ cup uncooked rice
¼ cup finely chopped celery
1 cup milk or half-and-half
¼ cup flour
Salt and pepper
Sliced green onion, snipped watercress, or snipped parsley

1. Put cauliflowerets, stock, rice, and celery into a large saucepan. Bring to boiling; simmer until cauliflower is crisp-tender and rice is cooked (about 10 minutes).
2. Gradually add milk to flour, blending until smooth; stir into soup. Bring to boiling, stirring constantly until thickened. Season to taste.
3. Sprinkle each serving with green onion, watercress, or parsley.
6 SERVINGS

Creamed French Cauliflower Soup: Follow recipe for French Cauliflower Soup; strain soup after Step 1. Purée vegetables and rice in an electric blender. Return vegetables and stock to saucepot. Continue with Step 2. Stir in **¼ cup white wine** and either **½ teaspoon basil** or **¼ teaspoon dill weed.** Garnish as suggested.

Chicken Soup Tortellini

2 quarts water
1 broiler-fryer chicken (about 2½ pounds)
1 onion, sliced
2 teaspoons fresh minced parsley or 1 teaspoon dried parsley
1½ teaspoons salt
1 teaspoon rosemary or

chervil
⅛ teaspoon pepper
1 cup sliced celery with leaves
1 cup sliced fresh mushrooms
½ cup dry white wine
32 tortellini (see recipe)

1. Place water, chicken, onion, parsley, salt, rosemary, and pepper in a large saucepan. Bring to boiling; simmer covered 1 hour, or until chicken is tender.
2. Remove chicken; cool. Discard chicken skin. Remove meat from bones and chop fine. Reserve for tortellini filling.
3. Bring stock to boiling; stir in remaining ingredients. Simmer 15 minutes, or until tortellini are done. (If using frozen tortellini, simmer about 30 minutes.)
8 TO 10 SERVINGS

Baked Minestrone

Tortellini

Dough:
2 eggs
2 egg whites
2 tablespoons olive or vegetable oil
2 teaspoons salt
3 cups all-purpose flour

Filling:
2½ cups finely chopped chicken
¼ cup grated Parmesan cheese
2 egg yolks

1. Prepare dough by combining eggs, egg whites, oil, and salt in a bowl. Gradually add flour, mixing well until mixture forms a soft dough. Turn onto a floured surface and knead in remaining flour to form a very stiff dough.
2. Wrap dough in waxed paper; let rest 10 minutes.
3. Combine chicken, cheese, and egg yolks in a bowl. Set aside.
4. Divide dough in quarters. Roll each quarter into a large circle as thin as possible. Cut into about 32 (2-inch) rounds.
5. For each tortellini, place about 1 teaspoon chicken mixture in center of round. Moisten edges with water. Fold in half; seal edges. Shape into rings by stretching the tips of half circle slightly and wrapping the ring around your index finger. Gently press tips together (tortellini may be frozen at this point).
6. Cook as directed in recipe for Chicken Soup Tortellini.
ABOUT 128 TORTELLINI

Baked Minestrone

1½ pounds lean beef for stew, cut in 1-inch cubes
1 cup coarsely chopped onion
2 cloves garlic, crushed
1 teaspoon salt
¼ teaspoon pepper
2 tablespoons olive oil
3 cans (about 10 ounces each) condensed beef broth
2 soup cans water

1½ teaspoons herb seasoning
1 can (16 ounces) tomatoes (undrained)
1 can (15¼ ounces) kidney beans (undrained)
1½ cups thinly sliced carrots
1 cup small seashell macaroni
2 cups sliced zucchini
Grated Parmesan cheese
1 can (6 ounces) pitted ripe olives (unstrained)

1. Mix beef, onion, garlic, salt, and pepper in a large saucepan. Add olive oil and stir to coat meat evenly.
2. Bake at 400°F 30 minutes, or until meat is browned, stirring occasionally.
3. Turn oven control to 350°F. Add broth, water, and seasonings; stir. Cover; cook 1 hour, or until meat is tender.
4. Stir in tomatoes, kidney beans, olives, carrots, and macaroni. Put sliced zucchini on top. Cover; bake 30 to 40 minutes, or until carrots are tender.
5. Serve with grated cheese.
10 TO 12 SERVINGS

Vegetable Medley Soup

8 slices bacon
½ cup chopped onion
½ cup sliced celery
5 cups water
1½ cups fresh corn or 1 package (about 10 ounces) frozen corn
½ cup sliced carrots
1 potato, pared and sliced
1 tablespoon salt
1 teaspoon sugar
¼ teaspoon crushed thyme or basil
1 cup fresh green beans, cut in 1-inch pieces
4 cups chopped peeled tomatoes (4 to 5 tomatoes)

1. Cook bacon until crisp in a Dutch oven or kettle. Drain off all but 2 tablespoons fat.
2. Sauté onion and celery in bacon fat.
3. Stir in water, corn, carrots, potato, salt, sugar, pepper, and thyme. Bring to boiling; simmer covered 30 minutes.
4. Stir in green beans; simmer 10 minutes, or until beans are crisp-tender.
5. Stir in tomatoes; heat 5 minutes.
ABOUT 6 SERVINGS

Dill Cabbage Soup

2 quarts beef stock
1 cup thinly sliced carrots
1 cup sliced celery
½ cup chopped onion
8 cups (about ½ head) thinly sliced cabbage
Salt and pepper to taste
3 tablespoons water
2 tablespoons flour
½ cup yogurt or dairy sour half-and-half
½ teaspoon minced dill or ¼ teaspoon dried dill weed
Minced parsley

1. Pour stock into a large saucepan. Add carrots, celery, and onion. Bring to boiling, reduce heat, and cook until vegetables are tender (about 10 minutes).
2. Add cabbage; continue cooking until crisp-tender (about 5 minutes). Season to taste with salt and pepper.
3. Stir water gradually into flour, stirring until smooth. Pour slowly into soup, stirring constantly. Bring to boiling; boil 1 minute.
4. Stir in yogurt and dill.
5. Garnish with parsley.
8 TO 10 SERVINGS

Cream of Turkey Soup

½ cup butter
6 tablespoons flour
½ teaspoon salt
Pinch black pepper
2 cups half-and-half
3 cups turkey or chicken broth
¾ cup coarsely chopped cooked turkey

1. Heat butter in a saucepan. Blend in flour, salt, and pepper. Heat until bubbly.
2. Gradually add half-and-half and 1 cup of broth, stirring constantly. Bring to boiling; cook and stir 1 to 2 minutes.
3. Blend in remaining broth and turkey. Heat; do not boil. Garnish with grated carrot.
ABOUT 6 SERVINGS

Frosty Cucumber Soup

1 large cucumber, scored with a fork
¼ teaspoon salt
Pinch white pepper
1½ cups yogurt
1¼ cups water
½ cup walnuts, ground in an electric blender
2 cloves garlic, minced
Green food coloring (optional)

1. Halve cucumber lengthwise and cut crosswise into very thin slices. Rub inside of a large bowl with cut surface of ½ clove garlic. Combine cucumber, salt, and pepper in bowl. Cover; chill.
2. Pour combined yogurt and water over chilled cucumber; mix well. If desired, tint with 1 or 2 drops of food coloring. Chill.
3. Combine walnuts and garlic; set aside for topping.
4. Ladle soup into bowls. Place soup bowls over larger bowls of crushed ice. Serve with walnut topping.
4 SERVINGS

Gazpacho

2 cans (6 ounces each) seasoned tomato juice
½ cucumber, coarsely sliced
1 tomato, quartered
¼ cup vinegar
¼ cup salad oil
1 tablespoon sugar
1 can or bottle (25.6 ounces)
seasoned tomato juice
½ cucumber, chopped
1 tomato, chopped
1 small onion, chopped
Minced parsley
Chopped hard-cooked egg
Chopped cucumber
Croutons

1. Pour the 12 ounces tomato juice into an electric blender. Add sliced cucumber, tomato, vinegar, oil, and sugar; blend.
2. Serve with bowls of parsley, hard-cooked egg, cucumber, and croutons.
4 SERVINGS

Pumpkin Patch Soup

3 cups canned pumpkin or fresh cooked puréed pumpkin
2 cups milk, half-and-half, or 1 can (13 ounces) evaporated milk
3 tablespoons maple syrup
1 teaspoon salt
½ teaspoon nutmeg
½ teaspoon cinnamon
¼ teaspoon cloves or allspice

Combine all ingredients in a large saucepan. Heat.
4 SERVINGS

Tomato Cooler Gazpacho

2 cans (about 10 ounces each) condensed tomato soup
2 soup cans water
1 large clove garlic, crushed
1 tablespoon lemon juice
5 to 10 drops Tabasco
½ teaspoon crushed basil
½ cup chopped cucumber
½ cup chopped green pepper
2 tablespoons sliced green onion

1. Combine ingredients; chill several hours.
2. Serve in chilled sherbet glasses or bowls with garnishes suggested in Gazpacho.
6 SERVINGS

Beef Barley Soup

2 quarts water
1 soup bone with meat
½ cup chopped celery tops
1 tablespoon salt
½ teaspoon pepper
½ cup uncooked regular barley
3 cups coarsely chopped

cabbage
1 cup sliced carrots
1 cup sliced celery
2 cups sliced parsnips
2 cups thinly sliced onion
1 can (12 ounces) tomato paste

1. Combine water, bone, celery tops, salt, and pepper in a Dutch oven. Bring to boiling; cover tightly and simmer 1 to 2 hours.
2. Remove bone from stock; cool. Remove meat from bone; chop. Return to stock.
3. Stir in barley; continue cooking 30 minutes.
4. Add remaining ingredients; simmer 30 minutes, or until vegetables are tender.
8 TO 10 SERVINGS

Sweet Pea Soup

1 small head lettuce, shredded (about 5 cups)
2 cups shelled fresh peas, or 1 package (10 ounces) frozen green peas
1 cup water
½ cup chopped leek or green onion
2 tablespoons butter

2 teaspoons chervil
1 teaspoon sugar
½ teaspoon salt
¼ teaspoon black pepper
1 can (about 10 ounces) condensed beef broth
¾ cup water
2 cups half-and-half

1. Put lettuce, peas, 1 cup water, leek, butter, chervil, sugar, salt, and pepper into a large saucepan; stir and bring to boiling. Cover and cook until peas are tender.
2. Press mixture through a coarse sieve or food mill and return to saucepan. Stir in broth and ¾ cup water.
3. Just before serving, stir half-and-half into mixture and heat.
6 SERVINGS

Alphabet Soup

½ pound ground beef
1 onion, chopped
5 cups water
1 can (16 ounces) tomatoes
3 potatoes, cubed
2 carrots, sliced
2 stalks celery, sliced
2 teaspoons salt
1 teaspoon Worcestershire

sauce
1 beef bouillon cube
¼ teaspoon garlic powder
¼ teaspoon pepper
3 sprigs fresh parsley, minced, or 2 tablespoons dried
1 cup uncooked alphabet macaroni

1. Brown meat in a large saucepan; drain off fat.
2. Add remaining ingredients, except macaroni. Bring to boiling; cover and simmer 1 hour.
3. Stir in macaroni; cook 20 minutes.
6 TO 8 SERVINGS

Tomato-Lentil Soup

2 cups chopped carrots
1 cup chopped onion
1 cup sliced celery
2 tablespoons margarine, melted
1 clove garlic, crushed
1¼ cups (½ pound) dried

lentils
2 quarts water
1 tablespoon salt
1 can (6 ounces) tomato paste
¼ teaspoon crushed dill weed or tarragon

1. Sauté carrots, onion, and celery in margarine in a large saucepan until tender.
2. Add garlic, lentils, water, and salt. Simmer 2 hours, or until lentils are tender.
3. Add tomato paste and dill weed; stir.
6 TO 8 SERVINGS

Split Pea Soup with Ham Bone

2 cups dried green split peas
1½ quarts water
1 ham bone (about 1½ pounds)
1 onion, sliced
1 cup sliced celery

1 cup grated carrot
2 teaspoons salt
1 teaspoon crushed basil
¼ cup butter or margarine
¼ cup flour
2 cups milk

1. In a large saucepan, combine peas, water, bone, onion, celery, carrot, salt, and basil. Bring to boiling; simmer 1½ to 2 hours.
2. Stir flour into melted butter in a separate saucepan; cook until bubbly. Gradually add milk, stirring constantly. Bring to boiling; cook 1 minute.
3. Stir white sauce into soup.
8 SERVINGS

French Onion Soup

5 medium onions, sliced (4 cups)
3 tablespoons butter or margarine
1½ quarts beef broth

½ teaspoon salt
⅛ teaspoon pepper
Cheese Croutons (see recipe below)

1. Sauté onions in melted butter in a large saucepan. Cook slowly, stirring until golden (about 10 minutes).
2. Blend in beef broth, salt, and pepper. Bring to boiling, cover, and simmer 15 minutes.
3. Pour soup into warm soup bowls or crocks. Float a cheese crouton in each bowl of soup.
6 SERVINGS

Cheese Croutons

6 slices French bread, toasted
2 tablespoons butter or

margarine
¼ cup (1 ounce) grated Gruyère or Swiss cheese

1. Spread one side of each bread slice with butter. If necessary, cut bread to fit size of bowl. Sprinkle cheese over buttered toast.
2. Place under broiler until cheese melts.

Vegetable Oyster Soup

4 cups chopped head lettuce
2 cups chopped spinach
1 cup chopped carrots
½ cup chopped onion
1½ cups chicken broth or 1 can (about 10 ounces) chicken broth
1 can (10 ounces) frozen oysters, thawed

2 tablespoons butter
2 tablespoons flour
1¼ teaspoons salt
2 cups milk
1 teaspoon lemon peel
1 tablespoon lemon juice
Freshly ground pepper
Lemon slices

1. Put lettuce, spinach, carrots, onion, ½ cup chicken broth, and oysters into a 3-quart saucepan. Cover and cook until carrots are just tender (about 5 minutes).
2. Turn half of cooked mixture into an electric blender container and blend a few seconds; repeat. Set vegetable mixture aside.
3. Melt butter in a saucepan. Stir in flour and salt. Gradually add milk and remaining 1 cup chicken broth, stirring until smooth. Bring to boiling, stirring occasionally, and cook until thickened. Add vegetable mixture, lemon peel and juice, and pepper; heat to desired serving temperature, stirring occasionally.
4. Serve garnished with lemon slices.
ABOUT 7 CUPS

Tomato-Cheese Soup

1 can (about 10 ounces) condensed tomato soup
1 soup can milk
1 cup (4 ounces) shredded

Cheddar, American, or Colby cheese
¼ teaspoon finely crushed basil (optional)

1. Turn soup into a large saucepan; gradually blend in milk. Stir until hot and blended.
2. Mix in cheese and, if desired, basil.
3 SERVINGS

Chinese Cabbage Soup

2 cups cooked chicken, cut into strips (about 1 chicken breast)
7 cups chicken broth
6 cups sliced Chinese cab-

bage (celery cabbage)
1 teaspoon soy sauce
1 teaspoon salt
¼ teaspoon pepper

Combine chicken and chicken broth; bring to boiling. Stir in remaining ingredients; cook only 3 to 4 minutes, or just until cabbage is crisp-tender. (Do not overcook.)
6 SERVINGS

Note: If desired, lettuce may be substituted for the Chinese cabbage. Reduce cooking time to 1 minute.

Volhynian Beet Soup

¼ cup dried navy or pea beans
2 cups water
2 cups Bread Kvas (below)
2 cups meat broth, bouillon, or meat stock
6 medium beets, cooked and peeled

1 can (16 ounces) tomatoes (undrained)
1 small head cabbage (about 1½ pounds)
1 small sour apple
Salt and pepper
1 tablespoon butter (optional)
Sour cream

1. Bring beans and water just to boiling in a large kettle. Remove from heat. Let stand 1 hour. Then boil for 20 minutes, or until beans are tender. Add kvas and meat broth.
2. Slice beets. Mash tomatoes or make a purée by pressing through a sieve or using an electric blender. Add beets and tomatoes to beans.
3. Cut cabbage into sixths; remove core. Pare apple, if desired; core and dice. Add cabbage and apple to beans.
4. Season to taste with salt and pepper. Stir in butter, if desired. Cook soup over medium heat 30 minutes.
5. To serve, spoon a small amount of sour cream into each bowl. Ladle in hot soup and stir.
ABOUT 2½ QUARTS

Bread Kvas

1 quart hot water
1 pound beets, pared and

sliced
1 rye bread crust

1. Pour hot water over beets in a casserole. Add bread. Cover with a cloth. Let stand 3 to 4 days.
2. Drain off clear juice and use as a base for soup.
ABOUT 3 CUPS

Corn Soup II

2 tablespoons butter or margarine
½ cup chopped onion
2 cups (17-ounce can) cream-style corn
1 cup canned tomato sauce

3 cups chicken stock, canned chicken broth, or 3 cups water plus 3 chicken bouillon cubes
1 cup cream
Salt and pepper

1. Melt butter in a large saucepan. Add onion and cook until soft. Add corn, tomato sauce, and stock. Bring to boiling, reduce heat, and simmer about 10 minutes to blend flavors, stirring frequently.
2. Remove from heat and stir in cream. Season to taste with salt and pepper. Serve hot.
6 TO 8 SERVINGS

BREADS

Basic White Bread

5½ to 6 cups flour	1 cup milk
2 packages active dry yeast	1 cup water
2 tablespoons sugar	2 tablespoons oil
2 teaspoons salt	Oil or butter

QUICK MIX METHOD

1. Combine 2 cups flour, yeast, sugar, and salt in a large mixing bowl.
2. Heat milk, water, and 2 tablespoons oil in a saucepan over low heat until very warm (120° to 130°F).
3. Add liquid to flour mixture; beat on high speed of electric mixer until smooth, about 3 minutes. Gradually stir in more flour to make a soft dough.
4. Turn onto lightly floured surface and knead until smooth and elastic (5 to 10 minutes).
5. Cover dough with bowl or pan; let rest 20 minutes.
6. For two loaves, divide dough in half and roll out two 14x7-inch rectangles; for one loaf roll out to 16x8-inch rectangle.
7. Roll up from narrow side, pressing dough into roll at each turn. Press ends to seal and fold under loaf.
8. Place in 2 greased 8x4x2-inch loaf pans or 1 greased 9x5x3-inch loaf pan; brush with oil.
9. Let rise in warm place until double in bulk (30 to 45 minutes).
10. Bake at 400°F 35 to 40 minutes.
11. Remove from pans immediately and brush with oil; cool on wire rack.
ONE 2-POUND LOAF OR TWO 1-POUND LOAVES

CONVENTIONAL METHOD

1. Heat milk, sugar, oil, and salt; cool to lukewarm.
2. In a large bowl, sprinkle yeast in warm water (105° to 115°F); stir until dissolved.
3. Add lukewarm milk mixture and 2 cups flour; beat until smooth.
4. Beat in enough additional flour to make a stiff dough.
5. Turn out onto lightly floured surface; let rest 10 to 15 minutes. Knead until smooth and elastic (8 to 10 minutes).
6. Place in a greased bowl, turning to grease top. Cover; let rise in warm place until double in bulk (about 1 hour).
7. Punch down. Let rest 15 minutes.
8. Follow same shaping and baking instructions as Quick Mix Method.

You'll want to try these flavor variations to the Basic White Bread for something different. Shaping variations are also included.

Cheese Bread: Add **1 cup (4 ounces) shredded Cheddar cheese** before the last portion of the flour.

Onion Bread: Omit the salt and add **1 package (1⅜ ounces) dry onion soup mix** to the warm milk.

Mini Loaves: Divide dough into 10 equal pieces. Shape into loaves. Place in 10 greased 4½x2½x1½-inch loaf pans. Cover; let rise until double in bulk (about 20 minutes). Bake at 350°F 20 to 25 minutes.

Braided Egg Bread: Reduce milk to ½ cup. Add **2 eggs** with warm liquid to the flour mixture. Divide dough into 3 equal pieces. Form each into a rope, 15x12 inches. Braid. Tuck ends under. Place on a greased baking sheet or 9x5x3-inch loaf pan. Cover and let rise and bake the same as basic recipe.

French Bread: Omit the milk and oil and use **2 cups water.** Divide dough in half. Roll each half into 15x12-inch rectangle. Beginning at long side, roll up tightly. Seal seams. Taper the ends. With a sharp knife, make ¼-inch deep diagonal cuts along loaf tops. Cover. Let rise until less than double in bulk (about 20 minutes). Brush with water. Bake at 400°F 15 minutes, then reduce to 350°F and bake 15 to 20 minutes longer. For crisper crust, put pan of hot water in bottom of oven and 5 minutes before loaf is done, brush with glaze of **1 beaten egg white** and **1 tablespoon cold water.**

Whole Wheat Bread

¼ cup warm water (105°F for dry yeast, 95°F for compressed yeast)	to 105° or 95°F
	1 cup honey
1 package yeast, active dry or compressed	2 tablespoons olive oil
	2 tablespoons salt
1½ cups scalded milk, cooled	6 to 6½ cups whole wheat flour

1. Pour water into a bowl; add yeast and stir until dissolved. Add milk, honey, olive oil, and salt. Stir with a wooden spoon until well blended.
2. Stir in 4 cups of flour, 1 cup at a time. Beat until dough is smooth and elastic. Mix in another cup of flour. The dough will be very stiff.
3. Measure another cup of flour; sprinkle half of it on a board. Turn dough onto the board. Knead dough, adding flour to board until the dough no longer sticks. Continue kneading until dough is not sticky (about 8 minutes).
4. Put dough into a greased bowl about three times the size of the dough. Turn dough to grease surface lightly. Cover bowl with a towel and let rise in a warm place for about 2 hours, or until double in bulk. Test by inserting a finger about ½ inch into dough. If indentation remains, the dough is ready to shape.
5. Punch dough down; squeeze out air bubbles and shape into a smooth ball. Let rise again in warm place for about 30 minutes.
6. Divide into equal portions for 2 loaves. Form each into a smooth oval loaf. Let stand covered for 15 minutes.
7. Place the loaves seam side down in 2 greased 9x5x3-inch loaf pans. Cover with a towel and let rise in warm place until almost double in bulk (about 1 hour).
8. Bake at 375°F about 30 minutes, or until crust is medium brown.
9. Turn out of pans at once. Cool on wire racks.
2 LOAVES

100% Whole Wheat Bread

4¼ to 4¾ cups whole wheat flour
2 packages active dry yeast
1 tablespoon salt
¾ cup milk
¾ cup water
2 tablespoons oil
2 tablespoons honey
1 egg (at room temperature)
Oil

1. Combine 1¾ cups flour, yeast, and salt in a large mixing bowl.
2. Heat milk, water, oil, and honey over low heat until very warm (120° to 130°F).
3. Add the liquid and egg to flour mixture; beat until smooth, about 3 minutes on high speed of electric mixer.
4. Gradually stir in more flour to make a soft dough.
5. Turn onto a lightly floured surface and knead until smooth and elastic (5 to 8 minutes).
6. Cover dough with bowl or pan; let rest 20 minutes.
7. Roll out to 16x8-inch rectangle.
8. Roll up from narrow side, pressing dough into roll at each turn. Press ends to seal and fold under loaf.
9. Place in a greased 9x5x3-inch loaf pan; brush with oil.
10. Let rise in a warm place (80° to 85°F) until double in bulk (30 to 45 minutes).
11. Bake at 375°F 35 to 40 minutes.
12. Remove from pans immediately and brush with oil or butter; cool on wire rack.
1 LOAF

Delicatessen Rye Bread

2 to 2¾ cups all-purpose or unbleached flour
2 cups rye flour
2 teaspoons salt
2 packages active dry yeast
1 tablespoon caraway seed
1 cup milk
¾ cup water
2 tablespoons molasses
2 tablespoons oil

1. Combine 1¾ cups all-purpose flour, salt, yeast, and caraway seed in a large mixing bowl.
2. Heat milk, water, molasses, and oil in a saucepan over low heat until very warm (120° to 130°F).
3. Add liquid gradually to flour mixture, beating on high speed of electric mixer; scrape bowl occasionally. Add 1 cup rye flour, or enough to make a thick batter. Beat at high speed 2 minutes. Stir in remaining rye flour and enough all-purpose flour to make a soft dough.
4. Turn dough onto a floured surface; knead until smooth and elastic (about 5 minutes).
5. Cover with bowl or pan and let rest 20 minutes.
6. Divide in half. Shape into 2 round loaves; place on greased baking sheets. Cover; let rise until double in bulk (30 to 45 minutes).
7. Bake at 375°F 35 to 40 minutes, or until done.
2 LOAVES

Freezer Oatmeal Bread

12 to 13 cups all-purpose flour
4 packages active dry yeast
2 tablespoons salt
2 cups milk
2 cups water
½ cup honey
¼ cup vegetable oil
2 cups uncooked oats
½ cup wheat germ
Oil

1. Combine 2 cups flour, yeast, and salt in a large mixing bowl.
2. Heat milk, water, honey, and oil in a saucepan until very warm (120° to 130°F).
3. Add the liquid gradually to flour mixture, beating 3 minutes on high speed of electric mixer until smooth. Stir in oats, wheat germ, and enough remaining flour to make a soft dough.
4. Turn dough onto a floured surface; knead until smooth and elastic (8 to 10 minutes).
5. Divide dough into quarters. Shape each quarter into a loaf, and either place in an 8x4x2-inch loaf pan or on a baking sheet. Freeze just until firm. Remove from pan. Wrap tightly in aluminum foil or freezer wrap. Dough will keep up to 2 weeks.
6. To bake, remove wrapping and place dough in a greased 8x4x2-inch loaf pan. Thaw in refrigerator overnight or at room temperature 2 hours. Brush with oil and let rise in a warm place until double in bulk (about 2 hours).
7. Bake at 400°F 30 to 35 minutes, or until done.
4 LOAVES

Freezer Whole Wheat Bread: Follow recipe for Freezer Oatmeal Bread, substituting **5 cups whole wheat flour** for 5 cups all-purpose flour.

Freezer White Bread: Follow recipe for Freezer Oatmeal Bread, omitting oats and wheat germ and increasing flour by about 1 cup.

Orange Soda Bread

3½ cups all-purpose flour
1 teaspoon salt
1 teaspoon sugar
1 teaspoon baking powder
1 cup buttermilk
½ cup fresh orange juice
1 egg
1 cup raisins
1 tablespoon grated orange peel

1. Combine flour, salt, sugar, and baking soda in a bowl. Make a well in the center and pour in buttermilk and orange juice; mix well.
2. Add egg, raisin, and orange peel; beat until smooth (dough will be sticky).
3. Knead lightly on a well-floured surface. Shape into a round loaf and put into a well-greased 9-inch round layer cake pan. Cut an X across the top of loaf.
4. Bake at 350°F 40 minutes, or until a cake tester inserted in center comes out clean. Serve warm.
1 LOAF

Basic White Bread (page 119)

Quick Applesauce Bread

2¼ cups Basic Oats Mix (page 157)
1 cup sugar
1 teaspoon cinnamon
1 cup canned sweetened applesauce
1 egg
½ cup milk
½ cup raisins

1. Combine Oats Mix, sugar, and cinnamon in a bowl. Add applesauce, egg, milk, and raisins; stir until mixed.
2. Turn batter into a greased and floured 8½x4½x2½-inch loaf pan.
3. Bake at 350°F 55 to 60 minutes.
4. Remove from pan and cool completely on a rack before slicing.
1 LOAF BREAD

Oregano and Kefalotyri Cheese Bread

3 to 3½ cups all-purpose flour
2 tablespoons sugar
1½ teaspoons salt
2 packages active dry yeast
¾ cup milk
¼ cup water
¼ cup shortening
1 egg
3 tablespoons oregano
¼ teaspoon garlic powder
½ cup grated kefalotyri cheese
1 teaspoon mint
2 tablespoons basil
¼ cup instant minced onion
1 tablespoon sesame seed

1. Combine 1 cup flour, sugar, salt, and dry yeast in a large bowl.
2. Heat milk, water, and shortening in a saucepan until warm. (Shortening will not melt completely.) Add milk mixture and egg to flour mixture. Beat until smooth.
3. Mix oregano, garlic powder, cheese, mint, basil, onion, and sesame seed. Stir into dough. Gradually add more flour to form a stiff dough.
4. Turn into a greased loaf pan. Cover with a towel. Let rise in a warm place until double in bulk (about 1 hour).
5. Bake at 350° about 40 minutes, or until golden brown.
1 LOAF

Church Bread

1 package active dry yeast
2½ cups warm water (105° to 115°)
6 cups all-purpose flour
1 teaspoon salt
Prosphoron seal

1. Sprinkle yeast over ¼ cup warm water; stir until dissolved.
2. Combine 5½ cups of flour and salt in a large bowl and make a well in the center. Pour in yeast and remaining warm water. Mix with a wooden spoon.
3. Sprinkle remaining flour over a board. Knead 10 minutes, adding as little flour as possible to the board. Dough will be sticky.
4. Put dough into a large bowl, cover with a cloth, and let rise in a warm place until double in bulk.
5. Sprinkle board with a little flour, punch dough down, and knead 15 minutes. (Dough should be firm and smooth.)
6. Form into a large round loaf and place in a heavily floured 12-inch round pan. Lightly flour the top of the loaf. Flour the phosphoron seal. Press seal down firmly in the center to make a sharp impression and leave on the dough.
7. Cover and allow to rise in a warm place until double in bulk. Remove seal.
8. Bake at 350°F for 1 hour. Remove from pan to cool.
1 LOAF

Quick Applesauce Bread

Corn Bread I

2 eggs
2 cups buttermilk
3 tablespoons shortening, melted
1½ teaspoons salt
2½ cups cornmeal
1 teaspoon baking powder
½ teaspoon baking soda

1. Beat eggs until light. Add buttermilk and melted shortening; mix well.
2. Mix dry ingredients together. Add to egg mixture; beat until smooth. Pour into a greased 9-inch square baking pan.
3. Bake at 375°F about 25 minutes. Serve hot.
ABOUT 16 PIECES

Greek Christmas Bread

2 envelopes active dry yeast
2 cups scalded milk, cooled to 105° to 115°F
1 cup sugar
1 teaspoon salt
4 eggs (or 8 yolks), well beaten
½ cup unsalted butter, melted
7½ to 8 cups all-purpose flour
1½ teaspoons cardamom, pounded, or 1 teaspoon mastic
½ cup dried golden currants
¾ cup chopped walnuts
2 egg whites, beaten
3 to 4 tablespoons sugar

1. Sprinkle yeast over 1 cup warm milk in a small bowl; stir until dissolved. Set aside.
2. Reserve 2 teaspoons sugar for pounding with mastic, if using. Put sugar into a bowl and add salt, eggs, remaining 1 cup milk, and butter; mix well.
3. Put 7 cups flour into a large bowl. Stir in cardamom, or pound mastic with 2 teaspoons sugar (so it will not become gummy) and add. Make a well and add dissolved yeast, egg mixture, currants, and nuts; mix well.
4. Knead dough on a floured board, adding the remaining 1 cup flour as required. Knead dough until smooth (5 to 6 minutes).
5. Place dough in a greased bowl. Turn until surface is completely greased. Cover. Set in a warm place until double in bulk.
6. Punch dough down. Form into two round loaves and place in buttered 10-inch pans.
7. Cover and let rise again in a warm place until double in bulk.
8. Bake at 375°F 15 minutes. Remove from oven and brush with beaten egg whites, then sprinkle with sugar. Return to oven. Turn oven control to 325°F and bake about 35 to 40 minutes, or until bread is done.
2 LOAVES

Dark Rye Bread

2 cups milk, scalded
2 tablespoons butter
2 tablespoons sugar
1 teaspoon salt
1 package active dry yeast
½ cup lukewarm water
4 cup rye flour
2½ cups whole-wheat flour
2 tablespoons caraway seed

1. Pour scalded milk over butter, sugar, and salt in a large bowl; stir. Cool.
2. Dissolve yeast in lukewarm water.
3. Add softened yeast and 3 cups rye flour to milk mixture. Beat thoroughly, then beat in remaining rye flour.
4. Cover and let rise in warm place until doubled in bulk. Turn onto well-floured surface. Knead in whole-wheat flour and caraway seed. Knead until dough is smooth.
5. Divide dough in half and shape into 2 round or oblong loaves. Place round loaves in greased round pans; oblong loaves in greased loaf pans. Cover and let rise in warm place until doubled in bulk.
6. Bake at 450°F 15 minutes; reduce heat to 350°F and bake 35 to 40 minutes longer. Brush with melted butter 5 minutes before done if a more tender crust is desired.
2 LARGE LOAVES

Polish Christmas Bread

5 eggs
2 cups confectioners' sugar
2¼ cups all-purpose flour
¾ cup finely chopped walnuts
⅔ cup raisins
4 ounces candied orange peel, finely chopped
2 teaspoons baking powder
½ teaspoon salt
1 cup butter or margarine (at room temperature)
1 tablespoon grated lemon peel
1 teaspoon vanilla extract
3 tablespoons vodka or brandy

1. Beat eggs with sugar 5 minutes at high speed of electric mixer.
2. Mix nuts, raisins, and orange peel with 2 tablespoons flour. Mix remaining flour with baking powder and salt.
3. Cream butter, lemon peel, and vanilla extract until fluffy. Beat in vodka. Add egg mixture gradually, beating constantly. Add flour mixture and beat 5 minutes. Fold fruit-nut mixture into the batter. Turn into a generously greased and floured 9x5x3-inch loaf pan or 1½-quart ring mold.
4. Bake at 350°F 1 hour.
5. Cool cake in pan on wire rack 10 minutes. Turn cake out onto rack; cool completely.
6. Wrap in plastic wrap. Store 1 or 2 days to mellow. Sprinkle with confectioners' sugar, if desired.
1 LOAF

Corn Bread II

1 cup all-purpose flour
1 cup yellow cornmeal
2 teaspoons baking powder
½ teaspoon baking soda
1 teaspoon salt
1 cup milk
2½ teaspoons lime juice
1 egg, beaten
2 tablespoons lard, melted

1. Combine flour, cornmeal, baking powder, baking soda, and salt in a bowl.
2. Mix milk and lime juice; add to dry ingredients along with egg and lard. Mix well, but do not beat. Pour into a greased 11x7x1½-inch baking pan.
3. Bake at 450°F 15 to 20 minutes, or until it is brown and tests done. Cool slightly and cut into squares.
ABOUT 8 SERVINGS

Whole Wheat-Oatmeal Bread

2¼ cups milk
¼ cup butter or margarine
1 tablespoon salt
¼ cup firmly packed brown
  sugar
2½ to 2¾ cups all-purpose

flour
2 cups whole wheat flour
2 packages active dry yeast
2 cups uncooked oats
⅔ cup wheat germ

1. Heat milk, butter, salt, and sugar in a saucepan until lukewarm. Pour liquid into a large mixer bowl. Add 1 cup all-purpose flour and 1 cup whole wheat flour; beat 2 minutes at medium speed of electric mixer. Add remaining whole wheat flour and yeast; beat 2 minutes at medium speed. Stir in oats, wheat germ, and enough additional all-purpose flour to make a soft dough.
2. Turn dough onto a floured surface; knead until smooth and elastic (about 10 minutes). Round dough into a ball. Place in a greased bowl; lightly grease surface of dough. Cover; let rise in a warm place until nearly double in bulk (about 1 hour).
3. Punch dough down; shape into 2 large or 8 miniature loaves. Place in greased 8x4x2½-inch or 4x3x2-inch loaf pans. Let rise in a warm place until nearly double in bulk.
4. Bake at 375°F 45 minutes for large loaves or 30 minutes for miniature loaves. Remove from pans immediately; cool on wire rack.
2 LARGE LOAVES OR 8 MINIATURE LOAVES

Easter Egg Bread

2 packages active dry yeast
½ cup warm water
1 cup all-purpose flour
⅓ cup water
¾ cup butter or margarine
1 tablespoon grated lemon
  peel

1½ tablespoons lemon juice
¾ cup sugar
1 teaspoon salt
2 eggs, well beaten
3¾ to 4¼ cups all-purpose
  flour
6 colored eggs (uncooked)

1. Soften yeast in the warm water in a bowl. Mix in the 1 cup flour, then the ⅓ cup water. Beat until smooth. Cover; let rise in a warm place until doubled (about 1 hour).
2. Cream butter with lemon peel and juice. Add beaten eggs in halves, beating thoroughly after each addition.
3. Add yeast mixture and beat until blended. Add about half of the remaining flour and beat thoroughly. Beat in

enough flour to make a soft dough.
4. Knead on floured surface until smooth. Put into a greased deep bowl; turn dough to bring greased surface to top. Cover; let rise in a warm place until doubled.
5. Punch down dough; divide into thirds. Cover; let rest about 10 minutes.
6. With hands, roll and stretch each piece into a roll about 26 inches long and ¾ inch thick. Loosely braid rolls together. On a lightly greased baking sheet or jelly-roll pan shape into a ring, pressing ends together. At even intervals, gently spread dough apart and tuck in a colored egg. Cover; let rise again until doubled.
7. Bake at 375°F about 30 minutes. During baking check bread for browning, and when sufficiently browned, cover loosely with aluminum foil.
8. Transfer coffee cake to a wire rack. If desired, spread a confectioners' sugar icing over top of warm bread.
1 LARGE WREATH

Family Wheat Bread

5 to 6 cups all-purpose or
  unbleached flour
2 packages active dry yeast
1 tablespoon salt
2 cups milk

½ cup water
¼ cup oil
3 tablespoons honey
3 eggs
2 cups whole wheat flour

1. Combine 2½ cups all-purpose flour, yeast, and salt in a large mixing bowl.
2. Heat milk, water, oil, and honey in a saucepan until very warm (120° to 130°F).
3. Add liquid to flour mixture and beat until smooth. Add eggs and continue beating about 3 minutes on high speed of electric mixer.
4. Stir in whole wheat flour and enough all-purpose flour to make a soft dough.
5. Turn dough onto a floured surface; allow to rest 10 minutes for easier handling. Knead until smooth and elastic (about 8 minutes). Let rest 20 minutes.
6. Divide dough in half. Roll each half into a 14x9-inch rectangle. Shape into loaves. Place in greased 9x5x3-inch loaf pans.
7. Cover with plastic wrap. Refrigerate 2 to 24 hours.
8. When ready to bake, remove from refrigerator. Let stand at room temperature 10 minutes.
9. Bake at 400°F 40 minutes, or until done.
2 LOAVES

Variations: Substitute 1 cup any one of the following ingredients for 1 cup of the whole wheat flour: **uncooked oats, cornmeal, cracked wheat, soybean grits, millet, wheat germ, ground sunflower seeds, bran, crushed shredded wheat cereal,** or any flour of your choice.

French Bread (page 119)

Cornmeal French Bread

1 cup cooked cornmeal
  mush (see recipe)
2 packages active dry yeast
½ cup warm water
1 cup milk, scalded

1 tablespoon sugar
2½ teaspoons salt
4¾ to 5¼ cups all-purpose
  flour

1. Prepare cornmeal mush; cool slightly.
2. Dissolve yeast in warm water.
3. Pour scalded milk over sugar and salt in a large bowl. Add mush and mix well; cool to lukewarm. Beat in 1 cup flour. Mix in yeast and enough additional flour to make a soft dough.
4. Turn dough onto a lightly floured surface. Knead until smooth and satiny (about 10 minutes).
5. Put dough into a greased bowl; turn to grease top. Cover; let rise in a warm place until double in bulk (about 1 hour).
6. Punch dough down; cover and let rest 10 minutes. Form into a long thin roll on greased baking sheet. With a sharp knife, cut diagonal ¼-inch-deep slits about 2½ inches apart across the top. Brush top of loaf with salt water (**1 table-spoon salt** dissolved in **¼ cup water**). Cover; let rise until double in bulk (about 45 minutes).
7. Pour boiling water into a pie pan to a ½-inch depth; set on bottom rack of oven.
8. Bake at 400°F 15 minutes; turn temperature control to 350°F and bake 30 to 35 minutes longer. About 5 minutes before bread is finished baking, baste with salt water.
1 LARGE LOAF

Cornmeal Mush: Heat **3 cups water** to boiling in a saucepan. Mix **1 cup cornmeal, 1 teaspoon salt,** and **1 cup cold water.** Pour cornmeal mixture into boiling water, stirring constantly. Cook until thickened, stirring frequently. Cover; continue cooking over low heat 10 minutes.
4 CUPS

Anadama Batter Bread

1 package active dry yeast
¼ cup warm water
1 cup cornmeal
2 teaspoons salt
½ teaspoon baking soda
⅓ cup dark molasses

3 tablespoons shortening
¾ cup boiling water
1 egg
2¼ cups all-purpose flour
Melted butter

1. Dissolve yeast in warm water.
2. Combine cornmeal, salt, baking soda, molasses, and shortening in a large mixer bowl. Stir in boiling water; cool to lukewarm.
3. Add softened yeast, egg, and 1 cup flour to cornmeal mixture; beat 2 minutes on medium speed of electric mixer or 300 vigorous strokes with a wooden spoon. Stir in remaining flour.
4. Spread batter in a well-greased 2-quart casserole. Cover; let rise in a warm place until nearly double in bulk (1 to 1½ hours).
5. Bake at 350°F about 40 minutes. Remove from casserole immediately. Brush top lightly with melted butter; cool.
1 LOAF

Cheddar Cornbread

1 cup yellow cornmeal
1 cup all-purpose flour
1 tablespoon baking powder
1 teaspoon salt
2 cups shredded Cheddar
  cheese (8 ounces)
1 cup milk

¼ cup melted butter or
  margarine or vegetable oil
1 egg
4 slices crisply cooked
  bacon, crumbled
1 green pepper, sliced
  (optional)

1. Combine cornmeal, flour, baking powder, salt, and 1 cup cheese in a mixing bowl.
2. Combine milk, butter, and egg in a separate bowl; beat well.
3. Add liquid ingredients to dry ingredients; stir just until flour is moistened. Pour into a greased 9-inch round layer cake pan. Sprinkle with remaining cheese and bacon. Top with green pepper rings, if desired.
4. Bake at 425°F 25 minutes, or until done.
ABOUT 8 SERVINGS

Pleasin' Pumpkin Bread

3½ cups all-purpose flour
3 cups sugar
2 cups cooked mashed
  pumpkin
1 cup vegetable oil
⅓ cup water
4 eggs

2 teaspoons baking soda
1½ teaspoons salt
2 teaspoons cinnamon
½ teaspoon nutmeg
¼ teaspoon cloves
¼ teaspoon ginger

1. Put flour, sugar, baking soda, salt, and spices into a large mixing bowl; mix well. Add pumpkin, oil, water, and eggs; beat until well blended.
2. Divide batter equally into 2 greased 9x5x3-inch loaf pans.
3. Bake at 350°F 70 minutes, or until done.
4. Cool before wrapping.
2 LOAVES

Anadama Batter Bread

Peasant Black Bread

Peasant Black Bread

3½ cups rye flour
½ cup unsweetened cocoa
¼ cup sugar
3 tablespoons caraway seed
2 packages active dry yeast
1 tablespoon instant coffee
(powder or crystals)
2 teaspoons salt

2½ cups hot water (120°-130°F)
¼ cup vinegar
¼ cup dark molasses
¼ cup vegetable oil or
melted butter
3½ to 4½ cups unbleached
or all-purpose flour

1. Thoroughly mix rye flour, cocoa, sugar, caraway, yeast, coffee, and salt in a large mixing bowl.
2. Stir in water, vinegar, molasses, and oil; beat until smooth.
3. Stir in enough unbleached flour to make a soft dough.
4. Turn onto a floured surface. Knead until smooth and elastic (about 5 minutes).
5. Place in an oiled bowl; turn to oil top of dough. Cover; let rise in warm place until doubled (about 1 hour).
6. Punch dough down. Divide in half; shape each half into a ball and place in center of 2 greased 8-inch round cake pans. Cover; let rise until double in bulk (about 1 hour).
7. Bake at 350°F 40 to 45 minutes, or until done.
2 LOAVES

Aspen Batter Bread

4 cups all-purpose flour
2 tablespoons sugar
1 package active dry yeast
1 teaspoon salt
¼ teaspoon ginger

1 can (13 ounces) evaporated
milk
½ cup hot water
2 tablespoons vegetable oil

1. Combine 2 cups flour, sugar, yeast, salt, and ginger in a large mixing bowl.

2. Heat milk, water, and oil until very warm (120° to 130°F).
3. Stir in liquid with flour mixture; beat 2 minutes by hand or with electric mixer. Cover; let rise 15 minutes.
4. Beat in remaining flour by hand. Pour into 2 greased 1-pound coffee cans. Cover with greased plastic lids; let rise in a warm place until dough rises to top of cans (or until lids pop off), about 35 minutes. Remove lids.
5. Bake at 375°F 40 to 45 minutes, or until done. Place on wire racks to cool slightly before removing loaves from cans.
2 LOAVES

Beer-Cheese Bread with Raisins

1 cup raisins (5 ounces)
1 can or bottle (12 ounces)
beer
2½ cups all-purpose flour
¾ cup sugar
1 tablespoon baking powder

½ teaspoon baking soda
½ teaspoon salt
4 ounces Cheddar cheese,
finely shredded
¼ cup oil
1 egg

1. Heat raisins and beer to simmering. Remove from heat; let stand about 10 minutes.
2. Combine dry ingredients. Add cheese; stir to coat.
3. Mix oil and egg. Add to dry ingredients, along with beer and raisins. Beat just until blended.
4. Turn into a greased and floured 9x5x3-inch loaf pan.
5. Bake at 350°F 1 hour. Turn out on a rack to cool. Cool thoroughly before slicing.
1 LOAF

Green
Chili
Cornbread

Ground Nut Bread

3 cups all-purpose flour
1½ cups whole wheat flour
2 packages active dry yeast
2 teaspoons salt
1¾ cups hot tap water (120°
   to 130°F)
¼ cup honey

2 tablespoons vegetable oil
1 cup rolled oats
1 cup ground unsalted nuts
½ cup ground unsalted
   hulled sunflower seeds
½ cup cornmeal

1. Mix flours.
2. Combine 1¾ cups flour mixture, yeast, and salt in a large mixing bowl.
3. Add water, honey, and oil to flour mixture; beat until smooth, about 3 minutes on high speed of electric mixer.
4. Stir in oats, nuts, sunflower seeds, cornmeal, and enough more flour to make a soft dough.
5. Turn dough onto a floured board; knead until smooth and elastic (5 to 8 minutes).
6. Place in an oiled bowl; turn to oil top of dough. Cover; let rise in a warm place until double in bulk (about 1 hour).
7. Punch dough down. Divide in half, then each half in thirds. Form each piece into a rope 12 to 15 inches long. For each loaf, braid 3 pieces together. Tuck ends under; place in 2 greased 9x5x3-inch loaf pans or on greased baking sheets. Cover; let rise until double in bulk (about 1 hour).
8. Bake at 375°F 35 to 40 minutes, or until done.
2 LOAVES

Green Chili Cornbread

4 ounces sharp Cheddar
   cheese (2 cups shredded)
2 green onions, trimmed and
   cut in 1-inch pieces
1 can (4 ounces) whole
   green chilies, drained and
   seeded
1 cup milk
1 egg

¼ cup vegetable oil
1¼ cups cornmeal
¾ cup flour
¼ cup sugar
1 tablespoon baking powder
½ teaspoon salt
1 can (8 ounces) whole
   kernel corn

1. Using **shredding disc** of food processor, shred cheese and set aside.
2. Using **steel blade,** process the green onions until finely chopped.
3. Add green chilies to green onions in bowl and process, in quick on/off motions, until finely chopped and set aside.
4. With **plastic blade** in bowl, add milk, egg, and oil, and process until blended. Add cornmeal, flour, sugar, baking powder, and salt and mix together for a few seconds. Add corn, green onions, and chilies.
5. Pour half of batter into a greased 9-inch square baking pan. Sprinkle with half of cheese. Repeat, using remaining batter and cheese.
6. Bake at 400°F about 35 to 40 minutes, or until lightly browned. Serve warm cut in squares.
8 TO 12 SERVINGS

Refrigerator Rye Bread

3 to 3½ cups unbleached or all-purpose flour	or grated orange peel
¼ cup firmly packed brown sugar	2 cups hot water
	¼ cup molasses
2 packages active dry yeast	2 tablespoons softened butter or margarine
1 tablespoon salt	3 cups rye flour
1 tablespoon caraway seed	Cornmeal

1. Combine 2 cups unbleached flour, brown sugar, yeast, salt, and caraway seed in a large mixing bowl.
2. Heat water, molasses, and butter until very warm (120° to 130°F).
3. Add liquid gradually to flour mixture and beat about 3 minutes on high speed of electric mixer. Stir in rye flour and enough unbleached flour to make a soft dough.
4. Turn dough onto a floured surface; knead until smooth and elastic (about 5 minutes). Let rest 20 minutes.
5. Divide dough in half. Shape into 2 long narrow loaves by rolling and stretching dough as for French Bread (see page 119). Place on a greased baking sheet sprinkled with cornmeal. Cover with plastic wrap or waxed paper; refrigerate 2 to 24 hours.
6. When ready to bake, remove plastic wrap carefully. Let rise in a warm place while oven is preheating, about 15 minutes. Brush loaves with water.
7. Bake at 400°F 40 minutes, or until done.
2 LOAVES

Dilly Cottage Batter Bread

2½ cups all-purpose flour	cheese (at room temperature)
1 package active dry yeast	
1 tablespoon instant minced onion	½ cup hot tap water (120° to 130°F)
1 teaspoon salt	1 egg (at room temperature)
½ teaspoon dill weed, thyme, or rosemary	1 tablespoon honey
1 cup creamed cottage	1½ cups all-purpose flour

1. Combine 1 cup flour, yeast, onion, salt, and dill weed.
2. Add cottage cheese, water, egg, and honey to flour mixture; beat 3 minutes by hand or with electric mixer.
3. Beat in remaining flour. Cover; let rise in a warm place until double in bulk (about 1 hour).
4. Stir batter down; pour into a well-greased 1½-quart round casserole. Let rise in a warm place until light (30 to 40 minutes).
5. Bake at 375°F 50 to 55 minutes, or until done.
1 LOAF

Oklahoma Oatmeal Bread

1 cup evaporated milk	sugar
2 tablespoons vegetable oil	1 teaspoon baking soda
1 tablespoon vinegar	½ teaspoon salt
1 cup uncooked oats	1 cup raisins or chopped nuts
1 cup all-purpose flour	
1 cup firmly packed brown	

1. Beat milk, oil, and vinegar in a mixing bowl until smooth.
2. Add oats, flour, brown sugar, baking soda, and salt; mix until well blended.
3. Stir in raisins or nuts.
4. Turn into a greased 9x5x3-inch loaf pan or two 7x4x2-inch loaf pans.
5. Bake at 350°F 50 to 60 minutes, or until done.
6. Cool before wrapping.
1 LARGE LOAF OR 2 SMALL LOAVES

Quick Buttermilk Bread

1¾ cups all-purpose flour	1½ cups uncooked oats
2 teaspoons baking powder	1 cup buttermilk
¾ teaspoon baking soda	½ cup vegetable oil
1 teaspoon salt	2 eggs, beaten
⅓ cup firmly packed brown sugar	½ cup chopped pecans

1. Mix flour, baking powder, baking soda, and salt in a bowl. Stir in brown sugar and oats. Add remaining ingredients; stir only until dry ingredients are moistened.
2. Pour batter into a greased 9x5x3-inch loaf pan.
3. Bake at 350°F 50 to 55 minutes. Cool on wire rack about 10 minutes. Remove from pan; cool thoroughly.
4. Wrap and store. (Bread will slice better if stored a day before slicing.)
1 LOAF

Quick Buttermilk Bread

4. Punch dough down; divide in half. Proceed, following directions below for desired shape.

5. Cover; let rise in a warm place until double in bulk (about 1 hour). If making sheaf, make diagonal snips with scissors along the bent portion of stalks above the twist. If desired, gently brush sheaf with beaten egg.

6. Bake on lowest rack position at 400°F about 20 minutes for sheaves and 25 to 30 minutes for loaves, or until done. Remove from baking sheets and cool on wire racks.
2 LOAVES OR 1 SHEAF

To make round loaves: Shape each half of dough into a smooth round ball. Press each ball slightly to flatten into rounds 6 inches in diameter. Place on greased baking sheets.

Harvest Bread

1½ cups milk
⅓ cup margarine
2 tablespoons honey
2 tablespoons light molasses
2 teaspoons salt
2 large shredded wheat biscuits, crumbled

½ cup warm water (105° to 115°F)
2 packages active dry yeast
2 cups whole wheat flour
¼ cup wheat germ
2 to 3 cups all-purpose flour

1. Heat milk; stir in margarine, honey, molasses, salt, and shredded wheat biscuits. Cool to lukewarm.

2. Measure warm water into a large warm bowl. Sprinkle in yeast; stir until dissolved. Add lukewarm milk mixture and whole wheat flour; beat until smooth. Stir in wheat germ and enough all-purpose flour to make a stiff dough.

3. Turn dough onto a lightly floured surface; knead until smooth and elastic (8 to 10 minutes). Place in a greased bowl; turn to grease top. Cover; let rise in a warm place until double in bulk (about 1 hour).

To Make Wheat Sheaf: Divide one half of dough into 18 equal pieces. Roll 2 pieces into 12-inch ropes. Twist ropes together; set aside. Roll 8 pieces into 18-inch ropes and roll remaining 8 pieces into 15-inch ropes. Place one 18-inch rope lengthwise on center of a greased baking sheet, bending top third of rope off to the left at a 45-degree angle. Place a second 18-inch rope on sheet touching the first rope but bending top third off to the right. Repeat procedure using two more 18-inch ropes, placing them along outer edges of straight section and inside bent sections so that ropes are touching. Repeat, using two of the 15-inch ropes. Repeat, starting with the long ropes, placing them on top of the arranged long ropes and slightly spreading out ropes forming bottom of sheaf. Fill in by topping with the remaining 15-inch ropes, making shorter bends in two uppermost ropes. Cut twist in half. Arrange twists side by side around center of sheaf, tuck ends underneath. Repeat with remaining half of dough.

Mushroom Bread

¼ cup margarine	¼ teaspoon pepper
½ pound mushrooms, finely chopped	½ cup warm water (105° to 115°F)
1 cup finely chopped onion	2 packages active dry yeast
2 cups milk	1 egg
3 tablespoons molasses	1 cup wheat germ
4 teaspoons salt	8 to 9 cups all-purpose flour

1. Melt 2 tablespoons margarine in a large skillet over medium heat. Add mushrooms and onion; sauté until onion is tender and liquid has evaporated. Cool.
2. Heat milk; stir in molasses, salt, and pepper. Cool to lukewarm.
3. Measure warm water into a large warm bowl. Sprinkle in yeast; stir until dissolved. Add lukewarm milk mixture, egg, wheat germ, and 2 cups flour; beat until smooth. Stir in enough additional flour to make a stiff dough.
4. Turn dough onto a lightly floured surface; knead until smooth and elastic (8 to 10 minutes). Place in a greased bowl; turn to grease top. Cover; let rise in a warm place until double in bulk (about 1 hour).
5. Meanwhile, use four 30-ounce fruit cans to prepare Mushroom Pans (see below).
6. Punch dough down; turn onto lightly floured surface.

To Make Mushrooms: Divide dough onto 4 equal pieces. Shape each piece into a smooth round ball. Place in prepared Mushroom Pans. Let rise in a warm place until double in bulk (about 1 hour). With fingertips, gently press lower edge of mushroom cap down to meet foil-covered collar. Reshape cap if necessary. If desired, brush mushrooms with a mixture of 1 egg beaten with 1 tablespoon water. Bake on lowest rack position at 400°F about 40 minutes, or until done. Carefully remove from pans and cool on wire racks.

To Make Loaves: Divide dough in half. Roll each half to a 14x9-inch rectangle. Shape into loaves. Place in 2 greased 9x5x3-inch loaf pans. Cover; let rise in a warm place until double in bulk (about 1 hour). Bake at 400°F about 45 minutes, or until done. Remove from pans and cool on wire racks.
4 MUSHROOMS OR 2 ROUND LOAVES

Mushroom Pans: Cut 4 heavy cardboard squares 2 inches wider than can opening. Trace can opening in center of squares and cut out. Cover rings with foil. Place rings over cans so they fit tightly around opening. Grease cans and foil collars well.

Mushroom Bread

Carrot Brown Bread

3 cups whole wheat flour	½ cup water
4 cups unbleached or all-purpose flour	¼ cup vegetable oil
2 packages active dry yeast	2 tablespoons honey
2 teaspoons salt	2 tablespoons molasses
2 cups milk	1 cup grated carrot

1. Mix flours.
2. Combine 2 cups flour mixture, yeast, and salt in a large mixing bowl.
3. Heat milk, water, oil, honey, and molasses in a saucepan until very warm (120° to 130°F).
4. Add liquid gradually to flour mixture, beating 3 minutes on high speed of electric mixer.
5. Stir in carrot and enough more flour to make a soft dough.
6. Turn dough onto a floured surface; allow to rest 10 minutes for easier handling. Knead until smooth and elastic (5 to 8 minutes).
7. Place dough in an oiled bowl; turn to oil top of dough. Cover; let rise in a warm place until double in bulk (about 1 hour).
8. Punch dough down; divide in half. Either shape into 2 round loaves and place on a greased baking sheet, or shape into 2 loaves and place in 2 greased 9 x 5 x 3-inch loaf pans. Cover; let rise until double in bulk (about 30 minutes).
9. Bake at 375°F 40 to 45 minutes, or until done.
2 LOAVES

Italian Bread

Italian Bread

1 package active dry yeast	5 to 5½ cups sifted all-
2 cups warm water	purpose flour
1 tablespoon salt	

1. Soften yeast in ¼ cup warm water. Set aside.
2. Combine remaining 1¾ cups water and salt in a large bowl. Blend in 3 cups flour. Stir softened yeast and add to flour mixture, mixing well.
3. Add about half the remaining flour to the yeast mixture and beat until very smooth. Mix in enough remaining flour to make a soft dough. Turn dough onto lightly floured surface. Allow to rest 5 to 10 minutes. Knead 5 to 8 minutes, until dough is smooth and elastic.
4. Shape dough into a smooth ball and place in a greased bowl, just large enough to allow dough to double. Turn dough to bring greased surface to the top. Cover bowl with waxed paper and a towel. Let stand in warm place (about 80°F) until dough is doubled (1½ to 2 hours).
5. When dough has doubled in bulk, punch down with fist. Knead on a lightly floured surface about 2 minutes. Divide into 2 equal balls. Cover with towel and let stand 10 minutes.
6. Roll each ball into a 14x8-inch rectangle. Roll up lightly from wide side into a long, slender loaf. Pinch ends to seal. Place loaves on a lightly greased 15x10-inch baking sheet. Cover loaves loosely with a towel and set aside in a warm place until doubled.
7. Bake at 425°F 10 minutes. Turn oven control to 350°F and bake 1 hour, or until golden brown.
2 LOAVES

Note: To increase crustiness, place shallow pan on the bottom of the oven and fill with boiling water at the beginning of the baking time.

Colonial Bread

2 cups whole wheat flour	2 packages active dry yeast
2½ cups unbleached or all-	1 tablespoon salt
purpose flour	2½ cups hot tap water (120°
¾ cup rye flour	to 130°F)
½ cup yellow cornmeal	¼ cup vegetable oil
⅓ cup firmly packed brown	1 egg
sugar	

1. Blend flours and cornmeal. Combine 2½ cups flour mixture, sugar, yeast, and salt in a large mixing bowl.
2. Stir water, oil, and egg into flour mixture; beat until smooth, about 3 minutes on high speed of electric mixer.
3. Gradually stir in enough more flour mixture to make a soft dough.
4. Turn dough onto a floured surface; knead until smooth and elastic (5 to 8 minutes).
5. Place in an oiled bowl; turn to oil top of dough. Cover; let rise in a warm place until double in bulk (about 1 hour).
6. Punch dough down. Divide in half; shape into loaves. Place in 2 greased 9x5x3-inch loaf pans. Cover; let rise until double in bulk (about 30 minutes).
7. Bake at 375°F 35 to 40 minutes, or until done.
2 LOAVES

Irish Soda Bread with Currants

4 cups sifted all-purpose	¼ cup butter or margarine
flour	⅔ cup dried currants,
2 tablespoons sugar	plumped
2 teaspoons baking soda	½ cup white vinegar
1½ teaspoons salt	1 cup milk

1. Mix flour, sugar, baking soda, and salt in a bowl. Cut in the butter with pastry blender or two knives until particles resemble rice kernels. Lightly mix in currants.
2. Mix vinegar and milk. Add half of the liquid to dry ingredients; blend quickly. Add remaining liquid and stir only until blended.
3. Turn dough onto floured surface. Lightly knead dough about 10 times and shape into a round loaf. Place on greased baking sheet.
4. Bake at 375°F 35 to 40 minutes.
1 LARGE LOAF SODA BREAD

Irish Soda Bread

Greek Easter Bread

2 packages active dry yeast
½ cup warm water
½ cup milk, scalded and cooled
1 cup unsalted butter, melted and cooled to lukewarm
4 eggs, slightly beaten
1 egg yolk
¾ cup sugar
1 tablespoon anise seed, crushed
1 teaspoon salt
7 cups all-purpose flour
1 egg white, slightly beaten
¼ cup sesame seed

1. Blend yeast with warm water in a large bowl and stir until dissolved. Add milk, butter, eggs, egg yolk, sugar, anise seed, and salt; blend thoroughly. Add flour gradually, beating until smooth.
2. Turn dough onto a lightly floured board and knead for 10 minutes, or until dough is smooth and elastic.
3. Place dough in a lightly oiled large bowl, turning dough to coat surface. Cover and let rise in a warm place for about 2 hours, or until double in bulk. Test by inserting a finger about ½ inch in dough. If indentation remains, the dough is ready to shape.
4. Punch dough down. Knead on unfloured board to make a smooth ball. Cut off four pieces, each the size of a large egg. Place remaining dough in a greased round pan, 10 inches in diameter and 2 inches high. Shape small pieces into twists about 4½ inches long. Arrange the twists from the center of the dough so they radiate out to the edge. Brush the loaf lightly with beaten egg white. Sprinkle with sesame seed. Cover loaf lightly and set in a warm place until double in bulk (about 1½ hours).
5. Bake at 375°F for 30 minutes, or until a wooden pick inserted in center of loaf comes out clean. Transfer to wire rack to cool.
1 LARGE LOAF

Note: For Easter, place a red egg in center of the dough in pan. Shape small pieces of dough into loops and place a red egg in the center of each.

New Year's Day Bread: Follow recipe for Greek Easter Bread; substitute **grated peel of 1 large orange** for the anise seed. Wrap a coin in foil and knead into the dough. Proceed as directed.

Island Bread

2 packages active dry yeast
1½ cups warm water (105°
  to 115°F)
¼ cup packed dark brown
  sugar
2 tablespoons honey
3 cups whole wheat flour
¼ cup olive oil

2 tablespoons grated orange
  peel
1 tablespoon grated lemon
  peel
2½ teaspoons salt
1 teaspoon anise seed,
  crushed
2 cups all-purpose flour

1. Dissolve yeast in warm water; stir in brown sugar, honey, and whole wheat flour. Beat with a wooden spoon until smooth. Cover and let rise in a warm place until almost double in bulk (about 2 hours).
2. Stir in oil, orange and lemon peels, salt, and anise seed. Gradually add 1¾ cups all-purpose flour, beating vigorously. Cover for 10 minutes.
3. Sprinkle remaining ¼ cup flour on a board and work it in. Put dough on board, cover, and let rise until double in bulk. Shape into a round loaf; put onto a well-greased cookie sheet.
4. Let rise until dough is double in bulk.
5. Bake at 375°F 45 minutes. Turn out of pan immediately and cool on a rack.
1 LOAF

Jiffy Beer Bread

Jiffy Beer Bread

3 cups self-rising flour
3 tablespoons sugar

1 can or bottle (12 ounces) beer

1. Mix self-rising flour and sugar; make a well in center.
2. Add beer. Stir until just blended.
3. Turn into a greased 9x5x3-inch loaf pan.
4. Bake at 350°F 50 minutes, or until done. Turn out immediately. Cool on a rack.

Fruit Bread, Milan Style

2 packages active dry yeast
¼ cup warm water
1 cup butter, melted
1 cup sugar
1 teaspoon salt
2 cups sifted all-purpose flour
½ cup milk, scalded and cooled to lukewarm

2 eggs
4 egg yolks
3½ cups all-purpose flour
1 cup dark seedless raisins
¾ cup chopped citron
½ cup all-purpose flour
1 egg, slightly beaten
1 tablespoon water

1. Dissolve yeast in the warm water.
2. Pour melted butter into large bowl of electric mixer. Add the sugar and salt gradually, beating constantly.

3. Beating thoroughly after each addition, alternately add the 2 cups flour in thirds and lukewarm milk in halves to the butter mixture. Add yeast and beat well.
4. Combine eggs and egg yolks and beat until thick and piled softly. Add the beaten eggs all at one time to yeast mixture and beat well. Beating thoroughly after each addition, gradually add the 3½ cups flour. Stir in raisins and citron.
5. Sift half of the remaining ½ cup flour over a pastry canvas or board. Turn dough onto floured surface; cover and let rest 10 minutes.
6. Sift remaining flour over dough. Pull dough from edges toward center until flour is worked in. (It will be sticky.) Put dough into a greased deep bowl and grease top of dough. Cover; let rise in a warm place (about 80°F) about 2½ hours.
7. Punch down dough and pull edges of dough in to center. Let rise again about 1 hour.
8. Divide dough into halves and shape each into a round loaf. Put each loaf into a well-greased 8-inch layer cake pan. Brush surfaces generously with a mixture of slightly beaten egg and water. Cover; let rise again about 1 hour.
9. Bake at 350°F 40 to 45 minutes, or until golden brown. Remove to wire racks to cool.
2 LOAVES

Fruit Bread, Milan Style

Corn Bread III

1 cup all-purpose flour	1 cup milk
1 cup yellow cornmeal	2½ teaspoons lime juice
2 teaspoons baking powder	1 egg, beaten
½ teaspoon baking soda	2 tablespoons lard, melted
1 teaspoon salt	

1. Combine flour, cornmeal, baking powder, baking soda, and salt in a bowl.
2. Mix milk and lime juice; add to dry ingredients along with egg and lard. Mix well, but do not beat. Pour into a greased 11x7x1½-inch baking pan.
3. Bake at 450°F 15 to 20 minutes, or until it is brown and tests done. Cool slightly and cut into squares.

ABOUT 8 SERVINGS

Zucchini Bread

2 cups sugar	1 teaspoon baking soda
1 cup vegetable oil	1 teaspoon cinnamon
3 eggs	2 cups shredded unpeeled
1 teaspoon vanilla extract	zucchini
3 cups all-purpose flour	1 cup chopped nuts
1 teaspoon salt	

1. Beat sugar, oil, eggs, and vanilla extract in a mixing bowl until fluffy.
2. Mix flour, salt, baking soda, and cinnamon. Add to egg mixture and stir until blended.
3. Stir in zucchini and nuts.
4. Turn into a greased 9x5x3-inch loaf pan.
5. Bake at 350°F 1 hour and 20 minutes, or until done.
6. Cool before wrapping.

1 LOAF

Poppy Seed Cheese Bread

1 cup shredded Cheddar cheese (about 4 ounces)	1 egg
	¼ cup chopped onion
1 cup all-purpose biscuit mix	1 tablespoon poppy seed
⅓ cup milk	

1. Combine ½ cup cheese and biscuit mix in a mixing bowl.
2. Add milk; stir just until flour is moistened. Pat dough over bottom of a greased 8- or 9-inch pie plate.
3. Combine remaining cheese, egg, and onion. Spread over biscuit dough. Sprinkle with poppy seed.
4. Bake at 425°F 15 to 20 minutes.

ABOUT 6 SERVINGS

Rhubarb Bread

1½ cups firmly packed brown sugar	1 teaspoon salt
	1 teaspoon baking soda
⅔ cup vegetable oil	1½ cups finely chopped
1 cup buttermilk	rhubarb
1 egg	½ cup chopped nuts
1 teaspoon vanilla extract	2 tablespoons sugar
2½ cups all-purpose flour	

1. Beat brown sugar, oil, buttermilk, egg, and vanilla extract in a mixing bowl.
2. Mix flour, salt, and baking soda. Add to brown sugar mixture and stir until blended.
3. Stir in rhubarb and nuts.
4. Turn into 2 greased 8x4x2-inch loaf pans. Sprinkle 1 tablespoon sugar over each.
5. Bake at 325°F 1 hour, or until done.

2 LOAVES

Corn Bread III

Piquant Cheese Loaf

7 to 7½ cups sifted enriched
  all-purpose flour
1 teaspoon sugar
1 tablespoon salt
2 packages active dry yeast
1 cup plain yogurt
½ cup water
2 tablespoons margarine

6 eggs (at room temperature)
½ pound muenster cheese,
  shredded (about 2 cups)
2 cups julienne cooked ham
  (optional)
1 egg, slightly beaten
1 tablespoon milk

1. Mix 1½ cups flour, sugar, salt, and undissolved yeast thoroughly in a larger mixer bowl.
2. Combine yogurt, water, and margarine in a saucepan. Set over low heat until very warm (120-130°F); margarine does not need to melt. Add liquid mixture gradually to dry ingredients while beating at low speed of electric mixer. Beat at medium speed 2 minutes, scraping bowl occasionally. Add 6 eggs, 1 cup flour, and 1½ cups shredded cheese. Beat at high speed 2 minutes, scraping bowl occasionally. Stir in enough of the remaining flour to make a stiff dough.
3. Turn dough onto a lightly floured surface. Knead 8 to 10 minutes, or until dough is smooth, elastic, and shows small blisters under surface when drawn tight.
4. Form dough into a ball and place in greased deep bowl; turn to bring greased surface to top. Cover; let rise in a warm place until double in bulk (about 1 hour).
5. Punch down dough; turn onto lightly floured surface. Divide in half. If using ham, knead 1 cup ham strips into each half. Shape each half into a ball and place on a greased cookie sheet. Cover; let rise again until double in bulk (about 1 hour).
6. Combine eggs and milk; brush over loaves. Sprinkle with remaining ½ cup cheese.
7. Bake at 350°F about 30 minutes. Remove from cookie sheets and place on wire racks to cool.

2 LOAVES BREAD

Greek Sesame Bread

Greek Sesame Bread

2 packages active dry yeast	pieces
1 cup lukewarm water	1 egg
1 cup milk, scalded	5½ to 6 cups flour
3 tablespoons sugar	Cornmeal
1 tablespoon salt	2 tablespoons half-and-half
4 tablespoons butter, cut in	3 tablespoons sesame seed

1. Add yeast to lukewarm water and stir until dissolved.
2. In a 1-quart measuring cup, combine scalded milk, sugar, salt, and butter and stir until dissolved. Cool to lukewarm.
3. Using **steel blade** of food processor, lightly beat egg. Add egg and yeast mixture to cooled milk mixture.
4. Aside, measure half of flour (3 cups flour). Using **steel blade,** put 2 cups of flour into the bowl and add half of liquid ingredients. Process a few seconds until thoroughly blended. Add remaining cup of flour, ¼ cup at a time, until dough forms into a slightly sticky, smooth ball around edge of bowl, usually after 2½ to 2¾ cups flour. Let ball of dough spin around bowl for 20 to 30 seconds to knead the dough. Turn ball of dough onto floured board, knead for a minute by hand, and form into a neat ball.
5. Transfer dough to a greased bowl and rotate to coat all sides. Cover with a towel and place in a warm, draft-free place to rise for 1½ to 2 hours, or until double in bulk.
6. Repeat procedure, using remaining flour and liquid ingredients. Combine two balls of dough only if making one large loaf.
7. When double in bulk, punch down and turn dough onto lightly floured board; form into ball again. Place each ball of dough into a well-greased 9-inch round cake pan, lightly

sprinkled with cornmeal.
8. Brush each loaf with half-and-half and sprinkle with sesame seed. Cover and put into a warm, draft-free place to rise for 1½ to 2 hours.
9. Bake at 350°F for 40 minutes, or until loaves are crusty.
TWO 9-INCH ROUND LOAVES

Triple Treat Bread

4½ cups all-purpose or unbleached flour	milk
2 cups whole wheat flour	2 packages active dry yeast
1 cup rye flour	1 tablespoon salt
½ cup firmly packed brown sugar	2 cups hot tap water (120° to 130°F)
½ cup instant nonfat dry	¼ cup vegetable oil

1. Mix flours.
2. Combine 2 cups flour mixture, sugar, dry milk, yeast, and salt in a large mixing bowl.
3. Stir water and oil into flour mixture; beat until smooth, about 3 minutes on high speed of electric mixer. Stir in enough remaining flour to make a soft dough.
4. Turn dough onto a floured surface; knead until smooth and elastic (5 to 8 minutes).
5. Place in an oiled bowl; turn to oil top of dough. Cover; let rise in a warm place until double (about 45 minutes).
6. Punch dough down. Divide in half; shape into loaves and place in 2 greased 9x5x3-inch loaf pans. Cover; let rise until double in bulk (about 30 minutes).
7. Bake at 375°F 35 to 40 minutes, or until done.
2 LOAVES

Mozzarella Egg Bread

7 to 8 cups all-purpose flour	1 cup plain yogurt
2 packages active dry yeast	2 cups shredded mozzarella cheese (8 ounces)
1 tablespoon sugar	½ cup hot water (120° to 130°F)
1 tablespoon salt	
6 eggs (at room temperature)	

1. Combine 2 cups flour, yeast, sugar, and salt in a mixing bowl.
2. Stir eggs, yogurt, 1½ cups cheese, and water into flour mixture; beat until smooth, about 3 minutes on high speed of electric mixer.
3. Stir in enough more flour to make a soft dough.
4. Turn dough onto a floured surface; knead until smooth and elastic (5 to 8 minutes).
5. Place in an oiled bowl; turn to oil top of dough. Cover; let rise in a warm place until double in bulk (about 1 hour).
6. Punch dough down. Divide in half; shape into loaves, and place in 2 greased 9x5x3-inch loaf pans. Cover; let rise until double, about 30 minutes. Top loaves with remaining cheese.
7. Bake at 375°F 30 minutes, or until done.
2 LOAVES

Mozzarella Egg Bread

Date Nut Bread

Garlic Bread

1 loaf French bread
½ cup butter or margarine, softened

¼ teaspoon garlic powder or garlic salt

1. Slice bread almost through to bottom crust at 1-inch intervals.
2. Thoroughly combine butter and garlic powder. Spread on both sides of each bread slice.
3. Place on baking sheet.
4. Bake at 350°F 15 to 20 minutes, or until hot and crispy.
ABOUT 1 DOZEN SLICES

Grandma Louise's Banana Loaf

1 cup sugar
½ cup shortening
1 cup mashed fully ripe bananas (2 to 3 bananas)
1 egg

¼ cup buttermilk
1¾ cups all-purpose flour
1½ teaspoons baking powder
1 teaspoon baking soda
½ teaspoon salt

1. Combine sugar, shortening, bananas, egg, and buttermilk in a mixing bowl; beat well.
2. Blend remaining ingredients, add to banana mixture, and mix until blended (about 1 minute).
3. Turn into a greaed 9x5x3-inch loaf pan.
4. Bake at 350°F 45 to 50 minutes, or until done.
1 LOAF

Date Nut Bread

½ cup warm water
2 packages active dry yeast
1¾ cups warm milk
2 tablespoons sugar
1 tablespoon salt
3 tablespoons margarine
5 to 5½ cups sifted enriched

all-purpose flour
1 cup whole wheat flour
1 cup chopped dates
½ cup chopped pecans
1 teaspoon ground cinnamon
Peanut Oil
Margarine (optional)

1. Measure warm water into a warm large bowl. Sprinkle in yeast; stir until dissolved. Add warm milk, sugar, salt, and margarine. Stir in 2 cups all-purpose flour. Beat with rotary beater until smooth (about 1 minute). Add 1 cup all-purpose flour; beat with rotary beater until smooth (about 1 minute). Add 1 cup all-purpose flour; beat vigorously with a wooden spoon until smooth (about 150 strokes). Stir in whole wheat flour, dates, pecans, cinnamon, and enough of the remaining all-purpose flour to make a soft dough.
2. Turn dough onto a lightly floured surface. Knead 8 to 10 minutes, or until dough is smooth, elastic, and shows small blisters under surface when drawn tight. Cover with plastic wrap, then a towel. Let rest 20 minutes.
3. Punch dough down. Divide into 3 equal portions. Roll each into a 12x7-inch rectangle. Shape into loaves. Place in 3 greased 7x4x2-inch loaf pans. Brush loaves with oil. Cover pans loosely with plastic wrap. Refrigerate 2 to 24 hours.
4. When ready to bake, remove loaves from refrigerator. Uncover dough carefully. Let stand uncovered 10 minutes at room temperature. Puncture with a greased wooden pick or metal skewer any gas bubbles which may have formed.
5. Bake at 400°F about 35 minutes. Remove from pans immediately, place on wire racks to cool, and, if desired, brush with margarine.
3 LOAVES BREAD

Whole Wheat Pear Bread

2 to 3 fresh Bartlett pears
2 tablespoons shortening
1 teaspoon grated lemon
  peel
⅔ cup firmly packed light
  brown sugar
½ cup honey
2 tablespoons lemon juice
⅓ cup water
1 egg, beaten
1 cup sifted enriched all-
  purpose flour
1 teaspoon baking soda
1 teaspoon salt
½ teaspoon ground
  cinnamon
¼ teaspoon ground cloves
1 cup whole wheat flour
1 cup chopped walnuts

1. Core pears, but do not peel. Cut lengthwise slices from one pear and reserve to decorate top. Dice enough remaining pears to measure 1 cup.
2. Mix shortening, grated lemon peel, and brown sugar in a bowl. Add honey, lemon juice, water, and egg; mix well.
3. Sift all-purpose flour, baking soda, salt, cinnamon, and cloves; stir in whole wheat flour. Add flour mixture to liquid mixture; stir just enough to moisten flour. Mix in walnuts and diced pears. Turn into a greased 9x5x3-inch loaf pan and arrange reserved pear slices crosswise along center.
4. Bake at 325°F 70 to 75 minutes.
5. Cool bread 10 minutes in pan on wire rack; remove from pan and cool completely before slicing or storing.

1 LOAF BREAD

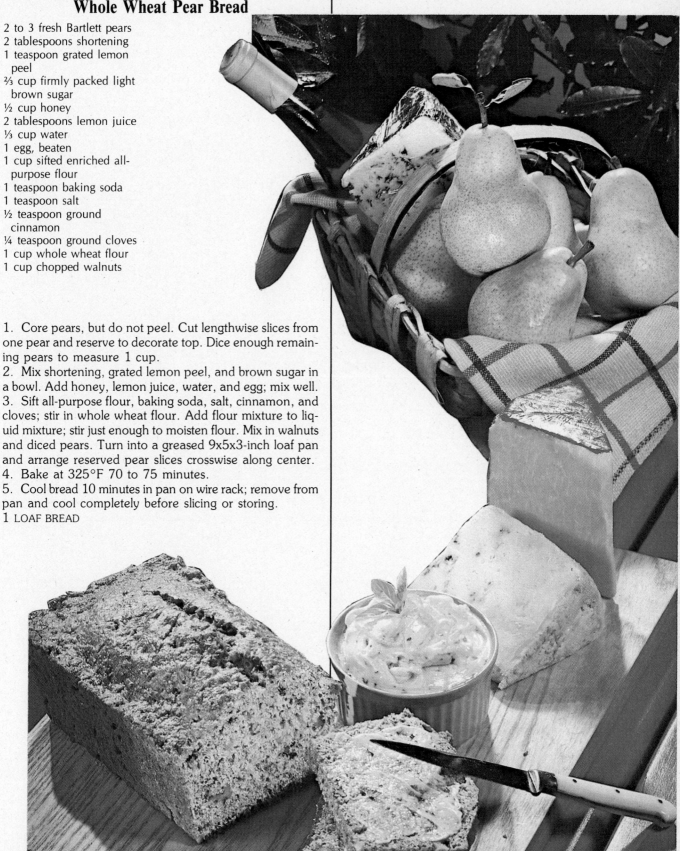

Flavorful Herb Bread

¾ cup warm milk
2 tablespoons melted bacon fat or butter
2 tablespoons sugar
1½ teaspoons salt
1 package active dry yeast
¼ cup warm water (105° to 115°F)
1 egg
¼ cup chopped chives
2 tablespoons minced parsley
1 teaspoon crushed oregano
3 to 3½ cups all-purpose flour

1. Heat milk, bacon fat, sugar, and salt; cool to lukewarm.
2. Sprinkle yeast over warm water in a large mixing bowl; stir until dissolved.
3. Add the liquid, egg, chives, parsley, and oregano to yeast. Stir in 2 cups flour, beating until smooth. Add enough more flour to make a stiff dough.
4. Turn dough onto floured surface; knead until smooth and elastic (10 minutes).
5. Place in a greased bowl, turning to grease top of dough. Cover; let rise in a warm place until double in bulk (1 to 1½ hours).
6. Punch dough down. Shape into a round loaf. Place in a greased 9-inch pie pan. Cover; let rise until double in bulk (about 30 minutes).
7. Bake at 400°F 10 minutes; reduce to 375°F and bake 20 to 25 minutes longer, or until bread is well browned.
1 LOAF

Bran-New Batter Bread

1 cup all-purpose flour
1 package active dry yeast
2 teaspoons salt
½ cup hot water
½ cup milk
½ cup vegetable oil
⅓ cup honey
2 eggs
1 cup whole bran cereal
½ cup wheat germ
1½ cups all-purpose flour

1. Combine 1 cup flour, yeast, and salt in a large mixing bowl.
2. Heat water, milk, oil, and honey until very warm (120° to 130°F).
3. Add liquid and eggs to flour mixture and beat about 3 minutes at high speed of electric mixer.
4. Beat in bran cereal, wheat germ, and remaining flour by hand. Divide mixture into 2 well-greased 1-pound coffee cans. Cover with greased plastic lids and let rise in a warm place until dough rises almost to top of cans (about 35 minutes). Remove lids.
5. Bake at 375°F 35 minutes, or until done. Place on wire racks. Cool loaves slightly, then remove from cans and place on racks to cool.
2 LOAVES

Hearty Potato Bread

6½ to 7½ cups flour
2 packages active dry yeast
2 tablespoons sugar
1 tablespoon salt
2¼ cups hot potato water
1 cup warm unseasoned mashed potatoes
2 tablespoons oil

1. Combine flour, yeast, sugar, and salt in a large mixing bowl.
2. Add potato water (see Note), potatoes, and oil to flour mixture; beat about 3 minutes on high speed of electric mixer.
3. Stir in enough more flour to make a soft dough.
4. Turn dough onto a floured surface; knead until smooth and elastic (5 to 8 minutes).
5. Place in an oiled bowl; turn to oil top of dough. Cover; let rise in a warm place until double in bulk (about 1 hour).
6. Punch dough down. Divide in half; shape into loaves and place in 2 greased 9x5x3-inch loaf pans. Cover; let rise until double in bulk (about 45 minutes).
7. Bake at 375°F 40 to 45 minutes, or until done.
2 LOAVES

Note: To make potato water, cook 2 pared, cut-up potatoes until tender in about 3 cups water. Drain, reserving water. Mash potatoes and cool for bread.

Here's-To-Your-Health Bread

4½ cups all-purpose or unbleached flour
3 cups whole wheat flour
1 cup uncooked oats
½ cup wheat germ
2 packages active dry yeast
2 teaspoons salt
2½ cups hot tap water (120° to 130°F)
1½ cups (12 ounces) creamed cottage cheese (at room temperature)
½ cup molasses or honey
2 tablespoons vegetable oil
1 cup raisins

1. Mix flours and oats.
2. Combine 3 cups flour mixture, wheat germ, yeast, and salt in a large mixing bowl.
3. Add water, cottage cheese, molasses, and oil to flour mixture; beat until smooth, about 3 minutes on high speed of electric mixer.
4. Stir in raisins and enough more flour to make a soft dough.
5. Turn dough onto a floured surface; let rest 10 minutes for easier handling. Knead until smooth and elastic (5 to 8 minutes).
6. Place in an oiled bowl; turn dough to oil top. Cover; let rise in a warm place until double in bulk (about 1 hour).
7. Punch dough down. Divide dough in thirds; shape into loaves and place in 3 greased 9x5x3-inch loaf pans. Cover; let rise until double in bulk (about 30 minutes).
8. Bake at 375°F 30 to 35 minutes, or until done.
3 LOAVES

Indian Flat Bread

1 cup all-purpose flour
1 package active dry yeast
2 teaspoons salt
1 cup hot water (120°-130°F)
¼ cup buttermilk or yogurt
1 egg (at room temperature)
2 tablespoons vegetable oil
1 tablespoon honey or sugar
2 to 3 cups all-purpose flour
Melted butter (optional)
Cornmeal or sesame or poppy seeds (optional)

1. Combine 1 cup flour, yeast, and salt in a mixing bowl.
2. Stir in water, buttermilk, egg, oil, and honey; beat until smooth.

3. Stir in enough remaining flour to form a soft, sticky dough.
4. Turn onto a floured surface; continue to work in flour until dough is stiff enough to knead. Knead until smooth and elastic, but still soft (3 to 5 minutes).
5. Place in an oiled bowl, turning once to oil top of dough. Cover; let rise until double in bulk (about 45 minutes).
6. Punch dough down. Shape into 16 equal balls. Let rest 5 minutes. Roll out each ball to a ¼-inch-thick round. If desired, brush with melted butter and sprinkle with cornmeal, sesame, or poppy seeds. Set on baking sheets.
7. Bake at 450°F 5 to 8 minutes.
16 ROUND LOAVES

Pocket Bread

2 cups all-purpose flour
2 packages active dry yeast
2 tablespoons sugar or honey
2 teaspoons salt
2½ cups hot water (120°-
130°F)
¼ cup vegetable oil
5½ to 6 cups all-purpose flour

1. Combine 2 cups flour, yeast, sugar, and salt in a large mixing bowl.
2. Stir in water and oil; beat until smooth.
3. Stir in enough remaining flour to make a soft dough.
4. Turn onto a floured surface; continue to work in flour until stiff enough to knead. Knead until smooth and elastic (about 5 minutes).
5. Place in an oiled bowl; turn to oil top of dough. Cover; let rise in a warm place until double in bulk (about 45 minutes).
6. Punch dough down. Divide in half. Divide each half into 10 equal pieces. Roll each piece into a ball. Let dough rest 5 minutes. Roll balls into 3- or 4-inch rounds, ⅛ inch thick. Place on greased baking sheets. Cover; let rise 30 minutes (see Note).
7. Bake at 450°F 5 to 8 minutes, or until puffed and brown.
20 POCKET BREADS

Note: Avoid punching or creasing dough after rolling, or bread will not puff properly.

Sourdough Starter

2 cups flour
1 package active dry yeast
1 tablespoon sugar
2 cups warm potato water (105° to 115°)

1. Combine flour, yeast, and sugar in a nonmetal mixing bowl. Stir in potato water.
2. Cover; let stand in a warm place (80° to 85°F) for 48 hours.
3. Store in covered jar in refrigerator.

To use in recipe: Stir well before use. Pour out required amount called for in recipe and use as directed.

To replenish remaining starter: Mix in 1 cup each flour and warm water until smooth. Let stand in warm place a few hours until it bubbles again before covering and replacing in refrigerator.

Note: Use in recipe or remove 1 cup starter and replenish every week.

Golden Sourdough Bread

1 package active dry yeast
1¼ cups warm water
¼ cup firmly packed brown sugar
2 teaspoons salt
⅓ cup butter or margarine
3½ to 4 cups all-purpose flour
1½ cups sourdough starter (above)
3½ cups uncooked oats

1. Soften yeast in ¼ cup warm water. Pour remaining 1 cup water over sugar, salt, and butter in a large bowl. Stir in 2 cups of flour, sourdough starter, oats, and softened yeast. Stir in enough additional flour to make a stiff dough.
2. Knead dough on a floured surface until smooth and elastic (about 10 minutes). Round dough into a ball; place in a greased bowl. Lightly grease surface of dough. Cover; let rise in a warm place until nearly double in bulk (about 1 hour).
3. Punch dough down; shape into 2 round loaves. Place on greased cookie sheets. Let rise in a warm place until nearly double in bulk (about 40 minutes). Slash tops with sharp knife or kitchen shears.
4. Bake at 400°F 35 to 40 minutes. Cool on wire racks.
2 LOAVES

Golden Sourdough Bread

San Francisco Sourdough French Bread

1 cup sourdough starter (page 119)	5 to 6 cups all-purpose flour
1½ cups warm water	1 tablespoon salt
2 tablespoons sugar	½ teaspoon baking soda

1. Combine starter, water, sugar, and 3 cups flour in a large nonmetal mixing bowl. Cover with plastic wrap or a towel; let stand at room temperature 12 hours or overnight.
2. Combine salt, soda, and 1 cup flour. Stir into dough; beat until smooth.
3. Stir in enough remaining flour to make a soft dough.
4. Turn dough onto a floured surface; continue to work in flour until dough is stiff enough to knead. Knead until smooth and elastic (5 to 8 minutes).
5. Shape dough into a long, narrow loaf by rolling and stretching dough as for French Bread (page 119). Place on a greased baking sheet. Cover; let rise in a warm place until double in bulk (1½ to 2 hours).
6. With a sharp knife, slash top ½ inch deep at 2-inch intervals. Brush loaf with **water.**
7. Bake at 375°F 30 to 35 minutes.

1 LOAF

Note: For a browner and shinier crust, brush before baking with a mixture of **1 egg white** and ⅓ **cup water** instead of only water.

Sourdough Sam's Skillet Loaves

1 cup sourdough starter	¼ cup vegetable oil
2½ cups warm water	1 tablespoon salt
2 tablespoons honey or sugar	1 teaspoon baking soda
7 to 7½ cups all-purpose flour	6 tablespoons butter
	4 tablespoons cornmeal

1. Combine starter, water, honey, and 5 cups flour in a large nonmetal mixing bowl. Cover with plastic wrap or a wet towel; let stand at room temperature 12 hours or overnight.
2. Stir in oil. Combine salt, soda, and 1 cup flour. Stir into dough; beat until smooth.
3. Stir in enough remaining flour to make a soft dough.
4. Turn dough onto a floured surface; continue to work in flour until dough is stiff enough to knead. Knead until smooth and elastic (about 5 minutes).
5. Divide dough in half. Roll each into a 10-inch round (see Note).
6. For each loaf, melt 3 tablespoons butter in a heavy 10-inch cast-iron skillet with heat-resistant handle. Sprinkle with 2 tablespoons cornmeal. Place dough in skillet. Turn over to coat top with butter and cornmeal. Let rise 15 minutes.
7. Bake at 400°F 25 to 30 minutes, or until done.
8. Serve hot with **butter** and **honey.**

2 LOAVES

Note: If you don't have 2 skillets, simply allow the second dough circle to rise while the first bakes – it will just have a lighter texture.

Sweet and Sourdough Granola Bread: Prepare dough as in Sourdough Sam's Skillet Loaves. After dividing dough in half, roll out each half into a 16x6-inch rectangle. Brush each with **2 tablespoons melted butter** and sprinkle with half the Granola Cinnamon Filling. Beginning with narrow end of rectangle, roll up tightly as for jelly roll; seal edges. Place loaves in 2 greased 9x5x3-inch loaf pans. Cover; let rise until double in bulk (45 to 60 minutes). Bake at 350°F 40 to 45 minutes.

Granola Cinnamon Filling: Combine **1 cup granola,** ½ **cup firmly packed brown sugar,** ½ **cup chopped dates or raisins** (optional), and **1 teaspoon cinnamon.**

Sourdough Apple Kuchen: Prepare dough as in Sourdough Sam's Skillet Loaves. After dividing dough, roll out each half into a 10-inch round. Place dough in 2 greased 9- or 10-inch springform pans. Press dough about 1½ inches up sides of pan. Fill each kuchen with a mixture of **2 cups finely sliced pared apples,** ½ **cup firmly packed brown sugar,** ¼ **cup all-purpose flour,** and **1 teaspoon cinnamon.** Sprinkle with ¼ **cup sliced almonds.** Dot with 2 tablespoons butter. Let rise 30 minutes. Bake at 375°F 40 to 45 minutes, or until done.

Basic Dinner Rolls

4 to 4¾ cups all-purpose flour	1 cup milk
2 tablespoons sugar	½ cup water
2 packages active dry yeast	¼ cup butter or margarine
1 teaspoon salt	1 egg (at room temperature)
	Melted butter (optional)

1. Combine 1½ cups flour, sugar, yeast, and salt in a mixing bowl.
2. Heat milk, water, and butter until very warm (120° to 130°F).
3. Add liquid and egg to flour mixture; beat until smooth, about 3 minutes.
4. Stir in enough remaining flour to make a soft, sticky dough.
5. Turn dough onto a floured surface; continue to work in flour until dough can be kneaded. Knead until smooth and elastic, but still soft (about 5 minutes).
6. Cover dough with bowl or pan. Let rest 20 minutes.
7. Shape dough as desired. Cover and let rise until double in bulk (about 15 minutes).
8. Bake at 425°F about 12 minutes. Cool on wire rack. Brush with butter if desired.

2 TO 2½ DOZEN ROLLS

Pan Rolls: Divide dough into 24 equal pieces by first dividing dough in half and then each half into 12 equal pieces. Roll into balls. Place in a greased 13x9x2-inch baking pan. Brush with melted butter, if desired.

Cloverleaf Rolls: Pinch off bits of dough; roll into 1-inch balls. For each roll, place 3 balls in a greased muffin-pan well.

Crescents: Divide dough in half. Roll each half into a 12-inch round about ¼ inch thick. Brush with **2 tablespoons melted butter.** Cut into 12 wedges. For each crescent, roll up wedge beginning at side opposite the point. Place point-side down on a greased baking sheet; curve ends.

Snails: Roll dough into a rectangle ¼ inch thick. Cut off strips ½ inch wide and 5 inches long. Roll each piece of dough into a rope about 10 inches long. Wind into a flat coil, tucking ends under. Place on greased baking sheet.

Figure Eights: Shape strips of dough ½ inch wide and 5 inches long into 10-inch ropes as in Snails (above). For each roll, pinch ends of rope together and twist once to form a figure 8. Place on greased baking sheets.

Twists: Follow procedure for Figure Eights, giving each 8 an additional twist.

Bowknots: Roll dough into a rectangle ¼ inch thick. Cut off strips ½ inch wide and 5 inches long. Roll each strip into a smooth rope 9 or 10 inches long. Gently tie into a single or double knot. Place on a greased baking sheet.

Parker House Rolls: Roll dough ¼ inch thick. Brush with **3 or 4 tablespoons melted butter.** Cut with a 2½-inch round cutter. With a knife handle, make a crease across each circle slightly off center. Fold larger half over the smaller, pressing edges to seal. Place on a greased baking sheet or close together in a greased 13x9x2-inch baking pan.

Braids: Form several ropes, ½ inch in diameter. Braid 3 ropes into a long strip; cut into 3-inch strips. Pinch together at each end. Place on a greased baking sheet.

Butterflies: Divide dough in half. Roll each half into a 24x6-inch rectangle about ¼ inch thick. Brush with **2 tablespoons melted butter.** Starting with long side, roll up dough as for jelly roll. Cut off 2-inch pieces. With handle of knife, press crosswise at center of each roll, forming a deep groove so spiral sides become visible. Place on a greased baking sheet.

Fantans or Butterflake Rolls: Roll dough into a rectangle ¼ inch thick. Brush with **3 or 4 tablespoons melted butter.** Cut into 1-inch strips. Stack 6 or 7 strips; cut each into 1½-inch sections. Place on end in greased muffin-pan wells.

Cloverleaf Rolls

Croissants

1 cup milk	115°F)
1 tablespoon oil	2¾ to 3 cups all-purpose
1 tablespoon sugar	flour
½ teaspoon salt	1 cup (½ pound) butter,
1 package compressed or ac-	softened
tive dry yeast	1 egg yolk
¼ cup warm water (105° to	1 tablespoon milk

1. Heat 1 cup milk, oil, sugar, and salt in a saucepan; cool to lukewarm.
2. Dissolve yeast in warm water in a large bowl. Add milk mixture and 1 cup flour; beat until smooth. Stir in enough remaining flour to make a soft dough.
3. Turn dough onto a floured surface; continue to work in flour until dough can be kneaded. Knead until smooth and elastic (about 5 minutes).
4. Shape dough into a ball and place in an oiled bowl; turn to oil top of dough. Cover; let rise in a warm place until double in bulk (about 45 minutes).
5. Punch dough down. Roll out on floured surface to form a rectangle about ¼ inch thick.
6. Cut butter in slices (just soft enough to spread but not melted). Spread over center one-third section of rectangle. Fold each extending side of butter, pressing together the open edges to seal. Roll out again until rectangle is ⅜ inch thick. Turn dough occasionally, flouring surface lightly to prevent sticking. Fold in thirds again to make a squarish rectangle. Roll dough and fold again in the same manner. Wrap dough in waxed paper or foil; chill 30 minutes. If at any time dough oozes butter and becomes sticky while rolling, chill until butter is more firm.
7. Roll and fold again 2 more times exactly as directed before. Chill dough again another 30 minutes.
8. Roll dough into a rectangle about ⅛ inch thick. Cut into strips 6 inches wide. Cut triangles out of each strip to measure about 6x8x6 inches. Roll up each triangle of dough from a 6-inch edge, pinching tip to seal. Shape each roll into a crescent. Place, point down, 1½ inches apart on ungreased baking sheet.
9. Cover; let rise until double in bulk (30 to 45 minutes).
10. Brush each roll with mixture of egg yolk and 1 tablespoon milk.
11. Bake at 425°F 15 minutes, or until brown. Remove from baking sheet and cool on wire rack. Serve warm.
ABOUT 1½ DOZEN CROISSANTS

Cloverleaf Rolls

2 packages active dry yeast	½ cup sugar
¼ cup lukewarm water	1 teaspoon salt
1 cup milk	2 eggs
8 tablespoons butter (1 stick),	5 cups flour
cut in 5 pieces	¼ cup melted butter

1. Add yeast to lukewarm water and stir until dissolved; set aside to cool.
2. Scald milk, remove from heat, and add butter, sugar, and salt; stir to dissolve. Cool to lukewarm.
3. Using **steel blade** of food processor, beat eggs until frothy.
4. In a 1-quart measuring cup, combine yeast mixture, milk mixture, and beaten eggs and stir thoroughly.
5. Aside, measure half of flour (2½ cups). Using **steel blade,** add 2 cups flour and half of liquid ingredients; process until blended.
6. Add remaining ½ cup of flour, ¼ cup at a time, and process until dough forms itself into a fairly smooth ball. Then let ball of dough spin around the bowl for about 20 to 30 seconds to thoroughly knead the dough.
7. Turn dough onto lightly floured board, knead by hand for a minute, and form into a neat ball. Transfer to a greased bowl and rotate to coat all sides.
8. Cover with a damp cloth and place in a warm, draft-free place to rise until double in bulk (about 1½ hours).
9. Repeat procedure, using remaining ingredients.
10. When double in bulk, punch the dough down. Let it rest for 15 minutes. Break off dough and form into balls the size of a walnut.
11. Roll each ball in melted butter.
12. Grease muffin-pan wells and place 3 balls in bottom of each well.
13. Cover loosely with a towel and let rise again in a warm, draft-free place until doubled in bulk (about 1 hour).
14. Bake at 400°F about 15 minutes. Serve warm.
36 ROLLS

Croissants

Brioche

½ cup butter
⅓ cup sugar
½ teaspoon salt
½ cup undiluted evaporated milk
1 package active dry yeast

¼ cup warm water
1 egg yolk
2 eggs
3¼ cups all-purpose flour
1 egg white, unbeaten
1 tablespoon sugar

1. Cream the butter with the ⅓ cup sugar and salt in a large bowl. Beat in the evaporated milk.
2. Soften yeast in the warm water.
3. Beat egg yolk with the 2 eggs until thick and piled softly. Gradually add to the creamed mixture, beating constantly until fluffy. Blend in the yeast.
4. Add the flour, about ½ cup at a time, beating thoroughly after each addition. Cover; let rise in a warm place until doubled, about 2 hours.
5. Stir down and beat thoroughly. Cover tightly with moisture-vaporproof material and refrigerate overnight.
6. Remove from refrigerator and stir down the dough. Turn onto a lightly floured surface and divide into two portions, one using about three fourths of the dough, the other about one fourth.
7. Cut each portion into 16 equal pieces. Roll each piece into a smooth ball. Place each large ball in a well-greased muffin-pan well (2¾ x1¼ inches). Make a deep indentation with finger in center of each large ball; then moisten each depression slightly with cold water. Press a small ball into each depression.
8. Cover; let rise again until more than doubled, about 1 hour.
9. Brush tops of rolls with a mixture of the egg white and 1 tablespoon sugar.
10. Bake at 375°F about 15 minutes, or until golden brown.
16 BRIOCHES

Crusty Hard Rolls

3½ to 4½ cups all-purpose flour
2 packages active dry yeast
1 tablespoon sugar
1½ teaspoons salt
1 cup hot tap water (120° to

130°F)
2 tablespoons vegetable oil
1 egg white
1 egg yolk
1 tablespoon water

1. Combine 1 cup flour, yeast, sugar, and salt in a large mixer bowl. Stir in water, oil, and egg white; beat until smooth, about 3 minutes on high speed of electric mixer. Gradually stir in more flour to make a soft dough.
2. Turn dough onto a floured surface; knead until smooth and elastic (3 to 5 minutes).
3. Cover with bowl or pan and let rest about 20 minutes.
4. Divide into 18 equal pieces. Form each into a smooth oval; place on a greased baking sheet. Slash tops lengthwise about ¼ inch deep. Let rise until double in bulk (about 15 minutes).
5. Brush with a mixture of egg yolk and 1 tablespoon water.
6. Bake at 400°F 15 to 20 minutes. For a crisper crust, place a shallow pan of hot water on lowest oven rack during baking.
1½ DOZEN ROLLS

Kaiser Rolls: Follow recipe for Crusty Hard Rolls, only flatten each of the 18 pieces of dough into 4- to 4-½-inch rounds. For each roll, lift one edge of the round and press it into center of circle. Then lift the corner of the fold and press it into the center. Continue clockwise around the circle until 5 or 6 folds have been made. Let rise and bake as directed above.

Poppy Seed Rolls

Dough:
2 packages active dry yeast
½ cup warm water
4½ cups all-purpose flour
¾ cup sugar
½ teaspoon salt
½ cup butter or margarine
2 eggs
2 egg yolks
½ cup sour cream
1 teaspoon vanilla extract

chased already ground in gourmet shops)
2 tablespoons honey
2 teaspoons lemon juice or vanilla extract
¼ cup raisins, steamed
2 egg whites
½ cup sugar
¼ cup finely chopped candied orange peel
2 teaspoons grated lemon peel

Filling:
2 tablespoons butter
10 ounces poppy seed, ground twice (may be pur-

Icing:
1 cup confectioners' sugar
2 tablespoons lemon juice

1. For dough, soften yeast in warm water in a bowl.
2. Mix flour with sugar and salt. Cut in butter with a pastry blender or two knives until mixture has a fine, even crumb.
3. Beat eggs and egg yolks; mix with yeast, then stir into flour mixture. Add sour cream and vanilla extract; mix well.
4. Knead dough on floured surface for 5 minutes. Divide in half. Roll each half of dough into a 12-inch square. Cover.
5. For filling, melt butter in a large saucepan. Add poppy seed. Stir-fry 3 minutes.
6. Add honey, lemon juice, and raisins to poppy seed. Cover and remove from heat; let stand 10 minutes.
7. Beat egg whites with sugar until stiff, not dry, peaks form. Fold in orange and lemon peels. Gently fold in poppy seed mixture.
8. Spread half of filling over each square of dough. Roll up, jelly-roll fashion. Seal edges. Place on greased baking sheets. Cover. Let rise until doubled in bulk, about 1½ hours.
9. Bake at 350°F about 45 minutes. Cool.
10. For icing, blend sugar and lemon juice until smooth. Spread over rolls.
2 POPPY SEED ROLLS

Bran Rolls

¾ cup whole bran cereal
⅓ cup sugar
1½ teaspoons salt
½ cup margarine
½ cup boiling water
½ cup warm water

2 packages active dry yeast
1 egg, beaten
3¼ to 3¾ cups sifted enriched all-purpose flour
Margarine, melted

1. Combine bran cereal, sugar, salt, and margarine in a bowl. Add boiling water; stir until margarine is melted. Cool to lukewarm.
2. Measure warm water into a warm large bowl. Sprinkle in yeast; stir until dissolved. Mix in lukewarm cereal mixture, egg, and enough of the flour to make a stiff dough.
3. Turn dough onto a lightly floured surface; knead 8 to 10 minutes, or until smooth and elastic. Form dough into a ball and place in a greased deep bowl; turn to bring greased surface to top. Cover; let rise in a warm place until double in bulk (about 1 hour).
4. Punch dough down; divide in half. Divide each half into 12 equal pieces. Form each piece into a smooth ball. Place in greased muffin-pan wells, 2½x1½ inches, or in 2 greased 8-inch round cake pans. Brush rolls with melted margarine. Cover; let rise again until double in bulk (about 30 minutes).
5. Bake at 375°F 20 to 25 minutes. Remove from pans and place on wire racks. Serve warm.
2 DOZEN ROLLS

Hurry-Up Dinner Rolls

2½ to 3 cups all-purpose flour
2 tablespoons sugar
1 package active dry yeast
½ teaspoon salt
¾ cup hot water (120° to

130°F)
1 egg (at room temperature)
2 tablespoons vegetable oil
2 tablespoons melted butter or margarine

1. Combine 1 cup flour, sugar, yeast, and salt in a bowl. Stir in water, egg, and oil; beat until smooth. Cover; let rise in a warm place 15 minutes.
2. Stir in enough remaining flour to make a soft, sticky dough.

3. Turn dough onto a floured board; continue to work in flour until dough can be kneaded. Knead until smooth and elastic (about 3 minutes).
4. Divide dough into 16 pieces; shape into balls. Place in a greased 9-inch square pan. Brush tops with melted butter. Cover; let rise 20 minutes.
5. Bake at 425°F 8 to 10 minutes.
16 ROLLS

Potato Pan Rolls

½ cup milk
1 tablespoon sugar
¾ teaspoon salt
2 tablespoons margarine
½ cup warm water (105° to 115°F)
1 package active dry yeast

1 egg
½ cup mashed potatoes (at room temperature)
3½ to 4½ cups all-purpose flour
Flour for dusting

1. Heat milk; stir in sugar, salt, and margarine. Cool to lukewarm.
2. Measure warm water into a large warm bowl. Sprinkle in yeast; stir until dissolved. Stir in lukewarm milk mixture, egg, mashed potatoes, and 2 cups flour. Beat until smooth. Stir in enough additional flour to make a soft dough.
3. Turn dough onto a lightly floured surface; knead until smooth and elastic (8 to 10 minutes). Place in a greased bowl; turn to grease top. Cover; let rise in a warm place until double in bulk (about 1 hour).
4. Punch dough down; turn out onto a lightly floured surface. Divide in half. Divide each half into 16 equal pieces; form into smooth balls. Place in 2 greased 9-inch round layer cake pans. Cover; let rise in a warm place until double in bulk (about 1 hour).
5. Dust rolls with flour.
6. Bake at 375°F about 25 minutes, or until done. Remove from pans and cool on wire racks.
32 ROLLS

Potato Pan Rolls

Cottage Cheese Rolls

¼ cup warm orange juice
 (105° to 115°F)
1 package active dry yeast
1 cup (8 ounces) creamed
 cottage cheese
2 teaspoons caraway seed
1 tablespoon sugar
1 teaspoon grated orange

peel
1 tablespoon grated onion
1 teaspoon salt
¼ teaspoon baking soda
1 egg, slightly beaten
2⅓ cups sifted all-purpose
 flour

1. Put orange juice into a warm large bowl. Sprinkle yeast over orange juice and stir until dissolved.
2. Heat cottage cheese in a small saucepan just until lukewarm. Stir cheese into yeast mixture. Add remaining ingredients except flour; mix well. Beat in flour gradually until completely blended, scraping down sides of bowl as necessary; beat vigorously about 20 strokes (dough will be sticky and heavy).
3. Cover bowl with a clean towel; let rise in a warm place about 1 hour, or until double in bulk.
4. Stir dough down. Divide evenly among 12 greased 2½-inch muffin pan wells. Cover with towel; let rise again 35 minutes, or until double in bulk.
5. Bake at 350°F 25 minutes, or until rolls are golden brown and sound hollow when tapped.
6. Remove from pans and serve while hot.
12 ROLLS

Cottage Cheese Rolls

Brown-and-Serve Rolls

9 to 10 cups all-purpose
 flour
½ cup sugar
2 packages active dry yeast

1 tablespoon salt
2 cups warm water
1 cup milk
½ cup butter or margarine

1. Stir together 3 cups flour, sugar, yeast, and salt in a large mixer bowl.
2. Heat water, milk, and butter until very warm (120° to 130°F).
3. Add liquid ingredients to flour mixture; beat until smooth, about 3 minutes on high speed of electric mixer.
4. Gradually stir in enough more flour to make a soft dough.
5. Turn out onto a floured surface; knead until smooth and elastic (5 to 8 minutes).
6. Shape dough into a ball, place in an oiled bowl, and turn to oil top of dough. Cover; let rise in a warm place until double in bulk (30 to 45 minutes).
7. Punch dough down. Divide in half. Shape each half into rolls (see page 149 for different shapes). Let rise in a warm place until double in bulk (30 to 45 minutes).
8. Bake at 375°F 20 to 25 minutes, or just until rolls begin to change color. Cool in pans 20 minutes. Finish cooling on wire racks. Wrap tightly in plastic bags and refrigerate up to 1 week, or freeze up to 2 months. Before serving, place rolls on ungreased baking sheet.
9. Bake at 400°F 10 to 12 minutes.
ABOUT 4 DOZEN ROLLS

Sweet Rolls

2 packages active dry yeast
½ cup warm water
½ cup sugar
½ teaspoon salt
1 tablespoon anise seed
½ cup butter or margarine,
 melted

3 eggs, at room temperature
3¾ to 4¾ cups all-purpose
 flour
1 egg yolk
2 tablespoons light corn
 syrup

1. Sprinkle yeast over water in a large warm bowl. Stir until yeast is dissolved. Add sugar, salt, anise seed, melted butter, eggs, and 2 cups of flour; beat until smooth. Stir in enough additional flour to make a soft dough.
2. Turn dough onto a lightly floured surface; knead until smooth and elastic (8 to 10 minutes).
3. Put dough into a greased bowl; turn to grease top. Cover; let rise in a warm place until double in bulk (about 1 hour).
4. Punch dough down and turn onto lightly floured surface; roll into a 12-inch square. Cut into fourths and cut each square into 4 triangles.
5. Allowing space for rising, place triangles on greased cookie sheets. Cover; let rise in warm place until double in bulk (about 1 hour).
6. Beat egg yolk and corn syrup together until blended. Generously brush over triangles.
7. Bake at 350°F 10 to 15 minutes. Serve warm.
16 LARGE ROLLS

Pumpkin Spice Rolls

3½ to 4½ cups all-purpose flour
¼ cup firmly packed brown sugar
1 package active dry yeast
1 teaspoon salt
½ teaspoon cinnamon
¼ teaspoon nutmeg
⅛ teaspoon cloves
⅛ teaspoon ginger
1 cup milk
¼ cup water
¾ cup canned pumpkin
¼ cup vegetable oil
1 egg
2 tablespoons melted butter

1. Combine 1½ cups flour, brown sugar, yeast, salt, and spices in a large mixer bowl.
2. Heat milk, water, pumpkin, and oil in a saucepan until very warm (120° to 130°F).
3. Add liquid and egg to flour mixture and beat until smooth, about 3 minutes on high speed of electric mixer.
4. Stir in enough remaining flour to make a soft dough.
5. Turn dough onto floured board; continue to work in flour until dough is stiff enough to knead. Knead until smooth and elastic (about 5 minutes).
6. Cover with bowl or pan; let rest 20 minutes.
7. Shape into 2-inch balls; place each ball in a greased muffin-pan well. Brush with melted butter. Cover; let rise until double in bulk (about 20 minutes).
8. Bake at 375°F 20 minutes, or until done.
2 DOZEN ROLLS

Better Batter Rolls

3 cups all-purpose flour
1 package active dry yeast
1 teaspoon salt
1 cup hot water
¼ cup vegetable oil
¼ cup honey
1 egg

1. Combine 2 cups flour, yeast, and salt in a mixer bowl. Add water, oil, honey, and egg; beat until smooth, about 2 minutes on medium speed of electric mixer or 300 vigorous strokes by hand.
2. Beat in remaining flour by hand. Cover; let rise until double in bulk (about 30 minutes).
3. Fill greased muffin-pan wells half full. Let rise until double in bulk (about 30 minutes).
4. Bake at 400°F 10 to 12 minutes.
2 DOZEN ROLLS

Savory Biscuit Bread

1½ cups all-purpose flour
1 tablespoon baking powder
½ teaspoon salt
½ teaspoon paprika
½ teaspoon celery salt
¼ teaspoon pepper
¼ teaspoon poultry seasoning
¼ cup shortening
½ cup milk (about)

1. Combine flour, baking powder, and seasonings in a mixing bowl. Cut in shortening until mixture resembles rice kernels.
2. Stir in milk with a fork just until flour is moistened.
3. Pat into a greased 8-inch round layer cake pan.
4. Bake at 450°F 10 to 15 minutes, or until done.
6 SERVINGS

Biscuits Port-au-Prince

2 cups sifted all-purpose flour
2 teaspoons baking powder
1 teaspoon salt
5 tablespoons vegetable shortening
¾ cup milk

1. Combine flour, baking powder, and salt in a bowl. Cut in shortening with pastry blender or two knives until mixture resembles small peas.
2. Make a well in center of mixture and add milk. Stir with fork until dough holds together.
3. Knead on a lightly floured board 30 seconds. Roll dough to ½-inch thickness. Cut with a floured 1½-inch cutter.
4. Place on greased baking sheets about 1 inch apart.
5. Bake at 425°F 15 to 20 minutes, or until golden brown.
ABOUT 2 DOZEN BISCUITS

Sunshine Corn Muffins

1½ cups all-purpose flour
1½ cups yellow cornmeal
1 tablespoon baking powder
⅛ teaspoon salt
1 cup milk
½ cup honey
½ cup vegetable oil
2 eggs

1. Combine dry ingredients in a mixing bowl.
2. Combine remaining ingredients in a separate bowl; beat well.
3. Add liquid ingredients to dry ingredients; stir just until flour is moistened. Spoon into 24 greased muffin-pan wells.
4. Bake at 400° 15 to 20 minutes, or until wooden pick inserted in muffin comes out clean.
2 DOZEN

Sunshine Cornbread: Follow recipe for Sunshine Corn Muffins, except pour mixture into a greased 9-inch square pan. Bake at 400°F 30 minutes, or until done.
6 SERVINGS

Bran-Oatmeal Muffins

¾ cup bran cereal
¾ cup milk
¼ cup butter or margarine
¼ cup molasses
1 egg
1 cup all-purpose flour
2 tablespoons sugar
1 teaspoon baking powder
½ teaspoon baking soda
½ teaspoon salt
1 cup uncooked oats

1. Combine bran cereal and milk to soften.
2. Beat butter and molasses together in a bowl. Add egg and mix well. Add bran-milk mixture.
3. Mix flour, sugar, baking powder, baking soda, and salt. Add dry ingredients to bran mixture; stir just until moistened. Stir in oats.
4. Spoon mixture into 12 greased medium-sized muffin-pan wells.
5. Bake at 400°F 15 to 18 minutes, or until golden-brown.
1 DOZEN

Biscuits

2 cups all-purpose flour
1 tablespoon baking powder
1 teaspoon salt
⅓ cup butter or shortening
¾ cup milk

1. Combine flour, baking powder, and salt in a mixing bowl. Cut in butter with pastry blender or 2 knives until mixture resembles rice kernels.
2. Stir in milk with a fork just until mixture clings to itself.
3. Form dough into a ball and knead gently 8 to 10 times on lightly floured board. Gently roll dough ½ inch thick.
4. Cut with floured biscuit cutter or knife, using an even pressure to keep sides of biscuits straight.
5. Place on ungreased baking sheet, close together for soft-sided biscuits or 1 inch apart for crusty ones.
6. Bake at 450°F 10 to 15 minutes, or until golden brown.
ABOUT 1 DOZEN

Southern Buttermilk Biscuits: Follow recipe for Biscuits, substituting **buttermilk** for the milk and adding ¼ **teaspoon baking soda** to the dry ingredients and reducing baking powder to 2 teaspoons.

Drop Biscuits: Follow recipe for Biscuits, increasing milk to 1 cup. Omit rolling-out instructions. Simply drop from a spoon onto a lightly greased baking sheet.

Basic Oats Mix, Oatmeal Biscuits, Oatmeal Muffins

Basic Oats Mix

6 cups sifted all-purpose flour
¼ cup (4 tablespoons) baking powder
4 teaspoons salt
1⅓ cups shortening
2 cups quick or old-fashioned oats, uncooked

1. Sift flour, baking powder, and salt together into large bowl. Cut in shortening until mixture resembles coarse crumbs. Stir in oats.
2. Store mixture in an airtight container in a cool, dry place until ready to use.
9¾ CUPS MIX

Oatmeal Muffins

2 cups plus 2 tablespoons Basic Oats Mix (next column)
¼ cup sugar
1 cup milk
1 egg, beaten

1. Combine Oats Mix and sugar in a bowl. Add milk and egg; stir until just blended.
2. Fill 12 greased 2½-inch muffin-pan wells ⅔ full.
3. Bake at 400°F about 20 minutes, or until golden brown.
12 MUFFINS

Oatmeal Biscuits

2 cups Basic Oats Mix (above)
⅔ cup cold milk

1. Combine Oats Mix and milk in a bowl; stir with a fork to a soft dough.
2. Turn dough onto a lightly floured surface. Knead with fingertips 10 times. Roll out to ½-inch thickness. Cut with a floured 2-inch round cutter. Put onto an ungreased cookie sheet.
3. Bake at 450°F 8 to 10 minutes.
ABOUT 16 BISCUITS

Scones

1⅔ cups all-purpose flour	½ teaspoon salt
1 tablespoon sugar	½ cup shortening
1½ teaspoons baking powder	½ cup buttermilk
½ teaspoon baking soda	

1. Combine flour, sugar, baking powder, baking soda, and salt in a mixing bowl. Cut in shortening with pastry blender or two knives until mixture resembles rice kernels.
2. Stir in buttermilk with a fork until mixture clings to itself.
3. Form dough into a ball and knead gently about 8 times on a floured surface. Divide dough in half; roll each into a round about ½ inch thick. Cut each round into 6 wedge-shaped pieces. Place on ungreased baking sheets.
4. Bake at 450°F 8 to 10 minutes. Serve warm.
1 DOZEN

Maple Tree Muffins

2 cups all-purpose flour	½ cup pure maple syrup or
1 tablespoon baking powder	maple-blended syrup
½ teaspoon salt	1 egg
½ cup chopped nuts	¼ cup vegetable oil
⅔ cup milk	

1. Combine flour, baking powder, salt, and nuts in a mixing bowl.
2. Combine remaining ingredients in a separate bowl; beat well.
3. Add liquid ingredients to dry ingredients; stir just until flour is moistened. Spoon into 12 greased muffin-pan wells.
4. Bake at 400°F 15 to 20 minutes, or until a wooden pick inserted in muffin comes out clean.
1 DOZEN

Lemon Chiffon Muffins

½ cup softened butter or	(about 1 lemon)
margarine	1 cup all-purpose flour
½ cup sugar	1 teaspoon baking powder
Grated peel of 1 lemon	¼ teaspoon salt
(about 1 tablespoon)	¼ cup chopped nuts
2 tablespoons milk	1 tablespoon sugar
2 eggs, separated	1 teaspoon nutmeg
3 tablespoons lemon juice	

1. Cream butter, sugar, lemon peel, milk, and egg yolks in a mixing bowl until light and fluffy. Beat in lemon juice.
2. Combine flour, baking powder, and salt in a separate bowl. Add to batter and mix just until blended.
3. Beat egg whites until soft peaks form; fold into batter.
4. Spoon into 12 greased muffin-pan wells. Sprinkle with a mixture of nuts, sugar, and nutmeg.
5. Bake at 375°F 15 to 20 minutes, or until done.
1 DOZEN

Dakota Bran Muffins

1 cup all-purpose flour	1 cup milk
1 tablespoon baking powder	1 egg
½ teaspoon salt	¼ cup vegetable oil
1½ cups ready-to-eat bran	¼ cup honey or sugar
flakes	

1. Combine dry ingredients in a mixing bowl.
2. Combine remaining ingredients in a separate bowl; beat well.
3. Add liquid ingredients to dry ingredients; stir just until flour is moistened. Spoon batter into 12 greased muffin-pan wells.
4. Bake at 400°F 20 to 25 minutes, or until golden brown.
1 DOZEN

Raised Cornmeal Muffins

5 to 5¼ cups sifted enriched	½ cup shortening
all-purpose flour	2 eggs
½ cup sugar	1 cup enriched yellow
1 tablespoon salt	cornmeal
2 packages active dry yeast	Butter or margarine, melted
2¼ cups milk	

1. Mix 2¾ cups flour, sugar, salt, and undissolved yeast thoroughly in a large mixer bowl.
2. Put milk and shortening into a saucepan. Set over low heat until very warm (120-130°). Add liquid mixture gradually to dry ingredients while mixing until blended. Beat 2 minutes at medium speed of electric mixer, scraping bowl occasionally. Mix in eggs and 1¾ cups flour, or enough to make a batter. Beat at high speed 2 minutes, scraping bowl occasionally. Blend in cornmeal and enough of the remaining flour to make a smooth, thick batter.
3. Cover; let rise in a warm place until double in bulk (1 to 1½ hours).
4. Beat batter down. Cut against side of bowl with a large spoon enough batter at one time to fill each greased 2½- or 3-inch muffin-pan well two-thirds full, pushing batter with a rubber spatula directly into well. Cover; let rise again until almost double in bulk (about 30 minutes).
5. Bake at 400°F about 20 minutes. Brush tops with melted butter. Remove from pan and serve piping hot.
1½ TO 2 DOZEN MUFFINS

Note: If desired, mix 1 teaspoon crushed herb, such as chervil, oregano, rosemary, or thyme with flour before adding to batter.

New England Blueberry Muffins

1 cup sugar	2 cups all-purpose flour
½ cup softened butter or	2 teaspoons baking powder
margarine	½ teaspoon salt
2 eggs	1 to 1½ cups fresh or frozen
½ cup milk	blueberries

1. Combine sugar, butter, eggs, and milk in a mixing bowl; beat well.
2. Blend flour, baking powder, and salt; add and mix until blended (about 1 minute). Fold in blueberries.
3. Spoon into 12 well-greased muffin cups, filling almost to the top of the cup.
4. Bake at 375°F 20 to 25 minutes.
12 LARGE MUFFINS

Biscuits and Muffins (pages 157-158)

English Muffins

3 to 3½ cups all-purpose flour
2 tablespoons sugar
1 package active dry yeast
1 teaspoon salt
¾ cup hot milk (120° to 130°F)
1 egg (at room temperature)
2 tablespoons vegetable oil
Cornmeal

1. Combine 1 cup flour, sugar, yeast, and salt in a mixer bowl.
2. Stir in milk, egg, and oil; beat until smooth, about 3 minutes on high speed of electric mixer.
3. Stir in enough remaining flour to make a soft dough.
4. Turn out onto floured board; knead until smooth and elastic (5 to 8 minutes).
5. Cover with bowl; let rest 20 minutes.
6. Roll out to ½-inch thickness. Cut into 3- or 4-inch rounds. Sprinkle with cornmeal. Cover; let rise until double in bulk (about 45 minutes).
7. Bake in a greased heavy skillet or on a griddle on top of the range over low heat 20 to 30 minutes, or until golden brown, turning once. Cool and store in an airtight container or plastic bag.
8. To serve, split with knife or fork. Toast. Serve hot.
ABOUT 1 DOZEN MUFFINS

Brooklyn Bagels

4 to 5 cups all-purpose flour
1 package active dry yeast
2 teaspoons salt
1½ cups hot water (120° to 130°F)
2 tablespoons honey or sugar
1 egg white
1 teaspoon water

1. Combine 1 cup flour, yeast, and salt in a bowl.
2. Stir in hot water and honey; beat until smooth, about 3 minutes. Stir in enough remaining flour to make a soft dough.
3. Turn out onto a floured surface; continue to work in flour until dough is stiff enough to knead. Knead until smooth and elastic (about 5 minutes).
4. Cover with bowl. Let rest 15 minutes.
5. Divide into 12 equal parts. Shape each into a flattened ball. With thumb and forefinger poke a hole into center. Stretch and rotate until hole enlarges to about 1 or 2 inches. Cover; let rise about 20 minutes.
6. Boil water in a large shallow pan, about 2 inches deep. Reduce heat. Simmer a few bagels at a time about 7 minutes. Remove from pan; drain on a towel about 5 minutes. Place on a baking sheet; brush with mixture of egg white and water.
7. Bake at 375°F 30 minutes, or until done.
8. To serve, split and toast. Spread with **butter** and **jam** or **cream cheese.**
1 DOZEN BAGELS

Basic Sweet Dough

4 to 5 cups all-purpose flour
2 packages active dry yeast
1 teaspoon salt
¾ cup milk
½ cup water
½ cup melted butter
½ cup sugar
1 egg

1. Stir together 1¾ cups flour, yeast, and salt in a large mixer bowl.
2. Heat milk, water, butter, and sugar until very warm (120° to 130°F).
3. Add liquid ingredients to flour mixture; beat until smooth, about 2 minutes on electric mixer.
4. Add egg and ½ cup more flour and beat another 2 minutes.
5. Gradually add enough more flour to make a soft dough.
6. Turn out onto floured board; continue to work in flour until dough can be kneaded. Knead until smooth and elastic, but still soft (about 5 minutes).
7. Cover; let rest about 20 minutes.
8. Shape, let rise, and bake as directed in recipes that follow.

Cinnamon Rolls: Roll dough into a 13x9-inch rectangle. Spread with **2 tablespoons softened butter** or **margarine.** Sprinkle with mixture of **½ cup firmly packed brown** or **white sugar** and **2 teaspoons cinnamon.** Beginning with long side, roll dough up tightly jelly-roll fashion. Cut roll into 12 (1-inch) slices. Place slices in a greased 13x9x2-inch baking pan or greased muffin cups. Bake at 375°F 15 to 20 minutes.
1½ DOZEN

Glazed Raised Doughnuts: Follow recipe for Basic Sweet Dough. Roll out to about ½-inch thickness. Cut with doughnut cutter or make into shape of your choice, such as squares, twists, long johns, doughnut holes, or bismarcks. Let rise, uncovered, until light, 40 to 50 minutes. Fry in deep hot oil (375°F) 3 to 4 minutes, turning once. Drain on paper towels. Dip in a glaze of **1½ cups confectioners' sugar, 2 tablespoons warm water,** and **1 teaspoon vanilla extract.**

Apricot Crisscross Coffeecake: For one large coffeecake, roll dough into a 15x12-inch rectangle. For two small coffeecakes, divide dough in half. Roll each half into a 12x8-inch rectangle. Combine **½ cup apricot preserves, ½ cup raisins,** and **½ cup sliced almonds.** Spread half the filling lengthwise down the center of each rectangle. Make about 12 slashes, each 2 inches long, down the long sides of each coffeecake. Fold strips alternately over filling, herringbone fashion. Cover; let rise until double in bulk (50 to 60 minutes). Bake at 375°F 20 to 25 minutes for small coffeecakes and 35 to 40 minutes for large coffeecake.

Apple Strudel

3 cups sifted all-purpose flour
½ teaspoon salt
1 egg, beaten
1 tablespoon cooking oil
1 cup lukewarm (80°F to 85°F) water
Cooking oil (not olive oil)
1 cup butter
½ cup all-purpose flour
Confectioners' sugar or Vanilla Confectioners' Sugar (page 164)
Sweetened Whipped Cream (page 164)
4 medium-size (about 1½ pounds) cooking apples

2 tablespoons vanilla extract
2 tablespoons brown sugar
2 tablespoons sugar
1½ teaspoons cinnamon
½ teaspoon allspice
2 tablespoons brown sugar
1 cup (about 4 ounces) walnuts
2 teaspoons grated lemon peel
2 tablespoons butter
¾ cup (about 2 slices) fine dry bread crumbs
2 tablespoons dark seedless raisins
3 tablespoons currants

1. Generously butter 2 baking sheets.
2. **For Strudel Dough**—Put 3 cups sifted all-purpose flour and salt into a large bowl and make a well in center.
3. Add egg and 1 tablespoon cooking oil and mix well.
4. Stirring constantly to keep mixture a smooth paste, add water gradually.
5. Mix until a soft dough is formed (the dough will be sticky). Turn dough out onto a lightly floured pastry board. Hold dough high above board and hit it hard against the board about 100 to 125 times, or until the dough is smooth and elastic and leaves the board easily. (After 15 or 20 times it will no longer stick.)
6. Knead slightly and pat into a round. Lightly brush top of dough with cooking oil.
7. Cover dough with an inverted bowl and allow it to rest 30 minutes.
8. Meanwhile, see filling recipe; prepare apples, bread crumbs, nuts and sugar mixture.
9. Melt butter and set aside to cool.
10. Cover a table (about 48x30 inches) with a clean cloth, allowing cloth to hang down, and sprinkle with flour (most in center of cloth).
11. Place dough on center of cloth and roll into a 12-inch square. If necessary, sprinkle more flour under dough so it does not stick. Keep dough square. Using a soft brush, lightly brush off any flour on top and brush with cooking

oil. (The oil aids in preventing formation of holes during stretching.)
12. With palms of hands down, reach under the dough to its center (dough will rest on backs of hands) and lift slightly, being careful not to tear dough. To stretch dough, gently and steadily pull arms in opposite directions. Lower dough to table as you walk slowly around table pulling one side and another, but not too much in one place. Keep dough close to table. (Dough should not have any torn spots. If some should appear, do not try to patch them.) Keep pulling and stretching dough, draping it over edge of table. Continue until dough is as thin as tissue paper and hangs over edges of table on all sides. With kitchen shears, trim off thick outer edges. Allow stretched dough to dry 10 minutes. Avoid drying too long as it becomes brittle.
13. Drizzle dough with about ¼ cup of the cooled melted butter. Sprinkle the bread crumbs over dough as directed in recipe for filling. Cover dough with remaining ingredients for the filling.
14. **For Rolling and Baking**—Fold overhanging dough on three sides over the filling. Drizzle the filling with ½ cup of the cooled melted butter. Beginning at narrow folded end of dough, grasp the cloth with both hands, holding it taut; slowly lift cloth and roll dough over filling. Pull cloth toward you; again lift cloth and, holding it taut, slowly and loosely roll dough. Cut Strudel into halves, and lifting each half on cloth, gently roll onto the baking sheets. Brush off excess flour from the roll; cut off ends of roll. Brush top and sides of Strudel with some of the melted butter.
15. Bake at 350°F 35 to 45 minutes, or until Strudel is golden brown. Baste and brush about 4 times during baking with melted butter. When Strudel makes a crackly sound on touching it is done. (Strudel should not be smooth.)
16. Remove to cooling rack; cool slightly. Sift Confectioners' sugar or Vanilla Confectioners' Sugar over top of strudel.
17. Remove to a cutting board. Cut Strudel into 2-inch slices and serve warm with **Sweetened Whipped Cream.**
12 SLICES

18. **For Filling**—Wash, quarter, core and pare apples.
19. Cut apples into slices about ⅛ inch thick and put into a bowl with vanilla extract and 2 tablespoons brown sugar.
20. Toss lightly to coat slices evenly. Set aside for at least 30 minutes, tossing occasionally.
21. Mix together sugar, cinnamon, and allspice.
22. Blend in 2 tablespoons brown sugar.
23. Chop walnuts finely and set aside.
24. Grate lemon peel and set aside.
25. Heat a skillet over medium heat. Add butter and melt quickly.
26. Toss bread crumbs in the butter until browned and thoroughly coated.
27. Sprinkle the bread crumbs evenly over one-half the stretched and slightly dry dough.
28. Drain the apples and cover crumbs evenly with the slices. Sprinkle lemon peel over apples. Toss evenly over apples the nuts and raisins and currants.
29. Sprinkle sugar mixture over nuts and fruits. Drizzle with melted butter.

Apple Strudel

Vanilla Confectioners' Sugar

Confectioners' sugar
1 vanilla bean, about 9
inches long

1. Set out a 1- to 2-quart container having a tight-fitting cover. Fill with sugar.
2. Remove vanilla bean from air-tight tube, wipe with a clean, damp cloth and dry.
3. Cut vanilla bean into quarters lengthwise; cut quarters crosswise into thirds. Poke pieces of vanilla bean down into the sugar at irregular intervals. Cover container tightly and store on pantry shelf.
4. Use on cookies, cakes, tortes, rolled pancakes or wherever a sprinkling of confectioners' sugar is desired.

Note: The longer sugar stands, the richer will be the vanilla flavor. If tightly covered, sugar may be stored for several months. When necessary, add more sugar to jar. Replace vanilla bean when aroma is gone.

Sweetened Whipped Cream

1 cup chilled whipping cream
¼ cup sifted confectioners'
sugar
1 teaspoon vanilla extract

1. Place a rotary beater and a 1-quart bowl in refrigerator to chill.
2. Using chilled bowl and beater, beat until cream stands in peaks when beater is slowly lifted upright.
3. Beat sugar and vanilla extract into whipped cream with final few strokes until blended.
4. Set in refrigerator if not used immediately.
ABOUT 2 CUPS WHIPPED CREAM

Austrian Almond Bread

Austrian Almond Bread

5 to 5½ cups all-purpose flour
2 packages active dry yeast
1 cup milk
½ cup sugar
½ cup shortening or butter
¼ cup butter
2 teaspoons salt
2 eggs (at room temperature)

½ cup golden raisins
½ cup candied mixed fruit, chopped
½ cup chopped blanched almonds
Almond Icing (see recipe)
Candied fruit and nuts for decoration (optional)

1. Combine 2 cups flour and yeast in a large mixer bowl.
2. Heat milk, sugar, shortening, water, and salt in a saucepan over low heat until very warm (120° to 130°F), stirring to blend. Add liquid to flour-yeast mixture and beat until smooth, about 3 minutes on medium speed of electric mixer. Blend in eggs. Add 1 cup flour and beat 1 minute. Stir in fruit and almonds; add more flour to make a soft dough.
3. Turn dough onto a lightly floured surface; knead until smooth and satiny (5 to 10 minutes). Cover dough and let rest 20 minutes. Divide dough in half.

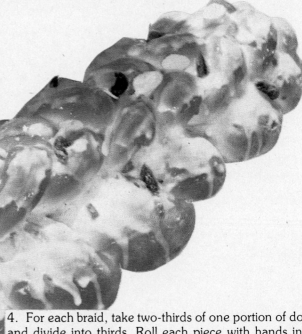

4. For each braid, take two-thirds of one portion of dough and divide into thirds. Roll each piece with hands into a 15-inch strand. Braid strands on lightly greased baking sheet. Divide remaining third into thirds; form three 18-inch strands. Braid strands loosely; place on first braid, pressing in lightly. Tuck ends of top braid under ends of bottom braid. Brush with oil. Let rise in a warm place until double in bulk (about 45 minutes).
5. Bake at 350°F 25 to 30 minutes, or until golden brown. Remove from baking sheets to wire rack. While braids are still slightly warm, ice with almond icing. Decorate with candied fruit and nuts, if desired.
2 LARGE LOAVES

Almond Icing: Put **1½ cups confectioners' sugar, 2 tablespoons milk,** and **1 teaspoon almond extract** into a small bowl; stir until smooth.

Russian Kulich

Russian Kulich

5 cups all-purpose flour
2 packages active dry yeast
1 cup milk
½ cup sugar
¼ cup oil
2 teaspoons salt
2 eggs (at room temperature)
2 teaspoons grated lemon peel
½ cup chopped blanched almonds
¼ cup raisins
¼ cup chopped candied citron
¼ cup chopped candied orange peel
¼ cup chopped candied cherries
½ cup confectioners' sugar
1 tablespoon milk
Candied fruit (optional)

1. Combine 1 cup flour and yeast in a large mixer bowl.
2. Heat 1 cup milk, sugar, oil, and salt in a saucepan over low heat until very warm (120° to 130°F), stirring to blend. Add liquid to flour-yeast mixture and beat until smooth, about 2 minutes on medium speed of electric mixer. Beat in eggs, lemon peel, almonds, raisins, and candied fruit. Add 1 cup flour and beat 1 minute on medium speed. Stir in more flour to make a soft dough.
3. Turn dough onto a lightly floured surface and knead until smooth and satiny (8 to 10 minutes). Shape into a ball and place in a lightly greased bowl; turn to grease surface. Cover; let rise in a warm place until double in bulk (about 1½ hours).
4. Punch dough down; divide into 2 or 3 equal portions and shape into balls. Let rest 10 minutes.
5. Grease generously two 46-ounce juice cans or three 1-pound coffee cans. Place dough in cans, filling about half full; brush with oil. Let rise until double in bulk (about 1 hour).
6. Bake at 350°F 30 to 35 minutes, or until golden brown. Immediately remove from cans and cool.
7. Blend confectioners' sugar and 1 tablespoon milk until smooth; ice top of loaves. Decorate with candied fruit, if desired.
2 LARGE OR 3 MEDIUM LOAVES

Kugelhupf

3 to 4 cups all-purpose flour
2 packages active dry yeast
1 cup milk
1 cup raisins
½ cup water
½ cup sugar
½ cup butter
1 teaspoon salt
3 eggs (at room temperature)
2 teaspoons rum extract
Butter, softened
⅓ cup ground almonds
Sifted confectioners' sugar
Candied fruits and nuts
Corn syrup

1. Combine 2 cups flour and yeast in a large mixer bowl.
2. Heat milk, raisins, water, sugar, ½ cup butter, and salt in a saucepan over low heat until very warm (120° to 130°F), stirring to blend; add to flour-yeast mixture and beat until smooth, about 3 minutes on medium speed of electric mixer. Blend in eggs and rum extract; add ½ cup flour and continue to beat 2 minutes. Add enough flour to make a thick batter. Cover; let rise in a warm place until double in bulk and batter is bubbly (about 1 hour).
3. Stir batter down. Spoon into two 1½-quart or three 1-quart turk's-head or other fancy molds that have been buttered and dusted with ground almonds. Cover; let rise in a warm place until double in bulk (about 30 minutes).
4. Bake at 325°F 1 hour for 1½-quart loaves or 45 minutes for 1-quart loaves. If necessary to prevent excessing browning, cover during the last 10 minutes of baking. Unmold on wire racks. Dust with confectioners' sugar. Decorate with candied fruits and nuts that have been dipped in corn syrup.
2 LARGE OR 3 SMALL LOAVES

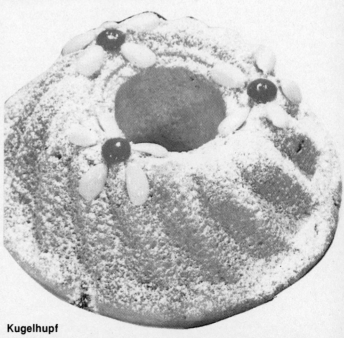

Kugelhupf

King's Bread Ring

2 packages active dry yeast
  or 2 cakes compressed
  yeast
½ cup warm water (hot for
  dry yeast, lukewarm for
  compressed)
½ cup milk, scalded
⅓ cup sugar
⅓ cup shortening

2 teaspoons salt
4 cups all-purpose flour
  (about)
3 eggs, well beaten
2 cups chopped candied
  fruits (citron, cherries, and
  orange peel)
Melted butter or margarine
Confectioners' Sugar Icing

1. Soften yeast in water.
2. Pour hot milk over sugar, shortening, and salt in large bowl, stirring until sugar is dissolved and shortening melted. Cool to lukewarm. Beat in 1 cup of the flour, then eggs and softened yeast. Add enough more flour to make a stiff dough. Stir in 1½ cups candied fruits, reserving remainder to decorate baked ring.
3. Turn dough onto a floured surface and knead until smooth and satiny. Roll dough under hands into a long rope; shape into a ring, sealing ends together. Transfer to a greased cookie sheet. Push a tiny china doll into dough so it is completely covered. Brush with melted butter.
4. Coveer with a towel and let rise in a warm place until double in bulk (about 1½ hours).
5. Bake at 375°F 25 to 30 minutes, or until golden brown.
6. Cool on wire rack. Frost with Confectioners' Sugar Icing and decorate with reserved candied fruit.

1 LARGE BREAD RING

Confectioners' Sugar Icing: Blend **1⅓ cups confectioners' sugar, 4 teaspoons water,** and **½ teaspoon vanilla extract.**

Refrigerator Sweet Dough

5 to 6 cups all-purpose flour
2 packages active dry yeast
½ cup sugar
1½ teaspoons salt
1 cup milk

½ cup water
½ cup butter or margarine,
  softened
2 eggs

1. Stir 1¾ cups flour, yeast, sugar, and salt together in a large mixer bowl.
2. Heat milk, water, and butter to very warm (120° to 130°F).
3. Add liquid to dry ingredients and beat until smooth, about 2 minutes on electric mixer.
4. Add eggs and ½ cup flour and continue beating another 2 minutes.
5. Gradually stir in enough additional flour to make a soft dough.
6. Turn out onto floured board; continue to work in flour until dough can be kneaded. Knead until smooth and elastic, but still soft (5 to 8 minutes).
7. Cover with plastic wrap, then with a towel.
8. Let rest 20 minutes.
9. Divide in half and shape as desired.
10. Brush with oil. Cover with plastic wrap.
11. Refrigerate 2 to 24 hours. When ready to bake, remove from refrigerator and let stand 10 minutes.
12. Bake at 375°F 20 to 30 minutes.

13. Remove from pans and cool on rack.

2 COFFEECAKES

Cinnamon Slice Coffeecake: Follow shaping instructions as in Cinnamon Rolls (page 161), only omit 13x9x2-inch pan. Instead, place 6 slices, cut-side down, on bottom of a greased 10-inch tube pan. Place 6 more slices cut-side against outer side of pan. Cover first layer with remaining 6 rolls. Bake at 375°F 20 to 25 minutes.

Cinnamon Discs: Combine **¾ cup firmly packed brown sugar, ¾ cup white sugar, ½ cup finely chopped pecans,** and **1 teaspoon cinnamon.** Divide dough in half. Roll each half into a 12-inch square. Melt **½ cup butter.** Brush dough with 2 tablespoons of the butter. Sprinkle with ⅓ cup sugar mixture. Roll up jelly-roll fashion; pinch to seal edges. Cut into 1-inch slices. Place on greased baking sheets at least 3 inches apart. Cover with waxed paper. Flatten each to about 3 inches in diameter. Let rise 15 minutes. Flatten again. Brush with remaining butter; sprinkle with remaining sugar mixture. Cover with waxed paper; flatten again. Bake at 400°F 10 to 12 minutes.

2 DOZEN

Bubble Bread: Divide dough into 20 equal pieces; shape into balls. Combine **½ cup sugar or firmly packed brown sugar, ½ cup finely chopped nuts,** and **1 teaspoon cinnamon.** Melt **½ cup butter or margarine.** Roll balls in butter, then in sugar mixture. Arrange balls in a well-greased 10-inch tube pan. Cover; let rise until double in bulk (45 to 60 minutes). Bake at 350°F 30 to 35 minutes.

Orange Bubble Ring: Shape dough into 20 balls as for Bubble Bread. Roll each ball in **½ cup melted butter** and then a mixture of **½ cup sugar** and **1 tablespoon grated orange peel.** Arrange and bake as above.

Streusel Coffeecake

Coffeecake:
2 cups all-purpose biscuit
  mix
½ cup sugar
⅔ cup beer
1 egg, slightly beaten

Topping:
½ cup flour
⅓ cup sugar
1 teaspoon cinnamon
⅓ cup butter or margarine

1. For coffeecake, combine biscuit mix and sugar. Mix beer and egg.
2. Add beer mixture to dry mixture. Stir lightly, just until moistened. Turn into a greased 9-inch round cake pan.
3. For streusel topping, combine flour, sugar, and cinnamon. Cut in butter until crumbly. Sprinkle over coffeecake batter.
4. Bake at 400°F 25 minutes. Serve warm or cooled.

1 COFFEECAKE

Tomato-Cheese Pizza

½ package active dry yeast	8 ounces mozzarella cheese,
1 cup plus 2 tablespoons	thinly sliced
warm water	½ cup olive oil
4 cups sifted all-purpose	¼ cup grated Parmesan
flour	cheese
1 teaspoon salt	1 teaspoon salt
3 cups drained canned	½ teaspoon pepper
tomatoes	2 teaspoons oregano

1. Soften yeast in 2 tablespoons warm water. Set aside.
2. Pour remaining cup of warm water into a large bowl. Blend in 2 cups flour and 1 teaspoon salt. Stir softened yeast and add to flour-water mixture, mixing well.
3. Add about 1 cup flour to yeast mixture and beat until very smooth. Mix in enough remaining flour to make a soft dough. Turn dough onto a lightly floured surface and allow to rest 5 to 10 minutes. Knead 5 to 8 minutes, until dough is smooth and elastic.
4. Shape dough into a smooth ball and place in a greased bowl just large enough to allow dough to double. Turn dough to bring greased surface to top. Cover with waxed paper and let stand in warm place (about 80°) until dough is doubled (about 1½ to 2 hours).
5. Punch down with fist. Fold edge towards center and turn dough over. Divide dough into two equal balls. Grease another bowl and place one of the balls in it. Turn dough in both bowls so greased side is on top. Cover and let rise again until almost doubled (about 45 minutes).
6. Roll each ball of dough into a 14x10-inch rectangle, ⅛ inch thick. Place on two lightly greased 15½x12-inch baking sheets. Shape edges by pressing dough between thumb and forefinger to make a ridge. If desired, dough may be rolled into rounds, ⅛ inch thick.
7. Force tomatoes through a sieve or food mill and spread 1½ cups on each pizza. Arrange 4 ounces of mozzarella cheese on each pizza. Sprinkle over each pizza, in the order given, ¼ cup olive oil, 2 tablespoons grated Parmesan cheese, ½ teaspoon salt, ¼ teaspoon pepper, and 1 teaspoon oregano.
8. Bake at 400°F 25 to 30 minutes, or until crust is browned. Cut into wedges to serve.

6 TO 8 SERVINGS

Mushroom Pizza: Follow Tomato-Cheese Pizza recipe. Before baking, place on each pizza 1 cup (8-ounce can) drained **mushroom buttons.**

Sausage Pizza: Follow Tomato-Cheese Pizza recipe. Before baking, place on each pizza 1 pound **hot Italian sausage** (with casing removed), cut in ¼-inch pieces.

Anchovy Pizza: Follow Tomato-Cheese Pizza recipe. Omit mozzarella and Parmesan cheeses, decrease amount of oregano to ¼ teaspoon, and top each pizza with **anchovy fillets,** cut in ¼-inch pieces.

Miniature Pizzas: Follow Tomato-Cheese Pizza recipe. After rolling dough, cut dough into 3½-inch rounds. Shape edge of rounds as in Tomato-Cheese Pizza recipe. Using half the amount of ingredients in that recipe, spread each pizza with 2 tablespoons sieved canned tomatoes. Top with a slice of mozzarella cheese. Sprinkle cheese with ½ teaspoon olive oil, ½ teaspoon grated Parmesan cheese, and a few grains salt and pepper. Bake at 400°F 15 to 20 minutes, or until crust is browned.

ABOUT 24 MINIATURE PIZZAS

English Muffin Pizzas: Split 12 **English muffins** and spread cut sides with **butter or margarine.** Toast under the broiler until lightly browned. Top each half as for Miniature Pizza. Bake at 400°F 5 to 8 minutes, or until tomato mixture is bubbling hot.

24 PIZZAS

Pancakes

1½ cups sifted all-purpose	2 egg yolks, beaten
flour	1⅓ cups milk
1 tablespoon sugar	2 tablespoons butter or
1½ teaspoons baking powder	margarine, melted
¼ teaspoon salt	2 egg whites

1. Start heating griddle or heavy skillet over low heat.
2. Mix flour, sugar, baking powder, and salt in a bowl.
3. Combine egg yolks, milk, and butter. Add liquid to flour mixture and beat until blended.
4. Beat egg whites until rounded peaks are formed. Spread beaten egg whites over batter and fold gently together.
5. Test griddle; it is hot enough for baking when drops of water sprinkled on surface dance in small beads. Lightly grease griddle, if so directed by manufacturer.
6. Pour batter onto griddle into pools about 4 inches in diameter, leaving at least 1 inch between cakes. Turn pancakes as they become puffy and full of bubbles. Turn only once.
7. Serve hot.

ABOUT 12 PANCAKES

Buttermilk Pancakes: Follow recipe for Pancakes; substitute ½ **teaspoon baking soda** for the baking powder and **buttermilk** for the milk. Do not separate eggs. Beat eggs with buttermilk and proceed as in step 3 above.

Cornmeal Pancakes: Follow recipe for Pancakes. Decrease flour to ¾ cup. Mix ¾ **cup yellow cornmeal** into dry ingredients.

Rye Pancakes: Follow recipe for Buttermilk Pancakes. Decrease flour to ¾ cup and mix in ¾ **cup rye flour.** Blend **3 tablespoons molasses** into buttermilk-egg mixture.

Blueberry Pancakes: Follow recipe for Pancakes; gently fold **2 cups rinsed and drained blueberries** into batter after folding in beaten egg whites.

Tomato-Cheese Pizza

Waffles

2 cups sifted all-purpose
  flour
1 tablespoon sugar
1 tablespoon baking powder
½ teaspoon salt

3 eggs, well-beaten
2 cups milk
½ cup butter or margarine,
  melted

1. Mix flour, sugar, baking powder, and salt in a bowl.
2. Combine eggs, milk, and melted butter. Add liquid mixture to flour mixture; beat just until batter is blended.
3. Heat waffle baker. Pour enough batter into waffle baker to allow spreading to within 1 inch of edges. Lower cover and bake waffle; do not raise cover during baking. Lift cover and loosen waffle with a fork. Serve hot.
ABOUT 4 LARGE WAFFLES

Buttermilk Waffles: Follow recipe for Waffles; substitute **buttermilk** for milk. Decrease baking powder to 2 teaspoons and add **1 teaspoon baking soda.**

Wheat Germ Pecan Waffles: Follow recipe for Waffles; decrease flour to 1½ cups. Stir **½ cup toasted wheat germ** into the flour mixture. Sprinkle **3 tablespoons coarsely chopped pecans** onto the batter before baking each waffle.

Cheese Waffles: Follow recipe for Waffles. When batter is smooth, blend in **½ cup shredded cheese.**

Chocolate Waffles: Follow recipe for Waffles. Generously sprinkle **semisweet chocolate pieces** over batter before closing waffle baker.

Popovers

3 eggs
1 cup milk
2 tablespoons vegetable oil

½ teaspoon salt
1 cup sifted all-purpose flour

1. Beat eggs in a mixing bowl. Beat in milk, oil, and salt.
2. Beat in flour until mixture is smooth and well blended.
3. For best results, preheat iron popover pan after thoroughly coating pan wells with shortening or oil. Pour batter into 8 popover-pan wells or 8 greased heat-resistant custard cups.
4. Bake at 400°F 35 to 40 minutes, or until popovers are puffed and golden brown. Serve hot with butter.
8 POPOVERS

Note: For a crispier popover, make slit in side of each baked popover to allow the steam to escape. Return popovers to oven for 10 minutes with the heat turned off.

Croutons for Fruit Soups

4 stale dinner rolls or slices
  baba or bread
½ cup whipping cream

2 tablespoons butter or
  margarine
¼ cup confectioners' sugar

1. Cut rolls into 1-inch cubes.
2. Dip cubes in cream; quickly sauté in butter.
3. Dust with confectioners' sugar.
ABOUT 14 TO 18

Buttermilk Coffeecake

1 cup sugar
½ cup butter or margarine,
  softened
2 eggs
1 teaspoon vanilla extract
2 cups all-purpose flour
1 teaspoon baking powder
1 teaspoon baking soda
½ teaspoon salt

1 cup buttermilk

Topping:
1 cup chopped nuts
1 cup sugar
⅓ cup firmly packed brown
  sugar
1 teaspoon cinnamon
½ cup butter or margarine

1. Cream sugar and butter; beat in eggs and vanilla extract until well blended.
2. Combine flour, baking powder, baking soda, and salt.
3. Add buttermilk and flour mixture alternately to sugar mixture, beating well after each addition.
4. For topping, combine nuts, sugar, brown sugar, and cinnamon. Cut in butter.
5. Sprinkle half of topping mixture in bottom of a greased and floured 13x9x2-inch baking pan. Pour in batter. Cover with remaining topping.
6. Bake at 350°F 25 to 30 minutes.
7. Serve warm.
1 COFFEECAKE

Quick Strips

1 loaf unsliced white bread
½ cup butter or margarine,
  melted
¼ teaspoon garlic salt

Grated Parmesan cheese,
  sesame seed, or poppy
  seed

1. Cut flour 1¼-inch slices from loaf of bread. Cut each slice into 1-inch strips.
2. Combine butter and garlic salt in a 13x9x2-inch baking pan.
3. Toss bread strips in butter; sprinkle with cheese.
4. Bake at 350°F 20 minutes.
ABOUT 20 STRIPS

Sesame Seed Twists

2 cups biscuit mix
¼ cup chilled butter
3 tablespoons melted butter

2 tablespoons sesame seed
1 egg yolk
1 teaspoon milk

1. Prepare biscuit mix as directed on package for rolled biscuits. Roll out on a lightly floured surface into a 12-inch square.
2. Thinly slice 3 tablespoons of butter and place on half of dough; fold other half over it. With rolling pin, gently seal open edges. Repeat procedure, using remaining chilled butter. Fold other half over, forming a 6-inch square.
3. Roll dough into a 12-inch square. Divide in half. Set one half in refrigerator.
4. Brush surface with melted butter. Sprinkle with some of the sesame seed. Cut into twelve 6x1-inch strips. Twist each strip and place on an ungreased baking sheet. Brush with mixture of egg yolk and milk. Sprinkle with more sesame seed. Repeat with other half.
5. Bake at 425°F 10 minutes.
2 DOZEN TWISTS

Drop Doughnuts

4 eggs
1 cup buttermilk
2 teaspoons vanilla extract
1 teaspoon grated lemon or
  orange peel (optional)

3 cups all-purpose flour
1½ teaspoons baking powder
Cooking oil for deep frying
Honey
Cinnamon

1. Beat eggs; stir in buttermilk, vanilla extract, and grated peel. Combine flour and baking powder. Stir into the egg mixture. Cover with a cloth. Let stand at room temperature for 1 hour.
2. In a deep fryer, heat oil to 375°F. Drop batter by the tablespoon. Cook 4 minutes, or until doughnuts are golden brown. Drain on paper towels. Drizzle with honey and sprinkle with cinnamon. Serve hot.
ABOUT 30 DOUGHNUTS

Note: Batter keeps well in the refrigerator. Bring to room temperature before cooking.

Crispy Breadsticks

1 cup whole wheat flour
1 package active dry yeast
1 tablespoon sugar
1 teaspoon salt

⅔ cup hot water
2 tablespoons vegetable oil
1 to 1¼ cups all-purpose
  flour

1. Stir together whole wheat flour, yeast, sugar, and salt in a mixing bowl.
2. Blend in water and oil; beat until smooth.
3. Stir in enough flour to form a soft dough.
4. Turn onto a floured surface; continue to work in flour until dough is stiff enough to knead. Knead until smooth and elastic (about 5 minutes), working in as much flour as possible. (The more flour, the crispier the bread sticks.)
5. Cover with bowl; let rest about 30 minutes.
6. Divide dough in quarters. Divide each quarter into 8 equal pieces. For ease in shaping, allow dough to rest about 10 minutes. Roll each piece with palms of hands into 10-inch lengths.
7. Place on greased baking sheets about ½ inch apart. If desired, brush with a mixture of 1 egg white and 1 teaspoon water.
8. Bake at 325°F 20 minutes, or until golden brown and crispy.
32 BREAD STICKS

Drop Doughnuts

Parmesan Bread Fingers

2½ cups all-purpose biscuit mix
1 package active dry yeast
½ teaspoon salt
⅔ cup hot water

¼ cup butter or margarine, melted
¼ cup grated Parmesan cheese

1. Combine biscuit mix, yeast, and salt in a bowl.
2. Stir in water until mixture clings to itself.
3. Turn dough onto a floured surface. Knead 8 to 10 times.
4. Roll out into a 13x9-inch rectangle.
5. Brush half of butter in a 13x9x2-inch baking pan. Place dough in pan, pressing to fit. Cut crosswise into 16 strips, then lengthwise in half.
6. Brush with remaining butter and sprinkle with cheese. Cover; let rise 15 minutes.
7. Bake at 425°F 15 minutes. Turn off oven; allow sticks to remain in oven 15 minutes.

32 BREAD FINGERS

La Verde Slices

1 loaf Italian bread, cut diagonally in 1-inch slices
½ cup softened butter or margarine

2 tablespoons finely chopped green pepper
2 tablespoons finely chopped onion

1. Broil bread slices until golden brown on each side.
2. Combine butter, green pepper, and onion. Spread on one side of each slice.
3. Broil until lightly browned.

ABOUT 1 DOZEN SLICES

Pasta, Grains & DUMPLINGS

Meat-Stuffed Manicotti

2 tablespoons olive oil
½ pound fresh spinach, washed, dried, and finely chopped
2 tablespoons chopped onion
½ teaspoon salt
½ teaspoon oregano
½ pound ground beef
2 tablespoons fine dry bread crumbs
1 egg, slightly beaten
1 can (6 ounces) tomato paste
8 manicotti shells (two thirds of a 5½-ounce package), cooked and drained
1½ tablespoons butter, softened (optional)
1 to 2 tablespoons grated Parmesan or Romano cheese (optional)
Mozzarella cheese, shredded

1. Heat olive oil in a skillet. Add spinach, onion, salt, oregano, and meat. Mix well, separating meat into small pieces. Cook, stirring frequently, until meat is no longer pink.
2. Set aside to cool slightly. Add bread crumbs, egg, and 2 tablespoons tomato paste; mix well. Stuff manicotti with mixture. Put side by side in a greased 2-quart baking dish. If desired, spread butter over stuffed manicotti and sprinkle with the grated cheese.
3. Spoon remaining tomato paste on top of the manicotti down the center of the dish. Sprinkle mozzarella cheese on top of tomato paste. Cover baking dish.
4. Bake at 425°F 12 to 15 minutes, or until mozzarella melts.
4 SERVINGS

Egg Noodles Abruzzi

1 tablespoon butter
¼ cup olive oil
1 pound ground lamb
2 green peppers, chopped
1 teaspoon salt
¼ teaspoon pepper
½ cup dry white wine
2 large tomatoes, peeled and coarsely chopped
1 pound egg noodles

1. Heat butter and oil in a large skillet. Stir in lamb and green peppers; season with salt and pepper. Brown the meat slightly, stirring occasionally.
2. Add wine and simmer until liquid is almost evaporated. Stir in tomatoes and simmer mixture 30 minutes, or until sauce is thick.
3. Cook noodles according to package directions; drain. Place noodles on a hot platter, pour sauce over noodles, and serve.
4 TO 6 SERVINGS

Meat-Stuffed Manicotti

Green Noodles in Pastry

1 unbaked deep 9-inch pie shell
6 large mushrooms, cleaned and sliced
2 tablespoons butter
12 ounces green noodles
1 tablespoon butter
¼ cup grated Parmesan cheese
1 cup Bolognese Meat Sauce (see page 52)
1½ cups Cream Sauce (see page 53)
1 mushroom cap
6 to 8 mushroom halves
1 tablespoon butter, melted
Grated Parmesan cheese

1. Thoroughly prick bottom and sides of pie shell. Bake at 450°F about 7 minutes, or until lightly browned; set aside.
2. Sauté mushrooms in 2 tablespoons butter 3 minutes. Cook noodles according to package directions and drain.
3. Combine noodles, mushrooms, 1 tablespoon butter, ¼ cup cheese, meat sauce, and 1 cup Cream Sauce. Turn mixture into pie shell. Spread remaining ½ cup Cream Sauce over top. Put mushroom cap in center and surround with mushroom halves. Drizzle melted butter over all and sprinkle with additional cheese.
4. Bake at 400°F about 8 minutes, or until heated through and top is slightly browned.
ABOUT 6 SERVINGS

Pasta with Potatoes

2 white onions, chopped
2 tablespoons olive oil
2 tablespoons butter
1 pound potatoes, pared and diced
2 pounds very ripe tomatoes, peeled and coarsely chopped
1½ teaspoons salt
½ teaspoon freshly ground pepper
1 tablespoon minced Italian parsley
1 pound lumachine
6 tablespoons grated Romano cheese

1. Sauté onions in oil and butter until soft. Stir in potatoes and simmer, covered, 15 minutes.
2. Stir in tomatoes, salt, pepper, and parsley. Simmer, covered, 25 minutes, then uncovered 10 minutes, stirring often.
3. Cook lumachine according to package directions; drain. Add to tomatoes and potatoes; mix well. Blend in 4 tablespoons cheese.
4. Serve immediately in hot soup bowls with remaining cheese sprinkled on top.
6 TO 8 SERVINGS

Basic Noodle Dough

4 cups sifted all-purpose flour
½ teaspoon salt
4 eggs
6 tablespoons cold water

1. Mix flour and salt in a bowl; make a well in center, Add eggs, one at a time, mixing slightly after each addition. Add water gradually, mixing to make a stiff dough.
2. Turn dough onto a lightly floured surface and knead until smooth.
3. Proceed as directed in recipes.

Green Noodles in Pastry

Pasta with Beans Sorrento Style

2 cups dried Great Northern beans
5 cups water
1 teaspoon salt
1 cup chopped celery
1 cup chopped onion
3 tablespoons olive oil
1 teaspoon salt
6 ripe tomatoes, peeled and diced
1 tablespoon chopped Italian parsley
4 fresh basil leaves, chopped or 1 teaspoon dried basil
½ pound conchigliette

1. Rinse beans and put into a heavy saucepot or kettle. Add water and bring rapidly to boiling; boil 2 minutes and remove from heat. Cover; set aside 1 hour.
2. Stir 1 teaspoon salt into beans, cover, and bring to boiling. Cook until beans are nearly done, but still firm (about 2 hours). Drain and set aside.
3. Sauté the celery and onion in olive oil until soft. Sprinkle in 1 teaspoon salt, then stir in tomatoes, parsley, and basil.
4. Simmer 15 minutes, uncovered. Add the beans to tomato mixture; stir well. Cook the conchigliette according to package directions, drain, and stir into bean mixture. Serve in hot soup bowls.
4 TO 6 SERVINGS

Green Noodles

¼ pound spinach
3 cups sifted all-purpose flour
½ teaspoon salt
3 eggs
6 quarts water
1 tablespoon salt
¾ cup grated Parmesan cheese
½ teaspoon salt
¼ cup butter

1. Wash spinach and put into a heavy saucepan. Do not add water; cook only in moisture remaining on leaves from washing. Partially cover and cook 5 minutes, stirring occasionally with a fork.
2. Drain spinach, pressing out water, and chop finely.
3. Mix flour and ½ teaspoon salt in a bowl; make a well in center. Add eggs, one at a time, mixing slightly after each addition. Add the chopped spinach and mix well.
4. Turn dough onto a lightly floured surface and knead until smooth, adding flour if needed for a stiff dough.
5. Divide dough in half. Lightly roll each half into a rectangle, about ⅛ inch thick. Cover; let stand 1 hour. Beginning with a narrow end, gently fold over about 2 inches of dough and continue folding over so final width is about 3 inches. (Dough must be dry enough so layers do not stick together.) Beginning at a narrow edge, cut dough into strips ¼ inch wide. Unroll strips and arrange on waxed paper on a flat surface. Let stand until noodles are dry (2 to 3 hours).
6. Bring water to boiling in a large saucepot. Add 1 tablespoon salt. Add noodles gradually. Boil rapidly, uncovered, 8 to 10 minutes, or until tender.
7. Drain noodles and put a third of them into a greased 2-quart casserole. Top with a third each of the cheese and remaining salt. Dot with a third of butter. Repeat layering twice.
8. Bake at 350°F 15 to 20 minutes, or until cheese is melted.
ABOUT 8 SERVINGS

Skillet Franks 'n' Noodles

1 pound frankfurters, cut in half diagonally
½ cup chopped onion
½ teaspoon basil or oregano leaves, crushed
2 tablespoons butter or margarine
1 can (10¾ ounces) con-densed cream of celery or mushroom soup
½ cup milk
½ cup chopped canned tomatoes
2 cups cooked wide noodles
2 tablespoons chopped parsley

1. In a skillet, brown frankfurters and cook onion with basil in butter until tender.
2. Stir in remaining ingredients. Heat, stirring occasionally.
4 TO 6 SERVINGS

Rice Noodles

1½ cups cooked rice
2 eggs
1 tablespoon butter or margarine
¼ teaspoon salt

1. Combine all ingredients. Beat until well mixed.
2. Drop by small spoonfuls into **boiling soup or broth.** Cook until noodles float, about 3 minutes.
ABOUT 2 CUPS

Homemade Noodles

3 cups semolina
3 eggs
3 tablespoons olive oil (do not substitute)
1½ teaspoons salt
1½ teaspoons warm water

1. Combine all ingredients in a mixing bowl and work with fingers until dough holds together and can be shaped into a ball. A few drops of water may be added, if necessary, but do not let dough get sticky.
2. Knead dough on a board until smooth and shiny. Cover and let rest 15 minutes. Divide dough into 4 portions. Roll out each portion into a paper-thin sheet.
3. Lay sheets on a linen cloth and allow to dry for 1 to 2 hours.
4. Loosely fold sheets over jelly-roll fashion. Cut strips no more than ¼ inch wide. Holding in place, cut again at right angles, the same width, to make square noodles. Noodles may be cooked right away or dried.
5. To dry, transfer to a large tray, and spread on a linen surface for about 3 days, turning occasionally.
6. To cook, bring a large quantity of water, with **salt** and **2 tablespoons oil** added, to a rolling boil. Add noodles and boil until they have doubled in size (about 5 minutes).
7. Serve hot with **browned butter** or **tomato sauce.** Sprinkle with **grated kefalotyri cheese.**
ABOUT 2 POUNDS NOODLES

Chiffon Noodles

2 eggs, separated
2 tablespoons flour
¼ teaspoon salt

1. Beat egg whites and salt until stiff, not dry, peaks form.
2. Beat yolks separately just until frothy. Fold into whites. Fold in flour.
3. Gently spoon onto **boiling soup or broth.** Cover; cook 2 minutes. Turn; cook a few seconds longer.
4. To serve, break into separate portions with a spoon.
ABOUT 4 SERVINGS

Pasta Dough for Tortellini

3½ cups all-purpose flour
1 teaspoon salt
2 eggs, beaten
1 tablespoon olive oil
Warm water (about ½ cup)

1. Put flour on a board and sprinkle with salt. Make a well and add eggs and oil. Mix well until a soft smooth dough is formed. Add warm water gradually, if necessary, to soften dough. Knead 5 to 10 minutes until dough is smooth and elastic. Cover with a bowl for 30 minutes.
2. Divide dough in quarters. Roll each quarter into a round as thin as possible. Cut into 2-inch rounds.
3. For each tortellini, place ¼ to ½ teaspoon filling in center of round. Moisten edges with water. Fold in half; seal edges. Shape into rings by stretching the tips of half circle slightly and wrapping the ring around your index finger. Gently press tips together.
4. Cook as directed.
ABOUT 12 DOZEN TORTELLINI

Lasagne

Tomato Meat Sauce (see page 50)
3 tablespoons olive oil
1 pound ground beef
1 pound lasagne noodles, cooked and drained
¾ pound mozzarella cheese, thinly sliced
2 hard-cooked eggs, sliced
¼ cup grated Parmesan cheese
½ teaspoon pepper
1 cup ricotta

1. Prepare sauce, allowing 4½ hours for cooking.
2. Heat olive oil in a skillet. Add ground beef and cook until browned, separating into small pieces.
3. Spread ½ cup sauce in a 2-quart baking dish. Top with a layer of noodles and half the mozzarella cheese. Spread half the ground beef and half the egg slices on top. Sprinkle on half the Parmesan cheese and ¼ teaspoon pepper. Top with ½ cup ricotta.
4. Beginning with sauce, repeat layering, ending with ricotta. Top ricotta with ½ cup sauce. Arrange over this the remaining lasagne noodles. Top with more sauce.
5. Bake at 350°F about 30 minutes, or until mixture is bubbling. Let stand 5 to 10 minutes to set the layers. Cut in squares and serve topped with remaining sauce.
6 TO 8 SERVINGS

Beaten Noodles

1 tablespoon butter or margarine (at room temperature)	2 egg yolks
2 whole eggs	3 tablespoons flour
	¼ teaspoon salt

1. Beat butter until fluffy. Beat in whole eggs and egg yolks, one at a time. Mix in flour and salt.
2. Spoon into **boiling soup or bouillon.** Cover; cook 2 minutes. Turn. Cover and cook a few seconds longer.
3. To serve, break noodles into separate portions with a spoon.
ABOUT 6 SERVINGS

White Clam Sauce for Linguine

12 ounces enriched linguine	¼ to ½ teaspoon salt
¼ cup olive oil	Few grains pepper
½ cup chopped onion	3 cans (8 ounces each) minced clams, drained; reserve 1½ cups liquid
¼ cup snipped parsley	
3 cloves garlic, minced	
2 tablespoons flour	

1. Cook linguine following package directions; drain and keep hot.
2. Meanwhile, heat oil in a large skillet. Add onion, parsley, and garlic; cook about 3 minutes, stirring occasionally.
3. Mix in flour, salt, and pepper; cook until bubbly. Add reserved clam liquid gradually, while blending thoroughly. Bring rapidly to boiling, stirring constantly, and boil 1 to 2 minutes. Mix in the minced clams and heat; do not boil.
4. Serve clam sauce on the hot linguine.
6 SERVINGS

Fettuccine Alfredo

1 pound green noodles	basil
Boiling salted water	1 clove garlic, minced
2 tablespoons olive oil	Grated Parmesan cheese
1 teaspoon chopped fresh	Butter

1. Cook noodles in boiling salted water until just tender; drain.
2. In a chafing dish, heat olive oil, basil, and garlic. Toss the noodles in hot oil with a fork until they are very hot.
3. Sprinkle generously with Parmesan cheese, adding a generous piece of butter, and toss again a moment before serving.
ABOUT 8 SERVINGS

Fettuccine al Burro Alfredo: Cook egg noodles in boiling salted water until barely tender, *al dente;* drain thoroughly. Bring quickly to the table in a heated serving bowl and rapidly toss and twirl with a generous amount of unsalted butter and finely grated Parmesan or Romano cheese so that the butter and cheese melt so quickly that the fettuccine can be served piping hot.

Green Lasagne

½ pound spinach	1 teaspoon salt
4 cups all-purpose flour	2 large eggs, beaten

1. Wash spinach and place in heavy saucepan. Do not add water; cook only in moisture remaining on leaves from washing. Partially cover and cook 5 minutes, stirring occasionally with a fork.
2. Drain spinach, press out the water, chop it, and force it through a sieve; or drain, press out water, and purée in an electric blender. It should retain its fresh green color and become a smooth purée. If the purée is very wet, heat it in the saucepan, about a minute, over very high heat to evaporate some of the moisture. Allow it to cool.
3. Sift the flour and salt into a large mixing bowl. Make a well in the center of the flour and put the beaten eggs and puréed spinach in it. Mix gradually with one hand, or with a fork, until the paste is well blended. If the mixture is too dry, add some water until it forms a ball. If the dough is too sticky, add more flour.
4. Knead the dough at least 12 minutes, until it is smooth and elastic. Divide dough in 4 pieces and roll out to $\frac{1}{16}$-inch thick. Cut the sheets of dough into 4x2-inch rectangles, or longer, if desired. The dough may also be cut in squares. Let cut pieces of dough dry on towels for an hour. If not using immediately, store at room temperature.
ABOUT 1¼ POUNDS PASTA

Green Noodles: Follow recipe for Green Lasagne. Roll the sheets of dough up and cut in ¼-inch-wide strips. Unroll and place on towels for half an hour to dry. Place in **boiling salted water** and cook 5 minutes; drain. Served tossed with **butter,** or any sauce desired.

Spaghetti Sicilian Style

½ cup olive oil	sweet basil
2 cloves garlic, peeled and quartered	1 tablespoon capers
½ medium-size eggplant, pared and diced	4 anchovy fillets, cut in small pieces
6 large ripe tomatoes, peeled and coarsely chopped	12 ripe olives, pitted and halved
2 green peppers	1 teaspoon salt
1 tablespoon chopped fresh basil or ½ teaspoon dried	¼ teaspoon pepper
	1 pound spaghetti

1. Heat olive oil in a skillet; stir in garlic. Remove garlic from oil when brown. Stir eggplant and tomatoes into skillet; simmer 30 minutes.
2. Cut peppers vertically in half; remove membrane and seeds. Place peppers under broiler, skin side up, to loosen skins. Peel off skin, slice peppers, and add to tomato mixture.
3. Stir basil, capers, anchovies, olives, salt, and pepper into tomato mixture. Cover the skillet and simmer 10 minutes, or until sauce is well blended and is thickened.
4. Cook spaghetti according to package directions and drain. Immediately pour sauce over spaghetti and serve.
ABOUT 6 SERVINGS

Ravioli

Tomato Meat Sauce (see page 50)
3 cups (about 1½ pounds) ricotta
1½ tablespoons chopped parsley
2 eggs, well beaten
1 tablespoon grated Parmesan cheese
¾ teaspoon salt
¼ teaspoon pepper
Basic Noodle Dough (see page 181)
7 quarts water
2 tablespoons salt
Grated Parmesan or Romano cheese

1. Prepare Tomato Meat Sauce.
2. Mix ricotta, parsley, eggs, 1 tablespoon grated Parmesan, ¾ teaspoon salt, and pepper.
3. Prepare noodle dough. Divide dough in fourths. Lightly roll each fourth ⅛ inch thick to form a rectangle. Cut dough lengthwise with pastry cutter into strips 5 inches wide. Put 2 teaspoons filling 1½ inches from narrow end in center of each strip. Continuing along strip, put 2 teaspoons filling at 3½-inch intervals.
4. Fold each strip in half lengthwise, covering mounds of filling. To seal, press the edges together with the tines of a fork. Press gently between mounds to form rectangles about 3½ inches long. Cut apart with a pastry cutter and press cut edges of rectangles with tines of fork to seal.
5. Bring water to boiling in a large saucepot. Add 2 tablespoons salt. Add ravioli gradually; cook about half of ravioli at one time. Boil, uncovered, about 20 minutes, or until tender. Remove with slotted spoon and drain. Put on a warm platter and top with Tomato Meat Sauce. Sprinkle with grated cheese.
ABOUT 3 DOZEN RAVIOLI

Ravioli with Meat Filling: Follow recipe for Ravioli. Prepare sauce. Omit ricotta and parsley. Heat **2 tablespoons olive oil** in a skillet. Add **¾ pound ground beef** and cook until no pink color remains. Cook **½ pound spinach** until tender (see step 1 of Green Noodles, page 181); drain. Mix spinach and ground beef with egg mixture. Proceed as directed.

Spaghetti à la King Crab

Parmesan Croutons
2 cans (7½ ounces each) Alaska king crab or 1 pound frozen Alaska king crab
2 tablespoons olive oil
½ cup butter or margarine
4 cloves garlic, minced
1 bunch green onions, sliced
2 medium tomatoes, peeled and diced
½ cup chopped parsley
2 tablespoons lemon juice
¼ teaspoon thyme
½ teaspoon salt
1 pound enriched spaghetti

1. Prepare Parmesan Croutons; set aside.
2. Drain canned crab and slice. Or, defrost, drain, and slice frozen crab.
3. Heat olive oil, butter, and garlic in a saucepan. Add crab, green onions, tomatoes, parsley, lemon juice, basil, thyme, and salt. Heat gently 8 to 10 minutes.
4. Meanwhile, cook spaghetti following package directions; drain.
5. Toss spaghetti with king crab sauce. Top with Parmesan Croutons. Pass additional grated Parmesan cheese.
ABOUT 6 SERVINGS

Parmesan Croutons: Put **3 tablespoons butter** into a shallow baking pan. Set in a 350°F oven until butter is melted. Slice **French bread** into small cubes to make about 1 cup. Toss with melted butter. Return to oven until golden (about 6 minutes). Sprinkle with **2 tablespoons grated Parmesan cheese** and toss.

Pasta with Fresh Tomatoes and Artichoke Hearts

For each serving:
1 medium ripe tomato, peeled, seeded, and diced
2 cooked artichoke hearts, cut in half
1 teaspoon oregano
½ teaspoon basil
1 garlic clove, crushed in a garlic press
Salt and pepper to taste
1 tablespoon wine vinegar
3 tablespoons olive oil
½ cup macaroni, cooked according to package directions
Mizithra cheese, cut in slices, for garnish
Kalamata olives for garnish

1. Combine all ingredients except macaroni and garnishes in a bowl. Cover and marinate several hours.
2. Turn macaroni onto a plate. Cover with marinated mixture. Garnish with cheese and olives. Serve cool.

Egg Pasta Dough for Manicotti

4 cups all-purpose flour
4 eggs, beaten
1½ teaspoons salt
2 teaspoons olive oil
Warm water (about ½ cup)

1. Put flour onto a board, make a well in center, and add eggs, salt, and olive oil. Mix until a soft dough is formed, adding warm water as needed.
2. Knead about 10 minutes until dough is smooth and elastic. Add more flour if dough is too soft.
3. Divide dough in quarters. Roll each quarter into as thin a sheet as possible. Cut the sheets into 3-inch squares. Dry on cloth or cloth-covered board for 1 hour before using.
ABOUT 1¾ POUNDS DOUGH

Spaghetti à la King Crab

Stuffed Pasta Rings in Cream

½ turkey breast (about 2½ pounds), boned
4 slices prosciutto
1 medium-size veal sweetbread, blanched and cleaned
¼ pound lean pork
¼ pound lean beef
7 tablespoons butter
¼ pound Parmesan cheese,
grated
2 egg yolks, beaten
Pinch grated nutmeg
Pinch ground cinnamon
Salt and pepper
Pasta Dough for Tortellini (see below)
4 quarts chicken broth
1 cup whipping cream

1. Cut turkey breast, prosciutto, sweetbread, pork, and beef into pieces.
2. Melt 4 tablespoons of the butter in a large skillet. Sauté meats until sweetbread pieces are cooked. Remove from heat and cool.
3. Put meat mixture through a meat grinder twice, so it is very finely ground. Place the ground meat in a large bowl and stir in half the cheese, the egg yolks, nutmeg, cinnamon, and salt and pepper to taste. Blend well.
4. Prepare Pasta Dough for Tortellini, using turkey mixture for filling. Set aside on a cloth, cover with another cloth, and allow to dry 30 minutes.
5. Bring the chicken broth to a gentle simmer, not a violent boil or the pasta will break apart. Melt the remaining 3 tablespoons butter in a large saucepot over low heat.
6. Carefully drop filled tortellini, a few at a time, into the gently simmering broth. Simmer until cooked through, but still a little firm (about 10 minutes). Remove, using a slotted spoon, and place in melted butter in saucepot. When all the tortellini are cooked and in the saucepot, pour in the whipping cream and sprinkle remaining cheese over tortellini. Stir gently with a wooden spoon until sauce is smooth.
7. Serve immediately in heated soup bowls. Accompany with additional grated Parmesan cheese.
ABOUT 8 SERVINGS

Note: A 2-pound frozen boneless turkey roast (thawed) may be substituted for the turkey breast.

Macaroni in Browned Butter with Grated Cheese

1 pound macaroni
1 cup butter
½ cup freshly grated
kefalotyri or Parmesan cheese (or more to taste)

1. Cook macaroni according to directions on the package, adding **¼ cup cooking oil** and **1 tablespoon salt**. Drain. Rinse under hot water.
2. Brown butter in a saucepan, stirring constantly.
3. Return the macaroni to the pot in which it was cooked, or place it in a warm serving dish. Drizzle the browned butter over it. With two spoons lift the macaroni to coat all the strands evenly. Cover with freshly grated kefalotyri. Serve at once.
4 TO 6 SERVINGS

New Peas in Rice Ring

1 package (6 or 6¾ ounces) seasoned wild and white rice mix
3 pounds fresh peas
Butter

1. Cook rice mix according to package directions.
2. Meanwhile, rinse and shell peas just before cooking to retain their delicate flavor. Cook covered in boiling salted water to cover for 15 to 20 minutes or until peas are tender. Drain and add just enough butter so peas glisten.
3. Butter a 1-quart ring mold. When rice is done, turn into the mold, packing down gently with spoon. Invert onto a warm serving platter and lift off mold.
4. Spoon hot peas into center of rice ring just before serving.
ABOUT 6 SERVINGS

Rice and Beans

2 quarts water
2 cups dried red beans, rinsed
1 can (13¾ ounces) beef broth
Water
1 tablespoon salt
8 parsley sprigs
3 scallions or green onions, chopped
3 garlic cloves
¼ teaspoon dried rosemary
3 tablespoons peanut oil
2 cups rice

1. Bring water to boiling. Add red beans and cook covered for 1½ hours.
2. Drain beans, reserving liquid, and set aside. Add beef broth and enough water to bean liquid to equal 4¾ cups liquid. Set aside.
3. In a mortar, pound together to form a paste the salt, parsley, scallions, garlic, and rosemary.
4. Heat oil and seasoning paste in a Dutch oven over medium heat. Put rice in Dutch oven and stir until well coated with oil. Add reserved liquid and bring to a boil, stirring. Add beans and again bring to a boil. Reduce heat, cover, and cook undisturbed for 20 minutes.
5. Remove cover, stir, and cook about 5 minutes longer, or until no liquid remains.
8 TO 10 SERVINGS

Baked Rice Balls

1½ pounds ground beef
1 small onion, chopped
1 can (6 ounces) tomato paste
¾ cup water
1 teaspoon salt
⅛ teaspoon pepper
1 tablespoon chopped parsley
6 cups cooked rice, hot
½ cup grated Romano cheese
¼ cup butter
2 to 2½ cups all-purpose flour
2 eggs, slightly beaten
3 eggs, slightly beaten
2 cups fine dry bread crumbs
1 can (8 ounces) tomato sauce

1. Brown ground beef with onion in a skillet. Add tomato paste, stir, and cook 5 minutes. Add water, salt, pepper, and parsley. Mix well and cool about 15 minutes.
2. Combine rice, cheese, butter, 1 cup flour, and 2 eggs. Mix until butter is melted and ingredients are well blended.
3. With well-floured hands, shape some rice into a small ball. Flatten slightly and top with 1 tablespoon of the meat mixture. Top with more rice to cover meat, and make into a ball size of a small orange.
4. Hold the ball over a shallow pan filled with about 1 cup flour; add more flour when needed. Sprinkle rice ball with flour while gently packing and turning in palm of hand.
5. Carefully dip ball in beaten eggs, then roll gently in bread crumbs to coat. Repeat with remaining rice. Place finished rice balls in a jelly-roll pan or baking sheet lined with aluminum foil.
6. Bake at 350°F 30 minutes. While rice balls are baking, stir tomato sauce into meat sauce and heat. Serve sauce over baked rice balls.
7 OR 8 SERVINGS

Cracked Wheat Pilaf

3 tablespoons butter
1¼ cups cracked wheat
3 cups stock, heated
Salt and pepper to taste

Melt butter in a large saucepan, add wheat, and cook over low heat, tossing lightly with a fork until lightly browned. Add stock, cover, and simmer about 30 minutes until wheat is done. Season with salt and pepper.
4 SERVINGS

Lemon Rice with Egg

1¾ cups chicken broth
¾ cup uncooked long grain rice
1 egg
1 tablespoon lemon juice
¼ cup grated Parmesan cheese

1. Bring broth to boiling in a saucepan. Stir in rice; cover tightly. Cook 15 to 20 minutes, or until rice is tender and liquid is absorbed.
2. Place egg, lemon juice, and cheese in a bowl; beat until foamy. Stir into rice over low heat. Serve immediately.
ABOUT 4 SERVINGS

Baked Rice Balls

Caribbean Rice

4 parsley sprigs	2 tablespoons peanut oil
3 peppercorns	2 cups rice
2 garlic cloves	4½ cups chicken broth
2 scallions or green onions, cut in pieces	1 bay leaf
1½ teaspoons salt	1 green hot pepper or ½ teaspoon cayenne or red pepper
½ teaspoon thyme	

1. In a mortar, pound parsley, peppercorns, garlic, scallions, salt, and thyme to a paste. Set aside.
2. Heat oil in a large, heavy saucepan; add rice. Stir until all the rice is coated with oil and turns chalky.
3. Add seasoning paste and chicken broth; bring to a boil. Reduce heat and add bay leaf and pepper. Cover saucepan and cook undisturbed for 20 minutes.
4. Remove the cover; continue to cook over low heat for 5 minutes, or until no liquid remains.
5. Discard bay leaf and whole pepper. Fluff rice and serve.
8 SERVINGS

Rice and Avocado: Follow recipe for Caribbean Rice. Place **cubed avocado** on top of the rice for the last 5 minutes of cooking. Mix in avocado when rice is fluffed.

Coconut and Rice: Follow recipe for Caribbean Rice, using **brown rice** and an additional **½ cup chicken broth.** Add **1 cup freshly grated coconut** along with bay leaf and pepper. Proceed as directed.

Saffron Rice: Steep **½ teaspoon Spanish saffron** in **2¼ cups boiling water** until it turns bright orange. Strain. Follow recipe for Caribbean Rice, using saffron water in place of some of the chicken broth to cook the rice.

Gnocchi

Tomato Meat Sauce (see page 50)	quartered
3 medium (about 1 pound) potatoes, pared and	1¾ cups sifted all-purpose flour
	Grated Parmesan cheese

1. Prepare sauce, allowing 4½ hours for cooking.
2. While sauce is cooking, place the potatoes in enough boiling salted water to cover. Cook, covered, about 20 minutes, or until tender when pierced with a fork. Drain.

Dry potatoes by shaking in pan over low heat.
3. Mash or rice the potatoes with a potato masher, food mill, or ricer that has been scalded with boiling water. Keep the potatoes hot.
4. Place the flour in a bowl, make a well in the center, and add the mashed potatoes. Mix well to make a soft dough. Turn dough onto lightly floured surface and knead 5 to 8 minutes until it is smooth and elastic.
5. Break off small pieces of dough and, using palms of hands, roll to pencil thickness. Cut into ¾-inch pieces. Curl each piece by pressing lightly with the index finger and pulling the finger along the dough toward you. Gnocchi may also be shaped by pressing each piece with a lightly floured fork.
6. Gradually add the gnocchi to 3 quarts boiling water, cooking about half at a time. Boil rapidly, uncovered, 8 to 10 minutes, or until gnocchi are tender and float to the surface.
7. Drain gnocchi in a colander or large sieve, and mix with 2 cups Tomato Meat Sauce, top with remaining sauce, and sprinkle generously with cheese. Serve immediately.
ABOUT 6 SERVINGS

Liver Mounds

¾ pound chicken, turkey, or capon livers	⅓ cup minced onion
1 cup milk	⅓ cup fine dry bread crumbs
1 tablespoon butter or margarine	3 eggs, separated
	½ teaspoon salt

1. Soak livers in milk in a glass or pottery bowl 3 hours in refrigerator. Drain livers, discarding milk. Mince livers.
2. Melt butter in skillet. Add onion and stir-fry until golden. Remove from heat.
3. Combine minced liver, onion with butter, bread crumbs, and egg yolks. Mix until thoroughly combined.
4. Beat egg whites with salt until stiff, not dry, peaks are formed. Fold into liver mixture.
5. Spoon liver mixture into well-greased muffin-pan wells. Grease a piece of brown paper or waxed paper on one side. Place paper, greased side down, on top of muffin pan.
6. Bake at 350°F 25 to 35 minutes. Remove at once from pan. Serve hot with **piquant sauce** or in **chicken broth.**
ABOUT 6 SERVINGS

Egg Barley

1 egg	Dash salt
3 tablespoons grated Parmesan cheese (optional)	1 cup all-purpose flour (about)

1. Beat egg with cheese (if desired) and salt, then add flour until a thick dough forms.
2. On a floured surface, knead in more flour until a stiff, dry dough forms.
3. Grate dough onto waxed paper. Let dry 1 to 2 hours.
4. Cook in **boiling soup** about 5 minutes, or until egg barley floats.
ABOUT 1 CUP DRY; ABOUT 1¾ CUPS COOKED

Fiesta Zucchini-Tomato Casserole

1½ quarts water
2 packets dry onion soup mix
4 ounces enriched spaghetti, broken
⅓ cup butter or margarine
⅔ cup coarsely chopped onion
1 cup green pepper strips
2 or 3 zucchini (about ¾ pound), washed, ends trimmed, and zucchini cut in about ½-inch slices
4 medium tomatoes, peeled and cut in wedges
¼ cup snipped parsley
1 teaspoon seasoned salt
⅛ teaspoon ground black pepper
⅔ cup shredded Swiss cheese

1. Bring water to boiling in a saucepot. Add onion soup mix and spaghetti to the boiling water. Partially cover and boil gently about 10 minutes, or until spaghetti is tender. Drain and set spaghetti mixture aside; reserve liquid.*
2. Heat butter in a large heavy skillet. Add onion and green pepper and cook about 3 minutes, or until tender. Add zucchini; cover and cook 5 minutes. Stir in tomatoes, parsley, seasoned salt, and pepper. Cover and cook about 2 minutes, or just until heated.
3. Turn contents of skillet into a 2-quart casserole. Add drained spaghetti and toss gently to mix. Sprinkle cheese over top. If necessary to reheat mixture, set in a 350° oven until thoroughly heated before placing under broiler.
4. Set under broiler with top about 5 inches from heat until cheese is melted and lightly browned.

6 TO 8 SERVINGS

*The strained soup may be stored for future use as broth or for cooking
vegetables, preparing gravy or sauce, as desired.

Fluffy Dumplings

2 cups Basic Oats Mix (page 157)
1 cup milk

Thoroughly combine Oats Mix and milk. Spoon onto boiling stew. Cook, uncovered, over low heat 10 minutes; cover and cook 10 minutes longer.

10 TO 12 DUMPLINGS

Potato Dumplings

2 cups hot mashed potatoes
⅓ cup fine dry bread crumbs
2 egg yolks
¾ teaspoon salt
¼ teaspoon pepper
⅓ cup all-purpose flour
2 egg whites, beaten until stiff, but not dry

1. Mix ingredients in a large bowl in the order given.
2. Place on floured board and roll to pencil thickness. Cut into 2- or 3-inch strips.
3. Drop into **boiling salted water.** Cook until dumplings float to top.

Croquettes: Sauté **½ cup chopped onion** in **2 tablespoons butter.** Proceed as in recipe for Potato Dumplings; add onion to potatoes. Roll strips in **fine dry bread crumbs.** Pan-fry in **butter** until golden brown.

Fluffy Dumplings

Denim Dumpling Dinner

Chicken Mixture:
2 broiler-fryer chickens (3 pounds each), rinsed
6 cups boiling water
1 tablespoon salt
1 medium onion, sliced
1½ cups cut celery (½-inch pieces)
¾ cup cut carrot (½-inch pieces)
2 cups cold water
¾ cup all-purpose flour

Dumplings:
2 packages (12 ounces each) frozen shredded hash brown potatoes, thawed
1 cup shredded sharp Cheddar cheese (about 4 ounces)
⅔ cup all-purpose flour
2 teaspoons salt
¼ teaspoon pepper
2 eggs, slightly beaten

1. Put chicken, boiling water, and salt into a saucepot. Bring to boiling, reduce heat, and simmer covered 2 to 3 hours, or until tender.
2. Remove chicken from bones, leaving in large pieces. Set aside.
3. Skim fat from broth; measure broth and add enough water to make 4 cups. Return to saucepot and add vegetables; cover and simmer until vegetables are tender, 15 to 20 minutes.
4. Add cold water to flour, stirring until well blended. Gradually add water and flour mixture to hot vegetables in saucepot, stirring constantly. Bring to boiling; simmer 3 minutes, stirring constantly. Return chicken to mixture; heat thoroughly.
5. Meanwhile, for dumplings, turn hash brown potatoes into a bowl and separate with a fork; add cheese, flour, salt, pepper, and eggs and mix with fork.
6. Put half of hot chicken mixture into each of two 13½x8¾x1¾-inch baking dishes or into one 15½x9½x2¼-inch roaster. Drop dumpling mixture by tablespoonfuls onto hot chicken mixture. Cover dishes with aluminum foil.
7. Bake at 350°F 30 minutes, or until dumplings are done.
8. Sprinkle with snipped parsley before serving.
ABOUT 12 SERVINGS

Egg Drops

2 eggs, beaten
¼ teaspoon salt
1 tablespoon water
⅓ cup all-purpose flour

1. Combine all ingredients and stir until smooth.
2. Hold spoonfuls of batter about 12 inches from **boiling soup**; pour slowly from end of spoon. Let boil 2 to 3 minutes, until egg drops float.
ABOUT 4 SERVINGS

String Dumplings: Prepare Egg Drops batter. Pour almost continuously from a cup or spoon into boiling soup to form long "strings." Break apart after cooking.

Fish Dumplings

1 onion, minced
1 tablespoon butter or margarine
1 pound cooked fish or 2 cups flaked cooked fish
1 slice white bread, soaked in water and squeezed
2 eggs
¾ teaspoon salt
2 tablespoons fine dry bread crumbs
1 teaspoon dill weed
1 teaspoon chopped parsley
2 tablespoons flour

1. Fry onion in butter until golden.
2. Flake or chop fish very fine. Or, grind fish with the onion.
3. Mix fish with bread and eggs. Season with salt and pepper. Stir in bread crumbs, dill and parsley.
4. Form balls about 1½ inches in diameter. Roll in flour.
5. Cook in **boiling water** until dumplings float, about 4 minutes.
4 TO 6 SERVINGS

Denim Dumpling Dinner

Stuffed Pancakes

4 eggs
1 cup all-purpose flour
½ teaspoon salt
¾ cup water
Cooking oil

½ cup freshly grated
Parmesan or Romano
cheese
1 cup minced prosciutto
1 cup chicken broth

1. Beat eggs well in a medium-size mixing bowl. Gradually add flour and salt; mix well. When the mixture is smooth and creamy, add water, more if needed to make a thin batter.
2. Heat a 5-inch skillet and brush with oil. Pour in 2 tablespoons batter, spreading over bottom of skillet to form a thin pancake. As soon as bubbles appear on the top, turn and brown other side.
3. Continue making pancakes, greasing the skillet between each one. Combine cheese with prosciutto; sprinkle each pancake with about 1½ tablespoons of the mixutre. Roll up pancakes tightly and place side by side in a shallow baking dish.
4. Bring chicken broth to boiling and pour over rolled pancakes. Cover the dish and set in a hot place (a heated oven with the heat turned off) for a few minutes, so the broth will be partially absorbed. Serve immediately.
16 FILLED PANCAKES

Pierogi

2 cups all-purpose flour
2 eggs
½ teaspoon salt

⅓ cup water
Filling (see pages 193-194)

1. Mound flour on a bread board and make a well in the center.
2. Drop eggs and salt into well. Add water; working from the center to outside the flour mound, mix flour into liquid in center with one hand and keep flour mounded with other hand. Knead until dough is firm and well mixed.
3. Cover dough with a warm bowl; let rest 10 minutes.
4. Divide dough into halves. On floured surface, using half of dough at a time, roll dough as thin as possible.
5. Cut out 3-inch rounds with large biscuit cutter.
6. Place a small spoonful of filling a little to one side on each round of dough. Moisten edge with water, fold over and press edges together firmly. Be sure they are well sealed to prevent the filling from leaking out.
7. Drop pierogi into **boiling salted water**. Cook gently 3 to 5 minutes, or until pierogi float. Lift out of water with perforated spoon.
1½ TO 2 DOZEN

Note: The dough will have a tendency to dry. A dry dough will not seal completely. Work with half the dough at a time, rolling out a large circle of dough and placing small mounds of filling far enough apart to allow for cutting. Then cut with biscuit cutter and seal firmly.

Never put too many pierogi in cooking water. The uncooked will stick together and the cooked get lumpy and tough.

Little Ears

2 cups all-purpose flour
½ cup water
1 egg

⅛ teaspoon salt
Filling (see pages 193-194)

1. Mound flour on a bread board and make a well in the center. Place remaining ingredients in the well. Mix flour into liquid in center until a dough is formed. Knead thoroughly.
2. Roll dough very thinly on a floured surface. Cut into 2-inch squares.
3. Put a spoonful of filling in center of each square. Fold so that the corners meet in the middle. Press together with fingers to seal. Fold in half diagonally, so the square becomes a triangle. Seal edges. Then bring the 2 long ends of triangle together; press firmly to seal.
4. Drop into **boiling soup**. Cook until the little ears float.
ABOUT 3 DOZEN

Beef Filling

1 large onion, halved and
sliced
2 tablespoons margarine or
shortening
1¾ cups ground cooked beef
¾ cup cooked rice

2 teaspoons instant bouillon
or meat extract
3 tablespoons hot water
1 tablespoon chopped fresh
parsley
Salt and pepper

1. Stir-fry onion in margarine in a large skillet until golden. Stir in meat and rice.
2. Dissolve bouillon in hot water. Add to meat mixture with parsley and salt and pepper to taste.
ABOUT 2½ CUPS

Mushroom Filling

1½ cups chopped
mushrooms
½ cup chopped onion
2 tablespoons butter or

margarine
¼ teaspoon salt
⅛ teaspoon pepper
2 egg yolks or 1 egg, beaten

1. Stir-fry mushrooms and onion in butter until onion is soft. Remove from heat.
2. Stir in remaining ingredients.
ABOUT 1 CUP

Sauerkraut Filling

⅓ cup chopped onion
1 tablespoon butter or
margarine

1½ cups finely chopped
sauerkraut
2 tablespoons sour cream

1. Stir-fry onion in butter in a saucepan 3 minutes.
2. Rinse and drain sauerkraut. Add to onion and cook 2 minutes.
3. Remove from heat. Stir in sour cream.
ABOUT 1½ CUPS

Sausage Filling

10 ounces Polish sausage
(kielbasa), skinned and
chopped
½ cup grated cheese or

chopped mushrooms
¼ cup fine dry bread crumbs
1 egg

Combine all ingredients thoroughly.
ABOUT 2 CUPS

Raw Potato Dumplings

2 cups grated raw potatoes
2 eggs
1 teaspoon salt
½ cup fine dry bread crumbs

1½ cups all-purpose flour
(about)
Boiling salted water

1. Rinse potatoes in cold water; drain well.
2. Combine potatoes in a large bowl with eggs, salt, crumbs, and enough flour to make a stiff dough.
3. Using a wet spoon, drop tablespoonfuls of dough into boiling salted water.
4. Cook until dumplings float to the top. Dumplings should be about 1½x½ inches when done.
ABOUT 6 SERVINGS

Yeast Pierogi

4 eggs
1 tablespoon melted butter
1 teaspoon salt
1 package active dry yeast
¼ cup warm water
1 cup sour cream

1 tablespoon sugar
1½ teaspoons grated lemon
peel (optional)
4 cups all-purpose flour
(about)
Filling (see pages 193-194)

1. Beat eggs with melted butter and salt until thick and fluffy.
2. Dissolve yeast in warm water in a large bowl. Let stand 10 minutes.
3. Add egg mixture to yeast. Beat in sour cream, sugar, and, if desired, lemon peel. Stir in flour, 1 cup at a time, until dough is firm but not stiff.
4. Turn dough on floured surface; knead 3 minutes. Place dough in a greased bowl. Cover with plastic wrap. Let rise in a warm place until doubled, about 1 hour.
5. Roll out dough to ⅜-inch thickness on floured surface. Cut into 3-inch rounds.
6. Place a spoonful of filling a little to one side of each round. Moisten edges. Fold over and seal. Place on greased baking sheet.
7. Bake at 350°F about 20 to 35 minutes, or until golden brown.
ABOUT 3 DOZEN

Cheese & Eggs

Crêpes Benedict

12 eggs
Salt
Pepper
2 tablespoons butter or
  margarine

8 thin slices boiled ham,
  heated
8 dinner crêpes (page 36)
1 cup hollandaise (below)

1. Beat eggs with salt and pepper to taste.
2. Melt butter. Soft-scramble eggs in butter.
3. To assemble, put 1 slice of ham on each crêpe and spoon eggs on top. Fold crêpe and ham over eggs and serve topped with warm hollandaise.
8 FILLED CRÊPES

Hollandaise Sauce

2 egg yolks
2 tablespoons cream
¼ teaspoon salt
Few grains cayenne pepper

2 tablespoons lemon juice or
  tarragon vinegar
½ cup butter

1. In the top of a double boiler, beat egg yolks, cream, salt, and cayenne pepper until thick with a whisk beater. Set over hot (not boiling) water. (Bottom of double-boiler top should not touch water.)
2. Add the lemon juice gradually, while beating constantly. Cook, beating constantly with the whisk beater, until sauce is the consistency of thick cream. Remove double boiler from heat, leaving top in place.
3. Beating constantly, add the butter, ½ teaspoon at a time. Beat with whisk beater until butter is melted and thoroughly blended in.
ABOUT 1 CUP

Note: If necessary, the sauce may be kept hot 15 to 30 minutes over hot water. Keep covered and stir sauce occasionally.

Cheesy Potato Fondue

3 cups sliced pared potatoes
3 cups water
1 tablespoon butter
1 tablespoon flour
1½ cups milk
¾ cup coarsely grated
  Parmesan or Romano

cheese
2 egg yolks, fork beaten
¾ teaspoon salt
⅛ teaspoon cayenne pepper
Cooked ham, cut into cubes
Cherry tomatoes, halved
Zucchini

1. Cook potatoes in a small amount of water until soft (about 15 minutes). Drain, reserving the water; sieve or rice potatoes.
2. Melt butter in a large fondue saucepan. Add flour and cook 1 or 2 minutes without browning.
3. Stir in potatoes with reserved water and milk. Blend until smooth and simmer 10 minutes, stirring occasionally.
4. Stir in cheese and beat in egg yolks. Continue beating until mixture is smooth, hot, and thick. Stir in salt and cayenne.
5. Serve warm with ham, tomatoes, and zucchini for dippers.
4 TO 6 SERVINGS

Creamy Corn Dip

2 tablespooons butter or
  margarine
2 tablespoons finely chopped
  green pepper
¼ cup flour
¼ teaspoon salt
⅛ teaspoon cayenne pepper
1½ cups chicken broth
  (dissolve 1 chicken
  bouillon cube in 1½ cups

boiling water)
4 ounces Swiss cheese,
  shredded (about 1 cup)
1 can (8 ounces) cream-style
  corn
4 drops Tabasco
Party rye bread, buttered and
  toasted, or crusty French
  bread cubes

1. Heat butter in cooking pan of a chafing dish over medium heat. Add green pepper and cook until just tender, occasionally moving and turning with a spoon. Blend in flour, salt, and cayenne. Heat until mixture bubbles, stirring constantly.
2. Blend in chicken broth, cooking and stirring until sauce thickens.
3. Remove from heat. Add cheese all at one time, stirring until cheese is melted. Stir in corn and Tabasco.
4. Keep warm over hot water while serving.
ABOUT 6 SERVINGS

Crêpes Benedict

Buttermilk Fondue

1 pound Swiss cheese,
  shredded (about 4 cups)
3 tablespoons cornstarch
½ teaspoon salt
⅛ teaspoon white pepper

¼ teaspoon dry mustard
2 cups buttermilk
1 clove garlic, split in half
1 loaf dark rye bread, cut
  into 1-inch cubes

1. Toss cheese with a mixture of cornstarch, salt, pepper, and dry mustard. Set aside.
2. In a fondue saucepan, heat buttermilk with garlic over low heat. When hot, remove garlic and add cheese; stir constantly until cheese is melted.
3. Keep fondue warm over low heat while dipping bread cubes.
4 TO 6 SERVINGS

Rinktum Ditty with Beans

1 can (10¾ ounces) con-
  densed tomato soup
8 ounces sharp Cheddar
  cheese, shredded (about 2
  cups)
¼ teaspoon dry mustard
½ teaspoon Worcestershire

sauce
2 drops Tabasco
1 egg, slightly beaten
2 cups cooked and drained
  large white dried beans
Salt and pepper

1. Heat soup, cheese, and seasonings over hot water in cooking pan of chafing dish.
2. When cheese is melted, quickly add beaten egg, stirring constantly until smooth. Stir in the cooked, drained beans. Season to taste.
3. Heat over simmering water until piping hot and serve over **crisp hot toast.**

Note: If desired, cooked red or pinto beans may be substituted for white beans.

Cheese Rabbit Fondue

1 small clove garlic
2 cups beer
1 pound sharp Cheddar
  cheese, shredded (about 4
  cups)
3 tablespoons flour
1 teaspoon Worcestershire
  sauce

½ teaspoon dry mustard
2 tablespoons chopped
  chives or green onion top
  (optional)
1 loaf sourdough French
  bread, cut into 1-inch
  cubes

1. Rub inside of a nonmetal fondue pot with garlic; discard garlic. Heat beer in the pot until almost boiling.
2. Dredge cheese in flour and add about ½ cup at a time, stirring until cheese is melted and blended before adding more.
3. When mixture is smooth and thickened, stir in Worcestershire sauce and dry mustard.
4. Sprinkle chives on top and serve with bread cubes. Keep fondue warm while serving.
4 TO 6 SERVINGS

Tasty Rabbit

3 tablespoons butter or
  margarine
¼ cup flour
½ teaspoon dry mustard
1 teaspoon salt
¼ teaspoon pepper
2 cups milk

6 ounces Cheddar cheese,
  shredded (about 1½ cups)
¼ cup diced pimento
1 cup (3½ ounces) shredded
  diced beef
6 to 8 slices toast, buttered

1. Heat butter in cooking pan of a chafing dish. Remove from heat and blend in flour, dry mustard, salt, and pepper; heat and stir until bubbly.
2. Gradually add milk, stirring until smooth. Cook over medium heat, stirring constantly, until mixture thickens. Cook 1 to 2 minutes longer.
3. Place over simmering water and add cheese, stirring until melted. Stir in pimento and dried beef. Serve immediately over buttered toast.
6 TO 8 SERVINGS

Brunch Egg Casserole

2 cups unflavored croutons
1 cup (4 ounces) shredded
  Cheddar cheese
4 eggs
2 cups milk
½ teaspoon salt

⅛ teaspoon onion powder
½ teaspoon prepared
  mustard
Dash pepper
8 bacon slices, cooked,
  drained, and crumbled

1. Combine croutons and cheese. Place in bottom of a 10x6-inch baking dish.
2. Lightly beat together eggs, milk, salt, onion powder, mustard, and pepper. Pour over crouton-cheese mixture. Sprinkle bacon over top.
3. Bake, uncovered, at 325°F 55 to 60 minutes, or until set. Serve with **broiled tomato halves.**
6 SERVINGS

Welsh Rabbit with East Indian Flavor

1 tablespoon butter
1 pound sharp Cheddar
  cheese, shredded (about 4
  cups)
½ teaspoon Worcestershire
  sauce

½ teaspoon dry mustard
Few grains cayenne pepper
⅓ cup milk
2 tablespoons chutney
6 slices bread, toasted

1. Heat butter in cooking pan of a chafing dish over low heat. Add cheese all at one time and stir occasionally until cheese begins to melt.
2. Place over direct heat of chafing dish and blend in Worcestershire sauce, dry mustard, and cayenne pepper. Add milk gradually, stirring constantly until mixture is smooth and cheese is melted.
3. Spread a teaspoon of chutney over each slice of toast. Top with cheese mixture. Serve immediately. Top each serving with a poached egg, if desired.
6 SERVINGS

Yogurt Cheese

2 quarts yogurt   Honey (optional)
Salt to taste

1. Pour yogurt into a bag made of several thicknesses of cheesecloth. Suspend bag from a nail or sink faucet and drain several hours or overnight.
2. Remove cheese from bag. Chill.
3. To serve, sprinkle lightly with salt and spread on bread. Spoon honey over top.

Cottage Cheese Croquettes

3 tablespoons butter or margarine	1 cup elbow macaroni, cooked and drained
¼ cup flour	1 pound (2 cups) creamed cottage cheese
1 teaspoon salt	
Dash pepper	1½ cups corn-flake crumbs (more if needed)
½ teaspoon dill weed	
1 cup milk	3 eggs, slightly beaten
1 teaspoon instant minced onion	Oil for deep frying

1. In a 3-quart saucepan, melt butter. Blend in flour, salt, pepper, and dill weed.
2. Combine milk with onion. Add gradually to flour mixture, stirring constantly. Stir while cooking until thickened. Reduce heat and cook 2 minutes longer.
3. Stir in macaroni and cheese; mix well. Chill 1 to 2 hours, or until firm enough to handle.
4. Shape into 12 croquettes, coating with crumbs as soon as shaped. Dip in egg and again in crumbs.
5. Fill wok not more than half full with oil. Slowly heat oil to 375°F. Fry 3 croquettes at a time in hot oil or until golden brown. Remove to a baking sheet lined with paper towels to drain. When all croquettes are drained, remove paper towels.
6. Bake croquettes at 350°F 10 to 15 minutes. Serve hot.
6 SERVINGS

Note: If desired, fine dry bread crumbs can be substituted for the corn-flake crumbs.

Bacon 'n' Egg Croquettes

3 tablespoons butter or margarine	6 hard-cooked eggs, coarsely chopped
2 tablespoons chopped onion	8 slices bacon, cooked and finely crumbled
3 tablespoons flour	1 egg, fork beaten
½ teaspoon salt	2 tablespoons water
⅛ teaspoon pepper	⅓ cup fine dry bread or cracker crumbs
¾ teaspoon dry mustard	
¾ cup milk	Oil for deep frying

1. Melt butter in a saucepan; stir in onion and cook about 2 minutes, or until tender. Stir in a mixture of flour, salt, pepper, and dry mustard. Heat until bubbly. Add milk gradually, stirring constantly. Cook and stir until mixture forms a ball.
2. Remove from heat and stir in chopped eggs and crumbled bacon. Refrigerate about 1 hour, or until chilled.
3. Shape into 8 croquettes (balls or cones). Mix egg with water. Roll croquettes in crumbs, dip into egg, and roll again in crumbs.
4. Fill a large wok no more than half full with oil. Slowly heat to 385°F. Fry croquettes without crowding in the hot oil 2 minutes, or until golden. Remove croquettes with a slotted spoon; drain over fat and place on paper towel to drain.
4 SERVINGS

Herbed Egg Croquettes: Follow recipe for Bacon 'n' Egg Croquettes. Decrease mustard to ¼ teaspoon and bacon to 4 slices. Add ½ **teaspoon summer savory,** crushed, with mustard and **4 teaspoons snipped parsley** with chopped egg.

Maria's Filled Loaf

1 unsliced loaf white bread	liquid
2 tablespoons melted butter	Salt
	Pepper
Crab Meat Stew:	½ teaspoon parsley
2 tablespoons butter	12 ounces crab meat
3 tablespoons flour	6 tablespoons coarsely grated cheddar cheese
1½ cups milk and crab meat	

1. Cut off the top part of the bread and remove most of the dough from the lower part. Brush the crust with melted butter inside and out.
2. Heat butter and flour for the stew for a few minutes over low heat. Add milk and crab meat liquid and bring mixture to a boil for a few minutes. Reduce to low heat.
3. Season with salt, pepper, parsley and stir in the crab meat.
4. Fill the loaf with the stew and sprinkle the grated cheese on top. Bake in a 450°F oven for 8 to 10 minutes until it has turned light brown. Serve with a **green salad** and **lemon wedges.**
SERVES 6

Scrambled Eggs

6 eggs
6 tablespoons milk, cream, or undiluted evaporated milk
¾ teaspoon salt
⅛ teaspoon pepper
3 tablespoons butter or margarine

1. Beat the eggs, milk, salt, and pepper together until blended.
2. Heat an 8- or 10-inch skillet until hot enough to sizzle a drop of water. Melt butter in skillet.
3. Pour egg mixture into skillet and cook over low heat. With a spatula, lift mixture from bottom and sides of skillet as it thickens, allowing uncooked portion to flow to bottom. Cook until eggs are thick and creamy.

4 SERVINGS

Cheddar-Beer Omelet

⅓ cup beer
¼ teaspoon salt
⅓ teaspoon Tabasco
6 eggs
½ cup shredded Cheddar cheese
2 to 3 tablespoons butter

1. Combine beer, salt, and Tabasco in a bowl. Add eggs to mixture and beat with a rotary beater only until well blended, do not beat until frothy.
2. Place 1 tablespoon butter, more if needed, in a wok and heat. Pour in half the egg mixture and stir rapidly with a fork until mixture begins to set.
3. Sprinkle with half the cheese. When omelet is cooked but top is still moist, fold over both sides of omelet towards center and place on a warm platter while making other omelet.

4 TO 6 SERVINGS

Cheese-Tomato Supper Dish

⅔ cup butter or margarine
¼ cup minced onion
1 cup mushrooms, cleaned and sliced
2 tablespoons flour
½ teaspoon dry mustard
¼ teaspoon salt
Few grains cayenne pepper
½ cup milk
½ teaspoon Worcestershire
sauce
1 can (10¾ ounces) condensed tomato soup
¾ pound sharp Cheddar cheese, shredded (about 3 cups)
6 hard-cooked eggs, cut into quarters lengthwise
1 tablespoon minced parsley

1. Heat butter in cooking pan of chafing dish over medium heat. Add onion and mushrooms. Cook over medium heat, stirring occasionally, until mushrooms are tender. With a slotted spoon, remove mushrooms to a bowl; set aside.
2. Blend a mixture of flour, dry mustard, salt, and cayenne pepper into cooking pan. Heat until mixture bubbles and remove from heat.
3. Gradually add milk, Worcestershire sauce, and condensed soup while stirring. Place cooking pan over simmering water. Add cheese all at once, and stir until cheese is melted.
4. Blend in the hard-cooked eggs and reserved mushrooms. Garnish with parsley and serve with **toast fingers** or **bread sticks.**

ABOUT 8 SERVINGS

Poached Eggs

Eggs

1. Grease bottom of a deep skillet. Pour in water to a depth of 2 inches. Bring water to boiling; reduce heat to keep water at simmering point.
2. Break each egg into a saucer or small dish and quickly slip into water, holding the saucer close to the surface of the water. Cook 3 to 5 minutes, depending upon firmness desired.
3. Carefully remove egg with a slotted spoon or pancake turner. Drain by holding spoon on absorbent paper for a few seconds.
4. Season with **salt** and **pepper.** Serve immediately.

Shrimp-Walnut Rabbit

2 tablespoons butter or margarine
1 green onion including top, thinly sliced
1 cup thinly sliced celery
2 tablespoons flour
½ teaspoon salt
1 cup milk
Pinch cayenne pepper
2 tablespoons dry white wine
½ cup shredded sharp Cheddar cheese
1 cup cleaned cooked shrimp
½ cup coarsely chopped walnuts

1. In cooking pan of a chafing dish, melt butter. Stir in onion and celery. Cook 5 minutes over medium heat.
2. Blend in flour and salt. Add milk gradually. Cook over medium heat, stirring constantly, until mixture boils and is thickened.
3. Stir in cayenne, wine, and cheese. Add shrimp and walnuts. Heat thoroughly over simmering water; do not boil.
4. Serve in heated **patty shells.**

4 SERVINGS

Eggs Creole

¼ cup chopped onion
½ cup finely diced green pepper
1 tablespoon butter or margarine
1 can (8 ounces) tomato sauce
1 jar (4 ounces) whole
mushrooms, (undrained)
⅛ teaspoon thyme
¼ teaspoon salt
⅛ teaspoon pepper
4 eggs
English muffins, split, toasted, and buttered

1. Cook onion and green pepper in butter in cooking pan of a chafing dish over medium heat about 3 minutes.
2. Add tomato sauce, mushrooms, thyme, salt, and pepper to onion and green pepper; mix well. Heat to simmering.
3. Break eggs, one at a time, into a saucer and gently slip egg into the hot mixture.
4. Simmer, covered, over low heat about 5 minutes, then place over simmering water and heat, covered, until egg whites are set.
5. To serve, place an egg on each English muffin half and top with sauce.

4 SERVINGS

Croustade Basket

1 loaf unsliced bread   margarine
⅓ cup melted butter or

1. Neatly trim the crusts from top and sides of loaf. Using a sharp pointed knife, hollow out center, leaving 1-inch sides and bottom.
2. Brush inside and out with melted butter. Place on a baking sheet.
3. Toast in a 400°F oven 10 to 15 minutes, or until golden brown and crisp. Fill with **Scrambled Eggs** (double recipe), page 202, and serve with **Mushroom-Caraway Sauce,** opposite.

Miniature Croustades: Trim crusts from top and sides of loaf of unsliced bread; cut into cubes slightly larger than 1 inch. Using a serrated knife, hollow out centers. Brush cases inside and out with a mixture of **½ cup butter** and **¼ teaspoon garlic salt.** Set on a baking sheet. Toast in a 350°F oven 15 to 20 minutes, turning occasionally, until golden brown and crisp. Cool. Use as cases for appetizers.

Mushroom-Caraway Sauce

1 can (10½ ounces) condensed cream of mushroom soup
1 bottle (7 ounces) lemon-lime carbonated beverage
¼ cup heavy cream

¾ teaspoon caraway seed
¼ teaspoon onion salt
⅛ teaspoon freshly ground black pepper
1¾ teaspoons wine vinegar

1. Put mushroom soup into a heavy saucepan; stir until smooth.
2. Gradually add lemon-lime carbonated beverage and then cream, stirring constantly.
3. Blend in the remaining ingredients and heat until mixture begins to simmer.
ABOUT 2 CUPS

Peasant Omelette

4 to 5 slices thick bacon	Pepper
4 boiled potatoes	2 tomatoes, sliced
1 onion	2 ounces Swiss cheese,
4 eggs	grated
4 tablespoons milk	Parsley
Salt	

1. Chop the onion and cut the potatoes in cubes.
2. Brown the bacon, potatoes, and onion in a skillet.
3. Beat the eggs with milk. Add salt and pepper to taste and pour over the ingredients in the skillet.
4. Put sliced tomatoes on top and sprinkle with cheese. Make sure eggs are evenly distributed in the skillet. Cook until omelette is creamy on the surface. About 10 minutes.
5. Serve with cut parsley on top.

Eggs Pisto Style

1 large clove garlic	2 cups small cubes yellow
1 cup thinly sliced onion	summer squash
1 cup slivered green pepper	2 cups finely cut peeled ripe
½ cup olive oil	tomatoes
1 cup thin raw potato strips	2 teaspoons salt
1 tablespoon chopped	1 teaspoon sugar
parsley	⅛ teaspoon pepper
⅓ cup (2 ounces) diced	6 eggs, beaten
cooked ham	

1. Add garlic, onion, and green pepper to heated olive oil in a large wok; cook until softened, then remove garlic.
2. Add remaining ingredients except eggs to wok; cook over medium heat, stirring frequently, about 10 minutes, or until squash is just tender.
3. Pour beaten eggs into vegetables, and cook over low heat. With a spatula, lift mixture from bottom and sides as it thickens, allowing uncooked portion to flow to bottom. Cook until eggs are thick and creamy.

6 SERVINGS

Scrambled Eggs Deluxe

6 eggs	¼ cup finely shredded Ched-
6 tablespoons milk, cream,	dar cheese
or undiluted evaporated	3 tablespoons butter or
milk	margarine
¾ teaspoon salt	1 medium-size firm ripe
⅛ teaspoon pepper	tomato, peeled and cut into
½ teaspoon Worcestershire	small cubes
sauce	1 cup ¼- to ½-inch croutons

1. Beat eggs, milk, salt, pepper, and Worcestershire sauce together until blended. Stir in cheese.
2. Melt butter in wok over very low heat. Pour egg mixture into wok and cook over low heat. With a spatula, lift mixture from bottom and sides of wok as eggs cook, allowing uncooked portion to flow to bottom. Cook eggs until they are thick and creamy.
3. Before removing from heat, gently stir in tomato and croutons.

4 TO 6 SERVINGS

Cheese Tricorn Rolls

1 package active dry yeast	¼ cup plus 2 tablespoons
¼ cup warm water, 110°F to	shortening
115°F (If using compressed	1 tablespoon lemon juice
yeast, soften 1 cake in ¼	½ cup sugar
cup lukewarm water, 80°F	½ teaspoon salt
to 85°F)	1 egg
¼ cup warm water	1 egg white
¾ cup sifted all-purpose flour	2¼ cups sifted all-purpose
4 ounces sharp Cheddar	flour
cheese (about 1 cup,	Melted butter or margarine
grated)	

1. Two baking sheets will be needed.
2. Soften yeast in ¼ cup warm water.
3. Set aside.
4. Meanwhile, pour ¼ cup warm water into a large bowl.
5. Blend in ¾ cup sifted all-purpose flour.
6. Stir softened yeast and add, mixing well. Beat until very smooth. Cover bowl with waxed paper and a clean towel and let stand in warm place (about 80°F) 1½ to 2 hours.
7. Meanwhile, grate cheese and set aside.
8. Cream shortening and lemon juice until blended.
9. Add gradually, creaming until fluffy after each addition, a mixture of sugar and salt.
10. Beat egg and egg white until thick.
11. Add beaten eggs in thirds to sugar mixture, beating thoroughly after each addition. Add yeast mixture, mixing well.
12. Measure 2¼ cups sifted all-purpose flour.
13. Add about one-half the flour to yeast mixture and beat until very smooth. Blend in grated cheese, mixing thoroughly. Beat in enough of the remaining flour to make a soft dough. Turn dough onto a lightly floured surface and allow it to rest 5 to 10 minutes.
14. Knead.
15. Shape dough into a smooth ball and put into a greased deep bowl. Turn dough to bring greased surface to top. Cover with waxed paper and a clean towel and let stand in a warm place (about 80°F) until dough is doubled.
16. Grease the baking sheets.
17. Punch dough down with fist. Turn out onto a lightly floured surface, cover and allow dough to rest 5 to 10 minutes.
18. Roll dough ¼ inch thick. Cut into 3-inch squares. Crease each square diagonally across center by pressing with handle of knife or wooden spoon. Fold squares on creases to form triangles; press edges to seal. Place rolls on baking sheets and brush tops with melted butter or margarine.
19. Cover rolls with waxed paper and towel and let rise again until doubled.
20. Bake at 350°F 40 to 45 minutes, or until golden brown.

2 DOZEN TRICORN ROLLS

Baked Deviled Eggs

6 hard-cooked eggs	margarine
1¼ cups sour cream	¼ cup chopped pimento
2 teaspoons prepared mustard	1 can (10¾ ounces) condensed cream of mushroom soup
¼ teaspoon salt	
½ cup chopped green pepper	½ cup (2 ounces) shredded Cheddar cheese
¼ cup chopped onion	Paprika
2 tablespoons butter or	

1. Shell eggs and split in half lengthwise. Remove yolks; mash with fork. Combine with ¼ cup sour cream, mustard, and salt. Refill egg whites.
2. Sauté green pepper and onion in butter in a skillet. Stir in pimento, soup, and remaining 1 cup sour cream.
3. Pour into a 12x8-inch baking dish. Place deviled eggs on top, yolk side up. Sprinkle with cheese and paprika.
4. Bake, uncovered, at 325°F 25 minutes, or until heated through. Serve over **Holland rusks** with **hot cooked asparagus spears.**
6 SERVINGS

Cheese Mousse

¾ cup heavy cream	*Garnish:*
7 ounces cream cheese	Watercress
1 package unflavored gelatin	2 sliced cucumbers
½ teaspoon salt	6 radishes
½ teaspoon paprika	
1 tablespoon chopped chives	

1. Whip the heavy cream till stiff. Stir in the cream cheese until smooth and add half the cream to it.
2. Place the gelatin in 2 tablespoons water and dissolve over low heat. Stir the gelatin in the cream and cream cheese mixture and add the rest of the whipped cream. Add seasonings.
3. Pour the cheese cream into a water-rinsed ring mold. Place in refrigerature to set. Serve garnished with **watercress, cucumbers** and **radishes.**
SERVES 4

Cheese Soufflé I

¼ cup flour
¾ teaspoon salt
½ teaspoon dry mustard
⅛ teaspoon paprika
1⅔ cups (13-ounce can) evaporated milk

¼ teaspoon Tabasco
2 cups coarsely shredded sharp Cheddar cheese (about 8 ounces)
6 egg yolks, well beaten
6 egg whites

1. Blend the flour, salt, dry mustard, and paprika in a heavy saucepan. Add the evaporated milk gradually, then the Tabasco, stirring until smooth. Bring to boiling; stir and cook 1 to 2 minutes.
2. Add cheese all at one time and stir until cheese is melted. Remove from heat.
3. Pour sauce slowly into beaten egg yolks, beating constantly.
4. Beat egg whites until stiff, not dry, peaks are formed. Spoon the sauce over egg whites and fold together until just blended. Turn into an ungreased 2-quart soufflé dish (deep casserole with straight sides). About 1½ inches from edge of dish, draw a circle by inserting the tip of a spoon 1 inch into the mixture to form a "top hat."
5. Bake at 300°F 55 to 60 minutes, or until a knife inserted halfway between center and edge of soufflé comes out clean.
ABOUT 6 SERVINGS

Welsh Rabbit I

⅔ cup lukewarm beer (measured without foam)
1 pound sharp Cheddar cheese (about 4 cups, shredded)
1 tablespoon butter

½ teaspoon Worcestershire sauce
½ teaspoon dry mustard
Few grains cayenne pepper
Crisp toast slices

1. Have beer ready.
2. Shred Cheddar cheese and set aside.
3. Melt butter in top of a double boiler over simmering water.
4. Add cheese all at one time and stir occasionally until cheese begins to melt. Blend in Worcestershire sauce, dry mustard, and cayenne pepper.
5. As soon as cheese begins to melt, add very gradually, stirring constantly, ½ to ⅔ cup beer.
6. As soon as beer is blended in and mixture is smooth, serve immediately over crisp toast slices.

Welsh Rabbit II: Follow recipe for Welsh Rabbit. Substitute **milk** for the beer.

Welsh Rabbit III: Follow recipe for Welsh Rabbit. Substitute **process cheese food** or **sharp process Cheddar cheese** for the sharp Cheddar cheese and **milk** for the beer.

Glorified Welsh Rabbit: Follow recipe for Welsh Rabbit or either variation. Top each serving with a slice of **tomato**, two slices panbroiled **bacon** and a sprig of **parsley**.

Egg Foo Yong

1 cup finely diced cooked ham, roast pork, or chicken
1 cup drained canned bean sprouts
¾ cup chopped onion
1 tablespoon soy sauce
½ teaspoon monosodium glutamate

¼ to ½ teaspoon salt (reduce if using ham)
6 eggs, slightly beaten
Fat or cooking oil (about 2 tablespoons or enough to form an ⅛-inch layer)
Foo Yong Sauce

1. Mix ham, bean sprouts, onion, soy sauce, monosodium glutamate, and salt. Stir in eggs.
2. Heat fat in a large wok. Drop a fourth of the mixture into the hot fat to form a patty. Cook about 5 minutes, or until browned on one side; turn and brown other side.
3. Remove patty from wok; drain over fat a few seconds. Transfer to a warm heat-resistant platter; keep warm in a 200°F oven while cooking remaining patties.
4. Pour hot sauce over the patties and serve with **hot fluffy rice** and additional soy sauce.
4 SERVINGS

Foo Yong Sauce: Blend **2 tablespoons cornstarch, 1 tablespoon cold water, 2 teaspoons soy sauce,** and **1 teaspoon molasses** in a small saucepan. Stir in **1 cup chicken broth.** Bring to boiling, stirring constantly. Boil 3 minutes, or until sauce is thickened. Keep hot.
¾ CUP SAUCE

Spinach-Bacon Soufflé

2 cups firmly packed, finely chopped fresh spinach leaves (dry the leaves before chopping)
¼ cup finely chopped green onions with tops
½ pound sliced bacon, cooked, drained and crumbled
3 tablespoons butter or

margarine
¼ cup enriched all-purpose flour
½ teaspoon salt
¼ to ½ teaspoon thyme
1 cup milk
3 egg yolks, well beaten
4 egg whites
2 teaspoons shredded Parmesan cheese

1. Toss the spinach, green onions, and bacon together in a bowl; set aside.
2. Heat butter in a saucepan over low heat. Blend in flour, salt, and thyme. Stirring constantly, heat until bubbly. Add milk gradually, continuing to stir. Bring rapidly to boiling and boil 1 to 2 minutes, stirring constantly.
3. Remove from heat and blend spinach-bacon mixture into the sauce. Stir in the beaten egg yolks; set aside to cool.
4. Meanwhile, beat egg whites until rounded peaks are formed (peaks turn over slightly when beater is slowly lifted upright); do not overbeat.
5. Gently spread spinach-bacon mixture over the beaten egg whites. Carefully fold together until ingredients are just blended.
6. Turn mixture into an ungreased 2-quart soufflé dish (straight-side casserole); sprinkle top with Parmesan cheese.
7. Bake at 350°F 40 minutes, or until a knife comes out clean when inserted halfway between center and edge of soufflé and top is lightly browned. Serve immediately.
6 SERVINGS

Cheese Soufflé II

Cheese Soufflé II

½ pound sharp process
Cheddar cheese (about 2
cups, grated)
6 tablespoons butter or
margarine
6 tablespoons all-purpose
flour

¾ teaspoon dry mustard
½ teaspoon salt
⅛ teaspoon white pepper
⅛ teaspoon paprika
1½ cups milk
6 egg yolks
6 egg whites

1. Set out a 2-quart casserole; do not grease.
2. Grate Cheddar cheese and set aside.
3. Melt butter or margarine in a saucepan over low heat.
4. Blend in flour, dry mustard, salt, white pepper, and paprika.
5. Heat until mixture bubbles. Remove from heat. Add milk gradually, while stirring constantly.
6. Return to heat and bring rapidly to boiling, stirring constantly; cook 1 to 2 minutes longer. Cool slightly and add the grated cheese all at one time. Stir rapidly until cheese is melted.
7. Beat egg yolks until thick and lemon-colored.
8. Slowly spoon sauce into egg yolks while stirring vigorously.
9. Beat egg whites until rounded peaks are formed and whites do not slide when bowl is partially inverted.
10. Gently spread egg-yolk mixture over beaten egg whites. Carefully fold together until just blended. Turn mixture into casserole. Insert the tip of a spoon 1 inch deep in mixture, 1 to 1½ inches from edge; run a line around mixture.

(Center part of soufflé will form a "hat").
11. Bake at 300°F 1 to 1¼ hours, or until a silver knife comes out clean when inserted halfway between center and edge of soufflé.
12. Serve at once, while "top hat" is at its height.
8 TO 10 SERVINGS

Cheese-Bacon Soufflé: Follow recipe for Cheese Soufflé. Dice and panbroil until crisp 5 slices **bacon.** When bacon is crisped and browned, remove from skillet, set aside on absorbent paper to drain thoroughly. Substitute 3 tablespoons of the reserved **bacon fat** for 3 tablespoons butter or margarine. Fold bacon pieces into egg whites with sauce. Proceed as in recipe.

Shirred Eggs with Feta

1 tablespoon butter
2 eggs

¼ cup crumbled feta cheese
Dash pepper

1. Melt butter in a ramekin or baking dish. Add eggs. Sprinkle with cheese. Season with pepper.
2. Bake at 350°F about 10 minutes, or until eggs are done as desired.
1 SERVING

Beer Drinker's Deep-Pan Pizza

Crust:
1 cup warm beer (110° to 120°F)
4 tablespoons olive or salad oil
1 tablespoon sugar
1½ teaspoons salt
1 package active dry yeast
2¾ to 3¼ cups all-purpose flour
2 tablespoons cornmeal

Topping:
10 to 12 ounces mozzarella cheese, shredded or thinly sliced
1 can (6 ounces) tomato paste
½ cup beer
2 teaspoons oregano
1 teaspoon fennel seed (optional)
½ teaspoon sugar
¾ to 1 pound bulk pork or Italian sausage, broken up
½ cup grated Parmesan cheese

1. For crust, combine in a large bowl the warm beer, 2 tablespoons oil, sugar, salt, and yeast. Add 1½ cups flour; beat until smooth. Stir in enough additional flour to make a fairly stiff dough.
2. Turn dough out onto a lightly floured surface. Knead until smooth and elastic (about 5 minutes). Place dough in a greased bowl, turning once to grease top. Cover and let rise in warm place (85°F) until double in bulk (about 1 hour).
3. Punch dough down. (For 2 small pizzas, divide in half.) Using 2 tablespoons oil, coat a 14-inch round deep pizza pan. (Or use two 9-inch round cake pans.) Sprinkle with cornmeal. Pat dough into pan, pinching up a rim around the edge. Cover and let rise in a warm place until double in bulk (about 30 minutes).
4. For topping, mix tomato paste, beer, oregano, fennel seed, and sugar. Cover pizza dough evenly with mozzarella cheese; evenly spoon on tomato paste mixture. Sprinkle with sausage, then top with Parmesan cheese.
5. Bake at 450°F 15 to 20 minutes, or until crust is browned and sausage is cooked.
ONE LARGE OR 2 SMALL PIZZAS; 4 SERVINGS

Note: Alternate toppings could be (1) **1 can (4 ounces) sliced mushrooms, drained,** or (2) **8 anchovies** plus ⅓ **cup chopped ripe olives,** or (3) ½ **pound sliced pepperoni.** Omit or reduce the sausage, but include cheeses and tomato sauce.

Pizza

Dough:
1 package active dry yeast
½ teaspoon salt
2 tablespoons salad oil
½ cup warm water
1½ cups flour

Filling:
1 pound ground beef

3 tomatoes, sliced
1 teaspoon tarragon, or oregano
6 slices mozzarella cheese
½ cup Parmesan cheese, grated
1 can anchovy fillets (optional)

1. Crumble yeast in bowl and stir it with ½ teaspoon salt and 2 tablespoons oil. Add ½ cup warm water so that yeast dissolves thoroughly.
2. Mix in the flour and work the dough together. Set aside to rise for 30 minutes.
3. Roll out the dough and place on a cookie sheet.
4. Spread the ground beef on the dough and arrange the sliced tomatoes on top. Sprinkle with tarragon.
5. Put cheese slices on top of the tomatoes and sprinkle on a thick layer of the grated cheese. Anchovy fillets can also be put on the tomatoes before the cheese is added. Bake in a 450°F oven for 15 to 20 minutes until the cheese is melted, and the meat brown.
SERVES 4

Pear and Frozen Cheese Salad

4 ounces Roquefort or blue cheese (1 cup, crumbled)
½ cup chopped celery
3 ounces (1 package) cream cheese
¼ cup mayonnaise
1 tablespoon lemon juice
¼ teaspoon salt

⅛ teaspoon pepper
½ cup chilled whipping cream
4 chilled, ripe Bartlett pears
Lemon juice
Curly endive, watercress, or other salad greens
French dressing

1. Crumble Roquefort or blue cheese and set aside.
2. Prepare celery and set aside.
3. Beat cream cheese until fluffy.
4. Mix in mayonnaise and lemon juice, and a mixture of salt and pepper, stirring until thoroughly blended after each addition.
5. Stir in the crumbled cheese and chopped celery. Set mixture aside.
6. Using a chilled bowl and beater, beat whipping cream until cream is of medium consistency (piles softly).
7. Gently fold into cheese mixture. Turn into a chilled refrigerator tray. Put into freezing compartment of refrigerator and freeze until cheese mixture is firm.
8. When ready to serve, cut frozen cheese into 1-inch cubes.
9. For Bartlett Pear Salad – Rinse well, cut into halves and core Bartlett pears.
10. Brush cut sides of pears with lemon juice.
11. Place salad greens on each of 8 chilled salad plates.
12. Put one pear half, cut side up, on each plate. Place two or three frozen Roquefort or blue cheese cubes in hollow of each pear half. Or arrange greens, pear halves and cheese cubes on a large chilled serving plate.
13. Serve immediately with French dressing.
8 SERVINGS

Welsh Rabbit in Chafing Dish

¼ cup butter
8 cups shredded sharp Cheddar cheese (about 2 pounds)
2 teaspoons Worcestershire sauce

1 teaspoon dry mustard
Few grains cayenne pepper
4 eggs, slightly beaten
1 cup light cream or half-and-half

1. In a chafing dish blazer over simmering water, melt butter. Add cheese and heat, stirring occasionally, until cheese is melted. Mix in Worcestershire sauce, dry mustard, and cayenne pepper.
2. Blend eggs and cream; strain. Mix into melted cheese. Cook until thick, stirring frequently.
3. Garnish with **parsley sprigs.** Serve over toasted **English muffin halves.**
6 CUPS WELSH RABBIT

Royal Swiss Cheese Salad Bowl

½ pound natural Swiss cheese
French dressing

Bibb lettuce
Leaf lettuce
Watercress

1. Cut Swiss cheese into thin strips.
2. Put cheese into a shallow bowl and cover with French dressing.
3. Marinate in refrigerator 1 hour.
4. Wash, discard bruised leaves from bibb lettuce, leaf lettuce, and watercress, drain thoroughly and pat dry (using as much of each green as desired).
5. Arrange bibb and leaf lettuce in a large salad bowl. Fill center with watercress. Put salad bowl into plastic bag or cover with aluminum foil. Chill in refrigerator at least 1 hour.
6. Drain marinated cheese strips. Arrange in salad bowl on both sides of watercress. Serve with additional French dressing.

Shirred Eggs with Sausage and Cheese

Salami or bologna, thinly sliced
2 tablespoons butter or margarine

Swiss or Cheddar cheese, thinly sliced
6 eggs

1. Brown salami lightly in the butter in a skillet; reserve drippings in skillet.
2. Line a 9-inch pie plate with salami and add an even layer of cheese.
3. Break and slip eggs, one at a time, onto the cheese. Pour drippings over all. Season with **salt** and **pepper** and drizzle with **Worcestershire sauce.**
4. Bake at 325°F about 22 minutes, or until eggs are as firm as desired. Serve immediately with **parsley-buttered toast.**
6 SERVINGS

Fluffy Cheese Potatoes

6 medium-size (about 2 pounds) baking potatoes
1 tablespoon fat
2 ounces process Swiss cheese (about ½ cup, shredded)
4 tablespoons butter or margarine
½ cup hot milk or cream

¾ teaspoon salt
¼ teaspoon paprika
¼ teaspoon pepper
8 slices crisp, panbroiled bacon, crumbled
1 tablespoon finely chopped onion
Finely chopped parsley

1. Wash and scrub potatoes with a vegetable brush.
2. Dry potatoes with absorbent paper and rub with fat.
3. Place potatoes on rack in oven.
4. Bake at 425°F 45 to 60 minutes, or until potatoes are soft when pressed with the fingers (protected by paper napkin).
5. While potatoes bake, shred cheese and set aside.
6. Remove potatoes from oven. To make each potato mealy, gently roll potatoes back and forth on a flat surface. Cut large potatoes into halves lengthwise or cut a thin lengthwise slice from each smaller potato. With a spoon, scoop out inside without breaking skin. Mash thoroughly or rice. Whip in, in order, butter or margarine, milk or cream (adding gradually) and a mixture of salt, paprika, and pepper until mixture is fluffy.
7. Mix in the shredded cheese and bacon and onion.
8. Pile mixture lightly into potato skins, leaving tops uneven.
9. Return potatoes to oven for 8 to 10 minutes, or until thoroughly heated.
10. Sprinkle with parsley.
6 SERVINGS

Cheddar Cheese Potatoes: Follow recipe for Fluffy Cheese Potatoes. Substitute ⅓ cup grated **sharp Cheddar cheese** for the Swiss cheese.

Cheddar Cheese-Olive Potatoes: Follow recipe for Fluffy Cheese Potatoes. Substitute ⅓ cup grated **sharp Cheddar cheese** for the Swiss cheese. Omit the bacon and onion and add 8 to 10 **stuffed olives,** finely chopped, with the cheese. If desired, omit parsley and top potatoes with ⅓ cup crushed buttered **corn flakes** or **crumbs** before baking.

Eggnog Fondue

2 eggs, beaten
2 tablespoons sugar or honey
⅛ teaspoon salt
1½ cups milk
½ teaspoon vanilla extract

3 tablespoons arrowroot
3 tablespoons dark rum
Nutmeg
Fruitcake, cut into ¾-inch pieces

1. Beat together eggs, sugar, and salt. Stir in milk and vanilla extract.
2. Pour eggnog into a nonmetal fondue pot. Mix arrowroot with 1 tablespoon rum and stir into the eggnog.
3. Cook over medium heat until mixture thickens, stirring occasionally. Stir in remaining rum.
4. Keep fondue warm while dipping fruitcake pieces.
6 TO 8 SERVINGS

Eggs Florentine à l'Orange

1 tablespoon butter or margarine	1 teaspoon salt
½ cup chopped onion	⅛ teaspoon pepper
¼ pound mushrooms, cleaned and sliced	1 cup Florida orange sections*
1 package (10 ounces) frozen chopped spinach, thawed and drained	4 eggs Salt Pepper

1. Melt butter in medium saucepan. Add onions and cook until tender; add mushrooms and cook 5 minutes. Stir in spinach, salt, pepper, and orange sections.
2. Divide equally among 4 buttered ramekins or individual shallow baking dishes, making a depression in the center of each.
3. Bake in a 350°F oven 15 to 20 minutes, or until hot.
4. Add 1 egg to the depression in each dish; sprinkle with additional salt and pepper. Bake 7 to 10 minutes longer, or until egg white is set.
4 SERVINGS

*To section Florida oranges, cut off peel round and round spiral fashion. Go over fruit again, removing any remaining white membrane. Cut along side of each dividing membrane from outside to middle of core. Remove section by section over a bowl; reserve juice for other use.

French Omelet I

6 eggs	⅛ teaspoon black pepper
6 tablespoons milk or water	3 tablespoons butter or margarine
¾ teaspoon salt	

1. Beat the eggs, milk, salt, and pepper together until blended.
2. Heat an 8- to 10-inch skillet until just hot enough to sizzle a drop of water; melt butter in the skillet.
3. Pour egg mixture into skillet. As edges of omelet begin to thicken, draw cooked portions toward center with spoon or fork to allow uncooked mixture to flow to bottom of skillet, tilting skillet as necessary; do not stir.
4. When eggs are thickened but surface is still moist, increase heat to quickly brown the bottom of omelet. Loosen edges carefully and fold in half; slide onto a warm serving platter. If desired, garnish with sprigs of parsley.
4 TO 6 SERVINGS

Citrus Omelet: Follow recipe for French Omelet. Substitute **3 tablespoons lemon or orange juice** and **3 tablespoons water** for liquid.

Chicken Liver Omelet: Follow recipe for French Omelet. Just before serving, enclose in omelet ¼ **pound chicken livers** which have been coated with **seasoned flour** and browned in **butter or margarine** with **minced onion**.

Eggs Florentine à l'Orange

Puffy Cheese Omelet

4 ounces process Cheddar
cheese (about 1 cup,
grated)
2 tablespoons butter or
margarine

3 egg whites
3 tablespoons water
½ teaspoon salt
Few grains white pepper
3 egg yolks

1. Set oven temperature control at 350°F. Set out a heavy 10-inch skillet.
2. Grate Cheddar cheese and set aside.
3. Heat skillet until just hot enough to sizzle a drop of water. Heat butter or margarine in the skillet.
4. Meanwhile, beat egg whites until frothy.
5. Add water, salt, and white pepper to egg whites.
6. Continue beating until rounded peaks are formed. (The beaten egg whites should stand no longer than it takes to beat the yolks.)
7. Beat egg yolks until thick and lemon-colored.
8. Spread egg yolks over egg whites and gently fold together.
9. Turn egg mixture into skillet. Level surface gently. Cook ½ minute on top of range; lower heat and cook slowly about 10 minutes, or until lightly browned on bottom and puffy but still moist on top. Do not stir at any time.
10. Place skillet with omelet in the 350°F oven about 5 minutes. Remove and sprinkle all the grated cheese over top. Return to oven and continue until cheese is melted.
11. To serve, loosen edges with spatula, make a quick, shallow cut through center, and fold one side over. Gently slip omelet onto a warm serving platter. Or omit the shallow cut and folding, and using two forks, tear the omelet gently into wedges. Invert wedges on warm serving dish so browned side is on top.
3 SERVINGS

Cottage Cheese Omelet

6 eggs
6 tablespoons water or milk
¾ teaspoon salt
⅛ teaspoon pepper
1 cup cream-style cottage
cheese

2 tablespoons finely chopped
pimiento
1 tablespoon minced chives
3 tablespoons butter or
margarine

1. Set out a 10-inch skillet.
2. Beat eggs, water or milk, salt and pepper together until well blended but not foamy.
3. Mix cottage cheese, pimiento, and chives thoroughly and blend into egg mixture.
4. Heat skillet until just hot enough to sizzle a drop of water. Heat butter or margarine in skillet.
5. Pour egg mixture into skillet and reduce heat. As edges of omelet begin to thicken, draw cooked portions toward center with spoon or fork to allow uncooked mixture to flow to bottom of skillet. Shake and tilt skillet as necessary to aid flow of uncooked eggs. Do not stir.
6. When eggs no longer flow but surface is still moist, heat may be increased to brown bottom of omelet quickly. Loosen edges carefully and fold in half. Slide omelet onto a warm serving platter.
4 TO 6 SERVINGS

French Omelet II

6 eggs
6 tablespoons milk or water
¾ teaspoon salt

⅛ teaspoon pepper
3 tablespoons butter or
margarine

1. Set out an 8- to 10-inch skillet.
2. Beat together eggs, milk or water, salt and pepper until well blended but not foamy.
3. Heat skillet until just hot enough to sizzle a drop of water. Melt butter or margarine in skillet.
4. Pour egg mixture into skillet and reduce heat. As edges of omelet begin to thicken, with a spoon or fork draw cooked portions toward center to allow uncooked mixture to flow to bottom of skillet. Shake and tilt skillet as necessary to aid flow of uncooked eggs. Do not stir.
5. When eggs no longer flow but surface is still moist, the heat should be increased to brown quickly the bottom of omelet. Loosen edges carefully and fold in half. Slide omelet onto a warm serving platter.
6. If desired, fill omelet before folding with diced or shredded cooked meat or vegetables.
4 TO 6 SERVINGS

Mushroom Omelet: Drain, reserving liquid, contents of 8-ounce can **mushroom pieces and stems** (about 1 cup, drained). Cook mushrooms until lighty browned in a small skillet containing 3 tablespoons **butter** or **margarine**. Set aside and keep warm. Follow recipe for French Omelet, substituting **mushroom liquid** for milk or water. Spoon mushrooms over top of omelet just before folding.

Cheese Omelet: Follow recipe for French Omelet. Blend ¼ cup (1 ounce) grated **Swiss** or **Cheddar cheese** and 2 tablespoons minced **parsley** into egg mixture before pouring into skillet. Sprinkle an additional ¼ cup (1 ounce) grated **cheese** over omelet while it is cooking.

Jam or Jelly Omelet: Follow recipe for French Omelet. Just before folding omelet in half, spread omelet with ⅓ to ½ cup **apricot, strawberry** or **raspberry jam, orange marmalade, currant** or **cranberry jelly.**

Parsleyed Cheese Puff

1 cup milk
1½ teaspoons celery salt
3 cups soft ¼-inch bread
cubes
2 cups shredded Cheddar

cheese (about 8 ounces)
½ cup finely snipped parsley
4 egg yolks, well beaten
4 egg whites

1. Heat milk and celery salt over low heat until just hot.
2. Pour milk into a large bowl; immediately add bread cubes, cheese, and parsley; mix lightly.
3. Add beaten egg yolks and gently fold together.
4. Beat egg whites until stiff, not dry, peaks are formed. Gently fold with cheese mixture. Turn into a buttered 1½-quart casserole.
5. Bake at 325°F about 55 minutes, or until set. Garnish with **snipped parsley.**
ABOUT 6 SERVINGS

Swiss Cheese Fondue

1 tablespoon cornstarch
2 tablespoons kirsch
1 clove garlic, halved
2 cups Neuchâtel or other dry white wine
1 pound natural Swiss cheese, shredded (about 4 cups)
Freshly ground black pepper to taste
Ground nutmeg to taste
1 loaf French bread, cut into 1-inch cubes

1. Mix cornstarch and kirsch in a small bowl; set aside.
2. Rub the inside of a nonmetal fondue pot with cut surface of garlic. Pour in wine; place over medium heat until wine is about to simmer (do not boil).
3. Add cheese in small amounts to the hot wine, stirring constantly until cheese is melted. Heat cheese-wine mixture until bubbly.
4. Blend in cornstarch mixture and continue stirring while cooking 5 minutes, or until fondue begins to bubble; add seasoning.
5. Dip bread cubes in fondue. Keep the fondue gently bubbling throughout serving time.
ABOUT 6 SERVINGS

Cheese-Onion Pie

1 tablespoon bacon drippings or shortening
1 cup chopped onion
2 cups shredded cheese (about 8 ounces)
1 unbaked 9-inch pie shell
3 eggs, slightly beaten
¾ cup sour cream
½ teaspoon salt
Dash pepper

1. Using bacon drippings or shortening, stir-fry chopped onions until tender.
2. In bottom of pie shell, spread onion and shredded cheese.
3. Combine beaten eggs, sour cream, salt, and pepper in mixing bowl. Pour over onion-cheese mixture in pie shell.
4. Bake at 375°F 25 to 30 minutes, or until center is set. Do not overbake.
ONE 9-INCH PIE

Spinach-Cheese Bake

2 packages (10 ounces each) frozen chopped spinach
3 eggs, beaten
¼ cup enriched all-purpose flour
1 teaspoon seasoned salt
¼ teaspoon ground nutmeg
¼ teaspoon ground black pepper
2 cups (16 ounces) creamed cottage cheese
2 cups (8 ounces) shredded Swiss or Cheddar cheese

1. Cook spinach following package directions; drain.
2. Combine eggs, flour, seasoned salt, nutmeg, and pepper in a bowl. Mix in cottage cheese, Swiss cheese, and spinach.
3. Turn into a buttered 1½-quart casserole.
4. Bake at 325°F 50 to 60 minutes.
6 TO 8 SERVINGS

Cheese-Mushroom Scallop

1 4-ounce can sliced mushrooms (about ½ cup, drained)
½ pound sharp Cheddar cheese
6 slices white bread
2 tablespoons butter or margarine
Milk or cream (enough to make 1 cup liquid)
2 eggs
½ teaspoon salt
½ teaspoon paprika
⅛ teaspoon pepper

1. Grease a 1½-quart casserole.
2. Set mushrooms aside to drain, reserving liquid.
3. Cut Cheddar cheese into ½-inch slices.
4. Trim crusts from white bread and cut into thirds.
5. Arrange some bread fingers on bottom of casserole. Cover with a layer of one-half the cheese and mushrooms. Repeat layering; top with remaining bread fingers. Dot with butter or margarine.
6. Add milk or cream to reserved mushroom liquid.
7. Beat eggs until thick and piled softly. Add eggs to milk and mushroom mixture.
8. Beat salt, paprika, and pepper into the liquid.
9. Pour over layers in casserole.
10. Bake at 325°F 30 to 40 minutes, or until puffed and lightly browned.
ABOUT 6 SERVINGS

Swiss Cheese Fondue

VEGETABLES

Zucchini and Tomatoes au Gratin

2 zucchini (about 1 pound each)
3 ripe tomatoes
½ teaspoon salt
½ teaspoon pepper
½ teaspoon basil
1 cup grated cheese

1. Wash, dry and slice the zucchini. Place the slices in a greased ovenproof dish.
2. Cut the tomatoes in half and put them in the middle. Season with salt, pepper and basil and sprinkle on the cheese.
3. Bake in a 400°F oven for 15 to 20 minutes.
SERVES 4

Zucchini Boats

8 medium zucchini, washed and ends removed
1 medium tomato, cut in small pieces
¼ cup chopped salted almonds
1 tablespoon chopped parsley
1 teaspoon finely chopped onion
½ teaspoon seasoned salt
2 teaspoons butter, melted
¼ cup cracker crumbs

1. Cook zucchini in boiling salted water until crisp-tender, 7 to 10 minutes. Drain; cool.
2. Cut zucchini lengthwise into halves; scoop out and discard centers. Chop 2 shells coarsely; set remaining shells aside. Put chopped zucchini and tomato into a bowl. Add almonds, parsley, onion, and seasoned salt; mix well.
3. Spoon filling into zucchini shells. Mix butter and cracker crumbs. Sprinkle over filling. Set on a cookie sheet.
4. Place under broiler 4 inches from heat. Broil 3 minutes, or until crumbs are golden.
6 SERVINGS

Composed Vegetable Platter

1 large sweet red pepper, cut in 1-inch pieces
3 large green peppers, sliced
3 medium kohlrabi, pared, cut in half lengthwise, and sliced
6 carrots, sliced
Chicken Stock (page 48)
Herbed Mock Mayonnaise (page 49)

1. Simmer vegetables in a covered saucepan in 1 inch of stock just until tender (about 10 minutes). Drain.
2. Arrange red pepper pieces in center of a large round platter. Arrange remaining vegetables in circles around the red pepper. Pass the mayonnaise or spoon over vegetables.
3. The vegetable platter can be refrigerated and served cold as a salad.
8 SERVINGS

Note: You may desire to serve 2 or 3 sauces with the vegetable platter; Cucumber Sauce, and Green Onion Sauce (pages 44, 46) would be excellent.

Zucchini and Tomatoes au Gratin

Fresh Peas with Basil

2 tablespoons butter or margarine
½ cup sliced green onion with tops
1½ cups shelled fresh peas (1½ pounds)
½ teaspoon sugar
½ teaspoon salt
⅛ teaspoon ground black pepper
¼ teaspoon basil
1 tablespoon snipped parsley
½ cup water

1. Heat butter in a skillet. Add green onions and cook 5 minutes, stirring occasionally. Add peas, sugar, salt, pepper, basil, parsley, and water.
2. Cook, covered, over medium heat 10 minutes, or until peas are tender.
ABOUT 4 SERVINGS

Note: If desired, use 1 package (10 ounces) frozen green peas and decrease water to ¼ cup.

Cauliflower Italiana

2 packages (10 ounces each) frozen cauliflower
2 tablespoons butter or margarine
½ clove garlic, minced
2 teaspoons flour
1 teaspoon salt
1 can (16 ounces) tomatoes (undrained)
1 small green pepper, coarsely chopped
¼ teaspoon oregano

1. Cook cauliflower following package directions; drain.
2. Meanwhile, heat butter with garlic in a saucepan. Stir in flour and salt and cook until bubbly.
3. Add tomatoes with liquid and bring to boiling, stirring constantly; cook 1 to 2 minutes. Stir in green pepper and oregano.
4. Pour hot sauce over cooked cauliflower.
ABOUT 6 SERVINGS

Potato Volcano

9 or 10 medium potatoes
½ cup warm milk
1 tablespoon butter
1 teaspoon salt
½ teaspoon pepper
Grated nutmeg

Filling:
¼ pound butter

2 egg yolks
⅓ cup grated Cheddar cheese
½ teaspoon paprika
1 egg, beaten
1 tablespoon bread crumbs
1 tablespoon grated Cheddar cheese

1. Peel potatoes and boil in lightly salted water, then drain.
2. Mash the potatoes or put them through a food mill.
3. Beat in the warm milk and the butter. Season with salt, pepper and nutmeg.
4. Shape the mashed potatoes in an ovenproof dish into a volcano with a cavity in the middle like a crater.
5. **Make the Filling** – Melt the butter and stir in the cheese until melted. Add the egg yolks and simmer until thickened. Season with paprika.
6. Pour the filling into the center and brush the volcano with the beaten egg. Sprinkle on the bread crumbs and the grated cheese.
7. Bake in a 400°F oven for 10 minutes. Serve with fried **frankfurters** or **sausages** and **bacon strips**.
SERVES 6

Zucchini Squares

1 pound zucchini, shredded
2 teaspoons salt
4 ounces feta cheese, crumbled
2 eggs, beaten
2 teaspoons flour
2 teaspoons snipped fresh or 1 teaspoon crumbled dried mint leaves

¼ cup finely chopped green onion tops
¼ teaspoon freshly ground pepper
1 cup Low-Fat Yogurt (page 47)
1 teaspoon snipped fresh or ½ teaspoon crumbled dried mint leaves

1. Mix zucchini with 2 teaspoons salt. Let stand 10 minutes; rinse and drain well between paper toweling. Mix zucchini with remaining ingredients except yogurt and 1 teaspoon mint. Beat mixture well with a fork. Pour mixture into a lightly oiled 8-inch square baking pan.
2. Bake at 375°F 45 minutes. If further browning is desired, place under broiler 1 minute. Cut into squares to serve.
3. Mix yogurt and 1 teaspoon snipped mint. Serve over zucchini squares.
6 TO 8 SERVINGS

Note: **Dill weed** can be substituted for the mint in this recipe, using the same amounts.

Potato Volcano

Parsley-Buttered New Potatoes

18 small new potatoes
Boiling water
1½ teaspoons salt
2 tablespoons butter
1 tablespoon snipped parsley

1. Scrub potatoes and put into a saucepan.
2. Pour in boiling water to a 1-inch depth. Add salt; cover and cook about 15 minutes, or until tender. Drain and peel.
3. Return potatoes to saucepan and toss with butter and parsley.
ABOUT 6 SERVINGS

Note: Snipped chives, grated lemon peel, and lemon juice may be used instead of parsley.

Kraut with Apples

4 cups drained sauerkraut
2 apples, thinly sliced
½ cup apple cider
1 tablespoon light brown
sugar
2 tablespoons butter or
margarine

Mix all ingredients. Cover and simmer 5 minutes, or until apples are tender. Garnish with **apple wedges** and **parsley.**
ABOUT 8 SERVINGS

Zesty Beets

1 can or jar (16 ounces)
small whole beets
2 tablespoons butter or
margarine
2 tablespoons prepared
horseradish
½ teaspoon prepared
mustard
½ teaspoon seasoned salt

1. Heat beets in liquid; drain.
2. Add butter, horseradish, prepared mustard, and seasoned salt; stir gently.
ABOUT 4 SERVINGS

Potato Pancakes

Butter or margarine (enough,
melted, for a ¼-inch layer)
2 tablespoons flour
1½ teaspoons salt
¼ teaspoon baking powder
⅛ teaspoon ground black
pepper
6 medium potatoes, washed
2 eggs, well beaten
1 teaspoon grated onion
Applesauce or maple syrup,
warmed

1. Heat butter in a heavy skillet over low heat.
2. Combine flour, salt, baking powder, and pepper and set aside.
3. Pare and finely grate potatoes; set aside.
4. Combine flour mixture with eggs and onion.
5. Drain liquid from grated potatoes; add potatoes to egg mixture and beat thoroughly.
6. When butter is hot, spoon batter into skillet, allowing about 2 tablespoons for each pancake and leaving about 1 inch between cakes. Cook over medium heat until golden brown and crisp on one side. Turn carefully and brown on other side. Drain on absorbent paper. Serve with applesauce or maple syrup.
ABOUT 20 PANCAKES

Bavarian Carrots

1 pound carrots, pared and
cut in 2½-inch pieces
1 tablespoon sugar
3 slices bacon
1 large onion, peeled and
quartered
2 apples, pared, cored, and
quartered
½ cup chicken stock
½ teaspoon salt
⅛ teaspoon pepper
Pinch nutmeg

1. Place carrots horizontally in the feed tube and slice with **slicing disc.**
2. In a saucepan, cover carrots with water and add sugar; cook until barely tender. Drain thoroughly.
3. Meanwhile, in a large saucepan, cook bacon until crisp, reserving drippings. Drain well on paper towel. Using **steel blade,** process until coarsely chopped.
4. Still using **steel blade,** process onion until chopped. Sauté in bacon drippings until golden.
5. Slice apples with **slicing disc.** Add sliced apples and chopped bacon to onions and cook together for 5 minutes. Add cooked carrots and toss gently. Add chicken stock, salt, pepper, and nutmeg and simmer for 5 minutes.
6 SERVINGS

Greek-Style Carrots and Green Beans

1 pound carrots, pared and
cut in 2½-inch pieces
1 clove garlic
1 medium onion, peeled and
quartered
1 pound fresh green beans,
cleaned, trimmed, and cut
in 2½-inch pieces
2 tablespoons butter
2 tablespoons oil
1 can (15 ounces) tomato
sauce
¼ teaspoon cinnamon
½ teaspoon salt
¼ teaspoon pepper

1. Place carrots horizontally in the feed tube and slice with **slicing disc.** Set aside.
2. Using **steel blade,** mince garlic. Add onion and process until chopped.
3. In a saucepan, sauté green beans, sliced carrots, onion, and garlic in butter and oil about 15 minutes.
4. Add tomato sauce, cinnamon, salt, and pepper; simmer, partially covered, until vegetables are tender (about 30 minutes).
8 SERVINGS

Baked Sweet Potatoes in Foil

4 sweet potatoes
Vegetable shortening
4 teaspoons brown sugar
4 teaspoons butter or
margarine

1. Wash, scrub, and dry sweet potatoes. Rub shortening over entire surface of potatoes and wrap each loosely in aluminum foil. Seal open ends with a double fold.
2. Place on grill and bake about 45 minutes, or until tender. Turn several times for even baking.
3. Loosen foil. Make a slit in top of each. Put brown sugar and butter on top.
4 SERVINGS

Vegetables Polonaise

1½ pounds vegetables
(Brussels sprouts or savoy
cabbage or carrots or
cauliflower or green beans
or leeks)
1 cup boiling water
1 teaspoon salt
½ teaspoon sugar (optional)

2 tablespoons butter
¼ teaspoon salt
⅛ teaspoon pepper
1 tablespoon lemon juice
(optional)
2 tablespoons fine dry bread
crumbs

1. Choose one vegetable to prepare at a time. Trim and pare as necessary. (Leave Brussels sprouts and green beans whole. Cut cabbage into six wedges. Leave cauliflower whole or break into flowerets. Slice leeks.)
2. Cook vegetable, covered, in boiling water with 1 teaspoon salt and the sugar, if desired, until tender. Drain off water.
3. Melt butter. Stir in ¼ teaspoon salt, pepper, and lemon juice. Add bread crumbs. Sauté until golden. Spoon over top of vegetable.
ABOUT 4 SERVINGS

 ## Deep-Fried Zucchini

1¼ cups all-purpose flour
1 teaspoon salt
¼ teaspoon pepper
2 eggs, well beaten
¾ cup milk
1 teaspoon Worcestershire
sauce

1 tablespoon butter or
margarine, melted
Oil for deep frying
6 medium (about 2 pounds)
zucchini, cut in halves
crosswise and into 3¼-inch
sticks lengthwise

1. Blend flour, salt, and pepper in a bowl. Add a mixture of eggs, milk, Worcestershire sauce, and butter; beat just until smooth.
2. Heat oil in a fondue pot or a deep fryer to 365°F.
3. Dip zucchini sticks into batter, using a fork to coat evenly. Allow any excess coating to drip off.
4. Fry 2 to 3 minutes, or until golden brown. Lift from oil and drain a few seconds before removing to absorbent paper.
5. Sprinkle with salt.
6 SERVINGS

Mallow Sweet Potato Balls

3 cups warm mashed sweet
potatoes
Salt and pepper to taste
3 tablespoons melted butter
8 large marshmallows

1 egg
1 tablespoon cold water
1 cup almonds, blanched
and chopped
Oil for deep frying

1. Season potatoes and add butter. Mold potato mixture around marshmallows, forming 8 balls with a marshmallow in center of each.
2. Beat egg and mix with cold water. Dip sweet potato balls in egg and then in almonds.
3. Slowly heat oil in a wok to 365°F. When oil is hot, fry sweet potato balls until brown, turning occasionally.
8 SERVINGS

Mustard Relish Mold

1 cup cold water
2 envelopes unflavored
gelatin
6 eggs
1½ cups sugar
1½ tablespoons dry mustard
1¼ teaspoons salt
1½ cups vinegar

1 16-ounce can peas (about
1¾ cups, drained)
1 cup (about 2 medium-size)
grated carrot
1 cup chopped celery
1 tablespoon minced parsley
Curly endive or other crisp
greens

1. A 1½-quart mold will be needed.
2. Pour water into a small bowl.
3. Sprinkle gelatin evenly over cold water.
4. Let stand until softened.
5. Beat eggs slightly in top of a double boiler.
6. Blend in a mixture of sugar, mustard, and salt.
7. Add vinegar gradually, stirring constantly.
8. Cook over simmering water, stirring constantly, until mixture thickens. Remove from simmering water. Stir softened gelatin; add to egg mixture and stir until gelatin is completely dissolved. Cool, chill until mixture begins to gel (gets slightly thicker).
9. Meanwhile drain peas.
10. Lightly oil the mold with salad or cooking oil (not olive oil) and set it aside to drain.
11. Prepare carrot, celery, and parsley.
12. When gelatin is of desired consistency, blend in the vegetables. Turn into the prepared mold. Chill in refrigerator until firm.
13. Unmold onto chilled serving plate. Garnish with curly endive or other crisp greens.
ABOUT 12 SERVINGS

Apple-Stuffed Acorn Squash

2 acorn squash
2 tart apples
1½ teaspoons grated fresh
lemon peel
1 tablespoon fresh lemon
juice
¼ cup butter or margarine,

melted
⅓ cup firmly packed brown
sugar
Salt
Cinnamon
Apple and lemon slices for
garnish (optional)

1. Cut squash into halves lengthwise and scoop out seedy centers. Place cut side down in baking dish and pour in boiling water to a ½-inch depth. Bake at 400°F 20 minutes.
2. Pare, core, and dice apples; mix with lemon peel and juice, 2 tablespoons butter, and brown sugar.
3. Invert squash halves and brush with remaining 2 tablespoons butter; sprinkle with salt and cinnamon.
4. Fill squash halves with apple mixture. Pour boiling water into dish to a ½-inch depth; cover and bake 30 minutes.
5. Before serving, spoon pan juices over squash. If desired, garnish with apple and lemon slices.
4 SERVINGS

Beans Plaki

3 cups dried white beans
½ cup olive oil
2 medium onions, chopped
2 garlic cloves, crushed in a garlic press
1 can (8 ounces) tomato sauce or 1 cup Tomato Sauce (page 54)
2 celery stalks, diced
1 carrot, diced
1 bay leaf
1 teaspoon oregano
1 teaspoon sugar
Salt and pepper to taste
Wine vinegar

1. Place beans in a pot and cover with water. Bring to a boil. Simmer covered 2 to 3 hours, until just tender. Drain.
2. Heat oil in a saucepan, add onion, and cook until translucent. Add garlic, tomato sauce, celery, carrot, bay leaf, oregano, sugar, salt, and pepper. Simmer 5 minutes. (If sauce is too thick, add a little water.)
3. Add beans to sauce and simmer covered about 20 minutes, or until tender.
4. Serve hot or cold with a cruet of wine vinegar.
ABOUT 12 SERVINGS

Spinach-Cheese Bake

2 packages (10 ounces each) frozen chopped spinach
3 eggs, beaten
¼ cup enriched all-purpose flour
1 teaspoon seasoned salt
¼ teaspoon ground nutmeg
¼ teaspoon ground black pepper
2 cups (16 ounces) creamed cottage cheese
2 cups (8 ounces) shredded Swiss or Cheddar cheese

1. Cook spinach following package directions; drain.
2. Combine eggs, flour, seasoned salt, nutmeg, and pepper in a bowl. Mix in cottage cheese, Swiss cheese, and spinach.
3. Turn into a buttered 1½-quart casserole.
4. Bake at 325°F 50 to 60 minutes.
6 TO 8 SERVINGS

Beans Plaki

Spinach-Bacon Soufflé

2 cups firmly packed, finely chopped fresh spinach (dry the leaves before chopping)
¼ cup finely chopped green onions with tops
½ pound sliced bacon, cooked, drained, and crumbled
3 tablespoons butter or margarine
¼ cup enriched all-purpose flour
½ teaspoon salt
¼ to ½ teaspoon thyme
1 cup milk
3 egg yolks, well beaten
4 egg whites
2 teaspoons shredded Parmesan cheese

1. Toss the spinach, green onions, and bacon together in a bowl; set aside.
2. Heat butter in a saucepan over low heat. Blend in flour, salt, and thyme. Stirring constantly, heat until bubbly. Add milk gradually, continuing to stir. Bring rapidly to boiling and boil 1 to 2 minutes, stirring constantly.
3. Remove from heat and blend spinach-bacon mixture into the sauce. Stir in the beaten egg yolks; set aside to cool.
4. Meanwhile, beat egg whites until rounded peaks are formed (peaks turn over slightly when beater is slowly lifted upright); do not overbeat.
5. Gently spread spinach-bacon mixture over the beaten egg whites. Carefully fold together until ingredients are just blended.
6. Turn mixture into an ungreased 2-quart soufflé dish (straight-sided casserole); sprinkle top with Parmesan cheese.
7. Bake at 350°F 40 minutes, or until a knife comes out clean when inserted halfway between center and edge of soufflé and top is lightly browned. Serve immediately.
6 SERVINGS

Smothered Cabbage

2 small heads cabbage
2 tablespoons peanut oil
1 onion, minced
1 garlic clove, crushed in a garlic press
8 bacon slices
½ cup stock
Freshly ground pepper to
taste
3 drops Tabasco
1 tablespoon butter
1 tablespoon cornstarch
1 teaspoon tomato paste
1 teaspoon lime juice
Lime wedges

1. Remove wilted leaves from cabbage. Quarter and core cabbage.
2. Heat oil in a top-of-range casserole, add onion and garlic and sauté until golden. Add cabbage pieces and lay a bacon slice on each. Add stock, pepper, and Tabasco. Bring to a boil, reduce heat, and simmer covered 15 minutes; cabbage will still be a little crisp.
3. Meanwhile, mix butter and cornstarch.
4. Transfer cabbage to a heated platter. Mix tomato paste and lime juice into cooking liquid and bring rapidly to a boil, then add butter-cornstarch mixture and stir until liquid is slightly thicker.
5. To serve, pour sauce over cabbage. Accompany with lime wedges.
8 SERVINGS

Stuffed Tomatoes with Rice and Pine Nuts

Stuffed Tomatoes with Rice and Pine Nuts

8 large firm tomatoes with tops sliced off and reserved	½ cup water
Salt, pepper, and sugar to taste	½ cup chopped parsley
	½ cup dried currants
¾ cup olive oil	½ cup pine nuts
4 onions, minced	1 teaspoon mint
1 cup long-grain rice	Juice of 1 lemon
	2 cups water

1. Scoop out pulp from tomatoes and reserve. Sprinkle insides of tomatoes with salt, pepper, and sugar. Arrange in a baking dish.
2. Heat ¼ cup oil in a large skillet. Add onion, pulp, rice, water, parsley, currants, pine nuts, mint, and lemon juice. Simmer, covered, stirring occasionally, until liquid is absorbed. Cool slightly. Adjust seasonings.
3. Fill tomatoes with rice mixture. Replace tops and put into baking dish. Drizzle remaining olive oil between tomatoes. Add water.
4. Bake at 350°F about 40 minutes, or until rice is cooked; baste occasionally. If necessary, add a little water. Serve hot or chilled.

6 SERVINGS

French Fries in a Poke

Put partially thawed frozen French fried potatoes onto a large square of heavy-duty aluminum foil. Sprinkle with salt and pepper. Gather foil up around potatoes, partially closing at top. Set on the grill over hot coals and heat, shaking the package occasionally, 15 minutes, or until potatoes are hot to the touch.

Dilled Onion Packet

1 large Bermuda onion	½ teaspoon dill weed
1 teaspoon butter or margarine	Seasoned salt

1. Peel and partially core the onion (allow 1 for each serving). Put the butter and dill weed into cavity; sprinkle generously with the seasoned salt. Wrap in a square of heavy-duty aluminum foil.
2. Cook on grill 1 to 1½ hours. Serve topped with **sour cream.**

1 SERVING

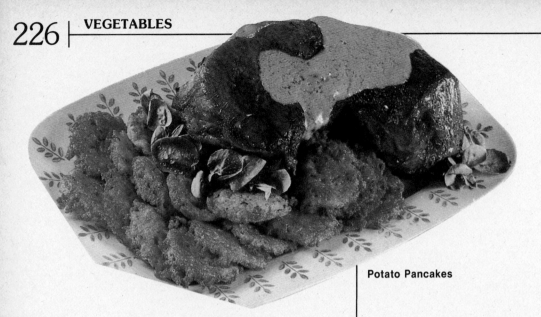

Potato Pancakes

Potato Pancakes

2 tablespoons all-purpose flour	grated)
	Fat (enough to make a layer
1½ teaspoons salt	¼ inch deep)
¼ teaspoon baking powder	2 eggs, well beaten
⅛ teaspoon pepper	1 tablespoon grated onion
6 medium-size (about 2 lbs.) potatoes (about 3 cups,	1 tablespoon minced parsley

1. Combine flour, salt, baking powder, and pepper. Set aside.
2. Wash, pare and finely grate potatoes. Set aside.
3. Heat fat in a heavy skillet over low heat.
4. Combine the flour mixture with eggs, onion and parsley.
5. Drain liquid that collects from grated potatoes; add potatoes to egg mixture and beat thoroughly with a spoon.
6. When fat is hot, spoon about 2 tablespoons of batter for each pancake into fat, leaving about 1-inch between pancakes. Cook over medium heat until golden brown and crisp on one side. Turn carefully and brown other side. Drain on absorbent paper.
7. Serve with **Sauerbraten** or as a main dish accompanied by **apple sauce.**
ABOUT 20 MEDIUM-SIZE PANCAKES

Potato Pancakes, King-Size: Use a large, heavy skillet. Heat 2 tablespoons **fat** in the skillet. Spoon about one-third of batter into skillet. Quickly spread batter evenly with spoon to cover bottom, making one large pancake. When golden brown and crisp, turn carefully. Add 2 tablespoons **shortening** and brown other side. Repeat for rest of batter.
3 LARGE PANCAKES

Kettle Patio Potatoes

Scrub long white baking potatoes. Cut each lengthwise into 4 or 5 slices. Place sliced potatoes on double-thick pieces of heavy-duty aluminum foil. Pour 1 tablespoon cream over each, dot with 1½ teaspoons butter, and sprinkle with ¼ teaspoon salt and few grains pepper. Seal securely, using drugstore fold and turning up ends. Set on grill to cook 45 to 60 minutes.

Ratatouille of Pumpkin

1 cup diced salt pork	6 dried Italian pepper pods
4 slices ham or Canadian bacon	or ½ green hot pepper
	2½ pounds pumpkin meat,
3 scallions or green onions including green tops, cut in pieces	pared and cubed
	2 cups stock or chicken broth
3 garlic cloves	3 tablespoons butter
5 parsley sprigs	¼ cup chopped parsley

1. Sauté salt pork and ham in a Dutch oven until brown.
2. In a mortar, pound together to a paste the scallions, garlic, parsley, and pepper pods.
3. Add pumpkin, seasoning paste, and stock to Dutch oven. Cover and simmer until pumpkin is tender enough to mash with a fork.
4. Remove cover and, stirring constantly, cook off most of the liquid, being careful that pumpkin does not stick. Add butter and stir until melted.
5. Serve sprinkled with parsley.

Zucchini Boats

8 medium zucchini, washed and ends removed	parsley
	1 teaspoon finely chopped onion
1 medium tomato, cut in small pieces	½ teaspoon seasoned salt
¼ cup chopped salted almonds	2 teaspoons butter, melted
1 tablespoon chopped	¼ cup cracker crumbs

1. Cook zucchini in boiling salted water until crisp-tender, 7 to 10 minutes. Drain; cool.
2. Cut zucchini lengthwise into halves; scoop out and discard centers. Chop 2 shells coarsely; set remaining shells aside. Put chopped zucchini and tomato into a bowl. Add almonds, parsley, onion, and seasoned salt; mix well.
3. Spoon filling into zucchini shells. Mix butter and cracker crumbs. Sprinkle over filling. Set on a cookie sheet.
4. Place under broiler 4 inches from heat. Broil 3 minutes, or until crumbs are golden.
6 SERVINGS

Cauliflower with Mustard Sauce

1 medium-size head
  cauliflower
1 cup heavy cream
¼ cup sugar
2 tablespoons dry mustard

2 teaspoons cornstarch
½ teaspoon salt
1 egg yolk, slightly beaten
¼ cup cider vinegar

1. **For Cauliflower** — Remove leaves, cut off all the woody base and trim any blemishes from cauliflower.
2. Rinse and cook the cauliflower 20 to 25 minutes, or until tender but still firm.
3. **For Mustard Sauce** — Meanwhile, set out cream. Scald in top of double boiler ¾ cup of the cream.
4. Sift together into a small saucepan sugar, mustard, cornstarch, and salt.
5. Add, stirring well, the remaining ¼ cup cream. Gradually add the scalded cream; stir constantly. Stirring gently and constantly, bring cornstarch mixture rapidly to boiling over direct heat and cook for 3 minutes.
6. Wash double-boiler top to remove scum.
7. Pour mixture into double-boiler top and place over simmering water. Cover and cook 10 to 12 minutes, stirring occasionally. Remove cover and vigorously stir about 3 tablespoons of this hot mixture into egg yolk.
8. Immediately blend into mixture in double boiler. Cook over simmering water 3 to 5 minutes. Stir slowly to keep mixture cooking evenly. Remove from heat. Add gradually, stirring in vinegar.
9. Drain the cauliflower and serve on a separate plate; pour the sauce over cauliflower.
4 SERVINGS

Stuffed Baked Sweet Potatoes

4 medium sweet potatoes,
  washed
1 small ripe banana, peeled
2 tablespoons butter or
  margarine

⅓ cup fresh orange juice
1 tablespoon brown sugar
1½ teaspoons salt
¼ cup chopped pecans

1. Bake sweet potatoes at 375°F 45 minutes to 1 hour, or until tender when tested with a fork.
2. Cut a lengthwise slice from each potato. Scoop out sweet potatoes into a bowl; reserve shells. Mash banana with potatoes; add butter, orange juice, brown sugar, and salt and beat thoroughly. Spoon mixture into shells. Sprinkle with pecans. Set on a cookie sheet.
3. Return to oven 12 to 15 minutes, or until heated.
4 SERVINGS

Artichokes with Creamy Dill Sauce

Cooked Artichokes
1 cup creamed cottage
  cheese
½ cup plain yogurt
1 tablespoon lemon juice
1 teaspoon instant minced

onion
1 teaspoon sugar
½ teaspoon dill weed
½ teaspoon salt
Few grains pepper
2 parsley sprigs

1. Prepare desired number of artichokes.
2. Meanwhile, combine cottage cheese, yogurt, lemon juice, onion, sugar, dill weed, salt, pepper, and parsley in an electric blender container. Blend until smooth. Chill.
3. Serve artichokes with sauce for dipping.
ABOUT 1½ CUPS SAUCE

Cooked Artichokes: Wash **artichokes.** Cut off about 1 inch from tops and bases. Remove and discard lower outside leaves. If desired, snip off tips of remaining leaves. Stand artichokes upright in a deep saucepan large enough to hold them snugly. Add **boiling water** to a depth of 1 inch. Add **salt** (¼ teaspoon for each artichoke). Cover and boil gently 30 to 45 minutes, or until stems can easily be pierced with a fork. Drain artichokes; cut off stems.

Stir-Fry Vegetables and Rice

1 cup brown rice
¼ cup vegetable oil
1 medium onion, thinly
  sliced
1 cup thinly sliced carrot
1 clove garlic, crushed
1 green pepper, coarsely

chopped
1 cup thinly sliced zucchini
1 cup thinly sliced
  mushrooms
2 cans (16 ounces) bean
  sprouts, drained
¼ to ⅓ cup soy sauce

1. Cook rice following package directions; set aside.
2. Heat oil in a large skillet. Add onion, carrot, and garlic; cook and stir over medium high heat about 2 minutes.
3. Add green pepper, zucchini, and mushrooms; cook and stir 2 to 3 minutes.
4. Stir in cooked rice, bean sprouts, and soy sauce. Cook and stir 1 to 2 minutes, or until thoroughly heated.
6 TO 8 SERVINGS

Tangy Green Beans

¾ pound fresh green beans,
  cut crosswise in pieces, or
  1 package (9 ounces)
  frozen cut green beans
½ teaspoon salt
¼ cup butter or margarine
1 medium onion, quartered

and thinly sliced
1 tablespoon wine vinegar
¼ teaspoon salt
⅛ teaspoon ground black
  pepper
¼ teaspoon dill weed
⅛ teaspoon crushed savory

1. Put beans and ½ teaspoon salt into a small amount of boiling water in a saucepan. Bring to boiling and cook, covered, until crisp-tender. Drain and set aside.
2. Heat 3 tablespoons butter in a skillet; add onion and cook 3 to 5 minutes. Mix in beans and cook about 4 minutes, or until thoroughly heated, stirring occasionally. Add remaining butter, wine vinegar, ¼ teaspoon salt, pepper, dill, and savory; toss over low heat until butter is melted.
ABOUT 4 SERVINGS

Braised Belgian Endives with Egg Butter

6 Belgian endives (1½ pounds)
2 tablespoons butter
½ teaspoon salt
½ cup water

Egg Butter:
¼ cup butter
1 hard-boiled egg
½ teaspoon salt

1. Wash the endives and cut away the bottom part. Cut in half lengthwise.
2. Sauté endives in butter in a skillet until they turn light golden brown.
3. Add salt and water and simmer, covered, for 10 minutes.
4. Meanwhile, make the Egg Butter. Stir the butter until soft. Chop the egg and mix with the butter. Season with salt.
5. Serve the endives with the egg butter and **lemon wedges,** if desired.
SERVES 4

Artichokes à la Four Thieves

8 artichokes
Boiling salted water

Four Thieves Sauce (page 43)

1. Wash artichokes under running water. Let them stand 10 minutes in cold salted water; drain.
2. With a sharp kitchen knife, remove stem and bottom leaves from each artichoke, and with kitchen shears snip ¼ inch off the top of each leaf.
3. Cook the artichokes uncovered in a pot of boiling salted water 30 minutes; drain and cool.
4. To serve, gently spread artichoke leaves to the sides and, with a grapefruit knife, remove the very small purplish leaves and the choke that covers the bottom, scraping it clean. Accompany with hot Four Thieves Sauce.
8 SERVINGS

Baked Zucchini

2 pounds zucchini
1 cup shredded mild Cheddar cheese
½ cup cottage cheese
4 eggs, beaten
¾ cup dry bread crumbs

3 tablespoons chopped parsley
1½ teaspoons salt
½ teaspoon pepper
3 tablespoons butter

1. Wash zucchini and slice crosswise into ¼-inch slices. (It is not necessary to peel zucchini, unless skin seems very tough.)
2. Combine cheeses, eggs, bread crumbs, parsley, salt, and pepper until evenly mixed. Layer into baking dish, alternating zucchini with sauce. Dot top with butter.
3. Bake at 375°F about 45 minutes, or until slightly set.
6 TO 8 SERVINGS

Flavor-Rich Baked Beans

1½ quarts water
1 pound dried navy beans, rinsed
½ pound salt pork
½ cup chopped celery
½ cup chopped onion
1 teaspoon salt

¼ cup ketchup
¼ cup molasses
2 tablespoons brown sugar
1 teaspoon dry mustard
½ teaspoon ground black pepper
¼ teaspoon ground ginger

1. Grease 8 individual casseroles having tight-fitting covers. (A 2-quart casserole with lid may be used.)
2. Heat water to boiling in a large heavy saucepan. Add beans gradually to water so that boiling continues. Boil 2 minutes. Remove from heat and set aside 1 hour.
3. Remove rind from salt pork and cut into 1-inch chunks; set aside.
4. Add pork chunks to beans with celery, onion, and salt; mix well. Cover tightly and bring mixture to boiling over high heat. Reduce and simmer 45 minutes, stirring once or twice. Drain beans, reserving liquid.
5. Put an equal amount of beans and salt pork chunks into each casserole.
6. Mix one cup of bean liquid, ketchup, molasses, brown sugar, dry mustard, pepper, and ginger in a saucepan. Bring to boiling. Pour an equal amount of sauce over beans in each casserole. Cover casseroles.
7. Bake at 300°F about 2½ hours. If necessary, add more reserved bean liquid to beans during baking. Remove covers and bake ½ hour longer.
8 SERVINGS

Sweet Potato Soufflé

2 cups hot mashed sweet potatoes
⅓ cup hot milk
⅓ cup amber rum
¼ cup butter

⅛ teaspoon nutmeg
Dash Tabasco
1 teaspoon grated lime peel
4 egg yolks, beaten
5 egg whites, stiffly beaten

1. Beat sweet potatoes, milk, rum, and butter together until smooth. Add nutmeg, Tabasco, lime peel, and beaten egg yolk; beat well. Fold in beaten egg white.
2. Pour into a well-greased 1½-quart soufflé dish. Set in pan of hot water.
3. Bake at 425°F 25 to 30 minutes. Serve at once.

Spinach with Tomato

2 packages (10 ounces each) fresh spinach
3 slices bacon
2 tablespoons bacon fat

½ cup chopped onion
1 cup chopped fresh tomato
¾ teaspoon salt
⅛ teaspoon pepper

1. Wash spinach thoroughly. Put spinach with water that clings to leaves into a large saucepan. Cook rapidly about 5 minutes, or until tender. Drain.
2. Meanwhile, fry bacon until crisp in a large skillet. Drain bacon, crumble, and set aside. Add onion to 2 tablespoons bacon fat in skillet and cook until soft. Add tomato, spinach, salt, and pepper. Heat thoroughly.
3. Garnish with sliced hard-cooked egg, if desired.
ABOUT 6 SERVINGS

Braised Belgian Endives with Egg Butter

Tuna-Stuffed Peppers

4 large green peppers
1 cup Medium White Sauce (page 49; use cream for milk)
1 teaspoon lemon juice
½ teaspoon paprika

1 7-ounce can tuna fish or 7¾-ounce can salmon
¼ cup (1-ounce) grated Parmesan or Cheddar cheese

1. Grease a 2-quart baking dish.
2. Rinse and slice stem ends from peppers.
3. With a knife or spoon, remove and discard white fiber and seeds. Rinse cavities. Drop into boiling salted water to cover and simmer 5 minutes. Remove peppers from water and invert. Set aside to drain.
4. Meanwhile, prepare medium white sauce.
5. Blend lemon juice and paprika into sauce and set aside.
6. Drain and flake tuna fish or salmon with a fork.
7. Combine with sauce; spoon mixture into peppers. Place in baking dish.
8. Bake at 350°F about 15 minutes. Just before serving, sprinkle with Parmesan or Cheddar cheese.
9. Other kinds of fish may be used, or combinations or several kinds.
4 SERVINGS

Rice-Stuffed Peppers: Follow recipe for Tuna-Stuffed Peppers. Substitute **Tomato Sauce** for Medium White Sauce. Substitute ½ **pound ground beef** for tuna fish. Brown ground beef in **2 tablespoons shortening,** breaking it into small pieces with fork or spoon.
Prepare ⅔ **cup package precooked rice** according to directions on package. Mix with sauce and browned meat. Heap mixture into peppers and bake as in Tuna Stuffed Peppers.

Fried Okra Pods

2 pounds large okra pods, washed and stems trimmed
Salt, pepper, and cayenne or red pepper to taste
1 egg yolk
1 tablespoon olive oil

1 cup dried bread crumbs
Oil for deep frying, heated to 365°F
Watercress and wedges of avocado and tomato for garnish

1. Cook okra in lightly salted boiling water 7 minutes. Drain and season.
2. Roll them in egg yolk beaten with oil, then in bread crumbs.
3. Fry the pods in heated oil until golden and drain on absorbent paper.
4. Serve surrounded with watercress, avocado, and tomato.

Green Tomatoes and Zucchini

2 tablespoons butter
1 large onion, chopped
¾ cup chopped, canned Mexican green tomatoes (tomatillos)
3 medium zucchini, thinly

sliced
½ teaspoon oregano
½ teaspoon salt
1 tablespoon water
¼ cup grated Parmesan cheese

1. Heat butter in a large skillet. Add onion and cook until soft. Add green tomatoes, zucchini, oregano, salt, and water; stir. Cover; bring to boiling, reduce heat, and cook until zucchini is crisp-tender (5 to 7 minutes).
2. Stir in cheese just before serving.
6 TO 8 SERVINGS

Braised Lettuce

8 small heads Boston lettuce or 16 heads Bibb lettuce
1 cup chicken broth
Juice of 1 lime

6 tablespoons butter
Salt and freshly ground pepper to taste

1. Rinse lettuce under cold running water; tie each head firmly with string.
2. Put lettuce into a skillet with broth, lime juice, butter, salt, and pepper. Bring to a boil, then cover, reduce heat, and simmer 15 minutes.
3. Remove cover, increase heat, and boil rapidly until no liquid remains and edges of lettuce are golden. Remove the string. Serve with roasts.

Barbecued Sweet Peppers

4 sweet red peppers
4 green sweet peppers

Peanut oil
French dressing

1. Core the peppers and cut each into three strips.
2. Coat both sides of pepper strips with oil; let them stand 40 minutes.
3. Brush pepper strips lightly with oil and place in a hinged grill. Barbecue 2 inches from ash-covered coals, allowing peppers to blister.
4. Chill and serve with French dressing as an antipasto or with other marinated vegetables.

Cauliflower à la Romagna

1 head cauliflower, washed
  and trimmed
⅔ cup fine dry bread crumbs
1 teaspoon grated Parmesan
  cheese
½ teaspoon salt
¼ teaspoon pepper
2 eggs, slightly beaten
¼ cup milk
Fat for deep frying heated to
  365°

1. Put whole cauliflower into a saucepan containing a 1-inch depth of boiling salted water. Cook, uncovered, 5 minutes. Cover and cook 15 to 20 minutes, or until cauliflower is tender. Drain, separate into flowerets, and set aside to cool.
2. Combine crumbs, cheese, salt, and pepper. Mix eggs and milk in a small bowl. Coat flowerets with egg mixture, then with crumbs.
3. Put only as many flowerets into fat at one time as will float uncrowded. Fry 2 to 4 minutes, or until golden brown; turn occasionally during frying.
4. Drain and serve hot.
ABOUT 4 SERVINGS

Florentine Spinach

2 pounds spinach
2 cups Medium White Sauce
  (page 49)
3 eggs, slightly beaten
3 tablespoons minced onion
½ teaspoon salt
½ teaspoon pepper

1. Wash spinach. Put into a large saucepan with only the water clinging to the leaves; cover. Cook rapidly about 5 minutes, or until tender. Drain well.
2. Prepare white sauce. Pour hot sauce into beaten eggs, stirring vigorously to blend. Set aside to cool to lukewarm.
3. Finely chop spinach. Combine spinach, sauce mixture, onion, salt, and pepper. Turn into a thoroughly greased 9-inch ring mold.
4. Set filled mold in a pan and pour hot water into pan to a depth of 1 inch.
5. Bake at 350°F 45 to 55 minutes, or until set.
6. Remove from oven; remove mold from water and let stand 5 minutes. Loosen spinach from mold and unmold onto a warm serving plate.
6 SERVINGS

Boiled Curly Endive with Lemon Juice and Olive Oil

2 bunches young curly
  endive
3 cups water
1 teaspoon salt
1 lemon, cut in wedges, or
  use wine vinegar
Olive oil

1. Slice endive in half lengthwise. Rinse several times to remove all traces of dirt. Cut stem 1 inch from bottom and discard.
2. Boil the endive in water with salt added in a covered pot until tender (about 20 to 25 minutes).
3. Serve with lemon juice and olive oil.
4 SERVINGS

Danish Cabbage

2 pounds cabbage	1 teaspoon caraway seed
3 cups boiling water	½ teaspoon salt
1 cup sour cream	½ teaspoon white pepper

1. Slice cabbage into small pieces and cook in boiling water covered 6 to 8 minutes until tender, but still crisp. Drain very well.
2. In the top of a double boiler toss cabbage with sour cream, caraway seed, salt and pepper. Cover and cook for 15 minutes.
6 SERVINGS

Tomato Cabbage

3 cups cabbage	1 cup tomato sauce
¾ cup boiling milk	½ teaspoon salt
4 slices bacon	½ teaspoon white pepper
1 small yellow onion, minced	2 teaspoon brown sugar

1. Cut cabbage into shreds.
2. Boil milk and gradually drop in cabbage. Boil for 2 minutes. Drain and discard milk.
3. Dice and sauté bacon. Remove bacon from pan and set aside.
4. Sauté onion in bacon fat. Add tomato purée, salt, pepper and brown sugar.
5. Bring sauce to a boil and add the cabbage and bacon. Serve very hot.
6 SERVINGS

Broccoli Florentine

1 pound broccoli, washed and trimmed	2 cloves garlic, sliced thin
2 tablespoons olive oil	¼ teaspoon salt
	¼ teaspoon pepper

1. Split the heavy broccoli stalks (over ½ inch thick) lengthwise through stalks up to flowerets. Put into a small amount of boiling salted water. Cook, uncovered, 5 minutes, then cover and cook 10 to 15 minutes, or until broccoli is just tender.
2. Meanwhile, heat oil and garlic in a large skillet until garlic is lightly browned.
3. Drain broccoli and add to skillet; turn to coat with oil. Cook about 10 minutes, stirring occasionally. Season with salt and pepper. Serve hot.
4 SERVINGS

Broccoli Roman Style: Follow recipe for Broccoli Florentine. Omit cooking broccoli in boiling water. Cook broccoli in oil only 5 minutes. Add **1½ cups dry red wine** to skillet. Cook, covered, over low heat about 20 minutes, or until broccoli is tender; stir occasionally.

Spinach Sautéed in Oil: Follow recipe for Broccoli Florentine; substitute **2 cups chopped cooked spinach** for broccoli. Add spinach, **1 tablespoon chopped pinenuts or almonds,** and **1 tablespoon raisins** to oil mixture.

Artichoke Pie

1 package (9 ounces) frozen artichoke hearts	Flour
	4 eggs
Lemon juice	½ teaspoon salt
2 tablespoons olive oil	Pinch pepper
1½ tablespoons butter	2 tablespoons milk or water

1. Thinly slice the artichoke hearts vertically and spread out on paper towels. Pat dry when thawed, and drizzle with lemon juice.
2. Heat olive oil and butter in a 10-inch skillet with an oven-proof handle. Coat artichoke heart slices with flour and brown on both sides in hot fat.
3. Beat eggs slightly. Mix in salt, pepper, and milk. Pour over artichoke slices in skillet.
4. Bake at 350°F 5 to 10 minutes, or until egg mixture is set.
4 SERVINGS

Asparagus Extraordinaire

1½ pounds fresh asparagus	Freshly ground pepper
1 medium sweet red pepper, cut in ¼-inch strips	¼ pound prosciutto or boiled ham, cut in 1x⅛-inch strips
Chicken Stock (page 48)	½ cup Mock Hollandaise Sauce (page 49)
Salt	

1. Break off and discard tough parts of asparagus stalks. Pare stalks. Simmer asparagus and pepper strips in 1 inch of stock in a covered skillet until tender (about 7 minutes); drain.
2. Arrange asparagus spears on a serving platter; arrange pepper strips over center of asparagus. Sprinkle lightly with salt and pepper. Arrange ham along sides of asparagus. Spoon hollandaise over all.
4 SERVINGS

Note: For a special luncheon entrée, increase amount of asparagus to 2 pounds and the ham to ½ pound. Arrange on individual plates; top each with a **poached egg.**

Green Onions with Mock Hollandaise

4 bunches green onions, cleaned and trimmed	⅔ cup Mock Hollandaise Sauce (page 49)
1¼ cups Chicken Stock (page 48)	¼ teaspoon freshly grated nutmeg
Salt	Orange wedges

1. Arrange green onions in a large skillet; pour stock over. Simmer until onions are tender (about 10 minutes). Drain; arrange onions on a platter; sprinkle lightly with salt.
2. Blend hollandaise and nutmeg. Serve over onions. Garnish platter with orange wedges.
4 TO 6 SERVINGS

Danish Cabbage and Tomato Cabbage

Stuffed Peppers

4 medium green peppers
¼ cup vegetable oil
1 onion, finely chopped
2 cloves garlic, minced
½ pound ground beef
½ teaspoon salt
½ teaspoon pepper
½ teaspoon thyme
½ cup drained stewed
   tomatoes
1 cup cooked rice
1 tablespoon parsley

1. Cut top off each pepper and remove seeds and veins. Blanch in boiling water for 3 to 4 minutes. Remove and let cool.
2. In a skillet, heat oil, add onion and garlic and sauté for 4 to 5 minutes.
3. Add meat, salt, pepper and thyme and cook until meat is browned.
4. In a large mixing bowl, combine the meat, tomatoes, rice and parsley.
5. Stuff each pepper with the meat mixture, place the top back on each and bake in a preheated 325°F oven for 20 to 25 minutes.
SERVES 4

Cooked Hearts of Palm

½ cup cubed salt pork
2 cups cubed heart of palm
1 cup chicken broth

1. Render salt pork in a Dutch oven. Add heart of palm and broth; simmer covered over medium heat until no liquid remains and heart of palm is tender.
2. Serve hot with Béchamel Sauce (page 52) or cold with **French dressing.**

Herbed Cabbage

3 cups shredded cabbage
1 large onion, sliced
½ teaspoon snipped fresh or
   ¼ teaspoon dried tarragon
   leaves
½ teaspoon snipped fresh or
   ¼ teaspoon dried basil
   leaves
2 teaspoons snipped fresh or
1 teaspoon dried marjoram
   leaves
¼ teaspoon freshly ground
   pepper
Chicken Stock (page 48)
2 teaspoons clarified butter
½ pound mushrooms, sliced
1 teaspoon salt
Snipped parsley

1. Place cabbage and onion in a medium saucepan; sprinkle with tarragon, basil, marjoram, and pepper. Pour in 1 inch of stock; simmer covered until cabbage is tender (about 10 minutes). Drain.
2. Heat butter in a medium skillet until bubbly; add mushrooms and cook 4 minutes, stirring occasionally. Stir mushrooms and salt into cabbage mixture. Sprinkle with snipped parsley. Serve with Mock Crème Fraîche (page 46) or yogurt, if desired.
4 TO 8 SERVINGS

Baked Cheddar Onions

6 medium onions
3 cups chopped carrots
1½ cups (6 ounces) shredded
   Cheddar cheese
1 teaspoon thyme
½ teaspoon salt
Chicken Stock (page 48)

1. Cut a thin slice off both ends of each onion; peel. Carefully scoop out inside of onions with a sharp knife or melon-baller, leaving a shell 2 or 3 rings thick. Chop onion centers; mix with carrots, cheese, thyme, and salt. Fill onions with mixture; place in a shallow baking pan. Pour ½ inch stock around onions.
2. Bake at 400°F 1 to 1¼ hours, or until onions are tender.
6 SERVINGS

Vegetable Kabobs

24 Brussels sprouts
2 small zucchini, each cut in
   6 pieces
Chicken Stock (page 48)
12 cherry tomatoes
12 mushrooms
Salt
1⅓ cups Cauliflower Sauce
   (page 47)

1. Simmer Brussels sprouts and zucchini in 1 inch of stock in a covered saucepan 5 minutes. Drain vegetables; cool.
2. Thread vegetables alternately on skewers. Sprinkle lightly with salt. Arrange kabobs in a shallow baking dish.
3. Bake at 400°F about 10 to 15 minutes, or until vegetables are tender; baste occasionally with stock. Serve hot sauce over kabobs.
6 SERVINGS

Stuffed Vegetables

6 turnips, kohlrabi,
   cucumbers, or celery roots
   (about 1½ pounds)
2 cups boiling water or
   chicken broth
1½ teaspoons salt
½ teaspoon sugar (optional)
¼ pound ground beef or
   pork
¼ cup sliced mushrooms
¼ cup chopped onion
1 tablespoon grated
   Parmesan cheese (optional)
¼ teaspoon salt
⅛ teaspoon pepper
1 egg, beaten
2 tablespoons fine dry bread
   crumbs

1. Trim and pare vegetables. Cook in boiling water with 1½ teaspoons salt and sugar, if desired, until tender.
2. Scoop out centers of vegetables until a thick, hollow shell is left.
3. Fry ground beef with mushrooms and onion in a skillet until onion is golden. Add cheese, salt, and pepper; mix well. Remove from heat. Blend in egg.
4. Mash scooped-out portion of vegetables. Combine with meat mixture.
5. Fill vegetable shells with stuffing. Sprinkle bread crumbs on top.
6. Place stuffed vegetables in a shallow casserole or baking dish.
7. Bake at 400°F 10 to 15 minutes, or until lightly browned on top.
6 SERVINGS

Spinach Casserole

4 packages (10 ounces each) frozen spinach, defrosted
7 slices day-old whole wheat bread with crusts removed
Water
¼ cup olive oil
3 garlic cloves, crushed in a garlic press
2 bunches scallions, minced
1 leek, minced
½ pound mushrooms
Salt and pepper to taste
2 tablespoons dill weed
1 tablespoon oregano
½ teaspoon cinnamon
1 tablespoon mint
6 eggs, beaten
¾ cup grated kefalotyri cheese
1½ cups water or chicken broth
1 cup freshly toasted coarse bread crumbs
Olive oil

1. Squeeze excess liquid from spinach. Sprinkle bread slices with water. Squeeze water out.
2. Heat olive oil in a large skillet. Sauté garlic, scallions, leek, and mushrooms for 3 minutes. Remove from heat. Add salt, pepper, dill, oregano, cinnamon, mint, and spinach. Sauté the mixture for 3 minutes. Add bread, eggs, cheese, and water; mix well.
3. Oil a 3½-quart baking dish and sprinkle bottom with bread crumbs. Pour in the spinach mixture.
4. Bake at 350°F 40 to 50 minutes, or until mixture is firm.
8 TO 12 SERVINGS

Sweet-Sour Red Cabbage II

1 head red cabbage (about 2 pounds)
1½ cups water
⅓ cup packed brown sugar
1 teaspoon salt
Dash pepper
¼ cup vinegar
¼ cup butter or margarine

1. Discard wilted outer leaves of cabbage. Cut into quarters, discarding core. Coarsely shred.
2. Place cabbage in a saucepan with water, brown sugar, salt, and pepper. Cover loosely and simmer 20 to 30 minutes, or until cabbage is tender and most of liquid has evaporated. Boil down without lid a few minutes, if necessary.
3. Add vinegar and butter; toss until butter is melted.
8 TO 10 SERVINGS

Smothered Green Peas or Salad Greens

2 packages (10 ounces each) frozen peas or 1¼ pounds escarole or endive, trimmed
1 teaspoon salt
2 cups boiling water
½ cup sour cream
1 teaspoon dill weed
2 tablespoons melted butter or bacon drippings
2 tablespoons flour
¼ teaspoon pepper
1 tablespoon chopped parsley

1. Add peas and salt to boiling water. Cover; remove from heat. Let stand 10 minutes. Drain.
2. Combine sour cream, dill weed, butter, flour, pepper, and parsley; mix well. Add to vegetables. Cover. Cook over medium-low heat 10 to 15 minutes, or until tender; stirring occasionally. Garnish with croutons, if desired.
4 TO 6 SERVINGS

Cucumbers in Sour Cream

3 cups sliced cucumbers
Salt
¼ cup chopped fresh dill or
2 tablespoons dill weed
1 cup sour cream or yogurt

1. Sprinkle cucumbers with salt. Let stand 30 minutes. Pat dry with paper towels.
2. Stir dill into sour cream. Add cucumbers; mix well.
4 TO 6 SERVINGS

Sauerkraut

1 pound sauerkraut, drained
5 slices bacon, diced
1½ cups water
1 tablespoon flour
½ cup sour cream (optional)

1. Rinse sauerkraut if mild flavor is desired. Drain well.
2. Fry bacon in a skillet until golden. Drain off 1 tablespoon fat; set aside.
3. Add sauerkraut to skillet. Fry 3 minutes, stirring often.
4. Add water. Cover and cook 45 minutes over medium heat.
5. Blend flour into reserved bacon fat. Stir into sauerkraut. Cook and stir over high heat 2 minutes. Stir in sour cream, if desired. Remove from heat.
ABOUT 4 SERVINGS

Potato Cakes

2 pounds potatoes
3 tablespoons grated kefalotyri cheese
2 tablespoons chopped parsley
Salt and pepper to taste
6 eggs, beaten
1 garlic clove, crushed in a garlic press
Flour for coating
Oil for frying

1. Boil potatoes in skins until tender. Peel and mash thoroughly. Mix in cheese, parsley, salt, pepper, eggs, and garlic. Shape into flat cakes. Coat with flour.
2. Heat oil in a skillet and add cakes, a few at a time. Fry until golden brown, turning once.
6 SERVINGS

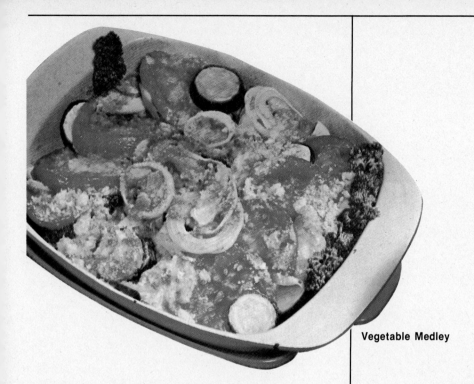

Vegetable Medley

Vegetable Medley

½ cup butter
2 cups (about ½ pound) sliced zucchini
1 cup chopped green pepper
1 cup chopped celery
¾ cup thinly sliced onion
2 cups cubed eggplant
½ teaspoon salt
1 cup coarse bread crumbs
3 medium tomatoes, sliced

1. Heat butter in a skillet. Add zucchini, green pepper, celery, and onion; sauté until just tender. Stir in eggplant and salt; spoon into a buttered 2-quart shallow casserole, leaving butter in skillet. Add crumbs to butter in skillet. Top vegetables with tomato slices and buttered crumbs.
2. Bake at 350°F about 30 minutes.
ABOUT 8 SERVINGS

Smothered Vegetables

1½ pounds potatoes, carrots, turnips, or celery roots
1 cup boiling water
1 teaspoon salt
4 teaspoons butter
4 teaspoons flour
¼ teaspoon pepper
1 tablespoon lemon juice (optional)
1 cup bouillon

1. Choose one vegetable to prepare at a time. Pare and slice or dice. Cook in boiling water with 1 teaspoon salt about 10 minutes, until crisp-tender. Drain.
2. Melt butter in a saucepan. Stir in flour, pepper, and, if desired, lemon juice. Gradually stir in bouillon. Add vegetable; stir to coat with sauce.
3. Cook, covered, 15 minutes, or until vegetable is tender. Garnish with Croutons if desired.
ABOUT 4 SERVINGS

Note: For extra flavor, dice **2 slices bacon.** Stir-fry until golden but not crisp. Substitute for butter.

Spinach with Rice

1 medium onion, finely chopped
3 tablespoons olive oil
1 pound fresh spinach, washed well and drained, or 2 packages (10 ounces
each) frozen leaf spinach, partially thawed
1 tablespoon tomato paste
¼ cup water
2 tablespoons long-grain rice
Salt and pepper to taste

1. In a saucepan, cook onion in olive oil until translucent. Add the spinach.
2. Mix tomato paste with the water and add along with rice; cover.
3. Simmer until rice is tender (about 20 minutes). Season with salt and pepper.
4 SERVINGS

Stuffed Tomatoes

4 medium tomatoes
⅓ cup chopped onion
2 tablespoons butter or margarine
½ pound ground beef or pork (optional)
1 cup cooked rice
1 tablespoon chopped fresh dill or 1 teaspoon dill weed
½ teaspoon salt
¼ teaspoon pepper
⅓ cup sour cream
Fine dry bread crumbs

1. Remove cores and seeds from tomatoes.
2. Sauté onion in butter. Add meat; cook until browned. Add rice, dill, salt, pepper, and sour cream; mix well.
3. Stuff tomatoes with rice mixture. Sprinkle bread crumbs on top. Place in a shallow casserole or baking dish. Cover.
4. Bake at 375°F 20 minutes. Remove cover. Continue baking until tender.
4 SERVINGS

Note: Green peppers may be substituted for tomatoes, if desired.

Sweet-Sour Red Cabbage I

1 head (about 2 pounds) red cabbage
Boiling salted water to cover (1 teaspoon salt per quart of water)
½ cup firmly packed brown sugar
1 tablespoon caraway seed
½ cup vinegar
¼ cup butter

1. Set out a heavy 3-quart saucepan.
2. Remove and discard wilted outer leaves from red cabbage.
3. Rinse, cut into quarters (discarding core), and coarsely shred (about 2 quarts, shredded). Put cabbage into the saucepan and add water to cover, brown sugar, caraway seed.
4. Cook 8 to 12 minutes, or until cabbage is just tender. Remove from heat and drain.
5. Add to cabbage vinegar and butter.
6. Toss together lightly to mix.
7. Serve immediately.
6 SERVINGS

Baked Carrot Ring

¾ cup butter
2 eggs, separated
½ cup packed brown sugar
1 teaspoon cinnamon
½ teaspoon nutmeg
½ teaspoon mint
Juice of ½ lemon
2 teaspoons water
1½ cups grated carrots
1 cup dried black currants
1 cup pine nuts
1 cup all-purpose flour
1 teaspoon baking powder
½ teaspoon baking soda
½ teaspoon salt
½ cup cracker meal

1. Using an electric mixer, cream butter, egg yolks, brown sugar, cinnamon, nutmeg, and mint until fluffy. Add lemon juice, water, carrots, currants, and pine nuts; blend thoroughly.
2. Mix flour, baking powder, baking soda, and salt. Add to carrot mixture.
3. Beat egg whites until fluffy. Fold into batter.
4. Grease a 9-inch ring mold or a square cake pan. Sprinkle with cracker meal. Pour in the batter.
5. Bake at 350°F 50 to 55 minutes.
6. Cool on wire rack. Place a serving dish over the top of carrot ring. Invert to unmold.
8 SERVINGS

Steamed Yellow Squash

1 can (10 ounces) plum tomatoes
1 large onion, minced
1 tablespoon minced parsley
1 teaspoon mint
1 teaspoon oregano
Salt and pepper to taste
1 cup chicken stock
3 tablespoons butter
2 pounds small yellow squash, sliced in half lengthwise

1. Combine all ingredients except squash.
2. Bring to a boil. Add squash.
3. Reduce heat and simmer about 15 minutes, or until squash is tender.
6 SERVINGS

Braised Leeks

¼ cup lemon juice
6 tablespoons olive oil
1½ cups chicken stock
1 teaspoon fennel seed, crushed
1 teaspoon coriander seed, crushed
½ teaspoon thyme
1 bay leaf
1 garlic clove, sliced
Salt and pepper to taste
9 medium leeks, white part only, split and cleaned, attached at the root

1. Combine lemon juice, olive oil, chicken stock, fennel seed, coriander seed, thyme, bay leaf, garlic, salt, and pepper in a skillet and bring to boiling. Simmer covered 15 minutes.
2. Arrange the prepared leeks in skillet in one layer. Simmer covered 20 to 30 minutes, or until tender.
3. Remove leeks carefully, arrange on serving platter, and pour liquid over.
3 SERVINGS

Bubble and Squeak

Cooked Corned Beef Brisket
6 medium-sized potatoes, pared
6 small whole white onions, peeled
1 pound small whole carrots, pared
2 pounds fresh Brussels sprouts, or 4 packages (10-ounces each) frozen Brussels sprouts
English Mustard Sauce, page 52

1. Bring the corned beef cooking liquid to boiling; add potatoes and onions and return to boiling. Cook 20 minutes. Add carrots and Brussels sprouts and return to boiling. Cook, partially covered, until tender, 10 to 15 minutes.
2. Serve corned beef with the vegetables and English Mustard Sauce.
6 SERVINGS

Polish Noodles and Cabbage

¼ cup butter or margarine
½ cup chopped onion
4 cups chopped or sliced
  cabbage
1 teaspoon caraway seed
½ teaspoon salt
⅛ teaspoon pepper
1 package (8 ounces) egg
  noodles
½ cup sour cream (optional)

1. Melt butter in a large skillet. Add onion; sauté until soft.
2. Add cabbage; sauté 5 minutes, or until crisp-tender. Stir in caraway seed, salt, and pepper.
3. Meanwhile, cook noodles in salted boiling water as directed on package. Drain well.
4. Stir noodles into cabbage. Add sour cream, if desired. Cook 5 minutes longer, stirring frequently.
6 TO 8 SERVINGS

Grilled Tomatoes with Rosemary and Dill

6 large ripe red tomatoes,
  cored and sliced in half
  horizontally
¼ cup olive oil
3 teaspoons rosemary
2 teaspoons dill
12 teaspoons grated
  kefalotyri cheese
Salt and pepper to taste

1. Arrange tomatoes, cut side up in a baking dish. Pour olive oil onto tomatoes, letting some fall into the dish.
2. Sprinkle with rosemary, dill, and cheese. Season with salt and pepper.
3. Broil until topping begins to brown (about 5 minutes).
6 SERVINGS

Stuffed Eggplant

¼ cup olive oil
2 large onions, minced
1 cup minced celery
1 carrot, thinly sliced
1 tablespoon long-grain rice
1 garlic clove, crushed in a
  garlic press
⅓ cup chopped parsley
1 teaspoon mint
½ teaspoon oregano
½ teaspoon thyme
1 can (8 ounces) whole
  tomatoes, drained
Salt and pepper to taste
1 firm ripe eggplant

1. Heat oil in a large skillet, add onion, and sauté. Remove from heat. Add celery, carrot, rice, garlic, parsley, mint, oregano, thyme, tomatoes, salt, and pepper. Cover. Simmer 10 to 15 minutes.
2. Cut off the stem end of the eggplant. Scoop out the center pulp. Sprinkle inside with salt. Set shell aside. Mash pulp and add to vegetables. Simmer, stirring occasionally, for 10 minutes.
3. Rinse inside of eggplant with a little water. Spoon in vegetable mixture. Replace top and secure with wooden picks.
4. Pour ½ cup water into a baking pan. Place eggplant on a trivet in pan.
5. Bake at 350°F 1 hour.
6. To serve, slice eggplant in half from top to bottom. Lay portions flat. Slice each lengthwise.
4 SERVINGS

Stewed Cauliflower

1 head cauliflower
½ cup olive oil
1 medium onion, chopped
1 garlic clove
1 bay leaf
1 tablespoons wine vinegar
¼ cup chopped parsley

1. Remove leaves from cauliflower and cut off tough end. Soak in cold salted water for 15 minutes. Rinse and drain. Keep whole or break into flowerets.
2. Heat olive oil in a saucepan. Add onion and cook until translucent. Add garlic, bay leaf, wine vinegar, parsley, cauliflower, and enough water to cover. Cover. Simmer, turning several times until tender (10 to 20 minutes).
3. Serve hot or cooled.
4 SERVINGS

Fried Eggplant

2 medium eggplants
Salt
¾ cup olive oil
¾ cup vegetable oil
2 cups all-purpose flour
Salt and pepper to taste

1. Slice eggplants horizontally ⅓ inch thick. Sprinkle both sides generously with salt. Arrange in a single layer in baking dish. Allow to stand 1 hour.
2. Squeeze each eggplant slice firmly between palms of hands or use a heavy weight wrapped in aluminum foil to press out excess liquid.
3. Heat oils together to smoking.
4. Meanwhile, season flour with salt and pepper. Dip each slice in the flour. Fry the eggplant slices until golden brown, turning once. Remove. Serve immediately.
ABOUT 6 SERVINGS

Simmered Zucchini

6 zucchini (5 inches long),
  cut in thick slices
1 cup water
½ cup olive oil
¼ cup wine vinegar
1 parsley sprig
1 garlic clove
Salt and pepper to taste

1. Combine all ingredients in a saucepan. Bring to a boil and reduce heat.
2. Simmer covered about 8 minutes, or until just tender.
3. Let cool in the liquid. Serve hot or chilled.
6 SERVINGS

Artichokes in White Wine

12 whole small onions,
  peeled
1 cup wine
1 cup water
¾ cup olive oil
Salt and pepper to taste
1 teaspoon sugar
1 teaspoon marjoram
1 bay leaf
4 parsley sprigs, minced
Juice of 1 lemon
8 artichokes, cleaned and cut
  in quarters

1. Combine all ingredients in a deep saucepan. Simmer covered until artichokes are tender.
2. Serve either hot or cold.
4 SERVINGS

Yams and Sweet Potatoes

Yams and Sweet Potatoes

Yams or sweet potatoes   Butter (optional)
Salt

Boil yams and serve plain sprinkled with salt and, if desired, topped with butter. Or barbecue yams on a grill 4 inches from ash-covered coals, turning frequently, until soft. Or bake yams until tender.

Okra with Tomatoes

2 pounds fresh okra
½ cup olive oil
1 large onion, minced
5 tomatoes, peeled, seeded, and coarsely chopped
3 garlic cloves, halved
1 teaspoon sugar
Salt and pepper to taste
Juice of 1 lemon

1. Wash okra and cut off any hard stems. Blanch in salted water for 3 minutes.
2. Heat olive oil. Add onion and cook until translucent. Add okra and cook until it begins to soften. Add tomatoes, garlic, sugar, salt, and pepper. Cook 2 to 3 minutes. Pour in enough water to cover. Cover and simmer about 1 hour, or until okra is tender. Stir in lemon juice. Serve hot.
8 SERVINGS

Green Beans with Tomatoes

2 pounds green beans or 3 packages (9 ounces each) frozen green beans
1 teaspoon salt
½ cup olive oil
1 can (20 ounces) tomatoes
(undrained)
1 medium onion, chopped
Juice of 1 lemon
1 teaspoon oregano, crushed
Salt and pepper

1. Wash green beans, cut off ends, and cut in half lengthwise. Bring a small amount of water to a boil. Add ½ teaspoon salt and the beans. Cover and cook about 20 minutes. Drain. If frozen beans are used, cook according to directions on the package.
2. Heat olive oil in a skillet. Add tomatoes, onion, lemon juice, oregano, and salt and pepper to taste. Simmer covered 10 minutes. Pour over beans. Simmer together an additional 10 minutes.
8 SERVINGS

Stewed Cabbage in Tomato Sauce

1 head cabbage
Boiling salted water
½ cup olive oil
1 medium onion, chopped
1 can (16 ounces) tomatoes (undrained)
1 celery stalk, diced
1 carrot, diced
1 bay leaf
1 teaspoon sugar
Salt and pepper to taste

1. Remove outer leaves from cabbage and trim off part of the core. Drop into boiling salted water to cover. Cook until just tender (about 8 minutes). Drain.
2. Meanwhile, heat olive oil in a saucepan and add onion; cook until translucent. Add tomatoes, celery, carrot, bay leaf, and sugar. Simmer 15 minutes.
3. Pour sauce over cabbage. Season with salt and pepper.
4 SERVINGS

Cauliflower in Béchamel Sauce

1 head cauliflower
Boiling water
Juice of 1 small lemon
2 cups Béchamel Sauce (page 52)
½ cup grated mizithra cheese
¼ cup fresh bread crumbs
¼ teaspoon ground allspice
Salt and pepper to taste

1. Remove leaves from the cauliflower and cut off tough end. Soak in cold salted water for 15 minutes. Rinse and drain. Keep whole or break into flowerets.
2. Boil enough water to cover cauliflower. Add lemon juice and the cauliflower. Cook until stalks are just tender (10 to 20 minutes). Drain.
3. Place cauliflower in a baking dish. Cover with Béchamel Sauce, sprinkle with cheese, bread crumbs, allspice, salt, and pepper.
4. Bake at 375°F 20 minutes.
4 TO 6 SERVINGS

Potatoes a la Huancaina

1½ pounds potatoes
4 hard-boiled eggs
1 (8 ounce) container cottage cheese
¼ cup sour cream
Juice of ½ lemon
2 tablespoons olive oil
½ teaspoon salt
½ teaspoon paprika
½ teaspoon crushed caraway seeds
½ teaspoon turmeric
½ teaspoon white pepper
¼ teaspoon cayenne
Lettuce leaves
1 large red onion, cut in rings
12 black olives
1 thinly sliced fresh chili pepper

1. Boil the potatoes in their skins. Peel them while still warm and let cool.
2. Peel the boiled eggs. Cut 2 eggs in wedges and separate yolks and whites of the other two.
3. Mash the two yolks and stir in the cottage cheese.
4. Mix the cottage cheese with the sour cream, lemon juice and oil. Whip the mixture till smooth.
5. Season with salt, paprika, caraway, turmeric, white pepper and cayenne.
6. Slice the potatoes and place the slices on a bed of lettuce leaves.
7. Pour on the cottage cheese mixture and garnish with egg wedges, onion rings, olives, sliced chili pepper and the two remaining hard-boiled egg whites cut into strips.
SERVES 4

Smothered Mixed Vegetables

8 small carrots, sliced	½ cup green peas
8 small potatoes	½ cup lima beans
4 medium white turnips, pared and sliced	2 tablespoons peanut oil
	1 large Spanish onion, sliced
4 medium tomatoes, peeled, seeded, and quartered	1 cup stock or beef broth
	¼ cup peanut oil
2 small chayote or zucchini, sliced	1 tablespoon salt
	Freshly ground pepper
1 green and 1 red sweet pepper, cut in strips	1 garlic clove, crushed in a garlic press
1 small eggplant (unpeeled), diced	4 dried Italian pepper pods or 1 pink hot pepper
Cauliflower chunks	1 tablespoon tomato paste

1. Arrange in a top-of-range casserole with lid the sliced carrot, potatoes, turnip slices, tomato quarters, sliced chayote, pepper strips, diced eggplant, cauliflower chunks, peas, and beans.

2. Heat 2 tablespoons oil in a skillet over medium heat. Add onion and sauté until golden. Add stock, ¼ cup oil, salt, pepper, and garlic; pour over vegetables in casserole. Lay pepper pods over vegetables; cover and cook covered over low heat 45 minutes.

3. Remove cover, increase heat, and cook off most of the liquid. Remove peppers and stir tomato paste into vegetable mixture. Serve with **pepper steak** or well-browned **spareribs** or **pork chops.**

Mixed Baked Vegetables

1 pound fresh green beans, ends snipped off and beans sliced vertically
2 large potatoes, pared and quartered
2 medium zucchini, pared and cut in ½-inch slices
4 celery stalks, cut in ½-inch slices
1 can (20 ounces) whole tomatoes, quartered, or 4

fresh tomatoes, peeled and cut in wedges
2 large onions, peeled and sliced
3 tablespoons olive oil
2 garlic cloves, crushed in a garlic press
½ cup chopped parsley
½ cup chopped dill
Salt and pepper to taste
Warm water

1. Oil a 2½-quart casserole. Arrange green beans, potatoes, zucchini, celery, tomatoes, and onions in layers, drizzling with oil and seasoning layers with garlic, parsley, dill, salt, and pepper. Add enough water to reach three fourths the depth of vegetables. Cover casserole.
2. Bake at 400°F about 15 minutes, or until liquid begins to simmer. Turn oven control to 325°F and bake 20 minutes longer. Remove cover and bake another 10 minutes. Adjust seasoning.
6 SERVINGS

Green Beans with Onion Rings

1 cup water
1 onion, thinly sliced
2 pounds green beans, ends snipped off and beans sliced
½ cup butter
Salt and pepper to taste
Lemon juice to taste

1. Bring water to boiling.
2. Separate onion slices into rings and add. Add green beans, butter, salt, pepper, and lemon juice.
3. Boil until beans are tender (about 20 minutes).
6 SERVINGS

Gingered Turnips

2 pounds yellow turnips, pared and cubed
1 tablespoon minced onion
1¼ cups Beef Stock (page 48)
½ teaspoon ground ginger
½ teaspoon sugar
2 teaspoons soy sauce

Combine all ingredients in a saucepan; simmer covered until turnips are tender (about 15 minutes). Drain; mash turnips with potato masher or electric mixer until fluffy; adding cooking liquid as needed for desired consistency.
6 SERVINGS

Macaroni Vegetable Medley au Vin

2 cups (8 ounces) elbow macaroni
1 package (10 ounces) frozen mixed vegetables
2 tablespoons butter or margarine
3 ounces fresh mushrooms, chopped
½ cup chopped onion
1 can (about 10 ounces) condensed cream of celery soup
1 soup can milk

2 teaspoons Worcestershire sauce
1 teaspoon salt
¼ teaspoon white pepper
1 teaspoon dry mustard
½ cup dry sherry or dry white wine
¼ cup chopped pimento
1 cup cooked peas
½ pound Swiss cheese, shredded
Chopped parsley
Pimento strips

1. Cook macaroni and frozen vegetables following directions on package. Drain and set aside.
2. Heat butter in a skillet; add mushrooms and onion. Cook, stirring occasionally, until onion is soft; set aside.
3. In a large bowl mix soup, milk, Worcestershire sauce, salt, white pepper, dry mustard, and wine. Add chopped pimento, peas, cheese, mushroom mixture, mixed vegetables, and macaroni; mix well. Turn into a greased 2½-quart casserole.
4. Bake at 300°F until thoroughly heated, about 30 minutes. Garnish with chopped parsley and pimento strips.
ABOUT 8 SERVINGS

Dilled Carrots

1 cup water
¼ cup white wine vinegar
1 medium onion, quartered
½ teaspoon salt
1 tablespoon dill
6 large carrots, pared and cut in thick slices

1. Bring water and vinegar to boiling. Put in onion, salt, dill, and carrots. Reduce heat and simmer 10 minutes. Cool.
2. Refrigerate in liquid until chilled.
3. Drain and serve cold.
4 TO 6 SERVINGS

Mushroom Cutlets

1 pound fresh mushrooms or 2 cups drained canned mushrooms
1 cup chopped onion
2 tablespoons butter
2 cups stale bread cubes
½ cup milk or water
3 eggs, beaten
1 tablespoon chopped parsley
½ teaspoon salt
¼ teaspoon pepper
Fine dry bread crumbs

1. Chop mushrooms. Sauté with onion in butter.
2. Soak bread cubes in milk 10 minutes. Add to mushrooms. Stir in eggs, parsley, salt, and pepper.
3. Shape into patties, using about 3 tablespoons for each. Coat with bread crumbs.
4. Fry in **butter** in a skillet until golden brown on both sides.
ABOUT 12 TO 14 CUTLETS

Baked Mushroom Mounds: Prepare Mushroom Cutlets as directed; add ¼ **teaspoon mace** along with salt. Spoon mushroom mixture into well-greased muffin pans. Dot tops with small pieces of **butter.** Bake at 350°F 15 to 20 minutes, or until set.

Cabbage Casserole

1 small head cabbage (1 pound)
2 carrots
1½ cups chicken stock or broth
5 peppercorns
1 (1 pound) can corn, drained
½ teaspoon salt
2 teaspoons soy sauce
4 hard-boiled eggs

1. Remove wilted leaves and cut the cabbage in strips. Pare the carrots and cut in slices.
2. Bring the chicken stock and peppercorns to a boil.
3. Add the cabbage and the carrots and boil, partially covered, for 15 minutes.
4. Add the corn and simmer until hot, about 5 minutes. Season with salt and soy sauce. Serve with egg halves. Garnish with chopped **parsley,** if desired.
SERVES 4

Cooked Vegetables with Garlic Mayonnaise

1 cup french-cut green beans, cooked
1 cup green peas, cooked
4 artichoke hearts, cooked
1 cup broccoli pieces, cooked
1 cup cauliflowerets, cooked
Paprika
Garlic Mayonnaise (page 53)
Parsley sprigs for garnish

1. Arrange vegetables in separate mounds in a serving dish, leaving a space in the center. Sprinkle with paprika.
2. Mound Garlic Mayonnaise in the center. Garnish with parsley.
6 TO 8 SERVINGS

Rice with Pine Nuts

¼ cup butter
1 small onion, minced
4 cups rice, cooked in chicken broth
¼ cup pine nuts
Juice of 1 lemon
1 teaspoon dill
½ teaspoon mint
Salt and pepper to taste

1. Melt butter in a saucepan.
2. Add onion and sauté until translucent. Add cooked rice, pine nuts, lemon juice, dill, mint, salt, and pepper. Heat thoroughly.
6 SERVINGS

Polish Beets

6 cooked beets, peeled
2 tablespoons butter
1 tablespoon flour
1 tablespoon vinegar
½ teaspoon salt
1 tablespoon sugar
¼ teaspoon caraway seed
½ cup sour cream

1. Grate the beets.
2. Melt butter in a saucepan; add flour and blend. Stir in vinegar, salt, sugar, and caraway seed.
3. Add beets. Cook over high heat 2 or 3 minutes. Stir in sour cream. Serve at once.
4 SERVINGS

Rice in Tomato Sauce

½ cup canned tomato sauce
1½ cups water
¼ cup butter
1 small onion, minced
Juice of 1 lemon
1 cup long-grain rice
Salt and pepper to taste

1. In a saucepan, combine tomato sauce, water, butter, onion, and lemon juice. Simmer covered until butter is melted.
2. Add rice. Continue simmering until the liquid is absorbed (about 20 minutes).
3. Season with salt and pepper.
4 TO 6 SERVINGS

Stuffed Artichokes or Tomatoes

4 cooked artichokes or 4 small tomatoes
¾ cup chopped onion
1 clove garlic, crushed
2 tablespoons butter
⅓ cup fine dry bread crumbs
1 tablespoon chopped fresh parsley
½ teaspoon dried basil leaves
½ teaspoon salt
¼ teaspoon pepper
1 tablespoon grated Parmesan cheese (optional)
4 teaspoons butter or margarine

1. Remove center leaves of artichokes; remove chokes. (Remove core from tomatoes and scoop out seeds; sprinkle inside with sugar and salt.)
2. Sauté onion and garlic in 2 tablespoons butter. Stir in bread crumbs, parsley, basil, salt, and pepper.
3. Fill vegetables with onion mixture. Sprinkle cheese on top. Set in a shallow casserole or baking dish. Place 1 teaspoon butter on top of each stuffed vegetable.
4. Bake at 375°F about 20 minutes, or until tender and browned on top.
4 SERVINGS

Mushrooms with Sour Cream

1 large onion, minced
2 tablespoons butter
1 pound fresh mushrooms, diced
1 tablespoon flour
½ teaspoon salt
¼ teaspoon pepper
½ cup whipping cream
½ cup dairy sour cream
¼ cup grated cheese (Parmesan, Swiss, or Cheddar)
2 tablespoons butter, melted

1. Sauté onion in 2 tablespoons butter in a skillet 5 minutes. Add mushrooms; sauté 5 minutes longer.
2. Blend flour, salt, and pepper with skillet mixture. Add whipping cream and sour cream gradually mixing thoroughly. Turn into 1-quart casserole. Top with cheese. Drizzle melted butter over top.
3. Bake at 350°F about 20 minutes, or until thoroughly heated.
4 TO 6 SERVINGS

Braised Cucumbers

¼ cup parsley, cleaned and
trimmed (2 tablespoons
chopped)
2 medium onions, peeled
and quartered
4 tablespoons butter
6 large cucumbers
2 tablespoons flour

½ cup chicken stock
Salt and pepper to taste
Pinch sugar
2 tablespoons lemon juice
1 teaspoon dried dill
½ cup sour cream
Dash nutmeg

1. Using **steel blade of food processor,** separately process parsley and onions until chopped. Set aside.
2. In a saucepan, sauté chopped onion in butter until transparent.
3. Pare cucumbers, cut in half lengthwise, and remove seeds. Cut into 3-inch lengths.
4. Add cucumbers to sautéed onions and cook until lightly browned. Add flour and cook for 2 minutes. Add chicken stock, salt, pepper, sugar, and lemon juice. Sprinkle with chopped parsley and dill and simmer for 10 minutes. Just before serving, add sour cream and nutmeg. Bring to a boil and reduce heat. Simmer for 5 minutes.

8 SERVINGS

Stewed Sauerkraut with Mushrooms

1 ounce dried mushrooms or
¼ pound fresh mushrooms
½ cup warm water
1 large onion, diced
2½ tablespoons butter or
shortening

1½ pounds sauerkraut, rinsed
and drained
⅓ cup water
2 tablespooons flour
Salt and pepper

1. Soak the dried mushrooms in ½ cup warm water 1 hour.
2. Sauté mushrooms and onion in butter in a skillet 3 minutes.
3. Add sauerkraut to mushrooms; cook and stir 10 minutes.
4. Blend ⅓ cup water into flour. Mix with sauerkraut and simmer 15 minutes. Season to taste with salt and pepper. Serve with **fish.**

ABOUT 6 SERVINGS

Sauerkraut with Dried Peas (for Christmas Eve)

1 cup dried split green or
yellow peas, rinsed
2⅔ cups boiling water
1 quart sauerkraut, rinsed
and drained

½ cup chopped mushrooms
3 cups water
Salt and pepper
1 can (2 ounces) anchovies,
drained

1. Combine peas and 2⅔ cups boiling water in a saucepan. Bring to boiling and boil 2 minutes. Remove from heat. Cover and let soak 30 minutes. Bring to boiling; simmer 20 minutes.
2. Cover sauerkraut and mushrooms with 3 cups water in a saucepan; cover and cook 1 hour.
3. Add cooked peas to sauerkraut mixture. Season to taste with salt and pepper; mix well. Turn into a buttered baking dish. Top with anchovies. Cover.
4. Bake at 325°F 30 minutes.

4 TO 6 SERVINGS

Sauerkraut with Dried Peas: Prepare Sauerkraut with Dried Peas; omit anchovies and baking. Fry **1 onion, chopped,** with **½ pound salt pork or bacon,** chopped, until lightly browned. Blend in **2 tablespoons flour** and add **1 cup sauerkraut cooking liquid.** Cook and stir until smooth. Mix with sauerkraut and peas; heat thoroughly.

French-Style Peas

2 cups shelled peas (see
Note)
8 small boiling onions, cut in
half
1 cup shredded lettuce
1 teaspoon sugar

2 teaspoons snipped parsley
2 teaspoons clarified butter
½ teaspoon salt
¼ teaspoon freshly ground
pepper
¾ cup water

Combine all ingredients except water; let stand 1 hour, stirring occasionally. Transfer mixture to a saucepan; add water. Simmer covered until peas and onions are tender (about 15 minutes). Serve hot.

4 SERVINGS

Note: Two packages (10 ounces each) frozen peas can be substituted in this recipe; do not mix with other ingredients. Add to saucepan during last 5 minutes of cooking.

Red Beets with Horseradish

3 cups cooked or canned red beets, drained and coarsely chopped
6 ounces prepared cream-

style horseradish
1 tablespoon brown sugar
1 teaspoon vinegar
¼ teaspoon salt

1. Combine all ingredients. Cover; refrigerate 3 days.
2. Serve with cold meats.
ABOUT 3 CUPS

Pickled Beets

3 cups sliced cooked or canned beets
1 tablespoon grated fresh horseradish or 4 teaspoons prepared horseradish

8 whole cloves or ½ teaspoon caraway seed
2 cups vinegar
1 tablespoon brown sugar
2 teaspoons salt

1. Layer beets in a glass or earthenware bowl, sprinkling layers with horseradish and cloves.
2. Boil vinegar with sugar and salt 2 minutes. Pour over the beets. Cover; refrigerate 24 hours.
ABOUT 3 CUPS

Whipped Carrots with Dill

1 pound carrots, sliced
Chicken Stock (page 48)
½ cup Mock Crème Fraîche (page 46)

2 tablespoons snipped fresh or 1 tablespoon dried dill weed
1 teaspoon salt

1. Simmer carrots in 1 inch of stock in a covered saucepan until tender (about 15 minutes); drain.
2. Purée in a food processor or blender with remaining ingredients. Return to saucepan; heat thoroughly.
4 SERVINGS

Stewed Okra and Tomatoes

1 pound okra, cut in 1-inch pieces
4 medium onions, chopped
4 large tomatoes, cored and chopped (see Note)
½ cup Beef Stock (page 48)
2 tablespoons fresh lemon

juice
½ teaspoon coriander seed, crushed
1 teaspoon salt
¼ teaspoon freshly ground pepper
Lemon wedges

1. Combine all ingredients except lemon wedges in a medium saucepan. Simmer covered over low heat 45 minutes.
2. Serve hot, or refrigerate and serve cold. Accompany with lemon wedges.
6 TO 8 SERVINGS

Note: If fully ripe fresh tomatoes are not available, use drained tomatoes from a 29-ounce can.

Whipped Carrots and Pears

1 pound carrots, sliced
Chicken Stock (page 48)
2 medium pears, pared, cored, and chopped
½ cup Creamy Fruit Mayon-

naise (page 53)
¼ teaspoon salt
1 teaspoon toasted sesame seed

1. Simmer carrots in 1 inch of stock in a covered saucepan until tender (about 10 minutes); drain.
2. Purée in a food processor or blender with pears, mayonnaise, and salt. Return to saucepan; heat thoroughly. Sprinkle with sesame seed.
6 SERVINGS

Squash and Tomatoes Parmesan

2 large yellow squash, pared and cut in thirds lengthwise
Chicken Stock (page 48)
¾ teaspoon salt
¼ teaspoon freshly ground pepper
1½ teaspoons snipped fresh or ¾ teaspoon dried basil leaves

1½ teaspoons snipped fresh or ¾ teaspoon dried oregano leaves
¼ teaspoon garlic powder
3 medium tomatoes, cut in thin slices
3 tablespoons freshly grated Parmesan cheese

1. Simmer squash in a large covered skillet in 1 inch stock until tender (about 8 minutes).
2. Remove squash to broiler pan. Sprinkle with half the salt, pepper, basil, oregano, and garlic. Top squash with tomato slices; sprinkle with remaining spices and cheese.
3. Broil 3 inches from heat until cheese browns (3 to 5 minutes).
6 SERVINGS

Broiled Tomatoes with Piquant Sauce

6 medium tomatoes, cut in half
Salt
Freshly ground pepper
1 hard-cooked egg, minced
1 egg, slightly beaten
1 tablespoon wine vinegar
1 tablespoon Worcestershire

sauce
1 teaspoon curry powder
½ teaspoon sugar
½ teaspoon dry mustard
3 tablespoons low-fat ricotta cheese
½ teaspoon salt
¼ cup water

1. Arrange tomatoes cut side up on a broiler pan. Season with salt and pepper. Broil 5 inches from heat 8 minutes.
2. Mix remaining ingredients except water in top of a double boiler. Cook and stir over simmering water 2 minutes; add ¼ cup water. Stir until sauce has thickened (about 3 minutes). Spoon sauce over tomatoes.
6 SERVINGS

Note: The sauce in this recipe can be served over any cooked vegetables. It is also delicious over steaks or roast beef.

Cabbage Rolls Paprikash

Cabbage Rolls Paprikash

8 large cabbage leaves
2½ cups diced cooked
 chicken
2 tablespoons chopped
 onion
½ cup finely chopped celery
¼ pound chopped fresh
 mushrooms
1 small clove garlic, minced
½ teaspoon salt
½ teaspoon thyme leaves
1 egg, beaten
2 tablespoons butter or
 margarine
6 tablespoons flour
2 cups chicken broth
2 cups sour cream
3 tablespoons paprika

1. Cook cabbage leaves 4 minutes in boiling salted water to cover. Drain and pat dry.
2. Mix chicken, onion, celery, mushrooms, garlic, salt, and thyme; stir in egg.
3. Place ½ cup of the chicken mixture in the center of each cabbage leaf. Fold sides of the cabbage leaf toward center, over filling, and then fold and overlap ends to make a small bundle. Fasten with wooden picks. Place in a 3-quart baking dish.
4. Heat butter in a large skillet. Blend in flour and heat until bubbly. Add chicken broth gradually, stirring until smooth. Blend in sour cream and paprika. Cook over low heat, stirring constantly, until thickened. Pour sauce over cabbage rolls. Cover baking dish.
5. Cook in a 350°F oven 35 minutes.
4 SERVINGS

Soy Pilaf with Fresh Vegetables

1½ cups chopped onion
½ cup soy grits or granules
 (see Note)
1 small eggplant, pared and
 cut in ½-inch cubes
1½ cups Chicken Stock
 (page 48)
½ teaspoon curry powder
¼ teaspoon salt
½ teaspoon paprika
½ teaspoon cumin
¼ teaspoon chili powder
⅛ teaspoon garlic powder
¼ teaspoon salt
2 medium tomatoes,
 chopped
1 green onion, chopped
1½ tablespoons lemon juice
¼ teaspoon salt
⅛ teaspoon freshly ground
 pepper
1 tablespoon snipped parsley

1. Spread onion in a 9x5x2-inch baking dish; sprinkle with soy. Layer eggplant over top. Mix stock with curry, salt, paprika, cumin, chili powder, and garlic; pour over eggplant.
2. Bake covered at 350°F 1 hour. Mound mixture on a serving platter; sprinkle with ¼ teaspoon salt.
3. While eggplant mixture is baking, mix tomatoes and remaining ingredients in a small bowl. Refrigerate covered. Spoon around pilaf on platter.
4 TO 6 SERVINGS

Note: Soy grits can be purchased in specialty or health food stores. They have a flavor similar to cracked wheat. Cracked wheat can be used in this recipe. You will need **2 cups cooked cracked wheat;** cook according to package directions.

Vegetable Mélange

1 medium eggplant, pared and cut in ¾-inch pieces
1 can (16 ounces) tomatoes, cut in thirds; use juice
4 stalks celery, cut in ¾-inch pieces
½ cup snipped parsley
½ cup dry vermouth
1½ teaspoons salt
¼ teaspoon freshly ground pepper
2 tablespoons snipped fresh or 1½ teaspoons dried fennel leaves
1 cup coarsely chopped onion
1½ cups coarsely chopped green pepper

1. Combine all ingredients except onion and green pepper in a Dutch oven; simmer covered 30 minutes.
2. Add onion and green pepper; simmer uncovered 20 minutes, stirring occasionally.
3. Serve in small bowls.
6 TO 8 SERVINGS

Note: Try different herb combinations in place of the fennel: **2 teaspoons snipped fresh basil** and **1 teaspoon snipped fresh oregano**, or **2 teaspoons curry powder** and **1 teaspoon cumin.**

Hash Brown Potatoes au Gratin

1 package (2 pounds) frozen chopped hash brown potatoes, partially defrosted
1½ teaspoons salt
Few grains pepper
¼ cup coarsely chopped green pepper
1 jar (2 ounces) sliced pimentos, drained and chopped
2 cups milk
¾ cup fine dry enriched bread crumbs
⅓ cup soft butter
⅔ cup shredded pasteurized process sharp American cheese

1. Turn potatoes into a buttered shallow 2-quart baking dish, separating into pieces. Sprinkle with salt and pepper. Add green pepper and pimentos; mix lightly. Pour milk over potatoes. Cover with aluminum foil.
2. Cook in a 350°F oven 1¼ hours, or until potatoes are fork-tender. Remove foil; stir potatoes gently. Mix bread crumbs, butter, and cheese. Spoon over top of potatoes. Return to oven and heat 15 minutes, or until cheese is melted.
ABOUT 6 SERVINGS

Vegetable-Stuffed Grapevine Leaves

1 small eggplant, pared and cut in ¼-inch cubes
Water
⅔ cup chopped onion
⅔ cup chopped celery
⅔ cup chopped carrot
1¼ teaspoons salt
¼ teaspoon freshly ground pepper
½ teaspoon poultry seasoning
½ teaspoon cinnamon
2 tablespoons snipped
parsley
2 teaspoons snipped fresh or 1 teaspoon dried mint leaves
1 jar (8 ounces) grapevine leaves preserved in brine*
Cold water
1 cup water
2 tablespoons fresh lemon juice
¾ cup Mock Hollandaise Sauce (page 49)

1. Simmer eggplant in 1 inch of salted water in a covered saucepan until tender (about 10 minutes); drain.
2. Process onion, celery, and carrot in a food processor or blender until finely ground; transfer mixture to mixing bowl. Mix in eggplant, salt, pepper, poultry seasoning, cinnamon, parsley, and mint. Spoon vegetable mixture into a 1-quart casserole.
3. Bake at 325°F 40 minutes; cool slightly.
4. Soak grapevine leaves in cold water 20 minutes; pat dry. Cover bottom of large skillet with four leaves. Place a rounded tablespoon of vegetable mixture on stem end of each leaf; roll up leaf, tucking in sides. Place filled leaf seam side down in skillet. Repeat with remaining leaves and vegetable mixture.
5. Pour 1 cup water and the lemon juice over rolls. Simmer covered 30 to 35 minutes. Serve hot, or refrigerate and serve cold. Pass hollandaise. This recipe can also be served as a first course.
8 SERVINGS (4 ROLLS EACH)

*Grapevine leaves can be purchased in a gourmet shop or in the specialty department of a supermarket.

Hash Brown Potatoes au Gratin

Vegetables Creole

4 slices bacon, diced
1 package (10 ounces) frozen french style green beans
1 package (10 ounces) frozen succotash
1 can (8 ounces) tomatoes
1 teaspoon dried minced

onion
1 beef bouillon cube
2 tablespoons Chili Sauce
2 tablespoons flour
8 dinner crêpes (see page 36)

1. Sauté bacon until crisp. Drain and reserve drippings. Add beans, succotash, tomatoes, onion, bouillon cube, and Chili Sauce to bacon pieces. Stir and cook until heated.
2. Stir flour into reserved bacon drippings. Stir into vegetable mixture. Simmer, stirring occasionally, until thick.
3. Assemble, using turnover method (see page 36); drain vegetables with a slotted spoon. Place filled crêpes, seam side down, on a baking sheet.
4. Bake at 375°F 10 minutes. Serve topped with remaining warmed sauce.

8 FILLED CRÊPES

Artichokes in Lemon

1 can (14 ounces) artichoke hearts
3 tablespoons lemon juice
2 tablespoons olive oil

1 clove garlic, peeled and finely chopped
¼ teaspoon salt
⅛ teaspoon pepper

1. Drain artichoke hearts and place in refrigerator to chill. Combine remaining ingredients and chill.
2. When ready to serve, stir lemon-olive oil mixture and pour over artichoke hearts.

6 APPETIZER SERVINGS

Cheese-Spinach Gnocchi

1½ cups milk
1 tablespoon butter
¼ teaspoon salt
Few grains ground nutmeg
¼ cup uncooked farina
½ cup well-drained cooked chopped spinach
1 egg, well beaten
1 tablespoon chopped onion,

lightly browned in 1 teaspoon butter
1½ cups shredded Swiss cheese
2 eggs, well beaten
¾ cup milk
1 tablespoon flour
1 teaspoon salt
Few grains ground nutmeg

1. Bring milk, butter, salt, and nutmeg to boiling in a saucepan. Add farina gradually, stirring constantly over low heat until mixture thickens.
2. Stir in spinach, egg, onion, and 1 cup shredded cheese; mix well. Remove from heat and set aside to cool slightly.
3. Drop mixture by tablespoonfuls close together in a well-greased 9-inch shallow baking pan or casserole. Sprinkle mounds with remaining cheese.
4. Combine remaining ingredients and pour over spinach mounds.
5. Bake at 350°F 35 to 40 minutes, or until topping is golden brown.

ABOUT 6 SERVINGS

Stuffed Eggplant

3 medium eggplants (about 3 pounds)
1½ teaspoons salt
1 cup boiling water
¼ cup butter
1 cup chopped onion
2 cups coarsely chopped peeled tomatoes
1 to 2 teaspoons salt
¼ teaspoon pepper
1 teaspoon dried basil

½ teaspoon oregano
2 cups chopped cooked ham
1 cup fine dry bread crumbs
¼ teaspoon oregano
¼ cup butter, melted
6 slices mozzarella cheese, halved
12 anchovy fillets
2 tablespoons chopped parsley

1. Cut the eggplants in half lengthwise. Make several cuts into the pulp, being careful not to pierce skin. Sprinkle cut sides with 1½ teaspoons salt. Let stand 30 minutes.
2. Pat eggplant halves dry with paper towels. Place flat-side down in a baking pan. Add boiling water.
3. Bake at 375°F, uncovered, 15 minutes, or until just tender. Cool on wire rack. Scoop out pulp, leaving ¼-inch-thick shell walls. Chop pulp coarsely and drain. Set pulp and shells aside.
4. Melt ¼ cup butter in a large skillet. Add the onion and sauté about 5 minutes, or until golden. Stir in tomatoes, 1 to 2 teaspoons salt, pepper, basil, ½ teaspoon oregano, ham, ½ cup of the bread crumbs, and the eggplant pulp. Simmer, covered, 5 minutes.
5. Fill eggplant shells with mixture, mounding slightly. Place in a shallow baking pan. Combine remaining ½ cup bread crumbs, ¼ teaspoon oregano, and melted butter; sprinkle over each eggplant.
6. Place 2 pieces cheese on top of each eggplant half. Lay 2 anchovy fillets on each half.
7. Bake at 375°F about 15 minutes, or until cheese melts and filling is heated through. Sprinkle each half with 1 teaspoon chopped parsley.

6 SERVINGS

Vegetable Omelet

3 tablespoons olive oil
½ cup chopped onion
½ cup sliced mushrooms
½ cup sliced zucchini
10 frozen artichoke heart halves, thawed

1 teaspoon salt
¼ teaspoon freshly ground black pepper
6 eggs
¼ cup canned tomato sauce

1. Heat oil in a 9-inch skillet with an ovenproof handle. Sauté onion 5 minutes. Add mushrooms, zucchini, and artichoke heart halves; cook 10 minutes over low heat. Sprinkle ½ teaspoon salt and ⅛ teaspoon pepper over vegetables.
2. Beat eggs with remaining ½ teaspoon salt and ⅛ teaspoon pepper; pour over vegetables. Spoon tomato sauce over the top.
3. Bake at 350°F 15 minutes, or until eggs are set. Cut in wedges and serve immediately.

4 TO 6 SERVINGS

Artichokes Basilicata Style

1 package (9 ounces) frozen artichoke hearts
1 tablespoon lemon juice
½ cup fine dry bread crumbs
1 tablespoon grated Parmesan or Romano cheese
1 teaspoon chopped fresh basil leaves or ½ teaspoon dried basil
1 egg
½ teaspoon salt
⅛ teaspoon pepper
½ cup olive oil

1. Slice aritchoke hearts vertically into thin slices. Spread out on paper towels to thaw. Sprinkle with lemon juice and let stand 30 minutes.
2. Combine bread crumbs, cheese, and basil. Beat egg with salt and pepper. Dip artichoke heart slices in egg, then roll in bread-crumb mixture.
3. Heat olive oil in skillet. Add artichoke heart slices and cook over low heat until browned. Serve while crisp.
3 OR 4 SERVINGS

Green Beans Basilicata Style

1½ pounds fresh green beans
1 teaspoon salt
2 quarts boiling water
¼ cup chopped onion
2 tablespoons olive oil
½ teaspoon salt
⅛ teaspoon pepper
2 tablespoons chopped fresh mint or basil leaves
3 tablespoons wine vinegar

1. Wash beans and break off ends. Leave whole or cut as desired.
2. Add 1 teaspoon salt to boiling water, stir in beans, cover, and bring to boiling. Cook 10 minutes, or until crisp-tender.
3. While beans are cooking, sauté onion in olive oil until transparent (about 8 minutes). When beans are done cooking, drain and add to onion. Season with ½ teaspoon salt and the pepper. Add mint leaves and vinegar; toss gently. Serve while hot.
4 TO 6 SERVINGS

Green Beans with Onions

8 to 12 small whole onions, peeled
1 pound green beans
¼ teaspoon salt
2 tablespoons olive oil
1 clove garlic, chopped
½ teaspoon salt
⅛ teaspoon pepper

1. Put onions in a small amount of boiling salted water in a saucepan. Cover and cook 15 to 20 minutes, or until onions are tender.
2. Meanwhile, wash beans, break off ends, and cut beans lengthwise into fine strips. Bring a small amount of water to boiling in a saucepan, add ¼ teaspoon salt and beans. Cover and cook 10 to 15 minutes, or until beans are tender. Drain.
3. Heat oil and garlic in a skillet until garlic is lightly browned. Add green beans and onions, season with salt and pepper, and cook 5 to 10 minutes, or until thoroughly heated, stirring occasionally.
ABOUT 4 SERVINGS

Stuffed Artichokes Sicilian

4 medium artichokes
1 teaspoon salt
⅔ cup fine dry bread crumbs
1 clove garlic, peeled and thinly sliced
1 teaspoon grated Parmesan cheese
1 teaspoon chopped parsley
1 teaspoon salt
¾ teaspoon pepper
2 cloves garlic, peeled and thinly sliced
1 tablespoon chopped parsley
2 cups boiling water
2 tablespoons olive oil

1. Cut off 1 inch from the top and base of each artichoke. Remove lower outer leaves. If desired, snip off tips of remaining leaves. Cover with cold water and add 1 teaspoon salt. Let stand 5 to 10 minutes. Drain upside down.
2. Mix together bread crumbs, 1 clove garlic, thinly sliced, cheese, 1 teaspoon chopped parsley, 1 teaspoon salt, and pepper. Set aside.
3. Spread leaves of drained artichokes open slightly. Place 3 slices garlic in each artichoke. Sprinkle bread crumb mixture between leaves and over top of artichokes. Sprinkle with chopped parsley.
4. Place artichokes close together in a 10-inch skillet so they will remain upright during cooking. Pour the boiling water in the skillet and sprinkle the artichokes with olive oil.
5. Cook, covered, about 30 minutes, or until artichoke leaves are tender.
4 SERVINGS

Asparagus Parmesan

1½ pounds asparagus
½ cup butter, melted
½ cup grated Parmesan or
Romano cheese
1 teaspoon salt
½ teaspoon pepper

1. Wash asparagus. Put into a small amount of boiling salted water in a skillet. Bring to boiling, reduce heat, and cook 5 minutes, uncovered; cover and cook 10 minutes, or until just tender.
2. Pour melted butter into a greased 1½-quart casserole. Put cooked asparagus into casserole and sprinkle with mixture of grated cheese, salt, and pepper.
3. Bake at 450°F 5 to 10 minutes, or until cheese is melted.
ABOUT 6 SERVINGS

Buttered Carrots

1½ pound carrots
1 teaspoon sugar
½ teaspoon salt
⅛ teaspoon pepper
3 tablespoons butter
¾ cup water
1 tablespoon chopped parsley

1. Pare carrots and cut into julienne strips. Place in a large, heavy saucepan with sugar, salt, pepper, butter, and water. Cover.
2. Bring to boiling, then simmer 10 to 15 minutes, or until carrots are tender and moisture is evaporated. Remove cover to evaporate moisture, if necessary.
3. Turn carrots into a serving bowl and sprinkle with parsley.
6 SERVINGS

Brussels Sprouts and Grapes

1½ pounds fresh Brussels
  sprouts, cut in half
1½ cups beer
2 teaspoons clarified butter
¼ teaspoon salt

⅛ teaspoon freshly ground
  white pepper
1 cup seedless white grapes
Snipped parsley

1. Simmer Brussels sprouts in beer in covered saucepan
until tender (about 8 minutes); drain.
2. Drizzle butter over sprouts; sprinkle with salt and pepper. Add grapes; heat thoroughly. Sprinkle with parsley.
4 TO 8 SERVINGS

Crispy French Fried Onion Rings

2 sweet Spanish onions
1 cup pancake mix
¾ cup beer

Oil for deep frying heated to
375°F
Salt

1. Peel onions and cut into ½-inch-thick slices; separate into rings.
2. Combine pancake mix and beer to make a smooth, thick batter.
3. Dip onion rings in batter and fry, a few at a time, in hot fat until golden brown. Drain on absorbent paper-lined baking sheets.
4. Keep fried onion rings hot in oven until all rings are fried.

Note: To freeze fried onion rings, leave onion rings on lined baking sheets, place in freezer, and freeze quickly. Then carefully remove rings to moisture-vaporproof containers with layers of absorbent paper between layers of onions. Cover container tightly and freeze. To heat frozen onion rings, place rings on a baking sheet and heat in a 375°F oven for several minutes.

Broccoli, Southern Style

1 medium onion, thinly
sliced
1 clove garlic, thinly sliced
2 tablespoons olive oil
1½ tablespoons flour
½ teaspoon salt
⅛ teaspoon pepper

1 cup chicken broth
4 anchovy fillets, chopped
½ cup sliced ripe olives
2 cups shredded process
Cheddar cheese
2 pounds broccoli, cooked
and drained

1. Cook onion and garlic in hot olive oil in a saucepan until onion is soft. Blend in a mixture of flour, salt, and pepper. Heat until bubbly.
2. Add chicken broth, stirring constantly. Bring to boiling and cook 1 or 2 minutes, or until sauce thickens.
3. Blend in anchovies, olives, and cheese. Pour sauce over hot broccoli.
ABOUT 6 SERVINGS

Italian Cauliflower

1 large head cauliflower,
washed and trimmed
2 tablespoons butter
½ clove garlic, minced
2 teaspoons flour

1 teaspoon salt
2 cups canned tomatoes
1 small green pepper, coarsely chopped
¼ teaspoon oregano

1. Separate cauliflower into flowerets. Put into a saucepan containing a small amount of boiling salted water. Cook, uncovered, 5 minutes. Cover and cook 8 to 10 minutes, or until cauliflower is tender. Drain if necessary and keep hot.
2. Heat butter with garlic; stir in flour and salt and cook until bubbly.
3. Add tomatoes and bring to boiling, stirring constantly; cook 1 to 2 minutes. Mix in green pepper and oregano.
4. Pour sauce over hot cauliflower.
ABOUT 6 SERVINGS

Baked Eggplant

4 eggplants (about ¾ pound
each)
½ cup olive oil

2 teaspoons salt
1 teaspoon pepper

1. Wash and dry eggplants; remove stems. Leave eggplant whole and unpeeled. Make a slit the length of each eggplant only to the center, not completely through to the other side.
2. In each slit, drizzle 1 tablespoon olive oil and season with ½ teaspoon salt and ¼ teaspoon pepper. Gently press eggplant together and rub completely with olive oil. Rub an 11x7-inch baking dish with olive oil. Place eggplants in dish.
3. Bake at 375°F about 30 minutes, or until eggplants are tender.
6 TO 8 SERVINGS

Eggplant Parmesan

Tomato Meat Sauce (page
50)
4 quarts water
1 tablespoon salt
3 cups (about 8 ounces)
noodles
1 eggplant (about 1 pound)
2 eggs, slightly beaten

¼ cup cream
3 tablespoons olive oil
⅔ cup fine dry bread crumbs
1 cup grated Parmesan
cheese
6 slices (3 ounces) moz-
zarella cheese

1. Prepare Tomato Meat Sauce.
2. Heat water in a large saucepan. Add salt, then noodles; stir with a fork. Boil rapidly, uncovered, 10 to 15 minutes, or until noodles are tender. Drain. Set aside.
3. Wash eggplant, pare, and cut into ½-inch-thick slices.
4. Combine eggs and cream.
5. Heat oil in a skillet. Dip eggplant into egg mixture, then into bread crumbs. Put eggplant slices into skillet and brown slowly on both sides.
6. Put a third of the drained noodles into a greased 2-quart casserole. Layer with a third of eggplant slices. Add 1 cup meat sauce. Sprinkle with a third of grated cheese. Repeat layers, ending with eggplant slices. Top with cheese slices. Cover casserole.
7. Bake at 350°F about 20 minutes. Remove cover and bake 10 to 15 minutes, or until cheese is lightly browned. Serve with remaining meat sauce.
ABOUT 6 SERVINGS

Apple-Stuffed Acorn Squash

2 acorn squash
2 tart apples
1½ teaspoons grated fresh
lemon peel
1 tablespoon fresh lemon
juice
¼ cup butter or margarine,

melted
⅓ cup firmly packed brown
sugar
Salt
Cinnamon
Apple and lemon slices for
garnish (optional)

1. Cut squash into halves lengthwise and scoop out seedy centers. Place cut side down in baking dish and pour in boiling water to a ½-inch depth. Bake at 400°F 20 minutes.
2. Pare, core, and dice apples; mix with lemon peel and juice, 2 tablespoons butter, and brown sugar.
3. Invert squash halves and brush with remaining 2 tablespoons butter; sprinkle with salt and cinnamon.
4. Fill squash halves with apple mixture. Pour boiling water into dish to a ½-inch depth; cover and bake 30 minutes.
5. Before serving, spoon pan juices over squash. If desired, garnish with apple and lemon slices.
4 SERVINGS

Apple-Stuffed Acorn Squash

Zucchini Parmesan I

2 tablespoons cooking oil
1 small clove garlic, minced
4 medium zucchini, thinly sliced
⅓ cup coarsely chopped onion
1 tablespoon chopped parsley

1 teaspoon salt
⅛ teaspoon pepper
¼ teaspoon oregano
¼ teaspoon rosemary
2 cups chopped peeled tomatoes
¼ cup grated Parmesan cheese

1. Heat oil in a large wok. Add garlic and stir-fry about 1 minute. Stir in zucchini, onion, and parsley. Sprinkle with a mixture of salt, pepper, oregano, and rosemary. Stir together and cover.
2. Heat about 5 minutes over medium heat. Stir in tomatoes and cook, uncovered, 1 to 2 minutes, or until tomatoes are thoroughly heated.
3. Turn mixture into a serving dish and sprinkle with cheese.
4 OR 5 SERVINGS

Mushrooms Parmesan

1 pound mushrooms with 1- to 2-inch caps
2 tablespoons olive oil
¼ cup chopped onion
½ clove garlic, finely chopped
⅓ cup fine dry bread crumbs

3 tablespoons grated Parmesan cheese
1 tablespoon chopped parsley
½ teaspoon salt
⅛ teaspoon oregano
2 tablespoons olive oil

1. Clean mushrooms and remove stems. Place caps open-end up in a shallow greased 1½-quart baking dish; set aside. Finely chop mushroom stems.
2. Heat 2 tablespoons olive oil in a skillet. Add mushroom stems, onion, and garlic. Cook slowly until onion and garlic are slightly browned.
3. Combine bread crumbs, cheese, parsley, salt, and oregano. Mix in the onion, garlic, and mushroom stems. Lightly fill mushroom caps with mixture. Pour 2 tablespoons olive oil into the baking dish.
4. Bake at 400°F 15 to 20 minutes, or until mushrooms are tender and tops are browned.
6 TO 8 SERVINGS

Anchovy-Stuffed Mushrooms: Follow recipe for Mushrooms Parmesan. Omit cheese. Mix in **4 anchovy fillets,** finely chopped.

Stuffed Onions

6 large onions
2 tablespoons butter
1 cup soft bread crumbs
2 tablespoons olive oil
¼ pound ground beef
2 cups soft bread crumbs
1 egg yolk

2 teaspoons chopped parsley
1 teaspoon salt
¼ teaspoon pepper
¼ teaspoon marjoram
2 tablespoons olive oil
1 tablespoon chopped parsley

1. Cut off root ends of onions; peel, rinse, and cut off a ½-inch slice from top of each.
2. Put onions in boiling salted water to cover in a large saucepan. Cook 10 to 15 minutes, or until onions are slightly tender. Drain well and cool.
3. Meanwhile, heat butter in a skillet. Stir in 1 cup bread crumbs. Turn into a small bowl and set aside.
4. With a sharp knife, cut down around onions, about ¼ inch from edge, leaving about 3 outside layers. With a spoon, scoop out centers and chop them.
5. Heat 2 tablespoons oil in skillet. Add chopped onion and ground beef to heated oil; cook until beef is browned.
6. Combine beef mixture with 2 cups bread crumbs, egg yolk, 2 teaspoons parsley, salt, pepper, and marjoram. Lightly fill onions with mixture.
7. Put filled onions into a greased 2½-quart casserole. Spoon buttered crumbs on top and sprinkle with remaining oil and parsley.
8. Bake at 350°F about 1 hour.
6 SERVINGS

Stuffed Peppers

4 green peppers
¼ cup olive oil
1 pound ground beef
1⅓ cups cooked rice
2 tablespoons minced onion
1 tablespoon minced parsley
½ teaspoon salt
¼ teaspoon pepper
1½ cups canned tomatoes,

sieved
¼ cup water
¼ cup minced celery
1 tablespoon olive oil
½ teaspoon salt
¼ teaspoon pepper
Mozzarella cheese, cut in strips

1. Rinse peppers and cut a thin slice from stem end of each. Remove white fiber and seeds; rinse. Drop peppers into boiling salted water to cover and simmer 5 minutes. Remove peppers from water; invert and set aside to drain.
2. Heat ¼ cup oil in a skillet. Add ground beef and cook until browned. Stir in cooked rice, onion, parsley, ½ teaspoon salt, and ¼ teaspoon pepper. Lightly fill peppers with rice-meat mixture, heaping slightly. Set in a 2-quart baking dish.
3. Mix tomatoes, water, celery, and remaining oil, salt, and pepper; pour around peppers. Put strips of cheese on each pepper.
4. Bake at 350°F about 15 minutes.
4 SERVINGS

Zucchini Parmesan II

8 to 10 small zucchini
   squash (about 2½ pounds)
3 tablespoons olive oil
⅔ cup coarsely chopped
   onion
¼ pound mushrooms, cleaned
   and sliced

⅔ cup grated Parmesan
   cheese
2 cans (6 ounces each)
   tomato paste
1 clove garlic, minced
1 teaspoon salt
⅛ teaspoon pepper

1. Wash and trim off ends of zucchini; cut crosswise into ⅛-inch-thick slices.
2. Heat olive oil in a large saucepan; add zucchini, onion, and mushrooms. Cover saucepan and cook vegetables over low heat 10 to 15 minutes, or until tender, stirring occasionally.
3. Remove vegetable mixture from heat; stir in about half the cheese. Combine tomato paste, garlic, salt, and pepper; pour into vegetable mixture, blending lightly but thoroughly. Turn mixture into a 2-quart casserole. Sprinkle with remaining cheese.
4. Bake at 350°F 20 to 30 minutes.
ABOUT 8 SERVINGS

Bananas à l'Antillaise

6 green-tipped bananas,
   peeled and halved
2 cups dry white wine
Salt to taste
2 tablespoons butter

2 tablespoons flour
⅛ teaspoon mace
⅛ teaspoon cloves
Cayenne or red pepper to
   taste

1. Put bananas into a saucepan with wine and salt. Bring to a boil, cover, and simmer 25 minutes.
2. Blend butter, flour, mace, cloves, and pepper.
3. Remove fruit from saucepan. Stir butter mixture into liquid in saucepan. Boil and stir 3 minutes.
4. Serve the fruit and sauce in a dish as an accompaniment to roast pork.

Baked Tomatoes, Genoa Style

4 firm ripe tomatoes, cut in
   halves and seeded
Sugar
¼ cup olive oil
2 cloves garlic, minced
1½ teaspoons salt

½ teaspoon pepper
1½ teaspoons marjoram,
   crushed
¼ cup finely snipped parsley
½ cup shredded Parmesan
   cheese

1. Put tomato halves, cut side up, in a shallow baking dish. Sprinkle lightly with sugar.
2. Mix olive oil, garlic, salt, pepper, and marjoram. Spoon an equal amount onto each tomato half. Sprinkle with parsley and cheese.
3. Bake at 350°F about 20 minutes, or until lightly browned.
4 SERVINGS

Deep-Fried Potatoes

Fat for deep frying heated to
   360°F
2 pounds potatoes (about 6

medium)
Salt

1. Start heating fat for deep frying.
2. Wash and pare potatoes. Trim off sides and ends to form large blocks. Cut lengthwise into sticks about ⅜ inch wide. Pat dry with absorbent paper.
3. Fry about 1 cup of potatoes at a time in hot fat until potatoes are tender and golden brown. Drain over fat, then put on paper toweling. Sprinkle with salt.
4. Serve hot.
ABOUT 4 SERVINGS

Zucchini Romano

8 small zucchini (about 1½
   pounds)
1 egg, fork beaten
½ cup shredded mozzarella
   cheese
3 tablespoons bottled Italian
   salad dressing

1/16 teaspoon black pepper
2 tablespoons melted butter
   or margarine
½ pound ground ham or
   veal
½ cup Tomato Sauce (page
   54)

1. Wash zucchini and trim ends. Slice off a narrow lengthwise strip. Using an apple corer, remove seeds to make a hollow about ¾ inch deep for each zucchini. Cover with boiling water, simmer about 5 minutes, and drain well.
2. Meanwhile, combine egg, cheese, dressing, pepper, and butter in a bowl. (If using veal, add ¼ teaspoon salt.) Lightly mix in meat. Fill zucchini with meat mixture, using about 3 tablespoons in each hollow.
3. Arrange zucchini, stuffed side up, in a single layer in an oiled shallow 1½-quart baking dish; spread tops with sauce. (Or omit sauce and brush tops with olive oil.)
4. Bake at 375°F about 15 minutes, or until meat is cooked. Serve hot.
8 SERVINGS

Fried Artichoke Hearts

¾ cup beer	8 canned artichoke hearts
½ teaspoon salt	¾ cup all-purpose flour
1 egg, beaten	Oil for deep frying

1. Mix beer, salt and egg.
2. Dip artichokes in beer batter, then in flour.
3. Fry in hot oil for 5 minutes until brown all over.
4. Drain on paper towels and serve hot with **lemon wedges.**

SERVES 4

Deviled Potatoes

8 medium potatoes
½ teaspoon turmeric
1 teaspoon salt
1 teaspoon garlic powder
2 tablespoons vegetable oil
1 tablespoon chopped
  yellow onion
½ teaspoon freshly grated
  ginger

½ teaspoon chopped fresh
  chili pepper
⅓ cup boiling water
½ teaspoon crushed
  coriander seeds
½ teaspoon aniseed
½ teaspoon poppy seeds

1. Peel the potatoes and cut each lengthwise in 8 slices.
2. Mix turmeric, salt and garlic powder. Sprinkle this on the potatoes, stir and let stand for about 15 minutes.
3. Heat half the oil and fry the potatoes half soft on low heat.
4. Heat the rest of the oil in another pan and brown the chopped onion, the chili pepper and the ginger. Pour on the boiling water.
5. Add the potatoes and let them absorb the liquid over low heat.
6. Sprinkle on the other seasonings and shake the potatoes in the pan. Taste and correct seasoning with salt if needed.
SERVES 4

Stuffed Baked Sweet Potatoes

4 medium sweet potatoes, washed
1 small ripe banana, peeled
2 tablespoons butter or margarine
⅓ cup fresh orange juice
1 tablespoon brown sugar
1½ teaspoon salt
¼ cup chopped pecans

1. Bake sweet potatoes at 375° 45 minutes to 1 hour, or until tender when tested with a fork.
2. Cut a lengthwise slice from each potato. Scoop out sweet potatoes into a bowl; reserve shells. Mash banana with potatoes; add butter, orange juice, brown sugar, and salt and beat thoroughly. Spoon mixture into shells. Sprinkle with pecans. Set on a cookie sheet.
3. Return to oven 12 to 15 minutes, or until heated.
4 SERVINGS

French-Fried Breadfruit

1 large heavy breadfruit
Oil for deep frying, heated to
365°F
Salt to taste

1. Cut the breadfruit into wedges about 1½ inches thick; discard the center. Soak the wedges in lightly salted water 30 minutes. Dry with absorbent paper.
2. Fry breadfruit wedges, a few at a time, in heated oil until golden (about 8 minutes). Drain on absorbent paper. Salt lightly and serve very hot where you would serve French-fried potatoes.

Basic Mexican Beans

1 pound dried pinto, pink, black, or red kidney beans
1 cup chopped onion
Water
Salt to taste

1. Wash beans well and put into a large saucepan. Add onion, then add enough water to cover beans completely. Cover, bring water to boiling, reduce heat, and simmer until beans are tender, about 3 hours. Add more water if needed, but add it gradually so water continues to boil.
2. When beans are tender, add salt to taste.
3. Use in recipes calling for cooked beans.
ABOUT 5 TO 6 CUPS COOKED BEANS

Soupy Beans: Beans prepared as above are sometimes served in soup bowls without further preparation, or with a sprinkling of grated cheese and chopped green onion.

Zucchini in Salsa Verde

Fat for deep frying
¼ cup olive oil
2 tablespoons wine vinegar
2 tablespoons minced parsley
1 clove garlic, crushed in a garlic press or minced
2 anchovy fillets, finely
chopped
Few grains black pepper
4 zucchini squash, washed and thinly sliced
Flour
Salt

1. Start heating the fat to 365°F.
2. Meanwhile, blend oil, vinegar, parsley, garlic, anchovies, and pepper in a small bowl and set mixture aside.
3. Coat zucchini slices slightly with flour. Fry in hot fat, turning frequently, until lightly browned (2 to 3 minutes). Remove from fat and drain. Sprinkle lightly with salt.
4. Put zucchini into a bowl; pour the sauce over it and toss lightly to coat well. Cover and set aside at least an hour before serving.
4 SERVINGS

Refried Beans

2 to 3 cups cooked beans (see Basic Mexican Beans, opposite), or use canned kidney beans)
½ cup lard or bacon drippings
1 cup chopped onion
1 clove garlic, minced
½ cup cooked tomatoes or tomato sauce
1 teaspoon chili powder
Salt and pepper

1. Mash beans with a potato masher with half of the lard or bacon drippings (drippings make the best-flavored beans).
2. Heat remaining lard or drippings in skillet. Add onion and garlic and cook until onion is soft, about 5 minutes. Add mashed beans and continue cooking until all fat is absorbed by beans, stirring constantly to prevent sticking. Stir in tomatoes, chili powder, and salt and pepper to taste.
3 TO 4 CUPS BEANS

Stuffed Sweet Peppers

4 red or green sweet peppers, halved lengthwise
Stock
1 cup cooked rice
2 cups cooked ground beef,
ham, or poultry
Shredded cheese
Tomato Sauce Creole (page 50)

1. Parboil pepper halves in stock to cover. Drain peppers and reserve stock.
2. Mix rice and meat; stuff peppers. Sprinkle tops with cheese. Arrange peppers in a baking dish; add reserved stock to dish.
3. Bake at 350°F 30 minutes, or until well browned. Serve in the baking dish and accompany with the sauce.
4 SERVINGS

Eggplant Pugliese Style

3 medium-size eggplants
  (about ½ pound each)
2 tablespoons olive oil
1 tablespoon chopped
  parsley
1 medium onion, chopped
1 clove garlic, peeled and
  chopped
1½ cups chopped cooked

meat (see Note)
½ cup fine dry bread crumbs
1 tablespoon chopped
  pinenuts or almonds
Salt and pepper
3 or 4 tablespoons olive oil
1 can (8 ounces) tomato
  sauce

1. Wash and dry eggplants; remove stems. Cut eggplants in half crosswise, and scoop out most of the pulp; reserve pulp.
2. Heat 2 tablespoons olive oil in a skillet. Sauté pulp, parsley, onion, and garlic. Add meat, bread crumbs, and pinenuts. Season with salt and pepper; set aside.
3. Heat 3 or 4 tablespoons olive oil in another skillet. Cook eggplant shells in hot oil until the skins start to brown. Fill each half with the meat mixture. Pour tomato sauce over each half and cover skillet.
4. Cook eggplant slowly 20 to 30 minutes, or until tender.
5. If desired, place eggplant in a serving dish, add more tomato sauce, and keep in warm oven until ready to serve.
4 TO 6 SERVINGS

Note: If desired, ¾ pound uncooked chopped beef, lamb, or pork may be used. Sauté with pulp, parsley, onion, and garlic until browned before combining with other ingredients.

Broccoli with Buttery Lemon Crunch

1½ pounds broccoli, washed
¼ cup butter or margarine
½ cup coarse dry enriched
  bread crumbs
1 tablespoon grated lemon
  peel

3 tablespoons butter or
  margarine
1 small clove garlic, crushed
  in a garlic press or minced
½ teaspoon salt
Few grains black pepper

1. Cook broccoli in a small amount of boiling salted water until just tender. (Cook uncovered 5 minutes, then cover and cook 10 to 15 minutes, or cook, covered, the full time and lift the lid 3 or 4 times during cooking.)
2. Meanwhile, heat ¼ cup butter in a large skillet; add bread crumbs and heat, stirring frequently, until well browned. Remove crumbs from butter with a slotted spoon and mix with the lemon peel.
3. Put 3 tablespoons butter, garlic, salt, and pepper into skillet; heat until butter is lightly browned. Add broccoli and turn gently until well coated with butter.
4. Arrange broccoli in a heated vegetable dish and pour remaining garlic butter over it. Top with the "lemoned" crumbs.
ABOUT 6 SERVINGS

Lima Beans New Orleans

1 package (10 ounces) frozen
  lima beans
1 tablespoon vinegar
2 tablespoons olive oil
½ teaspoon salt

Dash pepper
2 tablespoons chopped
  parsley
½ clove garlic, minced
1 teaspoon lemon juice

1. Cook lima beans following package directions; drain if necessary.
2. Add vinegar, olive oil, salt, pepper, parsley, and garlic to limas in saucepan. Heat thoroughly, then mix in lemon juice. Serve immediately.
4 SERVINGS

Brussels Sprouts in Herb Butter

2 pounds fresh Brussels
  sprouts
⅓ cup butter
1 tablespoon grated onion
1 tablespoon lemon juice

¾ teaspoon salt
¼ teaspoon thyme
¼ teaspoon marjoram
¼ teaspoon savory

1. Cook Brussels sprouts in boiling salted water until just tender.
2. Put butter, onion, lemon juice, salt, thyme, marjoram, and savory into a saucepan. Set over low heat until butter is melted, stirring to blend.
3. When Brussels sprouts are tender, drain thoroughly and turn into a warm serving dish. Pour the seasoned butter mixture over the Brussels sprouts and toss gently to coat sprouts evenly and thoroughly.
ABOUT 8 SERVINGS

Butter-Sauced Asparagus

2 pounds fresh asparagus,
  washed, or 2 packages (10
  ounces each) frozen
  asparagus spears, cooked

¼ cup butter
¼ cup chopped pecans
¼ cup finely chopped celery
1 tablespoon lemon juice

1. Put fresh asparagus into a small amount of boiling salted water in a skillet, bring to boiling, reduce heat, and cook 5 minutes, uncovered; cover and cook 10 minutes, or until just tender.
2. Meanwhile, heat butter in a small saucepan. Add pecans and celery and cook 5 minutes. Stir in lemon juice. Pour over asparagus and serve immediately.
ABOUT 6 SERVINGS

Vegetable-Rice Medley

Lagered Sauerkraut with Apples

1 can (16 ounces) sauerkraut
1 medium apple
¾ cup beer
1 tablespoon sugar
1 tablespoon butter
½ teaspoon caraway seed
Dash pepper

1. Rinse sauerkraut in a large strainer; drain. Slice apple but do not peel.
2. Place all ingredients in a saucepan. Simmer, uncovered, for about 30 minutes, stirring occasionally, until most of liquid has evaporated and apples are tender.
4 SERVINGS

Vegetable-Rice Medley

3 tablespoons butter or margarine
¾ cup chopped onion
1½ pounds zucchini, thinly sliced
1 can (16 ounces) whole kernel golden corn, drained
1 can (16 ounces) tomatoes
(undrained)
3 cups cooked enriched white rice
1½ teaspoons salt
¼ teaspoon ground black pepper
¼ teaspoon ground coriander
¼ teaspoon oregano leaves

1. Heat butter in a large saucepan.
2. Add onion and zucchini; cook until tender, stirring occasionally. Add corn, tomatoes with liquid, cooked rice, salt, pepper, coriander, and oregano; mix well.
3. Cover and bring to boiling; reduce heat and simmer 15 minutes.
ABOUT 8 SERVINGS

BEEF & VEAL

Marinated Beef

4 pound blade pot roast of beef (any beef pot roast may be used)
2 cups vinegar
2 cups water
1 large onion, sliced
¼ cup sugar
2 teaspoons salt
10 peppercorns
3 whole cloves
2 bay leaves

1 lemon, rinsed and cut into ¼-inch slices
2 tablespoons butter
¼ cup butter
¼ cup all-purpose flour
3 cups liquid (reserved cooking liquid and enough reserved marinade or hot water to equal 3 cups liquid)
½ cup thick sour cream

1. Have ready 4-pound pot roast of beef. Put the meat into a deep 3- or 4-quart bowl. Set aside.
2. Combine in a saucepan and heat, without boiling, vinegar, water, onion, sugar, salt, peppercorns, cloves, and bay leaves.
3. Pour hot mixture over meat in bowl and allow to cool. Add lemon.
4. Cover and set in refrigerator. Marinate for 4 days, turning meat once each day.
5. Set out a heavy 4-quart kettle or Dutch oven and a tight-fitting cover.
6. Remove meat from marinade and drain thoroughly. Strain and reserve marinade.
7. Heat butter in the kettle over low heat.
8. Add the pot roast and brown slowly on all sides over medium heat. Slowly add 2 cups of the reserved marinade (reserve remaining marinade for gravy). Bring liquid to boiling. Reduce heat; cover kettle tightly and simmer 2½ to 3 hours., or until meat is tender when pierced with a fork. Add more of the marinade if necessary. Liquid surrounding meat should at all times be simmering, not boiling.
9. Remove meat to a warm platter and keep warm. Pour cooking liquid from kettle and set aside for gravy. For gravy melt butter in the kettle. Blend in ¼ cup of flour.
10. Heat until butter-flour mixture bubbles and is golden brown, stirring constantly. Remove kettle from heat.
11. Add liquid gradually, stirring constantly.
12. Return to heat. Bring to boiling; cook rapidly, stirring constantly, until gravy thickens. Cook 1 to 2 minutes longer. Remove from heat. Stirring vigorously with a French whip, whisk beater, or fork, add sour cream to kettle in very small amounts.
13. Cook mixture over low heat about 3 to 5 minutes stirring constantly, until thoroughly heated; do not boil. Serve meat and gravy with potato pancakes.
8 TO 10 SERVINGS

Cold Roast Beef Vinaigrette

1½ pounds cooked medium-rare roast beef, sliced ¼ inch thick and cut in 2-inch-wide strips
3 stalks celery, cut in ¼-inch pieces
1 medium tomato, chopped
2 sweet red or green peppers, chopped in ¼-inch pieces
1 tablespoon finely chopped red onion
1 tablespoon olive oil
2 tablespoons wine vinegar
¼ cup Beef Stock (page 48)

2 teaspoons snipped fresh or 1 teaspoon dried basil leaves
1 teaspoon snipped fresh or ½ teaspoon dried coriander leaves (cilantro)
1 tablespoon snipped parsley
1 teaspoon salt
¼ teaspoon freshly ground Szechuan or black pepper*
1 teaspoon snipped fresh or ½ teaspoon dried oregano leaves
2 garlic cloves, finely minced
2 teaspoons Dijon mustard

1. Arrange beef in a shallow glass dish. Mix remaining ingredients and pour over meat. Refrigerate covered 8 hours or overnight.
2. Taste meat and marinade; adjust seasoning, if desired. Let stand at room temperature 45 minutes before serving. Serve beef slices topped with marinade.
4 TO 6 SERVINGS

*Lightly roast Szechuan pepper over medium heat in a skillet before grinding.

Spicy Steak Tartare

1 small green onion, cleaned, trimmed, and cut in 1-inch pieces
2 tablespoons fresh parsley, cleaned and trimmed (1 tablespoon chopped)
1 radish, cleaned and trimmed
½ pound beef (sirloin, tenderloin, or fillet), cut in

1-inch cubes
1 egg yolk
1 tablespoon lemon juice
1 tablespoon capers
Drop of Dijon mustard
Salt
Freshly ground black pepper to taste
3 drops Tabasco

Using **steel blade** of food processor, process green onion, parsley, and radish together until finely chopped. Add meat and remaining ingredients and process, using quick on/off motions, to desired consistency. Serve with triangles of **black bread.**

Cold Roast Beef Vinaigrette

Roast Beef Filet with Burgundy Sauce

1 beef loin tenderloin roast, center cut (about 4 pounds)	Spiced crab apples
Salt and pepper	*Burgundy Sauce:*
½ cup dry red wine, such as burgundy	½ cup warm water
	¼ cup flour
Sautéed mushroom caps	1 cup beef broth
Parsley-buttered potatoes	½ cup burgundy

1. Have butcher trim all but a thin layer of fat from meat and roll meat like a rib roast (but without adding fat).
2. Rub meat with salt and pepper and place in shallow roasting pan. Insert meat thermometer into center of thickest portion of roast.
3. Roast in a very hot oven, 450°F, about 45 to 60 minutes until thermometer registers 140°F (rare), basting twice with the wine after meat has cooked for 20 minutes.
4. Remove roast to heated serving platter. Garnish with sautéed mushroom caps, parsley-buttered potatoes, and spiced crab apples. Serve with Burgundy Sauce.
5. For sauce, pour off clear fat from drippings, saving ¼ cup.
6. Pour warm water into roasting pan; stir and scrape up all brown bits; strain.
7. Heat the reserved fat in a skillet; stir in flour. Slowly stir in strained liquid, beef broth, and burgundy. Cook and stir until sauce boils and thickens. Add a few drops of gravy coloring, if desired.

6 TO 8 SERVINGS

Mushroom-Beer Steaks

1 beef round steak, cut ½ inch thick (2 pounds)	(homemade, canned, or from bouillon cubes)
Flour for dredging	¼ cup ketchup
¼ cup shortening or cooking oil	½ teaspoon salt
2 large onions, sliced	¼ teaspoon pepper
2 garlic cloves, minced	1 bay leaf
1 can or bottle (12 ounces) beer	1 can (4½ ounces) mushroom stems and pieces
1 cup beef broth	¼ cup flour

1. Cut meat into 6 serving pieces. Pound with meat mallet.
2. Dredge meat in flour. Brown in shortening in a large skillet; set meat aside.
3. Add onion and garlic to skillet, adding more fat if needed. Sauté until golden. Remove.
4. To skillet add beer, broth, ketchup, salt, pepper, and bay leaf. Stir up brown bits.
5. Layer meat and onions in skillet. Cover and simmer 1 to 1½ hours, or until meat is tender. Drain mushrooms, reserving liquid. Add mushrooms during last 5 minutes.
6. Place meat, onions, and mushrooms on serving platter; cover with foil to keep warm. Measure liquid. If needed, add water to measure about 2 cups.
7. Mix ¼ cup flour, mushroom liquid, and just enough water to make a smooth paste. Stir into cooking liquid. Cook, stirring constantly, until thickened. Serve gravy over meat and a **noodle** or **potato** accompaniment.

6 SERVINGS

Creamy Baked Steak

1 pound beef round tip steak	1 can (10½ ounces) condensed beef broth
4 tablespoons flour	1 cup sour cream
½ teaspoon salt	2 tablespoons sherry
2 tablespoons vegetable oil	1 can (3 ounces) sliced mushrooms, drained
1 small onion, sliced	
1 garlic clove, minced	

1. Cut steak into serving-size pieces. Sprinkle with 1 tablespoon flour and the salt.
2. Brown meat in oil in a skillet. Add onion and garlic.
3. Combine beef broth with remaining 3 tablespoons flour. Stir into skillet. Cook, stirring constantly, until mixture thickens. Put meat and sauce into a 12x8-inch baking dish.
4. Bake, covered, at 350°F 30 minutes, or until steak is tender. Remove cover. Combine sour cream, sherry, and mushrooms. Stir into meat mixture in baking dish. Bake an additional 5 minutes, or until heated through.

2 OR 4 SERVINGS

Swiss Steak Mozzarella

2 pounds beef round steak, ½ inch thick	1¼ teaspoons salt
3 tablespoons flour	¼ teaspoon basil
½ cup butter or margarine	½ cup chopped green pepper
1 can (16 ounces) tomatoes, cut up	1½ cups (6 ounces) mozzarella cheese

1. Cut meat into serving-size pieces; coat with flour.
2. Melt butter in a skillet. Brown meat slowly on both sides. Put into a 12x8-inch baking dish.
3. Combine tomatoes, salt, basil, and green pepper. Pour over meat.
4. Bake, covered, at 350°F 1 hour, or until meat is tender. Remove cover. Sprinkle with cheese and bake an additional 5 minutes, or until cheese is melted.

8 SERVINGS

Yankee Steak

2 pounds beef round steak, ½ inch thick	2 medium onions, thinly sliced
½ cup flour	1 can (15 ounces) tomato sauce
2 teaspoons salt	⅛ teaspoon garlic powder
½ teaspoon pepper	
3 tablespoons vegetable oil	

1. Cut meat into serving-size pieces. Combine flour, salt, and pepper; pound into steak.
2. Heat oil in a skillet. Brown meat slowly on both sides. Place in a 13x9-inch baking dish. Top with onion slices.
3. Combine tomato sauce and garlic powder. Pour over meat.
4. Bake, covered, at 350°F 1 hour, or until meat is tender.

8 SERVINGS

Stuffed Flank Steak

6 slices dry bread, cut in quarters (1½ cups crumbs)
4 cubes (1 inch each) Parmesan cheese (½ cup grated)
½ cup fresh parsley, cleaned and trimmed (¼ cup chopped)
1 clove garlic
2½ medium onions, peeled and quartered
2 tablespoons butter
¼ pound mushrooms, cleaned and trimmed
¼ teaspoon tarragon
½ teaspoon pepper
1 egg
1 beef flank steak (about 2 pounds)
1 carrot, pared and cut in 1-inch pieces
1 stalk celery, cut in 1-inch pieces
½ cup red wine
1 cup beef stock

1. Using **steel blade** of food processor, separately process bread to coarse crumbs, Parmesan cheese to a fine powder, and parsley until chopped; remove from bowl.
2. Still using **steel blade** mince garlic. Add 2 onions and process until chopped.
3. In a skillet, heat butter and sauté onion and garlic until lightly browned.
4. Using **steel blade,** process mushrooms until chopped and add to skillet along with tarragon, salt, pepper, and parsley; cook a few minutes more.
5. Using **plastic blade** lightly beat egg. Add bread crumbs and mushroom mixture to bowl and process, with quick on/off motions, until blended.
6. Spread the mixture on the steak. Roll lengthwise in a jelly-roll fashion and tie with string at 1-inch intervals.
7. In a heavy skillet or Dutch oven, brown the meat on all sides and remove from pan.
8. Using **steel blade,** process carrot, celery, and remaining ½ onion together until finely chopped. Add to skillet, along with wine and beef stock. Place stuffed flank steak on top and cover tightly.
9. Bake at 350°F about 2 hours, or until tender.
10. When meat is done, remove from pan, and keep warm. Using **steel blade** process pan drippings until puréed. Add more water or milk to reach desired consistency.
11. Put steak on a platter and surround with cooked vegetables such as **sliced zucchini, julienne carrots,** and **frenched green beans**.
12. Cut steak into 1-inch slices and serve with gravy on the side.
4 TO 6 SERVINGS

Bachelor's Steak

2 small single-serving steaks (rib, rib eye, strip, T-bone)
1 garlic clove, halved
1 can (2 to 2½ ounces) sliced mushrooms
¼ to ⅓ cup beer
1 tablespoon flour
¼ teaspoon salt
Dash pepper

1. Rub meat with cut surface of garlic. Broil 2 to 3 inches from heat until as done as desired.
2. Meanwhile, drain mushroom liquid into measuring cup. Add enough beer to measure ⅔ cup total liquid.
3. Pour 2 tablespoons steak drippings into a saucepan; stir in flour, salt, and pepper until smooth. Stir in beer mixture. Cook, stirring constantly, until thickened and smooth. Add drained mushrooms; heat through.
4. Pour beer-mushroom sauce over steak and **potatoes**.
2 SERVINGS

Beefsteak à la Mexicana

2 pounds very thinly sliced tender beef (cubed steaks may be used)
Salt, pepper, and garlic salt
Fat
1 pound fresh tomatoes, peeled, cored, and chopped
1 cup chopped onion
4 jalapeño chilies, seeded and chopped

1. Sprinkle beef with salt, pepper, and garlic salt on both sides.
2. Pan-fry meat quickly in a small amount of hot fat in a skillet (about 2 minutes pers side). Smother with chopped tomatoes, onio, and chilies. Cover skillet and cook over low heat about 15 minutes. Serve at once.
4 TO 6 SERVINGS

Herbed Skirt Steak

1½ pounds lean beef skirt steak
2 teaspoons clarified butter
1 large yellow onion, finely sliced
½ cup Beef Stock (see page 48)
1 garlic clove, minced
¼ teaspoon freshly ground pepper
1½ teaspoons salt
½ cup Mock Crème Fraîche (see page 46)
¼ cup snipped fresh dill or 2 tablespoons dried dill weed

1. Slice steak in half lengthwise; cut pieces across the grain into paper-thin slices. Heat butter over high heat in a 12-inch skillet. Add meat slices, stirring quickly to coat meat with butter. Add onion; cook and stir 2 minutes. Add Beef Stock, garlic, pepper, and salt; simmer covered until onion is tender (about 3 minutes).
2. Stir ¼ cup pan juices into Mock Crème Fraîche. Stir mixture back into pan; stir in dill. Serve immediately.
4 TO 6 SERVINGS

Steaks with Herb Butter

¼ cup soft butter or
 margarine
2 tablespoons chopped green
 onion
1 tablespoon chopped chives
2 tablespoons chopped
 parsley

½ teaspoon dill weed
½ teaspoon salt
¼ teaspoon Tabasco
1 tablespoon lemon juice
4 beef rib steaks, 1½ inches
 thick

1. Combine butter, green onion, chives, parsley, dill, and salt. Add Tabasco and lemon juice gradually, beating until blended.
2. Place steaks on grill about 2 inches from hot coals. Grill steaks about 5 minutes on each side, or until done as desired.
3. Spread steaks with herb butter and serve immediately.
4 SERVINGS

Standing Rib of Roast Beef

3-rib (6 to 8 pounds) stand-ing rib roast of beef (have butcher saw across ribs near backbone so it can be removed to make carving easier)
1½ teaspoons salt
⅛ teaspoon pepper

1. Place roast, fat side up, in a shallow roasting pan. Season with a blend of salt and pepper. Insert meat thermometer so tip is slightly beyond center of thickest part of lean; be sure tip does not rest on bone or in fat.
2. Roast at 300° to 325°F, allowing 23 to 25 minutes per pound for rare; 27 to 30 minutes per pound for medium; and 32 to 35 minutes per pound for well done meat. Roast is also done when meat thermometer registers 140°F for rare; 160°F for medium; and 170°F for well done.
3. Place roast on a warm serving platter. Remove ther-mometer.
4. For a special treat, serve with *Yorkshire Pudding, below.*
8 TO 10 SERVINGS

Note: A rib roast of beef may be one of three cuts. From the short loin end of the rib section, a first-rib roast is cut. This is mostly choice, tender "rib eye" meat. From the center rib section, the center-rib roast is cut. It has less "rib eye" meat than the first-rib roast and is usually somewhat less expensive. From the shoulder end of the rib section, the sixth-and-seventh rib roast is cut. It has the least "rib eye" meat and is likely to be least tender of the three. It usually is the least expensive. When purchasing a rib roast, buy not less than two ribs for a standing roast; for a rolled rib roast, buy a 4-pound roast.

Rolled Rib Roast of Beef: Follow recipe for Standing Rib Roast of Beef. Substitute **rolled beef rib roast** (5 to 7 pounds) for the standing rib roast. Roast at 300°F, allow-ing 32 minutes per pound for rare; 38 minutes per pound for medium; and 48 minutes per pound for well done meat.

Yorkshire Pudding: Pour **¼ cup hot drippings** from roast beef into an 11x7x1½-inch baking dish and keep hot. Add **1 cup milk, 1 cup sifted all-purpose flour,** and **½ teaspoon salt** to **2 well-beaten eggs.** Beat with hand rotary or elec-tric beater until smooth. Pour into baking pan over hot drip-pings. Bake at 400°F 30 to 40 minutes, or until puffed and golden. Cut into squares and serve immediately.
ABOUT 8 SERVINGS

Steak with Mushroom Stuffing

1 small onion, finely chopped
2 shallots, finely chopped
2 tablespoons Beef Stock (see page 48)
½ pound mushrooms, cleaned and chopped
1 tablespoon brandy
3 grinds fresh or ¼ teaspoon ground nutmeg
¾ teaspoon salt
¼ teaspoon freshly ground pepper
2½ pounds lean beef sirloin steak, boneless
Snipped parsley

1. Simmer onion and shallots in stock until tender (about 5 minutes). Mix onion, shallots, mushrooms, brandy, nutmeg, salt, and pepper.
2. Trim excess fat from steak. Cut pocket in steak, cutting to, but not through opposite side and leaving 1 inch intact on each end. Fill pocket loosely with onion mixture; skewer opening with wooden picks.
3. Broil steak 3 inches from heat, 8 minutes on each side for medium rare, 10 minutes on each side for medium. Remove wooden picks. Sprinkle steak with parsley. Slice and serve.
8 SERVINGS

Slow Oven Beef Stew

2 pounds beef stew meat, cut in 1½-inch cubes
2 medium onions, each cut in eighths
3 celery stalks, cut in 1-inch diagonally sliced pieces
4 medium carrots, pared and cut in half crosswise and lengthwise
3 cups tomato juice
⅓ cup quick-cooking tapioca
1 tablespoon sugar
2 teaspoons salt
¼ teaspoon pepper
1 bay leaf
2 medium potatoes, pared and cut in ¼-inch-thick slices

1. Put all ingredients, except potatoes, into a 3-quart casserole.
2. Bake, covered, at 300°F 2½ hours. Remove bay leaf and stir in potatoes. Bake, covered, an additional 1 hour, or until meat and vegetables are tender.
8 SERVINGS

Beef 'n' Peppers

1 garlic clove, minced
1½ pounds lean beef, cut in 1-inch cubes
2 tablespoons shortening
1 cup sliced fresh
mushrooms
2 cans (10½ ounces each) brown gravy with onions
1 green pepper, cut in strips

1. Sauté garlic and beef in hot shortening in a skillet. Put into a 1½-quart casserole.
2. Combine mushrooms and gravy in skillet with drippings. Pour over meat.
3. Bake, covered, at 350°F 2 hours, or until meat is tender. Remove cover. Add pepper strips. Bake an additional 15 minutes, or until pepper is tender but still crisp. Serve over **hot, cooked rice** or **noodles.**
6 SERVINGS

Beef Wellington

3½- to 4-pound beef
tenderloin
1 can (2 to 3 ounces) liver
pâté or spread
Pastry (prepared from pie

crust mix or Buttery Pastry,
below)
1 egg yolk, fork beaten
1 teaspoon water

1. Set beef on a rack in a shallow roasting pan. Roast at
425°F 25 minutes (medium rare). Remove from oven and
cool completely.
2. Discard any fat on roast. Sprinkle with *salt* and *pepper*
and spread with liver pâté.
3. Meanwhile, prepare pastry (enough for the equivalent
of three 9-inch pie shells).
4. On a lightly floured surface, roll out pastry large enough
to wrap around the roast.
5. Place meat on one edge of pastry and bring other edge
over meat to cover completely; reserve extra pastry for
decorations. Moisten edges with water and pinch together
firmly. Place on a baking sheet. Cut out a few small holes
on top to allow steam to escape.
6. Cut out decorative shapes from reserved pastry. Moisten
underside of each with water and place on top. Brush entire surface of pastry with a mixture of egg yolk and water.
7. Bake at 425°F 30 to 35 minutes, or until pastry is golden
brown.
8. Let stand 5 to 10 minutes before carving into thick slices.
6 TO 8 SERVINGS

For Buttery Pastry: Prepare pastry as directed in step 3,
roll out on a lightly floured surface into an 18-inch square,
and dot the center portion with slivers of *butter* (6 tablespoons). Fold so the two sides meet in center and seal by
pressing edges with fingers. Fold ends to center and seal.
Wrap and chill 20 minutes. Roll out as directed in step 4.

Spicy Beef Strips

1½ pounds beef round steak
(¼ inch thick)
2 tablespoons cooking oil
1 clove garlic
2 beef bouillon cubes
1 cup boiling water
1 tablespoon instant minced
onion
½ teaspoon salt

Few grains cayenne pepper
¼ teaspoon chili powder
¼ teaspoon ground
cinnamon
¼ teaspoon ground celery
seed
2 tablespoons prepared
mustard

1. Cut round steak into 2x½-inch strips; set aside.
2. Heat cooking oil in a large wok. Add garlic and stir-fry
until browned. Remove the garlic.
3. Add the round steak strips, half at a time, and stir-fry
until browned.
4. Dissolve bouillon cubes in boiling water. Add to wok with
all the ingredients; stir to mix. Cover and simmer 25 to 30
minutes, or until meat is fork-tender.
5. Serve over **hot fluffy rice.**
6 SERVINGS

Sukiyaki

½ cup Japanese soy sauce
(shoyu)
½ cup sake or sherry
⅓ cup sugar
3 tablespoons cooking oil
1½ pounds beef tenderloin,
sliced 1/16 inch thick and
cut into pieces about
2½x1½ inches
12 scallions (including tops),
cut into 2-inch lengths
½ head Chinese cabbage
(cut lengthwise), cut into

1-inch pieces
½ pound spinach leaves, cut
into 1-inch strips
2 cups drained shirataki (or
cold cooked very thin long
egg noodles)
12 large mushrooms, sliced
lengthwise
12 cubes tofu (soybean curd)
1 can (8½ ounces) whole
bamboo shoots, drained
and cut in large pieces

1. Mix soy sauce, sake, and sugar to make the sauce; set
aside.
2. Heat oil in a wok and add enough sauce to form a
¼-inch layer in bottom of wok.
3. Add half the beef and stir-fry just until pink color disap-
pears; remove and stir-fry remaining meat, adding more of
the sauce if necessary. Remove meat and set aside.
4. Arrange all other ingredients in individual mounds in
skillet. Top with beef.
5. Cook until vegetables are just tender. Do not stir. Serve
immediately with bowls of **hot cooked rice.**
4 SERVINGS

Beef Chow Mein

2 to 4 tablespoons cooking
oil
1 pound beef tenderloin or
sirloin steak, cut into
3x½x⅛-inch strips
½ pound fresh mushrooms,
sliced lengthwise
2 cups sliced celery
2 green onions, sliced ½
inch thick
1 small green pepper, cut into narrow strips

1½ cups boiling water
1 teaspoon salt
⅛ teaspoon pepper
2 tablespoons cold water
2 tablespoons cornstarch
2 teaspoons soy sauce
1 teaspoon sugar
1 can (16 ounces) Chinese
vegetables, drained
2 tablespoons coarsely
chopped pimento

1. Heat 2 tablespoons oil in a large wok. Add beef and stir-
fry until browned evenly. Remove meat; set aside.
2. Heat more oil, if necessary, in wok. Stir in mushrooms,
celery, green onions, and green pepper; stir-fry 1 minute.
Reduce heat and blend in boiling water, salt, and pepper.
Bring to boiling; cover and simmer 2 minutes. Remove
vegetables; keep warm.
3. Bring liquid in wok to boiling and stir in a blend of cold
water, cornstarch, soy sauce, and sugar. Cook and stir 2
to 3 minutes. Reduce heat; mix in the browned beef,
vegetables, Chinese vegetables, and pimento. Heat
thoroughly.
4. Serve piping hot with **chow mein noodles.**
4 TO 6 SERVINGS

Nectarine Sukiyaki

1 tablespoon cooking oil
2 pounds beef sirloin steak, boneless, cut 1½ inches thick, sliced 1/16 inch thick, and cut into about 2½-inch pieces
2 large onions, cut in thin wedges
8 green onions (including tops), cut into 2-inch pieces

5 ounces fresh mushrooms, sliced lengthwise
1 can (5 ounces) bamboo shoots, drained and sliced
2 cups unpared sliced fresh nectarines
½ cup soy sauce
½ cup canned condensed beef broth
2 tablespoons sugar

1. Heat oil in a large wok. Add meat, 1 pound at a time, and stir-fry over high heat until browned. Remove meat and set aside.
2. Arrange vegetables and nectarines in mounds in wok; top with the beef. Pour a mixture of soy sauce, condensed beef broth, and sugar over all. Simmer 3 to 5 minutes, or until onions are just tender.
3. Serve immediately over **hot fluffy rice.**
6 TO 8 SERVINGS

Teriyaki

1 teaspoon ground ginger
⅓ cup soy sauce
¼ cup honey
1 clove garlic, minced
1 teaspoon grated onion
1 pound beef sirloin tip, cut into 2x½x¼-inch strips

2 to 3 tablespoons cooking oil
1 tablespoon cornstarch
½ cup water
⅛ teaspoon red food coloring

1. Blend ginger; soy sauce, honey, garlic, and onion in a bowl. Add meat; marinate about 1 hour.
2. Remove meat, reserving marinade, and brown quickly on all sides in the hot oil in a large wok. Remove meat from wok.
3. Stir a blend of cornstarch, water, and food coloring into the reserved marinade and pour into wok. Bring rapidly to boiling and cook 2 to 3 minutes, stirring constantly.
4. Add meat to thickened marinade to glaze; remove and drain on wire rack.
5. Insert a frilled wooden pick into each meat strip and serve with the thickened marinade.
ABOUT 24 APPETIZERS

Oven Beef Bake

2 pounds beef stew meat, cut in 1-inch cubes
1 can (10¾ ounces) condensed cream of mushroom

soup
1 can (10½ ounces) condensed onion soup
¼ cup dry vermouth

1. Put meat into a 2-quart casserole.
2. Combine mushroom soup, onion soup, and vermouth. Pour over meat.
3. Bake, covered, at 325°F 3 hours, or until meat is tender. Serve with **hot, cooked noodles.**
8 SERVINGS

 ## Multi-Vegetable Beef Stew

3 pounds lean beef for stew (1½-inch cubes)
⅓ cup flour
1 teaspoon salt
½ teaspoon pepper
Fat
6 small potatoes, pared
6 green onions with tops, sliced
3 large carrots, pared and cut in ½-inch pieces

3 large stalks celery, cut in ½-inch pieces
¼ pound green beans, ends trimmed and beans cut in 1-inch pieces
1 can (16 ounces) tomatoes (undrained)
1 can (about 10 ounces) condensed beef broth
½ cup dry red wine

1. Coat beef cubes with a mixture of flour, salt, and pepper; brown in fat in a large skillet.
2. Put browned meat into an electric cooker. Add vegetables, broth, and wine; mix well.
3. Cover and cook on Low 10 to 12 hours.
10 TO 12 SERVINGS

 ## Beef à la Fondue

2 teaspoons butter
1 tablespoon flour
½ cup dry white wine
8 ounces Swiss cheese, shredded (about 2 cups)

1½ pounds beef top sirloin steak, cut into bite-size pieces
Oil for deep frying
Sauces for dipping

1. Melt butter in top of a double boiler over boiling water. Remove from heat; add flour and part of wine, mixing to a smooth paste.
2. Add remaining wine; heat over water until thickened. Add cheese; heat until melted. Keep warm.
3. At serving time, fill a metal fondue pot half full with oil. Heat oil to 375°F. Cook a cube of beef in the hot oil and dip it into the cheese sauce, and then into other sauces and side dishes. **Horseradish sauce** (sour cream and horseradish), **tartar sauce, mustard sauce, chopped chives** and **chutney** are suitable sauces and accompaniments. These should be in small individual dishes clustered around each place setting.
4 SERVINGS

Pepper Steak Port-au-Prince

2 tablespoons peppercorns
8 beef sirloin steaks (4 pounds), about 2 inches thick
2 tablespoons peanut oil
2 tablespoons butter
1 onion, minced
Salt to taste
½ cup dry white wine
¼ cup beef stock
3 tablespoons butter
2 tablespoons chopped parsley
¼ cup amber rum

1. In a mortar, pound the peppercorns until coarsely crushed. With the heel of the hand, press peppercorns into the meat.
2. Heat oil, 2 tablespoons butter, and onion over high heat in a large skillet. Sauté steaks in the fat until meat is as done as desired. Season with salt. Transfer meat to a warm platter and keep hot.
3. Pour wine and stock into the skillet over high heat to deglaze. Add the remaining butter and parsley. Pour mixture over the meat.
4. Warm rum, ignite it, and pour it, still flaming, over the steak.
5. Serve immediately with Smothered Mixed Vegetables (see page 244).
8 SERVINGS

Savory Beef Stew

1½ pounds beef stew meat, boneless, cut in 1½-inch cubes
¼ cup flour
1 teaspoon salt
¼ teaspoon basil
¼ teaspoon savory or marjoram
⅛ teaspoon pepper
3 tablespoons vegetable oil
2 onions, sliced
1 can or bottle (12 ounces) beer
½ cup water
1 bay leaf
5 medium potatoes (1⅔ pounds)
1 pound carrots (8 to 10); or ½ pound each parsnips and carrots

1. Dredge meat in mixture of flour, salt, basil, savory, and pepper. Reserve excess flour. Brown meat in oil. Add onion, beer, water, and bay leaf. Cover and simmer 1½ hours.
2. Pare potatoes; cut into large cubes. Slice carrots and/or parsnips. Add vegetables to stew. If necessary, add a little more water.
3. Cover and simmer 1 hour more, or until meat and vegetables are tender. Make smooth paste of reserved flour mixture and a little water. Stir into stew during last 10 minutes of cooking.
6 SERVINGS

Pepper Steak Port-au-Prince

Goulash

1½ pounds boneless pot
   roast of beef, chuck or
   blade
2 beef bouillon cubes
2 cups boiling water
4 slices bacon
1½ cups (about 3 medium-
   size) chopped onion
1 tablespoon paprika
1½ teaspoons salt
¼ teaspoon freshly ground

pepper
⅛ teaspoon marjoram
¼ cup (about 1 small)
   chopped green pepper
¾ cup dry white wine
½ cup water
¼ cup all-purpose flour
1 tablespoon butter
½ teaspoon paprika
1 tablespoon water

1. Set out a Dutch oven or a heavy 3-quart sauce pot having a tight-fitting cover.
2. Set out boneless pot roast of beef, chuck or blade on wooden board and cut into 1½-inch pieces.
3. Dissolve bouillon cubes in boiling water. Set aside.
4. Dice bacon and place into the sauce pot. Cook slowly, stirring and turning frequently, until bacon is lightly browned. Remove bacon with slotted spoon from sauce pot to small bowl and set aside.
5. Add chopped onion to the bacon fat in the sauce and cook over medium heat until onion is almost tender, stirring occasionally. Remove onion with slotted spoon to bowl containing bacon and set aside.
6. Add meat to the bacon fat and slowly brown on all sides, stirring occasionally. Sprinkle evenly over the meat a mixture of paprika, salt, ground pepper and marjoram.
7. Stir in the bacon-onion mixture with chopped green pepper.
8. Slowly pour in the reserved meat broth and dry white wine.
9. Bring to boiling. Reduce heat, cover sauce pot and simmer 2 to 2½ hours, or until meat is tender when pierced with a fork. Remove meat with slotted spoon to hot serving dish. Thicken cooking liquid if desired.
10. *To Thicken Cooking Liquid* – Pour water into 1-pt. screw-top jar. Sprinkle flour into the liquid. Cover jar tightly and shake until mixture is well blended. Slowly pour one-half of the mixture into the sauce pot, stirring constantly. Bring to boiling. Gradually add only what is needed of remaining flour-water mixture for consistency desired. Bring to boiling after each addition. After final addition, cook 3 to 5 minutes longer.
11. Melt butter in a small skillet. Remove from heat. Blend in paprika. Stir in water. Immediately add to liquid in sauce pot, stirring until well blended. Pour this sauce over meat.
12. Serve immediately.
6 TO 8 SERVINGS

Stir-Fry Beef and Broccoli

2 pounds broccoli
2 pounds beef round or
   chuck, boneless
¼ cup olive oil
2 cloves garlic, minced
3 cups hot chicken broth
4 teaspoons cornstarch

¼ cup cold water
3 tablespoons soy sauce
1 teaspoon salt
2 cans (16 ounces each)
   bean sprouts, drained and
   rinsed

1. Cut broccoli into pieces about 2½ inches long and ¼ inch thick; set aside. Slice beef very thin and cut diagonally into 4x½-inch strips; set aside.
2. Heat 1 tablespoon olive oil with garlic in a large wok. Add half the beef and stir-fry until evenly browned. Remove cooked meat from the wok and stir-fry remaining beef, adding more olive oil, if necessary.
3. Pour 1 tablespoon olive oil in the wok. Add half the broccoli and stir-fry over high heat ½ minute. Remove cooked broccoli from the wok and stir-fry remaining broccoli ½ minute, adding more oil, if necessary.
4. Place all the broccoli in wok; cover and cook 3 minutes. Remove broccoli and keep warm.
5. Blend into broth a mixture of cornstarch, cold water, soy sauce, and salt. Bring to boiling, stirring constantly, and cook until mixture thickens.
6. Add bean sprouts, broccoli, and beef; toss to mix. Heat thoroughly and serve over **hot fluffy rice.**
8 SERVINGS

Chafing Dish Stroganoff

1 pound beef tenderloin,
   sirloin or rib, boneless, cut
   into 2x½x¼-inch strips
¼ cup flour
½ teaspoon salt
Pinch black pepper
3 tablespoons butter or
   margarine
¼ cup finely chopped onion

1 cup beef broth
1½ tablespoons butter or
   margarine
¼ pound fresh mushrooms,
   sliced lengthwise
½ cup sour cream
1½ tablespoons tomato paste
½ teaspoon Worcestershire
   sauce

1. Coat meat strips evenly with a mixture of flour, salt, and pepper.
2. Heat 3 tablespoons butter in a large heavy skillet. Add meat strips and onion. Brown on all sides over medium heat, turning occasionally. Add broth; cover and simmer about 20 minutes.
3. Heat 1½ tablespoons butter in cooking pan of a chafing dish over medium heat. Add mushrooms and cook until lightly browned and tender. Add meat and liquid to mushrooms.
4. Blending well after each addition, add a mixture of sour cream, tomato paste, and Worcestershire sauce in small amounts. Place over simmering water and continue cooking, stirring constantly, until thoroughly heated (do not boil).
ABOUT 4 SERVINGS

Dried Beef 'n' Noodles

1 cup diced celery
1 cup chopped onion
½ cup chopped green
 pepper
¼ cup shortening
2 tablespoons flour
2 cups milk
1 tablespoon Worcestershire

sauce
Dash Tabasco
½ cup (2 ounces) shredded
 American cheese
1 package (3 ounces) dried
 smoked beef, cut in pieces
2 cups cooked wide noodles
2 hard-cooked eggs, sliced

1. Sauté celery, onion, and green pepper in shortening in a skillet.
2. Stir in flour. Gradually add milk, stirring until thickened and smooth. Add Worcestershire sauce, Tabasco, and cheese, stirring until smooth. Stir in beef and noodles.
3. Put into a 1½-quart casserole. Top with hard-cooked egg slices.
4. Bake, covered, at 350°F 30 minutes, or until heated through.
4 SERVINGS

Old-World Short Ribs

3 to 4 pounds beef short ribs
2 tablespoons oil
1 medium onion, chopped
1 can (8 ounces) tomato
 sauce
1 can or bottle (12 ounces)
 beer

1 teaspoon caraway seed
½ teaspoon salt
⅛ teaspoon pepper
1 bay leaf
¼ cup flour
2 to 3 cups cooked noodles

1. Brown ribs slowly in oil in a Dutch oven or deep skillet. Remove as they are browned.
2. Add onion and sauté until golden. Add tomato sauce, 1¼ cups beer, and seasonings. Return ribs.
3. Cover and simmer 1½ hours, or until tender.
4. Place ribs on platter; keep warm. Skim fat from cooking liquid (there should be about 2 cups liquid). Stir in paste made from flour and remaining ¼ cup beer. Cook, stirring constantly, until thickened. Serve gravy over ribs and noodles.
4 SERVINGS

Szededine Goulash

2 pounds beef stew meat,
 cut in 1-inch pieces
¼ cup vegetable oil
2 cups sliced onion
1 garlic clove, minced
1 teaspoon salt
1 can (10 ounces) tomato
 purée

1 cup water
1 cup sour cream
2 teaspoons paprika
2 teaspoons caraway seed
1 can (16 ounces) sauerkraut,
 rinsed and drained
2 tablespoons snipped
 parsley

1. Brown beef in oil in a skillet. Add onion and garlic. Sauté about 5 minutes; drain off excess fat.
2. Add salt, tomato purée, and water. Put into a 2½-quart casserole.
3. Bake, covered, at 325°F 2 hours, or until meat is tender, stirring occasionally. Remove cover. Stir in sour cream, paprika, caraway seed, and sauerkraut. Bake an additional 15 minutes, or until heated through. Sprinkle with parsley.
8 SERVINGS

Stew with Cornbread Topping

1½ pounds beef stew meat,
 cut in ¾-inch cubes
2 tablespoons butter or
 margarine
2 medium onions, sliced
1 garlic clove, minced
2¼ cups water
1 can (8 ounces) tomato
 sauce
¼ bay leaf
2 teaspoons salt
¼ teaspoon pepper
4 carrots, cut in 1-inch

pieces
4 celery stalks, cut in 1-inch
 pieces
½ cup all-purpose flour
2 teaspoons baking powder
1 tablespoon sugar
1 teaspoon salt
1 cup cornmeal
1 egg, beaten
1 cup milk
2 tablespoons vegetable oil
1 tablespoon snipped parsley

1. Brown meat in butter in a skillet. Add onion and garlic, cooking until lightly brown. Stir in water, tomato sauce, bay leaf, 2 teaspoons salt, and the pepper. Put into a 2½-quart casserole.
2. Bake, covered, at 350°F 45 minutes. Remove bay leaf. Add carrots and celery. Bake, covered, an additional 25 minutes, or until meat and vegetables are tender.
3. Sift together flour, baking powder, sugar, and 1 teaspoon salt into a bowl. Mix in cornmeal. Add egg, milk, and oil. (Mix only until dry ingredients are moistened.)
4. Remove stew from oven. Pour topping over hot stew. Sprinkle with parsley.
5. Bake, uncovered, at 400°F 20 minutes, or until cornbread is golden brown.
6 SERVINGS

Steak Tartare with Vegetables

2 pounds beef sirloin steak,
 boneless
⅓ cup finely chopped leek
 or green onion
1½ teaspoons Worcestershire
 sauce
¼ teaspoon Tabasco
1 teaspoon Dijon mustard
½ teaspoon salt
Freshly ground Szechuan or
 black pepper
1 egg yolk, if desired
1 teaspoon drained capers
2 bunches parsley, stems
 removed

1 green pepper, cut in 1-inch
 pieces
1 sweet red pepper, cut in
 1-inch pieces
1 large zucchini, cut in
 ¼-inch slices
1 medium cucumber, cut in
 ¼-inch slices
12 medium mushrooms, cut
 in half lengthwise
1 large carrot, cut in ¼-inch
 slices
12 large red or white
 radishes, cut in half

1. Chop meat coarsely in a food processor (or have butcher grind meat coarsely 2 times). Place beef, leek, Worcestershire sauce, Tabasco, mustard, salt, and pepper in a mixing bowl; mix quickly and lightly with 2 forks. Taste; adjust seasonings.
2. Mound beef on a medium serving platter. Make an indentation in top of mound; slip egg yolk into indentation. Sprinkle beef with capers. Surround beef with a thick rim of parsley. Arrange vegetables on parsley. Serve immediately with knives for spreading beef mixture on vegetables.
8 SERVINGS

Note: For a party, this recipe would make about 48 appetizer servings.

Sauerbraten

1 beef round rump roast, boneless (about 3 pounds)	1 bay leaf
2 cups water	2 juniper berries (optional)
1 cup vinegar	1 tablespoon lard
1 teaspoon salt	¾ cup golden raisins
2 onions, peeled and sliced	5 or 6 gingersnaps, crumbled
1 carrot, pared and sliced	1 tablespoon grated apple
5 peppercorns	1 teaspoon salt
2 whole cloves	¼ teaspoon pepper
	1 cup sour cream

1. Trim excess fat from roast and put meat into a large glass bowl.
2. Combine water, vinegar, salt, onion, carrot, peppercorns, cloves, bay leaf, and juniper berries (if used) in a saucepan. Bring to boiling, then set aside to cool.
3. Pour cooled marinade over meat, cover, and refrigerate 2 or 3 days; turn meat over several times during marinating.
4. Remove meat from marinade and pat dry with paper towels. Reserve marinade.
5. Heat lard in a saucepot or Dutch oven; add meat and brown well on all sides. Put meat fat side up, in an electric cooker. Strain marinade into cooker.
6. Cover and cook on Low 8 to 10 hours.
7. Remove meat and keep warm. Turn cooker control to High.
8. Add raisins, gingersnap crumbs, apple, salt, and pepper to liquid in cooker; cook and stir until thickened. Blend in sour cream.
9. Cover and cook on High 30 minutes.
10. Slice meat and serve with gravy. Accompany with potato dumplings, if desired.
ABOUT 8 SERVINGS

Sauerbraten

Beef Stroganoff

1½ pounds well-trimmed beef loin top sirloin steak, boneless	2 tablespoons cornstarch
2 cups sliced mushrooms	1 can (about 10 ounces) condensed beef broth
3 tablespoons butter	½ teaspoon salt
1 shallot, chopped	Pepper to taste
¼ bay leaf	1 cup sour cream
¾ cup dry sherry	1 tablespoon finely chopped parsley

1. Broil steak until rare. Cool thoroughly, then cut into strips.
2. Sauté mushrooms in butter. Add shallot, bay leaf, and sherry; boil 5 minutes, until wine is reduced in volume to about half. Remove bay leaf.
3. Stir cornstarch into a little of the broth. Turn remaining broth over mushrooms, add cornstarch mixture, and cook-stir until sauce boils thoroughly and thickens. Add salt and pepper.
4. Just before serving, reheat sauce, then stir in sour cream and parsley and heat until simmering. Add steak strips and heat, but do not boil. Serve as soon as steak is thoroughly heated.
6 SERVINGS

Chinese Beef and Pea Pods

1½ pounds flank steak, thinly sliced diagonally across
grain
1 to 2 tablespoons cooking
oil
1 bunch green onions,
chopped (tops included)
1 or 2 packages (7 ounces
each) frozen Chinese pea
pods, partially thawed to
separate
1 can (10½ ounces) con-
densed beef consommé
3 tablespoons soy sauce
¼ teaspoon ground ginger
2 tablespoons cornstarch
2 tablespoons cold water
1 can (16 ounces) bean
sprouts, drained and rinsed

1. Stir-fry meat, a third at a time, in hot oil in a large wok
until browned. Remove from wok and keep warm.
2. Put green onions and pea pods into wok. Stir in a mixture of condensed consommé, soy sauce, and ginger. Bring
to boiling and cook, covered, about 2 minutes.
3. Blend cornstarch with water and stir into boiling liquid
in wok. Stirring constantly, boil 2 to 3 minutes. Mix in the
meat and bean sprouts, heat thoroughly.
4. Serve over **hot fluffy rice.**

6 SERVINGS

Pot Roast of Beef with Wine

3- to 4-pound beef pot roast,
boneless (rump, chuck, or
round)
2 cups red wine
2 medium onions, chopped
3 medium carrots, washed,
pared, and sliced
1 clove garlic
1 bay leaf
¼ cup all-purpose flour
2 teaspoons salt
¼ teaspoon pepper
3 tablespoons butter
2 cups red wine
1 cup cold water
¼ cup all-purpose flour

1. Put the meat into a deep bowl. Add wine, onions, carrots, garlic, bay leaf, pepper. Cover and put into refrigerator
to marinate 12 hours, or overnight; turn meat occasionally. Drain the meat, reserving marinade, and pat meat dry
with absorbent paper.
2. Coat meat evenly with a mixture of flour, salt, and
pepper.
3. Heat butter in a large saucepot; brown the meat slowly
on all sides in the butter. Drain off the fat. Add the marinade
and wine. Cover and bring to boiling. Reduce heat and simmer slowly 2½ to 3 hours, or until meat is tender.
4. Remove meat to a warm platter.
5. Strain the cooking liquid. Return the strained liquid to
saucepot.
6. Pour water into a screw-top jar and add flour; cover jar
tightly and shake until mixture is well blended.
7. Stirring constantly, slowly pour one half of the blended
mixture into liquid in saucepot. Bring to boiling. Gradually
add only what is needed of the remaining blended mixture
for consistency desired. Bring gravy to boiling after each
addition.
8. Serve meat with gravy.

8 TO 10 SERVINGS

Island-Style Short Ribs

4 pounds lean beef short ribs
½ cup soy sauce
⅓ cup sugar
2 tablespoons vinegar
1 tablespoon vegetable oil
1 teaspoon ginger
½ teaspoon lemon pepper
seasoning
¼ teaspoon garlic salt
1 large onion, finely
chopped
¼ cup butter or margarine
2 cups water

1. Cut meat from bones; reserve the bones. Trim off as
much fat as possible. Cut meat into cubes. Put meat into
a bowl.
2. Combine soy sauce, sugar, vinegar, oil, ginger, lemon
pepper seasoning, and garlic salt. Pour over meat. Cover
and refrigerate several hours or overnight.
3. Sauté onion in butter in a skillet. Remove onion; set
aside.
4. Cook meat in skillet about 10 minutes. Add onion,
marinade, and water. Put into a 2-quart casserole. Top with
bones.
5. Bake, covered, at 325°F 1½ hours. Remove bones and
bake, uncovered, an additional 30 minutes, or until meat
is tender. To serve, spoon broth over **hot, cooked rice.**

8 SERVINGS

Oriental One-Pot Meal

6 cups Beef Stock (see page
48)
¼ cup light soy sauce
⅓ cup beer
2 teaspoons sugar
¼ teaspoon freshly ground
Szechuan or black pepper*
½ teaspoon salt
2 cups sliced fresh
mushrooms
2 bunches green onions, cut
in ½-inch pieces
1 cup sliced bamboo shoots
1 cup sliced Chinese cab-
bage or bok choy**
1½ pounds lean beef sirloin
or rib eye steak, cut in
paper-thin slices

1. Mix stock, soy sauce, beer, sugar, pepper, and salt in
a 3-quart saucepan. Boil 3 minutes. Simmer vegetables in
stock mixture until vegetables are just tender (about 5
minutes). Divide vegetables among 6 shallow bowls; keep
warm in oven.
2. Cook half the beef slices in the simmering stock mixture
until rare to medium done (2 to 4 minutes). Divide meat
among bowls. Cook remaining meat; divide among bowls.
Serve hot stock mixture over meat and vegetables or in individual bowls for dipping.

6 SERVINGS

*Lightly roast Szechuan pepper over medium heat in a skillet
before grinding.
**Chinese cabbage can be purchased in Oriental or specialty
shops.

Spanish Beef Stew with Olives

2 tablespoons olive or salad oil
3½ pounds beef stew meat, cubed
1 teaspoon salt
⅛ teaspoon pepper
2 medium onions, sliced
2 large cloves garlic, crushed
2 cups beef broth
2 cups dry red wine
4 tomatoes, peeled and quartered
1 bay leaf
4 parsley sprigs
½ teaspoon thyme leaves
1½ cups pimento-stuffed olives
2½ pounds potatoes, pared and halved
2 tablespoons flour
3 tablespoons water
Parsley (optional)

1. Heat oil in a large kettle or Dutch oven. Add meat, a few pieces at a time, and brown well on all sides. Remove meat and season with salt and pepper. If drippings in kettle are too brown, drain off and add additional 2 tablespoons oil.
2. Add onions and cook until tender and lightly brown. Add garlic, broth, wine, one of the tomatoes, and herbs (tied in cheesecloth). Add browned meat and bring to boiling.
3. Cover and simmer, or bake in a 350°F oven, 2 hours, or until meat is tender. Add olives and potatoes and continue cooking 30 minutes.
4. Remove meat and vegetables to serving dish; keep warm. Drain cooking liquid into saucepan and skim off fat; bring to boiling.
5. Blend flour with water; stir into boiling liquid. Add remaining tomatoes and simmer 10 minutes. Pour liquid over meat and vegetables; top with tomatoes. Garnish with parsley, if desired.
8 TO 10 SERVINGS

Kidney Bean Rice Olympian

2 tablespoons olive oil
1½ pounds beef round steak, boneless, cut in 1-inch cubes
2 teaspoons salt
¼ teaspoon ground black pepper
2 large cloves garlic, crushed in a garlic press
2 cups beef broth
1 cup sliced celery
1 can (16 ounces) tomatoes, cut in pieces (undrained)
2 cans (16 ounces each) kidney beans (undrained)
1 large green pepper, diced
3 cups hot cooked rice
1 large head lettuce, finely shredded
3 medium onions, peeled and coarsely chopped

1. Heat olive oil in a large heavy skillet. Add meat and brown on all sides. Add salt, pepper, and garlic; pour in beef broth. Bring to boiling, reduce heat, and simmer, covered, about 1 hour.
2. Stir celery and tomatoes and beans with liquid into beef in skillet; bring to boiling and simmer, covered, 30 minutes. Add green pepper and continue cooking 30 minutes.
3. To serve, spoon rice onto each serving plate, cover generously with shredded lettuce, and spoon a generous portion of the bean mixture over lettuce. Top each serving with about 3 tablespoons chopped onion.
ABOUT 8 SERVINGS

Munich Beef

1 can or bottle (12 ounces) beer
1 medium onion, chopped
½ teaspoon salt
⅛ teaspoon pepper
1½ pounds beef chuck, boneless, cut in 1-inch cubes
4 medium carrots (¾ pound)
3 tablespoons flour
2 tablespoons currant or grape jelly
1 tablespoon grated orange or lemon peel
1 tablespoon lemon juice
4 cups cooked noodles

1. In a 2- to 2½-quart casserole, combine beer, onion, salt, and pepper. Add beef. Cover; marinate in refrigerator 10 to 24 hours, stirring occasionally.
2. Place casserole in oven (do not brown beef).
3. Bake at 300°F 1½ hours. Add carrots. Continue baking 1 hour longer, or until meat and carrots are tender.
4. Mix flour, jelly, peel, and lemon juice to a paste. Stir into stew. Bake 15 minutes more, stirring once or twice, until thickened and bubbly. Serve over noodles.
6 SERVINGS

Tenderloin Supreme in Mushroom Sauce

1 whole beef loin tenderloin roast (4 to 6 pounds)

Mushroom Sauce:
⅓ cup butter
¾ cup sliced mushrooms
¾ cup finely chopped onion
1½ tablespoons flour
¾ teaspoon salt
⅛ teaspoon pepper
⅛ teaspoon thyme
1½ cups beef broth
¾ cup red wine, such as burgundy
1½ teaspoons wine vinegar
1½ tablespoons tomato paste
1½ teaspoons chopped parsley

1. Place tenderloin on rack in roasting pan. Insert roast meat thermometer in center of meat so that tip is slightly more than halfway through meat.
2. Roast, uncovered, at 425°F 45 to 60 minutes. The roast will be rare when meat thermometer registers 140°F.
3. For Mushroom Sauce, heat butter in a skillet. Add mushrooms and cook over medium heat until lightly browned and tender, stirring occasionally. Remove mushrooms with a slotted spoon, allowing butter to drain back into skillet; set aside.
4. Add onion and cook 3 minutes; blend in flour, salt, pepper, and thyme. Heat until mixture bubbles. Remove from heat.
5. Gradually add, stirring constantly, beef broth, wine, and wine vinegar. Cook rapidly until sauce thickens. Blend in the mushrooms, tomato paste, and parsley. Cook about 3 minutes.
6. Serve slices of beef tenderloin with sauce spooned over individual servings.
16 TO 24 SERVINGS

Spanish Beef Stew with Olives

Fondue Bourguignonne

Sauces for dipping (three or
  more, below)
Cooking oil

1½ to 2 pounds beef
  tenderloin or sirloin, cut into 1-inch pieces

1. Prepare sauces and set aside until serving time.
2. Fill a metal fondue pot half full with oil. Heat oil to 375°F. Spear pieces of meat with dipping forks and plunge into hot oil, cooking until done as desired.
3. Dip cooked meat in desired sauce and transfer to plate. Place another piece of meat in hot oil to cook while eating cooked meat.
4 SERVINGS

Jiffy Sauces for Fondue Bourguignonne:

Onion-Chili: Combine ½ **envelope (about 1½ ounces) dry onion soup mix** and ¾ **cup boiling water** in a saucepan. Cover partially and cook 10 minutes. Adding gradually, mix in 1½ **tablespoons flour** mixed with ¼ **cup water**. Bring to boiling, stirring constantly; cook until thickened. Remove from heat; mix in **2 tablespoons chili sauce**.

Onion-Horseradish: Blend ½ **envelope (about 1½ ounces) dry onion soup mix, 1 tablespoon milk, 2 teaspoons prepared horseradish**, and desired amount of **snipped parsley** into **1 cup sour cream**.

Horseradish: Blend **3 tablespoons prepared horseradish, 1 teaspoon grated onion**, and ½ **teaspoon lemon juice** with **1 cup mayonnaise**.

Curry: Blend **1 tablespoon curry powder, 1 teaspoon grated onion**, and ½ **teaspoon lemon juice** with **1 cup mayonnaise**.

Mustard: Blend **1 tablespoon half-and-half** with **1 cup mayonnaise** and stir in **prepared mustard** to taste.

Caper: Mix **1 tablespoon chopped capers** and **1 cup bottled tartar sauce;** blend in **1 tablespoon half-and-half**.

Bearnaise: Blend **1 tablespoon parsley flakes**, ½ **teaspoon grated onion**, ¼ **teaspoon crushed tarragon**, and **1 teaspoon tarragon vinegar** into **hollandaise sauce** prepared from a mix according to package directions.

Barbecue: Blend **prepared horseradish** to taste with a **bottled barbecue sauce**.

Velvet Lemon Sauce

2 eggs
½ teaspoon salt
2 tablespoons lemon juice
½ cup butter, softened

Few grains white pepper
½ slice onion
½ cup hot water

1. Put eggs, salt, lemon juice, butter, pepper, and onion into an electric blender container. Blend until smooth. Add hot water, a little at a time, while blending.
2. Turn into top of double boiler. Cook over simmering water, stirring constantly until thickened (about 10 minutes).
ABOUT 1½ CUPS SAUCE

Paprika Sauce

2 tablespoons butter or
  margarine
2 tablespoons flour
½ teaspoon salt
⅛ teaspoon pepper

1 cup milk
1 teaspoon minced onion
Few grains nutmeg
2 to 3 teaspoons paprika

1. Heat butter in a saucepan. Blend in flour, salt, and pepper; heat and stir until bubbly.
2. Gradually add milk, stirring until smooth. Bring to boiling; cook and stir 1 to 2 minutes longer.
3. Blend in onion, nutmeg, and paprika.
ABOUT 1 CUP SAUCE

Fondue Bourguigonne

Beef Stew with Lentils or Lima Beans

5 pounds beef chuck roast
¼ cup olive oil
2 large onions, thinly sliced
4 celery stalks, chopped
2 large carrots, chopped
1½ pounds fresh tomatoes, peeled and diced
2 parsley sprigs, minced

1 pound dried lentils (or lima beans)
Salt and pepper to taste
3 garlic cloves, crushed in a garlic press
1 cup dry red wine
3 cups beef stock (or more if necessary)

1. Trim excess fat from beef roast. Cut meat into large cubes.
2. Heat oil in a large Dutch oven. Brown meat on all sides and remove to platter.
3. Put onions into the Dutch oven and cook until translucent. Pour off excess fat.
4. Return meat to the Dutch oven. Arrange vegetables, parsley, and lentils around the meat. Season with salt and pepper.
5. Combine garlic, wine, and stock in a saucepan. Bring to boiling. Pour over meat and vegetables. Cover. Simmer until meat is tender. (Meat should be covered with liquid throughout cooking.)
8 TO 10 SERVINGS

Note: This dish is tastier when made early and allowed to rest several hours or overnight, then reheated.

Full-Flavored Steak

Full-Flavored Steak

2½ tablespoons brown sugar
1½ tablespoons sugar
1 tablespoon ground ginger
1 clove garlic, crushed
½ cup soy sauce

1 tablespoon tarragon vinegar
3 pounds beefsteak (sirloin, porterhouse, T-bone, or rib), cut 1½ inches thick

1. Combine the sugars, ginger, garlic, soy sauce, and vinegar.
2. Put meat into a large shallow dish and pour soy sauce mixture over meat. Allow to marinate at least 30 minutes, basting frequently and turning once or twice.
3. When ready to grill, remove meat from marinade, reserving marinade.
4. Place steak on grill about 3 inches from coals. Brushing frequently with marinade, grill about 6 minutes, or until one side is browned. Turn and grill other side abut 6 minutes, or until done. (To test, slit meat near bone and note color of meat.) Serve immediately.
4 TO 6 SERVINGS

Beef Kabobs with Vegetables

3 tablespoons light brown sugar
¼ teaspoon dry mustard
1 cup soy sauce
½ cup water
3 tablespoons dry sherry
¼ teaspoon Tabasco
1 tablespoon grated onion
1 clove garlic, minced
1½ to 2 pounds beef sirloin, cut in 1½-inch cubes
Tomato wedges
Green pepper squares (about 1 to 1½ inches)
Small onions, peeled

1. Mix brown sugar, mustard, soy sauce, water, sherry, Tabasco, onion, and garlic in a bowl.
2. Place meat in glass baking dish, pour marinade over beef, and allow to marinate in refrigerator overnight. Remove meat and reserve marinade.
3. Alternate meat and vegetables on skewers.
4. Place kabobs on grill about 5 inches from hot coals. Brush generously with marinade. Grill 7 to 10 minutes, then turn and baste with more marinade. Continue cooking until meat is done as desired.
ABOUT 6 SERVINGS

Note: The beef often requires a longer cooking period than the vegetables. If desired, place all beef on 2 or 3 skewers, and place all vegetables on other skewers. Place vegetables on grill towards end of cooking time of beef. Meat and vegetables may be rearranged on skewers for serving.

Company Beef and Peaches

1 can (8 ounces) tomato sauce with onions
1 can (8 ounces) sliced peaches, drained; reserve syrup
¾ cup beef broth
2 tablespoons brown sugar
2 tablespoons lemon juice
1 tablespoon prepared mustard
1 teaspoon Worcestershire
sauce
1 clove garlic, minced
1 beef round bottom round roast or eye round roast, boneless (2 to 3 pounds)
Vegetable oil
Salt and seasoned pepper
2 tablespoons cold water
2 teaspoons cornstarch
Watercress or parsley

1. Turn the tomato sauce with onions into a bowl. Mix in the peach syrup (set peaches aside), beef broth, brown sugar, lemon juice, prepared mustard, Worcestershire sauce, and garlic. Set aside.
2. Cut meat across the grain into 6 to 8 slices, about ¾ inch thick.
3. Heat oil in a large skillet. Add the meat slices and brown on both sides. Sprinkle with salt and seasoned pepper. Pour the sauce mixture over the meat. Bring to boiling, reduce heat, and simmer, covered, about 1½ hours, or until meat is fork-tender; turn meat slices occasionally.
4. Overlap meat slices to one side of a heated serving platter.
5. Blend water and cornstarch; stir into sauce in skillet. Bring to boiling; cook about 1 minute. Mix in sliced peaches and heat thoroughly; spoon to the side of meat on the platter. Cover meat with sauce. Garnish with watercress.
6 TO 8 SERVINGS

Beef Kabobs with Vegetables

Sauerbraten Moderne

1 cup wine vinegar
1 cup water
1 medium onion, thinly sliced
2 tablespoons sugar
1 teaspoon salt
5 peppercorns
3 whole cloves
1 bay leaf
2 pounds beef round steak (¾ inch thick), boneless, cut in cubes
1 lemon, thinly sliced
2 tablespoons butter or margarine
1 can (10¾ ounces) beef gravy
1 can (3 ounces) broiled sliced mushrooms (undrained)
6 gingersnaps, crumbled (about ⅔ cup)
Cooked noodles

1. Combine vinegar, water, onion, sugar, salt, peppercorns, cloves, and bay leaf in a saucepan. Heat just to boiling.
2. Meanwhile, put meat into a large shallow dish and arrange lemon slices over it. Pour hot vinegar mixture into dish. Cover and allow to marinate about 2 hours.
3. Remove and discard peppercorns, cloves, bay leaf, and lemon slices; reserve onion. Drain meat thoroughly, reserving marinade.
4. Heat butter in a skillet over medium heat. Add meat and brown pieces on all sides. Stir 1 cup of the reserved liquid with the onion into skillet. Cover, bring to boiling, reduce heat, and simmer about 45 minutes.
5. Blend beef gravy and mushrooms with liquid into mixture in skillet. Bring to boiling and simmer, loosely covered, about 20 minutes longer, or until meat is tender.
6. Add the crumbled gingersnaps to mixture in skillet and cook, stirring constantly, until gravy is thickened. Serve over noodles.
6 TO 8 SERVINGS

Flemish Beef Stew

4 pounds beef chuck or round boneless, cut in 1-inch cubes
¼ cup oil
2 tablespoons parsley flakes
2 teaspoons each thyme, sugar, and salt
½ teaspoon pepper
2 garlic cloves, minced
2 bay leaves
2 cans or bottles (12 ounces each) beer
8 medium onions, sliced
¼ cup cornstarch

1. Brown meat in oil; place in a very large casserole or two medium ones, about 2½ quarts each. Add seasonings; stir to coat meat.
2. Add beer plus a little water, if needed, to almost cover meat. Cover casseroles.
3. Bake at 300°F 1½ hours.
4. Parboil onion half covered with water, stirring frequently, until soft. Stir into meat. Cover and continue baking 1 to 1½ hours, or until meat is tender.
5. Make a paste of cornstarch and a little water. Stir into casseroles. Return to oven about 10 minutes, stirring once or twice. Serve over **noodles.**
12 TO 14 SERVINGS

Braised Beef Corfu Style

Braised Beef Corfu Style

3 cups all-purpose flour
Salt and pepper to taste
1 teaspoon paprika
Olive oil for frying
4 pounds beef top round, cut
  in slices ¼ inch thick or
  less

4 garlic cloves, crushed in a
  garlic press
1 cup red wine vinegar
1½ cups water
1 teaspoon sugar
1 bay leaf
¼ cup chopped parsley

1. Season flour with salt, pepper, and paprika.
2. Heat olive oil in a skillet. Lightly dip meat slices in flour. Shake off excess. Brown meat on each side in the olive oil. Arrange in a casserole.
3. Combine garlic, vinegar, water, sugar, bay leaf, and parsley in a small saucepan; heat to boiling. Pour over the meat.
4. Bake at 325°F 1 hour, or until the meat is tender and almost all the liquid is absorbed.
5. Serve with **mashed potatoes.**
ABOUT 8 SERVINGS

Beef-on-Tomato Medallions

3 large ripe tomatoes
Salt
Freshly ground pepper
1 tablespoon vegetable oil
½ teaspoon sesame or
  walnut oil
2½ pounds lean beef sirloin
  steak, boneless, cut in

paper-thin slices
2 bunches green onions, cut
  in ¾-inch pieces
1 tablespoon light soy sauce
2 tablespoons dry white
  wine
¼ teaspoon sugar
½ teaspoon salt

1. Slice each tomato into 4 slices horizontally. Sprinkle with salt and pepper. Bake on a cookie sheet at 325°F until hot (about 15 minutes).
2. Heat vegetable and sesame oils in a wok or skillet until hot but not smoking. Add meat, stirring to coat pieces. Cook 1 minute. Add green onions. Cook and stir 1 minute. Mix soy sauce, wine, sugar, and ½ teaspoon salt; pour over meat. Cook and stir until meat is done (about 3 minutes).
3. Overlap 2 tomato slices at the side of each serving plate. Arrange meat mixture on plates, partially covering tomatoes.
6 SERVINGS

Note: Sesame and walnut oils can be purchased in specialty or gourmet shops. These oils have a delicate but distinct flavor which provides an interesting accent in this recipe. The oil can be omitted, or vegetable oil substituted.

Scandinavian Sailors' Beef Casserole

1½ to 2 pounds beef round
  steak, boneless, cut ½ inch
  thick
Flour
3 medium onions, sliced
¼ cup margarine, oil, or
  butter
6 medium potatoes, pared

and thickly sliced
1 teaspoon salt
¼ teaspoon pepper
1 can or bottle (12 ounces)
  beer
¼ cup minced parsley
  (optional)

1. Cut meat into 6 serving pieces. Dredge in flour. Pound to ¼-inch thickness.
2. Sauté onion in 2 tablespoons margarine in a large skillet; set aside.
3. In remaining margarine, brown meat on both sides in same skillet.
4. In a large casserole, layer meat, potatoes, and onion, sprinkling layers with salt and pepper.
5. Pour beer into skillet; stir up brown bits. Add to casserole.
6. Cover and bake at 350°F 1½ hours, or until meat is tender. Sprinkle with parsley. Serve with **pickled beets.**
6 SERVINGS

Mexican Beef Stew

2 pounds beef for stew, cut
  in 2-inch chunks
1 large onion, chopped
1 clove garlic, minced
1 green pepper, cut in strips
1 cup canned tomato sauce
1 canned chipotle chili,
  finely chopped
1 tablespoon vinegar

1½ teaspoons salt
1 teaspoon oregano
3 cups cubed pared potatoes
4 or 5 carrots, pared and cut
  in strips
Beef stock, or water plus
  beef bouillon cube
2 tablespoons flour

1. Put meat into a Dutch oven or large kettle. Add onion, garlic, green pepper, tomato sauce, chili, vinegar, salt, and oregano. Cover and bring to boiling; reduce heat and simmer 2½ hours, stirring occasionally.
2. Add potatoes and carrots to meat mixture. If more liquid seems needed, add up to 1 cup beef stock. Cover and cook about 30 minutes, or until meat and vegetables are tender.
3. Sprinkle flour over stew and stir in; continue to cook until sauce is thickened.
ABOUT 8 SERVINGS

Oriental Beef Stew

1¼ pounds boneless beef (round sirloin, sirloin tip, or rump), cut ½ inch thick
Seasoned instant meat tenderizer
3 tablespoons cooking oil
1 green pepper, cut in thin strips
1 sweet red pepper, cut in thin strips
2 celery stalks, cut lengthwise in thin strips, then into 2-inch pieces
2 small onions, thinly sliced
6 fresh mushrooms (about 2 ounces), sliced lengthwise through caps and stems
1 can (5 ounces) water chestnuts, drained and sliced
2 tablespoons cornstarch
2 teaspoons sugar
¾ teaspoon ground ginger
1½ cups water
3 tablespoons Japanese soy sauce (shoyu)
1 beef bouillon cube

1. Tenderize meat according to the directions; cut into 2x¼-inch strips.
2. Heat 1 tablespoon of the oil in a large skillet. Add beef strips and stir-fry over high heat about 2 minutes, or until well browned. Remove and set aside.
3. Add remaining oil and heat. Add vegetables and cook, turning frequently, about 3 minutes, or until vegetables are crisp-tender. Remove from heat and return meat to skillet.
4. In a saucepan, thoroughly blend cornstarch, sugar, and ginger; stir in water and soy sauce; add bouillon cube. Bring the mixture to boiling and boil 3 minutes, stirring frequently.
5. Pour sauce over meat and vegetables; toss lightly to coat well. Heat thoroughly. Serve immediately.
ABOUT 4 SERVINGS

Beef with Baby Onions

¼ cup olive oil
4 pounds beef shoulder, cut in large pieces
Salt and pepper to taste
1 can (16 ounces) tomatoes (undrained)
1 tablespoon tomato paste mixed with ½ cup water
5 garlic cloves, crushed in a garlic press
1 cup red wine
1 teaspoon sugar
1 tablespoon lemon juice
1 bay leaf
Pinch cinnamon
1 teaspoon oregano
¼ cup chopped parsley
3 tablespoons pickling spice (put in a tea infuser or wrapped and securely tied in cheesecloth)
3 pounds whole fresh baby onions, peeled

1. Heat oil in a large Dutch oven. Brown meat well on all sides. Season with salt and pepper.
2. Add tomatoes and diluted tomato paste. Cover and simmer 10 minutes.
3. Add remaining ingredients, except onions. Cover. Bring to a boil. Reduce heat. Simmer 2 to 3 hours until meat is tender.
4. Meanwhile, cut a small cross at the base of each onion. During the last ½ hour of cooking, add onions. Adjust salt and pepper.
5. Serve with **rice** or **pasta**.
8 SERVINGS

Oriental Beef Stew

Beef Burgundy

2 slices bacon
2 pounds beef round tip steak, cut in 2-inch cubes
2 tablespoons flour
1 teaspoon seasoned salt
1 package beef stew seasoning mix
1 cup burgundy
1 cup water
1 tablespoon tomato paste
12 small boiling onions
4 ounces fresh mushrooms, sliced and lightly browned in 1 tablespoon butter or margarine
16 cherry tomatoes, stems removed

1. Fry bacon in a Dutch oven; remove bacon. Coat meat cubes with a blend of flour and seasoned salt. Add to fat in Dutch oven and brown thoroughly. Add beef stew seasonings mix, burgundy, water, and tomato paste. Cover and simmer gently 45 minutes.
2. Peel onions and pierce each end with a fork so they will retain their shape when cooked. Add onions to beef mixture and simmer 40 minutes, or until meat and onions are tender. Add mushrooms and cherry tomatoes; simmer 3 minutes. Pour into a serving dish.
6 TO 8 SERVINGS

Note: If cherry tomatoes are not available, use canned whole peeled tomatoes.

Pot Roast Jardinière

1 beef chuck pot roast (4 pounds)
¼ cup prepared horseradish
1 tablespoon salt
1 medium tomato, chopped
1 cup Beef Stock (see page 48)
3 medium kohlrabi or turnips, pared and cut in ½-inch cubes
3 medium carrots, cut in ½-inch slices
1 pound fresh Brussels sprouts, cleaned*
1 teaspoon snipped fresh or ½ teaspoon dried thyme leaves
1 teaspoon snipped fresh or ½ teaspoon dried marjoram leaves
1 teaspoon snipped fresh or ½ teaspoon dried thyme leaves
1 teaspoon snipped fresh or ½ teaspoon dried marjoram leaves
1 teaspoon salt
½ teaspoon pepper
2 leeks, cut in 1-inch pieces
2 teaspoons arrowroot
Cold water

1. Rub meat on both sides with a mixture of horseradish and 1 tablespoon salt; place meat in a Dutch oven. Add tomato and stock to Dutch oven. Cover.
2. Cook in a 325°F oven about 3 hours, or until meat is tender.
3. Add vegetables, thyme, marjoram, 1 teaspoon salt, and ½ teaspoon pepper to Dutch oven during last 15 minutes of cooking time; cook just until vegetables are tender.
4. Remove meat and vegetables to platter. Skim fat from cooking liquid. If thicker sauce is desired, mix arrowroot with a little cold water and stir into liquid. Simmer, stirring constantly, until sauce is thickened. Pass sauce.
6 SERVINGS

*1 package (10 ounces) frozen Brussels sprouts can be substituted for the fresh. Add to Dutch oven for length of cooking time indicated on package.

Beef Pot Roast

1 beef round rump or chuck roast, boneless (3½ pounds)
3 tablespoons salad oil or ¼ pound salt pork, diced
Bouillon or meat broth (about 1½ cups)
1 bay leaf
2 onions, quartered
2 carrots, cut in pieces
½ teaspoon salt
½ teaspoon coarse pepper
Flour
Salt and pepper

1. Brown the beef in oil. Add ¼ cup bouillon, bay leaf, onions, carrots, salt, and pepper; cover and simmer 2½ hours, basting with additional bouillon to prevent burning.
2. Sprinkle flour over meat and turn it over. Sprinkle with more flour. If necessary, add more bouillon for the sauce. Cook uncovered 30 minutes. Serve the pot roast with **noodles** or **potatoes** and any kind of vegetables.
8 TO 10 SERVINGS

Pot Roast with Sour Cream: Prepare *Beef Pot Roast* as directed. Add **1½ cups sour cream** instead of bouillon after flouring the meat. Finish cooking as directed.

Pot Roast with Sour Cream and Pickles or Mushrooms: Prepare *Beef Pot Roast* as directed. Add **1½ cups sour cream** instead of bouillon after flouring the meat. Then stir in **⅔ cup chopped dill pickles** or **1 cup sliced mushrooms.** Finish cooking as directed.

Roast Beef with Wine

1 beef rolled rump roast (5 pounds or more)
Salt and pepper
2 garlic cloves, crushed in a garlic press
1 tablespoon oregano
2 tablespoons grated kefalotyri cheese
Chicken stock (about ¾ cup)
1 medium onion, quartered
½ cup red wine
1 package macaroni, cooked according to directions on package
1 cup grated kefalotyri cheese

1. Sprinkle beef roast with salt and generously cover with pepper. Slit the meat with a small sharp knife in several places on a diagonal slant about 1 inch deep.
2. Mix garlic, oregano, and 2 tablespoons cheese. Fill each incision with some of this mixture. Pinch to close incision.
3. Place beef on a trivet in a roasting pan. Pour enough stock into the pan to barely reach top of trivet. Add the quartered onion.
4. Roast at 325°F until done to taste. (A meat thermometer will register 140°F for rare, 160°F for medium, and 170°F for well-done meat.)
5. During the last 15 minutes of roasting, pour in wine.
6. Remove meat to a platter. Keep warm. Remove fat from pan juices. Toss in cooked pasta. Sprinkle with remaining cheese. Serve hot.
ABOUT 8 SERVINGS

Beef Stroganoff Turnovers

2 tablespoons butter or margarine
½ medium onion, minced
½ pound mushrooms, cleaned and sliced
1 pound skirt steak, cut in thin strips (sirloin, round, or flank can be substituted)
1 medium clove garlic, crushed in a garlic press
⅛ teaspoon cumin
⅛ teaspoon dill weed
⅛ teaspoon marjoram
1 teaspoon Worcestershire sauce
2 tablespoons ketchup
⅓ cup red wine
1 beef bouillon cube
Salt and pepper
8 ounces sour cream
6 dinner crêpes

1. Melt butter. Sauté onion and mushrooms. Add meat strips, garlic, cumin, dill weed, marjoram, Worcestershire sauce, and ketchup. Sauté until meat is browned. Stir in wine and bouillon cube. Simmer until meat is tender. Season with salt and pepper to taste. Stir in sour cream. Cook over low heat 5 minutes.
2. Using a slotted spoon, assemble by turnover method (page 36). Place on baking sheet.
3. Bake at 350°F 10 minutes. Serve topped with any remaining sauce.
6 TURNOVERS

Tournedos

6 slices beef loin tenderloin steak (1½ inches thick)
Salt and pepper to taste
½ cup butter
¼ cup flour
¾ cup dry white wine
½ cup chopped parsley
Juice of 1 lemon

1. Season meat with salt and pepper on both sides.
2. Melt butter in a heavy skillet. Add meat and brown quickly on each side. Remove to a dish.
3. Using a whisk, stir flour into pan juices. Cook, stirring constantly, over low heat for 2 minutes.
4. Stir in wine and cover. Simmer 5 minutes.
5. Add meat, parsley, and lemon juice. Simmer 5 minutes.
6 SERVINGS

Corned Beef Casserole

½ cup chopped onion
¼ cup chopped green pepper
2 tablespoons shortening
1 can (12 ounces) corned beef, cut up
¾ cup water
1½ cups ketchup
1 package (10 ounces) frozen peas, thawed
1½ cups (about 6 ounces) shell macaroni, cooked and drained

1. Sauté onion and green pepper in shortening in a skillet. Stir in remaining ingredients. Put into a 2-quart casserole.
2. Bake, covered, at 350°F 30 minutes, or until heated through.
6 SERVINGS

Corned Beef

6-pound beef brisket corned, boneless
2 teaspoons whole cloves
½ cup firmly packed light brown sugar
¼ cup sherry

1. Put the meat into a saucepot and add enough water to cover meat. Cover saucepot tightly and bring water just to boiling over high heat. Reduce heat and simmer about 4 hours, or until meat is almost tender when pierced with a fork.
2. Remove from heat and cool in liquid; refrigerate overnight.
3. Remove meat from liquid and set on rack in roasting pan. Stud with cloves. Put brown sugar over top and press firmly.
4. Roast at 325°F 1½ hours. After roasting 30 minutes, drizzle with sherry.
5. To serve, carve meat into slices.
ABOUT 12 SERVINGS

Easy Corned Beef Bake

½ package (6 ounces) noodles, cooked and drained
1 can (12 ounces) corned beef, cut up
1 cup (4 ounces) shredded
American cheese
¾ cup milk
¼ cup chopped onion
½ cup fine dry bread crumbs
2 tablespoons butter or margarine

1. Combine noodles, corned beef, cheese, milk, and onion. Put into a greased 1½-quart casserole.
2. Top with bread crumbs. Dot with butter.
3. Bake, covered, at 325°F 45 minutes, or until casserole is bubbly.
4 SERVINGS

Beef Slices with Sour Cream and Mushrooms

½ cup all-purpose flour
1 teaspoon salt
½ teaspoon pepper
2 pounds beef eye round, top round, or sirloin (cut in thin steaks)
3 tablespoons butter or fat
1 can (4 ounces) mushrooms
with liquid
1 cup water
6 medium potatoes, cooked; or 3 cups sauerkraut, drained
1 tablespoon flour
1 cup sour cream

1. Mix flour with salt and pepper. Coat meat with seasoned flour.
2. Melt butter in a large skillet or Dutch oven. Brown meat quickly on both sides.
3. Add mushrooms with liquid and water. Cover. Simmer 1 hour, basting occasionally with sauce.
4. Add potatoes to meat; cook 10 minutes, or until meat and potatoes are tender.
5. Blend flour into sour cream. Blend into sauce. Bring to boiling, then simmer 5 minutes.
6 SERVINGS

Beef Bourguignon

¼ cup flour
1 teaspoon salt
½ teaspoon freshly ground black pepper
2 pounds beef stew meat, cut in 2-inch cubes
¼ cup butter or margarine
1 medium onion, chopped
2 medium carrots, chopped
1 garlic clove, minced
2 cups dry red wine
1 can (6 ounces) mushroom crowns, drained, reserving liquid
1 bay leaf
3 tablespoons snipped parsley
½ teaspoon thyme
1 can (16 ounces) onions, drained

1. Combine flour, salt, and pepper; coat beef cubes.
2. Brown beef in butter in a skillet. Pour into a 2-quart casserole.
3. Add onion, carrots, and garlic to skillet. Cook until tender but not brown. Add wine, liquid from mushrooms, bay leaf, parsley, and thyme. Pour over meat.
4. Bake, covered, at 350°F 2½ hours. Remove cover. Add onions and mushroom crowns. Bake an additional 30 minutes, or until meat is tender.
8 SERVINGS

Carbonada Criolla

2 pounds veal for stew (1- to 1½-inch pieces)
½ cup flour
1 teaspoon salt
Lard for frying
2 cloves garlic, crushed
2 medium onions, peeled and chopped
2 green peppers, cut in strips
1 cup chopped celery
4 potatoes, pared and cubed
½ pound pared pumpkin meat, cubed (optional)
2 apples, pared and cut in wedges
¼ cup chopped parsley
1½ teaspoons salt
½ teaspoon thyme
¼ teaspoon marjoram
⅛ teaspoon cayenne pepper
6 peppercorns
1 bay leaf
1 cup white wine, such as sauterne
1 cup beef broth
1 can (about 8 ounces) whole kernel corn, drained
3 medium tomatoes, peeled and cut in wedges
2 peaches, peeled and cut in wedges
½ pound grapes, halved and seeded
½ pound zucchini, washed and thinly sliced

1. Coat veal with a mixture of flour and 1 teaspoon salt.
2. Heat a small amount of lard in a large skillet, add meat, and brown well on all sides.
3. Put browned meat into a large electric cooker.
4. Heat a small amount of lard in a skillet, add garlic, onion, and green pepper, and cook until partially tender. Turn contents of skillet into cooker. Add celery, potato, pumpkin (if used), apple, parsley, dry seasonings, wine, and broth; mix well.
5. Cover and cook on Low 8 to 10 hours.
6. Remove bay leaf. Add corn, tomatoes, peaches, grapes, and zucchini to mixture in cooker; stir.
7. Cover and cook on High 1 hour.
8. Accompany with **fluffy hot rice.**
ABOUT 10 SERVINGS

Short Ribs, Western Style

4 medium onions, peeled and quartered
2 teaspoons salt
¼ teaspoon ground black pepper
½ teaspoon rubbed sage
1 quart water
1 cup dried lima beans
3 tablespoons flour
1 teaspoon dry mustard
2 to 3 tablespoons fat
2 pounds beef rib short ribs, cut in serving-size pieces

1. Combine onions, salt, pepper, sage, and water in a large heavy saucepot or Dutch oven. Cover, bring to boiling, reduce heat, and simmer 5 minutes. Bring to boiling again; add lima beans gradually and cook, uncovered, 2 minutes. Remove from heat, cover, and set aside to soak 1 hour.
2. Meanwhile, mix flour and dry mustard and coat short ribs evenly.
3. Heat fat in a large heavy skillet and brown short ribs on all sides over medium heat. Add meat to soaked lima beans. Bring to boiling and simmer, covered, 1½ hours, or until beans and meat are tender.
ABOUT 6 SERVINGS

Carbonada Criolla

Beef Stew

3 tablespoons lard or vegetable oil
3 pounds lean beef, cut in ½-inch cubes
1 large onion, finely chopped
1 clove garlic, minced
3 fresh ripe tomatoes, peeled, seeded, and chopped
2 cans (4 ounces each) mild red chilies, drained and puréed
2 cups beef broth
2 teaspoons salt
⅛ teaspoon pepper
½ teaspoon oregano

1. Heat lard in a large skillet. Brown meat quickly on all sides. Remove beef from fat and set aside.
2. Add onion and garlic to fat in skillet; cook until onion is soft. Remove from fat and add to beef.
3. Cook tomato in fat in skillet, adding more fat if necessary. Return meat and onion to skillet. Add chili purée, beef broth, and seasonings; stir. Cover; bring to boiling, reduce heat, and cook over low heat about 2 hours, or until meat is tender.

6 TO 8 SERVINGS

Steamed Beef

3 to 4 pounds beef round rump or eye round steak
Salt and pepper
2 onions, sliced
1 cup each diced carrot, parsley root, and parsnips
1 cup green peas
½ cup sliced celery
½ cup asparagus stems (optional)
1 cauliflower or cabbage core, diced (optional)
2 tablespoons butter

1. Pound the meat. Sprinkle with salt and pepper. Let stand 30 minutes. Pound again.
2. In a steamer top, combine meat and vegetables. Add butter. Cook over gently boiling water about 3 hours, or until meat is tender.
3. Slice meat. Serve with the steamed vegetables.

6 TO 8 SERVINGS

Braised Veal with Lemon and Anchovies

6 thick slices veal shin, sawed through so marrow shows
½ cup flour
½ cup butter
1 cup dry white wine
¼ cup chicken or veal stock
1 can (16 ounces) tomatoes (undrained)
2 teaspoons salt
1 teaspoon ground pepper
1 teaspoon thyme
2 garlic cloves, crushed in a garlic press
1 teaspoon grated lemon peel
½ cup minced parsley
2 anchovies, minced

1. Roll veal shin slices lightly in flour.
2. Melt butter in a Dutch oven and add veal, browning on all sides. Add wine, stock, tomatoes, salt, pepper, thyme, and garlic. Cover. Simmer about 2 hours, or until meat is tender, adding a little liquid when necessary.
3. Sprinkle with lemon peel, parsley, and anchovies before serving.

3 SERVINGS

Roast Veal

3 pounds veal rump roast, boned, rolled, and tied
1 garlic clove
1 tablespoon dill
1 teaspoon oregano
Salt and pepper to taste
3 tablespoons butter
¼ cup water
¼ cup white wine
1 teaspoon rosemary

1. Rub roast with garlic, dill, and oregano. Season with salt and pepper.
2. Melt butter in a roasting pan. Brown veal well on all sides.
3. Place a rack under veal. Pour water and wine into bottom of pan. Add rosemary. Cover pan.
4. Roast in a 350°F oven 2 hours.
5. Serve with pan juices.

6 TO 8 SERVINGS

Veal Stew with Onions

Flour seasoned with salt, pepper, and paprika
6 veal shanks, cut in pieces
3 tablespoons olive oil
3 tomatoes, peeled, seeded, and cubed
2 tablespoons chopped parsley
1 cup water
1 tablespoon wine vinegar
2 garlic cloves, minced
1 teaspoon sugar
1 bay leaf
2 whole cloves
2 whole allspice
Pinch red pepper seed
2 pounds whole baby onions
Water

1. Put seasoned flour into a bag. Add shank pieces and shake to coat evenly.
2. Heat oil in a Dutch oven and brown meat on all sides. Add tomatoes, parsley, 1 cup water, wine vinegar, garlic, and sugar. Tie bay leaf, cloves, allspice, and red pepper seed in cheesecloth. Add to meat mixture. Cover and simmer 1 hour.
3. Meanwhile, peel onions. Cut a small cross on the bottom of each. Add to stew and pour in enough water to cover. Simmer until onions are tender (about 25 minutes). Discard spices. Serve hot with **rice** or **cracked wheat pilafi.**

3 OR 4 SERVINGS

Roasted Veal

1 veal leg round roast or shoulder arm roast (4 to 5 pounds)
Boiling water
3 tablespoons lemon juice
1 tablespoon salt
1 teaspoon pepper
½ cup butter, melted
Flour for dusting

1. Dip meat quickly in boiling water; drain well.
2. Mix lemon juice, salt, and pepper. Spread over surface of meat.
3. Place meat on a spit or rack in a roasting pan.
4. Roast at 400°F 20 minutes. Reduce heat to 325°F. Roast 55 minutes.
5. Baste with melted butter. Sprinkle flour over top. Roast 10 minutes longer, or until done as desired.

6 TO 8 SERVINGS

Beef Sirloin Tip Roast with Parmesan Barbecue Baste

1 sirloin tip roast (3½ to 5 pounds) Parmesan Barbecue Baste (below)

1. Place roast, fat side up, in a shallow roasting pan. Insert meat thermometer so bulb is centered in the thickest part. Do not add water. Do not cover.
2. Roast at 325°F. Roast is done when meat thermometer registers 140°F for rare; 160°F for medium; and 170°F for well done. Brush with Parmesan Barbecue Baste occasionally during the last 30 minutes cooking time.
3. For a 3½- to 5-pound roast, allow 35 to 40 minutes per pound. For a 6- to 8-pound roast, allow 30 to 35 minutes per pound.
4. For easier carving, allow roast to "stand" in a warm place 15 to 20 minutes after removal from oven. Since roast usually continues to cook after removal from oven, it is best to remove it about 5°F below the temperature desired.

Parmesan Barbecue Baste

¾ cup ketchup
½ cup chopped onion
¼ cup water
2 tablespoons Parmesan

cheese
1 tablespoon Worcestershire sauce

Combine ketchup, onion, water, Parmesan cheese, and Worcestershire sauce in small saucepan. Cook slowly, for 5 to 10 minutes, stirring occasionally.
MAKES 1 CUP SAUCE

Veal Parmigiano

1 pound veal steak or cutlet, thinly sliced
1 teaspoon salt
⅛ teaspoon pepper
1 egg
2 cups plus 2 teaspoons water
⅓ cup grated Parmesan cheese

⅓ cup fine dry bread crumbs
¼ cup shortening
1 medium onion, finely chopped
1 can (6 ounces) tomato paste
1 teaspoon salt
½ teaspoon basil
6 slices mozzarella cheese

1. Cut veal into 8 pieces; sprinkle with 1 teaspoon salt and the pepper.
2. Lightly beat together egg and 2 teaspoons water.
3. Combine Parmesan cheese and bread crumbs.
4. Dip veal in egg wash, then Parmesan mixture. Refrigerate at least ½ hour.
5. Brown veal on both sides in shortening in a skillet. Remove to a 1½-quart shallow baking dish.
6. Sauté onion in skillet. Stir in tomato paste, 1 teaspoon salt, and basil. Simmer 5 minutes. Pour three fourths of the sauce over veal. Top with mozzarella cheese. Pour remaining sauce over cheese.
7. Bake, uncovered, at 350°F 20 to 25 minutes, or until mixture is bubbly.
4 SERVINGS

Veal à la Nelson

3 ounces dried mushrooms (optional)
2 cups warm milk
3 slices bacon
1 pound fresh mushrooms, sliced
4 large onions, chopped
8 veal cutlets (about 3

pounds)
3 bouillon cubes
3 tablespoons flour
¼ cup butter or margarine, melted
1 cup sour cream
Salt and pepper
8 medium potatoes, cooked

1. Soak dried mushrooms in warm milk 2 hours.
2. Fry bacon in a large skillet. Add mushrooms and onion. Sauté until onion is soft. Add fried bacon, mushrooms, and onion to milk.
3. Sauté veal in drippings. Add oil, if needed.
4. Add milk mixture and bouillon cubes. Cover; simmer 1 hour.
5. Stir flour into melted butter. Blend in a small amount of cooking liquid. Stir into remainder of liquid in skillet. Cook and stir until sauce is smooth and thick. Then blend in sour cream. Season to taste with salt and pepper.
6. Add potatoes. Cook 10 to 15 minutes, or until potatoes are hot.
8 SERVINGS

Savory Veal Stew

3 pounds veal stew cubes
1½ teaspoons salt
½ teaspoon freshly ground pepper
2 garlic cloves
1 teaspoon caraway seed, lightly crushed
2 bay leaves
½ cup dry white wine
1 cup Beef Stock (page 48)
1 small head cabbage, cut in

8 wedges
3 leeks, cut in 3-inch pieces
¾ teaspoon salt
½ teaspoon freshly ground pepper
1 tablespoon arrowroot
Cold water
½ pound mushrooms, sliced
½ cup Mock Crème Fraîche, if desired (page 46)

1. Place veal in a 6-quart Dutch oven; sprinkle with 1½ teaspoons salt and ½ teaspoon pepper. Mix garlic, caraway, fennel, bay leaves, wine, and stock. Pour over veal. Simmer covered over low heat 2 hours.
2. Add cabbage and leeks to Dutch oven; sprinkle with ¾ teaspoon salt and ½ teaspoon pepper. Simmer covered until vegetables and veal are just tender (about 15 minutes). Remove veal and vegetables to a shallow serving dish; keep warm.
3. Skim fat from cooking liquid in Dutch oven. Discard bay leaves. Mix arrowroot with a little cold water. Stir into cooking liquid; simmer until thickened (about 3 minutes). Stir in mushrooms and Mock Crème Fraîche; simmer 1 minute. Pour thickened mixture over veal and vegetables. Sprinkle with **parsley**.
8 SERVINGS

Beef Sirloin Tip Roast with Parmesan Barbecue Baste

Veal Cutlets Valle d'Aosta

6 veal chops, boneless, 1 inch thick
6 thin slices fully cooked ham
6 slices fontina or mozzarella cheese
1 cup all-purpose flour
1 teaspoon salt
¼ teaspoon pepper
1 egg, beaten with 1 tablespoon water
Fine bread crumbs
¼ cup butter, more if needed

1. Butterfly chops by slicing through the chop almost all the way, and laying chop open so it is ½ inch thick; pound flat.
2. Place a slice of ham, then a slice of cheese, in the center of each chop. Moisten edges of chop and press together.
3. Dip each folded chop first in flour mixed with salt and pepper, then in beaten egg, and finally in the bread crumbs.
4. Heat the butter in a large skillet. Brown the chops slowly, about 5 minutes on each side or until done.

6 SERVINGS

Veal Scallops in Lemon Sauce

12 veal scallops (about 2 pounds)
¼ cup water
¼ teaspoon bottled brown bouquet sauce
2 teaspoons clarified butter
Salt
¾ cup dry white wine
¾ cup Chicken Stock (page 48)
⅓ cup finely chopped onion
1 garlic clove, minced
½ cup fresh lemon juice
¼ teaspoon freshly ground white pepper
½ teaspoon salt
1 tablespoon arrowroot
Cold water
1 tablespoon snipped parsley

1. Pound veal scallops with a mallet until thin and even in thickness. Brush both sides lightly with a mixture of water and brown bouquet sauce. Cook a few pieces of veal in hot butter in a skillet just until done (about 1 minute on each side). Sprinkle lightly with salt. Keep warm in oven while cooking remaining veal.
2. While veal is cooking, mix wine, stock, onion, and garlic in a small saucepan. Simmer until onion is tender (about 3 minutes). Stir in lemon juice, pepper, and salt.
3. Mix arrowroot with a little cold water. Stir into simmering stock mixture. Simmer, stirring constantly, until mixture thickens.
4. Arrange veal on warm plates. Pour sauce over. Sprinkle with parsley.

6 SERVINGS

Corned Beef in Grapefruit Juice

1 corned brisket of beef (about 4 to 5 pounds)
Water
1½ quarts grapefruit juice
1 large onion studded with 12 whole cloves
8 peppercorns
1 celery stalk with leaves, cut in thirds
1 bay leaf
1 tablespoon caraway seed
1 green pepper, sliced
10 carrots, pared and halved
8 small white onions
4 baking potatoes, pared and halved
1 green cabbage, cut in quarters

1. Put corned beef into a heavy kettle. Add water to cover. Bring to boiling and cover tightly. Reduce heat and simmer 1 hour.
2. Pour off water and add grapefruit juice and water to cover. Add onion studded with cloves, peppercorns, celery, bay leaf, caraway seed, and green pepper. Bring to boiling; reduce heat and simmer, covered, 2 hour.
3. Add carrots, onions, and potatoes; cook 30 minutes.
4. Add cabbage and cook 30 minutes.
5. Serve meat and vegetables on a platter.

8 SERVINGS

Stuffed Veal Breast

2½ pounds boneless breast of veal
Salt
Freshly ground pepper
1 large onion, chopped
2 tablespoons Chicken Stock (page 48)
½ pound fresh spinach, washed and stems removed*
¾ cup low-fat ricotta cheese
¼ cup grated Jarlsberg or Parmesan cheese
2 garlic cloves, minced
1 teaspoon snipped fresh or
½ teaspoon dried thyme leaves
1½ teaspoons snipped fresh or ¾ teaspoon dried basil leaves
½ teaspoon snipped fresh or ¼ teaspoon dried oregano leaves
2 tablespoons snipped parsley
1 teaspoon salt
¼ teaspoon pepper
½ cup dry white wine or Chicken Stock (page 48)

1. Trim excess fat from meat. Sprinkle meat lightly on both sides with salt and pepper.
2. Simmer onion in stock just until tender (about 5 minutes).
3. Place spinach with water clinging to leaves in a large saucepan; cook covered over medium heat just until wilted (about 3 minutes).
4. Drain onion and spinach well in a strainer, pressing moisture out with a wooden spoon. Mix onion, spinach, cheeses, garlic, thyme, basil, oregano, parsley, 1 teaspoon salt, and ¼ teaspoon pepper. Spoon mixture on surface of meat; roll up and tie with string at intervals. Place meat in a roasting pan. Pour wine over roast. Cover.
5. Roast in a 325°F oven about 1½ hours, or until tender.
6. Remove roast to a serving platter. Cover lightly with aluminum foil. Let stand 15 minutes before carving.

6 SERVINGS

*1 package (10 ounces) frozen spinach can be substituted for the fresh. Thaw and drain thoroughly in strainer.

Cooked Corned Beef Brisket

5 pounds corned beef brisket
1 onion, halved
1 clove garlic, halved
6 whole cloves
8 peppercorns
2 bay leaves
4 stalks celery, cut in pieces

1. Put corned beef into a large kettle; cover with cold water. Add remaining ingredients and bring to boiling. Cover and simmer 3½ to 4 hours, or until the beef is tender.
2. Remove beef from liquid. Slice and serve hot with **English Mustard Sauce,** (page 52).
8 TO 10 SERVINGS

Ossobuco

4 to 5 pounds veal shank
  crosscuts
Flour
⅓ cup olive oil
Salt and pepper
½ cup beef broth or bouillon
1 onion, chopped
1 clove garlic, crushed in a
  garlic press
1 medium carrot, sliced
1 leek, sliced
1 slice celery root
2 whole cloves
1 bay leaf
Pinch each of sage, thyme,
  and rosemary
½ cup white wine
1 can (28 ounces) whole
  tomatoes
1 tablespoon grated lemon
  peel

1. Dredge crosscuts with flour. Heat several tablespoons olive oil in a skillet. Brown the veal well, season with salt and pepper, and transfer to a heatproof casserole or Dutch oven. Handle gently so the marrow remains in the bones. Pour the broth into the casserole.
2. Add more oil to skillet, if needed. In hot oil, sauté onion, garlic, carrot, leek, and celery root over medium heat about 5 minutes.
3. Stir in the cloves, bay leaf, sage, thyme, and rosemary. Pour in the wine and continue cooking until wine is almost evaporated. Stir in tomatoes and grated lemon peel. Cook over medium heat several minutes.
4. Pour tomato mixture over meat in casserole. Cover tightly and simmer about 1½ hours, or until meat is tender. Remove veal to serving dish and keep hot.
5. Force vegetables and juice in casserole through a sieve or food mill. If the resulting sauce is thin, cook over high heat to reduce liquid. Season sauce if necessary. Pour sauce over meat or serve separately.
6. Serve with **rice** or **spaghetti** tossed with **melted butter** and topped with **grated Parmesan** or **Romano cheese.**
4 or 5 SERVINGS

Saltimbocca

4 large, thinly sliced veal
  cutlets
Salt and pepper
4 large, very thin slices ham
  or prosciutto
Dried sage leaves
Olive oil
¼ cup (2 ounces) Marsala

1. Place veal slices on a cutting board and pound with a mallet until very thin. Divide each slice into 2 or 3 pieces.
2. Season veal with salt and pepper.
3. Cut ham into pieces the same size as veal.
4. Place a sage leaf on each piece of veal and top with a slice of ham. Secure with a wooden pick.
5. Heat several tablespoons olive oil in a skillet; add the meat and cook slowly until golden brown on both sides. Remove meat to heated platter and keep warm.
6. Scrape residue from bottom of pan; add the Marsala and simmer over low heat several minutes. Pour over meat and serve.
4 SERVINGS

Scamorze-Crowned Veal with Mushrooms

2 pounds veal cutlets, cut
  about ½ inch thick
¼ cup lemon juice
½ teaspoon salt
1/16 teaspoon black pepper
¼ cup butter
½ cup flour
1 egg, beaten
½ cup fine dry bread crumbs
¼ pound mushrooms,
  cleaned and sliced
6 thin slices cooked ham
6 ounces scamorze cheese,
  cut in 6 slices
6 mushroom caps, browned
  in butter

1. Cut meat into 6 serving-size pieces; place on a flat working surface and pound both sides with a meat hammer. Put into a large, shallow dish.
2. Mix lemon juice, salt, and pepper together and spoon over veal. Cover and refrigerate 2 hours.
3. Heat butter in a large, heavy skillet. Coat veal pieces with flour, dip in egg, then in bread crumbs. Add to hot butter in skillet and fry about 5 minutes on one side, or until lightly browned.
4. Turn meat and arrange on each piece a layer of mushroom slices, a slice of ham, a slice of cheese, and a mushroom cap. Continue cooking about 5 minutes, or until second side is browned and cheese is melted.
5. Remove to a warm serving platter and serve immediately.
6 SERVINGS

 ## Embassy Veal Glacé

1½ teaspoons dry tarragon
  leaves
1 cup dry white wine
1½ pounds veal round steak
  (about ¼ inch thick)
3 tablespoons butter or
margarine
½ teaspoon salt
⅛ teaspoon pepper
½ cup condensed beef
  consommé
½ cup dry vermouth

1. Stir tarragon into white wine; cover and set aside several hours, stirring occasionally.
2. Cut meat into pieces about 3x2 inches. Heat butter in cooking pan of chafing dish until lightly browned. Add meat and lightly brown on both sides; season with salt and pepper.
3. Reduce heat and pour in tarragon-wine mixture with the consommé and vermouth. Simmer, uncovered, about 10 minutes, or until veal is tender.
4. Remove veal to a platter and cover.
5. Increase heat under pan and cook sauce until it is reduced to a thin glaze, stirring occasionally. Return veal to pan and spoon sauce over meat, turning meat once.
6. Cover and place over direct heat of chafing dish until warm.
ABOUT 6 SERVINGS

Rack of Veal with Peppercorn Sauce

1 veal rib roast (about 5 pounds)
1 teaspoon salt
Freshly ground white pepper
White wine
1⅓ cups Mock Béarnaise Sauce (page 49; double recipe)
2 tablespoons drained green peppercorns

1. Rub roast with salt and pepper; place in a roasting pan. Insert meat thermometer so tip is in center of meat, away from bone.
2. Roast uncovered in a 325°F oven to an internal temperature of 165°F (about 3 hours). Baste several times with white wine during last hour of roasting. Remove to a platter and cover loosely with aluminum foil; let stand 20 minutes before carving.
3. While roast is standing, make the sauce, adding peppercorns before heating. Pass sauce.
10 SERVINGS

Note: A boneless veal roast can also be used in this recipe. Roast as directed above, allowing about 35 minutes per pound.

Curried Veal and Vegetables

1 pound veal for stew (1-inch cubes)
2 cups water
1 teaspoon salt
3 medium carrots, pared and cut in quarters
½ pound green beans
2 large stalks celery, cut in
½-inch slices
3 tablespoons butter or margarine
2 tablespoons flour
½ teaspoon curry powder
¼ teaspoon salt
Cooked rice
Fresh parsley, snipped

1. Put veal into a large saucepan with water and 1 teaspoon salt. Cover, bring to boiling, reduce heat, and simmer 1 hour. Add carrots, green beans, and celery. Cover, bring to boiling, and simmer 1 hour, or until meat is tender.
2. Remove meat and vegetables from broth with a slotted spoon; set aside. Reserve broth.
3. Heat butter in a saucepan. Blend in flour, curry powder, and ¼ teaspoon salt. Heat until bubbly. Add reserved broth gradually, stirring until smooth. Bring to boiling, stirring constantly, and cook 1 to 2 minutes. Mix in meat and vegetables. Heat thoroughly.
4. Serve over rice. Sprinkle with parsley.
ABOUT 6 SERVINGS

Veal Scaloppine with Mushrooms

1 tablespoon flour
¾ teaspoon salt
Pinch pepper
1 pound veal cutlets
2 tablespoons cooking oil
4 ounces fresh mushrooms, quartered lengthwise
½ cup sherry
2 tablespoons finely chopped parsley

1. Combine flour, salt, and pepper; sprinkle over veal slices. Pound slices until thin, flat, and round, working flour mixture into both sides. Cut into ¼-inch-wide strips.
2. Heat oil in a large wok. Add veal strips and stir-fry over high heat until golden.
3. Sprinkle mushrooms on top and pour sherry over all. Simmer, uncovered, about 15 minutes, or until tender.
4. Toss with parsley and serve.
4 SERVINGS

Rack of Veal with Peppercorn Sauce

Veal Rollettes

2 cloves garlic, minced
1 tablespoon grated
 Parmesan cheese
2 teaspoons chopped parsley
½ teaspoon salt
¼ teaspoon pepper

1½ pounds veal round steak,
 cut about ½ inch thick
Mozzarella cheese, sliced
3 tablespoons olive oil
½ cup butter, melted
¼ cup water

1. Mix garlic, Parmesan cheese, parsley, salt, and pepper Set aside.
2. Cut veal into 4x3-inch pieces. Put 1 slice mozzarella cheese on each piece of meat. Top each with 1 teaspoon garlic-cheese mixture. Roll each piece of meat to enclose mixture; tie with string, or fasten meat roll with wooden picks or small skewers.
3. Heat oil in a skillet. Add meat rolls and brown slowly on all sides. Put meat into a greased 2-quart casserole. Mix butter and water; pour over meat. Cover casserole.
4. Bake at 300°F about 1 hour, or until meat is tender. Remove string, wooden picks, or skewers.
ABOUT 4 SERVINGS

Veal and Peppers Basilicata Style

2 tablespoons butter
1 tablespoon lard
1½ pounds boneless veal
 leg, rump, or shoulder
 roast, cut in 1-inch pieces
1 teaspoon salt
⅛ teaspoon pepper
1 medium-size onion, sliced

4 large ripe tomatoes
1 tablespoon chopped basil
 leaves or 1 teaspoon dried
 sweet basil
4 large firm green or red
 peppers
3 tablespoons olive oil

1. Heat butter and lard in skillet over medium heat. Add meat and brown on all sides. Stir in salt, pepper, and onion; cook 5 minutes.
2. Cut tomatoes in half, squeeze out seeds, chop pulp, and add with basil to meat. Cover and simmer 20 minutes.
3. Cut out stems, remove seeds, and clean peppers. Cut in quarters, lengthwise. Fry peppers in hot olive oil about 10 minutes, or until softened. Add to meat, cover, and simmer 30 minutes, or until meat is tender. Serve hot.
4 SERVINGS

Veal Chops Pizzaiola

¼ cup olive oil
6 veal rib or loin chops, cut
 about ½ inch thick
1 can (28 ounces) tomatoes,
 sieved

2 cloves garlic, sliced
1 teaspoon oregano
1 teaspoon salt
½ teaspoon pepper
½ teaspoon chopped parsley

1. Heat oil in a large, heavy skillet. Add chops and brown on both sides.
2. Meanwhile, combine tomatoes, garlic, oregano, salt, pepper, and parsley. Slowly add tomato mixture to browned veal. Cover and cook over low heat 45 minutes, or until meat is tender.
6 SERVINGS

Beefsteak Pizzaiola: Follow recipe for Veal Chops Pizzaiola. Substitute **2 pounds beef round steak,** cut about ¾ inch thick, for veal chops. Cook about 1½ hours.

Schnitzel with Spinach

2½ pounds veal cutlet
½ teaspoon salt
½ teaspoon pepper
2 pounds spinach
2 tablespoons butter
¼ teaspoon nutmeg
¾ cup beef bouillon
2 sprigs tarragon,
 chopped

Piquant Sauce:
1 large onion, chopped
3 tablespoons green pepper,
 finely chopped
1 tablespoon fresh tarragon
4 tablespoons tomato paste
½-¾ cup white wine
½-¾ cup heavy cream
⅛ teaspoon arrow root

1. Make sauce. Sauté onion, green pepper, tarragon and tomato paste in butter. Add wine and bouillon. Cook covered over low heat for 30 minutes. Strain sauce and return to saucepan. Add cream and arrow root and season with salt and pepper. Keep sauce warm.
2. Heat butter and sauté veal over low heat about 5 minutes. Add bouillon and continue to cook about 10 minutes. Turn a few times.
3. Chop and sauté spinach in butter. Season with salt and nutmeg.
4. Place spinach on serving dish and put veal on top. Pour sauce on top. Garnish with tarragon. Serve with cooked rice.
8 SERVINGS

Veal Scaloppine with Mushrooms and Capers

1 pound veal round steak,
 cut about ½ inch thick
½ cup flour
½ teaspoon salt
⅛ teaspoon pepper
¼ cup olive oil
½ clove garlic, minced
¼ pound mushrooms,
 cleaned and sliced

lengthwise
1 medium onion, thinly
 sliced
1¾ cups sieved canned
 tomatoes
¼ cup capers
1 teaspoon minced parsley
¼ teaspoon oregano

1. Put meat on a flat working surface and pound on both sides with a meat hammer. Cut into 1-inch pieces. Coat evenly with a mixture of flour, ½ teaspoon salt, and ⅛ teaspoon pepper.
2. Heat oil with garlic in a large skillet. Add veal and slowly brown on both sides.
3. Meanwhile, heat butter in a skillet. Add mushrooms and onion; cook until mushrooms are lightly browned.
4. Add mushrooms to veal along with tomatoes, capers, 1 teaspoon salt, ⅛ teaspoon pepper, parsley, and oregano; mix well.
5. Cover skillet and simmer about 25 minutes, or until veal is tender; stir occasionally.
ABOUT 4 SERVINGS

Veal Peasant Style

2 tablespoons butter	teaspoon dried basil leaves
1 tablespoon olive oil	¾ cup beef broth
1 cup finely chopped onion	2 tablespoons butter
⅓ cup finely chopped celery	1 pound fresh green peas,
1½ to 2 pounds veal, cubed	shelled, or 1 package (10
1 teaspoon salt	ounces) frozen green peas
¼ teaspoon pepper	3 carrots, diced
4 tomatoes, peeled and	½ teaspoon salt
coarsely chopped	¾ cup hot water
Several basil leaves or ¼	1 tablespoon minced parsley

1. Heat 2 tablespoons butter and the olive oil in a Dutch oven or large saucepot. Add onion and celery; sauté 3 or 4 minutes.
2. Add meat and brown on all sides. Season with 1 teaspoon salt and the pepper. Stir in tomatoes and basil. Cover Dutch oven.
3. Cook at 275°F 1¼ hours, or until meat is almost tender. Add broth, a little at a time, during cooking.
4. Heat 2 tablespoons butter in a saucepan. Stir in peas, carrots, ½ teaspoon salt, and water. Cook, covered, until vegetables are tender (about 15 minutes).
5. Skim off fat from the meat. Stir in the cooked vegetables and parsley. Continue cooking in oven until meat is tender.
6. Serve meat surrounded with the vegetables and **small sautéed potatoes** on a heated platter. Pour sauce over all.
6 TO 8 SERVINGS

Ham-and-Asparagus-Stuffed Veal Rolls

6 slices (1½ pounds) veal	2 tablespoons butter
cutlet, boneless	⅓ cup finely chopped
1 teaspoon salt	parsley
¼ teaspoon black pepper	2 cloves garlic, crushed
6 slices prosciutto	3½ ounces dried
6 slices Emmenthaler cheese	mushrooms, hydrated
6 white asparagus spears, 4	(soaked in water)
inches long	¼ cup beef gravy
¼ cup butter	3 cups cream
½ cup port wine	1 teaspoon salt

1. Pound veal cutlets until thin. Season with salt and pepper.
2. Place a slice of prosciutto, then a slice of cheese and an asparagus spear, over each veal slice. Roll into fingers; skewer or secure with twine.
3. Melt the ¼ cup butter in a large, heavy skillet. Add veal rolls; brown on all sides. Add port wine; cover and simmer about 10 minutes.
4. Meanwhile, melt the 2 tablespoons butter in a saucepan. Add and lightly brown the parsley and garlic. Mix in the mushrooms, beef gravy, and cream; simmer 5 minutes. Pour sauce over veal rolls; correct seasoning, using the remaining 1 teaspoon salt. Cover and simmer until meat is tender.
6 SERVINGS

Veal Parmesan

2 cups Tomato Meat Sauce	cheese
(see page 50)	3 eggs, beaten
1½ to 2 pounds veal round	1 teaspoon salt
steak, cut about ½ inch	¼ teaspoon pepper
thick	⅓ cup olive oil
1⅓ cups fine dry bread	6 slices (3 ounces) moz-
crumbs	zarella cheese
⅓ cup grated Parmesan	

1. Prepare Tomato Meat Sauce.
2. Put meat on a flat working surface and repeatedly pound on one side with meat hammer. Turn meat over and repeat process. Cut into 6 pieces.
3. Mix bread crumbs and grated cheese; set aside.
4. Mix eggs, salt, and pepper; set aside.
5. Heat oil in a large skillet. Coat meat pieces first with egg, then with crumb mixture. Add to oil in skillet and brown on both sides.
6. Put browned meat into an 11x7x1½-inch baking dish. Pour sauce over meat. Top with slices of mozzarella cheese.
7. Bake at 350°F 15 to 20 minutes, or until cheese is melted and lightly browned.
6 SERVINGS

Veal Cutlet in Wine with Olives

1½ pounds veal cutlets, cut	2 to 3 tablespoons butter or
about ¼ inch thick	margarine
¼ cup all-purpose flour	⅓ cup marsala
1 teaspoon salt	⅓ cup sliced green olives
¼ teaspoon pepper	

1. Place meat on flat working surface and pound with meat hammer to increase tenderness. Turn meat and repeat process. Cut into 6 serving-size pieces. Coat with a mixture of flour, salt, and pepper.
2. Heat butter in skillet over low heat. Brown meat over medium heat. Add marsala and green olives. Cover skillet and cook over low heat about 1 hour, or until meat is tender when pierced with a fork.
ABOUT 6 SERVINGS

German Veal Chops

4 veal loin or rib chops	1 bay leaf
Butter or margarine	½ teaspoon salt
2 medium onions, sliced	Dash pepper
1 cup dark beer	2 tablespoons flour

1. Brown veal in butter in a skillet; set meat aside. Sauté onion in same skillet until golden.
2. Add beer, bay leaf, salt, and pepper. Cover and simmer 15 minutes.
3. Transfer veal and onion to a platter. Make a paste of flour and a little water; stir into cooking liquid in skillet. Cook, stirring constantly, until thickened and smooth. Pour over veal and onion.
4 SERVINGS

Note: If you do not have dark beer, add ½ **teaspoon molasses** to light beer.

Puffy Veal Cutlets

1½ pounds veal round steak (cutlet), cut about ½ inch thick
¼ cup all-purpose flour
1 teaspoon salt
⅛ teaspoon pepper
1 egg yolk
4 tablespoons butter
1 egg white

1. Set out a large, heavy skillet having a tight-fitting cover.
2. Have steak ready.
3. Cut into 4 serving-size pieces. Coat cutlets with a mixture of flour, salt, and pepper. Set aside.
4. Beat egg yolk until thick and lemon-colored.
5. Set aside.
6. Heat butter in the skillet over low heat.
7. Meanwhile, using a clean beater, beat egg white until rounded peaks are formed.
8. Spread the egg yolk over the egg white and gently fold together.
9. Coat cutlets on one side with the egg mixture. Put cutlets into skillet egg-coated side down. Cook until lightly browned (about 15 minutes).
10. Spoon remaining egg mixture onto cutlets, being sure to cover tops and turn. Cover and cook over low heat about 20 minutes, or until meat is tender when pierced with a fork.
4 SERVINGS

Veal Cutlets with Fried Eggs: Do not separate egg; beat slightly and mix with **1 tablespoon milk.** After flouring cutlets, dip into the egg mixture and then coat with **1 cup (3 to 4 slices) fine, dry bread crumbs.** Cook; keep warm while preparing fried eggs.
1. Heat 1 to 2 tablespoons **butter** in a heavy skillet over low heat. Break into a saucer, one at a time, and slip into the skillet, **4 eggs.** Reduce heat and cook slowly about 4 minutes, or to desired stage of firmness. Baste eggs frequently with butter in skillet.
2. Arrange fried eggs on top of cutlets. Garnish platter with vegetables and diamonds of **crisp toast** topped with **smoked salmon, caviar** and cutouts of **hard-cooked egg white.**

Stuffed Veal Steak

4 veal loin top loin chops, 1 inch thick (about 1½ pounds)
1 cup dry white wine, such as chablis
½ cup sliced mushrooms
1 green pepper, cut in ½-inch pieces
½ cup butter or margarine
½ cup all-purpose flour
1 egg, fork beaten
½ cup fine dry bread crumbs
½ cup grated Parmesan cheese
4 slices prosciutto (Italian ham)
4 slices (4 ounces) Cheddar cheese

1. Make a cut in the side of each veal chop, cutting almost all the way through. Lay each open and pound flat. Marinate meat for 1 hour in wine.
2. While meat marinates, sauté mushrooms and green pepper in butter for about 10 minutes or until tender. Remove from skillet with slotted spoon, leaving butter in skillet. Set vegetables aside.
3. Dry veal on paper towel. Bread on one side only, dipping first in flour, then in beaten egg, and last in bread crumbs mixed with Parmesan cheese.
4. Lay a slice of prosciutto on one half of unbreaded side of veal. Fold other side over. Pan-fry for 6 minutes on one side in butter in skillet, adding more butter if needed. Turn veal, and remove skillet from heat.
5. Insert a slice of cheese, and ¼ of the mushroom-pepper mixture into the fold of each steak.
6. Return to heat and cook 6 minutes, or until meat is tender.
4 SERVINGS

Veal in Wine-Mushroom Sauce

1½ pounds thin veal cutlets
1 clove garlic, peeled and cut
1 tablespoon flour
¼ cup butter or margarine
½ pound mushrooms, thinly sliced
½ teaspoon salt
Dash white pepper
½ cup white wine, such as vermouth
1 teaspoon lemon juice (optional)
Snipped parsley

1. Pound meat to ¼-inch thickness. Rub both sides with garlic. Cut veal into 2-inch pieces and sprinkle with flour.
2. Sauté veal, a few pieces at a time, in hot butter in a large skillet, until golden brown on both sides.
3. Return all pieces to skillet. Top with mushrooms and sprinkle with salt and pepper.
4. Add wine and cook, covered, over low heat for 20 minutes, or until fork tender, adding 1 tablespoon or so water if necessary.
5. To serve, sprinkle with lemon juice, if desired, and parsley.
4 TO 6 SERVINGS

LAMB

Roast Leg of Lamb with Spicy Wine Sauce

1 cup dry red wine
¼ cup salad oil
1 onion, coarsely chopped
2 cloves garlic, minced
½ teaspoon Tabasco

2 teaspoons salt
1 lamb leg whole (6 to 8 pounds)
Parsley

1. Combine wine, oil, onion, garlic, Tabasco, and salt; pour over lamb. Cover and refrigerate 6 hours or overnight, turning occasionally.
2. Place lamb on rack in shallow roasting pan. Roast at 325°F about 25 minutes per pound, or until meat thermometer registers 160° to 170°F (medium); baste occasionally with marinade.
3. Garnish with parsley.
12 TO 16 SERVINGS

Roast Leg of Lamb with Spicy Wine Sauce

Lamb Shank in Parchment Paper

1 lamb shank per serving

For each serving:
1 garlic clove, peeled and slivered
1 slice hard mizithra cheese
1 small onion, sliced
1 small tomato, peeled and diced

1 teaspoon minced parsley
¼ teaspoon dill
¼ teaspoon mint flakes
½ teaspoon oregano
Juice of ½ lemon
Salt and pepper to taste
1 teaspoon olive oil
Parchment paper
Cotton string

1. Make several incisions in the meat, top and bottom. Insert sliver of garlic in each incision.
2. Place meat on a piece of parchment paper ample enough to seal meat and vegetables securely. Put cheese on meat, then arrange onion and tomato on top. Sprinkle with herbs, lemon juice, salt, and pepper. Drizzle with olive oil.
3. Wrap securely in parchment paper. Tie with string. Set in a roasting pan.
4. Bake at 350°F about 1½ hours, or until meat is done. Serve package unopened.

Note: Oiled brown paper may be substituted for the parchment paper.

Stuffed Lamb Breasts

5 strips bacon	½ teaspoon salt
½ cup finely chopped onion	¼ teaspoon pepper
6 cups bread cubes with crusts removed	3 eggs, well beaten
	½ cup milk
⅓ cup chopped pepperoni	2 lamb breasts with pockets (about 5 pounds)
3 tablespoons fresh parsley, or 1½ tablespoons dried parsley	Brown Sauce
	2 tablespoons cornstarch
1 teaspoon dried sweet basil	½ cup water

1. Cook bacon in skillet until crisp; drain, then crumble and set aside. Sauté onion in bacon fat until tender, but do not brown.
2. In large bowl, combine bread, onion, pepperoni, parsley, sweet basil, salt, pepper, and bacon. Toss lightly until well mixed.
3. In small bowl, mix beaten eggs and milk; then add to bread mixture and toss lightly until well mixed. Spoon half of stuffing into each lamb breast; then close opening with skewers. Place lamb breasts on rack in shallow roasting pan. Sprinkle lightly with additional salt and pepper.
4. Roast in a 350°F oven 15 minutes. Meanwhile make Brown Sauce. Generously baste lamb with Brown Sauce and continue to roast for 2 hours longer, or until lamb breasts are tender, basting lamb with Brown Sauce about every 15 minutes.
5. Remove lamb to heated platter. Skim fat from pan juice; stir in cornstarch dissolved in water. Cook over medium heat, stirring continuously, until thickened, adding more water if needed.
6. Carve lamb into slices and serve with pan gravy.

6 SERVINGS

Brown Sauce: In a 2-cup saucepan, mix **1½ cups water or bouillon** with **1 teaspoon prepared mustard, 1 teaspoon Worcestershire sauce, 1 teaspoon bottled steak sauce, ½ teaspoon celery salt, 1 bay leaf,** and **2 whole cloves.** Add **1 medium onion, halved,** and simmer over low heat for 15 minutes. Remove onion halves and place on top of lamb breasts. Baste meat with sauce.

Lamb Stew, Continental

2 pounds lamb shoulder, boneless, cut in 1½-inch cubes	1 bay leaf, crushed
	1 can (16 ounces) tomatoes (undrained)
2 tablespoons oil	1 can (8 ounces) tomato sauce
½ cup chopped onion	
½ teaspoon salt	2 cloves garlic
½ teaspoon basil	1 teaspoon sugar
½ teaspoon oregano	½ green pepper, cut in strips

1. Brown lamb cubes in oil in a large skillet. Add onion and cook, stirring frequently, until onion is soft. Drain off excess fat. Add salt, basil, oregano, bay leaf, tomatoes, tomato sauce, garlic, and sugar. Simmer covered 1½ hours.
2. Add green pepper, cover, and simmer 15 minutes, or until meat is tender.
3. Remove cover and cook, stirring as necessary, until sauce is reduced to desired consistency. Remove garlic.

ABOUT 6 SERVINGS

Saddle of Lamb with Artichoke Purée

1 (5 pounds) saddle of lamb (lamb loin roast)	8 to 10 thick grapevine leaves
2 tablespoons olive oil	8 artichoke bottoms, cooked
Salt and pepper	1 pound mushrooms, cooked
2 teaspoons oregano	2 tablespoons butter
4 garlic cloves, crushed in a garlic press	½ cup red wine
	½ cup water

1. Rub lamb with olive oil. Combine salt, pepper, oregano, and garlic. Rub over lamb. Cover with grapevine leaves. Seal with foil. Refrigerate overnight.
2. Purée artichoke bottoms and mushrooms. Combine with butter and heat.
3. Set roast in a roasting pan. Remove grapevine leaves and season with salt and pepper.
4. Roast in a 325°F oven 50 minutes. Remove from oven. Reserve juice in the pan. Separate each loin from the saddle in one piece. Cut the meat into slices. Spread each slice with some of the purée. Reassemble the loins and tie securely in place. Return the meat to the roasting pan and add wine and water. Continue roasting, basting frequently, for 15 minutes.
5. Remove to a serving platter and discard strings. Skim fat from the pan juices and strain juices over the meat.

ABOUT 10 SERVINGS

Lamb with Endive and Lemon Sauce

3 large bunches curly endive	2 tablespoons flour
1 quart water	2 cups water
3 tablespoons olive oil	Salt and pepper to taste
5 pounds lamb shoulder with bone, cut in large pieces	3 eggs
	Juice of 2 lemons
1 medium onion, minced	

1. Wash endive thoroughly under running cold water to remove grit. Cut off coarse stems. Bring 1 quart water to boiling in a large saucepot. Remove from heat and add endive. Let stand 3 minutes. Drain.
2. Heat olive oil in a large Dutch oven. Add meat and brown on all sides. Add onion. Cover and simmer, stirring occasionally.
3. Combine flour with 2 cups water in a bowl; stir well. Pour into meat. Season with salt and pepper. Add endive, cover, and continue cooking 1½ to 2 hours, or until meat is tender. (There should be enough stock for lemon sauce.)
4. To prepare sauce, beat eggs in a bowl and, beating constantly with a whisk, add lemon juice in a steady stream. Take 1 cup stock from meat and add, a tablespoon at a time, beating constantly.
4. Pour sauce over meat and endive. Heat; do not boil.

6 SERVINGS

Roast Leg of Lamb with Orzo

1 lamb leg (6½ to 7 pounds)
4 large garlic cloves, peeled and cut in half lengthwise
¼ cup oregano, crushed
1 tablespoon salt
2 tablespoons freshly ground pepper
Juice of 2 lemons

1 pound orzo (a pasta)
¼ cup cooking oil
1 tablespoon salt
1 cup boiling water
2 medium onions, quartered
¾ cup shredded or grated kefalotyri cheese

1. First prepare the lamb by placing it on a large sheet of aluminum foil. With a small, sharp knife, make eight 1-inch-deep diagonal incisions on the top and bottom of the lamb. Into each incision, insert half a garlic clove. Press meat back to cover incisions.
2. Combine oregano, 1 tablespoon salt, and the pepper. Rub this all over the lamb. Fold the four sides of foil up to form a cuff. Pour on lemon juice. Seal the foil and refrigerate at least 6 hours, or preferably overnight.
3. Place leg of lamb on a rack in a roasting pan.
4. Roast in a 450°F oven 20 minutes. Turn oven control to 350°F. Roast until meat is cooked as desired; a meat thermometer inserted in the leg will register 160°F for medium and 170°F to 180°F for well-done meat.
5. Remove from roasting pan to a carving board. Keep warm. When ready to serve, slice meat on the diagonal. Save the pan drippings to use for making gravy.
6. Prepare orzo by boiling it according to directions on the package, adding cooking oil and 1 tablespoon salt. Drain. Rinse under hot water.

7. To make gravy for the orzo, remove the fat from the pan drippings. Add boiling water while stirring with a spoon to loosen drippings on bottom of the pan. Add onions.
8. Bake at 350°F 15 minutes.
9. Pour the gravy with onions into a blender and purée. Return to the roasting pan. Combine the orzo with the gravy. Toss quickly. Serve with shredded kefalotyri as an accompaniment to the lamb.
6 TO 8 SERVINGS

Lamb Olé

1 package chili seasoning mix
2 tablespoons flour
2 teaspoons salt
4 lamb shanks
3 tablespoons cooking oil
1 can (28 ounces) tomatoes

(undrained)
1 can (15 ounces) chili style beans
1 can (15 ounces) golden hominy (optional)
2 tablespoons cornmeal

1. Combine 2 tablespoons chili seasoning mix, flour, and salt. Place in a large plastic bag; add shanks to bag and shake to coat with flour mixture.
2. Heat oil in a large skillet; add shanks and brown on all sides.
3. Place lamb in casserole dish; mix tomatoes with remaining chili seasoning; pour over shanks.
4. Bake at 325°F 1 hour. Remove casserole from oven; skim off fat. Add beans, hominy (if desired) and cornmeal to casserole, stirring gently to combine.
5. Return to oven and continue to bake 1½ hours, or until sauce is slightly thickened and lamb is tender.
4 SERVINGS

Lamb Olé

Braised Lamb Shanks

3 tablespoons olive oil
6 lamb shanks
Salt and pepper to taste
1 can (16 ounces) tomatoes
  (undrained)
2 cups red wine
¼ cup dried oregano
2 bay leaves
¼ cup minced parsley
2 garlic cloves, minced
2 onions, quartered

1. Heat olive oil until it begins to smoke. Brown lamb shanks on all sides. Season with salt and pepper. Add tomatoes, wine, oregano, bay leaves, parsley, garlic, and onion. Cover. Simmer 2 to 2½ hours, or until meat is fork tender.
2. Remove from heat. Cool. Skim off fat. Reheat and serve hot.
6 SERVINGS

Lamb Stew with Eggplant

2 pounds lean lamb
  shoulder, cut in large
  pieces
1 cup flour seasoned with
  salt and pepper
2 tablespoons olive oil
1 large onion, minced
3 large tomatoes, peeled and
  diced
¾ cup water
1 bay leaf
Salt and pepper to taste
3 cups water
2 medium eggplants, cut in
  large cubes
2 garlic cloves, crushed in a
  garlic press
1 tablespoon tomato paste

1. Dip lamb lightly in flour.
2. Heat oil in a large skillet. Add meat and brown on all sides. Remove meat with a slotted spoon.
3. Put onion in the oil and sauté until translucent.
4. Return meat to skillet. Add tomatoes, water, and bay leaf. Season with salt and pepper. Bring to boiling. Reduce heat and simmer, covered, for 1½ hours.
5. Meanwhile, bring water to a boil in a saucepan. Add eggplant and simmer 5 minutes (to remove bitter taste). Pour off water.
6. Add eggplant, garlic, and tomato paste to meat. Stir to blend. Cover. Simmer about 40 minutes, or until meat is tender.
4 TO 6 SERVINGS

Lamb Chops with Oregano

2 lamb chops (rib or loin)
  per serving

For each serving:
1 tablespoon oregano
Salt to taste
1 lemon, cut in half
1 tablespoon olive oil
  (optional)
Pepper to taste

1. An hour before cooking, sprinkle lamb chops with oregano. Season with salt. Set aside.
2. Place lamb chops on a broiler rack and broil 7 minutes on each side.
3. Remove from broiler and squeeze lemon juice over the chops. Drizzle with salt. Season with pepper.

Lamb-Stuffed Zucchini with Lemon Sauce

8 medium straight zucchini
1 pound ground beef round
  or lamb
½ cup long-grain rice
1 small onion, minced
2 tablespoons chopped
  parsley
1 teaspoon chopped mint
Salt and pepper
Water (about 2 cups)

Sauce:
2 egg yolks
Juice of 2 lemons
½ cup broth

1. Remove the ends and scrape the skins off the zucchini. With a corer, scoop out the zucchini centers and discard. Soak the zucchini in cold water.
2. Meanwhile, mix meat with rice, onion, parsley, mint, salt, and pepper. Drain zucchini and stuff with meat mixture.
3. Arrange stuffed zucchini in a single layer in a Dutch oven. Add enough water to half cover the zucchini. Bring the water to a boil, reduce heat, and simmer, covered, about 35 minutes.
4. Before serving, beat egg yolks until frothy. Slowly add lemon juice, beating constantly. Add broth, tablespoon by tablespoon, beating constantly. Heat thoroughly, but do not boil. Pour over zucchini. Serve immediately.
4 SERVINGS

Roast Baby Lamb's Head

1 head per serving, split in
  half and tied with a string
  to keep brains intact
Juice of 1 lemon
2 tablespoons olive oil
1 tablespoon oregano or
  more to taste
Salt and pepper to taste

1. Soak head in cold salted water for 1 hour. Drain. Pat dry. Cut string and place halves in a shallow pan, brains up.
2. Combine lemon juice, olive oil, oregano, salt, and pepper. Drizzle over head.
3. Roast in a 350°F oven for about 20 minutes, basting frequently until brains are tender. Remove brains with a spoon and keep warm. Continue roasting about 45 minutes more, or until other parts are tender.

Lamb Kidneys in Wine Sauce

4 lamb kidneys
Water
1 tablespoon wine vinegar
3 tablespoons flour
¼ cup butter
1½ cup white wine
1 bay leaf
1 garlic clove
2 tablespoons minced parsley
2 teaspoons oregano
½ teaspoon cumin
Salt and pepper to taste

1. Soak kidneys in cold water and vinegar for 15 minutes. Drain. Remove opaque skin and cut out the core. Slice kidneys thinly.
2. Dip slices in flour.
3. Melt butter in a skillet. Sauté the kidneys until browned on both sides. Add wine, bay leaf, garlic, parsley, oregano, cumin, salt, and pepper. Cover and simmer 20 minutes.
4 SERVINGS

Lamb Casserole

2 pounds lamb (cut in 1-inch
  cubes)
¼ cup oil
2 onions, chopped
1 clove garlic, minced
½ pound peas

½ pound string beans
6 carrots, scraped
½ head cauliflower
3 cups stewed tomatoes
¼ cup red wine

1. In a skillet heat the oil and brown the lamb on all sides.
2. Add onions and garlic and heat until onions are soft.
3. In a separate saucepan blanch the peas, string beans, carrots and cauliflower.
4. In a 2 quart casserole combine the wine, tomatoes and meat and bake in a 325°F oven for 1 hour.
5. Add the vegetables and continue cooking covered for another 15 minutes.

6 SERVINGS

Lamb and Pork in Cognac

⅓ cup cognac	chopped
1⅔ cups dry white wine	3 carrots, finely chopped
½ teaspoon ground mace	1 medium yellow onion,
¼ teaspoon ground	finely chopped
cinnamon	2 teaspoons salt
½ teaspoon salt	½ pound baby carrots
1½ pounds lean lamb stew	½ pound fresh broccoli
cubes	½ pound baby white onions
1½ pounds lean pork stew	Chicken Stock (page 48)
cubes	Salt
3 stalks celery, finely	Freshly ground pepper

1. Mix cognac, wine, mace, cinnamon, and ½ teaspoon salt; pour over meat cubes in a shallow glass bowl. Refrigerate covered 6 hours or overnight; stir occasionally. Drain meat, reserving ¾ cup marinade.
2. Mix chopped vegetables and layer them in bottom of a Dutch oven; pour reserved marinade over and simmer on top of range 5 minutes. Layer meat cubes over vegetables and sprinkle with 2 teaspoons salt. Cover Dutch oven.
3. Bake at 350°F 1½ to 2 hours, or until meat is tender.
4. Simmer vegetables in 1 inch of stock until just tender (about 15 minutes). Season with salt and pepper.
5. Remove meat from Dutch oven with a slotted spoon to a shallow serving dish; arrange attractively with vegetables.
6 SERVINGS

Hunter-Style Lamb with Fettuccine

2 pounds lamb (leg, loin, or	1 teaspoon rosemary,
shoulder), trimmed and cut	crushed
in 1½-inch cubes	1 teaspoon basil, crushed
¾ to 1 teaspoon pepper	¼ teaspoon sage, crushed
2 tablespoons butter	½ cup red wine vinegar
2 tablespoons olive oil	½ to ¾ cup chicken broth
4 anchovies, chopped	2 teaspoons flour
1 clove garlic, minced	8 ounces fettuccine noodles,
1 medium green pepper,	cooked and drained
cleaned and cut in pieces	Grated Parmesan cheese
Olive oil	Minced parsley

1. Season lamb with salt and pepper.
2. Heat butter and 2 tablespoons oil in a large, heavy skillet; add meat and brown on all sides.
3. Meanwhile, cook anchovies, garlic, and green pepper in a small amount of oil in a small saucepan about 5 minutes. Add rosemary, basil, sage, and vinegar; mix well. Cook and stir until boiling.
4. Remove lamb from skillet with a slotted spoon; set aside. Add enough chicken broth to drippings in skillet to make ¾ cup liquid. Add herb-vinegar mixture and bring to boiling, stirring to blend. Return lamb to skillet, cover tightly, and simmer over low heat about 40 minutes, or until tender.
5. Combine flour with a small amount of water to make a smooth paste. Add to liquid in skillet; cook and stir until mixture comes to boiling; cook 1 to 2 minutes.
6. Serve on a heated serving platter surrounded with fettuccine tossed with grated Parmesan cheese. Sprinkle with parsley.
ABOUT 6 SERVINGS

Lamb and Grilled Corn on the Cob

For each spit take 3-4 pieces	6 mushrooms
boned lamb	1 tomato quartered

1. Marinate the meat for 2-3 hours. Put the meat on the skewers alternately with mushrooms and tomato wedges. Grill for about 15 minutes. Brush with the marinade. Serve with **boiled rice** and **roasted slivered almonds.**

Grilled Corn on the Cob: Place fresh or frozen corn on the cob on a skewer and put it right on the coals. Grill for about 15 minutes, and serve with creamed butter.

Smothered Lamb Chops

6 lamb rib chops	1½ cups beef bouillon
2 tablespoons butter or	2 tablespoons snipped
margarine	parsley
4 medium red potatoes,	¼ cup buttered bread
pared and thinly sliced	crumbs
2 large onions, sliced	

1. Brown lamb chops on both sides in butter in a skillet. Place in a 2-quart shallow baking dish.
2. Arrange potatoes over chops and onions over potatoes. Season lightly with **salt.** Pour bouillon over all.
3. Bake, covered, at 375°F 1 hour, or until chops and vegetables are tender. Combine parsley and bread crumbs. Remove cover from casserole. Sprinkle with the parsley-bread crumbs. Bake, uncovered at 450°F 10 minutes, or until crumbs are lightly browned.
6 SERVINGS

Roast Leg of Lamb, Italian Style

1 lamb leg (5 to 6 pounds);	peel
do not remove fell	1½ teaspoons salt
Garlic cloves, cut in slivers	¼ teaspoon pepper
⅓ cup olive oil	1 teaspoon rosemary
1 tablespoon grated lemon	

1. Cut several small slits in surface of meat and insert a sliver of garlic in each.
2. Place lamb, skin side down, on rack in a roasting pan. Brush meat with olive oil. Sprinkle with lemon peel and a mixture of salt, pepper, and rosemary. Insert meat thermometer so tip is slightly beyond center of thickest part of meat; be sure that it does not rest in fat or on bone.
3. Roast, uncovered, at 325°F 2 to 3¼ hours, allowing 25 to 35 minutes per pound. Meat is medium done when thermometer registers 160°F and is well done at 170°F-180°F.
4. Remove meat to a warm serving platter. Garnish with parsley sprigs, if desired.
8 TO 10 SERVINGS

Lamb Curry

1½ pounds boneless lamb shoulder, cut in ¾-inch cubes
2 tablespoons shortening
1 teaspoon salt
1 teaspoon paprika
¼ teaspoon pepper
1 large onion, sliced
1 cup sliced celery
2¼ cups water
1 teaspoon curry powder
¼ cup flour
1 cup uncooked white rice

1. Brown lamb in shortening in a large saucepan. Sprinkle with salt, paprika, and pepper. Add onion, celery, and 2 cups water. Cover and simmer 1 hour, or until tender.
2. Combine curry powder, flour, and remaining ¼ cup water. Gradually add to saucepan, stirring until thickened and smooth.
3. Meanwhile, prepare rice according to package directions. Press rice in bottom and up sides of a 2-quart casserole. Pour lamb mixture into rice shell.
4. Bake, covered, at 350°F 20 minutes, or until casserole is bubbly. Serve with **chopped peanuts, shredded coconut,** and **chutney**.
6 SERVINGS

Fruited Lamb Roast

½ pound dried pears or apples
½ pound dried apricots
½ cup golden raisins
1 teaspoon finely minced ginger root or ½ teaspoon ground ginger
1 tablespoon grated orange
peel
Juice of 1 orange
1 cup plus 2 tablespoons bourbon
Apple cider (about 3 cups)
1 lamb leg, boneless (about 4 pounds)
Salt

1. Place pears, apricots, raisins, ginger root, orange peel, orange juice, and ½ cup bourbon in a medium saucepan. Pour in enough apple cider to cover fruits. Simmer uncovered 20 minutes; cool.
2. Trim roast of excess fat. Lay roast flat in a shallow glass casserole. Drain fruit. Add ½ cup bourbon to drained juice; add enough apple cider to measure 2 cups. Pour juice mixture over roast. Refrigerate roast covered 8 hours or overnight. Refrigerate fruits covered.
3. Remove roast from marinade; salt lightly on both sides. Arrange one third of the fruit on surface of meat; roll up and tie with string at intervals.
4. Place roast on rack in a roasting pan. Insert meat thermometer so tip is in center of roast.
5. Roast uncovered in a 325°F oven to an internal temperature of 175°F (about 2 hours). Add remaining fruit to roasting pan during last half hour of cooking.
6. Place roast and half the fruit on a serving platter. Cover lightly with aluminum foil. Let stand 20 minutes before carving.
7. Purée remaining fruit in a blender or food processor with 2 tablespoons bourbon and enough apple cider to make a sauce consistency. Heat thoroughly; serve with the roast.
8 TO 10 SERVINGS

Roast Leg of Lamb I

1 teaspoon salt
½ teaspoon ground black pepper
1 teaspoon seasoned salt
½ teaspoon ground marjoram
¼ teaspoon dry mustard
⅛ teaspoon ground
cardamom
1 lamb leg, whole (about 6 pounds)
2 cloves garlic, cut in slivers
½ teaspoon ground thyme
Orange peel, cut in slivers
Fresh mint sprigs (optional)

1. Mix salt, pepper, seasoned salt, marjoram, dry mustard, and cardamom; rub over lamb. Cut about 16 deep slits in roast. Toss garlic and thyme together. Insert garlic in each slit along with a sliver of orange peel.
2. Place lamb, fat side up, on a rack in a shallow roasting pan. Insert meat thermometer in center of thickest portion of meat.
3. Roast, uncovered, in a 325°F oven 2½ to 3 hours. Meat is medium done when thermometer registers 175°F and is well done at 180°F.
4. Remove meat thermometer. Place roast on a warm serving platter. Put a paper frill around end of leg bone and garnish platter with mint, if desired.
ABOUT 10 SERVINGS

Roast Leg of Lamb II

Vinegar
1 lamb leg, whole
Garlic cloves, slivered
Salt and pepper

1. Soak a towel with vinegar; wrap around the leg of lamb. Let stand overnight.
2. Remove towel. Trim off fell, if necessary, and excess fat. Make small slits in fat cover on meat. Push a sliver of garlic into each slit.
3. Place lamb, fat side up, on rack in a roasting pan. Sprinkle with salt and pepper.
4. Roast in a 325°F oven until done as desired. Allow 30 minutes per pound for medium; 35 minutes per pound for well-done.
ABOUT 8 TO 12 SERVINGS

Lamb Mayan Style

2 pounds boneless lamb for stew, cut in 2-inch chunks
½ cup chopped onion
1 clove garlic, minced
1 cup canned tomatoes, chopped
1 teaspoon salt
¼ teaspoon pepper
Water
1 cup pepitas
1 tablespoon annatto seeds
2 tablespoons oil
1 tablespoon lemon juice

1. Put lamb, onion, garlic, tomatoes, salt, and pepper into a Dutch oven or heavy saucepot; mix well. Add water to cover. Bring to boiling, reduce heat, cover, and simmer until meat is tender (about 2 hours).
2. Meanwhile, combine pepitas and annatto seeds in an electric blender and blend until pulverized.
3. Fry mixture in a small amount of hot oil in a small skillet 2 or 3 minutes, stirring constantly. Stir into the sauce with meat. Stir in lemon juice. Serve with **cooked rice**.
6 SERVINGS

Lamb Shish Kebob

¾ cup dry red wine
¼ cup lemon juice
3 tablespoons olive oil
1 teaspoon salt
Freshly ground pepper to taste
2 garlic cloves, crushed in a garlic press
1 onion, minced
Bay leaf
2 tablespoons oregano,
crushed
3 pounds leg of lamb, boneless, cut in 1½-inch cubes
Green peppers, cored and cut in squares
Baby onions, peeled and left whole
Large mushroom caps
Tomato wedges

1. Make a marinade of wine, lemon juice, olive oil, salt, pepper, garlic, onion, bay leaf, and oregano in a large bowl and add lamb cubes. Cover securely and refrigerate at least 6 hours. Turn lamb several times while marinating.
2. Remove meat from marinade and place on skewers with green pepper squares, onions, mushroom caps, and tomato wedges.
3. Barbecue over hot coals or broil about 20 minutes, or until done; baste with marinade during cooking.
8 TO 10 SERVINGS

Elegant Leg of Lamb

1 lamb leg, whole (about 6 pounds)
2 garlic cloves, each sliced in 3 pieces
1 tablespoon Dijon mustard
1 tablespoon strong coffee
2 teaspoons ground ginger
1 cup strong black coffee
¼ cup white port wine
1 cup Chicken Stock (page 48)
4 teaspoons arrowroot
Cold water
2 teaspoons butter, if desired

1. Trim excess fat from roast. Cut 6 small slits in the roast and insert garlic slices. Rub mixture of mustard, 1 tablespoon coffee, and ginger over entire surface of roast.
2. Place in a shallow roasting pan. Insert meat thermometer so that tip is in center of meat, away from bone and fat.
3. Roast in a 325°F oven to an internal temperature of 175°F (about 3 hours). Mix 1 cup coffee and wine; baste roast with mixture several times during last hour of roasting time.
4. Remove roast to meat platter. Cover loosely with a tent of aluminum foil.
5. Carefully spoon fat from roasting pan. Add remaining basting mixture and stock to roasting pan. Heat to boiling, stirring to incorporate meat particles from pan. Mix arrowroot with a little cold water. Stir into stock mixture. Simmer, stirring constantly, until mixture thickens. Stir butter into gravy just before serving.
6 TO 8 SERVINGS

Party Lamb Chops

6 lamb loin chops, about 2 pounds
½ teaspoon salt
⅛ teaspoon pepper
2 tablespoons butter
2 tablespoons prepared mustard
1 can (16 ounces) quartered hearts of celery
1 cup tomato juice
½ cup dry white wine, such as sauterne
¼ cup finely chopped parsley

1. Sprinkle chops with salt and pepper.
2. Brown chops on both sides in butter in skillet. Spread mustard on chops.
3. Add celery and liquid from can, tomato juice, and wine. Cover and simmer 1 hour over low heat until chops are tender. Place chops on platter and keep warm.
4. Pour pan juices into blender and whirl until smooth, or beat with a rotary beater in small bowl. Pour back into skillet and reheat until bubbly and thick. Spoon over chops. Sprinkle chops with parsley.
6 SERVINGS

Lamb Chops with Dill Sauce

3 tablespoons butter margarine
½ cup chopped onion
4 lamb shoulder arm chops, cut ½ inch thick
2 tablespoons water
1 tablespoon vinegar
1 teaspoon salt
¼ teaspoon pepper
1 bay leaf
2 tablespoons butter or

margarine
2 tablespoons flour
¼ teaspoon salt
Few grains pepper
½ cup beef broth
1 tablespoon chopped fresh dill
½ cup dry white wine, such as chablis or sauterne
2 tablespoons vinegar

1. For chops, melt butter in a large heavy skillet with a tight-fitting cover. Add onion to fat and cook slowly, stirring occasionally, about 5 minutes. Remove onion from skillet with slotted spoon to small dish and set aside.
2. Cut through fat about every inch on outside edges of lamb chops. Be careful not to cut through to lean meat. Place chops in skillet; slowly brown both sides.
3. Meanwhile, combine water, vinegar, salt, pepper, and bay leaf; slowly add this mixture to the browned lamb. Return onion to skillet. Cover skillet and simmer 25 to 30 minutes, or until lamb is tender when pierced with a fork. If needed, add small amounts of water as lamb cooks.
4. For sauce, melt butter in small skillet over low heat. Blend flour, salt, and pepper into butter until smooth. Heat mixture until bubbly and lightly browned. Remove skillet from heat. Gradually add a mixture of the broth and fresh dill, stirring constantly.
5. Bring rapidly to boiling, stirring constantly; cook 1 to 2 minutes longer. Remove sauce from heat and gradually add wine and vinegar, stirring constantly. Serve the sauce over lamb chops.
4 SERVINGS

Orange-Ginger Lamb Chops

4 lamb leg sirloin or shoulder chops
1 tablespoon oil
¾ teaspoon salt
¼ teaspoon ginger
Dash pepper

1 orange, peeled
1 small to medium onion
1 can or bottle (12 ounces) beer
2 tablespoons sugar
1 tablespoon cornstarch

1. Brown chops in oil in a skillet; pour off fat. Mix salt, ginger, and pepper. Sprinkle over chops.
2. Cut off a thin slice from each end of orange. Cut remainder of orange into 4 slices. Remove seeds. Repeat with onion; do not separate into rings.
3. Top each chop with an orange slice, then an onion slice. Add 1¼ cups beer. Cover and simmer 30 minutes, or until meat is tender.
4. Transfer chops topped with orange and onion to a platter.
5. Mix sugar, cornstarch, and remaining ¼ cup beer. Add to liquid in skillet. Cook, stirring constantly, until thickened. Add dash of salt, if desired. Strain into a sauceboat. Accompany chops with rice, pouring sauce over both.
4 SERVINGS

Lamb and Rice

3 tablespoons butter or margarine
½ cup chopped onion
½ cup diced green pepper
1 can (10½ ounces) tomato purée
1 teaspoon bottled brown bouquet sauce

¼ cup ketchup
1 can (8¼ ounces) diced carrots
2 cups ground cooked lamb
1 teaspoon salt
1 cup packaged precooked rice
1 cup chicken bouillon

1. In cooking pan of a chafing dish, melt butter. Stir in onion and green pepper; cook over medium heat until vegetables are lightly browned.
2. Stir in remaining ingredients and cover. Cook over low heat 10 minutes, or until thoroughly heated and rice is tender.
3. Place over simmering water to keep warm.
4 TO 6 SERVINGS

Company Affair Lamb Chops

3 tablespoons butter
3 tablespoons flour
1 cup rich beef stock
¼ cup diced smoked pork loin, Canadian style bacon, or lean ham
1 tablespoon butter
¼ cup sherry

2 tablespoons minced green pepper
6 slices eggplant, cut ½ inch thick; unpeeled
Olive oil
6 lamb loin chops
6 broiled mushroom caps

1. Melt butter in saucepan; add flour and cook until lightly browned. Gradually add beef stock and cook sauce until smooth and thick.
2. Combine bacon and butter in skillet and fry at least 2 minutes. Add sherry and green pepper and add to sauce.
3. Brush eggplant with olive oil and broil until lightly browned.
4. Broil lamb chops so that they are pink and juicy inside and crisply browned on outside.
5. Pour hot sauce over eggplant slices and place one lamb chop on each slice of eggplant. Garnish with a mushroom cap.
6 SERVINGS

Lamb Chops Burgundy

8 lamb loin or rib chops, cut 1½ to 2 inches thick
½ cup burgundy
¼ cup olive oil
⅔ cup chopped red onion

½ clove garlic, minced
¼ teaspoon salt
3 peppercorns, crushed
½ teaspoon cumin seed, crushed

1. Put lamb chops into a shallow dish.
2. Combine burgundy, olive oil, red onion, garlic, salt, peppercorns, and cumin in a screw-top jar and shake to blend.
3. Pour marinade over meat. Cover and set in refrigerator to marinate about 2 hours, turning chops occasionally.
4. Remove chops from marinade and place on broiler rack. Set under broiler with tops of chops 3 to 5 inches from heat. Broil 18 to 22 minutes, or until meat is done as desired; turn once and brush occasionally with remaining marinade. To test, slit meat near bone and note color of meat.
8 SERVINGS

Piquant Lamb Kabobs

1½ pounds boneless lamb (leg or sirloin), cut in 1-inch cubes
18 fresh medium mushrooms (about ½ pound)
¾ cup beer
1 can (6 ounces) pineapple juice (¾ cup)
2 tablespoons oil
2 teaspoons soy sauce
1 garlic clove, quartered
18 cherry tomatoes (about 1 pint)
18 green pepper squares (1 large pepper)
4 to 5 cups cooked rice

1. Place lamb cubes and whole mushrooms in a ceramic casserole.
2. Combine beer, pineapple juice, oil, soy sauce, and garlic. Pour over lamb and mushrooms. Add a little more beer, if needed.
3. Cover and refrigerate at least 6 hours, or overnight.
4. On each of 6 long skewers, alternate lamb cubes with mushrooms, cherry tomatoes, and green pepper squares. Use 3 each of the vegetables for each skewer.
5. Broil 3 inches from heat to desired doneness (about 10 to 15 minutes), turning once or twice. Watch that vegetables do not overcook.
6. Heat marinade to pass as sauce. Serve kabobs on or with rice.
6 SERVINGS

Lamb Crown Roast with Mint Stuffing

8 slices enriched white bread, toasted and cubed
1 unpared red apple, cored and diced
1½ tablespoons coarsely chopped mint or 1½ teaspoons dried mint flakes
¾ teaspoon poultry
seasoning
½ teaspoon salt
6 tablespoons butter
½ cup chopped celery
¼ cup chopped onion
½ cup water
1 lamb rib crown roast (5 to 6 pounds)

1. Combine toasted bread cubes, apple, mint, poultry seasoning, and salt in a large bowl.
2. Heat butter in a saucepan. Mix in celery and onion and cook about 5 minutes. Pour over bread mixture along with water; toss lightly.
3. Place lamb on a rack, rib ends up, in a shallow roasting pan. Fill center with stuffing.
4. Roast in a 325°F oven about 2½ hours, or until a meat thermometer registers 175° to 180°F (depending on desired degree of doneness).
5. Place roast on a heated serving platter. Prepare gravy, if desired. Accompany with Parsley-Buttered New Potatoes (page 221) and Butter-Sauced Asparagus (page 264).
ABOUT 8 SERVINGS

Oven Lamb Stew

2 pounds lean lamb shoulder, boneless, cut in 2-inch cubes
1¾ teaspoons salt
¼ teaspoon thyme, crushed
1 bay leaf
4 whole allspice
2 tablespoons chopped parsley
1 clove garlic, minced
¼ small head cabbage, shredded
2 leeks, thinly sliced
2 medium onions, sliced
1 cup sliced raw potatoes
4 cups water
8 small onions
4 carrots, cut in 2-inch pieces
2 white turnips, quartered

1. Put lamb into a Dutch oven. Season with salt, thyme, bay leaf, allspice, parsley, and garlic. Add cabbage, leeks, sliced onions, and potatoes. Pour in water. Cover tightly and bring rapidly to boiling.
2. Cook in a 350°F oven about 1½ hours, or until meat is tender.
3. About 30 minutes before cooking time is ended, cook whole onions, carrots, and turnips separately in boiling salted water until tender. Drain.
4. Turn contents of Dutch oven into a food mill set over a large bowl. Return meat to the Dutch oven and add the cooked onions, carrots, and turnips. Discard bay leaf and allspice; force the vegetables through food mill into the bowl containing cooking liquid (or purée vegetables in an electric blender). Heat with meat and vegetables.
6 TO 8 SERVINGS

Lamb Kabobs

1½ pounds lamb (leg, loin, or shoulder), boneless, cut in 1½-inch cubes
½ cup vegetable oil
1 tablespoon lemon juice
2 teaspoons sugar
½ teaspoon salt
½ teaspoon paprika
¼ teaspoon dry mustard
⅛ teaspoon ground black
pepper
¼ teaspoon Worcestershire sauce
1 clove garlic, cut in halves
6 small whole cooked potatoes
6 small whole cooked onions
Butter or margarine, melted
6 plum tomatoes

1. Put lamb cubes into a shallow dish. Combine oil, lemon juice, sugar, salt, paprika, dry mustard, pepper, Worcestershire sauce, and garlic. Pour over meat. Cover and marinate at least 1 hour in refrigeraor, turning pieces occasionally. Drain.
2. Alternately thread lamb cubes, potatoes, and onions on 6 skewers. Brush pieces with melted butter.
3. Broil 3 to 4 inches from heat about 15 minutes, or until lamb is desired degree of doneness; turn frequently and brush with melted butter. Shortly before kabobs are done, impale tomatoes on ends of skewers.
6 SERVINGS

PORK

Ham Loaf en Brioche

Brioche Dough:
1 package (13¾ ounces) hot roll mix
¼ cup warm water
⅓ cup milk
⅓ cup butter or margarine
2 tablespoons sugar
3 eggs, beaten

2 eggs, beaten
2 cups fine soft bread crumbs
¾ cup California Sauterne
½ teaspoon dry mustard
½ teaspoon salt
¼ teaspoon pepper
½ cup coarsely chopped ripe olives
¼ cup diced pimento
1 tablespoon instant minced onion

Ham Loaf:
2 cups ground cooked ham
1 pound ground veal or lean beef

1. For brioche dough, combine yeast from packet in hot roll mix with warm water.
2. Scald milk and cool to lukewarm.
3. Cream butter and sugar. Add eggs and yeast; mix well. Stir in flour mixture from mix alternately with milk, beating until smooth after each addition. Cover tightly; let rise in a warm place until light (about 1 hour). Stir down and set in refrigerator until thoroughly chilled.
4. Meanwhile, prepare ham loaf.
5. For ham loaf, combine all ingredients and mix well. Turn into a greased fluted brioche pan, about 8½ inches across top and about 1-quart capacity; pack into pan and round up center.
6. Bake at 350°F 1 hour. Cool in pan about 10 minutes, then turn out of pan and cool thoroughly.
7. Divide chilled brioche dough in half. Roll each portion into a round about 10 inches in diameter. Turn cooled ham loaf upside down and fit a round of dough over bottom and sides. Trim off excess dough. Holding dough in place, quick-ly invert loaf and fit other round of dough over top and sides. Trim edges evenly.
8. Place dough-wrapped loaf in a well-greased brioche pan a size larger than one used for ham loaf, about 9½ inches in diameter across top and about 2-quarts capacity.
9. Shape dough trimmings into a ball and place on top of loaf. Let rise in a warm place about 30 to 45 minutes, or until dough is light.
10. Set on lowest shelf of 375°F oven. Bake 10 to 15 minutes, or until top is browned. Place a piece of brown paper or aluminum foil over top of loaf. Continue baking about 25 minutes, or until nicely browned and baked through (test brioche with wooden pick).
11. Turn loaf out of pan and serve warm or cold, cut in wedges.

ABOUT 8 SERVINGS

Barbecued Spareribs à la Marinade

Barbecued Spareribs à la Marinade

1 package 15-minute meat
 marinade
⅔ cup cold water
4 pounds pork spareribs

1. Combine meat marinade and water in a large shallow pan; blend thoroughly.
2. Put ribs into marinade. Pierce all surfaces of meat deeply and thoroughly with fork to carry flavor deep down. Marinate only 15 minutes, turning several times. Remove meat from marinade; reserve for basting.
3. Place ribs on grill 4 to 6 inches from hot coals. Cook until crispy brown, about 1 hour, turning and brushing with marinade frequently. Use kitchen shears to cut ribs into pieces for serving.
ABOUT 6 SERVINGS

Danish Pork Chops

2 pounds pork chops
Salt
Pepper
1 teaspoon curry
1 pound lean bacon
2 tart apples
2 yellow onions
1 cup plain yogurt
Paprika powder
1 teaspoon butter

1. Cut bacon, onions and apples in strips.
2. Sauté in butter over low heat.
3. Brown the chops in butter.
4. Pour on the yogurt, cover and fry the chops slowly for 5 minutes.
5. Distribute the fried bacon, onions and apples on the chops and serve with boiled rice and a green salad.
6 SERVINGS

Pork Casserole

14 ounces pork fillet
5 ounces chicken liver
1 garlic clove
3 onions
3 tablespoons butter or margarine
Dash freshly ground pepper
1 bayleaf (crushed)
Dash thyme
4 orange slices
4 carrots
½ cup bouillon and ¾ cup red wine or 1¼ cup bouillon
Chopped parsley

1. Thaw chicken livers (if you use frozen) and chop. Cut pork in ¼-inch thick slices.
2. Chop peeled onion and crush garlic. Peel carrots and cut in pieces.
3. Brown meat, onion and liver separately in butter and then add carrots, seasonings and orange slices with peel left on.
4. Pour bouillon and red wine on mixture and cook over low heat for 20 minutes. Add liver for last 10 minutes of cooking time. Stir carefully.
5. Serve garnished with **chopped parsley**.
4 SERVINGS

Pork and Green Tomato Sauce

2½ pounds lean pork, cut in 1-inch cubes
1 tablespoon vegetable oil
1 onion, chopped
2 cloves garlic, minced
1 can (12 ounces) Mexican green tomatoes (tomatillos), drained and chopped
2 cans (4 ounces each) green
chilies, drained, seeded, and chopped
1 tablespoon dried cilantro leaves
1 teaspoon marjoram
1 teaspoon salt
½ cup water
Cooked rice
Sour cream

1. Brown meat in oil in a large skillet. Push meat to sides of skillet; add onion and garlic and cook until onion is soft. Add green tomatoes, chilies, cilantro, marjoram, salt, and water; mix well. Cover; bring to boiling, reduce heat, and cook until meat is tender (about 2 hours).
2. Serve with rice and top with dollops of sour cream.
6 TO 8 SERVINGS

Neapolitan Pork Chops

2 tablespoons olive oil
1 clove garlic, minced
6 pork rib or loin chops, cut about ¾ to 1 inch thick
1 teaspoon salt
¼ teaspoon pepper
1 pound mushrooms,
cleaned and sliced
2 green peppers, cleaned and chopped
½ cup canned tomatoes, sieved
3 tablespoons dry white wine

1. Heat oil in a large, heavy skillet. Add garlic and cook until lightly browned.
2. Season chops with salt and pepper. Put chops in skillet and brown on both sides.
3. Add mushrooms, green pepper, sieved tomato, and wine. Cover and cook over low heat about 1 hour, or until tender.
6 SERVINGS

Saukerkraut with Pork

2 pounds pig's feet or ham hocks
2 pounds neck bones or spareribs
3 tablespoons lard or margarine
1 large onion
1 clove garlic, crushed
1½ quarts boiling water
1 green pepper, diced
4 whole allspice
1 bay leaf
½ teaspoon celery seed
1 quart (about 2 pounds) sauerkraut
¼ cup barley
1 small apple, chopped
½ teaspoon caraway seed
2 teaspoons salt
½ teaspoon pepper

1. Brown all meat in lard in a large kettle.
2. Add onion and garlic. Fry 1 minute.
3. Add boiling water, green pepper, allspice, bay leaf, and celery seed. Cover; cook 1 hour or until meat is tender.
4. Remove meat; cool. Boil until broth is reduced to 3 cups.
5. Discard bones and gristle from meat. Drain and rinse sauerkraut.
6. Cook barley in the broth 15 minutes. Add meat, sauerkraut, apple, caraway seed, salt, and pepper. Cook 45 minutes longer.
7. Serve with potato dumplings, if desired.
ABOUT 6 SERVINGS

Roast Suckling Pig

1 suckling pig, about 25 to 30 pounds
Salt and pepper
1½ pounds stale bread, diced
1½ cups milk
2 eggs
2 apples, sliced
2 onions, diced
⅓ cup chopped parsley
1 potato
Melted lard or salad oil
1 small whole apple
Parsley sprigs or small fruits and leaves

1. Wipe pig, inside and out, with a clean damp cloth. Sprinkle entire cavity with salt and pepper. If necessary to make pig fit into pan (and oven) cut crosswise in half just behind shoulders.
2. Put bread into a large mixing bowl. Add milk and let soak 20 minutes. Add eggs, sliced apples, onion, and parsley; mix well.
3. Spoon stuffing into cavity of pig. (There will not be enough stuffing to entirely fill cavity.)
4. Use metal skewers to hold cavity closed and lace with string.
5. Set pig belly side down in roasting pan. Tuck feet under body. Cover tail, snout, and ears with foil. Place whole potato in mouth.
6. Roast at 375°F 8 to 10 hours. Baste frequently with melted lard. When pig is done, juices run golden and skin is a crackling, translucent, golden-chocolate brown.
7. Set pig on platter. Remove potato from mouth; replace with apple. Make a wreath of parsley sprigs for neck or to cover joint behind shoulders.
ABOUT 25 SHOULDERS

Ham Mousse on Medallions

6 slices boiled ham, cut ⅓ inch thick (about 1½ pounds)
2 teaspoons unflavored gelatin
1 cup cold water
2 cups low-fat ricotta cheese
3 tablespoons snipped parsley

1½ tablespoons snipped fresh or 2 teaspoons crumbled dried tarragon leaves
2 teaspoons Dijon mustard
⅛ teaspoon salt
Dash freshly ground pepper
Parsley sprigs
Radish roses

1. Cut two 2½-inch circles from each slice ham; refrigerate covered. Mince remaining ham pieces; refrigerate covered.
2. Sprinkle gelatin over cold water in a saucepan; let stand 5 minutes. Set over low heat until dissolved (about 3 minutes), stirring occasionally.
3. Pour gelatin into a food processor or blender; add ricotta cheese, snipped parsley, tarragon, mustard, salt, and pepper. Process until mixture is smooth; transfer mixture to a medium mixing bowl. Stir in minced ham; refrigerate covered until mixture has set (about 1 hour).
4. Place 2 ham circles in each of 6 individual plates. Mound mousse by heaping tablespoonfuls on circles. Garnish with parsley and radish roses.
6 SERVINGS

Note: This recipe will make 12 first-course servings.

Pork Roast Stuffed with Liver

1 teaspoon fennel seed
2 cloves garlic, peeled
1 teaspoon salt
½ teaspoon sugar
½ teaspoon coarsely ground pepper
¾ teaspoon rubbed sage

Boneless pork loin or loin end roast (about 3 pounds)
½ pound pork, lamb, or beef liver, cut in slices ⅓ inch thick
1 tablespoon cornstarch
1 cup cool beef broth

1. Using a mortar and pestle, crush the fennel seed. Add the garlic, salt, sugar, pepper, and sage. Crush until mixture becomes a rough paste.
2. Open pork roast and lay flat side down; cut the meat if necessary to make it lie flat. Rub surface of the roast with about half the garlic paste. Lay liver strips lengthwise over meat.
3. Roll the roast tightly lengthwise with seasoned surface inside. Tie with heavy string at 2-inch intervals. Rub remaining garlic paste on outside of roast. Place roast on a rack in a shallow baking pan.
4. Cook, uncovered, at 375°F until meat thermometer inserted in thickest part of the roast registers 170°F (about 1½ hours). Transfer roast to a serving platter and keep warm.
5. Remove rack from roasting pan and place pan over direct heat. Stir together the cornstarch and broth until blended. Stir into drippings in roasting pan. Cook over medium heat, stirring constantly, until sauce boils and thickens. Pour sauce into a serving bowl.
6. To serve, cut and remove strings from roast, and cut meat into thin slices.
ABOUT 8 SERVINGS

Pork Pot Roast

1 pork shoulder arm picnic or pork loin roast, boneless (3 pounds)
2 tablespoons butter or lard
2 tomatoes, peeled and cored
1 celery root
1 parsley root
1 onion, sliced
2 sprigs parsley

2 tablespoons spices to taste: allspice, caraway seed, whole cloves, juniper berries, dried marjoram leaves, peppercorns (tie in cheesecloth)
¼ cup water
½ cup bouillon or meat broth
½ cup Madeira, Marsala, or sherry

1. Rub meat with salt and pepper. Let stand 1 hour.
2. Brown meat in butter in a large, heavy skillet. Add vegetables, parsley, spice bag, and water. Cover tightly. Cook over medium heat 1½ hours, stirring as necessary and turning meat occasionally.
3. Sprinkle a small amount of flour over top of meat. Pour bouillon and wine over meat. Simmer 15 minutes.
4. Slice and arrange meat on a warm platter. Strain sauce and pour over meat.
6 TO 8 SERVINGS

Canadian-Style Bacon and Peaches

Roast Canadian-Style Bacon:
2 pounds smoked pork loin Canadian-style bacon (in one piece)
10 whole cloves

Orange-Spiced Peaches:
½ cup firmly packed brown sugar
⅓ cup red wine vinegar

1 tablespoon grated orange peel
2 tablespoons orange juice
1 teaspoon whole cloves
½ teaspoon whole allspice
1 can (29 ounces) peach halves, drained; reserve 1½ cups syrup
Mustard Sauce

1. Remove casing from the meat and place, fat side up, on a rack in a shallow roasting pan. Stud with cloves. Insert a meat thermometer into bacon so bulb is centered. Roast, uncovered, at 325°F about 2 hours, or until thermometer registers 160°F.
2. For Orange-Spiced Peaches, stir brown sugar, wine vinegar, orange peel, orange juice, cloves, allspice, and peach syrup together in a saucepan. Bring to boiling; reduce heat and simmer 5 minutes. Mix in peaches and heat 5 minutes.
3. Remove from heat and allow peaches to cool in syrup. Refrigerate until ready to serve.
4. Shortly before meat is roasted, prepare Mustard Sauce.
5. Remove meat from oven and place on heated serving platter. Remove thermometer. Arrange peaches on platter. Accompany with Mustard Sauce in a bowl.
ABOUT 8 SERVINGS

Mustard Sauce: Mix **1 cup firmly packed brown sugar, 2 tablespoons prepared mustard, 1 tablespoon butter or margarine, 3 tablespoons cider vinegar** in a saucepan. Stir over low heat until sugar is dissolved; heat thoroughly, stirring occasionally.
⅔ CUP SAUCE

Pork Loin Roast

1 pork loin roast (4 to 6 pounds)	Salt and pepper
	Spiced crab apples

1. Have the butcher saw across the rib bones of roast at base of the backbone, separating the ribs from the backbone. Place roast, fat side up, on a rack in an open roasting pan. Season with salt and pepper. Insert meat thermometer in roast so the bulb is centered in the thickest part and not resting on bone or in fat.

2. Roast in a 350°F oven about 2½ to 3 hours, or until thermometer registers 170°F; allow 30 to 40 minutes per pound.

3. For easy carving, remove backbone, place roast on platter, and allow roast to set for 15 to 20 minutes. Garnish platter with spiced crab apples, heated if desired.

8 TO 10 SERVINGS

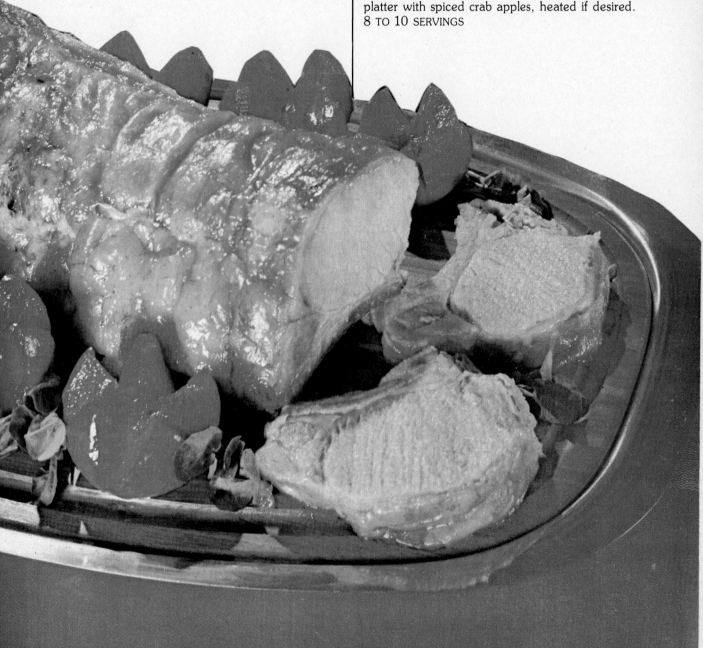

German Pork Roast in Spicy Beer Sauce

1 rolled pork loin roast,
  boneless (3 to 3½ pounds)
2 to 3 cups beer
1 cup chopped onion
2 teaspoons grated lemon
  peel
2 teaspoons sugar
1 teaspoon tarragon
1 teaspoon salt
¼ teaspoon each pepper,
  cloves, ginger, and nutmeg
3 bay leaves
1 carrot, diced
1 celery stalk, diced
¼ cup flour

1. Place meat in a deep dish just large enough to hold it. Combine 1 can (1½ cups) beer, onion, peel, and seasonings; pour over meat. Add a little more beer, if needed, to just cover meat. Marinate in refrigerator 1 to 2 days, turning occasionally.
2. Strain marinade, reserving solids and liquid. Place solids, carrot, and celery in bottom of a roasting pan. Place meat on top. Add a little liquid.
3. Roast in a 350°F oven 1 hour. Pour one quarter of remaining marinade liquid over meat. Continue roasting for 1 to 1½ hours more, basting occasionally with drippings and more marinade, until meat thermometer registers 170°F.
4. Mix flour and ⅓ cup marinade or beer to a smooth paste. Place roast on a platter; keep warm. Skim fat from cooking liquid. Strain, pressing solids; add flour mixture and ½ cup beer plus water, if needed, to measure 2 cups total liquid. Cook in roasting pan or a saucepan, stirring constantly, until thickened. (For 3 cups gravy, use more beer and water plus 6 tablespoons flour.) Serve sauce over meat slices.
8 SERVINGS

Ham Steak Barbecue

1 smoked ham slice, 1½
  inches thick
1 teaspoon grated grapefruit
  peel
1 cup grapefruit juice
¼ cup soy sauce
2 tablespoons salad oil
2 tablespoons sugar
1 teaspoon oregano
½ teaspoon salt
¼ teaspoon pepper
2 tablespoons chopped
  parsley
¼ cup chopped green onion

1. Put ham slice into a shallow dish. Mix remaining ingredients and pour over ham. Cover and refrigerate 2 hours.
2. Remove ham from marinade and place on grill over hot coals. Grill 25 minutes on one side, basting with marinade; turn and grill 20 minutes longer. Remove from grill and serve with Grapefruit Sauce (below).
ABOUT 6 SERVINGS

Grapefruit Sauce

½ cup sugar
2 tablespoons cornstarch
¼ teaspoon salt
¾ cup water
1¼ cups grapefruit juice
1 grapefruit, sectioned and
  sections halved

1. Mix sugar, cornstarch, and salt in a saucepan. Gradually add water and grapefruit juice, stirring to blend. Cook over low heat, stirring constantly, until mixture thickens and comes to boiling. Simmer 1 minute.
2. Remove from heat and stir in grapefruit pieces.
ABOUT 2½ CUPS SAUCE

Pork Chops Piquant

4 pork loin chops, 1 inch
  thick
¼ cup water
¼ teaspoon bottled brown
  bouquet sauce
½ teaspoon salt
Freshly ground pepper
½ cup Chicken Stock

(page 48)
¼ cup dry white wine
1 green pepper, chopped
1 medium yellow onion,
  chopped
2 tablespoons capers,
  drained
Watercress or parsley sprigs

1. Trim excess fat from chops. Brush chops lightly with a mixture of water and brown bouquet sauce. Brown chops lightly on both sides in a nonstick skillet over medium heat. Sprinkle with salt and pepper.
2. Add stock and wine. Simmer covered 30 minutes. Skim fat from liquid. Stir in green pepper, onion, and capers. Simmer uncovered 10 to 15 minutes until vegetables are just tender. Taste vegetables and sauce; adjust seasoning.
3. Serve vegetables and sauce over chops; garnish with watercress.
4 SERVINGS

Perugia Ham and Cheese Pie

2 cups all-purpose flour
½ teaspoon salt
¼ cup butter or margarine
2 eggs
3 tablespoons milk
1½ cups minced cooked

ham
½ cup shredded Swiss
  cheese
½ cup diced Bel Paese
  cheese
1 egg yolk, slightly beaten

1. Combine flour and salt in a bowl. Cut in butter with pastry blender or two knives until pieces are small. Add eggs and stir in milk to form a soft dough. Knead dough lightly; divide in two equal portions.
2. Roll out one portion on a lightly floured surface into a rectangle large enough to line the bottom and sides of an 11x7-inch baking pan. Place dough in pan and cover with ham and cheese.
3. Bring dough on sides of pan down over the meat and cheese. Roll out the remaining dough to form an 11x7-inch rectangle and place on top of filling. Press edges of top crust with a fork to seal to bottom crust. Prick top with fork in several places, and brush with egg yolk.
4. Bake at 425°F 10 minutes. Turn oven control to 350°F and bake 10 minutes. Cut into rectangles and serve warm.
6 TO 8 SERVINGS

Lomo of Pork with Pineapple

1 tablespoon lard or oil
3 pounds pork loin,
  boneless, cut in 2-inch
  chunks
1 cup chopped onion
2 cups pineapple chunks (1
  15¼-ounce can) with juice
1 cup beef stock, or 1 cup
  water plus 1 beef bouillon

cube
¼ cup dry sherry
⅓ cup sliced pimento
1 fresh tomato, peeled and
  chopped
½ teaspoon chili powder
Salt and pepper
2 tablespoons flour

1. Heat lard in a large, heavy skillet. Add meat and brown

well on all sides. Add onion and cook about 5 minutes, or until soft.
2. Add pineapple with juice, beef stock, sherry, pimento, tomato, and chili powder to the skillet; stir until well mixed. Bring to boiling, reduce heat to simmering, and add salt and pepper to taste. Cover and simmer until meat is tender, about 1½ hours; stir occasionally to prevent sticking.
3. Just before serving, sprinkle flour over simmering sauce and stir in; cook and stir until sauce is thickened. Serve over **hot rice.**
6 TO 8 SERVINGS

Whole Lomo of Pork in Tomato Sauce

1 pork loin roast, boneless (3
  to 4 pounds)
1 can (6 ounces) tomato
  paste
¼ cup chopped onion
1 canned chipotle chili, very
  finely chopped; or 2 teaspoons chili powder

1 clove garlic, minced
1 teaspoon salt
¼ teaspoon pepper
1½ cups chicken stock, or
  1½ cups hot water plus 2
  chicken bouillon cubes
1 cup sour cream

1. Put pork loin into a shallow baking pan; if necessary, cut in half so meat will fit into pan.
2. Combine tomato paste, onion, chili, garlic, salt, and pepper in a saucepan. Stir in chicken stock. Cook about 5 minutes.
3. Pour liquid over meat in pan.
4. Bake at 325°F about 1¼ hours. Occasionally spoon sauce over meat during baking, and check to see if additional water is needed to prevent drying.
5. When meat is tender, remove to serving platter.
6. Stir sour cream into sauce remaining in pan; warm slightly but do not boil. Pour over meat on platter.
7. To serve, slice meat about ¾ inch thick.
10 TO 12 SERVINGS

Breaded Pork Chops with Beer Gravy

4 pork chops, cut ½ to ¾
  inch thick
1 egg
1 tablespoon water
½ cup fine cracker crumbs
  (from about 12 saltines
½ teaspoon salt

¼ teaspoon paprika
2 tablespoons oil
¾ cup beer
2 tablespoons flour
¾ cup beef bouillon
1 tablespoon ketchup

1. Dip chops in a mixture of egg and water, coating both sides. Mix crumbs, salt, and paprika. Dip egg-coated chops in this mixture, coating both sides well.
2. Brown chops slowly in oil, cooking about 15 minutes. Reduce heat; add ¼ cup beer. Cover and simmer 20 to 30 minutes, or until done.
3. Make a paste of flour and a little remaining beer. Place chops on platter. Stir flour paste, rest of beer, bouillon, and ketchup into cooking liquid. Cook, stirring constantly, until thickened. Season to taste, if desired. (Makes enough gravy to pour over meat and potatoes.)
4 SERVINGS

Glazed Roast Ham

10-pound whole smoked
  ham

1. Place ham on a rack in a shallow roasting pan. Roast at 300° to 325°F about 2 hours; remove from oven.
2. Cut off rind (if any) and score fat. Insert a **whole clove** in the center of each diamond.
3. Spread with one of **Glazes for Ham** (below), and continue roasting about 1 hour, or until internal temperature reaches 160°F.
ABOUT 20 SERVINGS

Glazes for Ham

Cider: Combine and mix thoroughly **¾ cup packed brown sugar**, **½ teaspoon dry mustard**, and **2 tablespoons maple syrup**. Spread glaze over ham. Occasionally baste ham with about **¾ cup apple cider**.

Apricot (using apricot jam): Combine **¾ cup apricot jam**, **¾ cup honey**, and **2 tablespoons lemon juice** or **cider vinegar**. Spread glaze over ham.

Apricot (using dried apricots): Pour **1⅓ cups apple cider** over **8 ounces dried apricots** in a bowl. Cover and refrigerate overnight. Purée apricot mixture in an electric blender or force through a food mill. Stir in a mixture of **6 tablespoons brown sugar**, **½ teaspoon ground cinnamon**, **½ teaspoon ground allspice**, and **¼ teaspoon ground cloves**. Spread ham generously with mixture before heating. Heat remaining sauce and serve as an accompaniment to the ham.

Mustard Glaze: Mix thoroughly in a small bowl **1 cup packed brown sugar**, **1 tablespoon flour**, and **1 teaspoon dry mustard**. Stir in **2 tablespoons cider vinegar** to form a smooth paste.

Jelly or Jam: Dilute **1 cup quince or elderberry jelly, jam or orange marmalade** with **⅓ cup very hot water**.

Brown Sugar: Heat together in a saucepan, stirring until sugar is dissolved, **1 cup packed brown sugar** and **⅔ cup light corn syrup**. If desired, **⅔ cup spiced fruit juice or ginger ale** may be substituted for the corn syrup.

Pork Roast with Olives and Rice

7-pound pork loin roast
3 cloves garlic, slivered
1½ cups chicken broth
¾ cup dry vermouth
½ teaspoon ground sage

¼ teaspoon pepper
¾ cup sliced pimento-stuffed
   olives
Special Gravy, *below*
Saffron Rice, *below*

1. Score fat side of pork roast; insert garlic in slits. Place, fat side up, in a shallow roasting pan. Insert a meat thermometer in roast so that tip rests in thickest part of the meat.
2. Combine broth, vermouth, sage, and pepper; pour over meat.
3. Roast at 325°F until meat thermometer registers 170°F, basting occasionally. Total cooking time will be about 2½ hours. The last hour of cooking time, add ½ cup of the sliced olives to liquid in pan.
4. Transfer roast to a heated platter; keep warm.
5. Remove olives; reserve to add to rice along with remaining olives. Use liquid for the gravy.
6. Spoon the Saffron Rice onto platter around the roast. Accompany with the gravy.
ABOUT 12 SERVINGS

Special Gravy: Skim excess fat from reserved liquid. Measure liquid and add enough water to make 1¾ cups. Return liquid to pan or pour into a saucepan and bring to boiling. Stir a blend of **2 tablespoons cornstarch** and **¼ cup water** into boiling liquid; boil 1 to 2 minutes, stirring constantly. Pour into a gravy boat.
ABOUT 2 CUPS GRAVY

Saffron Rice: In a large saucepan, combine **1 quart chicken broth, 2 cups uncooked white rice, 2 tablespoons butter or margarine, ½ teaspoon salt,** and **¼ teaspoon crushed saffron.** Bring to boiling, stirring with a fork. Cook, covered, over low heat 15 to 20 minutes, or until rice is tender. Toss reserved olives with rice.
ABOUT 8 CUPS

Bavarian Casserole

2 celery stalks, chopped
1 medium onion, chopped
3 tablespoons butter or
   margarine
½ teaspoon salt
¼ teaspoon sage
¼ teaspoon sugar

⅛ teaspoon pepper
1 cup beer
4 cups pumpernickel bread
   cubes (5 slices)
2 cups cubed cooked pork
   (10 ounces)

1. Sauté celery and onion in butter until soft; stir in seasonings. Add beer.
2. Place bread and pork in a 1½-quart casserole. Add beer-vegetable mixture. Stir lightly.
3. Cover and bake at 375°F 30 to 35 minutes.
4 SERVINGS

Pork Roast with Olives and Rice

Savory Spareribs

4 pounds pork spareribs
1 can or bottle (12 ounces)
   beer
½ cup honey

2 tablespoons lemon juice
2 teaspoons salt
1 teaspoon dry mustard
¼ teaspoon pepper

1. Cut spareribs into 2-rib sections.
2. Combine remaining ingredients in a shallow glass or ceramic baking dish. Add ribs. Marinate in refrigerator at least 24 hours, turning and basting occasionally.
3. Arrange ribs in a single layer in a large baking pan; reserve marinade.
4. Bake at 350°F 1½ hours, turning once and basting frequently with marinade.
4 TO 6 SERVINGS

Golden Pork Chop Bake

6 pork chops, 1 inch thick
2 tablespoons shortening
½ cup sliced celery
1 garlic clove, minced
2 cans (10¾ ounces each)
   condensed golden

mushroom soup
1⅓ cups water
1⅓ cups packaged pre-
   cooked rice
½ cup chopped tomato

1. Brown pork chops on both sides in shortening in a skillet. Remove chops from skillet; drain off excess fat.
2. Sauté celery and garlic in skillet. Combine with remaining ingredients. Spoon into a 2-quart shallow baking dish.
3. Arrange chops on top of rice mixture.
4. Bake, covered, at 350°F 1 hour, or until chops are tender.
6 SERVINGS

Luxemburg Stew

2 pounds boneless veal
   shoulder or stew meat, cut
   in 1-inch cubes
⅓ cup flour
6 tablespoons butter or
   margarine
1 large onion, sliced
2 cans (16 ounces each)
   tomatoes, broken up
1 can or bottle (12 ounces)

beer
6 whole cloves
1 teaspoon salt
½ teaspoon thyme
¼ teaspoon crushed
   rosemary
¼ teaspoon paprika
8 gingersnaps
2 tablespoons lemon juice

1. Dredge veal in flour. Brown in ¼ cup butter in a saucepot. Remove meat.
2. Add remaining 2 tablespoons butter and onion to saucepot. Sauté until golden.
3. Add veal, tomatoes with liquid, beer, and seasonings. Cover and simmer 1 hour.
4. Moisten gingersnaps with a little water; crush. Stir into meat. Simmer 5 minutes more. Add lemon juice; mix well.
5. Serve over **rice** or **noodles** or with **potatoes.**
8 SERVINGS

Note: Poultry or lean pork could be substituted for veal.

Pork Chops with Ham and Cheese

2 pork chops
¼ teaspoon salt
⅛ teaspoon pepper or ⅛ teaspoon paprika
½ teaspoon tarragon, oregano or rosemary
3 slices bayonne ham
2 slices cheese, cheddar
1 pound can ratatouille
1 to 2 tablespoons dry red or white wine

1. Brown pork chops about 20 minutes and season. Place ham and grated cheese on top.
2. Heat vegetables and add wine. Place in ovenproof dish with pork chops on top. Bake at 475°F for 5 to 10 minutes.
2 SERVINGS

Lagered Ham and Noodle Casserole

1 medium green pepper, chopped
1 medium onion, chopped
¼ cup butter or margarine
3 tablespoons flour
½ teaspoon dry mustard
½ teaspoon salt
Dash pepper
⅓ cup instant nonfat dry
milk
1 can or bottle (12 ounces) beer
1 cup shredded Cheddar cheese (4 ounces)
8 ounces medium noodles, cooked and drained
2 cups diced cooked ham (⅔ pound)

1. For sauce, slowly sauté green pepper and onion in butter until soft and almost tender. Stir in flour and seasonings.
2. Mix dry milk and ⅓ cup beer.
3. Gradually add remaining beer to flour mixture. Cook, stirring constantly, until thickened and bubbly. Add cheese; stir until melted. Remove from heat; add beer-milk mixture.
4. Combine sauce, cooked noodles, and ham. Turn into a 2½-quart casserole.
5. Bake at 350°F 20 minutes, or until heated through and bubbly.
6 SERVINGS

Northwoods Pork Chop

1 package (2¾ ounces) instant wild rice
¼ cup chopped celery
¼ cup chopped green pepper
¼ cup chopped onion
6 tablespoons butter or margarine
4 pork chops, ¾ inch thick
¼ cup flour
2 cups milk
½ teaspoon salt
⅛ teaspoon pepper
½ cup (2 ounces) shredded American cheese

1. Prepare wild rice according to package directions.
2. Sauté celery, green pepper, and onion in 4 tablespoons butter in a skillet. Combine with wild rice. Put into a 1½-quart shallow baking dish.
3. Brown pork chops on both sides in skillet. Place on top of wild rice mixture.
4. Melt remaining 2 tablespoons butter in skillet. Blend in flour. Gradually add milk, stirring until thickened and smooth. Add salt and pepper. Pour over pork chops.
5. Bake, covered, at 350°F 1 hour, or until chops are done. Sprinkle with cheese.
4 SERVINGS

Fruited Pork Roast, Scandinavian Style

1 pork rolled loin roast, boneless (3 to 3½ pounds)
8 to 10 pitted dried prunes
1 can or bottle (12 ounces) beer
½ teaspoon ginger
1 medium apple, pared and chopped
1 teaspoon lemon juice
½ teaspoon salt
Dash pepper
¼ cup flour

1. Make pocket down center of roast by piercing with a long, sharp tool such as a steel knife sharpener; leave string on roast. (Alternate method: Remove string. Using strong knife, cut pocket in pork by making a deep slit down length of loin, going to within ½ inch of the two ends and within 1 inch of other side.)
2. Meanwhile, combine prunes, beer, and ginger in a saucepan; heat to boiling. Remove from heat; let stand 30 minutes.
3. Mix apple with lemon juice to prevent darkening. Drain prunes, reserving liquid; pat dry with paper towels. Mix prunes and apple.
4. Pack fruit into pocket in pork, using handle of wooden spoon to pack tightly. (With alternate method of cutting pocket, tie with sring at 1-inch intervals. Secure with skewers or sew with kitchen thread.)
5. Place meat on rack in a roasting pan.
6. Roast at 350°F 2 to 2½ hour, allowing 40 to 45 minutes per pound. During last 45 minutes of roasting, spoon fat from pan; baste occasionally with liquid drained from prunes.
7. Transfer meat to a platter. Skim fat from cooking liquid; measure liquid. Add a little water to roasting pan to help loosen brown bits; add to cooking liquid. Add salt, pepper, and enough additional water to measure 2 cups total. Make a paste of flour and a little more water. Combine with cooking liquid. Cook, stirring constantly, until thickened. Pass in a sauceboat for pouring over meat slices.
8 SERVINGS

Calico Ham Bake

1 pound cooked ham
1 package (10 ounces) sharp Cheddar cheese
1 medium green pepper,
chopped
4 eggs, beaten
2 cups milk

1. Grind ham and cheese together. Combine with green pepper, eggs, and milk. Put into a greased 8-inch square baking dish.
2. Bake, uncovered, at 325°F 1 hour, or until browned. Cut into squares to serve.
6 SERVINGS

Ham in Rye Crust

Dough:
1 package active dry
 yeast
½ cup warm water
⅓ cup caraway seed
¾ cup water
2 tablespoons molasses
3 cups rye flour (about)

Topping for ham:
½ cup firmly packed brown
 sugar
1 teaspoon dry mustard
¼ teaspoon cloves

1 canned full cooked ham (5
 pounds)

1. For dough, dissolve yeast in ½ cup warm water and add caraway seed; let stand 10 minutes.
2. Stir in ¾ cup water, molasses, and half of the flour.
3. Turn out dough onto floured surface. Knead in remaining flour to make a stiff dough. Cover with plastic wrap. Let rest 20 minutes.
4. Mix brown sugar with mustard and cloves.
5. Remove gelatin and wipe ham with paper towels.
6. Roll out dough on a floured surface to form a 28x10-inch rectangle.
7. Sprinkle about 1 tablespoon brown sugar mixture in center of dough. Place ham on sugar mixture. Sprinkle remaining sugar mixture over top of ham.
8. Fold dough over top of ham, cutting out corners to fit with only one layer of dough. Pinch edges to seal.
9. Set dough-wrapped ham on rack in pan lined with foil.
10. Roast at 350°F 1½ to 1¾ hours, or until meat thermometer reaches 140°F. Remove from oven; let rest 10 minutes.
11. To serve, remove crust and discard. Slice ham.
12 TO 15 SERVINGS

Charcoal-Roasted Pig

3 garlic cloves, crushed in a
 garlic press
2 cups dry white wine
Juice of 2 lemons
1 tablespoon salt
¼ cup oregano
2 tablespoons crushed

peppercorns
1 piglet (12 to 15 pounds)
 with eyes, tongue, and feet
 removed
½ cup olive oil
1 tablespoon paprika

1. Make a marinade by combining garlic, wine, lemon juice, salt, oregano, and peppercorns. Refrigerate 1 hour.
2. Score pig several places with a knife. Rub interior cavity and exterior surface with marinade. Allow to marinate 12 hours in refrigerator.
3. Crush aluminum foil into a firm, thick ball and put in mouth to keep open. Cover ears with foil so they will not burn. Pull front feet forward and tie together. Pull hind feet backwards and tie together. Cover feet loosely with foil.
4. Attach pig to revolving spit and roast, basting frequently with a mixture of oil and paprika, until skin is brown and crisp and meat is tender (about 5 hours). In the last hour, remove foil so ears and feet can brown.
5. Remove pig from spit. Set on a platter. Put an apple or other piece of fruit in its mouth. Pour off fat from pan juices and serve.
8 TO 10 SERVINGS

Ham Wrap-Arounds

8 slices cooked ham, about
 ¼ inch thick
2 packages (10 ounces each)
 frozen broccoli spears,
 cooked and drained
3 cups cubed French bread,
 toasted*

1½ cups dry white wine
3 cups (12 ounces) shredded
 Swiss cheese
3 tablespoons flour
2 teaspoons prepared
 mustard
⅛ teaspoon garlic powder

1. Wrap ham slices around broccoli spears. Place in a 12x8-inch shallow baking dish. Sprinkle with bread cubes.
2. Heat wine in a saucepan. Mix cheese and flour. Gradually add to wine while stirring until smooth. Stir in mustard and garlic powder. Pour sauce over all in dish.
3. Bake, uncovered, at 350°F 30 minutes, or until heated through.
8 SERVINGS

*To toast cubed french bread, place on a baking sheet and put into a 350°F oven about 10 minutes.

Sausage-Green Bean Casserole

3 cups hot, cooked mashed
 potatoes
1 pound pork sausage links,
 cooked and drained
1 cup (4 ounces) shredded
 American cheese
1 package (9 ounces) frozen

cut green beans, cooked
 and drained
1 can (8 ounces) small whole
 onions, drained
1 tablespoon chopped
 pimento

1. Layer half of the mashed potatoes, half of the sausage, and half of the cheese in a 1½-quart casserole.
2. Combine green beans, onions, and pimento. Spoon over cheese. Top with remaining potatoes, sausage, and cheese.
3. Bake, covered, at 350°F 30 minutes, or until heated through.
6 SERVINGS

Hearty Sausage Supper

1 jar (16 ounces) applesauce
1 can (14 ounces) sauerkraut,
 drained
⅓ cup dry white wine
2 tablespoons firmly packed
 brown sugar
1 can (16 ounces) small

white potatoes, drained
1 can (16 ounces) small
 whole onions, drained
1 ring (12 ounces) Polish
 sausage, slashed several
 times
1 tablespoon snipped parsley

1. mix applesauce, sauerkraut, wine, and brown sugar. Put into a 2½-quart casserole.
2. Arrange potatoes and onions around edge of casserole. Place sausage in center.
3. Bake, covered, at 350°F 45 to 50 minutes, or until heated through. Sprinkle with parsley.
4 SERVINGS

Sausage in Polish Sauce

2 onions, sliced
3 tablespoons butter or margarine
Ring Polish sausage (about 1½ pounds)
1½ cups bouillon or meat broth
12 ounces beer
2 tablespoons flour
1 tablespoon vinegar
2 teaspoons brown sugar
¾ teaspoon salt
¼ teaspoon pepper
4 to 6 boiled potatoes

1. Sauté onion in 2 tablespoons butter until golden. Add sausage, bouillon, and beer. Simmer 20 minutes.
2. Blend flour into remaining 1 tablespoon butter. Stir into broth. Add vinegar, brown sugar, salt, and pepper.
3. Add potatoes. Cook over medium heat 10 to 15 minutes.
4. Slice sausage into 2-inch chunks to serve.
4 TO 6 SERVINGS

Pork Slices in Mole Verde

½ cup finely chopped onion
¼ cup finely chopped blanched almonds
2 tablespoons vegetable oil
2 cans (10 ounces each) Mexican green tomatoes (tomatillos)
1 tablespoon minced fresh coriander (cilantro) or 1 teaspoon dried coriander
1 to 3 tablespoons minced
canned green chilies
2 cups chicken stock, or 2 cups water plus 2 chicken bouillon cubes
6 to 8 slices cooked pork loin roast
Salt
Small lettuce leaves
Whole pickled mild chilies
Sour cream

1. Combine onion, almonds, and oil in a saucepan. Cook over medium heat until onion is soft.
2. Turn contents of cans of green tomatoes into an electric blender and blend until smooth (or force green tomatoes through a sieve).
3. Add purée to onion mixture and stir in coriander, chilies (to taste), and stock. Bring to boiling, reduce heat, and simmer, uncovered, until reduced to 2½ cups; stir occasionally.
4. Arrange meat in a large skillet, sprinkle with salt to taste, and pour sauce over meat. Cover, bring slowly to boiling, reduce heat, and simmer about 10 minutes, or until thoroughly heated.
5. Arrange sauced meat on a platter. Garnish with lettuce and chilies. Accompany with sour cream.
6 TO 8 SERVINGS

Wild Rice-Ham Rolls

1½ cups uncooked wild rice
½ cup sliced green onion
¼ cup snipped parsley
¼ pound fresh mushrooms, sliced
¼ cup butter or margarine
¼ cup flour
½ teaspoon salt
¼ teaspoon pepper
¼ teaspoon nutmeg
½ cup dry white wine
2 cups milk
8 slices cooked ham, about ¼ inch thick

1. Prepare wild rice according to package directions. Add ¼ cup green onion and the parsley.
2. Sauté remaining ¼ cup green onion and mushrooms in butter in a skillet. Stir in flour, salt, pepper, and nutmeg. Gradually add wine, then milk, stirring until thickened and smooth.
3. Combine 1 cup sauce with 2 cups wild rice. Divide evenly on top of each ham slice. Spoon remaining rice on bottom of a lightly greased 12x9-inch shallow baking dish.
4. Roll up ham rolls to enclose filling. Place seam side down on rice in casserole. Spoon remaining sauce over ham rolls.
5. Bake, uncovered, at 350°F 20 minutes, or until heated through.
8 SERVINGS

Polish Sausage

1½ pounds lean boneless pork
½ pound boneless veal
1 teaspoon salt
¼ teaspoon pepper
1 clove garlic, crushed
1 tablespoon mustard seed
¼ cup crushed ice
Casing

1. Cut meat into small chunks. Grind meat with seasonings and ice; mix well.
2. Stuff meat mixture into casing.
3. Smoke in a smoker, following manufacturer's directions. Or, place sausage in a casserole; cover with water. Bake at 350°F until water is dissolved, about 1½ hours. Roast 10 minutes.
ABOUT 2 POUNDS

Ham and Cheese Casserole Bread

⅔ cup chopped onion
3 tablespoons vegetable oil
2 cups all-purpose biscuit mix
1 cup chopped cooked ham
2 eggs
⅔ cup milk
1 teaspoon prepared mustard
1½ cups (6 ounces) shredded Cheddar cheese
2 tablespoons sesame seed
2 tablespoons snipped parsley
3 tablespoons butter or margarine, melted

1. Sauté onion in 1 tablespoon oil in a skillet.
2. Combine biscuit mix and ham.
3. Blend the remaining 2 tablespoons oil, eggs, milk, mustard, onion, and ¾ cup cheese. Stir into ham mixture. Spoon into a greased 1½-quart round casserole. Sprinkle with remaining ¾ cup cheese, sesame seed, parsley, and butter.
4. Bake, uncovered, at 350°F minutes, or until done. Cut into wedges to serve.
6 SERVINGS

Pork Slices in Mole Verde

Ham 'n' Chicken Specialty

6 green onions with tops, finely chopped
¼ pound fresh mushrooms, sliced lengthwise
¼ cup butter
1½ cups cooked ham pieces
1 cup cooked chicken pieces
½ teaspoon salt
½ teaspoon pepper
½ teaspoon celery salt
1 cup sour cream
1 cup creamed cottage cheese
1½ cups thin spaghetti pieces (1½ inches), cooked and drained
1 cup shredded sharp Cheddar cheese

1. Cook green onion and mushrooms until just tender in hot butter in a large skillet or saucepan. Mix in ham, chicken, and a mixture of salt, pepper, and celery salt; heat thoroughly.
2. Blend sour cream and cottage cheese. Add to spaghetti and toss lightly until thoroughly mixed. Add ham mixture and toss lightly.
3. Turn into buttered 1½-quart casserole or baking dish. Top evenly with shredded cheese.
4. Broil 3 inches from source of heat about 15 minutes, or until mixture is bubbly and cheese is delicately browned. Garnish with **parsley.**
ABOUT 6 SERVINGS

Ham Di Parma

8 ounces spaghetti, cooked and drained
¾ cup shredded Parmesan cheese
6 ounces mushrooms, sliced lengthwise
2 tablespoons grated onion
⅓ cup butter or margarine
¼ cup flour
2 cups cream
¾ cup dry white wine
1 pound cooked ham, cut in strips
⅓ cup sliced green olives
1 pimiento, cut in thin strips
¼ teaspoon oregano, crushed
⅛ teaspoon black pepper

1. Toss spaghetti with ½ cup cheese; keep hot.
2. Cook mushrooms and onion 5 minutes in hot butter in a large skillet. With a slotted spoon, remove mushrooms; set aside.
3. Blend flour into butter in skillet. Remove from heat and gradually add cream, stirring constantly. Bring to boiling; cook 1 minutes. Blend in wine, ham strips, olives, pimiento, oregano, and pepper.
4. Put hot spaghetti into a large shallow baking dish. Spoon hot creamed ham mixture over spaghetti. Sprinkle with remaining Parmesan cheese.
5. Broil 4 to 6 inches from source of heat until lightly browned and thoroughly heated.
ABOUT 8 SERVINGS

He-Man Casserole

½ cup chopped green onion
½ cup chopped green pepper
½ cup chopped celery
6 tablespoons butter or margarine
6 tablespoons flour
Dash pepper
1 cup chicken broth
1½ cups milk
4 cups cubed cooked ham
1 package (10 ounces) frozen peas, thawed
4 cups hot, cooked mashed potatoes (stiff)
1 egg, beaten
1 cup (4 ounces) shredded Cheddar cheese

1. Sauté onion, green pepper, and celery in butter in a saucepan. Stir in flour and pepper. Gradually add broth and milk, stirring until thickened and smooth.
2. Mix with ham and peas. Put into a 3-quart casserole.
3. Combine potatoes, egg, and cheese. Spoon around edge of casserole mixture.
4. Bake, uncovered, at 375°F 45 minutes, or until mixture is bubbly.
8 SERVINGS

Ham Napoli Ring

3 eggs
1½ cups milk
1 teaspoon salt
8 ounces noodles, cooked and drained
⅓ cup butter
½ cup sliced fresh mushrooms
¼ cup flour
½ teaspoon salt
2 cups milk
Cooked ham (enough to yield 1 cup pieces)
½ cup ripe olive pieces
¼ cup toasted, blanched almonds, coarsely chopped
2 tablespoons chopped parsley

1. Beat eggs slightly. Blend in 1½ cups milk and 1 teaspoon salt. Mix in cooked noodles. Turn mixture into a buttered 9-inch ring mold. Set in a pan containing boiling water to a depth of 1 inch.
2. Bake at 325°F 1½ hours, or until a knife inserted in center of mixture comes out clean.
3. Heat butter in a heavy saucepan. Add mushrooms and cook, stirring occasionally, until mushrooms are lightly browned and tender. With slotted spoon, remove mushrooms and set aside.
4. Blend flour and salt into butter in pan. Heat until bubbly. Gradually add remaining 2 cups milk, stirring to blend. Bring to boiling, stirring constantly; cook 1 to 2 minutes.
5. Stir in ham, olives, mushrooms, almonds, and parsley; heat thoroughly.
6. Unmold noodle ring onto hot platter and fill with creamed mixture. Garnish with **ripe olives, radish fans,** and **sprigs of parsley.**
6 SERVINGS

Chicken-Ham Napoli Ring: Follow recipe for Ham Napoli Ring. Substitute **cooked chicken** for half of ham and **chicken broth** for half of milk.

Neapolitan Pork Chops

2 tablespoons olive oil
1 clove garlic, minced
6 pork loin rib chops, cut
about ¾ to 1 inch thick
1 teaspoon salt
¼ teaspoon pepper

1 pound mushrooms
2 green peppers
½ cup canned tomatoes,
sieved
3 tablespoons dry white
wine

1. 1. Heat oil in large heavy skillet, add minced garlic and cook until lightly browned.
2. Season pork chops with a mixture of the salt, and pepper. Place in skillet and slowly brown chops on both sides.
3. While chops brown, clean and slice mushrooms and chop green peppers; set aside.
4. When chops are browned, add the mushrooms and peppers. Stir in tomatoes and wine, cover skillet and cook over low heat 1 to 1½ hours, depending on thickness of chops. Add small amounts of water as needed. Test the chops for tenderness by piercing with a fork.
6 SERVINGS

Smoked Sausage Dinner

1 medium onion, chopped
½ cup chopped green
pepper
2 tablespoons butter or
margarine

1 pound smoked sausage,
cut in ½-inch pieces
1 can (16 ounces) tomatoes,
cut up
1 cup uncooked noodles

1. Sauté onion and green pepper in butter in a skillet. Add sausage and brown lightly; drain off excess fat.
2. Stir in remaining ingredients. Put into a 1½-quart casserole.
3. Bake, covered, at 375°F 45 minutes, or until noodles are tender, stirring once.
4 SERVINGS

Roast Loin of Pork I

3½-pound (8 ribs) pork loin
roast
1½ teaspoons onion salt

½ teaspoon marjoram,
crushed
¼ teaspoon pepper

1. Rub roast with a mixture of the salt, marjoram, and pepper. Secure roast on spit. Insert meat thermometer. Adjust spit about 8 inches above prepared coals, placing aluminum foil pan under pork to catch drippings. If using a gas-fired grill, adjust flame size following manufacturer's directions.
2. Roast until meat thermometer registers 170°F or until meat is tender. About 30 minutes before roast is done, score surface.
3. Place roast on a warm serving platter. Garnish with parsley.

Note: To roast in the oven, place pork loin, fat side up, on a rack in a shallow roasting pan. Roast, uncovered, at 325°F about 2½ hours.

Ham and Asparagus Casserole

3 tablespoons butter or
margarine
3 tablespoons flour
½ teaspoon dry mustard
1½ cups milk
1½ cups (6 ounces) shredded
Cheddar cheese
2 cups cubed cooked ham

1 package (10 ounces) frozen
cut-up asparagus, cooked
and drained
⅛ teaspoon onion powder
Dash Tabasco
½ cup toasted slivered
almonds

1. Melt butter in a saucepan. Stir in flour and mustard. Gradually add milk, stirring until thickened and smooth. Add cheese, stirring until smooth.
2. Combine with ham, asparagus, onion powder, and Tabasco. Put into a 1½-quart casserole. Sprinkle with almonds.
3. Bake, uncovered, at 350°F 20 minutes, or until heated through.
4 SERVINGS

Roast Loin of Pork

Super Sausage Supper

1 cup chopped onion
1 garlic clove, minced
3 carrots, pared and thinly sliced
2 tablespoons shortening
1 jar (32 ounces) sauerkraut, drained
2 cups apple cider
½ cup dry white wine
¼ teaspoon pepper
3 parsley sprigs
1 bay leaf
1 package (12 ounces) pork

sausage links, cooked and drained
1 package (5 ounces) tiny smoked sausage links
2 links (8 ounces each) Polish sausage, cooked and drained
2 cans (16 ounces each) small white potatoes, drained
1 apple, cored and cut in chunks

1. Sauté onion, garlic, and carrot in shortening in a skillet. Add sauerkraut, apple cider, wine, pepper, parsley, and bay leaf. Bring to a boil; reduce heat and simmer 15 minutes.
2. Stir in remaining ingredients. Remove bay leaf. Put into a 3-quart casserole.
3. Bake, covered, at 350°F 1 hour.
8 SERVINGS

Pork Sausage with Orange Peel

2 pounds pork shoulder, ground
½ pound fat back, ground
Grated peel of 1 navel orange
2 garlic cloves, crushed in a garlic press
1 tablespoon minced parsley
1 tablespoon oregano

2 teaspoons salt
2 teaspoons anise seed
2 teaspoons coriander, ground
1½ teaspoons allspice, ground
1 teaspoon pepper
1 long casing, cut in 7- to 8-inch pieces

1. Combine pork shoulder, fat back and remaining ingredients, except casings, in a bowl and mix thoroughly. Cover and refrigerate several hours.
2. Rinse casings thoroughly in lukewarm water. Tie one end of a casing and stuff by pushing meat through a funnel inserted in the untied end; tie other end. Continue until all the meat and casings have been used.
3. Poach sausages in boiling water for 1 hour. Cool. Cut into slices and fry in a skillet until browned.

Note: If desired, omit casing, form sausage into patties, and fry until cooked.

Saucy Stuffed Peppers

6 medium green peppers
1½ pounds pork sausage meat
1 cup quick or old-fashioned oats, uncooked
⅔ cup tomato juice

1 can (10¾ ounces) condensed tomato soup
¼ cup milk
1 teaspoon Worcestershire sauce
⅛ teaspoon oregano

1. Cut ¼-inch slice from the top of each green pepper; remove seeds. Cook green peppers in **boiling water** about 5 minutes; drain.
2. Brown sausage in a skillet until lightly browned; drain off excess fat. Combine meat, oats, and tomato juice.
3. Fill green peppers with meat mixture. Stand upright in a 1½-quart shallow baking dish; add a small amount of **water.**
4. Bake, uncovered, at 350°F 45 to 50 minutes, or until done.
5. Serve with sauce made by heating together the soup, milk, Worcestershire sauce, and oregano.
6 SERVINGS

 ## Spit-Roasted Canadian Bacon

1 (1½-pound) piece smoked pork loin Canadian style bacon

⅔ cup bottled barbecue sauce
⅓ cup grape jelly

1. Secure meat on a spit and follow manufacturer's instructions for using rotisserie.
2. Beat barbecue sauce and grape jelly together.
3. Grill meat over medium coals, brushing with sauce every 15 minutes, for about 1½ hours, or until meat is heated throughout and reaches an internal temperature of 140°F; this internal temperature is for fully cooked pork.
4. Serve with the sauce, if desired.
ABOUT 6 SERVINGS

Note: A smoked pork shoulder may be prepared the same way; cook to 170°F.

Spit-Roasted Canadian Bacon

Super Sausage Supper

Orange-Glazed Pork Loin

1 pork loin roast (3 to 5 pounds)
3 tablespoons butter
½ cup lightly packed brown sugar
1 can (6 ounces) frozen
orange juice concentrate
½ cup water
2 teaspoons cornstarch
1 cup seeded and halved green grapes

1. Score fat on pork roast at 1-inch intervals. Place roast, fat side up, on grill directly over drip pan prepared from 3 thicknesses of heavy-duty aluminum foil. Insert meat thermometer through fat into very center of the meat. Place cover on kettle-type grill, adjust dampers, and cook at low heat (approximately 350°F) until meat thermometer registers 170°F (allow 20 to 30 minutes per pound).
2. For sauce, heat butter in a 1-quart saucepan. Stir in brown sugar. Add orange concentrate and stir until smooth. Remove ¼ cup sauce and baste roast during last 20 minutes of cooking time.
3. To complete sauce, stir water into cornstarch. Add gradually to remaining orange juice mixture. Cook, stirring constantly until thickened. Cook 8 minutes. Add grapes. Serve hot with pork.
6 TO 12 SERVINGS

Apple-Covered Ham in Claret

2 smoked ham center slices, fully cooked, about ¾ inch thick (about ½ pound each) or 1 large center cut 1½ inches thick
½ teaspoon dry mustard
3 to 4 medium Golden
Delicious apples, cored and cut in rings
4 orange slices
¾ cup dry red wine, such as claret
½ cup packed brown sugar
Parsley sprigs

1. Place ham slices in large shallow baking dish. Sprinkle each slice with ¼ teaspoon mustard.
2. Cut unpared apple rings in half and place around outer edge of ham, slightly overlapping slices.
3. Place two orange slices in center of each ham slice.
4. Pour wine over top of ham and fruit. Then sprinkle entire dish with brown sugar.
5. Cover; cook in a 350°F oven 45 minutes. Serve on platter or from baking dish, and garnish with parsley.
6 TO 8 SERVINGS

Orange-Glazed Pork Loin

Apple-Covered Ham in Claret

Chinatown Chop Suey

1¼ pounds pork, boneless
1 pound beef, boneless
¾ pound veal, boneless
3 tablespoons cooking oil
1 cup water
3 cups diagonally sliced celery
2 cups coarsely chopped onion

3 tablespoons cornstarch
¼ cup water
¼ cup soy sauce
¼ cup bead molasses
1 can (16 ounces) bean sprouts, drained and rinsed
2 cans (5 ounces each) water chestnuts, drained and sliced

1. Cut meat into 2x½x¼-inch strips. Heat oil in a large wok. Stir-fry ½ pound of meat at a time, browning pieces on all sides. Remove the meat from the wok as it is browned. When all the meat is browned, return it to the wok. Cover and cook over low heat 30 minutes.
2. Mix in 1 cup water, celery, and onions. Bring to boiling and simmer, covered, 20 minutes.
3. Blend cornstarch, the ¼ cup water, soy sauce, and molasses. Stir into meat mixture. Bring to boiling and cook 2 minutes, stirring constantly. Mix in bean sprouts and water chestnuts; heat.
4. Serve on **hot fluffy rice.**
8 SERVINGS

Dutch Sausage with Gravy

1 pound bulk pork sausage
1 to 2 tablespoons water
1 small onion, minced

1 tablespoon flour
1 cup beef broth

1. Shape sausage into 4 to 6 flat cakes. Put sausage cakes into a skillet. Add water; cover tightly and cook slowly about 5 minutes. Remove cover and cook slowly until well browned on both sides.
2. Remove cakes to cooking pan of a chafing dish and keep warm.
3. Drain off all but 3 tablespoons fat from skillet. Brown onion in the fat. Stir in flour and cook 1 minute. Stir in broth; simmer 5 minutes.
4. Pour gravy over sausage cakes and heat thoroughly.
4 TO 6 SERVINGS

Ham à la Cranberry

2 cups sugar
¼ teaspoon salt
2 cups water
1 pound (about 4 cups) cranberries, washed and sorted

2 teaspoons grated lemon peel
6 cups cubed cooked smoked ham or luncheon meat
½ cup seedless raisins (optional)

1. Combine sugar, salt, and water in a saucepan and heat to boiling. Boil, uncovered, 5 minutes. Add cranberries and continue to boil, uncovered, without stirring, about 5 minutes, or until skins pop.
2. Turn cranberry sauce into cooking pan of a chafing dish. Blend in lemon peel, ham, and raisins, if desired. Cook over direct heat until mixture starts to bubble; stir occasionally.
3. Place over simmering water to keep mixture hot. Serve over **toast triangles, patty shells,** or **hot biscuits.**
8 TO 10 SERVINGS

Sausage, Hominy, and Tomato Scramble

1 pound bulk pork sausage
½ cup fine dry bread crumbs
⅔ cup undiluted evaporated milk
½ teaspoon rubbed sage
¼ cup flour

2 cans (16 ounces each) tomatoes
1 can (20 ounces) hominy, drained
1 teaspoon salt
¼ teaspoon rubbed sage

1. Combine sausage, bread crumbs, evaporated milk, and ½ teaspoon sage. Mix well and shape into 16 balls. Roll balls in flour to coat, reserving remaining flour.
2. In cooking pan of a chafing dish, brown meatballs over low heat, turning frequently.
3. Remove all but 3 tablespoons of the fat from the pan. Stir in reserved flour, tomatoes, hominy, salt, and sage; blend well.
4. Cook, covered, over low heat about 15 minutes, or until sauce is thickened. Keep warm over chafing dish burner until ready to serve.
6 TO 8 SERVINGS

Calico Supper Pie

1 can (10 biscuits) refrigerator biscuits
2 cups diced cooked ham
1 large tomato, sliced
¼ cup chopped green onion
1 cup (4 ounces) shredded Cheddar cheese

2 eggs, separated
½ cup milk
2 tablespoons flour
¼ cup (1 ounce) grated Parmesan cheese
1 tablespoon snipped parsley

1. Separate dough into biscuits. Place in a 9-inch deep pie pan; press over bottom and up sides to form crust. Sprinkle with ham. Top with tomato, green onion, and Cheddar cheese.
2. Beat egg yolks. Stir in milk and flour. Pour over cheese.
3. Beat egg whites until soft peaks form. Fold in Parmesan cheese and parsley. Spread over pie. Cover edge of crust with foil.
4. Bake at 350°F 25 minutes. Remove foil. Bake an additional 10 minutes, or until crust is golden brown. Let stand a few minutes before serving.
6 SERVINGS

Sausage in Beer

1 can or bottle (12 ounces) beer
3 medium onions, thinly sliced
2 medium carrots, thinly sliced
1 teaspoon Worcestershire

sauce
½ teaspoon salt
8 bratwurst, knockwurst, Polish sausage, or large frankfurters
8 frankfurter buns

1. Put beer, onion, carrot, Worcestershire sauce, and salt in a saucepan. Heat to boiling. Cover, reduce heat, and simmer 15 minutes.
2. Add sausage. Cover and simmer 15 minutes more, stirring occasionally.
3. Place sausages in buns. Using a slotted spoon, lift vegetables from liquid and place on sausages.
8 SERVINGS

bone side almost to fat, making a pocket.
2. Sauté onion and celery in butter in a skillet. Combine with bread crumbs, salt, and poultry seasoning. Stuff into pockets in chops.
3. Brown chops in shortening in skillet. Place in a 10x8-inch baking dish.
4. Add soup and water to drippings in skillet. Stir to dissolve brown particles. Pour over chops.
5. Bake, covered, at 350°F 1 hour, or until chops are tender.
4 SERVINGS

Ham Steak with Parsley Sauce

2 bunches parsley, washed and stems removed
¼ cup dry white wine
1 center-cut smoked ham steak, ¾ inch thick (about

1½ pounds)
⅔ cup Mock Hollandaise Sauce (page 49)
Salt
Freshly ground white pepper

1. Line bottom of a shallow baking dish with half the parsley; drizzle with half the wine. Lay ham steak on parsley. Cover ham with remaining parsley; drizzle with remaining wine. Lightly cover baking dish.
2. Bake at 325°F about 30 minutes, or until ham is thoroughly heated.
3. Make Mock Hollandaise Sauce while ham is baking; keep warm.
4. Place ham on platter; cover lightly with aluminum foil. Purée cooked parsley in a blender or food processor; stir mixture into Mock Hollandaise Sauce. Season sauce with salt and pepper. Heat sauce thoroughly; serve with ham.
3 OR 4 SERVINGS

Baked Stuffed Pork Chops

4 rib pork chops, 1 inch thick
1 tablespoon finely chopped onion
¼ cup diced celery
2 tablespoons butter or margarine
1 cup soft bread crumbs

½ teaspoon salt
⅛ teaspoon poultry seasoning
2 tablespoons shortening
1 can (10¾ ounces) condensed cream of mushroom soup
⅓ cup water

1. Trim excess fat from pork chops. Slit each chop from

Pork Braised with Celery in Egg and Lemon Sauce

¼ cup butter
4 pounds lean pork, cut in 2-inch cubes
1 large onion, minced
2 cups water
2 bunches celery (stalks only), cut in 1-inch pieces

Egg and Lemon Sauce:
¼ cup butter
3 tablespoons flour
2 cups pork stock
Juice of 2 lemons
3 eggs, separated
Salt and pepper to taste

1. Melt butter in a Dutch oven and sauté pork until golden brown. Add onion and cook until translucent. Add water. Cover and simmer 1 to 1½ hours or until meat is just tender. Add celery and simmer about 15 minutes, or until tender. Drain off 2 cups stock and strain. Keep meat warm.
2. To make sauce, melt butter in a saucepan; add flour and cook about 1 minute, stirring constantly; do not brown. Add pork stock and lemon juice. Simmer, stirring constantly, until sauce thickens.
3. Separate eggs. Beat whites until soft peaks form. Beat yolks until thick. Fold yolks into whites. Using a wire whisk, slowly add sauce to eggs. Pour over pork mixture. Heat and serve at once.
8 SERVINGS

Peach 'n' Pork Chop Barbecue

6 pork chops, cut 1 inch
  thick
1 tablespoon fat
¼ cup lightly packed brown
  sugar
1 teaspoon ground cinnamon
½ teaspoon ground cloves
1 can (8 ounces) tomato

sauce
6 canned cling peach halves,
  drained (reserve ¼ cup
  syrup)
¼ cup cider vinegar
1 teaspoon salt
¼ teaspoon pepper

1. Brown chops on both sides in hot fat in a large heavy skillet.
2. Meanwhile, blend a mixture of brown sugar, cinnamon, and cloves with tomato sauce, reserved peach syrup, and vinegar.
3. Place pork chops in cooking pan of chafing dish. Sprinkle with salt and pepper. Place a peach half on each chop. Pour sauce over all.
4. Cover skillet and simmer about 30 minutes, or until pork is tender; baste occasionally with the sauce.
6 SERVINGS

Roast Loin of Pork II

2 tablespoons flour
1½ teaspoons salt
1 teaspoon dry mustard or
  caraway seed
½ teaspoon sugar
¼ teaspoon black pepper
¼ teaspoon ground sage
1 pork loin roast (4 to 5
  pounds)

Topping:
1½ cups applesauce
½ cup brown sugar
¼ teaspoon cinnamon or
  allspice
¼ teaspoon mace
¼ teaspoon salt

1. Mix flour, salt, mustard, sugar, pepper and sage. Rub over surface of meat. Set meat fat side up in a roasting pan.
2. Roast at 325°F 1½ hours.
3. For topping, mix applesauce with brown sugar, cinnamon, mace, and salt. Spread on top of meat.
4. Roast about 45 minutes longer, or until done.
8 TO 10 SERVINGS

Polish Sausage with Red Cabbage

1 head red cabbage, sliced
  (about 2 pounds)
Boiling water
2 tablespoons butter
⅓ cup lemon juice
½ cup red wine or beef
  broth

½ teaspoon salt
¼ teaspoon pepper
¾ pound Polish sausage,
  diced
2 teaspoons brown sugar
1 tablespoon cornstarch or
  potato flour

1. Place cabbage in a colander. Pour boiling water over cabbage. Drain well.
2. Melt butter in a Dutch oven or large heavy skillet. Add cabbage. Stir in lemon juice. Cook and stir about 5 minutes, or until cabbage is pink. Add wine, salt, and pepper. Cover. Simmer over medium-low heat 45 minutes.
3. Mix sugar and cornstarch. Stir into simmering liquid. Bring to boiling, stirring constantly. Reduce heat; add sausage. Cover; cook 30 minutes.
ABOUT 4 SERVINGS

Pork Chops with Vegetables

3 tablespoons vegetable oil
8 lean pork chops
1 can (15 ounces) stewed
  tomatoes
1¾ cups water
1 cup minced celery

1 large green pepper, minced
1 medium onion, minced
1 bay leaf
1 thyme sprig
¼ teaspoon paprika
Salt and pepper to taste

1. Heat oil in a large deep skillet. Add chops and brown on both sides.
2. Turn stewed tomatoes into a bowl. Add water, celery, green pepper, onion, bay leaf, thyme, paprika, salt, and pepper; mix well.
3. Remove excess fat from skillet; add tomato mixture. Cover.
4. Bake at 325°F about 2 hours, or until tender. Serve pork chops with **pilafi** or **potatoes.** Pass gravy separately.
8 SERVINGS

MIXED, GROUND & SPECIALTY MEATS

Hamburger Favorites

1½ pounds ground beef	¼ teaspoon pepper
1½ teaspoons salt	1 tablespoon fat

1. Set out a large, heavy skillet.
2. Mix ground beef lightly with a mixture of salt and pepper.
3. Shape into 6 patties about ¾ inches thick or 8 patties about ½ inch thick.
4. Heat fat in skillet.
5. Put patties in skillet and cook over medium heat until brown on one side. Turn and brown other side. Allow 10 to 15 minutes for cooking thick patties and 6 to 10 minutes for cooking thin patties. Remove from skillet to warm serving platter; garnish with parsley.

4 TO 6 SERVINGS

Meatballs with Lemon Sauce

2 pounds lean beef, ground	garlic press
1 large onion, minced	½ cup flour
3 tablespoons minced parsley	2 cups water
2 tablespoons mint leaves	Salt to taste
½ cup long-grain rice	2 tablespoons butter
Salt and pepper to taste	Juice of 1 or 2 lemons
1 garlic clove, crushed in a	2 eggs, separated

1. Mix thoroughly meat, onion, parsley, mint, rice, salt, pepper, and garlic. Dip hands in flour. Shape meat into round balls about 1 inch in diameter.
2. Bring water and salt to boiling in a large Dutch oven. Add butter and meatballs in a single layer. Simmer covered 40 minutes.
3. Pour stock into a small bowl and add lemon juice. Beat egg yolks until frothy. In another bowl, beat whites until peaks form. Fold in yolks. In a thin stream, pour stock into eggs. Pour over meatballs. Serve hot.

6 SERVINGS

Sautéed Sweetbreads

4 pairs sweetbreads from milk-fed calves	5 tablespoons butter or olive oil for frying
Ice water	Flour seasoned with salt and pepper
2 teaspoons salt	
1 tablespoon lemon juice	

1. Soak sweetbreads in ice water mixed with salt for 1 hour. Drain.
2. Place sweetbreads in boiling water to cover. Add lemon juice and simmer 10 minutes. Drain. Plunge at once into ice water. Remove membranes and connective tissue, and split into 2 pieces.
3. Melt butter or heat olive oil in a skillet. Dip sweetbreads into flour. Fry until golden brown on all sides.

2 SERVINGS

Meatballs with Tomato Sauce

1 pound beef, freshly ground	Salt and pepper to taste
1 large onion, minced	1 cup flour for rolling
3 tablespoons long-grain rice	Olive oil for frying
1 garlic clove	2 tablespoons tomato paste mixed with 1 cup water or beef stock
½ cup minced parsley	
1 tablespoon basil	

1. In a large bowl, combine meat, onion, rice, garlic, parsley, basil, salt, and pepper. Dip hands in flour. Shape meat mixture into round balls about 1½ inches in diameter.
2. Heat oil in a skillet. Sauté the meatballs, turning to brown on all sides. Remove to a baking dish.
3. Pour tomato paste liquid into the skillet. Simmer 3 minutes, stirring and scraping constantly. Strain the juices over the meatballs and add as much water or beef stock as needed to half cover them. Loosely cover wth foil.
4. Bake at 350°F about 40 minutes. Once or twice during the cooking, turn meatballs with a wooden spoon. Serve hot with **pilafi** or **mashed potatoes.**

ABOUT 6 SERVINGS

Health Burgers

¼ cup toasted wheat germ	celery
3 tablespoons milk	2 tablespoons finely chopped onion
1 tablespoon ketchup	1 pound ground beef round
1 teaspoon salt	Hamburger buns
¼ teaspoon Tabasco	Onion rings
2 tablespoons finely chopped	

1. Mix wheat germ, milk, ketchup, salt, Tabasco, celery, and onion in a bowl. Add meat; mix lightly and thoroughly. Shape into 4 patties.
2. Place on greased grill about 4 inches from hot coals. Grill about 7 minutes on each side, or until meat is done as desired.
3. Serve on buns with onion rings.

4 SERVINGS

Health Burgers

Hungarian Pepperdish

4 large red or green pepper
1 pound ground pork or beef
1 onion, chopped
¾ cup tomatoes
1 clove garlic, chopped
1 teaspoon salt
½ teaspoon pepper
1 teaspoon paprika
¾ cup cooked, cold rice
4 tablespoons grated cheese
1¼ cups water

1. Clean peppers and cut off tops. Remove seeds and veins. Place in an ovenproof dish.
2. Mix meat, onions, tomatoes and seasonings. Mix in rice and fill peppers with mixture. Sprinkle with cheese.
3. Pour water in bottom of dish so peppers don't burn on the bottom. Bake in a 350°F oven about 30 minutes till peppers are soft. Serve warm with cold sour cream.
4 SERVINGS

Meat-Stuffed Cabbage

1 large head cabbage (about 4 pounds)
Water
1 tablespoon salt
Cheesecloth
2 pounds lean ground beef
2 bunches green onions, cut in ¼-inch pieces
1 garlic clove, minced
1 medium zucchini, finely chopped (reserve 8 thin slices for garnish)
1 large green pepper, chopped
1 egg, slightly beaten
1 cup fine soft bread crumbs made from whole-grain bread
1½ teaspoons snipped fresh or ¾ teaspoon dried basil leaves
2 teaspoons snipped fresh or 1 teaspoon dried thyme leaves
2 teaspoons snipped fresh or 1 teaspoon dried rosemary leaves
2 teaspoons salt
½ teaspoon freshly ground pepper
1 can (16 ounces) plum tomatoes (reserve liquid)
4 fresh mushrooms, cut in half, for garnish
Water

1. Place cabbage in a Dutch oven. Cover with boiling water; add 1 tablespoon salt. Simmer covered until outer leaves are softened but still firm (about 10 minutes). Drain cabbage; rinse with cold water. Have cheesecloth ready for wrapping stuffed cabbage.
2. Mix remaining ingredients, except the reserved zucchini slices and the mushrooms, until well blended.
3. Core cabbage and pull outside leaves back. Remove inside of cabbage carefully, leaving outside layer 5 or 6 leaves thick. Lay outer leaves on a double thickness of cheesecloth; fill leaves with meat mixture. Wrap stuffed cabbage tightly in cheesecloth; invert on another piece of cheesecloth so that the opening of the cabbage is on the bottom. Wrap cabbage securely, tying the cheesecloth into a handle at the top. Lift wrapped cabbage into Dutch oven. Pour reserved tomato liquid around cabbage. Cover.
4. Bake at 350°F to an internal temperature of 165°F (about 1½ hours). Check temperature by inserting a meat thermometer through leaves and into center of meat. Lift cabbage out of Dutch oven; let stand 10 minutes.
5. While cabbage is standing, place zucchini slices and

mushrooms in a medium saucepan. Simmer in a small amount of water until barely tender (about 3 minutes); drain.
6. Remove outside layer of cheesecloth from cabbage; place a pie plate on cabbage and invert. Remove remaining cheesecloth; place serving platter on cabbage and invert. Gently shape cabbage with hands if necessary. Garnish top of cabbage with zucchini slices and mushrooms. Cut into wedges and serve.
8 TO 10 SERVINGS

Cabbage Rolls with Mushroom Sauce

1 onion, chopped
1 clove garlic, crushed (optional)
2 tablespoons butter
¾ cup uncooked raw rice
½ pound ground beef or veal
½ pound ground pork
1 teaspoon salt
¼ teaspoon pepper
1 whole head cabbage (about 3 pounds)
Boiling water
2 cups beef broth or stock
1 can (about 10 ounces) condensed cream of mushroom soup

1. Sauté onion and garlic in butter in a large skillet, about 5 minutes. Add rice, meat, salt, and pepper. Stir-fry just to mix well. Remove from heat.
2. Remove core from cabbage. Place whole head in a large kettle filled with boiling water. Cover; cook 3 minutes. Remove softened outer leaves. Repeat until all leaves are softened and have been removed. Cut thick stem from each leaf.
3. Taking one large cabbage leaf at a time, spoon about 1 rounded tablespoonful of meat mixture in center of leaf. Cover with a small leaf. Tuck ends up and just over edge of filling; place one end of leaf over filling and roll up loosely. If desired, secure with a wooden pick. Repeat until all filling and leaves are used. Place cabbage rolls in a large casserole; do not make more than 2 layers.
4. Combine beef broth and mushroom soup; pour over cabbage rolls.
5. Bake at 350°F about 1½ hours.
8 TO 12 SERVINGS

Meatballs

Peel of 1 lemon, grated
1 sprig parsley
2 cloves garlic peeled
1 pound ground beef
1 teaspoon salt
¼ teaspoon pepper
Pinch grated nutmeg
1 slice bread, crumbled
Milk
1 egg, beaten
2 to 3 tablespoons olive oil or other cooking oil

1. Mince together grated lemon peel, parsley, and garlic.
2. Mix ground beef with salt, pepper, nutmeg, and lemon peel mixture.
3. Soak bread in a small amount of milk, squeeze dry, and add with egg to meat mixture. Blend well.
4. On a lightly floured surface, form mixture into patties about ½ inch thick and 1½ inches wide.
5. Place the patties in hot oil in a skillet. Brown about 2 minutes on each side. Drain and serve hot.
4 TO 6 SERVINGS

Caraway Meat Loaf

1 pound ground beef
1 cup soft bread crumbs
(from 2 slices white or rye
bread)
1 small onion, minced
⅔ cup beer

1 egg
½ teaspoon caraway seed
½ teaspoon salt
¼ teaspoon pepper
⅓ cup chili sauce

1. Combine beef, crumbs, onion, ⅓ cup beer, egg, caraway seed, salt, and pepper.
2. Shape into a loaf. Place in a roasting pan. (Or pack into a 7x3½x2-inch loaf pan.)
3. Bake at 350°F 45 minutes.
4. Simmer chili sauce and remaining ⅓ cup beer about 5 minutes; serve over slices of meat loaf.
4 SERVINGS

Frankfurter Kabobs

12 frankfurters, each cut in 3
or 4 pieces
12 whole mushrooms,
cleaned
3 medium tomatoes, cut in
quarters or eighths

1 cup Basic Molasses
Barbecue Sauce (below)
1 tablespoon prepared
mustard
1 to 2 tablespoons pineapple
syrup (optional)

1. Thread franks, mushrooms, and tomato pieces onto 8- to 10-inch skewers.
2. Combine sauce, mustard, and pineapple syrup, if used. Mix well and brush generously over kabobs.
3. Cook 5 to 6 inches above the hot coals, 3 to 4 minutes on each side; brush with the sauce several times during cooking.
6 KABOBS

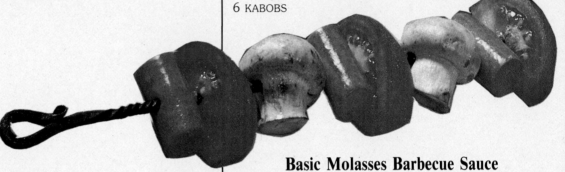

Basic Molasses Barbecue Sauce

¼ cup cornstarch
4 cups lemon juice (about 2
dozen lemons)
2 cups cooking oil
1 jar (12 ounces) light or
dark molasses

¼ cup salt
1 tablespoon black pepper
6 bay leaves, broken in
pieces
3 cloves garlic, minced

1. Combine cornstarch and lemon juice in a saucepan. Cook and stir over low heat until mixture bubbles and thickens. Cool.
2. Using rotary or electric beater, beat in remaining ingredients until thoroughly blended and thickened.
3. Store in refrigerator until needed.
ABOUT 2 CUPS SAUCE

Hunter's Stew

6 pounds diced cooked meat
(use at least ½ pound of
each of the following: beef,
ham, lamb, sausage, veal,
pork, venison or rabbit,
wild duck, wild goose, or
pheasant)*
5 ounces salt pork, diced
1 onion, minced
2 leeks, minced
2 tablespoons flour

1 pound fresh mushrooms,
sliced, or 3 cans (4 ounces
each) sliced mushrooms
(undrained)
1 to 2 cups water or
bouillon
6 pounds sauerkraut
2 teaspoons salt
1 teaspoon pepper
2 teaspoons sugar
1 cup Madeira

1. Fry salt pork until golden but not crisp in an 8-quart kettle. Add onion and leeks. Stir-fry 3 minutes. Stir in flour.
2. Add mushrooms with liquid and water to kettle; simmer 5 minutes.
3. Drain and rinse sauerkraut. Add to kettle along with cooked meat, salt, pepper, and sugar. Cover; cook over medium-low heat 1½ hours.
4. Stir in wine. Add more salt, pepper, and sugar to taste. Simmer 15 minutes; do not boil.
12 TO 16 SERVINGS

*If meat must be prepared especially for this stew, each piece should be braised separately. Put meat, poultry, or game into a Dutch oven with 1 carrot, 1 stalk celery, 1 onion, 1 parsnip, 1 clove garlic or 1 sprig parsley, 5 peppercorns, 1 cup water, and 1 cup wine. Simmer, covered, until meat is tender.

Note: When wine is added, chopped apples, heavy cream, and/or cooked small potatoes may also be added.

Jiffy Beer Chili

½ pound ground beef
½ cup chopped onion
(frozen, or 1 medium fresh)
1 can (6 ounces) tomato
paste
1 can or bottle (12 ounces)
beer

1 can (16 ounces) kidney
beans (undrained)
1 to 1½ teaspoons chili
powder
1 teaspoon sugar
1 teaspoon garlic salt
½ teaspoon oregano

1. Lightly brown ground beef and onion in a heavy medium saucepan; cook until onion is soft.
2. Add tomato paste and beer; stir up brown bits.
3. Add remaining ingredients. Cook slowly uncovered 10 to 15 minutes, or until onion is tender. Add a little water, if needed.
5 CUPS; 4 SERVINGS

Mixed Grill

1 pound lamb, pork, or veal
  kidneys
¼ cup butter or margarine
1 tablespoon lemon juice
½ teaspoon marjoram leaves
12 large mushroom caps

3 medium tomatoes, halved
6 knockwurst
Salt and pepper
2 tablespoons chopped
  parsley

1. Prepare kidneys by slicing in half crosswise and removing fat and connective tissue (if using veal kidneys, cut into chunks and remove fat and connective tissue).
2. Melt butter and add lemon juice and marjoram.
3. Place mushrooms, tomatoes, kidneys, and knockwurst on grill about 5 inches above medium coals. Brush with butter mixture and season with salt and pepper. Turning knockwurst and kidneys occasionally, grill 10 to 15 minutes, or until vegetables are fork tender and knockwurst browned. Kidneys should be slightly pink. Remove from grill and serve, sprinkling parsley over vegetables.
6 SERVINGS

Meat Casserole

2 pounds brisket of beef	2 teaspoons salt
¾ pound fresh ham or lean shoulder of pork	2 teaspoons paprika
4 large yellow onions	2 teaspoons freshly ground black pepper
2 ounces salad oil	3-4 cloves garlic, pressed
1 pound green peppers	1 bunch parsley
1 pound tomatoes	

1. Cut the meat in cubes 1x1-inches in size.
2. Chop the onions and fry in the oil.
3. Brown the meat cubes in the rest of the oil.
4. Cut the peppers in strips and the tomatoes in wedges and mix with the meat. Add the salt and the other seasonings.
5. Pour on cold water just to cover. Bring to boil and let boil until meat is tender, about 1 to 1½ hours. Serve the casserole sprinkled with chopped parsley.
8 SERVINGS

Cabbage Rolls

1 whole head cabbage (about 3 pounds)	¼ teaspoon pepper
Boiling water	5 slices bacon
1 pound ground beef	1 can (16 ounces) tomatoes or sauerkraut
½ pound ground veal	⅓ cup bouillon or meat broth
¾ cup chopped onion	½ teaspoon sugar
½ cup packaged precooked rice	¼ teaspoon salt
1 egg, beaten	¼ teaspoon pepper
1 teaspoon salt	

1. Remove core from cabbage. Place whole head in a large kettle filled with boiling water. Cover; cook 3 minutes. Remove softened outer leaves. Repeat until all large leaves have been removed (about 20 leaves). Cut thick center stem from each slice.
2. Sauté meat with onion 5 minutes. Remove from heat. Stir in rice, egg, 1 teaspoon salt, and ¼ teaspoon pepper.
3. Place 3 tablespoons meat mixture on each cabbage leaf. Roll each leaf, tucking ends in toward center. Fasten securely with wooden picks. Place each roll seam side down in a large skillet or Dutch oven.
4. Lay bacon slices over top of cabbage rolls.
5. Mix tomatoes, bouillon, sugar, ¼ teaspoon salt, and ¼ teaspoon pepper. Pour over cabbage rolls.
6. Cover; simmer about 1 hour, turning occasionally.
ABOUT 10 SERVINGS

Shepherdess' Pie

1½ cups Béchamel Sauce	pepper
1 medium onion, minced	1 teaspoon vinegar
1 egg, beaten	1 pound coarsely ground lamb or lean beef
¼ cup fresh cracker crumbs	4 cups mashed potatoes
¼ cup chopped parsley	½ cup grated kefalotyri cheese
1 teaspoon salt	1 teaspoon paprika
1 teaspoon thyme	
¼ teaspoon ground red	

1. Combine ¾ cup Béchamel Sauce, onion, egg, cracker crumbs, parsley, salt, thyme, red pepper, and vinegar.
2. Combine sauce with meat, tossing with 2 forks to mix lightly. Spoon mixture into a baking dish. Level top lightly with the back of the spoon. Make an indentation in the center.
3. Bake at 350°F 30 minutes, removing fat as it collects in the indentation.
4. Combine potatoes with remaining sauce.
5. Remove meat from oven when done. Sprinkle with cheese. Cover with potatoes. Sprinkle with paprika. Bake 20 minutes.
4 SERVINGS

Béchamel Sauce: Melt **¼ cup butter.** Whisk in **3 tablespoons flour.** Cook, stirring constantly, for 1 minute. Slowly pour in **1½ cups milk,** scalded. Cook, stirring constantly, until mixture coats a wooden spoon.

Mexican Meatballs

Sauce:

1 clove garlic, minced	½ pound ground pork
¼ cup oil or lard	¼ pound ground cooked ham
1 cup tomato sauce	½ cup chopped onion
2 cups beef broth, or 2 cups water plus 2 beef bouillon cubes	2 slices dry bread
	¼ cup milk
1 teaspoon salt	1 egg
½ teaspoon oregano	1½ teaspoons salt
½ teaspoon cumin (comino)	¼ teaspoon pepper
2 chipotle chilies, chopped	2 canned chipotle chilies, chopped
	2 hard-cooked eggs, coarsely diced (optional)

Meatballs:
1 pound ground beef

1. For sauce, cook onion and garlic in hot oil in a large skillet until onion is soft. Add remaining sauce ingredients and heat to boiling, stirring constantly. Reduce heat and let simmer while preparing meatballs.
2. For meatballs, combine beef, pork, ham, and onion.
4. Beat egg slightly and add salt, pepper, and chopped chilies. Add egg mixture and bread-milk mixture to meat; mix well.
5. Form into balls about 1½ inches in diameter. If desired, press a chunk of hard-cooked egg into center of each meatball.
6. Put meatballs into simmering sauce; cover and simmer 1 hour.
25 TO 30 LARGE MEATBALLS (OR ABOUT 75 SMALL APPETIZER-SIZE MEATBALLS)

Easy Hunter's Stew

¼ cup all-purpose flour
1 teaspoon paprika or caraway seed
2 tablespoons butter or margarine
1 pound lean beef, cubed
1 pound lean pork, cubed
2 pounds sauerkraut, rinsed and drained
2 medium onions, sliced

12 ounces kielbasa (Polish sausage) or 6 smokie link sausages, cut in 1-inch pieces
1 can (4 ounces) sliced mushrooms (undrained)
½ cup dry white wine
Chopped parsley (optional)
Small boiled potatoes (optional)

1. Combine flour and paprika; coat meat pieces.
2. Heat butter in a Dutch oven or saucepot. Add meat and brown on all sides. Add sauerkraut, onion, sausage, musrooms, and wine; mix. Cover and cook over low heat 1½ to 2 hours, or until meat is tender.
3. Remove meat and vegetables to serving platter. If desired, garnish with parsley and serve with small boiled potatoes.
6 TO 8 SERVINGS

Chili con Carne with Beans

1 pound boneless beef, cut in 1-inch cubes
1 pound boneless pork, cut in 1-inch cubes
3 tablespoons lard
1 cup beef broth
1 teaspoon salt
1 to 2 tablespoons chili powder
2 cloves garlic, minced

2 tablespoons lard
1 large onion, coarsely chopped
3 fresh tomatoes, peeled, seeded, and cut in pieces
1 can (16 ounces) white beans, drained
1 can (15 ounces) red kidney beans, drained

1. Brown meat in 3 tablespoons lard in a large skillet. Add broth; cover and cook 30 minutes.
2. Add salt, chili powder, and garlic; mix. Cook covered until meat is tender (about 1 hour).
3. Meanwhile, heat 2 tablespoons lard in a skillet. Add onion and tomato; mix well. Cover and cook until vegetables are soft. Purée vegetables.
4. Add purée and beans to meat; mix well. Heat thoroughly.
6 TO 10 SERVINGS

Green Chili Meat Loaf

1½ pounds ground beef
1 cup soft bread crumbs
1 cup canned undrained tomatoes
1 can (4 ounces) green chilies, drained,

seeded, and chopped
3 tablespoons dried onion flakes
1¼ teaspoons salt
¼ teaspoon garlic salt

1. Combine all ingredients thoroughly. Turn into a 9x5x3-inch loaf dish and press lightly.
2. Bake at 375°F 1 hour.
ABOUT 6 SERVINGS

Tomatoes Stuffed with Meat and Rice

12 large firm tomatoes
1 teaspoon sugar
½ teaspoon salt
¾ cup olive oil
2 onions, minced
1 garlic clove, crushed in a garlic press
1 pound lean ground beef or

lamb
¼ cup long-grain rice
¼ cup chopped parsley
1 teaspoon mint
½ teaspoon cinnamon
Salt and pepper to taste
½ cup water

1. Slice tops from tomatoes and save. Remove pulp and save. Sprinkle insides of tomatoes with sugar and salt.
2. Heat ¼ cup oil in a large skillet. Add onion and garlic and sauté until onion is translucent. Add meat and cook until no longer red. Add rice, seasonings, and tomato pulp. Simmer 10 minutes. Cool slightly.
3. Fill tomatoes two thirds full, leaving room for rice to expand. (If too much filling is added, tomatoes may break open.) Place in a baking dish. Put tops on tomatoes. Drizzle remaining olive oil between tomatoes. Add ½ cup water.
4. Bake at 350°F about 40 minutes, or until rice is tender, basting occasionally. (Add more liquid to dish, if necessary.)
12 SERVINGS

Stuffed Peppers: Follow recipe for Tomatoes Stuffed with Meat and Rice, substituting **green peppers** for tomatoes. Remove seeds from peppers and discard. Proceed as directed.

Taco Skillet Casserole

1½ pounds ground beef
½ cup chopped onion
1 clove garlic, minced
1 teaspoon salt
¼ teaspoon pepper
1 teaspoon chili powder (see Note)
2 cups canned tomato sauce

(see Note)
8 tortillas, cut into ½-inch strips
Oil for frying
½ cup shredded Monterey Jack or mild Cheddar cheese
Shredded lettuce

1. Crumble ground beef into a large skillet and brown well. If beef is very fat, pour off excess fat. Add onion and garlic and cook about 5 minutes, until onion is soft, stirring frequently. Stir in salt, pepper, chili powder, and tomato sauce and continue cooking over low heat about 15 minutes longer.
2. Meanwhile, in a separate skillet, fry tortilla strips in hot oil a few minutes until slightly crisped. Drain on absorbent paper. Stir tortilla strips into meat mixture and cook about 5 minutes longer, stirring frequently to prevent sticking. Sprinkle with cheese. As soon as cheese melts, remove from heat and serve. Top each serving with shredded lettuce.
6 SERVINGS

Note: **2 cups canned taco** or **enchilada sauce** may be substituted for chili powder and tomato sauce, if preferred.

Potato-Frosted Meat Loaf

1½ pounds ground beef
½ cup chopped onion
2 teaspoons salt
¼ teaspoon pepper
⅛ teaspoon oregano

⅔ cup quick or old-
 fashioned oats, uncooked
1 egg, beaten
½ cup milk
2 cups hot mashed potatoes*

1. Thoroughly combine all ingredients except mashed potatoes. Pack firmly into an 8½x4½x2½-inch loaf pan.
2. Bake at 350°F about 1 hour. Drain off excess fat. Let stand a few minutes; remove from pan.
3. Place on broiler rack. Frost loaf with mashed potatoes.
4. Place under broiler 5 to 7 inches from heat 2 to 3 minutes. Serve immediately.
8 SERVINGS

*Four medium-size potatoes will yield about 2 cups mashed potatoes.

Empanadas

Picadillo:
½ pound coarsely chopped
 beef
½ pound coarsely chopped
 pork
½ cup chopped onion
1 small clove garlic, minced
½ cup chopped raw apple
¾ cup chopped canned
 tomatoes
¼ cup raisins

¾ teaspoon salt
⅛ teaspoon pepper
Dash ground cinnamon
Dash ground cloves
¼ cup chopped almonds

Pastry:
4 cups all-purpose flour
1¼ teaspoons salt
1⅓ cups lard or shortening
⅔ cup icy cold water (about)

1. For picadillo, cook beef and pork together in large skillet until well browned. Add onion and garlic and cook until onion is soft. Add remaining ingredients, except almonds, and simmer 15 to 20 minutes longer until flavors are well blended.
2. Stir in almonds. Cool.
3. For pastry, mix flour and salt in a bowl. Cut in lard until mixture resembles coarse crumbs. Sprinkle water over flour mixture, stirring lightly with a fork until all dry ingredients hold together. Divide dough in four portions.
4. On a lightly floured surface, roll one portion of dough at a time to ⅛-inch thickness.
5. Using a 5-inch cardboard circle as a pattern, cut rounds of pastry with a knife. Place a rounded spoonful of filling in center of each round. Fold one side over filling to meet opposite side. Seal by dampening inside edges of pastry and pressing together with tines of fork.
6. Place empanadas on a baking sheet. Bake at 400°F 15 to 20 minutes, or until lightly browned. Or fry in **fat for deep frying** heated to 365°F until browned (about 3 minutes); turn once.
24 TO 30 EMPANADAS

Dried Lima Casserole

1 pound dried lima beans
1 large onion, sliced
¼ cup lard or oil
¼ pound chorizo or Italian-
 style sausage meat

¼ pound diced ham
1 cup canned enchilada
 sauce
½ cup shredded Monterey
 Jack

1. Soak lima beans in water to cover for 1 hour. Bring to boiling, reduce heat, and cook until tender; add more water if necessary.
2. Meanwhile, cook onion in lard until soft (about 5 minutes). If using sausage in casing, remove from casing and add to onion, crumbling slightly. Cook and stir until well browned. Add ham and enchilada sauce; cover and cook about 30 minutes.
3. Skim off excess fat. Add cooked beans and continue cooking about 15 minutes longer to blend flavors. Sprinkle with cheese just before serving.
6 TO 8 SERVINGS

Note: This skillet-type casserole dish can be transferred to a baking dish before the cheese is sprinkled on top. It may then be refrigerated for later serving. Heat in a 350°F oven 20 to 30 minutes, or until bubbling.

Saucy Ham Loaf

Meat loaf:
1½ pounds ground cooked
 ham
½ pound ground veal
½ pound ground pork
2 eggs, fork beaten
½ teaspoon salt
⅛ teaspoon ground black
 pepper
½ teaspoon ground nutmeg
½ teaspoon dry mustard
¼ teaspoon ground thyme
¼ cup finely chopped onion
½ cup finely chopped green
 pepper

2 tablespoons finely chopped
 parsley
¾ cup soft enriched bread
 crumbs
¾ cup apple juice

Sauce:
⅔ cup packed light brown
 sugar
2 teaspoons cornstarch
1 teaspoon dry mustard
1 teaspoon ground allspice
⅔ cup apricot nectar
3 tablespoons lemon juice
2 teaspoons vinegar

1. Combine ham, veal, and pork with eggs, salt, pepper, nutmeg, dry mustard, and thyme in a large bowl. Add onion, green pepper, and parsley and toss to blend. Add bread crumbs and apple juice; mix thoroughly but lightly. Turn into a 9x5x3-inch loaf pan and flatten top.
2. Bake at 350°F 1 hour.
3. Meanwhile, prepare sauce for topping. Blend brown sugar, cornstarch, dry mustard, and allspice in a small saucepan. Add apricot nectar, lemon juice, and vinegar. Bring rapidly to boiling and cook about 2 minutes, stirring constantly. Reduce heat and simmer 10 minutes to allow flavors to blend.
4. Remove meat loaf from oven; pour off and reserve juices. Unmold loaf in a shallow baking pan. Spoon some of the reserved juices and then the sauce over loaf. Return to oven 30 minutes.
5. Place loaf on a warm platter and garnish as desired.
8 TO 10 SERVINGS

Silly Dogs

1 pound (about 10) skinless
  franks
Water to cover
10 buns, hot dog and
  hamburger
Mustard, ketchup, pickle
  relish

1. Cut franks with a sharp knife to make the following shapes:
   – Along one side, cut slits halfway into frank and ¼ inch apart up to middle. Turn frank over; repeat with opposite side from middle to end. – Cut frankfurter in long quarters, making 4 separate strips.
   – Make 3 parallel slits at each end of frankfurter, cutting toward center. Leave 1 inch in center of frank uncut.
   – Cut frankfurter in half crosswise. Cut deep slits along one side of each half, ¼ inch apart.
2. Bring water to a boil. Pour over franks in a saucepan removed from heat. Cover and let stand 7 minutes. Franks will curl up into Silly Dog shapes.
3. Serve franks that have curled into a circle in hamburger buns; straight ones in hot dog buns. Serve with condiments.
ABOUT 10 SERVINGS

English Meat Patties

1 pound ground beef
½ cup fine dry bread
  crumbs
½ cup beer
1 small onion, finely minced
½ teaspoon salt
Dash pepper and garlic
  powder
Oil

Gravy:
2 tablespoons drippings
2 tablespoons flour
½ cup beer
½ cup water
1 teaspoon Worcestershire
  sauce
¼ teaspoon salt
Dash pepper

1. Combine beef, crumbs, beer, onion, salt, and pepper. Shape into 4 patties.
2. Pan-fry in a very small amount of oil in a skillet, pouring off drippings as they accumulate. Turn once, carefully, and cook until as done as desired. Place patties on a platter; keep warm.
3. For gravy, pour off drippings from skillet; return 2 tablespoons. Stir in flour. Add beer; stir until smooth. Add water and seasonings. Cook, stirring constantly, until thickened; stir up brown bits. After gravy boils, reduce heat and simmer 2 to 3 minutes to mellow beer flavor.
4 SERVINGS

Brewerburgers: Follow recipe for English Meat Patties; omit gravy. If desired, broil or grill over coals.

Spanish Take-Along Casserole

1½ pounds ground beef
½ cup chopped onion
¼ cup chopped green
  pepper
¼ cup chopped celery
1 can (8 ounces) pizza sauce
2 cups (about 4 ounces)
  medium noodles, cooked
  and drained
1 teaspoon salt
1 carton (16 ounces) cream-
  style cottage cheese

1. Brown ground beef, onion, green pepper, and celery in a skillet; drain off excess fat. Combine with remaining ingredients.
2. Put into a 2-quart casserole. (If desired, cover and refrigerate until ready to finish.)
3. Bake, covered, at 350°F 30 minutes, or until heated through. Garnish with **green pepper rings.**
6 TO 8 SERVINGS

Savannah Beef and Noodles

1 pound chopped beef
1 cup chopped onion
1 can (28 ounces) tomatoes
  (undrained)
2 teaspoons salt
2 teaspoons chili powder
1 teaspoon Worcestershire
  sauce
3 cups cooked noodles
1 can (5¾ ounces) pitted
  ripe olives, sliced
2 cups (8 ounces) shredded
  Cheddar cheese

1. Brown ground beef and onion in a skillet; drain off excess fat. Add tomatoes, salt, chili powder, and Worcestershire sauce; simmer 30 minutes.
2. Alternate layers of half the noodles, half the meat mixture, and half the ripe olives in a 2½-quart casserole; repeat layers. Top with shredded cheese.
3. Bake, covered, at 350°F 30 minutes, or until heated through.
   6 TO 8 SERVINGS

Silly Dogs

Sataras

Sataras

½ pound beef for stew (1- to 1½-inch cubes)
½ pound lamb for stew (1- to 1½-inch cubes)
½ pound pork cubes (1- to 1½ inches)
2 tablespoons butter or margarine
3 onions, peeled and chopped
4 green peppers (seedy centers discarded), cut in pieces
1 clove garlic, crushed
1 tablespoon paprika
1 teaspoon salt
1 teaspoon cumin seed, crushed
1 cup water
3 medium tomatoes, peeled and cut in pieces
1 cup sour cream

1. Brown meat on all sides in butter in a skillet. Add onion, green pepper, garlic, and paprika; stir. Cook 3 or 4 minutes.
2. Turn contents of skillet into an electric cooker. Sprinkle with salt and cumin. Add water to skillet; heat and stir to loosen browned particles. Pour into cooker; stir.
3. Cover and cook on Low 8 to 10 hours.
4. Add tomato and sour cream to stew; mix.
5. Cover and cook on High 30 minutes.
6. Serve hot with **fluffy hot rice** and **fresh vegetable salad.**
6 TO 8 SERVINGS

Applesauce-Topped Beef and Sausage Loaf

Meat Loaf:
1 pound ground beef
½ pound pork sausage
½ cup dry bread or cracker crumbs
½ cup beer
1 small onion, minced
1 egg, slightly beaten
½ teaspoon salt
¼ teaspoon each sage, thyme, and garlic powder
⅛ teaspoon pepper

Topping and Sauce:
1⅓ cups applesauce
¼ cup beer

1. For meat loaf, mix ingredients. Shape into an elongated loaf. Place in a shallow roasting pan.

2. Bake at 350°F 50 minutes.
3. Spoon fat from pan. Spread ⅓ cup applesauce over meat loaf. Bake 10 minutes longer.
4. For sauce, heat 1 cup applesauce and beer to simmering; serve over meat loaf slices.
6 SERVINGS

Red-Topper Meat Loaf

Meat loaf:
2 tablespoons butter or margarine
¾ cup finely chopped onion
¼ cup chopped green pepper
1½ pounds lean ground beef
½ pound bulk pork sausage
1 cup uncooked oats, quick or old fashioned
2 eggs, beaten
¾ cup tomato juice
¼ cup prepared horseradish
2 teaspoons salt
1 teaspoon dry mustard

Topping:
1 to 3 tablespoons brown sugar
1 teaspoon dry mustard
¼ cup ketchup

1. For meat loaf, heat butter in a skillet. Mix in onion and green pepper; cook about 5 minutes, or until onion is soft.
2. Meanwhile, lightly mix beef, sausage, and oats in a large bowl. Combine eggs, tomato juice, horseradish, salt, and dry mustard, add to meat mixture and mix lightly. Turn into a 9x5x3-inch loaf pan and press lightly.
3. For topping, mix brown sugar with dry mustard and blend in ketchup. Spread over meat loaf.
4. Bake at 375°F about 1 hour. Remove from oven and allow meat to stand several minutes before slicing.
ABOUT 8 SERVINGS

Taco Casserole

1 pound ground beef
1 package (1.25 ounces) taco seasoning mix
1 cup water
1 can (15 ounces) refried beans with sausage
2 cups shredded lettuce
¼ cup chopped onion
1 tablespoon chopped green

chilies
1 cup (4 ounces) shredded Cheddar cheese
Nacho-flavored tortilla chips
Chopped tomato
Sliced ripe olives
Sour cream
Taco sauce

1. Brown ground beef in a skillet; drain off excess fat. Add taco mix and water. Simmer, uncovered, until mixture is thickened (about 15 minutes).
2. Lightly grease bottom of an 11x7-inch baking dish. Spread refried beans evenly on the bottom. Sprinkle with shredded lettuce, onion, and chilies; top with ground beef mixture. (If desired, cover and refrigerate until ready to finish.)
3. Bake, uncovered, at 400°F 15 minutes. Sprinkle with shredded cheese and bake an additional 5 minutes, or until cheese is melted and mixture is heated through.
4. Remove from oven and garnish with tortilla chips.
5. Serve with chopped tomato, sliced olives, sour cream, and taco sauce in separate serving dishes.
6 SERVINGS

Cheese Ball Casserole

1 pound ground lean pork
½ pound smoked ham, ground
1 green pepper, finely chopped
1 small onion, finely chopped
3 cloves garlic, minced
2 tablespoons snipped parsley
1 can (16 ounces) tomatoes, well drained

2 tablespoons tomato juice
2 teaspoons sugar
½ teaspoon salt
¼ teaspoon pepper
½ cup dark seedless raisins
¼ cup chopped green olives
1 tablespoon capers
2 cups shredded tortillas
½ pound sharp Cheddar cheese, thinly sliced
1 egg, beaten
Tortillas

1. Cook pork in a skillet until no longer pink. Mix in remaining ingredients, except cheese, egg, and whole tortillas. Heat for about 20 minutes, stirring occasionally.
2. Meanwhile, cover bottom and sides of a 1½-quart casserole with overlapping cheese slices.
3. When meat mixture is heated, quickly stir in egg and spoon into lined casserole. Around edge of dish overlap small pieces (quarters) of tortillas and remaining cheese slices.
4. Set in a 325°F oven 15 minutes, or until cheese is bubbly.
5. If desired, garnish center with green pepper strips and parsley arranged to form a flower. Serve with warm tortillas.
8 SERVINGS

Baked Steak Patties

1 pound ground beef
½ pound pork sausage meat
2 cups cooked white rice
1 egg
6 bacon slices

1 package (1⅜ ounces) dry onion soup mix
3 cups water
2 tablespoons flour

1. Combine ground beef, sausage, rice, and egg. Shape to form 6 patties. Wrap each with a bacon slice; secure with wooden pick. Place in an 11x7-inch baking dish.
2. Bake, uncovered, at 350°F 30 minutes; drain off excess fat.
3. Meanwhile, combine soup mix and 2½ cups water in a saucepan. Cook, covered, 10 minutes.
4. Mix the remaining ½ cup water and flour until smooth. Gradually add to soup mixture, stirring until thickened.
5. Pour over steak patties and bake an additional 20 minutes. Remove picks before serving.
6 SERVINGS

Note: The gravy may be served with the steak patties or covered and refrigerated. Reheat and serve with mashed potatoes at the next evening's meal.

Beef and Rice Bake

1 pound ground beef
1 package (1⅜ ounces) dry onion soup mix
¾ cup uncooked white rice
1½ cups boiling water

1 can (16 ounces) tomatoes (undrained)
1 cup (4 ounces) shredded Cheddar cheese

1. Brown ground beef in a skillet; drain off excess fat. Combine with soup mix, rice, boiling water, and tomatoes. Put into a 2-quart casserole.
2. Bake, covered, at 350°F 45 minutes, or until rice is tender. Uncover; sprinkle with cheese. Bake an additional 5 minutes, or until cheese is melted.
6 SERVINGS

Party Beef Casserole

2 pounds ground beef
¾ cup chopped onion
1 garlic clove, minced
½ cup chopped green pepper
½ cup chopped celery
1 teaspoon salt
½ teaspoon pepper
1 can (15 ounces) tomato sauce
1 can (8 ounces) mushroom

stems and pieces, drained
1 can (6 ounces) tomato paste
½ cup sherry
2 tablespoons Worcestershire sauce
1 package (7 ounces) shell macaroni, cooked and drained
1 cup (4 ounces) shredded Cheddar cheese

1. Brown ground beef, onion, garlic, green pepper, and celery in a skillet; drain off excess fat. Combine with remaining ingredients, except shredded cheese. Put into a 3-quart casserole.
2. Bake, covered, at 350°F 45 minutes. Sprinkle with shredded cheese and bake an additional 5 minutes, or until heated through.
8 TO 10 SERVINGS

Pastichio

3 tablespoons olive oil
2 pounds ground beef or
  lamb
1 large onion, grated
Few parsley sprigs, chopped
1 tablespoon tomato paste
  mixed with ½ cup water
1 pound elbow macaroni,
  cooked according to
  directions on package and

drained
1 pound fresh kefalotyri
  cheese, grated

Béchamel Sauce:
½ cup butter, melted
7 tablespoons flour
1½ quarts milk, heated to
  lukewarm
10 eggs, separated

1. Heat oil in a large skillet. Add meat and onion and cook until meat is brown. Add chopped parsley and diluted tomato paste. Cover and simmer for 30 minutes. If any liquid remains, cook meat uncovered until liquid has evaporated.
2. Spread half the cooked macaroni in an 18x12-inch baking dish and cover wtih all the meat mixture. Sprinkle top with three fourths of the cheese. Form a layer with remaining macaroni.
3. Meanwhile, to make sauce, melt butter in a large saucepan. Add flour and mix with a whisk for several minutes. Gradually add milk while stirring; simmer until sauce thickens, stirring frequently.
4. Separate eggs. Beat whites in a bowl until they pile softly. Beat yolks in another bowl. Fold yolks and whites together, then fold in sauce. Spoon over meat and macaroni. Sprinkle with remaining cheese.
5. Bake at 325°F about 45 minutes, or until golden brown. Cool slightly before serving.
8 SERVINGS
Note: Pastichio may be prepared and baked in advance. To reheat, cover tightly with foil and heat in a 200°F oven.

Super Macaroni and Beef Bake

1 package (6 ounces) elbow
  macaroni
1 package (8 ounces) cream
  cheese
1 carton (16 ounces) cream-
  style cottage cheese

¼ cup sour cream
1½ pounds ground beef
3 cans (8 ounces each)
  tomato sauce
½ cup (2 ounces) grated
  Parmesan cheese

1. Cook macaroni in **boiling salted water** until just tender; rinse with cold water. Place half the macaroni in bottom of a greased 13x9-inch baking dish.
2. With mixer beat together cream cheese, cottage cheese, and sour cream; pour over macaroni. Sprinkle remaining macaroni over cheese mixture.
3. Brown ground beef in a skillet; drain off excess fat. Stir in tomato sauce. Evenly spread meat mixture over macaroni. Sprinkle with grated cheese.
4. Bake, uncovered, at 350°F 50 to 60 minutes, or until heated through.
8 SERVINGS

Note: This casserole is best when prepared a day in advance. Cover and refrigerate. Remove from refrigerator 1 hour before baking.

Sloppy Joe for a Crowd

2¼ pounds ground beef
2½ cups chopped onion
1 cup chopped green pepper
1 bottle (14 ounces) ketchup
¼ cup firmly packed brown
  sugar
¼ cup lemon juice
¼ cup vinegar

¼ cup water
2 teaspoons salt
1 teaspoon pepper
1 teaspoon Worcestershire
  sauce
½ teaspoon prepared
  mustard

1. Brown ground beef, onion, and green pepper in a skillet; drain off excess fat. Combine with remaining ingredients. Put into a large oven-proof Dutch oven.
2. Bake, covered, at 325°F 1½ hours. To serve, spoon over **toasted hamburger buns.**
16 SERVINGS

Oriental Meat and Vegetable Stew

2 tablespoons peanut oil or other cooking oil
½ pound mushrooms, cleaned and sliced lengthwise
½ pound roasted pork, cut in strips
½ pound cooked chicken, cut in strips
1 can (8½ ounces) sliced bamboo shoots, drained
1 cup diagonally sliced celery
8 green onions, sliced
2 cloves garlic, crushed
2 teaspoons sugar
½ teaspoon salt
⅛ teaspoon pepper
⅛ teaspoon ginger
3 to 4 teaspoons soy sauce
1 cup chicken broth
3 tablespoons sherry
1 tablespoon cornstarch

1. Heat oil in a large skillet. Add mushrooms; stir and cook until tender. Put mushrooms into an electric cooker. If desired, brown pork and chicken strips in oil in the skillet.
2. Add pork, chicken, bamboo shoots, celery, green onion, garlic, dry seasonings, soy sauce, and chicken broth to cooker; mix well.
3. Cover and cook on High 2 to 2½ hours.
4. Mix sherry and cornstarch. Stir into mixture in cooker.
5. Cover and cook on High 30 minutes.
6. Serve with **hot fluffy rice** or **Chinese noodles**.
ABOUT 6 SERVINGS

Beef and Pea Casserole

1 pound ground beef
1 medium onion, chopped
1 can (10¾ ounces) condensed tomato soup
⅓ cup water
2 cups cooked noodles
1 can (8 ounces) peas, drained*
1 can (4 ounces) sliced mushrooms, drained*

1. Brown ground beef and onion in a skillet; drain off excess fat. Combine with remaining ingredients. Put into a 2-quart casserole.
2. Bake, covered, at 350°F 30 minutes, or until heated through. To serve, sprinkle with **Parmesan cheese** and garnish with **pimento strips**.
6 SERVINGS

*The liquid from the peas or mushrooms may be substituted for the ⅓ cup water.

Mock Chop Suey Casserole

1 pound ground beef
¾ cup chopped onion
2 cups chopped celery
1 can (10¾ ounces) condensed cream of chicken soup
1 can (10¾ ounces) condensed cream of mushroom soup
½ cup uncooked white rice
2 cups boiling water
1 tablespoon soy sauce
1 can (5 ounces) chow mein noodles

1. Brown ground beef in a skillet; drain off excess fat. Combine with remaining ingredients, except chow mein noodles. Put into a 13x9-inch baking dish.
2. Bake, covered, at 350°F 45 minutes, or until rice is tender. Uncover; sprinkle with chow mein noodles. Bake an additional 10 minutes, or until noodles are heated through.
6 SERVINGS

Easy Beefy Casserole

1 pound ground beef
2 cans (16 ounces each) tomatoes (undrained)
1 can (16 ounces) whole kernel corn, drained
¼ cup sliced stuffed olives
½ cup chopped green pepper
1 teaspoon oregano
1½ tablespoons instant minced onion
1 teaspoon salt
½ teaspoon pepper
2 cups (about 4 ounces) uncooked noodles
¼ cup (1 ounces) grated Parmesan cheese

1. Brown ground beef in a skillet; drain off excess fat. Add remaining ingredients, except cheese. Put into a 2-quart casserole.
2. Bake, covered, at 350°F 25 minutes. Remove cover. Sprinkle with grated cheese and bake an additional 5 minutes, or until heated through.
6 SERVINGS

Oriental Meat and Vegetable Stew

Indian Rice and Meat Dish

Rice
1 tablespoon butter or
  margarine
1 cup long-grained rice
2-3 teaspoons curry
2 cups water
1 teaspoon salt

2 tablespoons butter or
  margarine
2 teaspoons curry
1 pound ground beef
1 teaspoon salt
½ teaspoon black pepper,
  freshly ground
1 small fresh cucumber
Chutney
3 eggs

1. Melt the butter or margarine in a saucepan. Stir in curry, then the rice until rice is well coated with curry. Pour on cold water, add salt and bring to a rapid boil while stirring. Put cover on saucepan and let rice boil over a very low heat for 20 minutes. Remove pan from heat and fluff it with two forks.
2. Meanwhile brown butter or margarine in a large, heavy frying pan. Put the ground beef in the pan, crumble it with a wooden fork and let meat brown while stirring. Season with salt, pepper and curry.
3. Rinse and cut the cucumber into ¼-inch long strips. Stir the cucumber strips into the meat mixture and stir carefully with two forks.
4. Stir in the rice and toss gently. Make 3 dents in the mixture and slip 3 eggs slowly into the dents. Let pan stand on a low heat covered until the eggs have set, about 10 minutes. Serve with **chutney** and a **fruit salad**.
SERVES 4

Italian-Style Meat Stew

¼ cup olive oil
1 pound lean beef for stew
  (1½-inch cubes)
1 pound lean lamb for stew
  (1½-inch cubes)
1 can (28 ounces) tomatoes
  (undrained)
1½ cups boiling water
1½ cups chopped onion
1 cup diced celery
2 teaspoons salt

½ teaspoon ground black
  pepper
4 large potatoes, pared and
  quartered (about 3 cups)
5 large carrots, pared and cut
  in strips (about 2 cups)
1 teaspoon basil, crushed
¼ teaspoon garlic powder
½ cup cold water
¼ cup enriched all-purpose
  flour

1. Heat oil in a large saucepot or Dutch oven; add meat and brown on all sides.
2. Add undrained tomatoes, boiling water, onion, celery, salt, and pepper to saucepot. Cover and simmer 1 to 1½ hours, or until meat is almost tender.
3. Add potatoes, carrots, basil, and garlic powder to saucepot; mix well. Simmer 45 minutes, or until meat and vegetables are tender when pierced with a fork.
4. Blend cold water and flour; add gradually to meat-and-vegetable mixture, stirring constantly. Bring to boiling and continue to stir and boil 1 to 2 minutes, or until sauce is thickened. (Leftover sauce may be served the following day on mashed potatoes.)
8 TO 10 SERVINGS

Indian Rice and Meat Dish

Easy Meatball Stroganoff

1 tablespoon instant minced
  onion
½ cup milk
1½ pounds ground beef
⅔ cup quick or old-
  fashioned oats, uncooked
1 teaspoon salt
¼ teaspoon pepper

¼ teaspoon dill weed
⅛ teaspoon garlic powder
1 egg, beaten
1 can (10¾ ounces) con-
  densed golden mushroom
  soup
½ cup sour cream

1. Combine onion and milk. Mix ground beef, oats, salt, pepper, dill weed, garlic powder, egg, and onion-milk mixture.
2. Shape to form 24 meatballs. Place in a shallow 10-inch casserole. Spoon soup over meatballs.
3. Bake, covered, at 350°F 35 minutes, or until meatballs are cooked through, stirring occasionally.
4. Uncover; blend in sour cream. Serve over **hot, cooked rice.**
6 SERVINGS

Texas Chili

2 pounds ground beef
2 medium onions, chopped
1 garlic clove, minced
3 tablespoons flour
2 tablespoons chili powder

2 teaspoons salt
½ teaspoon cumin
3 cups hot water
1 can (15½ ounces) kidney
  beans, drained

1. Brown ground beef, onion, and garlic in a skillet; drain off excess fat.
2. Combine flour, chili powder, salt, and cumin. Gradually stir in hot water. Combine with meat mixture. Pour into a 2½-quart casserole.
3. Bake, covered, at 350°F 1¼ hours. Remove cover. Add beans and bake an additional 15 minutes.
8 SERVINGS

Cheese, Beef, 'n' Macaroni Bake

2 pounds ground beef
½ medium onion, chopped
1 garlic clove, minced
1 jar (15½ ounces) spaghetti
  sauce
1 can (16 ounces) stewed
  tomatoes
1 can (3 ounces) mushroom

stems and pieces, drained
2 cups uncooked large
  macaroni shells
2 cups sour cream
1 package (6 ounces) pro-
  volone cheese slices
1 cup (4 ounces) shredded
  mozzarella cheese

1. Brown ground beef in a skillet; drain off excess fat. Add onion, garlic, spaghetti sauce, tomatoes, and mushrooms. Mix well and simmer 20 minutes.
2. Meanwhile, prepare macaroni shells according to package directions.
3. Put the macaroni shells into a 3-quart casserole. Cover with half the meat sauce. Spread meat with half the sour cream. Top with provolone cheese.
4. Repeat macaroni, meat, and sour-cream layers. Top with mozzarella cheese.
5. Bake, covered, at 350°F 35 to 40 minutes. Remove cover. Bake an additional 10 minutes, or until cheese is lightly browned.
8 TO 10 SERVINGS

Italian Spaghetti Bake

1 pound ground beef
½ cup chopped onion
1 can (16 ounces) tomatoes, drained
1 can (6 ounces) tomato paste
1 garlic clove, minced
1½ teaspoons salt
½ teaspoon oregano
½ teaspoon basil
¼ teaspoon whole marjoram
1 package (7 ounces) spaghetti
2 cups milk
3 eggs
Dash of pepper
1 cup (4 ounces) grated Parmesan cheese
1 cup (4 ounces) shredded mozzarella cheese

1. Brown ground beef and onion in a skillet; drain off excess fat. Stir in tomatoes, tomato paste, garlic, 1 teaspoon salt, oregano, basil, and marjoram.
2. Cook spaghetti in **boiling salted water** until just tender. Spread in bottom of a 13x9-inch baking dish.
3. Combine milk, eggs, pepper, and remaining ½ teaspoon salt. Pour over spaghetti. Sprinkle with Parmesan cheese. Spoon meat mixture over Parmesan cheese. Top with mozzarella cheese.
4. Bake, uncovered, at 350°F 40 to 45 minutes, or until heated through. Let stand 10 minutes. Cut into squares to serve.
8 SERVINGS

Biscuit-Topped Burger

1¼ pounds ground beef
3 tablespoons instant minced onion
½ cup chopped celery
1 can (8 ounces) tomato sauce
2 tablespoons sweet pickle relish
½ teaspoon chili powder
½ teaspoon horseradish
¼ teaspoon salt
1 can (10 ounces) refrigerator biscuits
1 cup (4 ounces) shredded Cheddar cheese
1 tablespoon snipped parsley
½ teaspoon celery seed

1. Brown ground beef, onion, and celery in a skillet; drain

off excess fat. Add tomato sauce, pickle relish, chili powder, horseradish, and salt. Simmer 2 minutes, or until heated through.
2. Spoon into an 11x7-inch baking dish.
3. Separate biscuits; then split each biscuit into 2 layers. Place half the biscuit halves over the meat mixture.
4. Combine cheese, parsley, and celery seed. Sprinkle over biscuit layer. Top with remaining biscuit halves.
5. Bake, uncovered, at 375°F 20 to 25 minutes, or until golden brown.
5 SERVINGS

Hominy-Beef Bake

2 pounds ground beef
3 medium onions, chopped
1 can (16 ounces) tomatoes (undrained)
1 can (16 ounces) whole white hominy, drained
1 can (16 ounces) whole kernel corn, drained
1 can (16 ounces) cream-style corn
1 cup sliced pitted ripe olives
2 cans (8 ounces each) tomato sauce
1 package (1.25 ounces) chili mix
1 package (6 ounces) corn tortillas, cut up

1. Brown ground beef and onion in a skillet; drain off excess fat.
2. Combine with remaining ingredients. Put into a 4-quart casserole.
3. Bake, covered, at 300°F 2 hours.
12 SERVINGS

Stuffed Cabbage Rolls

1 whole head cabbage (about 4 pounds)
Boiling salted water
1 onion, chopped
2 tablespoons oil
1½ pounds ground beef
½ pound ground fresh pork
1½ cups cooked rice
1 teaspoon salt
¼ teaspoon pepper
2 cans (about 10 ounces each) condensed tomato soup
2½ cups water

1. Remove core from cabbage. Place whole head in a large kettle filled with boiling salted water. Cover; cook 3 minutes, or until softened enough to pull off individual leaves. Repeat to remove all large leaves (about 30). Cut thick center stem from each leaf. Chop remaining cabbage.
2. Sauté onion in oil. Add meat, rice, salt, and pepper. Mix thoroughly. Place a heaping tablespoonful of meat mixture on each cabbage leaf. Tuck sides over filling while rolling leaf around filling. Secure with wooden picks.
3. Place half the chopped cabbage on bottom of a large Dutch oven. Fill with layers of the cabbage rolls. Cover with remaining chopped cabbage.
4. Combine tomato soup with water; mix until smooth. Pour over cabbage rolls. Cover and bring to boiling. Reduce heat and simmer 1½ hours.
5. Serve cabbage rolls with the sauce.
ABOUT 15 SERVINGS

Beef-Sour Cream Casserole

4 cups cooked noodles
1 cup (8 ounces) cream-style cottage cheese
1 package (8 ounces) cream cheese
¼ cup sour cream
⅓ cup instant minced onion
2 tablespoons butter or margarine, melted
1½ pounds ground beef
3 cans (8 ounces each) tomato sauce
½ teaspoon salt
1 teaspoon oregano
⅓ cup chopped green pepper
1 can (2 ounces) sliced mushrooms, drained

1. Put half the noodles into a 2-quart casserole.
2. Combine cottage cheese, cream cheee, sour cream, and onion. Spread over noodles. Cover with remaining noodles. Drizzle with butter.
3. Brown ground beef in a skillet; drain off excess fat. Add remaining ingredients. Pour over noodles. Cover and chill overnight.
4. Remove from refrigerator 1 hour before baking.
5. Bake, covered, at 375°F 45 minutes, or until heated through. To serve, sprinkle with **grated Parmesan cheese.**
8 SERVINGS

African Bobotie

3 slices day-old bread
1½ cups milk
2 medium onions, chopped
1 garlic clove, minced
½ cup slivered almonds
½ cup raisins
1 tablespoon sugar
1 teaspoon salt
1 teaspoon curry powder
⅛ teaspoon pepper
1 tablespoon vinegar
1 teaspoon lemon juice
1½ pounds ground beef
2 eggs

1. Soak bread in milk. Squeeze milk from bread, reserving milk. Combine all ingredients, except milk and 1 egg.
2. Press mixture into an 11x7-inch baking dish.
3. Add enough milk to reserved milk to make ¾ cup. Beat together milk and remaining egg. Pour over meat mixture.
4. Bake, uncovered, at 350°F 1 hour, or until golden brown and firm to the touch.
6 SERVINGS

Patchwork Casserole

Meatball Supper Pie

1 pound ground beef
½ cup quick or old-fashioned oats, uncooked
¼ cup chopped onion
1 teaspoon salt
¼ teaspoon pepper
¼ teaspoon thyme
1¼ cups milk
1 egg, beaten
1 tablespoon butter or
margarine
1 tablespoon flour
Dash ground red pepper
½ cup (2 ounces) grated Parmesan cheese
1 baked 9-inch pie shell
½ cup (2 ounces) shredded American cheese
1 tomato, cut in wedges

1. Combine ground beef, oats, onion, salt, pepper, thyme, ¼ cup milk, and egg. Shape to form 4 dozen small meatballs.
2. Brown meatballs in a skillet; drain off excess fat.
3. Melt butter in a saucepan. Stir in flour and red pepper. Gradually add remaining 1 cup milk, stirring until thickened and smooth. Stir in Parmesan cheese.
4. Place meatballs in pie shell. Pour cheese sauce over meatballs.
5. Bake, uncovered, at 375°F 20 minutes. Sprinkle with American cheese and top with tomato wedges. Bake an additional 5 minutes. Cut into wedges to serve.
6 SERVINGS

Patchwork Casserole

2 pounds ground beef
2 cups chopped green pepper
1 cup chopped onion
2 pounds frozen southern-style hash brown potatoes
2 cans (8 ounces each) tomato sauce
1 can (6 ounces) tomato paste
1 cup water
1 teaspoon salt
½ teaspoon basil
¼ teaspoon pepper
1 pound pasteurized process American cheese, thinly sliced

1. Brown the meat in a large skillet just until meat is no longer pink. Drain off excess fat. Add green pepper and onion; cook until tender, stirring occasionally. Add remaining ingredients except cheese; mix well.
2. Spoon half of meat-and-potato mixture into a 3-quart baking dish (13½x8¾-inch) or two 1½-quart casseroles. Cover with half of cheese. Spoon remaining meat-and-potato mixture into dish. Cover dish tightly with aluminum foil.
3. Bake at 350°F 45 minutes.
4. Cut remaining cheese into decorative shapes.
5. Remove foil from dish and arrange cheese in a patchwork design. Let stand about 5 minutes, or until cheese is softened.
12 TO 16 SERVINGS

Meat Loaf with Baked Potatoes

1 pound finely ground beef
1½ teaspoons salt
¼ teaspoon white pepper
⅛ teaspoon Jamaica pepper
4 potatoes, mashed
1 egg
3 ounces coarsely chopped parsley
1 can (7 ounces) sliced mushrooms in water

3 ounces milk

Trimmings:
4 medium potatoes
2 fresh cucumbers
½ pound grated carrots
½ pound grated white cabbage
¾ cup consommé

1. Preheat the oven to 325°F.
2. Work the ground beef with the seasonings. Add mashed potatoes, egg, parsley and mushrooms. Dilute with milk.
3. Shape into a loaf and place in an ovenproof dish and bake in the oven for about 60 minutes.
4. Add the consommé after 50 minutes.
5. Bake potatoes in the oven at the same time as the meat loaf. The potatoes will be ready when the meat loaf is. Serve with the vegetables.
SERVES 4

One 'n' One Casserole

1 pound ground beef
1 cup uncooked white rice
1 package (1⅜ ounces) dry onion soup mix
1 can (10¾ ounces) con-

densed cream of mushroom soup
2½ cups boiling water
½ cup sliced green onion tops

1. Brown ground beef in a skillet; drain off excess fat. Put into a greased 2-quart casserole. Sprinkle with rice and onion soup mix.
2. Combine mushroom soup and boiling water. Pour over rice.
3. Bake, covered, at 350°F 1 hour, or until rice is tender. Remove cover. Sprinkle with onion tops.
4 SERVINGS

Individual Burger Casseroles

1 pound ground beef
¼ cup finely chopped onion
1 teaspoon salt
¼ teaspoon oregano
2 tablespoons ketchup
1 cup plus 2 tablespoons milk

2 tablespoons butter or margarine
2 tablespoons flour
1 cup cooked mixed vegetables
2 slices American cheese, cut in 4 strips each

1. Combine ground beef, onion, ½ teaspoon salt, oregano, ketchup, and 2 tablespoons milk.
2. Divide into 4 equal portions. Evenly line bottom and sides of 4 individual casseroles with meat mixture.
3. Bake, uncovered, at 350°F 20 minutes, or until meat mixture is done. Pour off excess fat.
4. Meanwhile, melt butter in a saucepan. Stir in flour. Gradually add remaining 1 cup milk, stirring until thickened and smooth.
5. Add vegetables and remaining ½ teaspoon salt. Spoon into meat shells. Top each with crisscross of cheese strips.
6. Bake about 5 minutes or until cheese melts.
4 SERVINGS

Mediterranean Beef Casserole

1 can (20 ounces) pineapple chunks
1 cup uncooked white rice
1 teaspoon salt
1 pound ground beef
1 egg, lightly beaten
1 cup fine soft bread crumbs
1 tablespoon instant minced onion

1 teaspoon salt
⅓ cup milk
1 tablespoon vegetable oil
1 can (16 ounces) stewed tomatoes
½ teaspoon dill weed
2 tablespoons snipped parsley

1. Drain pineapple, reserving liquid. Add enough **water** to liquid to make 2½ cups.
2. Combine liquid, rice, and 1 teaspoon of the salt in a saucepan. Bring to a boil. Cover and simmer 25 minutes, or until rice is fluffy.
3. Combine ground beef, egg, bread crumbs, onion, 1 teaspoon salt, and milk. Shape to form 1-inch balls.
4. Brown meatballs in oil in skillet; drain off excess fat.
5. Add pineapple chunks, tomatoes, dill weed, and parsley. Put into a greased 2-quart casserole.
6. Bake, covered, at 375°F 25 minutes, or until meat is done. Serve over pineapple-rice.
6 SERVINGS

Cornbread Tamale Pie

1 pound ground beef
½ cup chopped onion
⅓ cup chopped celery
1 can (16 ounces) tomatoes (undrained)
1 can (12 ounces) whole kernel corn, drained
1 can (8 ounces) tomato sauce
1 tablespoon chili powder

1 teaspoon salt
¼ teaspoon pepper
¼ cup all-purpose flour
1½ teaspoon baking powder
½ teaspoon salt
¾ cup cornmeal
1 egg, beaten
½ cup milk
2 tablespoons vegetable oil

1. Brown ground beef, onion, and celery in a skillet; drain off excess fat. Add tomatoes, corn, tomato sauce, chili powder, 1 teaspoon salt, and the pepper; simmer 10 minutes.
2. Sift together flour, baking powder, and ½ teaspoon salt into a bowl. Mix in cornmeal. Stir in egg, milk, and oil. (Mix only until dry ingredients are moistened.)
3. Spoon hot meat mixture into a 2-quart casserole. Top with cornbread topping.
4. Bake, uncovered, at 425°F 15 minutes, or until topping is golden brown.
6 SERVINGS

Glazed Ham Loaf

Glazed Ham Loaf

1 cup firmly packed brown sugar	1 teaspoon Worcestershire sauce
¼ cup vinegar	1 cup milk
¼ cup water	2 eggs, beaten
1 teaspoon dry mustard	1 teaspoon dry mustard
2 cups ground cooked ham	¼ teaspoon salt
1 pound ground pork	¼ teaspoon pepper
1 cup (3 slices) fine, dry bread crumbs	2 tablespoons whole cloves

1. Set out a shallow baking pan.
2. *For Ham Glaze* – Mix brown sugar, vinegar, water and 1 teaspoon dry mustard thoroughly to form a smooth paste and set aside.
3. *For Ham Loaf* – Grind cooked ham.
4. Combine pork, bread crumbs, Worcestershire sauce, milk, eggs and a mixture of 1 teaspoon dry mustard, salt and pepper with ground ham and mix lightly.
5. Put meat mixture into baking pan and shape to resemble a ham. To score ham, draw knife point over meat surface forming a diamond pattern. Insert cloves in center of each diamond.
6. Pour glaze over ham loaf.
7. Bake at 350°F about 1½ hours. Baste with glaze frequently during baking.
6 TO 8 SERVINGS

Pineapple Upside-Down Ham Loaf: Follow recipe for Glazed Ham Loaf. Use a 9½x5¼x2¾-inch loaf pan instead of baking pan. Omit glaze. Spread in bottom of loaf pan a mixture of ⅔ **cup firmly packed brown sugar,** ¼ **cup vinegar** and **2 teaspoons dry mustard. Set out 3 pineapple slices.** Cut two into halves. Arrange slices over sugar mixture in an attractive pattern. Pack ham mixture lightly into pan. After baking, pour off excess liquid and unmold. Serve garnished with sprigs of **parsley** and **radish** roses.

Layered Hamburger Bake

1 pound ground beef	densed vegetable soup
1 medium onion, chopped	1 can (10¾ ounces) condensed cream of mushroom soup
4 medium potatoes, pared and sliced	
¼ teaspoon pepper	½ cup water
1 can (10½ ounces) con-	

1. Brown ground beef and onion in a skillet; drain off excess fat.
2. Put half of the potatoes into a greased 2-quart casserole. Top with half the meat mixture; repeat. Sprinkle with pepper.
3. Combine vegetable soup, mushroom soup, and water. Pour over meat.
4. Bake, covered, at 350°F 1 hour, or until potatoes are tender.
4 SERVINGS

Tamale Pie

1 cup cornmeal	½ cup chopped pitted ripe olives
1¾ teaspoons salt	
1 cup cold water	1 can (16 ounces) tomatoes (undrained)
2 cups boiling water	
1 pound ground beef	2 teaspoons chili powder
⅓ cup chopped onion	½ cup cubed sharp Cheddar cheese
2 tablespoons flour	

1. Combine cornmeal, 1 teaspoon salt, and cold water. Slowly pour into boiling water in a saucepan, stirring constantly. Cook until thickened, stirring frequently. Cover; continue cooking over low heat about 5 minutes. Stir occasionally.
2. Brown ground beef and onion in a skillet; drain off excess fat. Add flour, olives, tomatoes, chili powder, and remaining ¾ teaspoon salt.
3. Spread mush evenly in bottom of a greased 12x8-inch baking dish. Pour meat mixture over mush. Arrange cheese cubes over meat mixture.
4. Bake, uncovered, at 350°F 20 minutes, or until casserole is bubbly.
6 SERVINGS

Mexican Picadillo

½ cup fresh parsley, cleaned and trimmed (¼ cup chopped)
1 clove garlic
1 pound beef, cut in 1-inch cubes
1 pound pork, cut in 1-inch cubes
2 onions, peeled and quartered
1 green pepper, trimmed and cut in 1-inch pieces
1 tablespoon oil
1 apple, pared, cored, and quartered
1 stalk celery, trimmed and cut in 1-inch pieces
1 or more jalapeño peppers
1 can (28 ounces) whole tomatoes
½ cup raisins
½ cup dry red wine
⅛ teaspoon cinnamon
⅛ teaspoon cloves
⅛ teaspoon ginger
1½ teaspoons salt
¼ teaspoon pepper

1. Using **steel blade** of food processor, process parsley until chopped and set aside. Add garlic and process until minced. Add meat in ½-pound batches and process until finely chopped and set aside.
2. Still using **steel blade,** separately process onions and green pepper until chopped. In a large skillet, cook onion and green pepper in oil until soft. Add chopped meat and cook until no longer pink.
3. Still using **steel blade,** separately process apple and celery until chopped and add to meat mixture.
4. Drain jalapeño peppers and remove seeds. Using **steel blade,** process until finely chopped and add to meat mixture.
5. Drain tomatoes. Add juice to meat mixture and process tomatoes with **steel blade** until chopped. Add to meat.
6. Add remaining ingredients and simmer uncovered for 30 minutes longer until flavors are well blended and filling is slightly thickened.
7. Serve over a bed of **rice.**

8 SERVINGS

Potluck Meat Balls

1 pound ground beef (chuck or round)
1 egg, beaten
½ cup milk
1 cup fine soft bread crumbs
1 tablespoon instant minced onion
1 tablespoon minced parsley
¾ cup finely chopped toasted walnuts
1 teaspoon chili corne carne seasoning
1 teaspoon seasoned salt
⅛ teaspoon seasoned pepper
1 tablespoon cooking oil

1. Set out a large skillet.
2. Combine in a large bowl ground beef, egg, milk, bread crumbs, minced onion, minced parsley, and toasted walnuts.
3. Add a blend of chili con carne seasoning, salt, and pepper.
4. Toss with a fork until thoroughly mixed. Shape mixture into 1-inch balls.
5. Heat cooking oil in the skillet.
6. Add meat balls to hot oil and brown them on all sides over medium heat, shaking skillet occasionally to keep meat balls as round as possible. When balls are cooked to desired doneness, remove them from skillet and keep warm until ready to serve.
7. To serve, dip warm balls in **Spicy Ketchup Dip** (below) and in **finely chopped toasted walnuts.**
ABOUT 3 DOZEN SMALL MEAT BALLS

Spicy Ketchup Dip: Combine in a bowl and mix well **3 tablespoons brown sugar, ½ teaspoon dry mustard, ½ teaspoon ginger, 1 cup ketchup, 2 tablespoons soy sauce** and **1 tablespoon garlic-flavored wine vinegar**.
ABOUT 1¼ CUPS DIPS

Frankfurter Supper Bake

1 pound frankfurters
½ cup vegetable oil
1 large garlic clove, minced
8 slices bread, well toasted and cut in ½-inch cubes
1 cup diagonally sliced celery
2 tablespoons minced parsley
1 egg
¼ teaspoon salt
⅛ teaspoon pepper
2 cans (8 ounces each) tomato sauce with onions

1. Make diagonal slits at 1-inch intervals almost to bottom of each frankfurter. Set aside.
2. Mix oil and garlic and pour about half of mixture into a large skillet; heat thoroughly. Add about half of toast cubes and toss until all sides are coated and browned. Turn into a large bowl. Repeat heating oil; brown remaining toast cubes, and put into bowl along with celery and parsley.
3. Beat egg, salt, and pepper slightly. Add 1 can of tomato sauce; mix well. Pour over the crouton mixture; toss lightly.
4. Turn half of the mixture into a greased 1½-quart casserole. Put half of the franks onto the mixture. Brush franks with 1 teaspoon tomato sauce from remaining can. Repeat layers and brushing.
5. Bake, uncovered, at 350°F 45 minutes.
6. Heat remaining tomato sauce in a small saucepan and pour evenly over casserole mixture. Garnish with **parsley**.
6 SERVINGS

Franks and Scalloped Potatoes

6 medium potatoes, pared and thinly sliced
3 tablespoons finely chopped chives
3 tablespoons flour
1 teaspoon salt
¼ teaspoon pepper
3 tablespoons butter or margarine
2½ cups milk, heated
6 frankfurters, cut in pieces

1. Place one third of the potatoes in a greased 2½-quart casserole. Sprinkle with one third of the chives, one third of the flour, one third of the salt, and one third of the pepper. Dot with 1 tablespoon butter. Repeat twice. Pour milk over all.
2. Bake, covered, at 350°F 30 minutes. Remove cover. Stir in frankfurters. Bake, uncovered, an additional 50 minutes, or until potatoes are tender.
6 SERVINGS

Hot Dogs in Cornbread

1 package (8½ ounces) corn muffin mix
1 egg
⅓ cup milk
1 tablespoon instant minced onion
4 frankfurters, split in half lengthwise
1 teaspoon oregano
1 cup (4 ounces) shredded Cheddar cheese

1. Prepare corn muffin mix, using egg and milk, according to package directions. Stir onion into batter. Spread into a greased 1½-quart shallow baking dish.
2. Arrange frankfurters over batter. Sprinkle with oregano.
3. Bake, uncovered, at 400°F 15 minutes, or until golden brown. Sprinkle with cheese. Bake an additional 3 minutes, or until cheese is melted. Serve with **prepared mustard.**
4 SERVINGS

Hearty Sandwich Squares

2 cups pancake mix
1 can (11 ounces) condensed Cheddar cheese soup
1 teaspoon prepared mustard
1¼ cups milk
8 slices (1 ounce each) luncheon meat
4 slices (1 ounce each) American cheese
¼ cup chopped onion
¼ cup chopped green pepper

1. Combine pancake, mix, ¼ cup soup, mustard, and 1 cup milk.
2. Spread half the batter in a greased 8-inch square baking dish. Top with meat, cheese, onion, and green pepper. Spoon remaining batter over all.
3. Bake, uncovered, at 400°F 25 to 30 minutes, or until done. Cut into squares to serve. Heat together remaining soup and ¼ cup milk. Spoon over squares. Sprinkle with **snipped parsley.**
4 SERVINGS

Sausage-Stuffed Rouladen with Tomato-Beer Kraut

1 beef round steak, cut ½
  inch thick (about 2 pounds)
Flour
6 smoked link sausages
2 tablespoons oil
2 medium onions, sliced
1 can (16 ounces) sauerkraut,
  rinsed and drained
1 can (16 ounces) tomatoes
  (undrained)
1 can or bottle (12 ounces)
  beer
2 teaspoons caraway seed
1 teaspoon salt
¼ teaspoon pepper
3 tablespoons flour

1. Cut beef into 6 serving pieces approximately rectangular in shape. Dredge in flour. Pound on a floured board until as thin as possible. Roll each piece around a sausage. Fasten with wooden picks.
2. In a large skillet, brown meat in oil; set aside. Sauté onion in same skillet until golden.
3. Add sauerkraut, undrained tomatoes, beer, caraway seed, salt, and pepper. Stir. Add beef rolls. Cover and simmer 1½ to 2 hours, or until tender.
4. Transfer meat and vegetables to a serving platter, using slotted spoon. Make paste of flour and a little water; stir into cooking liquid. Cook, stirring constantly, until thickened. Pass gravy in sauceboat.
6 SERVINGS

Macaroni and Cheese with Franks

1 package (8 ounces) elbow
  macaroni, cooked and
  drained
2 cups (8 ounces) shredded
  Cheddar cheese
1 can (13 ounces) evaporated
  milk
1 small onion, finely
  chopped
⅛ teaspoon pepper
1 package (16 ounces)
  frankfurters, cut in 1-inch
  pieces

1. Combine all ingredients. Put into a 2½-quart casserole.
2. Bake, covered, at 350°F 30 minutes, or until heated through, stirring occasionally.
6 SERVINGS

Hamburger Stroganoff

1½ pounds lean ground beef
2 large onions, sliced
2 cans (10½ ounces each)
  condensed cream of
chicken soup
1 pint sour cream
1 teaspoon salt
Dash black pepper

1. Sauté ground beef and onions in a small amount of fat in cooking pan of a chafing dish until meat is well browned.
2. Stir in condensed soup, sour cream, salt, and pepper.
3. Cook, covered, over direct heat of chafing dish until thoroughly heated.
ABOUT 6 SERVINGS

Sausage-Stuffed Rouladen with Tomato-Beer Kraut

Pear-Topped Special

1 can (12 ounces) luncheon
  meat, shredded
2 medium onions, chopped
⅔ cup diced celery
⅓ cup slivered green pepper
4 medium potatoes, cooked,
  peeled, and cut in cubes
1 cup beef broth

½ teaspoon salt
Few grains pepper
1 can (29 ounces) pear
  halves, drained
Softened butter or margarine
¼ cup firmly packed brown
  sugar

1. Combine luncheon meat, onion, celery, green pepper, potato cubes, broth, salt, and pepper; toss lightly to mix. Turn into a buttered shallow 1½-quart baking dish.
2. Bake, uncovered, at 400°F 30 minutes. Arrange pear halves, cut side down, over top. Brush pears lightly with softened butter and sprinkle with brown sugar. Bake an additional 15 minutes.
ABOUT 6 SERVINGS

Deep-Fried Beef Pies

Pastry:
1 cup all-purpose flour
½ teaspoon salt
⅓ cup shortening
2 or 3 tablespoons cold
  water

Filling
¾ pound lean ground beef
2 tablespoons shortening
1½ teaspoons olive oil
1 teaspoon salt
¼ teaspoon black pepper
⅛ teaspoon cayenne pepper
1 ripe tomato, peeled and
  cut in pieces
⅓ cup finely chopped green

pepper
¼ cup finely chopped carrot
¼ cup finely chopped celery
¼ cup finely chopped onion
¼ cup finely chopped green
  onion
1 tablespoon chopped hot
  red pepper
1 tablespoon snipped parsley
1 tablespoon snipped
  seedless raisins
1 tablespoon chopped pitted
  green olives
1 tablespoon capers
¼ cup water
Oil for deep frying

1. To make pastry, sift flour and salt together into a bowl. Cut in shortening with pastry blender or two knives until pieces are the size of small peas.
2. Sprinkle water over mixture, a teaspoonful at a time, mixing lightly with a fork after each addition. Add only enough water to hold pastry together. Shape into a ball and wrap in waxed paper; chill.
3. To make filling, cook ground beef in hot shortening and olive oil in a large skillet, separating meat with a spoon. Remove from heat and drain off fat. Mix in remaining ingredients except the oil for deep frying. Cover and simmer 30 minutes.
4. Working with half the chilled pastry at a time, roll out ⅛ inch thick on a lightly floured surface. Using a lightly floured 4-inch cutter, cut into rounds. Place 1 tablespoon filling on each round. Moisten edges with cold water, fold pastry over, press edges together, and tightly seal.
5. Slowly heat the oil for deep frying in a wok to 375°F.
6. Fry one layer at a time in the heated oil until lightly browned on both sides (about 3 minutes.) Drain on absorbent paper.
ABOUT 16 PIES

Boulettes of Beef Stroganoff

1 pound ground beef round
  steak
1 egg, lightly beaten
⅓ cup fine fresh bread
  crumbs
¼ cup milk
¼ teaspoon grated nutmeg
¼ teaspoon each salt and
  freshly ground pepper
3 tablespoons paprika

¼ cup butter
¼ pound mushrooms, thinly
  sliced
⅓ cup finely chopped onion
¼ cup dry sherry
2 tablespoons brown sauce
  or canned beef gravy
¼ cup sour cream
¼ cup finely chopped
  parsley

1. Put the meat into a mixing bowl and add the egg.
2. Soak the crumbs in milk and add this to the meat. Add the nutmeg, salt, and pepper; mix well with the hands. Shape the mixture into balls about 1½-inches in diameter. There should be about 35 to 40 meatballs.
3. Sprinkle a pan with the paprika and roll the meatballs in it.
4. Heat the butter in a heavy skillet and cook the meatballs, turning gently, until they are nicely browned, about 5 minutes. Sprinkle the mushrooms and onion between and around the meatballs and shake the skillet to distribute the ingredients evenly. Cook about 1 minute and partially cover. Simmer about 5 minutes and add the wine and brown sauce.
5. Stir in the heavy cream. Partially cover and cook over low heat about 15 minutes. Stir in the sour cream and bring just to cooking without boiling. Sprinkle with parsley and serve piping hot with **buttered fine noodles** as an accompaniment.
4 TO 6 SERVINGS

Beef Polynesian

2 tablespoons cooking oil
1 pound lean ground beef
1 can (4 ounces) mushrooms,
  drained
½ cup golden raisins
1 package (10 ounces) frozen
  green peas

½ cup beef broth
1 teaspoon curry powder
1 tablespoon soy sauce
1 orange, sliced
½ cup salted cashews
Fried Rice

1. Heat oil in a large wok. Add ground beef and separate into small pieces; cook until lightly browned.
2. Add mushrooms, raisins, peas, broth, curry powder, and soy sauce. Break block of peas apart, if necessary, and gently toss mixture to blend.
3. Arrange orange slices over top. Cover loosely and cook over low heat 15 minutes.
4. Mix in cashews and serve with Fried Rice.
ABOUT 4 SERVINGS

Fried Rice: Cook ½ **cup chopped onion** in **2 tablespoons butter** until golden. Mix in **2 cups rice** and **2 tablespoons soy sauce**. Cook over low heat, stirring occasionally, 5 minutes. Stir in **1 slightly beaten egg** and cook until set.

Pâté à La Maison Grand Vefour

Dough
2 cups flour
1 egg
3 ounces water
7 ounces butter
salt

Filling
1 pound ground veal

1 pound ground pork
2 egg yolks
salt
pepper
chervil
tarragon
chopped parsley
½ pound cooked ham
Chopped truffles

1. Combine all ingredients for the dough and roll out to ⅓-inch thick.
2. For the filling make a mixture of the ground meat by grinding veal, and pork together, add egg yolks, and season with salt and pepper and the other spices.
3. Add the cooked ham and the truffles, and place the mixture on the dough.
4. Roll the dough around the mixture (save a little for decoration) and pinch it together at both ends. Place it on a baking sheet. Cut a small strip of the dough and make a band. Place it on top of the roll where the dough sides are overlapping. Seal the band with a beaten egg. This band will keep the dough sealed.
5. Put two "chimneys" of waxed paper in the roll. This will allow all the liquid to evaporate and the paté will be firm.
6. Bake in a medium hot oven (350°- 400°F) for about 1½ hours, for a paté of 4 pounds.
7. Remove the "chimneys." Cover the holes with small decorative lids made from leftover dough and brown.
SERVES 6

Rabbit Stew

2 rabbits, skinned, cleaned, and cut in four pieces each
1½ cups mild vinegar
1 cup water
1 large onion, quartered
2 teaspoons salt
1 teaspoon pepper
2 bay leaves
2 pounds whole baby onions
3 tablespoons olive oil

2 tablespoons tomato paste mixed with 1 cup water
1 cup red wine
1 garlic clove, crushed in a garlic press
1 bay leaf
⅛ teaspoon cinnamon
Salt and pepper to taste
Water to cover

1. Put rabbit pieces into a large bowl. Add vinegar, water, onion, salt, pepper, and bay leaves. Cover. Refrigerate 4 hours, turning occasionally. Pat dry.
2. Peel onions. Cut a small cross at the base of each (to keep onions whole during cooking).
3. Heat olive oil in a large Dutch oven and sear rabbits on all sides until reddened. Add all ingredients including onions and water to barely cover. Bring to a boil. Cover.
4. Bake at 250°F about 2 hours, or until rabbit is tender.
8 SERVINGS

Note: If a thick sauce is desired, pour the sauce into a saucepan and simmer uncovered for ½ hour. Pour over rabbit.

Parmesan Macaroni Casserole

1 package (8 ounces) cream cheese
½ teaspoon garlic salt
1 cup milk
½ cup (2 ounces) grated Parmesan cheese
1 can (12 ounces) luncheon

meat, chopped
½ cup sliced celery
¼ cup chopped green pepper
1 cup (4 ounces) elbow macaroni, cooked and drained

1. Soften cream cheese over low heat in a saucepan. Add garlic salt. Gradually add milk, stirring until smooth.
2. Stir in remaining ingredients. Put into a greased 1½-quart casserole.
3. Bake, covered, at 350°F 25 minutes, or until heated through and lightly browned.
6 SERVINGS

Sautéed Veal Brains in Browned Butter

4 veal brains
Juice of 2 lemons
1 teaspoon salt
½ cup flour seasoned with salt and pepper

½ cup butter
2 tablespoons chopped fresh dill
1 lemon, cut in wedges

1. Rinse brains thoroughly. Soak in water with ice cubes for 15 minutes. Drain; remove membranes.
2. Pour enough water into a saucepot to cover brains. Add lemon juice and salt; bring to boiling. Reduce heat and drop in brains. Simmer 15 minutes. Drain. Plunge into ice water to cool quickly.
3. Dip brains into seasoned flour.
4. Put butter into a skillet and heat until deep brown. Add brains and sauté briefly. Remove to a warm platter. Sprinkle with dill. Serve with lemon wedges.
4 SERVINGS

Cypriote Sausages

1 pound coarsely ground beef
1 pound coarsely ground pork
1 cup fresh bread crumbs
3 garlic cloves, crushed in a garlic press
2 teaspoons salt
2 teaspoons coriander
1 teaspoon cumin
1 teaspoon thyme

½ teaspoon paprika
¼ teaspoon ground red pepper
1 bay leaf, ground
1 egg
½ cup minced parsley
1 large onion, minced
2 tablespoons tomato paste mixed with ½ cup water
Flour for rolling
Oil for frying

1. Combine meats in a large bowl, tossing with 2 forks.
2. Combine remaining ingredients except flour and oil in a separate bowl. Toss with meat mixture.
3. Break off enough meat to form a 2-inch-long sausage. Lightly flour palms of hands. Roll meat into sausage shapes.
4. Heat oil to smoking in a skillet. Fry sausages until deep brown on all sides. Serve hot or cold.
20 TO 30 SAUSAGES

Pâté à La Maison Grand Vefour

Porcupine Beef Balls

Quick Tomato Sauce (below)
1 pound ground beef
½ cup uncooked rice
¼ cup minced onion
1 teaspoon salt
⅛ teaspoon pepper

1. Lightly grease a 2½-quart casserole having a tight-fitting cover.
2. Prepare and set aside Quick Tomato Sauce, adding ½ cup water.
3. Meanwhile, combine beef, rice, onion and a mixture of salt and pepper and mix lightly.
4. Shape into 1½-inch balls and put in casserole. Pour tomato sauce over meat balls.
5. Cover and bake at 350°F about 1 hour, or until visible rice is tender when pressed lightly between fingers.
6. To serve, garnish with parsley.
4 TO 6 SERVINGS

Porcupine Beef Balls with Mushrooms: Follow recipe for Porcupine Beef Balls. Substitute a mixture of **1¼ cups** (10½- to 11-ounce can) **condensed cream of mushroom soup** and **1 cup water** for the Quick Tomato Sauce.

Porcupine Beef Balls with Celery: Follow recipe for Porcupine Beef Balls. Add **½ teaspoon celery salt** with the seasonings in beef balls. Substitute a mixture of **1½ cups** (10½- to 11-ounce can) **condensed cream of celery soup** and **1 cup water** for the Quick Tomato Sauce.

Quick Tomato Sauce

2 tablespoons butter or margarine
¼ cup coarsely chopped celery
¼ cup coarsely chopped green pepper
2 tablespoons finely chopped onion
1¼ cups (10½- to 11-ounce can) condensed tomato
soup
¾ cup water
2 tablespoons lemon juice
1 teaspoon Worcestershire sauce
2 tablespoons brown sugar
1 teaspoon dry mustard
½ teaspoon salt
Few grains pepper

1. Heat butter or margarine in a small skillet.
2. Add chopped celery, green pepper and onion.
3. Cook, stirring frequently, until celery and green pepper

are tender. Remove from heat and add condensed tomato soup, water, lemon juice, Worcestershire sauce, brown sugar, dry mustard, salt and pepper slowly while stirring constantly.
4. Simmer, uncovered, about 5 minutes, or until sauce is heated thoroughly.
ABOUT 2½ CUPS SAUCE

Bacon Fry

1 pound sliced bacon, diced
4 eggs
1 cup milk
2 cups all-purpose flour
1 tablespoon sugar
2½ teaspoons baking powder
1½ teaspoons salt

1. Fry bacon just until golden in a 10-inch skillet. Remove ⅔ cup bacon and drippings.
2. Beat eggs with milk. Add 1 cup flour, sugar, baking powder, and salt. Beat until smooth. Beat in remaining flour.
3. Pour half of batter just in center of skillet over bacon and drippings. Tilt skillet slightly to spread batter. Cook until browned on bottom and set on top. Turn.
4. Sprinkle half the reserved bacon and 1 tablespoon drippings over top. Pour on half the remaining batter. Turn when bottom is browned.
5. Sprinkle remaining bacon and 2 tablespoons drippings on top. Pour on remaining batter. Turn when bottom is browned. Cook just until browned.
6. Cut into wedges for serving.
ABOUT 4 SERVINGS

Liver à la Nelson

1½ pounds sliced calf's liver
Milk
6 medium potatoes, pared
1 onion, sliced
½ cup sliced mushrooms
¼ cup butter
½ cup all-purpose flour
½ teaspoon salt
¼ teaspoon pepper
1 cup bouillon or meat broth
½ cup sweet red wine or Madeira

1. Soak liver 45 minutes in enough milk to cover.
2. Cook potatoes in boiling water until tender; cut in thick slices.
3. Sauté onion and mushrooms in butter in a large skillet until tender, about 5 minutes.
4. Mix flour with salt and pepper. Drain liver; pat dry with paper towels. Coat liver with seasoned flour.
5. Quickly brown liver in skillet with onion and mushrooms. Add sliced potatoes, bouillon, and wine. Cover. Simmer just until liver is tender, about 10 to 15 minutes.
6 SERVINGS

Moussaka

Fried Eggplant:
3 medium eggplants
Salt
2 cups flour (about)
Olive oil combined with
   vegetable oil for frying

Meat Filling:
¼ cup butter
2 pounds lean beef or lamb,
   ground
1 large onion, minced
¼ cup minced parsley
1½ teaspoons tomato paste
   mixed with ½ cup water

½ cup dry white wine
Salt and pepper to taste
3 egg whites, beaten until
   stiff
6 tablespoons fine bread
   crumbs

*Béchamel Sauce with Egg
Yolks:*
7 tablespoons butter
7 tablespoons flour
1½ quarts milk, scalded
3 egg yolks, beaten
1 cup grated kefalotyri
   cheese

1. Slice eggplants ¼ inch thick, and place on a large platter in a single layer. Sprinkle with salt on both sides. Let stand at least 30 minutes, or until liquid beads form on surfaces. Take each slice, squeeze well between both hands or press down with a heavy weight, being sure all liquid is squeezed out.

2. Dip each slice lightly in flour. Shake off excess. Heat oil in a large skillet. Fry eggplant, turning once, until golden brown. Drain on paper towels. Set aside.

3. For Meat Filling, melt butter in a large skillet; add meat and onion, and cook until browned. Add parsley, tomato paste and water, wine, salt, and pepper. Cook until all liquid has evaporated (about 30 minutes). Cool.

4. Beat egg whites until they form soft mounds. Fold in half the bread crumbs. Fold egg-white mixture into meat mixture.

5. For Béchamel Sauce, heat butter until melted. Stir in flour. Cook 4 minutes over low heat, stirring constantly; do not brown. Pour in warm milk slowly. Cook over low heat until sauce thickens. Cool. Stir in yolks with a whisk.

6. To assemble, oil an 18x12-inch baking pan. Dust with remaining bread crumbs. Line bottom of pan with 1 layer of eggplant. Cover with meat. Layer remaining eggplant on top. Sprinkle with cheese. Pour Béchamel Sauce over.

7. Bake at 350°F about 40 minutes, or until golden brown. Cool. Cut into squares and serve.

ABOUT 10 SERVINGS

Ham Mousse

1 tablespoon gelatin
¼ cup cold water
1½ cups chicken stock
3 cups ham, chopped
¼ cup celery, chopped
1 tablespoon onion, grated
½ cup mayonnaise
¼ cup sweet-sour pickles, chopped
3 tablespoons dill
½ teaspoon white pepper

1. Place gelatin in ¼ cup water. Add chicken stock and bring to a boil.
2. Chill mixture. When it is almost set add rest of ingredients.
3. Moisten a mold with cold water and add mixture. Chill until firm.
SERVES 10

Calf's Liver with Curried Onions

1 large yellow onion, sliced
¼ cup sherry
½ teaspoon curry powder
½ teaspoon salt
Freshly ground pepper
¼ cup golden raisins
2 teaspoons clarified butter
1 pound calf's liver
Clarified butter

1. Simmer onion slices in wine in a medium skillet until onion is tender and wine is absorbed (about 10 minutes). Stir in curry powder, salt, pepper, raisins, and 2 teaspoons butter.
2. While onion is cooking, brush liver slices very lightly with clarified butter.
3. Broil 4 inches from heat until lightly browned (about 3 minutes on each side). Serve with onion.
4 SERVINGS

Rabbit

1 rabbit (2 to 3 pounds), cut in pieces
Salt and pepper
Flour
¼ cup butter
1 cup chopped mushrooms
1 onion, sliced
1 clove garlic, sliced
1 cup meat stock
⅔ cup dry white wine*
½ teaspoon ground thyme
2 bay leaves

Sauce:
1 cup sour cream
1 teaspoon dried parsley flakes
¼ teaspoon nutmeg

*Or substitute ½ cup water and 1 tablespoon lemon juice

1. Sprinkle rabbit pieces with salt and pepper. Coat with flour.
2. Melt butter in a Dutch oven or flame-proof casserole. Add mushrooms, onion, and garlic. Add rabbit pieces and brown quickly. Remove garlic.
3. Mix stock with wine, thyme, and bay leaves. Add to rabbit.
4. Bake at 350°F or simmer about 1½ hours, or until rabbit is very tender.
5. Remove rabbit and place on heated platter. Stir sauce ingredients into broth in pan. Cook and stir just until sauce begins to simmer. Spoon over rabbit.
4 TO 6 SERVINGS

Boiled Tongue

1 beef tongue (about 3 pounds); fresh, smoked, or corned tongue may be used
Boiling water
¼ pound salt pork, diced
2 onions, quartered
2 bay leaves
1 celery root or 3 stalks celery
2 carrots
2 parsnips or turnips
1 fresh horseradish root (optional)
1 parsley root
2 sprigs fresh parsley
1 tablespoon salt
6 whole peppercorns

Sauce:
1 cup white wine
1 bouillon cube
1 tablespoon flour
2 tablespoons butter (at room temperature)
2 tablespoons prepared cream-style horseradish

1. Rinse tongue under cold, running water. Cook in enough boiling water to cover 1 hour.
2. Add salt pork, 1 onion, and 1 bay leaf. Cover; cook 1 to 2 hours, or until tongue is tender. Remove skin, fat, and gristle. Strain liquid.
3. Combine tongue, strained liquid, remaining onion, and bay leaf with vegetables, parsley, salt, and peppercorns. Cover; simmer until vegetables are tender, 30 to 45 minutes.
4. For sauce, purée vegetables in an electric blender or press through a sieve.
5. Combine 1½ cups cooking liquid, wine, and bouillon cube. Bring to boiling. Blend flour into butter; stir into boiling broth. Add vegetable purée and prepared horseradish. Cook and stir until sauce is smooth.
6. Slice tongue. Simmer in sauce 10 minutes.
ABOUT 8 SERVINGS

Liver and Onions, Italian Style

1½ pounds beef liver, sliced about ¼ to ½ inch thick
½ cup flour
1 teaspoon salt
⅛ teaspoon pepper
2 onions, thinly sliced
⅓ cup olive oil
½ cup Marsala

1. If necessary, remove tubes and membrane from liver; cut liver into serving-size pieces.
2. Coat liver with a mixture of flour, salt, and pepper; set aside.
3. Cook onions until tender in hot oil in a large skillet. Remove onions and add liver. Brown on both sides over medium heat.
4. Return onions to skillet; add the wine. Bring to boiling and cook 1 minute. Serve at once.
4 OR 5 SERVINGS

Liver and Onions with Mushrooms: Follow recipe for Liver and Onions, Italian Style. Add **1 cup drained canned whole mushrooms** with the Marsala.

Dolmas

6 medium green peppers
¾ pound ground lamb
1 onion, chopped
2 tablespoons olive oil
1½ cups cooked rice
1 teaspoon salt
¼ teaspoon each pepper,

oregano, and cumin seed
1 cup beef broth
2 teaspoons cornstarch
3 tablespoons tomato paste
1 teaspoon lemon juice
½ cup sour cream

1. Slice top from each green pepper. Remove white fiber and seeds.
2. Brown lamb and onion in hot oil in a skillet. Mix in rice and dry seasonings. Fill green peppers with meat mixture.
3. Put pepper tops in bottom of an electric cooker. Set filled peppers on top. Pour in broth.
4. Cover and cook on Low 6 hours.
5. Remove peppers to a serving dish.
6. Mix cornstarch, tomato paste, lemon juice, and sour cream; pour into cooker and stir to blend. Return peppers to cooker.
7. Cover and cook on High 30 minutes.
8. Serve sauce with stuffed peppers.
6 SERVINGS

Tripe and Vegetables Warsaw Style

2 pounds fresh tripe
1 pound beef or veal soup bones
Water
Salt
4 carrots, sliced
1 celery root, chopped, or 3 stalks celery, sliced
1 bunch green onions, sliced
1 tablespoon chopped fresh parsley
3 cups bouillon or meat broth
2 tablespoons butter or margarine
2 tablespoons flour
½ teaspoon salt
¼ teaspoon ginger
¼ teaspoon mace
¼ teaspoon marjoram
¼ teaspoon pepper
1 cup light cream or vegetable broth

1. Clean tripe well and rinse thoroughly under running cold water.
2. Combine tripe and soup bones with enough water to cover in a large kettle. Season with ½ teaspoon salt for each cup of water added. Cover. Bring to boiling; reduce heat and simmer 3 to 5 hours, or until tripe is tender.
3. Drain tripe; discard bones and cooking liquid. Cut tripe into very thin strips.
4. Cook tripe with vegetables and parsley in bouillon until vegetables are tender.
5. Melt butter in a saucepan. Stir in flour to make a smooth paste. Cook and stir until golden. Blend in a small amount of cooking liquid. Add ½ teaspoon salt and spices. Add cream gradually, stirring until smooth.
6. Drain vegetables and tripe. Stir into sauce. Simmer 5 minutes.
4 TO 6 SERVINGS

Tripe á la Creole

2 pounds tripe
1 lime, halved
Water
1 tablespoon wine vinegar
4 garlic cloves
1 green hot pepper or 3 dried Italian pepper pods
½ cup olive oil
2 large Spanish onions, sliced
1 cup cubed cooked ham
5 large tomatoes, peeled, seeded, and chopped
¼ cup amber rum
2 thyme sprigs
2 bay leaves

1. Wash tripe thoroughly in cold water; drain. Rub the cut surface of lime over entire tripe. Put into a large kettle, cover with water, and add salt and vinegar. Bring to a boil; simmer 5 hours, adding more water if necessary. (This step is generally done the day before tripe is served; tripe is left to cool in its water.)
2. Cut the tripe into 2-inch slices; set aside.
3. In a mortar, pound to a paste the garlic and green hot pepper; set aside.
4. Heat oil in a top-of-range casserole. Sauté onion, then add tripe, ham, tomato, rum, seasoning paste, thyme, and bay leaves. Simmer 20 minutes. Serve immediately.
6 TO 8 SERVINGS

Bollito Misto

1 fresh beef tongue (3 to 4 pounds)
1 calf's head, prepared for cooking, or 2 pounds veal neck
2 pounds beef (neck, rump, or chuck roast)
2 pig's feet or 1 pound cotechino or other uncooked pork sausage
1 stewing chicken (3 to 4 pounds)
4 medium carrots, pared and cut in 3-inch pieces
2 large stalks celery, cut in pieces
3 onions, peeled and quartered
4 turnips or parsnips, pared and quartered
2 tablespoons chopped parsley
1 teaspoon tarragon
1 teaspoon thyme
Water
Salt
Salsa Verde

1. Combine meats, chicken, vegetables, parsley, tarragon, and thyme in a large sauce pot. Pour in enough water to cover meat, and salt to taste.
2. Cover pot, bring to boiling, and simmer 3 to 4 hours, or until tongue is tender.
3. Remove skin from tongue. Slice meat, cut chicken in serving pieces, and arrange with vegetables on a large platter.
4. Serve with **boiled potatoes, cooked cabbage, beets, pickles** and Salsa Verde.
10 TO 12 SERVINGS

Note: A pressure cooker may be used. Follow manufacturer's directions for use of cooker and length of cooking time.

Salsa Verde: Finely chop **3 hard-cooked eggs**; set aside. Combine ½ **cup salad oil** and **3 tablespoons wine vinegar.** Add **sugar, salt,** and **pepper** to taste. Mix well and combine with the chopped eggs. Blend in **6 tablespoons chopped herbs** such as **dill, tarragon, chervil, parsley, sorrel** and **chives.** Refrigerate several hours to allow flavors to blend.

Liver-Apple Bake

1 pound sliced beef liver (about ¼ inch thick)
2 cups chopped apple
½ cup chopped onion
2 teaspoons seasoned salt
⅛ teaspoon ground black pepper
4 slices bacon, cut in thirds
Parsley sprigs

1. Remove tubes and outer membrane from liver, if necessary. Put liver slices into a greased shallow baking dish.
2. Combine apple, onion, seasoned salt, and pepper; toss to mix. Spoon over liver. Arrange bacon pieces over top. Cover dish.
3. Cook in a 325°F oven 1 hour. Remove cover and continue cooking about 15 minutes.
4. Garnish with parsley.
4 SERVINGS

Loin of Venison

2 pound boned loin of
  venison
3 tablespoons oil
¼ cup red wine
½ teaspoon black pepper
¼ cup cashews
⅓ cup raisins
2 tablespoons butter
Sauce
½ cup mushrooms, chopped
1½ teaspoons tomato paste
2 tablespoons oil
1 small yellow onion, diced

1 stalk celery, diced
1 red pepper, chopped
1 tablespoon flour
2½ cups beef stock
2 tablespoons parsley
1 bay leaf
½ cup red wine
2 tablespoons red wine
  vinegar
Salt
½ teaspoon pepper
½ cup heavy cream

1. Cut venison into slices about ¼-inch thick. Lay on a plate and sprinkle with 1 tablespoon oil and pepper. Cover and let stand for at least 1 hour.
2. Make sauce: Heat the oil, add onion, carrot, red pepper and celery and cook over a low heat until they start to brown.
3. Stir in the flour and continue cooking to a rich brown. Add ⅔ of the stock, the mushrooms, tomato paste, parsley and bay leaf and the wine. Bring mixture to a boil, stirring. Reduce heat and simmer with the lid half covering the pan for 20-25 minutes.
4. Add the remaining stock, bring to a boil again and skim. Strain sauce. Return to pan, add vinegar and continue to simmer 6-7 minutes.
5. Add cream and simmer for 5 minutes. Add nuts and raisins.
6. Heat remaining oil in a heavy frying pan and sauté venison over a high heat for about 4 minutes on each side. Arrange on a warm platter and pour warm sauce on top.
4 SERVINGS

Beef Liver à la Beauharnais

½ cup flour
1 tablespoon paprika
½ teaspoon salt
⅛ teaspoon freshly ground
  pepper
⅛ teaspoon cayenne or red
  pepper
1½ pounds beef liver, thinly

sliced
1 cup minced onion
3 tablespoons peanut oil
2 tablespoons butter
1 tablespoon chopped
  parsley
1 tablespoon lime juice

1. Combine flour, paprika, salt, and peppers. Coat liver slices with flour mixture. Set aside.
2. Sauté onion in oil over medium heat. When onion is translucent, add butter and liver slices. Cook liver about 5 minutes; do not overcook.
3. Arrange liver on a heated platter and sprinkle with parsley and lime juice. Garnish with **watercress.**
6 SERVINGS

Leg of Venison

Marinade:
1 bottle (⅘ quart) dry white
  wine
3 cups vinegar
2 cups olive oil or salad oil
1 cup sliced carrots
1 cup sliced onions
2 stalks celery, cut in pieces
2 cloves garlic, crushed
3 sprigs parsley
1 bay leaf
6 whole cloves
6 peppercorns

Venison and Sauce:
1 leg of venison (5 to 6
  pounds)
¼ cup oil
2 tablespoons butter
1 onion, diced
1 cup red wine
3 tablespoons sugar
6 whole cloves
1 cup sour cream
½ cup all-purpose flour
Salt and pepper

1. Combine all ingredients for marinade in a large crock. Soak the venison 2 or 3 days in the marinade. Remove and wipe dry with a cloth.
2. Heat oil and butter in a heavy skillet. Add venison; brown evenly on all sides. Fry onion in the same butter.
3. Strain 1 cup marinade. Add to skillet.
4. Place venison in a Dutch oven or roaster. Add liquid and onion from skillet. Add wine, sugar, and cloves.
5. Cover; simmer or bake at 350°F about 2½ hours, or until meat is tender.
6. Remove venison to carving board.
7. Make sauce by combining sour cream and flour. Gradually stir in 1 cup strained cooking broth. Return to Dutch oven; cook, stirring, until smooth and thick. Season to taste with salt and pepper.
8. To serve, carve venison; place slices on a warmed platter. Pour sauce over top.
8 TO 12 SERVINGS

Marinated Venison in Cream Gravy

1 venison roast, preferably
  from leg (4 to 5 pounds)
1 cup chopped onion
⅓ cup oil
2 cans or bottles (12 ounces
  each) beer
2 tablespoons lemon juice
2 teaspoons salt

1 teaspoon thyme
8 peppercorns
2 garlic cloves, minced
1 bay leaf
½ cup cream or half-and-half
  (about)
Flour

1. Place venison in a large glass bowl.
2. Sauté onion in oil. Stir in beer and seasonings. Pour over venison. Marinate in refrigerator 24 to 36 hours, turning occasionally.
3. Place venison and marinade in a Dutch oven. Cover.
4. Bake at 325°F 2½ hours, or until tender, basting several times. (Venison may be cooked a shorter time to rare, only if meat is from a young animal.)
5. Transfer venison to a platter. Strain cooking liquid; skim off most of fat. Measure liquid. Make a paste of cream and 2 tablespoons flour for each 1 cup cooking liquid. Combine the paste in a saucepan with liquid and cook, stirring constantly, until thickened. Season to taste. Serve in a sauceboat along with venison.
2 OR 3 SERVINGS PER POUND

Loin of Venison

Mixed Fry

½ pound calf's brains
2 cups water
1½ teaspoons vinegar or lemon juice
¼ cup flour
Salt
Pepper
½ pound liver (beef, lamb, veal, or calf), sliced ¼ to ½ inch thick
2 cups all-purpose flour
1½ cups milk
3 eggs, well beaten
2 tablespoons melted shortening
Oil for frying
6 artichoke hearts (canned in water), drained
2 zucchini, washed and cut crosswise in 1-inch slices
3 stalks celery, cut in 3-inch pieces

1. Wash brains in cold water. Combine with 2 cups water, vinegar, and ½ teaspoon salt in a saucepan. Bring to boiling, reduce heat, and simmer gently 20 minutes.
2. Drain the brains and drop in cold water. Drain again and remove membranes. Separate into small pieces and set aside.
3. Combine ¼ cup flour, ½ teaspoon salt, and pinch pepper. Coat the liver with the flour mixture, cut into serving-size pieces, and set aside.
4. Combine 2 cups flour with 1 teaspoon salt and ¼ teaspoon pepper; set aside. Combine milk, eggs, and shortening. Gradually add the flour mixture to the liquid, beating until smooth.
5. Fill a deep saucepan one-half to two-thirds full with oil. Heat slowly to 360°F. Dip pieces of meat and the vegetables in the batter and fry in hot oil, being careful not to crowd the pieces. Fry about 5 minutes, or until golden brown, turning occasionally.
6. Hold cooked pieces over the hot oil to drain before placing on paper towels. Place on a warm platter and serve immediately.
6 SERVINGS

Tongue in Almond Sauce

2 veal tongues (about 2½ pounds each)
1 medium onion, stuck with 2 or 3 cloves
1 stalk celery with leaves
1 bay leaf
6 peppercorns
2 teaspoons salt
Water

Almond Sauce:
2 fresh or dried ancho chilies

½ cup canned tomatoes with juice
½ cup whole blanched almonds
½ cup raisins
1 slice bread, torn in pieces
2 tablespoons lard or oil
2 cups tongue stock
Salt and pepper
¼ cup blanched slivered almonds

1. Put tongues, onion stuck with cloves, celery, bay leaf, peppercorns, and salt into a Dutch oven or kettle. Cover with water. Cover Dutch oven, bring to boiling, and cook until meat is tender, about 2 hours. Allow to cool in liquid.
2. Remove skin from cooled tongues, trim off roots, and slice meat into ½-inch slices. Strain stock in which meat was cooked and save, discarding onion, celery, and bay leaf. Return sliced meat to kettle.
3. For almond sauce, first prepare chilies.

Put chilies, tomatoes, the whole almonds, ¼ cup of the raisins, and the bread into an electric blender. Blend to a thick purée.
4. Heat lard in a skillet. Add the puréed mixture and cook about 5 minutes. Stir in tongue stock and remaining ¼ cup raisins. Cook about 5 minutes, stirring constantly. Season to taste with salt and pepper.
5. Pour sauce over sliced meat in Dutch oven and simmer until meat is heated through.
6. Transfer meat and sauce to platter and garnish with slivered almonds.
8 TO 10 SERVINGS

Oxtail Stew

½ cup enriched all-purpose flour
1 teaspoon salt
¼ teaspoon ground black pepper
3 oxtails (about 1 pound each), disjointed
3 tablespoons butter or margarine
1½ cups chopped onion
1 can (28 ounces) tomatoes,
drained (reserve liquid)
1½ cups hot water
4 medium potatoes, pared
6 medium carrots, pared
2 pounds fresh peas, shelled
1 tablespoon paprika
1 teaspoon salt
¼ teaspoon ground black pepper
¼ cup cold water
2 tablespoons flour

1. Mix ½ cup flour, 1 teaspoon salt, and ¼ teaspoon pepper in a plastic bag; coat oxtail pieces evenly by shaking two or three at a time.
2. Heat butter in a 3-quart top-of-range casserole. Add onion and cook until soft. Remove onion with a slotted spoon and set aside.
3. Put meat into casserole and brown on all sides. Return onion to casserole. Pour in the reserved tomato liquid (set tomatoes aside) and hot water. Cover tightly and simmer 2½ to 3 hours, or until meat is almost tender when pierced with a fork.
4. When meat has cooked about 2 hours, cut potatoes and carrots into small balls, using a melon-ball cutter. Cut the tomatoes into pieces.
5. When meat is almost tender, mix in potatoes, carrots, peas, paprika, 1 teaspoon salt, and ¼ teaspoon pepper. Cover and simmer 20 minutes. Stir in tomatoes and cook 10 minutes, or until meat and vegetables are tender. Put meat and vegetables into a warm dish.
6. Blend cold water and 2 tablespoons flour; add half gradually to cooking liquid, stirring constantly. Bring to boiling; gradually add only what is needed of remaining flour mixture for desired gravy consistency. Bring to boiling after each addition. Cook 3 to 5 minutes after final addition. Return meat and vegetables to casserole and heat thoroughly.
6 TO 8 SERVINGS

Meat Loaf à la Wellington

¾ pound medium mushrooms	2 eggs, slightly beaten
1½ pounds ground lean beef	2 teaspoons salt
¾ cup soft bread crumbs	¼ teaspoon black pepper
½ cup minced onion	⅓ pound liver sausage
⅓ cup ketchup	2 sticks pie crust mix
2 eggs, slightly beaten	Beaten egg for brushing

1. Rinse, dry, and trim stems of mushrooms. Reserve 6 whole mushrooms. Finely chop remaining mushrooms; put into a large bowl. Add beef, bread crumbs, onion, ketchup, eggs, salt, and pepper; mix lightly.

2. Shape half of the meat mixture into a 9x4-inch rectangle on a jelly-roll or shallow baking pan. Make a slight indentation lengthwise in center of meat rectangle. Place reserved mushrooms in well, stem ends down. Cover with remaining meat mixture; pat gently into shape, rounding top.

3. Bake at 350°F about 1 hour, or until done as desired.

4. Remove meat loaf from oven and set aside to cool.

5. Beat liver sausage with a fork and spread over top of meat loaf.

6. Prepare pie crust mix, following package directions. Roll out on a lightly floured pastry canvas into a rectangle about 18x12 inches. Center pastry over top of meat loaf; overlap bottom about ½ inch. Seal. Bring sides of pastry to bottom; overlap and seal, trimming ends if necessary. Place on a baking sheet. Brush top and sides with beaten egg. Use remaining scraps of pastry for making decoration for top; press firmly in place.

7. Bake at 400°F about 30 minutes, or until lightly browned. Let stand about 10 minutes before carving.

ABOUT 6 SERVINGS

Chili Dogs

1 pound ground beef
1 tablespoon chili seasoning
  mix
1 can (15 ounces) tomato

sauce with tomato bits
Water
12 skinless frankfurters
12 frankfurter buns

1. Brown ground beef in a skillet; drain. Add seasoning mix and tomato sauce; simmer until flavors are blended.
2. Meanwhile, bring water to boiling in a large saucepan. Add frankfurters, cover, remove from heat, and let stand 7 minutes.
3. Place frankfurters in buns; top with chili mixture.

12 CHILI DOGS

Savory Sweetbreads

1½ pounds sweetbreads
Cold water
¼ cup lemon juice
1 teaspoon salt
1½ cups beef broth
2 stalks celery with leaves,
  cut in 1-inch pieces
2 sprigs parsley
¼ teaspoon savory
¼ teaspoon thyme
⅛ teaspoon ground allspice

⅛ teaspoon ground nutmeg
⅓ cup butter or margarine
2 tablespoons flour
2 teaspoons dry mustard
⅛ teaspoon ground black
  pepper
1 tablespoon vinegar
¼ cup coarsely snipped
  parsley
Melba toast (optional)

1. Rinse sweetbreads with cold water as soon as possible after purchase. Put sweetbreads into a saucepan. Cover with cold water and add lemon juice and salt. Cover saucepan, bring to boiling, reduce heat, and simmer 20 minutes. Drain sweetbreads; cover with cold water. Drain again. (Cool and refrigerate if sweetbreads are not to be used immediately.) Remove tubes and membrane; reserve. Separate sweetbreads into smaller pieces and slice; set aside.
2. Pour broth into a saucepan. Add the tubes and membrane, celery, parsley, savory, thyme, allspice, and nutmeg. Bring to boiling and simmer, covered, 30 minutes. Strain broth, reserving 1 cup.
3. Heat butter in a skillet. Blend in flour, dry mustard, and pepper. Heat until bubbly. Add the reserved broth and vinegar while stirring until smooth. Bring to boiling, stirring constantly, and cook until thickened. Add the sweetbreads and parsley. Heat thoroughly.
4. Serve over Melba toast, if desired.

ABOUT 6 SERVINGS

POULTRY

Chicken with Tomatoes and Onions

2 broiler-fryer chickens
3 tablespoons olive oil
Juice of 1 lemon
2 teaspoons salt
½ cup butter

1 can (20 ounces) tomatoes
(undrained)
1 teaspoon pepper
1 tablespoon oregano
Salt

1. Rinse chickens well and pat dry with paper towels. Rub inside and out with a mixture of olive oil, lemon juice, and 2 teaspoons salt. Place in a large roasting pan.
2. Bake at 375°F 1 hour.
3. Melt butter in a saucepan. Add tomatoes, pepper, and oregano. Simmer 5 minutes.
4. Pour sauce over the chickens. Turn oven heat to 325°F and bake chickens an additional 45 minutes; baste frequently. Salt to taste.
4 SERVINGS

Note: Chicken with Tomatoes and Onions freezes very well.

Chicken Breasts with Yogurt Sauce

½ cup butter
6 chicken breasts, boned
Salt and pepper to taste
½ teaspoon paprika
6 fresh scallions, chopped
¼ cup minced parsley

2 cups chicken stock
Juice of 1 lemon
1 pound mushrooms, sliced
2 cups plain yogurt
1 cup coarsely ground
walnuts

1. Melt butter in a large skillet. Add chicken and season with salt, pepper, and paprika. Brown on both sides.
2. Add scallions, parsley, chicken stock, and lemon juice; bring to a boil. Reduce heat and simmer covered about 20 minutes, or until chicken is tender.
3. Remove chicken and arrange on a serving platter.
4. Add mushrooms to the stock. Simmer uncovered 3 minutes. Blend in yogurt and walnuts. (If sauce is too thick, dilute with a little stock or water.) Heat just to warm yogurt; do not boil.
5. Pour sauce over chicken.
6 SERVINGS

Braised Chicken with Tomatoes and Cheese

1 chicken (3 pounds), cut in
small pieces
¼ cup olive oil
Salt and pepper to taste
1 can (16 ounces) tomatoes
(undrained)
1 medium onion, minced
1 garlic clove, crushed in a

garlic press
2 tablespoons oregano
¼ teaspoon cinnamon
2 tablespoons whiskey
1 pound orzo (a pasta)
¼ cup vegetable oil
1 cup grated hard mizithra
cheese

1. Rinse chicken and pat dry with paper towels.
2. Heat olive oil in a large skillet. Add chicken pieces. Season with salt and pepper. Brown on all sides.
3. Mash tomatoes and add to skillet. Add onion, garlic, oregano, cinnamon, and whiskey. Cover and simmer about 30 minutes, or until done. Remove chicken pieces and keep hot.
4. Cook orzo according to directions on the package, adding vegetable oil to the water. Drain thoroughly and put into a deep serving dish. Add the sauce and toss lightly until orzo is coated completely. Adjust seasoning. Add the chicken. Toss again to combine.
5. Serve with grated cheese.
6 TO 8 SERVINGS

Broiled Chicken in Lemon Juice and Oregano

2 broiler-fryer chickens, cut
up
½ cup olive oil

Juice of 2 lemons
¼ cup oregano, crushed
Salt and pepper to taste

1. Rinse chicken pieces and pat dry.
2. In a bowl, make a marinade by combining olive oil with lemon juice and oregano. Dip each piece of chicken into the marinade. Season with salt and pepper. Marinate for several hours, or overnight if possible.
3. In a preheated broiler, place the chicken fleshy side down. Broil about 6 inches from heat about 15 minutes, or until brown, basting frequently. Turn once. Broil until done.
4 SERVINGS

Note: The marinade may be served as a gravy with cooked rice or noodles.

Broiled Chicken in Lemon Juice and Oregano

Country-Flavored Chicken Halves

1 package 15-minute chicken marinade
1 cup cold water
1 broiler-fryer (2½ to 3 pounds), cut in half

1. In a shallow pan, thoroughly blend chicken marinade and water. Place well-drained chicken in marinade; turn, pierce all surfaces of chicken deeply with fork. Marinade only 15 minutes, turning several times. Remove chicken from marinade and arrange skin side up in a shallow ungreased pan just large enough to accommodate the chicken.
2. Bake uncovered, at 425°F for 45 to 55 minutes, until thoroughly cooked.
4 SERVINGS

Chicken and Grapes

6 tablespoons butter
2 broiler-fryer chickens, cut in pieces
Salt and pepper to taste
3 scallions, chopped
1 cup dry white wine
Clusters of seedless white grapes
½ teaspoon paprika

1. Melt butter in a skillet. Add chicken and brown. Season with salt and pepper. Transfer chicken to a casserole.
2. Add scallions to the skillet and cook until browned. Add wine and heat. Pour over the chicken. Cover.
3. Bake at 350°F 30 minutes. Remove cover. Add grapes and bake an additional 5 minutes. Sprinkle with paprika.
4 TO 8 SERVINGS

Capon in Cream

1 capon or chicken (5 to 6 pounds)
Salt
2 cups chicken stock or broth
4 egg yolks
1 tablespoon melted butter
4 teaspoons flour
2 cups sour cream
1 teaspoon salt
¼ teaspoon pepper

1. Sprinkle cavity of bird with salt. Place in a large kettle.
2. Add stock to kettle. Cover. Simmer until just tender (about 1 hour). Allow to cool.
3. Meanwhile, cream egg yolks and butter; add flour and blend thoroughly. Stir in sour cream. Season with 1 teaspoon salt and pepper. Beat at high speed until stiff. Cook until thickened in top of a double boiler, stirring constantly to keep from curdling or sticking (handle like hollandaise sauce). Cool.
4. Make cuts in capon as for carving, but without cutting through. Place in a shallow baking pan. Fill cuts with sauce, then spread remainder over the whole surface of the bird.
5. Bake at 425°F about 20 minutes, or until sauce is browned.
6. Meanwhile, boil liquid in which chicken was cooked until it is reduced to 1 cup of stock.
7. To serve, pour stock over capon. Carve at the table.
ABOUT 6 SERVINGS

Chicken in Filo

1 stewing chicken, cut in pieces
½ cup unsalted butter
1 medium onion, minced
½ cup finely chopped leek
1 celery stalk, minced
1 garlic clove, crushed in a garlic press
2 tablespoons finely chopped parsley
2 tablespoons pine nuts
3 tablespoons flour
2½ cups chicken stock
½ cup cream
4 eggs, beaten until frothy
¼ teaspoon nutmeg
½ teaspoon dill
2 tablespoons white wine
Salt and pepper
1 package filo
Additional butter for filo

1. Rinse chicken pieces. In a large heavy Dutch oven, add ¼ cup butter. When hot, add the chicken. Cover. Cook, turning, without browning, for about 15 minutes.
2. Remove the chicken pieces and cool slightly. Remove bones and skin from chicken and discard. Chop chicken meat. Set aside.
3. Melt 2 tablespoons butter in a skillet. Add onion, leek, celery, garlic, parsley, and pine nuts. Sauté until vegetables are limp.
4. Melt remaining butter in a saucepan and blend in flour. Cook 2 minutes. Stir in stock. Simmer until sauce boils. Cool. Stir in cream, eggs, nutmeg, dill, chicken, vegetables, and wine, if sauce seems too thick. Season with salt and pepper.
5. Butter a 12x9x3-inch baking pan. Line it with 6 sheets of filo, brushing each with butter.
6. Spread chicken filling evenly over filo. Top with filo according to directions.
7. Bake at 350°F about 50 minutes, or until golden in color. Let stand 15 minutes before cutting into squares. Serve warm.
8 TO 10 SERVINGS

Broiled Chicken in Lemon Juice and Oregano

2 broiler-fryer chickens, cut up
½ cup olive oil
Juice of 2 lemons
¼ cup oregano, crushed
Salt and pepper to taste

1. Rinse chicken pieces and pat dry.
2. In a bowl, make a marinade by combining olive oil with lemon juice and oregano. Dip each piece of chicken into the marinade. Season with salt and pepper. Marinate for several hours, or overnight if possible.
3. In a preheated broiler, place the chicken fleshy side down. Broil about 6 inches from heat about 15 minutes, or until brown, basting frequently. Turn once. Broil until done.
4 SERVINGS

Note: The marinade may be served as a gravy with cooked rice or noodles.

Arroz con Pollo

2 pounds chicken parts
2 tablespoons salad oil
1 can (13½ ounces) chicken broth
1 can (16 ounces) tomatoes, cut up
½ cup chopped onion
2 medium cloves garlic, minced
1 teaspoon salt
¼ teaspoon saffron or turmeric
⅛ teaspoon pepper
1 bay leaf
1 package (10 ounces) frozen peas
1 cup uncooked regular rice
¼ cup sliced pimento-stuffed or ripe olives

1. In a skillet, brown chicken in oil; pour off fat. Add broth, tomatoes, onion, garlic, salt, saffron, pepper, and bay leaf.
2. Cover; cook over low heat 15 minutes. Add remaining ingredients.
3. Cover; cook 30 minutes more or until chicken and rice are tender; stir occasionally. Remove bay leaf.
4 SERVINGS

Roast Chicken with Potatoes

1 chicken (about 4 pounds)
Salt and pepper to taste
Juice of 1 lemon
¼ cup butter
¼ teaspoon paprika
1 cup water
5 medium potatoes, pared

1. Season chicken, inside and out, with salt, pepper, lemon juice, butter, and paprika. Place chicken on a rack in a baking dish.
2. Bake at 350°F about 1¼ hours, or until chicken is tender, basting occasionally. After the first 30 minutes of cooking, pour in water; add potatoes and baste with drippings.
3. Turn oven control to 400°F. Remove chicken to a platter and keep warm. Turn potatoes over in dish. Bake an additional 5 to 10 minutes.
5 SERVINGS

Chicken with Cheese

¼ cup butter
1 chicken (3 pounds), cut in pieces
1 medium onion, minced
Salt and pepper to taste
½ teaspoon rosemary
¼ teaspoon paprika
1 garlic clove, crushed in a garlic press
1½ cups chicken broth
⅓ pound kasseri cheese, cut in thin slices

1. Melt butter in a large skillet. Brown chicken on all sides. Add onion. Season with salt and pepper. Add rosemary, paprika, garlic, and chicken broth. Simmer, covered, about 40 minutes, or until chicken is tender.
2. Lay cheese slices on top of chicken. Simmer, covered, 5 minutes more. Serve at once.
2 TO 4 SERVINGS

Royal Chicken

⅓ cup butter
2 medium onions, chopped
1 cup sliced mushrooms
1 chicken or capon, cut in pieces
1 cup hot water
1 teaspoon salt
¼ teaspoon pepper
1 tablespoon flour
1 teaspoon paprika (optional)
1 cup sour cream or white wine

1. Melt butter in a large skillet. Add onion, mushrooms, and chicken pieces. Stir-fry until golden.
2. Add water, salt, and pepper.
3. Cover; cook over medium heat about 35 minutes, or until chicken is tender.
4. Blend flour, paprika (if desired), and sour cream. Stir into liquid in skillet. Bring just to boiling. Simmer 3 minutes.
ABOUT 6 SERVINGS

Smothered Stuffed Chicken

1 chicken (about 3 pounds)
½ teaspoon salt
⅛ teaspoon pepper
2 tablespoons butter
1¼ cups dry bread cubes or
pieces
¼ cup chopped onion
½ teaspoon dill weed
¼ cup hot milk
⅓ cup butter, melted

1. Sprinkle inside of chicken with salt and pepper. Tuck wing tips underneath wings. Chop liver.
2. Sauté liver in 2 tablespoons butter 2 minutes. Add bread cubes, onion, dill, and milk; mix.
3. Stuff chicken. Close and secure with poultry pins. Place in a ceramic or earthenware casserole.
4. Pour melted butter over chicken. Cover.
5. Bake at 350°F about 1 hour, or until chicken is tender.
6. If desired, remove cover. Baste. Increase temperature to 450°F. Bake 10 minutes to brown.
4 TO 6 SERVINGS

Capon Roasted in Salt

1 capon (about 5 pounds)
Salt
1 carrot, cut in 1-inch pieces
1 medium onion, cut in quarters
2 sprigs parsley
6 to 7 pounds coarse kosher salt
Watercress

1. Rinse capon; pat dry. Salt inside of cavity lightly; fill cavity with vegetables.
2. Line a deep Dutch oven (that will fit size of capon, allowing 1½ to 2 inches space on bottom, sides, and top) with heavy-duty aluminum foil, allowing 2 inches of foil to fold down over top edge of pan. Fill bottom of Dutch oven with a 1½-inch layer of salt. Place capon in Dutch oven. Carefully fill Dutch oven with salt, being careful not to get salt inside cavity of capon. Layer salt over top of capon.
3. Roast uncovered in a 400°F oven 2 hours. Remove from oven. Let stand 15 minutes.
4. Lay Dutch oven on its side. Using foil lining, gently pull salt-encased capon from Dutch oven. Break salt from capon, using an ice pick or screwdriver and hammer. Place capon on serving platter; remove vegetables from cavity. Garnish with watercress. Serve immediately.
4 SERVINGS

Honey-Glazed Filbert Roast Chicken

½ package herb-seasoned stuffing mix (2 cups)
1 cup toasted filberts, chopped
½ cup chopped celery
1 chicken liver, finely chopped
½ cup butter or margarine, melted
½ cup water
1 roaster-fryer or capon, about 5 pounds
½ cup honey
2 tablespoons soy sauce
1 teaspoon grated orange peel
2 tablespoons orange juice

1. Combine stuffing mix with the filberts, celery, chicken liver, butter, and water; toss lightly. Stuff cavity of chicken with the mixture, then tie chicken legs and wings with cord to hold close to body.
2. Place chicken, breast up, on rack in a shallow roasting pan. Roast at 325°F 2½ to 3 hours, or until chicken tests done. (The thickest part of drumstick feels soft when pressed with fingers and meat thermometer registers 180° to 185°F.)
3. Meanwhile, combine honey, soy sauce, and orange peel and juice. Brush chicken frequently with the mixture during last hour of roasting.

6 SERVINGS

Chicken Meringue

10 tiny boiling onions
2 stalks celery, cut in 1-inch pieces
1 large sweet red pepper, cut in ½-inch pieces
2 carrots, cut in ½-inch slices
2 cups Chicken Stock (page 48)
4 cups cubed cooked chicken
½ pound medium mushrooms, cut in half
½ pound fresh pea pods, or
1 package (10 ounces) frozen pea pods, thawed
2 tablespoons cornstarch
Cold water
Salt
Freshly ground pepper
4 egg whites
½ teaspoon salt
¼ teaspoon cream of tartar
1 tablespoon snipped fresh or 1½ teaspoons dried chervil leaves
2 tablespoons instant nonfat dry-milk solids

1. Simmer onions, celery, red pepper, and carrot in stock until just tender (about 8 minutes). Remove vegetables with slotted spoon and mix with chicken, mushrooms, and pea pods in a 2-quart casserole.
2. Mix cornstarch with a little cold water. Stir into stock; simmer, stirring constantly, until mixture thickens (about 4 minutes). Season to taste with salt and pepper. Pour over chicken in casserole.
3. Bake covered at 350°F 15 minutes.
4. Beat egg whites and ½ teaspoon salt until foamy. Add cream of tartar and chervil; continue beating, adding dry-milk solids gradually, until egg whites form stiff but not dry peaks. Spread meringue over casserole mixture, sealing to edges of casserole.
5. Bake at 350°F 12 to 14 minutes, or until meringue is lightly browned. Serve immediately.

4 TO 6 SERVINGS

Capon with Vegetable Dressing

1 capon (about 5 pounds)
½ can (10½-ounce size) condensed onion soup
1 medium eggplant, pared and cut in ½-inch cubes
1 cup chopped onion
1 cup chopped celery
1 cup chopped carrot
1½ to 2 teaspoons salt
¼ teaspoon freshly ground pepper
2 teaspoons poultry seasoning
¼ cup snipped parsley
2 eggs, beaten

1. Rinse capon; pat dry with paper toweling. Place capon on rack in a roasting pan. Pour onion soup over.
2. Roast in a 325°F oven about 2½ hours, or until capon is done; meat on drumstick will be very tender.
3. Remove capon to a serving platter; let stand 15 minutes before carving.
4. While capon is roasting, simmer eggplant in 1 inch of **salted water** until tender (about 10 minutes); drain.
5. Process onion, celery, and carrot in a food processor or blender until finely ground; transfer mixture to a mixing bowl. Mix in eggplant and remaining ingredients. Spoon vegetable mixture into a lightly oiled 2-quart casserole; do not cover.
6. Bake at 325°F 45 minutes. Remove to serving bowl.

4 SERVINGS

Note: Do not bake vegetable dressing in cavity of capon because the correct texture will not be obtained.
   This dressing is excellent served with pork.

Chicken Polish Style

1 chicken (2 to 3 pounds)
Salt
Chicken livers
¾ cup dry bread crumbs
1 egg
1 teaspoon dill weed
¼ teaspoon pepper
½ cup milk (about)
⅓ cup melted butter

1. Sprinkle the chicken with salt. Let stand 1 hour.
2. Chop the livers finely. Combine with bread crumbs, egg, salt to taste, dill, pepper, and as much milk as needed for a loose, sour-cream-like consistency.
3. Fill cavity of chicken with crumb mixture; truss. Place chicken in roasting pan.
4. Bake at 400°F about 45 minutes, or until chicken is tender. Baste often with melted butter.

ABOUT 4 SERVINGS

Chicken with Ham: Prepare Chicken Polish Style as directed. Substitute **6 ounces (1 cup) ground ham, ½ cup sliced mushrooms,** and **2 crushed juniper berries** for the chicken livers. Add **½ cup sherry** to pan drippings for a sauce.

Chicken Livers in Madeira Sauce

1 pound chicken livers
Milk
1 medium onion, minced
2 tablespoons chicken fat or
  butter
⅔ cup all-purpose flour
¾ teaspoon salt
⅔ cup chicken broth
½ cup Madeira

1. Cover chicken livers with milk; soak 2 hours. Drain; discard milk.
2. Sauté onion in fat.
3. Mix flour with salt. Coat livers with seasoned flour.
4. Add livers to onions. Stir-fry just until golden, about 5 minutes.
5. Stir in broth and wine. Cover. Simmer 5 to 10 minutes, or just until livers are tender.
4 SERVINGS

Curried Breast of Chicken Salad

6 cups bite-size pieces
  cooked chicken
1½ cups sliced celery
1 can (8½ ounces) water
  chestnuts, drained and cut
  in thirds
½ teaspoon salt
¼ teaspoon finely ground
pepper
1 cup Mock Mayonnaise
  (page 49)
1 teaspoon curry powder
2 tablespoons dry sherry
Lettuce leaves
Orange slices

1. Combine chicken, celery, water chestnuts, salt, and pepper.
2. Mix Mock Mayonnaise, curry, and sherry; stir gently into chicken mixture. Serve on lettuce-lined plates; garnish with orange slices.
6 SERVINGS

Chicken Livers Marsala

1 cup diced green pepper
½ cup finely chopped onion
⅔ cup water chestnuts,
  sliced in half
1½ cups Chicken Stock
  (page 48)
¼ cup Marsala wine
1½ pounds chicken livers,
  cut in half (discard
membrane)
2 teaspoons arrowroot
Cold water
½ teaspoon bottled brown
  bouquet sauce
Salt
Freshly ground pepper
Parsley sprigs

1. Simmer green pepper, onion, and water chestnuts in stock and wine until tender (about 5 minutes). Remove from stock with slotted spoon; keep warm. Add chicken livers to stock; simmer until livers are tender (about 8 minutes). Remove livers from stock with slotted spoon; add to vegetables are keep warm.
2. Mix arrowroot with a little cold water. Stir into stock. Simmer, stirring constantly, until it thickens (about 3 minutes). Stir brown bouquet sauce, vegetables, and livers into sauce. Season with salt and pepper to taste. Heat until hot. Spoon into ramekins. Garnish with parsley. Serve at once.
4 SERVINGS

Vegetable-Stuffed Chicken Breasts

3 whole large chicken
  breasts (about 3 pounds),
  boned, halved, and skinned
¾ pound cauliflower
¼ pound broccoli
Chicken Stock (page 48)
½ cup finely chopped celery
2 shallots, minced
½ teaspoon salt
Cauliflower Sauce (page 47)
  (do not add cheese or
  parsley)
3 ounces Swiss cheese,
  shredded
Snipped parsley

1. Rinse chicken breasts; pat dry. Pound with mallet until even in thickness; set aside.
2. Remove leaves and tough stalks from cauliflower and broccoli; separate into flowerets. Simmer covered in 1 inch of stock until tender (about 8 minutes). Coarsely chop the cauliflower and broccoli; mix with the celery, shallots, and salt.
3. Spoon mixture onto chicken breasts; roll up carefully and place seam side down in a lightly oiled shallow baking pan. Spoon Cauliflower Sauce over breasts.
4. Bake covered at 350°F 40 minutes. Uncover and bake 15 minutes. Sprinkle cheese over breasts; bake until cheese is melted (about 5 minutes). Arrange chicken on platter; sprinkle with parsley.
6 SERVINGS

Chicken en Cocotte

1½ cups sliced leeks, white
  part only
1 medium zucchini, cut in
  ¼-inch slices
2 large sweet red or green
  peppers, cut in ¼-inch
  slices
1 large green pepper, cut in
  ¼-inch strips
2 teaspoons snipped fresh or
  1 teaspoon finely crushed
  dried rosemary leaves
2 teaspoons snipped fresh or
  1 teaspoon finely crushed
dried thyme leaves
1½ teaspoons salt
⅓ cup dry sauterne or other
  white wine
1 roasting chicken (about 3
  pounds)
1 teaspoon clarified butter
Salt
1 small bunch parsley
1 cup 3-inch pieces, leek,
  green part only
1 tablespoon dry sauterne or
  other white wine

1. Arrange 1½ cups leeks, the zucchini, and peppers in bottom of a Dutch oven. Mix rosemary, thyme, and 1½ teaspoons salt; sprinkle one third of herb mixture over vegetables. Pour ⅓ cup sauterne over vegetables.
2. Rinse chicken and pat dry. Rub chicken with butter and sprinkle with remaining herb mixture. Lightly salt cavity of chicken. Stuff cavity with parsley and green part of leeks; sprinkle with 1 tablespoon sauterne. Place chicken in Dutch oven; cover with lid.
3. Bake at 325°F 2 hours, or until tender. Remove chicken to platter; discard parsley and leek from cavity. Surround chicken with vegetables.
4 SERVINGS

Sweet and Sour Chicken

Sauce:
¾ cup chicken stock
¼ cup brown sugar
¼ cup sugar
½ cup vinegar
¼ cup ketchup
1 tablespoon sherry
1 tablespoon cornstarch
2 tablespoons soy sauce
¼ cup pineapple juice

Chicken:
1 chicken breast, boned, skinned, and partially frozen
1 clove garlic
2 slices fresh ginger, each slice cut in quarters (1 teaspoon minced)
3 tablespoons peanut oil
1 green pepper, cut in 1-inch pieces
1 tomato, cut in 1-inch pieces
½ cup pineapple chunks, drained (reserving liquid)

1. For sauce, combine stock, sugars, vinegar, ketchup, and sherry in a saucepan. Bring to a boil, stirring to dissolve sugar.
2. Blend cornstarch, soy sauce, and pineapple juice. Stir into mixture in saucepan and cook over low heat until thickened.
3. For chicken, using **slicing disc** of food processor, slice meat. Set aside.
4. Using **steel blade,** mince garlic and ginger root by starting machine and adding ingredients through feed tube. Set aside.
5. Heat 2 tablespoons peanut oil in a wok. Add minced garlic and ginger root and stir-fry a few seconds. Add sliced chicken and stir-fry until just tender. Remove from pan and set aside.
6. Heat 1 tablespoon peanut oil in wok and stir-fry green peppers 2 to 3 minutes. Add tomato, pineapple, and chicken and stir-fry only to heat through.
7. Remove to a serving dish and spoon sauce over the top. Serve at once with **rice**.
4 SERVINGS

Mexican Chili Chicken Casserole

¼ cup instant minced onion
½ teaspoon instant minced garlic
⅓ cup water
1 can (17 ounces) whole kernel corn
2 tablespoons oil
1 can (16 ounces) tomatoes, drained and broken up
1 can (8 ounces) tomato sauce
4 teaspoons chili powder
1 teaspoon oregano leaves, crumbled
⅛ teaspoon salt
1 tablespoon cornstarch
½ cup pitted ripe olives, sliced
1½ pounds boned cooked chicken, chunked
8 bacon slices, cooked crisp

1. Combine minced onion and garlic with water; let stand for 10 minutes to rehydrate. Drain and reserve liquid from corn; set corn and liquid aside separately.
2. In a large saucepan, heat oil. Add onion and garlic; sauté for 5 minutes. Stir in tomatoes, tomato sauce, chili powder, oregano leaves, and salt.
3. Mix cornstarch with reserved corn liquid; stir into saucepan. Simmer, uncovered, for 15 minutes, stirring occasionally. Remove from heat; add olives.
4. In a large casserole, place in layers chicken, reserved corn, and sauce. Repeat procedure, ending with corn. Garnish with crisp bacon slices over top.
5. Bake at 400°F until casserole is bubbly (about 20 minutes).

8 SERVINGS

Chicken and Mushrooms in Sour Cream Sauce

2 frying chickens, cut in serving pieces
¼ cup oil
1 pound fresh mushrooms, cleaned and sliced
2 cups canned tomatoes with juice (16 ounce can)
2 canned green chilies, seeded
½ cup chopped onion
1 clove garlic, minced
1 cup chicken stock (or water plus chicken bouillon cube)
1½ teaspoons salt
1 cup sour cream

1. Brown chicken pieces in hot oil in a large skillet. Place chicken in Dutch oven or heavy saucepot.
2. Sauté mushrooms in oil remaining in skillet; spoon mushrooms over chicken.
3. Combine tomatoes, chilies, onion, and garlic in an electric blender and blend to a purée (if amount is too large for blender container, blend in two portions).
4. Pour purée into fat remaining in skillet in which chicken and mushrooms were cooked; bring to boiling and cook about 5 minutes. Stir in chicken stock and salt.
5. Pour sauce over chicken and mushrooms in Dutch oven. Cover and cook over low heat until chicken is tender (about 1 hour).
6. Just before serving, stir in sour cream and heat through, but do not boil.

6 TO 8 SERVINGS

Fried Chicken

1 frying chicken (about 3 pounds), cut in serving pieces
½ cup flour
1½ teaspoons salt
¼ teaspoon pepper
Olive oil
2 eggs, well beaten
¼ cup milk
1 tablespoon chopped parsley
½ cup grated Parmesan cheese
1 to 2 tablespoons water

1. Rinse chicken and pat dry with paper towels. To coat chicken evenly, shake 2 or 3 pieces at a time in a plastic bag containing the flour, salt, and pepper.
2. Fill a large, heavy skillet ½-inch deep with olive oil; place over medium heat.
3. Combine eggs, milk, and parsley. Dip each chicken piece in the egg mixture and roll in cheese. Starting with meaty pieces, place the chicken, skin-side down, in the hot oil. Turn pieces as necessary to brown evenly on all sides.
4. When chicken is browned, reduce heat, pour in water, and cover pan tightly. Cook chicken slowly 25 to 40 minutes, or until all pieces are tender. For crisp skin, uncover chicken the last 10 minutes of cooking.

3 OR 4 SERVINGS

Country Style Chicken

1 frying chicken (about 3 pounds), cut in serving pieces
2 tablespoons butter
2 tablespoons olive oil
1 medium-size onion, sliced
1 teaspoon salt
⅛ teaspoon pepper
1 pound zucchini
2 large green peppers
1½ tablespoons olive oil
1 teaspoon chopped basil leaves, or ¼ teaspoon dried sweet basil
½ cup dry white wine

1. In a large skillet, brown the chicken in butter and 2 tablespoons olive oil. Place onion around chicken; sprinkle with salt and pepper. Cover and cook slowly about 15 minutes.
2. While chicken is cooking, wash and cut zucchini in 1½-inch-thick slices. Wash peppers; remove stems and seeds. Rinse in cold water and slice lengthwise into 1-inch-wide strips.
3. In another skillet, heat 1½ tablespoons olive oil and sauté zucchini and peppers until soft (about 10 minutes). Sprinkle with basil. Transfer vegetables to skillet with chicken and pour in wine.
4. Simmer, covered, about 15 minutes, or until chicken is very tender and vegetables are cooked.

ABOUT 4 SERVINGS

Mexican Chili Chicken Casserole

Basque Chicken with Olives

1 broiler-fryer chicken, 3½ pounds ready-to-cook weight
Salt
¼ pound fresh mushrooms
1 medium onion
½ cup small pimento-stuffed olives
2 tablespoons olive oil
1 tablespoon butter
2 cans (8 ounces each) tomato sauce
½ cup dry white wine or chicken broth
10 small whole onions, peeled
2 sprigs parsley
½ teaspoon salt
⅛ teaspoon pepper
2 medium tomatoes, peeled and cut in wedges
1 medium green pepper, cut in strips
1 tablespoon olive oil

1. Set out a Dutch oven and a skillet.
2. Rinse and pat dry the chicken with absorbent paper.
3. Sprinkle body and neck cavities with salt and set aside.
4. Clean and slice the mushrooms; set aside.
5. Chop and set aside onion.
6. Set out olives.
7. Heat the olive oil and 1 tablespoon butter in Dutch oven.
8. Add the chicken to hot fat. Fry until golden on all sides, turning with two wooden spoons. Remove chicken from Dutch oven and set aside.
9. Add the mushrooms and onions to hot fat and stir occasionally until lightly browned. Add the tomato sauce, white wine or chicken broth, 10 small onions, and 2 sprigs parsley.
10. Return chicken to Dutch oven. Sprinkle with salt and pepper.
11. Simmer, covered, 1 hour, or until chicken is tender, basting occasionally; add olives 15 minutes before end of cooking time.
12. Transfer chicken to a large platter and tuck in neck skin; keep warm.
13. Simmer sauce uncovered 5 minutes.
14. Meanwhile, prepare 2 medium tomatoes and 1 medium green pepper.
15. Heat in the skillet 1 tablespoon olive oil. Add green pepper and cook, stirring occasionally, about 2 minutes. Gently mix in tomato wedges and heat thoroughly. Arrange green pepper strips and tomato wedges around chicken. Using a slotted spoon, lift olives, onions and mushrooms from sauce and arrange on platter.
16. Serve with hot **cooked rice** and remaining sauce.
4 TO 6 SERVINGS

Chicken Cacciatore

¼ cup cooking oil
1 broiler-fryer (2½ pounds), cut up
2 onions, sliced
2 cloves garlic, minced
3 tomatoes, cored and quartered
2 green peppers, sliced
1 small bay leaf
1 teaspoon salt
¼ teaspoon pepper
½ teaspoon celery seed
1 teaspoon crushed oregano or basil
1 can (8 ounces) tomato sauce
¼ cup sauterne
8 ounces spaghetti, cooked according to package directions

1. Heat oil in a large, heavy skillet; add chicken and brown on all sides. Remove from skillet.
2. Add onion and garlic to oil remaining in skillet and cook until onion is tender, but not brown; stir occasionally.
3. Return chicken to skillet and add the tomatoes, green pepper, and bay leaf.
4. Mix salt, pepper, celery seed, and oregano and blend with tomato sauce; pour over all.
5. Cover and cook over low heat 45 minutes. Blend in wine and cook, uncovered, 20 minutes longer. Discard bay leaf.
6. Put the cooked spaghetti onto a hot serving platter and top with the chicken and sauce.
ABOUT 6 SERVINGS

Chicken Breasts Regina

2 whole chicken breasts, skinned, boned, and cut in half
4 thin slices ham
4 thin slices liver sausage or liver pâté
Water
Flour
1 egg, beaten
Fine dry bread crumbs
3 tablespoons butter
Madeira Sauce (page 47)

1. Split chicken breast halves lengthwise, but not completely through. Open breast halves and pound until very thin.
2. Place a slice of ham, then a slice of liver sausage in center of each breast. Fold in half, enclosing the ham and liver sausage, moisten the edges with water, and press together.
3. Coat chicken breasts with flour, dip in beaten egg, and coat with bread crumbs.
4. Fry in butter in a skillet until golden brown on both sides. Serve with hot Madeira Sauce.
4 SERVINGS

Green Chicken

1 medium onion, coarsely chopped
1 clove garlic, peeled
1 cup (small can) salsa verde mexicana (Mexican green tomato sauce)
¼ cup (lightly filled) fresh parsley
1 teaspoon salt
¼ teaspoon pepper
2 frying chickens, cut in serving pieces

1. Put onion, garlic, salsa verde, and parsley into an electric blender. Blend until liquefied. Stir in salt and pepper.
2. Rinse chicken pieces and pat dry; arrange pieces in a heavy skillet. Pour green sauce over chicken. Cover; bring to boiling. Cook over low heat until chicken is tender, about 1 hour.
6 SERVINGS

Basque Chicken with Olives

Bouillon Cocq

1 meaty smoked ham hock	cut in chunks
1 capon (7 to 8 pounds)	2 carrots, pared and cut in
½ lime	chunks
½ orange	2 white turnips, pared and
2 tablespoons bacon	cut in chunks
drippings	2 onions studded with 8
1 tablespoon butter	whole cloves
1 tablespoon peanut oil	2 celery stalks, cut in pieces
3 quarts water	2 leeks, washed and cut in
Bouquet garni	chunks
1 pound cabbage, cut in	Salt, pepper, and cayenne or
chunks	red pepper to taste
4 small potatoes, pared and	Caribbean Rice (page 190)

1. Soak ham hock in cold water to remove excess salt. Drain.
2. Truss capon as for roasting. Rub skin with cut side of lime half, then cut side of orange half. Let stand to drain.
3. Heat bacon drippings, butter, and peanut oil in a deep soup kettle. Brown capon. Add ham hock, water, and bouquet garni; bring to a boil, reduce heat, and simmer 30 minutes, skimming twice.
4. Add vegetables and seasonings, bring to a boil, skim, then cook over low heat 30 minutes, or until vegetables and meats are tender.
5. Put the capon on a large platter and surround with drained vegetables and rice. Drink the broth from cups.

Piquant Chicken

1 frying chicken, cut in serv-	6 limes or 4 lemons, sliced
ing pieces	as thinly as possible
Butter or margarine	Salt and pepper

1. Brown chicken pieces in butter in a skillet.
2. Place chicken in an ovenproof casserole. Cover completely with lime or lemon slices. Sprinkle with salt and pepper. Cover tightly with foil.
3. Bake at 325°F about 1¼ hours, or until chicken is tender.

4 SERVINGS

Chicken with Anchovies

1 chicken (3 pounds), split in	1 tablespoon lemon juice
half	1 slice bacon, chopped
1 can (2 ounces) flat an-	Hot cooked rice
chovy fillets, cut in half	¼ cup sour cream
1 cup chicken broth	¼ teaspoon ginger

1. Slit the skin of the chickens, and insert anchovies in slits as in larding meat.
2. Put chicken, broth, lemon juice, and bacon into a flameproof casserole or Dutch oven. Cover; simmer about 1 hour, or until chicken is tender.
3. Spoon hot rice onto platter. Set chicken on rice.
4. Blend sour cream and ginger into liquid in casserole. Heat just until mixture bubbles; do not boil. Serve sauce over chicken.

4 TO 6 SERVINGS

Chicken or Turkey Mole Poblano I

1 jar (8 ounces) mole	Sugar and salt
poblano paste	3 cups diced cooked chicken
1 cup canned tomato sauce	or turkey
1 cup chicken stock or water	

1. Blend mole paste, tomato sauce, and stock in a large saucepan. Heat to boiling; add sugar and salt to taste. Reduce heat. Stir in chicken. Simmer about 10 to 15 minutes, stirring occasionally, to blend flavors.
2. To use as a tamale filling, the sauce must be fairly thick, so may be simmered until of desired consistency. Then spoon poultry pieces and sauce onto tamale dough spread on corn husk; use leftover sauce to serve over cooked tamales.
3. Or, Chicken or Turkey Mole Poblano may be served over **hot rice**.

ABOUT 4 CUPS FILLING (ENOUGH FOR 3½ DOZEN TAMALES)

Chicken or Turkey Mole Poblano II

6 ancho chilies, fresh or	1 tablespoon sugar
dried	¼ teaspoon anise
2 cups (16-ounce can)	¼ teaspoon cinnamon
cooked tomatoes	¼ teaspoon cloves
1 large onion, coarsely	¼ teaspoon coriander
chopped	¼ teaspoon cumin (comino)
1 clove garlic, peeled	1 cup chicken or turkey
½ cup salted peanuts or ½	stock
cup peanut butter	1 ounce (1 square)
1 tortilla or 1 piece of toast,	unsweetened chocolate
torn in pieces	Salt and pepper
⅓ cup raisins	3 cups diced cooked chicken
2 tablespoons sesame seed	or turkey
¼ cup oil	

1. Prepare chilies. Combine with tomatoes, onion, garlic, peanuts, tortilla, raisins, and sesame seed. Put a small amount at a time into an electric blender and blend to make a thick purée.
2. Heat oil in a large skillet. Add the purée and cook, stirring constantly, about 5 minutes. Stir in sugar, anise, cinnamon, cloves, coriander, cumin, and stock. Bring to boiling, reduce heat, and simmer. Add chocolate and continue simmering, stirring constantly, until chocolate is melted and blended into sauce. Add salt and pepper to taste. Stir in chicken pieces and simmer about 10 minutes.
3. To use as a tamale filling, the sauce must be fairly thick, so it may be simmered until desired consistency is reached. Then spoon poultry pieces and a little sauce onto tamale dough spread on a corn husk. Use leftover sauce to serve over cooked tamales.
4. Or, Chicken or Turkey Mole Poblano may be served over **hot rice**.

ABOUT 4 CUPS FILLING (ENOUGH FOR 3½ DOZEN TAMALES)

Chicken with Poached Garlic

1 broiler-fryer chicken (2½ to 3 pounds)
1 garlic clove, peeled and cut in half
Juice of 1 lime
Salt
Freshly ground white pepper
16 garlic cloves (unpeeled)
½ cup Chicken Stock (page 48)
¼ cup dry vermouth
Chicken Stock
2 teaspoons arrowroot
Cold water
¼ cup Mock Crème Fraîche (page 46)
1 tablespoon snipped parsley
Salt
Freshly ground white pepper

1. Rinse chicken; pat dry. Place in a roasting pan. Rub entire surface of chicken with cut garlic clove. Squeeze lime juice over chicken. Sprinkle cavity and outside of chicken lightly with salt and pepper. Place remaining garlic cloves around chicken; pour in ½ cup stock and ¼ cup dry vermouth.
2. Roast in a 325°F oven about 2½ hours, or until done; meat on drumstick will be very tender. Add stock if necessary to keep garlic covered. Remove chicken to platter. Cover loosely with aluminum foil. Let stand 20 minutes before carving.
3. Spoon fat from roasting pan. Add enough stock to pan to make 1 cup of liquid. Mix arrowroot with a little cold water; stir into stock. Simmer, stirring constantly, until thickened (about 3 minutes). Stir in Mock Crème Fraîche and parsley. Season to taste with salt and pepper. Pass sauce with chicken.
4 SERVINGS

Note: To eat garlic cloves, gently press with fingers; the soft cooked interior will slip out. The flavor of the poached garlic is very delicate.

Chicken with Rice

1 broiler-fryer chicken, (2 to 3 pounds), cut in pieces
¼ cup fat
½ cup chopped onion
1 clove garlic, minced
1 large tomato, chopped
3 cups hot water
1 cup uncooked rice
1 tablespoon minced parsley
2 teaspoons salt
½ teaspoon paprika
¼ teaspoon pepper
¼ teaspoon saffron
1 bay leaf

1. Rinse chicken and pat dry with absorbent paper.
2. Heat fat in a skillet over medium heat. Add onion and garlic; cook until onion is tender. Remove with a slotted spoon; set aside.
3. Put chicken pieces, skin side down, in skillet. Turn to brown pieces on all sides.
4. When chicken is browned, add tomato, onion, water, rice, parsley, and dry seasonings. Cover and cook over low heat about 45 minutes, or until thickest pieces of chicken are tender when pierced with a fork.
6 TO 8 SERVINGS

Marinated Chicken

2 broiler-fryer chickens, cut in serving pieces
1½ cups oil
1 cup cooked sliced carrots
2 large onions, sliced
2 stalks celery, cut in 2-inch pieces
1 clove garlic, minced
⅛ teaspoon thyme
⅛ teaspoon marjoram
1 small bay leaf
12 peppercorns
1 teaspoon salt
3 cups vinegar
Olives, radishes, pickled chilies

1. Brown chicken pieces in hot oil in a skillet. Place browned chicken in a Dutch oven or heavy kettle. Top with carrots, onions, celery, garlic, thyme, marjoram, bay leaf, peppercorns, and salt. Pour vinegar over all.
2. Simmer over low heat until chicken is tender (about 30 to 45 minutes).
3. Remove from heat and let cool to room temperature. Place in refrigerator and chill for at least 1 hour.
4. Garnish with olives, radishes, and chilies.
8 TO 10 SERVINGS

Chicken with Poached Garlic

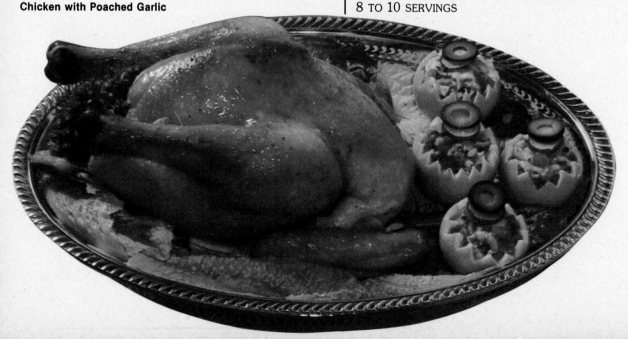

Chicken Tablecloth Stainer

2 frying chickens (about 2½ pounds each), cut in serving pieces
½ pound link sausages
½ cup canned pineapple chunks, drained
1 apple, pared, cored, and sliced
1 large, firm banana, sliced

Sauce:
2 fresh or dried ancho chilies and 2 fresh or dried pasilla chilies, or 1 tablespoon

chili powder
1 cup coarsely chopped onion
1 clove garlic
2 cups (16-ounce can) tomatoes with juice
½ cup whole blanched almonds
¼ teaspoon cinnamon
⅛ teaspoon cloves
2 cups chicken stock, or 2 cups water plus 2 chicken bouillon cubes
Salt and pepper

1. Put chicken pieces into a Dutch oven or heavy kettle.
2. Fry sausages in a skillet until browned. Put into Dutch oven with chicken. Arrange pineapple, apple, and banana over chicken.
3. For sauce, first prepare chilies. (If chilies are not available, substitute chili powder.) Combine chilies, onion, garlic, tomatoes, almonds, cinnamon, and cloves in an electric blender. Blend to a smooth purée.
4. Heat the fat remaining in the skillet in which the sausages were cooked. Add the blended sauce and cook about 5 minutes, stirring constantly. Stir in chicken stock. Season to taste with salt and pepper.
5. Pour sauce over chicken in Dutch oven. Cover and simmer over low heat 1 hour, or until chicken is tender.
6 TO 8 SERVINGS

Chicken Tablecloth Stainer

Martinique Stuffed Chicken in Rum

1 roaster chicken (about 4 pounds)
1 lime, halved
Salt and pepper
2 white bread slices with crusts trimmed
1 cup milk
1 package (3 ounces) cream cheese
2 tablespoons amber rum
½ cup chopped chicken

livers
2 pork sausage links, casing removed and meat chopped finely
1 scallion or green onion, chopped
1 tablespoon chopped parsley
⅛ teaspoon cayenne or red pepper
Salt and pepper (optional)

1. Rub chicken skin with the cut side of lime. Season with salt and pepper. Remove the fat deposits from the opening of the cavity. Set chicken and fat aside.
2. Soak bread in milk. Set aside.
3. Combine cream cheese, rum, chicken liver, sausage, scallion, parsley, and cayenne.
4. Squeeze bread and add to mixture; discard milk. Add salt and pepper, if desired. Mix well.
5. Stuff cavity of chicken with the mixture, then tie chicken legs and wings to hold close to body.
6. Place chicken, breast side up, on rack in a shallow roasting pan. Lay reserved fat across breast.
7. Roast in a 375°F oven about 2 hours.
8. Garnish with **watercress** and serve with Smothered Mixed Vegetables (page 244).
4 TO 6 SERVINGS

Chicken with Peas

3 broiler-fryer chickens (3 pounds each), cut in pieces
1 tablespoon lime juice
Salt and freshly ground pepper
¼ cup soybean oil
1 shallot
1 garlic clove

1 teaspoon dried thyme
1 green hot pepper or 3 dried Italian pepper pods
2 cups chicken stock
3 pounds fresh green peas, shelled
2 tablespoons butter
2 tablespoons cornstarch

1. Season chicken with lime juice, salt, and pepper.
2. Heat oil in a Dutch oven and sauté the chicken pieces until golden brown on all sides.
3. In a mortar, pound to a paste the shallot and garlic. Add seasoning paste, thyme, green hot pepper, 1 cup stock, and peas to the chicken. Reduce heat and simmer 25 minutes, or until chicken and peas are tender.
4. Remove chicken, peas, and hot pepper to a heated platter and keep hot. Add remaining stock to Dutch oven; bring to a boil. Mix butter and cornstarch and add to stock. Stir until sauce is slightly thicker. Add salt and pepper, if desired.
5. Garnish chicken with **chopped parsley** and serve sauce in a sauceboat.
ABOUT 10 SERVINGS

Squab with Peas: Follow recipe for Chicken with Peas, allowing ½ **squab per serving.** Carve birds and place meat on slices of **bread fried in butter.** Pour sauce over meat and croutons.

Quail with Peas: Follow recipe for Chicken with Peas, substituting **1 cup red wine** for the cooking stock. Allow **1 quail per serving.** Carve birds and place meat on slices of **bread fried in butter.** Pour sauce over meat and croutons.

Chicken and Dumplings

¼ cup butter or margarine
2 broiler-fryer chickens, cut in serving-size pieces
½ cup chopped onion
¼ cup chopped celery
2 tablespoons chopped celery leaves
1 clove garlic, minced
¼ cup enriched all-purpose flour
4 cups chicken broth
1 teaspoon sugar
2 teaspoons salt
¼ teaspoon ground black pepper
1 teaspoon basil leaves
2 bay leaves
¼ cup chopped parsley
Basil Dumplings
2 packages (10 ounces each) frozen green peas

1. Heat butter in a large skillet. Add chicken pieces and brown on all sides. Remove chicken from skillet.
2. Add onion, celery, celery leaves, and garlic to fat in skillet. Cook until vegetables are tender. Sprinkle with flour and mix well. Add chicken broth, sugar, salt, pepper, basil, bay leaves, and parsley; bring to boiling, stirring constantly. Return chicken to skillet and spoon sauce over it; cover.
3. Cook in a 350°F oven 40 minutes.
4. Shortly before cooking time is completed, prepare Basil Dumplings.
5. Remove skillet from oven and turn control to 425°F. Stir peas into skillet mixture and bring to boiling. Drop dumpling dough onto stew.
6. Return to oven and cook, uncovered, 10 minutes; cover and cook 10 minutes, or until chicken is tender and dumplings are done.
ABOUT 8 SERVINGS

Basil Dumplings: Combine **2 cups all-purpose biscuit mix** and **1 teaspoon basil leaves** in a bowl. Add **⅔ cup milk** and stir with a fork until a dough is formed. Proceed as directed in recipe.

Spiced Fruited Chicken

1½ teaspoons salt
¼ teaspoon pepper
¼ teaspoon cinnamon
¼ teaspoon cloves
2 cloves garlic, minced
2 frying chickens, cut in serving pieces
¼ cup oil
½ cup chopped onion
½ cup raisins
½ cup crushed pineapple
2 cups orange juice
½ cup dry sherry

1. Combine salt, pepper, cinnamon, cloves, and garlic. Rub into chicken pieces.
2. Heat oil in a heavy skillet. Brown chicken in hot oil. Place browned chicken in a Dutch oven or heavy saucepot.
3. Cook onion in remaining oil in skillet until soft (about 5 minutes).
4. Add onion to chicken along with raisins, pineapple, and orange juice. Add water, if needed, to just cover chicken. Bring to boiling, reduce heat, cover, and cook until chicken is tender (about 1 hour). Add sherry and cook about 5 minutes longer to blend flavors.
6 TO 8 SERVINGS

Braised Chicken and Onions

1 stewing chicken (about 4 pounds)
Papaya leaves
1 lime, halved
1 orange, halved
Salt and freshly ground pepper to taste
3 tablespoons soybean, olive, or peanut oil
3 tablespoons bacon
drippings
2 tablespoons water
24 small onions
2 cups chicken stock
2 tablespoons butter
2 tablespoons cornstarch
Chopped parsley
Chopped scallions or green onions

1. Truss chicken. Wrap in papaya leaves and refrigerate for 12 hours.
2. Rub the chicken with the cut sides of the lime and orange. Season with salt and pepper.
3. Heat oil and bacon drippings in a Dutch oven. Brown chicken. Add water and cover.
4. Cook in a 375°F oven about 2 hours, or until almost tender; turn occasionally and stir the juices. Add stock if more liquid is needed.
5. Add onions and continue cooking until onions are tender and well browned (about 30 minutes).
6. Place chicken and onions on a large serving platter. Carve bird.
7. Pour stock into Dutch oven and set over medium heat to deglaze. Mix butter and cornstarch and add to stock. Stir until sauce is slightly thicker.
8. Pour sauce over meat and sprinkle with chopped parsley and scallions. Serve with Caribbean Rice (page 190).
6 TO 8 SERVINGS

Chicken with Cashews

2 broiler-fryer chickens (about 2 pounds each), cut in pieces
1 lime, halved
Salt, freshly ground pepper, and cayenne or red pepper
½ cup peanut oil
4 shallots, minced
¾ cup dry white wine
½ cup chicken broth
1 cup split cashews
½ cup amber rum
2 tablespoons butter
2 tablespoons cornstarch

1. Rub chicken with the cut side of lime. Season with salt, pepper, and cayenne.
2. Heat oil in a Dutch oven and sauté the chicken until golden brown. Add shallots and brown. Add wine and chicken broth. Cover. Simmer over low heat 25 minutes. Add cashews and simmer about 10 minutes.
3. Remove chicken and cashews with a slotted spoon and keep warm. Remove excess fat from Dutch oven, leaving drippings. Deglaze with rum.
4. Mix butter and cornstarch and add to drippings. Cook over high heat, stirring constantly, until sauce is slightly thicker.
5. Pour sauce over chicken and nuts. Serve with Bananas à l'Antillaise and Guava Jelly (page 260).
6 SERVINGS

Roast Chicken Tarragon

1 broiler-fryer chicken (2½ to 3 pounds)
2 teaspoons clarified butter
2 teaspoons snipped fresh or 1 teaspoon dried tarragon leaves
Salt
2 carrots, cut in 1-inch pieces
1 small onion, cut in quarters
1 stalk celery, cut in 1-inch pieces

2 sprigs parsley
1¼ cups Chicken Stock (page 48)
1 tablespoon arrowroot
Cold water
½ teaspoon salt
¼ teaspoon freshly ground white pepper
2 teaspoons snipped fresh or 1 teaspoon dried tarragon leaves
2 tablespoons dry sherry

1. Rinse chicken; pat dry. Place in a roasting pan. Brush chicken with clarified butter; sprinkle with 2 teaspoons tarragon. Sprinkle cavity with salt; fill cavity with carrot, onion, celery, and parsley.

2. Roast in a 325°F oven about 2½ hours, or until chicken is done; meat on drumstick will be very tender. Remove chicken to a platter. Remove vegetables; reserve. Cover loosely with aluminum foil and let stand 20 minutes before carving.

3. Spoon fat from roasting pan. Heat stock to simmering in roasting pan, stirring to incorporate particles from pan. Mix arrowroot with a little cold water; stir into stock with salt, pepper, 2 teaspoons tarragon, and the sherry. Simmer, stirring constantly, until stock is thickened (about 5 minutes).

4. Slice chicken and arrange on platter. Garnish with reserved vegetables. Serve with sauce.

4 SERVINGS

Country Captain

1 broiler-fryer chicken (3 to 3½ pounds), cut in serving-size pieces
¼ cup enriched all-purpose flour
½ teaspoon salt
Pinch ground white pepper
3 to 4 tablespoons lard
2 onions, finely chopped
2 medium green peppers, chopped
1 clove garlic, crushed in a garlic press or minced
1½ teaspoons salt
½ teaspoon ground white pepper
1½ teaspoons curry powder
½ teaspoon ground thyme
½ teaspoon snipped parsley
5 cups undrained canned tomatoes
2 cups hot cooked rice
¼ cup dried currants
¾ cup roasted blanched almonds
Parsley sprigs

1. Remove skin from chicken. Mix flour, ½ teaspoon salt, and pinch white pepper. Coat chicken pieces.
2. Melt lard in a large heavy skillet; add chicken and brown on all sides. Remove pieces from skillet and keep hot.
3. Cook onions, peppers, and garlic in the same skillet, stirring occasionally until onion is lightly browned. Blend 1½ teaspoons salt, ½ teaspoon white pepper, curry powder, and thyme. Mix into skillet along with parsley and tomatoes.
4. Arrange chicken in a shallow roasting pan and pour tomato mixture over it. (If it does not cover chicken, add a small amount of water to the skillet in which mixture was cooked and pour liquid over chicken.) Place a cover on pan or cover tightly with aluminum foil.
5. Cook in a 350°F oven about 45 minutes, or until chicken is tender.
6. Arrange chicken in center of a large heated platter and pile the hot rice around it. Stir currants into sauce remaining in the pan and pour over the rice. Scatter almonds over top. Garnish with parsley.

ABOUT 6 SERVINGS

Spiced Fruited Chicken

12 pieces frying chicken (breasts, legs, and thighs)
1½ teaspoons salt
¼ teaspoon each pepper, cinnamon, and cloves
2 garlic cloves, minced
¼ cup oil
½ cup chopped onion
1 can (13¼ ounces) crushed pineapple
1⅓ cups orange juice (about)
½ cup raisins
½ cup dry sherry

1. Rub chicken with mixture of salt, pepper, cinnamon, cloves, and garlic. Brown in oil in a heavy skillet.
2. Place browned chicken pieces in an attractive range-to-table Dutch oven.
3. Lightly brown onion in oil remaining in skillet.
4. Drain pineapple, reserving liquid. Add enough orange juice to liquid to measure 2 cups.
5. Add onion, pineapple, raisins, and orange juice mixture to chicken. Cover and simmer about 45 minutes, or until chicken is tender.
6. Remove chicken. Add sherry; cook uncovered 15 minutes longer to cool down liquid. Return chicken; heat through.

12 SERVINGS

Chicken Fricassee with Vegetables

1 broiler-fryer chicken (about 3 pounds), cut in serving-size pieces
1½ teaspoons salt
1 bay leaf
Water
2 cups sliced carrots
2 onions, quartered
2 crookneck squashes, cut in halves lengthwise
2 pattypan squashes, cut in halves
Green beans (about 6 ounces), tips cut off
1 can (3½ ounces) pitted ripe olives, drained
1 tablespoon cornstarch
2 tablespoons water

1. Place chicken pieces along with salt and bay leaf in a Dutch oven or saucepot. Add enough water to just cover chicken. Bring to boiling; simmer, covered, 25 minutes until chicken is almost tender.
2. Add carrots and onions to cooking liquid; cook, covered, 10 minutes. Add squashes and green beans to cooking liquid; cook, covered, 10 minutes, or until chicken and vegetables are tender. Remove chicken and vegetables to a warm serving dish and add olives; keep hot.
3. Blend cornstarch and 2 tablespoons water; stir into boiling cooking liquid. Boil 2 to 3 minutes. Pour gravy over chicken.

ABOUT 4 SERVINGS

Chicken Polynesian Style

2 cups chicken broth
1 package (10 ounces) frozen mixed vegetables
½ cup diagonally sliced celery
1½ tablespoons cornstarch
½ teaspoon sugar
½ teaspoon seasoned salt
⅛ teaspoon ground black pepper
½ teaspoon Worcestershire sauce
1 small clove garlic, minced or crushed in a garlic press
1 tablespoon instant minced onion
1 can (6 ounces) ripe olives, drained and cut in wedges
Cooked chicken, cut in 1-inch pieces (about 2 cups)
Chow mein noodles
Salted peanuts
Soy sauce

1. Heat ½ cup chicken broth in a saucepan. Add frozen vegetables and celery; cook, covered, until crisp-tender. Remove vegetables and set aside; reserve any cooking liquid in saucepan.
2. Mix cornstarch, sugar, seasoned salt, and pepper; blend with ¼ cup of the chicken broth. Add remaining broth, Worcestershire sauce, garlic, and onion to the saucepan. Add cornstarch mixture; bring to boiling, stirring constantly. Cook and stir 2 to 3 minutes.
3. Mix in olives, chicken, and reserved vegetables; heat thoroughly, stirring occasionally.
4. Serve over chow mein noodles and top generously with peanuts. Accompany with a cruet of soy sauce.

ABOUT 6 SERVINGS

Chicken Italiano

2 whole chicken breasts
  (about 1 pound)
2 tablespoons oil
½ pound mushrooms,
  cleaned and chopped
1 can (16 ounces) stewed
  tomatoes
1 medium clove garlic,
  crushed in a garlic press

1 teaspoon oregano
½ teaspoon thyme
1 can (8 ounces) tomato
  sauce
⅓ cup grated Parmesan
  cheese
Salt and pepper
6 dinner crêpes

1. Bone chicken and cut into 1-inch strips.
2. Heat oil, sauté chicken and mushrooms until chicken turns white. Stir in stewed tomatoes, garlic, oregano, thyme, tomato sauce, and 3 tablespoons grated cheese. Add salt and pepper to taste. Simmer, uncovered, 5 minutes.
3. Using a slotted spoon, spoon onto crêpes. Assemble, using tube method (page 36), place on a baking sheet, and sprinkle tops of crêpes with remaining cheese.
4. Bake at 375°F until cheese browns (about 15 minutes). Serve immediately with any remaining sauce.
6 FILLED CRÊPES

Barbecued Chicken, Quail, or Guinea Fowl

Chicken, quail, or guinea
  fowl

Creole Barbecue Sauce (page
  52)

1. Split the birds in half and remove the backbone and neck.
2. Marinate birds overnight in Creole Barbecue Sauce.
3. Place bird halves on a grill 5 inches from glowing coals. Barbecue 25 minutes, turning several times and basting with the barbecue sauce.
4. Serve with **barbecued yams.**
ALLOW ½ BIRD PER SERVING

Chicken Livers and Mushrooms

2 pounds chicken livers,
  thawed if frozen
½ cup enriched all-purpose
  flour
1 teaspoon salt
¼ teaspoon ground white
  pepper

⅓ cup butter or margarine
1 cup orange sections, cut in
  halves
1 can (6 ounces) broiled
  mushrooms
Fresh parsley, snipped

1. Rinse chicken livers and drain on absorbent paper. Mix flour, salt, and peper; coat chicken livers evenly.
2. Heat butter in a large skillet, add chicken livers, and cook 10 minutes, or until livers are lightly browned and tender. Mix in orange sections; heat.
3. Meanwhile, heat mushrooms in their broth in a small skillet.
4. Arrange cooked chicken livers and heated orange sections on a hot platter. Top with mushrooms and sprinkle with parsley. Serve immediately.
ABOUT 6 SERVINGS

Chicken with Fruit

1 tablespoon flour
1 teaspoon seasoned salt
¾ teaspoon paprika
3 pounds broiler-fryer
  chicken pieces (legs, thighs,
  and breasts)
1½ tablespoons vegetable oil
1½ tablespoons butter or
  margarine
1 clove garlic, crushed in a
  garlic press or minced
⅓ cup chicken broth
2 tablespoons cider vinegar

1 tablespoon brown sugar
¼ teaspoon rosemary
1 can (11 ounces) mandarin
  oranges, drained; reserve
  syrup
1 jar (4 ounces) maraschino
  cherries, drained; reserve
  syrup
1 tablespoon water
1 tablespoon cornstarch
½ cup dark seedless raisins
Cooked rice

1. Mix flour, seasoned salt, and paprika. Coat chicken pieces.
2. Heat oil, butter, and garlic in a large heavy skillet. Add chicken pieces and brown well on all sides.
3. Mix broth, vinegar, brown sugar, rosemary, and reserved syrups. Pour into skillet; cover and cook slowly 25 minutes, or until chicken is tender.
4. Remove chicken pieces to a serving dish and keep warm; skim any excess fat from liquid in skillet. Blend water with cornstarch and stir into liquid in skillet. Add raisins, bring to boiling, stirring constantly, and cook about 5 minutes, or until mixture is thickened and smooth. Mix in orange sections and cherries; heat thoroughly.
5. Pour sauce over chicken and serve with hot fluffy rice.
ABOUT 6 SERVINGS

Chicken Mexicana

3 tablespoons vegetable oil
2 broiler-fryer chickens (2½
  to 3 pounds each), cut in
  serving-size pieces
2 cans (8 ounces each)
  tomato sauce
1 can (13¾ ounces) chicken
  broth
2 tablespoons (½ envelope)

dry onion soup mix
¾ cup chopped onion
1 clove garlic, minced
6 tablespoons crunchy
  peanut butter
½ cup cream
½ teaspoon chili powder
¼ cup dry sherry
Cooked rice

1. Heat oil in a large skillet. Add chicken and brown on all sides.
2. Meanwhile, combine tomato sauce, 1 cup chicken broth, soup mix, onion, and garlic in a saucepan. Heat thoroughly, stirring constantly.
3. Pour sauce over chicken in skillet. Simmer, covered, 20 minutes.
4. Put peanut butter into a bowl and blend in cream and remaining chicken broth; stir into skillet along with chili powder and sherry. Heat thoroughly. Serve with hot fluffy rice.
ABOUT 6 SERVINGS

Chicken Paprika with Spatzle

1 frying chicken, 2 to 3 pounds, ready-to-cook weight
1 quart hot water
1 small onion
3 parsley sprigs
2 teaspoons salt
3 peppercorns
1 bay leaf
8 slices bacon
¼ cup finely chopped onion
¾ cup all-purpose flour
1½ teaspoons salt
1½ teaspoon paprika
2 tablespoons fat

2 tablespoons all-purpose flour
1 cup reserved giblet broth
⅔ cup milk
1½ tablespoons paprika
1½ cups thick sour cream
2 quarts water
2 teaspoons salt
2⅓ cups sifted all-purpose flour
1 teaspoon salt
1 egg, slightly beaten
1 cup water
¼ cup butter or margarine, melted

1. For Chicken Paprika – Set out a deep, heavy 10-inch skillet (or a Dutch oven) having a tight-fitting cover.
2. Clean, rinse chicken and pat dry with absorbent paper.
3. Disjoint and cut into serving-size pieces. (If chicken is frozen, thaw according to directions on package.) Cut away and discard tough lining from gizzard. Slit heart; remove blood vessels. Refrigerate chicken and liver. Place cleaned gizzard, heart and neck into a saucepan and add water, onion, parsley sprigs, salt, peppercorns and bay leaf.
4. Bring water to boiling. Skim off and discard foam. Cover saucepan tightly and simmer 1 hour, or until giblets and neck meat are tender when pierced with a fork.
5. Shortly before end of cooking period, dice bacon and place into the skillet.
6. Cook slowly, stirring and turning frequently, until bacon is slightly crisp and browned. Add chopped onion.
7. Stirring occasionally, cook until onion is almost tender.
8. Meanwhile, coat chicken evenly by shaking 2 or 3 pieces at a time in a plastic bag containing a mixture of flour, salt and paprika.
9. With slotted spoon, remove bacon and onion from skillet, leaving bacon fat in skillet. Set aside.
10. Slightly increase heat under the skillet. Starting with meaty pieces of chicken, brown skin sides first. Put in less meaty pieces as others brown. To brown on all sides, turn chicken pieces as necessary with two spoons or tongs. When chicken is lightly and evenly browned, reduce heat.
11. Add cooked gizzard, heart and neck to the skillet with 1 or 2 tablespoons of the giblet broth. (Strain remainder of broth; reserve 1 cup and cool to lukewarm.) Cover skillet tightly. Add liver to skillet 10 to 15 minutes before end of cooking time. Cook chicken slowly 25 to 40 minutes, or until thick pieces are tender when pierced with a fork.
12. Meanwhile, melt fat in a small saucepan over low heat.
13. Blend flour into the fat.
14. Heat until mixture bubbles, stirring constantly. Remove from heat and add reserved giblet broth gradually, stirring constantly.
15. Return saucepan to heat and bring mixture rapidly to boiling, stirring constantly; cook 1 to 2 minutes longer. Gradually add milk and paprika to sauce, stirring constantly.
16. When thoroughly heated, remove saucepan from heat. Stirring vigorously with a French whip, whisk beater, or fork, add sour cream to the sauce in very small amounts.
17. Mix in the bacon and onion. Pour the sauce into the skillet over each piece of chicken. Cook the mixture over low heat, stirring sauce and turning chicken frequently, 3 to 5 minutes, until thoroughly heated; do not boil. Cover skillet tightly; turn off heat under chicken and let stand about 1 hour. About twice during hour spoon sauce over chicken. Reheat just before serving.
18. For Spatzle (Drop Noodles) – After setting chicken and sauce aside, bring to boiling water and salt in a 3- or 4-quart saucepan.
19. Meanwhile, sift together flour and salt and set aside.
20. Combine in a bowl and mix together egg and water.
21. Gradually add flour mixture to egg mixture, stirring until smooth. (Batter should be very thick and break from a spoon instead of pouring in a continuous stream.) Spoon batter into the boiling water by ½ teaspoonfuls, dipping spoon into water each time. Cook only one layer of noodles at one

time; do not crowd. After noodles rise to the surface, boil gently 5 to 8 minutes, or until soft when pressed against side of pan with spoon. Remove from water with slotted spoon, draining over water for a second, and place into a warm bowl. Toss noodles lightly with butter or margarine.
22. Place chicken onto a platter, leaving room at one end of platter for noodles. Cover chicken with sauce; sprinkle with paprika. Arrange noodles on platter. Garnish with parsley.
4 TO 6 SERVINGS

Stuffed Roast Capon

½ cup butter or margarine	bread cubes
1½ teaspoons salt	½ cup milk
¼ teaspoon ground black pepper	¼ cup chopped celery leaves
¼ teaspoon thyme	¼ cup chopped onion
¼ teaspoon marjoram	1 capon (6 to 7 pounds)
¼ teaspoon rosemary	Salt
1½ quarts soft enriched	Fat, melted

1. For stuffing, melt butter and mix in salt, pepper, thyme, marjoram, and rosemary.
2. Put bread cubes into a large bowl and pour in seasoned butter; lightly toss. Mix in milk, celery leaves, and onion.
3. Rub body and neck cavities of capon with salt. Fill cavities lightly with stuffing; truss bird, using skewers and cord.
4. Place, breast side up, on rack in a shallow roasting pan. Brush skin with melted fat and cover with a fat-moistened cheesecloth.
5. Roast in a 325°F oven 2½ hours, or until a meat thermometer inserted in center of inside thigh muscle registers 180°F to 185°F. For easier carving, allow capon to stand about 20 minutes after removing from oven. Serve on a heated platter.
6 TO 8 SERVINGS

Brewers' Chicken

1 broiler-fryer chicken (2 to 2½ pounds), cut up	1 tablespoon ketchup
12 small white onions; or 3 medium onions, sliced	½ teaspoon each thyme or rosemary, paprika, and salt
3 tablespoons cooking oil	1 bay leaf
¾ cup beer	½ cup milk or half-and-half
	3 tablespoons flour

1. In a large skillet, brown chicken and onions in oil, removing pieces as they brown. Pour off excess fat.
2. Add beer, ketchup, and seasonings to skillet. Stir up brown bits.
3. Return chicken and onions to skillet. Cover and simmer 30 to 35 minutes, or until tender.
4. With a slotted spoon, transfer chicken and onions to serving platter; keep warm. Boil down cooking liquid to about 1½ cups.
5. Stir milk into flour until smooth. Add to liquid in skillet. Cook, stirring constantly, until thickened and smooth. Strain, if desired.
4 SERVINGS

Broiled Marinated Chicken

1 broiler-fryer chicken (2 to 2½ pounds), cut up	2 tablespoons honey
1 can or bottle (12 ounces) beer	1 garlic clove, slivered
2 tablespoons lemon juice	½ teaspoon crushed rosemary
2 tablespoons oil	½ teaspoon salt
	⅛ teaspoon pepper

1. Place chicken in a shallow dish just large enough to hold pieces. Combine remaining ingredients; pour over chicken. Marinate in refrigerator at least 6 hours or overnight.
2. Grill or broil 6 to 8 inches from heat, basting often with marinade and turning, 30 to 40 minutes, or until tender.
4 SERVINGS

Crunchy Fried Chicken

1 cup all-purpose flour	½ cup beer
½ teaspoon salt	1 broiler-fryer chicken (2 to 2½ pounds), cut up
¼ teaspoon pepper	Cooking oil
2 eggs	

1. Mix flour, salt, and pepper. Beat eggs with beer; add to flour mixture. Stir until smooth.
2. Dip chicken in batter, coating pieces well. Chill 1 hour.
3. Fry chicken in hot oil ½ to 1 inch deep 15 minutes on one side. Turn; fry on other side 5 to 10 minutes, or until browned and done. Drain on absorbent paper.
4 SERVINGS

Roast Chicken with Orange-Beer Sauce

1 roasting chicken (4 to 5 pounds)	2 tablespoons lemon juice
Stuffing (optional)	2 tablespoons tomato paste or ketchup
Salt and pepper	2 teaspoons sugar
1 can or bottle (12 ounces) beer	¼ cup flour
½ cup orange juice	Fresh parsley and orange slices

1. Stuff chicken, if desired; truss. Rub with salt and pepper. Place in a roasting pan.
2. Combine 1 cup beer, orange juice, lemon juice, tomato paste, and sugar. Pour a little over chicken.
3. Roast, uncovered, at 375°F 2 to 2½ hours, or until done, basting occasionally with remaining beer mixture.
4. Transfer chicken to platter; keep warm. Skim fat from drippings; measure remaining liquid. If needed, add water to make 1½ cups. Make paste with flour and remaining ½ cup beer. Combine with liquid. Cook, stirring constantly, until thickened. Season with salt and pepper to taste.
5. Garnish chicken with parsley and orange slices. Pass sauce to pour over slices after carving.
6 SERVINGS

Ham-Bread Stuffing for Chicken: Combine **3 cups fresh bread cubes, ¼ pound ground ham, 1 small onion, minced, 2 tablespoons melted butter, ½ teaspoon salt, ¼ teaspoon sage, a dash pepper,** and just enough **beer** to moisten.

Chicken Tetrazzini

1 (3 pound) broiler chicken
2 cups water
1 cup dry white wine
2 carrots, cubed
1 medium finely chopped onion
2 parsley stalks
½ teaspoon thyme
1½ teaspoons salt

4 tablespoons butter
5 tablespoons flour
3 cups chicken stock
4 ounces light cream
6 ounces grated Parmesan cheese
1 cup sliced mushrooms
8 ounces ribbon macaroni

1. Place chicken in a casserole. Add water, wine, carrots, onion, parsley, thyme and salt. Bring to a boil, skim and let boil gently for about 40 minutes with casserole covered.
2. Strain the stock and save.
3. Skin and bone the chicken when cold. Cut the meat in slices.
4. Melt 3 tablespoons butter in a saucepan. Add the flour and stir. Add in turns 3 cups stock. Add the cream and heat for about 5 minutes. Stir in the Parmesan cheese, but save some for the top.
5. Preheat the oven to 350°F.
6. Melt the rest of the butter in a frying pan and brown the mushrooms lightly.
7. Bring 2 quarts of water with 3 teaspoons salt to a boil. Add the ribbon macaroni and boil until just soft, but no more.
8. Wash the macaroni and drain.
9. Mix mushrooms and macaroni and place at the bottom of a large ovenproof dish. Put the chicken on top. Pour on the sauce. Sprinkle with the remaining cheese.
10. Bake in the oven for about 15 minutes.
SERVES 6

African-Style Chicken

1 broiler-fryer chicken (2 to 2½ pounds), cut up
2 tablespoons peanut or other cooking oil
1 medium onion, chopped
1 garlic clove, minced
¾ cup beer
⅓ cup ground peanuts
1 tablespoon lemon juice

1 tablespoon honey
½ teaspoon salt
¼ to ½ teaspoon dried ground chili pepper or chili powder
¼ teaspoon ginger
3 tablespoons cream or milk
2 to 3 tablespoons flour
¼ cup flaked coconut

1. Brown chicken in oil in a heavy skillet; set aside.
2. Sauté onion and garlic in same skillet until golden. Add beer, peanuts, lemon juice, honey, and seasonings; mix.
3. Return chicken to skillet. Cover and simmer 35 to 40 minutes, or until tender.
4. Place chicken on a platter; keep warm. Measure cooking liquid. Make a paste of cream and flour, using 2 tablespoons flour per 1 cup cooking liquid. Add coconut. Cook, stirring constantly, until thickened. Pour part of sauce over chicken. Pass remainder to pour over **rice** or **potatoes.**
4 SERVINGS

Chicken and Rice in Beer

1 broiler-fryer chicken (2 to 2½ pounds), cut up
2 tablespoons oil
2 medium onions, chopped
1 garlic clove, minced
¾ cup uncooked rice (not instant)
½ green pepper, chopped

½ cup chopped fresh or canned tomatoes
1½ teaspoons salt
¼ teaspoon pepper
1 can or bottle (12 ounces) beer
2 bay leaves

1. Brown chicken in oil in a large skillet; set chicken aside.
2. In same skillet, sauté onion and garlic until golden.
3. Stir in rice, green pepper, tomatoes, 1 teaspoon salt, and pepper. Put mixture into a large, shallow baking dish.
4. Sprinkle chicken with ½ teaspoon salt; place on top of rice mixture.
5. Add beer to skillet; stir up brown bits. Pour over chicken and vegetables. Add bay leaves.
6. Cover tightly with foil or lid.
7. Bake at 375°F 40 to 60 minutes, or until chicken and rice are tender.
4 SERVINGS

Chicken Easy Oriental Style

¼ cup flour
1 teaspoon salt
¼ teaspoon pepper
4 chicken breasts, split in halves
¼ cup shortening
1 can (10¾ ounces) condensed cream of chicken

soup
¼ cup dry white wine
¼ cup milk
1 can (4 ounces) water chestnuts, drained and sliced
¼ teaspooon ground ginger

1. Combine flour, salt, and pepper; coat chicken with mixture.
2. Brown chicken in shortening in skillet. Place in a 13x9-inch baking dish.
3. Combine soup, wine, milk, chestnuts, and ginger. Pour over chicken.
4. Bake, covered, at 350°F 1 hour, or until chicken is tender. If desired, sprinkle with snipped parsley.
4 SERVINGS

Chicken and Tomato Casserole

1 broiler-fryer chicken (about 3 pounds), cut up
3 tablespoons shortening
½ cup chopped onion
¼ cup chopped green pepper
1 can (28 ounces) tomatoes

(undrained)
1 can (8 ounces) tomato sauce
1 can (6 ounces) tomato paste
1 teaspoon salt
1 teaspoon oregano

1. Brown chicken in shortening in a skillet. Place in a 2-quart casserole.
2. Sauté onion and green pepper in fat in skillet. Stir in remaining ingredients and pour over chicken.
3. Bake, covered, at 350°F 1 hour, or until chicken is tender. Serve with **hot, cooked spaghetti.**
4 SERVINGS

Chicken Tetrazzini

Chicken Novaes

2 jars (6 ounces each) tamales
1 can (4 ounces) sliced mushrooms, drained
2 cans (8 ounces each) tomato sauce
12 slices cooked chicken
2 cups cooked white rice
1 cup chopped green onion
2 cans (10¾ ounces each) condensed cream of chicken soup
1 cup (4 ounces) shredded Cheddar cheese
½ cup buttered bread crumbs

1. Remove paper from tamales. Cut in half crosswise and arrange in bottom of a 3-quart casserole.
2. Over the tamales, layer mushrooms, 1 can tomato sauce, chicken, rice and onion. Top with the remaining can of tomato sauce. Spoon chicken soup over all, inserting a knife so soup will seep through.
3. Combine cheese and bread crumbs. Sprinkle over top of casserole mixture.
4. Bake, covered, at 350°F 30 minutes, or until bubbly.
12 SERVINGS

Thyme-Chicken Casserole

4 chicken breasts, split in halves
1 teaspoon salt
¼ teaspoon pepper
¼ cup butter or margarine
1 can (10¾ ounces) condensed cream of mushroom soup
¼ cup dry white wine
1 can (4 ounces) sliced mushrooms, drained
¼ cup chopped green pepper
¼ teaspoon thyme
1 tablespoon instant minced onion

1. Season chicken with salt and pepper. Brown in butter in a skillet. Arrange, skin side up, in a 13x9-inch baking dish.
2. Blend soup into drippings. Slowly stir in wine. Add remaining ingredients; heat thoroughly. Pour over chicken.
3. Bake, covered, at 350°F 50 minutes. Remove cover and bake an additional 10 minutes, or until chicken is tender.
4 SERVINGS

Italian Baked Chicken

¼ cup butter or margarine, melted
1 tablespoon lemon juice
1 broiler-fryer chicken (about 3 pounds), cut up
1 package (1½ ounces)
spaghetti sauce mix
⅔ cup fine dry bread crumbs
½ to 1 cup half-and-half
1 cup (4 ounces) shredded mozzarella cheese

1. Combine butter and lemon juice. Dip chicken pieces in butter mixture.
2. Combine spaghetti sauce mix and bread crumbs; coat chicken pieces with mixture.
3. Place chicken pieces, skin side up, in a 1½-quart shallow baking dish. Pour half-and-half around and between chicken pieces.
4. Bake, covered, at 350°F 1 hour, or until chicken is tender. Top with cheese and bake 2 minutes, or until cheese is melted.
4 SERVINGS

Swiss Chicken Bake

6 chicken breasts, split in halves, boned, and skin removed
1½ cups (6 ounces) shredded Swiss cheese
1 can (10¾ ounces) condensed cream of chicken
soup
½ cup sherry
3 cups packaged herb stuffing mix
1 tablespoon butter or margarine

1. Place chicken breasts in a 13x9-inch baking dish. Sprinkle with cheese.
2. Combine soup and sherry; pour over Swiss cheese. Evenly spoon dressing over all. Dot with butter.
3. Bake, covered, at 350°F 1 hour, or until chicken is tender.
6 SERVINGS

Chicken Surprise

½ cup chopped onion
1 tablespoon butter or margarine
1 tablespoon cornstarch
¾ cup orange juice
2 tablespoons prepared
mustard
½ cup sherry
2 cups chopped cooked chicken
½ cup raisins
½ cup sliced celery

1. Sauté onion in butter in a skillet. Stir in cornstarch. Gradually add orange juice, mustard and sherry, stirring until thickened and smooth.
2. Place chicken, raisins, and celery in a 1-quart casserole. Pour sauce over all; mix.
3. Bake, covered, at 325°F 30 minutes, or until heated through. Serve in **chow mein noodle** or **patty shells** and garnish with **orange twists.**
4 SERVINGS

Chicken and Rice Valencia

1 broiler-fryer chicken (about 3 pounds), cut up
¼ cup olive oil
1 medium onion, finely chopped
1 medium green pepper, slivered
1 can (10 ounces) tomatoes (undrained)
1 bay leaf
¾ cup water
Dash ground saffron (optional)
1 cup drained stuffed olives
1 package (6 ounces) Spanish rice mix
½ cup chopped celery

1. Brown chicken pieces in olive oil in a skillet.
2. Add remaining ingredients, except rice and celery. Place in a 2-quart casserole.
3. Bake, covered, at 350°F 1 hour, or until chicken is tender.
4. Meanwhile, prepare rice according to package directions. Stir celery into rice. Spread on hot serving platter.
5. Remove bay leaf from chicken. Spoon chicken and sauce over rice.
4 SERVINGS

Crispy Chicken with Curried Fruit

1 cup corn flake crumbs
½ teaspoon salt
Dash pepper
1 broiler-fryer chicken (about
3 pounds), cut up
½ cup evaporated milk
Curried Fruit

1. Combine crumbs, salt, and pepper. Dip chicken pieces in milk. Roll in crumb mixture. Place chicken pieces in a 1½-quart shallow baking dish.
2. Bake, uncovered, at 350°F with Curried Fruit 1 hour, or until chicken is tender.
4 SERVINGS

Curried Fruit

1 can (16 ounces) peach halves, drained*
1 can (8½ ounces) pineapple chunks, drained*
4 maraschino cherries
¼ cup butter or margarine, melted
½ cup firmly packed brown sugar
1 tablespoon curry powder

1. Put fruits into a 1½-quart casserole. Combine butter, brown sugar, and curry powder. Spoon over fruits.
2. Bake, covered, at 350°F 1 hour. Serve with **hot, cooked rice.**
4 SERVINGS

*The drained liquids can be refrigerated and used in gelatin salads.

Skillet Chicken and Vegetables

1 can (about 10 ounces) condensed chicken broth
1 cup dry white wine, such as chablis
1 tablespoon instant minced onion
½ teaspoon salt
1 bay leaf
¼ teaspoon rosemary, crushed
6 half breasts of chicken
6 small carrots
6 small zucchini
2 tablespoons cornstarch
2 tablespoons cold water
3 tablespoons chopped pimento
2 tablespoons chopped parsley

1. Combine broth, wine, onion, salt, bay leaf, and rosemary in a large skillet. Heat to boiling.
2. Place chicken breasts in the boiling liquid; cover and simmer 20 minutes.
3. While chicken is cooking, pare carrots and cut in half lengthwise. Cut zucchini in half lengthwise. Add carrots and zucchini to the chicken; cover, and cook 15 minutes longer, or until chicken is tender and vegetables are crisp-tender.
4. Remove chicken and vegetables with a slotted spoon; keep warm.
5. Mix cornstarch with water and stir into liquid remaining in skillet. Cook, stirring until sauce boils thoroughly. Add pimento and parsley, and pour over chicken and vegetables. Serve immediately.
6 SERVINGS

Chicken Mac

1 package (7¼ ounces) macaroni and cheese dinner
1 tablespoon instant minced onion
2 tablespoons chopped celery
2 tablespoons chopped green pepper
1 garlic clove, minced
2 tablespoons butter or margarine
1 can (8¾ ounces) whole kernel corn, drained
1 can (10¾ ounces) condensed cream of chicken soup
1½ cups chopped cooked chicken or turkey
2 tablespoons snipped parsley
⅓ cup buttered bread crumbs

1. Prepare dinner according to package directions, except use ½ cup milk.
2. Sauté onion, celery, green pepper, and garlic in butter in a skillet. Combine with corn, soup, chicken, and prepared dinner. Put into a greased 1½-quart casserole.
3. Combine parsley and bread crumbs. Sprinkle over top of casserole mixture.
4. Bake, covered, at 350°F 25 minutes, or until heated through.
4 SERVINGS

Chicken Pie

1¼ cups water
1 cup milk
1 package (⅞ ounce) chicken gravy mix
1 package (10 ounces) frozen peas, thawed
2 tablespoons chopped pimento
2 cups cubed cooked chicken
1 tablespoon finely chopped onion
1 teaspoon snipped parsley
2 cups all-purpose biscuit mix

1. Combine ¾ cup water, milk, and gravy mix in a saucepan; bring to a boil.
2. Stir in peas, pimento, and chicken; heat thoroughly.
3. Stir onion, parsley, and remaining ½ cup water into biscuit mix, stirring until thoroughly moistened.
4. Pour hot chicken mixture into an 11x7-inch shallow baking dish. Roll or pat out dough to fit top of baking dish. Set on chicken mixture.
5. Bake, uncovered, at 450°F 10 to 12 minutes, or until topping is golden brown.
6 SERVINGS

Chicken Breasts with Sour Cream

8 chicken breasts, split in halves, boned, and skin removed
16 bacon slices
3 packages (3 ounces each)
smoked sliced beef
1 can (10¾ ounces) condensed cream of mushroom soup
2 cups sour cream

1. Roll each chicken breast in 1 bacon slice. (Another half bacon slice may be needed if the breast is a large one, so that all of it will be surrounded by the bacon.)
2. Shred beef and place in a 13x9-inch baking dish. Top with chicken breasts.
3. Combine soup and sour cream. Spoon over chicken breasts.
4. Bake, uncovered, at 275°F 3 hours, or until chicken is tender. Cover lightly with foil if it begins to get too brown.
8 SERVINGS

Chicken Artichoke Casserole

⅓ cup butter or margarine
¼ cup flour
1¾ cups milk
Dash ground red pepper
1 garlic clove, minced
¼ cup (1 ounce) shredded Cheddar cheese
1½ ounces Gruyère cheese,
cut up
2 cups chopped cooked chicken
1 can (4 ounces) button mushrooms, drained
1 can (14 ounces) artichoke hearts, drained

1. Melt butter in a saucepan. Stir in flour. Gradually add milk, stirring until thickened and smooth.
2. Add red pepper, garlic, and cheese, stirring until smooth. Blend in chicken, mushrooms, and artichoke hearts. Pour into a 2-quart casserole.
3. Bake, covered, at 350°F 30 minutes, or until heated through. Sprinkle with **paprika**.
6 SERVINGS

Chicken Bake

8 slices white bread, crusts removed
4 cups chopped cooked chicken or turkey
1 jar (4½ ounces) mushroom stems and pieces, drained
1 can (4 ounces) water chestnuts, drained and sliced
8 slices (1 ounce each) Cheddar cheese
¼ cup mayonnaise
4 eggs, well beaten
2 cups milk
1 teaspoon salt
2 cans (10¾ ounces each) condensed cream of mushroom soup
1 tablespoon chopped pimento
½ cup buttered bread crumbs

1. Place bread in a 13x9-inch baking dish. Top with chicken, mushrooms, water chestnuts, cheese, and mayonnaise.
2. Combine eggs, milk, and salt. Pour over all in casserole.
3. Mix soup and pimento; spread over top. Cover and refrigerate overnight.
4. Bake, covered, at 325°F 1 hour. Remove cover; sprinkle with bread crumbs and bake an additional 15 minutes, or until set. Let stand a few minutes before serving.
8 SERVINGS

Chicken-Chip Bake

2 cups chopped cooked chicken
2 cups sliced celery
1 can (8 ounces) pineapple chunks, drained
¾ cup mayonnaise
⅓ cup toasted slivered almonds
2 tablespoons lemon juice
2 teaspoons finely chopped onion
½ teaspoon salt
½ cup (2 ounces) shredded American cheese
1 cup crushed potato chips

1. Combine chicken, celery, pineapple, mayonnaise, almonds, lemon juice, onion, and salt. Put into a 1½-quart casserole. Sprinkle with cheese and potato chips.
2. Bake, uncovered, at 350°F 30 minutes, or until heated through.
4 TO 6 SERVINGS

Chicken-Green Noodle Casserole

½ cup chopped onion
½ cup slivered almonds
1 cup sliced fresh mushrooms
¼ cup butter or margarine
3 cups cooked spinach (green) noodles
1 cup milk
2 cans (10¾ ounces each) condensed cream of chicken soup
3 cups chopped cooked chicken
¼ teaspoon pepper
⅓ cup buttered bread crumbs

1. Sauté onion, almonds, and mushrooms in butter in a skillet. Combine with remaining ingredients, except bread crumbs. Put into a 2½-quart casserole.
2. Bake, covered, at 350°F 30 minutes. Remove cover. Sprinkle with bread crumbs and bake an additional 15 minutes, or until heated through.
8 SERVINGS

Chicken Breasts with Noodles

8 whole chicken breasts, flattened
Salt and pepper to taste
Dash of crushed marjoram
Butter to cover skillet
3 pounds fresh mushrooms
½ pound butter
12 ounces noodles
2 tablespoons butter
2 cups Medium White Sauce (see recipe)
1 cup cold milk
1 cup chicken broth
Hollandaise Sauce (see recipe)
½ cup dry white wine
Parmesan cheese, grated

1. Season chicken breasts with salt, pepper, and marjoram. Sauté in butter until breasts are fully cooked.
2. While chicken is cooking, wash mushrooms and cut into small pieces, then sauté in ½ pound butter.
3. Cook noodles until done; drain and work 2 tablespoons of butter gently into the noodles.
4. Make white sauce; add it to the cold milk and chicken broth. Cook mixture until thickened. Reserve while making hollandaise sauce.
5. Carefully blend hollandaise with white sauce mixture; stir in wine.
6. Butter a small roasting pan; place noodles in the bottom, add the mushrooms, and place chicken breasts on top of the mushrooms. Pour the sauce over all. Heat thoroughly in a 325°F oven about 45 minutes.
7. Remove from oven, sprinkle with grated Parmesan cheese and place under broiler to brown.
8 SERVINGS

Medium White Sauce: Melt **¼ cup butter or margarine** in a saucepan. Blend in **¼ cup flour, 1 teaspoon salt,** and **¼ teaspoon pepper.** Cook and stir until bubbly. Gradually add **2 cups milk,** stirring until smooth. Bring to boiling; cook and stir 1 to 2 minutes longer.
ABOUT 2 CUPS SAUCE

Hollandaise Sauce: Beat **4 egg yolks** in the top of a double boiler, then beat in **½ cup cream.** Cook and stir over **hot water** until slightly thickened. Blend in **2 tablespoons lemon juice.** Cut in **4 tablespoons cold butter,** a tablespoon at a time. Sauce will thicken.
ABOUT 1 CUP SAUCE

Chicken and Rice

2 cups cooked white rice
½ cup milk
2 tablespoons chopped pimento
1 can (10¾ ounces) condensed cream of celery soup
1 can (10¾ ounces) condensed cream of mushroom soup
1 broiler-fryer chicken (about 3 pounds), cut up
1 package (1⅜ ounces) dry onion soup mix

1. Combine rice, milk, pimento, celery soup, and mushroom soup. Pour into a greased 13x9-inch baking dish.
2. Dip chicken pieces in **milk,** then roll in onion soup mix. Arrange chicken pieces over rice mixture.
3. Bake, covered, at 30°F 1 hour, or until chicken is tender.
4 SERVINGS

Crumb-Crusted Duckling Halves

16 grapevine leaves
  preserved in brine*
2 ducklings (about 4½
  pounds each), cut in half
2 teaspoons salt
½ cup Chicken Stock (page
  48)
Juice of 1 lemon
Clarified butter
⅓ cup seasoned stuffing
  crumbs, slightly crushed
Cumberland Sauce (page 47)
  or Madeira Sauce (page 47)

1. Soak grapevine leaves in cold water 20 minutes. Pat dry. Set aside.
2. Using fingers and a sharp knife, remove skin and excess fat from ducklings (do not skin wings). Place ducklings breast side up on rack in a roasting pan; sprinkle with salt. Cover surface of ducks with grapevine leaves.
3. Roast in a 325°F oven about 2½ hours, or until ducklings are done; drumstick meat will feel soft. Baste ducklings every half hour with a mixture of stock and lemon juice.
4. Remove grapevine leaves. Brush ducklings very lightly with butter and sprinkle with crumbs. Broil 4 inches from heat until crumbs are browned (about 5 minutes). Remove ducklings to platter; let stand 10 minutes before serving. Serve with desired sauce.
4 SERVINGS

*Grapevine leaves can be purchased in a gourmet shop or in the specialty section of a supermarket.

Chicken Marengo

1 broiler-fryer chicken (2 to
  3 pounds)
⅓ cup all-purpose flour
1 teaspoon salt
¼ teaspoon pepper
¼ cup olive oil
1 clove garlic, crushed
3 tablespoons chopped
  onion
4 tomatoes, quartered
1 cup white wine
Herb Bouquet
1 cup (about 4 ounces) sliced
  mushrooms
2 tablespoons butter
½ cup sliced olives
½ cup chicken bouillon
2 tablespoons all-purpose
  flour

1. Disjoint chicken and cut into serving-size pieces. Rinse and pat dry with absorbent paper.
2. Coat chicken evenly with a mixture of flour, salt, and pepper.
3. Heat oil in a large skillet and brown chicken.
4. Add garlic, onion, tomatoes, wine, and Herb Bouquet to chicken; cover and simmer over low heat about ½ hour, or until thickest pieces of chicken are tender when pierced with a fork.
5. Sauté mushrooms in butter and add to chicken with olives.
6. Put bouillon and flour into screw-top jar; cover and shake well.
7. Remove chicken from skillet and discard Herb Bouquet. Gradually add bouillon-flour liquid to mixture in skillet, stirring constantly. Boil 3 to 5 minutes until mixture thickens.
8. Return chicken to sauce; cover and simmer 10 minutes. Arrange chicken on a hot platter. Cover with the sauce.
4 OR 5 SERVINGS

Bouquet: Tie neatly together **3 or 4 sprigs of parsley,** d ½ **bay leaf.**

Chicken Vesuvio

1 broiler-fryer chicken (2 to 3 pounds), cut in pieces
½ cup flour
1½ teaspoons salt
¼ teaspoon pepper
½ cup olive oil
2 tablespoons olive oil
1 clove garlic, sliced
2 tablespoons Marsala
½ teaspoon chopped parsley
Deep-Fried Potatoes

1. Coat chicken pieces with a mixture of flour, salt, and pepper.
2. Heat ½ cup oil in a large skillet. Add chicken pieces and brown on all sides. Put into a large, shallow baking dish.
3. Heat 2 tablespoons oil and garlic until garlic is lightly browned. Add Marsala and parsley; mix well. Pour over chicken in baking dish.
4. Bake at 325°F about 45 minutes, or until chicken is tender; turn once.
5. Prepare potatoes and place around edges of baking dish.
4 SERVINGS

Chicken Curry with Rice

⅔ cup butter or margarine
6 tablespoons chopped onion
6 tablespoons chopped celery
6 tablespoons chopped green apple
24 peppercorns
2 bay leaves
⅔ cup all-purpose flour
5 teaspoons curry powder
½ teaspoon sugar
¼ teaspoon nutmeg
5 cups milk
4 teaspoons lemon juice
1 teaspoon Worcestershire sauce
½ cup cream
¼ cup sherry
½ teaspoon Worcestershire sauce
6 cups cubed cooked chicken
Hot cooked rice

1. Heat butter in a heavy 3-quart saucepan over low heat. Add onion, celery, apple, peppercorns, and bay leaves, and cook over medium heat until lightly browned, occasionally moving and turning with a spoon.
2. Blend in flour, curry powder, sugar, and nutmeg; heat until mixture bubbles.
3. Remove from heat and add milk gradually, stirring constantly.
4. Return to heat and bring rapidly to boiling. Stirring constantly, cook until mixture thickens; cook 1 to 2 minutes longer.
5. Remove from heat; add lemon juice and 1 teaspoon Worcestershire sauce. Strain mixture through a fine sieve, pressing vegetables against sieve to extract all sauce. Set sauce aside.
6. Reheat the curry sauce and blend in cream, sherry, and ½ teaspoon Worcestershire sauce; add chicken and cook over medium heat 2 to 3 minutes, or until mixture is thoroughly heated. Serve with rice.
8 SERVINGS

Chicken à la Winegrower

2 slices bacon, diced
2 cloves garlic, halved
1 tablespoon butter or margarine
4 chicken legs (thighs and drumsticks)
1 cup chopped onion
½ cup dry white wine
2 tablespoons chopped parsley
2 tablespoons chopped
chives
1½ teaspoons salt
¼ teaspoon pepper
1 bay leaf
1 can (4 ounces) sliced mushrooms with liquid
1 cup chicken broth
2 tablespoons flour
Hot cooked rice
½ cup sour cream, warmed
Chopped parsley for garnish

1. Sauté bacon and garlic in butter until bacon is partially cooked. Discard garlic.
2. Add chicken and brown on all sides.
3. Stir in onion and sauté until transparent. Add ¼ cup wine and cook a few minutes, stirring to loosen browned particles.
4. Add parsley, chives, seasonings, mushrooms, and broth. Cover and cook over low heat for 30 minutes, or until chicken is tender. Remove chicken and keep warm. Discard bay leaf.
5. Blend flour with remaining wine. Stir into sauce and cook until thickened.
6. Serve chicken on beds of fluffy rice. Top with sauce and dollops of sour cream. Garnish with parsley.
4 SERVINGS

Brunswick Stew

1 chicken (about 4 pounds), disjointed
¼ cup cooking oil
1 cup coarsely chopped onion
¼ pound salt pork, chopped
4 tomatoes, peeled and quartered
2 cups boiling water
1 cup sherry
1 bay leaf
1 teaspoon Worcestershire sauce
1½ cups fresh lima or butter beans
½ cup sliced fresh okra
1½ cups fresh bread crumbs
2 tablespoons butter
Salt to taste

1. Sauté chicken in cooking oil until golden; remove chicken. Brown onion and salt pork in the same fat.
2. Put chicken, salt pork, onion, tomatoes, boiling water, sherry, bay leaf, and Worcestershire sauce into Dutch oven or saucepot. Cover and simmer 2 hours, or until chicken is tender.
3. After 1 hour, remove bay leaf; add beans and cook about 15 minutes. Add sliced okra; continue cooking about 15 minutes.
4. Sauté fresh bread crumbs in butter; stir into stew. Add salt to taste before serving.
8 SERVINGS

Chicken Vesuvio

Chicken à Seville

3 tablespoons butter or margarine
½ pound fresh mushrooms, cleaned and halved lengthwise
3 to 4 tablespoons olive or other cooking oil
3 pounds chicken pieces
1 cup uncooked rice
1 large clove garlic, minced
2 cups chicken broth or bouillon
12 very small white onions
1 cup small pimento-stuffed olives
1 cup dry white wine
¾ teaspoon oregano
½ cup toasted blanched almonds, sliced

1. Heat butter in a large skillet and stir in mushrooms. Cook until lightly browned, stirring occasionally. Remove from skillet and set aside. Pour oil into skillet and heat.
2. Coat chicken pieces with a blend of **flour, salt,** and **pepper.** Fry in hot oil until browned on all sides. Remove chicken and keep warm.
3. Mix rice and garlic with oil in skillet, then stir in 1 cup of the chicken broth. Turn contents of skillet into a shallow baking dish. Put onions, browned chicken, mushrooms, and olives into dish. Pour remaining broth and the wine over all. Sprinkle oregano over chicken.
4. Cook, covered, in a 375°F oven about 45 minutes, or until rice is tender. Remove from oven and top with the nuts.
ABOUT 6 SERVINGS

Breast of Chicken Savannah

4 large chicken breasts, split
2½ ounces (about ¼ cup) peanut butter
8 thin slices cooked ham
¼ cup sherry

Parmesan Sauce:
¼ cup flour
2 cups milk
½ teaspoon salt
6 tablespoons freshly grated Parmesan cheese
2 tablespoons firm butter

1. Lift skin on chicken breasts slightly, and spread a film of peanut butter on meat under skin; replace skin.
2. Place 1 slice of cooked ham over skin side of each breast.
3. Put sherry into a large casserole or braising pan. Add chicken pieces, ham side up; cover and cook in a 350°F oven 1 hour, or until pieces are tender.
4. Remove breasts from pan and keep warm while preparing Parmesan sauce; reserve ¼ cup pan drippings.
5. For sauce, put the pan drippings into a medium saucepan. Add flour; stir and heat until bubbly. Add milk gradually, stirring well; bring to boiling and cook 1 to 2 minutes.
6. Add salt and Parmesan cheese, stirring until cheese melts. Stir in butter, 1 tablespoon at a time.
7. Pour sauce over chicken and serve.
8 SERVINGS

Chicken and Wild Rice

¾ cup uncooked wild rice
4 cups chopped cooked chicken
1 cup sherry
1 cup chicken broth
1 small onion, chopped
1 can (8 ounces) mushroom slices, drained
¼ cup butter or margarine, melted
1 can (10¾ ounces) con-
densed cream of mushroom soup
1 can (10¾ ounces) condensed cream of chicken soup
2 packages (10 ounces each) frozen broccoli or asparagus spears, cooked and drained
1 cup (4 ounces) shredded Cheddar cheese

1. Cook wild rice according to package directions.
2. Combine rice with remaining ingredients, except broccoli and cheese.
3. Spread half the rice mixture in a 13x9-inch baking dish. Top with broccoli. Evenly spread remaining rice mixture over all.
4. Bake, uncovered, at 350°F 45 minutes, or until heated through. Sprinkle with cheese and bake an additional 5 minutes, or until cheese is melted.
8 SERVINGS

Roast Turkey with Pineapple-Stuffed Breast

1 turkey (10 to 12 pounds)
1½ tablespoons curry powder
2 teaspoons salt
⅓ cup minced onion
4 garlic cloves, minced
1 teaspoon minced ginger root
2 tablespoons vegetable oil
⅔ cup unsweetened pineapple juice
1 can (20 ounces) unsweetened crushed pineapple, drained
1½ cups minced cooked turkey or chicken
Unsweetened pineapple juice

1. Rinse turkey; pat dry. Carefully loosen skin over turkey breast by running fingers under the skin.
2. Mix curry powder; salt, onion, garlic, ginger root, vegetable oil, and ⅔ cup pineapple juice. Mix one quarter of the spice mixture with the drained pineapple and minced turkey. Spread pineapple mixture gently and evenly under skin of turkey breast with fingers. Place turkey in a roasting pan. Insert meat thermometer in thickest part of thigh. Brush remaining spice mixture over turkey breast.
3. Roast in a 325°F oven until thermometer registers 175°F (3½ to 4 hours); baste occasionally with pineapple juice. Remove turkey to serving platter; cover loosely with aluminum foil. Let stand 20 minutes before carving.
ABOUT 16 SERVINGS

Note: This recipe can be used for a roasting chicken of about 5 pounds. Use half the spice and pineapple mixtures; proceed as directed. Roast at 325°F about 2½ hours, or until chicken is tender; drumstick meat will feel very soft.

Canard à l'Orange

2 ducklings (4 to 5 pounds each)
2 teaspoons salt
½ teaspoon pepper
1 clove garlic, peeled and cut crosswise into halves
½ cup dry white wine
½ cup orange marmalade

Sauce:
2 tablespoons butter or margarine
1 can (13¾ ounces) condensed chicken broth
½ cup orange marmalade
¼ cup dry white wine
¼ cup orange juice
2 teaspoons cornstarch
2 teaspoons lemon juice
2 tablespoons slivered orange peel

1. If frozen, let ducklings thaw according to package directions. Remove giblets, necks, and livers from ducklings. Reserve livers for sauce; if desired, reserve giblets and necks for soup stock. Remove and discard excess fat. Wash, drain, and pat dry with paper toweling. Rub cavities with salt, pepper, and garlic. Fasten neck skin to back with a skewer. Tuck tail ends into cavities. Tie legs together and tuck wing tips under ducklings. Prick skin generously to release fat. Place ducklings, breast side up, on a rack in a large shallow roasting pan.

2. Roast at 350°F 2 to 2½ hours or until legs can be moved easily, basting several times during roasting and removing accumulated drippings about every 30 minutes. Remove ducklings from oven and spread surface with mixture of wine and marmalade. Return to oven and continue roasting for 10 minutes.

3. For sauce, melt butter in a skillet. Add duckling livers and sauté until lightly browned. Remove and chop livers. Add chicken broth, marmalade, wine, orange juice, and cornstarch blended with lemon juice. Cook, stirring constantly over low heat for 10 minutes or until sauce bubbles and thickens. Stir in chopped livers and orange peel.

4. Transfer ducklings to a heated platter. Remove skewers and twine. Garnish, if desired, with watercress and orange slices. Reheat sauce if necessary and serve with duckling.

8 SERVINGS

Chicken à la King

½ cup sliced fresh mushrooms
¼ cup butter or margarine
¼ cup flour
2 cups milk
1 teaspoon salt
1½ cups cooked noodles
2 cups chopped cooked chicken or turkey
¾ cup (3 ounces) shredded Cheddar cheese
1 cup cooked peas
1 tablespoon instant minced onion
2 teaspoons Worcestershire sauce
1 tablespoon ketchup
Dash Tabasco

1. Sauté mushrooms in butter in a skillet. Stir in flour. Gradually add milk, stirring until thickened and smooth. Stir in remaining ingredients. Put into a 2-quart casserole.
2. Bake, covered, at 350°F 30 minutes, or until heated through.
4 SERVINGS

Herb-Chicken with Mushrooms

2 tablespoons butter or margarine
1 broiler-fryer chicken (3 pounds), cut in quarters
¾ cup cider vinegar
¼ cup water
1 cup (about 3 ounces) sliced mushrooms
1 tablespoon finely chopped parsley
1 tablespoon finely chopped chives
1 teaspoon crushed tarragon
½ teaspoon thyme
½ teaspoon salt
¼ teaspoon black pepper
2 tablespoons flour
1½ cups chicken broth
½ cup sherry

1. Heat butter in a large skillet. Place chicken pieces, skin side down, in skillet and brown on all sides.
2. Meanwhile, pour a mixture of vinegar and water over the mushrooms. Let stand 10 minutes; drain.
3. When chicken is evenly browned, transfer pieces to a shallow baking dish. Sprinkle the seasonings over the chicken. Spoon drained mushrooms over the top; sprinkle evenly with flour. Pour broth and wine over all.
4. Bake at 325°F about 1 hour, or until tender.
ABOUT 4 SERVINGS

Roast Turkey with Anchovies

1 turkey (12 to 15 pounds)
5 slices bacon
1 large onion, minced
¾ pound veal (2 cups ground)
3 slices stale bread, cubed
⅓ cup milk or chicken broth
1 can (2 ounces) flat
anchovies
2 tablespoons butter
2 eggs, beaten
Grated peel and juice of 1 lemon
½ teaspoon pepper
⅔ cup melted butter

1. Rinse turkey with running water. Dry with paper towels.
2. Dice bacon. Fry until transparent. Add onion; stir-fry until golden. Stir in veal, bread cubes, and milk. Remove from heat.
3. Finely chop or mash anchovies. Mix in butter, lemon peel and juice, and pepper; beat until well combined. Add to meat mixture and stir until well blended. Stuffing should be of a paste consistency.

4. Spread stuffing in cavity of turkey. Truss.
5. Place turkey in roasting pan. If desired, insert meat thermometer in thickest part of breast.
6. Roast at 425°F about 3½ hours, basting frequently with melted butter and pan drippings. When done, leg of turkey moves easily and meat thermometer registers 180° to 185°F.
12 TO 18 SERVINGS

Stuffed Turkey

1 turkey (12 to 16 pounds)
Salt and pepper
Juice of 1 lemon
Stuffing (see below)
Melted butter
Gravy:
Flour
Chicken broth
White wine
Salt and pepper

1. Clean turkey. Sprinkle inside and out with salt and pepper, then drizzle with lemon juice.
2. Spoon desired amount of stuffing into cavities of turkey. Secure openings with skewers and twine.
3. Put turkey, breast side up, on a rack in a shallow roasting pan. Cover bird with a double thickness of cheesecloth soaked in butter.
4. Roast in a 325°F oven 4½ to 5½ hours, or until done (180°F to 185°F on a meat thermometer inserted in inside thigh muscle or thickest part of breast); baste with drippings several times during roasting.
5. For gravy, stir a small amount of flour with pan drippings. Cook until bubbly. Stir in equal parts of broth and wine. Season to taste with salt and pepper.
6. Put turkey on a platter and garnish with **watercress.** Accompany with gravy.
12 TO 16 SERVINGS

Stuffing

5 slices bacon, diced
1 onion, chopped
1 clove garlic, minced
3 pounds ground pork loin
½ cup tomato purée
¾ cup blanched almonds, chopped
½ cup ripe olives, coarsely chopped
6 jalapeño chilies, seeded
and chopped
3 carrots, pared and sliced
3 bananas, peeled and sliced
3 apples, pared, cored, and diced
¾ cup raisins
2 teaspoons sugar
Salt and pepper
Cinnamon

1. Fry bacon until brown in a large skillet. Remove bacon from fat; reserve. Brown onion and garlic in fat in skillet, then brown meat. Discard excess fat.
2. Add tomato purée, almonds, olives, chilies, carrots, fruit, sugar, and salt, pepper, and cinnamon to taste; mix well. Cook several minutes. Mix in bacon. Cool before stuffing turkey.

Turkey 'n' Dressing Bake

3 tablespoons butter or margarine	pepper
½ cup diced celery	1 egg, slightly beaten
¼ cup minced onion	2 tablespoons flour
3¼ cups chicken broth (dissolve 4 chicken bouillon cubes in 3¼ cups boiling water)	2 eggs, beaten
	⅛ teaspoon ground black pepper
	¼ teaspoon crushed leaf sage
5 cups coarse whole wheat bread crumbs; reserve ½ cup crumbs for topping	¼ teaspoon celery salt
	Thin slices of cooked turkey roast (see Note)
¼ cup snipped parsley	1 tablespoon butter or margarine, melted
½ teaspoon salt	
¼ teaspoon ground black	Parsley, snipped

1. Heat 3 tablespoons butter in a large skillet. Mix in celery and onion and cook about 5 minutes. Combine vegetables with 1¾ cups chicken broth, 4½ cups bread crumbs, ¼ cup parsley, salt, ¼ teaspoon pepper, and 1 egg. Mix lightly with a fork. Spoon the mixture over bottom of a shallow 2-quart baking dish; set aside.
2. Mix flour and ¼ cup cool broth in a saucepan until smooth; heat until bubbly. Add remaining broth gradually, stirring constantly. Cook and stir over medium heat until sauce comes to boiling; cook 2 minutes. Remove from heat and gradually add to eggs while beating. Blend in remaining pepper, sage, and celery salt.
3. Arrange the desired amount of turkey over dressing in baking dish. Pour the sauce over all.
4. Toss reserved bread crumbs with melted butter; spoon over top.
5. Bake at 350°F 30 to 40 minutes, or until egg mixture is set. Garnish generously with parsley.
6 SERVINGS

Note: Prepare frozen boneless turkey roast, following package directions.

Roast Stuffed Turkey

1 turkey (6 to 8 pounds)	2 tablespoons butter
1 package (7 ounces) herb-seasoned stuffing croutons	½ cup chopped celery
	½ cup chopped onion
½ cup melted butter	2 tablespoons chopped parsley
½ cup hot water or chicken broth	Melted butter

1. Rinse turkey with cold water; pat dry.
2. Turn stuffing croutons into a bowl; add ½ cup melted butter and toss gently. Stir in hot water or broth.
3. Heat 2 tablespoons butter in a skillet. Add celery and onion; cook until tender. Add to bowl with stuffing; add parsley and toss to mix.
4. Spoon stuffing into cavities of bird. Place turkey, breast side up, in a large electric cooker. Insert a meat thermometer in inner thigh muscle. Brush with melted butter.
5. Cover and roast at 300°F until meat thermometer registers 180° to 185°F, about 6 hours.
6 TO 8 SERVINGS

Note: If desired to enhance browning, place a piece of aluminum foil over turkey before covering with lid.

Turkey Croquettes

2 tablespoons butter	1 teaspoon salt
2 tablespoons minced shallot	¼ teaspoon freshly ground pepper
1½ tablespoons flour	
½ cup chicken broth	2 egg yolks
2 egg yolks, beaten	2 teaspoons cooking oil
2 cups ground turkey	Dry bread crumbs
1 tablespoon chopped parsley	Fat for deep frying, heated to 375°F

1. Melt butter in a skillet. Cook shallot over low heat until translucent. Stir in flour. Gradually add chicken broth, blending until smooth.
2. Remove from heat and beat 2 egg yolks. Add turkey, parsley, salt, and pepper; mix well.
3. Spread mixture on a platter and cool in refrigerator.
4. Shape mixture into small balls. Coat balls with a mixture of 2 egg yolks and oil and then roll in bread crumbs.
5. Fry in heated fat until golden. Drain on absorbent paper.
6. Serve with Tomato Sauce Creole (page 50).

Roast Turkey I

1 turkey, 10 to 12 pounds, ready-to-cook weight
Oyster Stuffing (see page 448)

2 teaspoons salt
Melted fat

1. Set out a shallow roasting pan with rack.
2. Clean turkey (and cut off neck at body, leaving skin).
3. (If turkey is frozen, thaw according to directions on package.) Rinse, drain and pat turkey with absorbent paper. Set aside.
4. Prepare Oyster Stuffing.
5. Rub cavities of turkey with salt.
6. Lightly fill body and neck cavities with stuffing. To close body cavity, sew or skewer and lace with cord. Fasten neck skin to back with skewer. Tie drumsticks to tail. Bring wing tips onto back. Brush skin thoroughly with melted fat.
7. Place breast up on rack in roasting pan.
8. If roast meat thermometer is used, place it in center of inside thigh muscle. When done, roast meat thermometer will register 190°F. Place fat-moistened cheesecloth over top and sides of turkey. Keep cloth moist during roasting by brushing occasionally with fat from bottom of pan.
9. Roast uncovered at 325°F 4 to 4½ hours, or until turkey tests done (thickest part of drumstick feels soft when pressed with fingers. Protect fingers with cloth or paper napkin.) Remove turkey from oven. Remove roast meat thermometer and keep turkey hot. Allow to stand about 20 minutes before serving. This makes it easier to carve the turkey and also allows time for last-minute preparations such as preparing gravy and garnishes.
10. Remove cord and skewers. Serve turkey on heated platter. Garnish with **parsley** and serve with **cranberry sauce**. If desired, put **paper frills** on drumsticks.
ABOUT 16 SERVINGS

Roast Half Turkey: Follow recipe for Roast Turkey. Use half or quarter turkey, 3½ to 5 pounds, ready-to-cook weight. Rub cut side with one half salt mixture. Skewer skin along cut sides to prevent shrinking. Tie leg to tail and wing flat against breast. Place skin-side up on rack. Roast at 325°F about 2 hours. Meanwhile, prepare **stuffing for half turkey.** Remove turkey from rack. Spoon stuffing onto a piece of aluminum foil and place on rack. Cover stuffing with half turkey. Roast 1 to 1½ hours longer, or until thickest part of drumstick feels soft when pressed with fingers. (Protect fingers with cloth or paper napkin.)
ABOUT 8 SERVINGS

Roast Turkey II

1 ready-to-cook turkey (10 to 12 pounds)
Oyster Stuffing
Salt
Melted fat
Gravy (favorite recipe)

1. Rinse bird with cold water. Drain and pat dry with absorbent paper or soft cloth.
2. Prepare oyster stuffing.
3. Rub body and neck cavities with salt. Fill lightly with stuffing. (Extra stuffing may be put into a greased covered baking dish or wrapped in aluminum foil and baked with turkey the last half hour of roasting time.)
4. Fasten neck skin to back with skewer and bring wing tips onto back. Push drumsticks under band of skin at tail, or tie with cord. Set, breast up, on rack in shallow roasting pan. Brush with melted fat.
5. If meat thermometer is used, insert it in center of inside thigh muscle or thickest part of breast meat. Be sure that tip does not touch bones. If desired, cover top and sides of turkey with cheesecloth moistened with melted fat. Keep cloth moist during roasting by brushing occasionally with fat from bottom of pan.
6. Roast, uncovered, at 325°F 4 to 4½ hours. When turkey is two-thirds done, cut band of skin or cord at drumsticks. Continue roasting until turkey tests done (the thickest part of the drumstick feels soft when pressed with fingers and meat thermometer registers 180° to 185°F).
7. For easier carving, let turkey stand 20 to 30 minutes, keeping it warm. Meanwhile, prepare gravy from drippings.
8. Remove cord and skewers from turkey and place on heated platter. Garnish platter as desired.

ABOUT 16 SERVINGS

Oyster Stuffing: Combine **3 quarts soft bread crumbs, 4 teaspoons salt, ½ teaspoon pepper, 1 pint to 1 quart small oysters,** whole or cut in small pieces, **¾ cup oyster liquor** (use turkey stock or milk if needed), **½ cup butter** or **turkey fat,** melted, mixing well.

Stuffing for a Small Turkey

½ cup butter
1 onion, minced
1 medium cooking apple, pared, cored and diced
1 pound mushrooms, sliced
2 medium potatoes, boiled, peeled, and diced
½ cup pine nuts
½ cup dried black currants
1 cup blanched almonds, sliced

2 pounds chestnuts, boiled and cleaned
4 cups prepared bread stuffing
2 cups or more chicken stock to make a moist stuffing
1 can (4½ ounces) pâté de foie gras
Salt and pepper to taste

1. Melt butter in a large deep skillet. Add onion, apple, and mushrooms; cook until tender.
2. Add potatoes, pine nuts, currants, almonds, chestnuts, stuffing, and stock. Heat thoroughly over low heat, adding more liquid if necessary.
3. Stir in pâté. Season with salt and pepper.
4. Cool completely. Stuff bird.

STUFFING FOR A SMALL TURKEY OR 2 CAPONS

Roast Turkey III

1 ready-to-cook turkey
  (reserve giblets)
1 lime, halved
1 orange, halved
Salt and freshly ground
  pepper
¼ cup olive oil
1 tablespoon tomato paste
1 garlic clove, crushed in a
  garlic press
1 quart water

1 large onion, sliced
4 parsley sprigs
1 bay leaf
2 teaspoons salt
Lettuce
Cherry tomato
Avocado half
Green pepper ring
2 tablespoons butter
2 tablespoons cornstarch

1. Rub the skin of the bird with the cut side of the lime and orange. Sprinkle salt and pepper over surface. Refrigerate 2 hours.
2. Combine oil, tomato paste, and garlic. Brush mixture over bird. Set on a rack in a shallow roasting pan.
3. Roast, uncovered, in a 375°F oven until turkey tests done (the thickest part of the drumstick feels soft when pressed with fingers, or meat thermometer inserted in the thickest part of inner thigh muscle registers 180°F to 185°F).
4. Meanwhile, prepare giblet broth. Put turkey neck and giblets (except liver), water, onion, parsley, bay leaf, and salt in a saucepan. Cover and simmer about 2 hours, or until giblets are tender. Add the liver the last 15 minutes of cooking. Strain.
5. Carve turkey and arrange meat on a bed of lettuce. Garnish with tomato, avocado, and green pepper.
6. Remove excess fat from roasting pan. Pour in 2 cups giblet broth to deglaze over medium heat.
7. Mix butter and cornstarch and add to broth. Stir until sauce is slightly thicker.
8. Serve sauce with turkey.

Roast Turkey with Herbed Stuffing

Cooked Giblets and Broth
4 quarts ½-inch enriched
  bread cubes
1 cup snipped parsley
2 to 2½ teaspoons salt
2 teaspoons thyme
2 teaspoons rosemary,
  crushed
2 teaspoons marjoram
1 teaspoon ground sage
1 cup butter or margarine

1 cup coarsely chopped
  onion
1 cup coarsely chopped
  celery with leaves
1 turkey (14 to 15 pounds)
Fat
3 tablespoons flour
¼ teaspoon salt
⅛ teaspoon ground black
  pepper

1. Prepare Cooked Giblets and Broth. Measure 1 cup chopped cooked giblets; set the broth aside.
2. Combine bread cubes, reserved giblets, and parsley in a large bowl. Blend salt, thyme, rosemary, marjoram, and sage; add to bread mixture and toss to mix.
3. Heat butter in a skillet. Mix in onion and celery; cook about 5 minutes, stirring occasionally. Toss with the bread mixture.
4. Add 1 to 2 cups broth (depending upon how moist a stuffing is desired), mixing lightly until ingredients are thoroughly blended.

5. Rinse turkey with cold water; pat dry, inside and out, with absorbent paper. Lightly fill body and neck cavities with the stuffing. Fasten neck skin to back with a skewer. Bring wing tips onto back of bird. Push drumsticks under band of skin at tail, if present, or tie to tail with cord.
6. Place turkey, breast side up, on rack in a shallow roasting pan. Brush skin with fat. Insert meat thermometer in the thickest part of the inner thigh muscle, being sure that tip does not touch bone.
7. Roast in a 325°F oven about 5 hours, or until thermometer registers 180°F to 185°F. If desired, baste or brush bird occasionally with pan drippings. Place turkey on a heated platter; for easier carving, allow turkey to stand about 30 minutes.
8. Meanwhile, leaving brown residue in roasting pan, pour remaining drippings and fat into a bowl. Allow fat to rise to surface; skim off fat and measure 3 tablespoons into roasting pan. Blend flour, salt, and pepper with fat. Cook and stir until bubbly. Continue to stir while slowly adding 2 cups reserved liquid (broth and drippings). Cook, stirring constantly, until gravy thickens; scrape pan to blend in brown residue. Cook 1 to 2 minutes. If desired, mix in finely chopped cooked giblets the last few minutes of cooking.
ABOUT 25 SERVINGS

Cooked Giblets and Broth: Put **turkey neck** and **giblets** (except liver) into a saucepan with **1 large onion,** sliced, **parsley, celery with leaves, 1 medium bay leaf, 2 teaspoons salt,** and **1 cup water.** Cover, bring to boiling, reduce heat, and simmer until giblets are tender (about 2 hours); add the liver the last 15 minutes of cooking. Strain through a colander or sieve; reserve broth for stuffing. Chop giblets; set aside for stuffing and gravy.

Turkey Pot Pie

2 cups chopped cooked
  turkey
2 cans (10¾ ounces each)
  condensed cream of celery
  soup
½ cup milk
½ teaspoon Worcestershire
  sauce

Dash pepper
6 cooked small onions
1 cup cooked cubed potato
1 cup cooked sliced carrot
⅓ cup shortening
1 cup self-rising flour
4 tablespoons cold water

1. Combine turkey, soup, milk, Worcestershire sauce, pepper, onions, potato, and carrot. Put into a 2-quart casserole.
2. Cut shortening into flour. Add water, a tablespoon at a time, mixing lightly until dough can be formed into a ball. (If necessary, add a little more water to make dough hold together.) Let rest 5 minutes.
3. Roll dough out on a lightly floured board or canvas to fit top of casserole. Cut slits to allow steam to escape. Adjust over filling; flute edges.
4. Bake, uncovered, at 425°F 20 minutes, or until pastry is golden brown.
6 SERVINGS

Duck Bigarade

2 limes, halved
1 ready-to-cook duck (about 5 pounds)
Salt, freshly ground pepper, and cayenne or red pepper
2 cups firmly packed brown sugar
1 cup water
2 teaspoons vanilla extract
½ cup orange peel strips
4 small oranges, halved and seeded
2 cups chicken broth
¼ cup orange juice
½ cup amber rum
¼ cup butter
¼ cup cornstarch

1. Squeeze lime juice over the entire duck. Season with salt, pepper, and cayenne. Place on a rack in a roasting pan.
2. Roast, uncovered in a 425°F oven 25 minutes. Turn oven control to 350°F and continue to roast 30 minutes.
3. Combine brown sugar, water, and vanilla extract in a large, heavy saucepan. Bring to a boil over high heat and boil about 6 minutes. Add orange peel and orange halves and continue boiling 1 minute. Remove from heat and cool. Set ¼ cup syrup aside in a small saucepan.
4. Transfer duck to a warm platter. Remove fat from roasting pan. Stir in chicken broth and orange juice to deglaze. Heat the rum, ignite it, and when flames die down, pour it into the chicken broth.
5. Heat the reserved syrup until it caramelizes. Add to chicken broth mixture and blend well.
6. Mix butter and cornstarch and add to roasting pan. Cook over medium heat, stirring constantly, until the gravy is slightly thicker.
7. Carve the duck. Sprinkle the glazed orange peel strips over the meat. Pour a little gravy over the meat. Serve remaining gravy separately. Arrange glazed orange halves around the duck, alternating with bouquets of **watercress**. Serve with Caribbean Rice (page 190).
4 SERVINGS

Smothered Duck in Caper Sauce

1 duck (5 to 6 pounds), cut up
1 clove garlic, crushed (optional)
Salt and pepper
3 tablespoons butter or bacon drippings
1 cup chicken or beef
bouillon
2 tablespoons water
2 teaspoons cornstarch
⅓ cup capers
2 teaspoons brown or caramelized sugar
1 tablespoon lemon juice

1. Rub duck with garlic. Sprinkle cavity with salt and pepper to taste. Let stand 1 to 2 hours.
2. Melt butter in a heavy skillet or Dutch oven. Add duck and brown quickly on all sides. Drain off fat, if desired.
3. Add bouillon. Cover. Simmer over medium heat about 1 hour, or until duck is tender.
4. Remove duck to a heated platter.
5. Blend water into cornstarch. Stir into hot liquid in Dutch oven. Add capers, cook and stir over high heat until sauce boils. Reduce heat. Add sugar and lemon juice. Stir just until sauce is thickened.
ABOUT 4 SERVINGS

Duck Bigarade

Turkey-Oyster Casserole

1 tablespoon butter
2 teaspoons grated onion
4 ounces mushrooms, sliced lengthwise
¼ cup butter
¼ cup enriched all-purpose flour
1 teaspoon salt
¼ teaspoon ground pepper
Few grains cayenne pepper
2 cups milk
1 egg yolk, slightly beaten
2 tablespoons chopped parsley
¼ teaspoon thyme
2 drops Tabasco
1 pint oysters (with liquor)
2 cups diced cooked turkey
Buttered soft enriched bread crumbs

1. Heat 1 tablespoon butter with onion in a skillet; add mushrooms and cook over medium heat until slightly browned, stirring occasionally. Set aside.
2. Heat ¼ cup butter in a saucepan over low heat. Stir in flour, salt, pepper, and cayenne; cook until bubbly. Add milk gradually, stirring until well blended. Bring rapidly to boiling and boil 1 to 2 minutes, stirring constantly.
3. Blend a small amount of the hot sauce into egg yolk and return to remaining sauce, stirring until mixed. Stir in parsley, thyme, and Tabasco.
4. Heat oysters just to boiling; drain. Add oysters, turkey, and the mushrooms to sauce; toss lightly until thoroughly mixed.
5. Turn mixture into a buttered shallow 1½-quart baking dish. Sprinkle with crumbs.
6. Heat in a 400°F oven about 10 minutes, or until mixture is bubbly around edges and crumbs are golden brown.
ABOUT 6 SERVINGS

Wild Duck, Goose, or Partridge

2 partridges, 1 duck, or 1 goose
12 peppercorns
1 onion, quartered
Salt
14 to 20 juniper seeds, ground or mashed
2 tablespoons bacon drippings or butter
½ cup water
2 cups sliced red cabbage
1 large onion, sliced
½ cup water
1 tablespoon cornstarch or potato starch
2 tablespoons water
½ teaspoon sugar
1 teaspoon vinegar
¾ cup red wine

1. Place partridges in a plastic bag with peppercorns and quartered onion. Refrigerate 3 days to age.
2. Discard peppercorns and quartered onion. Cut up bird. Sprinkle with salt and juniper. Let stand 1 hour.
3. Heat bacon drippings in a large skillet. Brown bird in the drippings; add ½ cup water. Cover and simmer 1 hour.
4. Add cabbage, sliced onion, and ½ cup water. Cover and simmer 30 minutes. Remove the meat to a warmed platter.
5. Mix the cornstarch with 2 tablespoons water to make a smooth paste. Stir into drippings in pan.
6. Stir in sugar and vinegar; bring to boiling. Cook and stir 2 minutes. Remove from heat. Stir in wine.
4 SERVINGS

Game Hens with Spicy Stuffing

3½ cups slightly dry bread cubes
½ cup chopped, drained sweet mixed pickles
½ cup diced dried figs
1 egg, slightly beaten
¼ teaspoon salt
⅛ teaspoon poultry

seasoning
½ cup chopped celery
¼ cup butter or margarine
4 frozen Rock Cornish game hens (1 pound each), thawed
2 tablespoons butter or margarine, melted

1. Toss together lightly in a bowl the bread cubes, pickles, figs, egg, salt, and poultry seasoning.
2. Sauté celery in ¼ cup butter 1 minute. Toss with bread mixture. Spoon into cavities of hens; truss and arrange securely on a spit.
3. Roast hens on rotisserie about 1 hour, or until well browned and tender, brushing occasionally with melted butter.
4 SERVINGS

Duck with Red Cabbage

1 head red cabbage, shredded
1 onion, chopped
Salt

6 ounces salt pork, diced
½ cup red wine or chicken broth
1 duck (5 to 6 pounds)

1. Put cabbage and onion in a bowl, sprinkle with salt, and let stand 10 minutes. Squeeze out liquid.
2. Fry salt pork in a skillet until golden. Add cabbage-onion mixture and wine. Cover and simmer 20 minutes.
3. Place duck in a roasting pan.
4. Bake at 425°F 30 minutes. Drain off fat. Spoon cabbage mixture over duck. Reduce oven temperature to 350°F. Bake about 45 minutes, or until duck is tender. Baste frequently.
ABOUT 4 SERVINGS

Ducklings with Green Peppercorn Sauce

2 ducklings (about 4½ pounds each)
1½ teaspoons salt
¼ teaspoon freshly ground pepper
1 teaspoon snipped fresh or

½ teaspoon dried crumbled rosemary leaves
Chicken Stock (page 48)
Green Peppercorn Sauce (page 46)

1. Rinse ducklings; pat dry. Place ducklings breast side up on rack in a roasting pan. Sprinkle with salt, pepper, and rosemary. Pierce breasts of ducklings with a fork several times.
2. Roast in a 350°F oven about 2½ hours, or until ducklings are done; drumstick meat will feel very tender. Baste ducklings occasionally with stock. Remove ducklings to a serving platter; let stand 15 minutes before carving.
3. Serve with the sauce.
6 TO 8 SERVINGS

Duckling with Fruit Salad

2 ducklings (about 4½ pounds each)
2 teaspoons salt
½ teaspoon freshly ground pepper
¾ teaspoon allspice
½ cup fruit juice
6 slices fresh or canned pineapple
6 preserved kumquats, thinly sliced
3 oranges, peeled and

segments removed
2 apples, sliced
2 papayas, peeled and sliced, if desired
2 bananas, sliced
1 pound white grapes
1 lime, cut in 6 wedges
1 lemon, cut in 6 wedges
1½ cups Low-Fat Yogurt
2 tablespoons snipped mint
Mint sprigs

1. Rinse ducklings; pat dry. Place ducklings breast side up on rack in a roasting pan. Sprinkle with salt, pepper, and allspice. Pierce breasts of ducklings with a fork several times.
2. Roast in a 350°F oven about 2½ hours, or until ducklings are done; drumstick meat will feel very soft. Baste ducklings occasionally with fruit juice. Remove ducklings to platter; let cool.
3. While ducklings are roasting, prepare fruits; refrigerate. Mix yogurt and snipped mint; refrigerate.
4. Carefully cut skin and fat from ducklings. Remove meat from carcass carefully, keeping meat in as large pieces as possible. Arrange duckling meat and fruits attractively on individual plates. Garnish with mint. Pass chilled yogurt sauce.
6 SERVINGS

Curried Duck Martinique

3 cups coarsely chopped cooked duck
3 cups sliced mushrooms
6 tablespoons butter, melted
1 cup diced apple
⅓ cup grated onion
1 garlic clove, crushed in a garlic press
3 tablespoons flour

1 tablespoon curry powder
½ teaspoon salt
¼ teaspoon freshly ground pepper
1 cup whipping cream
½ cup duck stock (made from cooking the carcass)
3 tablespoons Madeira or sweet sherry

1. Cook duck and mushrooms in half the melted butter in a skillet over low heat, until the duck is slightly browned and the mushrooms are tender. Remove from heat and cover.
2. Sauté apple, onion, and garlic in remaining butter in a large skillet until soft. Remove skillet from the heat and stir in flour, curry, salt, and pepper.
3. Place skillet over low heat and blend in cream, stock, and Madeira. Stir constantly until the mixture thickens. Stir in the duck and mushroom mixture.
4. Serve with **cooked white rice** tossed with 1 cup diced banana.
6 SERVINGS

Pheasant

1 Pheasant
1 to 1½ teaspoons salt
½ teaspoon black pepper
8 medium peeled raw
  potatoes
1 to 1½ teaspoons salt
3 tablespoons butter
¾ cup heavy cream
1 ounce apple cheese
2 teaspoon soy sauce
1 large bunch parsley sprigs

1. Rinse and wipe the pheasant inside and outside. Season with salt and pepper, half inside and half outside. Brown the pheasant quickly all around in a frying pan in half the butter. Wrap in aluminum foil.
2. Preheat the oven to 325°F.
3. Cut the peeled raw potatoes in slices and fry them lightly on both sides in the remaining butter in the pan. Later add the rest of the butter. Sprinkle some salt over each round of potato slices before they are transferred to an ovenproof deep dish or casserole.
4. Distribute the potato slices evenly on the bottom and up towards the edge of the casserole, place the pheasant in the middle and pour on the gravy from foil if there is any.
5. Cover the casserole immediately. Put the casserole in the oven and roast the pheasant for about 30 minutes.
6. Whip together cream, apple cheese and soy sauce. Taste and correct seasoning, adding more apple cheese if necessary.
7. Pour the cream mixture on pheasant and potatoes when the casserole has been in the oven for 20 minutes. Serve dish straight from the oven with the pheasant cut in four portion sizes, and garnish with fresh parsley sprigs.
4 SERVINGS

Rock Cornish Hens with Oranges and Almonds

1 Rock Cornish hen per
  serving

For each serving:
2 tablespoons butter, melted
2 tablespoons orange juice
Salt and pepper to taste
¼ teaspoon marjoram
¼ teaspoon thyme
½ garlic clove, crushed in a
  garlic press
½ navel orange with peel,
  cut in thin slices
2 tablespoons honey (about)
5 almonds, blanched,
  slivered, and toasted

1. Rinse hen well. Drain and pat dry. Place in a shallow baking dish. Drizzle inside and out with butter.
2. Combine orange juice, salt, pepper, marjoram, thyme, and garlic in a small bowl. Pour over and into the bird. Marinate 2 hours; turn occasionally.
3. Set bird on a broiler rack and put under broiler about 6 inches from heat. Broil 12 minutes on each side, or until tender, basting frequently with the marinade. During the last few minutes of broiling, arrange orange slices around the bird and drizzle with honey.
4. Garnish with almonds and serve at once.

Pot-Roasted Wild Duck

4 wild ducks (about 2
  pounds each)
Amber rum
8 limes, peeled
8 peppercorns, cracked
Papaya leaves
Bacon drippings
3 tablespoons soybean oil
12 shallots
⅓ cup amber rum
½ cup stock
1 carrot
1 garlic clove, crushed in a
  garlic press
1 thyme sprig
1 parsley sprig
1 green hot pepper
2 cups hot stock
2 tablespoons butter
2 tablespoons cornstarch
Salt and pepper to taste
8 slices bread, toasted
¼ cup butter

1. Wipe the duck with rum. Place 2 limes and 2 peppercorns in the cavity of each duck. Wrap the birds in papaya leaves to tenderize and refrigerate 12 hours.
2. Brush bacon drippings on each bird. Heat the oil in a Dutch oven and sauté ducks and shallots until the birds are brown on all sides.
3. Heat rum, ignite it, and pour it, while still flaming, over the birds. Add the ½ cup stock, carrot, garlic, thyme, parsley, and hot pepper. Cover Dutch oven.
4. Cook in a 475°F oven 30 minutes.
5. Cut the breasts in one piece and slice off remaining meat; reserve. Discard limes and peppercorns.
6. In a mortar, pound the carcasses until broken up. Pour the hot stock into the Dutch oven; add the broken carcasses and boil 10 minutes. Remove the hot pepper. Strain the stock and return to the Dutch oven.
7. Mix butter and cornstarch. Add to the stock; stir over medium heat until slightly thickened. Add salt and pepper to taste.
8. Fry toasted bread in butter until golden and crisp. Arrange meat on croutons. Pour sauce over all.
9. Garnish with Stuffed Sweet Peppers (page 263). Serve remaining sauce from a sauceboat.
8 SERVINGS

Hens in Wine

1 tablespoon rosemary
1 cup dry white wine
⅓ cup flour
1 teaspoon salt
½ teaspoon pepper
1 teaspoon snipped parsley
4 Rock Cornish hens,
  quartered
½ cup butter or margarine
1 pound small fresh
  mushrooms

1. Soak rosemary in wine 1 hour.
2. Combine flour, salt, pepper, and parsley. Coat hen quarters with flour mixture.
3. Brown hen quarters in butter in a skillet. Place in a 12x8-inch baking dish. Add wine mixture.
4. Bake, uncovered, at 350°F 30 minutes.
5. Meanwhile, sauté mushrooms in butter in skillet. Add to baking dish. Bake an additional 15 minutes, or until hen quarters are tender.
4 SERVINGS

Spit-Roasted Cornish Hens

Spit-Roasted Cornish Hens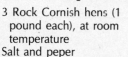

3 Rock Cornish hens (1 pound each), at room temperature
Salt and peper
½ cup olive oil, salad oil, or butter
¼ cup lemon juice

1 teaspoon salt
1 teaspoon marjoram
1 teaspoon thyme
½ teaspoon pepper
1 clove garlic, minced
2 tablespoons chopped chives

1. Season cavity of each hen with salt and pepper. Close neck and abdominal openings with skewers. Tie wings to bodies and tie legs together. Put a spit fork on rod. Dovetail hens and put second spit fork on rod. Insert spit forks in hens. Tighten screws with pliers. Attach spit with hens to rotisserie.
2. Combine the remaining ingredients and mix well. Start motor and brush hens with sauce. Roast over medium coals, about 6 inches from heat, until leg joints move easily and meat pulls away from leg bones, about 1 hour; brush frequently with sauce.
3. Split hens into halves with poultry shears or a sharp knife.
6 SERVINGS

Note: If using a gas-fired grill, sear hens for 2 minutes on high. Turn heat to medium and cook, brushing with sauce, until hens test done.

Glazed Duckling Gourmet

2 ducklings (about 4 pounds each), quartered (do not use wings, necks, and backs) and skinned
1½ teaspoons salt
¼ teaspoon ground nutmeg
3 to 4 tablespoons butter
1 clove garlic, minced
1½ teaspoons rosemary, crushed

1½ teaspoons thyme
1½ cups burgundy
2 teaspoons red wine vinegar
⅓ cup currant jelly
2 teaspoons cornstarch
2 tablespoons cold water
1½ cups halved seedless green grapes
Watercress

1. Remove excess fat from duckling pieces; rinse duckling and pat dry with absorbent paper. Rub pieces with salt and nutmeg.
2. Heat butter and garlic in a large skillet over medium heat; add the duckling pieces and brown well on all sides.
3. Add rosemary, thyme, burgundy, vinegar, and jelly to skillet. Bring to boiling; cover and simmer over low heat until duckling is tender (about 45 minutes). Remove duckling to a heated platter and keep it warm.
4. Combine cornstarch and water; blend into liquid in skillet; bring to boiling and cook 1 to 2 minutes, stirring constantly. Add grapes and toss them lightly until thoroughly heated.
5. Pour the hot sauce over duckling; garnish platter with watercress.
6 TO 8 SERVINGS

Wild Duck Pâté

2 wild ducks (about 4
  pounds each); reserve livers
¼ cup olive oil
Juice of 2 limes
1 garlic clove, halved
Water
1 carrot
1 leek
1 teaspoon salt
⅛ teaspoon pepper
1 cup port wine
2 bay leaves

1 small onion, minced
1 green hot pepper
⅛ teaspoon thyme
3 tablespoons olive oil
3 tablespoons butter
½ pound beef liver, cubed
¼ cup amber rum
1 egg
Lard
Truffles (optional)
Bay leaves and green hot
  peppers for garnish

1. Marinate the ducks for ½ hour in a mixture of ¼ cup oil and lime juice. Rub ducks with the cut surface of garlic clove.
2. Place birds in a Dutch oven and cover with water; add carrot, leek, salt, and pepper and bring to a boil. Simmer covered over low heat until birds are tender.
3. Remove birds from broth and cool. Reserve ¼ cup broth; store remaining broth for future use. Remove the meat from the carcasses, cutting the breast meat into long, even strips.
4. Mix port wine, bay leaves, onion, pepper, and thyme; marinate the breast meat for ½ hour. Set aside remaining duck meat.
5. Heat 3 tablespoons oil and butter in a medium skillet. Sauté duck livers and beef liver over high heat until golden. Warm the rum, ignite it, and pour it, still flaming, over the livers. Stir in ¼ cup of the reserved broth to deglaze the skillet.
6. Purée in an electric blender the liver mixture, reserved duck meat, and egg.
7. Coat heavily with lard 1 large terrine or loaf dish, or 2 small terrines or loaf dishes. Put in half the puréed mixture, then arrange the marinated strips of duck breast on top with slices of truffles, if desired. Cover with the remaining duck mixture, then with a thick coat of lard.
8. Garnish with bay leaves and green hot peppers. Cover terrine and place in a pan of hot water.
9. Bake at 375°F about 1½ hours.
10. Wipe clean the sides of the terrine. Cool and store covered in refrigerator up to a week.
11. To serve, remove bay leaves and peppers; slice pâté and accompany with salad.

Roast Rock Cornish Hen
with Wild Rice and Mushrooms

1½ cups water
½ teaspoon salt
½ cup wild rice
2 tablespoons butter or
  margarine
½ pound mushrooms, sliced
  lengthwise through caps
  and stems
1 tablespoon finely chopped

onion
3 tablespoons melted butter
  or margarine
2 tablespoons madeira
4 Rock Cornish hens, about
  1 pound each
2 teaspoons salt
¼ cup unsalted butter, melted
Watercress (optional)

1. Bring the water and salt to boiling in a deep saucepan.
2. Wash rice in a sieve. Add rice gradually to water so that

boiling will not stop. Boil rapidly, covered, 30 to 40 minutes, or until a kernel of rice is entirely tender when pressed between fingers. Drain rice in a colander or sieve.
3. While rice is cooking, heat 2 tablespoons butter or margarine in a skillet. Add the mushrooms and onion; cook, stirring occasionally, until mushrooms are lightly browned. Conbine mushrooms, wild rice, melted butter, and madeira; toss gently until mushrooms and butter are evenly distributed throughout rice.
4. Rinse and pat hens with absorbent paper. Rub cavities of the hens with the salt. Lightly fill body cavities with the wild rice stuffing. To close body cavities, sew or skewer and lace with cord. Fasten neck skin to backs and wings to bodies with skewers.
5. Place hens, breast-side up, on rack in roasting pan. Brush each hen with melted unsalted butter (about 1 tablespoon).
6. Roast, uncovered, in a 350°F oven; frequently baste hens during roasting period with drippings from roasting pan. Roast 1 to 1½ hours, or until hens test done. To test, move leg gently by grasping end bone; drumstick-thigh joint moves easily when hens are done. Remove skewers, if used.
7. Transfer hens to a heated serving platter and garnish with sprigs of watercress if desired.

4 TO 8 SERVINGS

Roast Duckling with Olives

1 duckling (about 4 pounds)
⅓ cup olive oil or other
  cooking oil
2 medium carrots, coarsely
  chopped
1 large onion, coarsely
  chopped
½ teaspoon salt
⅛ teaspoon seasoned pepper
¼ teaspoon rosemary
⅛ teaspoon savory

2 small stalks celery,
  chopped
3 sprigs parsley, chopped
1 small bay leaf
⅓ cup cognac
2 tablespoons tomato paste
2 cups hot chicken broth or
  bouillon
⅓ cup dry white wine
16 whole pitted green olives

1. Rinse, pat dry, and cut duckling into quarters. Remove any excess fat from pieces.
2. Heat oil in skillet; add duckling pieces and cook over medium heat until well browned on all sides. Remove pieces from skillet and keep warm.
3. Add carrots, onion, salt, seasoned pepper, rosemary, savory, celery, parsley, and bay leaf to skillet; continue cooking until carrots and onions are lightly browned. Drain off excess fat in skillet.
4. Return duck to skillet and pour cognac over it. Ignite and when flame ceases add a blend of tomato paste, chicken broth, and white wine. Cover skillet and cook in a 350°F oven about 1½ hours, or until duckling is tender.
5. Remove to heated serving platter and keep warm. Strain remaining mixture in skillet into a saucepan and add green olives. Heat until sauce is very hot and pour over duckling.

4 SERVINGS

Cornish Hens with Raisin Stuffing

4 Cornish hens (1 to 1½ pounds each)
16 grapevine leaves preserved in brine*
⅔ cup dark raisins
⅓ cup brandy
¾ cup cooked long-grain rice
1¼ cups finely chopped carrot
1¼ cups finely chopped celery
½ teaspoon cinnamon
1 tablespoon clarified butter
¼ teaspoon salt
⅛ teaspoon pepper
½ cup brandy

1. Rinse hens and pat dry; sprinkle lightly with salt.
2. Soak grapevine leaves in cold water 20 minutes. Pat dry. Set aside.
3. Simmer raisins in brandy 15 minutes; remove from heat and let stand 15 minutes. Stir in rice, carrot, celery, cinnamon, clarified butter, ¼ teaspoon salt, and the pepper. Spoon stuffing lightly into cavities of hens. Place hens on rack in a roasting pan. Cover breasts with grapevine leaves.
4. Roast in a 325°F oven 1¼ to 1½ hours, or until hens are tender. Baste with brandy during last ½ hour of roasting. Let hens stand 15 minutes before serving. Remove grapevine leaves.
4 SERVINGS

*Grapevine leaves can be purchased in a gourmet shop or in the specialty department of a supermarket.

Roast Goose with Sauerkraut Stuffing

1 goose (ready-to-cook 10 to 12 pounds)
1 tablespoon butter or margarine
2 large onions, chopped
6½ cups drained sauerkraut, snipped
2 medium apples, quartered, cored, and diced
1 small carrot, pared and shredded
2 medium potatoes, shredded (about 1½ cups)
½ cup dry white wine
1 to 2 tablespoons brown sugar
2 teaspoons caraway seed
½ teaspoon seasoned pepper
Salt

1. Singe and clean goose removing any large layers of fat from the body and neck cavities. Rinse thoroughly, drain, and pat dry with absorbent paper; set aside.
2. Heat butter in a skillet; add onion and cook until crisp-tender, 3 to 5 minutes.
3. Meanwhile, combine kraut, apple, carrot, and potato in a large bowl; toss until mixed. Add the onion, wine, and a blend of brown sugar, caraway seed, and seasoned pepper; toss again.
4. Rub cavities of goose with salt; lightly spoon stuffing into the body and neck cavities. Truss goose; set, breast side up, on a rack in a shallow roasting pan.
5. Roast, uncovered, in a 325°F oven about 3½ hours, or until goose tests done. Remove stuffing to a serving dish and accompany with slices of the roast goose.
ABOUT 8 SERVINGS

Rock Cornish Hens with Fruited Stuffing

1½ cups herb-seasoned stuffing croutons
½ cup drained canned apricot halves, cut in pieces
½ cup quartered seedless green grapes
⅓ cup chopped pecans
¼ cup butter or margarine, melted
2 tablespoons apricot nectar
1 tablespoon chopped parsley
¼ teaspoon salt
4 Rock Cornish hens (1 to 1½ pounds each), thawed if purchased frozen
Salt and pepper
⅓ cup apricot nectar
2 teaspoons soy sauce

1. Combine stuffing croutons, apricots, grapes, pecans, 2 tablespoons butter, 2 tablespoons apricot nectar, parsley, and ¼ teaspoon salt in a bowl; mix lightly.
2. Sprinkle cavities of hens with salt and pepper. Fill each hen with about ½ cup stuffing; fasten with skewers and lace with cord.
3. Blend ⅓ cup apricot nectar, soy sauce, and remaining butter. Place hens, breast side up, on a rack in a shallow roasting pan; brush generously with sauce.
4. Roast in a 350°F oven about 1½ hours, or until hens are tender and well browned; baste occasionally with sauce during roasting.
4 SERVINGS

Roast Goose with Prune-Apple Stuffing

2 cups pitted cooked prunes
1 goose (10 to 12 pounds, ready-to-cook weight)
Salt
6 medium (about 2 pounds) apples

1. Set out a shallow roasting pan with rack. Have prunes ready, reserving about 8 to 10 prunes for garnish.
2. If goose is frozen, thaw according to directions on package. Clean and remove any layers of fat from body cavity and opening of goose. Cut off neck at body, leaving on neck skin. Rinse and pat dry with absorbent paper. (Reserve giblets for use in gravy or other food preparation.) Rub body and neck cavities of goose with salt. Wash, core, pare and quarter apples.
3. Lightly fill body and neck cavities with the apples and prunes. To close body cavity, sew or skewer and lace with cord. Fasten neck skin to back with skewer. Loop cord around legs and tighten slightly. Place breast side down on rack in roasting pan.
4. Roast uncovered at 325°F 3 hours. Remove fat from pan as it accumulates during this period. Turn goose breast side up. Roast 1 to 2 hours longer, or until goose tests done. To test for doneness, move leg gently by grasping end of bone; drumstick-thigh joint should move easily. (Protect fingers with paper napkin.) Allow about 25 minutes per pound to estimate total roasting time.
5. To serve, remove skewers and cord. Place goose on heated platter. Remove some of the apples from goose and arrange on the platter. Garnish with the reserved prunes. For an attractive garnish, place cooked prunes on top of cooked apple rings, if desired.
8 SERVINGS

Roast Goose with Rice-and-Pickle Stuffing

3 cups cooked rice; or 1 package (6 ounces) seasoned white and wild rice mix, cooked following package directions
1 package (7 ounces) herb-seasoned stuffing croutons
2 medium navel oranges, pared and sectioned
2 onions, chopped
1 cup cranberries, rinsed, sorted, and chopped
1 cup sweet mixed pickles, drained and chopped
¼ cup sweet pickle liquid
½ to ¾ cup butter or margarine, melted
2 tablespoons brown sugar
1 goose (8 to 10 pounds)
1 tablespoon salt
¼ teaspoon ground black pepper
2 tablespoons light corn syrup
1½ cups orange juice
½ cup orange marmalade

1. Combine rice, stuffing croutons, orange sections, onions, cranberries, pickles and liquid, butter, and brown sugar in a large bowl; toss lightly until blended.
2. Rinse goose and remove any large layers of fat from the body cavity. Pat dry with absorbent paper. Rub body and neck cavities with salt and pepper.
3. Lightly spoon stuffing into the neck and body cavities. Overlap neck cavity with the skin and skewer to back of goose. Close body cavity with skewers and lace with cord. Loop cord around legs; tighten slightly and tie to a skewer inserted in the back above tail. Rub skin of goose with a little salt, if desired.
4. Put remaining stuffing into a greased casserole and cover; or cook in heavy-duty aluminum foil. Set in oven with goose during final hour of roasting.
5. Place goose, breast side down, on a rack in a large shallow roasting pan.
6. Roast in a 325°F oven 2 hours, removing fat from pan several times during this period.
7. Turn goose, breast side up. Blend corn syrup and 1 cup orange juice. Brush generously over goose. Roast about 1½ hours, or until goose tests done. To test for doneness, move leg gently by grasping end of bone; when done, drumstick-thigh joint moves easily or twists out. Brush frequently during final roasting period with the orange-syrup blend.
8. Transfer goose to a heated serving platter. Spoon 2 tablespoons drippings, the remaining ½ cup orange juice, and marmalade into a small saucepan. Heat thoroughly, stirring to blend. Pour into a serving dish or gravy boat to accompany goose.
6 TO 8 SERVINGS

Baked Pigeon

1 pigeon
Salt and pepper
1 strip bacon, diced
Melted butter

1. Soak the pigeon about 2 hours in cold water. Dry with paper towels.
2. Sprinkle cavity with salt and pepper.
3. Make small slits in skin; insert pieces of bacon. Place in a roasting pan.
4. Bake at 350°F 30 to 40 minutes, or until tender; baste often with butter.
1 SERVING

Ortolans on Croutons

8 ortolans
½ lime
Salt and freshly ground pepper
½ cup cubed salt pork
¼ cup amber rum
½ cup red wine
1 tablespoon butter
1 tablespoon cornstarch
8 white bread slices with crusts trimmed
¼ cup butter

1. Truss ortolans. Rub the skin with the cut side of the lime half. Season with salt and pepper.
2. Render the salt pork over high heat in a Dutch oven. Sauté ortolans for 6 minutes, or until well browned.
3. Heat rum, ignite it, and pour it, still flaming, over the birds. Place birds on a serving platter.
4. Pour wine into Dutch oven to deglaze. Mix 1 tablespoon butter and cornstarch and add to wine. Stir until sauce is slightly thicker.
5. Make croutons by frying bread slices in butter until brown on both sides.
6. Serve each ortolan on a crouton, top with a slice of sautéed liver pâté, if desired, and pour sauce over all.
8 SERVINGS

Wild Pigeons Perugian

3 pigeons or Rock Cornish hens
4 to 6 tablespoons olive oil
1 cup dry red wine
10 green olives
4 fresh sage leaves or ¼ teaspoon ground sage
½ teaspoon juniper berries
½ teaspoon salt
Dash pepper

1. Brown pigeons in 2 tablespoons hot olive oil in a Dutch oven, adding more oil if necessary. Stir in wine, 2 tablespoons olive oil, olives, sage, juniper berries, salt, and pepper.
2. Cook in a 300°F oven 50 to 60 minutes, or until pigeons are tender.
4 SERVINGS

Potted Pheasant

¾ cup all-purpose flour
½ teaspoon salt
¼ teaspoon pepper
1 pheasant, cut in pieces
½ cup butter
1 onion, quartered
1 stalk celery, cut up
2 cups meat stock or beef broth
3 whole allspice
½ cup whipping cream
2 tablespoons sherry

1. Mix flour with salt and pepper.
2. Coat each piece of pheasant with seasoned flour. Melt butter in a Dutch oven or flameproof casserole. Brown pheasant in butter. Add onion, celery, and 1 cup meat stock. Cover.
3. Bake at 350°F 40 minutes. Add remaining meat stock. Do not cover. Bake about 40 minutes longer, or until pheasant is tender.
4. Remove pheasant to heated platter. Strain broth; combine 1 cup broth to cream and sherry. Serve over the pheasant.
2 TO 4 SERVINGS

Guinea Stew

Salt and freshly ground
 pepper
1 guinea fowl (2½ to 3
 pounds)
1 lime, halved
¼ pound salt pork, cubed
4 parsley sprigs
2 scallions or green onions,
 chopped
2 garlic cloves
2 cloves
½ teaspoon salt
¼ cup soybean oil
½ cup amber rum
2 cups red wine
1 cup chicken stock
12 shallots
2 carrots, sliced
2 turnips, sliced
1 tablespoon butter
1 tablespoon cornstarch

1. Sprinkle salt, and pepper over bird and refrigerate over-night. The next day, rub the skin with the cut side of the lime. Cut bird into pieces.
2. Render salt pork over medium heat in a Dutch oven. When crisp, remove the cracklings.
3. In a mortar, pound to a paste the parsley, scallions, garlic, cloves, and salt. Add the seasoning paste and oil to the Dutch oven.
4. Sauté the meat until golden brown on all sides.
5. Heat rum, ignite it, and pour it, still flaming, over the meat. Add wine and stock; reduce heat, cover, and simmer 30 minutes.
6. Add shallots, carrots, and turnips. Simmer until meat and vegetables are tender.
7. Place meat and vegetables on a serving platter.
8. Mix butter and cornstarch; add to liquid in Dutch oven and stir over high heat until sauce is slightly thickened. Season with salt and pepper, if necessary. Pour sauce over meat and vegetables.
9. Serve with Caribbean Rice (page 190).
2 SERVINGS

Chicken Stew: Follow recipe for Guinea Stew, substituting **1 broiler-fryer chicken (about 2 pounds)** for guinea fowl.

Teal on the Spit

4 teals; reserve livers
1 orange, halved
8 chicken livers
1 tablespoon flour
¼ teaspoon garlic powder
Salt and pepper
2 tablespoons olive oil
4 bacon slices
2 tablespoons flour
2 tablespoons butter
1 can (13 ounces) clear consommé madrilène
1½ teaspoons lime juice
1½ teaspoons orange juice

1. Rub teals with cut sides of orange halves. Set aside.
2. Coat the teal livers and chicken livers with a mixture of 1 tablespoon flour, garlic powder, salt, and pepper. Heat oil and sauté the livers until golden brown.
3. Put the livers into the bird cavities. Wrap each bird in a slice of bacon, securing with skewers.
4. Spear birds on a spit and broil on the electric broiler about 25 minutes or, if charcoal is used, place the spitted bird 4 inches from the hot coals and turn often.
5. Brown 2 tablespoons flour in butter in a small saucepan over high heat. Add enough consommé madrilène to just moisten the mixture, stirring rapidly with a whisk. While it thickens, slowly pour in the remaining consommé in a thin stream. Boil rapidly, uncovered, stirring constantly for about

4 minutes, or until the sauce is reduced to ½ cup. Remove from heat and add lime juice and orange juice.
6. Serve teal with Stuffed Tomatoes with Rice and Pine Nuts (page 225) and the sauce separately.
4 SERVINGS

Barbecued Wild Game Birds

4 ready-to-cook wild game
 birds such as duckling,
 snipe, teal, or woodcock
Amber rum
6 peppercorns
4 parsley sprigs
3 garlic cloves
1 green hot pepper
1 tablespoon salt
1 tablespoon olive or peanut
 oil
1 cup red wine
Bacon drippings
Dry bread crumbs
Creole Barbecue Sauce (page
 52)

1. Brush surface of birds with rum. Split birds in half and pound with a meat hammer.
2. In a mortar, pound to a paste the peppercorns, parsley, garlic, pepper, and salt. Mix seasoning paste with olive oil and wine. Pour marinade over birds and refrigerate 12 hours.
3. Thoroughly drain bird halves. Brush with bacon drippings and coat with bread crumbs.
4. Barbecue bird halves in a hinged grill 4 inches from glowing coals about 10 minutes on each side, basting twice with Creole Barbecue Sauce; time depends on their size. Turn birds once and baste again.
5. Birds should be eaten on the rare side; when birds are pricked with a fork, a droplet of blood should surface slowly.
4 SERVINGS

Smothered Pigeons

3 tablespoons butter
2 pigeons (about 2 pounds)
3 onions, sliced
1 cup meat stock or broth
2 tart apples, cored and
 sliced
¼ cup sliced mushrooms
Juice of ½ lemon
⅓ cup Madeira
1 tablespoon butter or
 margarine (at room
 temperature)
1 tablespoon Browned Flour
1 cup sour cream

1. Melt butter in a large skillet. Sauté pigeons in butter 15 minutes. Remove pigeons.
2. Fry onions in the butter left in skillet until tender. Add stock, sliced apples, mushrooms, and lemon juice. Mix well and bring to boiling. Add wine.
3. Mix butter with flour until smooth. Stir into liquid in skillet. Cook and stir until mixture is thickened.
4. Dip pigeons in sour cream; return to skillet. Cook, covered, until tender.
2 SERVINGS

Browned Flour: Spread **1½ cups all-purpose flour** in a shallow baking pan. Place on lowest position for broiler. Broil and stir about 20 minutes, or until flour is golden brown. Stirring must be almost constant to prevent burning. If flour burns, skim off burned portion and continue browning remainder. Store in tightly covered container.
ABOUT 1⅓ CUPS

SEAFOOD

a baking dish.
3. Bake at 325°F 30 minutes.
4. Serve hot sealed in parchment.
1 SERVING

Fried Codfish in Garlic Sauce

4 frozen codfish fillets,
  thawed
Flour, seasoned with salt and
  pepper
Flour and water to make a
  thick paste (about 1¼ cups

water to 1 cup flour)
Oil for frying
Garlic and Potato Sauce (see
  below)
Lemon wedges

1. Pat fillets dry. Coat with seasoned flour. Dip in flour and water mixture.
2. Pour oil into a deep skillet and heat to smoking.
3. Put fillets in oil. Fry until golden brown, turning once.
4. Serve with Garlic and Potato Sauce and lemon wedges.
2 TO 4 SERVINGS

Garlic and Potato Sauce

1 pound potatoes, pared and
  cut in small pieces
4 garlic cloves, crushed in a
  garlic press

1 cup olive oil
¼ cup vinegar
Salt and freshly ground
  pepper

1. Boil potatoes until they can be pierced easily with a fork. Drain in a colander or on paper towels.
2. Mash potatoes in a potato ricer. Add garlic and then olive oil, a tablespoon at a time, beating well after each spoonful. Beat in vinegar. Season with salt and pepper to taste. If sauce is too thick, beat in a little warm water or move olive oil.
3. Serve with **fried** or **broiled seafood,** on **crackers** or **toasted bread,** or as a dip for **fresh vegetables.**
1 QUART SAUCE

Charcoal-Grilled Fish

Fish for grilling
¼ cup olive oil
Juice of 1 lemon

2 tablespoons oregano,
  crushed
Salt and pepper to taste

1. Fish suitable for grilling are trout, whitefish, bluefish, snapper, or mackerel.
2. Heat charcoal until white. Arrange grill so that it is about 4 inches from coals. Use a hinged basket grill for easier turning; oil it well to prevent fish from sticking.
3. Combine olive oil, lemon juice, oregano, salt and pepper.
4. Cool on one side about 7 minutes. Turn over and cook an additional 7 minutes.
5. Serve fish with remaining sauce.

Baked Halibut in Parchment Paper

1 tablespoon olive oil
Juice of ½ lemon
Pinch basil
Pinch oregano
1 halibut steak (or any other

preferred steak)
Salt and pepper
2 thin lemon slices
4 capers

1. Combine oil, lemon juice, basil, and oregano; spoon over both sides of the fish. Season with salt and pepper.
2. Place the fish on a piece of parchment paper. Lay lemon slices and capers on top of fish. Seal paper and tie. Put into

Russian Salmon Mound

Pastry:
4 cups flour
2 sticks butter, frozen and
   cut in 12 pieces
6 tablespoons shortening
1 teaspoon salt
12 tablespoons ice water

Salmon:
3 quarts water
2 cups dry white wine
1 large onion, peeled and
   quartered
2 stalks celery, trimmed and
   cut in 1-inch pieces
2 carrots, pared and cut in
   1-inch pieces
10 peppercorns
1 tablespoon salt
2½ pounds fresh salmon

Mushroom-Rice Filling:
8 tablespoons butter (1 stick)
½ cup uncooked rice

1¼ cups chicken stock
1 tablespoon dried dill
½ pound fresh mushrooms,
   cleaned and trimmed
3 tablespoons lemon juice
3 large onions, peeled and
   quartered
1½ teaspoons salt
¼ teaspoon pepper
3 hard-cooked eggs

Cream Sauce:
2 tablespoons buter
3½ tablespoons flour
2 cups milk, heated
¼ teaspoon salt
Dash pepper

Assembly:
2 tablespoons soft butter
1 egg yolk
1 tablespoon cream
1 tablespoon melted butter

1. To make pastry, using **steel blade** of food processor, place 2 cups flour, 1 stick butter cut in 6 pieces, 3 tablespoons vegetable shortening, and ½ teaspoon salt in a bowl. Process until butter and shortening are cut into flour. With machine on, add 6 tablespoons ice water through feed tube. Process until dough forms into a ball and remove from bowl.
2. Repeat procedure again, using same amounts of ingredients. Wrap both balls of dough in plastic wrap and place in refrigerator to chill while preparing remainder of recipe.
3. To cook salmon, combine 3 quarts water and wine in a large pot.
4. Using **steel blade,** chop onion, celery, and carrots together. Add to pot. Also add peppercorns and salt. Bring to boiling over high heat. Add salmon to liquid, reduce heat, and simmer for about 10 minutes until tender. Remove from pot and separate into small flakes with a fork. Also remove any bones and skin from fish. Set aside.
5. To make filling, melt 2 tablespoons butter in a saucepan,

add rice and cook 2 to 3 minutes until rice is coated with butter. Add chicken stock, bring to a boil, and cover. Reduce heat and cook about 20 minutes until tender and fluffy. Remove from heat and stir in dill with a fork. Set aside.
6. Slice mushrooms with **slicing disc.** Melt 2 tablespoons butter in a skillet, add mushrooms, and cook for 5 minutes. Transfer to a small bowl and toss with lemon juice; set aside.
7. Using **steel blade,** process onions until chopped. Melt 4 tablespoons butter in skillet, add chopped onion, and cook until soft, but not brown. Add mushrooms, salt, and pepper; set aside.
8. Using **plastic blade,** process hard-cooked eggs until finely chopped and set aside.
9. To make Cream Sauce, melt 2 tablespoons butter and add flour. Cook for a minute or two, remove from heat and add heated milk, stirring constantly with a whisk until smooth. Bring to boiling, add salt and pepper, and remove from heat.
10. In a large bowl, combine flaked salmon, mushroom-onion mixture, rice, chopped hard-cooked eggs, and Cream Sauce. Gently toss with two wooden spoons until thoroughly mixed. Adjust seasonings, adding more salt, pepper, and dill as desired.
11. To assemble, roll 1 ball of dough into a rectangle and trim to 15x8 inches. Coat a large cookie sheet with 2 tablespoons butter. Drape pastry around rolling pin and unroll over cookie sheet. Place filling in center, forming it into a mound and leaving a 2-inch border around edges. Using a pastry brush, coat border with a mixture of 1 egg yolk and 1 tablespoon cream.
12. Roll other ball of dough into a rectangle 18x11 inches. Roll it around rolling pin and place over salmon mound. Trim borders of dough so that they are even. Turn up border of dough to make a shallow rim around mound and decorate (crimp) at ½-inch intervals with dull side of a knife. Cut a 1-inch circle in center of mound and decorate top with leftover pastry. Brush entire loaf with egg yolk mixture. Pour 1 tablespoon melted butter in opening.
13. Bake at 400°F 1 hour, or until golden. Serve with a pitcher of **melted butter** or bowl of **sour cream.**
12 SERVINGS

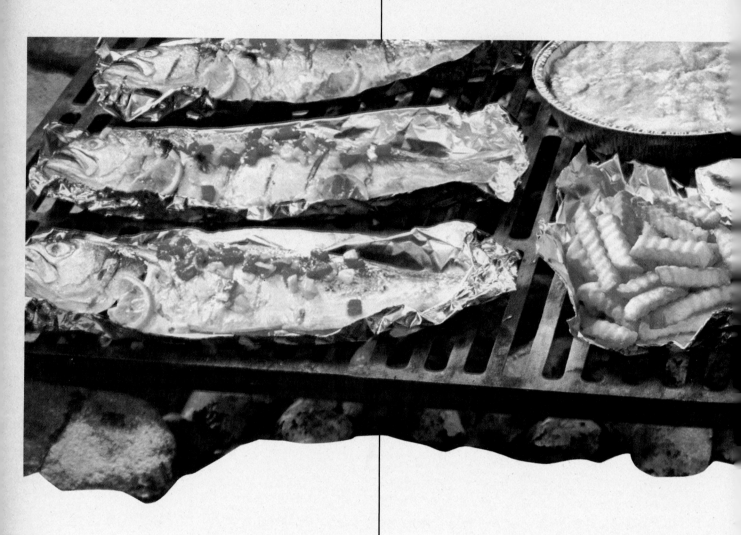

Savory Outdoor Baked Fish

Scale and clean fish, leaving whole. Place fish on individual sheets of heavy-duty aluminum foil and brush with melted butter or oil. Sprinkle with salt and pepper and drizzle with lemon juice. Top each fish with a teaspoonful of chopped tomato or pimento and garnish with lemon slices. Bring foil up over fish and seal with a double fold. Seal ends. Place on grill over a medium-hot fire and cook 10 minutes on a side for a small 1- to 1½-pound fish, 15 minutes on a side for 2- to 3-pound fish, and about 20 minutes on a side for 4- to 5-pound fish. Open foil; if fish flakes easily when tested with a fork, it is done. Serve with juices from bottom of package.

Fish Kebob

2 pounds swordfish or halibut with bones removed, cut in large cubes	1 teaspoon dill
	1 bay leaf
	Salt and pepper to taste
1 cup olive oil	Small whole onions, peeled
Juice of 2 lemon	Whole cherry tomatoes
1 teaspoon oregano	

1. Marinate fish in a mixture of the oil, lemon juice, oregano, dill, bay leaf, salt, and pepper for 2 hours, basting occasionally. Reserve marinade.
2. Alternate fish, onions, and tomatoes on skewers.
3. Broil, turning frequently, until done (about 5 minutes).
4. Heat marinade. Serve with Fish Kebob.

4 SERVINGS

Baked Fish à la Spetses

4 pounds fish fillets (turbot, whitefish, bass, mullet)
4 fresh tomatoes, peeled and sliced
¾ cup olive oil
1 cup white wine
2 tablespoons chopped parsley
1 garlic clove, crushed in a garlic press
Salt and pepper to taste
1 teaspoon basil (optional)
1 cup fresh bread crumbs
1 slice feta cheese for each portion

1. Put fillets into a baking dish.
2. In a bowl, combine tomatoes, olive oil, wine, parsley, garlic, salt, pepper, and basil. Pour over fillets. Sprinkle with bread crumbs.
3. Bake at 375°F 40 minutes.
4. Top fillets with feta cheese slices. Broil 1 or 2 minutes.
6 TO 8 SERVINGS

Poached Striped Bass

1 quart water
1 quart dry white wine
Juice of 3 lemons
2 cups olive oil
2 medium onions, quartered
1 large carrot, pared and left whole
2 celery stalks with leaves
2 leeks
Salt to taste
10 coriander seeds
8 whole peppercorns
1 bay leaf
4 parsley sprigs
1 thyme sprig
3 garlic cloves, peeled and left whole
5 pounds bass, cleaned, with gills removed and head and tail left on

1. Pour water, wine, lemon juice, and olive oil into a saucepot.
2. Wrap remaining ingredients, except fish, in cheesecloth and add. Bring to boiling and simmer covered 15 minutes.
3. Wrap fish in cheesecloth. Place in a fish poacher or a deep greased baking dish.
4. Pour in stock, discarding vegetables; cover and simmer 15 minutes. Remove from heat.
5. Let fish remain in the liquid for another 15 minutes. Lift out of pan and drain; reserve fish stock for other use. Remove cheesecloth and peel off skin.
6. Serve fish at room temperature with Vinegar and Oil Dressing with Tomato (below), Mayonnaise, or Garlic and Potato Sauce (page 463).
6 TO 8 SERVINGS

Vinegar and Oil Dressing with Tomato

1 tablespoon imported mustard (Dijon, preferably)
2 tablespoons red wine vinegar, or more to taste
½ cup olive oil
1 large tomato, peeled and diced
2 whole scallions, minced
2 tablespoons minced parsley
1 tablespoon chopped capers
1 teaspoon dill

Put mustard and vinegar into a small bowl. Add olive oil while stirring with a whisk. Add remaining ingredients, mix well. Refrigerate several hours before serving.
1¾ CUPS

Sole with Vegetables

2 tablespoons butter or margarine
1 large onion, diced
1 cup savory cabbage, shredded (optional)
1 leek, thinly sliced
1 large carrot, thinly sliced
1 stalk celery, thinly sliced
1 parsley root, thinly sliced
2 pounds sole or any white fish fillets
½ teaspoon salt
2 tablespoons water

Sauce:
2 tablespoons butter or margarine
2 tablespoons flour
1 cup chicken broth or fish stock
½ teaspoon salt
¼ teaspoon pepper
¼ cup sour cream

1. Melt butter in a Dutch oven or large skillet. Add vegetables and stir-fry 5 minutes.
2. Sprinkle fish fillets with salt. Place on the vegetables. Add water. Cover; simmer 15 minutes.
3. For sauce, melt butter in a saucepan. Stir in flour. Cook and stir until golden. Then gradually stir in broth. Cook, stirring constantly, until sauce boils.
4. Transfer the fish to a warm platter. Stir the sauce into the vegetables. Remove from heat. Season with salt and pepper; stir in sour cream. Pour over the fish.
ABOUT 6 SERVINGS

Seviche

1 pound pompano (or other mild-flavored fish fillets)
Juice of 6 limes (or lemons)
2 medium tomatoes, peeled and chopped
2 tablespoons finely chopped onion
1 or 2 canned jalapeño
chilies, seeded and finely chopped
¼ cup olive oil
1 tablespoon vinegar
¼ teaspoon oregano
Salt and pepper
Sliced green olives
Chopped parsley

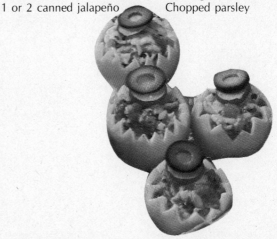

1. Wash the fish very well. Cut into small chunks or strips and place in a glass jar or glass bowl with cover. Pour lime juice over fish; cover and refrigerate about 6 hours. (Lime juice will "cook" raw fish until it is white and firm.)
2. At least a half hour before serving, add tomato, onion, chili, olive oil, vinegar, oregano, and salt and pepper to taste; stir gently until evenly mixed.
3. When ready to serve, garnish with sliced olives and parsley.
6 SERVINGS

Planked Fish Fillet Dinner

1 large fish fillet, weighing about 10 ounces (such as sole, flounder, whitefish, lake trout, or haddock)
1 tablespoon melted butter or margarine
Salt and pepper
Seasoned instant potatoes
2 broiled tomato halves
4 broiled mushroom caps (optional)
Lemon slices
Watercress or parsley

1. If fish is frozen, let thaw on refrigerator shelf or at room temperature. Brush seasoned plank lightly with melted butter.
2. Place fish fillet on plank and brush with remaining butter. Sprinkle lightly with salt and pepper. Bake at 350°F for 20 minutes, or just until fish flakes easily.
3. Remove from oven, and turn oven temperature up to 450°F. Pipe a border of hot mashed potatoes along sides of fish.
4. Return to oven for 10 minutes until potatoes are delicately browned. Place tomato halves and mushroom caps, if desired, on plank. Garnish with lemon slices and watercress. Serve at once.
2 SERVINGS

Trout in Grapevine Leaves

1 jar (32 ounces) grapevine leaves, drained
4 medium trout, cleaned, with heads and tails left on
2 tablespoons olive oil
2 tablespoons butter, melted
2 teaspoons oregano
1 teaspoon dill
Additional oil to brush outside of trout
Salt and pepper to taste
2 lemons, cut in wedges

1. Rinse grapevine leaves thoroughly under cold running water to remove brine.
2. Rinse trout; pat dry.
3. Drizzle 2 tablespoons olive oil and butter in trout cavities. Sprinkle with oregano and dill. Brush oil on outside of fish. Season inside and out with salt and pepper.
4. Wrap each trout in 5 or 6 grapevine leaves. Refrigerate 1 to 2 hours.
5. To charcoal-broil, adjust grill 4 inches from heated coals. Grease a rectangular, long-handled grill on all sides. Place fish in the grill, side by side. Grill one side about 8 minutes, turn, grill until fish flakes easily with a fork (about 8 minutes more).
6. Discard browned outer leaves. Serve trout in remaining leaves. Garnish with lemon wedges.
4 SERVINGS

Note: Trout may also be broiled under the broiler. For easy turning, use a long-handled grill.

Oyster Bisque Antoine's

2 tablespoons minced celery
2 tablespoons butter
3 tablespoons flour
¾ teaspoon salt
⅛ teaspoon white pepper
1 quart milk, scalded
2 cups oysters
¾ cup heavy cream, scalded
2 tablespoons sherry

1. In a heavy saucepan, cook the celery in butter until yellow in color. Stir in the flour, salt, and pepper; cook until bubbly. Blend in the scalded milk, cooking and stirring until thickened and smooth.
2. Heat the oysters in their liquor until the edges curl. Drain and reserve the liquor. Finely chop the oysters and rub them through a fine sieve or purée oysters in a blender.
3. Add the oysters to the white sauce alternately with the cream. Add sherry. (If bisque seems too thick, thin it with some of the oyster liquor.)
ABOUT 1½ QUARTS SOUP

Baked Fish with Tomatoes, Onions, and Parsley

½ cup olive oil
2 large onions, coarsely chopped
1 can (20 ounces) tomatoes (undrained)
½ cup white wine
½ cup chopped parsley
1 garlic clove, crushed in a garlic press
Salt and pepper to taste
3 pounds fish fillets (any firm fish such as turbot, bass, grouper, or red snapper may be used)

1. Heat olive oil in a saucepan. Add onion and cook until translucent. Add tomatoes, wine, parsley, garlic, salt, and pepper. Simmer covered 10 minutes.
2. Place fish in a large baking dish. Cover with sauce.
3. Bake at 350°F about 25 minutes, or until fish flakes easily when tested with a fork.
4 SERVINGS

Fish Casserole Haramogli

3 pounds whitefish, sole, or any other lean fish (head and tail removed), cut in 4 portions
5 cups fish stock
3 cups Béchamel Sauce (see page 49)
2 tablespoons minced parsley
1 teaspoon basil
1 garlic clove, crushed in a garlic press
4 cups cooked rice
½ cup freshly grated kefalotyri cheese

1. Wrap fish loosely in cheesecloth. Knot the ends. Heat fish stock until boiling. Add fish and simmer until done (about 10 minutes).
2. Remove fish from liquid and discard cheesecloth.
3. Mix Béchamel Sauce with parsley, basil, and garlic.
4. Turn rice into a casserole. Put fish on top. Top with Béchamel Sauce and cheese. Cover tightly with aluminum foil.
5. Set in a 300°F oven 12 to 15 minutes, or until thoroughly heated.
8 SERVINGS

Tuna for Two

1 can (2 ounces) sliced
mushrooms, drained
¼ cup sliced green onion
¼ teaspoon dill weed
2 tablespoons butter or
margarine
1 tablespoon lemon juice or
wine
1 can (7½ ounces)
semicondensed cream of

mushroom soup with wine
1 can (6½ or 7 ounces) tuna,
drained and flaked
1 tablespoon chopped
pimento
1 package (10 ounces) frozen
broccoli spears, cooked and
drained
2 tablespoons grated
Parmesan cheese

1. Sauté mushrooms, onion, and dill weed in butter in a saucepan. Stir in lemon juice, soup, tuna, and pimento.
2. Arrange broccoli spears in 2 or 3 individual casseroles. Spoon tuna mixture over broccoli. Sprinkle with Parmesan cheese.
3. Bake, uncovered, at 350°F 20 minutes, or until heated through.
2 OR 3 SERVINGS

Sea Chowder

¼ cup olive oil
3 garlic cloves
1 medium onion, quartered
2 bay leaves
Water to cover fish
1 cup dry white wine
Juice of 1 lemon
6 squid, cleaned and cut in

pieces
Salt and pepper to taste
2 tomatoes, peeled, seeded,
and diced
3 pounds fish (several kinds),
skinned and boned
1 pound shrimp, shelled and
deveined

1. Heat oil in a deep saucepan. Add garlic, onion, and bay leaves. Cook until onion is translucent.
2. Pour in water, wine, and lemon juice. Add squid. Season with salt and pepper. Cover and simmer 40 minutes.
3. Add tomatoes and fish; simmer 8 minutes. Add shrimp; simmer just until shrimp are cooked. Adjust seasonings. Serve at once.
6 SERVINGS

Baked Fish with Tomatoes, Onions, and Parsley

½ cup olive oil
2 large onions, coarsely
chopped
1 can (20 ounces) tomatoes
(undrained)
½ cup white wine
½ cup chopped parsley

1 garlic clove, crushed in a
garlic press
Salt and pepper to taste
3 pounds fish fillets (any firm
fish such as turbot, bass,
grouper, or red snapper
may be used)

1. Heat olive oil in a saucepan. Add onion and cook until translucent. Add tomatoes, wine, parsley, garlic, salt, and pepper. Simmer covered 10 minutes.
2. Place fish in a large baking dish. Cover with sauce.
3. Bake at 350°F about 25 minutes, or until fish flakes easily when tested with a fork.
4 SERVINGS

Fish au Gratin

1 cup chicken or vegetable
broth or stock
1 tablespoon flour
1 tablespoon butter or
margarine (at room
temperature)
½ teaspoon salt
¼ teaspoon parsley flakes
¼ teaspoon pepper
Pinch ground thyme
¼ cup whipping cream

1½ pounds sole, trout, pike,
or other white fish
3 tablespoons grated
Parmesan, Swiss, or
Gruyère cheese
2 tablespoons dry bread
crumbs
1 tablespoon melted butter
or margarine
1 teaspoon lemon juice
(optional)

1. Bring broth to boiling in a small saucepan. Blend flour into butter and stir into boiling broth. Cook and stir until thickened. Reduce heat. Stir in salt, parsley flakes, pepper, thyme, and cream.
2. Place fish in a well-buttered pan. Pour sauce over fish.
3. Bake at 375°F 15 minutes.
4. Mix cheese, bread crumbs, melted butter, and lemon juice (if desired). Sprinkle over fish in pan. Bake about 15 minutes longer, or until fish flakes easily.
4 TO 6 SERVINGS

Fish au Gratin with Tomatoes: Prepare Fish au Gratin as directed, except sprinkle ½ **cup chopped tomato** over top of fish before covering with sauce.

Fish au Gratin with Mushrooms: Prepare Fish au Gratin as directed, adding ½ **cup sliced mushrooms** to partially baked fish before topping with crumb mixture.

Fish au Gratin with Horseradish: Prepare Fish au Gratin as directed, adding **4 teaspoons prepared horseradish** to sauce along with cream.

Baked Leftover Fish

3 boiled potatoes, sliced
1½ cups diced cooked fish
¾ cup sliced cooked
cauliflower or mushrooms
(optional)
2 hard-cooked eggs, sliced
Salt and pepper

1 tablespoon flour
1 cup sour cream
¼ cup water
3 tablespoons bread crumbs
2 tablespoons grated
Parmesan cheese
2 tablespoons butter

1. Arrange layers of half the potatoes, fish, cauliflower, eggs, and remaining potatoes in a greased 1½-quart casserole. Lightly sprinkle salt and pepper over each layer.
2. Blend flour into sour cream; stir in water. Spoon over casserole mixture.
3. Mix bread crumbs, cheese, and butter together. Sprinkle over top of casserole.
4. Bake at 350°F 30 minutes.
ABOUT 4 SERVINGS

Solianka

Solianka

1 whole fish (about 1 pound)
1 package soup greens
1 teaspoon salt
2 cups boiling water
¼ cup butter or margarine
1 medium onion, peeled and thinly sliced
1 medium cucumber, pared and coarsely chopped (seeds discarded)
2 medium tomatoes, peeled and cut in pieces

1 teaspoon salt
¼ teaspoon white pepper
⅓ cup drained canned shrimp or lobster
⅓ cup drained canned mussels
1 gherkin, thinly sliced
5 pitted ripe olives, sliced
1 teaspoon capers
Thin lemon slices, halved
Fresh dill
Sour cream (optional)

1. Prepare fish fillets, cut in pieces, and refrigerate.
2. To prepare fish broth, put fish head, bones, and fins and soup greens into an electric cooker; add salt and boiling water.
3. Cover and cook on High 4 hours.
4. Heat butter in a skillet. Add onion and cook 5 minutes, stirring occasionally; do not brown.
5. Strain broth and return to cooker. Add onion, cucumber, tomato, salt, and pepper to broth; stir.
6. Cover and cook on High 30 minutes.
7. Add reserved fish, shrimp, mussels, gherkin, ripe olives, capers, lemon slices, and dill to cooker; mix.
8. Cover and cook on High 30 minutes.
9. Serve soup topped with sour cream, if desired.
ABOUT 6 SERVINGS

Fish in Horseradish Sauce

2 carrots
2 stalks celery (optional)
1 parsley root
1 onion, quartered
1 bay leaf
5 peppercorns
2 teaspoons salt
1½ quarts water
2 pounds carp, sole, or pike fillets

Horseradish Sauce:
3 tablespoons butter or

margarine
3 tablespoons flour
¾ cup prepared cream-style horseradish
½ teaspoon sugar
¼ teaspoon salt
⅔ cup sour cream
2 hard-cooked eggs, peeled and sieved

Garnish:
Shredded lettuce

1. Combine vegetables, dry seasonings, and water in a saucepot. Bring to boiling; simmer 20 minutes. Strain.
2. Cook fish in the strained vegetable stock 6 to 10 minutes, or until fish flakes easily.
3. Remove fish from stock. Arrange on serving platter and cover with plastic wrap. Chill.
4. Strain fish stock and reserve ¾ cup for horseradish sauce; cool.
5. For horseradish sauce, melt butter in a saucepan; blend in flour until smooth.
6. Add the cooked fish stock gradually, stirring constantly. Cook and stir until the sauce boils and becomes thick and smooth.
7. Remove from heat. Stir in horseradish, sugar, salt, sour cream, and eggs. Cool 15 minutes.
8. Pour the horseradish sauce over chilled fish. Garnish with shredded lettuce.
ABOUT 6 SERVINGS

Gefilte Fish

3 pounds fresh fish
(whitefish, carp, and/or
pike)
2 quarts water
2 teaspoons salt
½ teaspoon pepper
8 carrots, pared

4 medium onions, peeled
and cut to fit feed tube
2 eggs
6 tablespoons ice water
4 tablespoons matzoh meal
2 teaspoons salt
½ teaspoon pepper

1. Have fish filleted, reserving head, bones, and skin.
2. In a large pot, place water, 2 teaspoons salt, ½ teaspoon pepper, 7 carrots, head, bones, and skin of fish.
3. Using **slicing disc** of food processor, slice 3½ onions (cut remaining ½ onion in half and reserve). Add sliced onion to the pot, bring to a boil, lower heat, and simmer while fish is being prepared.
4. Cut fish into 2-inch pieces. Using **steel blade,** process fish in 1-pound batches to pastelike consistency. Remove to a large bowl and repeat 2 more times with remaining fish. After all fish has been processed, thoroughly mix together by hand to blend fish together.
5. Using **steel blade,** process remaining carrot and ½ onion together until finely chopped. Remove half of this mixture from the bowl.
6. Add half of fish mixture to the bowl. To this add 1 egg, 3 tablespoons ice water, 2 tablespoons matzoh meal, 1 teaspoon salt, and ¼ teaspoon pepper. Process, using quick on/off motions, until thoroughly blended. Remove mixture

from bowl and repeat procedure, using remaining ingredients.
7. Remove head bones, and skin of fish from stock.
8. With wet hands, shape fish into shapes the size of a small baking potato and place in fish stock. Simmer slowly 2 hours.
9. Remove fish balls with a slotted spoon and place on a lettuce-lined platter. Cool and chill. Cool fish stock and save for later use for storing leftover fish.
10. Garnish with pieces of cooked carrots left over from stock and serve with freshly made horseradish.
ABOUT 20 BALLS

Horseradish

½ cup horseradish root, cut
in 1-inch cubes

Beet juice

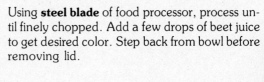

Using **steel blade** of food processor, process until finely chopped. Add a few drops of beet juice to get desired color. Step back from bowl before removing lid.

Steamed Red Snapper Oriental

3 red snapper (about 1½ pounds each), drawn and scaled
5 garlic cloves, finely sliced
Fish Stock (see page 48)
1 cup light soy sauce
½ cup dry white wine
3 tablespoons peanut or vegetable oil
1 tablespoon sesame oil

1 bunch green onions, tops only, cut in 2-inch matchstick-size pieces
½ teaspoon freshly ground Szechuan or black pepper*
3 zucchini slices
3 thin carrot slices
3 cloves
Lemon or lime slices
Watercress

1. Place fish on a piece of cheesecloth which is 18 inches longer than the fish. Using cheesecloth, lower fish onto rack in a fish steamer or large, deep roasting pan with 1½ inches of stock in bottom. Arrange garlic slices on fish. Simmer covered until fish is tender and flakes with a fork (about 40 minutes).
2. Using cheesecloth, lift fish from steamer to a heated platter. Remove cheesecloth from fish, carefully lifting fish with spatula and cutting cheesecloth with scissors if necessary.
3. Mix soy sauce, wine, and peanut and sesame oils in a small saucepan; heat to boiling. Drizzle 3 tablespoons soy mixture over fish; arrange green onion tops decoratively on fish. Sprinkle ground pepper over fish. Place zucchini and carrot slices over eyes of fish and secure with cloves. Arrange lemon slices and watercress around fish. Pass remaining soy mixture to spoon over individual servings.
4. If desired, let fish stand 45 minutes after poaching, then refrigerate until chilled (about 4 hours). Spoon hot soy mixture over fish and garnish as directed. Pass remaining soy mixture.
8 TO 10 SERVINGS

Note: Whole white fish, lake trout, or other lean fish can be substituted for the red snapper.

* Lightly roast Szechuan pepper over medium heat in skillet before grinding.

Northern Pike Polish Style

1 dressed northern pike, perch, or other white fish (2 pounds)
1 carrot
1 onion
1 stalk celery
10 peppercorns
1½ teaspoons salt
Water

Topping:
¼ cup butter
6 hard-cooked eggs, finely chopped
¼ cup lemon juice
1 tablespoon chopped fresh dill or parsley
¾ teaspoon salt
¼ teaspoon pepper

1. Put fish into a large kettle. Add carrot, onion, celery, peppercorns, and salt. Add enough water to cover. Cover; boil gently about 15 to 20 minutes, or until fish flakes easily.
2. Meanwhile, heat butter in a skillet. Add chopped eggs, lemon juice, dill, salt, and pepper. Cook 5 minutes, stirring frequently.
3. When fish is cooked, set it on a warm platter. Spoon topping over fish. Serve with boiled potatoes, if desired.
4 TO 6 SERVINGS

Pike or Carp Stuffed with Anchovies

1 can (2 ounces) flat anchovy fillets
1 pike (3 pounds) with milt and liver, or other white fish
¼ cup butter or margarine

(at room temperature)
2 eggs, separated
½ cup grated fresh bread
¼ cup melted butter for basting
1 cup sour cream

1. Cut half the anchovies in thin strips. Lard the fish with strips of anchovy.
2. Chop or mash remaining anchovies; cream with 2 tablespoons of butter. Divide in half.
3. For stuffing, beat egg yolks. Chop liver. Combine grated bread, egg yolks, milt, and liver. Add half of anchovy butter; mix well. Beat egg whites until stiff peaks are formed; fold into bread mixture.
4. Fill cavity of fish with stuffing. Close cavity with skewers or wooden picks. Place fish in roasting pan. Drizzle with half the melted butter.
5. Bake at 350°F 30 minutes. Baste with remaining melted butter. Bake 10 minutes longer. Spread remaining anchovy butter over fish. Top with sour cream. Continue baking until fish is tender and flakes easily.
6 TO 8 SERVINGS

Baked Fettuccine with Perch Florentine

White Sauce
12 small perch fillets
1 teaspoon salt
¼ teaspoon pepper
2 cups white wine
3 pounds spinach

1 pound fettuccine noodles, cooked according to package directions and drained
¼ cup grated Parmesan cheese

1. Prepare sauce, place a piece of waxed paper directly on surface, and keep warm.
2. Wash and dry the fillets; place in a saucepan. Sprinkle with salt and pepper and pour in the wine. Simmer 15 minutes, or less, being sure fish remains intact.
3. Wash spinach. Place in a saucepan only with water that clings to leaves from washing. Cover saucepan and cook rapidly about 5 minutes, or until tender. Drain well and chop.
4. Arrange half the spinach in a 3-quart baking dish. Place half the fettuccine over spinach, and top with 6 fillets. Repeat layering with remaining spinach, fettuccine, and fish. Pour the warm sauce over all and sprinkle cheese on top.
5. Bake at 400°F 20 minutes, or until top is browned. Serve 2 fillets per person on a mound of fettuccine and spinach.
6 SERVINGS

White Sauce: Melt **5 tablespoons butter** in a saucepan. Blend in **5 tablespoons flour, 1 teaspoon salt**, and ⅛ **teaspoon pepper**; heat until bubbly. Gradually add **2½ cups milk**, stirring until smooth. Bring to boiling and cook, stirring until smooth. Bring to boiling and cook, stirring constantly, 1 to 2 minutes. Stir in **pinch nutmeg**.
ABOUT 2½ CUPS SAUCE

Stuffed Fish Odette Mennesson

Stuffed Fish Odette Mennesson

1 large grouper or bluefish (4 to 5 pounds)	Odette Mennesson, chilled (below)
Court Bouillon for Fish and Shellfish (page 43)	1 cup crab meat
6 hard-cooked eggs	Parsley
2 cups Herbal Mayonnaise	Lime wedges and avocado slices for garnish

1. Have the fish split and boned without removing the head or tail.
2. Bring court bouillon to boiling in a large roasting pan. Wrap fish in cheesecloth and put into pan, leaving the ends of the cloth out of the pan. Poach 7 to 10 minutes, or until fish is thoroughly cooked.
3. Meanwhile, mash eggs with mayonnaise; mix in crab meat.
4. Gently remove fish from bouillon and transfer from cloth to a platter. Spoon crab mixture between the two halves of fish. Serve warm, or if desired, chill thoroughly.
5. To serve, arrange parsley around fish and garnish with slices of lime and avocado.

Herbal Mayonnaise Odette Mennesson

3 parsley sprigs	lettuce
3 basil sprigs	2 scallions or green onions
2 fennel or dill sprigs	2 hard-cooked eggs
6 watercress sprigs	1 cup Mayonnaise
3 leaves Boston or Bibb	

Stem herbs, watercress, and lettuce. Chop very finely along with scallions and eggs. Blend in Mayonnaise.
2 CUPS

Citrus Steamed Salmon and Shrimp

1½ pounds salmon fillets, cut in 2x1-inch pieces	1 teaspoon paprika
¾ pound uncooked shelled shrimp	1 teaspoon coriander seed, crushed
½ cup lemon juice	1 teaspoon cardamom seed, crushed (discard shells)
¼ cup lime juice	Parsley sprigs
¾ teaspoon salt	

1. Place salmon and shrimp in a shallow glass dish. Mix remaining ingredients except parsley and pour over fish. Refrigerate covered 30 minutes; stir twice.
2. Transfer fish and marinade to a large skillet. Simmer covered 4 minutes; stir and simmer uncovered 2 minutes. Add shrimp to skillet; simmer covered just until shrimp are done (about 3 minutes). Arrange fish and shrimp on a serving platter. Spoon pan juices over. Garnish with parsley.
6 TO 8 SERVINGS

Red Snapper Veracruz Style

¼ cup olive oil	¼ teaspoon pepper
1 cup chopped onion	2 pounds red snapper fillets
1 clove garlic, minced	¼ cup sliced pimento-stuffed olives
2 cups (16-ounce can) tomatoes with liquid	2 tablespoons capers
1 teaspoon salt	Lemon wedges

1. Heat oil in a large skillet. Cook onion and garlic in hot oil until onion is soft, about 5 minutes. Add tomatoes, salt, and pepper and cook about 5 minutes to blend flavors; slightly chop tomatoes as they cook.
2. Arrange red snapper fillets in a 3-quart baking dish. Pour sauce over fish. Sprinkle with olives and capers.
3. Bake at 350°F 25 to 30 minutes, or until fish can be flaked easily with a fork. Serve with lemon wedges.
ABOUT 6 SERVINGS

Red Snapper Veracruz Style

Planked Halibut Dinner

4 halibut steaks, fresh or thawed frozen (about 2 pounds)
¼ cup butter, melted
2 tablespoons olive oil
1 tablespoon wine vinegar
2 teaspoons lemon juice
1 clove garlic, minced
¼ teaspoon dry mustard
¼ teaspoon marjoram
½ teaspoon salt
⅛ teaspoon ground black pepper
2 large zucchini
1 package (10 ounces) frozen green peas
1 can (8¼ ounces) tiny whole carrots
Au Gratin Potato Puffs
Butter
Fresh parsley
Lemon wedges

1. Place halibut steaks in an oiled baking pan.
2. Combine butter, olive oil, vinegar, lemon juice, garlic, dry mustard, marjoram, salt, and pepper. Drizzle over halibut.
3. Bake at 450°F 10 to 12 minutes, or until halibut is almost done.
4. Meanwhile, halve zucchini lengthwise and scoop out center portion. Cook in boiling salted water until just tender.
5. Cook peas following directions on package. Heat carrots.
6. Prepare Au Gratin Potato Puffs.
7. Arrange halibut on wooden plank or heated ovenware platter and border with zucchini halves filled with peas, carrots, and potato puffs. Dot peas and carrots with butter.
8. Place platter under broiler to brown potato puffs. Sprinkle carrots with chopped parsley.
9. Garnish with sprigs of parsley and lemon wedges arranged on a skewer.
4 SERVINGS

Au Gratin Potato Puffs: Pare **1½ pounds potatoes;** cook and mash potatoes in a saucepan. Add **2 tablespoons butter** and **⅓ cup milk;** whip until fluffy. Add **2 slightly beaten egg yolks, ½ cup shredded sharp Cheddar cheese, 1 teaspoon salt,** and **few grains pepper;** continue whipping. Using a pastry bag with a large star tip, form mounds about 2 inches in diameter on plank. Proceed as directed in recipe.

Sole Véronique in Parchment

2 pounds sole fillets
¾ teaspoon salt
3 tablespoons snipped parsley
2 teaspoons minced lemon
peel
1½ cups seedless white grapes
⅔ cup dry white wine
Lemon wedges

1. Lay each fillet on a piece of parchment paper or aluminum foil, 12x12 inches. Sprinkle fillets with salt, parsley, and lemon peel. Divide grapes over fish; sprinkle with wine. Bring edges of parchment up, crime edges and seal; place on a jelly-roll pan.
2. Bake at 350°F 20 minutes.
3. Place parchment packets on individual plates; let each person open packet. Serve with lemon wedges.
4 SERVINGS

Stuffed Baked Fish

1 dressed pike, trout, or carp (4 to 5 pounds)
Salt and pepper
⅓ cup butter or margarine
2 onions, chopped
3 stalks celery, chopped
3 apples, cored and chopped
1 tablespoon chopped
parsley
1 cup sliced mushrooms
4 cups dry bread cubes
2 teaspoons sugar
½ teaspoon thyme
2 teaspoons lemon juice
3 eggs
1 cup water or wine

1. Sprinkle cavity of fish with salt and pepper.
2. For stuffing, melt ⅓ cup butter in skillet. Add onion and celery. Stir-fry until onion is transparent. Add apples, parsley, and mushrooms. Stir-fry 2 minutes longer.
3. Mix cooked vegetables with bread cubes, sugar, thyme, lemon juice, eggs, and water. Blend well.
4. Fill fish cavity with the stuffing. Close cavity with skewers or wooden picks. Place fish in a roasting pan and drizzle with **melted butter.**
5. Bake at 350°F about 40 minutes, or until fish flakes easily. Baste occasionally with additional melted butter.
ABOUT 8 SERVINGS

Cod Sailor Style

2 pounds cod steaks, about 1 inch thick
2 cups canned tomatoes, sieved
¼ cup chopped green olives
2 tablespoons capers
1 tablespoon parsley
1 teaspoon salt
½ teaspoon pepper
½ teaspoon oregano

1. Put cod steaks into a greased 1½-quart casserole.
2. Combine tomatoes, olives, capers, parsley, salt, pepper, and oregano in a saucepan. Bring to boiling and pour over cod.
3. Bake at 350°F 25 to 30 minutes, or until fish flakes easily when tested with a fork.
4 SERVINGS

Ancona Fish Stew

2 pounds assorted fish (mullet, sole, and halibut fillets)
1 large onion, thinly sliced
½ cup olive oil
2 teaspoons salt
½ teaspoon pepper
Pinch saffron
Water (about 2 cups)
Dry white wine (about 2 cups)

1. Cut fish fillets in 2½-inch pieces; set aside.
2. Sauté onion in olive oil until golden. Sprinkle in salt, pepper, and saffron. Add the fish and enough water and wine to cover the fish. Bring to boiling and cook over high heat 10 to 15 minutes.
3. Serve very hot in warmed soup bowls with crust of fried bread, if desired.
6 SERVINGS

Drunken Fish

1 whole red snapper or similar fish, or 5 pounds fish fillets
Flour, seasoned with salt and pepper
¼ cup oil
1 cup chopped onion
1 clove garlic, minced
6 fresh or dried ancho chilies
1½ cups canned tomatoes
2 tablespoons dried parsley
½ teaspoon oregano
½ teaspoon cumin (comino)
Salt and pepper
2 cups dry red wine
2 tablespoons capers

1. Dredge the fish with seasoned flour. Heat oil in a large skillet and brown fish on both sides. Remove fish from skillet and place in a shallow baking dish.
2. Add onion and garlic to oil remaining in skillet and cook until onion is soft, about 5 minutes.
3. Prepare chilies (see below); place in an electric blender and blend to a thick purée. Add to onion and garlic in skillet and cook about 5 minutes. Add tomatoes, parsley, oregano, and cumin. Bring to boiling, stirring constantly. Season to taste with salt and pepper. Stir in red wine and mix well.
4. Pour sauce over fish in baking dish.
5. Bake at 400°F about 30 minutes, or until fish flakes easily. Garnish with capers and serve.
6 TO 8 SERVINGS

How to prepare fresh chilies for cooking: Wash chilies and pat dry. If preparing a large number of big chilies, place on a broiler pan; place pan under broiler flame and roast chilies until well-blistered, turning to roast on all sides. For two or three chilies, or for the smaller varieties, roast in a small skillet over high heat until skins pop; chilies will be almost black. Remove from broiler or skillet and put into a plastic bag. Let stand a few minutes, then peel with sharp knife, beginning at the blossom end and working toward stem. Cut a slit in side of each chili and scoop out seeds and veins. If using for Chilies Rellenos, leave stems on to use as "handles." Otherwise, cut around stem with sharp knife and remove. *Note:* Wash hands with soap and water after handling fresh or dried chilies, as the small amount left on hands can burn if rubbed into eyes, or a small cut.

How to prepare dried chilies for cooking: Wash chilies and pat dry. Cut open and remove seeds, veins, and stems. Place in a small amount of water and boil until soft, about 10 minutes. Chop or blend as directed in recipe. Save water in which the chilies were boiled to use in whatever sauce you are preparing. Wash hands (see Note above).

How to use canned "Hot Peppers": These chilies may simply be chopped and used as they come from can or jar. To somewhat reduce the hotness, if desired, remove seeds and stems and rinse in cold water before chopping. Wash hands (see Note above).

Pickled Tuna

2 cans (6½ to 7 ounces each) tuna, drained
Juice of 2 limes or 1 lemon
¼ cup oil
1 medium onion, tinly sliced (about ½ cup)
2 canned jalapeño chilies, seeded and cut in thin
strips
1 clove garlic, minced
½ teaspoon oregano
½ teaspoon cumin (comino)
¾ cup wine or cider vinegar
Lettuce leaves
Sliced pimento-stuffed olives

1. Put tuna into a jar or bowl with lid; flake with fork. Pour lime juice over fish and let stand while preparing pickling mixture.
2. Heat oil in skillet. Add onion, chilies, and garlic; cook about 5 minutes, until onion is soft. Stir in oregano and cumin, then stir in vinegar. Bring to boiling.
3. Cover and refrigerate several hours. Serve on lettuce garnished with olive slices.
6 SERVINGS

Fillet of Sole in White Wine

2 pounds sole fillets
½ cup dry white wine
½ cup chopped onion
3 tablespoons butter, melted
2 bay leaves, crushed
1 teaspoon chopped parsley
½ teaspoon salt
¼ teaspoon pepper

1. Put fillets into a greased shallow 2-quart casserole.
2. Mix wine, onion, butter, and dry seasonings. Pour over fish. Cover casserole.
3. Bake at 375°F 25 minutes, or until fish flakes easily when tested with a fork.
6 SERVINGS

Poached Fish with Almonds

1 cup dry white wine
1 small can salsa verde mexicana (mexican green tomato sauce)
½ cup chopped onion
1 clove garlic, minced
Salt and pepper
2 pounds fish fillets (halibut, flounder, sole, or other white fish)
½ cup toasted slivered almonds
Lemon wedges

1. Combine wine, salsa verde, onion, and garlic in a large skillet. Season with salt and pepper to taste. Bring to boiling, reduce heat, and simmer about 10 to 15 minutes.
2. Place fish fillets in simmering sauce and cook until fish flakes easily with a fork, about 5 to 10 minutes.
3. Transfer fish to a heated platter, spoon some of the sauce over fish, and sprinkle with almonds. Serve with lemon wedges.
ABOUT 6 SERVINGS

Scrambled Eggs with Salt Cod

5 parsley sprigs
2 green onions, chopped
1 garlic clove, crushed in a garlic press
1 dried Italian pepper pod or 1 sliver green hot pepper
1½ cups shredded soaked salt cod
3 tablespoons peanut oil
1 cup hot milk
6 eggs

1. In a mortar, pound together to a paste the parsley, onion, garlic, and pepper pod. Mix this seasoning paste with the shredded cod.
2. Heat oil in a skillet, add fish mixture, and brown it, adding hot milk.
3. In another skillet, scramble eggs to a soft consistency while gradually adding the fish mixture.
4 SERVINGS

Stuffed Red Snapper

1 red snapper (about 5 pounds)
Salt and pepper to taste
½ lime
¼ cup flour
1 cup cooked rice
1 cup chopped raw shrimp
½ cup chopped green onion
(including top)
½ cup very thinly sliced celery
1 tablespoon grated ginger root
2 bacon slices
¼ cup dry white wine

1. Season red snapper inside and out with salt and pepper. Rub with cut side of lime. Sprinkle evenly with flour.
2. Combine rice, shrimp, onion, celery, and ginger root. Spoon into fish; skewer or sew the opening. Lay fish in a very heavily buttered baking pan. Score the top of fish in an attractive design to prevent it from buckling. Lay bacon slices over top.
3. Bake at 350°F 45 minutes, or until fish flakes. Transfer fish to a heated platter.
4. Deglaze baking pan with white wine. Pour liquid over fish.

Macadam of Cod Martinique

2 pounds salt cod
¼ cup olive oil
2 large onions, chopped
⅛ teaspoon cayenne or red pepper
Bouquet garni
1 garlic clove, crushed in a
garlic press
3 tomatoes, peeled, seeded, and cut in chunks
1 tablespoon olive oil
1 teaspoon lime juice
¼ cup chopped parsley
Caribbean Rice (page 190)

1. Soak cod in cold water overnight. The next day, drain, trim edges from fish, and coarsely shred fish.
2. Heat ¼ cup oil in a large skillet. Add onion and cod; cook until lightly browned. Add pepper, bouquet garni, garlic, and tomato; mix well. Cook covered over low heat 15 minutes. Add 1 tablespoon oil and the lime juice; mix well.
3. Transfer cod mixture to a serving platter and sprinkle with parsley. Serve with the rice.

Red Snapper Meuniere

2 red snappers (2 pounds each)
2 limes, halved
Salt and pepper to taste
½ cup flour
Peanut oil (about ¼ cup)
Butter (about 2 tablespoons)
5 drops Tabasco
¼ cup butter
1 tablespoon chopped parsley
1 tablespoon lime juice
Lime wedges for garnish

1. Have the fins and tails trimmed from fish, without removing the heads. Rub the fish with cut side of lime halves, squeezing gently to release the juice. Season with salt and pepper. Superficially slash the skin of the fish in a diamond design.
2. Put flour into a bag large enough to hold fish; put fish into bag and coat them evenly with flour.
3. Heat enough oil and butter to cover the bottom of a skillet large enough to hold both fish. When fat is sizzling, add Tabasco. Sauté fish about 12 minutes on each side, or until done, reducing the heat if necessary so as not to scorch them.
4. Meanwhile, cream ¼ cup butter with parsley.
5. Remove fish to a heated platter and keep warm. Discard all the fat in bottom of the skillet and add butter with parsley and the lime juice; stir until blended. Spoon over fish.
6. Garnish platter with lime wedges.
6 SERVINGS

Baked Fish with Shrimp Stuffing

1 dressed whitefish, bass, or lake trout (2 to 3 pounds)
Salt
1 cup chopped cooked shrimp
1 cup chopped fresh mushrooms
1 cup soft enriched bread crumbs
½ cup chopped celery
¼ cup chopped onion
2 tablespoons chopped
parsley
¾ teaspoon salt
Few grains black pepper
½ teaspoon thyme
¼ cup butter or margarine, melted
2 to 3 tablespoons apple cider
2 tablespoons butter or margarine, melted
Parsley sprigs

1. Rinse fish under running cold water; drain well and pat dry with absorbent paper. Sprinkle fish cavity generously with salt.
2. Combine in a bowl the shrimp, mushrooms, bread crumbs, celery, onion, parsley, salt, pepper, and thyme. Pour ¼ cup melted butter gradually over bread mixture, tossing lightly until mixed.
3. Pile stuffing lightly into fish. Fasten with skewers and lace with cord. Place fish in a greased large shallow baking pan. Mix cider and 2 tablespoons melted butter; brush over fish.
4. Bake at 375°F, brushing occasionally with cider mixture, 25 to 30 minutes, or until fish flakes easily when pierced with a fork. If additional browning is desired, place fish under broiler 3 to 5 minutes. Transfer to a heated platter and remove skewers and cord. Garnish platter with parsley.
4 TO 6 SERVINGS

Shrimp Kabobs

Shrimp Kabobs

Raw shrimp (about 2 pounds), shelled (leaving on tails) and deveined
1-inch strips green pepper (using 2 peppers)
Small cooked white onions (16-ounce can, drained)
12 whole mushrooms, cleaned
12 large pimento-stuffed olives
12 large pitted ripe olives
1 cup Basic Molasses Barbecue Sauce
1 tablespoon prepared horseradish
1 to 2 tablespoons pineapple syrup (optional)

1. Thread shrimp, green pepper, onions, mushrooms, and olives onto 8- to 10-inch skewers.
2. Combine sauce, horseradish, and pineapple syrup, if used. Mix well and brush generously over kabobs.
3. Cook 5 to 6 inches above the hot coals, 5 minutes on each side; brush with the sauce several times during cooking.
6 KABOBS

Basic Molasses Barbecue Sauce

¼ cup cornstarch
4 cups lemon juice (about 2 dozen lemons)
2 cups cooking oil
1 jar (12 ounces) light or dark molasses
¼ cup salt
1 tablespoon black pepper
6 bay leaves, broken in pieces
3 cloves garlic, minced

1. Combine cornstarch and lemon juice in a saucepan. Cook and stir over low heat until mixture bubbles and thickens. Cool.
2. Using rotary or electric beater, beat in remaining ingredients until thoroughly blended and thickened.
3. Store in refrigerator until needed.
ABOUT 2 QUARTS SAUCE

Crab-Stuffed Trout with Tarragon

2 large onions, finely chopped
¼ cup dry white wine
1 cup sliced fresh mushrooms
8 ounces fresh or 1 can (7¾ ounces) chunk crab meat, drained and flaked
1 tablespoon snipped fresh or 1½ teaspoons dried tarragon leaves
¼ cup snipped parsley
½ teaspoon salt
¼ teaspoon freshly ground white pepper
6 dressed trout (1 to 1½ pounds each)
1 tablespoon snipped fresh or 1½ teaspoons dried tarragon leaves
Lemon twists

1. Simmer onion in wine until tender (about 5 minutes). Mix 1½ cups cooked onion with the mushrooms, crab meat, 1 tablespoon tarragon, the parsley, salt, and pepper. Stuff trout with onion mixture.
2. Spread remaining onion in a shallow baking pan; arrange trout over onion.
3. Bake at 400°F about 20 minutes, or until fish is tender and flakes with a fork. Remove fish to serving platter. Sprinkle with 1 tablespoon tarragon and garnish with lemon twists.
6 SERVINGS

Veracruz Style Crab-Filled Fish Rolls

6 fish fillets (such as red snapper or sole), cut into long, thin slices
Juice of 1 lemon or lime
½ cup milk
2 tablespoons olive oil
½ cup chopped onion
1 clove garlic, minced
1 small tomato, peeled and chopped
1 teaspoon minced parsley
1 teaspoon salt
Dash of pepper
¼ pound crab meat, shredded
¼ pound shredded Monterey Jack
1 cup sour cream
1 egg yolk
¼ pound butter or margarine

1. Rinse fish; rub with lemon or lime juice; soak in milk.
2. Meanwhile, heat olive oil in a small skillet. Sauté onion and garlic in oil; add tomato and cook until no longer juicy. Remove from heat and stir in parsley, salt, and pepper. Add crab meat and ⅓ of the cheese and mix well.
3. Remove fish from milk and pat dry with paper towels. Place a small amount of crab meat filling on one end of fillet and roll up, as for a jelly roll. Place fish rolls in one layer in a greased baking dish.
4. Beat sour cream with egg yolk and pour over fish. Dot with butter. Sprinkle remaining cheese over top.
5. Bake at 350°F until golden brown and cheese is melted (about 20 minutes).
6 SERVINGS

Sole with Shrimp Pâté in Champagne

1 pound fresh asparagus, spears only (2-inch pieces)*
Fish Stock (see page 48)
8 sole fillets (about 3 pounds)
2 cups cooked, shelled shrimp
2 ounces Neufchatel cheese
2 teaspoons anchovy paste
1 cup champagne or Fish Stock
1 cup Mock Hollandaise Sauce (see page 49)
Lemon wedges

1. Simmer asparagus spears in 1 inch of stock 4 minutes; drain. Set aside.
2. Lay fillets on a flat surface. Purée shrimp with cheese and anchovy paste in a food processor or blender. Spoon shrimp mixture in center of fillets.
3. Arrange asparagus on shrimp mixture in center of fillets so spears are visible on sides; roll fillets and place seam side down in a large skillet. Pour champagne into skillet; simmer covered until fish is tender and flakes with a fork (about 5 minutes). Remove fish carefully with a slotted spoon to serving platter. Spoon hollandaise sauce over fillets; garnish with lemon wedges.
8 SERVINGS

*Frozen asparagus spears can be substituted for the fresh. Thaw and drain; do not cook.

Baked Fish with Red Sauce

2 pounds haddock fillets, cut in serving-size pieces*
1 teaspoon salt
¼ teaspoon freshly ground white pepper
1 lemon, thinly sliced
1 medium red onion, sliced
4 large sweet red peppers, cut in quarters
¼ cup dry vermouth
½ teaspoon salt
Dry vermouth
Watercress

1. Sprinkle haddock with 1 teaspoon salt and the pepper; place in a lightly oiled baking pan. Arrange lemon, onion, and peppers over fish. Pour ¼ cup vermouth over top.
2. Bake at 350°F about 20 minutes, or until fish is tender and flakes with a fork.
3. Place peppers and onion slices in a food processor blender container; discard lemon. Arrange fish on serving platter; keep warm.
4. Purée peppers, onion, and salt, adding additional vermouth, if needed, to make a thick sauce. Heat mixture thoroughly; spoon over fish. Garnish with watercress.
6 SERVINGS

*Flounder, halibut, or whitefish fillets, or poultry can be used in this recipe.

Sole with Shrimp Pâté in Champagne

Choose-a-Partner Tuna Casserole

2 cans (6½ or 7 ounces each) tuna in vegetable oil
1 teaspoon salt
Pasta or rice ingredient, cooked following package

directions
Frozen vegetable, thawed
Sauce
Extra ingredients (optional)

1. In a large bowl mix tuna, salt, cooked pasta or rice, thawed frozen vegetable, and sauce. Add one or more extra ingredients, if desired.
2. Turn into a greased 2-quart casserole; cover.
3. Bake at 350°F 50 to 60 minutes.
6 SERVINGS

CHOOSE A PASTA OR RICE INGREDIENT:

2 cups cooked elbow macaroni
1 cup cooked regular rice
4 cups cooked broad egg noodles
4 cups cooked large macaroni shells
3 cups cooked medium macaroni shells
4 cups cooked bow ties

CHOOSE A FROZEN VEGETABLE:

1 package (10 ounces) frozen chopped spinach
1 package (10 ounces) frozen chopped broccoli
1 package (9 ounces) frozen Italian green beans
1 package (10 ounces) frozen green peas
1 package (10 ounces) frozen mixed vegetables

CHOOSE A SAUCE:

1 can (about 10 ounces) condensed cream of mushroom soup plus 1 cup milk
1 can (about 10 ounces) condensed cream of celery soup plus 1¼ cups milk
1 can (about 10 ounces) condensed cream of chicken soup plus 1¼ cups milk
1 can (about 10 ounces) condensed cream of asparagus soup plus 1¼ cups milk
1 can (about 10 ounces) condensed Cheddar cheese soup plus 1¼ cups milk
1 can (16 ounces) seasoned stewed tomatoes

CHOOSE ONE OR MORE EXTRAS, IF DESIRED:

2 tablespoons grated Parmesan cheese
¼ cup shredded Swiss cheese
1 can (3 ounces) sliced mushrooms, drained
¼ cup sliced ripe olives
¼ cup chopped green pepper
¼ cup chopped onion
¼ cup chopped celery

SAMPLE CASSEROLE COMBINATIONS:

Tuna and Noodle Casserole Florentine: Use broad noodles, chopped spinach, mushroom soup, and Swiss cheese.

Tuna, Broccoli, and Macaroni Casserole: Use elbow macaroni, chopped broccoli, cheese soup, and chopped celery.

Tuna, Green Beans, and Rice Casserole: Use rice, Italian green beans, stewed tomatoes, and Parmesan cheese.

Salmon Bake

1 can (16 ounces) salmon, drained and flaked
1½ cups herb-seasoned stuffing croutons
2 tablespoons finely snipped parsley
2 tablespoons finely chopped onion
3 eggs, well beaten
1 can (10½ ounces) con-

densed cream of celery soup
½ cup milk
⅛ teaspoon ground black pepper
Lemon, thinly sliced and cut in quarter-slices
Parsley, snipped
Sour cream sauce (prepared from a mix)

1. Toss salmon, stuffing croutons, parsley, and onion together in a bowl. Blend eggs, condensed soup, milk, and pepper; add to salmon mixture and mix thoroughly. Turn into a greased 1½-quart casserole.
2. Bake at 350°F about 50 minutes. Garnish center with overlapping quarter-slices of lemon and parsley.
3. Serve with hot sour cream sauce.
ABOUT 6 SERVINGS

Sole with Tangerine Sauce

1 pound sole fillets
5 tablespoons butter or margarine
2 teaspoons finely shredded tangerine peel
½ cup tangerine juice
1 teaspoon lemon juice
1 tablespoon finely chopped parsley
1 tablespoon finely chopped green onion

1 bay leaf
1 tangerine, peeled, sectioned, and seeds removed
3 tablespoons flour
½ teaspoon salt
⅛ teaspoon ground black pepper
3 tablespoons butter or margarine
Parsley

1. Thaw fish if frozen.
2. Combine 5 tablespoons butter, tangerine peel and juice, lemon juice, 1 tablespoon parsley, green onion, and bay leaf in a saucepan. Bring to boiling and simmer over low heat until slightly thickened, stirring occasionally. Remove from heat; remove bay leaf and mix in tangerine sections. Keep sauce hot.
3. Mix flour, salt, and pepper; coat fish fillets. Heat 3 tablespoons butter in a skillet. Add fillets and fry until both sides are browned and fish flakes easily when tested with a fork.
4. Arrange fish on a hot platter and pour the hot sauce over it. Garnish with parsley.
ABOUT 4 SERVINGS

Creole Bouillabaisse

1 pound red snapper fillets
1 pound redfish fillets
2 teaspoons minced parsley
1 teaspoon salt
¾ teaspoon thyme
½ teaspoon allspice
⅛ teaspoon pepper
2 bay leaves, finely crushed
1 clove garlic, finely minced
  or crushed in a garlic press
2 tablespoons olive oil
1 large onion, chopped
1 cup white wine
3 large ripe tomatoes, peeled
  and cut in ¼-inch slices
3 or 4 lemon slices
1 cup hot Fish Stock (see
  below) or hot water
¾ teaspoon salt
⅛ teaspoon pepper
Dash cayenne pepper
Pinch of saffron
6 slices buttered, toasted
  bread

1. Thoroughly rub into fish fillets a mixture of parsley, salt, thyme, allspice, pepper, bay leaf, and garlic. Set fillets aside.
2. Heat olive oil in a large skillet over low heat; add onion and fillets. Cover and cook over low heat 10 minutes, turning fillets once.
3. Remove fish fillets from skillet; set aside and keep warm. Pour wine into skillet, stirring well; add tomato slices and bring to boiling. Add lemon slices, hot fish stock, salt, pepper, and cayenne pepper. Simmer about 25 minutes, or until liquid is reduced by almost one half.
4. Add fish fillets to skillet and continue cooking 5 minutes longer.
5. Meanwhile, blend several tablespoons of the liquid in which the fish is cooking with saffron. When fish has cooked 5 minutes, spread saffron mixture over fillets. Remove fillets from liquid and place on buttered toast. Pour liquid over fish. Serve at once.
6 SERVINGS

Fish Stock: Combine **1 quart water, 1 tablespoon salt, and 1 pound fish trimmings** (head, bones, skin, and tail) in a large saucepan. Cover and simmer 30 minutes. Strain liquid and use as directed.
ABOUT 1 QUART STOCK

Trout Amandine with Pineapple

6 whole trout
Lemon juice
Enriched all-purpose flour
6 tablespoons butter or
  margarine
Salt and pepper
2 tablespoons butter or
margarine
½ cup slivered blanched
  almonds
6 well-drained canned
  pineapple slices
Paprika
Lemon wedges

1. Rinse trout quickly under running cold water; dry thoroughly. Brush trout inside and out with lemon juice. Coat with flour.
2. Heat 6 tablespoons butter in a large skillet. Add trout and brown on both sides. Season with salt and pepper.
3. Meanwhile, heat 2 tablespoons butter in another skillet over low heat. Add almonds and stir occasionally until golden.
4. Sprinkle pineapple slices with paprika. Place pineapple in skillet with almonds and brown lightly on both sides. Arrange trout on a warm serving platter and top with pineapple slices and almonds. Garnish platter with lemon wedges.
6 SERVINGS

California Style Red Snapper Steaks

6 fresh or thawed frozen red
  snapper steaks (about 2
  pounds)
Salt and pepper
¼ cup butter or margarine,
  melted
1 tablespoon grated orange
  peel
¼ cup orange juice
1 teaspoon lemon juice
Dash nutmeg
Fresh orange sections

1. Arrange red snapper steaks in a single layer in a well-greased baking pan; season with salt and pepper.
2. Combine butter, orange peel and juice, lemon juice, and nutmeg; pour over fish.
3. Bake at 350°F 20 to 25 minutes, or until fish flakes easily when tested with a fork.
4. To serve, put steaks onto a warm platter; spoon sauce in pan over them. Garnish with orange sections.
6 SERVINGS

Two-Layer Salmon-Rice Loaf

Salmon layer:
1 can (16 ounces) salmon
2 cups coarse soft enriched
  bread crumbs
2 tablespoons finely chopped
  onion
½ cup undiluted evaporated
  milk
1 egg, slightly beaten
2 tablespoons butter or
  margarine, melted
1 tablespoon lemon juice
1 teaspoon salt

Rice layer:
3 cups cooked enriched rice

¼ cup finely chopped
  parsley
2 eggs, slightly beaten
⅔ cup undiluted evaporated
  milk
2 tablespoons butter or
  margarine, melted
¼ teaspoon salt

Sauce:
1 large onion, quartered and
  thinly sliced
¾ cup water
1 can (10¾ ounces) con-
  densed tomato soup

1. For salmon layer, drain salmon and remove skin. Flake salmon and put into a bowl. Add bread crumbs, onion, evaporated milk, egg, butter, lemon juice, and salt; mix lightly. Turn into a buttered 9x5x3-inch loaf pan; press lightly to form a layer.
2. For rice layer, combine rice with parsley, eggs, evaporated milk, butter, and salt. Spoon over salmon layer; press lightly.
3. Set filled loaf pan in a shallow pan. Pour hot water into pan to a depth of 1 inch.
4. Bake at 375°F about 45 minutes. Remove from water immediately.
5. Meanwhile, for sauce, put onion and water into a saucepan. Bring to boiling, reduce heat, and simmer, covered, 10 minutes. Remove onion, if desired. Add condensed soup to saucepan, stir until blended, and bring to boiling.
6. Cut loaf into slices and top servings with tomato sauce.
ABOUT 8 SERVINGS

Grilled Lobster

Avocado Voisin

4 tablespoons butter	1 cup milk
1½ tablespoons minced onion	1 egg yolk
1½ tablespoons minced celery	2 cans (about 6½ ounces each), crab meat, drained
¾ teaspoon curry powder	2 tablespoons chutney, finely chopped
¾ cup uncooked white rice	3 large avocados
1½ cups chicken or beef broth	Lemon juice
Salt	3 tablespoons grated Parmesan cheese
White pepper	Parsley and lemon wedges for garnish
1 small bay leaf	
2 tablespoons flour	

1. Melt 1½ tablespoons butter in skillet. Add onion and celery; cook until tender, about 4 minutes, stirring occasionally.
2. Add curry powder to vegetables and blend thoroughly. Stir in rice, mixing to coat each grain. Add broth, few grains each salt and white pepper, and bay leaf. Bring to boiling, cover, lower heat, and simmer until moisture is absorbed and rice is tender (about 20 minutes).
3. In a saucepan, melt 1½ tablespoons butter. Blend in flour and a few grains each salt and white pepper. Cook slowly for 5 minutes, not allowing mixture to brown. Remove pan from heat and stir milk gradually into flour mixture. Return pan to heat, cook until sauce is thickened (about 10 minutes), stirring constantly.
4. Beat a small amount of hot mixture into egg yolk, then return to mixture in saucepan. Heat just to boiling. Remove from heat, cover, and keep warm.
5. Sauté crab meat in 1 tablespoon butter 1 minute. Add chutney and mix well. Combine cooked rice and crab meat, tossing lightly to mix. Keep warm.
6. Halve avocados, remove seeds, and peel. Cut small slice from bottoms so that avocados will be flat. Put cut-off slices in avocado cavities, and brush cut surfaces of avocado with lemon juice.
7. Arrange avocado halves in a shallow baking dish. Pile crab-rice mixture into avocado halves. Spoon sauce over each stuffed avocado. Sprinkle with Parmesan cheese.
8. Bake at 300°F 10 to 15 minutes.
9. Garnish with parsley and lemon wedges.

6 SERVINGS

Grilled Lobster

1 live lobster (about 1½ pounds)	Tabasco Butter

1. Purchase a lobster for each serving. Live lobsters may be killed and dressed for cooking at the market. If prepared at home, place the lobster on a cutting board with back or smooth shell up. Hold a towel firmly over the head and claws. Kill by quickly inserting the point of a sharp heavy knife into the center of the small cross showing on the back of the head. Without removing knife, quickly bear down heavily, cutting through entire length of the body and tail. Split the halves apart and remove the stomach, a small sac which lies in the head, and the spongy lungs which lie between meat and shell. Also remove the dark intestinal line running through the center of the body. Crack large claws with a nutcracker or mallet.
2. Brush meat with Tabasco Butter. Place shell side down on grill about 5 inches from coals. Grill about 20 minutes, or until shell is browned. Baste frequently with butter. Serve in shell with remaining butter.

Tabasco Butter: Melt ½ cup butter and stir in ½ teaspoon Tabasco and 1 tablespoon lime juice.

Avocado Voisin

Fish Stew

Fish Stew

3 pounds fish fillets, skinned*
5 medium tomatoes, peeled and chopped
3 carrots, chopped
1 large onion, thinly sliced
2 teaspoons salt
¼ teaspoon freshly ground pepper

2 garlic cloves, minced
1 teaspoon fennel seed, crushed
1 tablespoon minced orange peel
1 cup dry white wine
1 quart Fish Stock (see page 48)

1. Cut fish into 1½-inch pieces. Set aside.
2. Simmer tomatoes, carrots, onion, salt, pepper, garlic, fennel, and orange peel in a mixture of wine and stock 15 minutes. Add fish to stock mixture; simmer covered until fish is tender and flakes with a fork (about 20 minutes).
3. Serve immediately in large shallow soup bowls.
8 SERVINGS (2 CUPS EACH)

*Flounder, haddock, cod, whitefish, halibut bass, or other fish can be used in this recipe. For maximum flavor and variety, select at least 3 kinds of fish.

Baked Flounder Superb

2 pounds flounder fillets
½ cup fine Melba toast crumbs
¼ cup butter or margarine, melted
⅔ cup minced green onion
2 tablespoons snipped parsley
½ teaspoon poultry seasoning
½ pound fresh or thawed

frozen sea scallops, chopped
1 can (4 ounces) mushroom stems and pieces, drained
2 tablespoons butter or margarine
2 tablespoons flour
¼ teaspoon salt
Few grains black pepper
1 cup milk
Shredded parmesan cheese

1. Thaw fish if frozen; cut fish into 12 pieces.
2. Toss crumbs and melted butter together in a bowl. Add green onion, parsley, poultry seasoning, scallops, and mushrooms; mix well.
3. Place a piece of flounder in the bottom of each of 6 ramekins. Spoon stuffing mixture over flounder and top with remaining flounder pieces.
4. Heat butter in a saucepan. Stir in flour, salt, and pepper and cook until bubbly. Add milk gradually, stirring until smooth. Bring rapidly to boiling; boil 1 to 2 minutes, stirring constantly.
5. Spoon sauce over flounder. Sprinkle with Parmesan cheese.
6. Bake at 350°F 20 to 25 minutes. If desired, set ramekins under broiler with tops about 3 inches from heat until lightly browned; watch carefully to avoid overbrowning.
6 SERVINGS

Stir-Fried Shrimp and Vegetables

¾ pound fresh bean sprouts
2 tablespoons cornstarch
2 teaspoons sugar
1½ cups water
2 tablespoons Japanese soy sauce
3 tablespoons white wine vinegar
½ teaspoon pepper
2 tablespoons sesame oil
1 teaspoon salt
1 cup diagonally sliced celery
6 green onions, sliced
diagonally into 1-inch pieces
1 cup thinly sliced fresh mushrooms
1 tablespoon sesame oil
2 cloves garlic, minced
1 teaspoon minced fresh ginger root
¾ pound cleaned and cooked shrimp
1 package (6 ounces) frozen snow peas, thawed and well drained

1. Blanch bean sprouts by turning half of them into a sieve or basket and setting in a saucepan of boiling water. Boil 1 minute. Remove from water and spread out on absorbent paper to drain. Repeat with remaining bean sprouts.
2. Blend cornstarch, sugar, water, soy sauce, vinegar, and pepper; set aside.
3. Heat 2 tablespoons sesame oil in a large wok. Stir in salt, celery, green onion, and mushrooms. Stir-fry vegetables about 1 minute. Add bean sprouts and stir-fry 1 minute more. Remove vegetables from wok.
4. Heat 1 tablespoon sesame oil. Add garlic and ginger root; stir-fry briefly. Add shrimp and snow peas; stir-fry 1 minute longer. Return other vegetables to wok and mix together. Stir-fry briefly to heat.
5. Push vegetables and shrimp up sides of wok. Stir cornstarch mixture into liquid in center of wok. Cook until thickened and combine with shrimp and vegetables. Serve immediately.

4 SERVINGS

Shrimp San Giusto

1 pound large uncooked shrimp
½ teaspoon salt
⅛ teaspoon pepper
1 bay leaf
3 tablespoons lemon juice
2½ cups water
1 bay leaf
1 thick slice onion
Pinch each salt, pepper, thyme, and oregano
2 tablespoons olive oil
1 tablespoon butter
½ cup finely chopped onion
1 clove garlic, finely chopped
1 teaspoon finely chopped parsley
Flour
⅓ cup dry white wine
1 large tomato, peeled, seeded, and chopped

1. Using scissors, cut the shells of the shrimp down middle of back; remove shells and set aside. Clean and devein shrimp.
2. Place cleaned shrimp in a bowl with salt, pepper, and a bay leaf; drizzle with lemon juice. Set shrimp aside to marinate 1 hour.
3. To make fish stock, place shrimp shells in a saucepan with water, a bay leaf, onion slice, salt, pepper, thyme, and oregano. Cover and simmer 30 minutes; strain.
4. Heat olive oil and butter in a skillet. Add chopped onion, garlic, and parsley; cook until soft. Coat marinated shrimp with flour, add to skillet with vegetables, and cook until lightly browned on both sides.
5. Add wine and simmer until it is almost evaporated. Stir in tomato and ½ cup or more of the strained fish stock. Simmer 15 to 20 minutes, or until the sauce is desired consistency.

3 TO 4 SERVINGS

Stir-Fried Shrimp and Vegetables

Marinated Shrimp with Mushrooms and Olives

1 pound fresh mushrooms, quartered
1 cup water
½ cup Italian salad dressing
2 tablespoons lemon juice
2 cloves garlic, halve
1¼ teaspoons salt
½ teaspoon thyme leaves
½ teaspoon peppercorns
⅛ teaspoon nutmeg
2 bay leaves
2 pounds medium shrimp, cooked and deveined
¾ cup small pimiento-stuffed olives

1. Combine all ingredients except the shrimp and in a large saucepan. Bring to boiling, reduce heat, cover and simmer 5 minutes.
2. Put shrimp and olives into a large bowl. Pour hot mixture into bowl and toss lightly to mix; cool. Refrigerate, covered, 6 to 8 hours, or overnight before serving.
3. To serve, pile generous amounts of the mixture with some of the marinade onto crisp **salad greens** on luncheon plates. Serve as a luncheon or supper entrée.
6 SERVINGS

Stuffed Squid

32 squid, cleaned and tentacles removed
¾ cup olive oil
1 large onion, chopped
1½ cups water
1 cup long-grain rice
½ cup chopped parsley
1 teaspoon mint
1 teaspoon basil
2 cloves garlic, crushed in a garlic press
½ cup pine nuts
¼ cup dried black currants
1 cup dry white wine
Salt and pepper to taste
Water
Juice of 2 lemons

1. Reserve squid. Rinse tentacles in cold water. Drain and mince finely.
2. In a large saucepan, heat 2 tablespoons of the oil, add onion and minced tentacles and cook over low heat until tentacles turn pink. Add water. Heat to boiling. Reduce heat, add rice, parsley, mint, basil, garlic, pine nuts, currants, and ½ cup of the wine.
3. Simmer until liquid is absorbed. Season with salt and pepper. Cool.
4. Using a teaspoon, stuff each squid cavity loosely with the rice mixture. Arrange squid in rows in a large baking dish. Combine the remaining wine and olive oil with enough water to reach half the depth of the squid. Season with additional salt and pepper. Cover.
5. Bake at 325°F about 40 minutes, or until squid is tender. Drizzle with lemon juice just before serving.
8 SERVINGS

Note: Stuffing may also be used as a side dish. Stuff 16 squid. Put remaining stuffing in a baking dish. Add a little water, salt, and pepper and cover. Bake at 325°F 30 minutes.

Tuna Fiesta

1 can (6½ to 7 ounces) tuna, drained and separated in large pieces
1 can (16 ounces) stewed tomatoes, drained
1 can (15¼ ounces) spaghetti in tomato sauce with cheese
1 tablespoon ketchup
1 teaspoon seasoned salt
½ cup (about 2 ounces) shredded sharp Cheddar cheese
Few grains paprika
Fresh parsley

1. Turn tuna, stewed tomatoes, and spaghetti into a saucepan. Add ketchup, seasoned salt, cheese, and paprika; mix well. Set over medium heat, stirring occasionally, until thoroughly heated (about 8 minutes).
2. Turn into a warm serving dish; garnish with parsley. Serve at once.
ABOUT 6 SERVINGS

Note: If desired, reserve cheese and paprika for topping. Mix remaining ingredients and turn into a greased 1-quart casserole. Top with the cheese and paprika. Set in a 350°F oven 20 minutes, or until thoroughly heated. Garnish with parsley.

Spiced Shrimp with Onions

4 quarts water
1 tablespoon salt
3 pounds raw shrimp, shelled and deveined
¾ cup white wine vinegar
1 cup olive oil
2 cups white wine
1 tablespoon salt
1 teaspoon pepper
2 jars whole baby onions, drained
3 garlic cloves
1 bay leaf
1 celery stalk, cut in half
Juice of 1 lemon

1. Bring water and 1 tablespoon salt to a rolling boil in a saucepot. Add shrimp. Boil 1 minute. Drain.
2. Combine remaining ingredients in a saucepot and bring to boiling. Simmer uncovered 5 minutes. Cool.
3. Pour onion mixture over shrimp. Refrigerate 6 to 8 hours.
4. Drain shrimp and onions and serve chilled.
6 TO 8 SERVINGS

Broiled Trout

Trout (8- to 10-ounce fish for each serving)
French dressing
Instant minced onion
Salt
Lemon slices
Tomato wedges
Mint sprigs or watercress

1. Remove head and fins from trout, if desired. Rinse trout quickly under cold running water; dry thoroughly. Brush inside of fish with French dressing and sprinkle generously with instant minced onion and salt. Brush outside generously with French dressing.
2. Arrange trout in a greased shallow baking pan or on a broiler rack. Place under broiler with top of fish about 3 inches from heat. Broil 5 to 8 minutes on each side, or until fish flakes easily; brush with dressing during broiling.
3. Remove trout to heated serving platter and garnish with lemon, tomato, and mint.

Marinated Shrimp with Mushrooms and Olives

Baked Shrimp

2 pounds large fresh
  uncooked shrimp
⅓ cup butter
1 teaspoon salt
4 cloves garlic, crushed in a
garlic press
¼ cup chopped parsley
2 teaspoons grated lemon
  peel
2 tablespoons lemon juice

1. Remove shells from shrimp, leaving shell on tail section. Remove vein down the back, wash under cold running water, and drain on paper towels.
2. Place butter in a 13x9-inch baking dish; heat in oven at 400°F until melted. Stir in salt, garlic, and 1 tablespoon parsley. Place shrimp in a single layer in the baking dish.
3. Bake at 400°F 5 minutes. Turn the shrimp and sprinkle with lemon peel, lemon juice, and remaining parsley. Continue baking about 15 minutes, or until tender.
4. Serve shrimp with sauce over **hot fluffy rice.**
ABOUT 6 SERVINGS

Bay Scallops with Cucumber Rings

2 pounds bay scallops or sea
  scallops, cut in thirds
1 tablespoon minced onion
½ cup minced celery
1 cup minced carrot
1½ cups Chicken Stock (see
  page 48)
½ teaspoon salt
2 large cucumbers, pared,
  sliced lengthwise, seeded,
  and cut in 1-inch slices
¼ cup dry white wine
1 tablespoon arrowroot
Cold water
Salt

1. Simmer scallops, onion, celery, and carrot in the stock until scallops are tender (about 4 minutes). Strain stock into a medium saucepan. Sprinkle ½ teaspoon salt over scallop mixture; keep warm.
2. Simmer cucumbers in stock until just tender (about 4 minutes). Remove cucumbers with slotted spoon; keep warm.
3. Heat remaining stock and wine to boiling. Mix arrowroot with a little cold water; stir into stock. Simmer, stirring constantly, until thickened (about 3 minutes). Season to taste with salt. Spoon half the cucumbers into a clear glass serving bowl. Arrange scallops on top. Spoon remaining cucumbers over scallops; pour sauce over. Serve immediately.
6 SERVINGS

Shrimp Giahni with Feta Cheese

1 medium onion, minced
½ cup olive oil
1 can (28 ounces) tomatoes
  (undrained)
4 ounces white wine
1 small bunch parsley, finely
  chopped
1 celery stalk, finely chopped
Salt and pepper
1 pound large shrimp,
  cleaned and deveined
¼ pound feta cheese,
  crumbled

1. Brown onion in oil. Add tomatoes, stirring until mixture reaches boiling. Lower heat and simmer, covered, 5 minutes. Add wine, parsley, celery, and salt and pepper to taste. Simmer 30 minutes.
2. While tomato sauce is simmering, parboil shrimp 2 minutes in **3 quarts boiling water** with **2 teaspoons salt.** Drain immediately.
3. Add shrimp to sauce. Simmer 1 minute. Garnish with feta.
6 SERVINGS

Broiled Salmon

6 salmon steaks, cut ½ inch
  thick
1 cup sauterne
½ cup vegetable oil
2 tablespoons wine vinegar
2 teaspoons soy sauce
2 tablespoons chopped green
  onion
Seasoned salt
Green onion, chopped
  (optional)
Pimento strips (optional)

1. Put salmon steaks into a large shallow dish. Mix sauterne, oil, wine vinegar, soy sauce, and green onion; pour over salmon. Marinate in refrigerator several hours or overnight, turning occasionally.
2. To broil, remove steaks from marinade and place on broiler rack. Set under broiler with top 6 inches from heat. Broil about 5 minutes on each side, brushing generously with marinade several times. About 2 minutes before removing from broiler, sprinkle each steak lightly with seasoned salt and, if desired, top with green onion and pimento. Serve at once.
6 SERVINGS

Coral Shrimp

½ cup finely chopped onion
1 tablespoon butter or
  margarine
2 cups Medium White Sauce
  (page 49)
1 to 2 teaspoons tomato
  paste
¼ cup dry white wine
½ teaspoon salt
¼ teaspoon white pepper
1 pound cooked medium
  shrimp (fresh or frozen)
12 crêpes (see page 36)

1. Sauté onion in butter until tender. Mix onion into white sauce. Stir in tomato paste, wine, salt, and pepper. Fold in shrimp.
2. Assemble, using tube method, (see page 36). Spoon extra sauce over crêpes. Garnish with **fresh tomato** and **Bibb lettuce.**
12 FILLED CRÊPES

Herbed Shrimp in Beer

2 pounds peeled raw shrimp
1½ cups beer
2 teaspoons lemon juice
2 garlic cloves, minced
2 tablespoons snipped chives
2 tablespoons snipped
  parsley
1½ teaspoons salt
½ teaspoon freshly ground
  pepper
Shredded lettuce
2 green onions, finely
  chopped

1. Combine all ingredients except lettuce and green onions in a bowl. Refrigerate covered 8 hours or overnight; stir occasionally. Drain; reserve marinade.
2. Broil shrimp 4 inches from heat until cooked and tender (about 2 minutes on each side; less time for small shrimp). Do not overcook or shrimp will become tough. Brush occasionally with marinade. Marinade can be heated and served for dipping, if desired.
3. Serve shrimp on shredded lettuce; sprinkle with chopped green onion.
6 SERVINGS

Pickled Octopus

1 small octopus (about 2
  pounds)
½ cup olive oil
¼ cup white wine vinegar
Juice of ½ lemon
1 tablespoon minced parsley
½ teaspoon marjoram
Salt and pepper to taste

1. Beat octopus with the flat side of a metal meat hammer 15 to 20 minutes; it will feel soft and excrete a grayish liquid.
2. Wash octopus thoroughly, drain, and cook in skillet without water until it becomes bright pink. Cut into bite-size pieces.
3. Make a salad dressing of the olive oil, vinegar, lemon juice, parsley, marjoram, salt, and pepper. Mix well.
4. Pour over octopus and store in the refrigerator in a covered container for 5 days before serving.
5. Serve cold as an appetizer.
4 TO 6 SERVINGS

Rice with Lobster Sardinian Style

2 large frozen lobster tails
⅔ cup minced onion
1 large clove garlic, minced
¼ cup olive oil
2 cans (16 ounces each)
  tomato purée
1 tablespoon chopped fresh
basil leaves, or 1 teaspoon
  dried basil
1 tablespoon mild honey
1 teaspoon salt
⅛ teaspoon pepper
4 cups hot cooked rice

1. Boil lobster tails according to package directions. Cool. Remove meat from shells and cut into chunks; set aside.
2. Sauté onion and garlic in olive oil 5 minutes. Stir in tomato purée, basil, honey, salt, and pepper.
3. Simmer sauce, covered, 45 minutes. If sauce becomes too thick while it is cooking, stir in ½ **cup water.**
4. Combine lobster with rice, pour hot sauce over rice, and serve.

Oysters Rockefeller

1 pint oysters
2 pounds fresh spinach,
  washed and stems
  removed*
1 cup instant nonfat dry-milk
  solids
2 tablespoons chopped
  onion
2 garlic cloves, minced
1 teaspoon salt
¼ teaspoon freshly ground
  pepper
⅛ teaspoon freshly ground
  nutmeg
2 egg whites
⅓ cup grated Jarlsberg or
  Parmesan cheese

1. Drain oysters; reserve liquor. Cook spinach in a covered saucepan with water clinging to leaves until tender (about 7 minutes); drain. Purée spinach with reserved liquor, the milk solids, onion, garlic, salt, pepper, nutmeg, and egg whites in a food processor or blender. Pour mixture into a saucepan; heat thoroughly.
2. Layer half the spinach mixture into large shell dishes or ramekins. Top with oysters; spoon remaining spinach mixture over oysters. Sprinkle with cheese. Set on a cookie sheet.
3. Bake at 400°F about 10 minutes, or until bubbly. Broil 1 to 2 minutes to brown tops. Serve immediately.
4 SERVINGS

Paella I

1 cup sliced carrots
1 small onion, sliced
2 bay leaves
1 tablespoon dried parsley
¼ teaspoon pepper
3 cups water
½ cup oil
2 broiler-fryer chickens, cut
  in serving pieces
2 cloves garlic, minced
1 green pepper, cut in thin
  strips
1 teaspoon crumbled saffron
1 can (12 ounces) clams or 8
  to 12 fresh clams
1½ cups uncooked rice
1 tablespoon salt
2 large tomatoes, peeled and
  chopped
1 can (8 ounces) artichoke
  hearts
1 pound cooked shrimp,
  shelled and deveined

1. Place carrots, onions, bay leaves, dried parsley, pepper, and water in saucepan; simmer over low heat about 20 minutes, or until carrots are tender.
2. Meanwhile, heat oil in a large Dutch oven or heavy kettle. Brown chicken pieces in oil, a few at a time, removing as they are well browned.
3. In same oil, sauté garlic, pepper strips, and saffron. Return chicken pieces to Dutch oven. Drain liquid from clams and add enough of this liquid to vegetable liquid to make 3 cups. Pour over chicken in Dutch oven. Bring to simmering and gradually stir in rice and salt.
4. Bake at 350°F 1 hour.
5. During last part of baking, prepare clams by cutting in half; chop tomatoes; cut artichoke hearts into quarters vertically. Add clams, tomatoes, shrimp, and artichoke hearts to chicken-rice mixture, and mix in carefully. Return to oven for 10 to 15 minutes more, or until heated through. Serve hot.
8 TO 10 SERVINGS

Paella II

1 cup olive or vegetable oil
1 broiler-fryer chicken (2 pounds), cut in pieces
½ cup diced boiled ham or smoky sausage
1 tablespoon minced onion
2 cloves garlic, minced
2 ripe tomatoes, peeled and coarsely chopped
1½ teaspoons salt
1½ pounds fresh shrimp, shelled and deveined
12 small clams in shells,

scrubbed
2 cups uncooked rice
1 quart hot water
1 cup fresh or frozen green peas
¼ cup coarsely chopped parsley
Few shreds saffron
1 rock lobster tail, cooked and meat cut in pieces
1 can or jar (7 ounces) whole pimentos

1. Heat oil in paellera or large skillet; cook chicken and ham about 10 minutes, turning chicken to brown on all sides. Add onion and garlic and cook 2 minutes. Add tomatoes, salt, shrimp, and clams; cover and cook 5 to 10 minutes, or until clam shells open. Remove clams and keep warm.
2. Add rice, water, peas, parsley, and saffron; mix well. Cover and cook, stirring occasionally, 25 minutes, or until rice is just tender. Mix in lobster, half of pimento, and the reserved clams in shells; heat until very hot. Serve garnished with remaining pimento.
8 TO 10 SERVINGS

Crab Meat Soup with Sherry

1 cup 1-inch celery pieces
1⅓ cups Fish Stock (see page 48)
2 cans (7¾ ounces each) crab meat, drained (reserve 1 cup flaked crab meat)
½ cup instant nonfat dry-milk solids
½ cup water

½ cup whole milk
¼ teaspoon salt
⅛ teaspoon ground mace
4 teaspoons arrowroot
Cold water
2 tablespoons dry sherry
3 tablespoons finely sliced celery for garnish

1. Simmer celery in stock in a covered saucepan 15 minutes. Place celery and stock in a food processor or blender; add 1 cup of flaked crab meat, the milk solids, water, milk, salt, and mace. Purée mixture; pour back into saucepan.
2. Heat crab mixture to simmering. Mix arrowroot with a little cold water; stir into crab mixture. Simmer, stirring constantly, until mixture has thickened. Stir in sherry and remaining crab meat. Heat thoroughly. Garnish with celery slices. Serve immediately.
4 SERVINGS (1½ CUPS EACH)

Gingered Scallops

3 cups Fish Stock (see page 48)
1 tablespoon minced fresh ginger root
2 tablespoons dry sherry
½ teaspoon ground ginger
1½ pounds bay scallops or

sea scallops, cut in ½-inch pieces
¾ cup chopped celery
2 teaspoons arrowroot
Cold water
Salt
Snipped parsley

1. Combine stock and ginger root in a medium skillet. Sim-

mer until stock is reduced to 1 cup (about 15 minutes). Strain stock and discard ginger root. Return stock to skillet; stir in sherry and ground ginger.
2. Simmer scallops and celery in stock until tender (about 4 minutes). Remove scallops with a slotted spoon to small shell dishes. Mix arrowroot with a little cold water; stir into stock. Simmer, stirring constantly, until sauce is thickened (about 2 minutes). Taste and season with salt. Spoon sauce over scallops; sprinkle with parsley.
4 SERVINGS

Note: This recipe will make 6 first-course servings.

Scampi Flamingo

½ cup butter
1 cup chopped celery
¼ cup chopped carrot
¼ cup chopped onion
¼ teaspoon thyme
2 pounds fresh shrimp with shells
3 tablespoons cognac

2 cups light cream
⅓ cup sherry
½ cup butter
½ teaspoon lemon juice
⅛ teaspoon ground nutmeg
¼ cup Béchamel Sauce (see page 49)

1. Heat ½ cup butter in a large skillet. Sauté vegetables with thyme until lightly browned. Add the shrimp and brown carefully.
2. Add cognac and flame it. Add cream, sherry, and sauce; cook 15 minutes.
3. Remove shrimp; shell and devein them; keep warm.
4. Add ½ cup butter, lemon juice, and nutmeg to sauce; cook about 5 minutes. Strain through a fine sieve and pour over the shrimp.
5. Serve sauce and shrimp with hot cooked rice.
ABOUT 4 SERVINGS

Fried Scampi

3 pounds fresh prawns or shrimp with shells
Fat for deep frying heated to 360°F
½ cup olive oil

4 cloves garlic, minced
1 teaspoon salt
½ teaspoon oregano
¼ teaspoon pepper
1 teaspoon chopped parsley

1. Wash prawns in cold water. Remove tiny legs, peel off shells, and devein prawns. Rinse in cold water, then pat dry with absorbent paper.
2. Put only as many prawns in fat as will float uncrowded one layer deep. Fry 3 to 5 minutes, or until golden brown. Drain over fat before removing to absorbent paper. Turn fried prawns onto a warm platter.
3. Heat oil in a skillet. Add garlic, salt, oregano, and pepper and cook until garlic is lightly browned. Pour sauce over prawns and sprinkle with parsley.
ABOUT 6 SERVINGS

Steamed Mussels in Wine Sauce

Steamed Mussels in Wine Sauce

2 pounds mussels
1 large onion, minced
1 large celery stak, minced
4 peppercorns
3 cups dry white wine
¼ cup butter (at room temperature)
1 tablespoon flour
1 teaspoon vinegar
1 tablespoon chopped parsley
1 garlic clove
Salt and pepper to taste

1. Scrub mussels well with a vegetable brush and rinse. Put into a kettle with onion, celery, peppercorns, and white wine. Cover and steam until they open, discarding any that are unopened.
2. Put mussels onto a deep platter. Cover and keep warm.
3. Strain liquid and simmer. Mix butter and flour together in a small bowl; stir into hot liquid. Add vinegar, parsley, garlic, salt, and pepper; continue to simmer until liquid is reduced by half.
4. To serve, pour sauce over mussels.
6 SERVINGS

Shrimp with Sesame Seed Sauce

½ cup plain pumpkin seed
3 tablespoons sesame seed
1 small clove garlic
2 tablespoons vegetable oil
¾ teaspoon chili powder
¼ teaspoon cinnamon
⅛ teaspoon cloves
¾ cup canned chicken broth
½ teaspoon salt
1½ tablespoons lime juice
1½ pounds hot cooked shelled shrimp

1. Combine pumpkin seed, sesame seed, garlic, and oil in a saucepan. Stir and cook over medium heat until sesame seed is light golden brown.
2. Remove from heat and stir in chili powder, cinnamon, and cloves. Turn into an electric blender and grind. Add broth and salt; blend.
3. Turn mixture into a saucepan, mix in lime juice, and heat over low heat, stirring in one direction, until thickened.
4. Arrange hot shrimp on a platter and spoon sauce over it. If desired, garnish with sliced green onion and lime wedges.
4 SERVINGS

African Rock Lobster en Casserole

6 (3 ounces each) frozen South African rock lobster tails
¼ cup butter or margarine
¼ cup flour
2 cups chicken broth
2 egg yolks, fork beaten
⅓ cup half-and-half
2 to 3 teaspoons Worcestershire sauce
1 teaspoon dry mustard blended with about 1
tablespoon cold water
1 or 2 packages (10 ounces each) frozen asparagus spears, cooked following package directions
1 package (8 ounces) spaghetti, cooked and drained
Parmesan-Romano cheese
¼ cup toasted slivered almonds

1. Drop frozen lobster tails into boiling salted water. Return to boiling and simmer 3 minutes.
2. Remove cooked lobster tails and place under running cold water until cool enough to handle. With scissors, cut along each edge of bony membrane on the underside of shell; remove meat.
3. Dice half of the meat and cut remainder into chunks; set aside.
4. Heat butter in a heavy saucepan; stir in flour. Cook until bubbly. Add broth gradually while blending thoroughly. Stirring constantly, bring rapidly to boiling and cook 1 to 2 minutes. Immediately blend about 3 tablespoonfuls into egg yolks and stir into the hot sauce. Cook 3 to 5 minutes, stirring constantly.
5. Blend in half-and-half, Worcestershire sauce, mustard, and diced lobster. Heat thoroughly.
6. Divide cooked asparagus equally among 6 individual casseroles. Spoon over spaghetti and hot lobster sauce. Generously shake cheese over all. Top with lobster chunks and almonds.
6 SERVINGS

African Rock Lobster en Casserole

Deep-Fried Squid

12 squid, cleaned, with their
   tentacles left on
Flour seasoned generously

with salt and pepper
Vegetable oil for deep frying
3 lemons, cut in wedges

1. Rinse the cleaned squid in cold water and pat dry with paper towels. Dip the squid into the seasoned flour and coat all surfaces evenly.
2. Heat the oil in a deep fryer to 375°F. Drop in the squid, a few at a time. Fry until golden brown (about 5 minutes). Transfer the squid with a slotted spoon to a baking dish lined with paper towels. Keep in a 200°F oven until all the squid are fried.
3. Remove paper; serve squid with lemon.
3 SERVINGS

Deep-Fried Squid

Patio Crab Casserole

¼ cup butter or margarine
2 cups chopped onion
1 pound frozen or 2 cans
   (7½ ounces each) Alaska
   king crab, drained and
   sliced
½ cup snipped parsley
2 tablespoons capers
2 tablespoons snipped chives
2 pimentos, diced

1½ cups corn muffin mix
⅛ teaspoon salt
1 egg, fork beaten
½ cup milk
1 cup cream-style golden
   corn
6 drops Tabasco
2 cups sour cream
1½ cups shredded extra
   sharp Cheddar cheese

1. Heat butter in a skillet. Add onion and cook until tender. Stir in crab, parsley, capers, chives, and pimentos; heat.
2. Meanwhile, stir corn muffin mix, salt, egg, milk, corn, and Tabasco until just moistened (batter should be lumpy). Turn into a greased shallow 3-quart dish and spread evenly to edges.
3. Spoon crab mixture and then sour cream over batter. Sprinkle cheese over all.
4. Bake at 400°F 25 to 30 minutes.
5. To serve, cut into squares.
ABOUT 12 SERVINGS

Scallops Gourmet

2 pounds scallops
1 cup boiling water
1 teaspoon salt
3 to 4 tablespoons lemon juice
1 medium onion, sliced
2 sprigs parsley
1 bay leaf
¼ cup butter or margarine
½ pound mushrooms, sliced
lengthwise
3 tomatoes, peeled and diced
2 tablespoons butter or margarine
2 tablespoons flour
¼ teaspoon garlic powder
8 patty shells, heated
Carrot curls

1. Rinse scallops under running cold water. Put scallops into a saucepan and pour boiling water over them. Stir in salt, lemon juice, onion, parsley, and bay leaf. Cook, covered, over low heat 5 minutes; drain and reserve 1 cup of the stock. If scallions are large, cut into smaller pieces. Set aside.
2. Heat ¼ cup butter in a skillet. Add mushrooms and cook until delicately browned and tender, stirring occasionally. Remove from skillet with slotted spoon; set aside. Add diced tomatoes to skillet and cook 5 minutes. Set aside.
3. Heat 2 tablespoons butter in a saucepan. Blend in flour; heat until bubbly. Add reserved stock gradually, stirring constantly. Continue to stir and bring rapidly to boiling; cook 1 to 2 minutes.
4. Add scallops, mushrooms, tomatoes, and garlic powder to sauce; heat thoroughly.
5. To serve, spoon scallop mixture into patty shells. Garnish with carrot curls.
ABOUT 8 SERVINGS

Savory Oysters

⅓ cup butter or margarine
1 can (4 ounces) sliced mushrooms, drained
⅓ cup chopped green pepper
½ clove garlic
2 cups coarse toasted enriched bread crumbs
1 quart oysters, drained
(reserve liquor)
¼ cup cream
1 teaspoon Worcestershire sauce
1 teaspoon salt
1 teaspoon paprika
⅛ teaspoon ground mace
Few grains cayenne pepper

1. Heat butter in a large skillet. Add mushrooms, green pepper, and garlic; cook about 5 minutes. Remove skillet from heat; discard garlic. Stir in toasted bread crumbs. Set aside.
2. Mix ¼ cup reserved oyster liquor, cream, and Worcestershire sauce.
3. Blend salt, paprika, mace, and cayenne.
4. Use about a third of crumb mixture to form a layer in bottom of a greased 2-quart casserole. Arrange about half of oysters and half of seasonings over crumbs. Repeat crumb layer, then oyster and seasoning layers. Pour the liquid mixture over all. Top with remaining crumbs.
5. Bake at 375°F 20 to 30 minutes, or until thoroughly heated and crumbs are golden brown.
6 TO 8 SERVINGS

Deviled Crab

Mustard Sauce:
2 tablespoons dry mustard
2 tablespoons water
2 tablespoons olive oil
1 tablespoon ketchup
¼ teaspoon salt
¼ teaspoon Worcestershire sauce

Crab meat mixture:
6 tablespoons butter
4 teaspoons finely chopped green pepper
2 teaspoons finely chopped onion
6 tablespoons flour
1 teaspoon salt
½ teaspoon dry mustard
1½ cups milk
1 teaspoon Worcestershire sauce
2 egg yolks, slightly beaten
1 pound lump crab meat, drained
2 teaspoons chopped pimento
2 tablespoons dry sherry
1 cup fine dry enriched bread crumbs
Paprika
Butter, melted

1. For Mustard Sauce, blend dry mustard, water, olive oil, ketchup, salt, and Worcestershire sauce in a small bowl; set aside.
2. For crab meat mixture, heat butter in a large heavy saucepan. Add green pepper and onion; cook until onion is golden in color.
3. Blend flour, salt, and dry mustard; stir in. Heat until bubbly. Add milk gradually, stirring until smooth. Stir in Worcestershire sauce. Bring rapidly to boiling; cook 1 to 2 minutes.
4. Remove mixture from heat and stir a small amount of hot mixture into the egg yolks; return to saucepan and cook 3 to 5 minutes, stirring constantly.
5. Stir in crab meat and pimento; heat thoroughly. Remove from heat and blend in sherry and the Mustard Sauce.
6. Spoon into 6 shell-shaped ramekins, allowing about ½ cup mixture for each. Sprinkle top with bread crumbs and paprika; drizzle with melted butter.
7. Set in a 450°F oven about 6 minutes, or until tops are lightly browned and mixture is thoroughly heated. Serve hot.
6 SERVINGS

Shrimp with Red Rice

¼ cup oil
½ cup chopped onion
1 clove garlic, minced
1 medium green pepper, seeded and sliced in ½-inch strips
1 pound shelled green shrimp
1 can (6 ounces) tomato paste
2½ cups water
1 teaspoon salt
¼ teaspoon pepper
¼ teaspoon marjoram
1 cup uncooked rice

1. Heat oil in a large, heavy saucepan. Add onion and garlic and cook until soft (about 5 minutes). Add green pepper and uncooked shrimp and cook until shrimp turn pink.
2. Stir tomato paste, water, and seasonings into shrimp mixture and bring to boiling. Add rice; mix well. Cover and simmer over very low heat until all liquid is absorbed by rice (about 25 to 30 minutes).
4 TO 6 SERVINGS

Seafood Kabobs

1 lobster tail (8 ounces), cut in 6 pieces
6 scallops
6 shrimp, peeled and deveined
12 large mushroom caps
½ cup olive oil
3 tablespoons soy sauce
1 tablespoon Worcestershire sauce
2 tablespoons white wine

vinegar
½ teaspoon grated lemon peel
2 tablespoons lemon juice
½ teaspoon ground pepper
2 teaspoons snipped parsley
18 (4-inch) pieces sliced bacon
12 (1-inch) squares green pepper
6 cherry tomatoes

1. Put lobster pieces, scallops, shrimp, and mushroom caps into a shallow dish.
2. Combine olive oil, soy sauce, Worcestershire sauce, vinegar, lemon peel, lemon juice, pepper, and parsley in a screwtop jar and shake vigorously. Pour the marinade over the seafood and mushroom caps and set aside for at least 2 hours.
3. Drain off marinade and reserve.
4. Wrap each piece of seafood in bacon. Thread pieces on skewers (about 10 inches each) as follows: green pepper, lobster, mushroom, scallop, mushroom, shrimp, and green pepper. Arrange on a broiler rack and brush with marinade.
5. Place under broiler 3 inches from heat. Broil 10 to 12 minutes, turning and brushing frequently with marinade. Add a cherry tomato to each skewer during the last few minutes of broiling.

6 SERVINGS

CAKES & TORTES

Génoise

1 cup sugar
6 eggs
2 teaspoons vanilla extract
Grated peel of 1 lime
1 cup all-purpose flour
¼ cup clarified butter

1. Combine sugar, eggs, vanilla extract, and grated peel in the top of a double boiler. Beat with an electric mixer over hot water for 15 minutes, or until light and fluffy. Remove from heat. Continue beating until mixture is cooled and has reached the ribbon stage. (The mixture should flow in ribbons and softly peak.)
2. Sift the flour onto the cooled mixture a fourth at a time; fold in gently after each addition. Fold in clarified butter.
3. Pour the batter into 2 greased and floured 9-inch round layer cake pans.
4. Bake at 325°F about 25 minutes, or until cake tests done.
5. Cool on racks. Frost cooled layers with **Rich Chocolate Frosting** (see page 576).
ONE 9-INCH LAYER CAKE

Cookout Lemon Cake

1 package (about 19 ounces) yellow cake mix
2 teaspoons grated lemon peel
¾ cup sugar
1 tablespoon lemon juice
½ cup melted butter

1. Prepare cake mix according to package directions, adding 1 teaspoon lemon peel. Turn into 2 well-greased 9-inch round pans.
2. Combine sugar with remaining lemon peel and spoon over batter in pans.
3. Combine lemon juice and butter. Pour over sugar.
4. Bake at 350°F about 30 minutes, or until cake tests done. Cake will have a crispy golden brown top.
5. Cool on racks. Leave cake in pans and wrap in foil to carry to cookout. If the day is cool, set pan on grill to warm over the coals before serving.
TWO 9-INCH CAKE LAYERS

Easter Baba

1 cup milk
3⅓ cups all-purpose flour
2 packages active dry yeast
¼ cup lukewarm water
⅔ cup sugar
2 teaspoons salt
15 egg yolks
1 teaspoon vanilla extract
¼ teaspoon almond extract
½ cup melted butter
¾ cup mixed chopped candied citron and orange and lemon peel
½ cup chopped almonds
⅓ cup raisins
Blanched almond halves
Fine dry bread crumbs

1. Scald milk; pour into a large bowl. Slowly add ¾ cup flour to hot milk and beat thoroughly. Cool.
2. Dissolve yeast in lukewarm water 5 minutes; add 1 tablespoon of the sugar. Let stand 5 minutes. Add to cooled milk mixture; beat well.
3. Cover; let rise until doubled in bulk.
4. Add salt to egg yolks. Beat until thick and lemon-colored, about 5 minutes. Add remaining sugar and extracts; continue beating. Combine egg mixture with milk mixture, beating thoroughly. Add remaining flour; mix well.
5. Knead 10 minutes in bowl. Add butter and continue kneading 10 more minutes, or until dough leaves the fingers. Add candied peel, almonds, and raisins; knead to mix well.
6. Let rise until doubled in bulk. Punch down and let rise again.
7. Generously grease a 12-inch fluted tube pan or turban mold. Press almond halves around sides and bottom of pan. Coat with bread crumbs.
8. Punch down dough and put into prepared pan. Dough should fill a third of pan. Let rise 1 hour, or until dough fills pan.
9. Bake at 350°F about 50 minutes, or until hollow sounding when tapped on top.
1 LARGE LOAF

Genoise

Sally Lunn with Strawberries

1 cup milk, scalded
½ cup sugar
2 teaspoons salt
½ cup butter or margarine, melted
1 package active dry yeast
½ cup warm water
3 eggs, beaten
5 cups all-purpose flour
½ teaspoon ground nutmeg
3 pints fresh strawberries, sliced and sweetened

1. Combine milk, ¼ cup of the sugar, salt, and butter; cool to lukewarm.
2. Soften yeast in the warm water in a large bowl. Blend with the milk mixture and eggs.
3. Gradually beat in the flour until smooth. Cover; let rise in a warm place until doubled, about 1 hour.
4. Stir dough down and turn into a greased and sugared 10-inch tube pan. Cover; let rise again until doubled, about 30 minutes.
5. Mix remaining ¼ cup sugar with the nutmeg and sprinkle over top of dough.
6. Bake at 400°F about 40 minutes. Remove from oven and cool 5 minutes. Turn out Sally Lunn and serve warm or cooled with the strawberries mounded in the center of the ring. Accompany with a bowl of **whipped cream** or a pitcher of **cream.**
ONE 10-INCH RING LOAF

Note: If desired, the strawberries may be left whole and unhulled to be dipped into the cream as they are eaten.

New Year's Day Cake

3½ cups all-purpose flour
2 teaspoons baking powder
1 cup softened unsalted butter
1 cup sugar
2 eggs (at room temperature)
1 egg yolk
Grated peel of 1 orange
¼ teaspoon nutmeg
(optional)
¼ cup cream
1 tablespoon cognac
1 silver coin, boiled and wrapped in foil
Blanched almonds (about 20)
1 egg white, beaten until frothy

1. Sift flour and baking powder; set aside.
2. Using an electric mixer, beat butter until fluffy. Add sugar gradually, beating 4 minutes. Add eggs and egg yolk, one at a time, beating after each. Add peel and nutmeg. Combine cream and cognac; add gradually while beating.
3. Add dry ingredients, using a wooden spoon to mix in well. Stir in coin.
4. Heavily grease a 10-inch round cake pan. Turn batter into pan. Press edge with fork tines to decorate. Arrange blanched almonds in a decorative pattern on top.
5. Bake at 350°F 15 to 20 minutes, or until cake is set. Pull out from oven, brush with egg white, and return to oven. Continue baking until a wooden pick inserted in the center comes out clean (about 20 minutes). Cool before serving.
8 TO 10 SERVINGS

Walnut Honey Cake

Syrup:
1 cup sugar
½ cup honey
1 cup water
1 teaspoon lemon juice
1 cinnamon stick

Cake:
¾ cup unsalted butter (at room temperature)
½ teaspoon grated orange peel
¾ cup sugar
3 eggs
1 cup all-purpose flour
1½ teaspoons baking powder
½ teaspoon cinnamon
¼ teaspoon salt
¼ cup milk
1 cup chopped walnuts

1. For syrup, bring all ingredients to a boil in saucepan. Simmer 20 minutes. Set aside to cool.
2. For cake, cream butter, orange peel, and sugar together until fluffy. Beat in eggs, one at a time, beating well after each addition.
3. Mix flour, baking powder, cinnamon, and salt. Fold flour mixture into butter mixture, alternating with milk. Stir in nuts.
4. Pour batter into a greased and floured 8-inch square pan.
5. Bake at 350°F 30 minutes, or until done.
6. Remove cake from oven, cool, and cut into diamonds while in the pan.
7. Pour syrup over cake. Cool. Refrigerate and let soak 24 hours before serving.
2 TO 3 DOZEN SERVINGS

Plum Cake

2⅓ cups all-purpose flour
2½ teaspoons baking powder
¾ teaspoon salt
1 cup sugar (reserve ¼ cup)
½ cup shortening
¾ cup milk
2 eggs
2 tablespoons fine dry bread crumbs
40 fresh plums (prune, Damson, or greengage), pitted and cut in half; or use 2 cans (30 ounces) whole purple plums, drained and pitted
3 tablespoons butter, cut in pieces
¼ teaspoon cloves

1. Combine flour, baking powder, salt, and ¾ cup sugar in a large mixing bowl. Add shortening, milk, and eggs. Beat at medium speed 4 minutes.
2. Grease bottom and sides of a 13x9x2-inch pan. Coat with bread crumbs.
3. Turn batter into prepared pan. Place plums on top, pushing one edge of each half down ¼ inch into batter. Dot with butter.
4. Combine remaining ¼ cup sugar and cloves; mix well. Sprinkle over plums.
5. Bake at 350°F about 40 minutes.
6. To serve, cut into pieces.
ABOUT 32 SERVINGS

Apple Cake: Prepare Plum Cake as directed, substituting 4 large apples, pared and thinly sliced, for the plums.

Pecan Snails

2 cups (about 7½ ounces) small pecan halves
1 cup milk or cream
1 package active dry yeast
¼ cup warm water, 105°F to 115°F (Or if using compressed yeast, soften 1 cake in ¼ cup lukewarm water, 80°F to 85°.)
½ cup sugar
1 teaspoon salt

5 cups sifted all-purpose flour
2 eggs, well beaten
½ cup butter, softened
⅔ cup butter
1 cup firmly packed brown sugar
¼ cup currants (omit, if desired)
1 tablespoon cinnamon

1. Twenty-four 2½-inch muffin-pan wells will be needed.
2. Coarsely chop 1 cup of the pecans, and set them all aside.
3. Scald milk or cream.
4. Meanwhile, soften the dry yeast in warm water. Set aside.
5. Put sugar and salt into a large bowl. Pour scalded milk over ingredients in bowl. Stir until sugar is dissolved. When mixture is lukewarm, blend in 1 cup sifted all-purpose flour, beating until smooth. Stir softened yeast and add, mixing well.
6. Measure 4 cups sifted all-purpose flour. Add about one-half of the flour to yeast mixture and beat until very smooth.
7. Beat in eggs. Vigorously beat in the ½ cup softened butter, 2 to 3 tablespoons at a time. Beat in enough remaining flour to make a soft dough. Turn dough onto lightly floured surface. Let stand 5 to 10 minutes.
8. Knead dough and form into a large ball; place it in a greased deep bowl. Turn dough to bring greased surface to top. Cover with waxed paper and towel and let stand in warm place (about 80°F) until doubled.
9. Punch down with fist; pull edges of dough in to center and turn completely over in bowl. Cover with waxed paper

and towel and let rise again until nearly doubled.

10. Lightly grease muffin-pan wells.

11. Meanwhile melt ⅔ cup butter. Put about 1 teaspoon of melted butter in bottom of each muffin-pan well. Reserve remaining butter for Pecan Snails.

12. Mix together brown sugar, currants, and cinnamon with the chopped nuts. Sprinkle 2 teaspoons of this mixture over butter in each muffin-pan well. Gently press 3 or 4 pecan halves onto mixture in each well.

13. Again punch down dough and form it into two balls. Roll each ball on lightly floured surface into a rectangle ¼ to ⅓ inch thick 6 to 8 inches wide and 12 inches long. Brush top surface of dough with remaining melted butter and sprinkle evenly with remainder of brown-sugar mixture. Beginning with longer side of rectangle, roll dough tightly into a long roll. Press edges together to seal. Cut each roll into 12 slices. Place one slice in each muffin pan well, cut side down. Cover muffin pans with waxed paper and towel and let dough rise until doubled.

14. Bake at 375°F 15 to 20 minutes. Invert muffin pans on cooling racks, leaving rolls in pan 1 minute. Remove rolls from pans and cool on cooling racks, glazed side up.

2 DOZEN PECAN SNAILS

Country Cheese Cake

Dough:
1¾ cups all-purpose flour
½ cup confectioners' sugar
¾ teaspoon baking pow-
  der
¼ teaspoon salt
¼ cup butter or margarine
3 egg yolks
3 tablespoons sour cream

Filling:
4 eggs
1 egg white
¾ cup sugar
1½ pounds farmer or pot
  cheese or ricotta
½ cup dairy sour cream
2 tablespoons grated orange
  peel
1 teaspoon vanilla extract

1. For dough, combine flour, sugar, baking powder, and salt in a bowl. With pastry blender, cut butter into flour mixture until coarse and crumbly.

2. Beat egg yolks into sour cream. Stir into flour mixture. Knead in bowl until dough is well mixed and holds its shape.

3. Refrigerate dough until easy to roll out, at least 1 hour.

4. Roll out dough on a floured surface to fit a 13x9x2-inch pan, about a 15x11-inch rectangle.

5. Line bottom of pan, fitting dough so it comes about ⅔ of the way up sides of pan.

6. For filling, beat eggs and egg white at high speed of electric mixer until thick. Gradually add sugar, beating at high speed until stiff, not dry, peaks form.

7. Press cheese through a sieve. Fold into beaten egg mixture. Add remaining ingredients. Mix gently but thoroughly. Turn filling into dough-lined pan.

8. Bake at 350°F about 40 minutes, or until set.

9. Cool before cutting into squares.

ABOUT 16 SERVINGS

Pasta Flora

½ cup unsalted butter (at
  room temperature)
2 eggs
1 teaspoon vanilla extract
1 cup sugar
3 cups all-purpose flour
1 tablespoon baking powder
1 pint jam or preserves
1 egg yolk, beaten with ½
  teaspoon water

1. Beat butter 4 minutes, using an electric mixer. Add eggs, vanilla extract, and sugar. Beat until fluffy. Mix flour and baking powder. Slowly work into mixture until well blended.

2. Divide dough into 2 parts; one a ball using three fourths of the total, and one using one fourth of the total.

3. Line the bottom of a 13x9-inch baking pan with the larger portion of the dough. Spread the preserves evenly over dough.

4. Roll the remaining quarter of the dough on a lightly floured board to fit the size of the pan. Cut into strips. Form a lattice over the preserves. Brush dough with the egg yolk and water.

5. Bake at 350°F about 45 minutes until pastry is golden brown or a wooden pick comes out clean when inserted. Cool. Cut into squares.

10 SERVINGS

Grandmother's Cheese Cake

Dough:
1¼ cups all-purpose flour
¾ teaspoon baking powder
¼ teaspoon salt
¼ cup butter or margarine
1 egg
3 tablespoons sour cream
⅓ cup confectioners' sugar

Filling:
6 eggs
2 cups confectioners' sugar

1½ teaspoons vanilla extract
1 pound farmer cheese or
  ricotta
⅔ cup melted butter
1½ cups unseasoned mashed
  potatoes
2 teaspoons baking powder
½ teaspoon nutmeg
½ teaspoon salt
¼ cup grated orange or
  lemon peel

1. For dough, combine flour, baking powder, and salt in a bowl. Cut in butter with a pastry blender.

2. Beat egg into sour cream. Stir into flour mixture. Stir in sugar. Knead dough until well mixed and smooth.

3. Roll dough on a floured surface into a rectangle. Line a 13x9x2-inch pan with dough, and bring dough part way up sides.

4. For filling, separate 1 egg and reserve the white. Beat remaining yolk and whole eggs with the sugar 5 minutes at high speed of electric mixer. Add vanilla extract. Beat at high speed until mixture piles softly.

5. Press cheese through a sieve. Blend cheese with butter; add potatoes, baking powder, nutmeg, and salt. Stir in orange peel. Fold into egg mixture. Turn into prepared crust in pan.

6. Bake at 350°F about 45 minutes, or until set. Cool.

7. Cool well before cutting.

ABOUT 32 PIECES

Delicate White Cake

2¾ cups sifted cake flour
1 tablespoon baking powder
¾ teaspoon salt
1 cup vegetable shortening
1½ teaspoons vanilla extract
1½ cups sugar

1 cup milk
8 egg whites
½ cup sugar
Rich Coconut Fruit Filling, below

1. Sift flour, baking powder, and salt together.
2. Cream shortening with the extract and the 1½ cups sugar, beating until mixture is fluffy.
3. Beating only until smooth after each addition, alternately add flour mixture and milk.
4. In a large bowl, beat egg whites until frothy; beating constantly, add remaining sugar gradually and continue beating until stiff shiny peaks are formed. Fold into cake batter.
5. Turn batter into three 9-inch layer cake pans which have been lined on bottoms with waxed paper.
6. Bake at 350°F 20 to 25 minutes, or until cake tests done.
7. Cool in pans 10 minutes before removing to wire racks to cool thoroughly. Spread the filling between and on top of cake layers. Store overnight or about 8 hours in a cool place before serving.
ONE 9-INCH 3-LAYER CAKE

Rich Coconut Fruit Filling

8 egg yolks, slightly beaten
1 cup sugar
½ cup butter (at room temperature)
⅓ cup bourbon
1⅓ cups flaked coconut

1 cup coarsely chopped pecans
¾ cup quartered candied cherries
¾ cup coarsely chopped seeded raisins

1. In a medium-sized saucepan combine the egg yolks, sugar, and butter. Cook over medium heat stirring constantly until sugar is dissolved and mixture is slightly thickened, 5 to 7 minutes.
2. Remove from heat and turn into a bowl. Cool slightly. Blend in the bourbon thoroughly.
3. Stir in the remaining ingredients. Cool thoroughly at room temperature before spreading on cooled cake layers.
3½ CUPS FILLING

Note: **2 tablespoons brandy flavoring** and **2 tablespoons water** may be substituted for the bourbon.

Delicate White Cake

Cross Cake

1 cup butter or margarine
1½ cups sugar
4 eggs
1 teaspoon vanilla extract
½ teaspoon salt
4 cups sifted cake flour

4 teaspoons baking powder
1⅓ cups milk
Basic Butter Frosting (below)
Butter Cream Decorating Frosting (see below)

1. Beat butter until softened. Gradually add sugar, creaming until fluffy. Add eggs, one at a time, beating thoroughly after each. Add vanilla extract and salt; beat well.
2. Mix flour with baking powder; alternately add with milk to creamed mixture, beating thoroughly after each addition.
3. Turn into a greased and floured 13x9x2-inch baking pan and spread evenly to edges.
4. Bake at 350°F about 45 minutes, or until top springs back when lightly touched.
5. Cool in pan on rack 5 minutes. Turn out onto rack; cool completely.
6. Cut out 3-inch squares from the two top corners of cake.
7. Cut out 6x2-inch rectangles from the two corners of the lower section of cake, leaving the cake in the form of a cross. Frost and decorate as desired.
1 CROSS CAKE

Basic Butter Frosting

6 tablespoons butter or margarine
1½ teaspoons vanilla extract

3 cups confectioners' sugar
1½ tablespoons milk or cream

1. Cream butter with vanilla extract. Add confectioners' sugar gradually, beating thoroughly after each addition.
2. Stir in milk and beat until frosting is of spreading consistency.
ABOUT 2 CUPS

Lemon Butter Frosting: Follow recipe for Basic Butter Frosting. Substitute **lemon juice** for milk and add **1½ teaspoons grated lemon peel.** If desired, add a few drops yellow food coloring.

Orange Butter Frosting: Follow recipe for Basic Butter Frosting. Substitute **1½ teaspoons grated orange peel** for the vanilla extract and **1½ to 2½ tablespoons orange juice** for the milk. If a deeper orange color is desired, mix 4 drops red food coloring and 3 drops yellow food coloring with orange juice.

Butter Cream Decorating Frosting

½ cup all-purpose shortening
¼ cup butter or margarine
1 teaspoon lemon extract

3 cups sifted confectioners' sugar

Beat shortening, margarine, and lemon extract together in an electric mixer bowl. Gradually beat in confectioners' sugar until frosting will hold the shape of a tube design.
ABOUT 2 CUPS

Basic Yeast Dough

2 cups milk
2 packages active dry yeast
½ cup warm water, 105°F to 115°F. (Or if using compressed yeast, soften 2 cakes in ½ cup lukewarm water, 80°F to 85°F.)
1 cup butter, softened
½ cup sugar
2 teaspoons salt
2 teaspoons grated lemon peel
9 to 10 cups sifted all-purpose flour
4 eggs, well beaten

1. Scald the 2 cups milk. Meanwhile, soften the 2 packages active dry yeast in ½ cup warm water. Set aside.
2. Put the butter, sugar, salt and grated lemon peel into a large bowl.
3. Immediately pour scalded milk over ingredients in bowl and stir mixture until butter is completely melted. When mixture has cooled to lukewarm, blend in the 2 cups sifted all-purpose flour, beating until smooth.
4. Stir softened yeast and add, mixing well.
5. Measure 7 to 8 cups sifted all-purpose flour. Add about one-half of the flour to the dough and beat until very smooth.
6. Add in thirds, beating well after each addition 4 eggs, well beaten. Then beat in enough of the remaining flour to make a soft dough. Turn dough onto a lightly floured surface and allow it to rest 5 to 10 minutes.
7. Knead dough. Form dough into a large smooth ball and place it in a lightly greased, deep bowl. Turn dough to bring greased surface to top.* Cover with waxed paper and towel; let stand in warm place (about 80°F) until dough is doubled, about 1½ hours.
8. Punch down dough with fist and turn out onto a lightly floured surface. Allow dough to rest 10 minutes before shaping.
9. Complete as directed in any of the following variations.
ENOUGH DOUGH FOR 4 COFFEE CAKES OR 4 DOZEN ROLLS

*This dough may be kept about 3 days in the refrigerator. Make sure dough is greased and well covered to keep surface of dough moist and elastic. Punch down dough occasionally as it rises. Remove amount of dough needed for a single baking and immediately return remainder to refrigerator. Proceed as directed in the desired variation.

Note: For bread, shape dough into 3 loaves. Place in greased 9x5x3-inch loaf pans. When dough is light, bake at 400°F about 50 minutes.

Apple Kuchen: To prepare 2 coffee cakes, use one-half of dough in basic recipe. Lightly grease two 9- or 10-inch square pans. Melt **¼ cup butter;** set aside. Wash, quarter, pare, core and thickly slice **4 cooking apples.** Divide dough in half and evenly press each half into pan. Press apple slices, rounded edges up, into dough forming three rows. Sprinkle each evenly with one half of a mixture of **½ cup sugar** and **½ teaspoon cinnamon** and drizzle with 2 tablespoons melted butter. Let rise in a warm place until doubled. Bake at 350°F 40 to 50 minutes, or until apples are tender and top is well browned. Remove coffee cakes from pans to cooling racks.

Filled Baba

Baba:
2 cups butter or margarine
  (at room temperature)
1 cup sugar
2 eggs
3 egg whites
2½ cups all-purpose flour

Custard:
3 egg yolks
¾ cup whipping cream
¾ cup sugar
¼ teaspoon salt

1. For baba, beat butter at high speed. Gradually add sugar, creaming until fluffy.
2. Beat in whole eggs and 2 egg whites. Stir in flour; mix well.
3. For custard, combine egg yolks, cream, sugar, and salt in the top of a double boiler or in a heavy saucepan. Cook and stir until custard is thickened. Set aside to cool a few minutes.
4. Generously grease muffin-pan wells; coat with fine dry bread crumbs. Line each with 1 tablespoon dough. Spoon in 2 tablespoons custard. Top with more dough.
5. Beat reserved egg white just until foamy. Brush top of each baba.
6. Bake at 350°F 20 to 25 minutes.
ABOUT 1½ DOZEN BABAS

Cream-Filled Chestnut Cake

1 pound chestnuts in the
  shell; or use 1¼ cups
  pecans, chopped
¾ cup butter
1 cup sugar
½ teaspoon vanilla extract

6 eggs, separated
1¼ cups all-purpose flour
1 teaspoon baking powder
½ cup milk
Chestnut Cream

1. Prepare chestnuts (see Note).
2. Cream butter with sugar and vanilla extract until fluffy. Mixing well after each addition, add the chestnut purée, then the egg yolks, one at a time.
3. Mix flour with baking powder, and add alternately with milk to the chestnut mixture, mixing well after each addition. Beat egg whites until stiff, but not dry. Fold into batter.
4. Turn mixture into 2 greased and floured 9-inch round layer cake pans.
5. Bake at 350°F about 25 minutes, or until done.
6. Let cool, then put layers together and decorate cake with chestnut cream.
ONE 9-INCH LAYER CAKE

Note: To prepare chestnuts, rinse chestnuts and make a slit on two sides of each shell. Put into a saucepan; cover with boiling water and boil about 20 minutes. Remove shells and skins; return chestnuts to saucepan and cover with boiling salted water. Cover and simmer until chestnuts are tender (10 to 20 minutes). Drain and finely chop.

Chestnut Cream: Prepare **¾ pound chestnuts** in the shell (see Note above); or use **1 cup pecans,** chopped. Whip **1 cup whipping cream** until thickened. Mix in ⅔ cup confectioners' sugar and ½ **teaspoon vanilla extract,** then chestnuts.

Haitian Upside-down Cake

Topping:
6 tablespoons butter, melted
½ cup firmly packed dark
  brown sugar
¼ cup light corn syrup
1 cup chopped pistachios or
  peanuts

Cake:
4 ounces (4 squares)

unsweetened chocolate
6 tablespoons butter
1¼ cups sugar
2 egg yolks
1 teaspoon vanilla extract
2 cups all-purpose flour
1 tablespoon baking powder
1½ cups milk
2 egg whites, beaten stiff, but
  not dry

1. For topping, blend butter, brown sugar, and corn syrup, then add nuts and mix well.
2. Spread nut mixture over bottom of a greased 13x9-inch baking pan.
3. For cake, melt chocolate over hot, not boiling, water.
4. Cream butter with sugar thoroughly. Beat in egg yolks, vanilla extract, and melted chocolate.
5. Sift flour with baking powder. Alternately add flour mixture with milk to the chocolate mixture, beating until blended after each addition. Fold in beaten egg white. Turn batter into pan over nut mixture.
6. Bake at 350°F about 45 minutes. Invert on a board or platter. If necessary, spread nut mixture evenly over the cake. Cool; serve cut in squares.
ONE 13x9-INCH CAKE

Pecan Cake

¾ cup cake flour
1 teaspoon baking powder
3 eggs, separated
⅔ cup sugar
1 tablespoon lemon juice
½ cup finely grated pecans
  (use blender or fine knife of

vegetable grater to get nuts
  very fine)
½ cup butter or margarine,
  melted
Pinch salt
Orange Glaze
Pecan halves for decoration

1. Blend flour and baking powder.
2. Beat egg yolks until thick and lemon colored in large bowl of electric mixer. Gradually beat in sugar. Beat in lemon juice and grated pecans, then gradually beat in flour mixture. Slowly beat in melted butter.
3. Beat egg whites with salt until stiff peaks form. Fold beaten egg whites into batter.
4. Pour batter into a greased and floured 9-inch round cake pan.
5. Bake at 350°F 30 to 35 minutes, or until cake tester inserted in center comes out clean.
6. Let cake cool 10 minutes before removing from pan. Cool completely on a wire rack, right side up.
7. Place cake on a serving plate and cover with hot orange glaze. Decorate with pecans halves.
6 TO 8 SERVINGS

Orange Glaze: Combine ½ **cup orange marmalade** and ¼ **cup sugar** in a small saucepan and cook until sugar is dissolved (2 to 3 minutes), stirring constantly. Use while still hot.

Chocolate Checkerboard Cake

2½ ounces (2½ squares) unsweetened chocolate
¾ cup butter
1 tablespoon vanilla extract
1½ cups sugar
3 cups sifted cake flour
1 tablespoon baking powder
¾ teaspoon salt
1 cup plus 2 tablespoons milk
3 tablespoons hot water
1½ tablespoons sugar
¾ teaspoon baking soda
4 egg whites
1 jar (16 ounces) apricot preserves, puréed in blender (or substitute raspberry jam, pressed through a sieve to remove seeds)
Chocolate Fudge Frosting

1. Melt chocolate in top of a double boiler.
2. Meanwhile, cream butter with vanilla extract and 1½ cups sugar in a bowl. Mix flour, baking powder, and salt; add alternately with milk to the creamed mixture, beating until blended. Spoon a little more than half of batter into a separate bowl. Set aside.
3. To batter in first bowl, add melted chocolate, hot water, remaining 1½ tablespoon sugar, and baking soda; mix well. (See Note.)
4. Beat egg whites until peaks are stiff, but not dry. Fold half into chocolate batter and half into white batter.
5. Divide chocolate batter evenly between 2 greased 8-inch round layer cake or square baking pans; then divide white batter between 2 greased 8-inch round layer cake or square baking pans.*
6. Bake at 350°F about 20 minutes, or until cake tests done. Cool 5 minutes in pans, then turn layers out on wire racks to cool. Assemble as directed below, putting sections and layers together with puréed jam. Refrigerate assembled cake until chilled, then frost with Chocolate Fudge Frosting.
ONE 4-LAYER 8-INCH CAKE

Note: If you have only 2 pans of either shape or size, bake the dark layers first, then empty the pans and bake the white layers. Remember, though, that beaten egg whites fall if left standing, so divide unbeaten whites in half. Beat first half, add to chocolate batter, and bake; when ready to bake white layers, beat second half of egg whites, fold into white batter, and bake as directed.

TO ASSEMBLE CHECKERBOARD CAKE

1. Depending on the size and shape of the cake baked, bake squares or circles on tracing paper and cut out shapes; then use them to make cardboard patterns.

2. Lay the large of the cardboard patterns (large square or circle) on each of the four layers (see illustration) and use a serrated knife to cut around it carefully. Remove these middle sections from each layer.

3. Lay the smaller of the cardboard patterns (small square or circle) on each middle section (the one just removed) and cut around it carefully; then remove all these center sections (see illustration).

4. There should be four outer borders, four middle pieces, and four center pieces. Set one dark border on a cake plate and spread cut surfaces with jam. Set middle section in place and spread cut surfaces with jam. Then set dark center section in place. Paint top of layer with jam. (See illustration.)

5. Set one light border on top of assembled layer and paint cut surfaces with jam. Insert dark middle section, paint with jam as before, and set light center in place. Cover this layer with jam, also. Repeat with remaining layers, using dark border for third layer and light border for top. Coat top of cake with a layer of jam.

*Four thin 8-inch round layers bake in the same length of time as 4 slightly thinner square layers. Or, if desired, you might bake the cake in 6 round layers for an elaborate checkerboard effect. Square layers are too thin to bake in 6 layers unless batter is increased.

Chocolate Fudge Frosting

3 ounces (3 squares) unsweetened chocolate, cut in pieces
2 cups sugar

⅔ cup milk
⅓ cup butter or margarine
4 teaspoons light corn syrup
2 teaspoons vanilla extract

1. Combine all ingredients except vanilla extract in a heavy 3-quart saucepan. Heat slowly, stirring until sugar is dissolved. Bring rapidly to boiling.

2. Set candy thermometer in place and cook, stirring occasionally, to 234°F (soft-ball stage; remove from heat while testing). Using a pastry brush dipped in water, wash down the crystals from sides of saucepan from time to time during cooking.

3. Remove from heat and cool to 110°F without stirring or jarring. Then mix in vanilla extract. Beat until of spreading consistency.

ABOUT 2 CUPS FROSTING

Zuppa Inglese

Italian Sponge Cake
½ cup rum
2 tablespoons cold water
Pineapple Cream Filling
(opposite)
Chocolate Cream Filling
chilled (opposite)
Whipped Cream (opposite)
Candied cherries

1. Trim corners of each of the sponge cake layers to form ovals. Save all pieces trimmed from cake. Place one layer on a platter; set other two aside.
2. Combine rum and water. Sprinkle a third of rum mixture over first cake layer and spread with desired amount of Pineapple Cream Filling. Top with second layer, sprinkle with half the remaining rum mixture, and spread with desired amount of Chocolate Cream Filling.
3. Place third layer on cake with waxed paper and chill several hours.
4. Make a square, diamond, or heart shape from leftover pieces of cake. Place on top of cake and frost cake with Whipped Cream. If desired, decorate with Whipped Cream using a No. 27 star decorating tip. Garnish with candied cherries.
5. Store dessert in refrigerator until ready to serve.
16 TO 20 SERVINGS

Italian Sponge Cake

5 egg yolks
½ cup sugar
2 tablespoons lemon juice
1 teaspoon grated lemon
  peel
1 teaspoon vanilla extract
½ teaspoon salt
5 egg whites
½ cup sugar
1 cup sifted cake flour

1. Combine egg yolks, ½ cup sugar, lemon juice, lemon peel, and vanilla extract. Beat 3 to 4 minutes with an electric mixer on medium-high speed; set aside.
2. Add salt to egg whites and beat until frothy. Gradually add ½ cup sugar, beating constantly until stiff peaks are formed.
3. Gently fold egg yolk mixture into beaten egg whites. Sift flour over the egg mixture, ¼ cup at a time, gently folding until just blended after each addition. Turn batter into a 9-inch tube pan (see Note).
4. Bake at 325°F 60 to 65 minutes, or until cake springs back when lightly touched or when a cake tester or wooden pick inserted comes out clean.
5. Invert and leave cake in pan until completely cooled.
ONE 9-INCH TUBE CAKE

Note: For Zuppa Inglese, pour batter into three 11x7x1½-inch baking pans. Bake at 325°F 30 to 35 minutes.

Pineapple Cream Filling

½ cup sugar
2 tablespoons cornstarch
⅛ teaspoon salt
½ cup cold milk
1½ cups milk, scalded
3 eggs, slightly beaten
1 can (20 ounces) crushed
  pineapple, drained
1 teaspoon vanilla extract

1. Combine sugar, cornstarch, and salt in a saucepan. Gradually add cold milk, stirring well. Slowly stir in the scalded milk.
2. Stirring gently and constantly, rapidly bring mixture to boiling over direct heat and cook 3 minutes. Pour into top of double boiler and place over simmering water. Cover and cook about 12 minutes, stirring three or four times.
3. Vigorously stir about 3 tablespoons hot mixture into the eggs. Immediately blend into mixture in double boiler. Cook over simmering water 3 to 5 minutes. Stir slowly so mixture cooks evenly. Remove from heat and cool.
4. Stir in pineapple and vanilla extract. Chill.
ABOUT 4 CUPS FILLING

Chocolate Cream Filling: Follow recipe for Pineapple Cream Filling. Add **1½ ounces (1½ squares) unsweetened chocolate** to milk before scalding. Beat smooth with a rotary beater. Increase sugar to ⅔ cup and omit the pineapple.
ABOUT 2½ CUPS FILLING

Whipped Cream

2 cups chilled whipping
  cream
6 tablespoons confectioners'
sugar
2 teaspoons vanilla extract

1. Beat whipping cream, 1 cup at a time, in a chilled 1-quart bowl using chilled beaters. Beat until cream stands in peaks.
2. Put whipped cream into a large chilled bowl. Fold or beat confectioners' sugar and vanilla extract into whipped cream until blended.
4 CUPS WHIPPED CREAM

Lamb Cake

2 cups sifted cake flour
¾ teaspoon baking powder
¼ teaspoon salt
¼ teaspoon mace
1 cup butter or margarine
1 cup plus 2 tablespoons
  sugar
2 teaspoons grated lemon
  peel
1½ teaspoons vanilla extract
½ teaspoon almond extract
4 eggs
1 tablespoon flour
2 tablespoons shortening
Seven-Minute Frosting (page
  577)
Shredded coconut

1. Sift together cake flour, baking powder, salt, and mace.
2. Cream butter. Gradually add sugar, creaming until fluffy. Add lemon peel and extracts.
3. Alternately beat in eggs and flour mixture.
4. Blend 1 tablespoon flour into shortening. Brush over both inside sections of a lamb mold.
5. Turn batter into face side of mold, filling it level. Spoon a small amount of batter into back side of mold, filling ears. Close and lock mold. Set on baking sheet.
6. Bake at 375°F 50 to 55 minutes.
7. Set mold on wire rack to cool 5 minutes. Remove back side. Cool 5 minutes longer. Turn out on rack to cool completely.
8. Frost with Seven-Minute Frosting. Coat with coconut.
1 LAMB CAKE

Easter Cheese Cake

Dough for Grandmother's
Cheese Cake (page 509)

Cheese Filling:
6 eggs
2¼ cups confectioners' sugar
1½ pounds farmer cheese or
ricotta
⅔ cup butter or margarine
(at room temperature)
½ teaspoon salt

1½ teaspoons vanilla extract
2 teaspoons grated lemon
peel
¼ cup finely chopped can-
died orange peel
⅓ cup raisins

Spread:
¾ cup thick raspberry jam or
strawberry preserves

1. Prepare dough for crust; line pan.
2. Beat eggs at high speed until thickened. Slowly beat in sugar, beating until mixture piles softly.
3. Press cheese through a sieve. Beat cheese with butter, salt, vanilla extract, and lemon peel.
4. Fold eggs into cheese mixture. Stir in orange peel and raisins.
5. Spread jam over bottom of prepared crust in pan.
6. Turn cheese mixture into pan.
7. Bake at 325°F 45 minutes to 1 hour or until a knife inserted near center comes out clean.
8. Cool well before cutting.
32 PIECES

Sherried Almond Torte

4 eggs, separated
½ cup sugar
1 cup sifted all-purpose flour
1 teaspoon baking powder
¼ teaspoon salt
⅓ cup melted butter or
margarine, cooled
1 teaspoon vanilla extract
½ teaspoon almond extract

(optional)

Sauce and Topping:
2 cups sugar
2 cups water
½ cup sherry
¾ cup toasted slivered
almonds

1. Beat egg whites until foamy; gradually add 4 tablespoons of the sugar and continue beating until soft peaks form.
2. Beat egg yolks with remaining 4 tablespoons of sugar. Gradually fold beaten yolks into beaten whites.
3. Sift flour, baking powder, and salt together. Sprinkle over egg mixture about ¼ cup at a time and fold in gently. Fold in butter, vanilla extract, and almond extract (if used).
4. Pour into a greased 9-inch square baking pan.
5. Bake at 375°F about 30 minutes, or until golden brown. Remove from oven and pierce all over with a long-handled kitchen fork or ice pick, making holes through to bottom.
6. Meanwhile, prepare sauce. Combine sugar and water in a saucepan and boil over low heat, stirring occasionally, to soft ball stage (234°F). Stir in sherry. Pour hot sauce over hot cake, sprinkle entire top with almonds as last third of sauce is poured over top. Let stand in baking pan until thoroughly cooled. Serve from pan, or remove to a serving plate.
8 TO 10 SERVINGS

Chocolate Pound Cake Loaf

3 cups sifted enriched all-
purpose flour
2 teaspoons baking powder
¼ teaspoon salt
½ cup cocoa, sifted
1 cup butter or margarine

½ cup lard
1 tablespoon vanilla extract
½ teaspoon almond extract
3 cups sugar
1 cup eggs (5 or 6)
1¼ cups milk

1. Lightly grease (bottom only) two 9x5x3-inch loaf pans. Line bottoms with waxed paper; grease paper. Set aside.
2. Combine flour, baking powder, salt, and cocoa and blend thoroughly. Set aside.
3. Cream butter and lard with extracts in a large bowl. Add sugar gradually, creaming thoroughly after each addition. Add eggs, one at a time, beating until fluffy after each addition.
4. Beating only until blended after each addition, alternately add dry ingredients in fourths and milk in thirds to creamed mixture.
5. Turn equal amounts of batter into prepared loaf pans. Spread batter evenly. (Top of baked cakes may have a slight crack down center.) Place pans on center of oven rack so that top of batter will be at center of oven.
6. Bake at 325°F about 65 minutes, or until cake tester inserted in center comes out clean.
7. Cool cakes in pans 15 minutes on wire racks. Loosen sides with a spatula and turn onto rack. Peel off paper, turn right side up, and cool completely.
TWO LOAF CAKES

Dutch Cocoa Loaf Cake: Follow directions for Chocolate Pound Cake Loaf except substitute **⅔ cup Dutch process cocoa** for the ½ cup cocoa and increase butter or margarine to 1½ cups; omit lard.

Citrus Bundt Cake

¾ cup butter
2 teaspoons grated lemon
peel
2 teaspoons grated orange
peel
1¾ cups sugar
3 eggs
3⅓ cups sifted enriched all-

purpose flour
1 tablespoon baking powder
½ teaspoon salt
1 cup milk
2 tablespoons lemon juice
2 tablespoons orange juice
⅓ cup sugar
Fruit sauce (optional)

1. Cream butter, grated peels, and 1¾ cups sugar until light and fluffy. Add eggs, one at a time, beating thoroughly after each addition.
2. Blend flour, baking powder, and salt. Mix into creamed mixture alternately with milk. Turn into a generously buttered 10-inch Bundt pan or angel food cake pan.
3. Bake at 325°F 60 to 75 minutes, or until a cake tester comes out clean. Remove from pan immediately and place on wire rack set over a shallow pan.
4. Combine fruit juices and ⅓ cup sugar in a small saucepan. Bring to boiling and boil 3 minutes. Drizzle over warm cake; cool completely before serving.
5. Slice and serve with a fruit sauce, if desired.
ONE 10-INCH BUNDT CAKE

Sherry-Coconut Chiffon Cake

Sherry-Coconut Chiffon Cake

2 cups sifted all-purpose flour	¼ cup California Sherry or Muscatel
1-1½ cups sugar	2 teaspoons vanilla extract
1 tablespoon baking powder	½ cup flaked coconut
1 teaspoon salt	1 cup egg whites (7 or 8)
⅔ cup cooking oil	½ teaspoon cream of tartar
2 egg yolks	Confectioners' sugar (optional)
½ cup water	

1. Sift flour, 1 cup sugar, baking powder, and salt into a bowl. Make a well and add, in order, oil, egg yolks, water, sherry, and vanilla extract. Beat to a smooth batter. Mix in coconut.
2. Pour egg whites into a very large mixing bowl. Sprinkle cream of tartar over egg whites. Whip until soft peaks are formed. Add remaining ½ cup sugar gradually, beating until very stiff peaks are formed. Do not underbeat (whites should be stiffer than for angel food cake or meringue).
3. Pour batter slowly over whites, gently folding with rubber spatula or large spoon just until blended.
4. Turn immediately into an ungreased 10x4-inch tube pan.
5. Bake at 325°F 1 hour and 10 minutes, or until top surface springs back when lightly touched with finger and cracks look dry.
6. Remove from oven and turn upside down. Cool completely in pan.
7. Loosen cake from sides and center tube. Turn pan over and hit edge sharply on table to loosen.
8. Put cake on a serving plate. If desired, sift confectioners' sugar over top.
ONE 10-INCH TUBE CAKE

Baba with Raisins

1 cup butter or margarine (at room temperature)	1½ cups all-purpose flour
1½ cups confectioners' sugar	1 cup cornstarch
4 eggs, separated	⅓ cup confectioners' sugar
¼ cup orange juice	½ teaspoon salt
4 teaspoons lemon juice	½ cup raisins
1 tablespoon grated orange or lemon peel	Fine dry bread crumbs
4 teaspoons baking powder	1 tablespoon whipping cream (optional)

1. Cream butter. Gradually add 1½ cups confectioners' sugar, beating at high speed of electric mixer. Beat in egg yolks, one at a time. Beat in orange juice, lemon juice, and orange peel.
2. Mix flour, cornstarch, and ⅓ cup confectioners' sugar.
3. With clean beaters, beat egg whites with salt until stiff, not dry, peaks form.
4. Fold half the flour mixture into the butter mixture. Fold in egg whites.
5. Add raisins to remaining flour mixture; mix well. Fold into batter.
6. Generously grease an 11-cup ring mold or baba pan. Coat with bread crumbs.
7. Turn batter into prepared pan. Brush top with cream.
8. Bake at 350°F about 40 minutes.
1 BABA

Cranberry Upside-Down Cake

Topping:	Cake:
¼ cup butter or margarine	1½ cups sifted enriched cake flour
⅔ cup sugar	2 teaspoons baking powder
1 tablespoon grated orange peel	½ teaspoon salt
½ teaspoon vanilla extract	½ cup butter or margarine
2 cups fresh cranberries, washed and coarsely chopped	1 teaspoon vanilla extract
⅓ cup sugar	½ cup sugar
	1 egg
	½ cup milk

1. For topping heat butter in a saucepan. Add ⅔ cup sugar, orange peel, and vanilla extract; blend thoroughly. Spread mixture evenly in an 8x8x2-inch pan.
2. Combine cranberries and ⅓ cup sugar. Spread over mixture in pan; set aside.
3. For cake, blend flour, baking powder, and salt; set aside.
4. Cream butter with vanilla extract. Add sugar gradually, creaming until fluffy after each addition. Add egg and beat thoroughly.
5. Beating only until smooth after each addition, alternately add dry ingredients in thirds and milk in halves to creamed mixture. Turn batter over cranberry mixture and spread evenly.
6. Bake at 350°F about 50 minutes.
7. Remove from oven and let stand 1 to 2 minutes in pan on wire rack. To remove from pan, run spatula gently around sides. Cover with a serving plate and invert; allow pan to remain over cake 1 or 2 minutes. Lift pan off. Serve cake warm or cool.
ONE 8-INCH SQUARE CAKE

Cream-Filled Walnut Torte

1½ cups walnuts
¾ cup superfine sugar
¾ cup sifted cake flour
9 egg whites
1 teaspoon cream of tartar
½ teaspoon salt
1½ cups superfine sugar
1½ teaspoons vanilla extract

1 package (about 3½ ounces) lemon pie filling
2 teaspoons grated orange peel
1¾ cups liquid (juice of 1 large orange plus water)
2 egg yolks, slightly beaten
1 cup heavy cream, chilled

1. Set out and grease three 8-inch layer cake pans; line bottoms with circles of waxed paper, foil, or greased brown paper.
2. Grate walnuts and combine in a bowl with ¾ cup superfine sugar, and sifted cake flour. Mix thoroughly and set aside.
3. Combine egg whites, cream of tartar and ½ teaspoon salt, beating until foamy. Beating constantly, add gradually 1½ cups superfine sugar. Continue beating until stiff peaks are formed. Add 1½ teaspoons vanilla extract. Fold in the walnut mixture, mixing gently until blended. Divide batter equally in the prepared pans; spread evenly.
4. Bake in a 325°F oven 40 minutes. Remove from oven to cooling racks. When cool, loosen sides of cake layers with spatula and remove from pans. Peel off waxed paper immediately.
5. Combine lemon pie filling, grated orange peel, and 1¾ cups liquid in a heavy saucepan. Blend thoroughly and stir in egg yolks. Cook and stir over medium heat until mixture comes to a full boil. Cover and set aside to cool.
6. Beat heavy cream until soft peaks are formed. Fold into cooled filling. Spread the filling evenly on top of each and stack layers. Refrigerate several hours before serving.

ONE 9-INCH TORTE

Note: If desired, decorate torte with Meringue Mushrooms. To prepare, remove about ⅔ cup of the meringue before folding in the walnut-flour mixture in the torte. Cover a baking sheet with foil and spoon 6 rounds about 1¼ inches in diameter on the foil. Spoon onto foil 6 tiny rounds to use for mushroom stems. Dust tops of larger mounds with unsweetened cocoa. Set aside while baking meringue layers. When layers are removed from oven reset temperature control to 275°F. Place "mushrooms" in oven and bake 1¼ hours. Turn off heat and let mushrooms remain in oven until cold. Stack large mounds on smaller ones and arrange on torte just before serving.

Strawberry Shortcake

1¾ cups all-purpose flour	½ cup lard, chilled
2 tablespoons sugar	¾ cup milk
1 tablespoon baking powder	Sweetened sliced ripe
½ teaspoon salt	strawberries

1. Blend the flour, sugar, baking powder, and salt in a bowl. Cut in the lard with a pastry blender or two knives until particles are about the size of coarse cornmeal. Make a well in the center and add milk all at one time. Stir with a fork 20 to 30 strokes.
2. Turn dough out onto a lightly floured surface and shape it into a ball. Knead lightly with the fingertips about 15 times.
3. Divide dough into halves. Roll each half about ¼ inch thick to fit an 8-inch layer cake pan. Place one round of dough in pan and brush with **melted butter or margarine.** Cover with the other round. Brush top with **milk.**
4. Bake at 425°F 15 to 18 minutes, or until top is delicately browned.
5. Split shortcake while hot and spread with **butter or margarine.** Arrange half of the strawberry slices over bottom layer. Spoon **whipped dessert topping, sour cream,** or **sweetened whipped cream** over berries. Cover with top layer and arrange remaining berries over it. Spoon additional topping over all.
ABOUT 6 SERVINGS

Note: **Orange or lemon marmalade** or **strawberry jam** may be thinly spread over layers before adding strawberries and topping.

Peach Shortcake: Follow recipe for Strawberry Shortcake. Substitute sweetened **fresh peach slices** for strawberries.

Sunshine Shortcake: Follow recipe for Strawberry Shortcake. Substitute **orange sections,** sliced **banana,** and **confectioners' sugar** for strawberries.

Christmas Cake

3 cups all-purpose flour	1 teaspoon salt
2 cups sugar	⅔ cup butter or margarine
2 teaspoons baking soda	2 cups buttermilk
1 teapsoon allspice	1 cup chopped dates, raisins,
1 teaspoon cinnamon	or mixed candied fruits
1 teaspoon nutmeg	½ cup chopped almonds or
1 teaspoon cloves	walnuts

1. Combine flour, sugar, baking soda, spices, and salt in a bowl. Cut in butter with pastry blender or two knives until particles resemble rice kernels. Add buttermilk; mix thoroughly. Mix in dates and nuts.
2. Turn batter into a generously greased and floured (bottom only) 9-inch tube pan or two 8x4x3-inch loaf pans.
3. Bake at 350°F about 1 hour, or until a wooden pick comes out clean.
4. Cool in pan on wire rack 15 minutes. Remove from pan and cool completely in wire rack.
1 TUBE CAKE

Light Fruitcake from Warsaw

5 eggs or 3 whole eggs plus	peel, finely chopped (about
3 egg whites	¾ cup)
1¾ cups confectioners' sugar	⅔ cup currants or raisins
¾ cup butter	⅔ cup finely chopped
1 teaspoon vanilla extract	walnuts
¼ cup milk or brandy	½ cup sliced dried figs
½ teaspoon salt	½ cup diced pitted dried
3 cups sifted cake flour	prunes
2 teaspoons baking powder	½ tablespoon cornstarch
3 ounces candied orange	

1. Beat eggs with sugar at high speed of electric mixer 7 minutes.
2. Cream butter with vanilla extract until fluffy. Beat in milk and salt.
3. Mix half of flour with baking powder. Add to creamed mixture and mix thoroughly. Fold in beaten eggs, then remaining flour.
4. Mix fruits and nuts with cornstarch. Fold into batter.
5. Butter an 11x7x3-inch loaf pan and sprinkle with bread crumbs. Turn batter into pan.
6. Bake at 350°F 50 minutes, or until a wooden pick comes out clean.
7. Cool before slicing.
1 FRUITCAKE

Orange Cake

1 cup butter	1 tablespoon grated orange
1 cup sugar	peel
3 egg yolks	¾ cup cashews, chopped
2 cups sifted all-purpose	3 egg whites
flour	Pinch salt
1 teaspoon baking powder	½ cup orange juice
1 teaspoon baking soda	½ cup corn syrup
1 cup milk	¼ cup rum
1 teaspoon lime juice	

1. Cream butter with sugar until light and fluffy. Beat in egg yolks.
2. Sift flour with baking powder and baking soda. Mix milk and lime juice. Add dry ingredients alternately with milk to creamed mixture, beating until blended after each addition. Mix in orange peel and cashews.
3. Beat egg whites and salt to stiff, not dry, peaks. Fold into batter.
4. Turn batter into a buttered and lightly floured 9-inch tube pan.
5. Bake at 350°F 40 minutes.
6. Mix orange juice, corn syrup, and rum. While cake is still hot in the pan, pour orange juice mixture over it.
ONE 9-INCH TUBE CAKE

Strawberry Shortcake

Chocolate Walnut Roll

2 tablespoons fine dry bread crumbs
1 cup walnuts, ground
¼ cup sifted cake flour
¼ cup unsweetened cocoa
1 teaspoon baking powder
½ teaspoon salt
¼ cup sugar
4 eggs
¼ teaspoon cream of tartar
½ cup sugar
2 tablespoons coffee beverage

1 cup heavy cream, chilled
2 tablespoons sugar
½ teaspoon vanilla extract
1 tablespoon brandy
¼ cup chopped walnuts
¼ cup chopped candied cherries (half red and half green)
2 ounces (2 squares) semisweet chocolate
2 teaspoons vegetable shortening
2 teaspoons light corn syrup

1. Set out a 15x10x1-inch pan. Line with greased waxed paper. To prevent sticking and for a slightly heavier crust, sprinkle greased paper with bread crumbs.
2. Sift together the cake flour, unsweetened cocoa, baking powder, salt and sugar. Combine with walnuts, mixing well.
3. Separate the eggs and beat egg whites with cream of tartar in large mixer bowl until foamy. Beating constantly, add ½ cup sugar gradually until very stiff peaks are formed.
4. Using same beater, beat the egg yolks until thick. Beat in coffee beverage.
5. Blend in the walnut-flour mixture. Turn batter over beaten egg whites and fold gently with spatula until no streaks of white remain. Turn into the baking pan and spread batter evenly into corners.
6. Bake at 400°F 10 minutes. Turn out onto sheet of waxed paper sprinkled with **granulated sugar** (about 2 tablespoons). Carefully peel off paper from cake. Cover cake with the pan and cool.
7. Meanwhile, prepare Walnut Cream Filling. Combine heavy cream, and 2 tablespoons sugar in a small mixer bowl. Beat until stiff peaks are formed, then blend in vanilla extract and brandy.
8. Fold in chopped walnuts and candied cherries. Spread cooled cake with the filling and roll up lengthwise. Place roll on serving plate.
9. Prepare Chocolate Glaze. Melt semisweet chocolate and vegetable shortening over hot water. Remove from heat and stir in light corn syrup.
10. Cool slightly, then spread over top and sides of cake roll. Decorate with **walnut halves** and **candied red cherries.**
1 CAKE ROLL

Brewmaster's Poppyseed Cake

Cake:
1 package (2-layer size) regular yellow cake mix
1 small package instant vanilla pudding and pie filling
4 eggs
1 cup beer

½ cup oil
¼ cup poppyseed

Glaze:
½ cup sugar
½ cup beer
¼ cup butter

1. Place cake mix, dry pudding, eggs, beer, oil, and poppyseed in an electric mixer bowl. Blend on low speed. Then beat on medium speed for 2 minutes.
2. Turn into a well-greased and floured 10-inch Bundt or tube pan.
3. Bake at 350°F 50 to 55 minutes, or until done.
4. Cool in pan 15 minutes. Turn out on rack.
5. To prepare glaze, boil ingredients for 5 minutes. Prick warm cake with skewer in many places. Brush warm glaze generously over top and sides. Cool. (If desired, sift confectioners' sugar over top; cake needs no frosting.)
1 LARGE CAKE; 16 SERVINGS

Chocolate Walnut Roll

Date Spice Cake

2¼ cups sifted enriched all-purpose flour
2 teaspoons baking powder
¼ teaspoon baking soda
½ teaspoon salt
2 teaspoons ground nutmeg
2 teaspoons ground ginger
⅔ cup shortening
1 teaspoon grated orange peel
1 teaspoon grated lemon peel
1 cup sugar
2 eggs
1 cup buttermilk
1 cup chopped dates

1. Grease a 9x9x2-inch pan. Line with waxed paper cut to fit bottom; grease paper. Set aside.
2. Blend flour, baking powder, baking soda, salt, nutmeg, and ginger.
3. Beat shortening with orange and lemon peels. Add sugar gradually, creaming until fluffy after each addition.
4. Add eggs, one at a time, beating thoroughly after each addition.
5. Beating only until smooth after each addition, alternately add dry ingredients in fourths and buttermilk in thirds to creamed mixture. Mix in dates. Turn batter into prepared pan.
6. Bake at 350°F about 45 minutes.
7. Remove from oven. Cool 5 to 10 minutes in pan on wire rack. Remove cake from pan and peel off paper; cool cake on rack.
ONE 9-INCH SQUARE CAKE

Raisin-Nut Spice Cake

3 cups sifted cake flour
2 teaspoons baking powder
1 teaspoon baking soda
½ teaspoon cinnamon
½ teaspoon nutmeg
¼ teaspoon ginger
¼ teaspoon salt
1 can or bottle (12 ounces) beer
1 cup raisins (5 ounces)
¾ cup butter or margarine
1 cup sugar
½ cup molasses
2 eggs
¾ cup chopped nuts (3 ounces)
Glaze

1. Sift dry ingredients together. Set aside.
2. Heat beer and raisins to simmering; let stand about 15 minutes to plump.
3. Cream butter and sugar until light and fluffy; add molasses.
4. Add eggs, one at a time, beating well after each addition.
5. Add dry ingredients alternately in thirds with beer drained from raisins, beating just until well blended. Stir in raisins and nuts.
6. Turn into a well-greased and floured 10-inch Bundt pan or angel food cake pan (nonstick pan preferred).
8. Let stand in pan about 10 minutes; invert onto cake rack. Cool. Cover with foil or store in airtight container. Cake slices better if made a day in advance.
9. Prepare a glaze by thinning **1 cup sifted confectioners' sugar** with **beer** or **milk**. Drizzle over cake shortly before serving.
1 LARGE CAKE; 16 SERVINGS

Nutmeg Cake

3 cups sifted cake flour
1 tablespoon baking powder
2 teaspoons nutmeg
½ teaspoon salt
¾ cup butter or margarine
2 teaspoons vanilla extract
1 cup granulated sugar
¾ cup packed brown sugar
2 whole eggs
2 egg whites
1 can or bottle (12 ounces) beer
Lemon-Beer Filling (below)
White frosting, any type

1. Sift dry ingredients together.
2. Cream butter with vanilla extract and sugars until light and fluffy. Add eggs and whites, one at a time, beating well after each adition (medium speed of mixer).
3. Alternately add sifted dry ingredients in thirds and beer in halves to creamed mixture, beating on low speed just until smooth after each addition.
4. Turn into 2 greased and waxed-paper-lined 9-inch round layer cake pans.
5. Bake at 350°F 30 to 35 minutes, or until cake tests done. Cool in pans about 10 minutes. Turn out onto wire racks. Cool completely before filling and frosting.
ONE 2-LAYER 9-INCH CAKE

Note: If not making a filling requiring egg yolks, use 3 whole eggs in batter.

Lemon-Beer Filling

½ cup sugar
2 tablespoons cornstarch
⅛ teaspoon salt
¾ cup beer
2 teaspoons grated lemon peel
2 tablespoons lemon juice
2 egg yolks

1. In top of a double boiler, combine sugar, cornstarch, and salt. Stir in beer. Cook over direct heat, stirring constantly, until thickened and clear.
2. Stir in lemon peel and juice.
3. Add a little hot mixture to egg yolks; return to double boiler top. Cook over hot water, stirring constantly, for 4 to 5 minutes. Cool before spreading on cake.
ABOUT 1 CUP

Carrot Cupcakes

1½ cups sifted enriched all-purpose flour
1 teaspoon baking powder
1 teaspoon baking soda
1 teaspoon ground cinnamon
½ teaspoon salt
1 cup sugar
¾ cup vegetable oil
2 eggs
1 cup grated raw carrots
½ cup chopped nuts

1. Blend flour, baking powder, baking soda, cinnamon, and salt. Set aside.
2. Combine sugar and oil in a bowl and beat thoroughly. Add eggs, one at a time, beating thoroughly after each addition. Mix in carrots. Add dry ingredients gradually, beating until blended. Mix in nuts.
3. Spoon into paper-baking-cup-lined muffin-pan wells.
4. Bake at 350°F 15 to 20 minutes.
ABOUT 16 CUPCAKES

Decorated Fruitcake

Fruitcake:
1½ cups (about 9 ounces) snipped dried figs
1 cup (about 6 ounces) snipped pitted dates
1 cup (about 5 ounces) dark seedless raisins
1 cup (about 5 ounces) golden raisins
1 cup (about 5 ounces) diced candied citron
1 cup (about 5 ounces) diced candied lemon peel
1 cup (about 5 ounces) diced candied orange peel
½ cup (about 3 ounces) diced candied pineapple
½ cup (about 3 ounces) halved red candied cherries
½ cup (about 2 ounces) currants
½ cup apricot brandy
½ cup orange juice
1 cup (4 ounces) blanched almond halves
4 cups sifted all-purpose flour
2 teaspoons baking powder
½ teaspoon salt
1 teaspoon ground cinnamon
½ teaspoon ground nutmeg
1 cup butter
1 teaspoon orange extract
2 cups sugar
6 eggs

Glaze:
⅓ cup sugar
½ cup water
½ cup dark corn syrup
Candied cherry halves
Whole almonds, blanched and split lengthwise

1. For fruitcake, combine fruits, brandy, and orange juice in a large bowl. (If desired, use either all brandy or all orange juice.) Cover tightly and set aside for 24 hours; stir occasionally.
2. Grease bottom and sides of a 10-inch tube pan. Line bottom and sides with greased parchment paper; set aside.
3. Add nuts to fruit. Sift flour with baking powder, salt, cinnamon, and nutmeg over fruit and nuts; toss until pieces are well coated.
4. Cream butter with orange extract and sugar in a large bowl; beat until lightly and fluffy. Add eggs, one at a time, beating thoroughly after each addition. (Mixture may be slightly curdled, but this will not affect the final product.) Using a spoon, thoroughly combine the creamed and fruit-nut mixtures. Spoon batter into prepared pan; spread evenly.
5. Bake at 300°F 2 hours and 40 minutes, or until cake tests done. Cool completely on wire rack before removing from pan. If desired, spoon ¼ cup apricot brandy or orange juice over cake as soon as it has finished baking.
6. When cool, remove from pan and peel off paper. If not to be served immediately, wrap and store in refrigerator.
7. Prepare Glaze when cake is cool and ready to serve. Combine sugar, water, and corn syrup in a small saucepan. Bring to boiling and boil for 2 minutes. Remove from heat and immediately brush on cake.
8. Arrange fruit and nuts on top of cake to form flowers. Use 5 almonds to form petals and a cherry half for center of each flower (see photo). Or decorate as desired. Immediately brush completed decorations with remaining glaze, and set aside to dry.
9. Wrap and refrigerate when glaze is dry. Slicing is easier when cake is cold.
6¾ POUNDS FRUITCAKE

Miniature fruitcakes: Follow recipe for Decorated Fruitcake; spoon batter into muffin pans. Bake at 300°F 45 minutes. Decorate cake with one flower, then glaze as above.

Chocolate-Beer Pudding Cake

Batter:
1½ cups all-purpose flour
¾ cup sugar
1 tablespoon unsweetened cocoa
1½ teaspoons baking powder
½ teaspoon baking soda
¼ teaspoon salt
¾ cup beer
⅓ cup oil
1 egg, slightly beaten

Syrup:
1 tablespoon unsweetened cocoa
¾ cup beer
⅓ cup packed brown sugar
⅓ cup granulated sugar

1. For batter, mix dry ingredients; make a well in center. Add beer, oil, and egg. Beat just until smooth.
2. For syrup, make a paste of cocoa and a little beer. Add remaining beer and sugars. Heat to boiling.
3. Pour batter into a greased 8-inch square baking pan. Drizzle syrup over top.
4. Bake at 350°F 40 minutes.
5. Cool about 5 minutes. Loosen sides of cake from pan; invert onto platter. Even out pudding layer with knife. Serve warm or cool.
6 TO 8 SERVINGS

Walnut Cake

2 cups (about 10 ounces) dark seedless raisins
⅔ cup sherry
4 cups sifted all-purpose flour
2 teaspoons baking powder
¼ teaspoon salt
1 teaspoon nutmeg
4 cups (about 1 pound)
walnuts
1¼ cups butter or margarine
2 teaspoons grated orange peel
2 cups sugar
6 eggs, well beaten
⅔ cup orange juice
½ cup molasses

1. Lightly grease a 10-inch tube pan. Line bottom with waxed paper cut to fit pan. Lightly grease paper.
2. Put raisins into a bowl. Pour sherry over raisins. Set aside.
3. Sift together flour, baking powder, salt, and nutmeg and set aside.
4. Chop walnuts and set aside.
5. Cream butter and orange peel until softened. Add sugar gradually, creaming until fluffy after each addition.
6. Add eggs gradually, beating thoroughly after each addition. Set aside.
7. Drain raisins, reserving liquid. Mix liquid with orange juice and molasses.
8. Alternately add dry ingredients in fourths and liquid in thirds to creamed mixture, beating only until smooth after each addition. Finally, blend in the raisins and walnuts. Turn batter into pan, spreading evenly to edges.
9. Bake at 275°F 2½ hours, or until cake tests done. Cool completely on cooling rack and remove from pan.
ONE 10-INCH TUBE CAKE

Decorated Fruitcake
Miniature Fruitcakes

Choo-Choo Cake

Choo-Choo Cake

1 package (2-layer size) yellow-cake mix	coloring
1 package (2-layer size) vanilla frosting mix	Decorating trims: large gumdrops, candy corn, candy covered chocolate drops
Few drops yellow food	

1. Prepare cake according to package directions. Bake in a greased and floured 13x9-inch baking pan. Cool. Cut 4 pieces of cake 4x2½ inches each. Remove from pan. Cut a piece 2x1 inches for smokestack.
2. Prepare frosting mix according to package directions, adding food coloring during mixing to give a pastel yellow color. Frost small pieces of cake on sides and top; frost smokestack and place on 1 car of train to make engine.
3. Cut a slice off large end of gumdrops for wheels. Use short pieces of wooden picks to secure to sides of cake.
4. Decorate tops of each car with candy covered chocolate drops.
5. Decorate smokestack with candy corn.
6. Press small end of a gumdrop into front of engine for light.
7. Place on tray to serve. Cut train cars in half to make 8 pieces. Frost remaining cake in pan with remaining frosting for extra servings.

Sherry Baba Ring

1 package active dry yeast	4 eggs
¼ cup warm water	2 cups all-purpose flour
¼ cup hot milk	Sherry Syrup
½ cup soft butter	Whipped cream
3 tablespoons sugar	Glacé fruits
1 teaspoon salt	

1. Soften yeast in water.
2. Combine hot milk, soft butter, sugar, and salt.
3. Beat eggs. Beat in yeast mixture, then butter mixture. Beat in flour thoroughly to make a smooth, thick batter.
4. Turn into a well-buttered 2-quart mold with tube center.

Let rise in a warm place until almost doubled in bulk, 1 to 1½ hours.
5. Bake at 375°F for 30 minutes, or until cake tests done. Make sherry syrup while baba is baking.
6. Remove baked baba from oven and allow to cool in pan 10 minutes. Turn baba onto a serving plate. Prick sides and top with tines of a fork. Slowly baste with sherry syrup. Let stand until syrup is almost absorbed.
7. Fill center of ring with slightly sweetened whipped cream and garnish with glacé fruits.
ABOUT 8 CUPS

Sherry Syrup: Simmer **1½ cups sugar** with **⅔ cup water** and **1 tablespoon grated orange peel** 10 minutes. Mix in **½ cup California Cream Sherry** and **¼ cup apricot-pineapple jam.** Simmer 5 minutes; cool.

Devil's Food Cake

2 cups sifted cake flour	¾ cup cocoa
1¾ cups sugar	⅔ cup soft shortening
½ teaspoon baking powder	1 cup water
1¼ teaspoons baking soda	1½ teaspoons vanilla
1 teaspoon salt	3 eggs (½ to ⅔ cup)

1. Sift flour, sugar, baking powder, soda, salt and cocoa together.
2. Add shortening, a little over half the water, and vanilla.
3. Beat vigorously with a spoon for 2 minutes (or with mixer at medium speed).
4. Add remaining water and eggs; beat vigorously with spoon 2 minutes (or with mixer at medium speed).
5. Turn into prepared pans; bake at 350°F. 30 to 40 minutes.
MAKES 2 9-INCH LAYERS

Mandarin-Glazed Cheese Cake

1⅔ cups graham cracker crumbs
5 tablespoons sugar
5 tablespoons butter or margarine, softened
1 package (3 ounces) lemon-flavored gelatin
1 cup very hot water
2 packages (8 ounces each) cream cheese, softened
1 teaspoon vanilla extract
½ cup sugar
1 cup chilled whipping cream
1 can (16 ounces) mandarin oranges, drained (reserve syrup)
2 teaspoons lemon juice
1 teaspoon unflavored gelatin

1. Combine graham cracker crumbs and 5 tablespoons sugar. Using a fork or pastry blender, blend in the butter. Using the back of a spoon, press crumb mixture in the bottom and sides of a buttered 8-inch springform pan.
2. Bake comb crust at 375°F 8 minutes. Cool.
3. Put lemon-flavored gelatin into a bowl. Add the very hot water and stir until gelatin is completely dissolved; cool. Chill, stirring constantly, until slightly thicker than thick unbeaten egg white.
4. While gelatin is chilling, combine cream cheese and vanilla extract. Gradually add remaining ½ cup sugar, beating until blended.
5. When gelatin is desired consistency, stir several tablespoons into the cream cheese mixture. Continue adding gelatin mixture slowly, stirring constantly until well blended.
6. Beat the whipping cream in a chilled bowl, using chilled beaters, until it piles softly. Gently fold into the gelatin-cheese mixture. Pour mixture into cooled crust. Chill until set (about 1 hour).
7. While cheesecake is chilling, pour the lemon juice into a small cup. Sprinkle the unflavored gelatin over the juice. Let stand about 5 minutes to soften.
8. Heat the reserved mandarin orange syrup until very hot. Add the softened gelatin and stir until completely dissolved. Cool. Chill gelatin mixture, stirring occasionally, until slightly thicker than thick unbeaten egg white.
9. Arrange mandarin orange segments on top of cheese cake. Spoon glaze evenly over orange segments. Chill until glaze is set.
12 TO 16 SERVINGS

Silver Cake

2¼ cups sifted cake flour
1½ cups sugar
3 teaspoons baking powder
¾ teaspoon salt
½ cup soft shortening
1 cup milk
1 teaspoon vanilla
¼ teaspoon almond extract
4-5 egg whites (⅔ cup)

1. Sift together into large bowl flour, sugar, baking powder and salt.
2. Add shortening, ⅔ cup of the milk, vanilla and almond extract.
3. Beat 2 minutes at medium speed on mixer or by hand (150 strokes per minute).
4. Scrape sides and bottom of bowl.
5. Add remaining milk and egg whites.
6. Beat 2 minutes as before.
7. Turn into 2 greased 9x11-inch layer pans.
8. Bake at 350°F 30 to 35 minutes.
MAKES 2 9-INCH LAYERS

Black Forest Torte

1½ cups toasted filberts, grated*	melted and cooled
¼ cup flour	6 tablespoons kirsch
½ cup butter or margarine	6 egg whites
1 cup sugar	Cherry Filling, below
6 egg yolks	3 cups chilled heavy cream
4 ounces (4 squares) semisweet chocolate,	⅓ cup confectioners' sugar
	Chocolate curls

1. Grease and lightly flour an 8-inch springform pan; set aside.
2. Blend grated filberts and flour; set aside.
3. Cream butter until softened. Beat in sugar gradually until mixture is light and fluffy. Add egg yolks, one at a time, beating thoroughly after each addition.
4. Blend in the chocolate and 2 tablespoons of the kirsch. Stir in nut-flour mixture until blended.
5. Beat egg whites until stiff, not dry, peaks are formed. Fold into batter and turn into the pan.
6. Bake at 375°F about 1 hour, or until torte tests done. (Torte should be about 1½ inches high and top may have a slight crack.)
7. Cool 10 minutes in pan on a wire rack; remove from pan and cool.
8. Using a long sharp knife, carefully cut torte into 3 layers. Place top layer inverted on a cake plate; spread with Cherry Filling.
9. Whip cream (1½ cups at a time) until soft peaks are formed, gradually adding half of the confectioners' sugar and 2 tablespoons of the kirsch to each portion.
10. Generously spread some of the whipped cream over the Cherry Filling. Cover with second layer and remaining Cherry Filling. Spread generously with more whipped cream and top with third torte layer. Frost entire torte with remaining whipped cream.
11. Decorate torte with reserved cherries and chocolate curls.
ONE 8-INCH TORTE

*To grate nuts, use a rotary-type grater with hand-operated crank.

Cherry Filling: Drain 1 jar (16 ounces) **red maraschino cherries,** reserving ½ cup syrup. Set aside 13 cherries for decoration; slice remaining cherries. Set aside. Combine reserved syrup and **4 tablespoons kirsch.** In a saucepan, gradually blend syrup mixture into **1½ tablespoons cornstarch.** Mix in **1 tablespoon lemon juice.** Stir over medium heat until mixture boils ½ minute. Mix in sliced cherries and cool.
1⅓ CUPS FILLING

Lemon Chiffon Cake

2¼ cups sifted cake flour or 2 cups sifted all-purpose flour	purpose flour)
	¾ cup cold water
1½ cups sugar	1 tablespoon grated lemon rind
3 teaspoons baking powder	1½ teaspoons vanilla
1 teaspoon salt	¼ teaspoon lemon extract
½ cup salad oil	7 egg whites
5 egg yolks, unbeaten (use 7 egg yolks when using all-	½ teaspoon cream of tartar

1. Sift first 4 ingredients together into large bowl; make a well in center.
2. Measure into this in order listed – salad oil, yolks, water, rind and extracts.
3. Beat with electric mixer (medium speed) or with spoon until smooth; set aside.
4. Beat egg whites with cream of tartar in large bowl until stiff peaks are formed.
5. Pour yolk mixture slowly over whites, folding gently until just blended (do not overmix).
6. Turn into ungreased 10-inch tube pan.
7. Bake at 325°F 55 minutes, then at 350°F 10 minutes.
8. Invert pan; let stand until cool.
MAKES 1 10-INCH TUBE CAKE

Spice Chiffon Cake. Follow recipe for Lemon Chiffon Cake except: omit lemon rind and lemon extract; sift only 1 cup sugar with dry ingredients; add **½ cup firmly packed brown sugar** to sifted dry ingredients; add **1 teaspoon cinnamon, ½ teaspoon each of nutmeg and allspice** and **¼ teaspoon cloves to dry ingredients.**

Orange Chiffon Cake. Follow recipe for Lemon Chiffon Cake except: substitute **¾ cup orange juice** for the cold water and **2 teaspoons grated orange rind for lemon rind.**

Mahogany Cake

½ cup firmly packed brown sugar	½ cup butter
	½ cup firmly packed brown sugar
½ cup milk	
½ cup cocoa	1½ teaspoons vanilla
2 cups sifted cake flour	3 egg yolks
1 teaspoon baking soda	½ cup milk
¼ teaspoon salt	

1. Combine first 3 ingredients in heavy saucepan, bring to boil, stir, set off heat.
2. Sift together flour, baking soda and salt.
3. In separate bowl cream together butter, brown sugar and vanilla until creamy and smooth.
4. Add egg yolks, one at a time to butter and sugar; beat after each addition until fluffy.
5. Add dry ingredients and the milk alternately in thirds; stir gently to blend smooth after each addition.
6. Add warm cocoa mixture; blend carefully.
7. Turn into 2 buttered 8-inch round layer cake pans.
8. Bake in 375°F (moderate) oven for 25-30 minutes.
9. Cool and frost with Chocolate Frosting (page 576).
MAKES 2 8-INCH LAYERS

Fruit-Glazed Layer Cake

Cake:
1 cup plus 2 tablespoons sifted cake flour
⅛ teaspoon salt
4 egg yolks
⅓ cup cool water
1 cup sugar
1 teaspoon orange extract
½ teaspoon lemon extract
4 egg whites
½ teaspoon cream of tartar
Vanilla Buttercream

Fruit Glaze:
1 tablespoon sugar
2 teaspoons cornstarch
⅓ cup apricot syrup
3 tablespoons pineapple syrup
1 tablespoon lemon juice
1 cup coarsely chopped walnuts
10 to 12 medium-size strawberries
1 slice canned pineapple
5 or 6 canned apricot halves (optional)
14 to 18 seedless grapes

1. For cake, blend flour with salt; set aside. Beat egg yolks until very thick and lemon colored. Add cool water a little at a time, beating well after each addition. Add sugar gradually, beating after each addition. Beat in extracts.
2. Sift the dry ingredients over egg mixture about one fourth at a time; after each addition gently fold in until blended.
3. Using a clean bowl and beaters, beat egg whites until frothy. Beat in cream of tartar. Continue beating until stiff, not dry, peaks form. Carefully fold beaten egg whites into the egg yolk mixture until just blended.
4. Turn batter into 2 ungreased 8-inch round layer cake pans and spread batter evenly.
5. Bake at 325°F about 25 minutes, or until cake tests done. Invert over wire racks (cake should not touch rack); cool layers about 1 hour before removing from pans.
6. Slice each layer in half horizontally, forming 4 layers. Place 1 layer on a serving plate. Spread top with ⅓ cup vanilla buttercream. Put second and third layers in place, frosting the tops of each layer. Put fourth layer on top and leave unfrosted. Use remaining buttercream to frost side of cake, smoothing as much as possible. Chill about 15 minutes.
7. For glaze, combine sugar and cornstarch in a small saucepan. Add apricot syrup, pineapple syrup, and lemon juice. Cook over medium-high heat, stirring constantly, until mixture thickens and begins to boil. Boil 1 minute; cool.

8. Gently press walnuts into buttercream on side of cake, a handful at a time. Place pineapple slice in center of top layer. Place a whole strawberry in center of the pineapple slice, and place grapes in a circle around the pineapple. If desired, cut apricot halves in half and place apricots end-to-end in a circle around the grapes. Place strawberry halves around edge of top layer.

9. Brush glaze over fruit, trying to keep glaze from drizzling down side of cake.

10. Using a pastry bag and tube 14 or 15 (star), fill with remaining buttercream. Pipe a shell border around top and bottom edges of cake. Chill briefly.
ONE 8-INCH LAYER CAKE

Note: Any combination of fruit may be used, but syrup from canned apricots and pineapple is needed for the glaze.

Vanilla Buttercream

4 egg yolks	2 teaspoons vanilla extract
½ cup sugar	1 cup chilled unsalted butter
½ cup hot half-and-half	

1. Put egg yolks and sugar into a bowl and beat until thick. Add hot half-and-half gradually, beating constantly. Pour into a saucepan. Cook and stir about 5 minutes, or until thickened.

2. Remove from heat and stir in vanilla extract. Pour into a bowl and beat 1 minute to cool slightly. Add butter, a small amount at a time, beating until butter is melted after each addition. Cool.
ABOUT 2 CUPS BUTTERCREAM

Chiffon Two-Egg Cake

2 eggs, separated	3 teaspoons baking powder
1½ cups sugar	⅓ cup cooking (salad) oil
2¼ cups sifted cake flour	1 cup milk
1 teaspoon salt	1½ teaspoons vanilla

1. Separate eggs and put whites into small mixer bowl.
2. Sift 1 cup of the sugar, the flour, salt and baking powder into large mixer bowl.
3. Pour in the oil, half of the milk and the vanilla.
4. Beat egg whites until frothy, then add remaining ½ cup sugar a little at a time, beating well after each addition.
5. Continue beating until very stiff peaks are formed.
6. Beat flour mixture on low speed of electric mixer 1 minute, scraping bowl with rubber spatula.
7. Add remaining milk and egg yolks; beat 1 minute longer.
8. Add egg-white mixture and fold in with rubber spatula until blended.
9. Turn batter into 2 greased 9-inch round layer pans (or 13x9-inch pan) and bake about 30 minutes for layers and 40 minutes for oblong cake.
10. Cool in pans about 5 minutes and remove to cooling racks.
MAKES 2 9-INCH LAYERS

Chocolate Loaf Cake

1½ cups sifted cake flour	½ teaspoon salt
1¼ cups sugar	⅔ cup shortening
½ cup cocoa	1 cup buttermilk
1 teaspoon baking powder	1 teaspoon vanilla
½ teaspoon baking soda	2 eggs

1. Sift first 6 ingredients together into a large bowl.
2. Cut in shortening with pastry blender.
3. Add buttermilk and vanilla; beat 2 minutes on low speed of electric mixer or 200 strokes by hand.
4. Add eggs and beat again 2 minutes.
5. Bake in a greased loaf pan 9x5x3 inches in a 350°F (moderate) oven 50-60 minutes.
MAKES 2 8-INCH LAYERS

Devil's Food Cake de Luxe

¾ cup boiling water	⅔ cup butter or margarine
3 squares (3 ounces) unsweetened chocolate	1½ cups firmly packed brown sugar
2¼ cups sifted cake flour	2 teaspoons vanilla
1 teaspoon baking soda	3 eggs, well beaten
1½ teaspoons baking powder	¾ cup buttermilk
1 teaspoon salt	

1. Combine boiling water and chocolate, stir until thick, set aside.
2. Sift together flour, soda, baking powder and salt.
3. Cream together shortening, sugar and vanilla until creamy and smooth.
4. Add eggs; beat until fluffy.
5. Add melted chocolate; stir to blend.
6. Add sifted dry ingredients and buttermilk alternately in one-thirds; beat gently after each addition.
7. Turn into 2 greased 8- or 9-inch round cake pans.
8. Bake in a 350°F (moderate) oven about 35-40 minutes.
MAKES 2 8 OR 9 INCH LAYERS

Chocolate Fudge Tweed Cake

2 cups sifted cake flour	¼ cup chopped walnuts
1 teaspoon baking powder	½ cup butter or margarine
½ teaspoon baking soda	1 cup firmly packed brown sugar
½ teaspoon salt	
1 bar (4 ounces) sweet cooking chocolate, coarsely grated	1¼ teaspoons vanilla
	2 eggs, beaten slightly
	¾ cup milk

1. Sift together flour, baking powder, soda and salt.
2. Add coarsely grated chocolate and nuts; mix carefully with a fork.
3. Cream together butter or margarine, brown sugar and vanilla until creamy and smooth.
4. Add eggs; beat until fluffy.
5. Add dry ingredients alternately with milk, each in one-thirds; beat after each addition.
6. Pour into 2 greased 8-inch layer pans.
7. Bake at 375°F about 25 minutes.
8. Fill and frost with Rich Chocolate Frosting (page 576).
MAKES 2 8-INCH LAYERS

Dobos Torte

Caramel Topping:
¾ cup sugar
Chocolate Buttercream

½ cup finely chopped
 walnuts
Torte Layers

1. Prepare Torte Layers. When they are cool, choose the flattest and most perfect one and lay it in the center of a large sheet of waxed paper. Butter a large knife and layer it to the side of the waxed paper along with a spatula.
2. For Caramel Topping, put sugar into a heavy, light-colored skillet and set over low heat. Stir constantly with a wooden spoon until sugar liquefies. Continue stirring until liquid turns a golden brown.
3. Pour syrup over torte layer on waxed paper, and use spatula to work syrup out to edges of layer. Spread quickly as caramel hardens in a short time.

4. With a buttered knife, cut caramelized layer into 8 equal wedges.

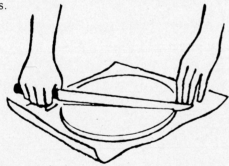

5. To assemble torte, place 1 torte layer on serving place and cover with ⅓ cup Chocolate Buttercream. Lay second layer on top of first and cover with same amount of buttercream. Repeat, layering and frosting until 7 layers are covered with frosting.
6. Frost sides and torte and press chopped nuts into frosting around sides. Arrange caramel-covered wedges in a circle on top of cake a spoon a dab of buttercream under each wedge to prop it up (see illustration). Then pipe a rosette in center of cake top. Refrigerate until serving time. Serve slightly chilled. Cake will taste better if allowed to ripen in refrigerator for 12 hours before serving and will keep for several days in the refrigerator.

ONE 8-INCH TORTE

Torte Layers

6 egg yolks
¾ cup sugar
1 cup all-purpose flour
⅛ teaspoon baking powder

⅛ teaspoon salt
3 tablespoons water
6 egg whites

1. Cut eight 8-inch circles from parchment paper, and set them on cookie sheets – as many as will fit into your oven. (Or, if desired, place parchment paper circles on inverted layer cake pans.) Grease and flour parchment paper circles well.
2. Beat egg yolks with sugar in large bowl of electric mixer until thick. Add flour, baking powder, and salt and beat again. Then add water and mix until well combined.
3. Meanwhile, beat whites until stiff, but not dry, and fold them into batter (there should be about 5 cups).
4. Ladle a scant cup batter onto each prepared circle; use spatula to spread batter as evenly as possble. (Don't worry if spread batter looks thin or holey; this will bake out to some extent.)
5. Bake at 300°F 10 to 12 minutes, or until edges become crisp and golden. Remove layers from oven and slide them, still attached to parchment paper, onto wire racks. When slightly cooled, carefully peel off paper.
6. Meanwhile, grease and flour the second batch of parchment paper circles and cover them with batter. As soon as first batch comes out of the oven, place second batch on cookie sheets and bake. Repeat with remaining batter until all is used. You will have 8 layers.

8 TORTE LAYERS

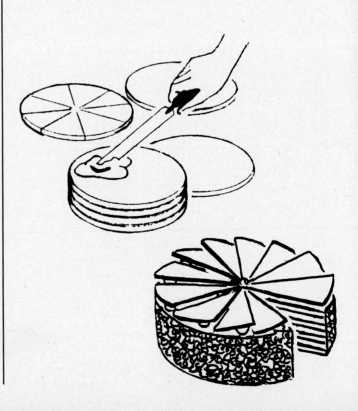

Chocolate Buttercream

1 cup (6 ounces) semisweet chocolate pieces
½ ounce (½ square) unsweetened chocolate
1½ cups unsalted butter

1¼ cups sugar
2 egg yolks
2 tablespoons rum (or 1 teaspoon rum extract)
⅛ teaspoon salt

1. Melt chocolate pieces and unsweetened chocolate in top of a double boiler. Cool over cold water.
2. Beat butter in large bowl of electric mixer until fluffy. Add sugar gradually, beating thoroughly to incorporate, and then add egg yolks, rum, and salt. Beat in cooled chocolate.
3. If necessary, refrigerate soft, freshly made frosting until of proper consistency to spread. Buttercream frosting will keep for several days in a covered container in the refrigerator.

ABOUT 4 CUPS BUTTERCREAM

Spiced Red Devil's Food Cake

1¾ cups sifted cake flour
1½ cups sugar
½ teaspoon salt
1 teaspoon baking soda
1 teaspoon cinnamon
½ teaspoon allspice
¼ teaspoon powdered cloves
½ cup shortening

1¼ teaspoons vanilla
1 cup buttermilk or sour milk
2 eggs
½ teaspoon red food coloring
3 squares (3 ounces) unsweetened chocolate, melted

1. Sift together flour, sugar, salt, baking soda and spices into a large bowl.
2. Add shortening, vanilla and ⅔ cup buttermilk.
3. Beat 2 minutes with electric mixer (or by hand with 150 strokes per minute).
4. Add remaining buttermilk, eggs, red food coloring and chocolate.
5. Beat as before.
6. Turn into 2 greased 8-inch layer pans or 1 9x9x2-inch pan.
7. Bake at 350°F 25 to 30 minutes for layers or 35 minutes for square pan.
8. Cool.
9. Frost with Nutmeg Butter Frosting (page 576).
MAKES 2 8-INCH LAYERS OR 1 9x9-INCH SQUARE

Mocha Sweet Cake

1 bar (4 ounce) sweet cooking chocolate
½ cup boiling water
1 cup butter, margarine or other shortening
2 cups sugar
1 teaspoon vanilla
4 egg yolks
2½ cups sifted cake flour

3 tablespoons instant coffee
1 teaspoon baking soda
½ teaspoon salt
1 cup buttermilk
4 egg whites, stiffly beaten
Mocha Cream Frosting
Coffee Whipped Cream Frosting
½ cup chopped pecans

1. Melt chocolate in water in a saucepan over low heat; cool.
2. Cream butter, sugar and vanilla together.
3. Add egg yolks, one at a time, beating well after each addition.
4. Blend in the chocolate.
5. Sift flour, soda, salt and instant coffee together.
6. Add to creamed mixture alternately with buttermilk, beating until blended after each addition.
7. Fold in beaten egg whites.
8. Turn into 3 8-inch layer pans, bottoms lined with greased waxed paper.
9. Bake at 350°F for 30 minutes, or until cake springs back when press lightly.
10. Spread Mocha Cream Frosting (page 578) between layers and on top.
11. Spread sides with Coffee Whipped Cream Frosting (page 578), and sprinkle with chopped pecans.
MAKES 3 8-INCH LAYERS

Dark Chocolate Fudge Cake

2 cups sifted cake flour
2 cups sugar
2¼ teaspoons baking powder
1 teaspoon salt
¼ teaspoon baking soda
¼ cup shortening

1½ cups milk
1½ teaspoons vanilla
2 eggs
4 squares (4 ounces) unsweetened chocolate, melted

1. Sift together flour, sugar, baking powder, salt and soda into large bowl.
2. Add shortening, 1 cup milk and vanilla.
3. Beat 2 minutes with electric mixer (or by hand with 150 strokes per minute).
4. Scrape down sides and bottom of bowl.
5. Add remaining milk, eggs and melted chocolate.
6. Beat 2 minutes as before.
7. Pour into 2 greased 8-inch or 9-inch layer pans.
8. Frost with Chocolate Frosting (page 576).
MAKES 2 8 OR 9 INCH LAYERS

Pecan Chocolate Fudge Cake. Mix ⅔ **cup chopped pecans** into batter and turn into one 10-inch square pan. Bake 40 to 45 minutes or until cake test done.

Sour Cream Chocolate Cake

3 squares (3 ounces) unsweetened chocolate, melted
½ cup double-strength coffee
2 cups sifted cake flour
½ teaspoon salt

1 teaspoon baking soda
1½ cups sugar
1 cup sour cream
2½ teaspoons vanilla
2 eggs, well beaten

1. Combine chocolate and coffee; cool.
2. Sift flour, salt and soda together.
3. Combine sugar, sour cream and vanilla; beat in eggs.
4. Blend in chocolate mixture.
5. Add dry ingredients in thirds, beating until smooth.
6. Bake in greased pans at 350°F. for 35 minutes.
MAKES 2 8-INCH LAYERS

Spanish Cocoa Cake

2 cups sifted cake flour
4 tablespoons cocoa
½ teaspoon salt
2 teaspoons baking soda
⅓ cup shortening

1 cup sugar
2 egg yolks
1 teaspoon vanilla
1⅓ cups buttermilk

1. Sift flour, cocoa, salt and baking soda together 3 times.
2. Cream shortening with sugar until fluffy.
3. Add egg yolks and vanilla and beat thoroughly.
4. Add dry ingredients and milk alternately in thirds, blending after each addition.
5. Pour into greased 8x8-inch pan; bake at 325°F 45 to 55 minutes.
MAKES 1 8x8-INCH CAKE

Chocolate Marble Cake

Part 1	Part 2
2⅓ cups sifted cake flour	2 squares (2 ounces)
2¼ teaspoons baking powder	unsweetened chocolate,
¼ teaspoon salt	melted
½ cup shortening	½ teaspoon baking soda
1 cup sugar	3 tablespoons sugar
1 egg, well beaten	2 tablespoons shortening
2 egg yolks	¼ teaspoon salt
1 teaspoon vanilla	¾ cup hot water
¾ cup milk	

1. Sift first 3 ingredients together.
2. Cream shortening and sugar until fluffy.
3. Add egg, egg yolks and extract and beat thoroughly.
4. Add dry ingredients and milk alternately in thirds, beating after each addition.
5. Combine ingredients in Part 2 in order given; blend.
6. Divide batter as follows: leave ⅓ of batter white; to other ⅔, add chocolate mixture; blend.
7. Drop batter by tablespoons into greased 9x9-inch pan, alternating white and chocolate batters.
8. Bake at 350°F. 30 to 35 minutes.

MAKES 1 9x9-INCH CAKE

Yeast Chocolate Cake

2 squares (2 ounces)	2 eggs, well beaten
unsweetened, chocolate	1 package active dry yeast
2 cups sifted cake flour	¼ cup warm water (110° to
1 teaspoon salt	115°F)
½ cup shortening	⅔ cup milk
1½ cups sugar	¾ teaspoon baking soda
½ teaspoon vanilla	2 tablespoons warm water

1. Melt chocolate and cool.
2. Sift flour and salt together.
3. Cream shortening, sugar and vanilla extract together well.
4. Add eggs; beat until light and fluffy.
5. Soften yeast in ¼ cup warm water.
6. Beat into creamed mixture with melted chocolate.
7. Add dry ingredients alternately with milk, beating only until smooth after each addition.
8. Cover and refrigerate at least 6 hours.
9. Remove batter from refrigerator and set aside.
10. Grease 2 8-inch round layer cake pans.
11. Mix baking soda and 2 tablespoons warm water together.
12. Quickly add to batter. Blend well and turn into greased pans.
13. Bake at 350°F 20 to 30 minutes.
14. Cool 5 minutes before removing to pans in cooling racks.
15. Fill cake with Orange Filling (page 575).

MAKES 2 8-INCH LAYERS

Cherry-Chocolate Cupcakes

1 package (9½ ounce)	2 cups sifted confectioners'
chocolate fudge cake mix	sugar
½ cup chopped, red	1 tablespoon maraschino
maraschino cherries	cherry syrup
¼ cup butter, softened	½ teaspoon vanilla

1. Prepare cake mix according to package directions; fold in cherries.
2. Turn into 10 greased cupcake pan wells.
3. Bake at 350°F 20 to 25 minutes.
4. Beat butter, sugar, syrup and extract together until fluffy for frosting.
5. Frost cupcakes and top each with a cherry, if desired.

MAKES 10 CUPCAKES

Marble Tube Cake

3½ cups sifted cake flour	2 cups sugar
3 teaspoons baking powder	4 eggs, well beaten
½ teaspoon salt	1 cup milk
1 cup butter or margarine	¼ cup cocoa
1 teaspoon almond extract	1 teaspoon rum flavoring

1. Sift flour, baking powder and salt together.
2. Cream butter and almond extract together.
3. Gradually add 1½ cups sugar, creaming well after each addition.
4. Add eggs and beat until light and fluffy.
5. Add dry ingredients alternately with milk, beating just until blended after each addition.
6. Blend remaining ½ cup sugar and cocoa together.
7. Divide batter in half and add cocoa mixture and rum extract to half the batter; blend well.
8. Grease bottom of a 10-inch pan; line with waxed paper.
9. Spoon batters in alternate layers into pan; cut through gently with a spatula to marble the batters.
10. Bake at 350°F. 60 minutes.
11. Cool 15 minutes; remove to rack.

MAKES 1 10-INCH TUBE CAKE

Mint Chocolate Chip Cake

1½ cups sifted cake flour	2 eggs, separated
2 teaspoons baking powder	½ cup milk
¼ teaspoon salt	1 teaspoon vanilla
½ cup shortening	½ cup semiweet chocolate
1 cup sugar	pieces

1. Sift flour, baking powder and salt together.
2. Cream shortening with ⅓ cup sugar until fluffy.
3. Beat yolks with ⅓ cup sugar until very thick.
4. Blend into creamed mixture.
5. Add dry ingredients and milk alternately in thirds, beating after each addition.
6. Beat egg whites until foamy; beat in remaining ⅓ cup sugar gradually, beating until stiff peaks are formed.
7. Fold into batter with extract and chocolate pieces.
8. Turn into 2 8-inch greased pans. Bake at 350°F 25 to 30 minutes.
9. Frost with Peppermint Frosting (page 578).

MAKES 2 8-INCH LAYERS

Nectarine Chiffon Cake

1½ cups sliced unpared fresh nectarines
1 tablespoon lemon juice
2¼ cups sifted cake flour
1½ cups sugar
1 tablespoon baking powder
1 teaspoon salt
½ cup salad oil
5 egg yolks (unbeaten)
1 teaspoon vanilla extract
¼ teaspoon almond extract
1 cup egg whites (7 or 8)
½ teaspoon cream of tartar

1. Put about half of nectarines at a time into an electric blender container and blend until puréed, stopping blender often and pushing nectarines into blades with a rubber spatula. Turn out into a measuring cup; blend remainder of fruit (should be 1 cup pulp)*. Mix with lemon juice.
2. Sift flour with 1 cup sugar, baking powder, and salt into a mixing bowl. Add oil, egg yolks, nectarine pulp, vanilla and almond extracts to flour mixture; beat to a smooth batter.
3. With clean beaters, beat egg whites with cream of tartar until frothy. Gradually add remaining ½ cup sugar, beating to a stiff meringue; do not underbeat. Pour batter slowly over egg whites, folding in carefully and thoroughly. Turn into an ungreased 10-inch tube pan. Set pan on lowest rack of oven.
4. Bake at 325°F 55 minutes. Turn oven control to 350°F and continue baking 15 minutes, or until a pick inserted in center of cake comes out clean and dry.
5. Invert pan and let cake hang upside down until cooled. Loosen sides and around tube with spatula, and rap pan sharply on counter to remove cake.
ONE 10-INCH TUBE CAKE

*If blender is not available, chop nectarines finely so peel is in small pieces, and crush with a fork to obtain moisture needed.

Nectarine Chiffon Cake

Semisweet Chocolate Cake

1 cup sifted cake flour
1¼ teaspoons baking powder
½ teaspoon baking soda
¼ teaspoon salt
1 cup semisweet chocolate pieces
½ cup butter
4 egg yolks
⅔ cup sugar
½ cup milk
1 teaspoon vanilla
2 egg whites

1. Sift first 4 ingredients together.
2. Combine chocolate pieces and butter and melt over hot water.
3. Cool 10 minutes.
4. Beat egg yolks and ⅓ cup of the sugar until thick.
5. Add dry ingredients alternately with milk, blending after each addition.
6. Blend in chocolate and vanilla.
7. Beat egg whites until frothy; add ⅓ cup sugar gradually, beating until stiff peaks are formed.
8. Fold into chocolate mixture.
9. Turn into greased pans and bake at 375°F 25 minutes.
10. Cool.
11. Fill and frost with Mocha Seven-Minute Frosting (page 577).
MAKES 2 8-INCH LAYERS

Indio Cream Cake

1 package (1 pound 3 ounces) chocolate cake mix
Indio Cream Filling
Whipped cream
Dates

1. Prepare cake mix according to package directions, using milk instead of water.
2. Turn into 2 greased 9-inch layer pans.
3. Bake at 350°F 30 minutes; cool.
4. Place one layer on serving plate, spread with Indio Cream Filling, top with second layer.
5. Garnish with whipped cream and dates.
6. Chill ½ hour or longer.
MAKES 2 9-INCH LAYERS

Indio Cream Filling

1 cup fresh dates, pitted
1 cup heavy cream
¼ teaspoon cinnamon
Dash nutmeg
1 tablespoon rum or ¼ teaspoon rum flavoring
½ teaspoon grated lemon rind
1 tablespoon chopped candied ginger

1. Slice dates.
2. Whip cream, adding next 4 ingredients during last minute of beating.
3. Fold in dates and ginger.

Snow Queen Doll Cake

Doll Cake   White Buttercream (page 569)

1. A china (or plastic) doll head and bust will be needed.
2. Lay the 8-inch sponge cake layer on a serving plate. With a long, sharp, serrated knife, split bowl-cake into 2 layers and set aside.
3. Prepare buttercream and spread over top and sides of cake layer on plate. Lay bottom half of bowl-cake over frosted layer and spread with icing; top with upper layer of bowl-cake and cover with icing. Meanwhile, with cupcake upside down, press doll torso into it carefully until doll stands without support.
4. Set cupcake (with doll) on top of cake and cover cake with frosting, using more frosting to keep doll upright, if necessary. Smooth frosting over sides of cake and assemble the skirt, using a spatula dipped often in hot water to make skirt as smooth as possible.
5. Drop tube 28 or 29 (star) into a pastry bag and fill bag with buttercream. Pipe stars over entire surface, starting at top and piping straight rows all the way to base of cake. Stars should touch but not be crowded.
6. Remove pastry tube from bag and drop tube 14 or 15 (star) into bag. Fill again with icing and pipe a border row of shells around bottom of dress. Refrigerate until serving time.
1 SNOW QUEEN DOLL CAKE

Doll Cake

5 egg yolks   1¼ cups sifted cake flour
1¼ cups sugar   5 egg whites
⅓ cup water   ½ teaspoon cream of tartar
1¼ teaspoons vanilla extract   ⅛ teaspoon salt

1. Beat egg yolks, half of the sugar, water, and vanilla extract together in large bowl of an electric mixer until very thick. Sift flour over batter and fold in carefully.
2. Beat egg whites with cream of tartar and salt until they form soft peaks. With beaters still running, add remaining sugar gradually, continuing to beat until meringue is thick. Fold into batter.
3. Grease the bottom and sides of an 8-inch round layer cake pan and line it on the bottom with greased parchment paper. Grease a 1½-quart oven-proof bowl (7 to 8 inches in diameter at top) and a 6-ounce glass custard cup. Cut small parchment paper rounds to fit in bottom of each; grease the parchment paper and put in place.
4. Divide the batter (there should be about 8¼ cups) into pans as follows: 4 cups into bowl, ⅔ cup into custard cup, and remaining batter into cake pan.
5. Bake at 350°F 25 minutes. Then lay a piece of foil over top of bowl and remove custard cup from oven. Allow another 10 minutes in oven for cake layer (a total of 35 minutes) and allow another 20 minutes for bowl cake (a total of 45 minutes). Cool cupcake upright on wire rack 10 minutes.
6. With a knife, loosen cake from custard cup and turn out on wire rack. Remove paper and finish cooling. Turn layer cake pan and bowl upside down on wire racks to cool as they come from the oven. Do not remove cakes from pans until they fall out by themselves or until they have cooled enough to be loosened easily from sides. Peel off paper and cool completely.

Raisin Cake

5¼ ounces butter or margarine at room temperature	rum
	½ to ¾ cup raisins
3 eggs	2 cups all-purpose flour
2 teaspoons lemon peel, grated	2 teaspoons baking powder
	½ cup milk
2 tablespoons lemon juice or	Bread crumbs
	Confectioners' sugar

1. Beat butter and sugar until foamy. Add eggs one at a time, beating vigorously after each.
2. Then add lemon peel, lemon juice, raisins mixed with 2 tablespoons flour, remainder of flour mixed with baking powder and milk.
3. Butter baking dish and sprinkle with bread crumbs. Pour in batter and bake in 350°F oven for 50 to 60 minutes. Sprinkle with confectioners' sugar after cooling.

Banana Chocolate Cake

2¼ cups sifted cake flour	2 squares (2 ounces) unsweetened chocolate, melted
1 teaspoon baking powder	
¾ teaspoon baking soda	
1 teaspoon salt	1 teaspoon vanilla
⅔ cup shortening	1 cup mashed ripe bananas
1½ cups sugar	½ cup buttermilk
2 eggs	

1. Sift first 4 ingredients together.
2. Cream shortening with sugar.
3. Add eggs, one at a time, beating well after each addition.
4. Beat in chocolate and extract.
5. Add dry ingredients alternately with banana and buttermilk, blending after each addition.
6. Turn into 2 greased 9-inch pans; bake at 350°F 30 to 35 minutes.
MAKES 2 9-INCH LAYERS

Chocolate Buttermilk Cake

1 cup butter	3 cups sifted cake flour
1 teaspoon vanilla	1½ teaspoons baking soda
1¾ cups sugar	1 teaspoon salt
2 eggs	2 cups buttermilk
½ cup cocoa	

1. Cream butter, vanilla and sugar together.
2. Add eggs, one at a time, beating thoroughly after each addition; beat until light and fluffy.
3. Stir cocoa, flour, soda and salt together.
4. Add to creamed mixture alternately with buttermilk, blending well.
5. Turn into 3 greased 9-inch round layer pans.
6. Bake at 350°F 25 to 30 minutes.
7. Let stand 5 minutes, then remove.
8. When cool, frost with Browned Butter Frosting (page 577).
MAKES 3 9-INCH LAYERS

Fudge Cake

5 eggs	½ cup shortening
4 squares (4 ounces) unsweetened chocolate	1½ teaspoons vanilla
	3 cups sifted cake flour
2½ cups sugar	1½ teaspoons baking soda
1¾ cups milk	½ teaspoon salt
¼ cup butter	

1. Beat 1 egg and combine with chocolate, 1 cup sugar and ¾ cup milk in a saucepan.
2. Cook over low heat, stirring until chocolate melts and mixture thickens.
3. Cool to lukewarm.
4. Cream butter, shortening, vanilla and 1½ cups sugar together.
5. Add remaining eggs, one at a time, beating well after each addition.
6. Sift flour, soda and salt together.
7. Add to creamed mixture alternately with remaining milk, beating until smooth after each addition.
8. Blend in the chocolate mixture.
9. Grease and line bottoms of 3 9-inch round layer pans with greased waxed paper.
10. Turn batter into pans.
11. Bake at 350°F 30 to 35 minutes.
12. When cool, frost with Fudge Frosting (page 576).
MAKES 3 9-INCH LAYERS

Party Cakes

2 cups plus 2 tablespoons sifted cake flour	½ cup soft shortening
	1 cup milk
1½ cups sugar	¾ teaspoon vanilla
3½ teaspoons baking powder	¼ teaspoon almond extract
1 teaspoon salt	4 egg whites, unbeaten

1. Sift together into a bowl the flour, sugar, baking powder and salt.
2. Add the shortening, milk and flavorings.
3. Beat 2 minutes on medium speed of electric mixer or 300 strokes by hand.
4. Scrape sides and bottom of bowl occasionally with rubber spatula.
5. Add egg whites and beat 2 minutes, scraping the bowl.
6. Turn batter into greased 15½x10½x1-inch jelly-roll pan, spreading evenly into corners.
7. Bake at 350°F about 20 minutes, or until surface springs back when touched with fingers. Cool.
8. Cut cake into oblongs, squares, circles, diamonds, crescents or any desired shape.
9. Spread top and sides with Butter Frosting (page 576).
MAKES ABOUT 50

To Decorate Cakes. Color some of the frosting and decorate cakes using decorating tubes. Hollow out some of the cakes; fill hollows with jam. Press chopped nuts, grated chocolate or toasted coconut into sides of frosted cakes. Rounds may be used as the bases upon which to stack rounds with centers cut out. The holes may be filled before frosting or decorating the entire pastry.

Dark Chocolate Cake

4 squares (4 ounces)
  unsweetened chocolate
¼ cup butter
2 cups sugar
2 egg yolks, unbeaten

2 cups sifted cake flour
¾ teaspoon salt
1¾ cups milk
1 teaspoon vanilla
1 teaspoon baking soda

1. Melt chocolate and butter over low heat; cool.
2. Beat in sugar. Add yolks and 1 cup milk; beat to blend.
3. Add flour and salt; blend until flour is dampened.
4. Beat 1 minute (or 150 strokes).
5. Add vanilla and ½ cup milk; beat until smooth.
6. Combine soda with ¼ cup milk; stir into batter.
7. Pour into greased 13x9 inch pan and bake at 350°F 45 minutes.
8. Frost with Fluffy Peppermint Frosting (page 577).
MAKES 1 13x9-INCH CAKE

Irresistible Chocolate Cake

2½ cups sifted cake flour
½ teaspoon baking soda
½ teaspoon salt
1½ teaspoons baking powder
⅛ teaspoon nutmeg
¾ cup butter or margarine
1½ teaspoons vanilla

1½ cups sugar
2 eggs, beaten
3 squares (3 ounces)
  unsweetened chocolate,
  melted
1¼ cups cold water

1. Sift together first 5 ingredients.
2. Cream together butter, vanilla and sugar until creamy.
3. Add eggs; beat until fluffy.
4. Add chocolate; blend well.
5. Add dry ingredients and water alternately in thirds; beat after each addition.
6. Pour into 2 greased 9-inch layer pans.
7. Bake at 350°F 30 to 35 minutes.
MAKES 2 9-INCH LAYERS

White Cake

2½ cups sifted cake flour
2½ teaspoons baking powder
½ teaspoon salt
½ cup shortening
1½ cups sugar

1 teaspoon vanilla
¼ teaspoon almond extract
1 cup milk
½ cup (about 4) egg whites

1. Sift flour, baking powder and salt together.
2. Cream shortening with sugar and flavorings until creamy.
3. Add sifted dry ingredients and milk alternately in small amounts, beating well after each addition.
4. Beat egg whites until stiff peaks are formed; fold into batter.
5. Turn into 2 8- or 9-inch greased layer pans.
6. Bake at 350°F 30 to 35 minutes.
7. Cool 5 minutes, then remove to racks.
8. When cool, spread Fig Filling (page 575) between layers.
9. Frost sides and top with Caramel Frosting (page 577).
10. Decorate sides of cake with shaved almonds.
MAKES 2 8 OR 9-INCH LAYERS

Lady Baltimore Cake

3½ cups sifted cake flour
4 teaspoons baking powder
½ teaspoon salt
1 cup butter or margarine
2 cups sugar

1 teaspoon vanilla
1 cup milk
1 cup (about 8 to 10) egg whites

1. Sift first 3 ingredients together.
2. Cream butter, sugar and extract together until light and fluffy.
3. Add dry ingredients alternately with milk, mixing until blended.
4. Beat egg whites until stiff, but not dry, peaks are formed.
5. Fold into batter.
6. Grease 3 round 8-inch layer pans; turn batter into pans.
7. Bake at 375°F 25 minutes, or until cake tests done.
8. Cool 5 minutes before turning onto cooling racks.
9. Cool and spread Lady Baltimore Filling (see page 577) between layers. Cover sides and top with reserved frosting.
MAKES 3 8-INCH LAYERS

Whipped Cream Cake I

2 cups sifted cake flour
½ teaspoon salt
3 teaspoons baking powder
1½ cups sugar
1 cup heavy cream

1 teaspoon vanilla
1 teaspoon almond extract
4 egg whites
½ cup cold water

1. Sift flour, salt, baking powder and 1 cup sugar together.
2. Whip cream until stiff. Add flavorings.
3. Beat egg whites until foamy; add remaining ½ cup sugar gradually, beating constantly until stiff peaks are formed.
4. Fold whipped cream into egg whites.
5. Add dry ingredients alternately with water in small amounts, folding until blended after each addition.
6. Turn batter into 2 round 9-inch pans (bottoms lined with waxed paper).
8. Bake at 350°F. 25-30 minutes.
MAKES 2 9-INCH LAYERS

Whipped Cream Cake II

1½ cups sifted cake flour
1 cup sugar
2 teaspoons baking powder
¼ teaspoon salt

1 cup heavy cream
2 eggs, well beaten
1½ teaspoons vanilla
¼ teaspoon lemon extract

1. Sift the flour, sugar, baking powder and salt together.
2. Whip cream until stiff peaks are formed.
3. Fold into well-beaten eggs with the flavorings.
4. Sift dry ingredients over mixture, ¼ at a time, folding until blended after each addition.
5. Line bottoms of 2 round 8-inch layer pans with waxed paper.
6. Turn batter into pans.
7. Bake at 350°F 30 minutes.
MAKES 2 8-INCH LAYERS

Chocolate-Almond Torte

1 package (4½ ounces)
  chocolate instant pudding
  and pie filling
2 cups milk

¼ teaspoon almond extract
12 dessert crêpes (below)
Blanched almond halves

1. Prepare instant pudding and pie filling following package directions and using 2 cups milk; stir in almond extract.
2. Divide pudding on crêpes and spread evenly. Stack the crêpes and decorate with almonds. Cut in wedges and serve.
6 SERVINGS

Dessert Crêpes

1 cup all-purpose flour
¼ cup sugar
Pinch salt
3 eggs

1½ cups milk
2 tablespoons melted buttter
  or oil
2 tablespoons brandy

1. Sift flour, sugar, and salt. Add eggs, one at a time, beating thoroughly. Gradually add milk, melted butter or oil, and brandy, beating until smooth. (Or mix in an electric blender until smooth.)
2. Let batter stand 1 hour before cooking crêpes.
ABOUT 18 CRÊPES

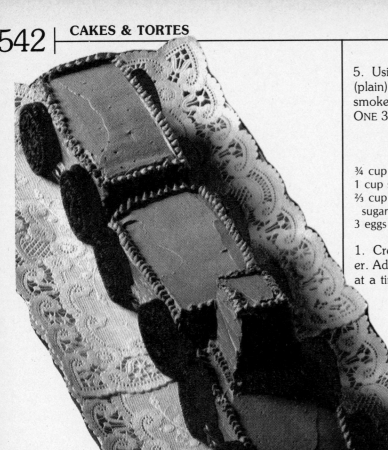

5. Using a large pastry bag filled with frosting, and tube 4 (plain), pipe a border around the edge of train and smokestack (see photo).

ONE 3-CAR TRAIN CAKE

Three-Egg Cake

¾ cup butter
1 cup sugar
⅔ cup firmly packed brown
 sugar
3 eggs

2¾ cups sifted cake flour
2¾ teaspoons baking powder
¼ teaspoon salt
1 cup milk
1½ teaspoons vanilla extract

1. Cream butter until fluffy in large bowl of an electric mixer. Add sugars, beating until well combined. Add eggs, one at a time, beating well after each addition.

2. Sift flour with baking powder and salt. Add to batter in fourths alternately with milk and vanilla extract, beginning and ending with flour. When thoroughly combined, spoon into a well-greased 9-inch square baking pan that has been lined on the bottom with greased parchment paper. Smooth top with a spatula, pushing batter into the corners.
3. Bake at 350°F 40 minutes, or until cake tests done. Turn out on wire rack and cool completely. Peel off paper.

Browned Butter Frosting

½ cup butter
4 cups confectioners' sugar
½ cup half-and-half (more if

needed)
1 tablespoon dark corn syrup
1 teaspoon vanilla extract

1. Melt butter in a heavy saucepan over low heat. Continue heating until it turns deep golden brown, watching carefully so it does not burn. Remove from heat and stir in confectioners' sugar, half-and-half, corn syrup, and vanilla extract.
2. Beat well, using an electric mixer or wire whisk. Frosting must be creamy and soft, yet stiff enough to spread on cake. Beat in additional confectioners' sugar or half-and-half as needed to reach desired consistency.

Train Cake

Three-Egg Cake, chilled
Browned Butter Frosting (see Note)
12 round, flat cookies or candies, 1 to 2 inches in diameter, to be used for wheels (sandwich cookies,

party mints, red-hot dollars, or lollipops with sticks removed may be used)
3 licorice sticks, halved
1 large marshmallow half (cut crosswise)
2 red gumdrops

1. Invert the cake so it is bottom side up. Cut 3 pieces of cake 5x3½ inches each, and cut 1 piece 3x1½ inches for smokestack.
2. Cover the top and sides of the pieces with Browned Butter Frosting, spreading as smoothly as possible with a metal spatula dipped frequently in hot water. Place smokestack on one car of train to make engine.
3. Arrange cars to form a train on a serving platter.
4. Immediately, before frosting begins to set, press or prop round cookies in place on both sides of cars to form wheels. Connect wheels with licorice sticks for "axles." Press sticky side of marshmallow half on front of first car, making a headlight. Place a gumdrop on each side of marshmallow.

Hazelnut Torte with Strawberry Whipped Cream

Graham cracker crumbs
(about 3 tablespoons)
2 cups sugar
½ teaspoon ground allspice
1 teaspoon grated lemon
peel
4 cups (about 1 pound)
filberts or hazelnuts, grated
in rotary-type grater

6 egg yolks (½ cup)
6 egg whites (¾ cup)
¼ teaspoon salt
1 tablespoon light corn syrup
1 teaspoon water
1 egg white, slightly beaten
Strawberry Whipped Cream,
(page 578)

1. Thoroughly grease a 6½-cup ring mold and coat evenly with graham cracker crumbs; set aside.
2. Blend sugar, allspice, and lemon peel in a large bowl; mix in filberts until completely blended.
3. Beat egg yolks until thick and lemon colored. Using a fork, blend into nut mixture.
4. Using a clean bowl and beater, beat the egg whites with the salt until stiff, not dry, peaks are formed. Blend into nut mixture. Turn into prepare mold; spread evenly using the back of a spoon.
5. Bake at 350°F 45 to 55 minutes.
6. Remove torte from oven (leave oven on); cool 10 to 15 minutes on a wire rack. Loosen torte from mold and turn out onto an ungreased baking sheet.
7. Blend corn syrup and water; brush over top of torte. Brush entire torte with egg white. Return torte to oven for 5 minutes.
8. Transfer to cake plate. Serve warm or at room temperature with Strawberry Whipped Cream.
ONE 9-INCH TORTE

Angel Food Cake

1 cup sifted cake flour
1¼ cups sugar
1 cup egg whites (8-10 eggs)
1 teaspoon cream of tartar

½ teaspoon salt
1 teaspoon vanilla
¼ teaspoon almond extract

1. Sift flour and ¼ cup sugar together 4 times.
2. Beat egg whites, cream of tartar and salt until frothy throughout.
3. Add remaining sugar in small amounts and beat after each addition, preferably with a rotary beater. Egg whites

should have fine, even texture and be stiff enough to hold a peak but not be dry.
4. Add flavorings.
5. Sift ¼ of flour at a time over mixture and fold in lightly.
6. Pour into 9-inch ungreased tube pan; cut through batter with spatula to remove large air bubbles.
7. Bake in moderate oven (375°F) 35-40 minutes.
8. Invert pan and let cake stand until cold.
MAKES 1 9-INCH TUBE CAKE

Meringue Angel Food Cake

1½ cups sugar
½ cup water
1¼ cups egg whites (10-12
eggs)
1 teaspoon cream of tartar

¼ teaspoon salt
1 teaspoon vanilla
¼ teaspoon almond extract
1 cup sifted cake flour

1. Cook sugar in water to 234°F or until syrup spins a long thread.
2. Beat egg whites until frothy throughout.
3. Add cream of tartar with salt and continue beating until egg whites hold a peak.
4. Pour syrup slowly over beaten egg whites and continue beating until mixture is cold.
5. Add flavoring. Fold in flour.
6. Cut through batter with spatula to remove large air bubbles.
7. Bake in ungreased tube pan in 375°F oven 35-40 minutes.
8. Invert pan and let cake hang in pan until cold.
MAKES 1 9-INCH TUBE CAKE

Hazelnut Torte with Strawberry Whipped Cream

Nutcake

5¼ ounces almonds
3 eggs
¾ cup sugar
½ teaspoon baking powder

Filling:
1 package pineapple mousse

½ cup heavy cream

Garnish:
½ can pineapple slices
½ cup heavy cream
1 teaspoon vanilla sugar
Green citron pieces

1. Grind almonds. Beat eggs and sugar until foamy. Add almonds and baking powder.
2. Butter a baking dish well and sprinkle with bread crumbs. Pour in batter. Bake cake in 350°F oven about 40 minutes.
3. Remove cake from baking dish when cooled and sprinkle with pineapple juice.
4. Prepare pineapple mousse according to package directions and place on top of cake. Garnish with pineapple slices, citron pieces and whipped cream.
14 SERVINGS

Dream Cake

8 eggs, separated
½ teaspoon cream of tartar
½ teaspoon salt

1 tablespoon lemon juice
1 cup sugar
¾ cup sifted cake flour

1. Beat egg yolks and salt until very thick and lemon colored; beat in juice and add sugar gradually, beating until thick enough to hold a soft peak.
2. Using clean beater, beat egg whites until frothy, then add cream of tartar and beat until stiff but not dry peaks form.
3. Fold egg whites and flour into egg yolk mixture.
4. Pour into ungreased 10-inch tube pan and bake at 350°F 40 minutes.
5. Invert pan; let cake hang until cold.
MAKES 1 10-INCH TUBE CAKE

Chocolate Angel Food Cake

¾ cup sifted cake flour
4 tablespoons cocoa
1¼ cups egg whites (10-12 eggs)

½ teaspoon salt
1 teaspoon cream of tartar
1¼ cups sifted sugar
1 teaspoon vanilla

1. Sift the flour and cocoa together 4 times.
2. Beat the egg whites and salt together until foamy throughout; add cream of tartar and continue beating until stiff enough to hold a peak, but not dry.
3. Fold in sugar lightly, 2 tablespoons at a time, until all is used.
4. Fold in vanilla.
5. Sift small amount of flour over mixture and fold in quickly but lightly; continue until all is used.
6. Pour batter into ungreased 9-inch tube pan and cut through batter with spatula to remove large air bubbles.
7. Bake in 375°F oven 35-45 minutes.
8. Invert pan and let cake hang in pan until cold.
MAKES 1 9-INCH TUBE CAKE

Yolk Sponge Cake

3¼ cups sifted cake flour
3 teaspoons baking powder
1 teaspoon salt
1 teaspoon vanilla

1½ teaspoons lemon extract
12 egg yolks (about 1 cup)
2 cups sugar
1 cup hot water

1. Sift flour and baking powder together 4 times.
2. Add salt and flavorings to yolks and beat with rotary beater until very thick.
3. Add sugar and hot water alternately in 4 portions, beating until very thick after each addition.
4. Fold in about ¼ of flour mixture at a time.
5. Pour into ungreased tube pan and bake in moderate oven (350°F) 1 hour.
6. Invert pan and let cake hang in pan until cold.
MAKES 1 10-INCH TUBE CAKE

Chocolate Sponge Cake

¾ cup sifted cake flour
¼ teaspoon salt
4 tablespoons cocoa

1 tablespoon lemon juice
5 eggs, separated
1 cup sifted sugar

1. Sift flour, salt and cocoa together 4 times.
2. Add lemon juice to beaten egg yolks and beat with rotary egg beater until very thick.
3. Beat egg whites until foamy; add sugar gradually, beating constantly until stiff peaks are formed.
4. Fold in the egg yolks, then flour mixture in small amounts.
5. Turn into ungreased 9-inch tube pan; cut through batter to remove large air bubbles.
6. Bake at 350°F 50-60 minutes.
7. Invert pan and let cake hang until cold.
MAKES 1 9-INCH TUBE CAKE

Meringue Sponge Cake

½ cup water
1¼ cups sugar
6 eggs, separated
¼ teaspoon salt

1 teaspoon cream of tartar
1 tablespoon lemon juice
1⅛ cups sifted cake flour

1. Boil water and sugar together to 238°F or until a small amount of the syrup forms a soft ball when dropped into cold water.
2. Beat egg whites and salt until stiff but not dry, pour syrup slowly over whites, add cream of tartar and beat until cool.
3. Add juice.
4. Beat egg yolks until very thick; fold into egg-white mixture.
5. Fold in flour.
6. Bake in ungreased 9-inch tube pan in moderate oven (350°F) 45 minutes.
7. Invert pan and let cake hang in pan until cold.
MAKES 1 9-INCH TUBE CAKE

Chocolate-Ricotta Cheese Cake

Pastry Dough:
2 cups flour
½ cup sugar
7 tablespoons soft butter
3 tablespoons shortening
3 egg yolks
1 whole egg
1 teaspoon grated lemon peel

Filling:
½ cup uncooked rice
2 ounces (2 squares) unsweetened chocolate
1 pound ricotta cheese
1½ cups sugar
1 teaspoon grated lemon peel
3 egg yolks
¼ teaspoon cinnamon
1 teaspoon vanilla extract
2 egg whites

1. For pastry dough, using **steel blade,** put all ingredients into the bowl and process until thoroughly blended.
2. Place two thirds of dough in a 9-inch springform pan. Using your fingers, spread it carefully over bottom and approximately 1½ inches up the sides. Chill shell and remaining dough while preparing filling.
3. For filling, cook rice, rinse it with cold water, and set aside to cool.
4. Melt chocolate in a double boiler and cool.
5. Using **steel blade,** add ricotta to the bowl and process until smooth. Add 1 cup sugar, grated lemon peel, egg yolks, cinnamon, the melted chocolate, and vanilla extract; process until creamy.
6. Using a mixer, beat 2 egg whites with remaining ½ cup sugar until stiff. Add to ricotta mixture and fold together. Fold in cooked rice.
7. Pour filling into pan. Roll out remaining dough on a floured board. Cut into 1-inch strips and arrange in lattice fashion on top.
8. Bake at 350°F 1 hour and 10 minutes, or until cake is firm and lattice is golden. Cool before serving.
ONE 9-INCH CHEESE CAKE

Orange Sponge Cake

2 cups sifted cake flour
2 teaspoons baking powder
¼ teaspoon salt
5 egg yolks
1⅞ cups sugar
½ cup water
1 tablespoon grated orange rind
½ cup orange juice
4 egg whites

1. Sift first 3 ingredients together.
2. Beat egg yolks and sugar until thick; add water gradually and beat well.
3. Mix orange rind with juice.
4. Fold dry ingredients into egg yolk mixture alternately with orange juice.
5. Fold in stiffly beaten egg whites.
6. Turn into ungreased 9-inch tube pan; cut through batter with spatula to remove large bubbles.
7. Bake at 350°F 50-60 minutes.
8. Invert pan and cool cake.
9. Frost with Orange Butter Frosting (page 576).
MAKES 1 9-INCH TUBE CAKE

Sunshine Cake

1½ cups sifted cake flour
1 teaspoon baking powder
½ teaspoon salt
6 egg yolks
1½ cups sugar
1 teaspoon lemon extract
1 teaspoon grated lemon rind
⅓ cup cold water
6 egg whites
½ teaspoon cream of tartar

1. Sift the flour, baking powder and salt together; set aside.
2. Beat egg yolks, then beat in the sugar gradually; continue beating until very thick and lemon-colored.
3. Beat in lemon extract and rind.
4. Blend in dry ingredients alternately with water.
5. Beat egg whites with cream of tartar until stiff peaks are formed.
6. Fold egg-yolk mixture into whites.
7. Bake at 325°F about 1 hour.
9. Invert pan and let cake hang until cold.
MAKES 1 10-INCH TUBE CAKE

Chocolate-Ricotta Cheese Cake

Filled Holiday Coffee Cake

2 packages active dry yeast
1 cup milk, scalded and
  cooled to warm
4 cups all-purpose flour
½ cup sugar
1 teaspoon salt

1 cup firm butter
2 eggs, beaten
1 teaspoon vanilla extract
Vanilla Butter Filling
1 cup chopped nuts
Confectioners' Sugar Icing

1. Soften yeast in the cooled milk.
2. Mix flour, sugar, and salt in a large bowl. Cut in the butter with a pastry blender until particles are the size of rice kernels. Mixing well after each addition, add the yeast, then the mixture of eggs and extract.
3. Cover bowl with plastic wrap. Chill several hours or overnight.
4. Before removing dough from refrigerator, prepare Vanilla-Butter Filling. Spread 2 tablespoons filling over bottom and sides of each of two 9x5x3-inch loaf pans.
5. Divide dough into halves. On a lightly floured surface, roll each portion into an 18x10-inch rectangle. Spread each with half of remaining filling and sprinkle with half of nuts. Cut rectangle into three 10x6-inch strips. Starting with long side, roll up each strip and twist slightly. Braid three rolls together and place one braid in each pan, being sure to tuck ends under. Brush tops with **melted butter**.
6. Cover; let rise in a warm place until doubled, about 1½ hours.
7. Bake at 350°F 45 to 50 minutes. Immediately remove from pans and cool on wire racks.
8. Spread coffee cakes with Confectioners' Sugar Icing. Before icing is set, decorate top with **marzipan fruit, glazed dried apricots,** and **preserved kumquats.**
2 FILLED COFFEE CAKES

Confectioners' Sugar Icing: Blend **1 cup confectioners' sugar, 1 tablespoon softened butter, 1 teaspoon light corn syrup,** and **1 tablespoon hot water.**

Vanilla-Butter Filling: Cream ¾ cup butter. Add 1½ cups sifted confectioners' sugar gradually, beating until light and fluffy. Blend in 1 teaspoon vanilla extract.

True Sponge Cake

1 cup sifted cake flour
¼ teaspoon salt
1 teaspoon grated lemon rind
1½ tablespoons lemon juice
1 cup sugar
5 eggs, separated

1. Sift flour and salt together 4 times.
2. Add lemon rind and juice to beaten egg yolks and beat until very thick.
3. Beat egg whites until stiff but not dry; fold in sugar in small amounts. Fold in the egg yolks.
4. Sift ¼ of the flour at a time over surface and fold in.
5. Bake in ungreased 9x9 inch tube pan in 350°F oven 55 to 60 minutes.
6. Invert pan and let cake hang in pan until cold.
MAKES 1 9-INCH TUBE CAKE

Ladyfingers

⅓ cup sifted flour
⅛ teaspoon salt
2 eggs, separated
½ cup sifted confectioners' sugar
½ teaspoon vanilla

1. Sift flour and salt together.
2. Combine egg yolks and sugar; beat until thick and lemon-colored.
3. Fold in the dry ingredients.
4. Beat egg whites until stiff; fold into batter with the vanilla.
5. Put batter into pastry bag filled with plain tube.
6. Force through tube onto baking sheet covered with heavy paper.
7. Sprinkle lightly with confectioners' sugar.
8. Bake at 325°F 12 to 18 minutes.
9. Remove to cooling racks at once. For double ladyfingers, immediately brush bottoms of baked fingers with slightly beaten egg white and press together in pairs.
MAKES ABOUT 12 PAIRS LADYFINGERS

Moss Rose Cake

2 cups sifted cake flour
½ teaspoon salt
2 teaspoons baking powder
4 eggs
2 cups sugar
½ teaspoon almond extract
1 cup hot milk

1. Sift flour, salt and baking powder together.
2. Beat eggs and add the sugar gradually, beating until very thick and lemon-colored.
3. Beat in the flavoring.
4. Sift dry ingredients over egg mixture, about ¼ at a time, folding gently until just blended after each addition.
5. Add hot milk all at one time and quickly mix until batter is smooth.
6. Pour into 3 lightly greased 8-inch round pans and bake at 375°F 15 to 20 minutes, or until cake springs back when touched lightly.
7. Let cool about 10 minutes in pans before removing to racks.
MAKES 3 8-INCH LAYERS

Hot Water Sponge Cake

1 cup sifted cake flour
1½ teaspoons baking powder
¼ teaspoon salt
2 eggs
1 cup sugar
½ tablespoon lemon juice
6 tablespoons hot water

1. Sift flour, baking powder and salt together.
2. Beat eggs until very thick and lemon-colored.
3. Add sugar gradually, beating constantly until thick enough to hold a soft peak.
4. Beat in lemon juice.
5. Add hot water gradually beating until very thick.
6. Fold in flour.
7. Bake in 2 lightly greased round 8-inch layer pans at 350°F 25-30 minutes.
MAKES 2 8-INCH LAYERS

Linzer Torte

1 cup unblanched almonds
1½ cups sifted flour
½ teaspoon cinnamon
⅛ teaspoon powdered cloves
¼ teaspoon salt
⅔ cup butter or margarine
⅔ cup sugar
2 egg yolks, beaten
1 teaspoon grated lemon rind
1 cup raspberry or apricot jam

1. Put almonds through medium blade of food chopper.
2. Sift together flour, spices and salt.
3. Cream butter and sugar together until creamy.
4. Add egg yolks, nuts and rind; beat unti fluffy.
5. Stir in dry ingredients.
6. Knead until very well mixed.
7. Press ¾ of dough against sides and bottom of 8-inch pie pan.
8. Fill with jam.
9. Form remaining dough into eight 8-inch strips ½-inch thick.
10. Make lattice top over jam, 4 strips dough each way.
11. Bake in a 350°F (moderate) oven 20-30 minutes.
12. Cool; if desired, garnish top with whipped cream.
MAKES 1 8-INCH TORTE

Hot Milk Sponge Cake

1 cup sifted cake flour
1 teaspoon baking powder
¼ teaspoon salt
3 eggs, well beaten
1 cup sugar
2 teaspoons lemon juice
6 tablespoons hot milk

1. Sift first 3 ingredients together.
2. Add sugar gradually to eggs, beating until thick.
3. Add lemon juice.
4. Sift dry ingredients over mixture, about ¼ at a time, folding to blend.
5. Add milk and quickly blend until smooth.
6. Turn into 2 lightly greased 9-inch layer pans.
7. Bake at 375°F 15 minutes or until cake tests done.
8. Frost.
MAKES 2 9-INCH LAYERS

Baba

1 package active dry yeast
½ cup milk, scalded and cooled
½ cup sugar
2 cups all-purpose flour
½ cup butter (at room temperature)
4 eggs
½ teaspoon salt

½ teaspoon cinnamon
¼ teaspoon mace
1 tablespoon grated lemon peel
½ cup raisins, chopped almonds, or chopped candied fruits (optional)
Lemon Icing (page 578) or honey

1. Dissolve yeast in milk 10 minutes. Add 1 tablespoon of the sugar and ½ cup of the flour; mix well. Cover. Let rise until doubled.
2. Cream butter, gradually adding remaining sugar. Beat until fluffy. Beat in 3 whole eggs, 1 at a time. Beat in 1 egg yolk; reserve remaining egg white.
3. Mix remaining flour with salt and spices. Beat into butter mixture. Stir in lemon peel and raisins.
4. Beat yeast mixture into butter mixture. Beat until batter is silky, about 10 to 15 minutes.
5. Turn into a well-greased and floured 10-inch baba or tube pan. Cover. Let rise until tripled in bulk, about 1½ hours.
6. Beat remaining egg white until foamy. Brush over top of baba.
7. Bake at 350°F about 40 minutes, until baba sounds hollow when tapped.
8. Cool on rack 10 minutes. Remove from pan. Drizzle with icing or brush with honey, if desired.
1 BABA

Baba au Rhum: Prepare Baba as directed. Set in cake pan or shallow casserole. To prepare Rum Sauce: Boil ⅓ **cup water, ⅓ cup sugar,** and ⅓ **cup apricot jam** with **1 teaspoon lemon juice** 5 minutes. Add ½ **cup rum.** Bring just to simmering. Pour over baba. With wooden pick, poke holes in baba. Continue pouring syrup over baba until all syrup is absorbed.

Blueberry Orange Cheese Cake

1½ cups graham cracker crumbs
2 tablespoons sugar
½ teaspoon cinnamon
½ teaspoon nutmeg
6 tablespoons butter, melted
4 cups cream-style cottage cheese
Heavy cream
6 eggs
1½ cups sugar
½ cup all-purpose flour
3 tablespoons thawed frozen orange juice concentrate
1 teaspoon vanilla extract
⅛ teaspoon salt
1 cup sour cream
2 tablespoons confectioners' sugar
1 cup dry-pack frozen blueberries, thawed

1. Set out a 9-inch springform pan.
2. To prepare crust, combine graham cracker crumbs, sugar, cinnamon and nutmeg in a bowl.
3. Stir in butter.
4. Press the mixture on bottom and about three-fourths up sides of the springform pan. Chill crust while preparing the filling.
5. Drain cottage cheese (reserving the cream), press through a coarse sieve and set aside.
6. Measure reserved cream in a measuring cup for liquids and fill to 1-cup level with heavy cream.
7. In a large mixing bowl, beat eggs until very thick.
8. Add sugar, beating until light and fluffy.
9. Blend in the sieved cottage cheese, the cream and flour, orange juice concentrate, vanilla extract, and salt. Mix well and turn filling into crumb-lined pan.
10. Bake at 350°F oven 1 hour and 10 to 20 minutes. (Cheese cake is done when a metal knife inserted in center comes out clean.)
11. While cake is baking, prepare topping. Combine sour cream, confectioners' sugar and blueberries in a small bowl.
12. When cake tests done, turn off heat. Open oven door and gently spread cake with topping mixture. Cool in oven until cake is of room temperature. Chill.
ONE 9-INCH CHEESE CAKE

Note: Syrup-pack canned or frozen blueberries, drained, may be used in topping.

Mocha Cake

1½ cups eggs (whole)
1¼ cups sugar
½ teaspoon vanilla
¼ teaspoon almond extract
2 cups sifted cake flour
¼ cup butter, melted

1. Heat eggs and sugar over hot water, beating constantly with a rotary beater until very light and fluffy, about 10 minutes. (Do not allow water to boil.)
2. Remove from heat; add extracts and beat until cold.
3. Fold in flour gradually, then blend in melted butter.
4. Turn into 3 greased 9-inch layer pans.
5. Bake at 325°F 30 minutes.
6. When cool, fill and frost with Mocha Cream Frosting (page 578, use 1½ times the recipe).
MAKES 3 9-INCH LAYERS

Pineapple Feather Cake

1½ cups sifted cake flour
1 teaspoon baking powder
6 eggs, separated
¼ teaspoon salt
1½ cups sugar
½ cup pineapple juice
1 tablespoon lemon juice

1. Sift flour and baking powder together 4 times.
2. Beat egg whites and salt until stiff but not dry.
3. Add ¾ cup sugar, about 2 tablespoons at a time, beating well after each addition.
4. Beat egg yolks, add remaining sugar and fruit juices and beat until thick and lemon-colored.
5. Fold flour, about ¼ of it at a time, into yolk mixture, folding just enough to moisten flour.
6. Fold in egg white mixture.
7. Pour into ungreased tube pan.
8. Cut through batter with spatula to remove large air bubbles.
9. Bake in slow oven (325°F) 50 to 60 minutes.
10. Invert pan and let cake hang in pan until cold.
MAKES 1 10-INCH TUBE CAKE

Daffodil Cake

¾ cup egg whites (about 6)
¼ teaspoon salt
¾ teaspoon cream of tartar
1 cup sifted sugar
¾ cup sifted cake flour
¼ teaspoon vanilla
¼ teaspoon grated orange rind
3 egg yolks, well beaten
1½ tablespoons sugar

1. Beat egg whites with salt and cream of tartar until foamy; add 1 cup sugar, 2 tablespoons at a time, beating after each addition. Beat until stiff peaks are formed.
2. Fold in flour gradually.
3. Divide batter into 2 parts. Add vanilla extract to one.
4. Beat egg yolks, orange rind and remaining sugar together until thick. Blend into remaining batter.
5. Drop from tablespoon into ungreased tube pan, alternating batters.
6. Bake at 350°F 45 to 55 minutes.
7. Invert pan and let cake hang until cool.
MAKES 1 9-INCH TUBE CAKE

Easy Twin Tortes

Coffee Torte
½ recipe Basic Frosting
½ teaspoon instant coffee
Apricot jam or preserves
1 12-ounce pound cake
Candied cherries and citron

1. Blend instant coffee into frosting.
2. Cut pound cake lengthwise into thin layers about ¼ inch thick.
3. Spread each layer, except one, with jam, putting layers back together as they are spread.
4. Secure at each end with a wooden pick.
5. Frost sides and top of cake with coffee frosting.
6. Decorate with candied cherries and citron into holly berries and leaves.
SERVES 12

Linda's Favorite Cheese Cake

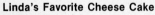

Linda's Favorite Cheese Cake

Crust:
1 cup flour
¼ cup sugar
1 teaspoon grated lemon peel
½ teaspoon vanilla extract
8 tablespoons butter, cut in 6 pieces
1 egg yolk

Filling:
4 packages (8 ounces each) cream cheese, cut in quarters
5 eggs
1¼ cups sugar
3 tablespoons flour
1 teaspoon grated lemon peel

1. For crust, using **steel blade** of food processor, place all ingredients in the bowl and process until mixture is thoroughly blended. Using your hands, pat onto bottom and sides of a 9-inch springform pan.
2. Bake at 400°F 10 to 15 minutes, or until lightly browned.
3. For filling, using **steel blade,** add 1 package cream cheese and 1 egg to the bowl and process until smooth. Add another package of cream cheese and another egg and process until smooth. Add last package of cream cheese and another egg and process until smooth. Add last two eggs and remainder of ingredients and process until smooth and creamy.
4. Pour cheese mixture into baked crust.
5. Bake at 325°F 1 hour, or until firm. Cool and top with Strawberry Glaze.
ONE 9-INCH CHEESE CAKE

Chocolate Torte

½ recipe Basic Frosting
2 squares (2 ounces) semisweet dipping chocolate
Evaporated milk
Raspberry jam or preserves
1 12-ounce pound cake

1. Melt chocolate over hot, not boiling water.
2. Gradually blend chocolate into frosting.
3. If frosting is too stiff, add a small amount of evaporated milk until of spreading consistency.
4. Continue as for Coffee Torte.
5. Decorate loaf with silver dragées.
SERVES 12

Basic Frosting. Cream **¼ cup butter** until softened; add **1 pound confectioners' sugar, sifted,** alternately with **⅓ cup plus 1 tablespoon evaporated milk.** Beat after each addition until smooth and creamy.

Prize Chocolate Cake

4 squares (4 ounces) unsweetened chocolate
1 cup milk
1 cup sifted cake flour
¼ teaspoon salt
2 teaspoons baking powder
4 eggs separated
1⅔ cups sugar
1 teaspoon vanilla

1. Cook chocolate (cut in pieces) and milk over low heat until thickened, stirring constantly; cool.
2. Sift flour, salt and baking powder together.
3. Beat egg yolks, sugar and extract together until thick.
4. Add dry ingredients and chocolate mixture alternately, beating well after each addition.
5. Fold in stiffly beaten egg whites.
6. Turn into greased 9x9-inch pan; bake at 350°F 35-40 minutes.
MAKES 10 9x9-INCH SQUARE CAKE

Ribbon Cake

3 cups sifted cake flour
4 teaspoons baking powder
½ teaspoon salt
¾ cup shortening
1¾ cups sugar
1 teaspoon vanilla
4 eggs, separated
1 cup water
Red food coloring
1 tablespoon molasses
¼ teaspoon ground mace
¼ teaspoon powdered cloves
½ teaspoon cinnamon
½ cup chopped dates or raisins
⅓ cup chopped figs or nuts

1. Sift flour, baking powder and salt together.
2. Cream shortening, sugar and vanilla together until creamy.
3. Add unbeaten egg yolks one at a time; beat well after each addition.
4. Add dry ingredients and water alternately in thirds, beating well after each addition.
5. Fold in egg whites, beaten until stiff but not dry.
6. Divide batter into 3 equal portions, leave 1 portion uncolored, tint second portion pink with food coloring and add remaining ingredients to third portion.
7. Pour each portion into greased 9-inch pan and bake in moderate oven (350°F) 30 to 35 minutes.
8. When cool put layers together with jelly or icing, with dark layer on bottom, uncolored in center and pink on top.
MAKES 3 9-INCH LAYERS

Velvety Chocolate Cake

2¾ cups sifted cake flour
2 teaspoons baking powder
1 teaspoon baking soda
¼ teaspoon salt
¾ cup butter or margarine
1 cup packed brown sugar
⅔ cup granulated sugar

3 eggs
3 ounces (3 squares) unsweetened chocolate, melted and cooled
1 can or bottle (12 ounces) beer

1. Sift dry ingredients together.
2. Cream butter and sugars until very light and fluffy.
3. Add eggs, one at a time, beating thoroughly at medium speed of electric mixer. Beat in chocolate.
4. Add sifted dry ingredients alternately with beer, beating at low speed until blended after each addition.
5. Turn into 2 greased and waxed-paper-lined 9-inch round layer cake pans.
6. Bake at 350°F 35 minutes, or until done. Cool in pans 10 minutes; turn out on wire racks. When cool, frost with favorite icing.
ONE 2-LAYER 9-INCH CAKE

Tri-Colored Party Cake

½ cup butter
1¼ cups sugar
1 teaspoon vanilla
3 eggs, separated
2 cups sifted cake flour

2 teaspoons baking powder
¼ teaspoon salt
⅔ cup milk
Red and green food coloring

1. Cream butter, sugar and vanilla together; add egg yolks, one at a time, beating well after each addition.
2. Sift flour, baking powder and salt together; add to creamed mixture alternately with milk.
3. Fold in stiffly beaten egg whites.
4. Divide the batter into 3 equal parts.
5. Color ⅓ light pink, ⅓ light green, and leave ⅓ yellow.
6. Turn into 3 greased 8-inch pans; bake at 375°F 15-20 minutes.
7. Remove from pans; cool.
8. Frost with Rich Chocolate Frosting (page 576).
MAKES 3 LAYERS

Mallow White Cake

2 cups sifted cake flour
2 teaspoons baking powder
½ teaspoon salt
½ cup shortening

1½ cups sugar
1 teaspoon vanilla
¾ cup water
4 egg whites

1. Sift flour, baking powder and salt together.
2. Cream shortening with sugar and vanilla until creamy.
3. Add sifted dry ingredients and water alternately in thirds, beating well after each addition.
4. Beat egg whites until stiff but not dry and fold into batter.
5. Pour into 2 greased 8-inch pans; bake at 350°F 30-35 minutes.
MAKES 2 8-INCH LAYERS

Anniversary Cake

3 cups sifted cake flour
½ teaspoon salt
4½ teaspoons baking powder
¾ cup butter
½ teaspoon almond extract
2 teaspoons vanilla

1¼ cups sugar
1 cup milk
¾ cup egg whites (about 6)
⅛ teaspoon salt
¾ cup sugar

1. Sift first 3 ingredients together.
2. Cream butter, extracts and 1¼ cups sugar together until light and fluffy.
3. Add dry ingredients alternately with milk in thirds, beginning and ending with dry ingredients and blending well after each addition.
4. Using clean beater, beat egg whites and ⅛ teaspoon salt together until foamy; add ¾ cup sugar gradually, beating well after each addition; beat until stiff peaks form.
5. Fold into cake batter.
6. Turn into 3 greased 8-inch layer pans; bake at 375°F 25-30 minutes.
7. When cool, put layers together with 1½ recipes of Lemon Filling (page 575); frost with Seven-Minute Frosting (page 577).
8. Sprinkle with toasted sliced, blanched almonds.
MAKES ONE 3-LAYER 8-INCH CAKE

Velvety Chocolate Cake

Cherry Fruitcake

1½ cups sifted all-purpose flour
1½ cups sugar
1 teaspoon baking powder
1 teaspoon salt
2 packages (7¼ ounces each) pitted dates
1 pound diced candied pineapple
2 jars (16 ounces each) red maraschino cherries, drained
18 ounces (about 5½ cups) pecan halves
6 eggs
½ cup dark rum
½ cup light corn syrup

1. Grease two 9x5x3-inch loaf pans; line with aluminum foil, allowing a 2-inch overhang; grease the foil.
2. Sift flour, sugar, baking powder and salt into a large mixing bowl.
3. Add dates, pineapple, maraschino cherries and pecan halves to flour mixture and toss until coated.
4. Beat eggs in a bowl until thick.
5. Blend in rum.
6. Pour over fruit mixture and toss until thoroughly mixed. Turn into prepared loaf pans, pressing mixture with spatula to pack tightly.
7. Bake at 300°F about 1¾ hours, or until wooden pick inserted in center of loaves comes out clean.
8. Remove from oven to cooling rack and allow to cool 15 minutes before removing loaves from pans. Peel off foil and while still warm brush loaves with **corn syrup.**
9. Cool thoroughly before serving or storing.
2 LOAVES FRUITCAKE

1-2-3-4 Cake

3 cups sifted cake flour
3 teaspoons baking powder
¼ teaspoon salt
1 cup shortening
2 cups sugar
1 teaspoon vanilla
4 eggs, separated
1 cup milk

1. Sift flour, baking powder and salt together.
2. Cream shortening with sugar and vanilla until creamy.
3. Add beaten egg yolks and beat thoroughly.
4. Add sifted dry ingredients and milk alternately in small amounts, beating well after each addition.
5. Beat egg whites until stiff but not dry and fold into batter.
6. Pour into 3 greased 9-inch pans and bake in moderate oven (375°F) about 30 minutes.
MAKES 3 9-INCH LAYERS

Coconut Cake. Spread **Lemon Filling** (page 575) or **Orange Filling** (page 575) between layers. Cover top and sides of cake with **Seven-Minute Frosting** (page 577) and sprinkle generously with **coconut.**

Circus Birthday Cake. Spread **Orange Marmalade Filling** between layers. Cover top and sides of cake with **Marshmallow Seven-Minute Frosting** (page 577). Arrange a circle of **animal crackers** upright on top of cake and another circle around bottom of cake. Place tiny candles on top of cake.

Lord Baltimore Cake

2½ cups sifted cake flour
½ teaspoon salt
3 teaspoons baking powder
¾ cup butter or margarine
½ teaspoon lemon extract
1 teaspoon vanilla
1¼ cups sugar
7 or 8 egg yolks (⅔ cup)
¾ cup milk

1. Sift together flour, salt and baking powder.
2. Cream together butter, flavorings and sugar until mixture is like whipped cream.
3. Beat egg yolks with rotary beater or electric mixer until very thick and very light colored.
4. Add to butter mixture and beat at least 5 minutes.
5. Add dry ingredients alternately with milk in thirds; beat well after each addition.
6. Pour into 3 greased 9-inch layer pans; bake at 375°F 20-25 minutes.
7. When cool, fill with Lord Baltimore Filling (page 577) and frost with reserved frosting.
MAKES 3 9-INCH LAYERS

Heavenly Torte

3 cups sifted cake flour
4 teaspoons baking powder
1 teaspoon salt
1 cup butter or margarine
1 teaspoon grated lemon rind
¼ teaspoon lemon extract
1 teaspoon vanilla
2 cups sugar
4 eggs
1 cup milk
½ cup finely chopped pecans

1. Sift first 3 ingredients together.
2. Cream butter with rind, extracts and sugar until fluffy.
3. Add eggs, one at a time, beating vigorously after each addition.
4. Add dry ingredients alternately with milk, blending after each addition.
5. Stir in nuts.
6. Turn batter into 3 greased 8-inch layer pans; bake at 375°F 25 to 30 minutes.
7. When cool, fill and frost with Heavenly Torte Filling (page 576).
MAKES 3 8-INCH LAYERS

Nut Loaf Cake

1½ cups sifted cake flour
2 teaspoons baking powder
¼ teaspoon salt
½ cup shortening
1 cup sugar
1 teaspoon vanilla
2 eggs, separated
½ cup milk
1 cup chopped nutmeats

1. Sift flour, baking powder and salt together.
2. Cream shortening with sugar and vanilla until creamy.
3. Add egg yolks and beat thoroughly.
4. Add sifted dry ingredients and milk alternately in small amounts, beating well after each addition.
5. Add nuts and fold in stiffly beaten egg whites.
6. Pour into greased 8x4x3-inch loaf pan and bake in moderate oven (350°F) 50 minutes.
MAKES 1 8x4x3-INCH LOAF

Cherry Fruitcake

Toasty Pineapple Angel Delight

½ cup butter, softened
½ cup firmly packed brown sugar
Dash cinnamon
1 loaf angel food cake, cut

into 6 slices
6 pineapple rings
¾ cup sour cream
6 maraschino cherries

1. Cream the butter, brown sugar and cinnamon together.
2. Place cake slices on broiler rack and toast on one side under broiler heat.
3. Spread butter mixture generously on untoasted side, spreading it over edges of cake.
4. Place a pineapple ring on buttered side and dot pineapple with any remaining butter mixture.
5. Broil about 2 minutes, or until golden.
6. Serve immediately topped with sour cream and a maraschino cherry.
SERVES 6

Graham Cracker Cream Cake

1 cup sifted cake flour
2 teaspoons baking powder
¼ teaspoon salt
1 cup fine graham cracker crumbs

½ cup shortening
½ cup sugar
2 eggs, beaten
1 cup milk
1 teaspoon almond extract

1. Sift first 3 ingredients together; mix with crumbs.
2. Cream shortening and sugar; beat in eggs.
3. Add dry ingredients and liquids alternately.
4. Bake in greased 8-inch pans at 350°F 30 minutes.
5. Fill with Cream Filling (page 576).
MAKES 2 8-INCH LAYERS

Chocolate Frost 'n' Fill

2 squares (2 ounces) unsweetened chocolate, cut up
2 cups milk
½ cup sugar
½ cup flour

⅛ teaspoon salt
2 eggs, slightly beaten
1 cup butter
1 teaspoon vanilla
1 cup confectioners' sugar

1. Combine chocolate and milk in a saucepan.
2. Cook over low heat until chocolate is melted, stirring occasionally.
3. Blend sugar, flour and salt together in a bowl; stir in a small amount of the milk mixture and return to saucepan.
4. Continue cooking and stirring until mixture thickens.
5. Add a small amount of the mixture to eggs and blend well.
6. Return to saucepan and cook 2 minutes, stirring constantly.
7. Remove from heat; chill.
8. Cream butter and vanilla; then blend in confectioners' sugar.
9. Add chocolate mixture and beat only until blended.
10. Split each cake layer crosswise into 2 layers.
11. Spread frosting between the layers and on sides and top of cake.
WILL FROST AND FILL 1 9-INCH CAKE

Yellow Butter Cake

½ cup butter
1¼ cups sugar
1 teaspoon vanilla
3 eggs

2 cups sifted cake flour
2 teaspoons baking powder
¼ teaspoon salt
⅔ cup milk

1. Cream butter, sugar and vanilla together.
2. Add eggs, one at a time, beating thoroughly after each addition.
3. Beat until light and fluffy.
4. Sift flour, baking powder and salt together.
5. Add to creamed mixture alternately with milk, bending after each addition.
6. Turn into 2 buttered, 8 or 9 inch round cake pans.
7. Bake at 375°F 25 to 30 minutes.
8. Remove from oven; let stand 5 minutes and remove layers onto cooling racks. Cool completely.
9. Frost with Chocolate Frost 'n' Fill (below).
MAKES 2 8- OR 9-INCH LAYERS

Banana Layer Cake

2¼ cups sifted cake flour
2½ teaspoons baking powder
¼ teaspoon baking soda
½ teaspoon salt
½ cup shortening

1 cup sugar
1 teaspoon vanilla
2 eggs
1 cup mashed ripe bananas
2 tablespoons milk

1. Sift flour, baking powder, soda and salt together.
2. Cream shortening with sugar and vanilla until creamy.
3. Add eggs one at a time; beat thoroughly after each is added.
4. Combine bananas and milk.
5. Add sifted dry ingredients and milk mixture alternately in small amounts, beating thoroughly after each addition.
6. Pour into 2 greased 8-inch pans and bake in a 375°F (moderate) oven 25-30 minutes.
7. Spread Seven-Minute Frosting (page 577) between layers and on top and sides of cake.
MAKES 2 8-INCH LAYERS

Blitz Torte

½ cup butter
1 teaspoon vanilla
½ cup sugar
4 egg yolks, well beaten
1 cup sifted cake flour

1 teaspoon baking powder
3 tablespoons milk
3 egg whites
½ cup sugar
¾ cup chopped pecans

1. Cream butter, vanilla and ½ cup sugar together.
2. Add egg yolks.
3. Sift flour and baking powder together; add alternately with milk.
4. Spread batter evenly in bottom of 11x7x1½-inch pan.
5. Beat egg whites until frothy; add ½ cup sugar, 2 tablespoons at a time; beat well after each addition.
6. Beat until stiff peaks are formed.
7. Spread on top of the batter.
8. Sprinkle with nuts and sugar; bake at 325°F 35 to 40 minutes.
MAKES 24 PIECES

Chocolate Torte

8 eggs, separated
1¼ cups sugar
¾ cup all-purpose flour
¼ cup fine dry bread crumbs
¼ teaspoon salt
2 ounces (2 squares)
  semisweet chocolate, grated
1½ teaspoons vanilla extract
Filling (see below)
Frosting (see below)

1. Beat egg yolks until very thick and lemon-colored, about 5 minutes. Gradually beat in sugar.
2. Combine flour, bread crumbs, and salt. Add chocolate and mix thoroughly but lightly.
3. Add flour mixture to egg yolks and sugar in 4 portions, folding until well mixed after each addition.
4. With clean beaters, beat egg whites with vanilla extract until stiff, not dry, peaks are formed. Fold into flour mixture.
5. Turn into a well-greased 10-inch springform pan or deep, round layer cake pan.
6. Bake at 325°F 50 to 60 minutes. Remove from pan and cool completely.
7. Split cake in half.
8. Spread filling on bottom half. Replace top. Spread frosting over sides and top. Refrigerate 4 hours or longer for torte to mellow.
ONE 10-INCH TORTE

Filling: Whip **½ cup whipping cream** until cream piles softly. Fold in **¼ cup ground almonds or walnuts** and **3 tablespoons sugar**.

Frosting: Melt **4 ounces (4 squares) unsweetened chocolate** and **3 tablespoons butter** together in a saucepan. Remove from heat. Stir in **1 tablespoon brandy**. Add **2 to 2½ cups confectioners' sugar** and **2 to 3 tablespoons milk or cream** until frosting is of spreading consistency.

Walnut Torte I

10 ounces walnuts (3½ cups grated)	1 cup sugar
½ cup flour	1 teaspoon grated lemon peel
½ teaspoon instant coffee	1 teaspoon vanilla extract
½ teaspoon cocoa	Mocha Butter Frosting
6 eggs, separated	

1. Grease bottoms of two 8-inch round layer cake pans. Line bottoms with waxed paper and grease waxed paper. Set aside.
2. Using **shredding disc** of food processor, shred walnuts. Set ¾ cup walnuts aside. Remove shredding disc and insert **steel blade.** Add flour, coffee, and cocoa to bowl and process remaining walnuts to a fine powder. Remove from bowl and set aside.
3. Using **steel blade,** process egg yolks, ½ cup sugar, and lemon peel until very thick and lemon colored (about 2 to 3 minutes). Add vanilla extract and process until blended.
4. Using a mixer, beat egg whites until frothy. Gradually add ½ cup sugar, beating well after each addition. Beat until rounded peaks are formed and egg whites do not slide when bowl is tipped. Gently spread egg-yolk mixture over beaten egg whites. Spoon a fourth of flour-walnut mixture over egg mixture and gently fold with a few strokes until batter is only partially blended. Repeat with second, third, and fourth portions and fold until just blended. Do not overmix!
5. Gently turn batter into prepared pans.
6. Bake at 350°F 25 to 30 minutes, or until torte tests done. Cool before removing from pan. Run spatula gently around sides of pan. Cover with wire rack. Invert and remove pan. Remove waxed paper and turn right side up.
7. Fill layers with frosting. Frost top and sides of cake and sprinkle top with remaining chopped walnuts. Chill to firm frosting.
ONE 8-INCH TORTE

Mocha Butter Frosting

4 ounces sweet chocolate	¾ cup butter
1 tablespoon instant coffee	½ cup confectioners' sugar
2 tablespoons water	

1. In the top of a double boiler, melt chocolate with coffee and water. Remove from heat and cool.
2. Using **steel blade** of food processor, cream butter. Add cooled chocolate mixture and confectioners' sugar. Process until smooth.

Blueberry Torte

1⅓ cups sifted cake flour	4 eggs, separated
2 teaspoons baking powder	⅓ cup milk
¼ teaspoon salt	½ cup sugar
⅓ cup shortening	1½ cups blueberries
⅔ cup sugar	2 tablespoons sugar
1 teaspoon vanilla	

1. Sift first 3 ingredients together.
2. Cream shortening with sugar and vanilla until creamy.
3. Add egg yolks, one at a time; beating vigorously after each addition.
4. Add sifted dry ingredients and milk alternately in thirds, blending after each addition.
5. Turn batter into 2 greased 8-inch round pans.
6. Bake at 350°F 15 minutes.
7. Meanwhile beat egg whites until foamy; add ½ cup sugar gradually, beating well after each addition; beat until stiff peaks are formed.
8. Spread over hot cake layers and return quickly to 300°F oven; bake 20 minutes longer, or until topping is lightly browned.
9. Cool and remove from pans.
10. Mash about ¼ cup of the berries with 2 tablespoons sugar and mix with whole berries.
11. Spread between cake layers. Chill.
SERVES 8

Cherry Topsy-Turvy Cake

1½ cups sifted flour	½ cup evaporated milk
1½ teaspoons baking powder	½ cup water
¼ teaspoon salt	1 can (1 pound 1 ounce)
½ cup butter	red, tart pitted cherries
1 teaspoon vanilla	½ cup sugar
1 cup sugar	¼ teaspoon red food
1 egg	coloring

1. Sift flour, baking powder and salt together.
2. Cream butter, vanilla and 1 cup sugar together.
3. Add egg; beat until light and fluffy.
4. Combine evaporated milk and water.
5. Add alternately with dry ingredients to creamed mixture; blend after each addition.
6. Turn batter into a greased 8x8-inch baking pan.
7. Combine contents of can of cherries with ½ cup sugar in a saucepan.
8. Bring to boiling, stirring occasionally.
9. Remove from heat; add red food coloring; blend well.
10. Spread cherries over uncooked cake batter in even layer.
11. Spoon hot cherry juice over cherries.
12. Bake in a 350°F (moderate) oven about 45 minutes, or until cake tests done.
13. Let cool about 10 minutes and turn onto serving plate.
14. If desired, garnish with Whipped Lemon Topping.
SERVES 9

Whipped Lemon Topping. Whip **½ cup icy cold undiluted evaporated milk** until stiff peaks are formed. Beat in **2 tablespoons lemon juice.** Fold in **½ cup sifted confectioners' sugar.**

Brownie Fruitcake, Irish Fruitcake, White Walnut Fruitcake, Banana Walnut Fruitcake (page 562), Double Walnut Fruitcake.

White Walnut Fruitcake

1½ cups walnuts (7 ounces)
1½ cups halved candied cherries (12 ounces)
1 cup diced candied pineapple (6 ounces)
¾ cup diced candied orange peel (4 ounces)
¾ cup diced candied lemon peel (4 ounces)
¾ cup diced citron (4 ounces)
¾ cup brandy
2 cups sifted all-purpose flour
¾ teaspoon baking powder
1 teaspoon salt
1 teaspoon mace
¾ cup butter or margarine
1 cup sugar
4 eggs, separated
1 tablespoon grated orange peel
½ teaspoon cream of tartar
Confectioners' sugar
Angelica or citron strips
Candied cherries

1. Chop walnuts coarsely and set aside.
2. Combine candied fruits and peels in a bowl. Pour ½ cup brandy over fruit, stir to moisten, cover, and let stand several hours or overnight.
3. Line bottom and sides of a 9-inch tube pan with one thickness of greased brown paper and one of greased waxed paper.
4. Sift flour with baking powder, salt, and mace.
5. Cream butter and sugar until light and fluffy. Beat in egg yolks and grated peel. Add dry ingredients alternately with remaining ¼ cup brandy to creamed mixture, mixing well after each addition. Mix in walnuts and brandied fruit.
6. Beat egg whites with cream of tartar until stiff, not dry, peaks are formed. Fold into fruit mixture. Spoon into prepared pan and spread level.
7. Place a shallow pan of hot water on oven floor. Set filled tube pan on lowest rack of oven.
8. Bake at 300°F about 2½ hours, or until cake tests done. Cool cake in pan.
9. To decorate, sift confectioners' sugar lightly over top of cake. Decorate with strips of angelica or citron and candied cherries.
ONE 4½-POUND FRUITCAKE

Brownie Fruitcake

1½ cups walnuts (7 ounces)
1 cup halved candied cherries (8 ounces)
1 cup diced mixed candied fruits (8 ounces)
1 cup sliced dates (5 ounces)
½ cup hot coffee
¼ cup unsweetened cocoa
1¾ cups sifted all-purpose flour
¼ teaspoon baking soda
¾ teaspoon salt
¼ teaspoon cinnamon
⅛ teaspoon cloves
½ cup butter or margarine
1 teaspoon vanilla extract
1¼ cups packed brown sugar
2 eggs
4 to 6 walnut halves
Candied cherry halves
Angelica, citron, or candied pineapple strips

1. Chop walnuts coarsely; combine with candied fruits and dates.
2. Stir coffee and cocoa together; set aside to cool.
3. Line bottom and sides of an 11x4½x2¾-inch loaf pan with one thickness of greased brown paper and one of greased waxed paper, allowing paper to extend about 1 inch above sides and ends of pan.
4. Sift flour with baking soda, salt, and spices.
5. Cream butter, vanilla extract, and brown sugar well. Add eggs, one at a time, beating thoroughly after each addition (mixture will look curdled). Blend in flour mixture alternately with cocoa mixture. Stir in chopped walnuts and fruits. Turn into prepared pan. Arrange walnut halves on top.
6. Place a shallow pan of hot water on oven floor. Set filled loaf pan on lowest rack of oven. Put a piece of brown paper on paper lining pan.
7. Bake at 300°F 2 to 2¼ hours, or until cake tests done. Cool in pan.
8. To decorate, arrange cherry halves and angelica strips between walnut halves.
ONE 3¾-POUND FRUITCAKE

Irish Fruitcake

1½ cups walnuts (7 ounces)
¾ cup dark seedless raisins (4 ounces)
¾ cup golden raisins (4 ounces)
¾ cup currants (3 ounces)
¾ cup diced citron (4 ounces)
¾ cup diced candied orange peel (4 ounces)
¾ cup halved candied cherries (6 ounces)
½ cup Irish whiskey or bourbon
1 tablespoon molasses
1 teaspoon grated lemon
peel
2 cups sifted all-purpose flour
½ teaspoon baking powder
1 teaspoon salt
1 teaspoon cinnamon
½ teaspoon nutmeg
½ teaspoon allspice
¾ cup butter or margarine
1 cup packed brown sugar
3 eggs
Confectioners' sugar
Water
Green food coloring
Green decorator sugar
Walnut halves

1. Chop walnuts coarsely and set aside.
2. Combine raisins, currants, and candied fruits and peels with ⅓ cup whiskey, molasses, and lemon peel. Mix well,

cover, and let stand overnight.
3. The next day, sift flour with baking powder, salt, and spices.
4. Cream butter and brown sugar well. Add eggs, one at a time, beating thoroughly after each addition (mixture will look curdled). Blend flour mixture into creamed mixture. Add fruits and walnuts and mix well.
5. Turn into a well-greased 9-inch Bundt pan.
6. Place a shallow pan of hot water on oven floor. Set filled Bundt pan on lowest rack of oven.
7. Bake at 300°F about 1¾ hours, or until cake tests done. Let cool 10 minutes in pan, then invert cake onto wire rack and spoon remaining whiskey slowly over cake so it soaks in. Cool cake completely.
8. To decorate, mix a small amount of confectioners' sugar with enough water to thin to pouring consistency. Tint lightly with food coloring; drizzle over top of cake. Sprinkle with green sugar and arrange walnut halves on top.
ONE 3¾-POUND FRUITCAKE

Double Walnut Fruitcake

2½ cups walnuts (12 ounces)
1 cup candied pineapple chunks (6 ounces)
1 cup halved candied cherries (8 ounces)
1 cup sliced dates (5 ounces)
½ cup golden raisins (3 ounces)
1½ cups sifted all-purpose flour
1 teaspoon baking powder
1 teaspoon salt
⅔ cup butter or margarine
1 teaspoon vanilla extract
1 cup packed brown sugar
3 eggs
Confectioners' sugar
Water
Mixed candied fruits and peels

1. Chop 1 cup walnuts coarsely; combine with candied fruits, dates, and raisins.
2. Grate remaining 1½ cups walnuts with Mouli grater (or put into an electric blender, ¼ cup at a time, and blend to a fine meal).
3. Sift flour with baking powder and salt.
4. Cream butter, vanilla extract, and brown sugar well. Add eggs, one at a time, beating thoroughly after each addition (mixture will look curdled). Blend in flour mixture and grated walnuts. Mix in walnut-fruit mixture.
5. Turn into a well-greased 11x4½x2¾-inch loaf pan or other pan with 2-quart capacity.
6. Place a shallow pan of hot water on oven floor. Set filled loaf pan on lowest rack of oven.
7. Bake at 300°F about 2 hours, or until cake tests done. Cool in pan 30 minutes, then turn cake out onto wire rack to cool.
8. To decorate, mix a little confectioners' sugar with enough water to thin to pouring consistency. Drizzle over top of cake. Pile candied fruits down center.
ONE 3½-POUND FRUITCAKE

Banana Walnut Fruitcake

1½ cups walnuts (7 ounces)
2 cups mixed candied fruits (1 pound)
1¾ cups sifted all-purpose flour
1 teaspoon baking powder
¼ teaspoon baking soda
1 teaspoon salt
¼ teaspoon nutmeg
⅔ cup butter or margarine
¾ cup sugar
2 eggs
1 cup mashed banana (3 small bananas)
Confectioners' sugar (optional)

1. Chop walnuts coarsely. Chop candied fruits finely and combine with walnuts in a bowl; set aside.
2. Sift flour with baking powder, baking soda, salt, and nutmeg.
3. Cream butter and sugar well. Add eggs, one at a time, beating thoroughly after each addition. Blend in flour mixture alternately with mashed banana.
4. Pour batter over fruit-walnut mixture and blend well.
5. Turn into a well-greased tube pan (about 2-quart capacity).
6. Place a shallow pan of hot water on oven floor. Set filled tube pan on lowest rack of oven.
7. Bake at 300°F about 1¼ hours, or until a wooden pick inserted in center comes out clean and dry. Cool 15 minutes in pan, then invert cake onto wire rack to cool.
8. Serve plain or with a light sifting of confectioners' sugar.
ONE 3-POUND FRUITCAKE

Crushed Pineapple Upside-Down Cake

3 tablespoons butter or margarine
⅔ cup firmly packed brown sugar
1½ cups (no. 2 can) drained crushed pineapple; reserve
½ cup syrup
Maraschino cherries
Walnut halves
⅓ cup shortening
1 teaspoon vanilla
½ cup sugar
1 egg
1¼ cups sifted flour
½ teaspoons baking powder
Whipped cream

1. Melt butter in 8-inch square pan or 9-inch round pan or oven-proof skillet.
2. Sprinkle with brown sugar.
3. Spread pineapple over mixture.
4. Decorate with cherries and walnuts.
5. Cream shortening, vanilla and sugar together.
6. Add egg; beat vigorously.
7. Add sifted dry ingredients alternately with pineapple syrup: mix until blended after each addition.
8. Spread over pineapple.
9. Bake in 350°F (moderate) oven 50 to 60 minutes.
10. Let cool 10 minutes, then turn out upside-down on plate.
11. Serve warm with whipped cream.
SERVES 6 TO 8

Marigold Cake

2¼ cups sifted cake flour
½ teaspoon salt
2½ teaspoons baking powder
½ cup shortening
1¼ cups sugar
1 teaspoon vanilla
3 eggs
⅔ cup milk
Bananas

1. Sift flour, salt and baking powder together.
2. Cream shortening, sugar and vanilla until creamy.
3. Add eggs one at a time; beat well after each is added.
4. Add sifted dry ingredients and milk alternately in small amounts; beat well after each addition.
5. Pour into 3 greased 8-inch layer pans.
6. Bake at 350°F 25 to 30 minutes. Cool.
7. Prepare a double recipe of Lemon Filling (page 575); fill layers.
8. Add a layer of sliced bananas to bottom layers and cover with lemon filling.
9. Frost cake with Divinity Frosting (page 577) and top with sliced bananas.
SERVES 12

Currant Fruitcake

2 cups all-purpose flour
1 teaspoon baking powder
½ teaspoon salt
¼ teaspoon nutmeg
1 cup dried currants
¼ cup candied orange peel, chopped
¼ cup candied lemon peel, chopped
¼ cup candied cherries,
halved
¼ cup candied apricots, chopped
¾ cup dark raisins
½ cup light raisins
¾ cup butter
⅔ cup sugar
3 eggs
½ cup blanched almonds, sliced

1. Preheat oven to 325°F. Grease a 9-inch tube pan.
2. Sift flour, baking powder, salt and nutmeg.
3. Mix currants, orange peel, lemon peel, apricots, cherries and raisins.
4. Beat butter and sugar until light and fluffy. Add eggs one at a time beating well after each addition.
5. Gradually add flour mixture and beat until well mixed.
6. Stir in fruit mixture until well mixed. Turn in prepared pan. Sprinkle with almonds. Gently press into top.
7. Bake 60 to 65 minutes till cake tester comes out clean. Cool on wire rack. Remove from pan after 15 minutes.

Lemon Meringue Cake

4 egg yolks
½ cup sugar
¼ cup water
1 teaspoon lemon extract
1 cup sifted cake flour
4 egg whites

½ teaspoon cream of tartar
⅛ teaspoon salt
½ cup sugar
Lemon Curd Buttercream
Italian Meringue

1. Grease bottom and sides of a 15x10x1-inch jelly-roll pan. Line bottom with parchment paper and grease the paper. Set aside.
2. In large bowl of an electric mixer, beat the egg yolks with ½ cup sugar, water, and lemon extract until very thick. Stir in flour until just blended.
3. Beat egg whites with cream of tartar and salt until soft peaks are formed. Gradually add ½ cup sugar, continuing to beat until stiff peaks are formed. Fold egg yolk mixture into meringue until blended. Turn batter into prepared pan and spread evenly.
4. Bake at 350°F 20 to 25 minutes, or until cake tests done. Turn out onto wire rack to cool. Peel off paper.
5. When cake is cool, cut into two 10x7½ inch pieces, forming 2 layers. Place 1 layer on an ovenproof serving plate.
6. Beat Lemon Curd Buttercream to soften, if necessary. Spread ⅔ cup over top of bottom layer. Place second layer on top. Cover top and sides of cake with remaining buttercream. Refrigerate until chilled (about 30 minutes).
7. Using a large pastry bag and tube 6 or 7 (plain), fill (below) with Italian Meringue. Cover top and sides of chilled cake with meringue snails (see illustration).
8. Bake at 400°F 5 to 8 minutes (oven must be preheated), or until meringue peaks are lightly browned. Remove from oven and chill immediately. Serve cold.

ONE 10x7-INCH LAYER CAKE

Note: This cake may be made as a single layer. Do not cut cake in half. Cover top and sides with frosting and make a double recipe of meringue to cover chilled cake.

Lemon Curd Buttercream

¼ cup butter
5 egg yolks
1 cup sugar
1 tablespoon grated lemon

peel
5 tablespoons strained fresh
lemon juice
½ cup butter

1. Combine ¼ cup butter, egg yolks, sugar, lemon peel, and juice in top of a double boiler. Cook over boiling water, stirring slowly but steadily with a wooden spoon until it is slightly thicker (about 10 minutes). Continue cooking over

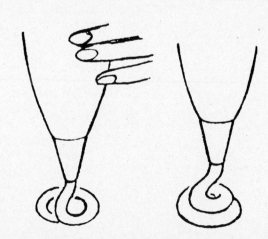

boiling water, stirring occasionally, until curd becomes thick (about 20 minutes). Add more boiling water to double boiler as necessary. Remove from heat and cool.

2. Beat ½ cup butter in a mixing bowl, using an electric mixer, until fluffy. Beating constantly, add cooled lemon mixture, ¼ cup at a time, beating until all has been added and buttercream is well mixed.

3. Refrigerate buttercream in a covered container until ready to use. This will keep at least 2 weeks. Before using, allow to soften to room temperature and beat for a moment, if necessary, to make more spreadable.

1¾ CUPS BUTTERCREAM

Italian Meringue

1⅓ cups sugar	4 egg whites
⅔ cup water	⅛ teaspoon salt
¼ teaspoon cream of tartar	⅛ teaspoon lemon extract

1. In a small, heavy saucepan, combine sugar, water, and cream of tartar, stirring over low heat until sugar is dissolved.
2. Cover saucepan and bring mixture to boiling. Boil gently 5 minutes. Uncover and put candy thermometer in place. During cooking, wash sugar crystals from sides of pan with a pastry brush dipped in water. Cook without stirring until mixture reaches 240°F.
3. While syrup is cooking, beat egg whites, using electric mixer, until peaks are stiff, but not dry. Beating constantly, pour hot syrup over beaten egg whites in a thin, steady stream (do not scrape pan).
4. After all the hot syrup is added, add salt and lemon extract. Continue beating 4 minutes, or until meringue stiffens. Use immediately.

Pineapple Crown Cheesecake

1¼ cups fine graham cracker crumbs	3 eggs
2 tablespoons butter, melted	1 teaspoon vanilla
1 cup plus 2 tablespoons sugar	1 pint sour cream
2 packages (8 ounces each) cream cheese	1 can (8¾ ounces) pineapple tidbits, drained
	¼ cup currant jelly

1. Grease a 9-inch springform pan; sprinkle sides with 2 tablespoons crumbs.
2. Combine remaining crumbs with butter and 2 tablespoons sugar.
3. Press mixture into bottom of pan.
4. Beat cream cheese and 1 cup sugar together.
5. Beat in eggs, one at a time, until fluffy.
6. Fold in extract and room-temperature sour cream.
7. Turn into pan.
8. Bake at 375°F 30 minutes.
9. Turn off heat; leave cake in oven 1 hour.
10. Chill.
11. To serve, garnish with pineapple and jelly.
SERVES 10

Super Turban Cake

2¼ cups sifted all-purpose flour	½ cup sugar
2¼ teaspoons baking powder	4 egg yolks (⅓ cup), well beaten
½ cup butter	¾ cup milk
1 tablespoon grated lemon peel	4 egg whites (½ cup)
1 teaspoon vanilla extract	½ cup sugar
	Chocolate Glaze (see below)

1. Sift the flour and baking powder together; set aside.
2. Cream butter with lemon peel and vanilla extract. Add ½ cup sugar gradually, creaming until fluffy after each addition. Add the beaten egg yolks in thirds, beating well after each addition.
3. Beating only until smooth after each addition, alternately add dry ingredients in thirds and milk in halves to creamed mixture.
4. Beat the egg whites until frothy. Add ½ cup sugar gradually, beating well after each addition; beat until stiff peaks are formed. Gently fold into batter. Turn into a greased and floured 12-cup fluted tube pan. Top with 6 layers of paper toweling.
5. Put pan into a large electric cooker.
6. Cover and cook on High 2½ to 3½ hours, or until cake tester inserted in center comes out clean.
7. Cool cake on wire rack. Loosen cake from pan by running a small spatula carefully around the tube and edge of cake. Spread warm Chocolate Glaze over the cake. Allow 2 to 3 hours for glaze to set.
8 TO 10 SERVINGS

Chocolate Glaze: Melt **4 ounces semisweet chocolate pieces** in a heavy saucepan over low heat. Remove from heat and stir in **¼ cup butter** until blended.

Super Turban Cake

Old English Cheesecake

Crust:
1¼ cups all-purpose flour
¼ cup sugar
⅓ cup butter or margarine
4 tablespoons cold beer

Filling:
½ cup golden raisins (2½ ounces), chopped
⅓ cup almonds (2 ounces), finely chopped
1 tablespoon grated lemon peel
1 pound cottage cheese
½ cup flour
4 eggs
1 cup sugar
¾ cup beer
⅛ teaspoon nutmeg

1. For crust, mix flour and sugar; cut in butter until crumbly. Add beer 1 tablespoon at a time, stirring with a fork. Shape dough into a ball. Chill.
2. Roll out on floured surface to a 13- to 14-inch circle. Fold in quarters. Gently unfold in a 9-inch springform pan. (1½ inches up sides if using a 10-inch pan). Prick all over with fork.
3. Bake at 425°F 10 minutes. Prick again and press to sides. Bake 10 minutes more, or until slightly golden.
4. For filling, mix chopped raisins, almonds, and peel.
5. Process cottage cheese, flour, and eggs until smooth, using food processor or electric blender. (Do in several batches in blender.)
6. Add sugar, beer, and nutmeg; blend until smooth. Stir in raisin mixture. Pour into cooled shell.
7. Bake at 300°F 1¼ to 1½ hours, or until set. Cool to room temperature for serving. Dust with **confectioners' sugar** and top with **whole unblanched almonds.**
8 TO 10 SERVINGS

Orange Angelic

1 large angel food cake
Orange sections
½ pint heavy cream, whipped
Orange Velvet Sauce

1. Place cake on a large serving plate.
2. Arrange orange sections in a ring around cake and fill center with additional sections.
3. Spoon whipped cream around top of cake, letting some flow down the sides about every 2 inches.
4. Drizzle the sauce over whipped cream.
SERVES 12

Orange Velvet Sauce. Mix together in saucepan: **1½ cups sugar, 2½ tablespoons cornstarch, ¼ teaspoon salt, 1½ cups orange juice, 2 tablespoons lemon juice, 3 tablespoons grated orange rind** and **3 tablespoons butter.** Blend well. Bring to a rolling boil, stirring occasionally. Boil 1 minute, stirring constantly. Slowly beat ½ of hot mixture into 4 slightly beaten egg yolks. Pour back into saucepan and blend. Cook 3 minutes, stirring constantly. Chill before serving.

Apple Upside-Down Cake

¼ cup butter or margarine
¾ cup light brown sugar
2½ cups (1 pound, 4-ounce can) sliced apples
¾ teaspoon ground mace
2 teaspoons lemon juice
⅓ cup shortening
⅔ cup sugar
1 teaspoon vanilla
1 egg, well beaten
1½ cups sifted flour
2 teaspoons baking powder
¼ teaspoon salt
⅔ cup milk

1. Melt butter in 8x8-inch pan; sprinkle with brown sugar.
2. Drain apples; arrange overlapping wedges on sugar.
3. Sprinkle with mace and lemon juice.
4. Cream shortening, sugar and vanilla together.
5. Add egg and beat vigorously.
6. Add sifted dry ingredients alternately with milk.
7. Pour batter over fruit.
8. Bake at 325°F about 1 hour; cool 5 minutes, then turn upside-down on serving plate.
SERVES 8

Cranberry Upside-Down Cake

3 tablespoons butter
1½ cups sugar
2 cups cranberries
1½ cups sifted cake flour
1½ teaspoons baking powder
¼ teaspoon salt
¼ cup shortening
1 teaspoon vanilla
1 egg, beaten
½ cup milk
Whipped cream

1. Melt butter in 8x8-inch pan.
2. Add a mixture of 1 cup sugar and the berries.
3. Sift dry ingredients together.
4. Cream shortening with remaining sugar and vanilla; beat in the egg.
5. Add dry ingredients and milk alternately in thirds.
6. Pour batter over berries.
7. Bake at 350°F 40 to 45 minutes.
8. Cool 5 minutes and invert on plate.
9. Serve with whipped cream.
SERVES 8

Apple Spice Upside-Down Cake

¼ cup butter, softened
½ cup firmly packed brown sugar
2 cups thinly sliced apples
¼ cup shortening
¼ teaspoon nutmeg
½ teaspoon cinnamon
¼ teaspoon allspice
¾ cup sugar
1 egg
1¼ cups sifted flour
1½ teaspoons baking powder
¼ teaspoon salt
½ cup milk
Whipped Cream

1. Blend butter with brown sugar; spread on bottom of 8x8-inch pan.
2. Arrange apple slices over sugar.
3. Cream shortening with spices and sugar; beat in the egg.
4. Add sifted dry ingredients alternately with milk.
5. Pour over apples; bake at 350°F 45 minutes, or until done.
6. Serve upside-down with whipped cream.
SERVES 8

Old English Cheesecake

Basket Cake

Feather Sponge Cake	semisweet chocolate
Cream Filling	Marzipan
White Buttercream	Green paste food coloring
2 ounces (2 squares)	Red tinted sugar

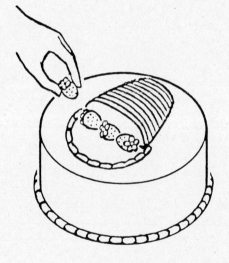

1. Use a long, serrated knife to slice each cake layer in half horizontally. Lay 1 cake layer half on a serving plate and cover with cream filling. Top with another layer and cover with cream filling. Continue with remaining layers. Frost top and sides of cake with White Buttercream. Dip a decorating comb in hot water, shake off excess drops, and "comb" cake sides evenly.

2. Melt chocolate. Add to remaining buttercream. Blend well; refrigerate.

3. Divide Marzipan in half. Press one half into a basket shape which is 4 inches long, 2½ inches wide at top of basket, 1½ inches wide at base, 1 inch high at top with a flattened base.

4. Add green food coloring to about 2 tablespoons marzipan for leaves. Shape remaining marzipan into 6 strawberries. Roll marzipan strawberries in red sugar; coat thoroughly. Using tube 67 (leaf), pipe leaves onto each strawberry.

5. Place basket-shaped marzipan on top of cake. Lay marzipan strawberries on cake.

6. Spread chocolate-flavored buttercream over marzipan basket. Then pipe weaving over basket, using tube 19 (see illustration). Place pine shells on cake for basket handle. Using a large pastry bag filled with chocolate-flavored buttercream and tube 19, pipe a shell border around bottom of cake.

1 BASKET CAKE

Feather Sponge Cake

1⅔ cups sifted cake flour
¼ teaspoon salt
3 egg yolks
½ cup cold water
1½ cups sugar

1 teaspoon orange extract
½ teaspoon lemon extract
3 egg whites
¾ teaspoon cream of tartar

1. Sift flour and salt together. Set aside.
2. In a large mixing bowl, beat egg yolks until very thick. Add water; continue beating until mixture is very light. Gradually add sugar and extracts. Fold in flour and salt.
3. In a separate bowl, beat egg whites until frothy; add cream of tartar and beat until soft peaks are formed.
4. Fold yolk mixture into egg whites.
5. Spoon batter into two 10-inch round layer cake pans which have been lined on bottom with greased parchment paper.
6. Bake at 325°F 25 to 30 minutes, or until cake tests done.
7. Invert cakes onto wire racks to cool. Peel off paper. When cake is cool, remove from pans.

Cream Filling

¼ cup cold milk
2 tablespoons cornstarch
4 egg yolks
¾ cup sugar
⅛ teaspoon salt
1¾ cups milk, scalded

2½ teaspoons unflavored gelatin
5 teaspoons water
1½ teaspoons vanilla extract
½ cup whipping cream

1. Mix cold milk with cornstarch in a small bowl, using a wire whisk so that no lumps remain.
2. Mix egg yolks, sugar, and salt in a small, heavy saucepan. Add hot milk to egg yolk mixture, a little at a time, stirring constantly until well combined. Set over low heat and stir in cornstarch mixture. Cook and stir 4 or 5 minutes, or until custard thickens and coats the spoon. Remove from heat.
3. Meanwhile, soften gelatin in water in top of a double boiler, then set over boiling water until melted. Stir gelatin into hot custard and mix well. Then set custard aside to cool, stirring often to allow steam to escape so custard will not become watery.
4. When cool, stir in vanilla extract. Whip cream and fold into custard. Spoon custard into a covered container and store in refrigerator until needed.

White Buttercream

2½ cups sugar
1 cup water
2½ tablespoons corn syrup
¼ teaspoon cream of tartar
¼ teaspoon salt

5 egg whites
4 teaspoons vanilla extract
½ teaspoon almond extract
1⅔ cups butter

1. In a heavy saucepan combine sugar, water, corn syrup, cream of tartar, and salt. Cover and simmer gently for 5 minutes.
2. Remove cover and cook until syrup reaches 246°F.
3. Beat egg whites at high speed until stiff but not dry. While still beating, pour the hot syrup into egg whites in a thin, steady stream. After all the syrup has been added, continue beating 2 or 3 minutes, or until frosting stiffens a little. Add extracts and continue beating until well mixed.
4. Beat 1⅔ cups butter until very soft. Add the icing, ¼ cup at a time, beating well after each addition. Cover and refrigerate until ready to use.
5½ CUPS

Marzipan

¼ cup canned almond paste
2 teaspoons light corn syrup
3 tablespoons (scant) marsh-

mallow creme
⅔ cup confectioners' sugar
(more if needed)

Mix almond paste, corn syrup, marshmallow creme, and confectioners' sugar together with fingers in a bowl, until well combined and smooth; knead in a little extra confectioners' sugar if paste is sticky. There will be about 10 tablespoons marzipan paste.

Baked Meringue Spice Cake

2 cups sifted cake flour
3 teaspoons baking powder
¼ teaspoon salt
1 teaspoon cinnamon
½ teaspoon powdered cloves
½ cup shortening
1 cup firmly packed brown sugar

1 egg plus 1 egg yolk, beaten
¾ cup milk

Meringue
2 egg whites
1 cup brown sugar
½ cup chopped nuts

For Cake:
1. Sift first 5 ingredients together.
2. Cream shortening with sugar until fluffy.
3. Add beaten egg and egg yolk and beat thoroughly.
4. Add sifted dry ingredients alternately with milk in thirds; beat well after each addition.
5. Pour into greased 11x7-inch pan.

For Meringue:
1. Beat egg whites until frothy; add sugar 1 tablespoonful at a time, beating until stiff.
2. Spread over batter, sprinkle with nuts.
3. Bake at 350°F. 45-50 minutes.
MAKES 1 11x7-INCH CAKE

Sour Cream Spice Cake

2¼ cups sifted cake flour	½ teaspoon powdered cloves
¾ teaspoon baking soda	1⅔ cups sugar
1 teaspoon baking powder	1 cup butter, melted
¼ teaspoon salt	1 cup sour cream
2 teaspoons cinnamon	3 eggs
1 teaspoon nutmeg	1 teaspoon vanilla

1. Sift first 7 ingredients together.
2. Mix lightly with sugar in large bowl.
3. Add butter, sour cream, eggs and vanilla all at one time; beat with a wooden spoon until thoroughly blended.
4. Pour batter into 2 greased 9-inch round layer pans.
5. Bake at 350°F 25 to 30 minutes.
6. Cool 5 minutes; remove from pans.
7. Frost with Orange Butter Frosting (page 576).
8. Top with nut halves.
MAKES 2 9-INCH LAYERS

Huckleberry Upside-Down Cake

2 cups cooked huckleberries	¼ cup shortening
1 tablespoon butter	½ cup sugar
½ cup brown sugar	1 egg, beaten
1 cup flour	¼ cup milk
¼ teaspoon salt	2 drops almond extract
1 teaspoon baking powder	

1. In a saucepan, combine huckleberries, butter and brown sugar and heat for 10 minutes.
2. Sift flour, salt, and baking powder together.
3. Cream shortening with sugar; add egg and mix thoroughly.
4. Add sifted dry ingredients alternately with milk and almond extract.
5. Turn huckleberries into greased 8x8-inch pan and cover with batter.
6. Bake in 350°F oven 45 minutes.
7. Loosen cake from sides and turn onto plate.
MAKES 1 8x8-INCH CAKE

Cherry Pecan Upside-Down Cake

1 cup butter	¼ teaspoon salt
2 cups sugar	1 teaspoon vanilla
1 cup pecans, chopped	2 eggs, well beaten
2 cups pitted tart cherries, well drained	⅔ cup milk
	Whipped cream
2½ cups sifted cake flour	Fresh cherries
3 teaspoons baking powder	

1. Melt ⅓ cup butter in 10-inch skillet; stir in ½ cup sugar.
2. Blend in nuts and cherries.
3. Sift dry ingredients together.
4. Cream remaining butter and sugar together; add vanilla and eggs and beat thoroughly.
5. Add dry ingredients and milk alternately in thirds blending after each addition.
6. Pour over mixture in skillet.
7. Bake in 350°F oven 50 to 60 minutes.
8. Let cool 5 minutes and turn onto plate.
9. Serve with whipped cream garnished with fresh cherries.
SERVES 12

Apple Lane Cake

1 cup butter or margarine, softened	⅔ cup milk
	8 egg whites (reserve yolks for filling)
1 teaspoon vanilla extract	½ cup shredded pared Red or Golden Delicious apples
1½ cups sugar	
2½ cups all-purpose flour	Apple Filling
2 teaspoons baking powder	White Frosting
¼ teaspoon salt	

1. Cream butter, vanilla extract, and sugar in a large bowl. Mix flour, baking powder, and salt. Blend into creamed mixture alternately with milk.
2. Beat egg whites until stiff, but not dry. Stir a little beaten egg white into batter. Stir in shredded apple. Fold batter into remaining egg whites. Turn into 3 greased and floured 9-inch round layer cake pans.
3. Bake at 350°F 20 to 25 minutes, or until cake tester inserted in center comes out clean. Cool 10 minutes; turn out of pans and cool completely on wire racks.
4. Spread Apple Filling between layers and on top of cake. Frost sides of cake with White Frosting. Refrigerate until ready to serve.
10 TO 12 SERVINGS

Apple Filling

8 egg yolks	melted and cooled
1 cup sugar	1 teaspoon vanilla extract
¼ teaspoon salt	1 cup chopped pecans
½ cup bourbon	2 cups chopped Red or
½ cup butter or margarine,	Golden Delicious apples

1. Beat egg yolks, sugar, and salt in a large bowl until light and thick. Gradually beat in bourbon, then butter.
2. Pour mixture into a heavy 2-quart saucepan. Cook, stirring constantly, until thickened (about 10 minutes). Remove from heat; stir in vanilla extract and pecans. Chill.
3. When ready to use, stir in apples.

White Frosting

½ cup sugar	2 egg whites
¼ cup light corn syrup	1 teaspoon vanilla extract
2 tablespoons water	

1. Mix sugar, corn syrup, and water in a small saucepan. Cover and bring to boiling over medium heat. Uncover and heat to 242°F; do not stir.
2. While syrup is heating, beat egg whites until stiff peaks form. Gradually beat hot syrup into egg whites, beating until stiff enough to spread. Beat in vanilla extract.

Indonesian Striped Spice Cake

¾ cup plus 2 tablespoons
  butter
1½ cups sugar
8 egg yolks
1 teaspoon vanilla extract
1¼ cups all-purpose flour
½ teaspoon salt
2½ teaspoons cinnamon
1¼ teaspoons nutmeg

1 teaspoon ginger
½ teaspoon cardamom
¼ teaspoon allspice
¼ teaspoon cloves
⅛ teaspoon mace
8 egg whites
Melted butter (about ¾ cup)
Confectioners' sugar for
  sprinkling

1. Grease bottom of a 9-inch springform pan and line the bottom with a circle of waxed or parchment paper cut to fit; grease paper.
2. Cream butter with sugar until well blended; add yolks and vanilla extract and beat well. Then add flour and salt and beat until well mixed.
3. Spoon half of batter into a separate bowl and add a blend of the spices; mix well.
4. Beat egg whites until peaks are stiff, but not dry. Divide in half and fold half into each portion of batter.
5. Spoon 1 cup of dark batter onto bottom of prepared pan to form a thin layer.
6. Set pan on lowest rack of oven.
7. Bake at 325°F about 20 minutes, or until layer tests done.
8. Remove pan from oven and use a pastry brush to spread a very thin layer of melted butter over top of baked layer. Then spoon 1 cup light batter over top of baked layer and return to oven until layer tests done (about 20 minutes). Brush top with melted butter as before.
9. Continue to alternate light and dark layers, brushing each baked layer with melted butter, until all batter is used and

cake is 6 layers thick. When last layer is added, return cake to oven and bake until center tests done and cake top is nicely browned (25 to 30 minutes).
10. Remove side of springform and set cake on wire rack to cool. When cool, remove springform bottom and wrap cake in foil, securing tightly. Store wrapped cake in a container with a tight-fitting lid and allow it to ripen for 2 days before serving.
11. At serving time, place cake on a serving plate and dust top with confectioners' sugar, if desired. Serve, cut in small pieces. Cake will keep up to 2 weeks if stored as directed.
ONE 9-INCH CAKE

Banana Spice Cake

2¾ cups sifted flour
2 teaspoons baking powder
1 teaspoon baking soda
1 teaspoon salt
¼ teaspoon powdered cloves
1½ teaspoons cinnamon
¾ teaspoon nutmeg

⅔ cup shortening
1⅓ cups sugar
2 eggs, well beaten
1⅔ cups mashed bananas (4
  to 5 bananas)
2 teaspoons vanilla

1. Sift flour, baking powder, soda, salt and spices together.
2. Cream shortening with sugar until fluffy.
3. Add eggs and beat thoroughly.
4. Add sifted dry ingredients and bananas alternately in thirds; beat well after each addition.
5. Stir in vanilla.
6. Pour into 2 greased 8- or 9-inch pans and bake in moderate oven (350°F) about 35 minutes.
MAKES 2 8- OR 9-INCH LAYERS

Date Delight Cake

1½ cups sugar	1 teaspoon cinnamon
1 cup salad oil	1 teaspoon allspice
3 eggs	1 cup buttermilk
2 cups sifted flour	1 cup chopped walnuts
1 teaspoon baking soda	1 cup chopped pitted dates
1 teaspoon salt	1 teaspoon vanilla
1 teaspoon nutmeg	

1. Combine sugar, oil and eggs in large mixing bowl.
2. Beat mixture until smooth and creamy.
3. Sift flour, soda, salt and spices together.
4. Add alternately with buttermilk to creamed mixture.
5. Beat until smooth.
6. Blend in nuts, dates and vanilla.
7. Turn batter into a greased 13x9x2-inch pan.
8. Bake in a 300°F (slow) oven for 55 to 60 minutes.
9. Cool cake in pan.
10. Spread with Buttermilk Frosting (page 577).
MAKES 1 13x9-INCH CAKE

Boiled-Raisin Spice Cake

3 cups raisins	1 teaspoon nutmeg
3 cups water	½ cup butter
2 cups sifted flour	1½ cups sugar
1 teaspoon baking soda	2 eggs
½ teaspoon salt	Nutmeg Butter Frosting
2 teaspoons cinnamon	

1. Cover raisins with water.
2. Bring to boil and simmer 20 minutes.
3. Drain and reserve 1 cup liquid.
4. Cool raisins and liquid.
5. Sift together flour, soda, salt and spices.
6. Cream butter and sugar together until light and fluffy.
7. Add eggs, one at a time; beat vigorously after each addition.
8. Stir in dry ingredients alternately with raisin liquid.
9. Stir in the raisins.
10. Turn into greased 13x9-inch pan.
11. Bake at 350°F 60 to 70 minutes.
12. Cool in pan.
13. Frost with Nutmeg Butter Frosting (page 576).
MAKES 1 13x9-INCH LAYER

Applesauce Cake

1¾ cups sifted cake flour	¼ teaspoon powdered cloves
1 teaspoon baking soda	½ cup shortening
½ teaspoon salt	1 cup sugar
1½ teaspoons cinnamon	1 egg, beaten
1 teaspoon allspice	1 cup unsweetened
1 teaspoon nutmeg	applesauce

1. Sift flour, soda, salt and spices together 3 times.
2. Cream shortening with sugar until fluffy.
3. Add egg and beat thoroughly.
4. Add sifted dry ingredients and applesauce alternately in

small amounts, beating well after each addition.
5. Pour into greased 9x9-inch pan. Bake at 350°F 45 to 50 minutes.
6. Frost with Caramel Fudge Frosting (page 576).
MAKES 1 9-INCH CAKE

Variation: Omit allspice and cloves; reduce cinnamon to 1 teaspoon and nutmeg to ½ teaspoon. Add **1 cup chopped raisins** and **½ cup chopped nuts.**

Maple Apple Upside-Down Cake

1½ cups sifted flour	¼ cup shortening
2 teaspoons baking powder	¾ cup sugar
¼ teaspoon salt	2 eggs, separated
3 tablespoons butter	½ cup milk
½ cup maple syrup	½ cup grated apple
2 cups thinly sliced apples	

1. Sift first 3 ingredients together.
2. Melt butter in an 8x8-inch cake pan, add maple syrup, remove from heat.
3. Place apple slices in rows in syrup mixture.
4. Cream shortening and ½ cup sugar together, add egg yolks, beat well.
5. Add dry ingredients and milk alternately in thirds, beating after each addition.
6. Stir in grated apple.
7. Beat egg whites until frothy; beat in remaining sugar gradually until stiff peaks form.
8. Fold into batter; spread over apples.
9. Bake at 350°F about 45 minutes.
10. Cool 5 minutes and invert on plate.
SERVES 8

Spice Marble Cake

2 cups sifted cake flour	⅔ cup milk
2 teaspoons baking powder	1 teaspoon cinnamon
¼ teaspoon salt	½ teaspoon powdered cloves
½ cup shortening	½ teaspoon nutmeg
1 cup sugar	2 tablespoons molasses
2 eggs, well beaten	

1. Sift flour with baking powder and salt.
2. Cream shortening and sugar until fluffy.
3. Add eggs and beat thoroughly.
4. Add sifted dry ingredients and milk alternately in thirds; beat well after each addition.
5. Divide batter into 2 parts.
6. To one part, add spices and molasses.
7. Drop by tablespoons into greased 8x8-inch pan alternating light and dark mixtures.
8. Bake at 350°F about 40 minutes.
MAKES 1 8x8-INCH CAKE

Variation: Drop batter into fluted paper cups in muffin-pan wells and bake 25 minutes.

Walnut Torte II

12 eggs, separated	Fine dry bread crumbs
1 cup sugar	2 to 3 tablespoons brandy or
½ pound finely ground	rum
walnuts	Filling
⅓ cup all-purpose flour	Frosting
½ teaspoon salt	Chopped walnuts

1. Beat egg yolks until thick and lemon-colored. Add sugar gradually, beating at high speed until mixture is very thick and piles softly.
2. Fold in ground walnuts and flour; mix thoroughly.
3. Beat egg whites with salt until stiff, but not dry, peaks form. Fold beaten egg whites into egg yolk mixture.
4. Generously grease two 10-inch cake layer pans or one 10-inch springform pan. Line with waxed paper. Grease paper. Coat with bread crumbs.
5. Turn batter into prepared pans.
6. Bake at 350°F about 25 minutes.
7. Remove layers from pans. Cool on racks 15 minutes. (Cut single, high cake, from springform pan, into 2 layers. Layers shrink slightly as they cool.) Sprinkle each layer with brandy. Cool completely.
8. Meanwhile, prepare filling and frosting.
9. Spread filling over 1 layer. Set second layer on top.
10. Spread frosting over top and sides of torte. Frosting is runny and will run down sides. Let stand 30 minutes. Pat chopped walnuts around sides of torte.
11. Refrigerate until ready to serve.
ONE 10-INCH TORTE

Filling: Whip **1 cup whipping cream** until it is very thick and piles softly. Gradually beat in **¾ cup sugar,** then **½ teaspoon vanilla extract** and, if desired, **2 tablespoons brandy or rum.** Fold in **1 cup finely ground walnuts,** a small amount at a time, until blended.
ABOUT 2 CUPS

Frosting: Beat **1 egg** until thick and foamy. Beat in **2 tablespoons melted butter or margarine, 2 tablespoons brandy or rum, pinch salt,** and about **2½ cups sifted confectioners' sugar.** Add enough confectioners' sugar to make frosting of thin spreading consistency.

Pineapple Upside-Down Cake

½ cup butter
1 cup firmly packed brown
  sugar
1 No. 2 can sliced pineapple
Large whole pecans
1 cup sifted cake flour
1 teaspoon baking powder
⅛ teaspoon salt
3 eggs, separated
1 cup sugar
5 tablespoons pineapple
  juice
Whipped cream

1. Melt butter in 9x9x2-inch pan.
2. Spread brown sugar evenly in pan.
3. Arrange pineapple slices on sugar, filling in spaces with pecans.
4. Sift flour, baking powder and salt together.
5. Beat egg yolks until light, adding sugar gradually.
6. Add pineapple juice and sifted dry ingredients alternately to egg-yolk mixture; mix until blended after each addition.
7. Fold in stiffly beaten egg whites.
8. Pour batter over pineapple in pan.
9. Bake in a 375°F (moderate) oven 30 to 35 minutes.
10. Let cool 10 minutes, then turn out on serving plate.
11. Serve with whipped cream.
MAKES 1 9x9-INCH CAKE

Rhubarb Upside-Down Cake

4 cups cut rhubarb
1 cup sugar
1 cup quartered
  marshmallows
1¾ cups sifted flour
2 teaspoons baking powder
⅛ teaspoon salt
½ cup shortening
1 cup sugar
⅓ teaspoon almond extract
⅓ teaspoon vanilla
2 eggs, separated
½ cup milk

1. Cook rhubarb, covered, in a heavy saucepan over low heat until juice begins to run.
2. Remove from heat, add 1 cup sugar and marshmallows; stir until marshmallows are melted.
3. Pour into greased 9x9-inch cake pan.
4. Sift flour, baking powder and salt together.
5. Cream shortening with 1 cup sugar and extracts.
6. Add egg yolks; beat vigorously.
7. Beat in dry ingredients and milk alternately in thirds.
8. Fold in stiffly beaten egg whites.
9. Pour over rhubarb mixture; bake at 350°F 40 to 50 minutes.
10. Loosen cake from sides and turn onto cake plate.
SERVES 8

Lemon Butter Filling

4 egg yolks, beaten
1 cup sugar
1 teaspoon cornstarch
2 tablespoons butter
1 teaspoon grated lemon rind
¼ cup lemon juice

1. Mix sugar and cornstarch and add to egg yolks.
2. Add butter, lemon rind and juice; cook over low heat, stirring frequently until thickened.
FILLING FOR 2 LAYERS

Molasses Cupcakes

2½ cups sifted cake flour
2½ teaspoons baking powder
1 teaspoon cinnamon
½ teaspoon salt
½ cup shortening
1½ teaspoons vanilla
¾ cup sugar
2 eggs, well beaten
½ cup molasses
¾ cup milk

1. Sift first 4 ingredients together.
2. Cream shortening, vanilla and sugar together until fluffy.
3. Add eggs and beat vigorously.
4. Beat in the molasses.
5. Alternately add dry ingredients in fourths, milk in thirds, to creamed mixture, beating only until smooth after each addition.
6. Fill paper baking cups or greased muffin-pan wells ½ full.
7. Bake at 350°F 25-30 minutes.
8. When cool, frost with Lemon Butter Frosting (page 576).
MAKES 12 CUPCAKES

Orange Filling

2 tablespoons butter
¼ cup sugar
2 eggs, beaten
1 tablespoon grated orange
rind
1 tablespoon lemon juice
½ cup orange juice

1. Combine all ingredients and mix well.
2. Cook mixture over very low heat, stirring constantly, until thickened.
3. Chill.
FILLING FOR 2 LAYERS

Lemon Filling

¾ cup sugar
2 tablespoons cornstarch
⅛ teaspoon salt
½ cup water
1 egg, beaten
1 tablespoon grated lemon
rind
1 tablespoon butter
¼ cup lemon juice

1. Mix first 4 ingredients together.
2. Bring to boiling, stirring constantly.
3. Boil 2 minutes.
4. Stir some into egg; return to hot mixture and cook 3 minutes.
5. Stir in the rind, butter and juice. Cool.
FILLS 2 LAYERS

Fig Filling

2 cups dried figs
1 cup crushed pineapple
3 cups water
¼ teaspoon salt
2 cups sugar

1. Rinse figs in hot water and drain.
2. Clip off stems and cut figs into thin strips.
3. Combine with pineapple and water and cook about 10 minutes.
4. Add salt and sugar and cook, stirring occasionally, until figs are tender and mixture is very thick.
5. Cool.
FILLING FOR 3 9-INCH LAYERS

Heavenly Torte Filling

¼ cup sugar
1 tablespoon cornstarch
2 egg yolks, beaten
2 cups sour cream

½ teaspoon lemon or orange extract
1 teaspoon vanilla

1. Blend sugar and cornstarch together in top of double boiler.
2. Stir in egg yolks, mixing well.
3. Blend in sour cream and cook over simmering water until mixture coats a spoon.
4. Add flavorings and cool.
FILLING FOR 3 LAYERS

Cream Filling

⅓ cup sugar
3 tablespoons cornstarch
¼ teaspoon salt
2 egg yolks

2 cups milk, scalded
2 tablespoons butter
1 teaspoon vanilla

1. Combine sugar, cornstarch and salt very thoroughly.
2. Add egg yolks and beat well.
3. Add a little of the milk slowly, mix and return mixture to remaining hot milk.
4. Cook over boiling water, stirring constantly, until mixture thickens.
5. Add butter, cool and add vanilla.
FILLING FOR 3 LAYERS

Rich Chocolate Frosting

½ cup butter
1 teaspoon vanilla
1 pound confectioners' sugar, sifted
2 egg whites (or 1 whole

egg)
⅛ teaspoon salt
2 squares (2 ounces) unsweetened chocolate, melted

1. Cream butter, vanilla and ⅓ cup sugar together; beat in egg whites (or egg) and salt.
2. Beat in remaining sugar and chocolate until of spreading consistency.
WILL FROST 2 8-INCH LAYERS

Fudge Frosting

2 cups sugar
2 tablespoons corn syrup
3 squares (3 ounces) unsweetened chocolate

½ cup milk
1 teaspoon vanilla
2 tablespoons butter

1. Cook sugar, corn syrup, chocolate and milk (stirring constantly) to 232°F or until a small amount of the syrup forms a very soft ball when dropped into cold water.
2. Remove from heat, add vanilla and butter.
3. Cool to lukewarm.
4. Beat until creamy.
WILL COVER TOPS AND SIDES OF 2 8-INCH LAYERS

Butter Frosting

½ cup butter
3 cups confectioners' sugar
4 tablespoons cream or

evaporated milk
1 teaspoon vanilla

1. Cream butter.
2. Add remaining ingredients and continue creaming until mixture is well blended and fluffy.
WILL COVER TOPS AND SIDES OF 2 8-INCH LAYERS

Lemon Butter Frosting. Add ½ teaspoon grated lemon rind and use equal parts of lemon juice and cream; omit vanilla.

Orange Butter Frosting. Add 1 tablespoon grated orange rind and use orange juice instead of cream.

Pineapple Butter Frosting. Add 1 tablespoon grated orange rind and use orange juice instead of cream.

Pineapple Butter Frosting. Use ⅓ cup crushed pineapple with juice instead of cream.

Nutmeg Butter Frosting. Reduce butter to 2 tablespoons, sugar to 2 cups, cream to 2 tablespoons. Add dash nutmeg to mixture.

Caramel Fudge Frosting

2 cups firmly packed brown sugar
1 cup granulated sugar

1 cup sour cream
1 tablespoon butter
1 teaspoon vanilla

1. Combine sugars and sour cream.
2. Cook, stirring constantly, to 238°F.
3. Add butter and vanilla and cool to lukewarm.
4. Beat until thick enough to spread.
WILL FROST 2 (9-INCH) LAYERS

Bride's Butter Frosting

⅔ cup butter
1½ teaspoons vanilla
¼ teaspoon almond extract
6 cups sifted confectioners'

sugar
1 egg white, unbeaten
3 to 6 tablespoons cream

1. Cream butter and extracts together; beat in sugar gradually until creamy.
2. Add egg white; beat until fluffy.
3. Blend in enough cream until of spreading consistency.

Chocolate Frosting

½ cup butter
3 squares (3 ounces) unsweetened chocolate
¼ teaspoon confectioners' sugar sifted

5 tablespoons cream or evaporated milk
1 egg white
1 teaspoon vanilla

1. Heat butter and chocolate over hot water until melted; add salt, sugar and cream, beating until smooth.
2. Stir in egg white and flavoring and beat until cool and thick enough to spread.
WILL FROST 3 9-INCH LAYERS

Divinity Frosting

1½ cups sugar	2 egg whites, stiffly beaten
6 tablespoons water	1 teaspoon vanilla
⅛ teaspoon cream of tartar	

1. Combine sugar, water and cream of tartar in a heavy 2-quart saucepan.
2. Cook syrup without stirring to 238°F (small amount forms a soft ball when dropped into cold water).
3. Pour ⅓ of the syrup in a fine stream over stiffly beaten egg whites while beating constantly.
4. Cook remainder of syrup to 248°F (small amount forms a firm ball when dropped into cold water).
5. Remove from heat and pour ½ of the remaining syrup in a fine stream into the mixture while beating constantly.
6. Cook remaining syrup to 268°F or the hardball stage.
7. Remove from heat and pour remaining syrup in a fine stream into the frosting, beating thoroughly.
8. Add flavoring and beat mixture until thick enough to spread.
WILL COVER TOPS AND SIDES OF 2 9-INCH LAYERS

Mint Divinity Frosting. While frosting is hot add **½ cup crused after-dinner mints** and enough vegetable coloring to tint frosting a very delicate green.

Lady Baltimore Filling. Double the recipe. Divide the frosting into halves. Reserve half; to other half add: **1 cup chopped seeded raisins, 1½ cups chopped nut meats, 1 cup chopped figs** and **½ teaspoon lemon extract.** Mix carefully and spread between layers of Lady Baltimore Cake (page 540). Spread reserved frosting over top and sides of cake.
WILL COVER 3 9-INCH LAYERS.

Lord Baltimore Filling. Double the recipe and divide frosting into halves. Reserve half; to other half add **½ cup dry macaroon crumbs, ¼ cup chopped blanched almonds, 12 candied cherries** (cut into quarters) and **2 teaspoons lemon juice.** Mix carefully and spread between layers of Lord Baltimore Cake (page 554). Spread reserved frosting over top and sides of cake.

Browned Butter Frosting

½ cup butter	6 cups sifted confectioners' sugar
1 teaspoon vanilla	
¼ teaspoon salt	⅓ to ½ cup cream

1. Brown butter lightly in a saucepan over low heat, stirring constantly.
2. Remove from heat; pour into mixing bowl.
3. Add vanilla, salt and ½ of confectioners' sugar; beat thoroughly.
4. Add remaining sugar alternately with cream, beating until of spreading consistency.
WILL FROST 2 9x9-INCH LAYERS

Note: To frost a 9-inch square cake, use one half of above recipe.

Seven-Minute Frosting

1½ cups sugar	2 teaspoons light corn syrup
⅓ cup water	¼ teaspoon salt
2 egg whites	1 teaspoon vanilla

1. Combine first 5 ingredients in double-boiler top; beat with rotary beater until blended.
2. Place over boiling water; beat constantly until mixture will hold a peak.
3. Remove from heat; add vanilla.
4. Beat until cool and thick enough to spread.
WILL FROST 2 9-INCH LAYERS

Beige Seven-Minute Frosting. Decrease sugar to ¾ cup and add **¾ cup firmly packed brown sugar.**

Fluffy Peppermint Frosting. Omit vanilla; add ¼ **teaspoon peppermint extract** and **several drops red food coloring** at end.

Mocha Seven-Minute Frosting. Increase corn syrup to 2 tablespoons, omit vanilla, add **2 tablespoons instant coffee** to sugar mixture. When frosting forms peaks, beat in **1 tablespoons maple extract.**

Marshmallow Frosting. Add **16 marshmallows,** cut into quarters, into hot cooked frosting beating until fluffy.

Buttermilk Frosting

1 cup sugar	½ teaspoon vanilla
½ cup buttermilk	½ cup butter or margarine
½ teaspoon baking soda	

1. Combine ingredients in saucepan.
2. Cook over medium heat, stirring constantly, to 230°F or until a small amount of the syrup forms a very soft ball when dropped into cold water.
3. Remove from heat; cool 5 minutes.
4. Beat until mixture begins to thicken.
WILL FROST 1 13x9-INCH CAKE

Caramel Frosting

2 cups brown sugar	¾ cup cream
1 cup granulated sugar	1 egg white
⅛ teaspoon baking soda	

1. Combine sugars, soda and cream.
2. Cook, stirring constantly, to 238°F or until a small amount forms a soft ball when dropped into cold water.
3. Cool to lukewarm without stirring.
4. Beat until creamy, add unbeaten egg white and beat until thick enough to spread.
WILL FROST 3 8-INCH LAYERS

Sweetened Whipped Cream

1 cup chilled whipping cream
¼ cup sifted confectioners'
sugar
1 teaspoon vanilla extract

1. Place a rotary beater and a 1-quart bowl in refrigerator to chill.
2. Using chilled bowl and beater, beat until cream stands in peaks when beater is slowly lifted upright.
3. Beat sugar and vanilla extract into whipped cream with final few strokes until blended.
4. Set in refrigerator if not used immediately.
ABOUT 2 CUPS WHIPPED CREAM

Rum Whipped Cream: Substitute **1 to 1½ tablespoons rum** for vanilla extract.

Strawberry Whipped Cream: Prepare 1½ times recipe. Slice **2 pints rinsed, hulled, fresh strawberries** (reserve a few whole berries for garnish, if desired). Fold berries into the cream.

Coffee Whipped Cream Frosting

¾ cup whipping cream
1½ tablespoons confectioners' sugar
1½ teaspoons instant coffee
½ teaspoon vanilla

1. Combine cream, sugar, coffee and vanilla in a chilled bowl.
2. Beat until soft peaks are formed.
WILL FROST 1 8x8-INCH CAKE

Peppermint Frosting

¼ cup crushed peppermint stick candy
½ cup milk
1 pound confectioners' sugar, sifted

1. Heat candy and milk over hot water until candy is melted.
2. Add enough sugar to make frosting thick enough to spread.
WILL FROST 2 8-INCH LAYERS

Mocha Cream Frosting

3 cups sifted confectioners' sugar
2 tablespoons cocoa
¼ teaspoon salt
⅓ cup shortening (use 2
tablespoons butter)
¼ teaspoon vanilla
¼ teaspoon instant coffee
¼ cup cold water

1. Sift sugar, cocoa and salt together.
2. Cream shortening and vanilla with ½ of the sugar.
3. Dissolve coffee in water; add alternately with remaining sugar, beating until of spreading consistency.
WILL FROST 2 9-INCH LAYERS

Lemon Icing

2 cups confectioners' sugar
2 to 3 tablespoons lemon
juice

Mix confectioner's sugar and lemon juice until smooth.

PIES

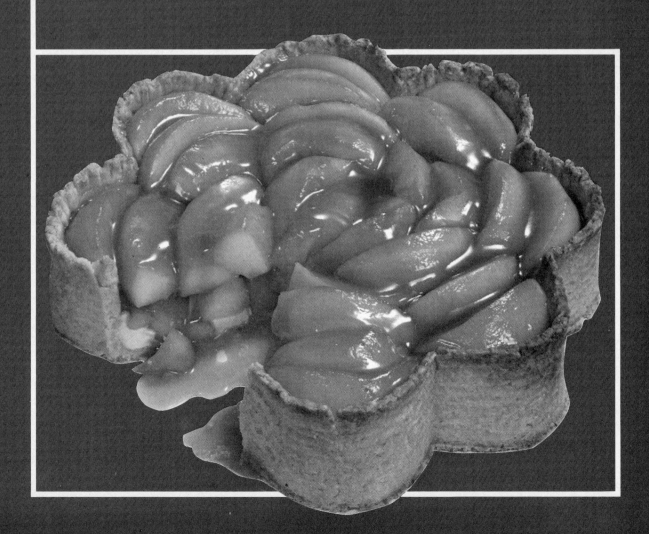

Pumpkin-Crunch Chiffon Pie

½ cup crunchy peanut butter
1 baked 9-inch pastry shell
  (page 610)
1 envelope unflavored
  gelatin
¼ cup cold water
1½ cups canned pumpkin
½ cup sugar

½ cup milk
3 egg yolks, well beaten
½ teaspoon each ginger,
  nutmeg, and cinnamon
¼ teaspoon salt
3 egg whites
1 cup chilled whipping
  cream, stiffly beaten

1. Using a spatula, spread the peanut butter on the bottom and sides of the pastry shell. Set aside.
2. Soften gelatin in the cold water and set aside.
3. Combine pumpkin, sugar, milk, egg yolks, spices, and salt in the top of a double boiler. Cook over medium heat 5 minutes. Stir in softened gelatin and cook 5 minutes more. Cool.
4. Beat the egg whites until soft peaks are formed. Gently fold egg whites into thoroughly cooled pumpkin filling. Pour mixture into pie shell. Chill until set.
5. To serve, cut in wedges and top each piece with a swirl of whipped cream.
8 TO 10 SERVINGS

Pineapple Volcano Chiffon Pie

2 envelopes unflavored
  gelatin
½ cup sugar
¼ teaspoon salt
3 egg yolks, fork beaten
½ cup water
1 can (20 ounces) crushed
  pineapple (undrained)
¼ teaspoon grated lemon
  peel

1 tablespoon lemon juice
3 egg whites
Frozen dessert topping,
  thawed, or whipped dessert
  topping
1 baked 9-inch graham
  cracker crust
1 can (8¼ ounces) crushed
  pineapple, drained

1. Mix gelatin, ¼ cup sugar, and salt in the top of a double boiler.
2. Beat egg yolks and water together. Stir into gelatin mixture along with undrained pineapple.
3. Set over boiling water. Thoroughly beat mixture and continue cooking 5 minutes to cook egg yolks and dissolve gelatin, stirring constantly.
4. Remove from water; mix in lemon peel and juice. Chill, stirring occasionally until mixture mounds slightly when dropped from a spoon.
5. Beat egg whites until frothy. Gradually add remaining ¼ cup sugar, beating until stiff peaks are formed. Fold into gelatin mixture.
6. Turn filling into crust; chill.
7. Garnish pie with generous mounds of the dessert topping. Spoon on remaining crushed pineapple to resemble "volcanoes."
ONE 9-INCH PIE

Glazed Strawberry Tart

⅓ cup sugar
3 tablespoons cornstarch
¼ teaspoon salt
⅓ cup instant nonfat dry
  milk
1½ cups milk
2 eggs, beaten
½ teaspoon grated lemon
  peel

½ teaspoon vanilla extract
¼ cup white grape juice
1 baked 9-inch pie or tart
  shell
2 pints ripe strawberries,
  rinse, hulled, and
  thoroughly dried
⅓ cup currant jelly
1 tablespoon sugar

1. Combine ⅓ cup sugar with the cornstarch and salt in a heavy saucepan; mix well.
2. Blend the nonfat dry milk with the milk and stir into the cornstarch mixture until smooth. Bring mixture to boiling, stirring constantly; boil 2 to 3 minutes, continuing to stir.
3. Vigorously stir about 3 tablespoons of the hot mixture into the eggs; return to mixture in saucepan. Cook and stir over low heat about 3 minutes, or until very thick.
4. Remove from heat and stir in lemon peel and vanilla extract. Cool slightly, then beat in the white grape juice with a hand rotary or electric beater until blended.
5. Spread the cooled filling in the completely cooled baked pie shell and refrigerate until thoroughly chilled. Top with the strawberries; set aside.
6. Heat jelly until melted and continue to cook about 5 minutes. Spoon over strawberries on the tart filling. Just before serving, sprinkle remaining 1 tablespoon sugar over the tart.
ONE 9-INCH TART

Apple Tart

½ cup butter
1 teaspoon grated lemon
  peel
1 teaspoon lemon juice
½ cup sugar
4 egg yolks, well beaten
2 cups all-purpose flour
¼ teaspoon salt

⅛ teaspoon baking soda
4 egg whites
½ teaspoon vanilla extract
⅔ cup sugar
¾ cup walnuts, finely
  chopped
2 large apples, coarsely
  shredded

1. Cream butter with lemon peel and juice. Gradually add ½ cup sugar, creaming well. Add egg yolks in halves, beating well after each addition.
2. Blend flour, salt, and baking soda. Add in thirds to creamed mixture, beating until blended after each addition. Chill thoroughly.
3. Beat egg whites with vanilla extract until frothy. Gradually add the ⅔ cup sugar, beating well; continue beating until stiff peaks are formed. Fold in nuts and apples.
4. Roll out two thirds of the dough and line bottom of a 13x9-inch baking pan. Turn nut-apple mixture into pan and spread evenly into corners.
5. Roll pieces of remaining dough into pencil-thin strips and arrange lattice-fashion over top. Press strips slightly into filling.
6. Bake at 325°F 35 to 40 minutes, or until lightly browned. Set aside on rack to cool completely. Cut into squares and, if desired, serve topped with small scoops of vanilla ice cream.
ONE 13x9-INCH TART

Fresh Lemon Meringue Pie

Filling:
1½ cups sugar
6 tablespoons cornstarch
¼ teaspoon salt
½ cup cold water
½ cup fresh lemon juice
3 egg yolks, well beaten
2 tablespoons butter or margarine
1½ cups boiling water

1 teaspoon freshly grated lemon peel
1 baked 9-inch pastry shell (page 610)

Meringue:
3 egg whites (at room temperature)
¼ teaspoon cream of tartar
6 tablespoons sugar

1. For filling, mix sugar, cornstarch, and salt together in a 2- to 3-quart saucepan. Using a wire whisk, gradually blend in cold water, then lemon juice, until smooth. Add egg yolks, blending very thoroughly. Add butter. Slowly add boiling water, stirring constantly with a rubber spatula.
2. Over medium to high heat, gradually bring mixture to a full boil, stirring gently and constantly with spatula. Reduce heat slightly as mixture begins to thicken. Boil gently 1 minute. Remove from heat and stir in lemon peel.
3. Pour hot filling into pastry shell. Let stand, allowing a thin film to form while preparing meringue.
4. For meringue, beat egg whites with an electric mixer several seconds until frothy. Add cream of tartar and beat on high speed until egg whites have just lost their foamy appearance. They should bend over slightly when beaters are withdrawn, forming soft peaks.
5. Reduce speed to medium while gradually adding sugar, about 1 tablespoon at a time. Return to high speed and beat until egg whites are fairly stiff, but still glossy. Soft peaks should be formed when beaters are withdrawn.
6. Place meringue on hot filling in several mounds around edge of pie. Push meringue to edge of crust to seal. Cover rest of filling by gently pushing meringue towards center of pie.
7. Bake at 350°F 12 to 15 minutes, or until golden brown. Cool on a wire rack at room temperature away from drafts for 2 hours before cutting and serving.
ONE 9-INCH PIE

Carrot-Apricot Tart

1 cup fresh or canned apricot halves, drained and cut into ¼-inch slices
1 pound baby carrots, cut in half lengthwise
½ teaspoon cinnamon
¼ cup carrot juice

2 eggs
½ cup instant nonfat dry-milk solids
¼ cup water
1 tablespoon brandy
¼ teaspoon nutmeg

1. Cover bottom of a 9-inch pie plate with apricots; arrange carrots in spoke design over apricots.
2. Mix remaining ingredients in a food processor or blender; pour over carrots.
3. Bake at 325°F about 45 minutes, or until set. Cool slightly. Cut into wedges to serve.
6 SERVINGS

Ricotta Pie

Pastry:
2 cups all-purpose flour
½ teaspoon salt
1 cup shortening
2 egg yolks, slightly beaten
1 to 2 tablespoons cold water

Filling:
1½ pounds ricotta
¼ cup flour

2 tablespoons grated orange peel
2 tablespoons grated lemon peel
1 tablespoon vanilla extract
⅛ teaspoon salt
4 eggs
1 cup sugar
2 tablespoons confectioners' sugar

1. To make pastry, combine flour with salt. Cut in shortening with a pastry blender until it is the size of small peas. Gradually sprinkle egg yolks over mixture; mix until thoroughly combined. Stir in just enough water to hold dough together.
2. Shape pastry into a ball and flatten on a lightly floured surface. Roll out to form a circle about 11 inches in diameter and ⅛ inch thick. Fit dough into a 9-inch round layer cake pan. (Handle dough carefully as it breaks easily.) Trim dough, leaving a ½-inch border around top of pan. Pinch dough between index finger and thumb to make it stand about ¼ inch high around edge; set aside.
3. For filling, combine cheese, flour, orange peel, lemon peel, vanilla extract, and salt; set aside. Beat eggs until foamy. Gradually add sugar, and continue beating until eggs are thick and pile softly. Stir eggs into ricotta mixture until well blended and smooth. Pour filling into pastry.
4. Bake at 350°F about 50 to 60 minutes, or until filling is firm and pastry is golden brown. Cool on wire rack. Sift confectioners' sugar over top before serving.
8 TO 10 SERVINGS

Cherry-Rhubarb Pie

1 can (16 ounces) pitted tart red cherries (water packed), drained
1 pound fresh rhubarb, sliced abut ⅛ inch thick
1¼ cups sugar

¼ cup quick-cooking tapioca
⅛ teaspoon baking soda
½ teaspoon almond extract
Few drops red food coloring
Pastry for a 2-crust 9-inch pie

1. Mix cherries, rhubarb, sugar, tapioca, baking soda, almond extract, and red food coloring; let stand 20 minutes.
2. Prepare pastry. Roll out enough pastry to line a 9-inch pie pan or plate; line pie pan. Roll out remaining pastry for top crust and slit pastry with knife in several places to allow steam to escape during baking.
3. Pour filling into pastry-lined pan; cover with top crust and flute edge.
4. Bake at 450°F 10 minutes. Turn oven control to 350°F and bake 40 to 45 minutes. Remove from oven and set on a wire rack. Serve warm or cooled.
ONE 9-INCH PIE

Apple Custard Tart

Crust:
1½ cups flour
1½ tablespoons sugar
¼ teaspoon salt
6 tablespoons frozen butter, cut in 5 pieces
2½ tablespoons shortening
4½ tablespoons ice water

Filling:
1½ pounds apples, pared, quartered, and cored

½ cup sugar
1 teaspoon cinnamon
½ teaspoon nutmeg
½ cup currants

Custard:
3 eggs
½ cup sugar
1 cup whipping cream
1 tablespoon vanilla extract
¼ cup flour

1. For crust, using **steel blade** of food processor, put flour, sugar, salt, frozen butter, and shortening in the bowl; process until crumbly.
2. With machine on, add ice water through feed tube and process until dough forms into a ball.
3. Roll out dough and line a 10-inch quiche pan, pressing dough lightly into bottom of pan. To reinforce the sides, gently life the edges of the dough and work it down the inside edge of the pan so as to make the sides thicker. Trim off excess dough by passing a rolling pin over the top of the pan.
4. With your thumbs, push the dough ⅛ inch above the edge of the pan. Prick the bottom with a fork. Line with foil or parchment paper and fill with dried beans or rice.
5. Bake at 400°F 10 minutes. Remove foil and beans and cook 8 to 10 minutes longer, or until lightly browned.
6. For filling, using **slicing disc,** slice enough apples to make about 3 cups.
7. Toss apple slices in a bowl with sugar, spices, and currants.
8. Arrange in partially baked shell; turn oven control to 375°F and bake 20 minutes, or until apples are almost tender.
9. Meanwhile, for custard, using **plastic blade,** beat eggs and sugar together until mixture is thick and pale yellow.
10. Add cream and vanilla extract and process. Add flour last and mix until blended and smooth.
11. Push apples gently down into tart and pour custard over top. Bake 30 minutes longer, or until puffy. Sprinkle with **confectioners' sugar** and serve warm.
ONE 10-INCH TART

Lemon-Beer Sponge Pie

1 unbaked 9-inch pie shell
4 eggs, separated
¾ cup sugar
¼ cup flour
3 tablespoons butter or margarine, softened

2 teaspoons grated lemon peel
1 can or bottle (12 ounces) beer
2 tablespoons lemon juice

1. Bake pie shell at 450°F 10 minutes.
2. Beat egg whites until foamy. Gradually add half of sugar, continuing beating until stiff peaks form.
3. In a separate bowl, beat remaining sugar, flour, butter, peel and egg yolks. Mix in beer and lemon juice.
4. Fold beaten egg whites into yolk mixture. Turn into partially baked pie shell.
5. Bake at 350°F about 50 minutes, or until set. Cool to room temperature before slicing.
ONE 9-INCH PIE

Peanuts-and-Beer Pie

Pastry for 9-inch pie shell
1 can or bottle (12 ounces) beer
1 envelope unflavored gelatin
½ cup packed brown sugar

3 eggs, separated
1 teaspoon vanilla extract
6 ounces salted peanuts (1¼ cups), chopped
¼ cup granulated sugar

1. Roll out pastry and fit into pie plate. Do not cut off excess pastry, but fold under and make high fluted sides. Prick bottom and sides thoroughly with fork.
2. Bake at 450°F 15 minutes, until light golden brown. Cool.
3. Pour beer into top of a double boiler; sprinkle with gelatin. Add brown sugar and slightly beaten egg yolks.
4. Cook over boiling water, stirring constantly, until slightly thickened and gelatin is dissolved (8 to 10 minutes). Add vanilla extract.
5. Chill until partially thickened. Stir in peanuts.
6. Beat egg whites until foamy. Gradually add granulated sugar, continuing beating until stiff peaks form. Fold in peanut-gelatin mixture. Turn into baked shell. Chill.
ONE 9-INCH PIE

Fresh Apricot Pie

Pastry for Lattice-Top Pie, (page 610)
1 cup sugar
⅓ cup all-purpose flour
⅛ teaspoon ground nutmeg

4 cups fresh apricots halved and pitted
2 tablespoons butter or margarine
2 tablespoons orange juice

1. Prepare a 9-inch pie shell and lattice strips for top crust; set aside.
2. Combine sugar, flour, and nutmeg; spoon some into pie shell. Arrange apricots, cut side up, over bottom of shell. Sprinkle with remaining sugar mixture. Dot with butter and drizzle with orange juice. Complete as directed for lattice-top pie.
3. Bake at 450°F and bake 30 to 35 minutes.
ONE 9-INCH PIE

Apple Pie

Pastry for 2-crust pie
6 to 8 tart cooking apples
1 tablespoon lemon juice
1 cup sugar
3 to 3½ tablespoons flour

1 teaspoon ground cinnamon
¼ teaspoon ground nutmeg
⅛ teaspoon salt
2 tablespoons butter or
   margarine

1. Prepare a 9-inch pie shell; roll out remaining pastry for top crust. Set aside.
2. Wash, quarter, core, pare, and thinly slice the apples. Turn into a bowl and drizzle with lemon juice. Toss lightly with mixture of sugar, flour, cinnamon, nutmeg, and salt.
3. Turn mixture into unbaked pie shell. Dot apples with butter. Complete as for a 2-crust pie.
4. Bake at 450°F 10 minutes; reduce oven temperature to 350°F and bake about 40 minutes, or until crust is lightly browned. Serve warm or cold.
ONE 9-INCH PIE

Applejack Apple Pie

Cheese Pastry for 2-Crust Pie,
   (page 610)
5 cups sliced pared apples
1 cup sugar
3 tablespoons cornstarch
¼ teaspoon salt
½ teaspoon ground nutmeg

¼ teaspoon ground
   cinnamon
⅓ cup applejack
4 teaspoons currant jelly
2 tablespoons butter or
   margarine

1. Prepare a 9-inch pie shell; roll out remaining pastry for top crust. Set aside.
2. Gently toss apples with a mixture of sugar, cornstarch, salt, nutmeg, and cinnamon. Pour a mixture of the applejack and jelly over apples and toss lightly.
3. Turn into the unbaked pie shell, heaping slightly at center; dot with butter. Completely as directed.
4. Bake at 450°F 10 minutes; reduce oven temperature to 350°F and bake 30 to 40 minutes, or until pastry is lightly browned. Serve slightly warm.
ONE 9-INCH PIE

Mrs. Eisenhower's Deep-Dish Apple Pie

Pastry for 1-crust pie
   (page 610)
6 tart apples
½ cup sugar
½ cup firmly packed brown
   sugar
½ teaspoon ground nutmeg

Grated peel of 1 lemon
   (about 1½ teaspoons)
Grated peel of 1 orange
   (about 2 teaspoons)
3 tablespoons butter or
   margarine

1. Prepare pastry and roll out slightly larger than overall size of baking dish to be used. Prick in a design. Set aside.
2. Pare and core apples; cut into eighths. Put into a greased deep 1½-quart baking dish.
3. Combine sugars, nutmeg, and lemon and orange peels; sprinkle mixture over the apples. Dot with butter. Cover with the pastry.
4. Bake at 425°F 40 to 45 minutes.
ABOUT 6 SERVINGS

Victoria Pie

5 large tart apples, cut in
   eighths, pared, and cored
½ cup water
½ cup dark seedless raisins
⅓ to ½ cup sugar
½ teaspoon ground
   cinnamon

1 unbaked 10-inch pie shell
½ cup sugar
4 ounces (½ cup) almond
   paste
6 egg yolks, beaten
⅓ cup heavy cream
Few grains salt

1. Combine apples and water in a saucepan; cover and cook until apples are just tender.
2. Add raisins and a mixture of ⅓ to ½ cup sugar and cinnamon; stir until sugar is dissolved. Cool slightly.
3. Turn apple-raisin mixture into pie shell.
4. Bake at 400°F 20 minutes.
5. Meanwhile, add the ½ cup sugar to almond paste gradually, beating thoroughly; add beaten egg yolks in thirds, beating well after each addition. Blend in the cream and salt.
6. Remove pie from oven; reduce oven temperature to 350°F. Spread almond mixture evenly over top. Return pie to oven and bake 10 to 15 minutes, or until top is lightly browned.
7. Remove to wire rack. Cool pie completely.
ONE 10-INCH PIE

Full-O'-Flavor Apple Pie

Pastry for 2-crust pie
   (page 610)
2 cans (20 ounces each)
   sliced apples packed in
   syrup
2 tablespoons lemon juice
½ cup firmly packed brown
   sugar
2 tablespoons flour

1 teaspoon ground cinnamon
¼ teaspoon ground nutmeg
⅛ teaspoon salt
2 tablespoons butter or
   margarine
½ cup confectioners' sugar
1 tablespoon light cream
¼ teaspoon vanilla extract

1. Prepare a 9-inch pie shell; roll out remaining pastry for top crust. Set aside.
2. Turn apples into a large bowl; lightly mix in the lemon juice. Add a mixture of brown sugar, flour, cinnamon, nutmeg, and salt; toss lightly.
3. Spoon the apple mixture into unbaked pie shell, heaping slightly at the center. Dot with butter. Complete as directed for 2-crust pie.
4. Bake at 450°F 10 minutes; reduce oven temperature to 350°F and bake 30 to 40 minutes, or until crust is lightly browned.
5. While pie is baking, prepare glaze by thoroughly mixing the remaining ingredients.
6. When pie is baked, remove from oven and set on wire rack. Using a pastry brush, evenly brush the glaze over top of pie. Serve warm or cool.
ONE 9-INCH PIE

Cherry-Berry-Peach Pie

3 cups sliced peeled peaches
1 cup fresh blueberries
1 cup halved and pitted fresh
  sweet cherries
1 tablespoon fresh lemon
  juice
¼ cup firmly packed light
  brown sugar

½ cup granulated sugar
3 tablespoons flour
⅛ teaspoon salt
¼ teaspoon cinnamon
Cheese Pastry for 2-Crust Pie,
  (page 610)
Milk
Granulated sugar

1. Combine the peaches, blueberries, and cherries in a large bowl. Sprinkle with lemon juice.
2. Stir together the brown sugar, ½ cup granulated sugar, flour, salt, and cinnamon. Gently stir into fruit, coating fruit evenly.
3. Roll out half the pastry and place in a 9-inch pie pan. Trim pastry so it extends 1 inch beyond rim of pan. Turn fruit into pan.
4. Roll out remaining pastry to form a rectangle about ⅛ inch thick and at least 10 inches long. Cut in ¾-inch strips, using a sharp knife or pastry wheel. Arrange strips in lattice fashion.
5. Trim strips even with edge of bottom crust. Moisten edge with water and fold edge of bottom crust over ends of strips. Flute as desired. Brush top with milk and sprinkle with ¼ to ½ teaspoon sugar.
6. Bake at 450°F 10 minutes. Turn oven control to 350°F and bake 45 to 50 minutes, or until pastry is brown and fruit is tender. Serve warm or cool.
ONE 9-INCH PIE

Branded Blackberry Pie

Pastry For Lattice-Top Pie,
  (page 610)
4 cups fresh ripe black-
  berries, rinsed and drained
1 cup sugar
3 tablespoons cornstarch
⅛ teaspoon salt

1 tablespoon grated orange
  peel
2 tablespoons butter or
  margarine
2 tablespoons blackberry-
  flavored brandy

1. Prepare an 8-inch pie shell and lattice strips for top crust; set aside.
2. Gently toss blackberries with a mixture of the sugar, cornstarch, salt, and orange peel.
3. Turn into unbaked pie shell, heaping berries slightly at center; dot with butter. Complete as directed for lattice-top pie.
4. Bake at 450°F 10 minutes; reduce oven temperature to 350°F and bake 25 to 30 minutes, or until pastry is lightly browned.
5. Drizzle brandy onto berries through lattice openings. Serve warm or cool.
ONE 8-INCH PIE

Saucy Strawberry Lattice Pie

Pastry for Lattice-Top Pie,
  (page 610)
1 quart firm ripe straw-
  berries, rinsed and hulled
1 cup sugar
3 tablespoons flour

½ teaspoon ground
  cinnamon
1 tablespoon lemon juice
3 tablespoons butter or
  margarine

1. Prepare a 9-inch pie shell; place in refrigerator to chill thoroughly.
2. Combine strawberries and a mixture of sugar, flour, and cinnamon in a large bowl. Let stand 5 minutes.
3. Meanwhile, roll out remaining pastry and cut lattice strips.
4. Mix lemon juice into strawberry mixture. Turn into chilled pie shell. Dot with butter. Top with pastry strips to form a lattice design; flute edge.
5. Bake at 450°F 10 minutes; reduce oven temperature to 375°F and bake 25 minutes, or until pastry is light brown.
6. Cool before serving.
ONE 9-INCH PIE

Fresh Red Raspberry Pie

Pastry for 2-crust pie,
  (page 610)
5 cups red raspberries
1 tablespoon orange juice

1 cup sugar
⅓ cup flour
¼ teaspoon salt

1. Prepare an 8-inch pie shell; roll out remaining pastry for top crust. Set aside.
2. Gently toss raspberries with orange juice and a mixture of the remaining ingredients.
3. Turn into unbaked pie shell, heaping slightly at center. Complete as directed for 2-crust pie.
4. Bake at 450°F for 10 minutes; reduce oven temperature to 350°F and bake 25 to 30 minutes, or until pastry is lightly browned.
ONE 8-INCH PIE

Fresh Blueberry Pie

Pastry for 2-crust pie,
  (page 610)
4 cups fresh blueberries
4 teaspoons lemon juice
¾ cup sugar
¼ cup flour
½ teaspoon ground

cinnamon
¼ teaspoon ground nutmeg
⅛ teaspoon salt
1 teaspoon grated lemon
  peel
2 tablespoons butter or
  margarine

1. Prepare an 8-inch pie shell; roll out remaining pastry for top crust; set aside.
2. Rinse and drain blueberries. Toss gently with lemon juice, then with a mixture of the sugar, flour, cinnamon, nutmeg, salt, and lemon peel.
3. Turn into unbaked pie shell, heaping berries slightly at center; dot with butter. Complete as directed for 2-crust pie.
4. Bake at 450°F 10 minutes; reduce oven temperature to 350°F and bake 30 to 35 minutes, or until crust is lightly browned. Serve warm or cool.
ONE 8-INCH PIE

Blueberry Lattice-Top Pie

1 package pie crust mix
4 cups fresh blueberries, washed and drained
1 cup sugar
¾ cup cold water
1 peeled orange, coarsely chopped
¼ cup cornstarch

1. Prepare pie crust following package directions. Roll out two-thirds of pie crust; line a 9-inch pie pan. Set aside.
2. Turn blueberries into a saucepan. Add sugar, ½ cup water, and orange; mix. Set over low heat and bring to boiling.
3. Mix cornstarch with remaining ¼ cup water. Stir into boiling mixture. Remove from heat. Cool.
4. Spoon cooled filling into pie crust.
5. Roll out remaining pie crust and cut into strips. Arrange strips in a lattice design over filling. Crimp edge of pie crust.
6. Bake at 400°F 35 to 40 minutes, or until browned. Cool.
ONE 9-INCH PIE

Strawberry Crumb Pie

6 cups halved fresh strawberries
¾ cup sugar
¼ cup quick-cooking tapioca
Pastry for High-Collared
1-Crust Pie, (page 610)
¼ cup packed light brown sugar
½ teaspoon ground cinnamon

1. Toss strawberries with sugar and tapioca; set aside.
2. Prepare pastry, reserving about ½ cup crumbs for topping, and make the pie shell. Turn strawberry mixture into shell. Cut an 8-inch round of aluminum foil and lay over filling.
3. Bake at 400°F 35 minutes.
4. Meanwhile, blend reserved flour mixture with brown sugar and cinnamon. Remove foil and sprinkle flour mixture evenly over pie. Continue baking 25 minutes, or until crust and topping are browned.
5. Cool on wire rack. Serve with **whipped cream.**
ONE 9-INCH PIE

Glazed Strawberry Pie

1 quart strawberries, rinsed and hulled
6 tablespoons sugar
1½ tablespoons cornstarch
6 tablespoons water
1 teaspoon lemon juice
3 or 4 drops red food coloring
3 ounces cream cheese
1 tablespoon orange juice
1 baked 9-inch pie shell

1. Reserve 2 cups whole strawberries. Crush remaining strawberries with a fork; set aside.
2. Mix sugar and cornstarch thoroughly in a saucepan. Blend in the water. Stirring constantly, bring to boiling and boil for 3 minutes, or until clear.
3. Remove from heat; stir in crushed strawberries, lemon juice, and food coloring. Cool mixture slightly by setting pan in a bowl of ice and water. Cover and set aside.
4. Beat the cream cheese until softened, then beat in the orange juice until blended. Spread over bottom of baked pie shell. Turn whole strawberries into shell. Pour cooled strawberry mixture over berries. Chill in refrigerator.
5. If desired, serve with a **cream topping.**
ONE 9-INCH PIE

Fresh Fig Pie

½ to ¾ pound fresh figs
¾ cup sugar
1 tablespoon grated orange peel
3 tablespoons lemon juice
1 unbaked 9-inch pie shell
2 tablespoons butter or margarine

1. Peel and slice figs (enough for 3 cups). Stir sugar, orange peel, and lemon juice into figs. Turn fruit into unbaked pie shell. Dot with butter.
2. Bake at 450°F 10 minutes; reduce oven temperature to 350°F and bake about 25 minutes.
ONE 9-INCH PIE

Lattice-Top Cherry Pie

¾ to 1 cup sugar
2½ tablespoons cornstarch
⅛ teaspoon salt
2 cans (16 ounces each) pitted tart red cherries, drained (reserve ¾ cup liquid)
1 teaspoon lemon juice
¼ teaspoon almond extract
4 or 5 drops red food coloring
Pastry for Lattice-Top Pie, (page 610)
1 tablespoon butter or margarine

1. Combine sugar, cornstarch, and salt in a heavy saucepan; stir in the reserved cherry liquid. Bring to boiling and boil 2 to 3 minutes, stirring constantly.
2. Remove from heat; stir in lemon juice, extract, and food coloring, then the cherries. Set aside.
3. Meanwhile, prepare an 8-inch pie shell and lattice strips for top crust; set aside.
4. When filling is cool, spoon into unbaked pie shell. Dot with butter. Complete as directed for lattice-top pie.
5. Bake at 450°F 10 minutes; reduce oven temperature to 350°F and bake about 35 minutes, or until pastry is lightly browned.
6. Remove pie to wire rack to cool.
ONE 8-INCH PIE

Cranberry-Orange Pie

Pastry for 1-crust pie, (page 610)
¼ teaspoon ground cinnamon
⅛ teaspoon ground ginger
⅛ teaspoon ground nutmeg
2¼ cups sugar
¼ teaspoon salt
¼ cup orange juice
2 tablespoons water

4 cups (1 pound) cranberries, rinsed and drained
2 tablespoons cold water
1 tablespoon cornstarch
2 tablespoons butter or margarine
1 teaspoon grated lemon peel
1 teaspoon grated orange peel

1. Prepare pastry, blending the ground spices into flour mixture; make a 9-inch pie shell and set aside.
2. Combine the sugar, salt, and orange juice with 2 tablespoons water in a saucepan. Stir over medium heat until sugar is dissolved; increase heat and bring to boiling.
3. Add cranberries; cook slowly 3 to 4 minutes, or until skins begin to pop.
4. Blend cold water with cornstarch; add gradually to hot cranberries, stirring constantly. Bring to boiling; stir and cook 3 minutes.
5. Remove from heat; stir in the butter and lemon and orange peels; cool.
6. Brush unbaked pie shell with **melted butter.** Turn filling into shell.
7. Bake at 450°F 10 minutes; reduce oven temperature to 350°F and bake about 20 minutes, or until pastry is lightly browned.
8. Garnish with **orange sections.** Cool.
ONE 9-INCH PIE

Grape Arbor Pie

Pastry for Lattice-Top Pie, (page 610)
3 cups Concord grapes
1 cup sugar
3 tablespoons cornstarch
¼ teaspoon salt

2 teaspoons grated orange peel
1 tablespoon orange juice
1 tablespoon lemon juice
1 tablespoon butter or margarine

1. Prepare an 8-inch pie shell and lattice strips for top crust; set aside.
2. Rinse and drain the grapes; slip off skins and chop; set aside in a bowl.
3. Bring skinned grapes to boiling in a saucepan; lower heat and simmer 5 minutes, or until seeds are loosened.
4. Drain pulp, reserving juice. Force pulp through fine sieve or food mill into bowl with chopped grape skins; set aside. Discard the seeds.
5. Thoroughly mix sugar, cornstarch, and salt in a saucepan. Stir in the reserved grape juice until well blended. Bring mixture to boiling; stir and cook 3 minutes.
6. Remove from heat; stir in the pulp mixture, orange peel, and the juices. Turn filling into unbaked pie shell. Dot with butter. Complete as directed for lattice-top pie.
7. Bake at 450°F 10 minutes; reduce oven temperature to 350°F and bake 20 to 25 minutes, or until pastry is lightly browned.
8. Cool on wire rack.
ONE 8-INCH PIE

Mango Pie

½ cup all-purpose flour
⅓ cup firmly packed dark brown sugar
Few grains salt
⅓ cup butter or margarine
1 unbaked 8-inch pie shell
4 cups sliced pared mangos (about two 1-pound

mangos)
4 teaspoons lime juice
½ cup sugar
¼ teaspoon salt
3 tablespoons quick-cooking tapioca
1 teaspoon grated lime peel

1. Combine flour, brown sugar, and salt in a bowl; cut in butter with a pastry blender until pieces are the size of small peas. Chill.
2. Bake pie shell at 450°F 5 minutes and set aside.
3. Sprinkle mango slices with lime juice. Gently toss with a mixture of the remaining ingredients.
4. Turn into partially baked pie shell, heaping slightly at center. Sprinkle crumb mixture evenly over the top of fruit mixture.
5. Bake at 450°F 10 minutes; reduce oven temperature to 350°F and bake 15 to 20 minutes, or until crumb topping is golden brown and fruit is tender.
6. Serve warm with **vanilla ice cream.**
ONE 8-INCH PIE

Fresh Peach-Plum Pie

Pastry for 2-crust pie (page 610)
2 cups sliced peeled ripe peaches
2 cups sliced ripe purple plums
2 to 4 teaspoons lemon juice
¼ teaspoon almond extract

1½ cups sugar
3 tablespoons quick-cooking tapioca
1 teaspoon grated lemon peel
¼ teaspoon salt
2 tablespoons butter or margarine

1. Prepare a 9-inch pie shell; roll out remaining pastry for top crust. Set aside.
2. Gently toss peaches and plums with the lemon juice and extract, then with a mixture of the sugar, tapioca, lemon peel, and salt.
3. Turn into unbaked pie shell, heaping slightly at center; dot with butter. Complete as directed for 2-crust pie.
4. Bake at 450°F 10 minutes; reduce oven temperature to 350°F and bake about 35 minutes, or until crust is lightly browned.
5. Serve warm.
ONE 9-INCH PIE

Fresh Peach Pie: Follow recipe for Fresh Peach-Plum Pie. Increase peaches to 4 cups and omit plums. Omit almond extract. Use **1¼ cups sugar.**

Fresh Plum Pie: Follow recipe for Fresh Peach-Plum Pie. Increase plums to 5 cups and omit the peaches. Omit almond extract. Decrease sugar to 1 cup; add **¼ cup firmly packed dark brown sugar.** Decrease lemon peel to ½ teaspoon.

Nectarine Lemon Pie

1¼ cups sugar
⅓ cup cornstarch
¼ teaspoon salt
1½ cups hot water
2 tablespoons butter
3 egg yolks, beaten
1 teaspoon grated lemon

peel
⅓ cup lemon juice
2 cups thinly sliced
  nectarines
1 baked 9-inch pastry shell
Mallow Meringue

1. Blend sugar, cornstarch, and salt in a saucepan. Stir in hot water and add butter. Cook over medium heat, stirring constantly, until mixture boils and is thickened.
2. Stir a small amount of hot mixture into egg yolks. Blend into mixture in saucepan. Cook and stir 2 or 3 minutes; do not boil.
3. Remove from heat and stir in lemon peel and juice. Cool slightly, then fold in sliced nectarines. Turn into baked pastry shell.
4. Top with Mallow Meringue and spread meringue evenly to pastry edge so filling is completely covered.
5. Bake at 450°F 1 to 2 minutes, or just until lightly tinged with brown.
6. Cool thoroughly before cutting. Decorate top with a few nectarine slices, if desired.
ONE 9-INCH PIE

Mallow Meringue: Beat **3 egg whites** with a few **few grains salt** until stiff. Beat in **1 cup marshmallow cream**, a heaping tablespoonful at a time, continuing to beat until mixture forms peaks that curve over slightly. Fold in **1 teaspoon vanilla extract.**

Glazed Peach Pie

2½ cups fresh peach slices
1 tablespoon lemon juice
¼ cup sugar
½ cup sugar
3 tablespoons cornstarch

2 tablespoons butter or
  margarine
⅛ teaspoon salt
⅛ teaspoon almond extract
1 baked 8-inch pie shell

1. Turn peach slices into a bowl. Drizzle lemon juice over them and mix lightly. Add ¼ cup sugar and toss gently. Set aside one hour.
2. Drain peaches, reserving syrup in a 1-cup measuring cup for liquids. Add enough water to syrup to measure one cup liquid.
3. Combine the ½ cup sugar and cornstarch in a saucepan. Stir in the reserved peach liquid until thoroughly blended. Stirring constantly, bring mixture to boiling; boil 3 minutes, or until thick and clear. Remove from heat.
4. Blend in the butter, salt, and extract. Add the peach slices and mix gently. Turn into baked pie shell; cool. If desired, serve with **whipped cream.**
ONE 8-INCH PIE

Fresh Pear Pie

Pastry for 2-crust pie,
  (page 610)
¾ cup sugar
3 tablespoons cornstarch
½ teaspoon ground nutmeg
Few grains salt

2 tablespoons lemon juice
4 large ripe pears, washed,
  quartered, cored, pared,
  and sliced (about 4 cups)
2 tablespoons butter or
  margarine

1. Prepare an 8-inch pie shell; roll out remaining pastry for top crust. Set aside.
2. Mix the sugar, cornstarch, nutmeg, and salt.
3. Sprinkle lemon juice over sliced pears and mix lightly; toss gently with the sugar mixture. Turn filling into pastry shell. Dot top with butter. Complete as directed for 2-crust pie.
4. Bake at 450°F 10 minutes; reduce oven temperature to 350°F and bake 30 to 35 minutes, or until crust is light golden brown.
5. Cool pie on wire rack.
ONE 8-INCH PIE

Almond-Crunch Pineapple Pie

Pastry for 2-crust pie,
  (page 610)
2 tablespoons sugar
3 tablespoons cornstarch
¼ teaspoon salt
1 can (20 ounces) crushed
  pineapple
2 tablespoons butter or
  margarine

1 tablespoon lime juice
1 tablespoon sugar
1½ teaspoons butter or
  margarine
¼ cup light corn syrup
1 teaspoon water
¾ cup sliced unblanched
  almonds

1. Prepare an 8-inch pie shell; roll out remaining pastry for top crust. Set aside.
2. Mix 2 tablespoons sugar, cornstarch, and salt in a saucepan; stir in undrained pineapple. Bring mixture to boiling over medium heat, stirring constantly. Boil until clear and thickened, 1 to 2 minutes. Stir in 2 tablespoons butter and lime juice.
3. Turn filling into the pie shell; cover with top crust. Seal and flute edges.
4. Bake at 425°F 20 minutes, or until pastry begins to brown.
5. Meanwhile, combine the 1 tablespoon sugar, 1½ teaspoons butter, corn syrup, and water in a small saucepan. Cook over low heat, stirring until sugar is dissolved and mixture boils.
6. Remove pie from oven. Sprinkle almonds over top crust. Spoon hot glaze evenly over nuts. Return pie to oven; bake about 8 minutes, or until topping is bubbly and lightly browned. Cool completely before cutting.
ONE 8-INCH PIE

Pear Meringue Pie

1 can (29 ounces) pear
  halves, drained
1 unbaked 8-inch pie shell
2 egg yolks, well beaten
½ cup sugar
2 tablespoons flour
½ teaspoon salt

1 cup sour cream
1 teaspoon vanilla extract
¼ teaspoon grated lemon
  peel
1 teaspoon lemon juice
Meringue II (page 608)

1. Slice pears to make about 4 cups slices; arrange in unbaked pie shell.
2. Beat into egg yolks a mixture of sugar, flour, and salt. Add a blend of sour cream, extract, and lemon peel and juice; mix thoroughly. Spread evenly over pears.
3. Bake at 350°F 50 to 55 minutes.
4. Cool to lukewarm on wire rack.
5. Prepare Meringue II and complete pie as directed in meringue recipe.

ONE 8-INCH PIE

Holiday Pear and Cranberry Pie

Pastry for 2-crust pie,
  (page 610)
3 fresh winter pears, cored
  (do not pare) and sliced
1½ cups fresh cranberries,
  rinsed and sorted

1 cup sugar
2 teaspoons grated orange
  peel
⅛ teaspoon salt
2 tablespoons quick-cooking
  tapioca

1. Using one half the pastry, line a 9-inch pie pan and flute the pastry edge. Roll out remaining pastry. Using a cutout of a pear tree with pears and a partridge, cut the tree from the pastry.
2. Combine pears and cranberries with remaining ingredients; mix well and spoon into pie shell. Carefully place the pear tree cutout over the pie filling.
3. Bake at 400°F about 40 minutes, or until fruit is tender and pie crust is light golden brown.

ONE 9-INCH PIE

Cream Pie

¾ cup sugar
3 tablespoons cornstarch
2 tablespoons flour
½ teaspoon salt
3 cups milk
3 egg yolks, slightly beaten

1 tablespoon butter or
  margarine
1½ teaspoons vanilla extract
1 baked 9-inch pie shell or
  crumb crust

1. Mix sugar, cornstarch, flour, and salt in a 1½-quart saucepan. Stir in one half of the milk, then a blend of remaining milk and egg yolks. Bring to boiling over medium heat, stirring vigorously. Reduce heat; stir and cook about 5 minutes.
2. Remove from heat; blend in butter and extract. Cool slightly.
3. Turn filling into the pie shell. Chill.

ONE 9-INCH PIE

Rosy Rhubarb Pie

Pastry for 2-crust pie,
  (page 610)
1 tablespoon quick-cooking
  tapioca
1¾ pounds fresh rhubarb
¼ cup grenadine
¾ cup sugar
½ cup flour

¼ teaspoon salt
1 teaspoon grated orange
  peel
2 tablespoons butter or
  margarine
Egg white, beaten
2 teaspoons sugar

1. Prepare a 9-inch pie shell; roll out remaining pastry for top crust. Sprinkle tapioca over bottom of pie shell. Set aside.
2. Wash rhubarb, trim off leaves and ends of stems, and cut into 1-inch pieces to make 6 cups. (Peel only if skin is tough.)
3. Toss rhubarb with grenadine, then with a mixture of sugar, flour, salt, and orange peel. Turn into pie shell, heaping slightly in center; dot with butter. Complete as directed for a 2-crust pie.
4. Brush top lightly with egg white, then sprinkle with the 2 teaspoons sugar.
5. Bake at 450°F 15 minutes; reduce oven temperature to 375°F and bake 20 to 25 minutes, or until golden brown.

ONE 9-INCH PIE

Toasted Coconut Pie

¾ cup sugar
¼ cup flour
¼ teaspoon salt
2 cups milk, scalded
3 egg yolks, fork beaten
2 tablespoons butter or

margarine
1 teaspoon vanilla extract
1 cup toasted flaked
  coconut*
1 baked 9-inch pie shell
Meringue I, (page 608)

1. Combine the sugar, flour, and salt in a heavy saucepan. Add scalded milk gradually, stirring constantly until mixture is thoroughly blended. Cook, stirring vigorously over medium heat until mixture thickens and comes to boiling; boil 1 to 2 minutes, stirring constantly.
2. Stir about ½ cup of the hot mixture into egg yolks; blend thoroughly and return to saucepan. Reduce heat; stir and cook about 5 minutes.
3. Remove from heat; stir in butter until thoroughly blended. Mix in the extract and toasted coconut; set aside to cool.
4. Turn filling into baked pastry shell; top with meringue and bake as directed in meringue recipe. Or, instead of meringue, spread with **whipped cream** before serving.

ONE 9-INCH PIE

*To toast coconut, spread in a shallow baking pan; heat in a 350°F oven about 10 minutes, or until coconut is golden brown, stirring occasionally.

Toasted Coconut-Banana Pie: Follow recipe for Toasted Coconut Pie. Decrease coconut to ¾ cup. Spread about one-third of cooled filling in bottom of pastry shell; slice **1 medium-size banana** over filling and cover with another third of filling. Slice a second banana over filling and cover with remaining filling. Top with meringue and bake as directed until lightly browned.

Almond Macaroon Pie

9 (1¾-inch) almond
  macaroon cookies
1 cup sugar
3 tablespoons flour
⅛ teaspoon salt
¼ cup cold milk
1 cup cream, scalded

3 egg yolks, slightly beaten
2 tablespoons butter or
  margarine
1 teaspoon almond extract
1 baked 9-inch pie shell
¼ cup blanched almonds,
  finely chopped

1. Heat cookies on a baking sheet in a 325°F oven for about 15 minutes; cool. Crush to make about ¾ cup fine crumbs.
2. Combine sugar, flour, and salt in top of a double boiler; mix well and stir in the cold milk. Gradually add the scalded cream, stirring constantly. Bring to boiling and cook 3 minutes.
3. Stir about ½ cup of hot mixture into beaten egg yolks; immediately blend into mixture in double boiler. Place over boiling water and cook about 5 minutes, or until thickened, stirring occasionally.
4. Remove from water. Blend in butter, extract, and macaroon crumbs; cool to lukewarm.
5. Turn filling into pie shell. To complete pie, top with **sweetened whipped cream** and sprinkle with chopped almonds.
ONE 9-INCH PIE

Double Lemon Meringue Pie

Pastry for 1-crust pie,
  (page 610)
1 teaspoon grated lemon
  peel
1½ cups sugar
7 tablespoons cornstarch
¼ teaspoon salt
½ cup cold water
1 cup boiling water

3 egg yolks, slightly beaten
2 tablespoons butter or
  margarine
1 teaspoon ground coriander
1 teaspoon grated lemon
  peel
½ cup lemon juice
Lemon Meringue (below)

1. Prepare pastry, mixing 1 teaspoon lemon peel with the dry ingredients. Line a 9-inch pie pan with pastry. Bake pie shell; cool.
2. Thoroughly mix sugar, cornstarch, and salt in a heavy saucepan. Stir in the cold water. Add the boiling water gradually, stirring constantly. Bring mixture to boiling; lower heat. Cook and stir about 10 minutes.
3. Stir about ½ cup of the hot mixture into beaten egg yolks. Immediately blend into mixture in saucepan. Stir and cook over low heat 3 minutes.
4. Blend in butter, coriander, and the lemon peel and juice. Cool.
5. Turn filling into pie shell. Top with meringue and bake as directed.
6. Cool on wire rack.
ONE 9-INCH PIE

Lemon Meringue: Beat **3 egg whites** and **1 teaspoon lemon juice** until frothy. Gradually add **6 tablespoons sugar,** beating constantly until stiff peaks are formed. Pile lightly over pie filling, sealing meringue to pastry edge. Bake at 350°F 15 minutes, or until meringue is delicately browned.

Shaker Sugar Pie

1 unbaked 9-inch pie shell
¾ cup firmly packed light
  brown sugar
¼ cup flour
2 cups cream

1 teaspoon vanilla extract
Few grains ground nutmeg
½ cup butter or margarine,
  softened

1. Prick pie shell and bake at 450°F 5 minutes. Set aside. Reduce oven temperature to 350°F.
2. Mix the brown sugar with flour until blended. Spoon over bottom of partially baked pie shell.
3. Combine the cream, extract, and nutmeg; pour over sugar in pie shell. Dot with the butter.
4. Bake at 350°F about 55 minutes, or until crust is lightly browned and filling is set.
ONE 9-INCH PIE

Dutch Apple Pie

3 to 4 (about 1 pound) tart
  cooking apples
1 unbaked 9-inch pie shell
1 egg, slightly beaten
1 cup whipping cream
1½ teaspoons vanilla extract
1 cup sugar
3 tablespoons flour
½ teaspoon cinnamon

¼ teaspoon nutmeg
⅛ teaspoon salt
4 teaspoons butter or
  margarine
½ cup walnuts, coarsely
  chopped
¾ cup shredded sharp Cheddar cheese

1. Wash, quarter, core, pare, and thinly slice apples. Turn slices into unbaked pie shell.
2. Blend the egg, cream, and vanilla extract. Gradually add a mixture of sugar, flour, nutmeg, cinnamon, and salt, mixing well. Pour over apples in pie shell. Dot with butter, sprinkle walnuts over top.
3. Bake at 450°F 10 minutes; turn oven control to 350°F and bake 35 to 40 minutes, or until apples are tender and top is lightly browned.
4. Remove from oven and sprinkle cheese over top. Serve warm.
ONE 9-INCH PIE

Lime Chiffon Pie

1 envelope unflavored
  gelatin
¼ cup cold water
4 egg yolks, slightly beaten
⅔ cup sugar
2 teaspoons grated lime peel
½ cup lime juice

¼ teaspoon salt
2 to 3 drops green food
  coloring
4 egg whites
½ cup sugar
1 baked 9-inch pastry shell

1. Soften gelatin in cold water; set aside.
2. Mix egg yolks, sugar, lime peel and juice, and salt in top of a double boiler. Cook over simmering water, stirring constantly, until mixture is slightly thickened.
3. Remove from water and blend in gelatin, stirring until gelatin is dissolved. Mix in the food coloring. Cool. Chill until mixture is partially set.
4. Beat egg whites until frothy; gradually add ½ cup sugar, beating constantly until stiff peaks are formed. Spread over gelatin mixture and fold together. Turn into pastry shell. Chill until firm.
ONE 9-INCH PIE

Banana Butterscotch Pie

¾ cup firmly packed brown
  sugar
5 tablespoons flour
½ teaspoon salt
2 cups milk
2 egg yolks, slightly beaten

2 tablespoons butter or
  margarine
1 teaspoon vanilla extract
3 ripe bananas
1 baked 9-inch pie shell

1. Mix the brown sugar, flour, and salt together in the top of a double boiler. Add milk gradually, stirring until mixture is thoroughly blended.
2. Place over boiling water and cook, stirring constantly until thickened.
3. Vigorously stir about 3 tablespoons of the hot mixture into egg yolks, then blend into mixture in double-boiler top. Cook over boiling water about 5 minutes, stirring constantly. Remove from water. Blend in butter and extract; set aside.
4. Turn half of the lukewarm filling into the pastry shell. Cut bananas into crosswise slices and arrange over filling. Turn remaining filling over bananas. Top with **whipped cream.**
ONE 9-INCH PIE

Strawberry Maple Cheese Pie

Pastry for High-Collared
  1-Crust Pie, (page 610)
4 ounces cream cheese
  softened

3 tablespoons maple syrup
½ cup sour cream
4 cups halved fresh
  strawberries

1. Prepare pie shell, bake, and cool.
2. Blend cream cheese with maple syrup; stir in sour cream. Pour into cooled pie shell, cover filling with waxed paper, and chill about 3 hours.
3. Drizzle strawberries generously with maple syrup; chill.
4. Top cheese filling with strawberries.
ONE 9-INCH PIE

Rich Dark Butterscotch Pie

5 tablespoons butter or
  margarine
⅓ cup flour
¾ cup firmly packed light
  brown sugar
¼ cup sugar
2 cups milk, scalded
3 egg yolks, beaten

¼ teaspoon salt
1 teaspoon vanilla extract
1 tablespoon firm butter or
  margarine
Meringue I (page 608)
1 baked 9-inch pie shell, or
  8 baked tart shells

1. Melt 5 tablespoons butter in a heavy saucepan. Over medium heat, stir in flour, forming a smooth paste. Stir in sugars. Heat, stirring constantly, until sugars are melted and mixture is smooth.
2. Stirring constantly, gradually add ½ cup of the hot milk; continue stirring until mixture boils. Add the remaining milk, ½ cup at a time, stirring constantly; bring to boiling after each addition.
3. Vigorously stir about 3 tablespoons of the hot mixture into the egg yolks. Immediately return to mixture in saucepan. Cook about 3 minutes, stirring constantly.
4. Remove from heat and stir in the salt, extract, and remaining butter. Set aside to cool.
5. Turn filling into the pastry shell. Top with meringue and bake as directed in meringue recipe.
6. Cool completely before serving.
ONE 9-INCH PIE

Mocha Cream Pie
with Crunchy Peanut Butter Topping

½ cup crunchy peanut butter
¾ cup confectioners' sugar
1 baked 9-inch pie shell
½ cup sugar
2 teaspoons flour
⅛ teaspoon salt
1 tablespoon instant coffee

1 can (14½ ounces)
  evaporated milk
2 eggs, fork beaten
2 tablespoons butter or
  margarine
½ teaspoon vanilla extract

1. Using a pastry blender or fork, mix peanut butter with confectioners' sugar until crumbly. Spread two thirds of mixture over bottom of pie shell; reserving remaining mixture for topping.
2. Combine sugar, flour, salt, and instant coffee in a heavy saucepan. Mix in evaporated milk. Bring mixture rapidly to boiling, stirring constantly. Cook and stir 2 minutes.
3. Gradually add about one third of hot mixture to beaten eggs, stirring constantly; blend into hot mixture. Cook and stir 5 minutes over low heat.
4. Remove from heat and stir in butter and extract. Pour filling over crumb mixture in pie shell. Sprinkle remaining crumb mixture on filling to form a border. Chill pie before serving.
5. If desired, serve with a **whipped dessert topping or sweetened whipped cream.**
ONE 9-INCH PIE

Lime Chiffon Pie

Blueberry Cookie Tarts

Blueberry Cookie Tarts

2 tablespoons cornstarch	washed and drained
½ cup confectioners' sugar	1 cup whipping cream
½ cup water	8 (3-inch) tart shells, baked
2 tablespoons lime juice	and cooled
2 cups fresh blueberries,	8 small cookies

1. Mix cornstarch and sugar in a saucepan. Stir in water and lime juice. Add ½ cup blueberries. Cook and stir until mixture comes to boiling; boil 1 minute. Cool.
2. Mix remaining blueberries into cooled mixture.
3. Whip cream and fold in filling. Spoon into tart shells. Top with cookies.
8 TARTS

Key Lime Pie

1 can (14 ounces) sweetened	coloring
condensed milk	1 baked 9-inch pie shell
3 egg yolks	3 egg whites
⅔ cup lime juice	⅓ cup sugar
1 or 2 drops green food	

1. Mix the condensed milk, egg yolks, lime juice, and food coloring until blended. Chill.
2. Turn mixture into baked pie shell.
3. Beat egg whites until frothy; add sugar gradually, beating well after each addition. Beat until stiff peaks are formed; spread the meringue over pie filling to edge of pastry.
4. Set in a 450°F oven about 5 minutes, or until meringue is delicately browned.
ONE 9-INCH PIE

Black Bottom Pie

½ cup sugar	melted and cooled
4 teaspoons cornstarch	2 teaspoons vanilla extract
½ cup cold milk	1 baked 10-inch pie shell
1½ cups milk, scalded	4 egg whites
4 egg yolks, slightly beaten	¼ teaspoon salt
1 envelope unflavored	¼ teaspoon cream of tartar
gelatin	½ cup sugar
¼ cup cold water	1 cup heavy cream, whipped
1 tablespoon rum extract	½ ounce (½ square)
1½ ounces (1½ square)	unsweetened chocolate
unsweetened chocolate,	

1. Blend ½ cup sugar and cornstarch in a saucepan. Stir in the cold milk, then the scalded milk, adding gradually. Bring rapidly to boiling, stirring constantly. Cook 3 minutes.
2. Turn mixture into a double-boiler top and set over boiling water. Vigorously stir about 3 tablespoons of hot mixture into egg yolks. Immediately blend into mixture in double boiler. Cook over simmering water, stirring constantly, 3 to 5 minutes, or until mixture coats a metal spoon. Remove double-boiler top from hot water immediately.
3. Soften gelatin in the cold water. Remove 1 cup of the cooked filling and set aside. Immediately stir softened gelatin into mixture in double boiler until completely dissolved. Cool until mixture sets slightly. Blend in rum extract.
4. Blend the melted chocolate and vanilla extract into the 1 cup reserved filling. Cool completely; turn into the baked pie shell, spreading evenly over bottom. Chill until set.
5. Beat egg whites with salt until frothy. Add cream of tartar and beat slightly. Gradually add remaining ½ cup sugar, beating well after each addition; continue beating until stiff peaks are formed. Spread over gelatin mixture and gently fold together. Turn onto chocolate filling in pie shell. Chill until firm.
6. Spread whipped cream over pie, swirling for a decorative effect. Top with chocolate curls shaved from the ½ ounces unsweetened chocolate. Chill until ready to serve.
ONE 10-INCH PIE

Lemon-Lime Meringue Pie

2 bottles (7 ounces each)
  lemon-lime carbonated
  beverage
¾ cup sugar
¼ cup cornstarch
¼ cup flour
½ teaspoon salt
3 egg yolks
⅓ cup sugar

⅓ cup lemon juice
¼ cup lime juice
1 teaspoon grated lemon
  peel
2 tablespoons butter or
  margarine
1 baked 9-inch pie shell
Meringue I, (page 608)

1. Heat lemon-lime carbonated beverage to boiling.
2. Combine the ¾ cup sugar, cornstarch, flour, and salt in a saucepan; add the hot beverage slowly, stirring until blended. Bring to boiling over medium heat, stirring constantly. Reduce heat; stir and cook 10 minutes.
3. Beat egg yolks and ⅓ cup sugar together. Stir about ½ cup of hot mixture into the egg yolks. Then blend into mixture in saucepan.
4. Add lemon and lime juice and cook over low heat until thickened, stirring constantly.
5. Remove from heat; stir in lemon peel and butter. Turn filling into pie shell; cool slightly.
6. Top with meringue and bake as directed in meringue recipe.
ONE 9-INCH PIE

Custard Pie

4 eggs
½ cup sugar
½ teaspoon nutmeg
¼ teaspoon salt

1½ cups milk, scalded
¾ cup cream, scalded
1 teaspoon vanilla extract
1 unbaked 8-inch pie shell

1. Beat the eggs slightly; add sugar, nutmeg, and salt and beat just until blended. Gradually add the scalded milk and cream, stirring constantly. Mix in the extract. Strain mixture into pie shell.
2. Bake at 450°F 10 minutes; reduce oven temperature to 350°F and bake 15 to 20 minutes, or until a knife inserted in custard halfway between center and edge comes out clean.
3. Cool on wire rack. Place in refrigerator until ready to serve.
ONE 8-INCH PIE

Slipped Custard Pie: Follow recipe for Custard Pie for amounts of ingredients. Prepare, bake, and set pie shell aside to cool. Lightly butter a second 8-inch pie pan. Prepare custard and strain into the pan. Set in pan of hot water. Bake at 325°F 25 to 30 minutes, or until custard tests done. Remove from water and cool. Run tip of knife around edge of pan; hold pan level and shake gently to loosen custard. Hold pan at a slight angle and slip the custard carefully into pie shell. Work quickly to avoid breaking custard. Set aside a few minutes.

Lemon-Raisin Pie

2 cups seedless raisins
2 cups water
½ cup sugar
3 tablespoons flour
¼ teaspoon salt
½ teaspoon ground
  cinnamon
¼ teaspoon ground cloves

2 eggs, beaten
2 tablespoons butter or
  margarine
1 teaspoon grated lemon
  peel
3 tablespoons lemon juice
1 baked 9-inch pie shell
¼ cup chopped walnuts

1. Combine raisins and water in a heavy saucepan and bring to boiling; lower heat and cook 10 minutes.
2. Thoroughly blend sugar, flour, salt, cinnamon, and cloves. Mix into hot raisins. Bring rapidly to boiling; cook and stir until thickened.
3. Stir a small amount of hot mixture into beaten eggs. Immediately blend with remaining hot mixture in saucepan. Cook and stir 3 minutes over medium heat.
4. Remove from heat. Stir in butter and lemon peel and juice. Turn filling into baked pie shell. Sprinkle walnuts in a circle on top. Cool.
5. Garnish with a border of **whipped cream.**
ONE 9-INCH PIE

Apricot Cheese Pie

1 cup dried apricots
1 unbaked 9-inch pie shell
3 eggs
½ teaspoon grated lemon
  peel
1 teaspoon lemon juice

¾ cup sugar
1 tablespoon flour
½ teaspoon salt
1½ cups creamed cottage
  cheese, sieved

1. Rinse and drain apricots; cut into small pieces and distribute over bottom of pie shell.
2. Combine eggs and lemon peel and juice; beat slightly. Gradually add a mixture of sugar, flour, and salt, beating constantly. Add the cottage cheese and mix until blended. Pour over apricots.
3. Bake at 375°F about 35 minutes, or until a knife inserted near center comes out clean.
4. Set pie on wire rack to cool before serving.
ONE 9-INCH PIE

Frau Moyer's Cheese Custard Pie

1 cup large-curd creamed
  cottage cheese
1 cup cream
½ cup confectioners' sugar
¼ teaspoon salt

¼ teaspoon ground nutmeg
5 egg yolks, slightly beaten
¼ cup butter, melted
5 egg whites
1 unbaked 9-inch pie shell

1. Force cottage cheese through a fine sieve into a bowl. Stir in the cream, confectioners' sugar, salt, nutmeg, beaten egg yolks, and melted butter.
2. Beat egg whites until stiff, not dry, peaks are formed. Fold into cheese mixture until blended. Turn into the pie shell.
3. Bake at 450°F 10 minutes. Reduce oven temperature to 350°F; bake about 20 minutes, or until custard tests done. Serve warm.
ONE 9-INCH PIE

Fruit-a-Plenty Pie

1 can (30 ounces) apricot halves
1 package (12 ounces) frozen pineapple chunks, thawed
1 package (8 ounces) cream cheese
2 tablespoons butter or margarine
1 cup all-purpose biscuit mix
½ cup sugar
2 tablespoons cornstarch
¼ teaspoon lemon juice
¼ teaspoon grated lemon peel
1 pint strawberries, rinsed and halved
1 bunch seedless grapes (about 1½ cups)

1. Drain apricots, reserving syrup. Drain pineapple chunks, reserving syrup. Set all aside.
2. To make crust, cut 3 ounces cream cheese (reserve remaining 5 ounces for use in cream cheese spread) and butter into biscuit mix until mixture resembles coarse crumbs; with hands form into a ball. Pat out dough on a lightly greased 12-inch pizza pan; flute edge. (Crust will be very thin.) Bake in a 425°F oven for about 8 minutes, or until crust is lightly browned; cool.
3. To make glaze, combine in a small saucepan ¼ cup sugar, cornstarch, and salt. Add 1 cup reserved apricot syrup, ½ cup reserved pineapple syrup, and lemon juice. Cook over medium-high heat, stirring constantly, until mixture thickens and begins to boil. Boil and stir 1 minute; cool.
4. To make cream cheese spread, stir remaining cream cheese, 2 tablespoons reserved apricot syrup, remaining ¼ cup of the sugar, and lemon peel until smooth; spread on cooled crust.
5. To assemble pie, arrange fruits in circles on cream cheese spread as follows: Place apricots around outer edge of pie, overlapping slightly. Next, make circle of halved strawberries, then circle of grapes, finally a circle of pineapple chunks. Arrange 3 apricot halves in center of pie. Brush some of the glaze over fruits. Cut pie into wedges; serve with remaining glaze mixture.
10 TO 12 SERVINGS

Strawberry-Glazed Cheese Pie

8 ounces cream cheese
½ cup sweetened condensed milk
¼ teaspoon vanilla extract
1 teaspoon grated lemon peel
2 tablespoons lemon juice
½ cup heavy cream,
whipped
1 baked 10-inch Graham Cracker Crumb Crust, (page 608)
1 package (16 ounces) frozen strawberries, thawed and drained (reserve syrup)
2 teaspoons cornstarch

1. Soften cream cheese in a bowl; beat in condensed milk, extract, and lemon peel and juice until thoroughly blended. Fold in the whipped cream. Turn mixture into baked pie shell; chill.
2. Stir ¾ cup of the reserved strawberry syrup into cornstarch in a saucepan. Cook and stir over medium heat until mixture comes to boiling; cook 3 minutes longer, or until mixture is clear. Cool about 10 minutes.
3. Gently mix in strawberries; spoon glaze over pie; chill thoroughly.
ONE 10-INCH PIE

Fruit-a-Plenty Pie

Florida Lime Pie

Crumb pie shell:
1½ cups corn flake crumbs
½ cup sugar
½ teaspoon ground cinnamon
½ cup butter, melted

Filling:
¼ cup lime juice
1 can (14 ounces) sweetened condensed milk
3 egg yolks, slightly beaten
Green food coloring
3 egg whites
2 tablespoons sugar
1 cup heavy cream, whipped

1. To prepare pie shell, combine the crumbs, sugar, and cinnamon in a bowl; stir in the butter and mix thoroughly.
2. Line a 9-inch pie pan with the mixture, pressing it firmly against bottom and sides. Chill about 20 minutes.
3. Combine the lime juice, condensed milk, and egg yolks; tint to desired color with food coloring.
4. Beat egg whites until frothy; add 2 tablespoons sugar and continue beating until stiff peaks are formed. Fold into yolk mixture until thoroughly blended. Turn into chilled shell.
5. Set in a 350°F oven about 20 minutes, or until lightly browned.
6. Cool pie and top with whipped cream; decorate as desired.
ONE 9-INCH PIE

Pecan-Topped Pumpkin Pie

1 unbaked 9-inch pie shell
1 can (16 ounces) pumpkin, about 2 cups
⅔ cup firmly packed light brown sugar
1 teaspoon ground cinnamon
½ teaspoon ground ginger
½ teaspoon ground nutmeg
⅛ teaspoon ground cloves
½ teaspoon salt
2 eggs, slightly beaten
2 cups cream, scalded
3 tablespoons butter or margarine
1 cup pecan halves
¼ cup firmly packed light brown sugar

1. Prepare pie shell; set aside.
2. For filling, combine pumpkin, ⅔ cup brown sugar, and a mixture of spices and salt in a bowl. Add the eggs and mix well. Gradually add the scalded cream, stirring until mixture is smooth. Pour filling into unbaked pie shell.
3. Bake at 400°F about 50 minutes, or until a knife inserted near center comes out clean. Cool on rack.
4. For topping, melt the butter in a small skillet. Add pecans; turn them with a spoon until coated with butter. Turn nuts into a bowl containing ¼ cup brown sugar; toss to coat thoroughly.
5. When pie is cool, arrange coated pecans, rounded side up, over the top in an attractive design. Place under broiler about 3 inches from source of heat. Broil 1 to 2 minutes.
ONE 9-INCH PIE

Very Blueberry Pie

Talbott Inn Orange Pie

¾ cup sugar
½ cup flour
¼ teaspoon salt
1 ¾ cups reconstituted frozen
   orange juice
2 egg yolks, slightly beaten

2 tablespoons lemon juice
1 tablespoon orange extract
1 baked 8-inch pie shell
2 egg whites
½ cup sugar
2 tablespoons water

1. Mix sugar, flour, and salt in the top of a double boiler. Stir in orange juice and cook over direct heat until thickened, stirring constantly.
2. Add a small amount of hot mixture to egg yolks; blend well and return to double boiler. Cook over boiling water about 5 minutes, or until mixture is thick. Remove from heat; add lemon juice and orange extract. Chill and turn into baked pie shell.
3. Beat egg whites, sugar, and water in top of double boiler until blended. Place over boiling water and beat 1 minute. Remove from heat and beat until meringue stands in peaks.
4. Pile over the pie and garnish with **orange sections** and **flaked coconut.**
ONE 8-INCH PIE

Very Blueberry Pie

½ cup cold water
⅓ cup all-purpose flour
Pinch salt
4 cups fresh blueberries,
   washed and drained

1 cup sugar
½ cup water
1 baked 10-inch pie shell
Sweetened whipped cream
   or whipped dessert topping

1. Mix cold water, flour, and salt until smooth.
2. Combine 1 cup of blueberries, sugar, and ½ cup water in a saucepan. Stir and bring to boiling. Add the flour mixture, stirring until mixture thickens. Cool.
3. Mix remaining blueberries into cooled mixture. Turn into pie shell. Chill.
4. To serve, garnish with whipped cream.
ONE 10-INCH PIE

Sour Cream-Apple Pie

1 can (20 ounces) sliced apples (packed in syrup)
½ cup firmly packed brown
  sugar
1 egg, slightly beaten
2 cups sour cream
3 tablespoons brown sugar
2 tablespoons flour

½ teaspoon ground
  cinnamon
⅛ teaspoon ground nutmeg
⅛ teaspoon ground mace
⅛ teaspoon salt
1 baked 9-inch Graham
  Cracker Crumb Crust,
  (page 608)

1. Toss apples gently with ½ cup brown sugar in a saucepan. Cook over medium heat until mixture bubbles; reduce heat and cook 5 minutes, stirring occasionally; remove from heat.
2. Blend beaten egg with sour cream and a mixture of remaining ingredients, except pie shell, until smooth.
3. Turn about one half of the sour cream mixture into pie shell; spread evenly.
4. Spoon apple mixture in an even layer over sour cream mixture; top with remaining sour cream mixture, spreading evenly.
5. Bake at 400°F 10 to 12 minutes, or until sour cream topping is set.
6. Cool on wire rack; chill thoroughly.
ONE 9-INCH PIE

Apple-Custard Pie

1½ cups thinly sliced pared
  apples
¼ cup sugar
¼ teaspoon ground
  cinnamon
¼ teaspoon ground nutmeg
1 unbaked 9-inch pie shell
¾ cup milk

½ cup cream
2 eggs, slightly beaten
½ cup sugar
⅛ teaspoon salt
1 teaspoon vanilla extract
1 cup small-curd creamed
  cottage cheese

1. Toss apples with ¼ cup sugar, cinnamon, and nutmeg. Turn into unbaked pie shell.
2. Bake at 425°F 15 minutes.
3. Meanwhile, scald milk and cream together.
4. Combine eggs with the remaining ingredients and beat only until blended. Add scalded milk and cream gradually, stirring constantly.
5. Remove pie from oven; reduce oven temperature to 325°F. Pour cheese mixture over apples in pie shell.
6. Return to oven and bake 45 minutes, or until mixture is "set" and lightly browned.
7. Serve slightly warm.
ONE 9-INCH PIE

Sour Cream-Raisin Pie

½ cup sugar
2 tablespoons flour
½ teaspoon ground
  cinnamon
¼ teaspoon ground nutmeg

¼ teaspoon salt
1 egg, well beaten
1½ cups sour cream
1½ cups dark seedless raisins
1 unbaked 9-inch pie shell

1. Combine sugar, flour, spices, and salt.
2. Combine the egg with sour cream; gradually add dry in-
gredients, blending thoroughly. Stir in raisins. Turn filling into unbaked pie shell.
3. Bake at 450°F 10 minutes; reduce oven temperature to 350°F and bake 20 to 25 minutes, or until a knife inserted near center comes out clean.
4. Serve slightly warm.
ONE 9-INCH PIE

Sour Cream-Date Pie: Follow recipe for Sour Cream-Raisin Pie. Omit spices and raisins. Stir **1 teaspoon grated lemon peel** into sugar mixture. Mix **2 cups date pieces** and **⅓ cup coarsely chopped pecans** into sour cream mixture.

Sweet Potato Pie

1½ cups sieved cooked
  sweet potatoes or yams
2 tablespoons butter or
  margarine, melted
1 teaspoon grated orange
  peel
½ cup firmly packed light
  brown sugar

1 teaspoon ground cinnamon
½ teaspoon ground ginger
½ teaspoon ground nutmeg
¼ teaspoon ground cloves
½ teaspoon salt
2 eggs, beaten
1½ cups milk, scalded
1 unbaked 9-inch pie shell

1. Combine sweet potatoes with melted butter, orange peel, and a mixture of the brown sugar, spices, and salt; mix until thoroughly blended.
2. Add eggs and beat well. Blend in scalded milk. Turn filling into unbaked pie shell.
3. Bake at 450°F 10 minutes; reduce oven temperature to 350°F and bake 30 to 35 minutes, or until a knife inserted near center comes out clean.
4. Set on wire rack to cool. Serve with **sweetened whipped cream** sprinkled with **¼ cup chopped unblanched almonds**.
ONE 9-INCH PIE

Kentucky Chess Pie

1 cup sugar
1 tablespoon flour
¼ teaspoon salt
2 egg yolks
1 whole egg
3 tablespoons water
1 teaspoon white vinegar

½ cup butter, melted
1 unbaked 8- or 9-inch pie
  shell

Meringue:
2 egg whites
2 tablespoons sugar

1. Mix the sugar, flour, and salt thoroughly.
2. Beat egg yolks with egg; beating constantly, slowly add the water, vinegar, and melted butter. Add dry ingredients and mix well. Turn into unbaked pie shell.
3. Bake at 350°F about 35 minutes, or until filling is "set."
4. Meanwhile, prepare meringue. Beat egg whites until foamy; add the sugar gradually, beating constantly until stiff peaks are formed.
5. Remove pie from oven; top with meringue and return to oven. Bake 12 to 15 minutes, or until meringue is lightly browned.
ONE 8- OR 9-INCH PIE

Rich Chocolate-Nut Pie

½ cup butter or margarine
1 teaspoon vanilla extract
1 cup sugar
3 eggs
¼ cup flour
⅓ cup cocoa

½ teaspoon salt
¼ cup dark corn syrup
¾ cup milk
¾ cup pecan halves
1 unbaked 9-inch pie shell

1. Cream the butter with the extract. Gradually add the sugar, creaming well after each addition. Add the eggs, one at a time, beating until fluffy after each addition.
2. Combine the flour, cocoa, and salt. Add to the creamed mixture, mixing well. Beat in the corn syrup and milk until thoroughly blended. Stir in the pecans. Pour the filling into unbaked pie shell.
3. Bake at 450°F 10 minutes; reduce oven temperature to 325°F and bake 40 to 45 minutes, or until the filling is set.
4. Serve slightly warm or cold with **unsweetened whipped cream.**

ONE 9-INCH PIE

Mince Pie

Pastry for 2-crust pie,
 (page 610)
3½ cups moist mincemeat
1¼ cups chopped apple

1 teaspoon grated lemon
 peel
1 tablespoon lemon juice

1. Prepare a 9-inch pie shell; roll out remaining pastry for top crust. Set aside.
2. Blend mincemeat and remaining ingredients in a saucepan; heat thoroughly. Cool slightly.
3. Turn filling into unbaked pie shell. Complete as directed for 2-crust pie.
4. Bake at 425°F 35 minutes. Cool on wire rack.

ONE 9-INCH PIE

Heavenly Lemon Pie

4 egg yolks
⅔ cup sugar
1 tablespoon grated lemon
 peel
⅓ cup lemon juice

4 egg whites
¼ teaspoon salt
½ cup sugar
1 baked 10-inch pie shell

1. In the top of a double boiler, beat the egg yolks with the ⅔ cup sugar until thoroughly blended; beat in the lemon peel and juice.
2. Cook and stir over simmering water 12 to 15 minutes, or until mixture is very thick. Turn into a bowl; cool.
3. Beat egg whites with salt until frothy; gradually add the ½ cup sugar, beating constantly until stiff peaks are formed.
4. Carefully spread egg-white mixture over the cooled lemon mixture and gently fold together. Turn filling into baked pie shell.
5. Bake at 450°F 5 minutes, or until filling is puffy and lightly browned. Serve while warm.

ONE 10-INCH PIE

Glazed Apple Tart in Wheat Germ Crust

Wheat Germ Crust (see
 recipe)
8 medium apples
1 cup red port
1 cup water
⅓ cup honey
2 tablespoons lemon juice

⅛ teaspoon salt
3 drops red food coloring
1 package (8 ounces) cream
 cheese
1 tablespoon half-and-half
1 tablespoon honey
1½ tablespoons cornstarch

1. Prepare crust and set aside to cool.
2. Pare, core, and cut apples into eighths to make 2 quarts.
3. Combine port, water ⅓ cup honey, lemon juice, salt, and food coloring in large skillet with a cover. Add half the apples in single layer, cover, and cook slowly about 5 minutes, until apples are barely tender. Remove apples with slotted spoon and arrange in a single layer in a shallow pan. Cook remaining apples in same manner. Chill apples, saving coking liquid for glaze.
4. Beat cream cheese with half-and-half and 1 tablespoon honey. Spread in even layer over bottm of cooled crust, saving about ¼ cup for decoration on top of tart, if desired.
5. Arrange apples over cheese.
6. Boil syrup from cooking apples down to 1 cup.
7. Mix cornstarch with 1½ tablespoons cold water. Stir into syrup, and cook, stirring, until mixture clears and thickens. Set pan in cold water, and cool quickly to room temperature. Spoon carefully over apples.
8. Chill until glaze is set before cutting.

ONE 10-INCH TART

Wheat Germ Crust

1½ cups sifted all-purpose
 flour
3 tablespoons wheat germ
3 tablespoons packed brown
 sugar

¾ teaspoon salt
⅛ teaspoon cinnamon
6 tablespoons shortening
2 tablespoons butter
2 tablespoons milk (about)

1. Combine flour, wheat germ, brown sugar, salt, and cinnamon in mixing bowl.
2. Cut in shortening and butter as for pie crust.
3. Sprinkle with just enough milk to make dough stick together.
4. Press dough against bottom and up sides of 10-inch spring-form pan to make shell 1¾ inches deep. Prick bottom. Set on baking sheet.
5. Bake at 375°F on lowest shelf of oven for about 20 minutes, or until golden.

ONE 10-INCH CRUST

Glazed Apple Tart in Wheat Germ Crust

Chocolate Eggnog Pie

9-inch pastry shell (page 610)
1 cup finely chopped toasted
    walnuts (see note)
¼ cup sugar
1 envelope unflavored
    gelatin
⅛ teaspoon salt
⅛ teaspoon mace or nutmeg
1 cup milk

1 ounce (1 square)
    unsweetened chocolate, cut
    fine
4 eggs
¼ cup sugar
½ cup heavy cream, chilled
2 tablespoons brandy or light
    rum
½ cup heavy cream, chilled

1. Set out a double boiler and a 9-inch pie pan. Prepare and bake 9-inch pastry shell.
2. Prepare and set aside walnuts (see note).
3. Combine in top of double boiler, mixing thoroughly ¼ cup sugar, gelatin, salt, mace or nutmeg.
4. Stir in milk and chocolate.
5. Heat over hot water until chocolate is melted.
6. Separate eggs. Beat egg yolks slightly. Using same beater, beat milk-chocolate mixture until smooth. Blend in the egg yolks and continue cooking over simmering water until slightly thickened, stirring occasionally. Remove from heat and cool. When mixture is completely cold and begins to gel, beat egg whites until foamy. Beating constantly, gradually add ¼ cup sugar.
7. Continue beating meringue until very stiff peaks are formed. Using same beater, beat heavy cream until soft peaks are formed.
8. Fold the meringue, whipped cream, and walnuts into gelatin mixture along with 2 tablespoons brandy or light rum.
9. Continue folding gently until well mixed and turn into baked pie shell. Refrigerate several hours to chill thoroughly.
10. When ready to serve, whip ½ cup heavy cream, chilled. Swirl over pie and decorate with walnut halves, chocolate candies and cherries.
ONE 9-INCH PIE

Note: To toast walnuts, drop kernels into rapidly boiling water; boil 2 minutes and drain. Spread in shallow baking pan and heat in 350°F oven 15 minutes, or until golden, stirring often.

Shoofly Pie

1 cup all-purpose flour
⅔ cup firmly packed dark
  brown sugar
¼ teaspoon salt
5 tablespoons butter or
  margarine

⅔ cup very hot water
5 tablespoons molasses
1 tablespoon dark brown
  sugar
½ teaspoon baking soda
1 unbaked 8-inch pie shell

1. Combine flour, ⅔ cup brown sugar, and salt in a bowl. Cut in butter until particles resemble rice kernels; set aside.
2. Blend hot water with the molasses, 1 tablespoon brown sugar, and baking soda.
3. Reserving 3 tablespoons crumb mixture for topping, stir molasses mixture into remaining crumb mixture. Pour into unbaked pie shell. Sprinkle reserved crumbs over filling.
4. Bake at 350°F 35 to 40 minutes, or until top springs back when touched lightly.

ONE 8-INCH PIE

Apple-Pecan Pie

2 tablespoons butter or
  margarine
1 teaspoon vanilla extract
1 cup firmly packed light
  brown sugar
3 eggs

1 cup coarsely chopped
  pecans
¾ cup dark corn syrup
½ cup thick applesauce
Few grains cinnamon
1 unbaked 9-inch pie shell

1. Cream butter with extract until softened; gradually add brown sugar, beating thoroughly. Add eggs, one at a time, beating thoroughly after each addition.
2. Blend in the pecans, corn syrup, applesauce, and cinnamon. Turn filling into unbaked pie shell.
3. Bake at 450°F 10 minutes; reduce oven temperature to 350°F and bake 35 to 40 minutes.
4. Cool on wire rack.

ONE 9-INCH PIE

Golden Raisin-Pecan Pie

1¾ cups sugar
3 tablespoons flour
¼ teaspoon salt
½ teaspoon ground nutmeg
3 egg yolks, well beaten
3 tablespoons butter or
  margarine, melted
½ cup undiluted evaporated

milk
2 tablespoons cider vinegar
1 teaspoon vanilla extract
⅔ cup chopped pecans
½ cup golden raisins
3 egg whites
1 unbaked 9-inch pie shell

1. Combine the sugar, flour, salt, and nutmeg; add to beaten egg yolks and blend thoroughly. Beat in the butter, evaporated milk, vinegar, and extract. Stir in the pecans and raisins.
2. Beat the egg whites until rounded peaks are formed, then fold into egg yolk mixture, blending thoroughly. Turn filling into pie shell.
3. Bake at 350°F 50 minutes, or until pastry is lightly browned.
4. Serve warm or cold.

ONE 9-INCH PIE

Bridge Pie

¾ cup butter or margarine
¾ cup sugar
2 egg yolks
¼ cup milk
¾ cup chopped pecans
1 cup coarsely chopped

dates
2 egg whites
1 unbaked 9-inch Graham
  Cracker Crumb Crust,
  (page 608)

1. Cream butter; gradually add sugar, beating thoroughly until light and fluffy. Add egg yolks and beat until smooth. Blend in the milk. Stir in pecans and dates.
2. Beat egg whites until stiff, not dry, peaks are formed; spread over date mixture and gently fold together. Turn filling into crust; spread evenly.
3. Bake at 350°F 35 to 40 minutes, or until "set."
4. Serve with **whipped cream.**

ONE 9-INCH PIE

Butternut Pie

3 eggs
1 cup sugar
1 teaspoon salt
1 teaspoon vanilla extract

1 cup maple syrup
1 cup coarsely chopped
  butternuts*
1 unbaked 9-inch pie shell

1. Beat the eggs, sugar, salt, and extract together until thick and piled softly. Beat in the maple syrup, then stir in butternuts. Pour the filling into unbaked pie shell.
2. Bake at 350°F about 40 minutes, or until a knife inserted near center comes out clean.

ONE 9-INCH PIE

*If butternuts are not available, substitute walnuts.

Cherry Chiffon Pie

2 cups stemmed, halved, and
  pitted dark sweet cherries
  (about 1 pound)
½ cup sugar
1 envelope unflavored
  gelatin
¼ cup cold water
2 tablespoons lemon juice

2 drops red food coloring
¼ cup sugar
½ cup heavy cream,
  whipped
2 egg whites
⅛ teaspoon salt
¼ cup sugar
1 baked 9-inch pie shell

1. Cut cherries into small pieces; mix with ½ cup sugar. Cover and let stand 1 hour to let syrup form.
2. Soften gelatin in cold water; set aside.
3. Drain cherries, reserving syrup; add enough water to cherry syrup to measure 1 cup; heat until very hot.
4. Remove from heat and immediately stir in softened gelatin until dissolved. Blend in lemon juice and food coloring; cool.
5. Chill until mixture is slightly thickened.
6. Beat the ¼ cup sugar into whipped cream with final few strokes.
7. Beat egg whites with salt until frothy; gradually add remaining ¼ cup sugar, beating constantly until stiff peaks are formed.
8. Mix cherries into slightly thickened gelatin. Spread whipped cream and beaten egg whites over gelatin; fold together.
9. Turn filling into pie shell. Chill until firm.

ONE 9-INCH PIE

Cherry Filbert Sundae Pie

Cherry Morency Sauce
Filbert Pastry, (page 608)
1 quart vanilla ice cream

¼ cup toasted filberts, coarsely chopped

1. Prepare and chill Cherry Morency Sauce.
2. Prepare and bake Filbert Pastry; set aside to cool.
3. Just before serving, scoop ice cream into pie shell. Sprinkle with filberts and pour ½ cup of the Cherry Morency Sauce over top. Serve immediately with remaining sauce.
ONE 9-INCH PIE

Cherry Morency Sauce: Drain **1 jar (8 ounces) red maraschino cherries.** Measure ⅓ cup of the cherries. Halve remaining cherries. Set aside. Add enough water to syrup to make ½ cup. Put syrup and the ⅓ cup of cherries into an electric blender container. Cover; blend about 20 seconds. Turn into a small saucepan and blend in **1½ teaspoons cornstarch.** Add **½ cup red currant jelly.** Stir over medium heat until jelly melts and sauce comes to boiling; boil 1 minute. Stir in the halved cherries and **1 tablespoon lemon juice.** Chill.
ABOUT 1⅓ CUPS SAUCE

Banana Chiffon Pie

1 cup undiluted evaporated milk
1 envelope unflavored gelatin
⅓ cup cold water
⅓ cup thawed frozen orange juice concentrate

½ cup sugar
¼ teaspoon salt
1 cup mashed fully ripe banana
2 tablespoons lemon juice
1 baked 9-inch pie shell

1. Pour evaporated milk into refrigerator tray and set in freezer until ice crystals form around edge.
2. Soften gelatin in cold water in a small saucepan. Stir over low heat until gelatin is dissolved.
3. Mix together the orange juice concentrate, sugar, and salt. Add the dissolved gelatin and stir until sugar is dissolved. Blend in the mashed banana. Chill until mixture is partially set.
4. Beat chilled evaporated milk until thick. Add lemon juice and continue beating until mixture is very stiff. Fold slightly thickened gelatin mixture into whipped evaporated milk. Pile mixture lightly into pie shell. Chill until firm.
5. Garnish with **banana slices** and, if desired, **orange slices.**
ONE 9-INCH PIE

Apricot-Nut Chiffon Pie

Apricot-Nut Pastry, below
1 envelope unflavored gelatin
½ cup sugar
⅛ teaspoon salt
¼ cup cold water
¼ cup orange juice
1¼ cups apricot nectar

1 tablespoon lemon juice
1 can (16 or 17 ounces) apricot halves, drained and sieved
½ cup heavy cream, whipped
⅔ cup chopped nuts

1. Prepare and bake Apricot-Nut Pastry; set aside.
2. Thoroughly mix gelatin, sugar, and salt in a saucepan. Blend in cold water and orange juice. Stir over low heat until gelatin is dissolved. Remove from heat. Blend in apricot nectar and lemon juice.
3. Chill mixture until slightly thicker than consistency of thick, unbeaten egg white. Beat with hand rotary or electric beater until light and fluffy. Blend in the sieved apricots. Fold in the whipped cream and nuts; turn filling into pastry shell. Chill until firm.
4. Serve topped with **whipped cream,** if desired.
ONE 9-INCH PIE

Apricot-Nut Pastry

7 tablespoons butter or shortening
3 tablespoons apricot nectar, heated
1 teaspoon milk

1¼ cups sifted all-purpose flour
½ teaspoon salt
¼ cup chopped nuts

1. Combine butter, hot apricot nectar, and the milk in a bowl; whip with a fork until mixture is smooth.
2. Sift flour and salt together into the butter mixture; stir quickly to a smooth dough.
3. Shape dough into a flat round and roll out between two 12-inch squares of waxed paper into a round about ⅛ inch thick.
4. Peel off top piece of paper and sprinkle dough with 2 tablespoons of the nuts, leaving a 1-inch border plain. Cover with the paper and gently roll nuts into dough.
5. Turn pastry over and repeat step 4.
6. Peel off top paper and fit pastry into a 9-inch pie pan; remove other piece of paper.
7. Flute pastry edge and generously prick shell with a fork.
8. Bake at 450°F 8 to 9 minutes, or until pastry is lightly browned; cool.
ONE 9-INCH PIE SHELL

Scandinavian Apple Pie

½ cup butter
1 cup flour
1 egg yolk
3 tablespoons water
8 medium apples

¾ cup sugar
1 egg, beaten
Vanilla sauce or whipped
 cream

1. Cut together the butter and flour with a knife until you have a grainy mixture, adding the egg yolk and water towards the end. Place the dough in the refrigerator for one hour.
2. Peel, core and slice the apples.
3. Roll out ⅔ of the dough and line an 8-inch pie plate. Layer the apples slices, sprinkling with sugar, in the pan. Roll out the rest of the dough and cut into strips. Arrange them lattice style on top of the pie.
4. Brush the pie with the beaten egg and bake in a 450°F oven for 30 minutes. Serve with vanilla sauce or whipped cream.

Meringue I

3 egg whites
⅛ teaspoon salt

6 tablespoons sugar

1. Beat egg whites with salt until frothy; gradually add sugar, beating constantly until stiff peaks are formed.
2. Pile meringue lightly over pie filling. Swirl with back of spoon; seal meringue to edge of crust.
3. Bake at 350°F about 15 minutes, or until meringue is delicately browned. Or, if serving pie soon after baking, bake at 450°F about 5 minutes.
TOPPING FOR ONE 9-INCH PIE

Meringue II: Follow recipe for Meringue I. Decrease egg whites to 2 and sugar to ¼ cup.
TOPPING FOR ONE 8-INCH PIE

Festive Meringue: Follow recipe for Meringue I or II. Before baking, sprinkle **slivered almonds** finely chopped, **crystallized ginger,** or finely chopped **candied cherries** over meringue.

Filbert Pastry

1⅓ cups sifted all-purpose
 flour
½ cup toasted filberts, finely
 chopped
¾ teaspoon salt

½ cup all-vegetable shortening (not oil)
¼ cup water
Sugar

1. Mix flour, filberts, and salt together in a bowl. Cut in shortening with pastry blender or two knives until mixture is crumbly.
2. Proceed as directed in Pastry for 1-Crust Pie, page 610, through step 6, except roll 1½ inches larger than pan.
3. Line inside of pie shell with a sheet of aluminum foil or waxed paper. Half fill with **dried beans or rice.**
4. Bake at 425°F 10 minutes. Remove beans and paper. Sprinkle shell lightly with sugar. Bake 5 minutes, or until pie shell is lightly browned. Cool.
ONE 9-INCH PIE SHELL

Pecan Pie

3 tablespoons butter or
 margarine
2 teaspoons vanilla extract
¾ cup sugar
3 eggs

½ cup chopped pecans
1 cup dark corn syrup
⅛ teaspoon salt
1 unbaked 9-inch pie shell
½ cup pecan halves

1. Cream butter with extract. Gradually add sugar, creaming well. Add eggs, one at a time, beating thoroughly after each addition.
2. Beat in chopped pecans, corn syrup, and salt. Turn into unbaked pie shell.
3. Bake at 450°F 10 minutes; reduce oven temperature to 350°F. Arrange pecan halves over top of filling. Bake 30 to 35 minutes, or until set. Cool on wire rack.
ONE 9-INCH PIE

Graham Cracker Crumb Crust

1⅓ cups graham cracker
 crumbs (16 to 18 crackers)
¼ cup sugar

¼ cup butter or margarine,
 softened

1. Mix cracker crumbs with sugar. Using a fork or pastry blender, blend butter evenly with crumb mixture.
2. With back of spoon, press crumb mixture firmly into an even layer on bottom and sides of an 8- or 9-inch pie pan. Level edges of the pie shell.
3. Bake at 375°F 8 minutes. Cool thoroughly before filling.
ONE 8- OR 9-INCH PIE SHELL

10-Inch Graham Cracker Crust: Follow recipe for Graham Cracker Crumb Crust. Increase crumbs to 1⅔ cups, sugar to 5 tablespoons, and butter to 5 tablespoons. Press into a 10-inch pie pan.

Nut-Crumb Crust: Follow recipe for Graham Cracker Crumb Crust. Decrease graham cracker crumbs to 1 cup and mix in ½ **cup finely chopped nuts.**

Cookie Crumb Crust: Follow recipe for Graham Cracker Crust. Substitute 1⅓ **cups cookie crumbs** (about twenty-four 2⅛-inch cookies, such as vanilla or chocolate wafers) for graham cracker crumbs. Omit sugar. Bake vanilla crumb crust at 375°F 8 minutes; bake chocolate crumb crust at 325°F 10 minutes. **For a 10-inch cookie crumb crust:** Increase cookie crumbs to 1¾ cups and butter to 5 tablespoons.

Pastry For 1-Crust Pie

1 cup sifted all-purpose flour
½ teaspoon salt
⅓ cup lard, vegetable
 shortening, or all-purpose

shortening
2 to 3 tablespoons cold
water

1. Sift flour and salt together into a bowl. Cut in shortening with pastry blender or two knives until pieces are the size of small peas.
2. Sprinkle the water over mixture, a teaspoonful at a time, mixing lightly with a fork after each addition. Add only enough water to hold pastry together. Work quickly; do not overhandle. Shape into a ball and flatten on a lightly floured surface.
3. Roll from center to edge into a round about ⅛ inch thick and about 1 inch larger than overall size of pan.
4. Loosen pastry from surface with spatula and fold in quarters. Gently lay pastry in pan and unfold it, fitting it to pan so it is not stretched.
5. Trim edge with scissors or sharp knife so pastry extends about ½ inch beyond edge of pie pan. Fold extra pastry under at edge, and flute.
6. Thoroughly prick bottom and sides of shell with a fork. (Omit pricking if filling is to be baked in shell.)
7. Bake at 450°F 10 10 to 15 minutes, or until crust is light golden brown.
8. Cool on rack.
ONE 8- OR 9-INCH PIE SHELL

Pastry for 2-Crust Pie: Double the recipe for Pastry for 1-Crust Pie. Divide pastry into halves and shape into a ball. Roll each ball as in master recipe. For top crust, roll out one ball of pastry and cut 1 inch larger than pie pan. Slit pastry with knife in several places to allow steam to escape during baking. Gently fold in half and set aside while rolling bottom crust. Roll second ball of pastry and gently fit pastry into pie pan; avoid stretching. Trim pastry with scissors or sharp knife around edge of pan. Do not prick. Fill as directed in specific recipe. Moisten edge with water for a tight seal. Carefully press edges to seal. Fold extra top pastry under bottom pastry. Flute.

Pastry for 1-Crust 10-Inch Pie: Follow master recipe. Increase flour to 1⅓ cups, salt to ¾ teaspoon, shortening to ½ cup, and water to about 3 tablespoons.

Pastry for Lattice-Top Pie: Prepare pastry as in recipe for Pastry for 2-Crust Pie. Divide pastry into halves and shape into two balls. Follow directions in master recipe for rolling pastry. Roll one pastry ball for bottom crust; fit gently into pie pan. Roll the second pastry ball into a rectangle about ⅛ inch thick and at least 10 inches long. Cut pastry with a sharp knife or pastry wheel into strips that are about ½ inch wide. Fill pastry shell as directed in specific recipe.

To Make a Lattice Top: Cross two strips over the pie at the center. Working out from center to edge of pie, add the remaining strips one at a time, weaving the strips under and over each other in crisscross fashion; leave about 1 inch between the strips. Or, if desired, arrange half the strips over top, twisting each strip several times. Repeat using remaining pastry strips and placing them diagonally to first strips. Trim the strips even with the edge of the pastry. Moisten the edge of pastry shell with water for a tight seal. Fold edge of bottom crust over ends of strips. Bake as directed in specific recipe.

Pastry for Little Pies and Tarts: Prepare master recipe. Roll pastry ⅛ inch thick and cut about ½ inch larger than overall size of pans. Carefully fit rounds into pans without stretching. Fold excess pastry under at edge. Flute. Prick bottom and sides of shell with fork. (Omit pricking if filling is to be baked in shell.) Bake at 450°F 8 to 10 minutes, or until light golden brown. Cool on wire rack.
THREE 6-INCH PIES, SIX 3-INCH TARTS, OR NINE 1½-INCH TARTS

Pastry for Rose-Petal Tarts: Double master recipe. Roll pastry ⅛ inch thick. Cut pastry into rounds, using 2½-inch round cutter. Place one pastry round in bottom of each 2¾-inch muffin-pan well. Fit 5 pastry rounds around inside of each well, overlapping edges. Press overlapping edges together. Prick bottom and sides well with fork. Bake at 450°F 8 to 10 minutes, or until light golden brown. Cool on wire rack. Carefully remove from pans.
SIX 2¾-INCH TARTS

Spice Pastry for 1-Crust Pie: Follow master recipe. Sift **2 tablespoons sugar, ¼ teaspoon cinnamon, ⅛ teaspoon ginger, and ⅛ teaspoon cloves** with flour and salt. Substitute **orange juice** for cold water.

Cheese Pastry for 1-Crust Pie: Follow master recipe. Cut in **½ cup (2 ounces) finely shredded Cheddar cheese** with the lard or shortening.

Cheese Pastry for 2-Crust Pie: Follow recipe for Pastry for 2-Crust Pie. Cut in **1 cup (4 ounces) finely shredded Cheddar cheese** with the lard or shortening.

Rolled Oat Pastry for 1-Crust Pie: Follow recipe for Pastry. I. Mix **½ cup uncooked rolled oats** with the flour. Increase shortening to ½ cup. Bake at 400°F 15 minutes or until crust is lightly browned.

Pastry Topping: Follow recipe for Pastry I. Roll out pastry 1 inch larger than overall size of baking dish or casserole and cut slits near center to allow steam to escape. Bake as directed in specific recipe.

DESSERTS

Frozen Chocolate Mousse

⅔ cup sugar
¼ cup water
4 ounces (4 squares) unsweetened chocolate
1½ teaspoons unflavored gelatin
¼ cup cold water

2 cups chilled whipping cream
½ cup confectioners' sugar
1 teaspoon vanilla extract
½ cup chilled whipping cream

1. Put sugar and ¼ cup water into top of a double boiler. Place over direct heat and stir until sugar is dissolved.
2. Set over simmering water and add chocolate. Heat until chocolate is melted. Remove from heat and set aside to cool.
3. Soften gelatin in cold water in a small saucepan. Stir over low heat until gelatin is dissolved.
4. Rinse a fancy 1½-quart mold with cold water and set aside to drain.
5. Beat whipping cream, 1 cup at a time, in a chilled bowl using a chilled rotary beater, until it piles softly. Beat the confectioners' sugar and vanilla extract into the whipped cream until blended.
6. Stir dissolved gelatin into chocolate mixture and gently mix chocolate into whipped cream until thoroughly blended. Spoon in mold, and place in freezer about 3 hours, or until firm.
7. Beat ½ cup whipping cream, using a chilled bowl and chilled beaters, until cream stands in stiff peaks when beater is lifted.
8. Just before ready to serve, remove mousse from freezer. To unmold, loosen top edge of mold with a knife. Wet a clean towel in hot water and wring it almost dry. Place a chilled serving plate on mold and invert. Wrap towel around mold for a few seconds only. Gently remove mold. If mousse does not loosen, repeat.
9. Force whipped cream through a pastry bag and a No. 27 star tube, to decorate center and sides of mousse.
10 TO 12 SERVINGS

Rolled Biscuits

3 cups Biscuit Mix (ingredients, page 157)

⅔ cup milk
Milk

1. Set out a baking sheet.
2. Measure biscuit mix into a mixing bowl.
3. Make a well in center of biscuit mix and add milk all at one time.

4. Stir with a fork until dough follows fork. Gently form dough into a ball. Turn onto lightly floured surface. To knead, fold opposite side of dough over toward you; press lightly with finger tips and turn dough quarter turn. Repeat 10 to 15 times.
5. Gently roll out dough from center to edge until about ½ inch thick. Cut dough with floured cutter or knife, using an even pressure to keep sides of biscuit straight. Place biscuits on baking sheet. Brush surface of biscuits with milk.
6. Bake at 450°F 10 to 15 minutes.
ABOUT 18 2-INCH BISCUITS

Applesauce Turnovers: Follow recipe for Rolled Biscuits. Roll dough into a rectangle about ¼ inch thick; cut into 4-inch squares. Place 1 tablespoon thick sweetened **applesauce** in center of each square. Fold diagonally in half, pressing edges together.
Applesauce may be sweetened with **honey** or **sugar** and flavored with **cinnamon. Jam, marmalade, preserves** or **jelly** may be substituted for applesauce.

Peach Cobbler: Drain contents of one 17-ounce can sliced **peaches,** reserving syrup (about 1½ cups peaches, drained). Set aside.
Combine **2 tablespoons sugar** with **1 tablespoon cornstarch** in a saucepan. Add gradually, and stir in reserved peach syrup. Bring to boiling and cook about 1 minute.
Add peaches, **1 tablespoon butter** or **margarine** and **½ teaspoon almond extract.**
Pour into shallow baking dish. Keep piping hot in oven while preparing one-half recipe **Drop Biscuits.** Add **1 tablespoon sugar** to mix. Drop by spoonfuls over fruit mixture and bake.

Frozen Chocolate Mousse

Danish Hearts

Puff Pastry:
1 cup flour
2 ounces sugar
1 egg yolk
3½ ounces butter

Filling:
6 ounces cream

2 egg yolks
½ tablespoon sugar
½ tablespoon corn flour

Decoration:
Confectioners' sugar
Cherries
Raspberries or strawberries

1. Blend flour, butter, egg yolk and sugar on a pastry board and work quickly into a dough.
2. Roll out the dough and line ⅔ of a greased heart-shaped pan with the paste.
3. Mix the ingredients for the filling and simmer on low heat until thickened. Let the cream cool.
4. Distribute the cream in the pans. Roll out the rest of the dough and put on top. Pinch the edges.
5. Bake the cakes in a 350°F oven for about 18 minutes. Remove the cakes and let them get cold.
6. Sift on the confectioners' sugar and decorate with berries.
MAKES 12

Strawberry Gelato

5 teaspoons unflavored
  gelatin
1½ cups sugar
4 cups milk
2 cups instant nonfat dry
  milk

2 packages (10 ounces each)
  frozen sliced strawberries,
  thawed
¼ cup kirsch
¼ teaspoon red food
  coloring

1. Thoroughly mix the gelatin and sugar in a large saucepan. Stir in the milk and then the nonfat dry milk. Stir over low heat until sugar and gelatin are dissolved. Set aside to cool.
2. Turn strawberries and kirsch into an electric blender container; add food coloring and blend until smooth. If necessary, strain through a fine sieve to remove seeds. Stir into cooled milk.
3. Pour into refrigerator trays and freeze until firm (2 to 3 hours).
4. Spoon the amount of ice cream to be served into a bowl; allow it to soften slightly and whip until smooth, using an electric mixer. Spoon into chilled stemmed glasses and serve immediately.
ABOUT 2 QUARTS GELATO

Strawberry-Banana Gelato: Follow recipe for Strawberry Gelato. Omit the frozen strawberries and kirsch. Combine **2 pints ripe strawberries,** rinsed, hulled, and crushed, with **¾ to 1 cup sugar** in a bowl. Mix and let stand about 1 hour. Turn half of the sweetened strawberries and **1 ripe banana,** peeled and cut in pieces, into an electric blender container; blend. Add remaining berries and blend thoroughly. Strain if necessary. Stir into cooled milk.
ABOUT 2½ QUARTS GELATO

Mint Gelato: Follow recipe for Strawberry Gelato. Reduce gelatin to 4 teaspoons and sugar to 1 cup. Omit strawberries, kirsch, and food coloring. Stir **2 teaspoons vanilla extract** and **½ teaspoon mint extract** into cooled milk.
ABOUT 1½ QUARTS GELATO

Bananas Foster Brennan's

1 tablespoon butter
2 teaspoons brown sugar
Dash ground cinnamon
1 firm ripe banana, cut

crosswise in 4 pieces
2 tablespoons warm rum
1 teaspoon warm banana
  liqueur

1. Heat butter, brown sugar, and cinnamon in a chafing dish; add banana and sauté until tender.
2. Pour rum and banana liqueur over banana and flame the spirit.
1 SERVING

Lemon Cream Chiffon Tarts

1¼ cups sugar
2 tablespoons cornstarch
1 envelope unflavored
  gelatin
¼ teaspoon salt
1 cup water
3 egg yolks
½ cup fresh lemon juice

2 tablespoons butter or
  margarine
1 cup whipping cream
1 teaspoon freshly grated
  lemon peel
3 egg whites
6 baked 4-inch tart shells
Satin Chocolate Sauce

1. Thoroughly combine 1 cup sugar, cornstarch, gelatin, and salt in a suacepan. Blend in water until smooth.
2. Beat egg yolks until light. Blend with lemon juice into mixture in saucepan. Add butter. Bring to boiling, stirring constantly; continue cooking 2 to 3 minutes. Remove from heat.
3. Stir filling vigorously while gradually adding ⅓ cup whipping cream and grated lemon peel. Immediately pour filling into a cool bowl. Chill until thickened, but not set. (Mixture should mound slightly when dropped from a spoon.)
4. Beat egg whites until soft peaks are formed. Add remaining ¼ cup sugar, beating until egg whites are stiff, but not dry. Whip remaining ⅔ cup whipping cream until stiff.
5. Gently fold egg whites and whipped cream into chilled mixture, mixing thoroughly. Spoon into tart shells. Chill until firm.
6. Drizzle the chocolate sauce over tarts before serving. Serve with additional sauce, if desired.
SIX 4-INCH TARTS

Note: Filling may be poured into a baked 9-inch pastry shell, if desired.

Satin Chocolate Sauce: Heat **½ cup semisweet chocolate pieces** with **½ cup light corn syrup** over low heat, stirring until chocolate is melted and sauce is smooth. Quickly blend in **¼ cup evaporated milk.** Heat 1 minute and cool.

Apricot Ice Cream

1 cup light cream
4 egg yolks
Grated rind from ½ lemon
3 ounces sugar
6 ounces dried and soaked
  apricots, diced

1 teaspoon gelatin
½ teaspoon vanilla
6 dried, finely chopped
  apricots
1 cup heavy cream, whipped

1. Beat the egg yolks in the cream in a heavy saucepan. Add grated lemon rind and sugar and whip the cream continuously while heating slowly. Remove from heat when cream starts to simmer, but go on whipping while it cools down.
2. Mix gelatin with 2 tablespoons hot water.
3. Add gelatin and vanilla to diced apricots. Chill until about to set.
4. Fold cream into gelatin mixture.
5. Freeze the cream for at least 3 hours and whip it a few times during that time. The apricot ice cream is spooned up in tall glasses and decorated with finely chopped dried apricots and whipped cream.
6 SERVINGS

Diples

2 eggs
1 egg yolk
1 tablespoon butter, melted
Grated peel of 1 orange
  (optional)
¼ cup orange juice
2 tablespoons lemon juice
Semolina (about 2½ cups)

½ teaspoon baking powder
½ teaspoon salt
Oil for deep frying (4 to 5
  inches deep)
Honey
Cinnamon
Chopped walnuts

1. Beat eggs and egg yolk until fluffy. Add melted butter, grated peel, orange juice, and lemon juice.
2. Mix 1 cup semolina with baking powder and salt. Stir into egg mixture. Add another cup semolina and mix well. Add remaining ½ cup semolina as necessary to make a soft dough. It will be a little sticky. Knead on a board until elastic and smooth.
3. Divide dough into 3 portions. Lighlty flour a large board and roll dough as thin as for noodles. Using a sharp knife, cut dough into 4-inch-wide strips. Cover dough until ready to fry.
4. Heat oil in a deep saucepan. When oil reaches 350°F, regulate temperature and drop in a piece of dough. Using two forks, turn in one end and roll up quickly to the other. Remove with a slotted spoon as soon as light gold in color. Drain on absorbent towels.
5. To serve, pour warm honey over the Diples and sprinkle with cinnamon and walnuts.
ABOUT 4 TO 5 DOZEN

Crème Magnifique

1 envelope unflavored
  gelatin
1 cup sugar
Few grains salt

2 cups whipping cream
1½ teaspoons vanilla extract
¼ teaspoon almond extract
2 cups sour cream

1. Mix gelatin, sugar, and salt in a heavy saucepan. Stir in whipping cream. Place over low heat and stir until gelatin is completely dissolved. Remove from heat and chill until mixture begins to gel, stirring occasionally.
2. Stir extracts with sour cream; blend with gelatin.
3. Turn into 8 individual molds. Chill until firm.
4. Unmold onto chilled dessert dishes and serve with thawed **frozen raspberries** or **strawberries.**
8 SERVINGS

Drop Yeast Doughnuts

2 packages active dry yeast
2 cups warm water (105°F
  to 115°F)
3 to 4 cups all-purpose flour
1 teaspoon salt

Vegetable oil or olive oil or
  a combination of the two
  for deep frying
Honey and cinnamon

1. Dissolve yeast in 1 cup warm water in a small bowl.
2. Add 1½ cups flour to yeast. Beat batter with a wooden spoon until smooth.
3. Cover with a towel and put into a warm place until batter is double in bulk.
4. Pour into a larger bowl, add remaining water, salt, and flour to make a thick but runny batter.
5. Cover with a towel and put into a warm place until batter is double in bulk and begins to bubble.
6. Half fill a deep fryer with oil. Heat just until smoking.
7. Drop batter by tablespoonfuls into oil; occasionally dip spoon in oil before dipping in batter. Cook until golden brown. Remove with a slotted spoon.
8. Drizzle with honey and sprinkle with cinnamon. Serve hot.
ABOUT 30

Whole Wheat Porridge with Currants and Almonds

5 cups whole wheat
Water
Salt, sugar, and cinnamon
1 cup coarsely ground

blanched almonds
½ cup dried currants
  (optional)

1. Place whole wheat in a large saucepan. Cover with cold water and let stand overnight.
2. The next day, drain wheat. Cover with fresh cold water. Simmer about 4 hours, or until tender, stirring frequently to prevent scorching and adding water as needed. Stock will become very thick.
3. Drain wheat stock into a saucepan. Add salt, sugar, and cinnamon to taste. Stir in almonds, currants, and 1 cup of the boiled wheat, if desired. Serve hot.
4 SERVINGS

Apricot Ice Cream

Baked Pineapple

1 large sugarloaf pineapple
1 banana, peeled and thinly sliced
¼ cup packed brown sugar
⅓ cup amber rum

1. Cut top from pineapple and remove pulp from inside the top. Reserve leafy top. With a grapefruit knife, remove the core and pulp from the pineapple, being careful to leave a ¼-inch layer of flesh inside the rind to keep juice in during baking.
2. Dice the pineapple pulp and mix with banana and brown sugar in a bowl. Warm rum, ignite it, and, when the flame subsides, pour over fruit mixture. Fill pineapple shell with fruit; replace top, moisten with water, and wrap in foil. Secure top with a few wooden picks. Set upright in oven in a deep casserole.
3. Bake at 350°F 25 minutes. Remove foil and serve hot.

Chocolate Custard

1 package (6 ounces) semisweet chocolate pieces
3 tablespoons half-and-half
3 cups milk
3 eggs
1 teaspoon vanilla extract
⅓ cup sugar
¼ teaspoon salt

1. Melt ⅔ cup chocolate pieces with half-and-half in top of a double boiler over hot (not boiling) water. Stir until smooth; spoon about 1 tablespoon into each of 8 custard cups or 10 soufflé dishes. Spread evenly. Put cups into a shallow pan; set aside.
2. Scald milk. Melt remaining ⅓ cup chocolate pieces and, adding gradually, stir in scalded milk until blended.
3. Beat together eggs, vanilla extract, sugar, and salt. Gradually add milk mixture, stirring constantly. Pour into chocolate-lined cups.
4. Set pan with filled cups on oven rack and pour boiling water into pan to a depth of 1 inch.
5. Bake, uncovered, at 325°F 25 minutes, or until a knife inserted halfway between center and edge comes out clean.
6. Set cups on wire rack to cool slightly. Refrigerate and serve when thoroughly cooled. Unmold and, if desired, garnish with whipped cream rosettes.
8 TO 10 SERVINGS

Figs with Mavrodaphne Wine

12 ripe figs
2 cups Mavrodaphne wine
2 cups whipping cream,
whipped
¼ cup walnuts

1. Peel figs. Prick each 3 or 4 times on sides and bottoms. Arrange figs in a dish and pour wine over them. Refrigerate for 2 hours, turning occasionally.
2. Remove figs to a serving platter. Reserve the wine. Arrange whipping cream around the figs. Garnish with walnuts. Serve wine separately.
4 SERVINGS

Chafing Dish Oeufs à la Neige

Meringues:
3 egg whites (at room temperature)
⅛ teaspoon salt
6 tablespoons sugar
¼ teaspoon vanilla extract

Custard:
6 egg yolks
¼ cup sugar
⅛ teaspoon salt
2½ cups milk
1½ teaspoons vanilla extract
Grated orange peel
Strawberries, sliced

1. Pour hot water to a depth of 2 inches in water pan of chafing dish. Heat to simmering.
2. To make meringues, beat egg whites and salt in a small bowl until frothy. Gradually beat in sugar, 1 tablespoon at a time. Continue to beat until stiff peaks form, beating in vanilla extract with last few strokes.
3. Drop meringue by heaping tablespoonfuls onto simmering water, poaching 6 at a time. Cover, and poach meringues 3 to 5 minutes, or until puffed and slightly dry to the touch. Remove from water using a slotted spoon and place in blazer pan.
4. Remove some of the poaching water so blazer pan will not touch water when set in place. Keep water warm.
5. To make custard, beat egg yolks in a heavy 2-quart saucepan. Stir in sugar and salt. Gradually stir in milk. Place over low heat and cook until custard coats a metal spoon, stirring constantly. Stir in vanilla extract.
6. Pour custard around meringues in blazer pan, allowing meringues to float. Sprinkle orange peel over meringues and garnish with strawberries.
7. Place blazer pan over warm water. Serve dessert warm; do not overheat or custard will curdle.
6 SERVINGS

Revani

1 cup unsalted butter
½ cup sugar
1 teaspoon grated lemon or orange peel
5 eggs
2 cups semolina
1 cup flour
1 tablespoon baking powder

Syrup:
3 cups sugar
1 quart water
1 cinnamon stick

1. Cream butter with sugar and grated peel. Beat together 5 minutes. Add eggs, one at a time, beating until well blended after each.
2. Combine semolina, flour, and baking powder. Add to creamed mixture and mix together by hand. Spread in a buttered 9-inch square pan.
3. Bake at 350°F 40 to 45 minutes. Cool 5 minutes.
4. While Revani is baking, prepare the syrup. Combine sugar, water, and cinnamon. Bring to boiling, reduce heat at once, and simmer covered 20 minutes.
5. Pour syrup over cake. Cool, then slice into squares. Serve plain or garnished with **whipped cream** and **toasted almonds** or accompanied with **fresh fruit**.
10 TO 12 SERVINGS

Kourambiethes

1 cup unsalted butter (at room temperature)	blanched almonds
2 egg yolks	2 cups all-purpose flour
1 tablespoon granulated sugar	1 teaspoon baking powder
1 cup coarsely chopped	Whole cloves
	Rosewater
	2 pounds confectioners' sugar

1. Beat butter until white in an electric mixer (about 10 minutes). Add egg yolks and sugar; beat well. Add chopped almonds and mix well. Blend flour and baking powder and mix in until blended.
2. Taking a small amount of dough, roll it between palms, shaping it into a ball. Continue until all dough has been used. Or, roll dough into a round log, about 1 inch in diameter; cut diagonally into 1-inch slices. Press a clove into center of each cookie.
3. Bake at 350°F 20 minutes. Remove from oven and sprinkle lightly with rosewater. Immediately sift confectioners' sugar over them, covering the tops and sides. Cool for 1 hour.
4. Using a spatula or fork, lift the cookies, being careful not to disturb the sugar, and place them in medium-size paper cupcake cups. Store cookies at least a day before serving.
ABOUT 30 COOKIES

Shredded Wheat Nut Dessert

3 cups sugar	½ cup sugar
1 quart water	2 teaspoons cinnamon
Grated peel of 1 lemon	2 pounds kataifi dough
2 whole cloves	1½ cups unsalted butter, melted
4 cups walnuts, coarsely ground	1 tablespoon rosewater

1. Combine 3 cups sugar, water, peel, and cloves in a saucepan. Bring to a boil. Reduce heat, cover, and simmer 20 minutes. Set aside to cool.
2. Combine nuts, ½ cup sugar, and cinnamon in a bowl. Set aside.
3. Take enough kataifi dough to pat into a 4x3-inch flat piece. Put 1 tablespoon of the nut filling in the center, fold dough over, and shape into a roll. Continue until all the filling and dough have been used.
4. Place rolls, 1 inch apart, in a greased large baking pan. Spoon melted butter over each roll.
5. Bake at 325°F about 40 minutes, or until golden brown. Remove from oven and sprinkle with rosewater. Pour cooled syrup over. Cool several hours before serving.
ABOUT 30

Kourambiethes

Copenhagen Pita

Syrup:	Filling:
3 cups sugar	5 eggs
1½ cups honey	2 cups sugar
5 cups water	1 teaspoon cinnamon
½ stick cinnamon	3 pieces zwieback, ground
	1½ cups almonds, blanched and ground
Cake:	
1½ cups butter	
1 cup confectioners' sugar	Topping:
5 eggs	1 package filo
1½ cups flour	1½ cups butter
1 tablespoon baking powder	
2 tablespoons cognac	

1. For syrup, combine sugar, honey, water, and cinnamon in a large saucepan. Bring to boiling. Reduce heat and simmer 20 minutes. Set aside to cool.
2. For cake, cream butter and confectioners' sugar. Add eggs, one at a time, beating well after each. Mix flour and baking powder and add to butter mixture. Add cognac and mix well.
3. Spread mixture evenly in a greased 18x12-inch baking pan. Set aside.
4. For filling, separate eggs. Beat yolks slightly, add sugar, and beat until light and fluffy.
5. Beat egg whites in another bowl until stiff, not dry, peaks are formed. Fold whites into yolk mixture. Combine cinnamon, zwieback crumbs, and almonds and fold into egg mixture. Spread evenly over layer in pan.
6. For topping, layer 10 sheets of filo over top, buttering after each layer has been added. Drizzle a little butter over top layer. Score topmost sheets into diamond shapes.
7. Bake at 350°F about 50 minutes, or until golden in color. Remove from oven and pour cooled syrup over.
8. Let stand several hours before serving.
ABOUT 60 PIECES

Apples in Blankets

1 pound apples, pared and cored	¼ cup buttermilk
2 eggs	Fat for deep frying heated to 365°F
⅓ cup sugar	Confectioners' sugar
Dash salt	Nutmeg or cinnamon (optional)
1¼ cups all-purpose flour	
⅓ cup sour cream	

1. Slice apples crosswise to make rings about ⅜ inch thick.
2. Beat eggs with sugar until thick and foamy. Add salt. Beat in small amounts of flour alternately with sour cream and buttermilk. Beat until batter is well mixed.
3. Coat apple slices with batter. Fry in hot fat until golden.
4. Drain on paper towels. Sprinkle with confectioners' sugar. Add a dash of nutmeg or cinnamon, if desired.
ABOUT 14

Koulourakia I

1 cup unsalted butter	4½ cups sifted cake flour
3 eggs	3½ teaspoons baking powder
2 egg yolks	Egg white, beaten
2 tablespoons cognac	Sesame seed, lightly toasted
2 cups confectioners' sugar	

1. Beat butter until light and fluffy. Add eggs and egg yolks, one at a time, beating well after each. Add cognac, then confectioners' sugar, beating well. Sift flour with baking powder and add to butter mixture; mix well.
2. Knead dough on a floured board until shiny.
3. Break off a small amount of dough and roll on a board to form a strip 5 to 6 inches long. Shape into a ring by joining the ends, or make a snail shape by winding up the strip. Place on a greased cookie sheet. Repeat with remaining dough.
4. Brush tops with beaten egg white. Sprinkle with sesame seed.
5. Bake at 350°F 20 to 25 minutes, or until done.
ABOUT 6 DOZEN

Baked Apples with Red Wine

8 apples, cored	½ teaspoon mace or nutmeg
Cherry or strawberry preserves	1 cup red wine
½ cup sugar	½ teaspoon vanilla extract

1. Place apples in a buttered casserole or baking dish. Fill each with preserves.
2. Blend sugar and mace; stir in wine and vanilla extract. Pour over apples. Cover.
3. Bake at 350°F 1 hour.
4. Chill 2 to 4 hours before serving.
8 SERVINGS

Turkish Delight

2 cups granulated sugar	⅛ teaspoon ground mastic
½ cup light corn syrup	2 tablespoons fresh lemon juice
½ cup cornstarch plus 3 tablespoons extra for dusting	¾ cup unsalted pistachios
3 cups water	Confectioners' sugar for rolling
1 tablespoon rosewater	

1. Combine granulated sugar and corn syrup in a saucepan and bring to boiling, stirring constantly. Cook for 30 seconds. Cool.
2. In another saucepan, combine ½ cup cornstarch with water. Simmer mixture until thick. Mix cornstarch into syrup and bring slowly to boiling. Stir to prevent lumps from forming. Reduce heat to very low and cook uncovered, stirring occasionally, until a candy thermometer registers 220°F. Stir in rosewater, mastic, lemon juice, and pistachios.
3. Pour the hot mixture into a square pan lined on bottom and sides with a heavy cotton cloth dusted with cornstarch. Spread mixture and dust top with cornstarch. Cover with a cloth and let it stand 24 hours.
4. Cut the layer into small squares with a sharp knife, roll the pieces in confectioners' sugar, and put into candy paper cups. This confection will keep for weeks.
ABOUT 3 DOZEN PIECES

Roast Chestnuts

4 pounds chestnuts

1. Cut a cross on the flat side of each chestnut with a small sharp knife, being careful not to damage nutmeat. Spread in a large baking pan.
2. Roast in a 425°F oven about 30 minutes, or until done; shake frequently. Serve hot.

Koulourakia I

Semisweet Chocolate Pudding

1 package (6 ounces)
  semisweet chocolate pieces
¼ cup water
½ cup firmly packed golden
  brown sugar
4 egg yolks
1 teaspoon vanilla extract

4 egg whites
1 cup chilled whipping
  cream
2 tablespoons golden brown
  sugar
Sliced almonds

1. Combine chocolate pieces, water, and ½ cup brown sugar in the top of a double boiler. Heat over simmering water until chocolate is melted. Beat until smooth. Cool.
2. Beat egg yolks with vanilla extract. Stir into chocolate mixture. Beat egg whites until stiff. Fold chocolate mixture into egg whites. Spoon into individual serving dishes. Chill 3 hours.
3. Combine whipping cream and 2 tablespoons brown sugar. Whip until stiff. Top pudding with the whipped cream and sprinkle with almonds.
6 SERVINGS

Black Bread Pudding

6 eggs, separated
½ cup sugar
¼ teaspoon salt
1 cup fine dry bread crumbs
  made from black bread
  (pumpernickel, rye, or

whole wheat bread)
¾ teaspoon cinnamon
¼ teaspoon cloves
2 tablespoons melted butter
Fine dry bread crumbs

1. Beat egg yolks at high speed in a small bowl until thick. Gradually beat in sugar. Continue beating at high speed until mixture is very thick and piles softly.
2. Using clean beaters and a large bowl, beat egg whites with salt until stiff, not dry, peaks form.
3. Fold bread crumbs, cinnamon, and cloves into beaten yolks. Then fold in 1 tablespoon melted butter. Fold in egg whites.
4. Brush a 2-quart soufflé dish or deep casserole with remaining 1 tablespoon melted butter. Coat dish with bread crumbs.
5. Gently turn soufflé mixture into prepared dish.
6. Bake at 350°F 25 to 30 minutes, or until set near center.
ABOUT 6 SERVINGS

Berry Compote

1 pint strawberries or
  raspberries
1 cup water

½ cup sugar
½ cup white dessert wine

1. Wash and hull berries. Put into a glass bowl.
2. Boil water with sugar 5 minutes. Pour over berries and add wine. Let stand 2 hours before serving. Chill, if desired.
4 SERVINGS

Raspberry Syrup

2 cups sugar
½ cup water

2 cups fresh or frozen
  raspberries

1. Combine sugar and water in a saucepan.
2. Bring to boiling; add raspberries. Boil 3 minutes. Remove from heat.
3. Line a strainer or colander with cheesecloth. Set over a bowl. Turn cooked berries into cloth-lined strainer. Let drain 2 hours.
4. Discard seeds and pulp. Return juice to saucepan. Boil about 12 minutes, or until reduced to half the original amount. Skim off foam.
5. Pour into a clean jar. Cover. Store in refrigerator. Serve with fruit compote, fresh fruits, or as a sauce for cake.
ABOUT 2 CUPS

Pear Compote

8 pears or 4 cups pitted dark
  sweet cherries
1½ cups wine
⅔ cup sugar
⅓ cup red currant jelly

½ teaspoon vanilla extract or
  1 tablespoon lemon juice
4 whole cloves
1 stick cinnamon

1. Pare pears, leaving whole with stems attached.
2. Combine wine, and remaining ingredients. Bring to boiling.
3. Add pears. Simmer until pears are transparent on the edges, about 45 minutes. (Boil cherries 2 minutes).
4. Remove fruit to serving dish.
5. Boil syrup until very thick, about 20 minutes. Pour over fruit.
6. Chill. Serve with whipped cream or soft dessert cheese, if desired.
8 SERVINGS

Fruit Compote in Spirits

2 pounds ripe peaches,
  pears, or apricots
1⅓ cups water

2 cups sugar
¾ cup white rum, vodka, or
  grain alcohol

1. Dip whole fruit, 1 piece at a time, in boiling water for a few seconds to loosen skin. Pull off skin; leave fruit whole.
2. Combine water with sugar in a saucepan. Boil 5 minutes.
3. Add fruits and simmer 3 minutes for small fruit, 5 minutes for large fruit.
4. Remove from heat. Skim off foam. Let stand overnight.
5. Remove fruit from syrup. Boil syrup 1 minute. Skim off foam. Pour syrup over fruit. Let stand overnight.
6. Remove fruits from syrup. Place in sterilized jars. Bring syrup to boiling; skim off foam. Add rum and pour over fruit. Seal.
7. Store in a cool, dry place at least 1 week before using.
6 TO 8 SERVINGS

Chocolate Fondue

4 packages (6 ounces each) milk chocolate pieces or semisweet chocolate pieces
2 cups (1 pint) light corn syrup
1 tablespoon vanilla extract
½ cup cream, brandy, or rum

Assorted dippers (marsh-mallows, strawberries with hull, apple slices, banana chunks, pineapple chunks, mandarin orange segments, cherries with stems, cake cubes, melon balls)

1. Combine chocolate pieces and corn syrup in a heavy saucepan. Heat and stir until chocolate melts and mixture is smooth.
2. Add vanilla extract (omit if using brandy or rum) and cream; stir until well blended. Turn into a fondue pot and keep hot.
3. To serve, surround fondue pot with small bowls of dippers. Provide fondue forks for guests to spear dippers, then dip into fondue.
ABOUT 4 CUPS

Dessert Puff with Fruit

4 eggs, slightly beaten
¾ cup skim milk
¾ cup flour
2 teaspoons sugar
¼ teaspoon salt

2 teaspoons clarified butter
4 cups assorted sliced fruits
1 cup Low-Fat Yogurt, (page 47)
Freshly ground nutmeg

1. Combine eggs, milk, flour, sugar, and salt; beat with a fork until blended but still slightly lumpy. Heat butter in a 10-inch skillet until bubbly and sides of skillet are hot; pour batter into skillet.
2. Bake at 425°F 20 minutes. Turn oven control to 350°F; bake until golden (10 to 15 minutes). (Do not open oven door during baking. Sides of puff will rise very high; the center will rise only slightly.) Remove from oven and cut into 8 wedges; place on individual plates.
3. Spoon ½ cup fresh fruit on each wedge. Dollop fruit with yogurt; sprinkle with nutmeg. Serve immediately.
8 SERVINGS

Squash and Apple Confection

3 large Golden Delicious apples
1 cup prune juice
1 cup water
¾ teaspoon ground ginger
3 eggs, beaten
1½ pounds acorn squash or

pumpkin, pared and sliced
Chicken Stock, (page 48)
3 tablespoons currants or dark raisins
1¼ cups Custard Sauce, (page 672)

1. Cut each apple into 12 slices; layer slices in a medium skillet. Pour prune juice, water, and ginger over. Simmer covered 5 minutes. Drain, pouring liquid into a small mixing bowl. Stir eggs into liquid.
2. Cook squash in 1 inch of stock in a covered saucepan until tender (about 5 minutes); drain.
3. Alternate half the apple and squash slices in rows in bottom of a lightly oiled 9x5x3-inch loaf pan. Sprinkle with currants; layer remaining apple and squash slices on top. Pour egg mixture over top. Place pan in larger baking pan; fill with 1 inch boiling water.
4. Bake at 375°F about 45 minutes, or until set. Cool to room temperature. Refrigerate covered 2 hours. Run knife around edge of plate; unmold on a platter. Slice; serve sauce over slices.
8 SERVINGS

Baked Sherried Bananas

6 medium bananas, cut in half lengthwise and crosswise
Pineapple juice
¼ cup sherry or pineapple

juice
1 tablespoon honey
¼ teaspoon ground ginger
1 tablespoon toasted sesame seed

1. Dip bananas in pineapple juice; arrange in a shallow casserole. Spoon sherry and honey over bananas; sprinkle with ginger.
2. Bake at 400°F 15 minutes. Serve in shallow bowls; sprinkle with sesame seed.
6 SERVINGS

Banana-Sweet Potato Bake

1 cup mashed cooked sweet potato or squash
2 medium bananas
1 cup water
½ cup instant nonfat dry-milk solids
2 egg yolks

2 tablespoons honey or sugar
½ teaspoon ground ginger
2 tablespoons dark rum, if desired
4 egg whites
1 cup Custard Sauce, (page 672)

1. Purée sweet potato, bananas, water, milk solids, egg yolks, honey, ginger, and rum in a food processor or blender. Pour into a mixing bowl.
2. Beat 4 egg whites until stiff but not dry peaks form. Fold into sweet potato mixture. Spoon into a lightly oiled 9x5x2-inch baking dish.
3. Bake at 325°F 45 minutes. Serve at room temperature, or refrigerate and serve cold. Cut into slices. Serve with Custard Sauce.
6 SERVINGS

Chocolate Fondue

Ice Cream with Cherries

1 pint vanilla ice cream
1 pint heavy cream
½ teaspoon almond extract
1 (1 pound) can red sour pitted cherries

1. Let vanilla ice cream soften.
2. Beat heavy cream, adding the almond extract, until it forms stiff peaks.
3. Fold the whipped cream into the soft ice cream and spoon into individual dishes.
4. Top with cherries and some of the juice.
5. Place in freezer and let dessert firm up before serving.
SERVES 6

Hot Apple-Raisin Compote

6 large apples, pared, cored, and cut in 1-inch pieces
½ cup golden raisins
1 stick cinnamon, broken in 3 pieces
⅔ cup water
1 tablespoon lemon juice
2 tablespoons bourbon
1 tablespoon chopped walnuts

1. Put apples, raisins, cinnamon stick, water, and lemon juice into a saucepan. Cook covered until apples are tender (about 10 minutes). Drain; discard cinnamon stick.
2. Add bourbon to saucepan; simmer until liquid is reduced by half. Purée 1 cup of the apples and raisins with liquid in a food processor or blender; pour mixture over remaining fruit and sprinkle with walnuts.
8 SERVINGS

Peaches and Cream

3 large ripe peaches, peeled
1½ teaspoons fresh lemon juice
½ cup long-grain rice
1 cup water
½ cup instant nonfat dry-
milk solids
½ cup 2% milk
2 to 3 tablespoons honey or sugar
¼ teaspoon almond extract
Mint sprigs

1. Purée 2 of the peaches in a food processor or blender; stir in lemon juice. Coarsely chop remaining peach.
2. Cook rice according to package instructions. Purée rice with remaining ingredients except almond extract and mint in a food processor or blender. Simmer rice mixture in a saucepan over medium heat 8 minutes; stir constantly. Remove from heat; stir in almond extract.
3. Spoon rice mixture and peach purée alternately into stemmed parfait glasses. Top with chopped peaches. Garnish with mint. Serve warm, or refrigerate until chilled.
6 SERVINGS

Note: Substitute pears, strawberries, or other fresh fruit if peaches are not available.

Baked Banana and Orange Compote

2 large navel oranges, peeled
½ teaspoon cinnamon
4 large bananas, peeled and
cut in 1½-inch pieces
½ cup orange juice
Cherries with stems

1. Cut oranges into ¼-inch slices; cut slices in half. Arrange orange slices in bottom of a shallow casserole; sprinkle with cinnamon.
2. Dip bananas in orange juice; arrange over oranges. Spoon remaining orange juice over fruit.
3. Bake at 400°F 15 minutes. Serve warm in compote dishes; garnish with cherries.
6 SERVINGS

White Port Granite

1 tray ice cubes (about 14)
¼ cup white port wine
Juice of 1 lemon
1½ to 2 tablespoons sugar
Lemon slices

1. Drop ice cubes, one at a time, into a food processor or blender, following manufacturer's directions. When ice is finely ground, add wine, lemon juice, and sugar. Process until ice is in small crystals.
2. Immediately spoon into stemmed glasses, garnish with lemon slices, and serve.
4 SERVINGS (ABOUT ⅔ CUP EACH)

Note: This recipe is excellent served as a first course.

Sliced Poached Pears in Wine

½ cup Mock Creme Fraîche (page 46)
¾ cup puréed cherries
⅛ teaspoon ground cloves
4 large firm-ripe pears
3 cups water
2 tablespoons lemon juice
2 large sticks cinnamon, broken in 1-inch pieces
1½ cups white or pink Chablis wine
¼ teaspoon ground cloves

1. Mix crème fraîche, cherries, and ⅛ teaspoon ground cloves. Refrigerate covered 1 hour.
2. Cut pears in half lengthwise; remove cores. Cut halves carefully into thin slices, keeping halves together. Dip pear halves into a mixture of water and lemon juice; place halves close together in a medium saucepan. Tuck cinnamon sticks around pears; pour wine over. Sprinkle pears with ¼ teaspoon ground cloves.
3. Simmer covered until pears are just tender (12 to 15 minutes). Cool slightly. Arrange pears in shallow dishes, fanning slices out slightly. Serve warm, or refrigerate and serve cold. Pass crème fraîche or spoon over pears.
8 SERVINGS

Note: This recipe is also excellent served with Custard Sauce (page 672).

Broiled Oranges

3 large navel oranges
3 tablespoons sweet

vermouth
36 black cherries with stems

1. Cut oranges in half; cut around sections with fruit knife. Drizzle vermouth over oranges.
2. Broil 3 inches from heat until oranges are hot through (about 5 minutes).
3. Place one cherry in center of each orange half. Arrange remaining cherries around oranges on plates.
6 SERVINGS

Basic Mousse with Variations

1 envelope unflavored
  gelatin
½ cup cold water
1 cup instant nonfat dry-milk
  solids

¼ cup sugar or honey
1 teaspoon vanilla extract
10 to 12 ice cubes
Mint sprigs or strawberries
  for garnish

1. Sprinkle gelatin over cold water in a saucepan; let stand 5 minutes. Set over low heat, stirring constantly until gelatin is dissolved (about 3 minutes).
2. Pour gelatin mixture into a food processor or blender container; add remaining ingredients except ice cubes. Process 10 seconds. Add ice cubes one at a time until mixture has consistency of heavy whipped cream.
3. Pour mixture into a serving bowl or individual stemmed glasses. Refrigerate until set (about ½ hour). Garnish with mint or strawberries.
6 SERVINGS

Note: Mousse can be unmolded, if desired. Run knife around side of bowl; dip briefly in hot water. Invert on serving plate.

Coffee Mousse: Follow recipe for Basic Mousse, adding **1 tablespoon instant coffee crystals** and **¼ teaspoon ground cinnamon** to ingredients.

Rum-Pineapple Mousse: Follow recipe for Basic Mousse, adding **1 tablespoon dark rum** to ingredients. When mousse is almost consistency of heavy whipped cream, add **1 cup crushed pineapple.** Continue adding ice cubes until desired consistency is achieved.

Ricotta Mousse: Prepare half the Basic Mousse recipe. When desired consistency is reached, add **1 tablespoon apple concentrate, 1 cup low-fat ricotta cheese,** and **¼ teaspoon cinnamon.** Turn food processor on and off 2 times so ingredients are just blended.

Fruit Mousse: Follow recipe for Basic Mousse, adding **1 cup sliced fruit or berries** to ingredients.

Fruit Concentrate Mousse: Follow recipe for Basic Mousse; omit sugar and add **3 tablespoons natural fruit concentrate** to ingredients. Garnish with slices of fresh fruit or **1 to 2 cups prepared fruit.**

Note: Natural fruit concentrates can be purchased in special-ty sections of the supermarket or in gourmet food shops. Many flavors, such as peach, apple, blackberry, and strawberry, are available.

Viceroy's Dessert

4 eggs, separated
¾ cup sugar
1 cup milk
1 cup dry sherry
1 teaspoon vanilla extract
Pinch salt
1 cup whipping cream
1 tablespoon confectioners'

sugar
2 tablespoons brandy
1 pound sponge cake or
  ladyfingers
Apricot preserves
Grated semisweet chocolate
Toasted slivered almonds

1. Place egg yolks and sugar in top of a double boiler; beat until evenly mixed, then beat in milk. Place over boiling water and cook until thickened, stirring constantly. Stir in ½ cup of the sherry and vanilla extract. Cool; set aside.
2. Beat egg whites with salt until stiff, not dry, peaks form. Beat cream with confectioners' sugar until stiff; stir in brandy. Fold egg whites into whipped cream mixture. Set aside.
3. Slice sponge cake into ½-inch-thick slices (or split ladyfingers). Spread with apricot preserves.
4. Arrange one layer in 2-quart serving dish (preferably glass, as the finished dessert is pretty). Sprinkle with some of remaining sherry. Spread with a layer of one-third of the custard mixture. Add another layer of cake, sprinkle with sherry, and spread with a third of the cream-egg-white mixture. Repeat layers until all ingredients are used, ending with a layer of cream-egg-white mixture.
5. Sprinkle with chocolate and almonds. Chill in refrigerator several hours.
6 TO 8 SERVINGS

St. Joseph's Day Cream Puffs

1 cup hot water
½ cup butter
1 tablespoon sugar
½ teaspoon salt
1 cup sifted all-purpose flour
4 eggs

1 teaspoon grated orange
  peel
1 teaspoon grated lemon
  peel
Ricotta filling; use one-half
  recipe (page 582)

1. Combine water, butter, sugar, and salt in a saucepan; bring to boiling. Add flour, all at once, and beat vigorously with a wooden spoon until mixture leaves the sides of pan and forms a smooth ball (about 3 minutes). Remove from heat.
2. Quickly beat in eggs one at a time, beating until smooth after each one is added. Continue beating until mixture is smooth and glossy. Add orange and lemon peel; mix thoroughly. Drop by tablespoonfuls 2 inches apart on a lightly greased baking sheet.
3. Bake at 350°F 15 minutes. Turn oven control to 350°F and bake 15 to 20 minutes, or until golden. Cool on wire racks.
4. To serve, cut a slit in side of each puff and fill with ricotta filling.
ABOUT 18 PUFFS

Pasta Flora

½ cup unsalted butter (at room temperature)
2 eggs
1 teaspoon vanilla extract
1 cup sugar

3 cups all-purpose flour
1 tablespoon baking powder
1 pint jam or preserves
1 egg yolk, beaten with ½ teaspoon water

1. Beat butter 4 minutes, using an electric mixer. Add eggs, vanilla extract, and sugar. Beat until fluffy. Mix flour and baking powder. Slowly work into mixture until well blended.
2. Divide dough into 2 parts; one a ball using three fourths of the total, and one using one fourth of the total.
3. Line the bottom of a 13x9-inch baking pan with the larger portion of the dough. Spread the preserves evenly over dough.
4. Roll the remaining quarter of the dough on a lightly floured board to fit the size of the pan. Cut into strips. Form a lattice over the preserves. Brush dough with the egg yolk and water.
5. Bake at 350°F about 45 minutes until pastry is golden brown or a wooden pick comes out clean when inserted. Cool. Cut into squares.
10 SERVINGS

Pasta Flora

Peach Sherbet

¼ pound well-ripened
 peaches
½ bottle white wine
8 ounces water

4 ounces sugar
Juice of 1 lemon
½ cup heavy cream
2 ripe peaches, sliced

1. Bring water and sugar to a boil and let boil for a couple of minutes.
2. Remove pits from peaches and cut fruit in thin slices. Place in a large bowl. Pour warm sugared water over peach slices and let cool. Add wine. Let stand overnight.
3. Strain peaches and mix or purée with wine and syrup in a blender. Add lemon juice.
4. Place bowl in freezer for 1 hour or until it starts to set. Remove from freezer at half hour intervals for three hours and beat rapidly each time.
5. Serve frozen sherbet immediately after last whipping in large wine glasses.
6. Top with whipped cream and fresh peach slices.
8 SERVINGS

Rum Cream

2 packages (3 ounces each)
 cream cheese, softened
3 egg yolks

⅓ cup sugar
2 tablespoons rum
Ladyfingers

1. Beat cream cheese until very light and fluffy; set aside.
2. Combine egg yolks and sugar, beating until very thick. Thoroughly blend in rum.
3. Pour egg-yolk mixture over cream cheese and fold in gently.
4. Fill 4 champagne or wine glasses to within ½ inch of rim. Chill 2 hours. Serve with ladyfingers.
4 SERVINGS

Neapolitan Fondant Roll

1 egg white
3 cups confectioners' sugar
1 teaspoon vanilla extract
4 tablespoons unsalted butter, softened

3 drops red food coloring
3 drops green foood coloring
½ cup finely chopped
 toasted almonds

1. Beat egg white until it forms soft peaks. Sift confectioners' sugar into egg white and combine thoroughly. Add vanilla extract; mix well. Cream butter until it is fluffy, add to the sugar mixture, and beat mixture until it is as fluffy as possible.
2. Divide creamed mixture into 3 equal parts. Blend red food coloring into one part, green into another, and leave remaining part white. Chill in refrigerator until firm enough to handle (about 1 hour).
3. With a spatula that has been dipped in cold water, shape the green part into a 7x3-inch rectangle on a piece of waxed paper. Spread the white part on the green, and the red on the white, forming a rectangle about ½ inch thick.
4. Using waxed paper, roll up rectangle from wide edge into a roll with the green on the outside. Chill 30 minutes, unwrap, and coat well with nuts. Rewrap in waxed paper, and chill in refrigerator 12 hours.
5. To serve, remove paper and cut in ¼-inch slices.
ABOUT 40 SLICES

Spumone

½ cup sugar
⅛ teaspoon salt
1 cup milk, scalded
3 egg yolks, beaten
1 cup whipping cream
½ ounce (½ square)
 unsweetened chocolate,
 melted
2 teaspoons rum extract
1 tablespoon sugar
⅛ teaspoon pistachio extract

2 drops green food coloring
½ cup whipping cream,
 whipped
1 maraschino cherry
1 tablespoon sugar
6 unblanched almonds, finely chopped
¼ teaspoon almond extract
½ cup whipping cream,
 whipped

1. Stir ½ cup sugar and salt into scalded milk in the top of a double boiler. Stir until sugar is dissolved.
2. Stir about 3 tablespoons of the hot milk into the egg yolks. Immediately return to double boiler top. Cook over boiling water, stirring constantly, about 5 minutes, or until mixture coats a spoon. Remove from heat and cool.
3. Stir in 1 cup whipping cream and divide mixture equally into two bowls.
4. Add melted chocolate to mixture in one bowl and mix thoroughly. Set in refrigerator.
5. Add rum extract to remaining mixture and pour into refrigerator tray. Freeze until mushy.
6. Turn into a chilled bowl and beat until mixture is smooth and creamy. Spoon into a chilled 1-quart mold and freeze until firm.
7. Fold 1 tablespoon sugar, pistachio extract, and food coloring into ½ cup whipping cream, whipped. Spoon over firm rum ice cream; freeze until firm.
8. When pistachio cream becomes firm, place the maraschino cherry in the center and return to freezer.
9. Fold 1 tablespoon sugar, chopped almonds, and almond extract into remaining ½ cup whipping cream, whipped. Spoon over firm pistachio cream. Freeze until firm.
10. When almond cream is firm, pour chocolate ice cream mixture into refrigerator tray and freeze until mushy.
11. Turn into a chilled bowl and beat until mixture is smooth and creamy. Spoon mixture over firm almond cream. Cover mold with aluminum foil or waxed paper. Return to freezer and freeze 6 to 8 hours, or until very firm.
12. To unmold, quickly dip mold into warm water and invert. Cut spumone into wedge-shaped pieces.
6 TO 8 SERVINGS

Sherried Holiday Pudding

1 package (14 ounces) gingerbread mix
¾ cup orange juice
¼ cup sherry
½ cup chopped walnuts
½ teaspoon grated orange peel
Golden Sherry Sauce (below)
Hard Sauce Snowballs (below)

1. Prepare gingerbread according to package directions using orange juice and sherry for liquid. Add walnuts and orange peel.
2. Turn batter into a well-greased 6-cup mold (batter should fill mold ½ to ⅔ full).
3. Bake at 350°F for 50 to 55 minutes, until pudding tests done. Serve warm with Golden Sherry Sauce and Hard Sauce Snowballs.
8 SERVINGS

Golden Sherry Sauce: Combine **½ cup each granulated and brown sugar (packed, ¼ cup whipping cream,** and **⅛ teaspoon salt** in saucepan. Heat slowly to boiling, stirring occasionally. Add **¼ cup sherry** and **1 teaspoon grated lemon peel.** Heat slightly to blend flavors.
ABOUT 1⅓ CUPS SAUCE

Hard Sauce Snowballs: Beat together **⅔ cup soft butter** or **margarine, 2 cups confectioners' sugar,** and **1 tablespoon sherry,** adding a little more sherry if more liquid is needed. Shape into small balls and roll in **flaked coconut.**
ABOUT 1½ CUPS OR 16 BALLS

Cheese and Fruit

Bel Paese — a soft, mild cheese of the North and often served with ripe cherries or plums.

Gorgonzola — the most popular of the dessert cheeses, a creamy, tangy cheese veined with green mold; often served with sliced fresh pears, ripe Italian bananas, or quartered apples.

Stracchino — a tangy goat's milk cheese of Milan which may be accompanied by any number of fruits including peaches and grapes.

Provolone — whether the pear-shape Provolone, round Provolette, or sausage-shape Provolone salami, this is a favorite when accompanied by quartered apples and small slices of watermelon.

Caciocavallo — typifying a tapering beet root, this smoked cheese is delicious when served as a dessert with small crackers.

Ricotta — a soft, bland pot cheese often used in baking, this can be served as a dessert when accompanied by berries and figs.

Stuffed Peaches

½ cup blanched almonds, finely chopped
½ cup macaroon crumbs (see Note)
¼ cup sugar
1 tablespoon chopped candied orange peel
6 large firm peaches
⅓ cup sherry or Marsala

1. Combine almonds, macaroon crumbs, 2 tablespoons sugar, and orange peel; set aside.
2. Peel peaches, cut in half, and remove pits. Lightly fill peach halves with almond mixture. Put two halves together and secure with wooden picks. Place in a 10x6-inch baking dish, pour sherry over peaches, and sprinkle with remaining sugar.
3. Bake at 350°F 15 minutes. Serve either hot or cold.
6 SERVINGS

Note: To make macaroon crumbs, grind enough Macaroons (below) in electric blender to make ½ cup crumbs.

Bread Pudding

2 cups firmly packed dark brown sugar
1 quart water
1 stick cinnamon
1 clove
6 slices toast, cubed
3 apples, pared, cored, and
sliced
1 cup raisins
1 cup chopped blanched almonds
½ pound Monterey Jack or similar cheese, cubed

1. Put brown sugar, water, cinnamon, and clove into a saucepan and bring to boiling; reduce heat and simmer until a light syrup is formed. Discard spices and set syrup aside.
2. Meanwhile, arrange a layer of toast cubes in a buttered casserole. Cover with a layer of apples, raisins, almonds, and cheese. Repeat until all ingredients are used. pour syrup over all.
3. Bake at 350°F about 30 minutes.
4. Serve hot.
6 SERVINGS

Sherried Holiday Pudding

Meringues

Meringues

6 egg whites
¼ teaspoon salt
¾ teaspoon cream of tartar
1½ cups sugar

Custard Filling, below
Cherry-Cinnamon Sauce
  (page 636)

1. Beat egg whites with salt and cream of tartar until frothy. Gradually add sugar, continuing to beat until stiff peaks are formed and sugar is dissolved.
2. Shape meringue shells with a spoon or force through a pastry bag and tube onto a baking sheet lined with unglazed paper.
3. Bake at 250°F 1 hour.
4. Transfer meringues from paper to wire racks to cool.
5. When ready to serve, spoon Custard Filling into meringue shells and top with Cherry-Cinnamon Sauce.
12 MERINGUE SHELLS

Custard Filling

½ cup sugar
2 teaspoons flour
¼ teaspoon salt

2 cups milk
6 egg yolks, beaten
1 teaspoon vanilla extract

1. Blend sugar, flour, and salt in a heavy saucepan. Stir in the milk. Bring to boiling; stir and cook 1 to 2 minutes.
2. Add a small amount of the hot mixture to egg yolks, stirring constantly. Blend into mixture in saucepan. Cook 1 minute.
3. Remove from heat and cool immediately by pouring custard into a chilled bowl and setting it in refrigerator or pan of cold water. Blend extract into cooled custard. Chill until serving time.
ABOUT 2½ CUPS FILLING

Almond Snow

2 cups milk
½ cup sugar
¼ cup ground blanched
  almonds

4 egg whites
Pinch salt
1 tablespoon kirsch
Toasted slivered almonds

1. Scald milk. Stir in sugar until dissolved. Add almonds. Cook over very low heat about 15 minutes. Cool.
2. Meanwhile, beat egg whites with salt until stiff, not dry, peaks form. Fold egg whites into milk mixture. Stir in kirsch.
3. Butter top of a double boiler; pour in mixture; cover. Cook over hot (not boiling) water until mixture is firm. Chill.
4. Unmold onto serving plate and stud with slivered almonds.
6 SERVINGS

Raspberry Mousse

5 packages (10 ounces each)
  frozen raspberries
2 packages unflavored
  gelatin
2 tablespoons lemon juice
5 whole eggs
4 egg yolks

½ cup sugar
3 tablespoons raspberry liqueur (optional)
2½ cups whipping cream
2 tablespoons confectioners'
  sugar

1. Drain raspberries, reserving juice. Using **steel blade,** process raspberries until puréed. Strain to remove seeds. Discard seeds and set purée aside.
2. In a saucepan, combine lemon juice and 6 tablespoons of reserved raspberry juice. Add gelatin and stir to soften. Stir over low heat until gelatin is dissolved. Let cool.
3. Using **steel blade,** add 5 whole eggs, 4 egg yolks, and sugar to bowl. Process for about 4 to 5 minutes, until very thick. Add raspberry purée and process until combined.
4. With machine on, add cooled gelatin mixture through the feed tube. Process until thoroughly blended. Add raspberry liqueur, if desired.
5 .Using a mixer, beat whipping cream until it begins to thicken. Add confectioners' sugar and continue to beat until it holds its shape. Remove one quarter of the whipped cream and save it to decorate the finished mousse.
6. Gently fold whipped cream and raspberry mixture together. Turn into a decorative crystal bowl.
7. Chill mousse until set, at least 2 hours, and decorate with remaining whipped cream put through a pastry bag.
10 TO 12 SERVINGS

Raspberry Mousse

Lemon Egg Fluff

3 envelopes unflavored
  gelatin
½ cup sugar
Few grains salt
1 cup water
10 egg yolks, beaten
1 can (6 ounces) frozen

lemonade concentrate,
  thawed
10 egg whites
½ cup sugar
Cherry-Cinnamon Sauce,
  below

1. Thoroughly blend gelatin, sugar, and salt in a heavy saucepan. Mix in water. Stir over low heat until gelatin is dissolved.
2. Gradually add a small amount of hot gelatin mixture to egg yolks, stirring constantly. Blend into mixture in saucepan; cook and stir 2 minutes without boiling.
3. Remove from heat. Stir in lemonade concentrate. Chill until mixture is slightly thickened.
4. Beat egg whites until frothy. Gradually add sugar, continuing to beat until stiff peaks are formed; fold in gelatin mixture. Turn into a 2½-quart tower mold and chill until firm.
5. Unmold onto a chilled serving plate and serve with Cherry-Cinnamon Sauce.
12 SERVINGS

Cherry-Cinnamon Sauce: Combine **½ cup sugar** and **2 tablespoons cornstarch** in a saucepan; mix thoroughly. Drain **1 can (about 16 ounces) tart red cherries,** reserving the liquid. Add cherry liquid and **3 tablespoons red cinnamon candies** to sugar mixture. Bring to boiling, stirring constantly; continue cooking until mixture is thickened and clear. Remove from heat. Stir in **1 tablespoon lemon juice** and the cherries. Cool.
ABOUT 2¼ CUPS SAUCE

Royal Eggs

¼ cup raisins
½ cup dry sherry
12 egg yolks
2 cups sugar
1 cup water
1 cinnamon stick
¼ cup slivered almonds

1. Soak raisins in ¼ cup of the sherry.
2. Beat egg yolks until they form a ribbon when poured from the beater.
3. Pour into a buttered shallow pan. Set this pan in another larger pan with about 1 inch of water in it.
4. Bake at 325°F about 20 to 25 minutes, or until set.
5. Remove from oven and cool on a wire rack.
6. Cut cooked, cooled eggs into cubes.
7. Meanwhile, combine sugar, water, and cinnamon stick in a saucepan and bring to boiling. Reduce heat and simmer about 5 minutes, stirring until all sugar is dissolved. Remove cinnamon stick.
8. Carefully place egg cubes in saucepan of sauce. Continue simmering over very low heat until cubes are well-saturated with the syrup. Add soaked raisins and remaining sherry. Sprinkle with slivered almonds.
6 SERVINGS

Coffee Liqueur Mold

1 envelope unflavored
  gelatin
¼ cup coffee liqueur
1 cup strong hot coffee
¼ cup sugar
1 cup whipping cream
Whipped cream (optional)
¼ cup chopped pecans
  (optional)

1. Soften gelatin in coffee liqueur. Dissolve in hot coffee. Add sugar and stir until dissolved. Cool to lukewarm. Stir in cream.
2. Pour into a mold. Chill until set.
3. To serve, turn out of mold onto serving plate. If desired, top with whipped cream and sprinkle with chopped pecans.
4 TO 6 SERVINGS

Quick Flan

¼ cup granulated sugar
4 eggs
1 can (14 ounces) sweetened
condensed milk
½ can water
1 teaspoon vanilla extract

1. Select a pan of at least 1-quart capacity which will fit inside pressure cooker. Spread sugar over bottom of pan. Heat over very low heat, stirring occasionally, until sugar melts and turns golden brown. Remove from heat.
2. Beat eggs in a bowl; beat in milk, water, and vanilla extract.
3. Pour milk-egg mixture into sugar-coated pan.
4. Place about 1 inch of water in pressure cooker. Place filled pan inside cooker. Lay a sheet of waxed paper over top of milk-egg mixture. Place cover on cooker and heat following manufacturer's directions; cook 10 minutes.
5. Cool, then chill before serving.
6 SERVINGS

Glazed Whole Oranges

 ## Glazed Whole Oranges

4 large navel oranges
3 tablespoons butter
¾ cup currant jelly
½ cup orange juice
1 tablespoon arrowroot
2 tablespoons cold water

1. Remove thin outer peel from three of the oranges with a vegetable peeler. Cut into very thin slivers and place in a small saucepan with enough water to cover. Cover saucepan.
2. Bring to boiling, reduce heat, and simmer 10 minutes. Drain and set peel aside. Cut remaining peel and white membrane from all four oranges.
3. Put butter and jelly in cooking pan of a chafing dish. Place over low heat and stir gently until melted. Stir in orange juice and cooked peel, reserving some to garnish oranges, if desired.
4. Place oranges in sauce. Cook about 5 minutes; spoon sauce over oranges occasionally. Mix arrowroot with cold water to form a smooth paste; stir into sauce.
5. Continue cooking until sauce thickens (about 5 minutes); spoon sauce over oranges while heating.
6. Serve oranges warm, covered with sauce, and sprinkle with reserved slivered peel, if desired.
6 TO 8 SERVINGS

Strawberry-Pear Flambée

2 packages (10 ounces each) frozen strawberries
1 cup sugar
6 tablespoons butter
½ cup orange juice
1½ teaspoons grated lemon peel
1 can (29 ounces) large pear halves, drained
⅓ cup cognac

1. Drain strawberries; reserve juice. Put berries through a sieve to purée. Add desired amount of reserved juice to sweeten and thin purée; set aside.
2. In cooking pan of a chafing dish, caramelize sugar with butter over medium heat. Stir in orange juice, lemon peel, and purée. Simmer sauce 1 to 2 minutes, stirring gently.
3. Place pears in sauce and roll in sauce until they are thoroughly heated and have a blush.
4. In a separate pan, heat cognac just until warm. Ignite the cognac and pour over the pears. Spoon the sauce over pears until the flames die out.
5. Serve the pears in dessert dishes with the sauce.
4 SERVINGS

Sherried Raisin-Rice Pudding

⅔ cup raisins
¼ cup sherry
1 cup uncooked rice
1 teaspoon grated lemon peel
Dash salt
1½ cups water
3 cups milk
1 cup sugar
½ teaspoon cinnamon
1 egg, beaten
Whipped cream (optional)

1. Soak raisins in sherry while preparing rest of pudding.
2. Put rice, lemon peel, salt, and water in a saucepan. Bring to boiling, reduce heat, cover, and cook over very low heat until all water is absorbed (about 10 to 15 minutes).
3. Stir in milk, sugar, and cinnamon and cook over very low heat, stirring frequently, until all milk has been absorbed.
4. Stir in soaked raisins, then beaten egg. Continue to heat 1 or 2 minutes, stirring constantly, until egg has cooked.
5. Turn pudding into a serving dish. Chill in refrigerator.
6. Serve with whipped cream, if desired.
6 TO 8 SERVINGS

Sopaipillas

2 cups sifted all-purpose flour
2 teaspoons baking powder
1 teaspoon salt
2 tablespoons shortening
⅔ to ¾ cup cold water
Oil or shortening for deep frying heated to 365°F
Cinnamon sugar

1. Sift flour, baking powder, and salt together into bowl. Cut in shortening until mixture resembles coarse crumbs. Sprinkle water over top and work in gradually until dough will just hold together (as for pie pastry).
2. Turn out on a lightly floured surface and knead gently about 30 seconds. Roll out as thin as possible. Cut into 2-inch squares.
3. Fry one or two at a time in heated fat, turning until puffed and golden brown on both sides.
4. Drain on absorbent paper. Sprinkle with cinnamon sugar while still hot.
2½ TO 3 DOZEN

Almendrado

1 tablespoon unflavored gelatin
½ cup sugar
1 cup cold water
4 egg whites
½ teaspoon almond extract
Red and green food coloring
1 cup finely ground almonds
Custard Sauce with Almonds

1. Mix gelatin and sugar in a saucepan. Stir in water. Set over low heat and stir until gelatin and sugar are dissolved. Chill until slightly thickened.
2. Beat egg whites until stiff, not dry, peaks are formed. Fold into gelatin mixture along with almond extract. Beat until mixture resembles whipped cream. Divide equally into 3 portions. Color one portion red, another green, and leave the last one white.
3. Pour red mixture into an 8-inch square dish or pan. Sprinkle with half of the almonds. Pour in white mixture and sprinkle with remaining almonds. Top with green layer. Chill thoroughly.
4. Cut into portions and serve with custard sauce.
12 SERVINGS

Custard Sauce with Almonds: Scald **2 cups milk.** Mix **4 egg yolks** and **¼ cup sugar** in the top of a double boiler. Add scalded milk gradually, stirring constantly. Cook over boiling water, stirring constantly until mixture coats a spoon. Remove from water and stir in **¼ teaspoon almond extract** and **½ cup toasted sliced almonds.** Cool; chill thoroughly. ABOUT 2½ CUPS

Fresh Pineapple and Almond Pudding

2 cups pared diced fresh pineapple
½ cup sugar
½ cup ground blanched almonds
½ cup dry sherry
4 egg yolks, beaten
¼ teaspoon cinnamon
1 dozen ladyfingers, or 12 (4x1-inch) slices sponge or angel food cake
½ cup orange marmalade
½ cup sour cream
1 tablespoon sugar
Toasted slivered almonds

1. Combine pineapple, ½ cup sugar, ground almonds, ¼ cup of the sherry, egg yolks, and cinnamon in a saucepan. Cook over low heat, stirring constantly, until thickened. Cool.
2. Meanwhile, split ladyfingers and spread with marmalade. (If using cake slices, they may be toasted lightly if very soft, but do not split before spreading with marmalade.)
3. Arrange half the spread ladyfingers or cake slices in bottom of a 1½-quart serving dish. Sprinkle with 2 tablespoons sherry. Spoon half the pineapple mixture on top. Repeat layers of ladyfingers, sherry, and pineapple mixture.
4. Set in refrigerator until well chilled (at least 1 hour).
5. Sweeten sour cream with 1 tablespoon sugar. Spread over top of chilled dessert. Decorate with toasted almonds.
6 TO 8 SERVINGS

Twelve-Fruit Compote

3 cups water
1 pound mixed dried fruits including pears, figs, apricots, and peaches
1 cup pitted prunes
½ cup raisins or currants
1 cup pitted sweet cherries
2 apples, peeled and sliced or 6 ounces dried apple slices

½ cup cranberries
1 cup sugar
1 lemon, sliced
6 whole cloves
2 cinnamon sticks (3 inches each)
1 orange
½ cup grapes, pomegranate seeds, or pitted plums
½ cup fruit-flavored brandy

1. Combine water, mixed dried fruits, prunes, and raisins in a 6-quart kettle. Bring to boiling. Cover; simmer about 20 minutes, or until fruits are plump and tender.
2. Add cherries, apples, and cranberries. Stir in sugar, lemon, and spices. Cover; simmer 5 minutes.
3. Grate peel of orange; reserve. Peel and section orange, removing all skin and white membrane. Add to fruits in kettle.
4. Stir in grapes and brandy. Bring just to boiling. Remove from heat. Stir in orange peel. Cover; let stand 15 minutes.
ABOUT 12 SERVINGS

Apricot-Filled Pastries

1 cup dried apricots
1 cup water
½ cup sugar
½ teaspoon vanilla extract
2 cups all-purpose flour
¾ teaspoon salt

½ teaspoon baking powder
⅔ cup lard
4 to 6 tablespoons icy cold water
Confectioners' Sugar Glaze

1. Put apricots and water into saucepan. Cover, bring to boiling, and cook 20 minutes.
2. Turn contents of saucepan into an electric blender; cover and blend until smooth.
3. Combine blended apricots and sugar in saucepan; cook until thick (about 5 minutes). Cool slightly; stir in vanilla extract.
4. Mix flour, salt, and baking powder in a bowl. Cut in lard until crumbly. Add cold water, 1 tablespoon at a time, tossing with a fork until dough holds together. Divide in half.
5. Roll each half of dough to a 14x10-inch rectangle on a lightly floured surface.
6. Line a 13x9x2-inch baking pan with one rectangle of dough. Spread apricot mixture evenly over dough. Place remaining dough on top; seal edges. Prick top crust.
7. Bake at 400°F 25 minutes, or until lightly browned around edges.
8. Cool slightly. Frost with confectioners' sugar glaze. Cool; cut in squares.
2 DOZEN FILLED PASTRIES

Confectioners' Sugar Glaze: Combine **1 cup confectioners' sugar** and **½ teaspoon vanilla extract.** Blend in **milk or cream** (about 3 tablespoons) until glaze is of spreading consistency.

Twelve-Fruit Compote

Mexican Custard

1 quart milk
1 cup sugar
3 or 4 cinnamon sticks

⅛ teaspoon salt
4 eggs
1 teaspoon vanilla extract

1. Combine milk, sugar, and cinnamon sticks in saucepan. Bring to scalding point, stirring constantly. Remove from heat and cool to lukewarm.
2. Meanwhile, beat eggs in a 1½-quart casserole. Gradually beat in milk-sugar mixture; stir in vanilla extract. Place in a shallow pan of water.
3. Bake at 325°F about 1 hour, or until custard is set.
4. Serve warm or cooled.
ABOUT 10 SERVINGS

Spiked Watermelon

1 large ripe watermelon   2 cups amber rum

1. Cut a hole 2½ inches wide and 2 inches deep in the watermelon rind. Pour rum through hole and replace rind.
2. Chill 24 hours. Serve ice-cold slices.

 ## Flaming Bananas

2 tablespoons butter or margarine
⅔ cup sugar

6 ripe bananas, peeled
½ cup rum

1. Melt butter in a chafing dish or skillet. Stir in sugar and heat until sugar melts.
2. Slice bananas lengthwise and add to butter-sugar mixture; turn to coat on all sides. Pour in rum and keep over medium heat.
3. Flame sauce by pouring a little rum into a teaspoon and holding it over flame of chafing dish or range until it flames; then use this flaming rum to light rum on top of bananas. Spoon flaming sauce over fruit several times.
4. Serve over **vanilla** or **chocolate ice cream.**
6 SERVINGS

 ## Pineapple Ablaze

1 cup packed brown sugar
1 cup water
6 fresh pineapple slices
6 raisin bread slices with crusts trimmed

½ cup unsalted butter
6 tablespoons coarsely ground cashews
1 teaspoon cinnamon
½ cup amber rum

1. Combine brown sugar and water in a saucepan. Bring to boiling and boil rapidly until reduced to half its volume. Add pineapple and poach for 6 minutes. Remove pineapple and keep syrup warm.
2. Fry bread slices in butter in a skillet until golden.
3. Lay these croutons in a circle in a chafing dish. Top with pineapple slices and sprinkle with cashews and cinnamon. Spoon half the syrup into chafing dish pan. Warm rum, ignite, and pour, still flaming, over all.
6 SERVINGS

Cherries Jubilee

1 package (16 ounces) frozen
  pitted tart cherries
⅓ cup sugar
¾ cup Cherry Heering
Dash salt
1 tablespoon cornstarch
1 tablespoon butter or

margarine
1 tablespoon grated lemon
  peel
18 dessert crêpes
¼ cup brandy
1 pint vanilla ice cream

1. Thaw cherries, drain, and reserve juice.
2. Combine juice (adding water to make 1 cup), sugar, ¼ cup Cherry Heering, salt, and cornstarch in chafing dish. Cook over medium heat, stirring constantly, until sauce begins to thicken. Stir in cherries, butter, and lemon peel. Simmer 3 minutes.
3. Using hot sauce method, fill chafing dish with crêpes.
4. Warm ½ cup Cherry Heering and brandy in saucepan. Pour in chafing dish and ignite. When flames die down, palce 3 crêpes on a plate, top with vanilla ice cream, and spoon warm sauce and cherries over all.
6 SERVINGS

Flaming Mangos

2 fresh mangos, or 12 slices
  canned mango, about ½
  inch thick

1 cup orange juice
2 tablespoons sugar
1 cup tequila

1. Wash and peel fresh mangos; cut each into 6 slices. Place in chafing dish or skillet. Pour orange juice over fruit and sprinkle with sugar. Heat to simmering, stirring gently to dissolve sugar and coat fruit. After 3 or 4 minutes, pour in tequila; keep over medium heat.
2. Flame sauce by pouring a little tequila into teaspoon and holding it over flame of chafing dish or range until it flames; then use this flaming tequila to light tequila on top of mangos.
3. Serve over **vanilla ice cream.**
6 SERVINGS

Pineapple Flan

3 cups pineapple juice
2 cups sugar
½ cup water

1 cup sugar
6 eggs
2 egg yolks

1. Combine pineapple juice and 2 cups sugar in a saucepan. Bring to a boil, then reduce heat and cook until a thin syrup is formed (about 5 minutes). Remove from heat, cool, and reserve.
2. Combine water and 1 cup sugar in a saucepan. Boil rapidly until it turns the color of maple syrup (5 to 7 minutes). Immediately remove from heat and pour it into a 1-quart mold, tilting mold until it is completely coated with caramel. Set aside to cool.
3. Beat eggs and yolks with the reserved pineapple syrup. Pour into mold. Set mold in a pan of hot water.
4. Bake at 325°F 1½ hours. Cool.
5. Chill thoroughly, then unmold on a serving platter.
ABOUT 12 SERVINGS

Pineapple Boat

1 small pineapple
2 cups whipping cream
1 cup sugar
1 tablespoon lime juice

½ cup whipped cream
  mixed with chopped flaked
  coconut
Chopped cashews

1. Cut pineapple in half lengthwise, a little off center. Remove pulp, keeping larger shell intact, and discard core. Chop pineapple finely or process in an electric blender. Measure 2 cups of pineapple and juice. Add to whipping cream along with sugar and lime juice.
2. Cut the leafy top off the pineapple shell and reserve for decoration. Spoon pineapple mixture into the shell and freeze until firm.
3. To serve, pipe large rosettes of the whipped cream around the shell and sprinkle with cashews. Decorate with leafy top.

Rum Pineapple Snow

1 small fresh fully ripe
  pineapple
4 egg whites
½ cup sugar

2 cups whipping cream
1 teaspoon vanilla extract
¾ cup amber rum
Ladyfingers

1. Pare pineapple and grate; keep grated pineapple separate from juice.
2. Beat egg whites until frothy; gradually add sugar while beating until meringue is thick and glossy.
3. Whip cream and blend in vanilla extract; fold into meringue along with as much grated pineapple and pineapple juice as meringue will hold and still pile softly.
4. Pour rum over ladyfingers and use to line sherbet glasses. Spoon in pineapple snow.

Pineapple Pyramids

2½ cups crushed Coconut
  Macaroons
3 tablespoons amber rum
3 cups whipping cream

⅓ cup sugar
¾ cup chopped cashews
12 pineapple slices
12 whole cashews

1. Sprinkle crushed macaroons with rum.
2. Whip cream with sugar, one half at a time, until it stands in peaks. Fold crumbs and chopped cashews into the whipped cream.
3. Place 1 pineapple slice on each dessert plate, mound cream mixture in a pyramid, and put a cashew on top of each.
12 SERVINGS

Rosé Baked Apples

Rosé Baked Apples

5 Rome Beauty or Golden Delicious apples	¼ teaspoon nutmeg
3 strips orange peel	½ cup lightly packed light brown sugar
¼ cup orange juice	Whipped cream or ice cream for topping
1 cup rosé wine	

1. Core apples and pare each about a quarter of the way down. Arrange in a large electric cooker.
2. Combine orange peel, juice, wine, nutmeg, and brown sugar and pour over apples.
3. Cover and cook on Low 3 to 4 hours.
4. Serve warm or cold with wine sauce; top with whipped cream or ice cream.
5 BAKED APPLES

Chestnuts with Coffee Cream

1 pound chestnuts	Coffee Cream (page 679)
3 tablespoons brown sugar	

1. Slit shells of chestnuts. Simmer chestnuts, in water to cover, 5 minutes. While the chestnuts are still hot, discard shells and skins. Put nuts into boiling water with brown sugar and cook 30 minutes, or until tender. Drain and chill.
2. To serve, pile chestnuts into sherbet glasses. Spoon Coffee Cream over them.

Pineapple Cream

1 pineapple, pared, sliced, and cored	6 tablespoons sugar
2 tablespoons amber rum	1 tablespoon flour
½ cup butter or margarine	6 egg yolks

1. Cube pineapple pulp and put with rum into the top of a double boiler over boiling water.
2. Beat remaining ingredients together about 5 minutes.
3. Pour the cream mixture over the pineapple cubes and mix well. Cook and stir over boiling water about 6 minutes, or until thickened.
4. Pour into small bowls or **pots de créme** cups and chill before serving.
ABOUT 3 CUPS

Coconut Milk

1 fresh coconut	2 cups boiling water

1. Open coconut, discarding liquid. With a sharp paring knife, remove the meat in chunks and grate it (see Note). Pour boiling water over grated coconut and let stand 4 hours.
2. Place a sieve over a bowl, turn grated coconut into sieve, and press out the liquid. Reserve grated coconut, if desired, to toast in the oven and use to decorate desserts and salads.
ABOUT 2 CUPS

Note: If you have an electric blender, coarsely chop coconut meat and process with boiling water a small amount at a time.

Purée of Breadfruit

1 breadfruit (1½ pounds), peeled and cubed	Salt, freshly ground pepper, and cayenne or red pepper to taste
1 cup whipping cream	

1. Cook breadfruit in lightly salted water until tender, drain.
2. Process breadfruit, a small amount at a time, with a small amount of cream, in an electric blender to make a purée. Mix in seasonings.

Note: If desired, force breadfruit through a food mill and beat in cream, slightly whipped, and the seasonings.

Spicy Peach Cobbler

1 can (29 ounces) sliced peaches, drained; reserve 1 cup syrup	2 tablespoons cider vinegar
½ cup firmly packed brown sugar	1 tablespoon butter or margarine
2 tablespoons cornstarch	1 cup all-purpose biscuit mix
⅛ teaspoon salt	½ cup finely shredded sharp Cheddar cheese
⅛ teaspoon ground cinnamon	2 tablespoons butter or margarine, melted
⅛ teaspoon ground cloves	¼ cup milk

1. Put drained peaches into a shallow 1-quart baking dish. Set aside.
2. Mix brown sugar, cornstarch, salt, cinnamon, and cloves in a saucepan. Blend in reserved peach syrup and vinegar; add 1 tablespoon butter. Bring mixture to boiling, stirring frequently; cook until thickened, about 10 minutes. Pour over peaches and set in a 400°F oven.
3. Combine biscuit mix and cheese. Stir in melted butter and milk to form a soft dough. Remove dish from oven and drop dough by heaping tablespoonfuls on top of hot peaches.
4. Return to oven and bake 20 minutes, or until crust is golden brown. Serve warm.
6 SERVINGS

Nectarine-Pineapple Sundae Sauce

1½ cups pared fresh nec-
  tarine slices
1 jar (12 ounces) pineapple
  sundae topping
¼ teaspoon mint extract or 1
  teaspoon rum or brandy extract (optional)

1. If desired, coarsely crush 1 cup of nectarines.
2. Mix nectarines with pineapple topping and, if desired, mint extract.
3. Cover and refrigerate until ready to use.

ABOUT 2½ CUPS SAUCE

Nectarine Ripple Ice Cream

1 cup sugar
¾ teaspoon unflavored
  gelatin
⅛ teaspoon salt
2 cups half-and-half
2 eggs, beaten
½ teaspoon vanilla extract
1 quart sliced fresh
  nectarines
1 tablespoon lemon juice
⅛ teaspoon yellow food
  coloring
2 drops red food coloring
1½ cups whipping cream,
  whipped until stiff

1. Combine ½ cup sugar, gelatin, and salt in a saucepan; mix well. Add half-and-half and heat to scalding over low heat, stirring occasionally. Add the beaten eggs gradually, stirring constantly. Continue to cook 5 minutes over low heat, stirring constantly, until mixture thickens slightly.
2. Remove from heat and stir in vanilla extract; chill.
3. Turn about 1 cup nectarines at a time into an electric blender and blend until particles are very fine, stopping blender and pushing fruit into blades with a rubber spatula. Turn out, then continue blending remainder of nectarines to measure 2 cups. (If blender is not available, cut up fruit and mash fine.) Stir in lemon juice and remaining ½ cup sugar.
4. Stir half of the nectarine mixture and the food coloring into chilled custard. Pour into trays and freeze until firm.
5. Turn frozen mixture into a chilled bowl, break mixture into small chunks, and beat with electric mixer at slow speed until smooth. Fold in whipped cream and return to trays. Set in freezer until almost firm, ½ to 1 hour.
6. Add the remaining nectarines, rippling them in, return to freezer, and freeze until firm.

ABOUT ½ GALLON ICE CREAM

Frozen Lemon Velvet

1 can (13 ounces) evaporated
  milk
2½ cups graham cracker
  crumbs
⅔ cup margarine, melted
2 packages (8 ounces each)
cream cheese, softened
1 cup sugar
2 tablespoons milk
2 tablespoons grated lemon
  peel
1 cup chopped walnuts

1. Pour evaporated milk into a refrigerator tray, and set in freezer until ice crystals form around edges.
2. Combine cracker crumbs and margarine. Turn into a 13x9-inch pan and press into an even layer.
3. Put cream cheese, sugar, milk, and lemon peel into a bowl; mix until smooth.
4. Turn icy cold evaporated milk into a chilled bowl and beat with a chilled beater until stiff peaks are formed. Fold whipped evaporated milk and nuts into cheese mixture; turn onto layer in pan and spread evenly. Freeze.
5. To serve, cut into squares and garnish with **lemon slices** and **graham cracker crumbs**.
16 TO 20 SERVINGS

Frozen Lemon Velvet

Cantaloupe Sherbet

2 cups ripe cantaloupe
  pieces
1 egg white
½ cup sugar
2 tablespoons fresh lime
  juice

1. Put melon pieces, egg white, sugar, and lime juice into an electric blender container. Cover and blend until smooth.
2. Turn into a shallow baking dish. Set in freezer; stir occasionally during freezing.
3. To serve, spoon into chilled dessert dishes.
ABOUT 1½ PINTS SHERBET

Pineapple Sherbet: Follow recipe for Cantaloupe Sherbet; substitute **2 cups fresh pineapple pieces** for cantaloupe.

Watermelon Sherbet: Follow recipe for Cantaloupe Sherbet; substitute **2 cups watermelon pieces** for cantaloupe and, if desired, decrease sugar to ¼ cup.

Banana Fan

4 ripe bananas
1 cup water
½ cup sugar
1 cup maraschino cherries
½ cup amber rum, warmed
  and flamed
1 cup whipped cream
¼ teaspoon vanilla extract

1. Peel bananas and halve them lengthwise. Arrange halves flat side down in the shape of an open fan on a round silver or glass dish.
2. Boil water and sugar together at a rolling boil 4 minutes. Add cherries, reduce heat, and simmer 2 minutes. Remove some of the cherries with a perforated spoon and arrange in a design on upper portion of fan.
3. Put the remaining fruit with syrup into an electric blender along with flamed rum; process until puréed. Or force mixture through a food mill. Spoon over upper part of fan.
4. Blend whipped cream and vanilla extract. Using a pastry bag and decorating tube, make a thick border around upper portion of fan to simulate lace. Serve well chilled.

Lemon Crunch Dessert

Lemon mixture:
¾ cup sugar
2 tablespoons flour
⅛ teaspoon salt
1 cup water
2 eggs, well beaten
1 teaspoon grated lemon
  peel
⅓ cup lemon juice

Crunch mixture:
½ cup butter or margarine
1 cup firmly packed brown
  sugar
1 cup all-purpose flour
½ teaspoon salt
1 cup whole wheat flakes,
  crushed
½ cup finely chopped
  walnuts
½ cup shredded coconut

1. For lemon mixture, mix sugar, flour, and salt in a heavy saucepan. Gradually add water, stirring until smooth. Bring mixture to boiling and cook 2 minutes.
2. Stir about 3 tablespoons of the hot mixture vigorously into beaten eggs. Immediately blend into mixture in saucepan. Cook and stir about 3 minutes.
3. Remove from heat and stir in lemon peel and lemon juice. Set aside to cool.
4. For crunch mixture, beat butter until softened; add brown sugar gradually, beating until fluffy. Add flour and salt; mix well. Add wheat flakes, walnuts, and coconut; mix thoroughly.
5. Line bottom of an 8-inch square baking dish with one third of the crunch mixture. Cover with the lemon mixture, spreading to form an even layer. Top with remaining crunch mixture.
6. Bake, uncovered, at 350°F 40 minutes, or until lightly browned. Serve warm or cold.
8 SERVINGS

Lemon Crunch Dessert

Grape Sherbet

2 envelopes unflavored gelatin
½ cup water
7 cups milk
4 cans (6 ounces each)

frozen grape juice concentrate, thawed
1 tablespoon lemon juice
½ cup sugar

1. Soften gelatin in water in a saucepan. Dissolve over low heat, stirring constantly. Pour gelatin into a large bowl and stir in milk.
2. Blend in grape juice concentrate, lemon juice, and sugar. Mix thoroughly.
3. Pour into metal pans, not more than three quarters full. Place in freezer until mushy. Turn into a chilled bowl and beat until fluffy. Return to metal pans and freeze until firm.
ABOUT 1 GALLON SHERBET

Note: If desired, sherbet may be frozen in an ice cream freezer. Follow manufacturer's instructions, using ¼ cup rock salt to 1 quart crushed ice, chilling sherbet mixture thoroughly before churning. Sherbet may be kept frozen 2 to 3 weeks packed in a plastic container.

Hawaiian Sherbet: Substitute **4 cans (6 ounces each) frozen red fruit punch concentrate** for grape juice concentrate.

Orange Sherbet: Substitute **4 cans (6 ounces each) frozen orange juice concentrate** for grape juice concentrate. Increase sugar to 1½ to 2 cups, sweetening to taste.

Lemonade Sherbet: Substitute **4 cans (6 ounces each) frozen lemonade concentrate** for grape juice concentrate. Increase sugar to 2 to 2½ cups, sweetening to taste.

Pineapple-Orange-Buttermilk Sherbet

1 quart buttermilk
2 cups milk
2 cups sugar
2 cups fresh orange juice
1 can (8 ounces) crushed

pineapple (undrained)
3 tablespoons fresh lemon juice
1 tablespoon vanilla extract

1. Combine buttermilk, milk, and sugar in a large bowl. Stir until sugar is dissolved.
2. Blend in orange juice, pineapple, lemon juice, and vanilla extract. (The mixture may appear curdled at this point.) Chill.
3. Pour mixture into refrigerator trays or metal pans, not more than three fourths full. Cover and freeze until mixture becomes firm around the edges.
4. Turn into a chilled bowl and beat or stir until smooth. Return to refrigerator trays and cover. Freeze until firm.
5. If not to be served soon after freezing, sherbet may be kept frozen in plastic containers 2 to 3 weeks.
ABOUT 1 GALLON SHERBET

Note: If desired, sherbet may be made in an ice cream freezer. Follow manufactuer's instructions and use ¼ cup rock salt to 1 quart crushed ice.

Strawberry-Rhubarb Sherbet

3 cups ½-inch pieces fresh rhubarb
3 cups sliced fresh strawberries
½ cup sugar

2 tablespoons lemon juice
6 cups milk
2 to 2½ cups sugar
¼ teaspoon salt

1. Combine rhubarb, 2 cups strawberries, and ½ cup sugar in a saucepan. Bring to boiling over medium heat, stirring frequently. Boil until rhubarb is tender (about 2 minutes).
2. Stir in remaining 1 cup strawberries. Purée in a blender or put through a food mill. Cool. Add lemon juice.
3. Combine the fruit purée, milk, 2 to 2½ cups sugar, and salt in a large bowl. Mix thoroughly. Pour into a metal pan, no more than three quarters full. Freeze until mushy. Turn into a chilled bowl and beat until fluffy. Return to metal pan. Freeze until firm.
3 TO 4 QUARTS SHERBET

Note: If desired, sherbet may be frozen in an ice cream freezer. Follow manufacturer's instructions, using ¼ cup rock salt to 1 quart crushed ice, chilling sherbet mixture thoroughly before churning. Sherbet may be kept frozen 2 to 3 weeks packed in a plastic container.

Strawberry Sherbet: Follow recipe for Strawberry-Rhubarb Sherbet. Use **6 cups strawberries** and omit rhubarb.

Grasshopper Sherbet

7 cups milk
1¼ cups sugar
¾ cup green crème de

menthe
½ to ¾ cup white crème de cacao

1. Combine milk, sugar, crème de menthe, and crème de cacao in a large bowl. Stir until sugar is dissolved. Chill.
2. Pour mixture into refrigerator trays or metal pans, not more than three fourths full. Cover and freeze until mixture becomes firm around the edges.
3. Turn into a chilled bowl and beat or stir until smooth. Return to refrigerator trays and cover. Freeze until firm.
4. If not to be served soon after freezing, sherbet may be kept frozen in plastic containers 2 to 3 weeks.
ABOUT 3 QUARTS SHERBET

Note: If desired, sherbet may be made in an ice cream freezer. Follow manufacturer's instructions and use ¼ cup rock salt to 1 quart crushed ice.

Clockwise from lower left:
Grasshopper Sherbet
Grape Sherbet
Pineapple-Orange-Buttermilk Sherbet
Strawberry-Rhubarb Sherbet

Almond Apples

4 medium apples
8 ounces almond paste
1 egg white

Grated rind of 1 lemon
1 egg yolk, beaten
Shredded almonds

1. Pare and core the apples and place in a greased oven-proof dish.
2. Grate the almond paste coarsely. Mix the almond paste with the egg white and lemon rind. Divide the mixture into four parts and shape each part into a round cake. Place a cake on each of the apples and press it down a little.
4. Brush with the egg yolk and sprinkle on the shredded almonds. Bake in a 400°F oven for 30 minutes or until the apples are soft and brown. Serve with **vanilla ice cream.**
SERVES 4

Quick Applesauce Whip

1 can (16 ounces)
 applesauce
½ teaspoon grated lemon
 peel
2 teaspoons lemon juice
½ teaspoon ground

cinnamon
3 egg whites
⅛ teaspoon salt
6 tablespoons sugar
Ground nutmeg

1. Combine applesauce, lemon peel, juice, and cinnamon.
2. Beat egg whites and salt until frothy. Add sugar gradually, beat well. Continue beating until rounded peaks are formed. Fold beaten egg whites into applesauce mixture.
3. Spoon immediately into dessert dishes. Sprinkle nutmeg over each serving.
ABOUT 6 SERVINGS

Coconut Chocolate Sauce

4 ounces (4 squares)
 semisweet chocolate
1½ cups Coconut Milk,

(page 644)
1 teaspoon vanilla extract

1. Combine chocolate and ¼ cup Coconut Milk in a saucepan. Stir over low heat until chocolate is melted. Gradually add the remaining Coconut Milk, stirring until smooth and blended.
2. Remove from heat and mix in vanilla extract.
ABOUT 2 CUPS

Purple Plum Crunch

5 cups pitted, quartered fresh
 purple plums
¼ cup firmly packed brown
 sugar
3 tablespoons flour
½ teaspoon ground
 cinnamon
1 cup enriched all-purpose

flour
1 cup sugar
1 teaspoon baking powder
¼ teaspoon salt
¼ teaspoon ground mace
1 egg, well beaten
½ cup butter or margarine,
 melted and cooled

1. Put plums into a shallow 2-quart baking dish or casserole.
2. Mix brown sugar, 3 tablespoons flour, and cinnamon; sprinkle over plums and mix gently with a fork.
3. Blend 1 cup flour, sugar, baking powder, salt, and mace thoroughly. Add to beaten egg and stir with a fork until mixture is crumbly. Sprinkle evenly over plums in baking dish. Pour melted butter evenly over the topping.
4. Bake at 375°F 40 to 45 minutes, or until topping is lightly browned. Serve warm.
6 TO 8 SERVINGS

Note: Other fresh fruits may be substituted for the plums.

Banana-Pineapple Ice Cream

2 cups mashed ripe bananas
 (about 5 medium)
1 cup sugar
1 teaspoon grated orange
 peel
1 teaspoon grated lemon
 peel

3 tablespoons lemon juice
2 tablespoons lime juice
1½ cups unsweetened
 pineapple juice
⅓ cup orange juice
2 cans (14½ ounces each)
 evaporated milk

1. Crushed ice and rock salt will be needed. Wash and scald cover, container, and dasher of a 3- or 4-quart ice cream freezer. Chill thoroughly.
2. Combine bananas, sugar, orange peel, lemon peel, lemon juice, and lime juice; blend thoroughly. Set aside about 10 minutes.
3. Stir fruit juices into banana mixture. Add evaporated milk gradually, stirring until well blended.
4. Fill chilled freezer container no more than two-thirds full with ice cream mixture. Cover tightly. Set into freezer tub. (For electric freezer, follow the directions.)
5. Fill tub with alternate layers of crushed ice and rock salt, using 8 parts ice to 1 part salt. Turn handle slowly 5 minutes. Then turn rapidly until handle becomes difficult to turn (about 15 minutes), adding ice and salt as necessary.
6. Wipe cover and remove dasher. Pack down ice cream and cover with waxed paper or plastic wrap. Replace lid. (Plug dasher opening unless freezer has a solid cover.) Repack freezer container in ice, using 4 parts ice to 1 part salt. Cover with heavy paper or cloth. Let ripen 2 hours.
ABOUT 2 QUARTS ICE CREAM

Molded Cheese Dessert

Molded Cheese Dessert

2 envelopes unflavord gelatin
1 cup cold water
1 cup double-strength coffee
1 pound pot cheese or low-fat cottage cheese
1 teaspoon vanilla extract
¼ cup sugar
2 bay leaves, broken in half
Mint leaves or watercress

1. Sprinkle gelatin over cold water in a small skillet; let stand 5 minutes. Heat, stirring occasionally, over low heat until dissolved (about 3 minutes). Pour gelatin mixture into a food processor or blender; add remaining ingredients except bay leaves and mint. Purée mixture.
2. Spoon mixture into a 1-quart mold. Push bay leaf pieces into mixture. Refrigerate covered 4 to 6 hours; unmold. Garnish with mint.
4 SERVINGS

Cream Puffs with Banana Slices

1 cup water
⅛ teaspoon salt
½ cup sweet butter
1 cup flour
3 eggs
1 egg yolk, beaten
4 bananas, sliced
2 cups heavy cream, whipped
Grated chocolate

1. Preheat oven to 350°F. Pour water and salt into a heavy saucepan. Cut the butter into small pieces and add to water. Heat over low heat, stirring with a wooden spoon, until mixture comes to a boil.
2. Put flour in all at once. Stir until blended and dough forms a ball. Remove dough to a bowl and beat in 3 eggs, one at a time. Continue beating until dough is very shiny. Refrigerate for 30 minutes.
3. Drop large tablespoons of dough 2 inches apart on an ungreased cookie sheet. Brush with beaten egg yolk.
4. Bake 35-40 minutes until puffed and golden brown. Cool puffs on a wire rack. Cut off tops and fill with whipped cream and banana slices. Sprinkle with grated chocolate.
SERVES 6

Ginger-Yam Mousse

1½ cups mashed cooked yams (about 3 medium yams)
1 cup sugar
2 teaspoons ground ginger
1 teaspoon ground nutmeg
½ teaspoon ground cinnamon
Few grains salt
3 egg yolks, fork beaten
2 cups milk
½ teaspoon grated lemon peel
½ teaspoon lemon juice
½ cup half-and-half
3 egg whites
¼ cup sugar
Whipped dessert topping
Toasted slivered almonds

1. Put mashed yams into a heavy saucepan. Blend 1 cup sugar, spices, and salt. Mix with yams, then mix in egg yolks and milk. Cook over medium heat, stirring constantly, until mixture is thick. Remove from heat when mixture just comes to boiling.
2. Cool, stirring occasionally. Blend in lemon peel, juice, and half-and-half.
3. Beat egg whites until frothy; add ¼ cup sugar gradually, continuing to beat until stiff peaks are formed. Fold into completely cooled yam mixture.
4. Turn into a 6½-cup ring mold, spreading evenly. Freeze until firm, about 3½ hours.
5. Allow mousse to soften slightly at room temperature before unmolding. Unmold onto a chilled plate. Spoon whipped dessert topping into center and sprinkle with almonds.
6 TO 8 SERVINGS

Raspberry Foam

4 egg whites
2 tablespoons sugar
1 cup heavy cream

1 (10 ounce) package frozen raspberries, thawed
½ teaspoon lemon juice

1. In a bowl whip the egg whites, adding the sugar slowly, until stiff peaks are formed.
2. Whip the cream until stiff and fold into the egg whites.
3. Let the raspberries thaw completely and then fold into the cream mixture (both berries and syrup). Add the lemon juice.
4. Divide into individual serving cups and chill until serving.
SERVES 4

Steamed Pumpkin Pudding

Pudding:
1¼ cups fine dry bread crumbs
½ cup enriched all-purpose flour
1 cup firmly packed brown sugar
1 teaspoon baking powder
½ teaspoon baking soda
½ teaspoon salt
½ teaspoon ground cinnamon
½ teaspoon ground cloves

½ cup salad oil
½ cup undiluted evaporated milk
2 eggs
1½ cups canned pumpkin

Lemon Nut Sauce:
½ cup butter or margarine
2 cups confectioners' sugar
¼ teaspoon salt
¼ teaspoon ground ginger
¼ cup lemon juice
½ cup chopped walnuts

1. Blend bread crumbs, flour, brown sugar, baking powder, baking soda, salt, cinnamon, and cloves in a large bowl.
2. Beat oil, evaporated milk, eggs, and pumpkin. Add to dry ingredients; mix until well blended.
3. Turn into a well-greased 2-quart mold. Cover tightly with a greased cover, or tie greased aluminum foil tightly over mold. Place mold on trivet or rack in a steamer or deep kettle with a tight-fitting cover.
4. Pour in boiling water to no more than one half the height of the mold. Cover steamer, bring water to boiling, and keep boiling at all times. If necessary, add more boiling water during cooking period.
5. Steam the pudding 2½ to 3 hours, or until a wooden pick inserted in center comes out clean.
6. For Lemon Nut Sauce, beat butter in a bowl. Blend confectioners' sugar, salt, and ginger; add gradually to butter, beating well. Add lemon juice gradually, continuing to beat until blended. Mix in walnuts.
7. Remove pudding from steamer and unmold onto a serving plate. Serve pudding with Lemon Nut Sauce.
ABOUT 12 SERVINGS

Note: If pudding is to be stored and served later, unmold onto a rack and cool thoroughly. Wrap in aluminum foil or return to mold and store in a cool place. Before serving, resteam pudding about 3 hours, or until thoroughly heated.

Raspberry Foam

Chocolate Peanut Butter Pudding

1 small package chocolate pudding and pie filling (not instant)
1 can (14½ ounces) evaporated milk
⅔ cup water

⅓ cup peanut butter
Slightly sweetened whipped cream (optional)
Chopped salted peanuts (optional)

1. Empty pudding mix into a saucepan, then stir in evaporated milk and water.
2. Cook and stir over moderate heat until thickened, about 5 minutes. Remove from heat and stir in peanut butter. Cover and chill.
3. To serve, spoon into dessert dishes. If desired, top with whipped cream and peanuts.
4 TO 6 SERVINGS

Zesty Beer Ice

1 envelope unflavored gelatin
2 cans or bottles (12 ounces each) beer

1 cup sugar
2 teaspoons grated lemon peel
½ cup lemon juice

1. Sprinkle gelatin over 1 can beer in a saucepan. Let stand 5 minutes to soften.
2. Add sugar. Cook over low heat just until dissolved.
3. Add remaining 1 can beer, lemon peel, and juice. Turn into a shallow pan.
4. Freeze until firm, stirring several times. Pack into a 1-quart covered container.
1 QUART

Raisin-Beer Pudding

2 eggs
1½ cups milk
½ cup sugar
¼ cup quick-cooking tapioca
¼ teaspoon nutmeg

⅛ teaspoon salt
1 can or bottle (12 ounces) beer
½ cup raisins

1. In a heavy 2-quart saucepan, beat eggs. Add milk, sugar, tapioca, nutmeg, and salt. Let stand 5 minutes.
2. Cook, stirring constantly, to simmering. Add beer gradually while stirring; add raisins. Cook and stir just to boiling.
3. Pour into dessert dishes.
ABOUT 1 QUART; 6 TO 8 SERVINGS

Baked Stuffed Apples

6 medium cooking apples (about 2 pounds)
½ cup raisins

½ cup packed brown sugar
1 teaspoon cinnamon
1 cup beer

1. Core apples. Remove 1-inch strip of peel around top.
2. Mix raisins, brown sugar, and cinnamon. Fill apple centers.
3. Place apples in a baking dish. Pour beer over.
4. Bake at 350°F 40 to 45 minutes, or until tender, basting occasionally.
5. Cool to room temperature, basting while cooling. Serve with its own sauce. If desired, add cream.
6 SERVINGS

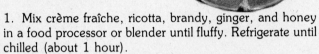

Fresh Fruit with Brandy Cream

½ cup Mock Crème Fraîche
(page 46)
¼ cup low-fat ricotta cheese
2 teaspoons brandy or
orange juice
¼ teaspoon ground ginger
2 teaspoons honey or sugar
3 cups assorted fresh fruit
2 teaspoons toasted sesame
seed (optional)

1. Mix crème fraîche, ricotta, brandy, ginger, and honey in a food processor or blender until fluffy. Refrigerate until chilled (about 1 hour).
2. Arrange fruit on individual plates. Spoon sauce over; sprinkle with sesame seed.
6 SERVINGS

Cherry-Pineapple Cobbler

1 can (21 ounces) cherry pie
filling
1 can (13¼ ounces) pineapple tidbits, drained
¼ teaspoon allspice

3 tablespoons honey
1 egg, slightly beaten
½ cup sour cream
1½ cups unflavored croutons

1. Combine cherry pie filling, pineapple tidbits, allspice, and 1 tablespoon honey. Put into a 1½-quart baking dish.
2. Blend egg, sour cream, and remaining 2 tablespoons honey. Stir in croutons. Spoon over cherry-pineapple mixture.
3. Bake, uncovered, at 375°F 30 minutes, or until heated through. If desired, top with ice cream.
8 SERVINGS

Buttery Baked Apples

8 medium baking apples,
cored
1 cup sugar
6 tablespoons butter or
margarine

1 tablespoon cornstarch
1 tablespoon cold water
½ teaspoon vanilla extract
½ cup milk

1. Put apples into a 1½-quart baking dish. Sprinkle with sugar. Dot with butter.
2. Bake, uncovered, at 450°F 20 minutes, or until fork-tender, basting occasionally.
3. Remove baking dish from oven and apples from baking dish.
4. Combine cornstarch, water, and vanilla extract; add to milk. Stir into liquid in baking dish. Return apples to baking dish.
5. Bake an additional 8 to 10 minutes, or until sauce is thickened. To serve, spoon sauce over each apple.
8 SERVINGS

Spicy Butterscotch Pudding

1 package (4-serving size)
butterscotch pudding and
pie filling (not instant)
⅔ cup instant nonfat dry
milk
1 teaspoon pumpkin pie

spice
1 cup beer
1 cup water
Whipped cream or thawed
frozen whipped dessert
topping

1. In a heavy saucepan, combine pudding mix, dry milk, and spice. Stir in beer and water.
2. Cook over medium heat, stirring constantly, until mixture boils.
3. Pour into 4 pudding dishes. Cover surfaces with plastic wrap. Chill until set. Serve topped with whipped cream or dessert topping.
4 SERVINGS

Hot Spicy Fruit Pot

1 can (16 ounces) pear
halves
1 can (16 ounces) peach
halves
1 can (16 ounces) purple
plums, halved and pitted
1 cup firmly packed brown
sugar
1 cinnamon stick

¼ teaspoon nutmeg
¼ teaspoon allspice
⅛ teaspoon ginger
¼ cup lemon juice
2 teaspoons grated orange
peel
2 tablespoons butter or
margarine

1. Drain fruits, reserving 1 cup liquid. Put fruit into a buttered 2-quart casserole.
2. Combine reserved liquid with remaining ingredients, except butter. Pour over fruit. Dot with butter.
3. Bake, covered, at 350°F 30 minutes, or until bubbly. Serve hot or cold. If desired, spoon over ice cream or cake.
8 SERVINGS

Indian Pudding

3 cups milk
½ cup cornmeal
1 tablespoon butter or
margarine

½ cup light molasses
½ teaspoon salt
½ teaspoon ginger
1 cup cold milk

1. Scald 2½ cups milk in top of double boiler over boiling water.
2. Combine cornmeal and the remaining ½ cup milk. Add to scalded milk, stirring constantly. Cook about 25 minutes, stirring frequently.
3. Stir in butter, molasses, salt, and ginger.
4. Pour into a greased 1½-quart baking dish. Pour the 1 cup cold milk over pudding.
5. Set in a baking pan. Pour boiling water around dish to within 1 inch of top.
6. Bake, covered, at 300°F about 2 hours. Remove cover and bake an additional 1 hour. Serve warm or cold with **cream** or **ice cream**.
6 SERVINGS

Currant-Apple Fritters

1 cup all-purpose flour | ½ cup chopped pared apple
1½ teaspoons baking powder | 2 eggs, slightly beaten
¼ teaspoon cinnamon | 1 teaspoon oil
¼ teaspoon salt | Fat for deep frying
½ cup beer | Confectioners' sugar
½ cup currants

1. Combine flour, baking powder, cinnamon, and salt. Add beer, currants, apple, eggs, and oil. Stir to blend well.
2. Drop by rounded teaspoonfuls into hot deep fat heated to 365°F. Fry until browned. Drain on paper towels.
3. Keep hot in oven until serving time. While still hot, roll in confectioners' sugar.
ABOUT 30 FRITTERS; 6 TO 8 SERVINGS

Mocha Pecan Snacks

¼ cup sugar | ½ cup chopped pecans
1 tablespoon instant coffee | 12 cocoa crêpes (below)
Dash salt | Unsweetened chocolate,
1 cup whipping cream | shaved or grated

1. Combine sugar, coffee, salt, and cream. Stir until well blended. Chill 30 minutes.
2. Whip cream until stiff. Fold in pecans.
3. Spread mixture over crêpes. Make three stacks of 4 crêpes each or stack as desired. Top with chocolate.
4. To serve, cut into wedges.
6 TO 9 SERVINGS

Beer Bread Pudding

1½ cups milk | ¼ teaspoon cinnamon
1 can or bottle (12 ounces) | ¼ teaspoon nutmeg
  beer | ¼ teaspoon salt
3 eggs | 4 cups dry bread cubes (6
½ cup packed brown sugar | slices)
½ teaspoon vanilla extract

1. Scald milk and beer.
2. Beat eggs with brown sugar, vanilla extract, cinnamon, nutmeg, and salt. Add scalded milk and beer gradually while stirring. Add bread.
3. Turn into a greased 1½- or 2-quart casserole. Set in a pan of boiling water.
4. Bake at 325°F 50 minutes, or until a knife inserted in center comes out clean. Serve hot or cold.
6 SERVINGS

Cocoa Crêpes

2 tablespoons cocoa | 1½ cup milk
1 cup all-purpose flour | 2 tablespoons melted butter
¼ cup sugar | or oil
Pinch salt | 2 tablespoons rum
3 eggs

1. Sift flour, cocoa, sugar, and salt. Add eggs, one at a time, beating thoroughly. Gradually add milk, melted butter or oil, and rum, beating until smooth. (Or mix in an electric blender until smooth.)
2. Let batter stand 1 hour before cooking crêpes.
ABOUT 18 CRÊPES

Baklava

Cherry Delight

1 package vanilla pudding
1 pint heavy cream whipped
with 1 tablespoon sugar

1 can (10 ounces) pitted red
cherries in syrup

Mix the vanilla pudding according to package directions and fold in the whipped cream, then the cherries with their syrup. Pour into individual serving dishes and chill for 2 to 3 hours before serving.
SERVES 6

Baklava

Syrup:
2 cups honey
2 cups sugar
3 cups water
2 whole cloves
1 stick cinnamon

Filling:
2 pounds chopped walnuts

or blanched almonds
1 tablespoon cinnamon

Filo:
¾ pound unsalted butter,
melted
2 packages filo

1. For syrup, combine all the ingredients in a large saucepan. Bring to a boil. Lower heat at once, cover, and simmer for 20 minutes. Remove from heat and cool to room temperature.
2. For filling, combine walnuts and cinnamon in a bowl. Set aside.
3. For filo, melt butter in a saucepan, being careful not to let it brown. Reheat it if it cools and does not spread easily.
4. Remove the layers of filo from their plastic wrapper and lay them flat on a large sheet of aluminum foil. Cover with another sheet of foil. (Filo must be kept completely covered at all times or it will dry out.)
5. Separate the filo layers one at a time. Brush with butter the bottom and sides of an 18x12-inch baking pan. Line the bottom of the pan with 4 filo layers, brushing each layer with melted butter before adding the next. After the fourth filo layer has been buttered, sprinkle it evenly with one third of the chopped nuts. Add 2 more filo layers, buttering each. Sprinkle with the remainder of the nuts. Cover with remaining filo, buttering each layer.
6. With a very sharp knife or a single-edge razor blade, using a ruler as a guide, cut into the topmost layers, tracing diamond shapes by making vertical cuts from one end of the pan to the other 1 inch apart, and diagonal cuts slightly less than ½ inch apart.
7. Bake at 250°F 1 hour and 50 minutes, or until golden. Cool 5 minutes. Pour the cooled syrup over it. Let stand overnight so syrup can be completely absorbed. Using a sharp knife, cut through each piece completely.
8. Remove the baklava slices with a fork to paper cupcake cups. Store no more than several weeks at room temperature. Baklava does not retain its crispness if stored in the refrigerator.
50 TO 60 PIECES

Cherry Delight

Tea Sherbet

2 cups boiling water
4 to 5 teaspoons tea (or tea bags)
4 ounces raisins
Juice of 1 lemon
½ cup sugar mixed with ¼ cup water
½ cup sugar
Few drops red food coloring
1 wedge lemon

1. Make strong tea by pouring the boiling water on the tea leaves. Steep for 3 to 5 minutes before straining. Add raisins and lemon juice. Add raisins and lemon juice.
2. Bring water and sugar to a boil and mix with the tea. Let cool, pour into a plastic bowl and put in the freezer.
3. Whip the sherbet at ½-hour intervals. After about 3 or 4 hours the sherbet will be frozen.
4. Serve in tall glasses decorated with sugar: Pour sugar on a plate. Add red coloring and stir until evenly blended. Rub the rim of the glass with lemon and dip into the colored sugar.
SERVES 4

Apple Cream

6 cups sliced apples (about 2 pounds)
½ cup sugar
1 teaspoon cinnamon
1 teaspoon nutmeg
¼ cup butter or margarine
⅔ cup sugar
1 egg
½ cup flour
½ teaspoon baking powder
½ teaspoon salt
1 cup whipping cream

1. Toss the apple slices with a mixture of the ½ cup sugar, cinnamon, and nutmeg. Spread evenly in bottom of a buttered 9-inch square baking dish.
2. Cream together butter and ⅔ cup sugar. Add egg and continue beating until mixture is light and fluffy.
3. Blend flour, baking powder, and salt; beat into creamed mixture until just blended. Spread evenly over apples.
4. Bake, uncovered, at 350°F 30 minutes. Pour cream over surface and bake an additional 10 minutes, or until topping is golden brown. Serve warm with cream, if desired.
8 SERVINGS

Bread Pudding

1 cup raisins
½ cup sherry
8 slices white bread
Butter
4 eggs
½ cup sugar
Dash salt
1 quart half-and-half
1½ teaspoons vanilla extract

1. Soak raisins in sherry 2 hours, stirring occasionally.
2. Trim crusts from bread and spread with butter. Place bread, buttered side down, in a 2½-quart casserole or soufflé dish.
3. Drain raisins and sprinkle over bread.
4. Beat remaining ingredients together. Pour over bread and let stand 30 minutes. Sprinkle with **cinnamon.**
5. Bake, covered, at 350°F 30 minutes. Remove cover and bake an additional 30 minutes, or until set.
8 SERVINGS

Baked Apricot Pudding

1 tablespoon confectioners' sugar
1¼ cups (about 6 ounces) dried apricots
1 cup water
1½ tablespoons butter or margarine
1½ tablespoons flour
¾ cup milk
4 egg yolks
½ teaspoon vanilla extract
4 egg whites
6 tablespoons granulated sugar
Whipped cream

1. Lightly butter bottom of a 1½-quart casserole and sift confectioners' sugar over it.
2. Put apricots and water into a saucepan. Cover; simmer 20 to 30 minutes, or until apricots are plump and tender. Force apricots through a coarse sieve or food mill (makes about ¾ cup purée).
3. Heat butter in saucepan. Stir in flour. Gradually add milk, stirring until thickened and smooth. Remove from heat.
4. Beat egg yolks and vanilla extract together until mixture is thick and lemon colored. Spoon sauce gradually into beaten egg yolks while beating vigorously. Blend in apricot purée.
5. Using clean beater, beat egg whites until frothy. Add sugar gradually, beating constantly. Continue beating until rounded peaks are formed. Spread apricot mixture gently over beaten egg whites and fold until thoroughly blended. Turn mixture into prepared casserole. Set casserole in a pan of very hot water.
6. Bake, uncovered, at 350°F 50 minutes, or until a knife inserted halfway between center and edge comes out clean. Cool slightly before serving. Top with whipped cream.
6 SERVINGS

Orange Liqueur Mousse

1 package (3 ounces) orange-flavored gelatin
1 cup boiling water
¼ cup cold water
¼ cup orange liqueur
1 cup whipping cream
Whipped cream (optional)
Shredded coconut (optional)

1. Dissolve gelatin in boiling water. Add cold water and cool mixture to room temperature. Stir in orange liqueur. Chill in refrigerator until mixture starts to thicken (about 30 minutes).
2. Whip cream until it piles softly. Gradually add gelatin mixture, stirring gently until evenly blended.
3. Pour into a mold. Chill until set.
4. Turn out of mold onto serving plate and top with additional whipped cream and coconut, if desired.
4 TO 6 SERVINGS

Watermelon and Pineapple Barbados

1 5-pound watermelon   chunks, with juice
1 can (1 pound) pineapple   ¾ cup dry white wine

1. Cut the watermelon in half. Scoop out the flesh and cut in squares.
2. Mix the pineapple juice with the wine. Mix the watermelon with the pineapple and pour the juice over the fruit. Refrigerate until well chilled (may be prepared the day before).
3. Serve the fruit in the watermelon shell.
SERVES 6 TO 8

Peach Meringue Pudding

2 cans (21 ounces each)
  peach pie filling
¼ cup butter or margarine,
  melted
½ teaspoon cinnamon

⅛ teaspoon nutmeg
⅛ teaspoon allspice
½ cup slivered almonds
3 egg whites
½ cup sugar

1. Combine peach pie filling, butter, cinnamon, nutmeg, allspice, and almonds. Put into a 1½-quart casserole.
2. Bake, uncovered, at 350°F 30 minutes, or until bubbly. Remove from oven.
3. Beat egg whites until stiff, but not dry. Gradually beat in sugar until glossy. Evenly spread over hot peaches. Sprinkle with **cinnamon.**
4. Bake an additional 12 to 15 minutes, or until lightly browned.
6 SERVINGS

Rice with Milk

1 cup uncooked rice
1 cup sugar
1 cinnamon stick
1 can (14 ounces) sweetened

condensed milk
1 quart milk
1½ teaspoons vanilla extract

1. Put all ingredients into a saucepan; stir. Bring to boiling, then reduce heat to low. Cover and cook until rice is tender, about 2 minutes; stir occasionally to prevent sticking. Remove cinnamon stick.
2. The dessert will be fairly runny. Serve hot or chilled.
6 TO 8 SERVINGS

Favorite Apple Pudding

6 or 7 medium firm, tart
  cooking apples, quartered,
  cored, pared, and cut in
  ⅛-inch slices
¾ cup firmly packed brown
  sugar
3 tablespoons flour
½ teaspoon salt
1 teaspoon cinnamon
¼ teaspoon nutmeg
3 tablespoonss butter or

margarine
1 teaspoon grated orange
  peel
¾ cup (3 ounces) shredded
  Cheddar cheese
5 slices white bread, toasted,
  buttered on both sides and
  cut in halves
¼ cup orange juice
½ cup buttered soft bread
  cubes

1. Arrange one third of the apple slices on bottom of a greased 2-quart casserole.
2. Thoroughly blend brown sugar, flour, salt, cinnamon, and nutmeg. Using a pastry blender or 2 knives, cut in butter and grated orange peel until mixture is in coarse crumbs. Mix in cheese.
3. Sprinkle one third of the sugar-cheese mixture over apples and cover with one half of the toast. Repeat layers. Cover the top with remaining apples and sugar-cheese mixture.
4. Pour orange juice over surface and top with the buttered bread cubes.
5. Bake, covered, at 425°F 30 minutes. Remove cover and bake an additional 10 minutes.
6 TO 8 SERVINGS

Berries and Cream

1 quart fresh, ripe strawberries, raspberries, or
  blueberries
1 cup chilled whipping

cream
3 tablespoons confectioners'
  sugar
1 teaspoon vanilla extract

1. Rinse and hull strawberries; dry thoroughly. Cover and chill.
2. Whip cream, using a chilled bowl and chilled beaters, until it forms soft peaks. Add sugar and vanilla extract and beat to form stiff peaks.
3. Spoon whipped cream into parfait glasses and layer with strawberries, ending with a strawberry on top.
6 SERVINGS

Brazilian Pudim Moka with Chocolate Sauce

3 cups milk
1 cup half-and-half
5 tablespoons instant coffee
2 teaspoons grated orange
  peel
4 eggs
1 egg yolk

½ cup sugar
½ teaspoon salt
1 teaspoon vanilla extract
Nutmeg
Chocolate sauce
Chopped Brazil nuts

1. Combine milk and half-and-half in top of a double boiler and heat over simmering water until scalded.
2. Add instant coffee and orange peel, stirring until coffee is dissolved. Remove from simmering water and set aside to cool (about 10 minutes).
3. Beat together eggs and egg yolk slightly. Blend in sugar and salt.
4. Gradually add coffee mixture, stirring constantly. Mix in vanilla extract. Strain through a fine sieve into eight 6-ounce custard cups. Sprinkle with nutmeg. Set cups in pan of hot water.
5. Bake, uncovered, at 325°F 25 to 30 minutes, or until a knife inserted in center of custard comes out clean.
6. Cool and chill. To serve, invert onto serving plates. Pour chocolate sauce over top and sprinkle with Brazil nuts.
8 SERVINGS

Cream Rolls

Filling:
2 cartons (15 ounces each) ricotta
2 teaspoons vanilla extract
½ cup confectioners' sugar
½ cup finely chopped candied citron
½ cup semisweet chocolate pieces

Shells:
3 cups all-purpose flour
¼ cup sugar
1 teaspoon cinnamon
¼ teaspoon salt
3 tablespoons shortening
2 eggs, well beaten
2 tablespoons white vinegar
2 tablespoons cold water
Oil or shortening for deep frying
1 egg white, slightly beaten
¼ to ½ cup finely chopped blanched pistachio nuts
Sifted confectioners' sugar

1. To make filling, beat cheese with vanilla extract. Add ½ cup confectioners' sugar and beat until smooth. Fold in candied citron and semisweet chocolate pieces. Chill thoroughly.
2. To make the shells, combine flour, sugar, cinnamon, and salt. Using a pastry blender, cut in shortening until pieces are the size of small peas. Stir in eggs; blend in vinegar and cold water.
3. Turn dough onto a lightly floured surface and knead until smooth and elastic (5 to 10 minutes). Wrap in waxed paper and chill 30 minutes.
4. Fill a deep saucepan a little over half full with oil. Slowly heat oil to 360°F.
5. Roll out chilled dough to ⅛ inch thick. Using a 6x4½-inch oval pattern cut from cardboard, cut ovals from dough with a pastry cutter or sharp knife.
6. Wrap dough loosely around cannoli tubes (see Note), just lapping over opposite edge. Brush overlapping edges with egg white and press together to seal.
7. Fry shells in hot oil about 8 minutes, or until golden brown, turning occasionally. Fry only a few at a time, being careful not to crowd them. Using a slotted spoon or tongs, remove from oil, and drain over pan before removing to paper towels. Cool slightly and remove tubes. Cool completely.
8. When ready to serve, fill shells with ricotta filling. Sprinkle ends of filled shells with pistachio nuts and dust shells generously with confectioners' sugar.
ABOUT 16 FILLED ROLLS

Note: Aluminum cannoli tubes or clean, unpainted wooden sticks, 6 inches long and ¾ inch in diameter, may be used.

Cheese-Stuffed Strawberries

Cheese-Stuffed Strawberries

½ cup low-fat ricotta cheese
1 teaspoon grated lemon
  peel
1 teaspoon fresh lemon juice

1 teaspoon honey or sugar
48 large strawberries
Mint sprigs (optional)

1. Mix cheese, lemon peel, lemon juice, and honey in a food processor or blender until fluffy; refrigerate until chilled (about 1 hour).
2. Gently scoop centers from strawberries with melon-baller or fruit knife. Fill with cheese mixture.
3. Arrange filled strawberries on small individual plates. Garnish with mint.
4 SERVINGS

Bananas with Royal Pineapple Sauce

3 tablespoons dark brown
  sugar
2 teaspoons cornstarch
1 can (8¼ ounces) crushed
  pineapple (undrained)
1 tablespoon butter
⅛ teaspoon almond extract

¼ teaspoon grated lemon
  peel
1 tablespoon lemon juice
¼ cup butter
4 firm bananas, peeled
2 tablespoons flaked coconut

1. Mix sugar and cornstarch in a saucepan. Add pineapple with syrup, 1 tablespoon butter, and almond extract; mix well. Bring to boiling, stirring constantly until thickened.
2. Remove from heat and stir in lemon peel and juice. Set the sauce aside.
3. Heat ¼ cup butter in a heavy skillet. Add bananas; turn them by rolling to cook evenly and brown lightly. (Do not overcook or fruit will lose its shape.)
4. Allowing one-half banana per person, serve at once topped with the warm pineapple sauce. Sprinkle with coconut.
8 SERVINGS

Pear and Apple Compote

2 cups water
⅔ cup water
6 pears, pared, cored,
  quartered
2 apples, pared, cored,

quartered
8 whole cloves
½ cup currant or gooseberry
  jelly

1. Bring water with sugar to boiling in a large saucepan. Boil 5 minutes.
2. Add fruits and cloves. Simmer until fruits are tender, about 7 to 10 minutes.
3. Remove fruits and place in a serving bowl. Discard cloves. Boil syrup until only 1 cup remains.
4. Blend syrup into jelly. Return to saucepan. Bring just to boiling. Pour over fruits. Let stand 1 hour before serving, or chill.
6 TO 8 SERVINGS

Italian Strawberry Water Ice

2 cups sugar
1 cup water
4 pints fresh ripe strawber-

ries, rinsed and hulled
⅓ cup orange juice
¼ cup lemon juice

1. Combine sugar and water in a saucepan; stir and bring to boiling. Boil 5 minutes; let cool.
2. Purée the strawberries in an electric blender or force through a sieve or food mill. Add juices to a mixture of the cooked syrup and strawberries; mix well.
3. Turn into refrigerator trays, cover tightly, and freeze.
4. About 45 minutes before serving time, remove trays from freezer to refrigerate to allow the ice to soften slightly. Spoon into sherbet glasses or other serving dishes.
ABOUT 2 QUARTS WATER ICE

Sherried Pears

8 pears, peeled and cored
1 cup sugar
½ cup water
1 cup sherry
½ cup orange juice
½ cup raisins
1 cup heavy cream, whipped
Peel of 2 oranges

1. Pour sugar and water into a large saucepan. Heat and stir until sugar is dissolved.
2. Place pears in pan. Cover and simmer about 30 minutes, until pears are soft.
3. Remove from heat and add sherry and orange juice. Mix gently and refrigerate until well chilled.
4. Serve with whipped cream, decorated with raisins and pieces of orange peel.
SERVES 8

Spicy Fruit Gelatin "with a Head"

1 can or bottle (12 ounces) beer
2 tablespoons packed brown sugar
1 stick cinnamon
4 whole cloves
1 package (3 ounces) orange-flavored gelatin
1 can (8¼ ounces) crushed pineapple
Water

1. Place beer, brown sugar, cinnamon, and cloves in a saucepan. Heat to boiling. Add gelatin; stir until dissolved.
2. Let stand at room temperature until lukewarm to mellow flavors. Remove spices.
3. Drain pineapple thoroughly, reserving liquid. Add water to liquid to measure ½ cup. Stir into gelatin mixture. Chill until partially thickened.
4. Fold in pineapple. Spoon into pilsner or parfait glasses. Chill until firm.
5. To serve, top with a "head" of whipped cream or prepared whipped topping.
4 OR 5 SERVINGS

Blueberry-Orange Parfaits

2 tablespoons cornstarch
1 cup sugar
½ teaspoon salt
2 cups orange juice
2 eggs, beaten
½ teaspoon grated lemon peel
2 tablespoons sugar
2 cups fresh blueberries
Whipped cream (optional)

1. Mix cornstarch, 1 cup sugar, and salt in a heavy saucepan. Add a small amount of the orange juice and blend until smooth. Stir in remaining orange juice.
2. Bring mixture to boiling, stirring constantly, and cook 3 to 5 minutes.
3. Stir about 3 tablespoons of the hot mixture into beaten eggs; immediately blend with mixture in saucepan.
4. Cook and stir about 3 minutes. Remove from water and cool. Stir in lemon peel. Chill.
5. Meanwhile, sprinkle 2 tablespoons sugar over blueberries and allow to stand at least 30 minutes. Spoon alternating layers of custard and blueberries in parfait glasses, beginning with a layer of custard and ending with blueberries. Top with whipped cream, if desired.
6 SERVINGS

Chocolate-Beer Pudding Cake

Batter:
1½ cups all-purpose flour
¾ cup sugar
1 tablespoon unsweetened cocoa
1½ teaspoons baking powder
½ teaspoon baking soda
¼ teaspoon salt
¾ cup beer
⅓ cup oil
1 egg, slightly beaten

Syrup:
1 tablespoon unsweetened cocoa
¾ cup beer
⅓ cup packed brown sugar
⅓ cup granulated sugar

1. For batter, mix dry ingredients; make a well in center. Add beer, oil, and egg. Beat just until smooth.
2. For syrup, make a paste of cocoa and a little beer. Add remaining beer and sugars. Heat to boiling.
3. Pour batter into a greased 8-inch square baking pan. Drizzle syrup over top.
4. Bake at 350°F 40 minutes.
5. Cool about 5 minutes. Loosen sides of cake from pan; invert onto platter. Even out pudding layer with knife. Serve warm or cool.
6 TO 8 SERVINGS

Marsala Custard

6 egg yolks
½ cup sugar
⅛ teaspoon salt
1 cup Marsala

1. In a bowl, beat egg yolks with sugar and salt until lemon colored. Stir in Marsala.
2. Cook in double boiler over simmering water. Beat constantly with rotary beater until mixture foams up and begins to thicken.
3. Turn into sherbet glasses and chill until serving time.
ABOUT 6 SERVINGS

Boiled Plantain

Green plantain
½ lime
Boiling salted water

1. Remove the skin and scrape the threads from plantain. Rub the fruit with the cut side of a lime.
2. Cook in boiling salted water 30 minutes.

Coconut Flan

Caramel Topping:
½ cup granulated sugar
2 tablespoons water

Custard:
2 cups milk

4 eggs
¼ cup sugar
⅛ teaspoon salt
½ teaspoon vanilla extract
⅓ cup shredded or flaked coconut

1. For caramel topping, heat sugar and water in a small skillet, stirring constantly, until sugar melts and turns golden brown.
2. Pour syrup into a 1-quart baking dish or 6 custard cups, tipping to coat bottom and part way up sides. Set dish aside while preparing custard.
3. For custard, scald milk. Beat eggs; beat in sugar, salt, and vanilla extract. Gradually beat scalded milk into egg mixture. Strain into prepared baking dish or custard cups. Sprinkle top with coconut.
4. Place baking dish in pan containing hot water which comes at least 1 inch up sides of dish.
5. Bake at 325°F about 45 minutes for individual custard cups, or 1 hour for baking dish.
6 SERVINGS

Stuffed Peaches

½ cup almond macaroon crumbs
6 large firm peaches
½ cup blanched almonds, chopped

2 tablespoons sugar
1 tablespoon chopped candied orange peel
⅓ cup sherry or Marsala
2 tablespoons sugar

1. Using an electric blender, grind enough almond macaroons to make ½ cup crumbs. Set crumbs aside.
2. Rinse, peel, and cut peaches into halves. Remove pit and a small portion of the pulp around cavity.
3. Combine and mix macaroon crumbs, chopped almonds, 2 tablespoons sugar, and orange peel.
4. Lightly fill peach halves with mixture. Put two halves together and fasten with wooden picks. Place in baking dish.
5. Pour sherry over peaches and sprinkle remaining sugar over peaches.
6. Bake at 350°F 15 minutes and serve either hot or cold.
6 SERVINGS

Individual Fruit Puddings

Pudding:
2 medium oranges
1½ cups sifted enriched all-purpose flour
1 teaspoon baking soda
¼ teaspoon salt
¼ teaspoon ground cinnamon
¼ teaspoon ground cloves
¼ teaspoon ground nutmeg
¼ cup shortening
1 cup firmly packed brown sugar
1 egg, well beaten
1 cup dark seedless raisins

½ cup pitted dates, cut in pieces
½ cup walnuts, coarsely chopped

Orange Sauce:
¾ cup sugar
2 tablespoons cornstarch
⅛ teaspoon salt
¾ cup orange juice
½ cup water
1 teaspoon grated orange peel
1 tablespoon butter or margarine

1. For pudding, grease eight 5-ounce custard cups. Set aside.
2. Peel oranges; slice into cartwheels, and cut into pieces; reserve juice as it collects.
3. Blend flour, baking soda, salt, cinnamon, cloves, and nutmeg. Set aside.
4. Beat shortening; add brown sugar gradually, beating until fluffy. Add egg and beat thoroughly.
5. Mix in the orange pieces, reserved juice, raisins, dates, and walnuts. Blend in the dry ingredients.
6. Fill custard cups about two-thirds full with mixture; cover tightly with aluminum foil. Set in a pan and fill pan with water to a 1-inch depth. Cover pan with aluminum foil.
7. Cook in a 325°F oven 2 hours.
8. For Orange Sauce, mix sugar, cornstarch, and salt in a saucepan. Add orange juice and water gradually, stirring constantly. Bring to boiling, stirring constantly until thickened; cook over low heat 6 to 8 minutes, stirring occasionally.
9. Remove from heat. Blend in orange peel and butter. Keep warm.
10. Unmold puddings while hot onto dessert plates and spoon sauce over each.
8 SERVINGS

Sherry Elegance

3 envelopes unflavored gelatin
1½ cups sugar
3 cups water
1 cup plus 2 tablespoons

sherry
¾ cup strained orange juice
⅓ cup strained lemon juice
9 drops red food coloring

1. Combine the gelatin and sugar in a large saucepan; mix well. Add water and stir over low heat until gelatin and sugar are dissolved.
2. Remove from heat and blend in remaining ingredients. Pour mixture into a 1½-quart fancy mold or a pretty china bowl. Chill until firm.
3. To serve, unmold gelatin onto chilled platter or serve in china bowl without unmolding. Serve with whipped cream or whipped dessert topping, if desired.
6 TO 8 SERVINGS

Pineapple-Berry Dessert

1 large pineapple
½ cup light rum or orange

juice
1 quart strawberries

1. Cut stem and end off pineapple; cut into quarters lengthwise. Remove core and pare; cut into ½-inch slices and place in a shallow glass dish. Pour rum over pineapple; refrigerate covered 4 hours, turning slices several times.
2. Arrange pineapple slices in overlapping pattern on a large platter.
3. Halve some of the strawberries and arrange on pineapple. Purée remaining strawberries in a food processor or blender and pour into a bowl. Serve with knife and fork.

Rhubarb Compote

1½ pounds rhubarb
¾ cup sugar
3 tablespoons butter
1 cup bread crumbs

2 ounces sliced almonds
¾ cup heavy cream, whipped

1. Rinse rhubarb and cut into 1-inch pieces. Place in an ovenproof dish and pour sugar on top. Cover with aluminum foil and bake in a 400°F. oven for 20 minutes. Remove from oven and let cool.
2. Heat butter in a skillet and brown bread crumbs and almonds. Let cool.
3. Place bread crumb mixture in the bottom of 4 dessert dishes. Spoon rhubarb on top and garnish with whipped cream.
SERVES 4

Vanilla Soufflé

1 tablespoon confectioners' sugar
¼ cup butter or margarine
3 tablespoons flour
1 cup milk

4 egg yolks
½ cup sugar
1 tablespoon vanilla extract
4 egg whites

1. Butter bottom of a 1½-quart soufflé dish (straight-sided casserole) and sift confectioners' sugar over it.
2. Heat butter in a saucepan. Stir in flour. Gradually add milk, stirring until thickened and smooth. Remove from heat.
3. Beat egg yolks, sugar, and vanilla extract together until mixture is very thick. Spoon sauce gradually into egg-yolk mixture while beating vigorously. Cool to lukewarm.
4. Using clean beater, beat egg whites until rounded peaks are formed. Spread egg-yolk mixture gently over egg whites and fold until thoroughly blended. Turn mixture into prepared soufflé dish. Set dish in a pan of very hot water.
5. Bake, uncovered, at 400°F 15 minutes. Turn oven control to 375°F and bake 30 to 40 minutes, or until a knife inserted halfway between center and edge comes out clean. Serve immediately.
6. Accompany with **pureed thawed frozen strawberries or raspberries.**
ABOUT 6 SERVINGS

Koulourakia II

3 cups sifted all-purpose flour
2 teaspoons baking powder
½ teaspoon salt
¾ cup unsalted butter
1 teaspoon anise flavoring

½ cup sugar
1 egg
¼ cup whipping cream
1 egg yolk, beaten, for brushing

1. Sift flour, baking powder, and salt together.
2. Cream butter with anise flavoring until fluffy. Add sugar and beat thoroughly. Add egg and beat well. Pour in whipping cream; mix thoroughly. Stir in flour mixture.
3. Knead dough on a floured board until shiny. Cover and refrigerate 2 hours.
4. Remove from refrigerator 30 minutes before rolling and baking. Break off a small amount of dough and roll on a board to form a strip 5 to 6 inches long. Shape into a ring by joining the ends, or make into a snail shape by winding up the strip. Place on a greased cookie sheet. Brush with egg yolk.
5. Bake at 350°F 20 to 25 minutes, or until done.
3½ DOZEN

Wine Fruit Compote

1 can (16 ounces) pear halves
1 can (16 ounces) cling peach halves
1 can (13½ ounces) pineapple chunks
½ lemon, thinly sliced and quartered

2 cups fruit juices and water
5 whole cloves
1 stick cinnamon
1 package (3 ounces) strawberry-flavored gelatin
2 teaspoons lemon juice
1 cup cherry kijafa wine

1. Drain fruit and reserve juice. Arrange fruit in a shallow 1½-quart dish. Scatter lemon slices over top.
2. Combine juices from fruit and water, cloves, and cinnamon in a saucepan. Heat to boiling. Simmer for 5 minutes. Strain.
3. Dissolve gelatin in the hot liquid. Add lemon juice and cherry wine. Pour over fruit. Chill 1 to 1½ hours, or until gelatin is only partly set. Baste fruit occasionally with gelatin mixture while chilling.
6 TO 8 SERVINGS

Port Wine Molds

1 envelope unflavored gelatin
1¼ cups sparkling water

½ cup ruby port
⅓ cup sugar

1. Soften gelatin in ½ cup of the sparkling water. Dissolve over hot water.
2. Combine remaining sparkling water, wine, and sugar; stir until sugar is dissolved. Mix in the gelatin.
3. Pour into 6 individual molds and chill until firm.
4. Unmold gelatin onto a chilled serving plate. Serve as a meat accompaniment.
6 SERVINGS

Rhubarb Compote

Banana Compote

½ cup sugar
½ cup apricot jam
1 cup water

6 ripe bananas
¼ cup unsalted butter

1. Combine sugar, jam, and water in a saucepan. Cook over medium heat until the syrup is heavy. Set aside.
2. Peel bananas and slice into ¼-inch pieces. Melt butter in a heavy skillet over medium heat and put in enough banana slices to cover bottom of skillet. Sauté until edges become golden. Pour reserved syrup over all bananas and boil uncovered over high heat until syrup is slightly thicker. Cool.
3. Pour into a crystal bowl, chill, and serve.

Raspberry Mousse

1 pound frozen raspberries
1 pint heavy cream
Sherry or port

1 package unflavored gelatine

1. Thaw the frozen berries, reserving a few for decoration.
2. Whip the cream until stiff.
3. Mash the raspberries with a fork and add a dash of sherry or port or sherry to the purée.
4. Fold in the gelatine and then the whipped cream. Arrange in glasses and decorate with the reserved raspberries.
Serves 4

Elegant Creamed Peaches

1 envelope plain gelatin
½ cup sweet red wine, such
   as port or muscatel
1 pint whipping cream
3 tablespoons powdered
   sugar
Dash salt

1 can (29 ounces) cling
   peach halves
½ cup glacé fruit
2 tablespoons roasted diced
   almonds
1 tablespoon honey
1 tablespoon sweet red wine

1. Combine gelatin and ½ cup wine in saucepan; place over low heat and stir until gelatin is dissolved.
2. Cool until mixture begins to thicken.
3. Whip cream with powdered sugar and salt.
4. Fold gelatin mixture into whipped cream. Spoon into 6 to 8 dessert dishes or 9-inch round pan.
5. Drain peaches; place cup-sides up in cream mixture.
6. Combine glacé fruit, almonds, honey, and 1 tablespoon wine. Spoon into peach cups. Chill.
6 TO 8 SERVINGS

New Orleans Holiday Pudding

3 cups boiling water
1¼ cups prunes
1 cup dried apricots
1 cup sugar
1 teaspoon ground cinnamon
1 teaspoon ground nutmeg
1 teaspoon ground allspice
1 cup orange juice
3 tablespoons ruby port
3 envelopes unflavored
   gelatin
1½ cups golden raisins,

plumped
2¼ cups candied cherries
⅓ cup diced candied citron
⅓ cup diced candied lemon
   peel
1½ cups walnuts, coarsely
   chopped
3 envelopes (2 ounces each)
   dessert topping mix, or 3
   cups whipping cream,
   whipped

1. Pour boiling water over prunes and apricots in a saucepan. Return to boiling, cover, and simmer about 45 minutes, or until fruit is tender. Drain and reserve 1 cup liquid. Set liquid aside until cold. Remove and discard prune pits.
2. Force prunes and apricots through a food mill or sieve into a large bowl. Stir in a mixture of the sugar, cinnamon, nutmeg, and allspice, mixing until sugar is dissolved. Blend in orange juice and wine; mix thoroughly.
3. Soften gelatin in the 1 cup reserved liquid in a small saucepan. Stir over low heat until gelatin is dissolved. Stir into fruit-spice mixture. Chill until mixture is slightly thickened, stirring occasionally.
4. Blend raisins, cherries, citron, lemon peel, and walnuts into gelatin mixture.
5. Prepare the dessert topping according to package directions or whip the cream. Gently fold into fruit mixture, blending thoroughly. Turn into 10-inch tube pan. Chill until firm.
6. Unmold onto chilled serving plate.
20 TO 24 SERVINGS

Custard Sauce

1 cup Low-Fat Yogurt,
   (page 47)
1 egg yolk

2 teaspoons honey or apple
   concentrate

Beat all ingredients until fluffy. Serve immediately or refrigerate until chilled.
ABOUT 1¼ CUPS

Ember-Baked Bananas

4 ripe bananas
Juice of ½ lemon
½ cup heavy cream or 1

tablespoon rum, brandy or
liquor, or 1 pint vanilla ice
cream

1. Preheat oven to 475°F or let a barbecue fire reduce to embers. Wrap unpeeled bananas in aluminum foil and place on rack in oven or on embers.
2. Leave bananas on fire until they are black and quite soft (about 15 minutes).
3. Slit peels lengthwise and drizzle on lemon juice. Top each banana with cream, liquor or ice cream.
SERVES 4

Sherried Holiday Pudding

1 package (14 ounces)
gingerbread mix
¾ cup orange juice
¼ cup sherry
½ cup chopped walnuts
½ teaspoon grated orange

peel
Golden Sherry Sauce (see recipe)
Hard Sauce Snowballs (see recipe)

1. Prepare gingerbread according to package directions using orange juice and sherry for liquid. Add walnuts and orange peel.
2. Turn batter into a well-greased 6-cup mold (batter should fill mold ½ to ⅔ full).
3. Bake at 350°F for 50 to 55 minutes, until pudding tests done. Serve warm with Golden Sherry Sauce and Hard Sauce Snowballs.
8 SERVINGS

Golden Sherry Sauce: Combine **½ cup each granulated and brown sugar (packed), ¼ cup whipping cream,** and **⅛ teaspoon salt** in saucepan. Heat slowly to boiling, stirring occasionally. Add **¼ cup sherry** and **1 teaspoon grated lemon peel.** Heat slightly to blend flavors.
ABOUT 1⅓ CUPS SAUCE

Hard Sauce Snowballs: Beat together **⅔ cup soft butter or margarine, 2 cups confectioners' sugar,** and **1 tablespoon sherry,** adding a little more sherry if more liquid is needed. Shape into small balls and roll in **flaked coconut.**
ABOUT 1½ CUPS OR 16 BALLS

Rosy Rhubarb Swirls

1½ cups sugar
1¼ cups water
⅓ cup red cinnamon candies
2 or 3 drops red food coloring
2¼ cups all-purpose flour
4 teaspoons baking powde

½ teaspoon salt
⅔ cup milk
⅓ cup half-and-half
3 cups finely diced fresh rhubarb (if tender do not peel)

1. Put sugar, water, and cinnamon candies into a saucepan. Stirring occasionally, cook over medium heat until candies are melted and mixture forms a thin syrup (about 10 minutes). Stir in food coloring.
2. Meanwhile, sift together into a bowl the flour, baking powder, and salt. Add a mixture of milk and half-and-half and stir with a fork only until dry ingredients are moistened. Turn onto a floured surface and knead lightly about 10 times with fingertips.
3. Roll dough into a 13x11x¼-inch rectangle. Spoon rhubarb evenly over dough. Beginning with longer side, roll dough and seal edges. Cut crosswise into 12 slices.
4. Pour syrup into a shallow baking dish and arrange rolls, cut side up, in syrup. Sprinkle with additional sugar (¼ to ⅓ cup) and top each roll with a small piece of **butter.**
5. Bake, uncovered, at 400°F 25 to 30 minutes. Serve warm with **half-and-half.**
12 SERVINGS

Vanilla Confectioners' Sugar

Confectioners' sugar
1 vanilla bean, about 9

inches long

1. Set out a 1- to 2-quart container having a tight-fitting cover. Fill with sugar.
2. Remove vanilla bean from air-tight tube, wipe with a clean, damp cloth and dry.
3. Cut vanilla bean into quarters lengthwise; cut quarters crosswise into thirds. Poke pieces of vanilla bean down into the sugar at irregular intervals. Cover container tightly and store on pantry shelf.
4. Use on cookies, cakes, tortes, rolled pancakes or wherever a sprinkling of confectioners' sugar is desired.

Note: The longer sugar stands, the richer will be the vanilla flavor. If tightly covered, sugar may be stored for several months. When necessary, add more sugar to jar. Replace vanilla bean when aroma is gone.

Coffee Extract

5 cups water

1½ cups ground coffee

1. Prepare a very strong coffee using water and ground coffee.
2. Pour brewed coffee into a large saucepan. Bring to a boil; simmer 30 minutes. Cool.
3. Store in a tightly covered container and use to flavor custard, buttercream, and ice cream.
ABOUT ½ CUP EXTRACT

Suet Pastry

½ pound beef suet
1 cup sifted all-purpose flour
½ teaspoon salt
2 cups sifted all-purpose flour
¼ cup milk
1 package active dry yeast
¼ cup warm water (110°F to 115°F If using compressed

yeast, soften 1 cake in ¼ cup lukewarm water, 80°F to 85°F)
1 tablespoon sugar
½ teaspoon salt
1 egg yolk
1 tablespoon lemon juice
Egg, slightly beaten

1. Set out 2 shallow baking sheets, having 4 sides; do not grease.
2. Have beef suet ready.
3. Break suet into small pieces, removing and discarding the membrane which coats it.
4. Sift together all-purpose flour and salt onto pastry board.
5. Press suet into flour with heel of hand until well blended. Shape suet mixture into a rectangle 2 inches thick; wrap in waxed paper and set aside in refrigerator.
6. Measure 1¾ to 2 cups all-purpose flour and set aside.
7. Scald milk.
8. Meanwhile, soften dry yeast in warm water.
9. Set aside.
10. Put sugar and salt into a bowl.
11. Immediately pour the scalded milk over ingredients in bowl. When mixture is lukewarm, blend in ¼ cup of the sifted flour, beating until smooth. Stir the softened yeast and add, mixing well. Add about one-half of the remaining flour to the dough and beat until very smooth. Beat in egg yolk and lemon juice.
12. Then beat in enough of the remaining flour to make a soft dough. Turn dough onto a lightly floured surface and let stand 5 to 10 minutes. Knead dough. Cover dough with inverted bowl and let rest about 15 minutes in warm place.

13. Lightly flour rolling pin. Roll dough on a lightly floured surface into a rectangle ½ inch thick around edges, leaving center slightly thicker.
14. Keep corners square, gently pulling dough into shape where necessary. With knife or spatula, loosen pastry from surface wherever sticking occurs; lift pastry slightly and sprinkle flour underneath.
15. Remove suet mixture from refrigerator; place on center of rolled dough. Fold edges of dough over suet mixture. Turn the dough upside down. Flatten with rolling pin, pressing down heavily while rolling. Make a rectangle about 14 inches long and 24 inches wide. Fold right third of dough over middle section. Fold left third over the right third. Let dough rest 5 minutes. Turn dough one quarter way around to have overlapping open edge away from you. Turn dough upside down. Again roll dough into rectangle about 14 inches long and 24 inches wide. Repeat folding, resting, turning one quarter way around and turning dough upside down. Follow directions for shaping dough into Crescents, Squares or Biscuits. Place pastries onto baking sheets. Brush each pastry with egg, slightly beaten.
16. Set pastry aside 15 minutes; brush again with some of remaining egg.
17. Bake at 350°F 20 to 30 minutes, or until golden brown.
ABOUT 3 DOZEN CRESCENTS OR SQUARES; ABOUT 2 DOZEN BISCUITS

Suet Pastry Crescents: Follow recipe for Suet Pastry. After second folding process, roll dough into 3-inch squares. Set out ⅔ cup thick **jam** such as apricot or strawberry. Spoon about ¾ teaspoon jam diagonally across center of each square. Starting at one of the corners, roll each square and turn ends slightly toward middle to form crescents. Press ends slightly with fingers to completely seal in jam. Place crescents, with overlapping edges underneath, about 1-inch apart onto baking sheets.

Suet Pastry Squares: Follow recipe for Suet Pastry Crescents but place jam at center of each square. Bring four corners of the square up toward center, pressing points together slightly with fingers to seal at the mid-point. Place squares about 1 inch apart onto baking sheets.

Suet Pastry Biscuits: Follow recipe for Suet Pastry. After second folding process, roll dough into a rectangle ½-inch thick. Score top of biscuit dough with sharp long-bladed knife by starting at upper left corner of rectangle and making diagonal cuts ⅛ inch deep and ¼ inch apart across dough. Repeat, starting at upper right corner. Cut biscuits with a lightly floured 2-inch biscuit cutter using an even pressure to keep sides of biscuits straight. Place biscuits about 1 inch apart onto baking sheets. Gather remaining dough by pushing pieces together without stacking. Avoid over-handling dough. Make top smooth with rolling pin. Make diagonal cuts across top of dough as before and cut out additional biscuits. Place onto baking sheets.

Note: Caraway seeds may be sprinkled onto top of biscuits just before baking.

Pear-Cheese Holiday Mold

1 can (29 ounces) pear halves
2 packages (3 ounces each) or 1 package (6 ounces) lime-flavored gelatin
½ teaspoon salt
2 cups boiling water
1 tablespoon lemon juice
1 package (8 ounces) cream cheese, softened
⅛ teaspoon ginger
½ cup chopped pecans

1. Drain pears, reserving syrup. Dice pears and set aside. Add enough water to reserved syrup to make 1½ cups liquid.
2. Dissolve gelatin and salt in boiling water. Add pear liquid and lemon juice. Chill half of the gelatin mixture until thickened. Stir in pears and pour into a 6-cup ring mold. Chill until set, but not firm.
3. Chill remaining gelatin until slightly thickened. Combine cream cheese and ginger. Gradually blend in gelatin and beat smooth. Stir in nuts and spoon into mold. Chill until firm (about 4 hours). Unmold onto a serving plate.

12 SERVINGS

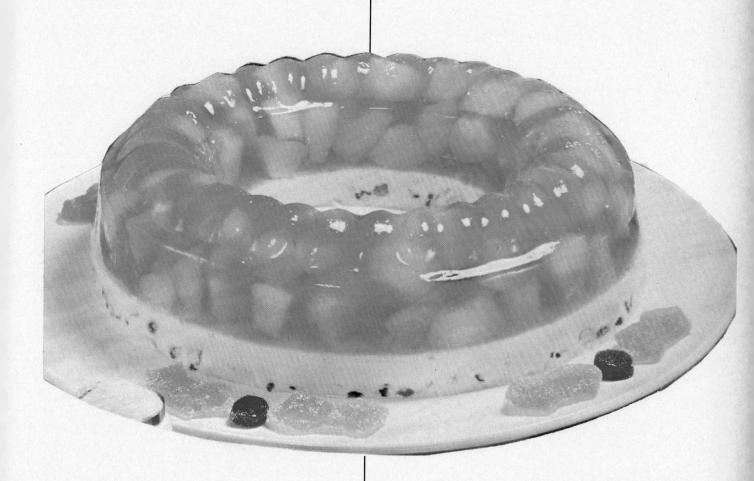

Applesauce

8 large sour, juicy apples	1 teaspoon cinnamon
½ cup water	½ teaspoon ground cloves
¾ cup sugar	

1. Wash, pare, quarter and core apples. Place them in a saucepan with water; cover tightly and simmer until tender.
2. Add sugar, cinnamon and cloves and cook a few minutes longer. Serve hot or cold.
SERVES 6

Peach Cobbler

1 can (29 ounces) sliced peaches	¾ cup beer
2 teaspoons lemon juice	1 cup all-purpose flour
¼ teaspoon cinnamon	1½ teaspoons baking powder
1½ tablespoons cornstarch	¼ teaspoon salt
	3 tablespoons shortening

1. Drain peaches, reserving syrup.
2. Lightly toss together peaches, lemon juice, and cinnamon. Arrange in a buttered shallow 1½-quart baking dish, 10x6 inches, or 8 inches square.
3. In a small saucepan, blend cornstarch, ¼ cup reserved syrup, and ¾ cup beer. Cook, stirring constantly, until thickened and clear. Pour over peaches.
4. Bake at 400°F 10 to 15 minutes, or until bubbly.
5. Meanwhile, mix flour, baking powder, and salt. Add ½ cup more reserved syrup (or use ½ cup beer plus 1 tablespoon sugar). Stir just until dough forms a ball.
6. Drop by large spoonfuls onto peaches. Continue baking 25 minutes.
8 SERVINGS

Sweetened Whipped Cream

1 cup chilled whipping cream	sugar
¼ cup sifted confectioners'	1 teaspoon vanilla extract

1. Place a rotary beater and a 1-quart bowl in refrigerator to chill.
2. Using chilled bowl and beater, beat until cream stands in peaks when beater is slowly lifted upright.
3. Beat sugar and vanilla extract into whipped cream with final few strokes until blended.
4. Set in refrigerator if not used immediately.
ABOUT 2 CUPS WHIPPED CREAM

Rum Whipped Cream: Substitute **1 to 1½ tablespoons rum** for vanilla extract.

Strawberry Whipped Cream: Prepare 1½ times recipe. Slice 2 pints rinsed, hulled, fresh strawberries (reserve a few whole berries for garnish, if desired). Fold berries into the cream.

Coffee Cream

4 cups milk	¾ cup sugar
2 tablespoons Coffee Extract, (page 675)	1 tablespoon butter or margarine
3 tablespoons cornstarch	¼ cup whipping cream
6 egg yolks, beaten	

1. Combine ½ cup of the milk, Coffee Extract, and cornstarch. Beat in egg yolks. Set aside.
2. Put the remaining milk, sugar, and butter into the top of a metal double boiler. Bring to a boil over direct heat.
3. Half fill the bottom of the double boiler with water; bring to boiling. Place the top of the double boiler over the bottom pan.
4. Add the reserved milk-and-egg mixture to the top pan while stirring. Cook over medium heat, stirring until the custard thickens and coats the spoon.
5. Cool custard, then add cream. Pour into a large bowl or individual custard cups. Serve chilled.

Rum Cream: Follow recipe for Coffee Cream, omitting Coffee Extract and cream. Heat **¼ cup amber rum** in a small saucepan. Ignite rum and stir it into the thickened custard. Serve chilled.

Dessert Cheese Plates

Wedges of Camembert   crackers
  cheese or Brie   Walnuts
Slices of Roquefort cheese   Green or red grapes
Sliced pumpernickel bread or

Place cheese on bread or crackers and arrange on plate with
walnuts and grapes.

Strawberry Pancakes

1 quart fully ripe strawberries
1¼ cups sifted all-purpose
  flour
⅛ teaspoon salt
2 eggs, well beaten
½ cup milk
½ teaspoon vanilla extract
2 egg whites
4 teaspoons sugar
2 tablespoons sugar
Confectioners' sugar

1. Set out a griddle or a heavy 10-inch skillet.
2. Wash and remove blemishes from strawberries.
3. Set 18 berries aside to garnish serving plates; hull and slice remaining berries, place them into refrigerator.
4. Sift together flour and salt into a bowl and set aside.
5. Beat with rotary beater to blend eggs, milk and vanilla extract.
6. Set griddle over low heat.
7. Make a well in center of dry ingredients. Add egg mixture, stirring batter only until blended; set batter aside.
8. Beat egg whites until frothy.
9. Add 4 teaspoons of sugar gradually, beating well after each addition.
10. Beat until stiff peaks are formed. Carefully fold egg whites into batter.
11. Test griddle; it is hot enough for baking when drops of water sprinkled on surface dance in small beads. Lightly grease griddle if manufacturer so directs. For each pancake pour about 1 cup of the batter onto griddle. Immediately tilt griddle back and forth to spread batter evenly. If necessary, use spatula to spread batter. Cook until pancake is puffy, full of bubbles and golden brown on underside. Turn only once and brown other side. Transfer pancakes to a warm platter and keep them warm by placing between folds of absorbent paper in a 350°F oven.
12. When all the pancakes are cooked, remove strawberries from refrigerator. Mix one-half of the sliced berries with sugar.
13. Spoon about ½ cup of the sweetened strawberries onto each pancake and roll. Place pancakes onto individual plates. Sprinkle each with confectioners' sugar.
14. Arrange remaining sliced strawberries over the top of pancakes. Garnish plates with leaf lettuce and the whole strawberries. Serve immediately.
3 SERVINGS

Boysenberry Ice

2 cans (16 ounces each)
boysenberries, drained
(reserve syrup)
2 tablespoons unflavored
gelatin
¼ cup sugar
¾ cup water
1 tablespoon lemon juice

1. Force drained boysenberries through a fine sieve; set aside.
2. Mix gelatin and sugar in a saucepan. Stir in water and set over low heat until gelatin and sugar are dissolved, stirring constantly.
3. Remove from heat and stir in 1½ cups of the reserved syrup, boysenberries, and lemon juice.
4. Pour into a 1-quart refrigerator tray and freeze until firm, stirring several times.
5. Serve in chilled sherbet glasses.
ABOUT 1 QUART ICE

COOKIES

Snowball Meltaways

1 cup butter
½ cup confectioners' sugar
1 teaspoon vanilla extract
2½ cups sifted all-purpose
flour
½ cup finely chopped pecans

1. In a heavy saucepan over low heat, melt and heat butter until light brown in color. Pour into a small mixing bowl; chill until firm.
2. Cream browned butter with confectioners' sugar and extract until light and fluffy. Gradually add flour, mixing until blended. Stir in the pecans. Chill several hours for ease in handling.
3. Shape into 1-inch balls. Place on ungreased cookie sheets.
4. Bake at 350°F about 20 minutes.
5. Remove to wire racks. While still hot, dust with **confectioners' sugar**

ABOUT 4 DOZEN COOKIES

Moravian Scotch Cakes

4 cups sifted all-purpose
flour
½ cup sugar
2 teaspoons caraway seed
1½ cups butter

1. Combine flour, sugar, and caraway seed in a bowl. Cut in butter until mixture becomes a soft dough (requires working beyond the stage when particles are the size of rice kernels); shape into a ball.
2. Roll a third of dough at a time ¼ inch thick on a floured surface. Cut into 2-inch squares. Transfer to lightly greased cookie sheets.
3. Bake at 325°F about 20 minutes.
4. Cool cookies; spread with Snowy Icing, *below*, and sprinkle with **colored sugar.**

ABOUT 3½ DOZEN COOKIES

Snowy Icing

1 cup sugar
¼ cup water
Few grains salt
1 egg white
1 teaspoon vanilla extract

1. Mix the sugar, water, and salt in a small saucepan; stir over low heat until sugar is dissolved.
2. Cook without stirring until mixture spins a 2-inch thread (about 230°F) when a small amount is dropped from a spoon.
3. Beat egg white until stiff, not dry, peaks are formed. Continue beating egg white while pouring hot syrup over it in a steady thin stream. After all the syrup is added, continue beating until icing is very thick and forms rounded peaks (holds shape).
4. Blend in extract.

ABOUT 2½ CUPS ICING

Hermits

1 cup dark seedless raisins
2½ cups sifted all-purpose
flour
¾ teaspoon baking soda
½ teaspoon salt
1 teaspoon ground cinnamon
½ teaspoon ground nutmeg
⅛ teaspoon ground cloves
¾ cup butter
1½ cups firmly packed
brown sugar
3 eggs
1 cup walnuts, chopped

1. Pour **2 cups boiling water** over raisins in a saucepan and bring to boiling; pour off water and drain raisins on absorbent paper. Coarsely chop raisins and set aside.
2. Sift flour, baking soda, salt, and spices together and blend thoroughly; set aside.
3. Cream butter; add brown sugar gradually, beating until fluffy. Add eggs, one at a time, beating thoroughly after each addition.
4. Add dry ingredients in fourths, mixing until blended after each addition. Stir in raisins and walnuts.
5. Drop by teaspoonfuls 2 inches apart onto lightly greased cookie sheets.
6. Bake at 400°F about 7 minutes.

ABOUT 8 DOZEN COOKIES

Snowball Meltaways

Chocolate Chip Cookies

1 cup sifted all-purpose flour
½ teaspoon baking powder
⅛ teaspoon baking soda
⅛ teaspoon salt
½ cup butter
1 teaspoon vanilla extract
¾ cup firmly packed light brown sugar
1 egg
1 package (6 ounces) semisweet chocolate pieces
½ cup chopped nuts

1. Blend flour, baking powder, baking soda, and salt.
2. Cream butter with vanilla extract. Add brown sugar gradually, creaming well. Add egg and beat thoroughly. Mix in dry ingredients, then chocolate pieces and nuts.
3. Drop batter by teaspoonfuls onto ungreased baking sheets.
4. Bake at 375°F 10 to 12 minutes.
5. Cool cookies on wire racks.
ABOUT 4 DOZEN COOKIES

Layered Chocolate Confections

Chocolate Layer
½ cup butter or margarine
2 ounces (2 squares) unsweetened chocolate
2 eggs
1 cup sugar
1 teaspoon vanilla extract
½ cup sifted all-purpose flour
½ cup chopped salted pecans

Cream Layer:
½ cup heavy cream
⅓ cup butter or margarine
1½ cups sugar
2 tablespoons brandy
2 ounces (2 squares) unsweetened chocolate, melted and cooled slightly

1. Chocolate Layer: Melt the butter and chocolate together; set aside to cool.
2. Beat eggs, sugar, and extract until thick and piled softly. Add cooled chocolate mixture and beat until blended. Stir in flour, then pecans. Turn into a greased 11x7x1½-inch baking pan and spread evenly.
3. Bake at 350°F about 25 minutes.
4. Cool in pan on wire rack.
5. Cream Layer: Combine cream, butter, and sugar in a heavy saucepan. Cook, stirring occasionally, over low heat until mixture reaches 236°F. Remove from heat; cool, undisturbed, to 110°F or just cool enough to hold pan on palm of hand. Turn into small bowl, add brandy, and beat until mixture is smooth and creamy. Spread on cooled chocolate layer. Chill slightly until top is firm to the touch. Spread melted chocolate over creamy layer. Chill thoroughly.
6. Cut into 1-inch squares. Place in bonbon cups to serve or pack in a gift box.
ABOUT 6 DOZEN CONFECTIONS

Note: A drop or two of **food coloring** may be blended with creamed mixture to harmonize with various party color schemes.

Left to right:
Holiday String-Ups
Swedish Jelly Slices (page 688)
Chocolate Chip Cookies
Sugared Cocoa Delights
Double Daisies (page 688)
Layered Chocolate Confections

Sugared Cocoa Delights

1¼ cups butter
1 teaspoon vanilla extract
1 cup confectioners' sugar
2 cups sifted all-purpose flour
½ cup unsweetened cocoa
¼ teaspoon salt
1 cup chopped pecans
Confectioners' sugar for coating

1. Cream butter with vanilla extract. Add confectioners' sugar gradually, creaming well.
2. Blend flour, cocoa, and salt; add to creamed mixture and mix well. Stir in pecans.
3. Pinch off small amounts of dough and place on ungreased cookie sheets.
4. Bake at 350°F about 15 minutes. Cool on wire racks. Coat with confectioners' sugar.
ABOUT 8 DOZEN COOKIES

Holiday String-Ups

1 cup butter
2 teaspoons vanilla extract
1½ cups sugar
2 eggs
3¼ cups sifted all-purpose
flour
1 teaspoon baking powder
½ teaspoon salt
Confectioners' Sugar Icing, below

1. Cream butter with extract; add sugar gradually, beating until fluffy. Add eggs, one at a time, beating thoroughly after each addition.
2. Sift flour, baking powder, and salt together; add to creamed mixture in fourths, mixing until blended after each addition. Chill dough thoroughly.
3. Roll a small amount of dough at a time ¼ inch thick on a floured surface; cut into a variety of shapes with cutters. Transfer to ungreased cookie sheets.
4. Insert 1-inch long pieces of paper straws or macaroni into top of each cutout, or press both ends of a piece of colored cord into the dough on the underside of each cutout.
5. Bake at 400°F 6 to 8 minutes.
6. Cool; gently twist out straws, leaving holes for ribbons or cord to be pulled through after decorating.
7. Prepare icing. Color with desired amount of **red** or **green food coloring.** Sprinkle with **decorative sugar.**
ABOUT 5 DOZEN COOKIES

Note: This versatile dough may be thinly rolled and baked cookies sandwiched together with filling.

Confectioners' Sugar Icing: Combine **1 cup confectioners' sugar** and **½ teaspoon vanilla extract.** Blend in **milk** or **cream** (about 1 tablespoon) until icing is of spreading consistency.
ABOUT 1 CUP

Chocolate String-Ups: Follow recipe for Holiday String-Ups. Blend in **2 ounces (2 squares) unsweetened chocolate,** melted and cooled, after the eggs are added. Mix in **1 cup finely chopped pecans** after the last addition of dry ingredients.

Swedish Jelly Slices

¾ cup butter
1 teaspoon grated lemon
  peel
¾ cup sugar
1 egg
1¾ cups sifted all-purpose
  flour
1½ teaspoons baking powder
¼ teaspoon salt
1 teaspoon ground coriander
½ teaspoon ground
  cardamom
1 jar (10 ounces) red cherry
  jelly
1 egg yolk
¼ cup sugar
2 teaspoons water
¼ cup finely chopped
  toasted blanched almonds

1. Cream butter with lemon peel. Add ¾ cup sugar gradually, creaming thoroughly. Add egg and beat well.
2. Blend flour, baking powder, salt, and spices; add to creamed mixture and mix well.
3. Chill dough until easy to handle.
4. On a floured surface, roll dough into a 12x8-inch rectangle. Cut into 12 (1-inch) strips.
5. Place strips 4 inches apart on greased cookie sheets; cookies will spread. Make a depression, ¼ inch wide and ¼ inch deep, lengthwise down the center of each strip of dough. Fill depression with jelly.
6. Bake at 375°F 10 minutes.
7. Meanwhile, combine egg yolk, ¼ cup sugar, and water and beat until thick.
8. Remove cookies from oven. Brush egg yolk mixture on hot cookies and sprinkle with almonds. Return cookies to oven and bake 5 minutes.
9. Cool cookies 5 minutes on cookie sheets. Add more jelly, if desired. Cut diagonally into 1-inch slices. Cool on wire racks.

ABOUT 7 DOZEN COOKIES

Double Daisies

1 cup butter
1½ teaspoons orange extract
1 cup confectioners' sugar
1 egg
2½ cups sifted all-purpose
  flour
1 teaspoon salt

Glaze and Frosting:
1 cup confectioners' sugar
2 tablespoons milk
½ teaspoon orange extract
Yellow food coloring
Cocoa

1. Cream butter with orange extract. Add confectioners' sugar gradually, creaming well. Add egg and beat thoroughly.
2. Mix flour and salt; add to creamed mixture and mix until well blended.
3. Chill dough thoroughly, 8 hours or overnight.
4. Using a small portion of chilled dough at a time, roll on a floured surface to ¼-inch thickness. Cut with floured large and small daisy cutters. Place on ungreased cookie sheets.
5. Bake at 375°F about 10 minutes, depending on size. Put on wire racks.
6. For glaze, combine confectioners' sugar, milk, and orange extract. Tint a pale yellow with food coloring.
7. Brush warm cookies with glaze. Cool.
8. Mix a small amount of cocoa and additional confectioners' sugar with remaining glaze to make the consistency of frosting.
9. Put a small amount of frosting on center of each large cookie. Top with a small one. Decorate top with a small amount of frosting.

ABOUT 2½ DOZEN COOKIES

Coconut Macaroons

⅔ cup (½ of a 14-ounce
can) sweetened condensed
milk
2 cups flaked coconut
½ to ¾ cup coarsely
chopped dry roasted
almonds
¼ cup chopped maraschino
cherries, drained
1½ teaspoons vanilla extract

1. Mix all ingredients thoroughly. Drop by rounded teaspoonfuls onto well-greased cookie sheet. To speed removal of cookies from cookie sheet, bake no more than 12 at a time.
2. Bake at 350°F 10 to 12 minutes, or until delicately browned.
3. Immediately loosen all cookies from cookie sheet and remove cookies to wire rack at once.

ABOUT 3 DOZEN COOKIES

Old-Fashioned Spice Cookies

2 cups sifted all-purpose flour	1 cup firmly packed brown sugar
¾ teaspoon salt	½ cup granulated sugar
½ teaspoon baking soda	1 egg
1 teaspoon cinnamon	2 tablespoons water
½ teaspoon nutmeg	2 cups uncooked rolled oats, quick or old-fashioned
¼ teaspoon cloves	¾ cup currants
1 cup soft vegetable shortening	

1. Blend flour, salt, baking soda, and spices in a bowl. Add shortening, sugars, egg, and water; beat with electric mixer until smooth (about 2 minutes). Stir in oats and currants.
2. Chill dough thoroughly.
3. Roll only a small portion of chilled dough at a time to ⅛-inch thickness on a pastry canvas or board lightly sprinkled with **confectioners' sugar.** Cut with a floured 3-inch round cutter. Put onto ungreased cookie sheets. Sprinkle with **granulated sugar.**
4. Bake at 375°F 8 to 10 minutes.

ABOUT 5 DOZEN COOKIES

Beginner Brownies

½ cup (1 stick) butter or margarine	2 eggs
2 squares (1 ounce each) unsweetened chocolate	1 teaspoon vanilla extract
	¾ cup all-purpose flour
1 cup sugar	½ cup chopped nuts (optional)

1. In the top of a double boiler, melt butter and chocolate together over water that is simmering, not boiling.
2. Meanwhile, use the butter wrapper to grease a square 8-inch baking pan. Shake in a little flour, then shake out excess.
3. When butter and chocolate have melted, remove the top from the double boiler and set it on the counter top to cool. Add sugar.
4. When mixture is room temperature, blend in eggs one at a time, beating well. Do this by hand or use the electric mixer.
5. Add vanilla extract. Stir in flour and if desired, chopped nuts. Stir only until ingredients are well mixed. Spread batter in prepared pan.
6. Bake at 350°F for 30 minutes, no longer. Remove from oven and place on a rack to cool. When room temperature, cut into 16 squares.

16 BROWNIES

Scandinavian Walnut Cookies

1 cup butter or margarine
½ cup sugar
1 teaspoon vanilla extract
2¼ cups sifted all-purpose
flour
½ cup finely chopped
walnuts

1. Cream butter, sugar, and vanilla extract together until well blnnded. Gradually blend in flour to make a stiff dough.
2. Mix in the walnuts; omit walnuts if preparing Finnish Bread. Shape and bake as below.

Finnish Bread: Using about 1 tablespoon of dough at a time, shape dough into small rolls about 2¼ inches long, and place on lightly greased cookie sheet. Brush tops of cookies with **slightly beaten egg white** and sprinkle with **½ cup chopped walnuts.** Bake at 350°F 15 to 18 minutes. ABOUT 30 COOKIES

Grandma's Jelly Cookies: Roll dough a little less than ¼ inch thick, and cut out rounds using a 2-inch cutter. Cut a circle from the center of half of the rounds. Place rounds on lightly greased cookie sheets and bake at 350°F 10 to 12 minutes. When completely cool, spread **¾ teaspoon tart jelly** on each of the solid rounds and top with a round with a cutout center. ABOUT 40 DOUBLE COOKIES

Walnut Balls: Shape dough into balls 1¼ inches in diameter. Chill thoroughly before baking, so balls will hold their shape. Bake at 350°F 25 minutes. Balls may be rolled in **powdered sugar** while hot, and again when cold. Or cool balls on wire rack and frost tops of balls with **powdered sugar frosting** when completely cooled. ABOUT 2½ DOZEN COOKIES

Frosted Triangles: Divide dough into 4 portions. Roll one portion of dough at a time into a strip 12 inches long and 1¾ inches wide. Transfer strip to a greased cookie sheet. Bake at 350°F 20 minutes. Cool slightly on cookie sheet, then carefully slide onto wire rack to cool completely. When cold, make a ruffle of frosting down the center of each strip, using your favorite buttercream frosting and a pastry bag fitted with a star tip. Cut into triangles when frosting is set. ABOUT 32 TRIANGLES

Jam Slices: Divide dough into four portions and roll into 12-inch strips as described for Frosted Triangles. Transfer strips to cookie sheet. With a finger, press a slight depression down the center of the entire length of the strip. Fill the depression using **2 tablespoons apricot jam** for each strip. Sprinkle each strip with **1 tablespoon finely chopped walnuts.** Bake at 350°F about 20 minutes. Cool slightly on cookie sheet, then slide carefully onto a wire rack, using broad spatulas. Cut in diagonal slices when cold. (*Note:* These cookies soften on standing, from moisture in jam, so are best eaten within a day or two of baking.) ABOUT 32 SLICES

Scandinavian Walnut Cookies

Wheat Germ Oatmeal Cookies

⅔ cup butter or margarine, softened
1 teaspoon vanilla extract
1 cup firmly packed brown sugar
½ cup granulated sugar
1 egg
¼ cup milk
1 cup sifted all-purpose flour
¾ teaspoon salt
½ teaspoon baking soda
¾ cup toasted wheat germ
½ cup walnuts, chopped
2½ cups uncooked rolled oats, quick or old-fashioned

1. Put butter, vanilla extract, sugars, egg, and milk into a bowl. Beat thoroughly.
2. Sift flour, salt, and baking soda together; add to creamed mixture and mix well. Stir in wheat germ, walnuts, and oats.
3. Drop by rounded teaspoonfuls onto greased cookie sheets.
4. Bake at 375°F 12 to 15 minutes. ABOUT 6 DOZEN COOKIES

Old-Fashioned Sugar Cookies

1 cup shortening
1 cup sugar
2 eggs, beaten
2 teaspoons vanilla
1 cup sour cream
5 cups cake flour
2 teaspoons baking powder
1¼ teaspoons salt
1 teaspoon soda

1. Cream shortening and sugar.
2. Add eggs and vanilla to sour cream.
3. Sift together the flour, baking powder, salt and soda and add alternately with the liquid to shortening and sugar mixture. Chill thoroughly.
4. Roll out on pastry cloth ¼ inch thick. Cut with large cutter, sprinkle with sugar and press in lightly.
5. Bake in moderate oven 375°F 15 minutes. 100 2½-INCH COOKIES

Pineapple-Raisin Cookies

1 cup firmly packed golden brown sugar
½ cup soft butter or margarine
1 egg
1 teaspoon vanilla extract
½ cup raisins
¾ cup canned crushed pineapple, undrained
2 cups all-purpose flour
1 teaspoon baking powder
½ teaspoon baking soda
½ teaspoon salt
½ cup chopped walnuts (optional)

1. Combine brown sugar, butter, egg, and vanilla extract in mixing bowl. Beat until fluffy.
2. Add raisins and pineapple; mix thoroughly.
3. Combine flour, baking powder, baking soda, and salt; add to the creamed mixture and mix well. Stir in nuts.
4. Drop the mixture by spoonfuls 2 inches apart on greased cookie sheets.
5. Bake at 375°F 12 to 15 minutes.
ABOUT 4 DOZEN COOKIES

Lemon Angels

Red, yellow, and green food coloring
1¾ cups flaked coconut
1 cup butter
1 teaspoon vanilla extract
1½ cups sifted confectioners' sugar
1 egg
2¼ cups all-purpose flour
½ teaspoon baking soda
¼ teaspoon salt
1 tablespoon grated lemon peel

1. To tint coconut, use 3 jars, one for each color. Blend 2 or 3 drops food coloring with a few drops of water in each jar. Put one-third of coconut into each jar; cover and shake vigorously until coconut is evenly tinted. Turn into shallow dishes and set aside.
2. Cream butter with vanilla extract in a bowl. Add confectioner's sugar gradually, creaming well. Add egg and beat thoroughly.
3. Blend flour, baking soda, and salt; add gradually to creamed mixture, mixing well. Stir in lemon peel.
4. Divide dough into thirds and chill until easy to handle.
5. For each third, roll teaspoonfuls of dough in one color of coconut, form balls, and place on ungreased cookie sheets.
6. Bake at 325°F 10 to 12 minutes. Remove immediately to wire racks to cool.
ABOUT 8 DOZEN COOKIES

Lemon Angels

Pineapple-Raisin Cookies

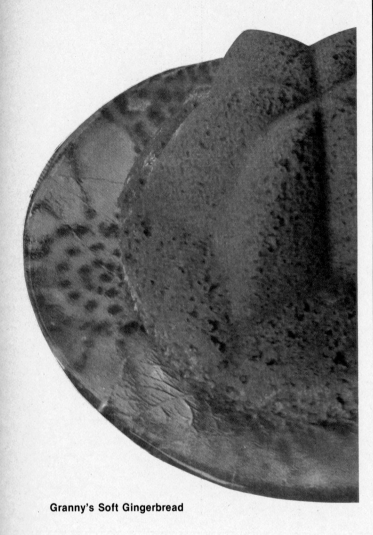

Granny's Soft Gingerbread

Surprise Bars

1 ounce (1 square) unsweetened chocolate	1 egg
½ cup graham cracker crumbs	¾ cup sifted all-purpose flour
2 tablespoons butter, melted	⅛ teaspoon baking soda
½ cup butter or margarine	⅛ teaspoon salt
½ teaspoon vanilla extract	¼ cup sour cream
½ cup sugar	¾ cup walnuts, coarsely chopped

1. Melt chocolate and set aside to cool.
2. Blend crumbs and melted butter; set aside.
3. Cream the ½ cup butter with the extract; add sugar gradually, beating until fluffy. Add egg and beat thoroughly.
4. Sift flour, baking soda, and salt together; add alternately to creamed mixture with sour cream, mixing until blended after each addition.
5. Divide mixture in half; blend cooled chocolate into one portion.
6. Turn chocolate mixture into a greased 8x8x2-inch baking pan and spread evenly. Cover with the crumbs and press lightly.
7. Stir walnuts into remaining portion; drop by spoonfuls over crumbs and carefully spread evenly.
8. Bake at 375°F 25 to 30 minutes.
9. While warm, cut into bars.

2½ DOZEN COOKIES

Wheat-Flake Bars

2 cups whole wheat cereal flakes	¾ cup plus 2 tablespoons butter or margarine, chilled
2 cups sifted all-purpose flour	½ cup orange marmalade
1 teaspoon baking powder	Glossy Orange Frosting, below
¾ cup firmly packed brown sugar	Semisweet chocolate pieces

1. Mix cereal, flour, baking powder and brown sugar in a bowl. Cut in butter until crumbly.
2. Press about two-thirds of the mixture in an even layer on the bottom of a 13x9x2-inch pan. Spread with marmalade; sprinkle remaining cereal mixture over marmalade.
3. Bake at 350°F about 30 minutes. Remove to a wire rack. Cool completely.
4. Frost with Glossy Orange Frosting. Cut into 3x1-inch bars. Decorate each bar with three semisweet chocolate pieces (points up).

3 DOZEN COOKIES

Glossy Orange Frosting: Beat **1 egg white** slightly; beat in **1½ cups confectioners' sugar.** Add **1 tablespoon melted butter** or **margarine,** ⅛ **teaspoon salt, 1 teaspoon vanilla extract,** and ¼ **teaspoon orange extract;** beat until smooth. Blend in, one drop at a time, orange food coloring (a mixture of about **2 drops** of **red** and **6 drops** of **yellow**) until frosting is tinted a light orange.

ABOUT 1 CUP FROSTING

Granny's Soft Gingerbread

½ cup butter	½ teaspoon ground cloves
2 eggs	1 teaspoon baking powder
1 cup dark brown sugar	1½ cups flour
2 teaspoons cinnamon	3 ounces heavy cream
1 teaspoon cardamom	3 ounces red raspberry jam
1 teaspoon ginger	Bread crumbs

1. Melt the butter and let it cool.
2. Beat eggs and sugar until fluffy.
3. Combine flour, spices and baking powder and stir into the batter together with cream and jam.
4. Finally add the melted butter.
5. Pour the batter into a well greased 1½ quart cake pan sprinkled with fine bread crumbs. Bake the cake in a 325°F oven for about 1 hour. Test with a skewer. Allow to cool 10 minutes; then remove from pan and place on cake rack.

Gumdrop Gems

1 cup vegetable shortening
¾ teaspoon vanilla extract
½ cup granulated sugar
½ cup firmly packed brown
  sugar
2 eggs, beaten
2 cups sifted all-purpose
flour
½ teaspoon baking soda
½ teaspoon salt
1½ cups uncooked rolled
  oats, quick or old-fashioned
48 small gumdrops

1. Cream shortening with vanilla extract. Add sugars gradually, creaming well. Add eggs and beat thoroughly.
2. Sift flour, baking soda, and salt together; add to creamed mixture and mix well. Stir in oats.
3. Shape dough into balls and put on greased cookie sheets. Make a hollow in each ball and place a gumdrop in each hollow.
4. Bake at 375°F 10 to 12 minutes.
4 DOZEN COOKIES

Molasses Butter Balls

1 cup butter
½ teaspoon vanilla extract
¼ cup molasses
2 cups sifted all-purpose
flour
½ teaspoon salt
2 cups pecans, finely
  chopped

1. Cream butter with extract; add molasses and beat well.
2. Blend flour and salt; add in fourths to creamed mixture, mixing until blended after each addition. Stir in the pecans.
3. Shape dough into 1-inch balls; place on lightly greased cookie sheets.
4. Bake at 350°F 12 to 15 minutes.
5. Cool slightly; roll in **confectioners' sugar.**
ABOUT 5 DOZEN COOKIES

Gumdrop Gems

Ginger Shortbread

1½ cups sifted all-purpose
  flour
1 teaspoon ground ginger
¼ teaspoon salt
½ cup butter or margarine
⅓ cup firmly packed brown
  sugar
1 tablespoon heavy cream

1. Sift flour, ginger, and salt together; set aside.
2. Cream butter; add brown sugar gradually, beating well. Add flour mixture gradually, mixing until well blended. Stir in cream.
3. Divide dough into halves. Place on an ungreased cookie sheet. Flatten into rounds about ½ inch thick. Mark into wedges. Flute the edges and prick centers with a fork.
4. Bake at 350°F about 20 minutes.
5. While still warm, cut into wedges.
2 SHORTBREAD ROUNDS

Overnight Cookies

2¼ cups sifted all-purpose
  flour
1 cup sugar
1 cup butter
½ cup cream
¼ teaspoon vanilla extract
⅛ teaspoon lemon extract

1. Sift flour and sugar together; cut in butter until particles are the size of rice kernels.
2. Combine cream and extracts; add gradually to flour mixture, mixing with a fork until well blended.
3. Chill dough until easy to handle.
4. Shape into two 1½-inch rolls. Wrap and chill overnight.
4. Cut each roll into ⅛- or ¼-inch slices. Transfer slices to ungreased cookie sheeets.
6. Bake at 350°F 9 to 12 minutes.
6 TO 8 DOZEN COOKIES

Mom's Sultanas

1 cup sifted all-purpose flour
¾ teaspoon baking powder
⅛ teaspoon baking soda
⅛ teaspoon salt
⅔ cup butter
2 teaspoons grated lemon
peel
½ cup sugar
1 egg
2 tablespoons lemon juice
1 cup uncooked rolled oats
½ cup golden raisins

1. Sift flour, baking powder, baking soda, and salt together; set aside.
2. Cream butter with lemon peel; add sugar gradually, creaming until fluffy. Add egg and beat thoroughly.
3. Alternately add dry ingredients with lemon juice, mixing until blended after each addition. Stir in rolled oats and raisins.
4. Drop by teaspoonfuls about 2 inches apart onto lightly greased cookie sheets.
5. Bake at 375°F 12 to 15 minutes.
ABOUT 4 DOZEN COOKIES

Frosted Ginger Bars

Frosted Ginger Bars

Bars:
½ cup butter or margarine
½ cup firmly packed brown
  sugar
1 egg
½ cup molasses
2 cups complete pancake
  mix
1½ teaspoons ginger
1½ teaspoons cinnamon

½ cup water

Frosting:
2 packages (3 ounces each)
  cream cheese
2 cups sifted confectioners'
  sugar
2 tablespoons lemon juice
1 tablespoon grated lemon
  peel

1. For bars, beat butter and brown sugar together until creamy. Add egg and beat well. Blend in molasses.
2. Blend pancake mix, ginger, and cinnamon; add to creamed mixture. Blend in water.
3. Turn batter into a greased and floured 15x10x1-inch jelly-roll pan and spread evenly.
4. Bake at 350°F about 20 minutes. Cool in pan on wire rack.
5. For frosting, beat cream cheese until fluffy. Add confectioners' sugar gradually, creaming until well mixed. Beat in lemon juice. Spread frosting over cooled bars. Sprinkle with grated lemon peel. Chill until frosting is set.
6. Cut into bars.
ABOUT 4 DOZEN COOKIES

Glazed Cinnamon Bars

1 cup butter or margarine
1 cup firmly packed golden
  brown sugar
1 egg, separated
1¾ cups all-purpose flour

1 tablespoon cinnamon
Pinch salt
½ cup unsifted powdered
  sugar
1 cup walnuts, chopped

1. Put butter, brown sugar, and egg yolk into a bowl; beat until creamy. Blend flour, cinnamon, and salt; add to creamed mixture and mix well. Spread in an even layer in a lightly greased 15x10x1-inch jelly-roll pan.
2. Beat egg white until frothy. Stir in powdered sugar. Brush mixture over layer in pan. Sprinkle with walnuts.
3. Bake at 350°F 30 to 35 minutes. While still hot, cut into bars. Remove from pan and cool on wire racks.
4 DOZEN COOKIES

Glazed Cinnamon Bars

Hazelnut Balls

2 egg whites
1 cup sugar

1½ cups (about 6 ounces)
  hazelnuts (filberts), grated

1. Beat egg whites until frothy; add sugar gradually, beating constantly until stiff peaks are formed.
2. Sprinkle hazelnuts over the egg whites and gently fold together just until blended.
3. Drop mixture by teaspoonfuls onto lightly greased cookie sheets. If necessary, work over each portion with the back of a spoon to round it.
4. Bake at 300°F about 25 minutes.
5. With a spatula, carefully remove cookies from cookie sheets to wire racks.
ABOUT 4 DOZEN COOKIES

Buttery Bitters Bars

1 cup butter or margarine
½ cup sugar
3 cups fine graham cracker
  crumbs (about 3 dozen
  square crackers)
2 cups firmly packed brown
  sugar
1 tablespoon flour

1 teaspoon baking powder
1 cup flaked coconut
1 cup coarsely chopped
  walnuts
1 tablespoon Angostura
  bitters
3 eggs, well beaten

1. Cut butter into a mixture of the ½ cup sugar and the crumbs until thoroughly blended. Press firmly into two ungreased 9x9x2-inch baking pans. Set aside.
2. Blend the brown sugar, flour, and baking powder. Mix in coconut and walnuts.
3. Combine bitters with beaten eggs, add to brown sugar mixture and beat thoroughly. Spread evenly over layer in each pan.
4. Bake at 350°F 35 minutes, or until top layer is set.
5. Cool in pan on rack. While still warm, cut into small bars. Coat lightly with **confectioners' sugar**.
8 TO 10 DOZEN BARS

Note: If desired, cut in 3-inch squares (omit confectioners' sugar) and serve with whipped dessert topping, whipped cream, or ice cream.

Walnut Bonnets

1 cup butter	¼ teaspoon baking powder
¾ cup sugar	1 cup finely chopped
1 egg	walnuts
1 teaspoon vanilla extract	3 tablespoons apricot jam
2½ cups sifted all-purpose	Glaze, below
flour	Candy sprinkles
½ teaspoon salt	

1. Beat butter, sugar, egg, and vanilla extract together until light and fluffy.
2. Combine flour with salt and baking powder and blend into creamed mixture. Divide dough into thirds.
3. Mix walnuts and jam into one third of dough.
4. Using the remaining plain dough, fill pastry bag fitted with a No. 4 star tube and press out rings onto lightly greased baking sheets, making rings about 2¼ inches in diameter.
5. Fill centers of rings with walnut dough, a rounded teaspoon for each.
6. Bake at 350°F about 15 minutes. Allow to cool.
7. If desired, brush centers with glaze and decorate with candy sprinkles.

ABOUT 3 DOZEN COOKIES

Glaze: Blend **1 cup sifted confectioners' sugar** with **1 tablespoon milk** and a drop or two of **vanilla extract.**

Walnut Cakes

1¼ cups sifted all-purpose	½ cup chopped walnuts
flour	1 to 1½ cups walnut halves
⅓ cup sugar	and large pieces
½ cup butter	Glaze, below
2 tablespoons milk	4 ounces (4 squares)
½ teaspoon vanilla extract	semisweet chocolate

1. Combine flour and sugar. Cut butter into mixture until particles are very fine.
2. Sprinkle milk and vanilla extract over mixture, and mix to a stiff dough. Mix in chopped walnuts.
3. Roll dough ¼ inch thick on a lightly floured surface, and cut into rounds. Place on ungreased cookie sheet.
4. Cover each cookie with walnut halves or large pieces, pressing the nuts lightly into the dough.
5. Bake at 350°F 15 minutes. Remove cookies to wire rack and place rack on a cookie sheet. Spoon tops with hot glaze, and allow cookies to cool.
6. Melt chocolate over warm, not hot, water and spread each cookie bottom with chocolate. Place cookies on waxed paper until chocolate is set.

1 DOZEN 3-INCH COOKIES, 2 DOZEN 2-INCH COOKIES, OR 3½ DOZEN 1½-INCH COOKIES

Glaze: Combine **⅓ cup firmly packed dark brown sugar** and **⅓ cup light corn syrup** in a small saucepan. Bring to boiling and use immediately.

Double Swirl Walnut Cookies

¾ cup shortening (half	1 teaspoon salt
butter)	2 ounces (2 squares)
1¼ cups sugar	unsweetened chocolate,
2 eggs	melted
1 teaspoon vanilla extract	2 tablespoons milk
2½ cups sifted all-purpose	⅔ cup walnuts, finely
flour	chopped
1 teaspoon baking powder	

1. Beat shortening, sugar, eggs, and vanilla extract together until fluffy.
2. Combine flour, baking powder, and salt; add to the creamed mixture and mix well.
3. Divide dough in half. To one half blend chocolate, milk, and ⅓ cup walnuts. To the remaining portion, mix in ⅓ cup walnuts. Wrap each half in waxed paper and chill thoroughly.
4. Roll the light dough on lightly floured surface to a 12x8-inch rectangle. Roll chocolate dough to same dimensions, and place light dough over chocolate dough, with shorter sides matching, longer side about ¼ inch from edge of chocolate. With a sharp knife, cut the dough in half crosswise, making two 6-inch sections for easier rolling.
5. Starting from the side with chocolate dough showing under the light dough, roll up the two together to the center. Turn over, and roll the dough from the other side to meet the first half. Wrap in waxed paper, plastic wrap, or foil, and place in freezer until dough is very firm.
6. Cut into ¼-inch slices and place on lightly greased cookie sheets.
7. Bake at 400°F 8 minutes. Leave cookies on cookie sheet for a minute, then remove carefully, using a broad spatula, and cool on wire racks.

ABOUT 4 DOZEN COOKIES

Note: If dough cracks on rolling, allow to stand at room temperature for a minute or two to warm up slightly. Cracks may be pinched together.

Pecan Dainties

1 egg white	1¼ cups chopped pecans
½ cup firmly packed brown	1½ tablespoons flour
sugar, sifted	

1. Beat egg white until frothy. Add brown sugar gradually, beating until very stiff peaks are formed. Fold in pecans and flour.
2. Drop by teaspoonfuls 2 inches apart onto lightly greased cookie sheets; shape into balls with the back of a spoon.
3. Bake at 350°F about 10 minutes.

ABOUT 4 DOZEN COOKIES

Left to right:
Walnut Bonnets
Walnut Cakes
Double Swirl Walnut Cookies

Moon Cakes

1¼ cup flour
7 ounces butter
1 teaspoon almond extract

For brushing:
Egg white

Decoration:
Granulated sugar

1. Work together flour and butter on a pastry-board. Add almond extract. Work the dough together and put it in a cold place to set.
2. Roll out the dough and cut out half moons with cookie cutters.
3. Brush the cakes with egg white, dip them in granulated sugar. Let the cakes stand about 15 minutes before baking them.
4. Bake the cakes in a 400°F oven for 6 to 8 minutes.
MAKES 100

Jam Cakes

8 ounces butter
4 ounces sugar
1¼ cups flour

Filling:
Raspberry Jam or Jelly

1. Work together the butter, sugar and flour quickly. Shape into a roll about 2 inches in diameter and put it in a cold place for a while.
2. Cut the roll in about 1-inch-thick slices with a sharp knife. Make a hole in the middle and fill it with jam or jelly.
3. Bake the cakes in a 350°F oven for about 10 minutes.

Cinnamon Hearts

7 ounces butter
3 ounces sugar
2 cups flour
1 egg yolk

Decoration:
Egg white
Cinnamon
Sugar

1. Mix flour and sugar and cut in butter on a pastry-board. Add the egg yolks and work the dough together quickly. Put in cold place for a while.
2. Roll out the dough and cut out cookie-cutter hearts. Brush them with lightly whipped egg white. Dip the cakes in a mixture of sugar and cinnamon. Bake in a 325°F oven for 10 to 12 minutes.
MAKES 75

Mint Diamonds

1 cup butter
1 teaspoon vanilla extract
1 cup firmly packed brown sugar
1 egg
2 cups sifted all-purpose flour

½ teaspoon baking powder
½ teaspoon salt
Creamy Pastel Frosting, (page 708)
Chocolate-Mint Glaze, (page 708)
½ cup pecans, chopped

1. Cream butter with extract; add brown sugar gradually, beating until fluffy. Add egg and beat thoroughly.
2. Sift flour, baking powder, and salt together; add to creamed mixture in fourths, mixing until blended after each addition. Turn mixture into ungreased 15x10x1-inch jelly roll pan and spread evenly.
3. Bake at 350°F 20 to 25 minutes; cool.
4. Spread the frosting quickly over cooled cookie base; spread glaze over frosting and sprinkle with nuts. Cool; cut into diamond shapes.
ABOUT 4 DOZEN COOKIES

Clockwise from bottom left:
Cinnamon Hearts
Jam Cakes
Moon Cakes

Spicy Ginger Crunchies

Spicy Ginger Crunchies

2¼ cups sifted all-purpose
    flour
2 teaspoons baking soda
1 teaspoon salt
1 teaspoon ground cinnamon
¾ teaspoon ground ginger

½ teaspoon ground cloves
¾ cup butter
1 teaspoon vanilla extract
1 cup sugar
1 egg
¼ cup molasses

1. Sift flour, baking soda, salt, and spices together; set aside.
2. Cream butter with extract; gradually add sugar, beating until light and fluffy. Add egg and molasses; beat thoroughly.
3. Gradually add dry ingredients to creamed mixture, mixing until blended. Chill several hours.
4. Shape dough into ¾-inch balls, roll in **sugar** and place 2 inches apart on greased cookie shets.
5. Bake at 375°F 7 to 8 minutes.
6. Immediately remove to wire racks to cool.

6 TO 7 DOZEN COOKIES

Date Perfections

¾ cup sifted all-purpose flour
¾ teaspoon baking powder
¼ teaspoon salt
2 eggs
¾ cup sugar

1½ cups dates, finely
    chopped
1 cup pecans, finely
    chopped
Lemon Glaze, (see page 710)

1. Sift flour, baking powder, and salt together; set aside.
2. Beat eggs and sugar together until mixture is thick and piled softly.
3. Fold in dry ingredients, dates, and pecans until blended. Turn into a greased 11x7x1½-inch baking pan and spread evenly into corners.
4. Bake at 325°F 30 to 35 minutes.
5. Immediately brush surface with Lemon Glaze. While warm, cut into squares.

ABOUT 2 DOZEN COOKIES

Note: Dried figs or apricots may be used instead of dates.

Cream Cheese Dainties

Apricot, Strawberry, or
  Mincemeat Filling, below
½ cup butter
1 package (3 ounces) cream

cheese
1 teaspoon sugar
1 cup all-purpose flour

1. Prepare desired filling or fillings and set aside.
2. Beat butter and cream cheese until well blended. Mix in sugar and then flour. Divide dough in half and chill thoroughly.
3. On a lightly floured surface, roll each half of dough to ¹⁄₁₆-inch thickness. Use floured 2-inch cookie cutters to cut about 3 dozen "bases."
4. Transfer bases to cookie sheets. Spoon about ¼ teaspoon filling in center of each cookie.
5. Cut remaining dough with the same size cutters. Use 1-inch cutters to cut out the centers. Top cookie bases with cut-out cookies or with 1-inch cutouts.
6. Bake at 375°F 6 to 8 minutes. Remove immediately to wire racks to cool.
ABOUT 5 DOZEN COOKIES

Apricot Filling: Mix **½ cup apricot preserves** with **½ teaspoon lemon extract.**

Strawberry Filling: Mix **½ cup strawberry preserves** with **½ teaspoon almond extract.**

Mincemeat Filling: Mix **½ cup prepared mincemeat** with **½ teaspoon orange extract.**

Note: If desired, make tart shells from dough. Roll dough to ¹⁄₁₆-inch thickness and cut out rounds with a 2¾-inch cookie cutter. Carefully line well-buttered 2¼x¾-inch tart pan wells with rounds of dough; prick with a fork. Bake at 375°F 8 to 10 minutes, or until lightly browned. Cool; remove from pans. Fill with fruit or cream filling.
ABOUT 3 DOZEN TART SHELLS

Pepparkakor

1 cup butter
1½ cups sugar
1 egg
1 tablespoon dark corn syrup
2¾ cups all-purpose flour
2 teaspoons baking soda

1 tablespoon cinnamon
2 teaspoons ginger
1 teaspoon ground cloves
Blanched almonds
Icing, below

1. Beat butter in a bowl until softened. Add sugar gradually, creaming well. Add egg and beat throughly. Blend in corn syrup.
2. Blend flour, baking soda, and spices; add to creamed mixture gradually, mixing until blended.
3. Chill dough until easy to handle.
4. Using a portion of the chilled dough at a time, roll dough on a lightly floured surface to ⅛-inch thickness. Cut with floured cookie cutters.
5. Transfer cookies to cookie sheets and decorate some with almonds.
6. Bake at 400°F 5 to 7 minutes. Remove immediately to wire racks.
7. Decorate cooled cookies with icing.
ABOUT 6 DOZEN COOKIES

Icing: Put **1 egg white** and **⅛ teaspoon almond extract** into a small bowl. Add **2 cups sifted confectioners' sugar** gradually to egg white while mixing; beat until smooth and glossy.

Butter Pecan Shortbread

Shortbread:
1 cup butter
½ cup firmly packed light
  brown sugar
2¼ cups all-purpose flour
½ cup finely chopped
  pecans

Decorator Icing:
2 tablespoons butter
¼ teaspoon vanilla extract
1 cup confectioners' sugar
Milk (about 1 tablespoon)
Red and green food coloring

1. To prepare shortbread, beat butter until softened; add brown sugar gradually, beating until fluffy. Add flour gradually, beating until well blended. Mix in pecans.
2. Chill dough until easy to handle.
3. On a lightly floured surface, pat and roll dough into a 14x10-inch rectangle about ¼ inch thick. Cut dough into 24 squares. Divide each square into 4 triangles.
4. Transfer triangles to ungreased cookie sheets.
5. Bake at 300°F 18 to 20 minutes, or until lightly browned. Remove to wire racks to cool.
6. To prepare icing, cream butter with vanilla extract in a small bowl. Add confectioners' sugar gradually, beating until blended. Blend in enough milk for desired consistency for icing. Color one third of icing red and two thirds green. Force icing through a decorator tube to make a holly decoration on each cookie.
8 DOZEN COOKIES

Clockwise from bottom left:
Cream Cheese Dainties
Pepparkakor
Butter Pecan Shortbread

Spritz

1 cup butter
1 teaspoon vanilla extract
½ cup sugar
1 egg yolk

2 cups sifted all-purpose
  flour
½ teaspoon baking powder
¼ teaspoon salt

1. Cream butter with extract; add sugar gradually, beating until fluffy. Add egg yolk and beat thoroughly.
2. Sift flour, baking powder, and salt together; add to creamed mixture in fourths, mixing until blended after each addition.
3. Follow manfacturer's directions, fill a cookie press with dough and form cookies of varied shapes directly onto ungreased cookie sheets.
4. Bake at 350°F 12 minutes.
ABOUT 5 DOZEN COOKIES

Chocolate Spritz: Follow recipe for Spritz. Thoroughly blend ¼ **cup boiling water** and **6 tablespoons cocoa**; cool. Mix in after addition of egg yolk.

Nut Spritz: Follow recipe for Spritz. Stir in ½ **cup finely chopped nuts** (black walnuts or toasted blanched almonds) after the last addition of dry ingredients.

Chocolate-Tipped Spritz: Follow recipe for Spritz. Dip ends of cooled cookies into Chocolate Glaze (below). If desired, dip into finely chopped **nuts,** crushed **peppermint stick candy,** or **chocolate shot.** Place on wire racks until glaze is set.

Marbled Spritz: Follow recipe for Spritz. Thoroughly blend **2 tablespoons boiling water** and **3 tablespoons cocoa**; cool. After the addition of egg yolk, remove a half of the creamed mixture to another bowl and mix in a half of the dry ingredients. Into remaining half of creamed mixture, stir cocoa mixture; blend in remaining dry ingredients. Shape each half of dough into a roll and cut lengthwise into halves. Press cut surfaces of vanilla and chocolate flavored doughs together before filling cookie press.

Spritz Sandwiches: Spread **chocolate frosting** or **jam** on bottom of some cookies. Cover with unfrosted cookies of same shape to form sandwiches.

Jelly-Filled Spritz: Make slight impression at center of cookie rounds and fill with ¼ **teaspoon jelly** or **jam** before baking.

Chocolate Glaze: Partially melt **3 ounces (½ cup) semisweet chocolate pieces** in the top of a double boiler over hot (not simmering) water. Remove from heat and stir until chocolate is melted. Blend in **3 tablespoons butter.**

English Toffee Bars

1 cup butter
1 cup sugar
1 egg yolk
2 cups sifted all-purpose
  flour
1 teaspoon ground cinnamon

1 egg white, slightly beaten
1 cup chopped pecans
2 ounces (2 squares)
  semisweet chocolate,
  melted

1. Cream butter; add sugar gradually, beating until fluffy. Beat in egg yolk.
2. Sift the flour and cinnamon together; gradually add to creamed mixture, beating until blended.
3. Turn into a greased 15x10x1-inch jelly roll pan and press evenly. Brush top with egg white. Sprinkle with pecans and press lightly into dough.
4. Bake at 275°F 1 hour.
5. While still hot, cut into 1½-inch squares. Drizzle with melted chocolate. Cool on wire rack.
5 TO 6 DOZEN COOKIES

Moji Pearls

¾ cup butter
½ teaspoon vanilla extract
⅓ cup sugar

1½ cups sifted all-purpose
  flour
⅛ teaspoon salt

1. Cream butter with extract; add sugar gradually, beating until fluffy.
2. Blend flour and salt; add in thirds to creamed mixture, mixing until blended after each addition. Chill dough until easy to handle.
3. Shape into 1-inch balls or into crescents (if desired, roll in sesame seed). Place about 2 inches apart on ungreased cookie sheets.
4. Bake at 325°F 20 minutes.
ABOUT 3 DOZEN COOKIES

Pecan Poofs: Follow recipe for Moji Pearls. Substitute ¼ **cup confectioners' sugar** for sugar. Decrease flour to 1 cup. Mix in **1 cup pecans,** finely chopped. Shape dough into balls or pyramids.

English Gingered Brandy Snaps

¼ cup butter or margarine
¼ cup sugar
2 tablespoons light corn
  syrup
1 teaspoon molasses
½ cup all-purpose flour
½ teaspoon ground ginger

⅛ teaspoon ground nutmeg
1 tablespoon brandy

Filling:
1 cup whipping cream,
  whipped
1 tablespoon sugar

1. Combine butter, sugar, corn syrup, and molasses in a medium saucepan. Heat mixture over medium heat just until butter is melted.
2. Combine flour, ginger and nutmeg in a small bowl. Stir this mixture into the butter mixture. Stir in the brandy.
3. Drop the mixture by teaspoonfuls 6 inches apart on greased cookie sheets.
4. Bake at 350°F 8 to 10 minutes. Let cool for 30 seconds. Ease cookies off the cookie sheets with a spatula; then immediately roll loosely around a 6-inch tapered metal tube with the upper surface of each brandy snap on the outside. Cool on wire racks.
5. Shortly before serving, whip cream, add sugar, and mix well. Using a pastry bag fitted with a star tip, fill the cavity in the rolled brandy snap from each end.
15 COOKIES

Note: If brandy snaps begin to harden before they are rolled, return them to the oven for 30 seconds to soften them.

Double-Quick Cookie Squares

30 square graham crackers
6 ounces semisweet
  chocolate pieces
½ cup grated coconut

1 can (14 ounces) sweetened
  condensed milk
½ cup chopped pecans

1. Crumble graham crackers into a bowl. Add chocolate pieces, coconut, and condensed milk; blend to moisten crackers. Turn into a lightly greased 9x9x2-inch baking pan. Top with pecans.
2. Bake at 325°F 30 minutes. (Cookies are moist and brown only slightly.)
3. Cool in pan on wire rack. Cut into squares.
3 DOZEN COOKIES

Choco-Honey Chews

1¾ cups honey-flavored
  graham cracker crumbs
1 can (14 ounces) sweetened
  condensed milk
2 tablespoons honey
1½ teaspoons grated orange

peel
2 tablespoons orange juice
1 cup semisweet chocolate
  pieces
¾ cup coarsely chopped
  pecans

1. Put crumbs into a bowl. Add the condensed milk, honey, and orange peel and juice; mix well. Stir in the chocolate pieces and pecans. Turn into a greased 13x9x2-inch baking pan and spread evenly.
2. Bake at 325°F 30 minutes.
3. While warm, cut into bars.
ABOUT 4 DOZEN COOKIES

Choco-Oat Bars

½ cup butter
½ cup peanut butter
1½ teaspoons vanilla extract
¾ cup firmly packed brown
  sugar
1 cup sifted all-purpose flour

½ teaspoon baking soda
¼ teaspoon salt
¼ cup water
1 cup uncooked rolled oats
6 ounces semisweet
  chocolate pieces

1. Cream butter with peanut butter and extract thoroughly; add brown sugar gradually, beating until fluffy.
2. Sift flour, baking soda, and salt together; add to creamed mixture alternately with water, mixing until blended after each addition. Stir in rolled oats.
3. Chill dough thoroughly.
4. Meanwhile, melt and cool chocolate.
5. Invert an 11x7x1½-inch baking pan onto a piece of waxed paper; mark around pan with a knife to form an outline without cutting through paper.
6. Divide the dough into halves; press half evenly into pan. Spread with cooled chocolate.
7. Pat remainder of dough evenly over marked oblong on waxed paper. Invert onto chocolate layer, press down gently and peel off paper.
8. Bake at 375°F 15 to 20 minutes.
9. Cool completely; cut into bars.
ABOUT 4½ DOZEN COOKIES

Peanut Butter Bars: Follow recipe for Choco-Oat Bars. Use a 15x10x1-inch jelly roll pan. Decrease brown sugar to ½ cup and add **½ cup sugar**. Add **1 egg** to creamed mixture and beat thoroughly. Increase flour to 1¼ cups. Substitute **1½ teaspoons baking powder** for baking soda. Omit water, oats, and chocolate pieces. Press all the dough into pan without chilling; bake. While warm, cut into bars.

Cinnamon Pecan Bars

½ cup butter
1 cup sugar
1 egg
½ cup all-purpose flour
1¼ teaspoons ground

cinnamon
¼ teaspoon salt
1 cup pecans, finely
  chopped

1. Cream butter; add sugar gradually, creaming thoroughly. Add egg and beat until fluffy.
2. Sift flour, cinnamon, and salt together. Add to creamed mixture and mix until blended. Stir in pecans. Turn into a greased 8x8x2-inch baking pan and spread evenly.
3. Bake at 350°F 40 minutes.
4. Cut into small bars while still warm; coat with **confectioners' sugar**.
ABOUT 2½ DOZEN COOKIES

Almond Cookies

Almond Cookies

¾ cup almonds
7 ounces margarine
½ cup sugar

1 egg
1½ cups flour

1. Blanch and grind almonds. Cream margarine and sugar and add almonds, egg and flour. Let dough rest.
2. Use a cookie press or pastry bag to squirt dough out in 4-inch-long pieces, and form into rings.
3. Bake in 400°F oven for about 7 minutes.
ABOUT 50 COOKIES

Graham Sensations

1¼ cups graham cracker crumbs
¼ cup sifted all-purpose flour
¼ teaspoon salt
1 can (14 ounces) sweetened condensed milk
¾ teaspoon vanilla extract

½ teaspoon grated lemon peel
½ cup flaked coconut
¾ cup coarsely chopped pecans
½ cup semisweet chocolate pieces

1. Blend crumbs, flour, and salt. Add condensed milk, extract, and lemon peel; mix well. Stir in remaining ingredients. Turn into a greased 13x9x2-inch baking pan and spread evenly.
2. Bake at 325°F 30 minutes.
3. While warm, cut into bars.
ABOUT 4 DOZEN COOKIES

Creamy Pastel Frosting

1½ cups sugar
½ cup cream

6 tablespoons butter
Food coloring

1. Put sugar, cream, and butter into a heavy saucepan; stir over low heat to dissolve sugar. Increase heat and bring to boiling; stir occasionally.
2. Put candy thermometer in place; continue cooking without stirring to 234°F.
3. Remove from heat; cool to 110°F, or until just cool enough to hold pan on palm of hand; do not stir.
4. Using food coloring to harmonize with the color scheme for the special occasion, blend 1 or 2 drops into sugar mixture and beat until frosting is of spreading consistency.
ABOUT 1½ CUPS

Chocolate-Mint Glaze: Melt **6 ounces (1 cup) semisweet chocolate pieces** with **½ teaspoon mint extract** over hot water. Cool slightly.

Black Walnut Dreams

2 tablespoons butter
5 tablespoons all-purpose flour
⅛ teaspoon baking soda
⅛ teaspoon salt
1 cup black walnuts, coarse-

ly chopped
2 eggs
¾ teaspoon vanilla extract
¼ teaspoon lemon extract
1 cup firmly packed brown sugar

1. Melt butter in a 8x8x2-inch baking pan; set aside.
2. Sift flour, baking soda, and salt together; stir in walnuts; set aside.
3. Beat eggs and extracts; add brown sugar gradually, beating until very thick. Blend in dry ingredients.
4. Turn into pan over melted butter; do not stir.
5. Bake at 350°F 25 to 30 minutes.
6. While warm, cut into squares and roll in **sugar.**
16 COOKIES

Peanut Butter Dreams

¼ cup butter
½ cup peanut butter
½ cup firmly packed light brown sugar
1 cup sifted all-purpose flour
2 eggs
1 teaspoon vanilla extract

1 cup firmly packed light brown sugar
⅓ cup sifted all-purpose flour
½ teaspoon baking powder
¾ cup flaked coconut
6 ounces semisweet chocolate pieces

1. Cream butter with peanut butter thoroughly; add ½ cup brown sugar gradually, beating until fluffy.
2. Add 1 cup flour in halves, mixing until blended after each addition. Press evenly into greased 9x9x2-inch baking pan.
3. Bake at 350°F 10 to 15 minutes, or until lightly browned.
4. Meanwhile, beat eggs, extract, and 1 cup brown sugar until thick. Add a mixture of ⅓ cup flour and the baking powder; beat until blended.
5. Stir in coconut and chocolate pieces. Spread evenly over partially baked layer in pan.
6. Return to oven and bake 30 minutes.
7. Cool completely and cut into squares or bars.
ABOUT 2 DOZEN COOKIES

Brandied Apricot Teacakes

8 ounces dried apricots, chopped
1 package (11 ounces) currants
½ cup boiling water
1 cup apricot brandy
½ cup butter
1½ cups firmly packed light brown sugar
3 eggs
2 cups all-purpose flour
½ teaspoon baking soda
½ teaspoon salt
1 teaspoon allspice
1 teaspoon cinnamon
1 teaspoon cloves
Confectioners' sugar

1. Put apricots and currants into a bowl; add water and brandy and mix well. Cover and let stand overnight.
2. Beat butter in a large bowl until softened. Add brown sugar gradually, creaming well. Add eggs, one at a time, and beat thoroughly after each addition.
3. Blend flour, baking soda, salt, and spices; add to creamed mixture gradually, mixing well. Blend in fruit mixture.
4. Set midget foil baking cups on baking sheets. Spoon a rounded tablespoonful of mixture into each cup.
5. Bake at 325°F about 30 minutes, or until a wooden pick inserted in cake comes out clean. Remove to wire racks to cool.
6. Before serving, sift confectioners' sugar over cakes.
ABOUT 5 DOZEN TEACAKES

Note: For smaller teacakes without baking cups, use well-buttered 1¾-muffin pan wells. Spoon 1 tablespoon mixture into each well. Bake at 325°F about 20 minutes.
ABOUT 7 DOZEN TEACAKES

Chewy Butterscotch Bars

Topping, below
1⅓ cups sifted cake flour
2 teaspoons baking powder
1 teaspoon salt
2 cups firmly packed brown sugar
½ cup corn oil
2 teaspoons vanilla extract
2 eggs
1 cup coarsely chopped pecans
1 cup flaked coconut

1. Prepare Topping; set over simmering water.
2. Sift flour, baking powder, and salt together; set aside.
3. Beat brown sugar, corn oil, and extract; add eggs, one at a time, beating thoroughly after each addition.
4. Stir in flour mixture until blended. Mix in pecans and coconut.
5. Turn into a well-greased 15x10x1-inch jelly roll pan and spread into corners. Drizzle hot topping over entire surface.
6. Bake at 350°F 30 minutes.
7. Cool 30 minutes in pan, cut into bars, and remove from pan.
ABOUT 2½ DOZEN COOKIES

Topping: Blend **¾ cup firmly packed brown sugar, 2 tablespoons butter, 3 tablespoons cream or evaporated milk,** and **¼ cup dark corn syrup** in a saucepan. Cook over medium heat, stirring occasionally, to 234°F. Remove from heat; blend in **1 teaspoon vanilla extract.**
ABOUT ⅔ CUP

Almond Awards

1 cup butter
2 teaspoons grated lemon peel
1 cup sugar
1 cup sifted all-purpose flour
½ teaspoon salt
1 cup almonds, finely chopped
½ cup heavy cream

1. Cream ½ cup of the butter with the lemon peel and ½ cup of the sugar. Blend flour and salt; add in halves, mixing until blended after each addition.
2. Turn into an 11x7x1½-inch baking pan and spread into an even layer.
3. Bake at 375°F 12 minutes.
4. Meanwhile, melt remaining ½ cup butter in a heavy saucepan; add almonds and remaining ½ cup sugar. Cook the mixture 3 minutes, stirring constantly.
5. Stir in cream and heat to boiling; cool slightly. Spoon topping over partially baked layer.
6. Return to oven and bake 20 minutes, or until light golden.
7. Cool completely; cut into squares or bars.
ABOUT 5 DOZEN COOKIES

Brandied Apricot Teacakes

Cookie Cigarettes

¼ cup egg whites
½ cup confectioners' sugar
⅓ cup sifted flour
3 tablespoons butter, melted and cooled
¾ teaspoon vanilla extract

1. Beat egg whites until frothy; add confectioners' sugar gradually, beating thoroughly after each addition; beat until stiff peaks are formed.
2. Fold in flour in halves. Blend in cooled butter and extract.
3. Quickly grease a preheated cookie sheet. Bake a trial cookie; if it is too brittle to roll, the batter needs a little more flour; if the cookie is thick and difficult to roll, add a little more cooled melted butter.
4. Drop mixture by heaping teaspoonfuls 4 inches apart onto hot cookie sheet; spread very thinly without making holes; bake only a few cookies at one time (they are difficult to roll when cool).
5. Bake at 400°F 2 to 3 minutes, or until edges are lightly browned.
6. Immediately remove from cookie sheet. Quickly roll each cooked around a pencil-thin wooden rod; place on wire rack. Remove rods when cooled.
7. Store in a tightly covered container.
ABOUT 2 DOZEN COOKIES

Note: These cookies may also be made using a krumkake iron. Spoon 1 teaspoonful of mixture onto heated iron, close iron, and bake for 1 minute over medium heat, turning once. Roll as directed.

Mansion Squares

½ cup butter
1 teaspoon vanilla extract
¾ cup firmly packed brown sugar
1 egg
1 cup sifted all-purpose flour
½ teaspoon baking powder
⅛ teaspoon baking soda
⅛ teaspoon salt
6 ounces semisweet chocolate pieces

1. Cream butter with extract; add brown sugar gradually, beating until fluffy. Add egg; beat well.
2. Sift flour, baking powder, baking soda, and salt together; add in thirds to creamed mixture, mixing until blended after each addition. Turn into greased 11x7x1½-inch baking pan. Top with chocolate pieces.
3. Bake at 350°F about 30 minutes.
4. While warm, cut into squares.
ABOUT 2 DOZEN COOKIES

Nut Mansion Squares: Follow recipe for Mansion Squares. Substitute **1 cup coarsely chopped filberts** for semi-sweet chocolate pieces.

Chocolate-Nut Mansion Squares: Follow recipe for Mansion Squares. Top with chocolate pieces immediately after removing from oven rather than before baking. When chocolate is softened, spread evenly over surface. Sprinkle with **1 cup filberts,** coarsely chopped.

Apricot Sours

⅔ cup butter, chilled
1½ cups sifted all-purpose flour
1 egg
½ cup firmly packed light brown sugar
¼ teaspoon vanilla extract
½ cup finely snipped apricots, cooked*
½ cup pecans, chopped
Lemon Glaze, below

1. Cut butter into flour until particles are the size of rice kernels. Press mixture evenly and firmly into a 13x9x2-inch baking pan.
2. Bake at 350°F 15 minutes.
3. Meanwhile, beat egg, brown sugar, and extract until thick; stir in a mixture of apricots and pecans.
4. Spread evenly over partially baked layer in pan.
5. Return to oven and bake about 20 minutes, or until lightly browned.
6. Remove from oven and immediately spread Lemon Glaze over top. When cool, cut into bars.
ABOUT 4 DOZEN COOKIES

*Put snipped apricots into a heavy saucepan with a small amount of water (3 to 4 tablespoons). Cover tightly and cook over low heat about 10 minutes, or until apricots are soft and liquid is absorbed. Cool.

Note: If packaged dried apricots are extremely soft, it may not be necessary to cook the apricots.

Lemon Glaze: Blend **¾ cup confectioners' sugar** with **2 tablespoons lemon juice.**

Dream Bars DeLuxe

1 cup sifted all-purpose flour
3 tablespoons confectioners' sugar
½ cup butter or margarine, softened
2 eggs
1½ teaspoons vanilla extract
1½ cups firmly packed light brown sugar
2 tablespoons flour
¼ teaspoon baking powder
⅛ teaspoon salt
¾ cup walnuts, chopped
½ cup flaked coconut

1. Blend 1 cup flour, confectioners' sugar, and butter. Press evenly into an 11x7x1½-inch baking pan.
2. Bake at 350°F 20 minutes; remove pan to wire rack.
3. Meanwhile, beat eggs with extract and brown sugar until thick.
4. Blend in a mixture of 2 tablespoons flour, baking powder, and salt; mix in ½ cup of the walnuts and ¼ cup coconut.
5. Spread evenly over partially baked layer in pan and sprinkle with a mixture of remaining nuts and coconut.
6. Return to oven and bake 25 minutes.
7. Cool completely; cut into bars.
ABOUT 3 DOZEN COOKIES

Cherry Jewels

Cherry Jewels

½ cup butter
1 teaspoon vanilla extract
¼ cup sugar
1 egg
1 teaspoon grated lemon peel
1 tablespoon lemon juice
1¼ cups sifted all-purpose flour
¾ cup finely chopped pecans
18 candied cherries, halved

1. Cream butter with extract and sugar until light and fluffy. Add the egg and lemon peel and juice; beat thoroughly. Gradually add flour, mixing until blended. Chill.
2. Shape dough into 1-inch balls, roll in chopped pecans and place on greased cookie sheets. Press a cherry half onto center of each ball.
3. Bake at 350°F 10 to 12 minutes.
4. Cool on wire racks.
3 DOZEN COOKIES

Wheatfield Bars

2 cups graham cracker crumbs
½ cup wheat germ
¼ teaspoon salt
1 can (14 ounces) sweetened
condensed milk
2 teaspoons vanilla extract
6 ounces semisweet chocolate pieces

1. Blend crumbs, wheat germ, and salt; mix in remaining ingredients.
2. Turn into lightly greased 8x8x2-inch baking pan and spread evenly.
3. Bake at 350°F about 35 minutes; avoid overbaking.
4. Cool; cut into bars.
ABOUT 1½ DOZEN COOKIES

Hi-Fi Brownies

½ cup butter or margarine
3 ounces (3 squares) unsweetened chocolate
2 eggs
1 cup sugar
1 teaspoon vanilla extract
1¼ cups sifted all-purpose
flour
½ teaspoon baking powder
½ teaspoon salt
1 cup pecans, chopped
5 ounces marshmallows, cut in small pieces
Chocolate Frosting, below

1. Melt butter and chocolate together; set aside to cool.
2. Beat eggs, sugar, and extract until thick and piled softly. Add cooled chocolate mixture and beat until blended.
3. Sift flour, baking powder, and salt together; add in thirds to egg-sugar mixture, mixing until blended after each addition. Stir in pecans. Turn into a greased 11x7x1½-inch baking pan and spread evenly.
4. Bake at 325°F 25 minutes.
5. Remove pan to wire rack. Immediately arrange marshmallow pieces over hot brownies.
6. Prepare Chocolate Frosting and spread over the brownies. Cut into 2x1-inch bars.
ABOUT 3 DOZEN COOKIES

Chocolate Frosting

½ cup (3 ounces) semisweet chocolate pieces
2 tablespoons butter or margarine
2 cups confectioners' sugar
⅛ teaspoon salt
½ teaspoon vanilla extract
3 tablespoons double-strength coffee
½ cup flaked coconut

1. Melt chocolate and butter together over hot water. Gradually add the confectioners' sugar, beating well after each addition.
2. Mix in salt and extract. Gradually add coffee, beating constantly. Continue to beat until mixture loses its gloss, about 2 minutes. Stir in coconut until well mixed.
ABOUT 1½ CUPS

Southern Brownies

3 tablespoons shortening
2 ounces (2 squares) unsweetened chocolate
2 egg yolks, well beaten
1 teaspoon vanilla extract
1 cup sugar
½ cup all-purpose flour
½ cup chopped nuts
2 egg whites

1. Melt shortening and chocolate together in a large saucepan; cool.
2. Stir in egg yolks, then extract, sugar, flour, and nuts.
3. Beat egg whites until stiff, not dry, peaks are formed. Blend into chocolate mixture.
4. Spread batter in a well-greased 8x8x2-inch pan.
5. Bake at 350°F 30 minutes, or until a wooden pick comes out clean.
6. Cool completely before cutting.
ABOUT 2 DOZEN COOKIES

Fudgy Brownies

Fudge Sauce, below
½ cup butter
1½ ounce (1½ square)
   unsweetened chocolate
2 eggs
1 cup sugar

¾ cup sifted all-purpose flour
½ teaspoon baking powder
⅛ teaspoon salt
¾ cup pecans, coarsely
   chopped

1. Prepare Fudge Sauce; set aside.
2. Melt butter and chocolate together; set aside to cool.
3. Beat eggs and sugar until thick and piled softly; add cooled chocolate mixture and beat until blended.
4. Sift together flour, baking powder, and salt; add in halves to chocolate mixture, mixing until blended after each addition.
5. Turn half of batter into a greased 9x9x2-inch baking pan and spread evenly.
6. Pour half of Fudge Sauce evenly over batter; remove remaining sauce from heat but allow to stand over hot water.
7. Spread remaining batter over sauce.
8. Bake at 350°F 35 to 40 minutes.
9. Set on wire rack 5 minutes; top with remaining sauce; sprinkle with pecans.
10. Broil 4 inches from source of heat 1 to 2 minutes, or until entire top is bubbly; do not allow sauce to burn. Cool completely before cutting into squares.
3 DOZEN COOKIES

Fudge Sauce

⅓ cup undiluted evaporated
   milk
⅓ cup sugar
4 teaspoons water
½ ounce (½ square)

unsweetened chocolate,
   grated
1½ teaspoons butter
¼ teaspoon vanilla extract
⅛ teaspoon salt

1. Combine evaporated milk, sugar, and water in the top of a double boiler; stirring constantly, bring to boiling. Boil 3 minutes.
2. Remove from heat; blend in remaining ingredients.
3. Set over simmering water until needed.
ABOUT ½ CUP SAUCE

Double Chocolate Squares: Follow recipe for Fudgy Brownies. Omit Fudge Sauce. Increase chocolate to 2 ounces (2 squares). After final addition of ingredients stir in pecans. Omit broiling; cool completely. If desired, spread with Chocolate Glaze II, *below;* decreasing butter to 1 tablespoon; arrange pecan halves on top. Leave in pan until glaze has become firm.

Chocolate Glaze II

4 ounces semisweet
   chocolate, melted
3 cups confectioners' sugar
4 teaspoons dark corn syrup

¼ cup cream
3 tablespoons boiling water
4 teaspoons butter
2 teaspoons vanilla extract

1. Mix all ingredients except extract in a heavy saucepan. Place over low heat and stir constantly until smooth; remove from heat.

2. Stir in extract; cool slightly.
ENOUGH TO GLAZE 3 DOZEN COOKIES

Luxury Mallow-Nut Brownies: Follow recipe for Double Chocolate Squares. Omit Chocolate Glaze and pecan halves. Melt **12 ounces semisweet chocolate pieces** and **2 tablespoons butter.** Cut **12 marshmallows** into quarters (or use 1⅓ cups miniature marshmallows) and stir into melted chocolate with ½ **cup coarsely chopped salted nuts,** such as pecans, pistachios, filberts, or almonds. Immediately spread over the baked brownies; cool.

Hazelnut Cookies

1½ cups flour
½ cup sugar
1 teaspoon ginger

½ cup butter or margarine
1 egg white
¾ cup shelled hazelnuts

1. Mix flour, sugar and ginger in a medium bowl.
2. Cut in butter, add egg white and whole shelled nuts.
3. Blend together and shape into a roll 1½ inches in diameter. Place in refrigerator for several hours or overnight.
4. Preheat oven to 400°F. Cut the roll in even slices with a very sharp knife. Bake on a cookie sheet for about 15 minutes.
ABOUT 3 DOZEN COOKIES

Hazelnut Cookies

Christmas Cookies

3 cups sifted flour
1 teaspoon baking powder
½ teaspoon salt
¾ cup butter

1½ cups sugar
2 eggs
1 teaspoon vanilla
Food coloring

1. Mix flour, baking powder and salt. Beat butter, sugar, eggs and vanilla until light and fluffy. Gradually stir in flour mixture. Mix until smooth and well combined.
2. Form dough into a ball and wrap in waxed paper. Refrigerate for several hours or overnight.
3. Preheat the oven to 375°F. Divide the dough in four parts. Roll out one part at a time, ⅛ inch thick, on a lightly floured surface. Flour cookie cutters and cut out different shapes. Place the cookie on a greased cookie sheet 2 inches apart. Bake 7 to 10 minutes. Decorate with food coloring.
ABOUT 3 DOZEN COOKIES

Dinah Shore Brownies

¾ cup butter or margarine
4 ounces (4 squares) unsweetened chocolate
3 eggs
1½ cups sugar

1½ teaspoons vanilla extract
¾ cup sifted all-purpose flour
½ cup coarsely chopped pecans

1. Melt butter and chocolate together; cool.
2. Beat eggs, sugar, and extract until thick and piled softly. Add cooled chocolate mixture and beat until blended.
3. Mix in flour, then pecans. Turn into a greased 8x8x2-inch baking pan and spread evenly.
4. Bake at 350°F about 35 minutes.
5. Cut into squares.
ABOUT 2 DOZEN COOKIES

Peanut Blonde Brownies

½ cup chunk-style peanut butter
¼ cup butter or margarine
1 teaspoon vanilla extract
1 cup firmly packed light brown sugar

2 eggs
½ cup sifted all-purpose flour
1 cup chopped salted peanuts
Confectioners' sugar

1. Cream peanut butter with butter and extract. Gradually add brown sugar, beating well. Add eggs, one at a time, beating until fluffy after each addition.
2. Add flour in halves, mixing until blended after each addition. Stir in peanuts. Turn into a greased 8x8x2-inch baking pan and spread evenly.
3. Bake at 350°F 30 to 35 minutes.
4. Remove pan to wire rack to cool 5 minutes before cutting into 2-inch squares. Remove from pan and cool on rack. Sift confectioners' sugar over tops.
16 BROWNIES

Triple-Treat Walnut Bars

½ cup butter or margarine
1 package (3 ounces) cream cheese
½ cup firmly packed dark brown sugar
1 cup whole wheat flour
⅓ cup toasted wheat germ
1 package (6 ounces) semisweet chocolate pieces
2 eggs

½ cup honey
⅓ cup whole wheat flour
⅓ cup instant nonfat dry milk
¼ teaspoon salt
¼ teaspoon ground cinnamon
¼ teaspoon ground mace
1½ cups chopped walnuts

1. Cream butter, cheese, and sugar in a bowl until light. Add 1 cup whole wheat flour and wheat germ and mix until smooth. Turn into a greased 13x9x2-inch pan; spread evenly.
2. Bake at 375°F 15 to 18 minutes, until edges are very lightly browned and top is firm.
3. Remove from oven and sprinkle with chocolate. Let stand about 5 minutes, or until chocolate softens, then spread it evenly over baked layer.
4. Combine eggs and honey; beat just until well blended. Add ⅓ cup whole wheat flour, dry milk, salt, cinnamon, mace, and walnuts; mix well. Spoon over the chocolate.
5. Return to oven and bake 18 to 20 minutes, or until top is set. Cool in pan, then cut into bars or diamonds.
ABOUT 3 DOZEN COOKIES

Lemon-Coconut Sours

⅓ cup butter, chilled
¾ cup sifted all-purpose flour
2 eggs
1 teaspoon grated lemon peel
½ teaspoon vanilla extract

1 cup firmly packed light brown sugar
¾ cup flaked coconut
½ cup pecans, coarsely chopped
Lemon Glaze, (page 710)

1. Cut butter into flour until thoroughly blended. Press evenly and firmly into an ungreased 13x9x2-inch baking pan.
2. Bake at 350°F 10 minutes.
3. Meanwhile, beat eggs, lemon peel, extract, and brown sugar until thick. Stir in coconut and pecans. Spread evenly over partially baked layer in pan.
4. Return to oven and bake about 20 minutes.
5. Immediately spread Lemon Glaze evenly over top. When cool, cut into bars or squares.
ABOUT 4 DOZEN COOKIES

Pineapple Bars: Follow recipe for Lemon-Coconut Sours. Substitute **unblanched almonds,** toasted and chopped, for pecans. Omit lemon peel and Lemon Glaze. Fold in **⅓ cup drained crushed pineapple** with coconut and almonds. Bake about 25 minutes.

Walnut Marshmallows

1½ cups walnuts
2 envelopes unflavored
 gelatin
1¼ cups water
2 cups granulated sugar
¼ teaspoon salt
1 teaspoon mint extract
3 to 4 drops green food
 coloring

1. Finely chop walnuts. Pour 1 cup of the nuts into a 9-inch square pan, and pat in an even layer.
2. Soften gelatin in ½ cup of the water. Combine remaining ¾ cup water with the sugar and salt, and cook until syrup reaches 234°F (soft ball stage). Add softened gelatin and let mixture stand until it cools to 130°F.
3. Add mint extract and food coloring. Beat at high speed with an electric mixer until very thick. Turn into the walnut-layered pan. Sprinkle remaining chopped walnuts on top. Let stand several hours or overnight.
4. Cut into squares and roll sides in any walnuts remaining in pan.
ABOUT 1½ POUNDS CANDY

Vanilla Marshmallows: Omit coloring and mint extract. Stir in **2 teaspoons vanilla extract.**

Peppermint Marshmallows: Substitute ¼ **teaspoon peppermint extract** for mint extract, and **red food coloring** for the green food coloring.

Walnut Toffee

2¼ cups walnut pieces
2 cups granulated sugar
½ cup water
½ cup light corn syrup
1 cup butter
1 package (6 ounces)
 semisweet or milk
 chocolate pieces (may use
 half of each)

1. Coarsely chop 1½ cups walnuts for the toffee. Finely chop the remaining walnuts and set aside for the topping.
2. Combine sugar, water, corn syrup, and butter. Bring to boiling, stirring until sugar is dissolved. Cover and cook 5 minutes. Uncover and boil to 300°F (hard crack stage). Remove from heat.
3. Stir in the coarsely chopped walnuts and quickly spread in a buttered 15x10x1-inch jelly-roll pan. Let stand until cooled.
4. Melt chocolate pieces over warm (not hot) water. Spread over cooled toffee. Sprinkle finely chopped walnuts over chocolate. Let stand until chocolate is set (about 30 minutes). Break into pieces.
ABOUT 2½ POUNDS CANDY

Walnut Brittle

2 cups sugar
1 cup light or dark corn
 syrup
½ cup water
1 teaspoon salt
2 tablespoons butter
3 cups coarsely chopped
 walnuts
2 teaspoons baking soda

1. Combine sugar, corn syrup, water, salt, and butter in a saucepan. Cook over moderate heat, stirring until sugar is dissolved. Cover and simmer 5 minutes to wash down sugar crystals from side of pan.
2. Uncover and boil to 300°F (hard crack stage).
3. While syrup is cooking, spread walnuts in a shallow pan and toast lightly in a 300°F oven. When candy reaches 300°F, quickly stir in the warm walnuts and baking soda. Turn at once into an oiled 15x10x1-inch jelly-roll pan (or two oiled cookie sheets if thinner brittle is desired) and spread thin.
4. Let stand until cold, then break into pieces.
ABOUT 2 POUNDS CANDY

Lime-Walnut Divinity

3 cups granulated sugar
1 cup water
¼ cup light corn syrup
¼ teaspoon salt
2 egg whites
1 package (3 ounces) lime-
 flavored gelatin
1 tablespoon lime juice
1 cup coarsely chopped
 walnuts

1. Combine the sugar, water, corn syrup, and salt in a large saucepan. Stir over moderate heat until sugar dissolves.
2. Cover saucepan and boil slowly 3 or 4 minutes, so steam will dissolve any sugar crystals on sides of pan. Uncover and boil over moderate heat until mixture reaches 248°F (firm ball stage).
3. When syrup reaches 248°F continue cooking, but beat egg whites until stiff. Gradually add gelatin, beating to form stiff peaks. Beat in lime juice. Set aside until syrup reaches 260°F (hard ball stage).
4. Begin beating the egg-white mixture and slowly pour in the hot syrup. Do not scrape sides of saucepan. Continue beating until mixture loses its gloss. Quickly stir in walnuts and drop by large teaspoonfuls onto waxed paper, or turn into an oiled 9-inch square pan.
5. Let candy stand until firm, then cut in squares. Store in a tightly covered container.
ABOUT 1 POUND CANDY

Note: For raspberry or strawberry divinity, use **raspberry-** or **strawberry-flavored gelatin,** and substitute **lemon juice** for lime juice.

Drop Mints

1 cup cream white fondant
4 drops peppermint oil
Few drops liquid food color

Place fondant in double boiler, add oil flavoring and food coloring. Heat just until melted. Turn off heat and remove from double boiler. Drop by teaspoonfuls onto a ribbed rubber-mat. Peel off when cool.

These mints are very attractive in pastel colors of pink, green, white, or yellow.

If candy becomes too thick to make smooth mints, place top candy pan back over hot water from double boiler until fondant becomes soft.

Golden Nut Bars

1 cup finely crushed round scalloped crackers
½ cup pecans, finely chopped
1 cup sugar
1 teaspoon baking powder
3 egg whites
¼ teaspoon salt

1. Blend crumbs, pecans, sugar, and baking powder.
2. Beat egg whites and salt until stiff, not dry, peaks are formed; fold in the crumb mixture, a small amount at a time.
3. Turn into an ungreased 11x7x1½-inch baking pan and spread evenly.
4. Bake at 350°F 25 minutes.
5. Cool completely before cutting into bars.
ABOUT 3 DOZEN COOKIES

Aristocrats

¾ cup butter
1 teaspoon vanilla extract
⅔ cup sugar
1 egg
2 cups sifted cake flour
⅔ cup apricot preserves
Pecan Topping

1. Cream butter with extract; add sugar gradually, creaming until fluffy. Add egg and beat thoroughly.
2. Add flour in fourths, mixing until blended after each addition.
3. Turn dough into a lightly greased 11x7x1½-inch baking pan and spread evenly. Spread the apricot preserves over dough.
4. Bake at 350°F 20 to 25 minutes, or until edges are lightly browned. Remove pan to wire rack (do not remove cookie layer from pan).
5. Prepare Pecan Topping and spread evenly over cooled cookie layer. Chill 2 to 3 hours.
6. Cut into strips, about 2½x¾-inch. Place strips about ½ inch apart on cookie sheets.
7. Bake at 375°F 15 minutes, or until topping is delicately browned.
ABOUT 4 DOZEN COOKIES

Pecan Topping: Beat **1 egg white** with ⅛ **teaspoon salt** until frothy. Add ⅔ **cup sugar** and **2 teaspoons flour** gradually, beating thoroughly after each addtion. Beat until stiff peaks are formed. Fold in ⅔ **cup pecans,** finely chopped.

Crown Jewels

Toppings, below
1 cup butter or margarine
½ teaspoon grated orange peel
½ cup sugar
2 hard-cooked egg yolks, sieved
2 cups sifted all-purpose flour

1. Prepare Toppings.
2. Cream butter with orange peel. Gradually add sugar, beating until fluffy.
3. Blend in sieved hard-cooked egg yolks. Add flour in fourths, mixing well after each addition.
4. Press dough firmly onto bottom of ungreased 15x10x1-inch jelly roll pan.
5. Bake at 350°F 20 minutes.
6. While still warm, spread with Date Topping and then Candied Fruit Topping. Cool thoroughly and cut into fancy shapes.
ABOUT 3 DOZEN COOKIES

Date Topping: Mix **1 cup (about 7 ounces) pitted dates,** finely chopped, with ¼ **cup orange juice** in the top of a double boiler. Heat, covered, over simmering water 10 minutes, stirring occasionally; cool.

Candied Fruit Topping: Mix ½ **pound (1⅔ cups) red and green candied pineapple,** finely chopped, ¼ **pound candied red cherries (⅔ cup),** finely chopped, **2 ounces candied orange peel (⅓ cup),** finely chopped, and ⅓ **cup rum** in the top of a double boiler. Heat, covered, over simmering water 30 minutes, stirring occasionally; cool slightly.

Lacy Almond Crisps

⅓ cup blanched almonds, grated
¼ cup sugar
2 teaspoons flour
3 tablespoons butter or margarine
1 tablespoon milk

1. Mix almonds, sugar, and flour in a bowl. Blend in butter and milk.
2. Drop batter by teaspoonfuls about 4 inches apart onto greased and lightly floured cookie sheets.
3. Bake at 350°F 6 to 7 minutes, or until golden brown.
4. Let set about 1 minute; carefully remove with a spatula to a wire rack. Cool completely. Store in an airtight container.
ABOUT 2 DOZEN 3-INCH COOKIES

Lacy Filbert Crisps: Follow recipe for Lacy Almond Crisps. Substitute ⅓ **cup filberts,** grated, for the almonds. Add ¼ **teaspoon ground mace.**

Chocolate Fudge

⅔ cup milk or cream
2 cups sugar
2 ounces (2 squares) unsweetened chocolate, chopped

2 tablespoons light corn syrup
2 tablespoons butter
1 teaspoon vanilla extract

1. Combine milk, sugar, chocolate, corn syrup, and butter in a saucepan and heat slowly, stirring until sugar is dissolved. Wash down any sugar crystals. Set candy thermometer in place. Cook, stirring occasionally, until the temperature reaches 236°F (soft-ball stage).
2. Add a **few grains salt** and the extract; cool, without stirring, to lukewarm (about 110°F).
3. Beat until creamy and mixture starts to lose its shine. Pour into buttered 8x8-inch square pan and mark into squares.
ABOUT 1¼ POUNDS

Note: If mixture becomes too stiff to pour, it may be kneaded, or a little **cream** may be added.

White Fudge: Follow recipe for Chocolate Fudge. Omit chocolate. Cook to 238°F.

Ribbon Fudge: Follow recipe for Chocolate Fudge. Add ½ **cup chopped nuts**; pour into deep square pan. Make a double recipe of White Fudge. When cooked to 236°F, turn half into another pan. To one add **1 or 2 drops red food coloring** and ½ **cup cut maraschino cherries.** When the White Fudge starts to set up, spread over Chocolate Fudge; when pink fudge is beaten, spread it over white layer.

Spicy Walnut Diamonds

2½ cups sifted all-purpose flour
2 tablespoons cocoa
1½ teaspoons baking powder
1 teaspoon salt
½ teaspoon ground nutmeg
¼ teaspoon ground cloves
2 cups firmly packed brown sugar

3 eggs
½ cup honey
½ cup butter or margarine, melted
1½ cups chopped walnuts (1 cup medium and ½ cup fine)
½ cup confectioners' sugar
2 to 3 teaspoons milk

1. Blend flour, cocoa, baking powder, salt, nutmeg, and cloves.
2. Combine brown sugar and eggs in a large bowl; beat until well blended and light. Add honey, butter, and flour mixture and mix until smooth.
3. Stir in the 1 cup medium walnuts, and spread evenly in a greased 15x10x1-inch jelly-roll pan. Sprinkle the ½ cup fine walnuts over top.
4. Bake at 375°F about 20 minutes, or just until top springs back when touched lightly in center. Cool in pan.
5. Mix confectioners' sugar and enough milk to make a smooth, thin glaze. Spread over cooled layer. Cut into diamonds or bars.
ABOUT 4 DOZEN COOKIES

Luscious Lemon Bars

1 cup sifted all-purpose flour
¼ cup confectioners' sugar
½ cup butter, chilled
1 cup sugar
2 tablespoons flour

½ teaspoon baking powder
3 eggs, well beaten
½ cup unstrained lemon juice

1. Blend the 1 cup flour and confectioners' sugar in a bowl. Cut in the butter until blended. Firmly and evenly press into an ungreased 9x9x2-inch baking pan.
2. Bake at 350°F about 15 minutes.
3. Meanwhile, combine sugar, 2 tablespoons flour, and baking powder; blend into beaten eggs along with the lemon juice.
4. Pour mixture over crust in pan. Return to oven and bake 25 minutes.
5. Remove to wire rack to cool. Spread a thin **confectioners' sugar icing** and top with **toasted sliced almonds**. Cut into bars.
ABOUT 3 DOZEN COOKIES

Almond Macaroons

½ pound almond paste, cut in pieces
⅓ cup (about 3) egg whites,

slightly beaten
¾ teaspoon vanilla extract
1 cup sugar

1. Work almond paste until softened. Add the egg whites gradually, mixing thoroughly.
2. Stir in extract. Add sugar in halves, mixing until blended after each addition.
3. Drop by rounded teaspoonfuls onto cookie sheets lined with unglazed paper (baking parchment or brown).
4. Bake at 300°F about 25 minutes.
ABOUT 3 DOZEN COOKIES

Cocoa Almond Bars Supreme

⅔ cup sifted all-purpose flour
⅓ cup Dutch process cocoa
½ teaspoon baking powder
¼ teaspoon salt
½ cup butter
¼ cup almond paste
1½ teaspoons vanilla extract
½ teaspoon almond extract

¾ cup sugar
1 egg
1 egg yolk
1 cup toasted blanched almonds, coarsely chopped
1 egg white
¼ teaspoon cream of tartar
¼ cup sugar

1. Blend flour, cocoa, baking powder, and salt; set aside.
2. Cream butter with almond paste and extracts until thoroughly blended. Add ¾ cup sugar gradually, beating until fluffy. Add egg and egg yolk; beat vigorously.
3. Mixing until blended after each addition, add dry mixture in thirds, then ½ cup of the almonds. Turn into a lightly grased 8x8x2-inch baking pan.
4. Beat egg white and cream of tartar until frothy. Add ¼ cup sugar gradually, continuing to beat until stiff peaks are formed. Fold in remaining almonds. Spread over batter in pan.
5. Bake at 350°F 35 to 40 minutes, or until meringue is lightly browned.
6. When thoroughly cooled cut into 2x1-inch bars.
2½ DOZEN COOKIES

Pastel Candied Fruit Peel

3 large grapefruit or 6 oranges (free from blemishes)
Water
2 packages (3 ounces each) or 1 package (6 ounces) fruit-flavored gelatin (any flavor)
2 cups water
1 cup sugar
1 large stick cinnamon
½ teaspoon whole cloves
1 cup sugar

1. Cut grapefruit in halves. Squeeze out juice, strain, and use as desired.
2. Cover grapefruit rinds with water in a saucepan. Cover pan and bring to boiling. Boil 15 minutes; drain. Using a spoon, carefully remove any remaining pulp and white membrane.
3. Using scissors or a sharp knife, cut the peel into thin strips, about ¼ inch wide, or cut into fancy shapes using hors d'oeuvres cutters. Place in a saucepan and cover with water. Boil, covered, 15 minutes, or until easily pierced with a fork. Drain.
4. Mix gelatin with 2 cups water and 1 cup sugar in a heavy 10-inch skillet. Add the fruit peel and slices, stirring to coat with the syrup. Bring to boiling. Reduce heat and continue cooking, stirring occasionally, until peels are translucent and syrup is almost absorbed (about 50 minutes). Remove from heat.
5. Lift peels from the skillet with a fork or slotted spoon and place in a single layer on wire racks over trays to drain. Let stand 1 hour or more until surface is dried. Sprinkle with 1 cup sugar (use more if needed) and toss lightly. Arrange pieces in a single layer on waxed-paper-lined trays. Let dry about 12 hours or overnight. Store in a tightly covered container.
ABOUT 1½ POUNDS

Banana-Bran Cookies

¾ cup sifted all-purpose flour
½ teaspoon baking powder
¼ teaspoon baking soda
¼ teaspoon salt
½ teaspoon ground cinnamon
⅛ teaspoon ground allspice
⅛ teaspoon ground cloves
1 cup bran flakes
½ cup mashed banana
⅓ cup butter
½ cup sugar
1 egg
¼ cup coarsely chopped pecans

1. Sift flour, baking powder, baking soda, salt, and spices together; set aside.
2. Combine bran flakes and the banana; set aside.
3. Cream butter; add sugar gradually, beating until fluffy. Add egg and beat thoroughly.
4. Add dry ingredients to creamed mixture alternately with the banana mixture, mixing until blended after each addition. Stir in pecans.
5. Drop by slightly rounded teaspoons onto greased cookie sheets.
6. Bake at 375°F 10 to 12 minutes.
ABOUT 4 DOZEN COOKIES

Chocolate Banana-Bran Cookies: Follow recipe for Banana-Bran Cookies. Stir in ½ **cup semisweet chocolate pieces** with the nuts.

Banana Spice Cookies: Follow recipe for Banana-Bran Cookies. Increase flour to ¾ cup plus 2 tablespoons. Decrease cinnamon to ¼ teaspoon. Omit allspice and bran flakes. Substitute **vegetable shortening** for butter. Increase pecans to ½ cup. Drop by tablespoonfuls onto the cookie sheets. If desired, frost cooled cookies with a **Butter Cream Frosting,** *see below,* flavored with a few drops **banana extract.**

Bran Flake Drops: Follow recipe for Banana-Bran Cookies. Increase baking powder to 1 teaspoon; omit baking soda. Omit banana; combine bran flakes with **¼ cup milk.**

Butter Cream Frosting

½ cup butter
½ teaspoon almond extract
5 cups confectioners' sugar
4 to 5 tablespoons milk or cream

Cream butter with extract. Alternately add confectioners' sugar and milk, beating thoroughly after each addition. Beat until of spreading consistency.

BEVERAGES

Rompope

1 quart milk
1 cup sugar
1 stick cinnamon
¼ cup finely ground almonds
1 teaspoon vanilla extract
8 egg yolks
1 cup light rum, brandy, or grain alcohol

1. Put milk, sugar, and cinnamon stick into a saucepan. Heat to simmering, and simmer gently, stirring constantly, about 10 minutes.
2. Remove from heat and remove cinnamon stick. Add almonds and vanilla extract.
3. Beat egg yolks until thick and lemon-colored. Gradually beat into milk. Return to heat and cook over low heat, stirring constantly, until mixture coats a spoon. Cool to room temperature.
4. Mix in rum and pour into a large bottle with screw lid. Refrigerate until ready to serve.
ABOUT 1½ QUARTS

Grapefruit Spritzer

1 can (6 ounces) frozen concentrated grapefruit juice, thawed
2½ to 3 cups chilled club soda

Pour concentrated grapefruit juice into a pitcher and add chilled club soda slowly; mix well.
ABOUT 4 SERVINGS

Spicy Iced Tea

1 cup water
1 cup sugar
⅛ teaspoon ground nutmeg
6 whole cloves
4 whole allspice
4 pieces (2 inches thick) stick cinnamon
3 tablespoons tea or 3 to 5 tea bags

1. Combine all ingredients except tea in a saucepan. Stir over low heat until sugar is dissolved. Cover tightly and simmer 20 minutes. Strain, cool, and chill thoroughly.
2. Bring 2 cups freshly drawn cold water to a full rolling boil in a saucepan. Remove from heat and immediately add the tea; stir. Let tea steep 5 minutes. Stir and drain into a pitcher containing 2 cups cold water. (Remove tea bags, if used, and omit straining.) Blend in the spiced syrup.
3. Pour into ice-filled glasses. Serve with thin slices of **lime** or **lemon.**
ABOUT 1 QUART

Tangy Cider Punch

½ cup water
¼ cup sugar
1 quart apple cider or juice
½ cup orange juice
¼ cup lemon juice

1. Cook water and sugar together in saucepan, stirring until sugar is dissolved. Boil 5 minutes; cool.
2. Combine cider, orange and lemon juices in a pitcher. Add cooled syrup and serve over ice cubes.
ABOUT 5 CUPS PUNCH

Note: For frozen "slush," put punch in freezer. When crystals start to form, remove from freezer and stir. Stir several times during freezing; serve semi-frozen in cups.

Sangría

⅓ cup lime juice
½ cup orange juice
½ cup sugar

1 bottle (⅘ quart) dry red wine
Ice cubes

1. Combine lime and orange juices with sugar; stir until sugar is dissolved. Stir into wine in a pitcher. Chill before serving.
2. To serve, pour over ice cubes in tall glasses.
ABOUT 1 QUART

Tía María

2 cups water
4 cups sugar
5 tablespoons instant coffee

1 tablespoon vanilla extract
1 bottle (⅘ quart) vodka or grain alcohol

1. Combine water and sugar in saucepan. Bring to boiling, reduce heat, and simmer about 20 minutes.
2. Remove from heat; stir in coffee and vanilla extract, then vodka.
3. Pour into a bottle with a screw lid and store 1 month before using.
ABOUT 5 CUPS

Glögg

1 cup (about 5 ounces) almonds
1 bottle (25 ounces) Aquavit
1 bottle (25 ounces) claret
6 2½-inch cinnamon sticks
1 cup (about 4 ounces) dark

seedless raisins
6 pieces candied orange or lemon peel
12 whole cloves
12 cardamom seeds, peeled
1 cup loaf sugar

1. Blanch almonds.
2. Empty aquavit and claret into a large saucepan or sauce pot.
3. Add the almonds, cinnamon sticks, raisins, orange or lemon peel, whole cloves and cardamom seeds.
4. Bring slowly to boiling. Reduce heat and simmer 10 minutes. Remove saucepan from heat. Put loaf sugar into a large sieve.
5. Place sieve over saucepan. Using a ladle or large spoon, pour some of the mixture from the saucepan over the sugar. Ignite the sugar with a match. Continue to pour the liquid over the sugar until the sugar has completely melted. The liquid will be flaming. If necessary, extinguish flame by placing cover over saucepan.
6. Serve Glögg hot in mugs or punch glasses. Be sure there are some raisins and almonds in each portion.
10 TO 15 RAISINS

Note: Glögg may be prepared days in advance and stored in bottles. When ready to serve, heat thoroughly (do not boil). Or if there is some Glögg left it may be stored for future use.

Wassail Bowl

12 small, firm baking apples (such as Jonathans)
¾ cup firmly packed brown sugar
¾ teaspoon nutmeg
¾ teaspoon cinnamon
2 tablespoons butter or margarine
1 cup sugar
1 cup water
2 cups water
1 tablespoon ginger

1 tablespoon nutmeg
6 whole cloves
6 whole allspice
2 2-inch sticks cinnamon
1 gallon apple cider
3 cups sugar
1½ cups firmly packed brown sugar
12 egg yolks
12 egg whites
1 cup brandy

1. *For Baked Apples* – Butter two baking dishes and insides of covers.
2. Wash and core apples.
3. Core by inserting corer in stem end; cut toward blossom end, pushing halfway into apple. Remove corer and insert in opposite end. Make a complete turn with corer in both ends. Remove all the core. Pare about 1-inch strip of peel at the stem end of each apple.
4. Arrange apples in baking dishes, pared sides up. Fill each with 2 to 3 teaspoons of a mixture of ¾ cup brown sugar, ¾ teaspoon nutmeg and ¾ teaspoon cinnamon, and top each with one-half teaspoon of butter or margarine.
5. Combine 1 cup sugar and water in a saucepan and bring to boiling.
6. Pour over apples in baking dish.
7. Cover and bake at 350°F 30 to 40 minutes or until tender when pierced with a fork. Baste every 5 minutes for first 15 minutes, and then every 15 minutes.
8. *For Wassail* – Stir 2 cups water, ginger, 1 tablespoon nutmeg, cloves, allspice and 2 2-inch sticks cinnamon together in saucepan.
9. Cover and bring to boiling; boil for 10 minutes.
10. Combine apple cider, 3 cups sugar, and 1½ cups brown sugar in 6-quart saucepan.
11. Simmer over low heat, stirring frequently. Stir in water-spice mixture and continue cooking 5 to 10 minutes.
12. Meanwhile, beat egg yolks until very thick and lemon-colored.
13. Beat egg whites until rounded peaks are formed.
14. Slide beaten egg whites into punch bowl. Pour beaten egg yolks over egg whites. Fold together. Add the hot mixture very slowly, stirring constantly. Stir in brandy.
15. Float Baked Apples in hot beverage. Serve hot.
ABOUT 50 SERVINGS

Note: For a Hot Cider Punch, omit Baked Apples, egg yolks and egg whites.

Pitcher of Sunshine

Mix equal amounts of chilled orange juice (either fresh or reconstituted frozen juice) with chilled champagne or ginger ale. If desired, garnish with orange slices and serve immediately in tall glasses.

Thanksgiving Wine Bowl

Thanksgiving Wine Bowl

2 cups apple cider or apple
  juice
½ cup sugar

2 sticks cinnamon
2 dozen whole cloves
2 quarts dry white wine

1. Combine cider and sugar in a large porcelain saucepan.
2. In a bag of cheesecloth, tie together cinnamon and cloves. Add to ingredients in saucepan and boil 5 minutes.
3. Remove spices from cider. Add wine. Cook only until mixture is thoroughly warm; do not boil.
4. Serve in heatproof punch bowl and ladle into heatproof punch cups with more cinnamon sticks for stirrers, if desired.
16 TO 20 SERVINGS

Peach Rum

3 pounds peaches, halved,
  pitted, and sliced
4 cups packed brown sugar

Grated peel of 1 lime
Amber rum (about 6 cups)

1. Put ingredients into a 1-gallon container; using enough rum to fill.
2. Seal container and place on a sunny window sill, occasionally turning it.
3. After 3 months, pour off the liquor and serve in small cordial glasses.
MAKES 3 QUARTS

Strawberry Thickmalts

2 pints ripe strawberries
1 quart vanilla ice cream,

softened
¼ cup malted milk powder

1. Set out an electric blender; set four tall glasses in refrigerator or freezer to chill.
2. Rinse and drain the strawberries.
3. Reserve a few whole strawberries to use for garnish. Hull the remaining berries and purée in the blender. Strain through a double thickness of cheesecloth to remove seeds.
4. Return purée to blender container and add the softened vanilla ice cream and malted milk powder.
5. Blend until smooth. Place blender container in freezer for about 1 hour.
6. Before serving the thickmalts, blend a few seconds until smooth. Spoon into the chilled glasses and serve with long-handled spoons.
7. Garnish malts with **whole strawberries.**
FOUR 8-OUNCE SERVINGS

Note: If desired, omit malted milk powder.

Strawberry Thickmelt

Lemonade

½ cup lemon juice 3 to 4 cups water
½ to ¾ cup sugar

1. Mix lemon juice and sugar. Stir until sugar melts. Add water.
2. Serve ice cold with crushed ice or ice cubes.
MAKES 1 QUART

Mixed Fruit Punch

1 can pineapple juice
1 can grapefruit juice
1 can frozen concentrated
 orange juice
4 to 6 cups water
Juice of 1 lemon

1 bottle club soda
1 to 2 lemons or oranges,
 sliced
1 package frozen strawberries or grapes

1. Mix all ingredients.

Frosty Sours

1 can (6 ounces) frozen
 orange juice concentrate
2 juice cans water
1 juice can bourbon
1 can (5¾ ounces) frozen

lemon juice
2 egg whites
¼ cup sugar
Orange slices
Mint slices

Combine all ingredients except orange slices and mint sprigs in an electric blender. Blend at low speed until smooth, then at high speed until frothy. Pour into ice-filled glasses. Garnish with orange slices and mint sprigs.
TEN 4-OUNCE SERVINGS

Sugar Syrup

4 cups sugar 1 cup water

1. Combine sugar and water in a saucepan. Stir over low heat until sugar is dissolved. Reduce heat and simmer until liquid is clear (about 3 minutes).
2. Cool and use as needed. Store in a glass jar in refrigerator.
ABOUT 3¼ CUPS

Rum Punch

Cracked ice
2 cups amber rum
¼ cup lime juice
2 jiggers grenadine

2 jiggers cane or maple
 syrup
1 jigger orgeat
5 dashes Angostura bitters

1. Half fill a pitcher with cracked ice and add ingredients.
2. Pour punch over cracked ice in highball glasses. Garnish with a stirrer of **peeled sugar cane,** if available.

Eggnog

6 egg yolks
¼ cup sugar
3 tablespoons rum extract
1 teaspoon vanilla extract

1½ cups chilled cream
6 egg whites
5 tablespoons sugar
Nutmeg

1. Beat egg yolks, sugar, rum extract and vanilla extract until very thick and lemon-colored.
2. Add chilled cream gradually and continue to beat until blended.
3. Set aside.
4. Beat egg whites until frothy.
5. Add sugar gradually, beating well after each addition.
6. Beat until very stiff peaks are formed.
7. Gently fold egg whites into egg yolk mixture until blended. Chill in refrigerator.
8. Pour into punch bowl and gently mix before serving. Ladle into serving cups and sprinkle lightly with nutmeg.
ABOUT 16 SERVINGS

Cranberry Nog: Follow recipe for Eggnog. Add 4 cups (2 pints) cranberry juice. Omit rum extract.

Holiday Eggnog

6 egg yolks
2 cups sugar
1 pint bourbon
1 cup Jamaica rum
1 cup brandy

3 pints heavy cream
1 pint milk
6 egg whites
Nutmeg

1. Beat egg yolks and sugar until very thick and lemon colored.
2. Slowly stir in bourbon, Jamaica rum and brandy.
3. Blend in heavy cream and milk.
4. Beat egg whites until stiff, not dry, peaks are formed.
5. Gently fold egg whites into egg yolk mixture. Pour into punch bowl, cover and chill in refrigerator.
6. Before serving, lightly sprinkle each portion with nutmeg.
ABOUT 25 SERVINGS

Belgian Hot Beer and Wine

1 can or bottle (12 ounces)
 beer
1½ cups white wine
⅓ cup sugar
1 cinnamon stick

Peel of ½ lemon, cut in
 strips
1 tablespoon cornstarch
½ cup warm milk
2 egg yolks

1. Heat beer, wine, sugar, cinnamon, and lemon peel for 10 to 15 minutes; do not simmer or boil.
2. In a heavy saucepan, mix cornstarch and milk; beat in egg yolks. Cook slowly, stirring constantly, until thickened.
3. Stir hot beer into egg mixture. Serve immediately in small punch cups.
3 CUPS; 6 SERVINGS

Fruit Punch

2 cups orange juice	thawed
2 cups pineapple juice	1 cup papaya juice
2 cups grapefruit juice	Sugar (optional)
2 cups grenadine or 1 small	Ice block
can frozen Samoa punch,	2 bottles ginger beer, chilled

1. Mix juices and sweeten to taste. Chill.
2. Pour chilled ingredients over ice block in a punch bowl. Just before serving, add ginger beer.
MAKES 3 QUARTS

Beer Nog

3 eggs
1 can or bottle (12 ounces) beer
1½ cups milk
⅓ cup sugar
⅛ teaspoon nutmeg

Beat eggs until frothy. Add remaining ingredients. Serve cold; or heat slightly for serving warm; do not simmer or boil. Sprinkle with nutmeg.

Cold Beer Punch

3 bottles or cans (12 ounces each) beer, chilled
¼ cup sherry
¼ cup brandy
¼ cup bar sugar or confectioners' sugar
3 tablespoons lemon juice
Few pieces lemon peel
Dash nutmeg

Mix all ingredients in a pitcher. Pour over ice in low glasses or punch cups. Sprinkle with nutmeg.
5 CUPS

Shandy Tang

½ cup beer or ale
½ cup lemon-lime soda
Ice cubes

Pour beer and soda over ice cubes in a tall glass. Stir lightly. May also be served without ice; have ingredients well chilled.
1 SERVING

American Colonial Flip

2 cans or bottles (12 ounces each) beer
½ cup gin, rum, or brandy
3 eggs
¼ cup sugar
Grated nutmeg

1. Heat beer and gin, if desired, but do not boil. Pour into a large pitcher.
2. Beat eggs with sugar until thick; pour into a second pitcher. Gradually add beer mixture to eggs, stirring constantly.
3. Froth by carefully and quickly pouring back and forth between the two pitchers. Pour into mugs.
3 OR 4 SERVINGS

Old-fashioned Posset

1½ cups milk
¼ cup sugar
¼ teaspoon cinnamon
1 can or bottle (12 ounces) ale or beer
2 to 3 toast squares or stars

1. Heat milk with sugar and cinnamon until sugar is dissolved.
2. Add ale; heat but do not simmer or boil.
3. Pour into 2 or 3 mugs. Float toast on top. If desired, increase recipe and serve from punch bowl.
2 OR 3 SERVINGS

Demitasse

Using ½ measuring cup water per serving, prepare Drip Coffee or any variation. Serve hot in demitasse or after-dinner cups.

Coffee for Twenty

Mix **½ pound regular grind coffee** with **1 egg and crushed egg shell.** Tie loosely in fine cheesecloth or put into a lightweight muslin bag. Put into a large kettle with **1 gallon freshly drawn cold water.** Cover tightly. Set over low heat and bring very slowly to boiling. Boil 3 to 5 minutes. Taste to test strength. Remove bag when coffee is desired strength. Cover kettle and let stand 10 to 15 minutes over low heat without boiling.

Café l'Orange

2 medium-sized oranges, sliced
Whole cloves
8 cups (coffee-cup size) hot
coffee
Sweetened whipped cream
Brown sugar
Ground cinnamon

1. Stud each orange slice with 4 cloves; pour hot coffee over them and allow to steep for 30 minutes. Discard orange slices and cloves.
2. Reheat coffee. Pour coffee into a handsome coffeepot or carafe.
3. Accompany with bowls of the whipped cream and brown sugar and a shaker of cinnamon so that guests may flavor their coffee as desired.
8 SERVINGS

Café Au Lait

For each cup of freshly brewed **coffee,** scald an equal measure of rich **milk.** Simultaneously pour hot coffee and hot milk into each cup. Sweeten if desired.

Boston Coffee: Serve **coffee** and **cream** in equal proportions.

Vienna Coffee: Serve **coffee** with **whipped cream.**

Hot Tea

Heat teapot thoroughly by filling with boiling water. Pour off water; put into pot **1 rounded teaspoon loose black tea** or **1 tea bag** for each cup of tea to be brewed, or use 1 large tea bag for about 4 cups tea. For each cup of tea, pour **1 cup briskly boiling freshly drawn water** into the teapot. Cover pot and allow tea to steep 3 to 5 minutes. Stir the brew and strain the tea into each teacup as it is poured or remove tea bag or bags before pouring.

Irish Coffee

24 ounces hot coffee	4 jiggers Irish whiskey
4 teaspoons sugar	2 jiggers Kahlua
1 cup heavy cream, whipped	Cocoa

1. Fill mugs ¾ full with coffee.
2. Add 1 teaspoon sugar for each mug.
3. Pour 1 jigger Irish whiskey and 1 jigger Kahlua into the coffee. Top with whipped cream. Sprinkle with cocoa.
SERVES 4

Hot Ginger Tea

4 tea bags	ginger, cut in very thin
2 pieces (3 inches each) stick	slices
cinnamon	3 to 4 tablespoons sugar
8 whole cloves	6 cups boiling water
2 large pieces crystallized	

1. Put the tea bags, cinnamon sticks, cloves, crystallized ginger, and sugar into a large teapot. Pour on boiling water; allow to steep 3 minutes. Remove tea bags and steep for 5 minutes.
2. To serve, pour tea into cups and float a quarter slice of **orange** in each cup.
ABOUT 8 SERVINGS

White Wine Cooler

White Wine Cooler

1 bottle dry white wine	1 cucumber, sliced
Ice	1 bottle (28 ounces)
1 lemon, sliced	sparkling water

Pour wine over ice and add lemon and cucumber. Mix in the soda just before serving.

Dressy Tea

1 quart freshly drawn water	2 rounded teaspoons tea or 2
½ cup sugar	prepared tea bags
4 whole cloves	1 cup orange juice
1 stick cinnamon	

1. Combine water, sugar, cloves, and cinnamon in a 2-quart saucepan. Set over medium heat and stir until sugar is dissolved. Increase heat and bring mixture to boiling.
2. Put tea into preheated teapot. Pour in the spice mixture. Cover and let tea steep 3 to 5 minutes.
3. Heat orange juice until hot. Strain tea and return to teapot. Mix in the hot orange juice. Serve with **lemon slices.**
ABOUT 6 SERVINGS

Hot Cocoa

5 to 6 tablespoons cocoa,	1 cup water
sieved	3 cups milk
5 to 6 tablespoons sugar	½ teaspoon vanilla extract
¼ teaspoon salt	

1. Mix cocoa, sugar, and salt in a heavy saucepan. Blend in the water. Boil gently 2 minutes over direct heat, stirring until slightly thickened.
2. Stir in the milk, heating slowly until scalding hot. Remove from heat. Cover and keep hot, if necessary, over hot water.
3. Just before serving, mix in the extract. Beat with hand rotary or electric beater until foamy. Serve steaming hot, plain or with **whipped cream, marshmallow cream,** or **marshmallows.**
6 SERVINGS

Hot Chocolate

2½ cups milk, scalded	¼ cup sugar
2 ounces (2 squares)	1 teaspoon vanilla extract
unsweetened chocolate,	Dash salt
quartered	

1. Rinse an electric blender container with hot water.
2. Put into container about ½ cup scalded milk, chocolate, sugar, extract, and salt. Cover and blend about 1 minute, or until smooth and color is even throughout.
3. Add remaining scalded milk and blend until thoroughly mixed. Serve immediately.
4 SERVINGS

Irish Coffee

Champagne Bowl

1 bottle Champagne, Canary wine or other sparkling wine
1 bottle club soda
3 ounces maraschino or curaçao liqueur
1 finely sliced lemon
Ice cubes

1. Mix wine, club soda and liqueur.
2. Add ice cubes, lemon slices and serve.

Mexican Chocolate I

4 ounces sweet chocolate
4 cups milk
1 teaspoon ground cinnamon

1. Combine all ingredients in a heavy saucepan. Cook over medium heat, stirring frequently, until chocolate is melted and mixture is heated.
2. Beat with a hand rotary beater or mix in an electric blender until frothy, about 1 minute. Serve steaming hot.
6 TO 8 SERVINGS

Mexican Chocolate II

2 ounces (2 squares) unsweetened chocolate
½ cup strong coffee
½ cup sugar
1 teaspoon ground cinnamon
$\frac{1}{16}$ teaspoon ground allspice
Few grains salt
3 cups milk
1½ teaspoons vanilla extract
Whipped cream

1. Heat chocolate and coffee together in a heavy saucepan, stirring until chocolate is melted and mixture is smooth. Cook 2 minutes, stirring constantly.
2. Mix in the sugar, cinnamon, allspice, and salt. Gradually add the milk, stirring until blended; heat thoroughly.
3. Remove from heat; blend in extract. Top each serving with whipped cream.
ABOUT 4 SERVINGS

Chocolate Java

3 ounces (3 squares) unsweetened chocolate
3 cups strong coffee
½ cup sugar
2 cups milk
4 egg yolks
¼ cup sugar
4 egg whites
¼ cup sugar

1. Combine chocolate, coffee, and ½ cup sugar in a saucepan. Set over low heat and stir constantly until chocolate is melted. Bring rapidly to boiling, stirring constantly. Reduce heat; cook and stir 3 minutes.
2. Remove from heat. Stir in the milk; chill thoroughly.
3. Beat egg yolks and ¼ cup sugar together until very thick. Gradually blend in the chilled chocolate mixture.
4. Beat egg whites until frothy; gradually add ¼ cup sugar, beating until rounded peaks are formed. Turn onto the chocolate mixture and slowly beat together until just blended. Chill. Serve topped with **Whipped Cream.**
ABOUT 10 SERVINGS

Iced Coffee

Using ½ measuring cup water per standard measure of coffee, prepare Drip Coffee, or any variation. Fill tall glasses to brim with ice cubes. Pour the hot coffee over the ice. Serve with **granulated** or **confectioners' sugar, sugar syrup, cream,** or **whipped cream** sprinkled with **ground cinnamon.**

Hot Apricot Nip

2 tablespoons sugar
4 whole cloves
1 piece (3 inches) stick cinnamon
1 cup water
1½ cups (12-ounce can) apricot nectar
2 tablespoons lemon juice

1. Combine sugar cloves, cinnamon stick, and water in a small saucepan. Cook and stir over low heat until sugar is dissolved. Increase heat to boiling and cook gently 5 minutes.
2. Add apricot nectar and continue to heat until very hot. Remove spices; stir in lemon juice and serve at once.
ABOUT 4 SERVINGS

Hot Spiced Cider

2 quarts apple cider
1 teaspoon whole cloves
1 teaspoon whole allspice
2 pieces (3 inches each) stick
cinnamon
½ cup firmly packed light brown sugar
Few grains salt

Bring all ingredients to boiling in a large saucepan; simmer, covered, 30 minutes. Remove spices. Serve hot, garnished with slices of unpared **red apples.**
ABOUT 2 QUARTS

Iced Cinnamon Coffee

4 cups strong coffee (use 2 to 4 teaspoons instant coffee to 1 cup boiling water)
1 piece (3 inches) stick cin-
namon, broken in pieces
½ cup heavy cream
Coffee Syrup.

1. Pour hot coffee over cinnamon pieces; cover and let stand about 1 hour.
2. Remove cinnamon and stir in the cream. Chill thoroughly.
3. To serve, pour into ice-filled glasses. Stir in desired amount of Coffee Syrup. If desired, top with **sweetened whipped cream** and sprinkle with **ground cinnamon.** Use **cinnamon sticks** as stirrers.
ABOUT 4 SERVINGS

Butterscotch Benchwarmer

4 cups milk
½ cup butterscotch pieces
Miniature marshmallows

1. Combine milk and butterscotch pieces in a 2-quart saucepan.
2. Heat until butterscotch pieces are melted, stirring occasionally.
3. Serve topped with marshmallows.
ABOUT 1 QUART BEVERAGE

Cheerleaders' Choice

½ cup water
¼ cup red cinnamon candies
¼ cup sugar
2 tablespoons whole cloves
⅛ teaspoon salt
4 cups milk
Cinnamon sticks

1. Combine water, cinnamon candies, sugar, whole cloves, and salt in a 2-quart saucepan.
2. Simmer over low heat about 5 minutes, stirring occasionally.
3. Add milk and heat to serving temperature.
4. Pour into four glasses with handles, or mugs. Serve with cinnamon sticks.
ABOUT 1 QUART BEVERAGE

Iced Orange Mocha

4 cups strong coffee (use 4 tablespoons instant coffee to 4 cups hot water)
2 medium-sized oranges, sliced
6 tablespoons sugar
3 tablespoons Dutch process cocoa
2 cups cold milk

1. Pour coffee over orange slices. Let stand 30 minutes.
2. Remove orange slices; thoroughly chill the coffee.
3. Combine the sugar and cocoa. Add ¼ cup of the milk; stir until smooth. Bring to boiling over direct heat and cook 1 to 2 minutes. Remove from heat. Add remaining milk gradually, blending well. Cover and chill until ready to use.
4. To serve, mix the chilled coffee and cocoa. Top each serving with **sweetened whipped cream,** sprinkled with a mixture of shaved **unsweetened chocolate** and grated **orange peel.**
6 TO 8 SERVINGS

Coffee Syrup

1 cup sugar
¾ cup water
1 teaspoon instant coffee
¼ cup boiling water

1. Combine sugar and the ¾ cup water in a saucepan. Stir over low heat until sugar is dissolved. Cover, bring to boiling, and boil 5 minutes. Remove from heat.
2. Dissolve instant coffee in boiling water. Stir into syrup. Cool; store covered in refrigerator.
ABOUT 1 CUP

Iced Tea

Cold-Water Method: For each **¾ cup (6 ounces) cold water** use **3 teaspoons tea** or **3 tea bags.** Measure tea into quart jar or other glass or china container; add measured cold water. Cover; set in refrigerator for 12 to 24 hours. Strain; pour over ice.

Hot Method I: Use **6 teaspoons (2 tablespoons) tea** or **6 tea bags** for each **1 pint (16 ounces) water.** Measure tea into quart jar or other glass or china container. Pour measured boiling water on top; let stand in warm place 5 minutes, strain, pour over ice.

Hot Method II: Use **3 teaspoons tea** or **3 tea bags** for each **1½ cups boiling water.** Make as directed under Hot Method I, let stand 5 minutes, strain, cover, and let cool for 2 to 3 hours without refrigeration before pouring over ice.

To serve with tea—Lemon wedges, crosswise slices of orange with whole cloves stuck in edges, fresh mint leaves, preserved ginger, or brandied cherries.

Lemonade

1 cup sugar
1 cup water
4 cups cold water
¾ cup lemon juice

1. Mix the sugar and 1 cup water in a saucepan. Stir over low heat until sugar is dissolved. Increase heat, cover, and boil 5 minutes. Remove from heat; cool.
2. Mix the cold water and lemon juice with the cooled syrup. Pour over chipped ice or ice cubes in tall glasses.
ABOUT 1½ QUARTS

Limeade: Follow recipe for Lemonade. Substitute **¾ cup lime juice** for lemon juice.

Orangeade: Follow recipe for Lemonade. Decrease lemon juice to ¼ cup (or substitute ¼ cup lime juice for lemon juice), decrease cold water to 1 cup, and mix in **3 cups orange juice.**

Black Velvet

Guinness stout, chilled   Champagne, chilled

Fill an 8-ounce highball glass half full with stout and half with champagne. Pour gently so it doesn't overflow. Proportion of stout may be decreased.
1 SERVING

Beer Bloody Mary

1 can or bottle (12 ounces) beer	juice
1 can (12 ounces) tomato	Dash Worcestershire sauce
	Dash Tabasco

Combine ingredients; pour over ice in old-fashioned glasses.
3 OR 4 SERVINGS

Holiday Eggnog

3 eggs, separated	¼ cup brandy or bourbon
½ cup sugar	1 cup whipping cream, whipped
2 cups milk	Nutmeg
1 can or bottle (12 ounces) beer	

1. Beat egg yolks with ¼ cup sugar until very thick. Gradually stir in milk, beer, and brandy.
2. Beat egg whites until foamy. Gradually beat in ¼ cup sugar, continuing beating until stiff peaks form.
3. Fold egg whites into yolk-beer mixture. Chill.
4. Just before serving, fold in whipped cream. Serve in small punch cups; sprinkle with nutmeg.
6 CUPS; 12 HALF-CUP SERVINGS

Ginger Ice Cooler

1 can (6 ounces) frozen lemonade concentrate, partially thawed	⅔ cup light corn syrup
	1 quart ginger ale, chilled

1. Blend lemonade concentrate with corn syrup, then ginger ale.
2. Pour into individual glasses over ginger ice (freeze additional ginger ale in ice cube trays and finely crush the ice).
1½ QUARTS

Raspberry Delight: Purée partially thawed **frozen red raspberries.** Blend with desired amount of Ginger Ice Cooler mixture. Strain if necessary. Serve thoroughly chilled in 4-ounce stemmed glasses. Omit ginger ice.

Strawberry Delight

Strawberry Delight

1 quart fresh strawberries	2 cups milk
2 pints vanilla ice cream	

1. Stem and wash the strawberries. Place them in a blender, food processor or bowl, reserving a few good berries for decoration.
2. Add half the ice cream together and the milk. Process for a minute until all ingredients are well mixed, or mash berries and ice cream with a fork and beat them rapidly, preferably with an electric beater, until all is well mixed.
3. Pour into 4 glasses with the rest of the vanilla ice cream. Decorate each with a strawberry. Serve immediately with long spoons.
SERVES 4

Banana-Lime Exotica

⅓ cup lime juice	½ large ripe banana
3 tablespoons confectioners' sugar	2 ice cubes

Put all ingredients into a chilled electric blender container. Cover and blend on high speed about 1 minute. Pour into an ice-filled glass.
1 SERVING

Black Velvet
Beer Bloody Mary
Holiday Eggnog

White Wine Bowl

1 bottle white wine
⅓ cup brandy
¾ cup lime juice
⅓ cup sugar
¼ cucumber, sliced

1 lemon, sliced
1 bottle (28 ounces)
    sparkling water
Ice cubes

Mix well everything except sparkling water and ice cubes, let stand 20 minutes, add sparkling water and ice and serve immediately.

Frothy Lemonade

1 cup water
¼ cup lemon juice
¼ cup honey

2 egg whites
Few grains salt
4 ice cubes

1. Put all ingredients except ice cubes into an electric blender container. Cover and blend until thoroughly mixed.
2. Add the ice cubes, one at a time, blending until mixed. Pour into glasses and spoon froth over top of each.
3 SERVINGS

Lemon-Cherry Cooler

4 cups water
½ cup sugar
1 package lemon-flavored
    soft drink mix
1 package cherry-flavored
    soft drink mix
1 can (6 ounces) frozen

orange juice concentrate,
    thawed
1 can (6 ounces) frozen
    pineapple juice concen-
    trate, thawed
1 bottle (12 ounces) spar-
    kling water, chilled

1. Combine water and sugar in a saucepan. Set over low heat and stir until sugar is dissolved. Bring to boiling and boil 2 minutes. Cool; chill.
2. Combine soft drink mixes and juice concentrates; beat with a rotary beater or mix in a blender. Stir in the chilled syrup. Pour over ice in a large pitcher. Add the sparkling water.
3. Mix well and pour into glasses. If desired, top each with a scoop of **vanilla ice cream.**
ABOUT 2 QUARTS

Lemon-Cranberry Nectar

1 cup chilled cranberry juice
    cocktail
¾ cup chilled apricot nectar
¾ cup water

1 can (6 ounces) frozen
    lemonade concentrate (not
    reconstituted)
Fresh ripe strawberries

1. Blend thoroughly the cranberry juice, apricot nectar, and water. Stir in lemonade concentrate until melted.
2. Pour into tall glasses over ice cubes or crushed ice.
ABOUT 3¼ CUPS

Lime-Rosemary Zing

1½ tablespoons crushed
    rosemary leaves
2½ tablespoons sugar
⅛ teaspoon salt

⅓ cup water
1½ cups apricot nectar
¾ cup lime juice
3 cups ginger ale, chilled

1. Combine rosemary, sugar, salt, and water in a small saucepan; simmer 2 minutes. Cool; strain. Blend with apricot nectar and lime juice; chill.
2. Blend ginger ale with chilled fruit juice mixture. Pour over crushed ice in tall glasses. Garnish each serving with spiral strips of **lime peel.**
ABOUT 5 CUPS

Peach Julep

½ cup sugar
1 tablespoon light brown
    sugar
2 tablespoons honey
1 cup water
2 whole cloves
1 piece (3 inches) stick

cinnamon
1 cup coarsely chopped
    peaches, puréed in an elec-
    tric blender, or forced
    through food mill or sieve
½ cup lemon juice
2 cups orange juice

1. Combine the sugars, honey, water, cloves, and cinnamon stick in a saucepan; heat, stirring constantly, until sugar is completely dissolved. Cool; remove cloves and cinnamon.
2. Blend peach purée, lemon juice, and orange juice into the cooled sugar syrup. Chill.
3. Serve in stemmed glasses.
ABOUT 12 SERVINGS

Purple Plum Cooler

2 cups purple plum juice*
2 cups sugar
1½ teaspoons cider vinegar

2⅔ cups sparkling water,
    chilled

1. Combine plum juice and sugar in a saucepan. Set over low heat and stir until sugar is dissolved; increase heat and simmer 10 minutes. Remove from heat and stir in vinegar. Cool; chill thoroughly.
2. Just before serving, pour sparkling water into chilled mixture.
ABOUT 5¼ CUPS

*Plum Juice: Rinse fresh **purple plums.** Cut into halves and remove pits. Put in kettle with **cold water,** allowing ¼ cup cold water to 1 quart firmly packed plums. Cover. Bring to boiling. Simmer at least 10 minutes, or until plums are soft. Strain through a jelly bag. Allow to hang several hours. Reserve the pulp for preparing purée. This juice may be frozen and used for jellymaking or may be sweetened for beverage use.

Wine Cup

2 bottles medium-dry white wine
3 bottles (28 ounces) sparkling water
½ cup rum
2 lemons, thinly sliced
Red and green cocktail cherries
Ice cubes

Mix the liquid ingredients in a large bowl. Add the lemons, cherries, and ice cubes.
MAKES 3 QUARTS

Minted Chocolate Refresher

3 ounces (3 squares) unsweetened chocolate
1 cup boiling water
¾ cup sugar
16 large marshmallows
½ teaspoon peppermint extract
1 quart milk
Mint sprigs

1. Melt chocolate in boiling water. Add sugar and stir until dissolved; pour into an electric blender container. Add marshmallows and extract; cover and blend until smooth.
2. Mix into milk; chill thoroughly.
3. Mix well before pouring over ice cubes in tall chilled glasses. Garnish each serving with a mint sprig.
ABOUT 6 CUPS

Wine Cup

Strawberry Fizz

8 large strawberries
Sugar
About ¾ cup milk
About ¼ cup (28 ounces) sparkling water

1. Cut 4 strawberries in half and place in a tall glass.
2. Sprinkle with a little sugar and fill the glass to ⅔ with icy cold milk.
3. Fill the glass to the rim with sparkling water and top with 4 whole strawberries.
SERVES 1

Peanut Butter — Milk Drink

¾ cup water
⅓ cup instant nonfat dry milk
1 tablespoon sugar
Few grains salt
2 tablespoons smooth peanut butter
⅛ teaspoon vanilla extract

Combine all ingredients in an electric blender container. Blend thoroughly. Serve chilled.
1 SERVING

Cantaloupe-Pineapple-Grapefruit Drink

2 cups diced ripe cantaloupe
¼ cup sugar
2 tablespoons lime juice
1 tablespoon lemon juice
Few grains salt
1 can (12 ounces) pineapple-grapefruit drink, chilled

1. Put the cantaloupe, sugar, lime and lemon juices, and salt into an electric blender container. Cover and blend thoroughly; chill.
2. Stir the blended mixture into the chilled fruit drink. To serve, pour over ice cubes or crushed ice in chilled glasses.
ABOUT 3 CUPS

Icy Nectarine-Plum Whirl

1 or 2 medium-sized firm ripe nectarines
2 or 3 medium-sized fresh red plums
½ cup sugar
½ cup cold milk
3 tablespoons lemon juice
1 cup crushed ice

1. Rinse, cut into halves, remove pits, and cut the nectarines and plums into pieces (enough to yield ½ cup each).
2. Put fruit into an electric blender container with the remaining ingredients. Cover and blend until thoroughly mixed. Serve immediately.
ABOUT 3 CUPS

Strawberry Fizz

Rhubarb Juice

2 pounds rhubarb
1 cup water
1 cup sugar

1. Wash the rhubarb and cut into 1-inch pieces. Place in a pot and pour on the water. Bring to a boil and let the rhubarb simmer until soft, about 10 minutes.
2. Strain the juice. Return to the pot and bring to a boil.
3. Stir in the sugar, bring to a boil and skim. Cool before serving.
YIELDS 1 QUART

Raspberry and Lime Swizzle

1 cup sugar
2 cups ripe red raspberries
1 cup lime juice
Lemon-lime carbonated
beverage, chilled
Watermelon Sherbet, *below*
Thin lime slices

1. Sprinkle sugar over berries in an electric blender container; let stand 1 hour. Blend thoroughly.
2. Add lime juice and chill at least 2 hours. Strain through a sieve.
3. Pour 1/4 cup of the raspberry syrup into each glass; add 1/2 cup lemon-lime carbonated beverage and stir. Top with a small scoop of Watermelon Sherbet. Garnish each glass with a thin slice of lime.
ABOUT 10 SERVINGS

Watermelon Sherbet: Mix **4 cups diced watermelon, 1/4 cup lemon juice, 1 cup sugar,** and 1/8 **teaspoon salt** together; chill 30 minutes; force through a sieve into a bowl. Soften **1 envelope unflavored gelatin** in 1/2 **cup cold water** in a small saucepan. Set over low heat until dissolved, stirring constantly. Stir into watermelon mixture. Turn into refrigerator trays and freeze until firm, stirring once.
ABOUT 3 CUPS SHERBET

Chocolate-Banana Shake

8 ripe bananas
6 cups cold milk
1 cup instant chocolate-
flavored drink mix
1 teaspoon vanilla extract
1 1/2 pints vanilla ice cream

1. Cut about one third of bananas into large pieces and put into an electric blender container. Add one third of each of the remaining ingredients; blend thoroughly. Pour into a chilled large pitcher. Repeat twice with remaining ingredients.
2. Pour into glasses and, if desired, top each with scoop of **vanilla ice cream.**
10 TO 12 SERVINGS

Milk and Honey

4 eggs
1/2 cup honey
1 cup instant nonfat dry milk
3 cups apricot nectar, chilled
1 1/3 cups orange juice, chilled
2 to 4 tablespoons lemon juice

1. Beat eggs until thick and piled softly; add honey gradually, beating constantly until blended.
2. Stir the dry milk into a mixture of apricot nectar and juices until dissolved. Add gradually to egg-honey mixture; beat until foamy. Chill and beat again before serving.
ABOUT 1 1/2 QUARTS

West Indian Chocolate Frost

2 cups milk
1/2 cup heavy cream
1 cup chocolate sauce or topping
4 teaspoons sugar
1 teaspoon vanilla extract
1 tablespoon instant coffee
1/2 teaspoon ground cinnamon
1/2 teaspoon ground cloves
1 pint vanilla ice cream

1. Combine all ingredients in an electric blender container; cover and blend. Chill thoroughly.
2. Beat slightly before pouring into tall glasses. Garnish with **chocolate curls.**

Frosted Coffee Shake

2 cups cold milk
2 tablespoons sugar
1 tablespoon instant coffee
1/2 pint vanilla or chocolate ice cream

Put milk, sugar, and instant coffee into an electric blender container. Cover and blend thoroughly. Add ice cream by spoonfuls and blend until mixed.
ABOUT 3 CUPS

Spanish Lemon and Lime

1 cup instant nonfat dry milk
1 quart icy cold milk
1/3 cup sugar
2/3 cup lime juice
1 pint lemon sherbet
1 quart crushed ice

1. Stir the dry milk into the cold milk until blended. Stir in the sugar until dissolved. Add the lime juice and sherbet and beat with hand rotary or electric beater until foamy.
2. Pour foamy beverage into a pitcher or individual glasses over part of the crushed ice. Garnish with **lemon and/or lime slices** and fresh **mint leaves,** along with the remaining ice. Serve with straws.
ABOUT 2 QUARTS

Red Wine Toddy

Red Wine Toddy

½ cup sugar
1 bottle Burgundy or other
  dry red wine
2 cloves

1 teaspoon grated lemon rind
1 cinnamon stick
½ cup Cognac or brandy
Lemon wedges

1. Place the sugar in a saucepan. Pour the wine into the pan and stir until the sugar dissolves.
2. Add cloves, lemon rind and cinnamon stick and heat almost to a boil.
3. Turn off heat, pour in Cognac and mix well. Place a spoon in each glass and a wedge of lemon. Wrap a napkin around each glass and pour in wine.
SERVES 4

Summer Sangría

1 lemon, sliced
1 orange, sliced
1 apple, sliced
½ canteloupe or other
  melon, cubed
1 pint strawberries, halved
1 bunch seedless grapes
1 bottle dry red Spanish

wine
1 bottle rosé wine
3 tablespoons sugar
6 tablespoons brandy
Ice cubes
1 bottle (28 ounces)
  sparkling water

1. Place the fruits, berries and grapes in a large bowl and pour on the wine, sugar and brandy.
2. Cover and marinate for at least 3 hours.
3. Add ice and sparkling water and serve.
SERVES 12

Summer Sangría

Indian Yoghurt Drink

2 cups yoghurt   ½ teaspoon honey
¼ cup water

1. Place yoghurt, water, honey and a couple of ice cubes in a blender or a bowl. Blend or whip vigorously with an electric beater. Serve immediately.
SERVES 2

Strawberry Shake

1 pint strawberries, rinsed   2 scoops vanilla or
1⅓ cups cold milk   strawberry ice cream
¼ cup sugar

Combine strawberries with the milk and sugar in an electric blender container. Cover and blend thoroughly. Add the ice cream and blend a few seconds.
3 SERVINGS

Strawberry Frost

1 pint ripe strawberries   2 tablespoons lemon juice
½ cup sugar   1 teaspoon vanilla extract
2 cups cold milk   ⅛ teaspoon salt
¼ cup cream   Vanilla ice cream

1. Crush strawberries; add sugar and 1 cup of milk; beat with hand rotary or electric beater until of a creamy consistency.
2. Gradually add remaining ingredients except ice cream, beating well.
3. Put 1 or 2 scoops ice cream into each chilled glass. Fill with strawberry mixture. If desired, garnish with **strawberries.**
ABOUT 5½ CUPS

Apricot Whirl

1 can (12 ounces) apricot   ¼ cup instant natural-
nectar   flavored malted milk powder
1 pint vanilla ice cream   2 tablespoons lemon juice

1. Pour apricot nectar into refrigerator tray; freeze until mushy.
2. Spoon apricot nectar and ice cream into an electric blender container; add malted milk powder and lemon juice. Cover and blend until smooth and creamy.
3. Pour into chilled glasses and serve immediately with straws.
ABOUT 3¾ CUPS

Homemade Chocolate Soda

1 small scoop chocolate or   ½ cup sparkling water or
vanilla ice cream   ginger ale
2 to 4 tablespoons sweet-   1 or 2 scoops softened ice
ened chocolate syrup   cream
½ cup cold milk

1. For each soda, blend a small scoop of ice cream and the chocolate syrup in a tall glass.
2. Add milk and sparkling water; mix thoroughly.
3. Float scoops of ice cream on top. Serve with straws and long-handled spoons.
1 SERVING

Homemade Lemon Soda: Follow recipe for Homemade Chocolate Soda. Use **vanilla ice cream** and substitute **2 tablespoons thawed frozen lemonade concentrate** for the chocolate syrup.

Homemade Peach Soda: Follow recipe for Homemade Chocolate Soda. Use **vanilla ice cream** and substitute ⅓ **cup mashed, sweetened ripe fresh peaches** for the chocolate syrup.

Homemade Pineapple Soda: Follow recipe for Homemade Chocolate Soda. Use **vanilla ice cream** and substitute ¼ **cup canned or frozen crushed pineapple** for the chocolate syrup.

Homemade Raspberry or Strawberry Soda: Follow recipe for Homemade Chocolate Soda. Use **vanilla ice cream** and substitute ¼ **cup crushed, sweetened red raspberries or strawberries** for the chocolate syrup.

Snappy Chocolate Soda

1 cup chocolate syrup   1 bottle (28 ounces) spar-
⅓ to ½ cup lemon juice   kling water, chilled
6 scoops vanilla ice cream

Combine the chocolate syrup and lemon juice. Divide evenly into six tall chilled soda glasses. Add a scoop of vanilla ice cream to each glass and fill with the chilled sparkling water, stirring to blend. Serve immediately.
6 SERVINGS

Cherry-Cola Soda, Blender Style

¾ cup cold cola beverage or   cherries
milk   4 large scoops vanilla ice
½ cup sugar   cream
1 pint pitted dark sweet   Cola beverage

1. Put the cola beverage and sugar into an electric blender container. Cover and turn on motor. Add cherries and then ice cream. Blend until thick and smooth.
2. Divide mixture among 8 tall glasses. Fill with cola beverage. Give a quick stir and top each with a scoop of **ice cream.**
8 TALL SERVINGS

Cranberry Juice

1 pint cranberries	3 cloves
2 cups water	¼ cup orange juice
¼ cup sugar	1 lime, sliced

1. Place cranberries and water in a heavy pan. Cook over medium heat about 5 minutes until skins pop.
2. Put berries through a strainer. Bring juice to a boil and add sugar and cloves. Cook for 2 minutes. Cool.
3. Add orange juice and chill. Garnish with slice of lime.
SERVES 4

Spicy Cranberry Punch

4 pieces (3 inches each) stick cinnamon, broken in pieces	cocktail
8 whole allspice	1 orange, sliced
18 whole cloves	6 bottles (7 ounces each) lemon-lime carbonated beverage, chilled
3 quarts cranberry juice	

1. Tie spices together in cheesecloth bag.
2. In a large saucepan, combine the cranberry juice cocktail, orange slices, and spice bag. Bring to boiling, reduce heat, and simmer about 20 minutes. Set aside to cool; discard spice bag and orange; chill cranberry juice.
3. Just before serving, pour into chilled punch bowl; add lemon-lime carbonated beverage and stir to blend. If desired, garnish with additional **orange slices.**
ABOUT 17 CUPS

Frosty Cola Apricade

¾ cup sugar	1½ cups lime juice
1½ cups water	¾ cup orange juice
3 cans (12 ounces each) apricot nectar	Cola Sherbet, *below*

1. Mix sugar and water; stir over low heat until sugar is dissolved. Cover, bring to boiling, and boil 5 minutes. Cool.
2. Blend the apricot nectar, lime juice, orange juice, and the cooled syrup. Chill thoroughly.
3. When ready to serve, pour fruit juice mixture into a chilled bowl. Serve in punch cups or mugs and top each serving with a scoop of Cola Sherbet.
ABOUT 2 QUARTS PUNCH

Cola Sherbet: Blend in a large bowl **¾ cup sugar, 1 cup carbonated cola beverage, 1 teaspoon grated lime peel, few grains salt,** and **1½ cups cream.** Stir until sugar is dissolved. Pour into a 1-quart refrigerator tray. Freeze until mixture is mushy. When mushy, turn into a chilled bowl and beat with a chilled beater until smooth. Immediately return mixture to refrigerator tray and freeze until firm, about 3 hours.
ABOUT 1½ PINTS SHERBET

Sparkling Punch

2 quarts apple cider	pineapple-orange juice concentrate
8 whole cloves	
2 pieces stick cinnamon	4 bottles (12 ounces each) lemon-lime carbonated beverage, chilled
6 whole allspice	
1 can (6 ounces) frozen	

1. Refrigerate 1 quart of the cider and pour remaining 1 quart into a saucepan with the spices. Cook 15 minutes and strain to remove spices.
2. Combine the spiced and chilled cider and fruit juice concentrate in a chilled punch bowl; blend well. Slowly pour in the carbonated beverage.
3. Add ice cubes or a fancy ice mold.
ABOUT 3 QUARTS PUNCH

Cranberry Punch

4 cups firm cranberries, rinsed	2 tablespoons lemon juice
4 cups water	4 cups pineapple juice, chilled
1½ cups sugar	1 cup orange juice, chilled

1. Combine cranberries and water in a saucepan. Cook over medium heat until cranberry skins pop.
2. Sieve cooked cranberries. Stir in sugar and lemon juice. Return to saucepan; bring to boiling and cook 2 minutes, stirring constantly. Immediately remove from heat; cool and chill thoroughly in refrigerator.
3. To serve, pour over ice cubes in a large pitcher or punch bowl. Stir in pineapple and orange juices. Serve in punch cups.
ABOUT 1½ QUARTS PUNCH

Iced Cardamom Coffee in Punch Bowl

½ cup instant coffee	cardamom
⅓ cup sugar	2 quarts boiling water
2½ teaspoons ground	

1. Mix the instant coffee, sugar, and cardamom in a heat-resistant bowl. Pour in boiling water and stir until sugar is dissolved. Cool or chill.
2. When ready to serve, pour coffee over an ice mold in a punch bowl. Ladle into punch cups and serve with a bowl of **sweetened whipped cream** and a crystal shaker of **ground cardamom** for guests to help themselves.
2½ QUARTS COFFEE

Chocolate Malted Milk

2 cups cold milk	4 scoops chocolate or vanilla ice cream
¼ cup Chocolate Syrup	
¼ cup malted milk powder	

Pour milk, Chocolate Syrup, and malted milk powder into an electric blender container. Cover and blend until frothy. Add the ice cream while motor is running. Blend only until mixed.
ABOUT 3 CUPS

Mexican Chocolate

2 ounces (2 squares) unsweetened chocolate
½ cup strong coffee
½ cup sugar
1 teaspoon ground cinnamon
¹⁄₁₆ teaspoon ground allspice
Few grains salt
3 cups milk
1½ teaspoons vanilla extract
Whipped cream

1. Heat chocolate and coffee together in a heavy saucepan, stirring until chocolate is melted and mixture is smooth. Cook 2 minutes, stirring constantly.
2. Mix in sugar, cinnamon, allspice, and salt. Gradually add milk, stirring until blended; heat thoroughly.
3. Remove from heat; blend in vanilla extract. Top each serving with whipped cream.
ABOUT 4 SERVINGS

Orange Honey Hero

4 cups milk
½ cup instant vanilla pudding mix
6 tablespoons thawed frozen orange juice concentrate
1 tablespoon honey

1. Combine milk, pudding mix, orange juice concentrate, and honey in a 2-quart saucepan and heat to serving temperature, stirring occasionally.
2. Pour into glasses with handles or mugs and garnish with **orange slices.**
ABOUT 5 CUPS BEVERAGE

MICROWAVE COOKING

Greek Meatballs

1 pound ground lamb
1 egg
⅓ cup cracker crumbs
⅓ cup soy sauce
½ cup water
¼ teaspoon ginger
¼ teaspoon garlic powder
⅛ teaspoon cumin
½ cup almonds or slivered almonds

1. In a medium mixing bowl, blend lamb, egg, and cracker crumbs. Add soy sauce, water, ginger, garlic powder, cumin, and pinenuts. Mix thoroughly. Shape in 1-inch meatballs.
2. Arrange 10 meatballs in a circle in a 9-inch glass pie plate. Cook, covered, 3 to 4 minutes, rotating dish one-quarter turn halfway through cooking time. Cook longer if needed.
3. Serve hot on wooden picks.
50 TO 60 MEATBALLS

Chicken-Stuffed Mushrooms

30 fresh medium mushrooms
1 can (4½ ounces) chicken spread
½ teaspoon seasoned salt
⅛ teaspoon pepper
1 tablespoon chopped parsley
½ cup chopped walnuts

1. Wash mushrooms quickly under cold water. Remove stems, and drain both stems and caps on paper towel.
2. In a small mixing bowl, blend chicken spread, seasoned salt, pepper, parsley, and walnuts. Stuff mushrooms; place stems in filling and secure with wooden pick.
3. Arrange mushrooms on a glass pie plate and cook, covered with waxed paper, 6 to 8 minutes, rotating dish one-quarter turn halfway through cooking time. Serve hot.
30 APPETIZERS

Conventional oven: Bake at 350°F 20 minutes.

Appetizer Kabobs

8 large precooked smoked sausage links
1 can (16 ounces) pineapple chunks, drained
1 tablespoon brown sugar
2 tablespoons soy sauce
1 tablespoon vinegar

1. Arrange sausage evenly around edge of roasting rack set in a glass dish or directly on glass plate and cook 2 to 3 minutes, rotating dish one-quarter turn halfway through cooking time. Drain sausage and cut each sausage link into 5 pieces.
2. Make kabobs, using 1 sausage piece and 1 pineapple chunk threaded on a round wooden pick. Arrange evenly in a large shallow dish.
3. In a 1-cup glass measure, blend brown sugar, soy sauce, and vinegar and pour over kabobs. Refrigerate 1 or 2 hours until serving time.
4. Arrange 20 kabobs on a large glass plate and cook 2 to 3 minutes, rotating dish one-quarter turn and spooning sauce over top halfway through cooking time.
5. Cook additional kabobs as needed. Serve warm.
40 APPETIZERS

Creamed Onion Soup

4 medium onions, sliced
½ cup butter
¼ cup flour
1 quart milk
2 cups chicken broth or 2 chicken bouillon cubes
dissolved in 2 cups boiling water
1 to 1½ teaspoons salt
1 egg yolk
1 tablespoon minced parsley
½ cup croutons

1. In a 3-quart casserole, sauté onions in butter 4 to 5 minutes, stirring every minute. Stir in flour and cook until sauce bubbles, about 1 minute.
2. Add milk slowly, stirring gently. Cook until slightly thickened, about 6 to 8 minutes, stirring every 2 minutes.
3. Add broth and cook 5 minutes, stirring twice.
4. Stir in salt to taste. Blend some of the hot soup with egg yolk and return to remaining soup. Cook 1 minute, stirring every 15 seconds.
5. Serve topped with minced parsley and croutons.
8 SERVINGS

Clam Chowder

4 slices bacon
1 can (8 ounces) minced clams
2 medium potatoes, pared and cubed
¼ cup chopped onion
1 can (16 ounces) whole tomatoes (undrained)
2 tablespoons flour
1 teaspoon salt
¼ teaspoon pepper
½ teaspoon oregano

1. Arrange bacon on the rack in a 2-quart glass baking dish. Cook 2 to 3 minutes, rotating dish one-quarter turn halfway through cooking time. Lift rack from dish; set bacon aside.
2. Drain clams, reserving liquor. Add clam liquor, potatoes, onion, and tomatoes to drippings in dish and cook, covered, 10 to 12 minutes, stirring halfway through cooking time.
3. Blend flour with ¼ cup hot liquid from dish. Stir salt, pepper, oregano, and clams into flour mixture. Add to liquid in dish, blending well. Cook, covered, 5 to 6 minutes or until mixture boils, stirring every 2 minutes.
4. Rest, covered, 5 minutes before serving. Garnish with cooked bacon.
4 SERVINGS

Stuffed Mushrooms

1 bunch green onions, chopped
¼ cup sour cream
½ teaspoon Worcestershire sauce
½ teaspoon oregano
½ cup bulk pork sausage
1 pound fresh mushrooms, washed, drained, and stemmed

1. In a 1-quart casserole, blend green onions, sour cream, Worcestershire sauce, oregano, and sausage. Cook 2 to 3 minutes, stirring halfway through cooking time.
2. Stuff mushroom caps with filling. Place stem in top of filling and secure in place with wooden pick.
3. Arrange 10 to 12 mushrooms evenly around the edge of a glass pie plate and cook, covered, 6 to 8 minutes.
4. Serve warm.
25 TO 30 APPETIZERS

Hot Tuna Canapés

1 can (6½ or 7 ounces) tuna
¼ cup mayonnaise
1 tablespoon ketchup
¼ teaspoon salt
Few grains cayenne pepper
2 teaspoons finely chopped onion
¼ teaspoon Worcestershire sauce
1 cucumber
Paprika (optional)
48 Melba toast rounds
12 pimento-stuffed olives, sliced

1. Drain and flake tuna. Add mayonnaise, ketchup, salt, cayenne pepper, onion and Worcestershire sauce.
2. Pare cucumber and slice paper-thin (if desired, sprinkle with paprika).
3. For each canapé, place cucumber slice on toast round, pile tuna mixture in center and top with olive slice.
4. Put 8 canapés in circle on 6 individual paper plates. For each plate, cook uncovered in microwave oven 30 to 60 seconds.

Frankfurter Reuben

12 slices rye bread
Butter
6 large frankfurters
⅓ cup Thousand Island dressing
1 cup sauerkraut, well drained
6 slices Swiss cheese

1. Toast bread, and butter each piece on 1 side. Split frankfurters in half lengthwise and place on buttered side of 6 slices toast. Spread dressing on frankfurters, and top each sandwich with about 2 tablespoons sauerkraut. Top each with slice of remaining bread, buttered side towards cheese.
2. Cook as follows, rotating one-quarter turn halfway through cooking time: 45 to 60 seconds for 1 sandwich; 2 to 2½ minutes for 3 sandwiches; and 3 to 4 minutes for 6 sandwiches.
3. Serve warm.
6 SERVINGS

Tomato-Leek Soup

2 tablespoons butter
2 leeks, chopped (about 2½ cups)
2 carrots, finely diced (about 1 cup)
2 tablespoons flour
2 beef bouillon cubes
2 cups boiling water
1 to 2 teaspoons sugar
¼ teaspoon salt
4 large ripe tomatoes (2 pounds), peeled and cut in pieces

1. Heat butter in a 2½-quart glass bowl about 30 seconds. Add leeks and carrots and heat 4 to 5 minutes, stirring halfway through cooking.
2. Stir in flour and heat 1 to 1½ minutes.
3. Dissolve bouillon cubes in water and stir into the vegetables. Bring to boiling, about 2½ to 3 minutes, stirring after every minute. Continue cooking 4 minutes, stirring after 2 minutes.
4. Stir in sugar, salt, and tomatoes. Heat 20 to 25 minutes, stirring every 5 minutes, until tomatoes are soft.
4 SERVINGS

Bacon Cheese-Melt Sandwiches

6 slices bacon, halved
4 slices bread
Butter
4 large tomato slices
4 pasteurized process American cheese slices

1. Arrange bacon on a roast rack set in a 2-quart glass baking dish. Cover with a paper towel. Cook in microwave oven 5 minutes.
2. Meanwhile, toast bread and lightly spread with butter.
3. Put toast on roast rack and top with bacon pieces. Put a tomato slice on each toast slice, and then a slice of cheese. Heat uncovered in microwave oven 2 minutes, or until cheese melts. Serve immediately.
4 SANDWICHES

Assorted Hot Rolls

Rolls (plain or sweet)

1. Place rolls in a napkin, terry towel, or napkin in a wooden bread basket.
2. Heat as follows: 1 roll, 10 to 15 seconds; 2 rolls, 20 to 30 seconds; 4 rolls, 40 to 60 seconds; and 6 rolls, 1 to 1¼ minutes. Always start with the shortest time, and heat longer if necessary.
3. Serve immediately while warm.

Quick Cheese Bread

2½ cups all-purpose biscuit mix
1 cup shredded sharp Cheddar cheese
1 tablespoon poppy seed
1 egg
1 cup milk

1. In a medium mixing bowl, blend biscuit mix, cheese, poppy seed, egg, and milk. Stir just to moisten. Pour into a buttered 8-inch square glass baking dish.
2. Cook 5 to 7 minutes, rotating dish one-quarter turn halfway through cooking time. Allow to stand 5 minutes. Center will be soft but will set with standing.
9 TO 12 SERVINGS

Note: A glass may be placed in the center of dish before pouring in batter to help the bread cook. A 9-inch round glass baking dish may also be used.

The bread may be browned under a conventional broiler for 1 to 2 minutes, but only if a glass ceramic baking dish is used, or the bread is transferred to a metal pan.

Quick Cheese Muffins: Follow recipe for Quick Cheese Bread. Line custard cups, paper drinking cups, or cupcaker with paper baking cups. Fill each cup half full with batter. Arrange 6 cups in a circle in microwave oven. Bake for 2 to 2½ minutes, rearranging cups halfway through cooking time.
ABOUT 1½ DOZEN MUFFINS

Pumpkin Bread

1½ cups sugar
⅓ cup salad oil
2 eggs
1 cup canned pumpkin
1½ cups all-purpose flour
¾ teaspoon salt
½ teaspoon cinnamon
½ teaspoon nutmeg
½ teaspoon cloves
½ teaspoon allspice
1 teaspoon baking soda
¼ teaspoon baking powder
½ cup coarsely chopped walnuts

1. In a large mixing bowl, blend sugar, oil, eggs, and pumpkin. When ingredients are well mixed, stir in flour, salt, cinnamon, nutmeg, cloves, allspice, baking soda, and baking powder, blending well. Stir in walnuts. Pour batter into an 8x4-inch glass dish.
2. Cook 12 to 14 minutes, rotating dish one-quarter turn every 4 minutes. Knife inserted in the center should come out clean when bread is done.
3. Rest 5 minutes and remove from pan. Serve either warm or cold with **butter** or **cream cheese**.
1 LOAF BREAD

Spicy Beef Dip

1 pound ground beef
½ cup chopped onion
1 clove garlic, minced
1 can (8 ounces) tomato sauce
¼ cup ketchup
¾ teaspoon oregano, crushed
1 teaspoon sugar
1 package (3 ounces) cream cheese
⅓ cup grated Parmesan cheese

1. In a 1½-quart casserole, sauté ground beef, onion, and garlic 4 to 6 minutes, stirring twice.
2. Spoon off excess fat. Stir in tomato sauce, ketchup, oregano, and sugar.
3. Cover and cook 5 to 6 minutes, stirring twice.
4. Add cream cheese and Parmesan cheese, and stir until cream cheese has melted. Serve warm.
ABOUT 3 CUPS DIP

Cheese and Bacon Sandwiches

12 slices wheat bread, toasted
6 slices process American cheese
12 slices bacon, cooked and cut in half
6 slices Swiss cheese

1. On each of 6 toast slices, place 1 slice American cheese, 4 bacon halves, and 1 slice Swiss cheese. Top with remaining pieces of toast.
2. Cook as follows, rotating one-quarter turn halfway through cooking time: 45 to 60 seconds for 1 sandwich; 2 to 2½ minutes for 3 sandwiches; and 3 to 4 minutes for 6 sandwiches.
3. Serve warm.
6 SANDWICHES

Canadian Mushroom Sandwiches

6 kaiser rolls
Butter or margarine, softened
1 tablespoon chopped un-
  cooked bacon
2 tablespoons chopped
  onion
1 jar (2 ounces) sliced
  mushrooms, drained
1 teaspoon snipped parsley

18 slices (about 1 pound)
  smoked pork loin Canadian-
  style bacon, cut ⅛ inch
  thick
6 slices (1 ounce each) Swiss
  cheese
6 thin green pepper rings
  Paprika

1. Split rolls; if desired, reserve tops to accompany open-faced sandwiches. Spread roll bottoms with butter.
2. Combine bacon, onion, mushrooms and parsley in a 2-cup glass measuring cup. Cook uncovered in microwave oven about 2 minutes, or until onion is tender; stir once.
3. Arrange 3 slices Canadian bacon on each buttered roll and top with mushroom mixture and 1 slice cheese. Place 1 green pepper ring on each cheese slice; sprinkle paprika inside ring.
4. Place sandwiches on paper towels or roast rack. Heat uncovered in microwave oven 4 to 6 minutes, or until cheese is bubbly and meat is hot.
6. Serve sandwiches garnished with a **cherry tomato** and a **pimento-stuffed olive** on each skewer.
6 OPEN-FACED SANDWICHES

Peanut Butter Coffee Cake

2 cups all-purpose biscuit
  mix
2 tablespoons sugar
¼ cup peanut butter, chunky
  or smooth

⅔ cup milk
1 egg
½ cup jelly or jam (optional)

1. Combine biscuit mix and sugar; cut in peanut butter with a fork. Stir in milk and egg; blend evenly. Pour into a buttered 9-inch glass dish. Swirl jelly through batter, if desired.
2. Cook 8 to 10 minutes, rotating dish one-quarter turn halfway through cooking time.
3. Rest 5 minutes before serving.
4 TO 6 SERVINGS

Cheese Rolls

8 hot dog buns or French rolls	½ cup grated Parmesan cheese
Soft butter	⅓ cup poppy seed

1. Slice each roll in half lengthwise. Spread all cut sides with soft butter.
2. In a glass pie plate, mix cheese and poppy seed. Press buttered sides of each roll in cheese mixture.
3. Wrap 4 rolls in paper towel, napkin, or terry towel and cook 45 seconds to 1 minute. Repeat procedure with remaining 4 rolls.
8 CHEESE ROLLS

Conventional oven: Bake at 350°F 10 to 12 minutes.

Note: Rolls may be cut smaller and served with salad or soup. Cheese rolls may be place under the broiler 1 minute for crisping before serving.

Fried Egg

Egg

1. Break egg into 10-ounce custard cup. Pierce yolk with a fork and cover with plastic wrap.
2. Cook as follows, rotating one-quarter turn halfway through cooking time: 1 egg, 25 to 35 seconds; 2 eggs, 1 minute to 1¼ minutes; 3 eggs, 1½ to 1¾ minutes; 4 eggs, 2 to 2¼ minutes. If a soft yolk is preferred, cook the shorter time. If a firmer yolk is desired, cook the longer time.
3. Rest, covered, 5 minutes before serving, if desired.

Note: If cupcaker is used, place a small amount of butter in the bottom of paper baking cup in each well. Break egg into each cup and cover with plastic wrap. Cook as directed for fried eggs in custard cup, but reduce cooking time 5 to 10 seconds for each egg.

Note: Never cook an egg in its shell in the microwave oven. Steam forms readily, and the egg might explode the shell.

Poached Egg

Egg	Water

1. Place ½ cup water in a 10-ounce custard cup and heat 30 seconds.
2. Break egg into hot water and cover with plastic wrap.
3. Cook, following times indicated for Fried Egg (above).
4. Rest, covered, 5 minutes before serving.

Bacon and Egg Turbans

6 slices bacon	2 tablespoons sour cream
6 eggs	

1. Arrange bacon on roasting rack in a 2-quart glass baking dish and cook as follows: 1 slice for 1 minute; 2 slices for 1½ minutes; 3 slices for 2½ minutes; 4 slices for 3 minutes; and 6 slices for 4 minutes. Limp, not crisp, bacon is desired.
2. Arrange a bacon slice in a circle in the bottom of a 6-ounce glass custard cup. Break egg in cup over bacon. Pierce yolk with fork, and top egg with 1 teaspoon sour cream.
3. Place cups in a circle on a 9-inch glass pie plate. Add 1 cup water to glass plate and cover with plastic wrap. Cook until done, as follows, rotating plate one-quarter turn halfway through cooking time: 1 egg, 1½ to 2 minutes; 2 eggs, 2 to 3 minutes; 3 eggs, 2½ to 3½ minutes; 4 eggs, 3 to 4 minutes; 6 eggs, 4 to 5 minutes.
4. Rest, covered, 1 minute after cooking. Invert custard cup on **buttered toasted English muffin** and serve immediately.
6 SERVINGS

Marvelous Eggs

3 tablespoons butter	½ teaspoon salt
1 tablespoon minced green onion	¼ teaspoon lemon juice
6 eggs, slightly beaten	1 package (3 ounces) cream cheese, cut in ½-inch cubes
⅓ cup milk	

1. In a 2-quart glass casserole, heat butter 30 seconds. Add onion and cook 2 minutes, stirring once. Stir in eggs, milk, salt, and lemon juice.
2. Cook, covered, 4 to 5 minutes, stirring every 2 minutes. When almost set, lightly fold in cream cheese.
3. Cook 1 minute longer, rest 5 minutes, and serve.
4 SERVINGS

Mushroom Eggs on Toast

1 pound fresh mushrooms, cleaned and sliced	1 cup milk
¼ cup butter	½ cup grated Parmesan cheese
4 slices hot buttered toast	¼ teaspoon dry mustard
2 tablespoons butter	4 poached eggs, (opposite)
2 tablespoons flour	Paprika (optional)

1. In a 1-quart glass casserole, cook mushrooms in ¼ cup butter 3 to 4 minutes, stirring halfway through cooking time. Cover each slice toast with one-fourth of the mushrooms.
2. In a 2-cup glass measure, heat 2 tablespoons butter 30 seconds. Stir in flour to blend. Stir in milk and cook 2 to 3 minutes, stirring every minute, until sauce becomes thick. Add cheese and dry mustard; stir to blend.
3. Place an egg on top of mushrooms on each toast slice and cover with sauce. Sprinkle with paprika, if desired.
3 OR 4 SERVINGS

Welsh Rabbit

1½ teaspoons butter	sauce
2 cups shredded pasteurized process sharp Cheddar cheese	¼ teaspoon dry mustard
	Few grains cayenne pepper
	⅓ cup milk
¼ teaspoon Worcestershire	Toast

1. Melt butter in a 1-quart glass casserole in microwave oven (about 15 seconds). Add cheese and heat uncovered in microwave oven about 1 minute, or until cheese begins to melt; stir after 30 seconds.
2. Add Worcestershire sauce, dry mustard and cayenne pepper to cheese. Add milk gradually, stirring constantly. Heat uncovered in microwave oven to serving temperature (1½ to 2½ minutes); stir occasionally.
3. Serve immediately on hot toast.

4 TO 6 SERVINGS

Confetti Eggs

2 tablespoons butter	4 eggs
½ cup diced ham	Dash Tabasco
2 green onions, including tops, chopped	½ teaspoon salt
	¼ teaspoon pepper

1. In a 2-quart casserole, cook butter, ham, and green onions 3 to 4 minutes, stirring every minute.
2. Add eggs, Tabasco, salt, and pepper; stir to blend.
3. Cook, covered, 3 to 4 minutes, stirring halfway through cooking time.
4. Rest, covered, 5 minutes.

3 OR 4 SERVINGS

Chili Burgers

2 pounds ground beef
1 medium onion, diced
1¼ cups diced celery
3 tablespoons vinegar
1 bottle (14 ounces) ketchup
1 can (8 ounces) tomato
  sauce
2 tablespoons dry mustard
½ cup water
¼ cup Worcestershire sauce
1½ teaspoons salt
½ teaspoon pepper
½ teaspoon chili powder
8 hamburger buns

1. In a 3-quart glass casserole, sauté ground beef, onion, and celery 6 to 8 minutes, stirring every 2 minutes. Drain off drippings.
2. Add vinegar, ketchup, tomato sauce, mustard, water, Worcestershire sauce, salt, pepper, and chili powder; stir to blend ingredients evenly.
3. Cook, covered, 8 to 10 minutes.
4. Heat buns wrapped in terry towel 1 to 1½ minutes.
5. Spoon mixture on heated buns.
6 TO 8 SERVINGS

Conventional oven: Bake at 350°F 1½ hours.

Note: This is a good mixture to make ahead and keep frozen.

Stromboli Sandwich

1 pound ground beef
2 tablespoons finely chopped
  onion
½ cup tomato sauce
½ cup ketchup
2 tablespoons grated
  Parmesan cheese
½ teaspoon garlic salt
¼ teaspoon oregano
½ teaspoon garlic powder
¼ cup butter
6 French rolls
6 slices mozzarella cheese

1. In a 1½-quart glass casserole, combine ground beef and onion. Cook 4 to 5 minutes, stirring halfway through cooking time. Spoon off drippings.
2. Stir in tomato sauce, ketchup, Parmesan cheese, garlic salt, and oregano. Cook, covered, 5 to 6 minutes, stirring halfway through cooking time.
3. In a 1-cup glass measure, combine garlic powder and butter; heat 30 seconds. Stir to blend. Pour melted butter evenly over inside of top half of each roll.
4. Divide meat mixture evenly and spread on bottom halves of each roll. Top with 1 slice mozzarella, place tops on buns, and wrap each in a napkin.
5. Cook as follows, rotating one-quarter turn halfway through cooking time: 30 to 45 seconds for 1 sandwich; 1½ to 2 minutes for 3 sandwiches; and 3 to 4 minutes for 6 sandwiches.
6. Serve warm.
6 SERVINGS

Tortilla Sandwiches

12 corn tortillas
Salad oil
6 slices Monterey Jack
  cheese

1. Fry tortillas in small amount of hot oil on range until limp. Fold in half and hold slightly open with tongs; continue to fry until crisp, turning to fry on both sides. Drain on paper towel.
2. Place ½ slice cheese in each tortilla. Arrange tortillas in shallow glass dish in microwave and cook 1 to 1½ minutes, rotating dish one-quarter turn halfway through cooking time.
3. Serve hot; reheat if needed.
12 SANDWICHES

Beefy Rice

1 beef bouillon cube
1¾ cups water
1 cup uncooked white rice
½ cup butter
1 teaspoon salt
1 tablespoon parsley flakes

1. In a 3-quart glass casserole, combine bouillon cube, water, rice, butter, and salt.
2. Cook, covered, 12 to 14 minutes, stirring halfway through cooking time.
3. Rest, covered, 10 minutes. Stir in parsley flakes.
4 TO 6 SERVINGS

Conventional oven: Bake at 375°F 1 hour.

Long Grain Rice

2½ cups water
1 cup long grain rice
1 teaspoon salt

1. In a covered 2-quart casserole, bring water to boiling, 5 to 6 minutes. Stir in rice and salt.
2. Cook, covered, 7 to 9 minutes, rotating dish one-quarter turn halfway through cooking time.
3. Rest, covered, 10 minutes before serving.
5 OR 6 SERVINGS

Cheese Fondue

½ pound Swiss cheese,
  shredded
2 tablespoons flour
½ teaspoon salt
¼ teaspoon garlic powder
¼ teaspoon nutmeg
¼ teaspoon white pepper
½ cup milk
2 tablespoons kirsch
  (optional)
French bread, cut in 1-inch
  cubes

1. In a 2-quart glass casserole, mix together the cheese, flour, salt, garlic powder, nutmeg, and white pepper. Add milk and, if desired, kirsch; stir to mix.
2. Cook, covered, 3 to 4 minutes, stirring once or twice. Rest, covered, 5 minutes.
3. Spear cubes of bread and dip in fondue. If fondue cools, reheat 1 to 2 minutes.
3 OR 4 SERVINGS

Acorn Squash

1 small acorn squash
1½ tablespoons butter
1½ teaspoons brown sugar
¼ teaspoon salt
⅛ teaspoon ginger

1. Pierce squash and place whole on dish or rack. Cook, 6 to 8 minutes, rotating dish one-quarter turn and turning over halfway through cooking time.
2. When done, cut in half and remove seeds.
3. Divide butter, brown sugar, salt and ginger in squash cavities. Cover with plastic wrap.
4. Cook in microwave oven at high temperature for 2 minutes. Allow to stand 5 minutes before serving.
2 SERVINGS

Quick Cheese Fondue

1 can (10½ ounces) condensed Cheddar cheese soup
⅓ cup milk
¼ teaspoon garlic powder
¼ teaspoon nutmeg
1½ cups shredded Swiss cheese

1. In a 4-cup glass measure, blend soup and milk; cook 3 to 4 minutes, stirring halfway through cooking time.
2. Add garlic powder and nutmeg; stir to blend. Blend in cheese.
3. Cook 2 to 3 minutes, stirring every minute, until cheese is melted.
4. Serve immediately while warm.
2 CUPS FONDUE

Confetti Rice Ring

4½ cups cooked rice
6 tablespoons butter or margarine
¾ cup snipped parsley
3 canned whole pimentos, drained and chopped

1. Prepare rice. While hot, stir in butter, parsley and pimento.
2. Pack rice mixture into a buttered 5-cup glass ring mold. Cover with plastic wrap.
3. Heat thoroughly in microwave oven (5 to 6 minutes). Uncover and allow to stand 3 minutes.
4. Unmold on a warm serving plate. Fill ring as desired.

Confetti Rice Ring

Cooked Fresh Broccoli

1 small bunch (1 pound) broccoli

1. Wash and remove dried leaves.
2. Add 2 tablespoons water and ½ teaspoon salt, if desired, to 1-quart glass dish.
3. Add broccoli to dish and cook, covered. Rotate dish one-quarter turn halfway through cooking time.
4 SERVINGS

Fresh Vegetable Medley

1 pound broccoli, cut in thin stalks	sliced ¼ inch thick
1 small head cauliflower (about 1 pound), cut in flowerets	5 or 6 fresh mushrooms, cleaned and cut in half
1 large zucchini, sliced ¼ inch thick	1 medium sweet red pepper, cut in strips
1 large crookneck squash, sliced ¼ inch thick	1 medium sweet green pepper, cut in strips
1 large pattypan squash,	¼ cup butter
	½ teaspoon garlic salt
	¼ teaspoon pepper

1. In a 2-quart glass baking dish or on a large glass serving platter, arrange broccoli around edge of dish; place cauliflower next to broccoli, and squash, mushrooms, and peppers alternately near the center of the dish.
2. In a 1-cup glass measure, combine butter, garlic salt, and pepper; heat 30 to 45 seconds. Drizzle butter over vegetables.
3. Cook, covered, 15 to 20 minutes or until vegetables are done as desired, rotating dish one-quarter turn every 5 minutes.
4. Rest, covered, 5 minutes before serving.
10 TO 12 SERVINGS

Fresh Vegetable Medley

Sweet-and-Sour Cabbage

1 small onion, chopped	diced
3 tablespoons butter	3 tablespoons vinegar
1 cup meat stock or water	1 tablespoon brown sugar
1 small head cabbage, shredded	¼ teaspoon allspice
	½ teaspoon salt
1 small tart apple, cored and	

1. In a 2-quart glass casserole, sauté onion in butter 2 minutes, stirring after 1 minute. Stir in stock, cabbage, and apple.
2. Cover casserole and cook 6 to 8 minutes, stirring halfway through cooking time.
3. Add vinegar, brown sugar, allspice, and salt to cabbage; mix well. Cook 3 to 4 minutes.
4. Rest, covered, 5 minutes before serving.
4 TO 6 SERVINGS

Cabbage au Gratin

1 medium head cabbage, shredded	1 cup milk
2 tablespoons butter	¾ cup shredded Cheddar cheese
2 tablespoons flour	¼ teaspoon dry mustard
½ teaspoon salt	Dash paprika

1. In a 3-quart glass casserole, cook cabbage, covered, 10 to 12 minutes, rotating dish one-quarter turn halfway through cooking time. Rest, covered, 5 minutes while preparing sauce.
2. In a 2-cup glass measure, heat butter 30 seconds. Stir in flour and salt; stir until smooth. Add milk gradually, stirring constantly. Cook 2 to 3 minutes, stirring after every minute until mixture boils.
3. Blend in cheese, dry mustard, and paprika. Cook 1 minute and stir well.
4. Drain liquid from cabbage. Add cheese sauce and stir to blend.
5. Rest, covered, 5 minutes before serving.
6 TO 8 SERVINGS

Cauliflower au Gratin

½ cup butter	wedges
1 medium head cauliflower, cut in flowerets	¼ cup seasoned bread crumbs
¼ teaspoon garlic salt	¼ cup grated Parmesan cheese
¼ teaspoon salt	½ cup shredded Swiss cheese
¼ teaspoon pepper	
2 large tomatoes, cut in	

1. In a 1½-quart glass casserole, heat butter 30 seconds. Add cauliflower, garlic salt, salt, and pepper, and stir to coat cauliflower with butter.
2. Cover cauliflower and cook 5 to 6 minutes, rotating dish one-quarter turn halfway through cooking time.
3. Arrange tomatoes on top of cauliflower and cook 2 minutes.
4. Add bread crumbs, Parmesan cheese, and Swiss cheese. Cook 1 to 2 minutes until cheese begins to melt.
5. Rest, covered, 5 minutes before serving.
3 OR 4 SERVINGS

Creamed Corn Casserole

2 tablespoons butter
1 egg
⅓ cup soda cracker crumbs
1 can (17 ounces) cream-
style corn
½ teaspoon salt
¼ teaspoon pepper

1. In a 1-quart glass casserole, heat butter 30 seconds. Add egg, cracker crumbs, corn, salt, and pepper; blend evenly.
2. Cook 4 to 6 minutes, stirring halfway through cooking time.
3. Rest 5 minutes before serving.
4 OR 5 SERVINGS

Eggplant Casserole

1 eggplant (about 1½ pounds)
Salt
Flour
½ cup salad oil for skillet
2 cans (8 ounces each)
tomato sauce
1 cup thinly sliced mozzarella cheese
½ cup grated Parmesan cheese

1. Peel eggplant and cut in ½-inch-thick slices. Sprinkle both sides with salt, and set aside 20 to 30 minutes.
2. Dip eggplant slices in flour. Brown eggplant in hot microwave browning dish or in hot salad oil in hot skillet on a conventional range. Drain slices on paper towel.
3. Pour 1 can tomato sauce in a 10-inch glass baking dish. Lay eggplant slices in sauce, and cover with other can of sauce. Place mozzarella cheese over the sauce and sprinkle Parmesan cheese on top.
4. Cover with waxed paper or lid. Cook 12 to 14 minutes, rotating dish one-quarter turn halfway through cooking time.
5. Rest, covered, 5 minutes.
4 TO 6 SERVINGS

Creamed Green Beans

1 jar (8 ounces) pasteurized process cheese spread
1 can (10½ ounces) condensed cream of mushroom soup
Tabasco
1 tablespoon soy sauce
1 medium onion, chopped
3 tablespoons butter
5 fresh mushrooms, cleaned and chopped
1 can (8 ounces) water chestnuts, drained and sliced
2 cans (16 ounces each) French-style green beans, drained
Slivered almonds

1. In a 4-cup glass measure, blend cheese spread, soup, Tabasco, and soy sauce. Cook 3 to 5 minutes, stirring halfway through cooking time.
2. In a 1½-quart glass casserole, cook onion and butter 3 to 4 minutes, stirring halfway through cooking time until onions are transparent. Stir in mushrooms and water chestnuts and cook 1 minute.
3. Add green beans and soup mixture to mushroom mixture; stir to blend. Garnish with almonds.
4. Cook 5 minutes, rotating dish one-quarter turn halfway through cooking time.
5. Rest 5 minutes before serving.
6 TO 8 SERVINGS

Orange-Glazed Carrots

6 to 8 medium carrots, pared and diagonally sliced
2 tablespoons butter
¼ cup brown sugar
2 tablespoons orange juice
1 teaspoon grated orange peel
1 teaspoon lemon juice
¼ teaspoon salt

1. In a 1½-quart glass casserole, combine carrots, butter, brown sugar, orange juice, orange peel, lemon juice, and salt.
2. Cover carrots and cook 10 to 12 minutes, stirring halfway through cooking time.
3. Rest, covered, 10 minutes before serving.
6 TO 8 SERVINGS

Spinach and Mushroom Salad

4 slices cooked bacon (page 776)
1 pound fresh spinach
2 hard-cooked eggs, finely chopped
½ pound fresh mushrooms, cleaned and sliced
2 teaspoons grated orange peel
⅔ cup orange juice
1 tablespoon lemon juice
⅓ cup bacon drippings
2 tablespoons soy sauce
½ teaspoon garlic powder

1. Crumble bacon into small pieces.
2. Wash spinach and remove tough stems. Dry with paper towel. Tear leaves into bite-size pieces and arrange in salad bowl.
3. Add eggs, mushrooms, and bacon. Cover tightly and refrigerate until serving time.
4. In a 1-quart glass measure, blend orange peel, orange juice, lemon juice, bacon drippings, soy sauce, and garlic powder. Cook 1 to 2 minutes, stirring every 30 seconds, until mixture boils.
5. Pour hot dressing over spinach just prior to serving.
4 TO 6 SERVINGS

Lamb Crown Roast with Apricot Stuffing

3 tablespoons butter
½ package (4 ounces) herb-seasoned stuffing mix
¼ cup water
3 tablespoons chopped
celery
3 tablespoons chopped dried apricots
1 lamb rib crown roast (5 to 6 pounds)

1. Melt butter in a 1-quart glass casserole in microwave oven. Add stuffing mix, water, celery and apricots; mix well.
2. Place lamb crown roast on a roast rack set in a 2-quart glass baking dish. Fill center cavity with stuffing. Cover with waxed paper. Roast in microwave oven 10 minutes.
3. Rotate dish one-half turn. Shield meat and ribs as needed with foil. Roast covered in microwave oven set at 160°F.
4. Remove roast from oven. Cover with foil and allow to stand 10 minutes before serving.
ABOUT 8 SERVINGS

Chinese Tomato Beef

2 pounds beef steak (sirloin, round, flank, or chuck)
2 tablespoons sugar
½ cup soy sauce
1 clove garlic, minced
¼ teaspoon ginger
3 tablespoons salad oil
2 large green peppers, cut in strips
3 green onions, cut in 1-inch pieces
2 large tomatoes, peeled and cut in wedges
2 tablespoons cornstarch
¼ cup water

1. Slice steak diagonally across the grain in ⅛-inch-thick slices. Meat will slice easier if placed in the freezer 30 minutes.
2. In a 2-cup glass measure, combine sugar, soy sauce, garlic, and ginger. Pour over meat in a 9-inch baking dish. Marinate at least 30 minutes, turning meat occasionally.
3. Preheat browning dish 6 minutes. Remove meat from marinade; reserve marinade. Add oil and meat to dish. Fry meat 5 to 6 minutes in microwave oven, stirring halfway through cooking time. Drain cooking juices into marinade.
4. Stir green pepper and onion into meat. Cook 3 to 4 minutes, stirring halfway through cooking time. Top with tomato wedges.
5. In a 1-cup glass measure, combine cornstarch and water, and blend with marinade. Cook 1 to 2 minutes, stirring halfway through cooking time, until thickened. Pour over meat and vegetables and heat 1 to 2 minutes.
6. Rest 5 minutes and serve over **hot fluffy rice.**
8 SERVINGS

Swiss Steak

1½ to 2 pounds beef round steak, cut in serving pieces and floured
2 tablespoons salad oil
1 can (10 ounces) condensed cream of mushroom soup
1 soup can water
½ teaspoon salt
Dash pepper
¼ teaspoon garlic powder
1 small onion, chopped
½ cup chopped green pepper

1. Brown meat in hot oil on range in a conventional skillet or in microwave oven. To brown in microwave oven, preheat browning skillet 6 minutes. Pour oil in hot pan and cook meat 1½ minutes, turn over, and cook for 1 minute. Place meat in a 2-quart glass casserole.
2. In a mixing bowl, blend soup with water, salt, pepper, and garlic powder. Pour over meat. Arrange onion and green pepper on top.
3. Cook, covered, 10 minutes; rest 5 minutes. Rotate dish one-quarter turn and cook 7 to 8 minutes; rest 5 minutes. Rotate dish one-quarter turn and cook 10 minutes.
4. Rest 10 minutes before serving.
6 TO 8 SERVINGS

Marinated Flank Steak

⅓ cup soy sauce
2 tablespoons vinegar
¼ cup minced onion
¼ teaspoon garlic powder
1½ teaspoons ground ginger
2 tablespoons sugar
2 pounds beef flank steak

1. In a 2-quart glass baking dish, blend soy sauce, vinegar, onion, garlic powder, ginger, and sugar. Dip meat in mixture and marinate 4 hours, turning occasionally.
2. Cut steak into serving pieces. Pound to tenderize.
3. Return to 2-quart dish with sauce and cook, covered, 12 to 14 minutes, rotating dish one-quarter turn halfway through cooking time.
4. Serve with **hot rice.**
6 OR 7 SERVINGS

Sukiyaki

1 pound beef sirloin steak, diagonally sliced in very thin long strips
2 cups celery, diagonally sliced in ½-inch pieces
2 medium onions, cut in wedges
1 bunch green onions, including tops, cut in 1-inch lengths
2 cups sliced fresh mushrooms
2 cans (5 ounces each) bamboo shoots, drained
½ cup soy sauce
¼ cup sugar
½ cup saké or beef stock

1. Stir-fry meat in conventional skillet on top of range, or using microwave oven, preheat browning dish 6 minutes, add meat, and fry 2 to 3 minutes until well browned.
2. In a 2-quart glass casserole, combine celery, onion, green onion, mushrooms, and bamboo shoots with meat. Cook, covered, 6 to 8 minutes, stirring halfway through cooking time. Rest, covered, 10 minutes.
3. In a 1-cup glass measure, blend soy sauce, sugar, and saké. Cook 1 minute, stirring halfway through cooking time.
4. Pour sauce over vegetables and stir to blend.
5. Serve hot over **fluffy rice.**
4 TO 6 SERVINGS

Teriyaki Steak

2 to 2½ pounds beef chuck or sirloin steak
¾ teaspoon ginger
2 tablespoons sugar
¼ cup salad oil
¼ cup soy sauce
2 tablespoons sherry
1 clove garlic, minced

1. Slice meat diagonally into ⅛-inch-thick strips. Meat will slice easier if placed in the freezer 30 minutes.
2. In a 2-cup glass measure, combine ginger, sugar, oil, soy sauce, sherry, and garlic. Stir to blend. Pour over meat strips and marinate from 1 hour to overnight.
3. Preheat browning dish 5 minutes. Reserving marinade, remove meat from marinade and add to hot dish: fry 2 to 3 minutes, stirring after every minute. (See Note.)
4. Pour marinade over meat and cook 4 to 5 minutes more, stirring after every minute.
5. Serve hot over **fluffy rice.**
4 TO 6 SERVINGS

Note: If desired, meat may be browned in a conventional skillet on top of the range, and then transferred to a 2-quart glass baking dish.

Beef Roast

5- to 6-pound beef roast (rib, rump, or chuck)

1. Place roast on roasting rack in a 2-quart glass baking dish. Shield protruding corners or bone ends with foil. Do not allow foil to touch inside walls of oven.
2. Cook, using the following times: for rare meat, 6 to 7 minutes per pound; for medium, 7 to 8 minutes per pound; and for well-done, 8 to 9 minutes per pound. Turn roast over and rotate the dish one-quarter turn halfway through cooking time.
3. Rest 10 to 15 minutes before carving and serving.
10 TO 12 SERVINGS

Favorite Meat Loaf

1¾ pounds ground beef	½ teaspoon pepper
¾ cup uncooked oats	1 cup tomato juice
¼ cup finely minced onion	2 eggs
¼ cup chopped celery	½ cup ketchup
1½ teaspoons salt	

1. In a large mixing bowl, combine ground beef, oats, onion, celery, salt, pepper, tomato juice, and eggs, blending evenly.
2. Turn mixture into a 9-inch glass pie plate with a glass, open end up, in center of dish, packing lightly.
3. Cook 6 to 8 minutes, rotating dish one-quarter turn halfway through cooking time.
4. Remove excess drippings. Pour ketchup over top, cover with waxed paper, and cook 6 to 8 minutes, rotating dish one-quarter turn halfway through cooking time.
5. Rest, covered, 10 minutes before serving.
4 TO 6 SERVINGS

German Meatball Stew

1½ pounds ground beef	2 tablespoons salad oil
1 egg	1 pound carrots, pared and
1½ teaspoons salt	sliced
½ teaspoon pepper	1½ cups beer or beef broth
1 large potato, pared and	1½ cups water
grated	¼ cup flour
½ teaspoon ginger	Fluffy Dumplings (optional)
2 large onions, sliced	

1. In a large mixing bowl, combine ground beef, egg, salt, pepper, potato, and ginger, blending evenly. Shape 24 meatballs.
2. Arrange meatballs evenly in a 2-quart glass baking dish. Cook 10 to 12 minutes, stirring halfway through cooking time.
3. In a 3-quart glass casserole, combine onions and oil and cook 2 minutes. Stir in carrots and cook, covered, 5 to 6 minutes.
4. Add meatballs, beer, and 1 cup water to casserole. Bring to boiling and cook 10 to 12 minutes, rotating one-quarter turn halfway through cooking time.
5. In a 2-cup glass measure, combine ½ cup water with flour and stir to blend. Stir flour mixture into liquid in stew. If desired, drop dumpling dough on stew. Cook, covered, 7 to 10 minutes, rotating one-quarter turn halfway through cooking time.
6. Rest, covered, 10 minutes before serving.

Fluffy Dumplings: In a small mixing bowl, combine **1½ cups all-purpose flour, 1 tablespoon baking powder, ½ teaspoon salt,** and **¼ cup chopped parsley.** Stir in **⅔ cup milk** until ingredients are moistened. Bring **2½ cups stock** to boiling. Drop dough by rounded teaspoonfuls onto boiling stock. Cook, covered, 7 to 10 minutes, rotating dish one-quarter turn halfway through cooking time. Rest 5 minutes before serving.
6 TO 8 SERVINGS

Rice-Stuffed Hamburger

1 pound ground beef	1 can (8 ounces) tomato
½ teaspoon salt	sauce
2 tablespoons chopped	2 cups cooked rice
onion	4 slices mozzarella cheese

1. In a mixing bowl, combine ground beef, salt, onion, and tomato sauce.
2. Spread half of mixture evenly over bottom of an 8-inch square glass dish. Lightly press rice onto meat. Layer cheese over rice. Spread remaining meat mixture on top.
3. Cook 6 to 8 minutes, rotating dish one-quarter turn halfway through cooking time. Spoon off drippings.
4. Rest 10 minutes before slicing.
4 TO 6 SERVINGS
Conventional oven: Bake at 375°F 30 to 40 minutes.

Many-Way Meatballs

1 pound ground beef	densed Cheddar cheese,
¼ cup dry bread crumbs	cream of celery, or cream
¼ cup minced onion	of mushroom soup
1 egg	½ cup water
¼ teaspoon salt	2 tablespoons parsley flakes
1 can (10½ ounces) con-	

1. In a mixing bowl, combine beef, bread crumbs, onion, egg, and salt. Shape into 16 meatballs, and place in a 2-quart baking dish.
2. Cook, covered, 5 to 6 minutes, stirring halfway through cooking time. Pour off drippings.
3. Stir in soup, water, and parsley. Cover and cook 6 to 8 minutes, stirring halfway through cooking time.
4. Rest 5 minutes before serving.
3 OR 4 SERVINGS

Sweet-and-Sour Meatballs

1 pound ground beef	chunks, drained (reserve
1 egg	juice)
1 tablespoon cornstarch	½ cup sugar
2 tablespoons finely minced	3 tablespoons cornstarch
green onion	1 tablespoon soy sauce
1 teaspoon salt	3 tablespoons vinegar
Dash pepper	4 cups cooked rice
1 can (16 ounces) pineapple	

1. In a medium mixing bowl, blend ground beef, egg, cornstarch, onion, salt, and pepper. Shape 1 tablespoon mixture around each pineapple chunk. Reserve remaining pineapple.
2. In a glass pie plate, arrange meatballs evenly around edge. Cook 5 to 7 minutes, stirring to rearrange meatballs halfway through cooking time.
3. In a 2-cup glass measure, blend sugar, cornstarch, soy sauce, vinegar, and reserved pineapple juice.
4. Cook sauce 2 to 3 minutes, or until mixture begins to boil, stirring after every minute.
5. Pour sauce and remaining pineapple chunks over meatballs, mixing gently.
6. Serve over cooked rice.
4 SERVINGS

Cheese Meat Loaf

2 slices bread	½ cup shredded Cheddar
⅓ cup milk	cheese
½ medium onion, chopped	1 teaspoon salt
2 eggs	¼ cup tomato sauce
1 pound ground beef	

1. Soak bread in milk.
2. In a large mixing bowl, combine bread, milk, onion, eggs, beef, cheese, and salt. Shape into loaf and place in glass loaf dish.
3. Cook 6 to 8 minutes, rotating dish one-quarter turn halfway through cooking time.
4. Pour tomato sauce over top and heat 1 minute.
5. Rest 10 minutes before slicing.
ABOUT 4 SERVINGS

Conventional oven: Bake at 375°F 1 hour.

Note: Loaf may be shaped in a ring for more even cooking.

Spareribs

1½ to 2 pounds lean	½ cup water
spareribs	2 cups Barbecue Sauce

1. In a covered 2-quart casserole, arrange spareribs in serving-size pieces toward edges of dish. Add ¼ cup water, cover, and cook 6 minutes, rotating dish one-quarter turn halfway through cooking time. Pour off water and drippings.
2. Add another ¼ cup water, cover, and cook again 6 minutes, rotating dish one-quarter turn halfway through cooking time. Pour off drippings.
3. Arrange spareribs in a 10-inch glass serving dish and cover with Barbecue Sauce.
4. Cook, uncovered, 4 to 5 minutes, rotating dish one-quarter turn halfway through cooking time.
5. Rest, uncovered, 5 minutes before serving.
4 SERVINGS

Bacon

Slices bacon

1. Arrange bacon on roasting rack or on crumpled paper towels in a 2-quart glass baking dish. Heat bacon 30 seconds to make separating slices easy. If there is more than 1 layer of bacon, placed crumpled paper towel between layers. Cover with paper towel to prevent spattering.
2. Cook until desired crispness is reached, using the following time guides: cook 1 slice bacon 1 to 1½ minutes; 2 slices, 2 to 2½ minutes; 4 slices, 4 to 4½ minutes; 6 slices, 5½ to 6 minutes; and 8 slices, 6 to 7 minutes. Rotate dish one-quarter turn halfway through cooking time.
3. To cook 1 pound of bacon, place separated slices in a glass baking dish. Heat about 4 minutes; rearrange bacon slices so cooked slices are in the center and uncooked pieces are near the edges. Continue cooking 4 to 5 minutes, or until done.

Broccoli 'n' Ham Roll-Ups

1½ pounds fresh broccoli	¼ cup Madeira
½ teaspoon salt	¼ cup half-and-half
3 tablespoons butter or	8 ounces fresh mushrooms,
margarine	cleaned and sliced
3 tablespoons flour	24 thin slices Swiss cheese
1 teaspoon prepared	(8 ounces)
horseradish	12 slices (1½ pounds)
¾ cup chicken broth	cooked ham

1. Wash and trim broccoli. Place with ½ cup water and salt in a 2-quart covered glass casserole. Cook in microwave oven for 8 to 10 minutes, stirring after 4 minutes. Drain. Allow to stand covered for 5 minutes.
2. Melt butter in a 1-quart glass measuring cup (30 seconds). Blend in flour. Add horseradish. Add broth and Madeira gradually, stirring until smooth. Cook uncovered in microwave oven 2½ to 3 minutes, or until thickened; stir twice.
3. Stir in half-and-half and mushrooms. Cook uncovered in microwave oven 1 minute.
4. Place 2 cheese slices and 2 broccoli spears on each ham slice. Roll up and place in a 3-quart glass baking dish. Pour sauce over all. Heat uncovered in microwave oven to serving temperature (6 to 8 minutes); rotate dish one-half turn once.
6 SERVINGS

Lamb Roast

5- to 6-pound lamb leg roast

1. Place roast, fat side down, on roasting rack in a 2-quart glass baking dish. Shield protruding corners or bones with foil. Do not allow foil to touch walls inside microwave oven.
2. Cook, using the following times: for medium, 7 to 8 minutes per pound; and for well-done, 8 to 9 minutes per pound. Turn roast over and rotate the dish one-quarter turn halfway through cooking time.
3. Rest 15 minutes before carving and serving.
8 TO 10 SERVINGS

Apple-Stuffed Pork Chops

1 cup bread crumbs	2 tablespoons butter
1 cup pared and cubed	1 teaspoon salt
cooking apples	4 to 6 medium pork chops

1. In a small mixing bowl, combine bread crumbs, apples, butter, and salt. Cook 2 to 3 minutes, stirring after every minute.
2. Cut a slit in each pork chop and stuff with bread-crumb mixture. Arrange in a 2-quart glass baking dish.
3. Cook, covered, 16 to 20 minutes, rotating dish one-quarter turn halfway through cooking time.
4. Rest, covered, 10 minutes before serving.
4 TO 6 SERVINGS

Cooked Ham

Fresh Ham

5- to 6-pound cook-before-eating ham

1. Place ham on roasting rack in a 2-quart glass baking dish. Shield protruding corners or shank end with foil. Do not allow foil to touch walls inside microwave oven.
2. Cook 40 to 50 minutes, allowing 8 to 9 minutes per pound. Turn ham over and rotate dish one-quarter turn halfway through cooking time.
3. Rest 10 to 15 minutes before carving or serving.
10 TO 12 SERVINGS

Cooked Ham: Follow recipe for Fresh Ham, but allow 6 to 7 minutes per pound cooking time, or 30 to 40 minutes for a 5- to 6-pound ham.

Fresh Pork Roast: Follow recipe for Fresh Ham, allowing 8 to 9 minutes per pound cooking time.

Breakfast Kabobs

8 ounces link pork sausage
6 ounces Canadian bacon, or
  12 ounces canned lunch-
  eon meat
1 can (8 ounces) pineapple

chunks, drained
16 maraschino cherries
Maple syrup
8 bamboo skewers

1. Cut each sausage link in 3 or 4 pieces. Cut bacon in small cubes.
2. Thread meat and fruit alternately on skewers. Arrange in a 2-quart glass baking dish and brush with maple syrup.
3. Cook, covered, 4 to 6 minutes, rotating one-quarter turn and basting with syrup halfway through cooking time.
4 TO 6 SERVINGS

Sausage Ring

1 pound bulk pork sausage
2 eggs
2 tablespoons minced onion

½ cup bread crumbs
2 tablespoons parsley flakes

1. In a 1-quart casserole, blend sausage, eggs, onion, bread crumbs, and parsley flakes. Mold into a ring and place a small glass, open end up, in the center of the ring.
2. Cook 5 to 6 minutes, rotating dish one-quarter turn halfway through cooking time.
3. Rest 5 minutes, remove glass from center, and invert ring on plate to serve. Center may be filled with **cooked rice** or **noodles.** If using for breakfast, center may be filled with **scrambled eggs.**
4 OR 5 SERVINGS

Note: Leftover Sausage Ring makes good sandwiches when reheated.

Glazed Ham Steak

½ cup buttermilk
1 smoked ham center slice,
  about 1 inch thick, cut in
  serving pieces
1 teaspoon dry mustard

1 teaspoon flour
¼ teaspoon pepper
2 egg yolks
1 cup buttermilk
Paprika

1. Generously brush ½ cup buttermilk on both sides of ham slice. Arrange on roasting rack in a 2-quart glass baking dish.
2. Cook 7 to 8 minutes, rotating dish one-quarter turn halfway through cooking time.
3. In a 2-cup glass measure, combine mustard, flour, pepper, and egg yolks, blending well. Slowly add 1 cup buttermilk, stirring until combined.
4. Cook 2 to 3 minutes, stirring every 30 seconds, until mixture thickens.
5. Spoon over individual ham portions, arranged in serving dish. Sprinkle with paprika. Reheat 1 to 2 minutes if needed.
6 TO 8 SERVINGS

Barbecued Meatballs

1 pound ground beef
1 egg
1 teaspoon anise seed
1 teaspoon salt
¼ teaspoon pepper
1 bottle (14 ounces) ketchup
¼ cup chopped onion
¼ cup vinegar

½ cup salad oil
¼ cup water
2 teaspoons Worcestershire
  sauce
½ teaspoon Tabasco
1 clove garlic, minced
1 teaspoon salt

1. In a medium mixing bowl, blend ground beef, egg, anise, 1 teaspoon salt, and pepper. Shape into 24 meatballs.
2. Arrange meatballs evenly toward outer edges of a 2-quart glass baking dish. Cook 5 to 6 minutes, rearranging meatballs in dish halfway through cooking time. Drain off juices.
3. In a 2-quart glass baking dish, combine ketchup, onion, vinegar, brown sugar, oil, water, Worcestershire sauce, Tabasco, garlic and 1 teaspoon salt. Cook sauce 4 minutes, stirring halfway through cooking time.
4. Add meatballs to sauce and cook 4 to 5 minutes, stirring halfway through cooking time.
5. Serve over **cooked rice** or **noodles**
4 TO 6 SERVINGS

Tangy Pork Chops

4 to 6 pork chops
Prepared mustard
1 can (10½ ounces) con-

densed cream of celery
  soup

1. Spread both sides of each pork chop with mustard and place in a 10-inch glass baking dish.
2. Cook pork chops 6 to 8 minutes, rotating dish one-quarter turn halfway through cooking time.
3. Remove drippings from pan. Pour soup over pork chops. Cook, covered, 5 to 6 minutes, rotating dish one-quarter turn halfway through cooking time.
4. Rest, covered, 5 minutes before serving.
4 TO 6 SERVINGS

Chicken Hawaiian

1½ cups sliced celery
1 green pepper, cut in strips
3 tablespoons butter
3 cups cubed cooked
  chicken
1 can (21 ounces) pineapple

pie filling
¼ cup soy sauce
2 teaspoons instant chicken
  bouillon
Chow mein noodles
Parsley (optional)

1. In a 2-quart glass casserole, blend celery, green pepper, and butter. Cook 3 to 4 minutes, stirring halfway through cooking time.
2. Add chicken, pie filling, soy sauce, and bouillon; mix well.
3. Cook, covered, 10 to 12 minutes, stirring halfway through cooking time.
4. Serve over chow mein noodles and garnish with parsley, if desired.
5 OR 6 SERVINGS

Microwave Fried Chicken

1 broiler-fryer (2½ to 3 pounds)
1 cup corn flake crumbs
¼ cup butter
Paprika

1. Wash chicken and coat with crumbs. In a 1-cup glass measure, heat butter 45 seconds.
2. On roasting rack in a 2-quart glass baking dish, arrange chicken with meatier pieces around edges of dish, and smaller pieces, such as wings, in the center. Pour a small amount of butter over each piece. Sprinkle with paprika.
3. Cook 10 to 12 minutes. Turn chicken pieces over and coat each piece with remaining butter and paprika. Cook 10 to 12 minutes.
4. Rest 5 minutes before serving.
4 TO 6 SERVINGS

Note: The chicken may be covered during cooking, which will steam the chicken, producing a soft, not crisp, skin. If the chicken is in a glass ceramic baking dish or is transferred to a metal pan, additional browning can be achieved by placing cooked chicken under a conventional broiler 1 to 2 minutes.

Chicken Enchiladas

1 onion, finely chopped
2 tablespoons butter
4 cups chopped cooked chicken or turkey
1 can (4 ounces) chopped green chilies
1 can (10½ ounces) condensed cream of chicken soup
12 frozen corn tortillas
1 can (10½ ounces) condensed cream of celery soup
1½ cups sour cream
1 pound Cheddar or Monterey Jack cheese, shredded

1. In a large glass mixing bowl, cook onion in butter 2 minutes, stirring halfway through cooking time. Blend in chicken, chilies, and cream of chicken soup.
2. Defrost tortillas until soft and easy to roll, about 1 minute. Spread about 3 tablespoons chicken mixture on each tortilla, roll, and secure with a wooden pick. Arrange in two 9-inch glass baking dishes.
3. In a small mixing bowl, blend cream of celery soup and sour cream. Pour over enchiladas.
4. Cook each dish 10 to 12 minutes, rotating one-quarter turn halfway through cooking time.
5. Sprinkle ½ pound of the cheese over top of each dish and heat for 1 minute.
6. Rest covered, 10 minutes. Remove wooden picks and serve.
6 TO 8 SERVINGS

Note: The enchiladas may be prepared through step 3, and then frozen immediately. Continue with steps 4 and 5 when casserole has been thawed and is ready to heat.

Chicken and Broccoli

2 packages (10 ounces each) frozen broccoli
3 chicken breasts, cooked and cut in serving pieces
1 can (10½ ounces) condensed cream of chicken soup
⅔ cup mayonnaise
½ cup milk
½ cup shredded Cheddar cheese
1 can (6 ounces) water chestnuts, drained and sliced
1 teaspoon lemon juice
½ teaspoon curry powder
½ cup chopped cashews
½ cup bread crumbs

1. Pierce broccoli packages and cook 6 to 8 minutes, rotating packages one-quarter turn halfway through cooking time.
2. Arrange broccoli evenly in bottom of a 2-quart baking dish and layer chicken on top.
3. In a small mixing bowl, blend soup, mayonnaise, milk, cheese, water chestnuts, lemon juice, curry powder, and cashews. Pour over chicken and broccoli. Sprinkle bread crumbs on top.
4. Cook 10 to 12 minutes, rotating dish one-quarter turn halfway through cooking time.
5. Rest, covered, 10 minutes before serving.
4 TO 6 SERVINGS

Creamed Chicken Casserole

4 chicken breasts, halved
1 can (10½ ounces) condensed cream of chicken soup
2 tablespoons brandy
½ cup sour cream
2 green onions, chopped
Dash pepper
¼ cup cashews
Parsley, chopped
Paprika

1. Wash chicken and pat dry. Arrange in a 2-quart baking dish. Cook 10 to 12 minutes, rotating one-quarter turn halfway through cooking time.
2. In a mixing bowl blend soup, brandy, sour cream, onion, pepper, and cashews. Pour over chicken.
3. Cook, covered, 12 to 15 minutes, rotating one-quarter turn halfway through cooking time.
4. Garnish with parsley or paprika, if desired.
4 SERVINGS

Chicken and Rice Dinner

¾ cup packaged precooked rice
1 can (10½ ounces) condensed cream of mushroom soup
1 can (4 ounces) mushroom
pieces (undrained)
¼ cup minced onion
1 can (13 ounces) evaporated milk
2 pounds chicken thighs and drumsticks

1. In a 3-quart glass casserole, blend rice, soup, mushrooms with liquid, onion, and milk. Cook, covered, 5 minutes, stirring halfway through cooking time.
2. Arrange chicken pieces in casserole. Cover, and cook 20 minutes, rotating dish one-quarter turn halfway through cooking time.
3. Rest, covered, 10 minutes before serving.
4 OR 5 SERVINGS

Roast Turkey

8- to 15-pound turkey
2 tablespoons butter
1 tablespoon bottled brown bouquet sauce

1. Clean and prepare turkey for cooking as directed on turkey wrapper. Place turkey, breast down on roasting rack in a glass baking dish; cover with waxed paper.
2. Estimate the total cooking time. For an 8- to 12-pound turkey allow 7 to 8 minutes per pound, and for a 12- to 15-pound turkey allow 6 to 7 minutes per pound. Cook the turkey for a fourth of the estimated cooking time.
3. Melt the butter in a custard cup and mix with the bottled brown bouquet sauce. Brush the turkey with the mixture. Cover the bottom half of wings and legs with small pieces of aluminum foil. Secure legs and wings close to body with string. Cover with waxed paper. Do not allow foil to touch inside walls of microwave oven.
4. Place turkey on its side and cook a fourth of estimated roasting time. Turn turkey on its other side and cook for another fourth of estimated roasting time. Cut strings to allow legs and wings to stand free, remove foil, place turkey breast up and cook until turkey reaches internal temperature of 175°F. Each time turkey is turned rotate dish one-quarter turn and baste with drippings. Remove drippings as they accumulate, or additional cooking time will be needed.
5. When cooking time is up, rest the turkey 15 to 20 minutes; temperature should reach 190°F. Return to oven for additional cooking if needed.
6. Garnish with green grapes and serve.
ABOUT 2 SERVINGS PER POUND

Note: If desired, turkey cavity may be filled with Apple Dressing. Follow Roast recipe, but add 6 minutes per pound to the cooking time.

Cranberry Sauce

2 cups sugar
1 cup water
1 pound fresh cranberries (4 cups)

1. Dissolve sugar in water in a 3-quart glass casserole. Stir in cranberries and cover dish.
2. Cook 8 to 10 minutes, stirring every 3 or 4 minutes, or until mixture boils and cranberries begin to pop.
3. Rest 10 minutes. Serve warm or chilled.
ABOUT 4 CUPS SAUCE

Dinner Chicken Wings

2 to 3 pounds chicken wings
1 teaspoon ginger
1 teaspoon dry mustard
1 tablespoon brown sugar
⅓ cup soy sauce
3 tablespoons salad oil
3 cloves garlic, quartered
2 tablespoons sesame seed

1. Clip wing tips from each wing. Divide each wing at the joint, in two pieces. Place wing pieces in a 2-quart glass baking dish.
2. In a mixing bowl, blend ginger, mustard, brown sugar, soy sauce, oil, and garlic. Pour over chicken pieces and marinate overnight.
3. Remove the garlic pieces from the marinade. Cook the chicken in marinade 12 to 14 minutes, rotating dish one-quarter turn halfway through cooking time.
4. Rest, covered with waxed paper, 10 minutes. Pour off marinade. Sprinkle chicken with sesame seed and heat 1 minute.
5 OR 6 SERVINGS

Note: Dinner Chicken Wings may be served with rice for a main dish or used as an appetizer.

Cranberry Chicken

1 broiler fryer (2½ to 3 pounds), cut in serving pieces
2 tablespoons lemon juice
3 tablespoons brown sugar
1 can (16 ounces) cranberry sauce

1. Arrange chicken pieces in a 2-quart glass baking dish with meatier pieces toward edge.
2. In a 1-cup glass measure, blend lemon juice, brown sugar, and cranberry sauce. Pour sauce evenly over chicken and cover dish with waxed paper.
3. Cook 20 minutes, basting with sauce and rotating dish one-quarter turn halfway through cooking time.
4. Rest, covered, 10 minutes before serving.
4 TO 6 SERVINGS

Chicken Cacciatore

1 broiler fryer, cut up (2½ to 3 pounds)
¼ teaspoon salt
¼ teaspoon dry mustard
3 tablespoons salad oil
1 tablespoon vinegar
¼ teaspoon pepper
½ cup ketchup or chili sauce
1 tablespoon parsley flakes

1. In a 2-quart glass baking dish, arrange chicken pieces with meatier pieces toward the edge.
2. In a 2-cup measure, combine salt, dry mustard, oil, vinegar, pepper, ketchup, and parsley flakes; stir to blend. Pour sauce over chicken.
3. Cook, covered, 20 minutes, rotating dish one-quarter turn halfway through cooking time.
4. Rest, covered, 10 minutes before serving.
5 OR 6 SERVINGS

Honey-Glazed Chicken

1 chicken (3 to 3½ pounds), cut in serving pieces	peel
2 tablespoons butter	1 teaspoon salt
⅓ cup honey	¾ teaspoon garlic powder
1 teaspoon grated orange	1 teaspoon dry mustard
	¼ teaspoon pepper

1. In a 2-quart glass baking dish, arrange chicken on a rack, if possible. Place meatier pieces in corners and small pieces in the center. Place giblets in the center tucked under back or wings. Cover with waxed paper.
2. Cook 15 minutes, rotating dish one-quarter turn halfway through cooking time.
3. In a 1-cup glass measure, heat butter 15 to 30 seconds. Add honey, orange peel, salt, garlic powder, dry mustard, and pepper; stir to blend. Heat mixture 30 seconds. Brush chicken pieces with honey-butter mixture.
4. Cook, uncovered, 4 minutes. Turn chicken pieces over and brush with remaining mixture. Return to oven and cook, uncovered, 3 to 4 minutes.
5. Remove chicken pieces to serving dish, pour drippings over chicken, and serve.
4 TO 6 SERVINGS

Conventional oven: Bake at 375°F 1¼ hours.

Apple Dressing

1½ cups finely chopped celery	1 teaspoon sage or thyme
⅔ cup finely chopped onion	½ to ¾ cup water
1 cup butter	12 cups dry bread cubes
1 teaspoon salt	3 cups pared and chopped apple

1. In a 3-quart glass casserole, sauté celery and onion in butter 2 to 3 minutes, stirring after every minute.
2. Mix together salt, sage, and water. Pour over bread cubes, tossing lightly to mix.
3. Add bread cubes to vegetable mixture. Stir in apple, blending evenly.
4. Stuff turkey just before roasting, or cook dressing in a 3-quart casserole dish 10 to 12 minutes, rotating dish one-quarter turn halfway through cooking time.
5. Rest 5 minutes before serving.
10 TO 12 SERVINGS

Note: This dressing is also good with pork chops. Extra dressing may be frozen and reheated later.

Chicken Livers and Mushrooms

1 to 1½ pounds chicken livers	¾ teaspoon salt
½ pound fresh mushrooms, thinly sliced	½ teaspoon pepper
¼ cup grated onion	½ cup burgundy
2 tablespoons chopped parsley	¼ cup butter
	6 slices toast or 3 English muffins, split and toasted

1. Dice livers coarsely. Combine with mushrooms, onion, parsley, salt, pepper, and wine in a large plastic bag. Marinate in refrigerator overnight.
2. In a 2-quart glass casserole, heat butter 30 to 45 seconds. Add chicken-liver mixture.
3. Cook, uncovered, 6 to 8 minutes, stirring every 2 minutes. Cover casserole and cook 3 to 4 minutes more.
4. Spoon onto toasted bread or muffins arranged on serving platter.
4 TO 6 SERVINGS

Yesterday's Turkey Casserole

¼ cup butter	2 chicken bouillon cubes
⅓ cup flour	¾ teaspoon salt
½ cup chopped onion	8 small fresh mushrooms, sliced
¾ cup thinly sliced celery	2 cups cooked diced turkey
1½ cups water	

1. In a 2-quart casserole, cook butter 30 to 45 seconds. Add flour; blend until smooth. Stir in onion, celery, water, bouillon cubes, and salt.
2. Cook 5 to 6 minutes, until mixture thickens. Stir once halfway through cooking.
3. Add mushrooms and turkey; stir to blend.
4. Cook, covered, 3 to 4 minutes, rotating dish one-quarter turn halfway through cooking time.
5. Serve over **toast, rice,** or **leftover stuffing.**
4 SERVINGS

Note: Chicken may be substituted for turkey. If no leftover cooked chicken is available, cook chicken breasts 7 minutes per pound. Cool chicken, remove meat from bones, and dice.

Turkey Tetrazzini

8 ounces uncooked spaghetti
¼ cup butter
¼ cup flour
1 teaspoon salt
¼ teaspoon nutmeg
2 cups turkey broth or 2 chicken bouillon cubes dissolved in 2 cups hot water
1 cup evaporated milk
¼ cup sherry

¼ cup grated Parmesan cheese
2 cups cubed cooked turkey or chicken
¼ pound green pepper, chopped
½ pound fresh mushrooms, sliced
1 egg yolk
½ cup slivered almonds

1. Cook spaghetti following package directions. Drain well.
2. In a 4-cup glass measure, heat butter 30 seconds. Blend in flour, salt, and nutmeg. Stir until mixture is smooth.
3. Stir broth and milk into flour mixture. Cook until mixture boils, 6 to 8 minutes, stirring after every minute. Blend sherry and cheese into sauce and add sauce to cooked spaghetti.
4. In a 2-quart glass casserole, combine spaghetti, turkey, green pepper, mushrooms, and egg yolk; blend thoroughly. Sprinkle with almonds.
5. Cook, uncovered, 6 to 8 minutes, rotating dish one-quarter turn halfway through cooking time. Rest 10 minutes before serving.
6 TO 8 SERVINGS

Conventional oven: Bake at 350°F 25 to 30 minutes.

Trout Amandine with Pineapple

2 tablespoons butter
1 package (2¼ ounces)
  slivered almonds
¼ cup (½ stick) butter
1 tablespoon lemon juice

6 whole cleaned and boned
  trout (about 8 ounces each)
6 drained canned pineapple
  slices

1. Put 2 tablespoons butter and almonds into a glass pie plate. Cook uncovered in microwave oven 5 to 6 minutes; stir every minute just until almonds are lightly toasted. Set aside.
2. Melt remaining butter in a 2-cup glass measuring cup in microwave oven (30 seconds). Add lemon juice.
3. Brush whole trout inside and out with lemon-butter mixture. Arrange fish around edge of a microwave-safe serving plate in a circular pattern. Fit a small piece of foil over each head to shield. Cover with plastic wrap.
4. Cook in microwave oven 6 to 7 minutes, or until fish flakes easily. (Be certain to check for doneness under shielded area.)
5. Remove from oven and allow to stand covered 2 minutes.
6. Meanwhile, arrange pineapple slices on toasted almonds. Cover with plastic wrap. Heat in microwave oven 2 minutes. Garnish fish with almonds and pineapple.
6 SERVINGS

Stuffed Flounder

¼ cup chopped green onion
¼ cup butter
1 can (4 ounces) chopped
  mushrooms
1 can (16½ ounces) crab
  meat, drained
½ cup cracker crumbs
2 tablespoons parsley flakes
½ teaspoon salt
¼ teaspoon pepper
2 pounds flounder fillets, cut

in serving pieces
2 tablespoons butter
2 tablespoons flour
¼ teaspoon salt
Milk
⅓ cup sherry
1 cup shredded Cheddar
  cheese
½ teaspoon paprika
1 teaspoon parsley flakes

1. In a 2-quart glass casserole, combine green onion and butter and cook 2 to 3 minutes, stirring after every minute.
2. Drain mushrooms and reserve liquid. Combine mushrooms, crab meat, cracker crumbs, 2 tablespoons parsley flakes, salt, and pepper with cooked onion. Spread mixture over fish fillets. Roll up each piece of fish and secure with a wooden pick. Place seam side down in a 10-inch glass baking dish.
3. In a 4-cup glass measure, heat butter 30 seconds. Stir in flour and salt.
4. Add enough milk to reserved mushroom liquid to make 1 cup. Gradually stir milk and sherry into flour mixture. Cook sauce 2 to 3 minutes, stirring every minute, until thickened. Pour sauce over flounder.
5. Cook flounder 6 to 8 minutes, rotating dish one-quarter turn halfway through cooking time.
6. Sprinkle cheese, paprika, and 1 teaspoon parsley flakes over fish. Cook 3 to 5 minutes, or until fish flakes easily with fork.
6 TO 8 SERVINGS

Fish with Caper Stuffing

1 dressed trout, pike, haddock, perch, or flounder
  (about 1½ pounds)
1 teaspoon salt
1 cup coarse dry bread
  crumbs
¼ cup capers
2 tablespoons finely chopped

green onion
2 tablespoons finely chopped
  parsley
1 egg, slightly beaten
2 to 4 tablespoons
  half-and-half
Lemon wedges

1. Rinse fish under cold water; drain well and pat dry with paper towels. Sprinkle cavity with salt and set aside.
2. Combine bread crumbs, capers, green onion, and parsley. Blend egg with 2 tablespoons half-and-half and pour over bread crumb mixture. Mix until moistened, adding additional half-and-half if necessary.
3. Lightly pile stuffing into fish. Fasten with wooden picks or secure with string. Place in an 11x7-inch baking dish. Cover with waxed paper.
4. Cook fish 8 to 10 minutes, or until fish flakes when tested with a fork; rotate dish one-quarter turn halfway through the cooking time. Allow to stand 2 minutes after cooking before serving. Garnish with lemon wedges.
4 SERVINGS

Crab-Stuffed Sole

3 tablespoons butter
3 tablespoons flour
1½ cups milk
⅓ cup sherry
½ teaspoon salt
1 cup shredded Swiss cheese
2 pounds sole fillets
Salt

Pepper
1 medium onion, minced
2 tablespoons butter
1 can (6½ ounces) crab meat
5 fresh mushrooms, cleaned
  and chopped
½ cup cracker crumbs
Parsley flakes

1. In a 4-cup glass measure, heat butter 30 seconds. Stir in flour, milk, sherry, and salt, blending well. Cook 2 to 3 minutes, stirring every minute until thickened. Stir in cheese and set aside.
2. Cut fish in serving pieces and sprinkle with salt and pepper.
3. In a 4-cup glass measure, cook onion in butter 2 to 3 minutes, stirring once, until tender. Add crab meat, mushrooms, and cracker crumbs; mix well.
4. Spread crab meat mixture evenly over each piece of fish. Roll up pieces of fish and secure with a wooden pick. Place seam side down in a 10-inch glass baking dish.
5. Cook, covered, 5 to 6 minutes, rotating dish one-quarter turn halfway through cooking time. Remove pan drippings and pour sauce over fish. Cook 2 to 3 minutes, sprinkle with parsley flakes, and serve.
6 TO 8 SERVINGS

Paprika Buttered Fish Fillets

1 package (1 pound) frozen fish fillets (perch, haddock, cod, or halibut), thawed
Flour
Salt and pepper
2 tablespoons butter
Paprika

1. Dip fillets in flour seasoned with salt and pepper coating well. Set aside.
2. Melt butter in an 11x7-inch baking dish. Dip fillets in butter and arrange in baking dish. Sprinkle with paprika.
3. Cook, uncovered, 2 to 4 minutes. Do not turn fish over, but do rotate dish one-quarter turn halfway through cooking time.
4. Serve garnished with **cooked asparagus spears** and **carrots.**
ABOUT 4 SERVINGS

Red Snapper à l'Orange

1 pound red snapper, cut in serving pieces
2 tablespoons orange juice
1 teaspoon grated orange
peel
1 tablespoon butter
½ teaspoon lemon juice

1. In a 2-quart glass baking dish, arrange fish evenly around edge.
2. In a 1-cup glass measure, blend orange juice, orange peel, butter, lemon juice, salt, and pepper. Heat 30 seconds and pour over fish.
3. Cook fish, covered, 5 to 6 minutes, rotating dish one-quarter turn halfway through cooking time.
4. Rest, covered, 5 minutes before serving. Garnish with parsley.
4 SERVINGS

Salmonburgers

1 can (16 ounces) salmon
½ cup chopped onion
¼ cup salad oil
⅓ cup dry bread crumbs
2 eggs, beaten
1 teaspoon dry mustard
½ teaspoon salt
½ cup dry bread crumbs

1. Drain salmon, reserving ⅓ cup liquid; set aside.
2. In a 2-cup glass measure, cook onion in oil 2 to 2½ minutes. In a large mixing bowl, combine onion, ⅓ cup dry bread crumbs, reserved salmon liquid, eggs, mustard, salt, and salmon; mix well. Shape into 6 patties.
3. Roll patties in ½ cup bread crumbs. Place on roasting rack in a 2-quart baking dish. Cook patties 5 to 6 minutes, rotating dish one-quarter turn halfway through cooking time. Rest 5 minutes before serving.
3 OR 4 SERVINGS

Salmon Ring: Follow recipe for Salmonburgers. Form mixture into a ring in a 1½-quart glass baking dish. Place a glass, open end up, in center of ring. Cook 5 to 6 minutes, rotating dish one-quarter turn halfway through cooking time. Rest 5 minutes before serving.

Paprika Buttered Fish Fillets

Cold Poached Salmon

2 cups water
½ fresh lemon, thinly sliced
½ medium onion, thinly sliced
6 whole cloves
1 bay leaf
1 stalk celery, cut in 1-inch pieces
1½ teaspoons salt
2 tablespoons lemon juice
3 tablespoons vinegar
4 salmon steaks or fillets

1. In a 2-quart glass baking dish, combine water, lemon, onion, cloves, bay leaf, celery, salt, lemon juice, and vinegar. Heat, covered, 5 to 6 minutes, stirring halfway through cooking time.
2. Arrange salmon in corners of baking dish. Cook, covered, 5 to 6 minutes, rotating dish one-quarter turn halfway through cooking time.
3. Gently turn fish over in liquid and rest, covered, 2 to 3 minutes. Fish should flake easily when tested with a fork. Add more cooking time if desired.
4. Remove fish from liquid. Serve hot or refrigerate 3 to 4 hours and serve cold with tartar sauce.
4 SERVINGS

Note: Halibut or other fish may be substituted for the salmon.

Sole Sauté Amandine

3 tablespoons flour
¾ teaspoon salt
¼ teaspoon pepper
1 pound sole or other white fish fillets
1 tablespoon oil
¼ cup butter
¼ cup sliced almonds
1 tablespoon fresh lemon juice
1 tablespoon chopped parsley

1. Combine flour, salt, and pepper in a shallow dish. Dip fillets into mixture, coating on all sides.
2. In a 10-inch glass dish, heat oil and 1 tablespoon butter 1 minute. Place fillets in dish and cover.
3. Sauté 4 to 5 minutes, turning fillets over and rotating dish one-quarter turn halfway through cooking time. Rest, covered, 5 minutes.
4. In a 1-cup glass measure, combine 3 tablespoons butter, almonds, and lemon juice. Cook and stir 1 to 2 minutes, until brown.
5. Pour sauce over fillets, sprinkle with parsley, and serve immediately.
3 OR 4 SERVINGS

Microwave Turbot

1 egg, slightly beaten
1 tablespoon lemon juice
½ teaspoon salt
Dash pepper
½ cup corn flake crumbs
1 pound turbot fillets, cut in serving pieces

1. In a small glass bowl, combine egg, lemon juice, salt, and pepper. Dip fish into mixture and coat with crumbs.
2. Arrange fish around edge of a 10-inch baking dish.
3. Cook, covered, 4 to 5 minutes, rotating dish one-quarter turn halfway through cooking time.
4 OR 5 SERVINGS

Note: Any white fish may be substituted for the turbot.

Year-Round Fruit Compote

1 cup dried apricots	unsweetened pineapple
1 cup golden raisins	chunks (undrained)
1 package (12 ounces) pitted	Lemon peel from ¼ lemon
prunes	1 cinnamon stick, broken in
1 can (20 ounces)	half

1. Put fruits, lemon peel and cinnamon sticks into a 1½-quart glass casserole. Cover with an all-glass lid or plastic wrap.
2. Cook in microwave oven 8 minutes; rotate dish one-quarter turn once.
3. Remove lemon peel and cinnamon before serving.
8 TO 10 SERVINGS

Lemon Meringue Pie

1½ cups sugar	peel
¼ teaspoon salt	3 egg yolks, slightly beaten
1½ cups boiling water	1 baked 9-inch pastry pie
2 tablespoons butter	shell
6 tablespoons cornstarch	3 egg whites
⅓ cup lemon juice	6 tablespoons sugar
1 tablespoon grated lemon	½ teaspoon lemon juice

1. In a 4-cup glass measure, combine 1½ cups sugar, salt, water, and butter. Cook 3 to 4 minutes, stirring halfway through cooking time until sugar is dissolved.
2. Blend cornstarch with 3 tablespoons water and stir into hot sugar mixture. Cook 2 to 3 minutes, stirring after every minute.
3. Stir in ⅓ cup lemon juice and lemon peel. Gradually add egg yolks, taking care to avoid overcooking them. Cook mixture 3 to 4 minutes, stirring after every minute. Cool and pour into pie shell.
4. Using an electric mixer, beat egg whites until stiff. Continue beating while adding 6 tablespoons sugar, 1 tablespoon at a time, until rounded peaks are formed. Beat in ½ teaspoon lemon juice.
5. Spread meringue evenly over cooked filling, sealing to edges of pie shell.
6. Bake in a conventional oven at 450°F 5 to 6 minutes, or until lightly browned.
6 OR 7 SERVINGS

Year-Round Fruit Compote

Lemon Meringue Pie

Strawberry Shortcake

2 cups all-purpose flour
¼ cup sugar
1 tablespoon baking powder
½ teaspoon salt
½ cup (1 stick) butter

¾ cup milk
Sweetened strawberries or
  other fresh fruit
Sweetened whipped cream

1. Line two 8-inch round glass cake dishes with 2 layers of paper towels cut to fit dish.
2. Combine flour, sugar, baking powder and salt in a bowl. Cut in butter until mixture resembles coarse crumbs. Add milk and mix only until the dry ingredients are moistened. Dough will be thick and lumpy.
3. Divide dough into two portions. Drop one-half of dough by teaspoonfuls into each lined cake dish. Spread evenly with moistened fingers.
4. Cook uncovered, one dish at a time, in microwave oven 2½ to 3 minutes, or until done.
5. Remove shortcake from dishes and peel off paper.
6. Serve shortcake warm, filled and topped with fruit and whipped cream.
6 TO 8 SERVINGS

Date Cake

Cake:
2 cups boiling water
½ cup chopped dates
2 teaspoons baking soda
1 cup butter
2 cups sugar
2 eggs
3 cups all-purpose flour
2 teaspoons vanilla extract

1 teaspoon salt

Topping:
3 tablespoons butter
1 cup brown sugar
¼ cup milk or cream
1 cup coarsely chopped
  walnuts

1. In a 4-cup glass measure, heat water about 5 to 6 minutes, to boiling. Stir in dates and sprinkle baking soda over water. Cool until just warm.
2. Cream butter with sugar and eggs. Add flour, vanilla extract, and salt to creamed mixture. Blend with date mixture and pour into a buttered 2-quart glass ceramic baking dish.
3. Cook 9 to 11 minutes, rotating dish one-quarter turn every 3 minutes.
4. Rest 5 minutes before removing from dish.
5. To make topping, heat butter 30 seconds in 2-cup glass measure. Add brown sugar, milk, and nuts. Blend ingredients evenly and spread on top of cake.
6. Place cake under conventional broiler 1 to 2 minutes, until mixture starts to bubble. Remove and serve warm.
20 TO 24 SERVINGS

Left to right:
Date Cake (page 790), Choco-Butterscotchies, Chocolate Marshmallow Devils, Almond Bark (page 792)

Choco-Butterscotchies

1 cup sugar
1 cup light corn syrup
1 cup peanut butter
6 cups oven-toasted rice cereal

1 package (6 ounces) semisweet chocolate pies
1 package (6 ounces) butterscotch-flavored pieces

1. In a large glass mixing bowl, blend together sugar and corn syrup. Cook 3 to 4 minutes until mixture is boiling.
2. Stir peanut butter into hot mixture. Add cereal; stir to blend well. Press mixture into a buttered 11x7-inch glass dish.
3. In a 2-cup glass measure; heat semisweet chocolate and butterscotch-flavored pieces 2 to 2½ minutes. Stir to blend well.
4. Spread melted mixture over cereal pressed in dish. Cool about 30 minutes. Cut into 1½-inch squares, then cut each square diagonally, forming triangular pieces.
ABOUT 5 DOZEN PIECES

Chocolate Marshmallow Devils

1 package (6 ounces) semisweet chocolate pieces
15 wooden skewers
15 large marshmallows
¾ cup crushed corn chips

1. In a 2-cup glass measure, heat chocolate pieces 3 to 4 minutes, stirring well after heating.
2. Place wooden skewer in center of each marshmallow. Dip marshmallow in melted chocolate, spread with knife to coat evenly, and roll in corn chips until well covered. Chill, remove skewers, and serve.
15 COATED MARSHMALLOWS

Pineapple Upside-Down Cake

2 tablespoons butter
1 can (8 ounces) crushed
  pineapple
½ cup firmly packed brown

sugar
6 maraschino cherries
1 package (9 ounces) yellow
  cake mix

1. Heat butter 30 seconds in an 8-inch round glass baking dish.
2. Drain pineapple, reserving juice.
3. Blend together butter, brown sugar, and drained pineapple; spread evenly in bottom of pan. Arrange maraschino cherries in bottom of pan.
4. Prepare cake mix as directed on package, substituting the reserved pineapple juice for water. Pour batter evenly over pineapple mixture.
5. Cook 5 to 7 minutes, rotating dish one-quarter turn halfway through cooking time. Rest 5 minutes until cake pulls away from sides of pan.
6. Invert onto serving dish.
6 TO 8 SERVINGS

Note: If desired, pineapple slices may be used. Blend the melted butter and the brown sugar in baking dish and arrange slices on top. Other fruits, such as apricots or peaches, may be used, also.

Almond Bark

¾ cup blanched whole
  almonds
1 teaspoon butter

1 package (12 ounces)
  semisweet chocolate pieces

1. Place almonds and butter in a 9-inch glass pie plate. Cook 3 to 4 minutes, stirring after every minute. Add more time if needed to toast almonds.
2. In a 4-cup glass measure, heat chocolate pieces 2 to 4 minutes; stir to blend. Add almonds and mix well.
3. Pour onto waxed paper and spread to desired thickness. Chill about 1 hour until firm. Break into pieces.
ABOUT 1 POUND

Hot Spiced Apple Cider

2 quarts sweet apple cider
1 teaspoon whole cloves
1 teaspoon whole allspice
2 cinnamon sticks (about 3 inches each)
½ cup firmly packed light brown sugar
Few grains salt
Red apple slices

1. Combine apple cider, cloves, allspice, cinnamon sticks, brown sugar and salt in a heat-resistant glass punch bowl. Heat uncovered in microwave oven to boiling (15 to 20 minutes).
2. Stir cider. Remove spices. Serve hot, garnished with apple slices.
ABOUT 2 QUARTS

Hot Spiced Apple Cider

Hot Spiced Tea

4 teaspoons black tea leaves
2 teaspoons whole cloves
10 cups boiling water
½ cup orange juice
1 cup lemon juice
¾ cup sugar

1. Place tea leaves and cloves in teapot or large saucepan. Pour 5 cups boiling water over tea leaves and cloves. Steep 1 hour and strain.
2. In a deep, 4-quart glass bowl, combine orange juice, lemon juice, sugar, tea, and remaining 5 cups boiling water.
3. Heat, covered, 10 to 12 minutes, stirring every 4 minutes.
12 CUPS

Instant Spiced Tea: Combine **2 cups water, 2 tablespoons sugar, 1 teaspoon lemon juice, ½ cup orange juice, 2 teaspoons instant tea,** and **4 whole cloves** in a 4-cup glass measure. Heat 4 to 5 minutes, stirring halfway through cooking time, and serve immediately.
2 CUPS

Irish Coffee

3 tablespoons Irish whiskey
1½ to 2 teaspoons sugar
1 tablespoon instant coffee
Water
Whipped cream

1. Measure whiskey into an 8-ounce coffee mug. Stir in sugar and coffee. Fill mug with water until three quarters full.
2. Cook 1½ to 2 minutes. Stir to blend. Fill with whipped cream to brim, but do not stir in.
3. Serve immediately.
1 CUP

Hot Cocoa

¼ cup cocoa
3 tablespoons sugar
¼ cup water
3 cups milk
Dash salt

1. In a 1½-quart deep glass casserole, mix cocoa, sugar, and water. Cook 1 minute.
2. Slowly stir in milk, add salt, and mix well. Cook 6 to 8 minutes, stirring every 2 minutes.
3. Pour in mugs and serve hot.
3 CUPS

Hot Chocolate

2 ounces (2 squares)
  unsweetened chocolate
1 cup water
3 to 4 tablespoons sugar
Dash salt
3 cups milk
Marshmallows

1. Put chocolate and water into a 2-quart glass casserole and heat uncovered in microwave oven 4 to 5 minutes, or until chocolate melts.
2. Stir chocolate mixture; add sugar and salt. Stir in milk gradually and heat uncovered in microwave oven to boiling (4 to 6 minutes); stir occasionally.
3. Beat hot chocolate with rotary beater. Pour over marshmallows in mugs.
4 TO 6 SERVINGS

Orange Glaze

2 tablespoons thinly slivered
  orange peel
¼ cup orange juice
½ cup dark corn syrup
¼ teaspoon ginger
¼ teaspoon salt

1. In a 2-cup glass measure, blend orange peel, orange juice, corn syrup, ginger, and salt. Cook 1½ to 2 minutes, stirring every 30 seconds.
2. Pour over yellow cake or use as glaze for poultry.
ABOUT ¾ CUP

INDEX

795

798